ASSESSMENT IN REHABILITATION AND HEALTH

Elias Mpofu
University of Sydney

Thomas Oakland
University of Florida

Merrill
Upper Saddle River, New Jersey
Columbus, Ohio

This book is dedicated to those aspiring students who are working diligently to establish a rewarding and personally meaningful career as rehabilitation specialists. May the contents of this book assist these efforts. May you enjoy your work as much as we have enjoyed ours.

Library of Congress Cataloging-in-Publication Data

Assessment in rehabilitation and health/[edited by] Elias Mpofu, Thomas Oakland.— 1st ed.
    p.;   cm.
  Includes bibliographical references and index.
  ISBN–13: 978-0-205-50174-8
  ISBN–10: 0-205-50174-5
  1. People with disabilities—Functional assessment.   2. Disability evaluation.   I. Mpofu, Elias.   II. Oakland, Thomas.
  [DNLM: 1. Disability Evaluation.   2. Rehabilitation.   3. Treatment Outcome. W 925 A846 2010]
  RM930.8.A87 2010
  616.07'5—dc22   2008032841

Vice President and Editor in Chief: Jeffery W. Johnston
Publisher: Kevin M. Davis
Acquisitions Editor: Meredith D. Fossel
Senior Managing Editor: Pamela D. Bennett
Senior Project Manager: Mary Irvin
Editorial Assistant: Nancy Holstein
Senior Art Director: Diane Lorenzo
Cover Design: Candace Rowley
Cover Image: SuperStock
Operations Specialist: Susan Hannahs
Vice President, Director of Sales and Marketing: Quinn Perkson
Marketing Manager: Amanda L. Stedke
Marketing Coordinator: Brian Mounts

This book was set in Garamond by GGS Book Services, PMG. It was printed and bound by Hamilton Printing Company. The cover was printed by Phoenix Color Corp.

Pearson® is a registered trademark of Pearson plc
Merrill® is a registered trademark of Pearson Education, Inc.

Pearson Education Ltd., London
Pearson Education Singapore Pte. Ltd.
Pearson Education Canada, Ltd.
Pearson Education—Japan
Pearson Education Austrailia, Limited

Pearson Educationn North Asia, Ltd., Hong Kong
Pearson Educación de Mexico, S.A. de C.V.
Pearson Education Malaysia Pte. Ltd.
Pearson Education Upper Saddle River, New Jersey

Merrill
is an imprint of

www.pearsonhighered.com

10 9 8 7 6 5 4 3 2 1

ISBN-13:   978-0-205-50174-8
ISBN-10:   0-205-50174-5

PREFACE

This book serves many purposes. Assessment is the cornerstone of rehabilitation and health interventions. Thus, this book is designed to serve as a resource to assist neophytes as well as seasoned professionals when they are engaged in assessment methods to benefit clients in their rehabilitation. These professionals include those in communication sciences, community health, counseling, ethics, kinesiology, law, occupational therapy, physical therapy, physiotherapy, physical medicine, psychology, special education, and any others who contribute to assessment practices.

This book discusses assessment methods and technology used in rehabilitation and health. Assessment methods used in this context may include, yet differ from, some commonly used in psychology, counseling, and other behavioral areas. Some methods are highly structured (e.g., standardized norm-referenced methods); others are less so (e.g., bedside practices) and thus require considerable professional experience in their use.

The book discusses the multidisciplinary nature of assessment services delivered by professions engaged in rehabilitation and health. Multidisciplinary services can have two outcomes: They can enrich the breadth and range of assessment practices available to clients or they can be characterized by fragmentation within and between professional specialties, thus negating the possible benefits derived from a comprehensive understanding of the client's rehabilitation and health needs.

During my professional preparation as a rehabilitation professional—first at the University of Wisconsin–Madison (1995–99) and later as a rehabilitation services educator—I was surprised by the lack of a single textbook usable for educating preservice and inservice rehabilitation service professionals in current assessment practices that did not require extensive supplementary readings. This book is in response to that need. No other single textbook addresses the breadth and depth of assessment practices in rehabilitation and health found in this book.

FOR WHOM THE BOOK IS INTENDED

This book is designed to meet the needs of students in upper division and graduate courses that provide foundation knowledge and skills in rehabilitation and health assessment. It also is designed to be useful to seasoned service providers who want to refresh their assessment practices or retool their repertoire of skills for effective practice. The chapters of the book are referenced extensively, thus providing useful links to current scholarship that examines issues in greater detail. These links may be especially useful to advanced undergraduate and graduate students who seek ways to benefit from clinical as well as research experiences during their professional development. Doctoral students and established professionals engaged in research and other forms of scholarship on issues pertaining to assessment methods also are likely to find these links to be of value. Thus, this book is designed to appeal to a wide range of users engaged in rehabilitation and health assessment.

GOALS OF THE BOOK

This book has three main goals. Its first goal is to inform students and professionals engaged in assessment of state-of-the-art assessment practices in rehabilitation and health. The major goal of rehabilitation and health intervention served by assessment is to determine functional capacity and possible deterioration in functioning, and to make an effort to restore function (Dittmar, & Gresham, 1997; Stucki, Üstün, & Melvin, 2005). The success of rehabilitation and health interventions depends, in part, on the accurate use of measures, the valid interpretation of their data, and their correct applications to address significant treatment issues (Institute of Healthcare Improvement, 2006; McDowell, 2006).

A second goal is to showcase the diversity of assessment methods and applications used in rehabilitation and health. A broad range of health assessment procedures are discussed, including measures of workplace accommodations, compensation, occupational/physical functioning, and service user satisfaction.

A third goal is to highlight and provide guidance to assessment procedures and practices that require further research—particularly those that have not received sufficient attention in current practices, those that are emerging from recent developments in health service delivery, or those that are due to demographic changes in the client populations—or to identify new assessment needs to support appropriate interventions.

OUR APPROACH

We consider *professional issues* in rehabilitation and health assessment in part 1, Chapters 1–3. Chapter 1 provides grounding on the historical, current, and emerging practices in rehabilitation and health assessments. Chapter 2 considers the legal and ethical basis of rehabilitation and health assessment. Chapter 3 considers how diversity and qualities of test use influence outcomes for rehabilitation and health clients.

Types of assessments and technical and conceptual bases are considered in part 2, chapters 4–9, including a focus on assessment procedures and their psychometric qualities. Specific assessment applications are considered in chapters 10–13, including forensic rehabilitation, disability determination evaluations, and workplace accommodations.

Assessment of *client development and adjustment* is considered in part 3, chapters 14–22. Measures are featured that assess personal qualities that influence client development and adjustment in rehabilitation, including intelligence (chapter 14), adaptive behavior (chapter 15), neuropsychological assessment (chapter 16), achievement (chapter 17), and personality (chapter 18). Work plays a central role in adult life and significantly influences an individual's sense of well-being. Measures of *career or vocational development and adjustment* are considered in chapters 19 and 20 and those for transition outcomes in chapter 21. Assessment of disability-related attitudes is considered in chapter 22.

Assessment of *client functioning or participation* is featured in Part 4. The ultimate goal of rehabilitation health interventions is to facilitate clients' functioning or participation in typical activities within their community and to promote positive changes in the quality of their lives (National Institute on Disability and Rehabilitation Research: NIDRR, 1999; Seelman, 2000). Measurement of physical functioning and performance, independent living, and occupational functioning is considered in chapters 23, 24, and 28. Measurement of participation of those with speech and communication disorders and visual impairments is discussed in chapters 25 and 26. Measurement of quality of life in patients with a chronic illness or disability is discussed in chapter 27. Measurement of consumer satisfaction of rehabilitation and health services is discussed in chapter 30. The closing chapter, 31, comments on the promises and prospects in rehabilitation and health assessment.

All authors wrote using a common outline. Thus, readers are likely to conceptualize assessments described in the various chapters using a common framework. The author's use of a common outline facilitates a succinct digest of professional history; current issues, practices, and developments; as well as needed research in each area of rehabilitation and health assessment. The authors were selected carefully based on their expertise in the specific assessment practices and drawn from diverse backgrounds in rehabilitation and health, including communication and speech disorders, engineering, law, neuropsychology, occupational therapy, psychology, rehabilitation counseling, physiotherapy, and public health. We believe this book presents state-of-the-art perspectives on the assessment procedures in rehabilitation science and practice.

INSTRUCTIONAL FEATURES

Authors used illustrative materials and instructional features to support users in their learning: discussion boxes, research boxes, case studies, and self-check questions.

Discussion boxes describe a current hot issue, dilemma, or controversy pertinent to the topic discussed in the chapter followed by questions to encourage users to demonstrate an understanding of the nature of the issue and to propose how it might be resolved. Research boxes briefly describe illustrative, historically significant or current research on pertinent assessment issues, thereby highlighting evidence for specific assessment procedures. Self-check questions are offered to assist users to verify their understanding of the core assessment issues of each chapter. Case studies assist users in applying learned concepts in real-world settings.

CONCEPTUAL FRAMEWORK

Authors generally applied the *International Classification of Disability, Functioning, and Health* (ICF: WHO, 2004) as a framework to promote an understanding of specific assessment procedures within the broader context of assessment needs in various domains of functioning. The ICF provides a common language used by rehabilitation and health professionals to address client issues in functional terms. Use of functional terms also enhances the utility and clarity of communication between rehabilitation and health professionals and their clients in an effort to relate assessment procedures directly to aspects of their health functioning.

The attempt to address ICF domains in rehabilitation and health assessments is not new. However, the mapping of specific assessment features to the ICF model in a manner that promotes applications that address specific rehabilitation and health care needs is new. The omission by others to directly address assessment needs within the ICF is somewhat surprising in that the ICF originally was proposed almost 30 years ago.

REVIEWERS

We would like to thank the following reviewers who were a great help in finalizing the text of this book: Kathleen M. Deidrick, Ph.D., Department of Health Psychology, University of Missouri–Columbia, Columbia, MO; Patrick L. Dunn, Ph.D., CRC, University of Tennessee–Knoxville, TN; Dothel W. Edwards, Jr., Ph.D., Fort Valley State University, GA; Amy L. Freeland, Ph.D., Western Michigan University, MI; Steven R. Hinderer, M.D., Rehabilitation Institute of Michigan, MI; James Patrick, Ph.D., Thomas University, GA; John Wadsworth, Ph.D., The University of Iowa, IA; William Stiers, Ph.D., ABPP, Johns Hopkins University School of Medicine, Baltimore, MD, Richard T. Roessler, Ph.D., CRC, University of Arkansas, Fayetteville, AR.

References

Dittmar, S. S., & Gresham, G. E. (Eds.). (1997). *Functional assessment and outcomes measures for the rehabilitation health professional*. Gaithersburg, MD: Aspen.

Institute of Health Improvement (2006). Patient-centered care: General. Retrieved on April 19, 2006, from http://www.ihi.org/IHI/Topics/PatientCenteredCare/PatientCenteredCareGeneral/

McDowell, I. (2006). *Measuring health: A guide to rating scales and questionnaires*. New York: Oxford Press.

NIDRR (1999). National Institute on Disability and Rehabilitation Research Long-Range Plan (1999–2003). Retrieved on November 16, 2006, from http://www.ncddr.org/new/announcements/lrp/fy1999–2003/execsum/index.html

Seelman, K. (2000). Rehabilitation research and training centers on functional assessment and the evaluation of rehabilitation outcomes. Accomplishments to date and goals for the future: Introduction. *Journal of Rehabilitation Outcomes Measurement, 4*(4), 1.

Stucki, G., Üstün, T. B., & Melvin, J. (2005). Applying the ICF for the acute hospital and early post-acute rehabilitation facilities. *Disability and Rehabilitation, 27*, 349–352.

World Health Organization (WHO) (2004). *International Classification of Functioning, Disability, and Health (ICF)*. Available at http://www.who.int/icidh.

Elias Mpofu & Thomas Oakland
October, 2007

ABOUT THE AUTHORS

Elias Mpofu, Ph.D., CRC is associate professor and head of discipline for rehabilitation counselling in the Faculty of Health Sciences at the University of Sydney, Australia. Formerly professor of rehabilitation services at the Pennsylvania State University, he is a recipient of three national research awards in rehabilitation: Mary Switzer Distinguished Research Award, National Council on Rehabilitation Education Researcher of the Year Award, and the American Rehabilitation Counseling Association Research Award. Dr. Mpofu has 12 years of research and test development experience in educational and rehabilitation settings, and has expertise with the use of the *International Classification of Functioning, Disability and Health* (ICF) to develop rehabilitation assessment. He has led a number of multidisciplinary research teams in applying the ICF and modern test theory to rehabilitation outcomes measurement. His measurement related publications include those in peer-refereed journals such the *British Journal of Educational Psychology, Educational and Psychological Measurement*, and *Personality and Individual Differences*, and book chapters in titles such as the *Comprehensive Handbook of Behavioral Assessment* Vols. 1 & 2 (M. Hersen, Ed.), *International Handbook of Intelligence* (R. Sternberg, Ed.), and *International Handbook of Creativity* (J. Kaufman & R. Sternberg, Eds.). Dr. Elias Mpofu was a keynote speaker on equitable assessment practices at the annual conference of the International Test Commission in October 2004. Dr. Mpofu's primary teaching assignment at The Pennsylvania State University was rehabilitation assessment.

Thomas Oakland, Ph.D. ABPP, ABPN is University of Florida Research Foundation professor. He is president of the International Foundation for Children's Education, president-elect of the International Association of Applied Psychology's Division of Psychological Assessment and Evaluation, and past president of the International School Psychology Association and the International Test Commission. He has worked in more than 40 countries. Dr. Oakland has authored or edited seven books, more than 140 chapters and articles, and six psychological tests. He was a coauthor of *Standards for Educational and Psychological Testing* and the 2002 APA code of ethics. He is a licensed psychologist, board certified in school psychology and neuropsychology, and has an active clinical and forensic practice. His interests center on psychological and educational characteristics of children and youth, cultural diversity, international issues, and professionalism. He is the recipient of distinguished service awards from APA's Division of School Psychology and the International School Psychology Association and received the 2002 National Association of School Psychology's Legend Award. Dr. Oakland received APA's 2003 Award for Distinguished Contributions to the Advancement of Psychology Internationally.

CHAPTER AUTHORS

Reginald J. Alston, Ph.D., is professor and associate head in the Department of Kinesiology and Community Health at the University of Illinois at Urbana–Champaign. His primary research interests are racial disparities in rehabilitation outcomes and psychosocial adjustment for African Americans with disabilities. Dr. Alston has published extensively in the leading journals of rehabilitation counseling and has directed research funding from NIH, NSF, and NIDRR. As evidence of his national reputation for scholarship, he received the James F. Garrett Award for a Distinguished Career in Rehabilitation Research from the American Rehabilitation Counseling Association in 2007. Dr. Alston is a former editor of the *Journal of Applied Rehabilitation Counseling* and a former board member for the American Rehabilitation Counseling Association (ARCA) and the Council on Rehabilitation Education (CORE).

Amy J. Armstrong, Ph.D., CRC, is an associate professor in the Department of Rehabilitation Counseling at Virginia Commonwealth University. She has been involved in advocacy, education and employment issues related to individuals with disabilities for 25 years. She has extensive experience providing national personnel training on disability-related issues, employment of marginalized populations, leadership and motivational topics. Her interests include the employment of individuals with significant disabilities, advocacy, welfare and poverty issues, building community liaisons, leadership and personal/professional transformation. She received an M.A. in Rehabilitation Counseling from Michigan State University and a Ph.D. in Education from VCU.

Nicholas Benson, Ph.D., is assistant professor at Florida International University in the Department of Educational and Psychological Studies. His responsibilities include coordinating the School Psychology Program, teaching graduate level courses, and advising students. His research interests center on the assessment of psychological and educational characteristics.

Norman L. Berven, Ph.D., is a professor and chair of the Rehabilitation Psychology Program at the University of Wisconsin–Madison. He is a certified rehabilitation counselor (CRC), is licensed in Wisconsin as a psychologist and as a professional counselor (LPC), and is a fellow in the American Psychological Association. He has received the James Garrett Award for a Distinguished Career in Rehabilitation Research from the American Rehabilitation Counseling Association (ARCA), the ARCA Distinguished Professional Award, nine ARCA Research Awards, the American Counseling Association (ACA) Research Award, and distinguished alumni awards from the rehabilitation programs at the University of Wisconsin–Madison and the University of Iowa. His research interests include assessment, individual and group counseling, education and training of professionals, and psychiatric rehabilitation.

Malachy Bishop, Ph.D., CRC, is associate professor and coordinator of the Rehabilitation Counseling Program in the Department of Special Education and Rehabilitation Counseling at the University of Kentucky. He completed his doctoral study in rehabilitation psychology at the University of Wisconsin–Madison. He conducts research in the areas of quality of life, adaptation to disability and chronic illness, and the psychosocial aspects of living with neurological conditions including multiple sclerosis, brain injury, and epilepsy. He has authored over 40 articles, several book chapters, and an edited book.

Carrie Bruce, M.A., CCC-SLP, ATP, is a research scientist at the Center for Assistive Technology and Environmental Access (CATEA) at Georgia Tech and an investigator for the Rehabilitation Engineering Research Center on Workplace Accommodations (Work RERC). Ms. Bruce is also a licensed speech–language pathologist and an assistive technology practitioner who has been working in the field of rehabilitation for over 10 years. She is distinguished for her work in examining environmental design issues related to accessibility and in investigating assessment methodologies that measure the environment's impact on participation.

Shane S. Bush, Ph.D., ABPP, ABPN, is the director of Long Island Neuropsychology, P.C. and is a clinical assistant professor in the Department of Psychiatry and Behavioral Science, State University of New York at Stony Brook School of Medicine. He is board certified in clinical neuropsychology and rehabilitation psychology by the American Board of Professional Psychology and is board certified in neuropsychology by the American Board of Professional Neuropsychology. He is a fellow of the American Psychological Association's Divisions of Neuropsychology and Rehabilitation Psychology and is a fellow of the National Academy of Neuropsychology. He is an editorial board member of *The Clinical Neuropsychologist, Applied Neuropsychology, Archives of Clinical Neuropsychology*, and *Journal of Head Trauma Rehabilitation*. He has published five books and two special journal issues on ethical issues and one book on geriatric neuropsychology. He has also published articles, chapters, and position papers on ethical and professional issues and has presented on professional ethics at national conferences.

Frederick M. Capps, Ph.D., M.S., LPC, AAC, is founder of A New Direction Counseling & Training, where he specializes in addictive processes, EMDR, and grief and trauma resolution counseling for individuals, families, and groups. He also provides training for professionals in the counseling field, as well as clinical supervision. Dr. Capps has written the substance-abuse counseling curriculum for Del Mar College in Corpus Christi, Texas, and is a past president of the Texas Association of Addiction Professionals (formerly known as TAADAC).

Linda Chamberlain, Psy.D., is a licensed psychologist and coordinator of the Center for Addiction and Substance Abuse (CASA) at the Counseling Center for Human Development, the University of South Florida in Tampa, Florida. Dr. Chamberlain coauthored a book on the treatment of problem gambling entitled *Best Possible Odds* and has written numerous articles and book chapters on the dynamics and treatment of addictions and on family therapy. Dr. Chamberlain has presented workshops and counselor training through the American Counseling Association and the American Psychological Association, and has been an invited speaker at local, national, and international conferences on addictions.

Christine J. Chapparo, Ph.D., OTR, is a Senior Lecturer, Acting SubDean, Undergraduate Coursework and Students in the Faculty of Health Sciences, The University of Sydney. She is a member of the Faculty's Clinical and Rehabilitation Sciences Research Group and her research interests focus on the ability of adults and children to participate in occupational performance life roles.

Cara Conway Jones, M.A., is a third year graduate student in the School Psychology Training Program at George Mason University. She is currently working as school psychology intern in Fairfax County, VA and will receive her Certificate of Advanced Graduate Studies (CAGS) specialist degree in School Psychology in May, 2009. Her research interests include cognitive processing and fair assessment.

David R. Cox, Ph.D., ABPP, is a licensed psychologist who is board certified through the American Board of Professional Psychology in Rehabilitation Psychology and is a fellow of the National Academy of Neuropsychology. He is executive officer of the American Board of Professional Psychology and president of Neuropsychology & Rehabilitation Consultants, P.C. in Chapel Hill, North Carolina. Dr. Cox has served as a consultant to the Social Security Administration Disability Determination Services and holds an academic appointment as Courtesy Professor of Clinical and Health Psychology at the University of Florida. He has previously held appointments on the staff and faculty of the University of California San Diego, Duke University Medical Center, and The University of North Carolina at Chapel Hill. Dr. Cox has been awarded the Karl F. Heiser Presidential Award of the American Psychological Association for his legislative, public policy, and advocacy efforts on behalf of the profession of psychology and the populations served by psychologists.

John E. Crews, DPA, is Lead Scientist, Disability and Health Branch, Centers for Disease Control and Prevention. He has thirty years of experience in vision rehabilitation and disability research, including work in vision impairment and aging; his research interests include caregiving as well as health disparities among people with disabilities. He has over eighty publications, including two books: *Vision Loss in an Aging Society* (2000) and *The Multiple Dimensions of Caregiving and Disability* (2009). He serves on the Editorial Board of the *Journal of Visual Impairment and Blindness* and the National Commission on Vision and Health.

Ralph M. Crystal, Ph.D., CRC, LPC, is Wallace Charles Hill Professor of Rehabilitation Education at the University of Kentucky. His research interests are in forensic rehabilitation and program evaluation. Dr. Crystal was coordinator of the rehabilitation counseling program at Kentucky for 24 years. Previously, he was research director of a rehabilitation research institute at the University of Michigan and on the faculty of the Michigan rehabilitation education program. He has published in the areas of rehabilitation assessment, program evaluation, and forensic rehabilitation and was editor for 9 years of the *Rehabilitation Professional*. Dr. Crystal maintains a private forensic rehabilitation practice and has worked in a rehabilitation facility.

Scott L. Decker, Ph.D., is an Assistant Professor in the Department of Counseling & Psychological Services at Georgia State University. He is the coauthor of the Bender-Gestalt II Second Edition and has authored multiple publications on visual-motor assessment. His primary area of research is applications of neuropsychological assessment in an educational context. He teaches courses on cognitive and academic assessment as well as interventions and biopsychology. He is an editorial board member of *Psychology in the Schools*.

Jeffrey Ditterline, M.Ed., is a predoctoral fellow in the College of Education at the University of Florida, where he is a student in the School Psychology Program. He has coauthored book chapters and journal publications on the topics of adaptive behavior and child psychopharmacology. Jeffrey also is the lead author of several encyclopedia entries on various topics in special education. His research interests include the emotional development of students, qualities that determine early school success, roles of parents and communities in education, and adaptive behavior profiles of students with various disabilities. Jeffrey is a student member of the American Psychological Association, National Association of School Psychologists, and Florida Association of School Psychologists and has presented at local, state, and national conferences.

Michelle Donelly, BAppSc, GradCert EdStudies, M.A., Ph.D., is a lecturer in occupational therapy at the University of Sydney. Her various research interests include: understanding the development of networks of support in the lives of people with disabilities; features of enabling environments in supported accommodation; use of civil legal tribunals by people with disabilities; understanding the meaning of people's experiences related to personal care, inclusive schooling and open employment; and advocacy.

Agnieszka M. Dynda, Psy.D., earned her doctoral degree from the APA accredited program in school psychology at St. John's University in Queens, NY. She is currently a practicing school psychologist in Great Neck, NY and an adjunct professor in the Department of Psychology at St. John's University. Dr. Dynda conducts research and publishes on various topics, notably nondiscriminatory assessment of culturally and linguistically diverse students. She is bilingual/bicultural (Polish).

Oliver W. Edwards, Ph.D., is a faculty member in the Department of Child, Family, and Community Sciences at the University of Central Florida where he has been recognized as a Distinguished Researcher. He is the author of numerous scholarly research articles and book chapters. His research addresses the differential effects of ethnicity and IQ. In addition, he investigates the positive youth development of children raised by their grandparents. Dr. Edwards presents workshops to national and international audiences on these topics.

Alice S. Erickson, M.S., CRC, is completing her doctoral degree (all but dissertation) at the University of Kentucky, Department of Special Education and Rehabilitation Counseling. She has over 15 years of experience in career and rehabilitation counseling in multiple settings and has spent an additional 10 years as an employer advisory council coordinator for the state of California. Her area of interest is workforce maintenance for adults with late onset disabilities. Her dissertation interest is in factors that support older workers with arthritis in successful employment.

Cynthia Faulkner, Ph.D., is an associate professor of social work at Morehead State University. Dr. Faulkner received her BSSW from Kansas State University in 1984, MSW from the University of Kansas in 1989, and Ph.D. in social work from the University of Texas at Arlington in 2001. Dr. Faulkner has over 15 years of practice experience in multiple settings including substance abuse treatment and is a Licensed Clinical Social Worker (LCSW).

Samuel Faulkner, Ph.D., is an associate professor of social work at Morehead State University. Dr. Faulkner's research interests include employee cohesion, challenge courses, and substance abuse. His research includes work with substance abusers, families (with a focus on adolescents and foster families), and employees.

James Micheal Ferrin, Ph.D., CRCC, CVE, (deceased) was an assistant professor and coordinator of fieldwork for the graduate program in rehabilitation counseling, Department of Rehabilitation Counseling & Disability Studies, at Langston University. Dr. Ferrin served as a rehabilitation counseling professional and educator for over 20 years with experience in private and public sector rehabilitation. He received his Ph.D. in rehabilitation psychology from the University of Wisconsin–Madison in 2002. Dr. Ferrin authored over 20 articles in professional journals. He served on the Northeast Oklahoma Disability Task Force and Department of Veterans Affairs Homeless Program. Dr. Ferrin was also a pilot, SCUBA Diving Instructor, and international folk dance instructor.

Elda E. Garcia, Ph.D., M.S., LCDC, SWA, is a consultant for data analysis, monitoring, and evaluation of at-risk programs for the Corpus Christi Independent School District's Office of Research, Testing, and Evaluation and a research assistant at Texas A&M University–Corpus Christi. She is a licensed chemical dependency counselor and a licensed social worker associate. In addition to her work with at-risk youth, she has worked with terminally ill children, adults, women, families, and the elderly. She is well-versed in the areas of criminal justice, residential treatment, and medical social work.

Alan L. Goldberg, Psy.D., ABPP; J.D., adjudicates claims for the Disability Determination Services Administration in Tucson, AZ, where he also maintains a private practice devoted to rehabilitation and forensic issues. He is a licensed psychologist in Arizona and California, is board certified in rehabilitation psychology by the American Board of Professional Psychology, is a fellow of the American Psychological Association, and is a member of the State Bar of Arizona.

Sam Goldstein Ph.D., is an assistant clinical professor of psychiatry at the University of Utah and clinical director of the Neurology, Learning, and Behavior Center in Salt Lake City, Utah. Author, coauthor or editor of 26 books, two dozen book chapters, and nearly two dozen peer-reviewed articles, he is editor-in-chief of the *Journal of Attention Disorders* and coeditor-in-Chief of the *Encyclopedia of Child Behavior and Development*. He is codeveloper of four psychological tests.

Debra A. Harley, Ph.D., is professor and chair of the Department of Special Education and Rehabilitation Counseling at the University of Kentucky. Her primary interests are cultural and gender issues, substance abuse, and ethics. Dr. Harley has published extensively in top tier journals of rehabilitation counseling and is coeditor of the book, *Contemporary Mental Health Issues Among African Americans*. She received the Educator of the Year Award from the National Council on Rehabilitation Education in 2006. Dr. Harley is former editor of the *Journal of Applied Rehabilitation Counseling* and the *Journal of Rehabilitation Administration*, and a board member of the Commission on Rehabilitation Counselor Certification (CRCC).

Robert Heard, Ph.D., is a psychologist and Senior Lecturer in the discipline of Behavioural and Community Health, Faculty of Health Sciences, The University of Sydney. He is a research advisor and mentor to higher degree students and staff in the faculty, and heads curriculum development and in various areas of research design and methods.

Anne Hillman, Ph.D, has primary research interests in people with chronic illness living in the community, and in particular to occupational role development and role partnerships. She is a lecturer at the University of Sydney, Faculty of Health Sciences, and currently is a Senior Research Fellow working as part of a team investigating the informal networks that support adults with disabilities.

Ev Innes, Ph.D., MHPEd, BAppSc(OT), AccOT, MHFESA, is a senior lecturer in occupational therapy in the Faculty of Health Sciences, The University of Sydney. Dr. Innes is on the editorial board of *WORK: A Journal of Prevention, Assessment and Rehabilitation*, represents health professionals on the New South Wales Workers' Compensation and Workplace Occupational Health and Safety Council, and is a member of the Department of Veterans' Affairs Technical Advisory Committee on Rehabilitation, the Research Committee of the WorkCover NSW Research Centre of Excellence, and the Faculty of Health Sciences' Occupational Performance Research Team. Ev's research interests are in the areas of work-related assessments, work-related injuries, and occupational rehabilitation/return-to-work programs.

Cynthia L. Jew, Ph.D., is the director of the Pupil Personnel Services Counseling program and an assistant professor at the University of Redlands (Redlands, CA). Her professional research interest is in resiliency. She is the author of Resiliency Skills and Abilities Scale (RSAS). Dr. Jew is a licensed psychologist and a certified school psychologist.

Joy Jansen, M.Ed., is a doctoral candidate at the University of Idaho. Her studies are focused in adult education with a cognate in neuropsychological deficiencies, specifically ADHD. As an instructor at the University of Idaho, she taught classes focusing on special education issues to pre-service teachers. Ms. Jansen has also worked as a learning specialist in the office of Disability Services at the University of Idaho and the University of North Carolina at Chapel Hill.

Kurt L. Johnson, Ph.D., received his master's degree in rehabilitation counseling and his Ph.D. in rehabilitation psychology. He is a professor in the Department of Rehabilitation Medicine in the School of Medicine at the University of Washington in Seattle. He is head of the Division of Rehabilitation Counseling and director of the U.W. Center on Technology and Disability Studies. Dr. Johnson's research has focused on multiple sclerosis, psychosocial and employment issues around disability, the measurement of rehabilitation outcomes such as fatigue and pain, and technology and disability.

Diana Joyce, Ph.D., NCSP, is a licensed psychologist and school psychologist with considerable experience in behavioral intervention programs in public schools. She has an Assistant Scholar faculty appointment at the University of Florida and serves as a faculty-in-residence at P.K. Yonge Developmental Research School collaborating on consultation-based school psychology services for K–12 students. Her research interests include assessment and effective intervention/ treatment for emotional and behavior disorders in children and adolescents. She is the recipient of the 2007 Junior Faculty of the Year Award from the Psychological Corporation and Trainers in School Psychology, as well as a 2008 recipient of the Scholarship of Engagement Award from the University of Florida, College of Education.

Harrison D. Kane, Ph.D., is an assistant professor in the Department of Counseling, Educational Psychology, and Special Education at Mississippi State University. He has several years experience in private practice, specializing in the assessment and diagnosis of learning problems in underserved youth. Dr. Kane's research interests include test development, multicultural issues in education and psychology, and the nature/structure of intelligence. He serves on the editorial boards of several international journals and is the founder of the International Society for the Study of Individual and Group Differences.

Gabor I. Keitner, M.D., is a professor of psychiatry at The Warren Alpert Medical School of Brown University and director of adult psychiatry at Rhode Island Hospital. His clinical work focuses on the inpatient treatment of severe forms of psychiatric disorders, and he is a supervisor for individual and family therapy for residents in the Brown Psychiatry Residency Program. Dr. Keitner's research interests are comprehensive treatments for mood disorders including pharmacotherapy, psychotherapy and family therapy, and pharmacological clinical trials. He is an international authority on family therapy and combined

(biological and psychosocial) treatments and investigates the effectiveness of disease management models for difficult to treat depressions and bipolar disorders.

Lynn C. Koch, Ph.D., CRC, is an associate professor and coordinator of the Rehabilitation Education and Research Program at the University of Arkansas–Fayetteville. Her research interests include client expectations, the psychosocial and vocational impact of emerging disabilities, qualitative inquiry, and reflective rehabilitation counseling practice. She has written more than 70 professional articles on these and related topics.

Frank J. Lane, Ph.D., is an assistant professor of psychology at Illinois Institute of Technology in Chicago, Illinois. Dr. Lane received his B.A. in psychology from Saint Leo College in 1984, MHS from the University of Florida in 2000, and Ph.D. in rehabilitation science from The University of Florida in 2006. Dr. Lane has over 10 years of clinical and administrative experience working with individuals with traumatic brain injury and substance abuse issues. He is a Certified Rehabilitation Counselor (CRC) and a Licensed Clinical Professional Counselor (LCPC). Dr. Lane's research interests include societal attitudes and contact theory as it relates to persons with disabilities.

Vivian M. Larkin, Ph.D., MSW, CRC, is a semiretired university educator, administrator, and researcher with more than 30 years of experience. The primary focus of her work has been in the areas of higher education administration, program development/implementation, teaching, outreach, and service. She is currently a senior lecturer at the University of Wisconsin–Madison in the Department of Rehabilitation Psychology & Special Education. Recent accomplishments include inductee into Omicron Delta Kappa National Leadership Honor Society; recipient of Auburn University Alumni Association's Minority Achievement Award; visiting editor for the *Rehabilitation Engineering & Assistive Technology Society of North America Journal* (RESNA); immediate past editor of the *Vocational Evaluation and Career Adjustment Program Journal* (VECAP); and invited expert panelist at the 2004 National Summit on Disability and Distance Education with the National Center on Disability and Access to Education. Dr. Larkin has also worked in medical settings and state human resource agencies, principally as a human service administrator. She has conducted research and published in the areas of vocational assessment, aging and disabilities, and rural community transition services.

Jeanne M. LeBlanc, Ph.D., ABPP (Rp), R. Psych., has a private practice in Vancouver, British Columbia, with an emphasis upon rehabilitation and neuropsychological assessment. Research interests include ecological validity of neuropsychological assessment, models of effective interdisciplinary cognitive rehabilitation, as well as outcome related to interdisciplinary intervention for those with concussions. Dr. LeBlanc is a diplomate in rehabilitation psychology, and has been an invited speaker at national and international conferences in respect to functional neuropsychological aspects of brain injury and disability.

Gloria K. Lee, Ph.D., CRC, is an assistant professor at the Department of Counseling, School and Educational Psychology at Buffalo State University of New York. Her research interests are on the psychosocial adjustment of caregivers and individuals with chronic pain and chronic illness, and psychosocial adjustment of caregivers of children with autism spectrum disorders. She is a consultant and research member of the Autism Spectrum Disorder Research Consortium, focusing on research and treatment for families and children with the spectrum disorders. She was the awardee of the American Rehabilitation Counseling Association Research Award in 2008.

Richard G. Long, Ph.D., COMS, has worked for 32 years in the education and rehabilitation of individuals with blindness and low vision. He has served this field as a teacher, counselor, program administrator, federal government researcher, and college professor. His primary focus in the last half of his career has been on the orientation and mobility of visually impaired individuals. Since beginning his college teaching career at Western Michigan University in 1998, Dr. Long has been principal investigator of a large, multisite research project focused on intersection design and the orientation and mobility of persons with blindness. He has published many book chapters and articles in transportation engineering, human factors psychology and rehabilitation journals. He currently maintains his leadership role with his NIH-funded bioengineering research project while serving as Associate Dean for the College of Health and Human Services at Western Michigan University. Dr. Long holds the Master of Science degree in rehabilitation counseling from the University of Tennessee and the Ph.D. in special education from Vanderbilt University.

Lynda R. Matthews, Ph.D., MRCAA, is a qualified rehabilitation counselor who specializes in psychiatric and psychosocial rehabilitation for people with post-traumatic mental health conditions. She is the manager of the Bachelor of Health Sciences at the University of Sydney, a member of the faculty of Health

Sciences' Mental Health and Occupational Performance Research Teams, and a member of the International Disability Management Research Network. Dr. Matthews has been appointed to a number of state and national government bodies responsible for the review and development of mental health and rehabilitation policies and guidelines. She is a past president of the Australasian Society for Traumatic Stress Studies and is secretary of the Rehabilitation Counselling Association of Australasia.

David McIntosh, Ph.D., HSPP, ABPP, is the David and Joanna Meeks Distinguished Professor in Special Education and Professor-Educational Psychology at Ball State University. He is Board Certified by the American Board of Professional Psychology. He research focuses on the identification and treatment of autism spectrum disorders, psychological assessment, and treatment of child disruptive behavior disorders.

Jack A. Naglieri, Ph.D., is professor of psychology at George Mason University and a senior research scientist at the Devereux Foundation's Institute for Clinical Training and Research. He is a fellow of APA Division 16 and recipient of APA Division 16's 2001 Senior Scientist Award. He has more than 250 publications including a number of tests such as the Cognitive Assessment System, Devereux Scales of Mental Disorders, Wechsler Nonverbal Scale of Ability, and Naglieri Nonverbal Ability Test–Second Edition; and books, including *Essentials of CAS Assessment, Helping Children Learn: Instructional Handouts for Parents and Teachers*, and *Essentials of WNV Assessment*.

Peter J. O'Donnell, M.A., NCC, NBCDCH, BCIAC, CSP, is the director of Psychology, Behavioral Medicine and Neuropsychology at HEALTHSOUTH Nittany Valley Rehabilitation Hospital in Pleasant Gap, Pennsylvania. Additionally, he serves as a consultant at an inpatient forensic mental health unit in a state correctional facility. Mr. O'Donnell has over 24 years of clinical experience in various settings. He is on faculty in the Department of Psychology, College of Arts & Sciences, for the University of Phoenix. He is both a licensed psychologist and licensed professional counselor in Pennsylvania and has obtained board certifications such as National Certified Counselor from the National Board for Certified Counselors; Certified Sports Psychologist, Diplomate status, from the National Association of Sports Psychologists/National Institute of Sports Professionals' National Register; Certified Diplomate in Clinical Hypnotherapy from the National Board for Certified Clinical Hypnotherapists; and Senior Fellow of the Biofeedback Certification Institute of America. He currently is a doctoral student in the Department of Psychology with specialization in Health Psychology/Behavioral Medicine at Northcentral University. His areas of expertise and interest are with various aspects of individuals' with disabilities, pain management, and forensic mental health.

Kate O'Loughlin, BA, Ph.D., is a senior lecturer in the discipline of behavioural and community health sciences, The University of Sydney. As a health sociologist, she teaches in the areas of patient–practitioner relations, occupational health and rehabilitation, and research methods. Her research interests are in healthy ageing, professional practice in health care settings, self and identity, and health policy. She is currently engaged in research related to ageing and the life course, professional practice, and changes in self and identity in the illness experience. Her supervision of HRD students is in the areas of professional practice in health care and occupational health and injury management.

Charles D. Palmer, Ph.D., is an associate professor & program coordinator of rehabilitation counseling in the Department of Counseling, Educational Psychology and Special Education at Mississippi State University. Dr. Palmer is a Certified Rehabilitation Counselor, sits on CORE's Commission on Standards and Accreditation and is president of the National Rehabilitation Counseling Association. He has published in national journals and presented at numerous national and regional conferences on topics ranging from self-employment options for people with disabilities to ethical problem-solving in rehabilitation. Dr. Palmer is particularly interested in reducing barriers to employment experienced by people who have disabilities.

John Joseph Peregoy, Ph. D., is a member of the Flathead Nation. He is current chair of the Council of National Psychological Associations for the Advancement of Ethnic Minority Issues (CNPAAEMI) for the American Psychological Association. He is past president of the Society of Indian Psychologists (SIP). John serves on the editorial board of the *Journal for Counseling and Development*. His consulting firm, Consulting, Diversity, and Educational Services (CDES) provides consultation in program design, research, evaluation, and development. CDES also provides diversity training, team building, and coaching. Dr. Peregoy is a licensed professional clinical counselor in the Commonwealth of Kentucky and a licensed school counselor (K–12) in the state of Utah.

Gary W. Peterson, Ph.D., is professor emeritus and formerly clinical training director for the academic program, Psychological Services in Education, College of Education, Florida State University. He also served as chair of the Department of Educational Psychology and Learning Systems. He continues to serve as a volunteer senior research associate in the Center for the Study of Technology in Counseling and Career Development. He has authored several books and more than 50 professional articles. His research interests include career problem-solving and decision-making, career assessment, and test construction. He is also a licensed psychologist in Florida.

Margaret Sherrill Luther Pitcairn, Ph.D., is adjunct and visiting assistant professor in the Department of Counseling and Educational Psychology at Texas A&M University—Corpus Christi. She has many years of professional and clinical experience in private practice, foster care, and program development and implementation in a community nonprofit setting. Dr. Pitcairn's research interests include family interventions; substance abuse and treatment; violence and victimization (including physical abuse/assault, sexual abuse/assault, neglect, domestic violence, and witnessing maltreatment); resilience and prevention; Latino culture; at-risk youth, foster care, and juvenile justice; program development; community and personal supportive resources; and ethics.

Steven R. Pruett, Ph.D., is a rehabilitation psychology postdoctoral researcher in the Department of Physical Medicine and Rehabilitation at The Ohio State University. He has worked in rehabilitation for many years as a clinician, educator, and researcher. His publications and research interests include the topics of psychosocial aspects of disability, and rehabilitation outcomes.

Judy Ranka, MA, BSc, OTR has an academic appointment in the discipline of occupational therapy at the University of Sydney where she teaches in the undergraduate and postgraduate programs. Her primary research interests are in ecological assessment of peoples' performances of everyday tasks and routines and the information processing behaviors that support that performance; and occupational therapy theory development and the management of reach, grasp, and release disorders that arise from stroke and their impact on task performance.

Eric Rossen, Ph.D., NCSP, is a nationally certified school psychologist with Prince George's County Public Schools in Maryland. Dr. Rossen also remains active teaching at the college level and through his clinical work in the private sector. His research interests include the assessment of emotional intelligence and its ability to predict important academic and mental health outcomes.

Elizabeth Ruff is a doctoral student in the combined doctoral program in counseling psychology and school psychology, Florida State University. She also received the M.S./Ed.S. degree in counseling and human systems at the same institution. She is currently a career counselor and an instructor of an undergraduate course in career development in the University Career Center. She is also involved in a behavioral health center at a local hospital and as a counselor in female corrections focusing on career development and anxiety reduction. Her research has focused on a creating a comprehensive database of research relating to RIASEC theory, and on increasing career information-seeking behavior through a model-reinforced video.

Christine E. Ryan, Ph.D., is an assistant professor in psychiatry at The Warren Alpert Medical School of Brown University and the director of family research at Brown University and Rhode Island Hospital. She is the senior author of a book on family therapy, *Evaluating and Treating Families: The McMaster Approach*. Her research interests include the relationship between patients with mood disorders and family members, particularly as it relates to the long-term course of illness, research methods and designs of longitudinal treatment trials, caregiver stress and coping with ill family members, and the effectiveness of disease management models for difficult to treat depressions and bipolar disorders.

Jon Sanford, M. Arch., is Director of the Center for Assistive Technology and Environmental Access and an Adjunct Associate Professor of Architecture at Georgia Tech where he co-directs the Rehabilitation Engineering Research Center (RERC) on Workplace Accommodations funded by the National Institute on Disability and Rehabilitation Research (NIDRR). He is also a Research Architect at the Rehab R & D Center at the Atlanta VA Medical Center. Mr. Sanford is one of the few architecturally-trained researchers engaged in research and development related to accessible and universally designed environments and was one of the authors of Universal Design Principles.

Diane L. Smith, Ph.D., OTR/L, is an assistant professor in the Department of Kinesiology and Community Health at the University of Illinois at Urbana–Champaign. She is also a practicing occupational therapist and has worked in clinical, management, consulting, and academic settings for more than 25 years. Dr. Smith's primary research interests are in disability policy with an emphasis on disparities for women with disabilities, including access to health care, employment, and domestic violence. In addition, she is an advocate for an inclusive environment and removal of physical and attitudinal barriers for persons with disabilities. Dr. Smith has published in leading disability and rehabilitation journals and presented at national and international conferences. She is currently on the editorial board for the *American Journal of Occupational Therapy* and the *Journal of Rehabilitation*.

Robert L. Smith, Ph.D., is professor and chair of the Counseling and Educational Psychology Department, and doctoral program coordinator at Texas A&M University–Corpus Christi. He is the author of several books and more than 60 professional articles. His research interests include the efficacy of treatment modalities in individual psychotherapy, family therapy, and substance abuse counseling. Dr. Smith is a diplomate fellow in psychopharmacology with the International College of Prescribing Psychologists.

Stephen Southern, Ed.D., is professor and chair in the Department of Psychology and Counseling at Mississippi College. Dr. Southern's work integrates the roles of clinician, supervisor, consultant, administrator, and educator. As a clinical consultant to several hospitals and residential treatment centers, Southern designed, implemented, and evaluated group treatment programs for individuals and families recovering from addiction. He is a member of the editorial board of the *Journal of Addictions & Offenders* and coeditor of *The Family Journal: Counseling and Therapy for Couples and Families*.

Mary E. Stafford, Ph.D., is a Nationally Certified School Psychologist and a licensed psychologist. She is an associate professor of school psychology at the University of Houston Clear Lake, where she teaches courses in assessment of and interventions for children with emotional and behavioral disorders and in biological bases of behavior. Dr. Stafford has served as the chair of the ethics committee for the International School Psychology Association (ISPA) for 6 years and is the current editor for the ISPA newsletter, the *World*Go*Round*. She has presented numerous workshops and symposia focused on ethical standards for school psychologists and counselors. Her research interests include resiliency and the effect of mobility on children's learning.

Patricia Stevens, Ph.D., is the director of the Women's Center for Lifelong Learning and the Reentry Student Center at Utah State University. She is a clinical member and approved supervisor with the American Association for Marriage and Family Therapy and a nationally certified counselor. Dr. Stevens is past president of the International Association of Marriage and Family Counselors and president-elect of the Association for Aging and Adult Development. She continues to have a small private practice and focuses on substance abuse issues with individuals and families.

Connie Tait, Ph.D., is professor and chair at Central Connecticut State University in the Department of Counseling and Family Therapy. Her responsibilities include coordinating the school counseling program, teaching master's level courses, and advising students. Dr. Tait has worked extensively with schools doing consulting, training, research, and coordination of programs. Her research interests are youth in at-risk environments and resiliency.

Timothy N. Tansey, Ph.D., CRC, CVE, is an assistant professor in the Department of Counseling, Educational Psychology, and Special Education at Michigan State University. Dr. Tansey received his doctorate in rehabilitation psychology from the University of Wisconsin–Madison. He is a licensed psychologist. Dr. Tansey has served on the board of the National Council on Rehabilitation Education. His research interests include functional assessment and rehabilitation of persons with psychiatric disabilities and the training of rehabilitation counselors

Suzanne Tew-Washburn, Ph.D., SPHR, CRC, is an assistant professor of counseling and psychology and the coordinator of the Rehabilitation Counseling Graduate Program at Troy University–Phenix City. Dr. Tew-Washburn has over 25 years experience in rehabilitation counseling and disability studies. Prior to joining Troy University's faculty in 2006, she was an educator at Auburn University for 14 years, as well as the director of rehabilitation services at a community rehabilitation agency in Georgia for 10 years. Her professional credentials include national certifications as a Senior Professional in Human Resources (SPHR) and as a Certified Rehabilitation Counselor (CRC). Dr. Tew-Washburn has authored and managed numerous local, state, and federal grants in excess of 6 million dollars, and is currently a peer grant reviewer for the U.S. Department of Education. In 2005, she was a recipient of the Rehabilitation Services Administration Commissioner's Award for Excellence in Education and Training.

Darlene Unger, Ph.D., is an associate professor of language, learning, and specialized instruction at DePaul University. She has worked in the special education and rehabilitation field since 1988 holding faculty appointments at Cornell University, Kent State University, and Virginia Commonwealth University. Her clinical and instructional experiences have focused on the education of youth with moderate and intensive disabilities and the delivery of transition-focused education. Dr. Unger has also coordinated federally-funded research and training projects related to improving transition service delivery and employment outcomes for youth with disabilities, supported employment, and the efficacy of business and rehabilitation partnerships in facilitating employment and job retention for individuals with disabilities. Her publications include book chapters and journal articles on employer experiences with people with disabilities, supported employment, and the use of technology for teaching and learning. She has presented at state, national, and international conferences and serves on the executive board of the Council for Exceptional Children's Division of Career Development and Transition. Dr. Unger earned her doctoral degree in Education from Virginia Commonwealth University.

CONTENTS

PART
I

Foundations of Assessment

1

Testing and Assessment
History, Current Context, and Prevailing Issues

ELIAS MPOFU
University of Sydney

THOMAS OAKLAND
University of Florida

JAMES T. HERBERT
Pennsylvania State University

PETER J. O'DONNELL
HealthSouth Nittany Valley Rehabilitation Hospital

OVERVIEW

A primary goal of rehabilitative service is either to improve or maintain functioning or, at the very least, decrease its rate of deterioration (Agency for Healthcare Research & Quality Health Resources and Services Administration, 2001). An assessment of an individual's functioning in multiple-functional life situations (e.g., in one's home, work, school, and other community settings) may be required to achieve this goal (World Health Organization [WHO], 1999, 2001). Rehabilitation and health assessment data are needed to address three broad issues: whether an individual is benefiting from care, whether the science and practice of rehabilitation and health care services are improving, and whether the conditions that lead to more effective and efficient services can be identified (Institute of Health Improvement, 2006; Morrison, 2000; Petaschnick, 2000a). These issues form the core of assessment in rehabilitation and health as presented in this book. This chapter provides an overview on rehabilitation assessments to support treatment effectiveness and efficiency that will also lead to improved professional services and reduced costs. It also presents the *International Classification of Functioning, Disability, and Health* (ICF) as a framework for understanding rehabilitation and health assessment. The influences of context, process, and technology on assessment priorities, methods, and outcomes are also considered.

LEARNING OBJECTIVES
By the end of the chapter, readers should be able to:

- Outline the history in the development of rehabilitation and health measures
- Explain the importance of multidisciplinary approaches to rehabilitation and health assessment
- Identify and describe at least five ways in which rehabilitation and health assessment can be understood
- Describe and explain the application of the ICF to guide rehabilitation assessment
- Evaluate the evidence for assessment in rehabilitation and health

INTRODUCTION

A BRIEF HISTORY OF TEST DEVELOPMENT

Professionals who use tests and other assessment methods benefit from a history that has established the foundation for current practice. The birth of assessment in the behavioral sciences occurred in China at least 3,000 years ago (Hoi & French, 2003). Measures of problem solving, visual/spatial perception, divergent thinking, creativity, and other qualities that reflect important talents and behaviors were used somewhat commonly. Later, under the Sui dynasty (581–618), a civil service examination system was initiated consisting of three parts: regular examinations stressing classical cultural knowledge, a committee examination before the emperor stressing planning and administrative features, and a third examination on martial arts. Forms of this assessment system continued in China until the 20th century.

Modern test methods had their birth in the late 19th century in Western Europe. Wilhelm Wundt (1832–1920), after receiving his medical degree, established the first psychological laboratory in Leipzig, Germany, to study reaction time and other psychophysical qualities. He and his students pioneered in the development of various tests. Frances Galton (1822–1911), a biologist in England, developed a number of measures to examine individual differences and was the first to use a questionnaire to acquire data. Tests developed by Alfred Binet (1857–1911) and colleagues in Paris had a different goal—to classify children in need of special education services. These test development activities and those of others laid the foundation for the emergence of test use by rehabilitation specialists and others, especially following World War II.

Seventeen million service men and women served in World War II. Many returned with medical, physical, and psychological problems that required professional attention, including services provided by the Veterans Administration hospitals. The need for professionals trained to provide rehabilitation services, including the use of tests to diagnose and assist in treatment planning, became apparent. The federal government began funding professional preparation programs to provide needed personnel. Once prepared, these professionals recognized the need to use a wide range of tests and other assessment methods to assist their work. Testing companies recognized their market-place potential and began developing and marketing tests used by professionals providing counseling, occupational and physical therapy, physical medicine, speech and language therapy, and other services. Researchers and practitioners in medical, rehabilitation, and university settings also developed various assessment methods and trained others in their use. Current assessment resources for rehabilitation specialists in the United States exceed those available in other countries.

The success of these early efforts to develop and use tests provided confidence in our ability to measure important qualities in a reliable and valid fashion. Traditional uses of tests—to facilitate research, diagnose disorders, and assist in treatment planning—remain important. Over the years, other purposes have been added: to describe current characteristics and attainment, screen for special needs, assist in guidance and counseling, place persons in special programs, and evaluate progress. Tests also are used for various administrative and planning purposes as well as to credential and license professionals. Thus, those engaged in providing rehabilitation services are likely to find various uses for tests and will benefit from having a wide range of tests to assist them in their work.

HISTORY AND CURRENT STATUS OF ASSESSMENTS IN REHABILITATION AND HEALTH

A majority of measures currently used in rehabilitation were developed for specific patient populations, and their development matured within practice settings for those populations. Signature developments in medical rehabilitation and allied areas with regard to the assessment of disability, functioning, and health status are featured in the following discussion.

Measures of Physical Functioning and Performance

Historically, effectiveness in medical rehabilitation has been measured in terms of restoration of functional abilities, leading to independence in self-care, sphincter control, mobility, locomotion, and communication (Granger,

Albrecht, & Hamilton, 1979; McDowell, 2006). (See also chapter 23 this volume.) The *Barthtel Index, Functional Independence Measure* (FIM), *Functional Assessment Measure* (FAM), *Functional Assessment Inventory* (FAI), *Functional Status Index* (FSI), and the *Patient Evaluation Conference System* (PECS) are among the most commonly used rehabilitation outcome measures by medical and allied rehabilitation facilities for patient intake, treatment planning, and discharge. For example, the FIM and FAM were developed primarily for use with patients with traumatic brain injury (Uniform Data System for Medical Rehabilitation, 2004). The development of the FIM constituted a major success story in physical rehabilitation care (Uniform Data System for Medical Rehabilitation, 2004). The 18-item FIM is highly accepted by medical rehabilitation practitioners and is used by over 60% of medical rehabilitation facilities in the United States. (Hobart et al., 2001).

The development of the 30-item FAM, a combination of the original 18 items on the FIM and 12 additional items, occurred because cognitive, behavioral, and community functioning were seen as contributing significantly to a person's adjustment to acquired disability. Results from various studies indicate that the FIM provides a useful measure of functional performance, particularly for persons with traumatic brain injury (Corrigan, Granger, & Smith, 2000; Hamilton, Granger, Sherwin, Zielezny, & Tashman, 1987) and stroke (Smith, Bennett, Illig, Fiedler, Hamilton, & Ottenbacher, 2000). These functional assessment instruments also have been used routinely with patients with diverse disabling conditions, including those with multiple sclerosis, amputation, and spinal cord injury.

Measures of physical and functional performance are more successful in predicting functional abilities for discharge or outpatient care (Hobart et al., 2001) and less successful in identifying the patient's needs for community reintegration (Gurka et al., 1999; Liang, Fossel, & Larson, 1990; Simmons, Crepeau, & White, 2000). For example, a study by Liang et al. (1990) observed weak and inconsistent correlations between *FSI* ratings and patient psychological well-being at discharge. Liang and others concluded that the *FSI* and similar instruments were of limited value because they merely measure physician–technical success rather than the patient's ability to cope with a handicap and the quality of his or her life following a disability. Both the FIM and FAM have low ceiling effects (maximum performance is reached by a disproportionate number of patients) (Bajo, Hazan, Fleminger, & Taylor, 1999).

Instruments used in medical rehabilitation often are used to predict functional independence at discharge rather than for their intended purpose to evaluate social or global functioning (e.g., Dittmar, 1997; Finch, Brooks, Statford, & Mayo, 2002; Simmons et al., 2000). The use of measures to predict physical functional independence in medical rehabilitation is merited by the fact that social and global functioning builds on a successful physical rehabilitation regimen (Hobart et al., 2001). Furthermore, current trends toward drastic reductions in medical costs warrant the need for data from clinical and social rehabilitation outcome measures to help optimize treatment resource allocation (Fisher, 1997; Galynker et al., 1997). However, prioritizing patient technical competence in physical functioning may encourage practitioners in medical rehabilitation to be overly optimistic about patient outcomes because this information may give patients as well as significant others false hopes about life after discharge or postacute care.

DISCUSSION BOX 1.1

A high school-aged male who resides with his four younger siblings, visually impaired homemaker mother, and middle-aged father, was involved in a motor vehicle accident. The young man was working at a convenience store after school to assist his family after the factory that his father worked at for many years closed. The accident resulted in a spinal cord injury and paraparesis. He had a positive outlook during his treatment and now has become depressed as he faces the barriers in his environment. His town is small and no public transportation is available. His father has a back injury and is limited in how much physical assistance he can provide.

Questions

1. Discuss the potential environmental, vocational, and systemic issues that influence this young man's treatment and future.
2. Discuss the long-term treatment issues that may have been overlooked if only the immediate rehabilitation needs are considered.

Many functional assessment measures have been developed within the past 30 years for specific disability populations, including Alzheimer's disease (Oswald & Gunzelmann, 1992), arthritis (Jacobs, 1993; Meenan, 1986), psychiatric disability (Anthony & Farkas, 1982), brain injury (Hall, Hamilton, Gordon, & Zasler, 1993; Lezak, 1987; Livingston & Livingston, 1985), knee pathology (Irrgang, Snyder-Mackler, Wainner, Fu, & Harner, 1998), learning disabilities (McCue, 1989), multiple sclerosis (Granger, Cotter, Hamilton, Fiedler, & Hens, 1990), pediatric mental health (Hodges, Wong, & Latessa, 1998), stroke (Lai, Duncan, & Keighley, 1998), and visual impairment (Graves, 1990). The use of rehabilitation outcome measures with patient populations other than those on which they were calibrated may yield misleading results in the absence of supporting evidence for their general applicability (Hobart et al., 2001; Linn et al., 1999; Gurka et al., 1999). The development of objective measures of functional performance that can be used with many disability categories (e.g., spinal cord injury, amputations) and settings (e.g., acute care, homes, work places) constitutes a major challenge.

Functional assessment measures may be unreliable even when used with the same general disability population (Linn et al., 1999). This is due, in part, to measures that were not co-normed or codeveloped, thus limiting their generalized use across disability groups. Further, as applied to physical or motor functioning measures, reliability estimates are higher for these aspects than for psychosocial functioning or functioning in nonclinical settings (Gurka et al., 1999). The cut score (i.e., one that differentiates those who do and do not display success) for many of the existing measures of physical and functional performance is unknown (Bajo et al., 1999; Samsa et al., 1999). Empirically determined cut scores, differentiating wellness from unwellness, are important for monitoring client rehabilitation progress or response to rehabilitation therapies. Thus, a need exists for "future research to include outcome measures that map intraindividual change from premorbid status to current levels of functioning, rather than utilizing measures with fixed outcomes" (Gurka et al.,1999, p. 255). Little progress appears to have been made in the last decade in developing measures of rehabilitation outcome sensitive to patient's social or global functioning.

Measures of Global and Domain Specific Functioning

Rehabilitation professionals and consumers also need measures of functioning that reduce the burden of care and application by using a brief yet valid measure that supports individualized customer care. There is growing evidence that global measures of rehabilitation outcome may address this need better than disability-specific scales. Nevertheless, disability-specific scales remain relevant for some clinical purposes (Kelley-Hayes, 2000). For example, a sickness-impact scale could be a good screening instrument of general functioning, yet its clinical utility for intervention with specific patient populations may be limited. Scales designed for specific disability conditions may be more useful when used to inform clinical interventions.

Global Measures and Multiple Comparisons

As previously noted, most functional assessment measures are based on norms from one client group or particular setting and lack evidence for use with other client groups or conditions. Efforts to develop global measures that could be used across disability groups, settings, and situations are increasing in order to circumvent that limitation to clinical practice (Harvey et al., 1992; Fisher, 1997). The use of a global measure has clear advantage in helping rehabilitation clinicians to provide more systematic and comprehensive care. Regardless of their academic discipline, nurses, occupational and physical therapists, physicians, psychologists, recreational therapists, rehabilitation counselors, speech–language pathologists, and social workers could use the same criteria when evaluating individual client strengths and areas needing improvement. A valid measure with content that reflects commonly agreed-upon standards would allow practitioners to monitor performance in a uniform manner when assessing treatment effectiveness and efficiency (e.g., the relationship between a program's benefits and associated costs to the patient). A global assessment could provide a mechanism for compiling a database that meets information needs of administrators and clinicians (Granger, Hamilton, Keith, Zielezny, & Sherwin, 1986).

However, the use of multiple criteria included in global assessments may dilute the various criteria and thus introduce a lack of clarity. For example, global measures of health functioning may undersample aspects of health pertinent to specific conditions, resulting in the loss of important information to inform specific interventions (Kane, 1999). For example, a global assessment measure may be less sensitive to changes in health status than are measures that assess this condition specifically. A basic rule of rehabilitation outcomes measurement holds that, the more global the outcome measured, the more distant it is from the specific effects of the immediate treatment and more sensitive to effects from other intervening forces.

Instruments that assess multiple aspects of a person's life have been developed only within the last decade. An example of this development is the FAM (e.g. Alcott, Dixon, & Swann, 1997; Gurka et al., 1999; Hawley, Taylor, Hellawell, & Pentland, 1999; Hobart et al., 2001; Tesio & Cantagallo, 1998; Turner-Stokes et al., 1999; see also chapter 23 this volume). Within vocational rehabilitation, the FAI (Crewe & Athelstan, 1981) is one of the few functional assessment instruments to examine several domains related to employment outcomes. A growing body of literature in medical rehabilitation has examined community integration, return to work, and improvements in physical functioning. However, few global assessments focus on functional skills needed to obtain and sustain employment.

Measures of Community and Independent Living

People with chronic illness or disability consider participation in ordinary community activities (e.g., work and independent living) important to their well-being. Most rehabilitation outcome measures are relatively reliable when predicting a patient's physical function for discharge or outpatient care (Hobart et al., 2001) and are less reliable when predicting a patient's engagement in instrumental activities associated with independent daily living (Crewe & Dijkers, 1995; DeJong, 1981; Granger et al., 1990; Gurka et al., 1999; Korner-Bitensky, Mayo, & Poznanski, 1990; Liang et al., 1990; Simmons, Crepeau, & White, 2000). In contrast to service providers, consumers are more likely to be interested in their real-world functional status (Kane, Rockwood, Finch, & Philip, 1997).

Various measures for social, community, and independent living are available (see also chapters 24 and 29 this volume). For example, the *Community Integration Questionnaire* (Willer, 1994), *Craig Handicap Assessment and Reporting Technique (CHART)* (Whiteneck, Charlifue, Gerhart, Overholser, & Richardson, 1992), and the *Instrumental Activities of Daily Living* (Lawton, 1988) are three instruments used by service providers to measure community integration (Dittmar, 1997; Lawton, 1988; Willer, 1994). Measures of independent living that are sensitive to daily settings have been developed during the past two decades (Boschen & Gargano, 1996; see also chapter 24 this volume).

There are relatively few measures of vocational or employment outcomes (see also chapters 19 and 20 this volume). This is puzzling, given the 80-year history of interest among vocational rehabilitation specialists in patient vocational and employment issues. Earlier examples of vocationally oriented measures include the *Human Service Systems Scale* (Reagles & Butler, 1976), *Rehabilitation Service Satisfaction Questionnaire* (Muthard & Miller, 1968), *Rehabilitation Services Satisfaction Survey* (Tenth Institute on Rehabilitation Services, 1972), and *Measure of Employment Satisfaction* (Weiss, 1985). However, since their initial development, little on-going research has supported their use in vocational rehabilitation.

The study of vocationally oriented scales has been neglected, in part, because state and federal agencies use one criterion to assess successful vocational rehabilitation: whether a person obtains gainful employment for a period of at least 90 days. Although easy to evaluate, this criterion is insufficient in determining effectiveness of service delivery. For example, the use of this criterion overlooks nonjob placement outcomes (Backer, 1980).

The continued reliance on using employment as the outcome benchmark is problematic for various reasons, in-

---

DISCUSSION BOX 1.2

An elderly adult lived alone and had no relatives or support network. The individual had fallen and fractured her hip. She was taken to the hospital where orthopedic surgery was performed. She became delirious and confused, and she hallucinated. She also was deconditioned, weak, and unable to care for herself. She was transferred to a rehabilitation hospital. Her delirium after her surgery began to resolve, but underlying possible memory and abstract reasoning problems and possible dementia became more apparent to staff.

Questions

1. How much physical care, monitoring, and assistance might the patient need?
2. Consider her ability to live independently. How would that determination be made?
3. What other information and data would be helpful to determine her rehabilitation outcomes?

cluding: (a) the tendency to emphasize numbers of persons who achieve employment rather than examining the quality of employment achieved (e.g., salary level, employee benefits, employment satisfaction); (b) the inability to recognize clients who achieve meaningful improvements in their lives without obtaining employment; (c) limited feedback with respect to evaluating quality-of-life outcomes as opposed to simply obtaining employment; and (d) little attention devoted to nonemployment-related variables that nevertheless impact on achieving employment outcomes (e.g., activities of daily living, family support, reliable transportation, psychosocial adjustment, and financial disincentives for working). Although the public vocational rehabilitation service delivery system will continue to change, outcome measurement technology will not evolve as long as rehabilitation outcomes use the single criterion as its definition of success.

A more complete picture of vocational rehabilitation service delivery effectiveness would consider several outcomes, including income level, hours worked, employment benefits, opportunities for advancement, employee/employer satisfaction, physical and psychosocial improvements, enhancement of activities of daily living, capacity for change, and satisfaction with services provided. The First Institute on Rehabilitation Issues (Bassett, 1974) outlined several dimensions to be included as part of vocational outcome indicators. These were: (a) economic independence (e.g., a person can support himself financially without reliance on public support and social services); (b) physical functioning (e.g., reduction of symptoms, increased physical performance and endurance); (c) psychosocial functioning (e.g., client feelings related to personal adequacy and security, functioning ability, emotional stability, and social interaction); and (d) vocational functioning and potential (e.g., client develops realistic appraisal of vocational self and demonstrates skills necessary to achieve vocational objectives).

A BASIC DIAGNOSTIC–INTERVENTION MODEL AND FIVE INTERNATIONAL SOURCES USED TO DEFINE DISABILITIES AND DISORDERS

Professionals engaged in providing rehabilitation services often rely on assessment data to implement a four-pronged diagnostic–intervention model. Information is acquired to understand salient features of a patient's (1) history, including his or her family history, as well as (2) current conditions and qualities. This information is used (3) to establish interventions and (4) to make judgments as to probable outcomes (i.e., prognosis).

This diagnostic–intervention model may be applicable to three authoritative, comprehensive, and widely used diagnostic systems (Oakland, Mpofu, Gregoire, & Faulkner, 2007): the *Diagnostic and Statistical Manual of Mental Disorders*, 4th edition, text revision (DSM-IV-TR) (American Psychiatric Association [APA], 2000); its international edition (American Psychiatric Association, 1995); and the *International Classification of Diseases and Related Health Problems*, 10th edition (ICD-10; World Health Organization, 1992a). The disorders identified by the ICD-10 generally are consistent with those cited in and are cross-referenced to the DSM's international version (APA, 1995).

In addition, the *International Statistical Classification of Disease and Related Health Problems* (ICIDH-2; World Health Organization, 1992b) and its revision, the *International Classification of Functioning, Disability and Health* (ICF; World Health Organization, 1999) promote the use of a unified and standard language framework to describe human functioning and disability components of health, including physical and mental health.

INTERNATIONAL CLASSIFICATION OF FUNCTIONING, DISABILITY, AND HEALTH (ICF)

The ICF provides an interdisciplinary classification system of three health-related components that impact functioning: body functions and structures, activities and participation, and contextual factors. These three components often are assessed in rehabilitation and health interventions and are discussed in many chapters in this book.

The ICF' emphasizies the importance of understanding a patient's health in light of the dynamic interaction among three broad components. Each influences the others. The term *functioning* generally is used to refer to all body functions, activities, and participation. See Table 1.1.

The term *body functions* refers to a person's physiological and psychological functions (e.g., sensory, neuromusculoskeletal, and mental functions). The term *body structure* refers to a person's anatomical parts (e.g., nervous, cardiovascular, and metabolic systems). Traditional health services focus on these qualities.

The term *activities* refers to tasks a patient is able to perform. Examples for adults include driving, banking, and cooking. The term *participation* refers to activities that become integrated into one's life. Examples for adults include going to work, visiting with family and friends, and refraining from embarrassing others. Activities and participation include the following nine

TABLE 1.1 Overview of the ICF

Two Parts: (A dynamic interaction)	Part 1: Functioning and Disability		Part 2: Contextual Factors	
Each Part Has Two Components:	**Body Functions and Structures**	**Activities and Participation**	**Environmental Factors**	**Personal Factors**
Domains (Contain the categories or units of classification of the ICF)	1. Body functions (including psychological functioning) 2. Body structures	Life areas (tasks, actions)	External influences on functioning and disability	Internal influences on functioning and disability
Constructs (Defined through use of qualifiers that modify the extent or magnitude of function or disability)	Change in body function (physiological) Change in body structure (anatomical)	Capacity: Executing tasks in a standard environment ("can do") Performance: Executing tasks in the current environment ("does do")	Facilitating or hindering impact of features of the physical, social, and attitudinal world	Impact of attributes of the person
Positive aspect	**Functioning** Functional and structural integrity Activities Participation		Facilitators	*Not classified in the ICF*
Negative aspect	**Disability** Impairment Activity limitation Participation restriction		Barriers/hindrances	

Note: Units of classification are situations, not people
(Adapted from WHO, 2001, p. 11).

domains (i.e., practical and meaningful sets of related physiological functions, anatomical structures, actions, tasks, or areas of life): learning and applying knowledge; general tasks and demands; communication; mobility; self-care; domestic life; interpersonal interactions and relationships; major life areas; and community, social, and civic life.

A *skill deficit* occurs when a person does not display a needed behavior. In contrast, a *performance deficit* occurs when a person has been and remains able to display a needed skill yet does not use it when needed. For example, a young adult who does not have the ability to dress him- or herself displays a skill deficit. In contrast, a young adult who has displayed the ability to dress him- or herself and does not do so regularly is described as having a performance deficit. Rehabilitation specialists work to promote the initial development of needed skills to help overcome skill deficits and work to promote the utilization

of needed skills to help overcome performance deficits. An understanding of a patient's activities and performance requires knowledge of body functions and structures as well as contextual factors that may be affecting them.

Contextual factors include both environmental and personal qualities. Environmental qualities include external influences that facilitate or hinder a person's physical, social, and attitudinal qualities, including the individual's home, workplace, school, and community (Institute of Health Improvement, 2006). Personal qualities include age, gender, race, and social class. They, too, may impact a person's attributes.

Applications of the ICF Model

The ICF classification system offers a template for professionals across disciplines and countries to assess patient functioning and to measure rehabilitation outcomes.

The system provides a framework for viewing behaviors from three broad and interactive components: body functions and structures, activities and participation, and contextual factors. A patient may display strengths and weaknesses in one, two, or all three components.

Thus, rehabilitation and health care services are enhanced by assessing body functions and structures, activities and participation, and contextual factors. Medical rehabilitation services traditionally have emphasized the assessment of body functions and structures. These remain important. The ICF model also emphasizes the importance of assessing a person's activities and participation as well as his or her environments in which health care may be provided. Knowledge of environmental qualities that may facilitate or impede functioning is important to intervention planning and evaluation.

Implementation of the ICF model requires more than knowledge of salient conditions in the three broad components of body functions and structures, activities and participation, and contextual factors. The model also requires an understanding of their *interactions*. Thus, assessing the reciprocal nature of these domains is critical to intervention planning and outcome evaluation within the ICF model.

Implementation of this model also requires the potential services of assessment specialists who represent a broad range of service providers, including nurses, occupational and physical therapists, physicians, psychologists, recreational therapists, rehabilitation counselors, speech–language pathologists, and social workers. Their work must result in understanding salient qualities in each of the three domains *as well as their interactions*. This last feature, their *interactions,* constitutes a serious challenge when implementing the ICF model. As noted in this chapter and others, few if any measures assess interactions among the three domains. Thus, the efforts of seasoned professionals skilled in working cooperatively with others are critical to the success of the ICF model. The ICF does not emphasize pathology or lead to a diagnosis. However, the ICF can be used as a companion to the World Health Organization's *International Statistical Classification of Diseases and Related Health Problems*, 10th edition (ICD-10; WHO, 1992a) when diagnosing disorders.

The ICD-10 provides a system for classifying and diagnosing health conditions, including diseases, disorders, and injuries based on etiology. In contrast, the ICF emphasizes a client's full and accurate description, not diagnosis, based on medical and social models of disability through biological, individual, and social perspectives of health. When a diagnosis is needed to obtain benefits, the ICD-10 may be used to classify a client's disability. The combined use of the ICF and ICD-10 provides for more comprehensive descriptions and is useful for program planning and intervention services. Efforts to enhance the use of the ICF model across health conditions and settings are ongoing. Many chapters in this volume reference the ICF framework and how it applies to assessment procedures for specific conditions.

FOUNDATIONAL INFORMATION ABOUT REHABILITATION ASSESSMENT

The National Institute on Disability and Rehabilitation Research (NIDRR) envisioned a broad view of rehabilitation assessments that includes "measures of medical rehabilitation effectiveness, long-term outcomes, consumer satisfaction with assistive technology, and assessments of community integration, independence, and the quality of life" (Seelman, 2000, p. 1). Traditional rehabilitation assessment practices tend to reflect and are specific to the major rehabilitation service provider specializations (e.g., health and medical care, community use and integration, vocational preparation) or types of disabilities commonly served (e.g., orthopedic, traumatic brain injury, spinal cord injury, stroke). Assessment developed within provider specializations at times is somewhat narrow and thus overlooks broader performance outcomes, including functional behaviors displayed in various settings and situations. Multidisciplinary approaches have been used to help overcome this industry segmentation.

Professionals who provide rehabilitation services, including assessment services, often consider the following questions: What are the assessment goals? What components of health should be measured? What is a realistic assessment process? From whom, how frequently, and where should data be acquired? What personal demographic and professional qualities influence outcomes? Intertwined in these questions are two main goals: to provide effective intervention services and to evaluate the patient following the receipt of the services (i.e., service outcomes). Some of these and other questions are daunting. Answers to them can have an important professional and fiscal impact.

Basic Terminology in Rehabilitation and Health Assessment

Personnel engaged in rehabilitation and health care can be expected to know commonly used terminology (Jennings & Staggers, 1999). For example, *rehabilitation outcome* has been defined as results associated with the treatment process (e.g., Slavin, 2001). Thus, rehabilitation outcomes refer to changes that result from services provided.

Data from outcome measures are used typically to examine one of three issues: the status of service recipients at various points during service delivery; studies designed to describe and compare outcome differences among groups that vary due to one or more variables (e.g., the nature and duration of the intervention, differences due to severity of the presenting problems, age, or gender); or variables that predict successful outcomes (Brown, Gordon, & Diller, 1983; Granger, Black, & Braun, 2006).

Program Aspects and Process Variables

This section considers key practices and influences in rehabilitation assessment for diagnosis, intervention, and evaluation: administrative and clinical aspects. Clinical assessment procedures occur within a care environment with administration systems that influence the quality of assessment and how the results of assessment will be used.

COLLECT ADMINISTRATIVE DATA   Administrative data are collected routinely, including a patient's demographic characteristics, service costs and payment, length of stay, number and duration of treatment sessions, services provided and by whom, other resources used, level of independence achieved at the conclusion of rehabilitation, and recidivism (Robertson & Pas Colborn, 1997). Most of these data are used to help understand the quality and effectiveness of a rehabilitation or health program, to obtain reimbursement, and to help protect an agency from law suits (see also chapter 2 this volume). The importance of documenting each stage of service should not be overlooked.

COLLECT PROCESS DATA   The effectiveness of outcomes may be evaluated by measuring process variables, including the initial severity of the disorder, the patient's initial and later physical responsiveness to interventions, as well as patient changes that document their self-views, expectations, values, and hopes—qualities known to influence the level of involvement in and thus the effectiveness of therapeutic interventions. The changes are recorded by noting patient actions and behaviors, including verbal and nonverbal expressions. Consideration of administrative, fiscal, and clinical indicators of performance also must be included in rehabilitation outcome assessment (Watts & Clement, 2000; see also chapter 12 this volume).

INFLUENCES OF STRUCTURE AND PROCESS ON ASSESSMENT   The term *structure* refers to individuals who provide rehabilitation services, resources used, and settings in which services occur (Dobrzykowski, 1997; Donabedian, 1980). Structural measures may include physical or organizational aspects of the rehabilitation setting (e.g., profit/nonprofit status, type of accreditation, geographic location, and/or staff organization aspects, staff/patient ratio, staff competence reviews; Watts & Clement, 2000).

The selection of outcome measures used by rehabilitation service providers is influenced by health care system policies and practices (Fuhrer, 1995). For example, changes in capitation systems used by health maintenance organizations impact current assessment services. Specifically, services for which a capitation system pays are more widely used, often resulting in the unique needs of patients with a nonreimbursable condition being overlooked. Assessment procedures that are reimbursed are prescribed by a health maintenance organization, with priority often given to those

---

DISCUSSION BOX 1.3

A young adult female involved in a motor vehicle accident sustains a brain injury. She sustains injuries to her frontal cortex as well as other areas and evidences memory impairments. The patient is able to ambulate and perform activities of daily living (ADLs) with monitoring, yet she is unable to make safe decisions, is impulsive, is unable to assess and perform financial tasks, is easily distractible, overwhelmed in situations that are overstimulating, and lacks insight and awareness into her

deficits. The current prevailing medical and payment model indicates she does not require rehabilitation because she can ambulate and perform ADLs, yet clearly she cannot function independently.

Questions

1. How might financial issues affect this patient?
2. How might her needs be assessed more effectively?

DISCUSSION BOX 1.4

John Blanco, a 7-year old African American child, had a high fever with a widespread rash during the late evening hours of an otherwise exciting Halloween evening. The Blancos, his biological parents, rushed him to an emergency hospital facility at a small Northeastern town. An early-to-middle career Caucasian physician assistant interviewed and examined John and his parents, who reported that John had been well during the day but presented symptoms late that night. They were concerned about the sudden onset and severity of the symptoms. Medical care included a brain scan, ostensibly to rule out any cerebral impact from the fever. The scan was outsourced to a radiological center in India for interpretation while the Blancos waited and John was under observation with bed rest. Two hours later, the brain scan report revealed no abnormalities. John was subsequently discharged by the physician on call and prescribed across the counter medications for skin irritation, pain, and fever relief.

A couple of weeks later, the Blancos received a bill of about $300 for the visit from their Health Maintenance Organization (HMO). The HMO explained the bill as necessary for an unwarranted visit to an emergency facility for a non-life-threatening condition. Furthermore, the HMO noted an observation by the treating hospital staff that the Blancos did not seem distressed by John's condition during the visit. The Blancos, after calling the HMO and being appraised of a lengthy appeal procedure, preferred to pay the bill to avoid extended wrangling with the HMO or its representatives.

Questions

1. Identify health outcome issues for the emergency treatment center, the HMO, and John and his family.
2. What is your view about impressionistic personal disposition evaluations by emergency hospital staff about the perceived lack of distress in the Blancos as the basis for denying a claim for medical services received?

for which there is research evidence. Ideally, assessment procedures that have evidence for their use and protect patients or consumers from poor quality of care are preferred. The U.S. Consumer Bill of Rights (1998) mandates that consumers of health services be empowered to participate in key decisions regarding their treatment. In this regard, rehabilitation customers (i.e., patients, people with disabilities, significant others) need greater direct access to information on and skills in using measures to monitor and evaluate functional health status.

The term *process* refers to activities that occur between rehabilitation practitioners and their clients/patients that influence clinical outcomes (Donabedian, 1980; Institute of Health Improvement, 2006). The influence of process variables on rehabilitation outcomes is founded on the belief that the quality of outcomes is directly attributable to the quality of care: Better care yields better outcomes. The measurement of process variables may include volume, frequency, and validation of diagnostic tests; services provided; timeliness of services; community resources; and staff turnover (Watts & Clement, 2000).

DISCUSSION BOX 1.5

You are working as a hospital administrator for an inpatient rehabilitation hospital unit that serves persons with acquired disabilities (e.g., amputation, spinal cord injury [SCI], stroke, and traumatic brain injury [TBI]). Your professional team wants to develop an outcome measure that will assess how well services that the unit provides impacts on improving patient quality of life. The hospital unit is comprised of nine areas that include occupational, physical and speech therapy, dietary, nursing, psychological, spiritual counseling, social services, and vocational rehabilitation. Address

the following questions as they relate to developing an outcome measure.

Questions

1. Develop at least one test item that you believe addresses a measurable aspect within each of the nine services provided. Share the nine items with your classmates for their reactions.
2. What types of criteria and measurement formats were used to assess these nine items?

Process measures provide the most direct indication of quality of care because their established use provides evidence of good patient care. As noted, the term *outcome* has been defined as results associated with the treatment process (e.g., Slavin, 2001). Thus, rehabilitation outcomes refer to changes that result from services provided.

The availability of measures that effectively assess the interaction between patients and their environments is limited due, in part, to the complexity of finding agreement on relevant outcomes and defining outcome terminology; to a lack of understanding the interrelationships among structure, process, and outcome variables; and to limited theoretical models that produce outcome measures. The National Institute on Disability and Rehabilitation Research believes these combined problems represent major challenges to the development of rehabilitation outcome measures (Seelman, 2000). Both the National Institute on Disability and Rehabilitation Research and the WHO advocate a broad view of outcomes, one that reflects all aspects of an individual's maximum participation within the community. Many of the outcomes important to clients participating in rehabilitation services are considered in this book.

EVIDENTIAL BASIS OF ASSESSMENT IN REHABILITATION AND HEALTH

MEASURE DEVELOPMENT HAS TENDED TO BE GUIDED BY PRACTICAL NEEDS RATHER THAN THEORY
Most assessment methods used in rehabilitation were developed as an outgrowth of practical clinical issues and thus lack a theoretical framework. The practice is still prevalent for practitioners to develop measures for specific purposes to assist in the provision of quality health care (Frytak, 2000) and assess treatment effectiveness (Haley & Jatte, 2000; McDowell, 2006). Except for some measures (e.g., those for physical and functional performance; see also chapter 23), assessments in rehabilitation and health largely have been developed singly and not codeveloped with complementary measures, thus limiting the building of a cumulative body of measurement data such as that obtained from the use of omnibus measures. Instead, specific structural (organizational/contextual) and process (clinical) issues have driven the development of assessment instruments.

For example, rehabilitation outcome assessment has focused on the need to document cost-effective treatment (Roper & Hackbarth, 1988); effectiveness of clinical treatments across health care organizations (Osborn, 1998); improvement in accountability in medical care (Kane, 1999); assessment of staff performance (Petaschnick, 2000a);

reimbursement for service (Cook & Kaplan, 1998); professional accountability (Jennings & Staggers, 1999); professional accreditation (Wilkerson, 2000); increase customer service, establish in-house benchmarking, and maintain managed care contracts, federal funding grants, and develop research initiatives (Petaschnick, 2000b).

This diversity of purposes for conducting outcome assessment has lead to fragmentation of assessments across rehabilitation settings, resulting in variations in item definitions, scale content, and coverage (Haley & Langmuir, 2000; Granger et al., 2006; Mpofu & Oakland, 2006). As noted previously, content domains that address rehabilitation-oriented movement and self-care activities are assessed somewhat extensively in many outcome measures. In contrast, health-oriented domains (e.g, learning and applying knowledge, communicating, providing domestic and interpersonal activities, and performing major life activities) have limited content coverage (Haley & Langmuir, 2000).

MEASURES UNDERSAMPLE ACTIVITY AND PARTICIPATION
Test content of most outcome measures tends to address a deficiency or disability, not participation or competence (Haley & Jatte, 2000; WHO, 2001). Some rehabilitation and health professionals select scales on somewhat narrow criteria (e.g, psychometric qualities, reputation, comprehensive coverage, and wide use by other rehabilitation professionals) (e.g., Deathe, Miller, & Speechley, 2002; Turner-Stokes & Turner-Stokes, 1997), not on their theoretical foundation or evidential support.

Research typically has focused more on medical rehabilitation and less on other important health-related aspects, including quality of life, patient satisfaction, and environmental factors. Some suggest that rehabilitation outcome research should examine the impact of clinical interventions and other intervening variables on specified rehabilitation outcomes as well as quality of life issues (see also chapters 27 and 29 in this volume). Quality of life should include biological and physiological variables (e.g., impairment, pain, organ system functioning); symptom status (e.g., patient perception of abnormal physical, emotional, cognitive status); functional status (i.e., person's ability to perform specific tasks); general health perceptions; and overall quality of life (degree of happiness/satisfaction with life) (Watts & Clement, 2000).

The construct of quality of life, while generating growing interest as an outcome measure, has been difficult to define conceptually and empirically (Felce & Perry, 1995; Djikers, 2003; Ware, 2003; see also chapter 27 this volume). Additionally, the measurement of satisfaction

RESEARCH BOX 1.1

Objective: Heinemann, Bode, Cichowski, and Kan (1998) investigated the reliability of patient satisfaction with medical rehabilitation settings.

Method: They compared patients' self-reported satisfaction with that reported by friends, family, and caregivers.

Results: Patients had significantly lower self-ratings of satisfaction compared to those by caregivers. Patients' self-ratings of satisfaction were closer to those of friends rather than family members and other caregivers.

Conclusion: Patients are the best informants on their satisfaction with rehabilitation care.

Questions

1. Explain what might account for the differences in satisfaction measures between patients, caregivers, or family members.
2. What criteria would you use in developing a satisfaction measure for patients? How might these criteria be different (or not) from those used by caregivers?

among patients following their receipt of services has been difficult due to poor conceptual and operational definitions, variations in measurement across health care organizations, poor psychometric properties of existing instruments, and data collection difficulties such as sampling and response rates (Olejnik, McKinley, Ellis, Buchanan, Kersey, & Clark, 1998; see also chapter 30 this volume). Although questionnaires are used as the major method to collect data, there is no universally accepted method of collecting customer satisfaction information (Boschen, 1996; McKinley et al., 1999; Niles, 1996). Despite problems with the construct of consumer satisfaction, it remains the most important indicator of quality among managed care organizations and hospitals. Moreover, consumer satisfaction should be evaluated within the various environments within which each person lives.

MEASURES CONSTRUCTED USING ITEM RESPONSE THEORY HAVE HIGH UTILITY Rehabilitation and health measures constructed using item response theory (IRT) often are superior in their efficiency of measurement compared to those developed using contrasting models of test development. IRT has a long history within educational measurement. However, its application in the health-care industry is relatively recent (Cella & Chang, 2000). IRT provides a method to determine the importance of a test item by knowing its contribution to estimating a person's ability on an underlying construct (Andrich, 1988; Rasch, 1980). Using IRT, a test item's difficulty and a person's ability are placed on a common scale (or metric) using log-odd units or logits. By placing them on a common scale, we are able to make reasonable comparisons across disability categories, settings, and situations. Therefore, logits allow test developers to consider each person's ability when responding to an individual item. Only items within a person's ability range are administered.

IRT based methods allow rehabilitation practitioners and researchers to: (a) evaluate people across a broad band of health conditions and cultural backgrounds, (b) yield useful individual patient level rather than group level data, (c) generate instruments with the appropriate number of items that provide relevant clinical data without overly taxing the test administrator or test taker, (d) develop several alternate and equivalent short forms to protect item integrity, (e) reliably measure differentiating abilities on a latent (underlying) construct, and (f) administer and score measures using computer testing specifically adapted to individual test taker needs (Hays, Morales, & Reise, 2000; Mpofu & Oakland, 2006). These qualities are possible with rehabilitation outcome measures developed using IRT methods.

MEASURES OF ENVIRONMENT AND UNIVERSAL ACCESS ARE UNDERDEVELOPED Environmental barriers represent formidable barriers to persons with disabilities participating fully in their communities (Maki & Riggar, 1997). This relationship between the physical environment and individual functioning is one that most outcome measures fail to address (see chapter 13 this volume). Although scales may demonstrate sound psychometric properties, they may not include items on environmental aspects (e.g., employment barriers, job market trends, workplace accommodations) (Vogel, Bishop, & Wong, 2001). The lack of attention to these outcomes presumes a patient lives in a "user friendly" environment (Steinfeld & Danford, 2000). However, "as the trend toward rehabilitation in community settings increases, the need for measures that factor in environment is apparent. Without understanding the role of the environment in enabling or disabling functional independence, it is difficult to measure the success of rehabilitation in suboptimal settings that might affect rehabilitation outcomes" (Steinfeld & Danford, 2000, p. 5).

In partial response to this criticism, the *Environmental Functional Independence Measure* was developed and shows promise as a useful measure in assessing environmental and person fit (Steinfeld & Danford, 2000; see also chapter 23 this volume). For example, people who experience both mild (e.g., attention deficit and hyperactivity disorder [ADHD] and severe (e.g. traumatic brain injury) forms of cognitive impairment may be unable to deal effectively with everyday cognition as demanded by the context in which they find themselves; may experience a number of stressful, frustrating, affective, and mood-related components with their disorder (e.g., anger associated with ADD); may have difficulty using current computer-based systems (e.g., those that are not designed using universal access principles that allow access for all persons regardless of ability) or tools to facilitate work,

entertainment, or pleasure; and may be unable to adapt quickly enough to changing dimensions or constraints within the contexts in which they function. In viewing these kinds of potential problems, rehabilitation technology that purports to enhance and improve cognitive readiness (and rehabilitation) must comprehensively address three important aspects of user interaction: understanding, usefulness, and usability. For example, the design and use of appropriate rehabilitation assessment technology require an understanding of interactions between a person and his or her environment (see also chapter 13). Rehabilitation assessment technology also must have utility in informing decisions to guide treatment or interventions and their evaluation. Usability of a rehabilitation assessment technology relates to general principals of human factors and human–computer interaction and often is determined at the "individual difference" level that exists when users interact with real interfaces. In turn, the objectives of assessment are not served when users cannot use the assessment products, services, or systems provided. Assessment systems not directly developed with user input are fraught with errors and unintended consequences, including a lack of universal access qualities.

Summary and Conclusion

Assessments conducted by rehabilitation and health providers constitute a complex process that spans several practice settings, including nurses, occupational and physical therapists, physicians, physical medicine and rehabilitation specialists, psychiatrists, psychologists, recreational therapists, rehabilitation counselors, speech–language pathologists, and social workers. Behavioral assessment devices within these subspecialties generally have been developed for use by subspecialties and for specific client populations. In contrast, multidisciplinary assessment practices are encouraged. Instruments useful for various client populations are becoming more available. The use of common assessment devices enhances communication for interdisciplinary interventions. The ICF provides a common language for the design and use of rehabilitation and health assessments.

Objective measures of participation that inform clinical decision-making and practice at the individual client level are needed. Most measures used in rehabilitation practice assess global indicators of physical functioning displayed in acute care settings, not the more realistic

daily life functions in a client's normal environments. These global indicators may predict physical functioning reliably yet overlook psychosocial functioning in other nonclinical settings. Almost all functional assessment measures are normed on one client or patient group, thus further reducing their broad utility. Application of measurement models that use item response theory techniques may lead to the development of efficient and objective assessment tools for behavioral health in rehabilitation and health settings across client populations and at various points during the rehabilitation process. Functional assessment instruments are needed that reliably measure changes as recipients of rehabilitation services move from one transition point to another in order to document rehabilitation progress within the context of rehabilitation interventions. Rehabilitation and health measures will continue to have limited value until they help us understand the interaction between patients' daily functioning and their environments. The application of universal design principles to rehabilitation and health assessments will result in measures with wider application or utility across patient populations.

Self-Check Questions

1. What are the relative advantages and disadvantages of using rehabilitation outcome measures on populations on which they were not developed?
2. Why is multidisciplinary assessment the gold standard in rehabilitation and health assessment?
3. What is the evidence for the use of behavioral measures in rehabilitation and health?
4. Discuss the concept of efficient measures and how that applies to rehabilitation and health assessment.
5. What instrument development strategies would result in responsive rehabilitation and health measures?

Case Study — The Case of Mr. Bonds

Referral and Identifying Information:

Mr. Bonds is a 56-year-old married obese white male from rural central Pennsylvania. He was seen initially after being admitted into a rehabilitation hospital (subacute care facility) under the services of Dr. A., physiatrist (physical medicine and rehabilitation specialist). He was followed while an inpatient and subsequently for ongoing outpatient individual and family therapy.

Presenting Problem & Background Information:

Past History: Mr. Bonds had presented to the acute care facility in an acute manner via ambulance after experiencing shortness of breath and chest pain. He was admitted and transferred to a tertiary care facility where he underwent coronary bypass graft surgery. His surgery was complicated by a cerebrovascular accident that resulted in difficulties with speech, right hemiparesis, and visual changes. He exhibited confusion and was agitated.

Family and Social History: Mr. Bonds has been married for 30 years and has two children from this marriage, a male aged 20, who is physically disabled, and a daughter aged 23, who recently graduated from a university, wed, and moved out of the area. His wife is a nurse at a small local hospital. He is one of six siblings, having been raised primarily on a farm. His siblings continue to reside within the county, and he has frequent contact with them. His parents are deceased, both dying of cancer at age 62. His father had a history of hypertension and cardiac disease. Maternal grandmother had numerous CVAs and had to be placed in a nursing home after the family had cared for her at home for many years.

Mental Status: When he was seen initially as an inpatient, he was disoriented to time and place, had decreased verbal fluency, and emotional lability. He evidenced decreased attention and concentration, as well as verbal and visual memory. Judgment was impaired. He acknowledged frustration, depression, and was quite tearful in discussing matters. He had acknowledged suicidal ideation and had verbalized such to staff. He had no plan or intent, but instead passively wished he had not survived the surgery. Score of the Geriatric Depression Scale–Short Version was indicative of moderate depression.

Psychiatric & Suicidal History: Psychological and psychiatric consultation occured while an inpatient as the result of his making statements of wanting to die to nursing staff. There was no previous history of mental health issues. There was no familial history of psychiatric disturbance reported. He had previous positive exposure to psychological evaluations with military and correction setting mandatory evaluations.

Medical History: Mr. Bonds has a history of essential hypertension, hyperlipidemia, non-insulin dependent diabetes mellitus, peripheral neuropathy, obesity, and lumbago.

Allergies: He has no known allergies.

Substance Use/Abuse: Mr. Bonds has both smoked and chewed tobacco. He has smoked since he was in the military and has chewed tobacco since high school. He drinks primarily beer with occasional hard liquor. Beer consumption has been six to twelve beers per night.

Educational & Military History: Mr. Bonds is a high school graduate. He indicated that he had some difficulties with mathematics when he was in school. He indicates that he struggled, but that because of his size and athletic ability he was passed along. He played high school football. He was a state runner up in wrestling in high school. He served in the military. He is a veteran of foreign conflict.

Religious Affiliation: Mr. Bonds had been raised as a member of the Lutheran denomination, but converted to

Roman Catholicism after meeting and marrying his wife. He attends services regularly and has been a member of several social organizations affiliated with the church.

Legal History: He has a history of one DUI (Driving Under the Influence) conviction.

Work History: Mr. Bonds has worked as a correctional officer at the state penitentiary for twenty years. He also has an excavating business and has raised beef cattle on the small farm where they live.

Recreation and Leisure Interests: Mr. Bonds had been an avid hunter. He enjoyed hunting with his family, and they had a hunting camp. He also enjoyed fly-fishing. Mr. Bonds enjoys woodworking. He is an active participant in various church and community activities. He has coached junior varsity wrestling at the local public school.

Medications: Previous medications: antihypertensive, ASA 81mg daily, statin. Current medications consist of coumadin, insulin, antihypertensive, statin, narcotic, thiamine and Librium.

QUESTIONS

The patient was treated at a facility that adheres to current practice guidelines; objective standardized assessments were used. Examples include but are not limited to: FIMS, NIS stroke scale, MMSE, BDI, and others. Should data be collected and compared? Should factors impacting care be identified that can enhance care and outcomes?

1. When and how is a determination made in transferring a patient from one facility to the next?
2. What is the likely impact on the family of the rehabilitation intervention?
3. What criteria or decisions may have been considered for determining his transfer from hospital to home?
4. What issues may have been addressed by a healthcare system that identified and treated potential risk factors, and for prevention?

References

Agency for Healthcare Research & Quality Health Resources and Services Administration (2001). *Health people 2010: Access to quality health services.* Author.

Alcott, D., Dixon, K., & Swann, R. (1997). The reliability of items of the Functional Assessment Measure (FAM): Differences in abstractness between FAM items. *Disability and Rehabilitation, 9,* 355–358.

American Psychiatric Association (1995). *Diagnostic and statistical manual of mental disorders, fourth edition (DSM-IV: International Version with ICD-10 Codes).* Washington DC: Author.

American Psychiatric Association (2000). *Diagnostic and statistical manual of mental disorders, fourth edition, text revision.* Washington DC: Author.

Andrich, D. (1988). *Rasch models for measurement.* Newbury Park, CA: Sage.

Anthony, W. A., & Farkas, M. (1982). A client outcome planning model for assessing psychiatric rehabilitation interventions. *Schizophrenia Bulletin, 8,* 13–38.

Backer, T. E. (1980). New directions in rehabilitation outcome measurement. In E. L. Pan, T. E. Backer, & C. L. Vash (Eds.), *Annual review of rehabilitation, Vol. 1* (pp. 193–230). New York: Springer Press.

Bajo, A., Hazan, J., Fleminger, S., & Taylor, R. (1999). Rehabilitation on a cognitive behavioral unit is associated with changes in FAM, not FIM. *Neuropsychological Rehabilitation, 3/4,* 413–419.

Basset, P. T. (1974). *Measurement of outcomes: A report from the study group on measurement of outcomes.* First Institute on Rehabilitation Issues; Denver, CO: irst IRI, West Virginia Research and Training Center.

Boschen, K. A. (1996). Correlates of life satisfaction, residential satisfaction and locus of control among adults with spinal cord injuries. *Rehabilitation Counseling Bulletin, 39,* 230–243.

Boschen, K. A., & Gargano, J. (1996). Issues in the measurement of independent living. *Canadian Journal of Rehabilitation, 10,* 125–135.

Brown, M., Gordon, W. A., & Diller, L. (1983). Functional assessment and outcome measurement: An integrative review. In E. L. Pan, T. E. Backer, & C. L. Vash (Eds.), *Annual review of rehabilitation, Vol. 3* (pp. 93–120). New York: Springer Press.

Cella, D., & Chang, C. (2000). A discussion of item response theory and its applications in health status assessment. *Medical Care, 38,* 11–72.

Cook, C., & Kaplan, S. (1998). Enhancing value outcomes management in outpatient rehabilitation. *Journal of Rehabilitation Outcomes Measurement, 2*(2), 62–65.

Corrigan, J. D., Granger, C. V., & Smith, K. (2000). Functional assessment scales: A study of persons with traumatic brain injury. *Journal of Rehabilitation Outcomes, 4*(4), 8–9.

Crewe, N. M., & Athelstan, G. T. (1981). Functional assessment in vocational rehabilitation: A systematic apprach to diagnosis and goal setting. *Archives of Physical Medicine and Rehabilitation, 62,* 299–305.

Crewe, N. M., & Dijkers, M. (1995). Functional assessment. In L. A. Cushman & M. J. Scherer (Eds), *Psychological* assessment in medical rehabilitation (pp. 101–144). Washington, DC: American Psychological Association.

Deathe, B., Miller, W. C., & Speechley, M. (2002). The status of outcome measurement in amputee rehabilitation in Canada. Archives of Physical Medicine and Rehabilitation, 83, 912–918.

DeJong, G. (1981). Environmental accessibility and independent living outcomes: Directions for disability policy and research. East Lansing, MI: The University Centers for International Rehabilitation.

Dittmar, S. (1997). Overview: A functional approach to the measurement of rehabilitation outcomes. In S. S. Dittmar & G. E. Gresham (Eds.), Functional assessment and outcomes for the rehabilitation health professional (pp. 1–8). Gaithersburg, MD: Aspen.

Djikers, M. P. (2003). Individualization in quality of life measurement: Instruments and approaches. Archives of Physical Medicine and Rehabilitation, 84, 3–14.

Dobrzykowski, E. A. (1997). The methodology of outcomes measurement. Journal of Rehabilitation Outcomes Measurement, 1(1), 8–17.

Donabedian, A. (1980). Exploration in quality assessment and monitoring: Vol. I: The definition of quality and approaches to its assessment. Ann Arbor, MI: Health Administration Press.

Felce, D., & Perry, J. (1995). Quality of life: Its definition and measurement. Research in Developmental Disabilities, 16, 51–74.

Finch, E., Brooks, D., Statford, P. W., & Mayo, N. (2002). Physical rehabilitation outcome measures: A guide to enhanced clinical decision making (2nd ed.). Hamilton, Ontario: Canadian Physiotherapy Association.

Fisher, W. P. (1997). Physical disability construct convergence across instuments: Towards a universal metric. Journal of Outcomes Measurement, 1, 87–113.

Frytak, J. (2000). Measurement. Journal of Rehabilitation Outcomes Measurement, 4(1), 15–31.

Fuhrer, M. J. (1995). Research forum-conference report: An agenda for medical rehabilitation outcomes research. Academy, 7, 35–39.

Galynker, I., Prikhojan, A., Phillips, E., Focseneanu, M., Ieronimo, C., & Rosenthal, R. (1997). Negative symptoms in stroke patients and length of hospital stay. The Journal of Nervous and Mental Disease, 185, 616–621.

Gierl, M. L., Henderson, D., Jodoin, M., & Klinger, D. (2001). Minimizing the influence of item parameter estimaton errors in test development: A comparison of three selection procedures. The Journal of Experimental Education, 69, 261–279.

Granger, C. V., Albrecht, G. L., & Hamilton, B. B. (1979). Outcome of comprehensive medical rehabilitation: Measurement by PULSES profile and the Barthel Index. Archives of Physical Medicine and Rehabilitation, 60, 145–154.

Granger, C. V., Black, T., Braun S. L. (2006). Quality and outcome measures for medical rehavilitation. In R. L. Braddom (Ed.), Physical Medicine & Rehabilitation, (3rd ed.), (pp. 151–164). Elsevier.

Granger C. V., Black T., & Braun, S. L. (in press). Quality and outcome measures for medical rehabilitation. In: R. L. Braddom (Ed.), Physical medicine & rehabilitation (3rd ed.). Elsevier.

Granger, C. V., Cotter, A. C., Hamilton, B. B., Fiedler, R. C., Hens, M. M. (1990). Functional Assessment Scales: A study of persons with multiple sclerosis. Archives of Physical Medicine & Rehabilitation, 71, 870–875.

Granger, C. V., Hamilton, B. B., Keith, R. A., Zielezny, M., & Shewin, F. S. (1986). Advances in functional assessment for medical rehabilitation. Topics in Geriatric Rehabilitation, 1(3), 59–74.

Graves, W. H. (1990). Vocational capacity with visual impairments. In S. Scheer (Ed.), Multidisciplinary perspectives in vocational assessment of impaired workers (pp. 155–166). Rockville, MD: Aspen.

Gurka, J. A., Felmingham, K. L., Baguley, I. J., Schotte, D. E., Crooks, J., & Marosszeky, J. E., (1999). Utility of the Functional Assessment Measure after discharge from inpatient rehabilitation. Journal of Head Trauma and Rehabilitation, 14, 247–256.

Hahn, E. A., & Cella, D. (2003). Health outcomes assessment in vulnerable populations: Measurement challenges and recommendations. Archives of Physical Medicine and Rehabilitation, 84 (Supplement 2), 535–542.

Haley, S. M., & Jatte, A. M. (2000). RRTC for measuring rehabilitation outcomes: Extending the frontier of rehabilitation outcome measurement and research. Journal of Rehabilitation Outcomes, 4(4), 31–41.

Haley, S. M., & Langmuir, L. (2000). How do current postacute functional assessments compare with the activity dimension of the International Classification of Functioning and Disability (ICIDH-2)? Journal of Rehabilitation Outcomes Measurement, 4(4), 51–56.

Hall, K. M., Hamilton, B. B., Gordon, W. A., & Zasler, N. D. (1993). Characteristics and comparisons of functional assessment indices: Disability Rating Scale, Functional Independence Measure and Functional Assessment Measure. Journal of Head Trauma Rehabilitation, 8, 60–71.

Hamilton, B. B., Granger, C. V., Sherwin, F. S., Zielzny, M., & Tashman, J. S. (1987). A uniform national data system for medical rehabilitation. In M. J. Fuhrer (Ed.), Rehabilitation outcomes. Analysis and measurement (pp. 137–147). Baltimore: Brookes.

Harvey, R. F., Silverstein, B., Venzon, M. A., Kilgore, K. M., Fisher, W. P., Steiner, M., & Harley, J. P. (1992). Applying psychometric criteria to functional assessment in medical rehabilitation: III. Construct validity and predicting level of care. Archives of Physical Medicine and Rehabilitation, 73, 887–892.

Hawley, C. A., Taylor, R., Hellawell, D. J., & Pentland, B. (1999). Use of the functional assessment measure (FIM + FAM) in head injury rehabilitation: A psychometric analysis. *Journal of Neural Psychiatry, 67,* 749–754.

Hays, R. D., Morales, L. S., & Reise, S. (2000). Item response theory and health outcomes measurement in the 21st century. *Medical Care, 38,* 28–42.

Heinemann, A. W., Bode, R., Cichowski, K. C., Kan, E. (1998). Measuring patient satisfaction with medical rehabilitation. In E. A. Dobrzykowski (Ed.), *Essential readings in rehabilitation outcomes measurement: Application, methodology, and technology* (pp. 92–103). Gaithersburg, MD: Aspen.

Hobart, J. C., Lamping, D. L., Freeman, J. A., Langdon, D. W., McLellan, D. L., Greenwood, R. J., & Thompson, A. J. (2001). Evidence-based measurement: Which validity scale for neurologic rehabilitation? *Neurology, 57,* 639–644.

Hodges, K., Wong, M. M., & Latessa, M. (1998). Use of the Child and Adolescent Functional Assessment Scale (CAFAS) as an outcome measure in clinical settings. *The Jouranl of Behavioral Health Services & Research, 25,* 325–336.

Hoi, S., & French, J. (2003). A history of the development of psychological and educational testing. In C. Reynolds & R. Kamphaus, R. (Eds.), *Handbook of psychological and educational assessment of children: Intelligence, aptitude, and achievement* (2nd ed.). New York: Guilford Press

Institute of Health Improvement (2006). Patient-centered care: General. Retrieved on April 19, 2006, from http://www.ihi.org/IHI/Topics/PatientCenteredCare/PatientCenteredCareGeneral/

Irrgang, J. J., Snyder-Mackler, L., Wainner, R. S., Fu, F. H., & Harner, C. D. (1998). Development of a patient-reported measure of function of the knee. *The Journal of Bone and Joint Surgery, 80-A,* 1132–1145.

Jacobs, J. W. (1993). Measurement of functional ability and health status in the arthritic patient. *Patient Education and Counseling, 20,* 121–132.

Jennings, B. M., & Staggers, N. (1999). The language of outcomes. *Journal of Rehabilitation Outcomes Measurement, 3*(1), 59–64.

Kane, R. L. (1999). Approaching the outcomes question. *Journal of Rehabilitation Outcomes Measurement, 3*(1), 50–58.

Kane, R., Rockwood, T., Finch, M., & Philip, I. (1997). Consumer and professional ratings of the importance of functional status components. *Health Care Financing Review, 19,* 11–22.

Kelly-Hayes, M. (2000). Stroke outcomes measurement: New developments. *Journal of Outcomes Measurement, 4,* 57–63.

Korner-Bitensky, N., Mayo, N E., & Poznanski, S. G. (1990). Occupational therapists' accuracy in predicting sensory, perceptual–cognitive, and functional recovery poststroke. *The Occupational Therapy Journal of Research, 10,* 237–248.

Lai, S. M., Duncan, P. W., & Keighley, J. (1998). Prediction of functional outcome after stroke: Comparison of the Orpington Prognostic Scale and the NIH Stoke Scale. *Stroke, 29,* 1838–1842.

Lawton, M. P. (1988). Instrumental Activities of Daily Living (IADL) scale. Self-rated version. Incorporated in the Philadelphia Geriatic Center. Multilevel Assessment Instrument (MAI). *Psychopharmacological Bulletin, 24,* 789–791.

Lezak, M. D. (1987). Relationship between personality disorders, social disturbance, and physical disability following traumatic brain injury. *Journal of Head Trauma Rehabilitation, 2(1),* 57–59.

Liang, M. H., Fossel, A. H., & Larson, M. G. (1990). Comparison of five health status instruments for orthopedic evaluation. *Medical Care, 28,* 632–642.

Linn, R. T., Blair, R. S., Granger, C. V., Harper, D. W., O'Hara, D. W., & Maciura, E. (1999). Does the Functional Assessment Measure (FAM) extend the Functional Independence Measure (FIM) Instrument? A Rasch analysis of stroke inpatients. *Journal of Outcome Measurement, 3(4),* 339–359.

Livingston, M. G., & Livingston, H. M. (1985). The Glasgow Assessment Schedule: Clinical and research assessment of head injury outcome. *International Rehabilitation Medicine, 7,* 145–149.

Maki, D. R. & Riggar, T. F. (1997). Rehabilitation counseling: Concept and paradigms. In D. R. Maki and T. F. Riggar (Eds.), *Rehabilitation Counseling Profession and Practice* (pp. 3–31). New York: Springer.

McCue, M. (1989). The role of assessment in the vocational rehabilitation of adults with specific learning disability. *Rehabilitation Counseling Bulletin, 33,* 18–37.

McDowell, I. (2006). *Measuring health: A guide to rating scales and questionnaires* (3rd ed.). New York: Oxford.

McKinley, C. O., Ellis, R. A., Buchanan, J. R., Clark, K. G., Kersey, G. E., Olejnik, S., & Somerindyke, J. L. (1999). Developing a customer satisfaction model to measure performance. *Journal of Rehabilitation Outcomes Measurement, 3(1),* 1–10.

Meenan, R. F. (1986). New approaches to outcome assessment: The AIMS questionnaire for arthritis. *Advances in Internal Medicine, 31,* 167–185.

Morrison, M. H. (2000). Will rehabilitation move to the next level in outcomes management? *Journal of Rehabilitation Outcomes Measurement, 4(4),* 49–50.

Mpofu, E., & Oakland, T (2006). Assessment of value change in adults with acquired disabilities. In M. Hersen (Ed.), *Clinician's handbook of adult behavioral assessment* (pp. 601–630). New York: Elsevier Press.

Muthard, J. E., & Miller, L. A. (1968). *The Rehabilitation Counselor Rating Scale.* Studies in Rehabilitation Counselor Training, No. 6. Joint Liaison Committee of the Council of State Administrators of vocational Rehabilitation and the Rehabilitation Counselor Educators.

Niles, N. (1996). Using qualitative and quantitative patient satisfaction data to improve the quality of cardiac care. *Joint Commission Journal on Quality Improvement, 22,* 323–334.

Oakland, T., Mpofu, E., Gregoire, G., & Faulkner, M. (2007). An exploration of learning disabilities in four countries: Implications for test development and use in developing countries. *International Journal of Testing, 7,* (1). 53–70.

Olejnik, S., McKinley, C. O., Ellis, R. A., Buchanan, J. R., Kersey, G. E., & Clark, K. G. (1998). Construct validation of customer satisfaction inventories. *Journal of Rehabilitation Outcomes Measurement, 2*(5), 30–38.

Osborn, C. E. (1998). Developing instruments for assessment of patient outcomes. *Journal of Rehabilitation Outcomes Measurement, 2*(6), 18–25.

Oswald, W. D., & Gunzelmann, T. (1992). Functional rating scales and psychometric assessment in Alzheimer's Disease. *International Psychogeriatrics, 4,* 79–88.

Petaschnick, J. (2000a). Rehabilitation outcomes survey overview: Obstacles hinder collection and use of outcomes data; despite difficulties, data proves useful. *Journal of Rehabilitation Outcomes Measurement, 4*(3), 35–42.

Petaschnick, J. (2000b). Outcomes data brings problems to the forefront; solutions not always simple. *Journal of Rehabilitation Outcomes Measurement, 4*(3), 51–53.

President's Advisory Commission on the Consumer Protection and Quality in the Health Care Industry. (1998). *Quality first: Better health care for all Americans (Consumer's Bill of Rights).* Washington, DC: Author.

Rasch, G. (1980). *Probabilistic models for some intelligence and attainment tests.* Chicago: University of Chicago Press.

Reagles, K.W. & Butler, A. S. (1976). The Human Service Scale: A New Measure for Evaluation. *Journal of Rehabilitation 42*(3), 34–38.

Robertson, S. C., & Pas Colborn, A. (1997). Outcomes research for rehabilitation: Issues and solutions. *Journal of Rehabilitation Outcomes Measurement, 1*(5), 15–23.

Roper, W. L., Hackbarth, G. M. (1988). Commentary. HCFA's agenda for promoting high-quality care. *Health Affairs, 7*(1), 91–98.

Samsa, G., Edelman, D., Rothman, M. I., Williams, G. R., Lipscomb, J., & Matchar, D. (1999). Determining clinically important differences in health status measurement: A general approach with illustrations to the Health Utilities Index mark II: *Pharmacoeconomics, 15,* 141–155.

Seelman, K. (2000). Rehabilitation research and training centers on functional assessment and the evaluation of rehabilitation outcomes. Accomplishments to date and goals for the future: Introduction. *Journal of Rehabilitation Outcomes Measurement, 4*(4), 1.

Simmons, D. C., Crepeau, E. B., & White B. P. (2000). The predictive power of narrative data in occupational therapy. *American Journal of Occupational Therapy, 54,* 471–476.

Slavin, M. D. (2001). How effective is rehabilitation? *Paraplegia News, 55*(9), 12.

Smith, P. M., Bennett Illig, S., Riedler, R. C., Hamilton, B. B., & Ottenbacher, K. J. (2000). Intermodal agreement of follow-up telephone functional assessment using the Functional Independence Measure in patients with stroke. *Journal of Rehabilitation Outcomes Measurement, 4(4),* 9–15.

Steinfeld, E., & Danford, G. S. (2000). Measuring handicapping environments. *Journal of Outcome Measurement, 4,* (4) 5–8.

Stineman, M. G., Shea, J. A., Jette, A., Tassoni, C. J., Ottenbacher, K. J., Fiedler, R., Granger, C. V. (1996). The Functional Independence Measure: Tests of scaling assumptions, structure and reliability across 20 diverse impairment categories. *Archives of Physical Medicine and Rehabilitation, 77,* 1101–1108.

Stucki, G., Ustun, B., & Melvin, J. (2005). Applying the ICF for acute hospital and early post-acute rehabilitation facilities. *Disability and Rehabilitation, 27,* 349–352.

Tenth Institute on Rehabilitation Services. (1972). *Program evaluation—A beginning statement.* Washington, DC: U.S. Department of Health, Education and Welfare, Social and Rehabilitation Service, Rehabilitation Service Administration.

Tesio, L., & Cantagallo, A. (1998). The functional Assessment measure (FAM) in closed traumatic brain injury outpatients: A Rasch based psychometric study. *Journal of Outcome Measurement, 2(2),* 79–96.

Turner-Stokes, L., Nyein, K., Turner-Stokes, T., & Gatehouse, C. (1999). The UK FIM + FAM: Development and evaluation. *Clinical Rehabilitation, 13,* 277–287.

Turner-Stokes, L., & Turner-Stokes, T. (1997). The use of standardized outcome measures in rehabilitation centers in the UK. *Clinical Rehabilitation, 11,* 306–313.

Uniform Data System for Medical Rehabilitation (2004). *Guide for the Uniform Data Set for Medical Rehabilitation (Adult FIM).* Buffalo, NY: Author.

Vogel, L., Bishop, E., & Wong, M. (2001). Using the functional assessment inventory (FAI) to measure vocational rehabilitation outcomes. *Journal of Rehabilitation Outcomes Measurements, 2(2),* 48–54.

Ware, J. (2003). Conceptualization and measurement of health-related quality of life: Comments on an evolving field. *Archives of Physical Medicine and Rehabilitation, 84,* 43–51.

Watts, J. H., & Clement, D. G. (2000). Conceptual framework for rehabilitation outcomes research. *Journal of Rehabilitation Outcomes Measurement, 4*(2), 55–61.

Weiss, D. J. (1985). Adaptive testing by computer. *Journal of Consulting and Clinical Psychology, 53(6),* 774–789.

Whiteneck, G. C., Charlifue, S. W., Gerhart, K. A., Overholser, J. D., & Richardson, G. N. (1992). Quantifying handicap: A new measure of long-term rehabilitation outcomes. *Archives of Physical Medicine and Rehabilitation, 73,* 519–526.

Willer, B. (1994). The community integration questionnaire: A comparative examination. *American Journal of Physical Medicine and Rehabilitation, 73,* 103–111.

Wilson, M. (1989). Saltus: A psychometric model of discontinuity in cognitive development. *Psychological Bulletin, 105,* 276–289.

Wilkerson, D. (2000). Rehabilitation outcomes and accreditation. *Journal of Rehabilitation Outcomes Measurement, 4* (4), 42–48.

World Health Organization (1992a). *The International Classification of Diseases and Related Health Problems,* Tenth Edition. Geneva, Swithzerland: Author.

World Health Organization (1992b). *International statistical classification of diseases and related health problems:* Tenth revision. Geneva: Author.

World Health Organization (WHO) (1999). *ICIDH-2: International classification of impairments, disabilities and handicaps: A manual of classification relating to the consequences of disease.* Geneva, Switzerland: Author.

World Health Organization (WHO) (2001). *Literature review on the role of environmental factors in functioning and disability.* Geneva, Switzerland: Author. Available at http://www.who.int/icidh/env_fact/index.html.

Legal and Ethical Considerations in Rehabilitation and Health Assessment

SHANE S. BUSH

Long Island Neuropsychology, P.C., Lake Ronkonkoma, NY
Stony Brook University School of Medicine

OVERVIEW

All rehabilitation and health services begin with assessment. Legal and ethical requirements and guidelines provide the parameters within which appropriate assessments occur. Health care professionals have multiple legal and ethical obligations that exist to protect and to advance the interests and well-being of patients, families and other consumers, and the public. However, even the most ethically conscious and well-intentioned clinicians face ethical dilemmas. The close interdisciplinary collaboration that is a strength of rehabilitation services is also a source of unique ethical challenges. Positive ethics require proactive efforts to anticipate challenges and to take steps to avoid or prepare to address such challenges. Although the answers to some ethical questions are straightforward and the solutions easily implemented, more complex ethical dilemmas place greater demands on the clinician's decision-making skills and use of resources. An ethical decision-making model provides a structured means of organizing one's thoughts, resources, and options so that clinicians can make appropriate decisions based on the relevant laws, ethical principles, and their own values.

LEARNING OBJECTIVES

By the end of the chapter, readers should be able to:

- Describe ethical issues of critical importance to rehabilitation and health assessment
- Explain the difference between positive ethics and disciplinary ethics
- Describe three essential ethical and legal resources relevant to rehabilitation and health assessment
- Explain the value of an ethical decision-making model

INTRODUCTION

All rehabilitation and health services begin with assessment. Although assessments can take many forms, the overarching goal of understanding the status, needs, or desires of the consumer (e.g., patient, client, examinee) is consistent. Adequate assessment allows the health care professional to move forward with the provision of services and the achievement of goals. Legal and ethical requirements and guidelines provide the parameters within which appropriate assessments occur.

The primary purposes of the present chapter are to (1) provide a general overview of ethical and legal resources relevant to health care professionals, (2) describe ethical challenges commonly encountered by health care professionals, (3) review resources available for ethical and legal decision-making, (4) present an ethical decision-making model, and (5) demonstrate the application of the ethical decision-making model through a case illustration. To achieve these goals, an emphasis is placed on clarifying the differences between, and convergence among, the ethical, legal, and professional contributions to complex cases. The chapter is intended to apply to general assessment practices across health care and rehabilitation contexts and disciplines, although there is greater representation of the psychology literature than that of any other single discipline.

LEGAL AND ETHICAL CONSIDERATIONS AND GOALS IN ASSESSMENT

This section addresses shared values and the protection and promotion of consumer and patient welfare. The ability of clinicians to understand and appreciate the values held by patients and consumers and to use that knowledge to protect and promote patient and consumer welfare is essential to ethical and legal practice.

Shared Values

Consumers of health care and health promotion services make assumptions, albeit with varying degrees of awareness, about the services they will receive and the professionals who provide the services. Such assumptions are made before the consumers are seen by the health care professional. With the exception of individuals with substantially compromised cognitive functioning, most people within a given society who seek the services of a health care professional share certain ideas about what to expect from the services they seek and the professionals who provide the services. Even patients or consumers who have significant cognitive deficits are likely to have similar expectations when receiving health care services prior to the onset of the cognitive deficits.

At a basic level, the assumptions made by patients or consumers about health care, health promotion, and health care professionals include the following: (1) The professionals providing the services are competent to do so; (2) the potential risks and benefits of various options will be explained to me or to those making decisions on my behalf if I lack the capacity to make the decisions; (3) I (or my proxy) may make an informed decision to accept or refuse services; (4) the health care professional's guiding principle is to do more good than harm; (5) needed services will be available; and (6) personal privacy will be maintained. These basic assumptions represent the shared values of Western societies, values which have long helped to define acceptable relationships between health care professionals and members of a society. These shared values become law and/or are incorporated in ethics codes of health care professions, tailored to meet the relatively unique, though overlapping, needs of each discipline. Thus, values guide our choices and actions in both our personal and professional lives (see also other chapters in this book).

As health care professionals, we must understand the values that society places on health-related services and must be intimately aware of the unique applications of these values to our own discipline and the disciplines of those professionals with whom we regularly collaborate. The shared values of society and our professions, the unique values of the consumers of our services, and our own values combine to influence the manner in which we provide our services (see also chapter 3).

Protecting and Promoting Consumer and Public Welfare

Shared values in the form of ethical and legal requirements serve the primary purposes of providing protection for and promoting the welfare of consumers of rehabilitation and health services, the public, and the reputation of the health care professions. Ethical and legal requirements protect and promote welfare by providing clinicians with descriptions of appropriate behavior. Although legal requirements are enforceable, professional ethics codes may be aspirational or enforceable, depending on the nature of the code and the jurisdiction in which the clinician practices. For example, the American Psychological Association's (APA) *Ethical Principles of Psychologists and Code of Conduct* (American Psychological Association [APA], 2002) is comprised of two main sections: aspirational general principles and enforceable ethical standards. However, its ethical standards are enforceable only for those psychologists who are members of the American Psychological Association or for those who practice in a state that has adopted the APA Ethics Code as its rules of professional conduct. The Code's ethical standards are not enforceable for psychologists who are not members of the American Psychological Association and do not practice in a jurisdiction that is governed by the code. Nevertheless, despite some controversial sections, the APA Ethics Code, including its standards, provides a model of appropriate professional behavior for all psychologists.

THEORIES, GUIDELINES, AND RESOURCES

This section provides overviews of positive ethics, principle-based ethics, and ethical and legal guidelines and resources. The promotion of ethical and legal conduct is maximized by considering bioethical principles and ethical and legal resources in the context of a personal commitment to the pursuit of ethical ideals.

Positive Ethics

Laws and ethical *requirements* establish a minimum level of professional responsibility. In contrast, ethical *principles* and professional *guidelines* often are described as *aspirational*, rather than enforceable requirements reflecting a high level of professional responsibility. Although a distinction is made between enforceable standards and aspirational principles or guidelines, it is difficult to conceive of situations in which clinicians would be justified in choosing a lesser standard of ethical responsibility and thus a lesser degree of protection of the rights of consumers, the public, and the health care professions. Health care professionals should strive to maintain a level of professional responsibility that is consistent with the highest standards of ethical and legal practice.

A primary goal of positive ethics is to shift the emphasis from misconduct and disciplinary actions to the active promotion of exemplary behavior (Handelsman,

Knapp, & Gottlieb, 2002; Knapp & VandeCreek, 2004, 2006). Knapp and VandeCreek (2006) further stated:

> A complete education in ethics requires consideration of the perspectives or processes by which psychologists can maximize their adherence to moral principles. It means going beyond the minimal standards found in the *APA* Ethics Code and trying to uphold the moral principles that form the foundation of the Ethics Code. (p. 11)

Some clinicians may choose not to pursue ethical ideals because maintaining a high standard of ethical practice often requires time and expense beyond that required by minimum enforceable ethical and legal standards. For example, in New York State, psychologists are not required to participate in continuing education; that is, they are on the honor system with regard to maintaining professional competence. As a result, clinicians vary widely in the degree to which they remain informed about advances in the knowledge, skills, and procedures that are the foundation of clinical practice. Although those clinicians who choose the least expensive and time-intensive options, if any, of professional development may maintain a minimum level of competence, it seems likely that they and their patients will derive less benefit from those efforts than will the clinician who is a member of professional organizations, receives and reads journals, attends conferences, and engages in other forms of structured continuing education on a consistent basis. Thus, although there are legal and ethical mandates to maintain competence in one's professional activities, participation in formal continuing education programs is left to the discretion of the New York-based clinician. Psychologists in New York wishing to pursue ethical ideals will actively and regularly seek both formal and informal avenues of continuing education. "The pursuit of ethical ideals requires an allocation of time and effort that only a personal commitment to such ideals can support...a personal commitment to ethical ideals is a primary responsibility and obligation of all practitioners" (Bush & Martin, 2006; p. 64).

Principle-Based Ethics

A variety of philosophical systems is relevant for ethical decision-making in health and rehabilitation settings. Such systems include virtue ethics, utilitarianism, deontological ethics, and principle-based ethics. These systems provide organization for the shared values or a common morality (Knapp & VandeCreek, 2006) of a society. As important components of the society, the health and rehabilitation professions rely on philosophical systems to serve as the foundation of their ethics codes.

Principle-based ethics, although developed nearly a century ago (Ross, 1930/1998), have gained popularity and fairly widespread acceptance among health care professionals in more recent years based in large part on the writings of Beauchamp and Childress (2001). Because of the reliance on principle-based ethics by clinicians in many health care professions, there is a familiarity and a common language that helps facilitate interdisciplinary communication regarding ethical matters. As a result, principle-based ethics, and not other philosophical systems, are described in this chapter.

Beauchamp and Childress identified four core ethical principles: respect for autonomy, nonmaleficence, beneficence, and justice. *Respect for autonomy* refers to the right of competent patients to make the decisions that govern their lives, as long as the decisions do not negatively impact the rights of others. This principle departs from the paternalistic approach traditionally encountered in medicine by which the health care professional is assumed to know what is in the patient's best interests and what interventions should be administered. Respect for patient autonomy is based on the premise that a competent, well-informed patient can choose to accept or decline examination or treatment options and should be included in the decision-making process.

The principle of *nonmaleficence* addresses the importance of doing no harm. Although this principle may initially seem obvious, determinations regarding what constitutes harm or which individual, organization, or system is owed such an obligation can be difficult to make in a given case. *Beneficence* as an ethical principle refers to a moral obligation to take action to advance the welfare of others. Beneficence encompasses the promotion of the rights and health of others as well as defense of the rights of others and the prevention of harm.

Justice refers to "fair, equitable, and appropriate treatment in light of what is due or owed to persons" (Beauchamp & Childress, 2001, p. 226). Justice has two components: distributive justice and formal justice. *Distributive justice* refers to the equitable distribution of health care resources. *Formal justice* refers to equal treatment for those who are equals and unequal treatment for those who are not equals. Challenges to the successful application of the principle of justice lie in defining what is equitable and determining which

individuals or groups are equals. Health care professionals must consider these questions in the unique contexts in which ethical problem-solving occurs.

Two additional moral principles, although identified as applicable to mental health professionals (Knapp & VandeCreek, 2006), also appear relevant for health care and rehabilitation professionals across various disciplines: fidelity and general beneficence. *Fidelity* (Bersoff & Koeppl, 1993; Kitchener, 1984) refers to the obligation to be truthful and faithful, keep promises, and maintain loyalty. *General beneficence* (Knapp & VandeCreek, 2006) refers to the clinician's responsibility to the public at large (i.e., society). As an example, these authors describe the responsibility of psychologists to protect future consumers of psychological evaluation services by safeguarding the integrity of psychological tests.

The biomedical ethical principles described above can provide valuable guidance in determining the most appropriate course of action in many instances in which ethical standards do not seem to provide the needed direction to resolve an ethical challenge, or when ethical standards conflict with each other or with jurisdictional laws. However, instances arise in which these biomedical ethical principles conflict with each other. For example, respect for patient autonomy conflicts with beneficence or general beneficence when patients report an intention to harm themselves or others. Although, in this example, the relative importance of the principles is clear, in other situations, it is difficult to determine which principle must be given greater weight, leaving the clinician to make such judgments. In such instances, use of an ethical decision-making model can be particularly helpful.

Ethics Codes

All professional health care and rehabilitation organizations have ethics codes that describe acceptable professional conduct, and most of the ethics codes are readily available on the Internet. The ethics codes of the different disciplines vary somewhat in the degree to which they address specific or general behaviors or provide enforceable standards or aspirational principles. However, the ethics codes strive to present the shared values of their discipline. Because of the common morality of Western societies, there is considerable overlap among ethics codes. Nevertheless, because each discipline contributes uniquely to health care and rehabilitation assessment, the various ethics codes are particularly important for helping clinicians apply professional ethics to their unique aspects of practice. For example, physicians and others with prescription privileges or psychologists and others who administer standardized psychological or neurocognitive tests will find different professional activities emphasized in their codes of ethics. Knowledge of ethics codes of colleagues in different disciplines can be informative when addressing ethical challenges and attempting to better understand the values and motivations of colleagues.

With regard to assessment services, the *APA Ethical Principles of Psychologists and Code of Conduct* (APA, 2002) can be a valuable resource for clinicians of all health care disciplines. In Ethical Standard 9 (Assessment), clinicians can obtain information about (1) bases for assessments, (2) use of assessments, (3) informed consent in assessments, (4) release of test data, (5) test construction, (6) interpreting assessment results, (7) assessment by unqualified persons, (8) obsolete tests and outdated test results, (9) test scoring and interpretation services, (10) explaining assessment results, and (11) maintaining test security.

Professional Guidelines and Resources

Ethics codes typically provide clinicians with minimum acceptable standards of professional behavior and serve as the basis for possible disciplinary action. As a result, clinicians tend to be aware of and are more or less familiar with the code of ethics of their profession. However, professional organizations, or specialties within professions, also commonly provide additional guidelines to assist clinicians with avoiding or addressing ethical conflicts. For purposes of illustration, the following guidelines and resources developed by or primarily for psychologists are provided. However, the American Medical Association, the American Congress of Rehabilitation Medicine, and other professional organizations also provide numerous resources of interest and relevance to clinicians of related health care and rehabilitation disciplines. Although agreement is not always apparent between guidelines or between guidelines and ethics codes, the clinician will be well served by seeking a convergence of opinions or positions from multiple sources, keeping in mind that some resources carry more weight than others.

The American Psychological Association (APA) has published numerous position papers and guidelines on various aspects of assessment, including the assessment of special populations such as the elderly. The *Guidelines for the Evaluation of Dementia and Age-related Cognitive Decline* (APA, 1998) and the *Guidelines for Psychological Practice with Older Adults* (APA, 2004) are two such examples.

The *Standards for Educational and Psychological Testing* (SEPT) (American Educational Research Association, American Psychological Association, and National Council on Measurement in Education, 1999) also address many of the testing-related ethical issues that are addressed in the APA *Ethical Principles of Psychologists and Code of Conduct* (2002) and provide additional information and examples that are not available in the more general APA Ethics Code. These standards are relevant for clinicians of all disciplines that administer psychological or neurocognitive tests.

The National Academy of Neuropsychology has published (www.nanonline.org) a variety of position papers pertaining to ethical and professional challenges commonly encountered in the assessment of individuals with known or suspected neurocognitive deficits, including informed consent, third-party observers, release of raw test data, and symptom validity assessment.

The Association of State and Provincial Psychology Boards (2005) provides a *Code of Conduct* that has been adopted by many state licensing boards as their rules of professional behavior and thus are applied in judicial contexts. Although its *Code of Conduct* is "non-optional" and "coercive" (i.e., not advisory or aspirational) for those practitioners to whom this Code applies, the Code nevertheless may serve as a professional resource for practitioners not directly governed by the Code.

The *International Classification of Functioning, Disability and Health* (ICF; World Health Organization, 2001) provides a biopsychosocial framework for conceptualizing health-related functional status. The ICF includes 11 basic ethical guidelines intended to reduce the risk of disrespectful or harmful use of the system (Petersen, 2005). The ethical guidelines address three core ethical topics: respect and confidentiality, clinical use of the ICF, and social use of the ICF information. Although these guidelines were developed in the context of the ICF, they encompass underlying general bioethical principles and therefore may serve as a reference in multiple rehabilitation and health care contexts.

In addition to published ethics codes and professional guidelines, colleagues constitute a primary resource for ethical and legal information and guidance. Consultation with colleagues may occur through professional organizations or personal contact with informed colleagues. Most major professional organizations have ethics committees that provide information and advice to members of their profession, although some provide consultation only to members of the association. Consultation with the association that has provided the ethics code for the profession can be particularly advantageous because of the added confidence of compliance with the ethics code. It is important to document all consultations with ethics committees. Such documentation can demonstrate, if requested by an investigatory body, the clinician's investment in determining an appropriate solution to an ethical dilemma.

Informal consultation with colleagues also may be very helpful. Colleagues who are experienced with, and particularly knowledgeable about, ethical and legal matters, such as those who have served on ethics committees or written or presented on related topics, often are excellent sources of information and direction. In addition to colleagues, professional liability insurance carriers typically have representatives available to advise clinicians regarding ethical and legal matters, usually from a risk management perspective.

Institutional Guidelines and Requirements

Many institutions in which health care and rehabilitation services are provided offer standards or guidelines for appropriate professional behavior. For example, most hospitals have ethics committees and legal departments that define, enforce, and provide education and guidance regarding appropriate professional conduct. Professionals who provide services in such settings should regularly avail themselves of such resources to (1) minimize the potential for ethical misconduct, (2) explore possibilities for pursuing ethical ideals, and (3) better prepare themselves for addressing ethical questions or challenges when they arise. The availability of access to institutional ethical and legal resources can be an advantage of working in such settings.

Jurisdictional Laws

State and federal laws govern the practice of health care providers and are essential resources for health care providers. The applicability of jurisdictional laws is addressed in the Jurisdictional Relevance section later in this chapter.

Conflicts Between Ethical and Professional Resources

Practitioners may expect congruence between the various ethical and professional requirements and guidelines. However, discrepancies between them are encountered with some frequency. For example, the APA Ethics Code (Ethical Standard 9.04, Release of Test Data) states, "... Pursuant to a client/patient release, psychologists provide test data to the client/patient or other persons identified in the release. Psychologists may refrain from releasing test data to protect a client/patient or others from substantial harm or misuse or misrepresentation of the data or the test, recognizing that in many instances

release of confidential information under these circumstances is regulated by law." In contrast, the Ethics Code of the Canadian Psychological Association (1991), the SEPT, and the National Academy of Neuropsychology (2000a, 2000b, 2003) take the position that, with the exception of a court order, raw test data should be released only to other professionals with the necessary education and training to appropriately interpret the data (see Appendix A for additional reading on this topic).

When faced with discrepancies between requirements (i.e., standards) and guidelines, clinicians should consider the source of each resource and weigh the importance of each accordingly. An ethical requirement established by the primary professional association of a discipline typically carries more weight than a position paper by a special interest organization. When confronted with conflicting ethical and/or professional requirements, the use of an ethical decision-making model, such as the one described in the present chapter, often helps to clarify the preferred course of action. As is described below, the ethical decision-making process includes consultation with colleagues who are experienced in addressing ethical issues as well as reliance on multiple other ethical, legal, and professional resources.

HISTORY OF RESEARCH AND PRACTICE

To the extent possible, rehabilitation and health care professionals select assessment procedures and base their assessment conclusions on scientific evidence. For example, neurocognitive tests must have adequate psychometric properties, including reliability, validity, positive predictive power, and negative predictive power. Similarly, conclusions derived from such tests must be based on peer-reviewed research pertaining to brain-behavior relationships and the interaction between neurocognitive functioning and factors such as emotional state and physical pain. In contrast to those aspects of assessment for which a body of research exists, there is relatively little empirical investigation of ethical questions related to assessment. Although many ethical issues do not readily lend themselves to empirical investigation, the lack of financial resources to support such studies also contributes to the meager research on ethical issues associated with assessment.

Because empirical investigations of ethical issues in rehabilitation and health assessment are rare, scholarly writings remain the primary source of ethical information when applying ethics codes and laws to specific aspects of practice. Occasional journal articles, special issues of journals (e.g., *Applied Neuropsychology, 13*(2), 2006; *Journal*

DISCUSSION BOX 2.1

Investigations of the potential impact of the presence of third parties (i.e., individuals other than the examiner and patient) on assessment results constitute an emerging body of scientific literature related to ethical issues in assessment. Potential negative impacts include poorer performance on certain neurocognitive tasks and threats to the security of assessment methods. The potential problems associated with third party observers have been discussed for at least ten years (McCaffrey et al., 1996). The National Academy of Neuropsychology published a position paper on the topic in 2000. However, only in the past few years has empirical evidence been available to support the impression of many clinicians that having third parties, including audio and video recording devices, in the assessment setting significantly affects performance on neurocognitive tests (see McCaffrey, Lynch, & Yantz, 2005, for a comprehensive overview). Despite this emerging literature, the benefits of having a third party present during the assessment may outweigh the potential negative effects. For example, if a young child is unwilling to cooperative without a parent present, the clinician may need to allow the parent to be present in order to obtain some sense of the child's ability levels. Similarly, in some situations an interpreter may need to be present to facilitate communication between the clinician and the patient. When the presence of a third party is unavoidable, the clinician must consider the potential impact of the third party on the patient's performance, limit or modify conclusions as needed, and describe the potential or known impact of the third party on the patient's performance in the assessment results.

Questions

1. What are two negative effects of having third parties present during neurocognitive assessments?
2. What are two advantages to having third parties present during assessments?

---

of Head Trauma Rehabilitation, 4(1), 1989; *Journal of Head Trauma Rehabilitation, 12*(1), 1997; *Neuro-Rehabilitation,* (2), 1996; *Rehabilitation Psychology, 41*(1),1996), and book chapters provide the core writings on rehabilitation ethics. In addition, many professional organizations (e.g., American Medical Association, American Psychological Association) provide position papers to supplement ethics codes. In the past few years, rehabilitation and health care-related ethics books have been published that integrate and summarize the available literature pertaining to specific disciplines (e.g., Bush, 2005; Bush & Drexler, 2002; Hanson, Kerkhoff, & Bush, 2005). Despite the limited availability of empirical support for ethical positions, the experiences and perspectives of learned colleagues have long served as the primary sources of education and problem-solving for ethical matters.

Professional ethics evolve. New versions of ethics codes are published periodically, with old standards maintained, revised, or eliminated, and new standards added. The dynamic nature of professional ethics codes and guidelines is due to many factors, including gradual changes in shared values, professional–political influences, legal matters, changes in professional activities stemming from technological advances, and, at times, the biases of the individuals or groups in positions of influence. Continued and expanded empirical studies of ethical issues are needed to reduce the influence on ethical resources of groups or individuals with personal agendas that may not be consistent with the best interests of patients, society, or the health care professions. Additional funding of ethics research may help generate novel and creative studies of ethical issues that have been considered beyond the realm of empirical investigation.

CRITICAL RESEARCH TOPICS

Many ethical questions could benefit from empirical research. Some critical research topics relevant to rehabilitation and health care assessment include the following: (1) professional competence; (2) informed consent; (3) third-party observers; (4) demographic factors and normative data; (5) test security; (6) misuse of test materials; (7) the impact of patient and situational factors (e.g., pain, medications, fatigue, and symptom validity) on assessment results; (8) test accommodations for individuals with sensory and motor deficits; (9) computerized assessment (broadly defined); and (10) incremental and ecological validity. Many different avenues of research could spring from these general topics. Most of these topics have been studied to some degree, but further research would be of value to rehabilitation professionals and consumers.

CULTURAL AND PROFESSIONAL ISSUES

Ethnic, cultural, and linguistic factors are essential influences on patient behavior in health care settings. With the exception of some purely biomedical tests, the results of

RESEARCH BOX 2.1

Many rehabilitation patients have sensory and/or motor deficits that prohibit standardized administration of neurocognitive tests. As a result, in such circumstances clinicians must adapt the test administration to accommodate the needs of the patient unless the purpose of the evaluation is to assess sensory–motor functioning. However, the APA Ethics Code (2002) states that clinicians must select tests whose validity and reliability have been established for use with members of the population tested, and test administration should be adapted based on research or other evidence supporting such adaptations (ES 9.02, Use of Assessments). A dilemma for clinicians exists because of the extremely limited research to support test adaptations.

For example, with patients who have hemiparesis involving the dominant upper extremity, tests of constructional or graphomotor ability must be completed with the nondominant hand. However, few studies have examined the intermanual equivalence on such tests in healthy adults or rehabilitation patients. The following study by Bush and Martin (2004) illustrates some research done on this topic.

Objective: To examine intermanual differences on the copy task of the Rey Complex Figure Test (RCFT) in order to assess the validity of using nondominant hand performance from persons with impaired dominant hand functioning.

Method: Fifty-eight healthy community dwelling adults completed the Rey Complex Figure Test with their dominant and nondominant hands in a counterbalanced order. Intermanual differences were compared.

Results: Intermanual differences were not significant [$t(57) = 1.70, p = 0.10$].

Conclusions: Use of the nondominant hand to complete the RCFT appears to be an acceptable alternative when the dominant hand is not functional. However, caution should be exercised in extrapolating these findings to persons with neurological impairment.

Overall, clinicians are advised to seek research to support any deviations from standardized test administration. When such research does not exist, clinicians should carefully consider whether the needed adaptation will provide a valid measure of the construct being examined; conclusions should be tempered accordingly. See Caplan and Shechter (2005) for further review of this topic.

Questions

1. In addition to the example provided above, what types of adaptations to test administration are likely to be needed in rehabilitation contexts, and what research exists to support such adaptations?
2. What additional research is needed to further establish the validity and reliability of a testing adaptation that is commonly used in your practice context? Describe the study's objective and methods in detail.

---

assessment procedures may be influenced by these factors. However, the extremely variable experiential, attitudinal, and behavioral differences that distinguish patients among and within ethnic and cultural groups challenge clinicians to reach accurate and meaningful assessment conclusions (Brickman, Cabo, & Manly, 2006; Byrd & Manly, 2005).

Although the ethical clinician considers ethnic, cultural, and linguistic factors when performing assessments and interpreting assessment results, the specific impact of these factors on the assessment of any given patient often is difficult, if not impossible, to discern. The psychological and neuropsychological assessment literature offers clinicians a foundation for deciding whether one should conduct assessments of persons whose cultural background differs from that of the dominant U.S. culture (Fletcher-Janzen, Strickland, & Reynolds, 2000; Nell, 2000; Samuda, 1998; Sandoval, Frisby, Geisinger, Ramos-Greiner, & Scheuneman 1998).

When assessing patients who do not share the clinician's language, clinicians may, in some contexts, consider using interpreters. The requirements of APA Ethical Standard 9.03 (Informed Consent in Assessments) subsection (c) are relevant across rehabilitation and health care disciplines. This standard states the following:

> Psychologists using the services of an interpreter obtain informed consent from the client/patient to use that interpreter, ensure that confidentiality of test results and test security are maintained, and include in their recommendations, reports, and diagnostic or evaluative statements, including forensic testimony, discussion of any limitations on the data obtained. (p. 13)

In addition to cultural factors, professional issues must be considered when anticipating or addressing ethical

DISCUSSION BOX 2.2

The development of demographically adjusted normative data (e.g., Heaton, Miller, Taylor, & Grant, 2004; Lucas et al., 2005) and the development or adaptation of Spanish language versions of multiple tests (e.g., Ardila, Rodriquez-Menendez, & Rosselli, 2002) and test batteries (e.g., Artiolo i Fortuny, Hermosillo, Heaton, & Pardee, 2000) for use in neurocognitive evaluations have advanced the assessment possibilities for non-White, non-English-speaking patients. The use of more culturally appropriate assessment methods and norms results in more accurate conclusions about patients' functioning in their life contexts. However, such cultural considerations may mask impairments, disabilities, or handicaps encountered by patients when required to interact with others outside of their cultural group or function in the dominant U.S. culture. Even with the advances in the assessment of persons from diverse cultures, the clinician must consider factors that are unique to each patient, such as cultural experience and level of acculturation, quality of education, stereotype threat (i.e., perception that one's performance will confirm a negative stereotype about one's group), and cultural values that may not correspond to those of the dominant U.S. culture (Byrd & Manly, 2005).

Questions

1. What are three cultural issues that you consider in your clinical assessments, and how does the above information impact or reinforce your practices?

challenges. A primary professional issue involves the impact of managed care on the selection and use of assessment procedures. Clinicians must base their diagnoses, opinions, and recommendations on information and techniques sufficient to substantiate their findings (Ethical Standard 9.01, Bases for Assessments; APA, 2002). Clinicians must be allowed to select the assessment methods that they consider to be appropriate for a given patient based on their education, training, and experience, and on their understanding of evidence-based assessment research.

However, managed care companies exert various degrees of control over the assessment methods and procedures employed by clinicians. The control may occur through selective reimbursement of certain assessment methods or through an overall cap on the number of units or hours of assessment that will be covered. Such situations place the clinician in a bind: Limit the assessment performed or risk not being paid for what is considered a medically necessary service. This bind may be alleviated in some contexts by informing the patient of the assessment options and the restrictions placed on payment for assessment services by managed care, and by providing the patient with the option of paying the balance. However, regardless of the payment issue, the clinician must perform an appropriate assessment.

INTERDISCIPLINARY APPLICATION

Interdisciplinary collaboration, comfort, and familiarity are advantageous for patients and professionals. Interdisciplinary collaboration allows for the provision of complementary services, including the integration of wide ranging expertise. However, such familiarity at times threatens ethical practice. In this author's experience, the greatest threat to ethical practice occurs with the temptation or invitation to engage in behaviors beyond one's area of professional competence.

Clinicians may become so familiar with the assessments performed by health care colleagues that they feel confident performing all or portions of such assessments themselves and independently. In fact, some busy clinicians may seek the assistance of colleagues from other less qualified disciplines to help perform needed assessments. However, in order to avoid harming patients and bringing discredit to their profession and institution, health care professionals must conduct assessments only within the boundaries of their competence, based on their education, training, and supervised experience. Furthermore, they must not promote the use of assessment techniques by unqualified persons. Interdisciplinary cooperation and communication will minimize the likelihood of ethical misconduct and will advance the pursuit of ethical ideals.

JURISDICTIONAL RELEVANCE

Jurisdictional Laws

State and federal laws govern the practices of health care providers. Whereas violations of the ethical standards of professional organizations can result in censure or, with serious matters, expulsion from the organization, violations of law can result in the loss of one's license to practice and criminal prosecution, including possible fines and incarceration. Nevertheless, many health care professionals are more familiar with their professional ethics codes than they are with the laws governing their practice. Fortunately for such professionals, ethics codes often are more conservative than laws; that is, they provide protections for consumers and the public that go beyond the requirements of law. As a result, professionals who follow their code of ethics also are likely to comply with laws.

However, this is not always true and should not be assumed. In some jurisdictions, licensing or certification boards may adopt, in whole or in part, the ethics code of a given discipline for that discipline's legally mandated rules of professional conduct. This practice reduces the potential for conflict between ethical and legal requirements. In psychology, some states have adopted the APA Ethical Principles of Psychologists and Code of Conduct, others have adopted the Association of State and Provincial Psychology Boards Code of Conduct, and still others have drafted their own requirements for professional conduct. Individual practitioners are required to be familiar with the laws governing their professional conduct.

Federal laws also exist to protect the rights of consumers of health care services. For example, in the United States, the Health Insurance Portability and Accountability Act of 1996 (HIPAA; U.S. Department of Health and Human Services, 2003) grants patients certain rights to privacy and to review and amend medical records. Clinicians should consult their state laws and institutional resources and determine HIPAA's applicability to their practices.

The Americans With Disabilities Act (ADA; 1990) was created to provide legislative support for the prevention of discrimination against people with disabilities and for the promotion of participation in society by individuals with disabilities. The ADA addresses five areas: employment, public services, public accommodations, transportation, and telecommunications. Although the ADA originally was considered to be landmark civil rights legislation, the ADA has been interpreted somewhat narrowly by the U.S. Supreme Court (Gostin, 2003). Health care professionals, particularly those providing rehabilitative services, "need to have a thorough understanding of the Americans With Disabilities Act to be effective advocates for their patients' vocational reentry and to meet their professional responsibilities under the principles of beneficence and justice" (Hanson, Kerkhoff, & Bush, 2005; p. 179).

Conflicts Between Ethical and Legal Resources

Ethical and legal requirements governing professional conduct generally are congruent. However, discrepancies between some ethics codes and laws exist, thus requiring clinicians to be familiar with both ethics and laws. For example, the assessment of persons with disabilities at times requires that accommodations be made in order for the construct of interest to be assessed most accurately. The Rehabilitation Act of 1973 prohibits the flagging of accommodations; that is, the examiner must not identify the use of, or reason for, testing accommodations. In contrast, when the reliability and validity of tests administered with accommodations have not been established, the APA Ethics Code requires examiners to describe the strengths and limitations of test results and interpretation and to identify any significant limitations on their interpretations (Ethical Standards 9.02, Use of Assessments, and 9.06, Interpreting Assessment Results). Such description of limitations requires the examiner to identify or "flag" the patient's disability. According to the SEPT (Standard 10.11), in the absence of established comparability between test scores obtained with and without an accommodation, ". . . specific information about the nature of the modification should be provided, if permitted by law, to assist test users to properly interpret and act on test scores." In contrast, the following Comment section states that the report should contain no reference to the existence or nature of the test taker's disability. Caplan and Shechter (2005) noted, "As worded, this standard seems to us to be a 'Catch 22,' imposing a considerable burden on the psychologist to describe and justify the modification that directly stemmed from the disability without naming the disability" (p. 100). Mehrens and Ekstrom (2002) took the position that, while "flagging" per se should be minimized, it is important to describe in reports any accommodations and modifications made to standardized test administration, unless doing so would violate federal laws.

When conflicts between ethical and legal requirements are encountered, clinicians should make known their commitment to professional ethics and attempt to resolve the matter in a manner that is consistent with their code of ethics. The first obligation for health care providers is to meet both ethical and legal requirements. If an ethically preferable solution or compromise cannot be reached, clinicians should ultimately yield to the legal authority. When conflicts between legal requirements are encountered, clinicians should consider which law offers the greatest protection of safety or other relevant rights and consult legal counsel as needed.

AN ETHICAL DECISION-MAKING PROCESS

Decision-Making Models

Determining an optimal course of ethical behavior can be difficult, particularly when adherence to one ethical principle conflicts with another principle. In such instances, use of an ethical decision-making model can be of particular value. A number of models have been proposed in the psychology literature for use when facing questions about one's own activities or the activities of colleagues (e.g., Bush, Connell, & Denney, 2006; Deiden & Bush, 2002; Haas & Malouf, 2002; Kitchener, 2000; Knapp & Vandecreek, 2003; Koocher & Keith-Spiegel, 2008).

An 8-stage model was proposed to address limitations noted with existing models (Bush, Connell, & Denney, 2006). The model consists of the following steps: (1) identify the problem, (2) consider the significance of the context and setting, (3) identify and utilize ethical and legal resources, (4) consider personal beliefs and values, (5) develop possible solutions to the problem, (6) consider the potential consequences of various solutions, (7) choose and implement a course of action, and (8) assess the outcome and implement changes as needed. The application of this model aids clinicians in avoiding ethical misconduct and pursuing ethical ideals. Writing down the steps taken during the resolution of ethical challenges may facilitate the decision-making process and may be of value if evidence of one's commitment to ethical practice is ever requested by an adjudicative body.

Documentation

The importance of documenting the efforts made and the steps taken throughout the ethical decision-making process cannot be overstated. Such documentation can help structure one's approach to the decision-making process, clarify options, facilitate reasoning, and avoid redundant efforts. In addition, having documentation of one's ethical decision-making efforts and commitment to ethical practice is critical if evidence of one's efforts and commitment is later requested by an ethics committee or professional regulatory body.

Documentation that follows the outline of the ethical decision-making model presented above and includes the details of the specific situation would likely satisfy an adjudicating body. Descriptions of the resources consulted and the reasoning underlying one's choice of action can be particularly important. In addition to promoting and demonstrating ethical conduct in a given situation, documentation of one's ethical decision-making process can facilitate future problem-solving in similar cases and serve as a valuable resource for colleagues facing similar challenges.

AREAS FOR FURTHER STUDY

Compared to most other areas of health care assessment, little research has been done on ethical issues. Despite the existence of scholarly writings on various aspects of assessment, there is a need for more quantitative research regarding ethical aspects of assessment. As described previously in this chapter, the following are some aspects of assessment ethics that need further study: (1) professional competence; (2) informed consent; (3) third-party observers; (4) demographic factors and normative data; (5) test security; (6) misuse of test materials; (7) the impact of patient and situational factors (e.g., pain, medications, fatigue, and symptom validity) on assessment results; (8) test accommodations for individuals with sensory and motor deficits; (9) computerized assessment (broadly defined); and (10) incremental and ecological validity. Investigation of these general topics could take many directions. Although some ethics topics do not readily lend themselves to empirical investigation, creative researchers supported with the necessary resources may be able to devise ways to study these research topics.

Summary and Conclusion

Health care professionals have multiple ethical obligations that exist to protect and advance the interests and well-being of patients, families and other consumers, and the public. These ethical obligations are consistent with the values and personal commitments of most health care professionals. However, even the most ethically conscious and well-intentioned clinicians face ethical dilemmas. The close interdisciplinary collaboration that constitutes a strength of rehabilitation services also is a source of unique ethical challenges. Positive ethics require proactive efforts to anticipate challenges and to take steps to avoid or prepare to address such challenges.

Although the answers to some ethical questions are straightforward and the solutions easily implemented, more complex ethical dilemmas place greater demands on the clinician's decision-making skills and use of resources. An ethical decision-making model provides a structured means of organizing one's thoughts, resources, and options so that clinicians can make appropriate decisions based on the relevant laws, ethical principles, and their own values.

The maintenance of ethical competence requires an ongoing commitment to increasing one's (1) understanding of ethical and legal issues encountered in rehabilitation and health assessment, (2) familiarity with the application of an ethical decision-making model, (3) appreciation of the multiple resources that can aid in ethical decision-making, and (4) personal investment in pursuing the highest ethical ideals. Rehabilitation and health care teams are encouraged to regularly include ethical and legal issues among their inservice and grand rounds topics. Through ethical clinical assessment, we have the privilege and responsibility of providing increased understanding of the neurocognitive, psychosocial, and physical strengths and limitations of individuals struggling to recover from or adapt to some of the most significant changes of their lives.

Self-Check Questions

1. What is a primary goal of positive ethics?
2. With regard to positive ethics, what is a primary responsibility and obligation of all practitioners?
3. List the four general bioethical principles described by Beauchamp and Childress.
4. List 3 to 5 additional ethical and professional resources that are specific to your discipline and professional activities.
5. Identify 3 to 5 additional areas of ethical or legal conflict or controversy in need of additional research specific to your assessment methods and measures.
6. Describe two specific avenues of research that would help clarify ethical and legal practices in your clinical setting(s).

Case Study

Kerri, a young occupational therapist, is new to the facility and to the outpatient brain injury rehabilitation program. Having recently completed her education and clinical training, she is eager to join the treatment team. While walking through the OT gym one day, Dr. A. Mazed, a neuropsychologist, notices Kerri reviewing a familiar line-drawn design with a patient. The design, Rey Complex Figure, is a commonly used neuropsychologist test. He observes Kerri providing the patient feedback on his performance and instruction on how to improve.

Analysis

Identify the Problem(s): Dr. Mazed observed a neuropsychological test being used inappropriately by a well-meaning rehabilitation colleague. Use of assessment measures as treatment materials invalidates their further use for assessment purposes. In addition, if the examining clinician is unaware that the assessment measure has been invalidated for a given patient, the measure may be used clinically, with the resulting inaccurate results misleading all those involved and possibly placing the patient at risk for harm. For example, if the results of one or more invalidated measures contribute to decisions to return to activities such as cooking, independent living, or driving, the patient could unintentionally end up in potentially dangerous situations.

Consider the Significance of the Context and Setting: The outpatient brain injury rehabilitation program treats hundreds of patients each year. The test may be administered many times to patients while in the program and after discharge, for both clinical and legal purposes. Inappropriate use of assessment measures may result in diagnostic errors and inappropriate recommendations and determinations for thousands of individuals within the span of a few years. An unknown percentage of those individuals will be harmed in some way because of the unintentional misuse of assessment measures.

Identify and Utilize Ethical and Legal Resources: Kerri believed she was practicing in a manner consistent with the ethical principle of beneficence and was promoting the recovery of her patient's visuospatial abilities. However, using tests as treatment materials violates the primary principle of nonmaleficence, whether done intentionally or unintentionally. As a neuropsychologist, Dr. Mazed has an ethical obligation (APA Ethical Standard 9.11, Maintaining Test Security) to educate colleagues about the importance of maintaining test security. He may wish to provide an inservice to educate the team about test security, including standardized tests used by other disciplines, not just those used by neuropsychologists.

In addition to general bioethical principles and professional ethics codes, legal resources provide important information for this case. When purchasing psychological or neuropsychological tests, the terms and conditions identify the test materials as copyrighted trade secrets. The purchaser agrees to protect the trade secrets by maintaining test security, only copying test forms for the purpose of conveying the information to another qualified professional, or in response to a subpoena or court order. Copying test stimuli for use as therapeutic material is a violation of copyright law. Both Kerri and Dr. Mazed should consult colleagues to obtain objective opinions about how to handle complex ethical and legal issues.

Consider Personal Beliefs and Values: Kerri and Dr. Mazed both want to do what is in the best interests of their patients and their professions. They have an appreciation of the impact that they have on the lives of others and want to do what they can to promote personal functions and safety while not allowing their services to bring harm to others. Dr. Mazed knows that he must address the problem in ways that do not offend or upset Kerri. He knows that she is motivated and is off to a great start in the program. Thus, he does not want to jeopardize their professional relationship.

Develop Possible Solutions to the Problem: Dr. Mazed considers the following options: (1) interrupt the OT session and remove the test materials, informing Kerri that she should not use the design for treatment purposes; (2) approach Kerri after the treatment session and ask to speak with her about her use of the test materials; or (3) discuss the matter with Kerri's supervisor with whom Dr. Mazed has worked closely for years.

Consider the Potential Consequences of Various Solutions: Dr. Mazed believes that interrupting the treatment session would embarrass both the patient and Kerri, place Kerri in a defensive position, and reduce the chances for a successful resolution. He believes that approaching Kerri after the session may be a good option, although he does not know her well and is concerned about how she may react. She may prefer to get such feedback from her supervisor. Dr. Mazed thinks that his developing professional relationship with Kerri may be jeopardized if he "goes over her head" by discussing the matter with her supervisor before discussing it with her.

Choose and Implement a Course of Action: Dr. Mazed elects to discuss his concerns directly with Kerri. After the session, Dr. Mazed asks to speak to Kerri and inquires about her use of the Rey Complex Figure for treatment purposes. She states that she brought the design with her from her last internship site, where it was routinely used for treatment. She was practicing as she had been trained to do at the previous facility. She also states that she is planning to present this design as well as other tests that involve red and white blocks (e.g., those from the Wechsler tests of intelligence) at an upcoming OT inservice. Dr. Mazed then explains to Kerri the nature of the test and the importance of maintaining the security of all tests. He also offers to help find and develop other therapeutic options to address visuospatial skills.

Kerri is apologetic, assures Dr. Mazed that she will no longer use the tests, and accepts his offer to identify alternative treatment options. As he begins to leave, Dr. Mazed asks, "Didn't the neuropsychologist at your last facility notice you using these materials?" at which point Kerri replies, "Where do you think I got them?"

Assess the Outcome and Implement Changes as Needed: Dr. Mazed is pleased with Kerri's receptivity to his concerns. After their discussion, they share a commitment to ensuring that tests be used appropriately and that through their creativity and resourcefulness they can obtain or develop alternative treatment materials that will serve their patients well. They both will inform their colleagues of the need to develop alternative treatment materials.

However, Dr. Mazed learned that a colleague at another facility knowingly provides test materials for inappropriate uses. As a neuropsychologist, Dr. Mazed has an ethical obligation (APA Ethical Standard 1.04, Informal Resolution of Ethical Violations) to talk to the neuropsychologist at the other facility about the importance of maintaining test security (APA Ethical Standard 9.11, Maintaining Test Security) and the need to educate all therapists at his facility of the need to stop using test materials for therapeutic purposes. Dr. Mazed must obtain an assurance that such steps will be taken by the other neuropsychologist and follow up at a later date to ensure that tests are no longer being misused in that facility.

Discussion

In this case, one ethical principle does not compete with others, and ethics and laws do not differ. Instead, this case illustrates the ethical and legal risks that exist when different disciplines work closely together and become careless with tests and other assessment measures. This risk also occurs when one discipline relies on another as test extenders, such as when a speech–language pathologist agrees to perform memory testing for a neuropsychologist. Although such arrangements may facilitate treatment and maximize use of resources, extra attention must be paid by all parties to the manner in which the test materials will be used and protected.

This case also demonstrates the awkwardness that may exist when a clinician from one discipline must confront a clinician from another discipline about assessment and treatment practices. Such confrontations become much easier when a foundation of good will and collaboration has been established and lines of communication are open. This case is intended to help readers apply the ethical decision-making model and appreciate its value when anticipating or resolving ethical challenges.

References

American Educational Research Association, American Psychological Association, & National Council on measurement in Education (1999). *Standards for educational and psychological testing.* Washington, DC: American Educational Research Association.

American Psychological Association [APA] (2002). Ethical principles of psychologists and code of conduct. *American Psychologist, 57,* 1060–1073.

American Psychological Association (2004). Guidelines for psychological practice with older adults. *American Psychologist, 59,* (4), 236–260.

American Psychological Association, Presidential Task Force on the Assessment of Age-Consistent Memory Decline and Dementia (1998). *Guidelines for the evaluation of dementia and age-related cognitive decline.* Washington, DC: American Psychological Association.

Americans with Disabilities Act of 1990, Public Law Number 101-336, 104 Stat. 328.

Ardila, A., Rodriquez-Menendez, G., & Rosselli, M. (2002). Current issues in neuropsychological assessment with Hispanics/Latinos. In F. R. Ferraro (Ed.), *Minority and cross-cultural aspects of neuropsychological assessment* (pp. 160–179). Lisse, NL: Sweet & Zeitlinger.

Artiol i Fortuny, L., Hermosillo, D., Heaton, R. K., & Pardee, R. E. (2000). *Manual de Normas y Procedimienos para la Bateria Neuropsicologica en Espanol.* London: Psychology press.

Association of State and Provincial Psychology Boards (2005). *ASPPB Code of Conduct.* Retrived January 28, 2005 from www.asppb.org/.

Beauchamp, T.L., & Childress, J.F. (2001). *Principles of biomedical ethics* (5th ed.). New York: Oxford University Press.

Bersoff, D., & Koeppl, P. (1993). The relations between ethical codes and moral principles. *Ethics and Behavior, 3,* 345–357.

Brickman, A.M., Cabo, R., & Manly, J.J. (2006). Ethical issues in cross-cultural neuropsychology. *Applied Neuropsychology, 13,* 91–100.

Bush, S.S. (Ed.) (2005). *A casebook of ethical challenges in neuropsychology.* New York: Psychology Press.

Bush, S.S., Connell, M.A., & Denney, R.L. (2006). *Ethical issues in forensic psychology: Key concepts and resources.* Washington, DC: American Psychological Association.

Bush, S.S., & Drexler, M.L. (Eds.). (2002). *Ethical Issues in Clinical Neuropsychology.* Lisse, The Netherlands: Swets & Zeitlinger Publishers.

Bush, S. S., & Martin, T. A. (2004). Intermanual differences on the Rey Complex Figure Test. *Rehabilitation Psychology, 49*(1), 76–78.

Bush, S. S., & Martin, T. A. (2006). Introduction to ethical controversies in neuropsychology. *Applied Neuropsychology, 13*(2), 63–67.

Byrd, D.A., & Manly, J.J. (2005). Cultural considerations in neuropsychological assessment of older adults. In S.S. Bush & T.A. Martin (Eds.), *Geriatric neuropsychology: Practice essentials* (pp. 115–139). New York: Psychology Press.

Canadian Psychological Association (1991). *Canadian code of ethics for psychologists* (Rev. ed.). Ottawa, ON Canada: Author.

Caplan, B., & Shechter, J. (2005). Test accommodations in geriatric neuropsychology. In S.S. Bush & T.A. Martin (Eds.), *Geriatric Neuropsychology: Practice Essentials* (pp. 97–114). New York: Psychology Press.

Deidan, C., & Bush, S. (2002). Addressing perceived ethical violations by colleagues. In S.S. Bush & M.L. Drexler (Eds.), *Ethical issues in clinical neuropsychology* (pp. 281–305). Lisse, The Netherlands: Swets & Zeitlinger Publishers.

Fletcher-Janzen, E., Strickland, L., & Reynolds, C. (Eds). (2000). *Handbook of cross-cultural neuropsychology.* New York: Kluwer Academic/Plenum Publishers.

Gostin, L. O. (2003). The judicial dismantling of the Americans with Disabilities Act. *Hastings Center Report, 33*(2), 9–11.

Haas, L., & Malouf, J. (2002). *Keeping up the good work: A practitioner's guide to mental health ethics* (3rd ed.). Sarasota, FL: Professional Resource Press.

Handelsman, M., Knapp, S., & Gottlieb, M. (2002). Positive ethics. In R. Snyder & S. Lopez (Eds.), *Handbook of positive psychology* (pp. 731–744). New York: Oxford University Press.

Hanson, S., Kerkhoff, T., & Bush, S. (2005). *Health care ethics for psychologists: A casebook.* Washington, DC: American Psychological Association.

Heaton, R.K., Miller, S.W., Taylor, M.J., & Grant, I. (2004). *Norms for an expanded Halstead–Reitan battery: Demographically adjusted neuropsychological norms for African American and Caucasian adults.* Lutz, FL: Psychological Assessment Resources.

Kitchener, K. S. (1984). Intuition, critical evaluation and ethical principles: The foundations for ethical decisions in counseling psychology. *The Counseling Psychologist, 12,* 43–55.

Kitchener, K. S. (2000). *Foundations of ethical practice, research, and teaching.* Mahwah, NJ: Erlbaum.

Knapp, S., & VandeCreek, L. (2003). *A guide to the 2002 revision of the American Psychological Association's Ethics Code.* Sarasota, FL: Professional Resource Press.

Knapp, S., & VandeCreek, L. (2004). A principle-based analysis of the 2002 American Psychological Association ethics code. *Psychotherapy: Theory, research, practice, training, 41* (3), 247–254.

Knapp, S., & VandeCreek, L. (2006). *Practical ethics for psychologists: A positive approach.* Washington, D.C.: American Psychological Association.

Koocher, G., & Keith-Spiegel, P. (2008). *Ethics in psychology and the mental health professions* (3rd). New York: Oxford University Press.

Lucas, J.A., Ivnik, R.J., Willis, F.B., Ferman, T.J., Smith, G.E., Parfitt, F.C., et al. (2005). Mayo's Older African Americans Normative Studies: Normative data for commonly used clinical neuropsychological measures. *The Clinical Neuropsychologist, 19*, 162–183.

McCaffrey, R. J. (Guest Ed.) (2005). Third party observers. *Journal of Forensic Neuropsychology*, *4* (2), special issue.

McCaffrey, R. J., Fisher, J. M., Gold, B. A., & Lynch, J. K. (1996). Presence of third parties during neuropsychological evaluation: Who is evaluating whom? *The Clinical Neuropsychologist, 10*(4), 435–449.

McCaffrey, R. J., Lynch, J. K., & Yantz, C. L. (2005). Third party observers: Why all the fuss? *Journal of Forensic Neuropsychology, 4*, 1–16.

Mehrens, W. A., & Ekstrom, R. B. (2002). Score reporting issues in the assessment of people with disabilities: Policies and practices. In R. B. Ekstrom & D. K. Smith (Eds.) *Assessing individuals with disabilities in educational, employment, and counseling settings* (pp. 87–100). Washington, DC: American Psychological Association.

National Academy of Neuropsychology (2000a). Test security: Official statement of the National Academy of Neuropsychology. *Archives of Clinical Neuropsychology, 15*(5), 383–386.

National Academy of Neuropsychology Policy and Planning Committee (2000b). Handling requests to release test data, recording and/or reproductions of test data. *Official statement of the National Academy of Neuropsychology.* http://www.nanonline.org/paio/secappend.shtm.

National Academy of Neuropsychology Policy and Planning Committee (2003). *Test security: An update. Official statement of the National Academy of Neuropsychology.* http://nanonline.org/paio/security_update.shtm.

Nell, V. (2000). *Cross-cultural neuropsychological assessment: Theory and practice.* Mahway, NJ: Lawrence Erlbaum Associates.

Petersen, D. B. (2005). International classification of functioning, disability and health: An introduction for rehabilitation psychologists. *Rehabilitation Psychology, 50*, 105–112.

Ross, W. D. (1998). What makes right acts right? In J. Rachels (Ed.), Ethical theory (pp. 265–285). New York: Oxford University Press. (Original work published 1930)

Samuda, R. J. (1998). *Psychological testing of American minorities: Issues and consequences,* (2nd ed.). Thousand Oaks, CA: Sage Publications.

Sandoval, J. H., Frisby, C.L., Geisinger, K. F., Rames-Greiner, J., & Scheuneman, J. D. (Eds.). (1998). *Test interpretation and diversity: Achieving equity in assessment.* Washington DC: American Psychological Association.

U.S. Department of Health and Human Services. (2003). *Public Law 104-191: Health Insurance Portability and Accountability Act of 1996.* Retrieved November 24, 2003, from http://www.hhs.gov/ocr/hipaa.

World Health Organization (2001). *International classification of functioning, disability and health (ICF).* Geneva, Switzerland: Author.

3

Diversity, Fairness, Utility, and Social Issues

SAMUEL O. ORTIZ
AGNIESZKA M. DYNDA
St. John's University, Jamaica, NY

OVERVIEW

Issues of fairness in rehabilitation health and assessment are important in all professional services and become especially salient when working with individuals from diverse cultural, ethnic, and linguistic backgrounds. Because the very tools, procedures, instruments, standards, and diagnostic criteria may reflect culturally-bound expectations and ideas, fair and accurate assessment is critical. Historically, bias has been viewed as being inherent primarily within the assessment tools. However, contemporary views of bias have expanded the concept beyond misdiagnosis to include differences in intervention selection, treatment response, and overall outcomes. Current research demonstrates that the most important qualities related to fairness in assessment revolve around the individual's level of acculturation (or familiarity with the entire purpose and process of rehabilitation health) and their English language proficiency (i.e., a communication barrier may impede successful rehabilitation efforts). This chapter is designed to help professionals learn about these important issues and how to apply practices designed to reduce bias and increase fairness in assessment. This chapter does not establish standards for an equitable evaluation. Rather, its goal is to provide basic information that advances knowledge and understanding of fairness in assessment that may guide activities relevant to the provision of health and rehabilitation services and that may lead to nondiscriminatory and equitable outcomes for those individuals from diverse ethnic, cultural, and linguistic backgrounds.

LEARNING OBJECTIVES

By the end of the chapter, readers should be able to:

- Define the terms (a) *fairness* and *bias* as they apply to assessment in rehabilitation health, and (b) *acculturation* and *limited English proficiency* and explain the manner in which they pose difficulties in some assessment activities

- Explain the importance of fair and accurate assessment

- Describe the main qualities that may introduce bias in evaluation or testing

- Discuss the manner in which (a) acculturation affects evaluation of functioning; (b) language differences affect evaluation of functioning; and (c) how the accuracy or validity of assessment data may be undermined by qualities related to cultural, ethnic, and linguistic differences

- Apply practices designed to reduce bias in evaluation of functioning and describe various strategies and methods that may help reduce bias and increase fairness in assessment

INTRODUCTION

Assessment practices, including the use of tests, comprise significant and important services provided by rehabilitation and health promotion specialists. For example, test use may be central to the measurement of an individual's current level of functioning, formation of a diagnosis, development of recommendations for treatment, implementation of interventions, and evaluation of change, progress, or response to treatment. Because test data are used to guide these and other critical aspects of rehabilitation and health, they must be as reliable, valid, and as fair (unbiased) as possible (American Educational Research Association, American Psychological Association, & National Council on Measurement in Education, 1999).

TEST BIAS

In general, test bias has been defined traditionally as results that are obtained through testing that are influenced by qualities other than what the test is designed to measure or results that may lead to discriminatory (more or less favorable) predictions, conclusions, or outcomes for members of one group versus another (Reynolds & Carson, 2005; Sattler, 2001). For example, a test may require the use of blocks to create various patterns and is designed to measure an individual's visual conceptual processing ability. This test would likely show evidence of bias if used with individuals who have fine and/or sensory–motor difficulties. In such a case, the test may be measuring the fine and/or sensory–motor functioning more than visual conceptual processing, with the results likely to yield a discriminatory (in this case an underestimated) picture of one's actual ability. Similarly, a test that asks individuals to recall as many words as they can for animals that begin with the letter "S" may be used to evaluate functioning in long-term memory and retrieval. If the test were given to individuals who were not native English speakers and the expected responses had to be given in English, the test again may underestimate the actual functioning of members of this group because, in general, they will have less vocabulary development and thus fewer available words to retrieve that begin with the letter "S."

Let us assume the purpose of assessing word retrieval is to form a judgment as to a patient's prognosis for full recovery of long-term memory. Again, language difference may adversely influence conclusions. For example, as noted previously, nonnative English speakers have less vocabulary and thus a comparatively smaller word pool than native English speakers. Thus, the number of words they are able to retrieve over time remains relatively small and consistent, even if functioning improves—thus suggesting a poor prognosis. By comparison, the number of words a typical native English speaker is able to retrieve over time is likely to increase steadily as functioning improves, thus suggesting a better prognosis. Therefore, conclusions regarding prognosis may be discriminatory and biased against the group for whom English is not its native language. Thus, the interpretations would be unfair, inequitable, and inconsistent with the principles of nondiscriminatory assessment. A goal of testing is to produce results that lead to equity: Similar conclusions, outcomes, and predictions will occur regardless of personal qualities (e.g., gender, English proficiency, ethnic background) that largely should be irrelevant to the traits being measured.

RELIABILITY AND VALIDITY

Issues of reliability, validity, and fairness cut across all aspects of assessment and pertain to all individuals (see also chapter 7). Reliability addresses issues about a test's ability to assess a trait or other quality consistently. Reliability typically is thought to be a property of a test, either the consistency of its items to measure a trait or its consistency to obtain comparable scores each time it is used. Because reliability generally is an inherent characteristic of a test, it often is not a significant source of bias for tests that are carefully developed and that adhere to the accepted standards for development (American Educational Research Association, American Psychological Association, National Council on Measurement in Education, 1999; Cummins, 1984; Figueroa, 1983, 1990b; Jensen, 1974, 1976, 1980; Reynolds & Carson, 2005; Valdés & Figueroa, 1994).

Validity addresses issues about the accuracy with which something is measured (e.g., a trait,

DISCUSSION BOX 3.1

Issue

Bias has been defined historically as some inherent property or characteristic of a test or tool. Thus, bias was seen to exist in assessment only when it could be shown that a particular tool produced results that either did not measure the same construct or did not predict equally well for two groups.

Discuss how such traditional views of bias may tend to ignore other potentially discriminatory aspects of assessment such as intervention selection, decisions regarding treatment, or outcomes in rehabilitation. In addition, which type of bias is likely to be found in rehabilitation health and why?

ability, skill, knowledge, and level of functioning). More specifically, validity refers to "the degree to which accumulated evidence and theory support specific interpretations of test scores entailed by proposed uses of a test" (p. 184, AERA et al., 1999). Issues of validity lie at the core of test use. Validity evidence is needed when providing a defensible foundation for test selection, use, and interpretations.

Validity tends to be more problematic because one never can prove that a test is measuring only what one believes it is measuring (DeVellis, 2003). In addition, a test that is reliable may not be valid for the specific purposes for which it is used. For example, a ruler that yields consistent results in measuring various objects cannot be used to measure intelligence by measuring a person's hand. The ruler will provide consistent results yet will not be a valid measure of the trait we intend to measure: intelligence.

When developing tests, efforts are made to help ensure a test measures a desired construct adequately and that qualities irrelevant to the construct do not attenuate its measurement. Two broad qualities may jeopardize test validity and thus contribute to an unfair assessment: *construct underrepresentation* and *construct irrelevance*. Therefore, efforts that avoid *construct underrepresentation* (i.e., when a test fails to measure important aspects of the construct or trait) and *construct irrelevance* (i.e., when qualities extraneous to the construct or trait attenuate its measurement) are critical when developing tests (AERA et al., 1999; Messick, 1995).

When selecting and using tests, clinicians should determine whether the test is consistent with current theory and research that help define the trait being assessed. In general, tests with more items are better than those with fewer items

because they generally provide a more complete assessment of the trait and thus avoid construct underrepresentation. Clinicians also should review the test to determine whether it has sufficient depth so as to adequately measure the construct or trait (i.e., to insure the test does not underrepresent the trait or behavior being assessed). Additionally, the selected measure should assess only the trait, not extraneous qualities, so as to avoid construct irrelevance.

Construct-irrelevant variance may result in bias when a test measures qualities that largely are irrelevant to the intended construct (AERA et al., 1999; Messick, 1995). For example, you may want to use a test designed to evaluate visual perceptual abilities that requires an individual to examine missing or incorrect components in illustrations of various objects. However, because such illustrations will necessarily be culturally embedded objects (i.e., people, household appliances, vehicles), it will be difficult to determine whether low performance was due to dysfunction in visual processing (the relevant construct) or lack of cultural knowledge (an irrelevant construct).

Construct underrepresentation occurs when a test provides a measure of only a limited portion of a particular construct. Tests that display these qualities are subject to bias (AERA et al., 1999; Messick, 1995). For example, suppose your task is to evaluate the general memory functioning of an individual and the test you select does so by requiring an individual to recall one part of a previously learned but unrelated pair of items when the other part is presented. Such a task measures primarily associative memory, a component of long-term retrieval ability.

Although the test may provide a good measure of this narrow skill, it does not inform us about functioning in other areas of long-term memory such as naming facility, free recall memory, or meaningful memory. In addition, it does not provide any information related to other broad aspects of memory such as short-term skills, including memory span and working memory. Decisions regarding functioning or performance made on the basis of such limited data are likely to be biased and lead to inequitable outcomes.

HISTORY OF RESEARCH AND PRACTICE IN FAIRNESS IN ASSESSMENT

All tests developed within the context of a particular culture are necessarily artifacts of that culture and reflect its values and ideas, and beliefs of the individuals who developed them (Sanchez, 1934; Scarr, 1978). In the United States, the history of test development can be traced to work that revolved around intelligence testing. The pioneering efforts in psychometrics focused on ability testing. Those early influences continue to underlie test development. Moreover, individuals from diverse ethnic, cultural, and linguistic backgrounds were part of that early development and heralded fairness in assessment issues despite the fact that such issues were largely misunderstood for a long time.

Alfred Binet and Theodore Simon developed some scales that served as the impetus for test development in the United States. Their work in France was used to evaluate academic aptitude in school-age children. During the early part of the 20th century, psychologists in the United States adapted these scales, extended the questions upwards, and translated them into English (Goddard, 1913). Despite Binet's cautions against viewing his scales as anything but a practical device and not as a measure of intelligence, Goddard, Terman (1916), and others trumpeted their adapted scales as reliable, valid, and fair measures of intelligence (Gould, 1996). The assumption of fairness was drawn largely from the belief that such tests were scientifically objective in nature and therefore not subject to bias.

Tests emanated from French, British, German, North American, and other similarly European cultures (Kamphaus, 1993). Naturally, tests came to reflect the values of those who created them, including an emphasis on abilities they felt were characteristic of intelligence. These included verbal development, logic and reasoning ability, mathematics, and general knowledge. Therefore, the tests were not as objective or value free as some thought.

Research on test use with individuals from various diverse ethnic and cultural backgrounds, including many who were limited in English proficiency or who did not speak it at all, occurred early in the 20th century. Despite attempts to create tests that were fair with such populations (i.e., tests with no bias), the prevailing beliefs and values of test developers often made attempts to detect bias difficult despite its appearance. For example, in 1923, Brigham, the originator of the SAT, analyzed data from Robert Yerkes' work for the Department of the Army that examined the performance of nonnative English speakers (i.e., immigrants from other countries) on the Binet scale administered in English. Brigham found the mental age on the Binet scale increased as the length of residence in the United States also increased, reaching average levels after 16 to 20 years of residence in the United States, thus yielding strong evidence regarding the test's unfair qualities and the existence of bias. Brigham, on the other hand, attributed the pattern to a progressive decline in the average intelligence of immigrants in each of the preceding 5-year periods since 1902 (Brigham, 1923). That is, Brigham discounted the effect of being limited in English as well as being unfamiliar with the culturally-based content of the test as conditions that influenced test performance and hence the fairness of the results.

The consequences of this and other early research were twofold: the belief that (1) intelligence largely was a function of genetic inheritance related to one's ethnicity or race, as well as (2) bilingual individuals somehow had a mental handicap (Bialystok, 1991; Hakuta, 1986). Subsequent research has informed our understanding of fairness in assessment and largely has dispelled these notions.

The qualities that contribute to test bias remain somewhat poorly understood. Likewise, methods for making the testing and evaluation process fair and for ensuring equitable outcomes require additional resources. The following section discusses and compares different diagnostic models regarding fairness in assessment. The specific qualities and variables that influence fairness, particularly that relate to test bias, also will be presented for the purpose of guiding assessment practices in rehabilitation in the fairest manner possible.

FAIRNESS IN ASSESSMENT

Fairness becomes more salient and complex when a person's background is characterized by cultural or linguistic differences, as is common in individuals who are ethnically diverse. Tests used with individuals whose cultural experiences and knowledge as well as linguistic backgrounds differ from the dominant culture may lack suitable validity, thus increasing the possibility of drawing invalid, inequitable, and potentially discriminatory inferences from test data (Ortiz, 2002; Ortiz & Dynda, 2005; Rhodes, Ochoa & Ortiz, 2005). Contemporary views on nondiscriminatory assessment have extended the concept of fairness beyond the notion of bias in testing. For example, fairness also includes equitable treatment in the testing process (e.g., using the best or most appropriate test for all individuals regardless of race, social class, or economic status) and equality in outcomes from testing (e.g., equivalent rates of learning disability diagnoses and eligibility for special education services across various ethnically diverse groups) (AERA et al., 1999). This chapter focuses on issues that may affect the fairness of assessment and testing practices, broadly speaking, with culturally and linguistically diverse individuals.

The dramatic increase in the racial/ethnic composition of the United States during the past few decades has increased attention to issues of fairness across many areas of professional practice and public service delivery, including specialists engaged in providing rehabilitation services. Professionals in rehabilitation who are involved in assessment activities should not assume current methods and procedures used with populations that are relatively homogenous with respect to ethnicity and culture also are reliable, valid, and fair when used with more heterogeneous populations. Some are, whereas others are not. Both test users and test developers share responsibility for ensuring fairness in assessment (AERA et al., 1999). The application of knowledge in the foundations of fair testing will foster success in this endeavor.

The use of tests in rehabilitation may focus initially on issues critical to diagnosis of current functioning. Nevertheless, assessment should not be considered a one time endeavor and instead should be considered as an on-going process conducted for the purpose of informing diagnoses, interventions, and evaluating treatment effects. The importance of utilizing assessment data to inform intervention planning and evaluation should be underscored because this process helps to ensure and increase fairness.

Efforts to promote fairness and reduce bias occur through practices consistent with four conceptual diagnostic–intervention models used to guide assessment and intervention (Mercer and Ysseldyke (1977). Table 3.1 summarizes these models. The importance of these models lies in their links to intervention and recognition of the respective degree of bias inherent in each

approach. The models differ in terms of assumptions, techniques, and definitions of normality/abnormality.

Medical Model

The medical model is one of the most relevant models to rehabilitation and thus is discussed first. In this model, the definition of normal/abnormal is based on the presence of some biological or physiological pathology within the individual. The model assumes that the symptoms or functional limitations are due to the biological condition. Thus, sociocultural qualities (e.g. ethnicity and language dominance and proficiency) largely are irrelevant to the disease process. The medical model is a deficit-based model: It attempts to identify and locate deficiencies or problems due to biophysical causes that are rather independent of culture. Thus, unlike other models, one's culture, race/ethnicity, and language are not primary related to pathology.

The medical model relies on instruments and tools (e.g. heart rate, blood pressure, chemical analyses, scanning devices, measures of muscle strength and motor control) to measure these biologically determined symptoms. Scores from such instruments are interpreted relative to biologically based population norms and an individual's levels of functioning, or baselines established prior to and/or after the onset of a biological insult. An individual's cultural or linguistic background generally, but not always, has little influence on the presence of biological symptoms and thus has a relatively minor role when interpreting medical model data. Treatment is directed toward the amelioration or elimination of the symptomatology that is attributable to the biological condition. Assessment methods used in this model generally are fair and may lead to equitable outcomes provided they focus only on biological conditions.

Cultural, racial, and linguistic qualities are unlikely to affect the model significantly when the process is carried out as described and the focus remains strictly on aspects of biology. However, there may be cases that deviate from this policy. For example, the brains of individuals who learned English later (e.g., after age 10) may begin to fossilize language sounds and thus may appear to have difficulty enunciating certain English sounds—problems that may be attributed to oral–motor or hearing problems that in fact result from natural physiological processes. Assessment of progress and expectations for recovery following traumatic brain injury that results in loss of hearing or various types of stroke or palsy involving facial muscles (e.g., Bell's Palsy) may not be fair if qualities related to first and second language development are not considered.

TABLE 3.1 Four Models for Assessment and Evaluation

	Medical Model	**Social Deviance or Social System Model**	**Psychoeducational Process Model**	**Task Analysis Model**
Definition of Normal–Abnormal	Presence of biological pathology within the individual	Degree to which behavior of individual conforms to group expectations	Presence of intact or deficient abilities or processes within the individual	Degree of mastery of subject matter, no formal definition of normal or abnormal
Assumptions	Symptoms caused by biological condition; sociocultural characteristics irrelevant	Multiple definitions of normal behavior; not biologically determined	Deficient academic performance is caused by underlying psychoeducational process or ability deficits	Deficient academic performance due to interaction between task demands and individual mastery of demands
Characteristics	Deficit, but not culture bound	Social system and role bound	Culture bound	Culture bound
Properties of Statistical Distributions	n/a – relies on prevalence rates and epidemiological data	n/a – behavior conforms or does not	Theoretically normal distributions of abilities and processes	Dichotomous data, either demonstrates behavior or does not
Characteristics of Appropriate Measures	Instruments measure biologically determined symptoms	Focus on assessing social competence in performance of social roles	Norm-referenced	Criterion-referenced
Interpretation of Scores	Isolated, without sociocultural context	Role specific and system specific; cannot be generalized	Ordinal data; relative standing compared to similar peers in norm sample	Mastery of skills for tasks; not relative to others
Nature of Treatment or Intervention	Direct treatment to the individual's biology	Focus on socializing or teaching individual to perform socially expected behaviors	Compensatory or remedial	Test–teach–test process
Extent of Racially and Culturally Discriminatory Effect	Not biased if limited to biological conditions	May be biased if lack of opportunity to learn exists. Can lead to intervention in circumscribed situations.	May be biased if individual is not comparable to norm samples from tests	Not biased; focus is on the individual
Examples of Appropriate Measures	Chemical analyses, imaging techniques, physical examination, reflexes, vision, hearing, motor functioning	Achievement tests measure role in school; behavior rating and social competence scales measure role in society	Norm-referenced, cognitive ability/processing tests	Criterion-referenced measures of reading, writing, math, oral language, or subject area

Note: Information in this table is adapted from Mercer, J. R & Ysseldyke, J. (1977). Designing Diagnostic-Intervention Programs. In T. Oakland (Ed.), Psychological and Educational Assessment of Minority Children (pp. 70-90). New York: Bruner/Mazel Inc.

Social Deviance or Social System Model

The social deviance or social systems model defines normal/abnormal primarily as the degree to which an individual's behavior conforms to group expectations. This definition is founded upon the assumption that there may be multiple definitions of what distinguishes normal from abnormal behavior. The causes of normal and abnormal behavior must be viewed within a social context because they may not be due to biologically determined causes. Thus, the model focuses on expectations established for a person's behaviors within various social systems (e.g., those within one's home, workplace, school, and clinic setting) and roles (e.g., as a leader or follower, a parent or child, the preferred display of passive or assertive behaviors). The types of measures deemed to be appropriate are those that focus on assessing social competence in the performance of social roles. The results from these assessments tend to be system and role specific and may not generalize beyond the context within which they were examined. Treatment and intervention efforts focus on helping the patient acquire suitable social behaviors and to desist in performing socially unacceptable behaviors.

Work within this model may be biased if an individual has not been given sufficient opportunity to learn the systems' rules and the roles he or she is expected to perform. Moreover, the norms for these social systems and the preferred roles for individuals born outside the United States, who immigrated here, may differ from current prevailing national norms. The implications of the social systems model may be greatest on rehabilitation efforts, given the importance of one's social system and role definition to one's recovery. The model also is applicable to psychotherapeutic efforts that address behavior and social functioning.

Process Model

In the process model, the definition of normal/abnormal is based on the presence of intact or deficient processes, typically linguistic, psychological, and neuropsychological processes within the individual. The underlying principles revolve around the assumption that performance deficiencies are due to processing or ability deficits; that is, one or more linguistic or cognitive processing deficiencies cause the performance deficit. Processing deficits typically are thought to reflect the manner in which the brain receives and processes information, and displays behaviors. Thus, the model displays cybernetic qualities.

Tests and other methods used in this model rely on norms often nationally established, to judge whether a person displays deficiencies in one or more processes. Scores are interpreted in terms of an individual's relative standing compared to peers within the norm sample. Assessment methods used in this model may be biased if the individual being evaluated is not comparable to the norm sample against which performance is being compared. The reliance on the *assumption of comparability*, the belief that an individual is being compared to others with similar cultural experiences and linguistic background (Oakland, 1976, 1977; Salvia & Ysseldyke, 1991), often renders such comparisons unfair when the individual was not born or raised in the host culture or language of the test.

Data can be used to compare a person's scores with a group (i.e., norm-referenced interpretation) or in reference to one's own normative behavior (i.e., an ideographic or ipsative interpretation). For example, let's assume a person's test scores are very low to below average, relative to a mean of 10, and include the following scores: 1, 2, 3, 4, 5, 6, and 7. When used in a norm-referenced evaluation, these scores would be considered to be below average.

In an ideographic or ipsative interpretation, the clinician first determines a person's average or mean score (in this case 4), and then subtracts each individual score from this mean to determine those that may be lowest—revealing personal weaknesses (e.g., 1 and 2) and the highest—revealing personal strengths (e.g. 6 and 7). If used independently from norm-referenced analysis, this method can lead to bias in that it identifies *person-relative* strengths and weaknesses, not actual ones. Conversely, an individual with several strengths may be identified as having a weakness in an area despite the fact that functioning in that area is average when compared to peers. Therefore, if ipsative analysis is used, it is best to combine it with norm-referenced analysis to avoid bias.

Moreover, care is needed to ensure that a test's norms are representative of the individual being tested in terms of critical and relevant personal variables. That is, to simply compare performance to others of the same age is insufficient. Consider, too, whether the individual's peer-based norm group shares similar cultural and linguistic experiences to help ensure fairness in testing.

Task Analysis or Behavioral Model

The task analysis or behavioral model has no formal definition of normal/abnormal. Whether behavior is normal or abnormal depends on the degree desired behaviors have been displayed. This model assumes that behavioral

DISCUSSION BOX 3.2

Issue

When an ipsative approach is used to evaluate test results, an average score is calculated using scores from all subtests. Then each subtest score is subtracted from the average in order to identify areas where the individual scored higher (i.e., a personal strength), about the same, or lower (i.e., a personal weakness) than their own average. Discuss how this process differs from the use of a normative approach that compares performance against the standards set by testing numerous individuals of the same age in the general population. What are the advantages and disadvantages of both approaches, and what can be done to avoid the problems in using one or the other?

deficiencies are due to the ineffective interactions between task demands and individual mastery of those demands. In other words, the failure of an individual to display desired behaviors is due to limitations in learning and behavior acquisition (i.e., instructional methods have been ineffective or inappropriate), not due to inherent biological condition.

Measurement in this model tends to use criterion-referenced rather than norm-referenced tests. Scores from criterion-referenced tests characterize performance as essentially yes (the desired behavior was displayed) or no (they were not displayed). Thus, scores are interpreted in terms of mastery of skills, not relative to others.

Rehabilitation specialists commonly use a behavioral model to gauge the degree to which an intervention is promoting desired behaviors. They commonly establish a baseline for desired behaviors, attempt to promote the desired behaviors using scientifically based and empirically supported methods, test them again, promote them again—leading to a continuous chain of intervene–test–intervene sequences. The test content matches the desired behaviors.

Within this model, a person's cultural and linguistic characteristics generally are thought to be unimportant, given the model's strict focus on behavior. Thus, the model will not result in biased or discriminatory outcomes due to cultural, racial, or linguistic differences as long as behavioral expectations and intervention strategies reflect realistic developmental goals consistent with one's cultural or linguistic qualities. For example, to expect an individual who is limited in English proficiency to progress as rapidly as a native English speaker, when behavioral improvements require reading English, would be unreasonable. The advantages of having English as a native language would benefit the rate of development under these conditions.

RACE AND ETHNICITY VERSUS CULTURE AND LANGUAGE

What are the variables that practitioners should consider in their attempts to engage in unbiased assessment? At first, answers to this question may seem obvious. The first variable that leaps to mind may be race, followed closely by ethnicity. These two qualities differ. Race is a social construct, a term coined for the purpose of distinguishing people on the basis of appearance, notably skin color. Although there are few if any biological or scientific bases for the concept of race (Gould, 1996), the term continues to be popular and embedded in almost all aspects of human activity. Ethnicity refers to a more circumscribed group of people who share common values, traditions, and beliefs, personally or ancestrally, and whose ancestors usually come or came from the same geographic location. For example, the term *Black* implies a particular race and *Cuban* implies a particular ethnicity.

The vague and ambiguous nature of race can be seen in the fact that Cuba, like many Caribbean nations, has a tri-racial history that includes an aboriginal influence (the native Taino people who inhabited the island first); a Caucasian influence (from the Western European nations that colonized the island); and African/Black heritage (from the people taken from their homeland in Africa and brought to the island to work the sugar cane plantations). Thus, to characterize individuals as similar on the basis of race often is not useful. In contrast, knowledge of one's ethnicity, particularly if one is a recent immigrant, is likely to be much more practical and helpful.

However, race and ethnicity often are equated within the construct of culture. Although culture is closely related to ethnicity, culture is more than a specific ethnic identification. Culture helps define and shape what individuals believe, perceive, value, and know even as early as age 5 (Lynch & Hanson, 2004). Thus, culture is a broad term that encompasses the relatively unique and idiosyncratic experiences that belong and pertain to individuals who generally share belief systems, social mores, values, and certain types of knowledge. Moreover, these beliefs, behaviors, and knowledge are transmitted from generation to generation in the language particular to the culture (Lynch & Hanson, 2004; Valencia & Suzuki, 2001).

DISCUSSION BOX 3.3

Issue

Individuals who come from diverse ethnic or cultural backgrounds may have beliefs, values, and attitudes that possibly conflict with those that underlie rehabilitation health activities. For example, they may believe that improvement in one's health requires a religious component, or they may see rehabilitation as ignoring important aspects of their lives that they believe are necessary for better health (e.g., spirituality). Identify at least three beliefs, values, and attitudes that may adversely affect the manner in which services are received by them and discuss what could be done to prevent them from adversely affecting rehabilitation efforts.

Culture helps define individual beliefs: how people are likely to behave in a variety of contexts, what they have experienced, and what they know. Thus, culture, or rather differences in culture, may affect assessed behaviors. Tests and other assessment methods are by nature a reflection of the culture in which they were developed and reflect the beliefs, knowledge, and expectations of functioning or performance that are valued by the culture and individuals raised in the culture. Individuals raised completely or partly outside the culture favored by the test may not be as acculturated to their presumed peers and may be at a disadvantage for lack of comparable experiences.

One assumes "that the [individual] being tested has been exposed to comparable, but not necessarily identical, acculturation patterns relative to the standardization sample" (Oakland, 1977, p. 54). Therefore, the degree to which an individual's acculturation matches that of the individuals against whom functioning or performance will be compared is critical to fair test use. The more closely an individual's background matches that of the groups with whom comparisons are made, the more likely the test will be appropriate, the results valid, and conclusions less discriminatory.

Such differences in acculturation need not come from ethnic or sociocultural differences alone and can be due to a variety of personal qualities that affect acculturation (Ortiz, 2005). On the other hand, the presence of a particular factor does not automatically render a test inappropriate or invalid. "We must be sensitive to the fact that important differences exist with respect to child-rearing practices, expectations and aspirations, language experiences, and availability of and involvement in informal and formal learning experiences, and that these and other qualities may result in acculturation patterns that are not directly comparable to those that are more typical in the United States" (Oakland, 1977, p. 55).

Influence of Language

A person's language qualities also impact test performance directly and indirectly in several important ways. On the surface, the issues seem rather straightforward—if the individual being evaluated is unable to communicate with the evaluator, what confidence can there be in the obtained results? An inability to communicate during an evaluation significantly and adversely impacts the entire testing process. An examinee must be able to fully comprehend instructions in order to perform at one's best level. However, even when communication is established, either because the examinee speaks sufficient English or an interpreter is used in the process, problems associated with language are not entirely resolved. Some tests measure language directly (e.g. measures of vocabulary). Others rely on language somewhat indirectly (e.g., those that assess short-or long-term memory).

To attend to potential areas of bias, professionals must attend to a person's language, including their dominance, preference, and competence. *Dominance* refers to the better developed language of the two or more an individual may speak. The dominant language is the one more advanced and developed, and means that the individual has more proficiency, also known as *competence*, in that language that allows for better functioning and communication when using it.

However, although an individual may be more proficient in one language than another, this should not imply that the individual has a high degree of competence (i.e., proficiency or skill) in the better language. Persons may not be proficient in their dominant language. Likewise, an individual who has very high and equal competence in two languages displays no dominance and instead is competent or proficient in both.

Individuals usually demonstrate a *preference* for the language in which they are dominant because, through its use, they are better able to communicate their needs, thoughts, and experiences. Language preference often is determined by context. For example, an individual may use the less dominant language in situations where there is little choice, such as during an intake interview where the clinician speaks English only (Ochoa, 2005).

Many of us have experienced the need to use a second language to communicate. Unless we are very proficient (i.e., fluent) in that language, our use of it is slower, requires us to translate from the second language to our first language, requires considerably more energy and attention—qualities that impede our true language fluency. These and other language qualities may impede a person for whom English is their second language in their attempts to demonstrate the full extent of their abilities.

Their speed or completion time for a task may be reduced if persons must translate internally to comprehend what is said. A task may be accomplished incorrectly if they do not fully comprehend the instructions. They may lack the fluency to describe their thoughts accurately if they are expected to use expressive language. Thus, their performance may be lowered overall, particularly on language-embedded tests. Professionals who do not consider these qualities during assessment may misjudge the person's true behaviors and abilities, leading to bias and potentially unfair outcomes.

Language proficiency and culture may interact to impact test performance. Language and culture often are interwoven. Thus, a lack of experience and resulting development in culture and language create behavioral differences between those with weak and strong acculturation and English language proficiencies (Cummins, 1984; Figueroa, 1990b; Matsumoto, 1994; Ortiz, 2005; Valdés & Figueroa, 1994). For example, consider possible differences between two 40-year-old men. One was born and raised in the U.S. cultural mainstream, including life-long exposure to English. The other is an immigrant who came to the United States at age 30. Compared to the native born man, the immigrant is less likely to have had a comparable age-related level of acculturation and English immersion. Differences in English proficiency and acculturation-based knowledge may attenuate the immigrant's test performance, most likely for reasons other than lack of knowledge, skill, capacity, or ability (Flanagan & Ortiz, 2001; Rhodes et al., 2005; Valdés & Figueroa, 1994). Thus, to hold the immigrant to the same standard as the nonimmigrant may be unfair. Furthermore, individual rates of acculturation also vary within groups. For example, the rate of cultural accommodation is likely to be more rapid for a 20-year-old immigrant than a 60-year-old immigrant because the younger person is more likely to be engaged in society and to be more cognitively and socially active.

Construct irrelevance occurs when an examinee's level of English proficiency or acculturation affects his or her performance during testing. That is, the measured performance is not due to actual intrinsic ability deficits, but to extraneous qualities (e.g., English proficiency) that were not directly relevant to the construct being measured by the test. Thus, the reasons a native English speaker and a non-English speaker do not perform well can be very different. For example, whereas the former may well have a speech–language deficiency, the latter may simply have less exposure to and experience with English and thus diminished development due to having been raised in a different culture surrounded by a different language. Successful nondiscriminatory assessment methods are those that attend to these qualities in a systematic way.

METHODS FOR NONDISCRIMINATORY ASSESSMENT

Several methods exist to help overcome developmental differences, to decrease bias, and to increase the validity of testing with individuals whose cultural and linguistic backgrounds differ from the U.S. mainstream. Although each has some disadvantages, their potential benefits generally outweigh their limitations. Three methods described in this section represent the more common and traditional approaches to controlling or limited bias. The fourth is relatively new and offers a more systematic and research-based approach to nondiscriminatory assessment.

Use of Nonverbal Tests

The use of nonverbal tests, most commonly found in the measurement of intelligence, constitutes a common method to minimize bias in assessment. Nonverbal tests are specifically designed to reduce the linguistic demands on the examinee and the examiner. In some cases, tests may be administered using only nonverbal gestures or pantomime, thus eliminating the need for the examinee (and in some cases the examiner) to use oral language. Nonverbal tests hold immense intuitive appeal as a method to overcome the potential test bias when working with linguistically diverse individuals and often are believed to reduce cultural effects by relying less on culture-specific knowledge.

Tests that reduce verbal demands and cultural content promote nondiscriminatory assessment (McCallum & Bracken, 1997). However, practitioners are advised to remain cautious in their use because they may contain or require significant mainstream cultural knowledge.

Examples include puzzles of objects (car, boat, house) or tasks with visual stimuli (snow, printer, bread) (Flanagan & Ortiz, 2001; Flanagan, Ortiz, & Alfonso, 2007). In addition, although nonverbal tests assist in reducing the language demands inherent in the assessment process, they do not eliminate language entirely. For example, tests require some form of communication between the examiner and examinee (Figueroa, 1990b). In addition, persons completing nonverbal tasks may continue to use language while performing the tasks, albeit at a subvocal level. Compared to verbal tests of intelligence, nonverbal tests tend to measure fewer intellectual abilities, thus introducing bias related to construct underrepresentation (Flanagan, McGrew & Ortiz, 2000; Flanagan & Ortiz, 2001; Flanagan et al., 2007; McGrew & Flanagan, 1998). Additionally, the norms for nonverbal tests may be inappropriate.

Use of Translators in Testing

The use of a translator to assist in the test's administration constitutes another common and popular approach designed to reduce discrimination in testing. The translator provides a way for an examiner and examinee who differ in their language skills to communicate and thus to reduce the possibility that test performance may be attenuated by lack of English proficiency and comprehension.

Effective use of translators requires training and practice by both the examiner and translator (Lopez, 1997, 2002). Although the ability to bridge a potential communication gap makes this procedure a viable method for reducing a major threat to validity, examiners should refrain from using untrained individuals as translators, particularly family members of the examinee. Moreover, because tests generally are not normed with the use of translators, using one may raise questions about the validity of the testing process—an issue that may be especially important in forensic settings (Ortiz & Ochoa, 2005; Rhodes et al., 2005).

Use of Native-Language Tests

Efforts to address linguistic and bilingual issues have led to the development of native-language tests (e.g., those that are available in the examinee's native language). Although these tests may be of considerable value in decreasing potential bias, native-language tests have their own disadvantages and difficulties with validity. Their administration requires an examiner who is fluent in the language of the examinee. This may be a rare occurrence. Additionally, such tests are normed primarily on monolingual individuals who speak the native language and live in households and are educated in countries that speak the native language. Therefore, such tests are better designed for use with non-English speaking monolinguals of that language, not necessarily those who are bilingual and live in a largely English-speaking country. Moreover, their norms may not be suitable for use with all speakers of the language.

THE CULTURE–LANGUAGE TEST CLASSIFICATIONS AND INTERPRETIVE MATRIX

The number of possible conditions that may adversely affect fair and equitable evaluation is daunting. Thus, achieving a goal of nondiscriminatory assessment, while not easy, requires particular attention to an individual's level of acculturation and English language proficiency. These two qualities form the basis for an interpretive approach that may further assist practitioners in making valid and defensible inferences from test data and that are within the professional reach of all practitioners.

Fair and equitable assessment is accomplished through the application of a comprehensive and systematic assessment framework, not simply from the selection or use of a particular test or battery (Ortiz, 2002; Rhodes et al., 2005). However, when the use of standardized tests is deemed appropriate, the following approach may provide guidance for practitioners regarding test selection and interpretation. The approach, called the Culture–Language Test Classifications and Interpretive Matrix (Flanagan & Ortiz, 2001; Flanagan, Ortiz & Alfonso, 2007; Ortiz & Ochoa, 2005; Rhodes et al., 2005), is based on a long history of research that has demonstrated a consistent decline in performance for persons who are bilingual on tests that are more culturally based or language embedded (Brigham, 1923; Cummins, 1984; Goddard, 1913; Jensen, 1974, 1976; Mercer, 1979; Sanchez, 1934; Valdés & Figueroa, 1994; Vukovich & Figueroa, 1982).

Guided by this and other research, the Culture–Language Test Classifications and Interpretive Matrix was derived using a simple 3x3 matrix that can be used to evaluate the degree to which a test is culturally loaded and linguistically demanding, to select tests that may be more fair and equitable for use with culturally and linguistically diverse individuals, and to evaluate whether test performance was more likely due to cultural or linguistic differences versus a disorder. Table 3.2 shows the test classifications for one of the more common intelligence tests, the *Wechsler Adult Intelligence Scale* (3rd ed.; Wechsler, 1997).

TABLE 3.2 Culture–Language Test Classifications of Wechsler Adult Intelligence Scale—Third Edition

| | | **DEGREE OF LINGUISTIC DEMAND** | | |
		Low	**Moderate**	**High**
DEGREE OF CULTURAL LOADING	**Low**		Block Design (*Gv*) Symbol Search (*Gs*) Digit Span (*Gsm*) Coding (*Gs*)	
	Moderate	Object Assembly (*Gv*) Mazes (*Gv*) Picture Arrangement (*Gc/Gv*)	Arithmetic (*Gq*)	
	High	Picture Completion (*Gc/Gv*)		Information (*Gc*) Similarities (*Gc*) Vocabulary (*Gc*) Comprehension (*Gc*)

The letter in parentheses next to each subtest represent the broad ability measured by the subtest. In cases where two abilities are listed, the test demonstrates mixed loadings; *Gv*–Visual Processing, *Gs*–Processing Speed, *Gq*–Quantitative Knowledge, *Gsm*–Short Term Memory, *Gc*–Crystallized Intelligence.

The cells are arranged according to levels that correspond to low, moderate, and high linguistic demands (i.e., the degree to which the test measures linguistic development, contains language oriented requirements, or requires the examinee to use expressive or receptive language ability) as well as low, moderate, and high cultural loading (i.e., the degree to which the test requires acculturative knowledge, contains culture-specific elements, or relies on comprehension of culture-specific information). By arranging the test classifications in this manner, a pattern of performance can be discerned that follows the increasing attenuating effect that an individual's lack of acculturation and limited English proficiency have on test results.

Figure 3.1 provides a graphic representation of this expected pattern of performance for culturally and linguistically diverse individuals. The smaller arrows in Figure 3.1 represent the attenuating effects on performance for tests that have increasing cultural loadings (vertical direction) and for tests that have increasing linguistic demands (horizontal direction). However, their arrangement in this orthogonal manner does not imply that cultural loadings and linguistic demands are uncorrelated. Indeed, the large arrow running diagonally in Figure 3.1 is perhaps the most important one and represents the combined effect of acculturation and English proficiency on test performance. This pattern occurs

because, for culturally and linguistically diverse individuals, performance on tests classified in the upper left cell would be least attenuated by cultural or linguistic qualities, whereas performance on tests classified in the lower right cell would be most adversely affected. In general, those who are bilingual tend to score about one standard deviation below the mean on tests with the highest degree of linguistic demand and cultural loading (e.g., measures of vocabulary, comprehension, and verbal analogies) (Cummins, 1984; Jensen, 1980; Valdes & Figueroa, 1994). Thus, the Culture–Language Test Classifications is helpful to clinicians who may need to evaluate certain abilities because they are able to select tests that are as culturally and linguistically reduced and thus as fair as possible.

The Culture–Language Interpretive Matrix, an extension of the Culture–Language Test Classifications, allows practitioners to use actual test scores to evaluate performance and determine the extent to which results from a battery of tests were influenced primarily by cultural and linguistic qualities. The Culture–Language Interpretive Matrix uses the same structure as that for the Culture–Language Test Classifications except that it is blank and contains spaces for entering the names of the specific collection of tests a clinician administered in an assessment as well as their corresponding standard scores. In addition, a space is provided for the calculation of an

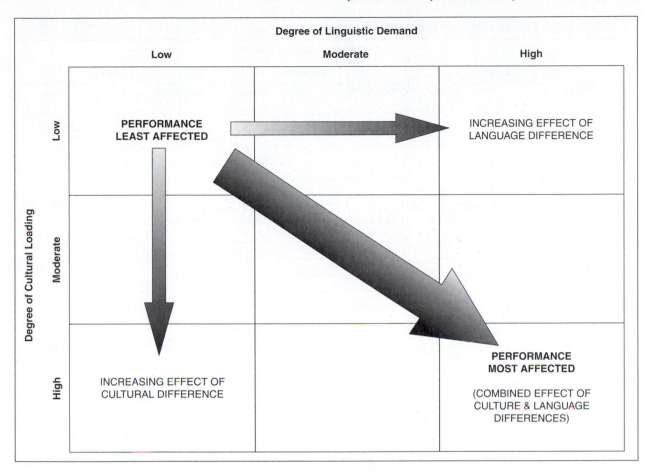

FIGURE 3.1 Pattern of Expected Test Performance for Culturally and Linguistically Diverse Individuals

average score for all test scores entered into each respective cell. An example of the matrix is provided in Table 3.3.

To use the matrix, an average or aggregate score is calculated based on any one or more of the tests that are classified in the same cell. If test scores from different batteries are used, clinicians should convert all scores to the same metric prior to conducting calculations (a mean of 100 and standard deviation of 15 are recommended). Once cell averages are determined, professionals then can examine the pattern of cell averages to determine whether the scores are attenuated systematically according to what would be expected for individuals who are culturally and linguistically diverse (refer to Figure 3.1). That is, the cell averages should be examined with respect to the presence of a pattern in which the highest test scores are found on tests within the low culture/low language cell (upper left), the lowest test scores are

found on tests within the high culture/high language cell (lower right), and the middle scores fall between the two extreme cells while also declining as the cultural loading and linguistic demand classifications increase.

For individuals with bicultural and bilingual backgrounds, the presence of this typical declining pattern of performance suggests that the low test scores are likely to be invalid because they were significantly influenced by cultural and linguistic differences. When the expected pattern of attenuation is not found (i.e., when there is no systematic decline in scores as a function of increasing cultural loading or linguistic demand), then the test results can be presumed to not be invalid due to cultural and linguistic influences. Although cultural and linguistic influences may be contributing, the lack of a typical declining pattern suggests other qualities may have affected test performance (e.g., a disability, motivation,

TABLE 3.3 The Culture-Language Interpretive Matrix

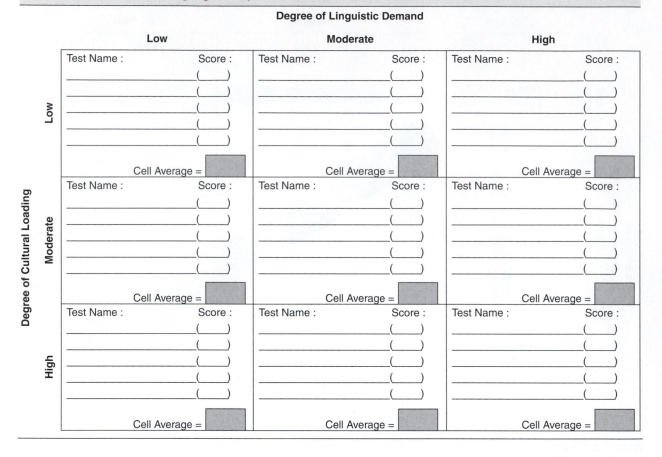

fatigue, emotional difficulties, improper administration and scoring).

When used in conjunction with other available data and framed within the context of the individual's unique cultural and linguistic background, the Culture–Language Interpretive Matrix can assist professionals in answering the difficult question regarding whether test performance was due more to difference than to disorders. The reader is referred to other sources for a more thorough discussion of these approaches (e.g., Flanagan, Ortiz, & Alfonso, 2007; Ortiz & Ochoa, 2005; Rhodes et al, 2005).

Except for the use of native language tests, the use of the other approaches presented here do not require a practitioner to be multilingual or familiar with all cultures. Competence in the assessment of individuals from diverse backgrounds does not necessarily require such skills. As noted by Ortiz and Flanagan (1998), "mere possession of the capacity to communicate in an individual's native language does not ensure appropriate, nondiscriminatory assessment of that individual. Traditional assessment practices and all their inherent biases can be quite easily replicated in any number of languages" (p. 426). The key to successful nondiscriminatory assessment lies in the application of a systematic approach and a solid understanding of the manner in which levels of acculturation and English language proficiency may combine to affect performance or functioning. Because the most significant problems are more likely to occur during the test interpretation phase, the Culture–Language Interpretive Matrix may be particularly valuable to practitioners by enabling them to directly and systematically evaluate the impact of language and acculturation on test performance (Flanagan et al., 2007; Ortiz & Ochoa, 2005; Rhodes et al., 2005).

LEGISLATIVE AND PROFESSIONAL ISSUES

Professionals providing rehabilitation services need to understand the definitions of disability in federal legislation (see the chapter 2 in this book). In the United States

RESEARCH BOX 3.1

Objective: To determine to what extent an individual's score on a test truly reflects the intended skill or ability rather than an extraneous variable such as lack of acculturation or limited English proficiency. Because cultural or linguistic differences may attenuate test results, fairness in testing rests on establishing the validity of the results.

Method: To evaluate the validity of test results, Ortiz and colleagues (Flanagan, Ortiz, & Alfonso, 2007; Ortiz & Dynda, 2005; Ortiz & Ochoa, 2005) developed an interpretive matrix arranged in a 3x3 format corresponding to low, moderate, and high classifications along the dimensions of cultural loading and linguistic demand. Performance on tests that primarily is influenced by these variables (rather than actual ability or skill) reveals a declining pattern of performance as the cultural content and linguistic demands of tests increase.

Results: By entering test scores in the matrix, a determination can be made regarding the degree to which culture and language affect test performance. If the scores are highest when using tests that have low cultural loading and linguistic demands, and lowest on tests that have high cultural loading and linguistic demands, then cultural and linguistic differences, not disability, are likely to be the primary

influence on test performance. Conversely, if the scores do not decline as described, then the individual's performance may be ascribed validly to actual ability or skill, and where deficiencies exist, to the possibility of a deficiency.

Conclusion: Ortiz and colleagues have been able to create a method for evaluating the validity of results obtained from tests by acknowledging that tests contain cultural elements and linguistic demands, to a greater or lesser extent, and by arranging tests along these two dimensions from low to high.

Questions

1. Explain why and how lack of acculturation and limited English proficiency will influence test performance.
2. What are some of the advantages and disadvantages when using the method developed by Ortiz and colleagues?
3. What additional research is needed to demonstrate the full utility and validity of this approach?
4. Design a research study that may help evaluate whether the approach is valid and useful for individuals who are culturally and linguistically diverse.

except for the Individuals with Disabilities Education Act (IDEA 2004), which addresses the needs of students with disabilities, definitions of disability and the antidiscriminatory protections afforded to individuals with disabilities are found in the Americans with Disabilities Act (ADA), first enacted in 1990. In general, the primary definition of disability under ADA is a person who has some type of physical or mental impairment that substantially limits one or more major life activities. A major life activity is an activity that an average person can perform with little or no difficulty. Examples are walking, seeing, hearing, speaking, breathing, learning, performing manual tasks, caring for oneself, working, sitting, standing, lifting, and reading. Assessments conducted by rehabilitation specialists may need to address whether clients meet the definition of disability due to an impairment that rises to a level that substantially limits one or more major life activities. Such decisions may ultimately determine whether an individual is entitled to protection under ADA.

ADA does not provide specific or objective criteria for what may constitute a substantial limitation in a major

life activity nor does it list all covered impairments. In addition, there is little guidance available on the possible correspondence between the International Classification of Functioning categories (World Health Organization, 2001, 2004) and the degree of one's impairment or limitation. These issues need to be resolved, including how cultural and linguistic qualities may influence perceptions of performance that may appear to indicate an impairment. Moreover, ADA is clear on the issue that cultural disadvantages (i.e., differences) are not considered impairments.

With respect to the last point, practitioners also are advised to consult the *Standards for Educational and Psychological Testing* (AERA et al., 1999). This reference established standards for test development and use and addresses issues pertaining to fair and nondiscriminatory test use. Thus, it is helpful in guiding almost all forms of assessment. Knowledge of and practices consistent with the *Standards* enhance one's defense of one's work, if challenged professionally or legally. Professionally developed and approved standards for nondiscriminatory assessment do not exist. Thus, the *Standards* serve as a useful resources for discussing these issues.

Most initial assessments conducted by rehabilitation specialists are likely to be consistent with the medical model. Many on-going assessments may be consistent with the behavioral model. The potential bias and discriminatory outcomes are less in these models than in the process model. Irrespective of the model used or the nature of the evaluation, assessment should remain grounded in methods that seek to reduce bias and promote fairness.

Summary and Conclusion

Tests are instruments designed, in part, to serve society and the individuals with whom they are used. Thus, professionals can be expected to be committed to this noble principle and not allow test use to jeopardize an individual's well-being. Commitment to this principle requires practitioners to understand when and how bias may operate (Flanagan et al., 2007; Ortiz & Dynda, 2005; Ortiz & Ochoa, 2005; Rhodes et al., 2005).

This chapter emphasized the importance of recognizing the following: Data are likely to be biased when tests are administered in English to those for whom English is not their first or dominant language or when tests are administered to individuals whose cultural background differs considerably from that of the group against whom performance is compared. Success in nondiscriminatory assessment largely is accomplished by recognizing the nature and sources of potential bias (notably linguistic and cultural differences), by utilizing each of the four evaluation models appropriately, along with best practice methods (e.g., nonverbal tests, use of interpreters, Culture–Language Test Classifications and Interpretive Matrix) designed specifically to reduce bias. Given the complex nature of linguistic- and acculturation-related variables, fair and equitable assessment is unlikely to occur simply or only by further perfection of assessment methods or tools. As Sattler (1992) notes:

> Probably no test can be created that will entirely eliminate the influence of learning and cultural experiences. The test content and materials, the language in which the questions are phrased, the test directions, the categories for classifying the responses, the scoring criteria, and the validity criteria are all culture bound (p. 579).

Self-Check Questions

1. Describe some reasons why fairness in evaluation is becoming an increasing concern for professionals in rehabilitation health.
2. Give at least one example of how bias may be introduced in rehabilitation health that is related to evaluation, treatment planning and selection, and outcome.
3. Define what is meant by the following terms: *ethnicity*, *acculturation*, and *English proficiency*.
4. Choose one of the four diagnostic–intervention models and describe how it differs from the other models.
5. Explain how some aspect of cultural difference may influence decisions that may impact rehabilitation services.
6. Describe at least one way in which fairness in the use of standardized tests may be achieved.
7. Describe how the Culture–Language Interpretive Matrix may be used to assist in determining the influence of cultural and linguistic influences on test performance.
8. List some advantages and disadvantages of using nonverbal tests.
9. Explain why an individual's language proficiency is important when attempting to comprehend test results.

Case Study—The Case of Carlos

Carlos, a 42-year-old man of Mexican descent whose native language is Spanish, immigrated to the United States at the age of 18 and began working and training as a brick mason. He recently suffered a head injury, mostly on the left side, after a fall from a one-story scaffold. He lost consciousness for several minutes and was brought to the hospital where he was treated for subdural hematoma. He was hospitalized for several days and appears to be recovering well physically. In fact, he has regained most of his premorbid functioning in all areas except balance and gross motor control for which he will likely require some rehabilitation. Whether the trauma he sustained also may have affected his cognitive functioning remains unclear.

His cognitive functioning was assessed by a neuropsychologist who used the *Wechsler Adult Intelligence Scale-III* (WAIS-III) as the main component of a battery of tests designed to evaluate general and specific cognitive abilities. Results from this testing are intended to be used in planning rehabilitation health services for Carlos. According to the neuropsychologist's findings, Carlos' Full Scale IQ appears to be low (FSIQ = 84); however, given his current occupation and educational background, she believes this may be due to his recent injury and not actual low ability. In addition, there is a large and statistically significant difference between his performance on the Processing Speed Index (PSI = 100) and his Verbal Comprehension Index (VCI=80), which could suggest a deficiency in his verbal abilities. The deficit is likely attributable to the effect of his head injury which was primarily on the speech–language (left) side of the brain, and therefore, rehabilitation is appropriate in his case and should focus on restoring functioning in this area.

The neuropsychologist noted that, although Carlos does not speak English very well, he seemed to understand the directions. Thus, she administered the test in English and believes that his conversational proficiency was such that the results are valid, but no other steps were taken to ensure the validity of the test scores.

When attempting to develop an appropriate rehabilitation program for Carlos, additional interviews were conducted with the assistance of his daughter who sometimes provided a translation of the questions as needed. According to Carlos, he feels that his language ability, in both English and Spanish, are really not any different following his injury. His major concern is that he feels less coordinated when walking but otherwise feels ok and believes he thinks, reasons, and speaks much as before the accident. His WAIS-III results were reviewed by using the Culture–Language Interpretive Matrix (the reader may wish to refer to Figure 3.1). Scores on tests that were low in cultural loading and linguistic demand (e.g., those that comprise the processing speed index such as digit–symbol coding and symbol search) were about average. However, as the tests became more culturally and linguistically demanding, Carlos' scores decreased. His lowest scores were on tests with the highest cultural loading and linguistic demands (e.g., the tests that comprise

the verbal comprehension index such as similarities, comprehension, and vocabulary). In addition, his lowest scores were within the ranges predicted by the Culture–Language Interpretive Matrix.

Thus, rehabilitation specialists concluded that, because the test results were very close to what would be expected of Carlos given his cultural and linguistic background, the scores were not likely to be valid reflections of actual verbal or language ability, particularly not in English. Rather, the pattern of Carlos' scores when evaluated within the matrix showed a clear and systematic decline as the cultural loading and linguistic demands of the tests increased. Thus, his low verbal scores were unlikely due to cognitive dysfunction and instead to result from his relative lack of acculturation and limited English proficiency. Consequently, his rehabilitation specialists decided he did not need cognitive rehabilitation related to language functioning and that his rehabilitation program should focus exclusively on his main complaints regarding general balance and gross motor control. Within a short period of time, and by not having to undergo needless speech–language rehabilitation, Carlos regained functioning at a level nearly commensurate with that before his injury, and he returned to work where he was able to resume his work and perform satisfactorily.

QUESTIONS

1. Because Carlos was able to understand the directions of the WAIS-III, the neuropsychologist assumed he fully understood what to do and therefore the results were valid. Why may this assumption not be true?

2. The neuropsychologist noted a large difference between Carlos' performance in language-related areas (low Verbal IQ) and visual–perceptual areas (higher visual-conceptual IQ) and concluded that such a discrepancy must indicate dysfunction. First, is the assumption that all individuals should have evenly developed abilities reasonable? And second, would such a pattern (low Verbal IQ/high visual-conceptual IQ) be unusual for normal individuals who are culturally and linguistically diverse?

3. The Culture–Language Interpretive Matrix predicts a systematic decline in test scores for culturally and linguistically diverse individuals without any disabilities. Describe test patterns for individuals who have a language-based disability as well as those with a global cognitive impairment.

References

American Educational Research Association, American Psychological Association, & National Council on Measurement in Education (1999). *Standards for educational and psychological testing.* Washington, DC: American Educational Research Association.

Bialystok, E. (1991). *Language processing in bilingual children.* New York: Cambridge University Press.

Brigham, C. C. (1923). *A study of American intelligence.* Princeton, NJ: Princeton University Press.

Cummins, J. C. (1984). *Bilingual and special education: Issues in assessment and pedagogy.* Austin, TX: PRO-ED.

DeVellis, R. F. (2003). *Scale development: Theory and applications* (2nd ed). Newbury Park, CA: Sage Publications.

Figueroa, R. A. (1983). Test bias and Hispanic children. *Journal of Special Education, 17,* 431–440.

Figueroa, R. A. (1990a). Assessment of linguistic minority group children. In C. R. Reynolds & R. W. Kamphaus (Eds.), *Handbook of psychological and educational assessment of children: Intelligence and achievement* (pp. 93–106). New York: Guilford Press.

Figueroa, R. A. (1990b). Best practices in the assessment of bilingual children. In A. Thomas & J. Grimes (Eds.), *Best practices in school psychology II* (pp. 671–696). Washington, DC: National Association of School Psychologists.

Flanagan, D. P., McGrew, K. S., & Ortiz, S. O. (2000). *The Wechsler intelligence scales and Gf-Gc theory: A contemporary approach to interpretation.* Boston: Allyn & Bacon.

Flanagan, D. P., & Ortiz, S. O. (2001). *Essentials of cross-battery assessment.* New York: Wiley.

Flanagan, D. P., Ortiz, S. O., & Alfonso, V.C. (2007). *Essentials of cross-battery assessment* (2nd ed.). New York: Wiley Press.

Goddard, H. H. (1913). The Binet tests in relation to immigration. *Journal of Psycho-Asthenics, 18,* 105–107.

Gould, S. J. (1996). *The mismeasure of man.* New York: W. W. Norton

Hakuta, K. (1986). *Mirror of language: The debate on bilingualism.* New York: Basic Books.

Jensen, A. R. (1974). How biased are culture-loaded tests? *Genetic Psychology Monographs, 90,* 185–244.

Jensen, A. R. (1976). Construct validity and test bias. *Phi Delta Kappan, 58,* 340–346.

Jensen, A. R. (1980). *Bias in mental testing.* New York: Free Press.

Kamphaus, R. W. (1993). *Clinical assessment of children's intelligence.* Boston: Allyn & Bacon.

Lopez, E. C. (1997). The cognitive assessment of limited English proficient and bilingual children. In D. P. Flanagan, J. L. Genshaft, & P. L. Harrison (Eds.), *Contemporary intellectual assessment: Theories, tests, and issues* (pp. 503–516). New York: Guilford Press.

Lopez, E. C. (2002). Best practices in working with school interpreters to deliver psychological services to children and families. In A. Thomas & J. Grimes (Eds.), *Best practices in school psychology IV* (pp. 1419–1432). Washington, DC: National Association of School Psychologists.

Lynch, E.W., & Hanson, M.J. (Eds.) (2004). *Developing cross-cultural competence: A guide for working with children and their families* (3rd ed.). Baltimore: Paul H. Brookes Publishing Co.

Matsumoto, D. (1994). *Cultural influences on research methods and statistics.* Pacific Grove, CA: Brooks/Cole.

McCallum, R. S., & Bracken, B. A. (1997). The Universal Nonverbal Intelligence Test. In D. P. Flanagan, J. L. Genshaft, & P. L. Harrison (Eds.), *Contemporary intellectual assessment: Theories, tests, and issues* (pp. 268–280). New York: Guilford Press.

McGrew, K. S., & Flanagan, D. P. (1998). *The intelligence test desk reference (ITDR): Gf-Gc cross-battery assessment.* Boston: Allyn & Bacon.

Mercer, J. R. (1979). *System of multicultural pluralistic assessment: Technical manual.* New York: The Psychological Corporation.

Mercer, J. R., & Ysseldyke, J. (1977). Designing diagnostic–intervention programs. In T. Oakland (Ed.), *Psychological and Educational Assessment of Minority Children* (pp. 70–90). New York: Brunner/Mazel Inc.

Messick, S. (1995). Validity of psychological assessment: Validation of inferences from persons' responses and performances as scientific inquiry into score meaning. *American Psychologist, 50,* 741–749.

Oakland, T. (Ed.) (1976). *Non-biased assessment of minority group children: With bias toward none.* Paper presented at a national planning conference on nondiscriminatory assessment for handicapped children. Lexington, KY.

Oakland, T. (Ed.) (1977). *Psychological and educational assessment of minority children.* New York: Brunner/ Mazel Inc.

Ochoa, S. H. (2005). Language Proficiency Assessment: The foundation for psychoeducational assessment of second-language learners. In R. Rhodes, S. H. Ochoa, & S. O. Ortiz, *Assessing culturally and linguistically diverse students: A practical guide* (pp. 137–152). New York: The Guilford Press.

Ortiz, S. O. (2001). Assessment of cognitive abilities in Hispanic children. *Seminars in Speech and Language, 22,* 17–37.

Ortiz, S. O. (2002). Best practices in nondiscriminatory assessment. In A. Thomas & J. Grimes (Eds.), *Best practices in school psychology IV* (pp. 1321–1336). Washington, DC: National Association of School Psychologists.

Ortiz, S. O. (2005). Acculturational factors in psychoeducational assessment. In R. Rhodes, S. H. Ochoa, & S. O. Ortiz, *Assessment of culturally and linguistically diverse students: A practical guide* (pp. 124–136). New York: The Guilford Press.

Ortiz, S. O., & Dynda, A. M. (2005). The use of intelligence tests with culturally and linguistically diverse populations.

In D. P. Flanagan & P. L. Harrison (Eds.), *Contemporary intellectual assessment* (2nd ed., pp. 545–556). New York: Guilford Press.

Ortiz, S. O., & Flanagan, D. P. (1998). Gf-Gc cross-battery interpretation and selective cross-battery assessment: Referral concerns and the needs of culturally and linguistically diverse populations. In K. S. McGrew & D. P. Flanagan, *The intelligence test desk reference (ITDR): Gf-Gc cross-battery assessment* (pp. 401–444). Boston: Allyn & Bacon.

Ortiz, S. O., & Ochoa, S. H. (2005). Intellectual Assessment: A nondiscriminatory interpretive approach. In D. P. Flanagan & P. L. Harrison (Eds.), *Contemporary intellectual assessment* (2nd ed., pp. 234–250). New York: Guilford Press.

Reynolds, C. R., & Carson A. D. (2005). Methods for assessing cultural bias in tests. In C. Frisby & C. R. Reynolds (Eds.) *Comprehensive handbook of multicultural school psychology* (pp. 795–823). John Wiley & Sons.

Rhodes, R., Ochoa, S. H., & Ortiz, S. O. (2005). *Assessment of culturally and linguistically diverse students: A practical guide.* New York: Guilford Press.

Salvia, J., & Ysseldyke, J. E. (1991). Assessment (5th ed). New York: Houghton Mifflin.

Sanchez, G. (1934). Bilingualism and mental measures: A word of caution. *Journal of Applied Psychology, 18,* 765–772.

Sattler, J. M. (1992). *Assessment of children* (3rd ed.). San Diego: Jerome M. Sattler.

Sattler, J. M. (2001). *Assessment of children: Cognitive applications* (4th ed.). San Diego: Sattler.

Scarr, S. (1978). From evolution to Larry P., or what shall we do about IQ tests? *Intelligence, 2,* 325–342.

Terman, L. M. (1916). *The measurement of intelligence: An explanation of and a complete guide for the use of the Stanford revision and extension of the Binet–Simon Intelligence Scale.* Boston: Houghton Mifflin.

Valdés, G., & Figueroa, R. A. (1994). *Bilingualism and testing: A special case of bias.* Norwood, NJ: Ablex.

Valencia, R. R., & Suzuki, L. A. (2001). *Intelligence testing and minority students: Foundations, performance factors, and assessment.* Thousand Oaks, CA: Sage Publications, Inc.

Vukovich, D., & Figueroa, R. A. (1982). *The validation of the system of multicultural pluralistic assessment: 1980-1982.* Unpublished manuscript, University of California at Davis, Department of Education.

Wechsler, D. (1997). *Wechsler Adult Intelligence Scale* (3rd ed.). San Antonio, TX: The Psychological Corporation.

World Health Organization (2001, 2004). International Classification of Disability, Functioning and Health. Available at http://www.cdc.gov/nchs/about/otheract/icd9/icfhome.htm

Yerkes, R. M. (1921). Psychological examining in the United States Army. *Memoirs of the National Academy of Sciences, 15.* 1–890.

Types of Assessments, Norms, and the Interpretation of Scores

4

Planning the Assessment Process

ROBERT M. GRAY
Advanced Neurobehavioral Health of Southern California–San Diego

CYNTHIA F. SALORIO
Kennedy Krieger Institute, Baltimore

OVERVIEW

This chapter reviews issues important to planning an assessment conducted in rehabilitation settings. Effective rehabilitation efforts begin with comprehensive goal-driven assessment, and assessment plays ongoing and critical roles throughout the rehabilitation process. The provision of quality assessment and evaluation services within the rehabilitation setting requires adequate planning and preparation that considers multiple consumer, setting, and assessor-related variables.

LEARNING OBJECTIVES

By the end of the chapter, readers should be able to:

- Identify important issues and information sources to consider when planning an assessment
- Identify personal factors specific to the individual consumer of rehabilitation services that can facilitate or impede the assessment process
- Identify environmental factors specific to the consumer's social and community setting that can facilitate or impede the assessment process
- Identify systemic factors specific to the rehabilitation setting that can serve to facilitate or impede the assessment process
- Identify how assessment goals and planning change dependent upon the stage of rehabilitation

INTRODUCTION

The International Classification of Functioning Disability and Health (ICF; World Health Organization [WHO], 2001) provides a framework for planning assessments. A distinction is made between *capacity*, the ability to perform a task under optimal conditions, and *performance*, what an individual can do in the current environment (WHO, 2001, p. 15.). As such, it is imperative to assess an individual's responses to task demands as well as the multiple contextual factors in which that response was displayed (Norton & Hope, 2001). Improvements in body function may not correspond to enhanced everyday performance; therefore, it is critical to assess aspects of function (including body function, activities, and participation), as well as the contextual factors (personal, environmental) that impact functioning and disability (Reed et al., 2005).

Health care providers working in rehabilitation settings are challenged to conceptualize the assessment process as more than a static procedure aimed at identifying a consumer's current level of function or impairment. Instead, the assessment process is dynamic and requires flexible application of multiple procedures designed to identify an individual's functional abilities accurately as well as factors that may potentially maximize participation in daily activities. Prior to initiation of an assessment or evaluation, information is needed regarding factors that may facilitate or impede treatment outcomes, including the ability and willingness to cooperate with health care professionals as well as the degree to which the consumer is able to participate in activities across multiple settings.

Assessment planning, whether at the referral, active rehabilitation, discharge, or follow-up stages, should be driven by the identification of desired functional outcomes. As Bickenback and colleagues (1999) note, the ICF encourages the use of assessment strategies that are linked to individual treatment goals. Planning an assessment with a sole emphasis on defining impairment or collecting test scores is likely to result in a misuse of valuable patient and clinician time and effort. Such data typically have limited application to promoting an understanding of the individual's functional capabilities in their daily life.

The development of assessment plans that view health as a "dynamic interaction between an individual's functioning and disability" (Peterson, 2005, p. 107) within the context of personal and environmental factors promotes a multidimensional and interactive approach that is continually guided by an awareness of how assessment contributes to advancing the individual's short- and long-term functional goals. Clinicians who keep functional goals in mind are likely to develop assessment plans that emphasize the adaptation and utilization of an array of tools and procedures in a flexible manner to obtain applicable results that lead to improvements in the lives of persons with disabilities, rather than plans driven by the use of standard procedures, tests, or diagnostic classification schemes (Eccleston et al., 2003, Wennemer et al., 2006).

The proposed model for assessment planning outlined in this chapter emphasizes the identification of personal and environmental factors specific to the consumer as well as an appreciation for how these factors change as the consumer progresses through the multiple stages of rehabilitation. An effective model also must consider multiple systemic factors (e.g., the setting, rehabilitation team composition, communication patterns) that serve to either support or obstruct the health care provider's ability to link assessment with functional goals, depending on how such factors either facilitate or interfere with the assessment process. Figure 4.1 summarizes primary factors for consideration when planning the assessment.

SYSTEMIC FACTORS

Setting Related Issues

Multiple systemic factors unique to the rehabilitation setting can serve to either support or obstruct the health care provider's ability to link assessment with functional goals. By identifying these qualities prior to development of the assessment plan, their impact can be considered during the planning process, thus enhancing consumer care.

Rehabilitation takes place in multiple settings, each with specific attributes that can impact the nature of the assessment process. Those providing acute care generally experience multiple constraints related to the consumer's

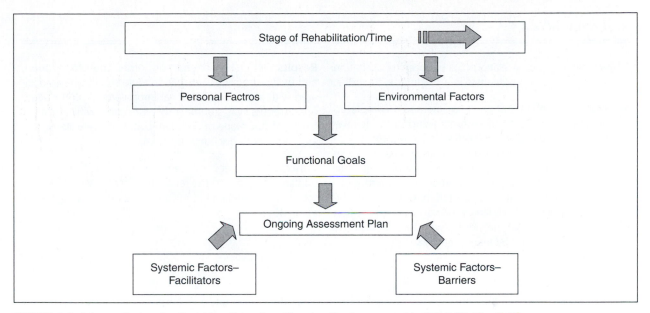

FIGURE 4.1 **Primary Factors for Consideration when Planning the Assessment in Rehabilitation Settings**

orientation and arousal level, such as frequent in-room visits from multiple providers and significant scheduling demands. Consumers in these settings generally experience disrupted sleep and wake cycles, are exposed to both sensory overstimulation and deprivation, may be on multiple medications that have a sedating effect, and thus may be prone to periods of confusion, fearfulness, and disorientation related to the intensive care unit (ICU) environment (Trovato et al., in press).

In contrast, settings that provide long term rehabilitation may be characterized by much different scheduling demands. However, in every rehabilitation setting, health care assessment specialists work in coordination with the rehabilitation team to educate allied health care professionals and staff regarding the importance of securing blocks of uninterrupted time to conduct assessments that are free from excessive noise or distraction. The physical settings often require modifications, including the use of bedside evaluations, adjustments in lighting, and use of portable assessment tools. Additionally, individuals who have sustained a neurological injury often are prone to distractibility and overstimulation and therefore are likely to perform differently on standardized tasks depending on the setting. For example, a 1:1 testing situation in a quiet office may produce test scores that differ considerably from those obtained from bedside testing characterized by constant background noise and interruptions from medical staff and/or roommates. The level of performance may differ dramatically depending on the setting, making it more difficult to assess capacity or the best possible

level of functioning (Reed et al., 2005). With some consumers, the nature and status of their injury or disability or their age may require family or other caretakers to be present to facilitate the assessment; whereas with other consumers, their presence may be disruptive. Accurate identification of scheduling issues is critical because the assessment must proceed according to the rehabilitation team's evaluation time lines that may call for prompt initial assessments as well as ongoing monitoring. Brevity of stay in the rehabilitation setting may have a considerable impact on scheduling as well.

Communication

The rehabilitation setting typically includes multiple providers, specialists, technicians, staff, and trainees, with a wide range of differences in training and expertise. Use of specialty terminology or nonuniform and inconsistent terminology when communicating referral needs and assessment findings can result in team confusion and substandard patient care. Regardless of the rehabilitation setting, health care providers can reduce ambiguity and confusion by improving communication. Characteristics that impact team functioning are strongly associated with rehabilitation outcomes. Thus, issues associated with communication should be identified and minimized prior to initiating the evaluation process (Strasser et al., 2005).

Referrals for assessment come from external and internal sources. For example, a consumer can be

---

RESEARCH BOX 4.1

Objective: To evaluate relationships between rehabilitation team functioning and outcomes in individuals with stroke.

Method: 530 rehabilitation team members completed questionnaires regarding team functioning in the following areas: communication, perceived effectiveness, physician involvement, physician support, teamness, utility of quality information, innovation, interprofessional relationships, order and organization, and task orientation. Functional improvement in rehabilitation, discharge to the home setting, and overall length of stay in rehabilitation were assessed in 1,688 individuals who had sustained a stroke and were served by team members.

Results: Better task orientation, order and organization, and utility of quality information were significantly associated with increased functional improvement. Better team effectiveness was significantly associated with a shorter length of stay. None of the team dynamics were statistically associated with discharge destination.

Conclusion: Aspects of team dynamics and communication are important to the rehabilitation process and are associated with rehabilitation functional outcomes. (Strasser et al., 2005.)

---

referred by a physician in the community or by rehabilitation team members. A referral for assessment may come in the form of a chart note, phone call, verbal request, or email. It may come directly from the referring source or indirectly from secondary or tertiary sources relaying the request. To reduce confusion and potential for miscommunication, clinicians should seek to identify the original referral source and review the reason for referral with that individual. A discussion with the referring individual will help clarify the purpose of the referral, address questions regarding how and when results are to be communicated to the referring individual and team members, reduce potential clinical overlap with other specialists, and provide an opportunity for enhanced understanding of what is considered an appropriate or inappropriate referral for a given specialist. All parties must be aware of how results will be shared with or communicated to the consumer. Issues regarding written or oral feedback and the use of direct (provider to the consumer) or indirect (provider to the team that then informs the consumer) feedback models should be established and identified prior to the assessment. Assessment data should be honored as sensitive and personal information, and clinicians must work together to ensure that the consumer is not provided contradictory, piecemeal, or confusing interpretation of assessment findings.

Role Clarification

As with any team endeavor, the rehabilitation team must work collectively to establish clear guidelines and expectations for those individuals who comprise the team. A rehabilitation setting characterized by a truly interdisciplinary team approach should result in minimal confusion

regarding roles and the purpose of referral as the team works together as a whole to establish and communicate a coordinated assessment and treatment plan.

However, a *multi-* rather than *inter-*disciplinary approach may feature various professionals conducting assessments targeting circumscribed areas of expertise in response to referral requests, but with a lack of understanding of how their findings should be integrated to meet the individual's overall functional goals. Team models in which assessment specialists act primarily as consultants potentially lead to confusion regarding who is the consumer of information and how to provide feedback regarding results (i.e., whether the assessment results are conveyed to the referring team leader or directly to the consumer). A clear understanding of communication roles between the rehabilitation team and the consumer and family/caretakers also assists in establishing an understanding of responsibility for continued care. Health care providers planning to deliver assessment services as part of a team should clarify their role as a team member to ensure that collaborative efforts are completed in an efficient manner and to reduce any potential overlap with related disciplines.

Provider Related Factors

The unique sets of skills, biases, strengths, and weaknesses each health care provider brings to the assessment constitute additional systemic qualities that impact assessment planning. Providers working in rehabilitation settings strive to maintain awareness and knowledge of the clinical characteristics of frequently occurring injuries, illnesses, and disabling conditions in accord with criteria established by their area of specialty training and expertise. Although assessment can center on answering questions regarding current capabilities (i.e., what an individual is able to do at a given time), *rehabilitation-referenced* assessment also often is focused on identifying capacity, whether new skills can be taught, and what compensatory strategies are most likely to be effective (Heinrichs, 1990). Thus, rehabilitation specialists must be knowledgeable of presenting symptoms, prognosis, and outcome data in relation to a variety of conditions and how various treatments (e.g., medications, surgery) can positively and negatively impact assessment findings and ultimately outcomes. A provider who establishes realistic expectations and proper attitudes can utilize the assessment process in a therapeutically supportive manner, working interactively with the consumer to help raise awareness of strengths and weaknesses and to recognize when compensatory techniques may be necessary. Rehabilitation providers recognize the need to practice within ethical boundaries and refer to appropriate specialists when conditions require the use of assessment tools or techniques outside of their area of expertise.

PERSONAL FACTORS

Consumers of assessment services are active participants, not passive recipients, in the assessment process. Many health care assessment specialists encounter written and verbal communication regarding evaluations that foster a view that assessment is something that is *done to* rather than *done with* a consumer. For example, consider the information relayed in the statement, "The patient was evaluated," versus "Ms. Smith participated in an evaluation." Careful consideration of and respect for multiple personal qualities are critical to developing meaningful functional goals and effective assessment plans.

Consumer Abilities and Limitation— Evaluating with Flexibility

Prior to launching a formal evaluation, the health care provider must obtain current information regarding the consumer's general orientation and functional communication abilities. Individuals who have experienced traumatic brain injury or cerebrovascular insult may be significantly disoriented and able to tolerate only brief bedside evaluations. The use of nonverbal assessment methods (e.g. pantomime instructions, pointing, recognition lists, multiple choice formats) or allowing the patient to utilize assisted communication techniques (e.g., dynavox, picture exchange communication system) may be needed. Consumers of rehabilitation services differ in

their auditory, visual, and motor-based abilities. Thus, selection of test procedures should be considered accordingly (e.g., use of eye gaze rather than pointing, motor free testing, reduced visual–spatial demands, reduced verbal demands, enlarged copies of testing materials). Fatigability and pain also are important considerations. The consumer may require frequent breaks and manage only brief periods of effort, thus necessitating a prioritized assessment plan. Regular breaks also may be needed for medical procedures (e.g. nursing evaluations, catheterization).

Many consumers, particularly those with brain injury, experience impaired self-awareness and insight, leading to potential conflicts when asked to identify appropriate rehabilitation and assessment goals (Korte & Wegener, 2004). Although family and health care providers may identify multiple areas of functional limitations, the consumer may deny any difficulties and reject the need for assessment or intervention services. Furthermore, consumers with impaired self-awareness may have "...limited capacity to utilize information about strengths and weaknesses to set goals and make plans" (Bergquist, & Malec 2002). The assessment plan may necessarily involve addressing the individual's self-awareness at the outset, as these characteristics can limit the ability to participate in the evaluation and benefit from evaluation/assessment outcomes.

Respecting the Individual's Dignity— Emotional & Cultural Considerations

Health care providers should strive to reduce a consumer's discomfort, stress, and fatigue. In addition to recognizing an individual's potential physical abilities and limitations, health care providers also should be attentive to the individual's personality qualities, including their emotional status (chapter 18 discusses personality assessment). Emotional dysregulation can result from the injury itself, particularly in cases involving central nervous system insults (e.g., Vasa et al., 2004). Consumers may demonstrate noncompliant and anxious behaviors when health care providers attempt to engage them in assessment-related activities. For example, during the acute recovery from a severe traumatic brain injury (TBI), an individual typically goes through a period of disorientation and confusion, termed post-traumatic amnesia (PTA), a condition similar to a state of delirium (American Psychiatric Association, 1994). Symptoms and signs can include impairment of the sleep–wake cycle, inattention, illusions and hallucinations, agitation, and disinhibition. The best treatment for this stage of recovery is increased environmental structure with a focus on safety and time (Ylvilsaker et al., 2006). As such, assessment of cognitive or other functional abilities during this stage may not be possible.

Emotional difficulties also may occur as reactions to emergent functional limitation, stress, and potential indignities due to loss of independent daily living skills. Such emotional reactions vary, including internalizing behavior characterized by social withdrawal and depression, and externalizing behavior characterized by poor frustration tolerance, agitation, and verbal aggression. Compared to the general population, consumers of rehabilitation services have higher rates of mood disturbances, especially anxiety and depression—rates that are similar to those who have other medical problems (Weissman & Myers, 1978; Rodin & Voshart, 1986; Richards, 1986). Mood disturbances after neurological injury are thought to arise from both the neurobiological changes related to the injury and the psychological adjustment to changes in abilities (Anderson, Catroppa, Haritou, Morse, & Rosenfeld, 2005; Felton & Revenson, 1984). Additionally, following their rehabilitation, substance abuse tends to be a significant problem in persons with TBI and spinal cord injury (SCI) (Heinemann, Schnoll, Brandt, Maltz, & Keen, 1988; Fann et al., 2004). Clinicians must plan and prepare to accurately describe and recognize a consumer's emotional status in order to distinguish whether the results are impacted by primary emotional or motivational factors (e.g., depression leading to psychomotor retardation or memory difficulties), by the primary injury factors, or both.

The assessment plan also must consider the consumer's personality characteristics that can impact adaptation, functional outcomes, mood, and quality of life after rehabilitation. Consumers who display more hope and agreeableness and lower levels of neuroticism and negative emotion generally demonstrate better outcomes (Elliott, Witty, Herrick, & Hoffman, 1991; Krause & Rohe, 1998). In contrast, consumers who use avoidance coping strategies generally display poor outcomes, including more pain (Elfstrom, Ryden Kreuter, Taft, & Sullivan, 2005; Frank et al., 1987; Kennedy et al., 2002; Turner, Jensen, Warms, & Cardenas, 2002).

Differing cultural views toward impairment, disability, and handicap dictate the need for differing approaches while developing functional goals and related assessment. Awareness and sensitivity to cultural variations also increase the health care provider's ability to deliver effective rehabilitation assessment and treatment services in a manner that respects the consumer's dignity, beliefs, and values. For example, one's religion and spirituality are considerably important to many consumers.

Thus, their impact should be considered during the assessment and intervention phases of rehabilitation in order to promote desired outcomes and maintain sensitivity to their importance in health promotion and recovery (Kilpatrick & McCullough, 1999).

When developing the assessment plan, health care providers will need to gather information regarding the consumer's ability to speak and comprehend oral language. When using written tests, the age or grade level of their reading recognition and comprehension should be screened. Consumers who are bilingual may appear to be sufficiently fluent in English but may be more competent in their native language. Furthermore, consumers who are bilingual generally are more fluent and accurate in their primary language after brain injury. Assessments conducted by trained clinicians who utilize the consumer's primary language or dual languages are preferred to the use of interpreters because important subtle clinical information may go unnoticed by an interpreter with minimal clinical skills (Artiola I Fortuny & Mullaney, 1998). Further information regarding the use of interpreters is available in the *Standards for Educational and Psychological Testing* (American Educational Research Association, American Psychological Association, & National Council on Measurement in Education, 1999).

On occasion, as a result of inadequate team communication, consumers, their families, and other caretakers receive limited or incorrect information and thus have limited awareness as to the reason for and the nature of needed assessment. Such conditions may lead to feelings of confusion, powerlessness, and invasiveness and thus negatively impact trust of the assessment specialist. Prior to engaging in any assessment, health care providers should ensure that they have appropriately discussed the purpose of the evaluation with the consumer or the caretaker and obtained informed consent as well as assent if needed.

ENVIRONMENTAL FACTORS

Assessing Environmental Variables

The ICF recognizes environmental factors as prominent aids to understanding the association between adaptation and disability (Scherer & Glueckauf, 2005). To ensure that assessment goals are relevant to the consumer's functional goals, assessment plans should emphasize identification and evaluation of contextual factors that can serve as *facilitators* and *inhibitors*, variables that may directly or indirectly impact performance and successful rehabilitation, and reintegration back into the individual's home setting. These variables often are dynamic and thus may alternate between an inhibitor or facilitator in response to the consumer's stage of rehabilitation and the nature of the interventions. For example, an assessment of a family's or caretaker's degree of support and stress may reveal limited initial support and high stress, thus serving as an inhibitor and placing the consumer at risk upon discharge. However, upon achieving targeted intervention goals, support may increase and stress levels decrease, thus now serving as a facilitator, leading to an improved prognosis for the consumer.

Using another example, when working with children with traumatic brain injury (TBI), knowledge of preinjury environmental conditions (e.g., family cohesiveness and overall family functioning) are robust predictors of longterm outcome (Rivara et al., 1994; Wade, Taylor, Drotar, Stancin, & Yeates 1996; Yeates et al., 1997). A family's

cohesiveness, resilience, support, maternal stress and coping, and reactions to injury or illness also predict the psychological adjustment of children with disabilities (Evans et al., 1987; Smith & Clark, 1995; Stein, Berger, Hibbard, & Gordan 1993; Rolland 1994; Wallander, Varni, Babani, Banis, & Wilcox, 1989; Werner & Smith, 1992).

Family structure and support can diminish and deteriorate in reaction to stress associated with the rehabilitation process. For example, rates of psychiatric disturbance and divorce increase after a family member has sustained a TBI (Wade et al, 1996, Rivara et al., 1992). Family support after TBI is impacted both by family's coping styles and by behavioral changes in the individual (Wells, Dywann, & Dumas 2005). Families characterized by chaos, social disengagement, social isolation, and active substance abuse display more difficulty providing social and emotional support for the family member with a disability (Glass & Maddox, 1992), are more

DISCUSSION BOX 4.1

Impact on the Family

Family environment significantly influences functional outcomes after an injury or illness that requires rehabilitation. However, family variables are not always assessed. Responsibility for caring for a family member with an injury or disability has a considerable impact on the caregiver and, in turn, the family's general functioning.

Stress associated with caring for a family member with a neurological injury, such as TBI, often is significant (Cameron, Cheung, Streiner, Coyte, & Stewart, 2006a; Verhaeghe, Defloor, & Grypdonck, 2005). For example, Cameron and colleagues reported that about 45% of caregivers of individuals after stroke were at risk for clinical depression. In addition, the stress of caregiving can be ongoing and often warrants professional services, even at 10–15 year follow-up (Verhaeghe et al.). Stress and injury-related burdens may increase over time, particularly in families caring for more severely injured individuals (Wade et al., 2006a). Notably, these effects do not apply only to acutely injured individuals. For example, caregivers of children with developmental limitations also report lower levels of stress and greater emotional well-being in situations where the child displays fewer behavior or cognitive difficulties and where the caregiver has a feeling of mastery (Raina et al., 2005).

Several studies examined caregiver burden and distress with neurobehavioral deficits and coping styles (see Wells et al., 2005 for review). Factors that have been found to impact the level of stress reported by the caregiver include amount of social support, feeling of mastery of the caregiving situation,

and level of behavior/cognitive difficulties displayed by the individual receiving care (Cameron et al., 2006a; Cameron, Herridge, Tansey, McAndrews, & Cheung, 2006b; Wells et al., 2005; Chronsiter & Chan, 2006). Additionally, mediators of these effects have been identified. The degree of social support for caregivers is an important mediator. For example, among family members responsible for caring for those with neurobehavioral disturbances, caregivers who feel little social support tend to express less satisfaction with life (Ergh, Hanks, Rapport, & Coleman, 2003). Furthermore, the impact of an individual's memory and behavior changes on their caregiver's mental health is exacerbated by the presence of family conflict (Clark et al, 2004).

In light of the increasing evidence that outcomes of the family, caregiver, and injured individual appear to be interrelated, several researchers have begun to design interventions to address some of the mediating factors associated with family burdens. For example, an online family problem-solving intervention was designed for families following pediatric TBI (Wade and colleagues, 2006b, 2006c). The intervention was intended to improve both child and family outcomes by integrating education regarding the cognitive/behavioral consequences of TBI with training in family communication, problem-solving, and conflict resolution. This intervention has had an initial promising impact on both child behavior (Wade, Carey, & Wolfe, 2006a) and reducing family and caregiver distress (Wade, Carey, & Wolfe 2006b).

vulnerable to stress associated with caring for that family member, and display increased risk for depression and social isolation (Grant, Elliott, Weaver, Glandon, & Giger, 2006). Thus the assessment of these mediating factors is critical.

Attitudes and expectations regarding injury, disease, illness, disability, and recovery impact rehabilitation outcomes. The rehabilitation team should consider these variables when developing assessment and rehabilitation plans. A consumer's occupational status, expected levels of support from his or her employer during the rehabilitation process, and the likelihood of returning to work also need to be considered. Although individuals with neurological injuries typically experience difficulty returning to work after rehabilitation, those who do return report a subjective well-being and higher life satisfaction (Storey, 2003; Vestling, Tufvesson, & Iwarsson, 2003; Johansson & Bernspang, 2003).

Identification of Compensatory Skills and Resources

Assessment planning must necessarily involve ensuring that information will be obtained regarding the consumer's ability to compensate for potential cognitive, physical, and emotional deficits. Interviews with family and other caretakers, along with a review of historical information and other records, aid in the identification of resources currently available to manage impairments. This information can provide a framework for further assessment and a review of functional goals tailored to take advantage of existing areas of strengths, including one's resiliency, and to shore up gaps or areas of weakness. For example, compensatory techniques and technological aids may focus on cognitive (e.g., calendars, notebooks, personal digital assistants, external prompts and cues, visual schedules) or physical (e.g., orthoses, prostheses, environmental modifications) impairments. Although consumers may be taught compensatory strategies in a hospital setting, many will have difficulty implementing these strategies when they return to school, home, work, and other community contexts in which they are needed. At the outset of assessment planning, providers should seek to identify external supports and resources that will be available after discharge. Environments that differ in the richness of support and resources can result in drastic differences in postrehabilitation outcome, and thus must be considered during all phases of the assessment and intervention process.

REHABILITATION STAGES

As indicated previously, assessment serves multiple purposes throughout the rehabilitation process, prompting referrals to address a variety of consumer needs at multiple stages of rehabilitation and recovery. A dynamic interactive relationship between the consumer and the rehabilitation team is required to accurately identify the stage of rehabilitation and how stage-related information impacts the attainment of short-and long-term consumer goals and subsequent assessment planning.

For example, prior to delivery of initial rehabilitation services, assessment goals may include the following: establishing an individual's eligibility for services; determining baseline functioning from which to compare progress, stability, or decline over time; linking strengths and weaknesses with treatment and intervention planning; determining available support networks and resources; or a combination of each of these. Clinicians planning assessment procedures select instruments and tools that are appropriately sensitive to change in domains of interest over time, including procedures that yield data amenable to tracking and monitoring. An assessment plan should provide a framework for data collection from various sources (e.g., the consumer, family members, other care providers, teachers, employers) and contexts (e.g., school, home, in 1:1 setting as well as in crowds, in familiar and unfamiliar settings) (Ylvilsaker et al., 2006). Table 4.1 provides some key methods of data collection that a clinician should consider when undertaking an assessment in the rehabilitation setting.

During the course of rehabilitation, the need to assess the consumer's capacity to benefit from differential treatment interventions or therapeutic approaches may become apparent. Serial (i.e., continuous, over time) assessments can inform the consumer and rehabilitation team about the consumer's degree of response to specific intervention techniques. For example, during the acute period of neurological recovery, attempts to conduct a comprehensive neuropsychological battery generally are not warranted. Serial assessments of basic abilities (e.g. alertness, personal orientation) provide greater utility in assisting the rehabilitation team in treatment planning and documenting the trajectory of recovery (Ewing-Cobbs, Levin, Fletcher, Miner, & Eisehberg, 1990; Levin, O' Donnell, & Grossman, 1979). In addition, clinicians must remain aware of practice effects. Many test instruments are prone to such effects and therefore become less useful when used repeatedly. Monitoring

TABLE 4.1 Obtaining Information Prior to the Rehabilitation Assessment: Potential Sources & Methods

Factor	Information Source/Method
Personal Factors	
Orientation	Staff interviews. Medical record review.
Abilities	Staff interview, medical chart/record review, school records, and brief consumer interview to determine functional abilities, sensory deficits, tolerance, fatigability, and awareness/denial of deficits. Historical record review and interview of consumer and family/significant others to determine primary language.
Emotional Functioning	Staff interview, medical chart/record review and brief consumer interview. Historical record review and interview of consumer and family/significant others to determine pre-rehabilitation emotional functioning.
Cultural Considerations	Historical record review and interview of consumer and family/significant others to determine view of rehabilitation/impairment, beliefs & acculturation.
Environmental Factors	
Support	Interview with consumer, family, significant others, historical record review, and use of rating scales to determine nature of social and family support.
Resources	Interview with consumer, employers, teachers, school personnel, and community health care providers to determine available environmental resources.
Compensatory Resources	Interview with consumer, family, significant others, employers, teachers, school personnel, and community health care providers to determine what compensatory mechanisms are in place to promote generalizability of rehabilitation goals.
Systemic Factors	
Setting Related Issues	Provider investigates rehabilitation setting to determine physical (room, lighting, noise) and systemic (visitor/medication schedules) variables/conditions.
Team Communication	Provider clarifies source of referral and identifies team approach to communicating results to client/team members.
Role Definition	Provider seeks to clarify role in rehabilitation team to minimize patient/team confusion or testing duplication.
Provider Related Factors	Adherence to professional training & continuing education standards appropriate for rehabilitation setting.

changes in environmental variables over the course of rehabilitation is important because external support can change in reaction to the consumer's progress, preconceived expectations, and response to educational interventions that enhance awareness of the consumer's strengths and weaknesses.

After the consumer is discharged from the rehabilitation setting, follow-up assessments often are necessary to monitor the patient's progress, establish changes in strengths and weaknesses, assist in predicting long-term outcomes or prognosis, and evaluate the suitability of the interventions within the patient's functional needs.

Summary and Conclusion

Adequate preparation according to the model proposed in this chapter allows for the development of assessment plans that address the consumer's functional goals in the context of a dynamic rehabilitation process. Health care providers planning an assessment in rehabilitation settings must recognize the supportive or obstructive impact of multiple systemic factors, and adjust assessment plans accordingly. Health care providers can improve the quality and effectiveness of the assessment, and enhance the quality of rehabilitation efforts overall through consideration and identification of important consumer, setting, and assessor-related variables prior to initiation of an assessment or evaluation.

Self-Check Questions

1. Name personal qualities that can facilitate or inhibit functioning after injury.
2. Name environmental qualities that can facilitate or inhibit functioning after injury.
3. Name systemic qualities that can facilitate or inhibit the assessment process.
4. Name five data sources a clinician can use to obtain a global picture of an individual's functioning prior to in-depth assessment.

5. Describe differences between interdisciplinary and multi-disciplinary rehabilitation teams.
6. Describe how an assessment plan may change depending on the stage of rehabilitation.

Case Study—Pediatric TBI

Bob, at age 7, sustained a severe traumatic brain injury as an unrestrained passenger involved in a motor vehicle collision. Nine days after the injury, he began to follow simple commands, and two days later he was admitted to a multidisciplinary inpatient rehabilitation program. During the acute phase of his rehabilitation, Bob was agitated and confused. Assessment was informal, aimed at monitoring alertness and orientation, and tracking periods of fatigue as well as conditions that promoted or impeded rehabilitation progress. For example, Bob was most alert in the mornings and was better able to participate in therapies on a 1:1 basis without the presence of other children or distractions in the therapy rooms.

Bob was assessed daily using the Children's Orientation and Amnesia Test (COAT, Ewing-Cobbs, et al., 1990). He remained disoriented and variable for approximately 28 days following admission (PTA, post-traumatic amnesia). Thus, the rehabilitation team initially focused on family support and education and physical rehabilitation, with limited teaching of compensatory strategies. Following resolution of PTA, Bob began to make progress in initiation, verbalization, impulse control, attention, and memory skill. The rehabilitation treatment team began to teach compensatory strategies for his cognitive difficulties.

Bob was reassessed twice following his discharge to update an understanding of his functioning and to assist with recommendations for ongoing intervention. Information was collected from Bob, his parents, and teacher through formal and informal measures. Bob continued to recover and show gains on standardized neuropsychological measures. Parents and teachers reported that Bob had difficulty attending, particularly on language-based activities, and that he appeared shy and reluctant to ask for assistance. They also reported difficulty understanding Bob due to his articulation difficulties. Behavioral observations during testing were consistent with these reports. Thus, accommodations were proposed, with smaller group instruction for language-based skills and a teacher's aide who assisted Bob more frequently. Bob's parents also practiced asking for clarification and slowing his rate of speech at home.

This case study exemplifies how awareness of multiple key factors, as described further below, allowed for planning and delivering flexible and appropriately goal-driven assessment services. Each of the factors impacted decisions regarding the type of assessment technique selected and the manner in which the assessment would be conducted.

Personal Factors

Bob had a history of language and learning disabilities prior to injury. His preinjury nonverbal IQ was average. Bob was described as a good-natured and hard-working child who enjoyed school. Preinjury behavior problems were not reported.

Environmental Factors

Bob had an intact family (2 parents, 2 brothers) that provided a high level of support and actively participated in the rehabilitation process. Bob lived in a rural area and attended the only public school in this area, one with limited special education resources. For one year, after inpatient rehabilitation, Bob attended a local school devoted exclusively to providing special education services. He then returned to his local public school with accommodations that were determined at a meeting attended by Bob's parents, his rehabilitation neuropsychologist, his rehabilitation special educator, and the principal and teachers at Bob's school.

Systemic Factors

During his inpatient rehabilitation, Bob was evaluated across setting to determine whether attention and impulsivity were more problematic in settings that were noisy, had many people and required change, as opposed to the 1:1 office testing setting and tutorial work in a quiet location at school. Team communication was critical at every stage of rehabilitation, particularly during PTA (when confusion and agitation frequently impeded Bob's ability to use compensatory strategies and fully participate in therapies).

Stage of Rehabilitation Issues

While in the inpatient setting, Bob was evaluated daily through the use of informal screening measures (i.e., COAT). He participated in a brief neuropsychological evaluation prior to his discharge from the inpatient setting, again at one-year postinjury, and then prior to entering middle school, to monitor recovery and update treatment recommendations and compensatory strategies. Bob will be re-evaluated prior to entering high school.

Assessment Plan

Body Functions, Structures and Impairments: Task performance measures progressed from following simple commands to general orientation and memory, based in part on the COAT data, to observational and informal assessment of basic cognitive skills (attention, memory, language, visual–spatial skill, executive functioning, intellectual functioning) to more standardized psychometric evaluation at follow-up.

Activities and Participation: Multidisciplinary assessment of Bob's abilities across multiple settings to complete daily tasks and to participate in the rehabilitation process was completed. Abilities and participation were assessed within the rehabilitation setting and then eventually in the community as tolerated. An understanding of preinjury ability and participation was necessary to set treatment goals.

Contextual Factors: Multiple environmental (school, home), family, and personal factors were assessed to determine barriers and facilitators to rehabilitation outcome and participation once Bob returned to the community.

References

American Educational Research Association, American Psychological Association, & National Council on Measurement in Education (1999). *Standards for Educational and Psychological Testing.* Washington, DC: American Educational Research Association.

American Psychiatric Association (1994). *Diagnostic and Statistical Manual of Mental Disorders (DSM-IV)*, 4th ed. Washington, DC: American Psychiatric Association.

Anderson, V. A., Catroppa, C., Haritou, F., Morse, S., & Rosenfeld, J. V. (2005). Identifying factors contributing to child and family outcome 30 months after traumatic brain injury. *Journal of Neurology, Neurosurgery and Psychiatry, 76*(3), 401–408.

Artiola I Fortuny, L., & Mullaney, H.A. (1998). Assessing patients whose language you do not know: Can the absurd be ethical? *The Clinical Neuropsychologist, 12,* 113–126.

Bergquist, T. F., & Malec, J. F. (2002). Neuropsychological assessment for treatment planning and research. In P. J. Eslinger, (Ed.), *Neuropsychological interventions* (pp. 38–58). New York: Guilford Press.

Bickenback, J. E., Chatterji, S., Badley, E. M., & Ustun, T. B. (1999). Models of disablement, universalism and the international classification of impairments, disabilities and handicaps. *Social Science and Medicine, 48,* 1173–1187.

Bruyere, S. M., Van Looy, S. A., & Peterson, D. B. (2005). The international classification of functioning, disability and health: Contemporary literature overview. *Rehabilitation Psychology, 50*(2), 113–121.

Cameron, J. I., Cheung, A. M., Streiner, D. L., Coyte, P. C., & Stewart, D. E. (2006a). Stroke survivors' behavioral and psychologic symptoms are associated with informal caregivers' experiences of depression. *Archives of Physical Medicine and Rehabilitation, 87,* 177–183.

Cameron, J. I., Herridge, M. S., Tansey, C. M., McAndrews, M. P., & Cheung, A. M. (2006b). Well-being in informal caregivers of survivors of acute respiratory distress syndrome. *Critical Care Medicine, 34*(1), 81–86.

Chronister, J. & Chan, F. (2006). A stress process model of caregiving for individuals with traumatic brain injury. *Rehabilitation Psychology, 51*(3), 190–201.

Clark, P. C., Dunbar, S. B., Shields, C. G., Viswanathan, B., Aycock, D. M., & Wolf, S. L. (2004). Influence of stroke survivor characteristics and family conflict surrounding recovery on caregivers' mental and physical health. *Nursing Research, 53*(6), 406–413.

Eccleston, C., Malleson, P. N., Clinch, J., Connell, H., & Sourbut, C. (2003). Chronic pain in adolescents: Evaluation of a programme of interdisciplinary cognitive behavioral therapy. *Archives of Disease in Childhood, 88,* 881–885.

Elfstrom, M. L., Ryden, A., Kreuter, M., Taft, C., & Sullivan, M. (2005). Relations between coping strategies and health-related quality of life in patients with spinal cord lesions. *Journal of Rehabilitation Medicine, 37*(1), 9–16.

Elliott, T.R., Witty, T. E., Herrick, S., & Hoffman, J. T. (1991). Negotiating reality after physical loss: Hope, depression, and disability. *Journal of Personality and Social Psychology, 61*(4), 608–613.

Ergh, T. C., Hanks, R. A., Rapport, L. J., & Coleman, R. D. (2003). Social support moderates caregiver life satisfaction following traumatic brain injury. *Journal of Clinical and Experimental Neuropsychology, 25*(8), 1090–1101.

Evans, R. L., Bishop, D. S., Matlock, A. L., Stranahan, S., Smith, G. G., & Halar, E. M. (1987). Family interaction and treatment adherence after stroke. *Archives of Physical Medicine and Rehabilitation, 68*(8), 513–517.

Ewing-Cobbs, L., Levin, H. S., Fletcher, J. M., Miner, M. E., & Eisenberg, H. M. (1990). The Children's Orientation and Amnesia Test: Relationship to severity of acute head injury and to recovery of memory. *Neurosurgery, 27*(5), 683–691.

Fann, J. R., Burington, B., Leonetti, A., Jaffe, K., Katon, W. J., & Thompson, R. S. (2004). Psychiatric illness following traumatic brain injury in an adult health maintenance organization population. *Archives of General Psychiatry, 61*(1), 53–61.

Felton, B. J., & Revenson, T. A. (1984). Coping with chronic illness: A study of controllability and the influence of coping strategies on psychological adjustment. *Journal of Consulting and Clinical Psychology, 53,* 343–353.

Frank, R. G., Umlauf, R. L., Wonderlich, S. A., Askinazi, G. S., Buckelew, S. P., & Elliott, T. R., (1987). Differences in coping styles among persons with spinal cord injury: A cluster–analytic approach. *Journal of Consulting and Clinical Psychology, 55*(5), 727–31.

Glass, T. A., & G. L. Maddox, (1992). The quality and quantity of social support: Stroke recovery as psycho-social transition. *Social Science & Medicine, 34*(11), 1249–1261.

Grant, J. S., Elliott, T., Weaver, M., Glandon, G., & Giger, J. (2006). Social problem-solving abilities, social support, and adjustment among family caregivers of individuals with a stroke. *Archives of Physical Medicine and Rehabilitation, 87*(3), 343–350.

Heinemann, A.W., Schnoll, S., Brandt, M., Maltz, R., & Keen, M. (1988). Toxicology screening in acute spinal cord injury. *Alcoholism, Clinical and Experimental Research, 12*(6), 815–819.

Heinrichs, R. W. (1990). Current and emergent applications of neuropsychological assessment: Problems of validity and utility. *Professional Psychology: Research and Practice, 12*(3), 171–176.

Johansson, U., & Bernspang, B. (2003). Life satisfaction related to work re-entry after brain injury, a longitudinal study. *Brain Injury, 17*(11), 991–1002.

Kennedy, P. C., Marsh, N., Lowe, R., Grey, N., Short, E., & Rogers, B. (2002). A longitudinal analysis of psychological impact and coping strategies following spinal cord injury. *British Journal of Health Psychology, 34,* 627–639.

Kilpatrick, S. D., & McCullough, M. E. (1999). Religion and Spirituality in Rehabilitation Psychology. *Rehabilitation Psychology, 44*(4), 388–402.

Korte, K. B., & Wegener, S. T. (2004). Denial of illness in medical rehabilitation populations: Theory, research and definition. *Rehabilitation Psychology, 49*(3), 187–199.

Krause, J., & Rohe, D. (1998). Personality and life adjustment after spinal cord injury: An exploratory study. *Rehabilitation Psychology, 43,* 118–130.

Levin H. S., O'Donnell V. M., & Grossman R. G. (1979). The Galveston Orientation and Amnesia Test: A practical scale to assess cognition after head injury. *Journal of Nervous and Mental Disorders 167,* 675–684.

Lezak, M. D. (1995). *Neuropsychological Assessment* (3rd ed.). New York: Oxford Press.

Mash, E. J., & Hunsley, J. (2005). Evidence-based assessment of child and adolescent disorders: Issues and challenges. *Journal of Clinical Child and Adolescent Psychology, 34*(3), 362–379.

Norton, P. J., & Hope, D. A. (2001). Analogue observational methods in the assessment of social functioning in adults. *Psychological Assessment, 13,* 59–72.

Peterson, D. B. (2005). International classification of functioning, disability and health: An introduction for rehabilitation psychologists. *Rehabilitation Psychology, 50*(2), 105–112.

Raina, P., O'Donnell, M., Rosenbaum, P., Brehaut, J., Walter, S. D., Russell, D., Swinton, M., Zhu, B., & Wood, E. (2005). The health and well-being of caregivers of children with cerebral palsy. *Pediatrics, 115*(6), 626–636.

Reed, G. M., Lux, J. B., Bufka, L. F., Trask, C. Peterson, D. B., Stark, S., Threats, T. T., Jacobson, J. W., & Hawley, J. A. (2005). Operationalizing the international classification of functioning, disability and health in clinical settings. *Rehabilitation Psychology, 50*(2), 122–131.

Richards, J.S. (1986). Psychologic adjustment to spinal cord injury during first postdischarge year. *Archives of Physical Medicine and Rehabilitation, 67*(6), 362–365.

Rivara, J., Fay, G., Jaffe, K., Polssar, N., Shurtleff, H., & Liao, S. (1992). Predictors of family functioning one year following traumatic brain injury in children. *Archives of Physical Medicine and Rehabilitation, 73,* 899–910.

Rivara, J., Jaffe, K., Polissar, N., Fay, G., Martin, K., Shurtleff, H., & Liao, S. (1994). Family functioning and children's academic performance in the year following traumatic brain injury. *Archives of Physical Medicine and Rehabilitation, 75,* 369–379.

Rodin, G., & K. Voshart (1986). Depression in the medically ill: An overview. *American Journal of Psychiatry, 143*(6), 696–705.

Rolland, J. (1994). *Families, illness and disability: An integrative treatment model.* New York: Basic Books.

Salorio, C., Brandys, E., Morozova, O., Pidcock, F., Trovato, M., Sadowsky, C., & Christensen, J. (2008). Neurorehabilitation.

In B. Capute & T. Accardo (Eds.), *Neurodevelopmental disabilities in infancy and childhood* (3rd ed.). Baltimore: Brookes Publishing.

Scherer, M. J., & Glueckauf, R. (2005). Assessing the benefits of assistive technologies for activities and participation. *Rehabilitation Psychology, 50*(2), 132–141.

Smith, D. S., & Clark, M. S. (1995). Competence and performance in activities of daily living of patients following rehabilitation from stroke. *Disability Rehabilitation, 17*(1), 15–23.

Stein, P., Berger, A., Hibbard, M., & Gordon, W. (1993). Interventions with the spouses of stroke survivors. In W. Gordon (Ed.), *Advances in stroke rehabilitation*, Andover, MA: Andover Medical, (pp. 242–257).

Storey, K. (2003). A review of research on natural support interventions in the workplace for people with disabilities. *International Journal of Rehabilitation Research, 26*(2), 79–84.

Strasser, D. C., Falconer, J. A., Herrin, J. S., Bowen, S. E., Stevens, A. B., & Uomoto, J. (2005). Team functioning and patient outcomes in stroke rehabilitation. *Archives of Physical Medicine and Rehabilitation, 86*(3), 403–409.

Trovato, M., Christensen, J., Salorio, C., Brandys, E., Sadowsky, C., & Suskauer S, Pidcock, F. (in press). Rehabilitation of children with critical illness. In D. Nichols (Ed.), *Rogers textbook of pediatric intensive care* (4th ed.). Philadelphia: Lippincott William & Wilkins.

Turner, J. A., Jensen, M. P., Warms, C. A., & Cardenas, D. D. (2002). Catastrophizing is associated with pain intensity, psychological distress, and pain-related disability among individuals with chronic pain after spinal cord injury. *Pain, 98* (1–2), 127–134.

Vasa, R. A., Grados, M., Slomine, B., Herkovits, E. H., Thompson, R. E., Salorio, C. F., Christensen, J. R., Wursta, C., Riddle, M. A., & Gerring, J. P. (2004). Neuroimaging correlates of anxiety after pediatric traumatic brain injury. *Biological Psychiatry, 55*(3), 208–216.

Verhaeghe, S., Defloor, T., & Grypdonck, M. (2005). Stress and coping among families of patients with traumatic brain injury: A review of the literature. *Journal of Clinical Nursing, 14*, 1004–1012.

Vestling, M., Tufvesson, B., & Iwarsson, S. (2003). Indicators for return to work after stroke and the importance of work for subjective well-being and life satisfaction. *Journal of Rehabilitation Medicine, 35*(3), 127–131.

Wade, S. L., Carey, J., & Wolfe, C. R. (2006a). The efficacy of an online cognitive-behavioral family intervention in improving child behavior and social competence following pediatric brain injury. *Rehabilitation Psychology, 51*(3), 179–189.

Wade, S. L., Carey, J., & Wolfe, C. R. (2006b). An online family intervention to reduce parental distress following pediatric traumatic brain injury. *Journal of Consulting and Clinical Psychology, 74*(3), 445–454.

Wade, S. L., Taylor, H. G., Drotar, D., Stancin, T., & Yeates, K. (1996) Childhood traumatic brain injury: Initial impact on the family. *Journal of Learning Disabilities, 29*, 652–666.

Wade, S. L., Taylor, H. G., Yeates, K. O., Drotar, D., Stancin, T., Minich, N. M., & Schluchter, M. (2006c). Long-term parental and family adaptation following pediatric brain injury. *Journal of Pediatric Psychology, 31*(10), 1072–1083.

Wallander, J. L., & Thompson, R. J. (1995). Psychosocial adjustment of children with chronic physical conditions. In M.C. Roberts (Ed.), *Handbook of pediatric psychology,* (2nd ed.). New York: Guildford Press.

Wallander, J. L., Varni, J. W., Babani, L., Banis, H. T., & Wilcox, K. T., (1989). Family resources as resistance factors for psychological maladjustment in chronically ill and handicapped children. *Journal of Pediatric Psychiatry, 14*, 157–173.

Wegener, S., Bechtold Kortte, K., Hill-Briggs, F., Johnson-Greene, D., Palmer, S., & Salorio, C. (2006). Rehabilitation Psychology Assessment and Intervention. In R. Braddom (Ed.), *Physical medicine and rehabilitation,* (3rd ed.). London: Elsevier.

Weissman, M. M., & J. K. Myers (1978). Affective disorders in a U.S. urban community: The use of research diagnostic criteria in an epidemiological survey. *Archives of General Psychiatry, 35*(11), 1304–11.

Wells, R., Dywann, J., & Dumas, J. (2005). Life satisfaction and distress in family caregivers as related to specific behavioural changes after traumatic brain injury. *Brain Injury, 19*(13), 1105–1115.

Wennemer, H. K., Borg-Stein, J., Gomba, L., Delaney, B., Rothmund, A., Barlow, D., Breeze, G., & Thompson, A. (2006). Functionally oriented rehabilitation program for patients with Fibromyalgia. *American Journal of Physical Medicine and Rehabilitation, 85*(8), 659–666.

Werner, E., & R. Smith (1992). *Overcoming the odds: High-risk children from birth to adulthood.* New York: Cornell University.

Wilson, B. (1989). Models of cognitive rehabilitation. In R. L. Wood & P. Eames (Eds.), *Models of brain injury rehabilitation* (pp. 117–141). London: Chapman & Hall.

World Health Organization (WHO) (2001). *ICF–International classification of functioning, disability and health.* Geneva: Author.

Yeates, K., Taylor, H. G., Drotar, D., Wade, S., Stancin, T., & Klein, S. (1997). Pre-injury environment as a determinant of recovery from traumatic brain injuries in school aged children. *Journal of the International Neuropsychological Society, 3*, 617–630.

Ylvilsaker, M., Adelson, D., Braga, L. W., Burnett, S. M., Glang, A., Feeney, T., Moore, W., Rummey, P., & Todis, B. (2006). Rehabilitation and ongoing support after pediatric TBI. *Journal of Head Trauma Rehabilitation, 20*(1), 95–109.

5

Types of Tests and Assessments

NICHOLAS BENSON
Florida International University

OVERVIEW

This chapter describes the methods (i.e., types of tests and assessments) available for assessment in rehabilitation and health. A general discussion of methods commonly used for assessments in rehabilitation and health settings is provided. Distinctions are made among structural, process, and outcome assessments. Types of tests and assessment methods used at the individual units of classification provided by the *International Classification of Functioning, Disability and Health* (ICF) are then described. The chapter concludes with a discussion of the types of tests and assessment methods used for structural, process, and outcome assessments.

LEARNING OBJECTIVES

By the end of the chapter, readers should be able to:

- Identify tests and assessment methods used at the individual units of classification provided by the International Classification of Functioning, Disability and Health
- Distinguish among structural, process, and outcome assessments
- Identify tests and assessment methods used for structural, process, and outcome assessments
- Evaluate the types of assessment methods used in health and rehabilitation settings

INTRODUCTION

The term *test* refers to methods used to examine or determine the presence of some phenomenon (VandenBos, 2007). The terms *test* and *assessment* are not synonymous. Assessment generally refers to qualitative judgments pertaining to the value of something or someone (VandenBos). In the context of rehabilitation and health, assessment is operationally defined as a comprehensive process used to gather information necessary for making decisions and accomplishing objectives related to promoting health, independent functioning, and well-being. Although tests are an integral part of the assessment process, tests are only one of several assessment methods.

The assessment process involves gathering historical data and formulating a description of current functioning. This information is used to clarify the referral question and develop assessment goals. Assessment goals derive from professionals' determinations regarding what aspects of an individual's functioning are worthy of examination and what outcomes are desired. Consistent with the World Health Organization's objective of attainment by all peoples of the highest possible level of health (World Health Organization, 2006), the all-encompassing goal of rehabilitation and health assessment is to prevent impairment and disability and promote health and well-being. Prevention and promotion are complementary processes, as any activity that promotes functioning prevents impairments and disability (Stachtchenko & Jenicek, 1990).

Assessment goals are dependent on the specific needs of the individual who is the subject of the evaluation as well as the specific needs of the evaluation setting. Assessment goals include, but are not limited to, diagnosis, treatment planning, Social Security Administration determination, resolving forensic disputes, and monitoring rehabilitation outcomes. Assessment goals are achieved using an integrative process that involves collecting, analyzing, and synthesizing data to make evidence-based conclusions.

Assessment in rehabilitation and health generally is comprehensive and involves collecting data about the components of functioning delineated in the *International Classification of Functioning, Disability and Health* (ICF; World Health Organization [WHO], 2001): body structures, body functions, activities and participation, environmental factors, and personal factors. The assessment process often is interdisciplinary, involving a team of rehabilitation professionals consisting of members such as physicians, nurses, physical therapists, occupational therapists, speech–language pathologists, psychologists, and social workers. This interdisciplinary assessment team collects data from multiple sources. Essential sources of information include but are not limited to family members, peers, teachers, friends, employees and employment history, and other records. Information may be gathered from these sources on multiple occasions using multiple methods.

This chapter describes the methods (i.e., types of tests and assessments) available for assessment in rehabilitation and health. Interviews are used most commonly to gather information in rehabilitation and health settings (Berven, 2001). Other important methods include reviews of historical records, behavioral observation, and testing.

ASSESSMENT METHODS

Interviews

An interview is a purposeful and planned meeting in which one person attempts to acquire information from another (VandenBos, 2007). In the context of rehabilitation and health, such information often includes a personal and family history, symptoms, complaints, as well as his or her perceptions of themselves and their functioning (Berven, 2001). The content and process of interviews depends on the interviewer's goals, skills, and theoretical orientation (see Chapter 10 for a more complete discussion of interviews).

Interviews may be structured, semistructured, or unstructured (Edelbrock & Costello, 1988). Structure helps to increase the reliability and thus the consistency of information together with its accuracy obtained between raters or over time. Structured interviews are designed to present a specific set of questions that examine a well-defined content using a standardized format (Sattler, 2002). Although semistructured interviews also include a set of questions for the interviewer, their content may vary in response to the goals (e.g., diagnosis, determining a client's needs, or ascertaining clients' perceptions of a rehabilitation provider) of the assessment

(Sattler, 1998). Unstructured interviews are open-ended and afford the interviewer the most flexibility to respond to the patient's unique situation (Sattler, 2002). These interviews typically lack a specific set of questions. The reliability and validity of information obtained through interviews should be scrutinized, supplemented, and thus verified by gathering information using other reliable methods (Berven, 2001).

Reviews of Historical Records

A patient's current functioning must be evaluated against the backdrop of his/her history. Impaired functioning may be related to the accumulation of a number of personal and environmental risk factors operating concomitantly (Sameroff & MacKenzie, 2003) or prior traumatic events. Knowledge of the incidence of physical and mental illness and other genetically linked diseases in first- and second-degree relatives is important, given familial-related proclivity for them. Many different moderator variables (e.g., health history, lifestyle) affect a patient's current functioning. Berg, Franzen, and Wedding (1987) suggest that, "Without knowledge of values for these moderator variables, it is virtually impossible to interpret even specialized, sophisticated test results" (p. 47).

Historical information (e.g., that examines premorbid conditions) may be particularly important for rehabilitation assessment when patients have experienced disease or trauma that may have negatively impacted their current functioning. This information often is critical to estimating the time to achieve recovery and expectations for its degree of success. Premorbid functioning is established best by review of historical records (Reynolds, 1997). Records that often are important include those from medical, psychiatric, neurological, neuropsychological, psychological, legal, educational, and family sources. The degree to which particular records are relevant to an assessment varies depending on the referral question and assessment goals. On many occasions, practitioners will find that a patient's historical records are less comprehensive than desired and need to be supplemented with interview data (see also chapter 10).

Behavioral Observations

Behavioral observations are used to elucidate patterns of behavior. This method requires careful attention to specifying what and how long the behaviors are observed, where and how observations are made, and how they are recorded. Behavioral observations can be qualitative or quantitative. For example, a practitioner may use qualitative observations to form a general impression of

cooperation and motivation during testing or to detect signs of pathology when formulating diagnoses. Practitioners may prefer to quantify their observations when they are comparing behavioral characteristics to some criteria (e.g., when comparing whether the number of times a patient completely dresses himself is consistent with program goals) or examining change over time (e.g., whether these occasions are increasing or decreasing).

Behaviors can be quantified based on four observable characteristics: frequency, duration, latency, and intensity (Salvia & Ysseldyke, 1998). Frequency is measured by counting the number of occurrences of a behavior during a fixed period of time. The frequency of a behavior can be measured only if the target behavior has a clear beginning and end and does not occur at such a high or low frequency that it is difficult to count. A behavior's duration is measured by recording the length of time a behavior occurs. Duration of a behavior can be measured only if the behavior has a clear beginning and end. Latency is measured by assessing the length of time that it takes for an individual to exert a behavior. Latency can be measured only if the behavior has a clear beginning. A behavior's intensity refers to the strength or force with which the behavior is expressed.

BEHAVIORAL RECORDING TECHNIQUES   Clinicians use many behavioral recording techniques. Narrative recording involves providing a continuous description of behavior in progress. The events described are organized in an antecedent-behavior-consequence sequence. Information gathered using this technique can be used to identify and operationally define behaviors being assessed, develop data collection procedures, and formulate behavioral goals (Sulzer-Azaroff & Mayer, 1991).

Permanent product recording is used to count real or concrete objects or outcomes (e.g., recording the number of books read) that result from a behavior. Event recording (e.g., tallying the number of times a specific behavior occurs during a specified time interval), duration recording (i.e., recording the length of time a behavior occurs), and interval time sampling (i.e., recording the presence or absence of a specific behavior during a specified time interval) are methods used to measure transitory behaviors, those behaviors that do not leave an enduring product (Sulzer-Azaroff & Mayer). The utility and efficiency of behavioral observation continue to be enhanced by advances in systems for coding behavior, computer technologies for recording and graphically displaying behavior, single-subject experimental designs, and statistical procedures for analyzing behavior.

BEHAVIOR ANALYSIS   Behavior analysis refers to systematic inquiry of environmental events that predict and maintain behavior (Skinner, 1953). Applied behavior analysis refers to the application of systematic inquiry to socially consequential behaviors identified by organizational or individual clients (Sulzer-Azaroff & Mayer). The overarching goal of applied behavior analysis is to promote learning and maintenance of desired behavior while preventing or reducing undesirable behavior.

The label *functional behavior assessment* is used to describe a set of processes used to identify environmental variables that maintain problem behavior. These processes include experimental analysis of problem behaviors (i.e., functional analysis), direct observation of behavior, interviews, and rating scales (O'Neill et al., 1997). Functional analysis methodology has developed to help identify environmental variables that maintain problem behavior and consequentially improve treatment selection (Hanley, Iwata, & McCord, 2003). This methodology involves making initial hypotheses about environmental events that predict and maintain problem behaviors, testing these hypotheses under controlled conditions in which some environmental variable is manipulated, and refining hypotheses until the functions of problem behavior are identified. Interviews, behavior observations, and rating scales often are used to improve the efficiency and comprehensiveness of the inquiry process used to identify functions of problem behavior.

FUNCTIONAL ASSESSMENT   The term *functional* has somewhat different meanings across academic disciplines. In the context of rehabilitation assessment, the term functional often is used to describe the performance of a meaningful task or critical life skill (e.g., dressing, toileting, grooming, cooking, eating, or conversing). Such meaningful tasks or critical life skills are defined as functional activities or activities of daily living (VandenBos, 2007).

Functional assessments are used to ascertain the extent to which individuals can perform meaningful tasks (Crewe & Dijkers, 1995). The task an individual must complete is analyzed, often with the goal of identifying smaller, teachable steps or actions needed to complete this task. Once these steps or actions have been identified, then an individual's functional capacities for completing a task are examined. The goal of this assessment is to determine the extent to which an individual can complete a meaningful task. This determination may lead to the selection of constructive or compensatory strategies. Constructive strategies are used to promote performance by building upon existing behaviors. Compensatory strategies are used

to promote performance by identifying effective accommodations.

Testing

Testing involves measuring samples of behavior and involves nomothetic and idiographic methods to examine data and other information. When using nomothetic methods, a person's qualities are compared with a suitable peer group (e.g., Are short- and long-term memories higher than, about the same as, or lower than those of his or her peers?). Thus, a nomothetic analysis involves interpersonal comparisons. In contrast, when using idiographic methods, one or more qualities of a person are compared with his or her other qualities (e.g., Is short-term memory better than long-term memory?) Thus, an ideographic analysis involves an intrapersonal comparison.

Many stable and meaningful attributes (i.e., traits) are difficult or impossible to measure through the use of casual observation processes (e.g., intellectual functioning, emotional functioning, or self-perceptions of quality of life). These qualities, often referred to as latent (i.e., unobservable) traits or constructs, are hypothetical concepts that emanate from "the informed scientific imagination of social scientists who attempt to develop theories for explaining behavior" (Crocker & Algina, 1986, p. 4). Testing is an efficient means of measuring these hypothetical concepts. Constructs are operationalized by identifying observable indicators that reflect the trait, constructing test items that are believed to adequately, albeit incompletely, represent the trait, and then assigning quantitative values to behavioral samples gathered from test performance (Crocker & Algina). For example, intelligence tests assess the latent trait of intelligence by using items that are believed to represent this trait. Test performance can be evaluated using norm-referenced, criterion-referenced, or qualitative interpretations. See Table 5.1.

In norm-referenced evaluations, an individual's test performance is compared to that of a reference group known as the normative sample (see also chapter 6). Raw test scores (e.g., the number of items correctly completed) have little interpretative value and thus must be converted to standard scores (e.g., z-score, Deviation IQ, T-score). Standard scores are derived after determining the normative sample's mean score and the deviation of scores around the mean (i.e., the test's standard deviation). Standard scores are used to interpret test performance by comparing one person's performance with his or her peers based on scores from the normative sample. The validity of these comparisons depends, in part, on the extent to which the characteristics of a normative

TABLE 5.1 Evaluating Test Performance: Interpretations and Examples

Evaluation	Interpretations	Examples
Norm-Referenced	Comparison of a patient's performance with the performance of his or her peers	• Intellectual functioning • Scholastic Aptitude Test scores
Criterion-Referenced	Comparison of a patient's performance with specific and absolute standards representing functional performance level of a task or skill	• Reading proficiency level • State licensing test for psychologists
Qualitative	Comparison of observations to expectations held by examiner	• Observation of marker symptoms for a syndrome • Test session observations that help explain test performance

sample are representative of the individual whose test results are interpreted (American Educational Research Association [AERA], American Psychological Association [APA], & National Council on Measurement in Education [NCME], 1999). Professionals must determine the specific meaning of test behaviors and normative performance and attempt to establish a set of logical connections between evidence and conclusions (AERA et al.).

In criterion-referenced evaluations, an individual's test performance is compared to functional performance levels—specific and absolute standards that reflect acquisition of a skill (e.g., identifying and describing specific two-dimensional shapes as circles, squares, triangles, or rectangles). Standards are established by logical analyses. Then tests are constructed to reflect these standards (Nitko, 1984). The usefulness of inferences derived from criterion-referenced interpretations depends on the extent to which scores derived from a criterion-referenced test

relate to external, real-world criteria. Examples of criterion-referenced interpretations include domain-referenced interpretations (e.g. comparing a person's performance to specific daily living skills) and cut score interpretations (i.e., a specified point on a measurement scale that serves as a performance standard such that scores at or above that point are interpreted or acted upon differently from scores below that point).

When interpreting a test, assessment specialists focus principally on the behaviors the test is designed to assess. However, when working with an individual patient, the specialist also will be provided with additional information, qualitative in nature, which also may be used when interpreting test data. Qualitative evaluations of test performance may include the person's test-taking behaviors (e.g., Was she cooperative and attentive?), his or her social and affective behaviors, the processes and strategies used by test takers, and patterns of errors.

DISCUSSION BOX 5.1

Psychologists frequently develop tests to measure psychological constructs, which refer to attributes (e.g., intelligence and personality) that are theoretically relevant to understanding human behavior but not directly observable. Although most tests are developed to measure existing constructs, occasionally tests are developed to measure novel constructs. The recent development of emotional intelligence tests provides an interesting example of the latter case. The zeitgeist for emotional intelligence emanated largely from the popularity of Daniel Goleman's (1995) book *Emotional Intelligence: Why it can matter more than IQ*. As the title suggests, emotional intelligence is proposed as a fundamental domain of psychological and social functioning. However, other scholars have con-

cluded that empirical, peer-reviewed research support for this assumption is negligible (e.g., Matthews, Zeidner, & Roberts, 2002; Schulte, Ree, & Carretta, 2004).

Questions

1. What types of evidence do you believe are needed to demonstrate the importance of emotional intelligence to psychological and social functioning?
2. Do you believe it is appropriate to measure emotional intelligence when assessing patients in rehabilitation and health settings?
3. What was the rationale for your decision?

Qualitative analysis can be used to identify strategies used by patients, specific skills they do and do not perform, and idiosyncratic behaviors that may be diagnostically useful. Qualitative information can help assessment specialists interpret test performance and understand how individual patients function (Lezak, 1995). Moreover, supplementing test scores with qualitative information may improve the link between assessment and intervention and ultimately lead to better outcomes for individual patients (Polkingborne & Gribbons, 1999).

STANDARDIZATION   Test standardization refers to a process that establishes the ways in which a test is administered and scored while minimizing the influence of extraneous qualities that could cloud attempts to assess the desired trait. Thus, when they are administered in a standardized fashion, tests provide equal opportunities for test takers to display the traits being assessed (Green, 1981).

Personnel in hospitals, clinics, or other units use nonstandardized tests to acquire data when existing standardized tests are not available, their scope is too broad, or the qualities needed to be addressed are specific to a few patients. For example, nonstandardized tests may be used to assess the gross motor strength, flexibility, and endurance displayed by patients engaged in physical rehabilitation. Practitioners need to deviate from using standardized administration methods when a patient's acute or chronic condition precludes their use (e.g., a patient is severely mentally retarded, blind, and/or deaf—for whom fewer standardized tests exist).

Standardized and nonstandardized tests have advantages and disadvantages. Standardized tests have clearly defined norms and have been subjected to empirical investigation and analyses that examine their reliability and validity—qualities not found in nonstandardized tests. Thus, practitioners have insight into the consistency as well as the appropriateness, meaningfulness, and usefulness of the specific inferences made from standardized test scores. Disadvantages of the standardization process include substantial time and monetary costs. Consequently, standardized tests are not available for every testing purpose. If standardized tests are not available, nonstandardized tests may be generated rather quickly by a practitioner and have the additional advantages of being tightly focused on particular skills of interest and of providing immediate feedback. Questions pertaining to their reliability and validity limit their use.

RATING SCALES   Rating scales provide an efficient way to acquire information. They typically contain a limited set of items that can be answered by having a respondent read and mark (i.e., rate) whether the qualities are displayed and, if so, how frequently. The assessment specialist informs the respondent why the information is needed and how to complete the rating scale. Thus, the specialist may spend little time administering the test.

A litany of rating scales is available to assist with rehabilitation and health assessment (McDowell and Newell, 2006). Many rating scales are standardized and normed, thus facilitating interpersonal comparisons. The accuracy of ratings scales may be attenuated due to response bias (e.g., a desire to show a behavior to be either higher or lower than it actually is). Thus, their data should be scrutinized and compared with other data that may be more objective (Witt, Heffer, & Pfieffer, 1990).

PROJECTIVE TECHNIQUES   Projective techniques are personality assessment procedures consisting of ambiguous stimuli or tasks designed to provoke responses that are used to make inferences about personality organization and function (VandenBos, 2007; see also chapter 18). Projective techniques vary widely. For example, they may require persons to tell stories in response to pictures, to draw, to form word associations, or to complete sentences.

DISCUSSION BOX 5.2

Testing accommodations are often necessary for individuals with disabilities. Appropriate accommodations may include providing a special setting or special scheduling for testing, revising test directions, changing item format, or modifying response methods.

Questions

1. What are some specific accommodations that may be appropriate for individuals with disabilities that impair auditory, visual, or motor functioning?

2. What impact might such accommodations have on the psychometric integrity of tests?

3. What types of information could be collected to aid with the interpretation of standardized test scores when accommodations are used?

Two of the most popular techniques include the *Rorschach* test and apperceptive tests. When completing the *Rorschach,* patients answer questions about what they perceive in pictures of ambiguously presented inkblots. Their responses are interpreted either by quantifying structural differences in their perception of the stimuli (e.g., Exner, 1986) or by qualitatively examining idiographic differences in their perception (e.g., Aronow, Reznikoff, & Moreland, 1994).

When using apperceptive tests, patients tell stories about their interpretations of pictures that depict scenes involving humans. Examiners interpret these responses in terms of content or structure, with the goal of identifying recurrent themes throughout responses—and thus in response to their prevailing life themes. Other projective techniques ask persons to draw pictures of themselves and their family members, complete word association tests (e.g., tell words a patient associates with other words such as love, anger, kind), and sentence completion tests (e.g., patients are presented with the beginning of sentences they must complete: "I wish my family would . . .").

Projective techniques may be used to form clinical impressions about an individual. The strength of these impressions should be examined by confirmatory evidence acquired from more widely used and valid measures. Their reliance on idiographic interpretation methods limits efforts to establish their validity. When used in the hands of a seasoned and skilled assessment specialist, projective measures often yield valuable information. However, when in the hands of less able professionals, their interpretations tend to be superficial and can be misleading.

Social psychological researchers recently have begun to develop implicit measurement techniques (Fazio & Olson, 2003). These techniques are similar to

---

RESEARCH BOX 5.1

Objective: Nock and Banaji (2007) developed an *indirect* clinical assessment method to detect and predict suicidal ideation and attempts. These authors indicated a need for such an indirect method because people with suicidal tendencies often are reluctant to disclose suicidal ideation or intent. The measure assesses reaction time to implicit associations between self-injury and self-relevance (i.e., associating stimuli pertaining to self-injury with themselves) and then examined the utility of this implicit measure for predicting suicide ideation and attempts.

Method: Participants included 89 (62% female) adolescents (38 nonsuicidal controls, 37 with a recent history of suicide ideation, and 14 with a recent history of attempting suicide). The adolescents rated a series of images as being either self-injurious or neutral as well as words as either self-relevant (e.g., I, mine) or other-relevant (e.g., they, them). Participants responded to these images and words while sitting alone at a desktop computer. Their reaction time was recorded (i.e., faster reaction times were assumed to demonstrate stronger associations between self-injury and self-relevance). Suicide ideation and attempts were assessed using multiple methods on two occasions (initially to establish a baseline and again six months later). The authors then compared performance on the implicit association test across groups (i.e., nonsuicidal, suicidal ideation, and suicidal attempt groups), examined the utility of the implicit association test for predicting suicidal ideation and attempts, and examined the

ability of the implicit association test to improve prediction of suicide ideation and attempts beyond significant demographic and psychiatric risk factors.

Results: Group differences in performance on the implicit association test were significant. Participants who had attempted suicide displayed a strong positive relationship between self-injury and self-relevance. Participants who had displayed suicidal ideation displayed a weak positive relationship between self-injury and self-relevance. Nonsuicidal participants showed a strong negative relationship between self-injury and self-relevance. In addition, the test data were found to strongly and consistently predict suicide ideation and attempts. Thus, the authors concluded the test data improve prediction of these outcomes well beyond the influence of known demographic and psychiatric risk factors.

Questions

1. Why might suicidal people be reluctant to disclose suicidal ideation or intent?
2. What are some potential explanations for the faster reaction times displayed by individuals who have attempted suicide?
3. What does this study demonstrate about the use of implicit measurement techniques to predict suicide outcomes?
4. What are some other possible uses of indirect clinical assessment methods researchers may want to investigate in future studies?

projective techniques, although the assumptions guiding their development differ. Projective techniques are based on psychodynamic theory and are believed to tap unconscious motives. Conversely, implicit measurement techniques are largely atheoretical and are intended to reduce response biases by using an indirect approach to measurement. Although respondents may be aware that they possess certain attitudes, drives, or motives, they are unaware that implicit measurement techniques are measuring these unobservable attributes. Implicit measurement techniques may be useful for gathering information that people are reluctant to disclose. Recent research pertaining to the prediction of suicidal ideation and attempts (Nock and Banaji, 2007) illustrates the potential of these techniques.

CATEGORIZATIONS OF TESTS AND ASSESSMENTS BASED ON FUNCTION AND UTILITY

Thousands of tests are available for use in health and rehabilitation settings. Lamentably, a general taxonomy for rehabilitation measures does not exist (Mermis, 2005). Given the absence of a general taxonomy for measures commonly used in rehabilitation practices, some system is needed that assigns the myriad of tests into a typology. The *Buros Mental Measurements Yearbook* describes and reviews many standardized tests. However, it does not provide much of the essential information needed by rehabilitation and health specialists when selecting tests.

Because assessment in rehabilitation and health is concerned with the assessment of functioning, tests and other assessment methods may be grouped to correspond to the units of classification delineated in the *International Classification of Functioning, Disability and Health* (ICF; WHO, 2001): body structures, body functions, activities and participation, environmental factors, and personal factors (see also chapter 1). Additionally, distinctions can be made between structural (i.e., examining how the functioning of interrelated components impacts service delivery), process (i.e., examining the sequence of operations that leads to service delivery), and outcome (i.e., examining the extent to which service delivery achieves desired benefits) assessment (Donabedian, 1966).

Tests and other assessment methods discussed in this chapter have been assigned according to their utility for assessing the various ICF units of classification and their function (i.e., structural assessment, process assessment, outcome assessment) in order to facilitate the description of the types of tests and assessments available for use in rehabilitation and health assessment. This process requires knowledge of the method's validity and thus narrows the scope of tests covered in the chapter to those with validity evidence that supports their application to standard functions of rehabilitation and health assessment.

Grouping tests and assessments into ICF units of classification should be useful to professionals when implementing the ICF. Notably, some useful tests or assessment techniques may be excluded from this chapter. The purpose of the following is to illustrate tests that may be useful for standard functions of rehabilitation and health assessment rather than to provide exhaustive coverage.

Body Functions

Body functions refer to the physiological functioning of body systems (including physiological and psychological functions). The primary assessment goal is to identify impaired and/or intact body functions (Erickson & McPhee, 1998). Criteria for impairment include loss or lack, reduction, addition or excess, or deviation of function. Impairment of body function is qualified in terms of two criteria: severity and location of impairment (i.e., right/left sides, front, back, proximal, distal, or multiple regions).

Interviews commonly are used to gather specific information pertaining to body function. Such information may include patient history and complaints as well as perceptions of functioning by one's self or family members. Medical professionals assess body functions, in part, by reviewing medical records, conducting physical examinations, analyzing specimens (e.g., blood and urine), and using medical imaging techniques.

Physical examinations are common to the assessment of body function. These examinations, which are completed by properly prepared and suitably licensed professionals, often include a review of body systems. Within the context of rehabilitation, neurological and musculoskeletal systems may receive the most attention while constitutional, head and neck, respiratory, cardiovascular, gastrointestinal, and genitourinary systems also generally receive special attention (Erickson & McPhee, 1998). These areas generally receive special attention because of their importance when diagnosing disease, defining the resulting disabilities and disorders, determining the consequences of impairment on functioning, and identifying existing strengths upon which to build during rehabilitation.

Assessment of the Senses

The assessment of body functions frequently involves examining sensory functioning and pain. Visual functioning often is assessed by ophthalmologists or optometrists. Visual acuity (i.e., the eye's ability to see details at near and far distances) can be examined using several types of visual acuity tests, some of which involve an eye chart. Visual field tests are used to check peripheral vision, the area that can be seen without shifting the gaze, while color vision tests are used to examine the ability to distinguish colors.

Audiologists typically use pure tone audiometry (i.e., a technique that involves having patients respond to sounds at different octave frequencies) and speech audiometry (i.e., an evaluation of a person's ability to hear and perceive speech) to examine auditory functioning. Auditory electrophysiological measures also may be used to examine infants or individuals suspected of sensorineural damage (i.e., damage that affects nerve cells in the cochlea).

Medical experts also may examine gustatory (i.e., taste), olfaction (i.e., smell), cutaneous (i.e., touch), kinesthetic (i.e., sense of movement and position of body parts), or vestibular (i.e., balance) senses. Pain may be assessed using interviews, physical examinations, or tests constructed to measure pain.

Assessment of Voice and Speech Functions

The assessment of body functions also may involve examining voice and speech functions (see also chapter 25). Interviews, clinical examinations, and tests commonly are used to assess the status of these qualities. Most assessment of these qualities would involve a combination of these three methods (Plante & Beeson, 2004).

Voice examinations may be used to determine the presence of voice disorders and may assess facial muscles, lips, teeth, soft and hard palate, tonsils, or pharynx (Barkmeier, 2004). Voice examinations also may include an endoscopy, a method that involves the use of fiberoptic equipment to look inside a client's nose and throat to examine nasal passages, soft palate, larynx, tonsils, or pharynx. Additionally, voice examinations may include respiration testing, acoustic measurements (e.g., spectograms of rate, loudness or intensity), and description of voice quality (e.g., hoarse).

A wide selection of standardized tests exists for evaluating speech production, articulation, fluency, and phonology. Speech production commonly is examined using the *Verbal Motor Production Assessment for Children* (Hayden & Square, 1999). Examples of tests commonly used to assess articulation include the *Goldman-Fristoe Test of Articulation-2* (Goldman & Fristoe, 2000) and the *Arizona Articulation Proficiency Scale* (3rd ed.) (Fudala, 2000). The *Stuttering Severity Instrument for Children and Adults* (3rd ed.) (Riley, 1994) is an example of a test that can be used to examine fluency. Examples of tests commonly used to assess phonology include the *Test of Phonological Awareness: Second Edition Plus* (Torgesen & Bryant, 2004) and the *Khan-Lewis Phonological Analysis* (2nd ed.) (Khan & Lewis, 2000).

Assessment of Global Mental Functions

Psychologists often are asked to assess global mental functions (see also chapter 14). Global mental functions include but are not limited to consciousness, orientation, intellectual, global psychosocial, temperament and personality, energy and drive, and sleep. These functions frequently are assessed during bedside screenings of neurocognitive function (see also chapter 16).

Bedside mental status screening measures are administered to provide objective indicators of need for further evaluation. All bedside mental status screening measures appear to yield high rates of false-positives (i.e., pathology is detected when in truth there is none) and false-negatives (i.e., pathology is not detected when pathology indeed exists). Thus, substantial neurobehavioral and clinical training is needed to accurately interpret their results (Wagner, Nayak, & Fink, 1995). These measures may be readministered to a patient multiple times to monitor change in mental functioning (Wagner, Nayak, & Fink, 1995). Examples of widely used measures include the *Mini-Mental State Exam* (Folstein, Folstein, & McHugh, 2001) and the *Neurobehavioral Cognitive Status Exam* (Kiernan, Mueller, Langston, & Van Dyke, 1987).

Supplementary measures may be used for process observation (Wagner, Nayak, & Fink). Examples include the *Clock Drawing Test* (Critchley, 1953) to assess cognitive formation and planning as well as motor control. The *Behavioral Dyscontrol Scale* (Paulson, 1977) is used to assess capacity to perform both novel and repetitive motor tasks. Additionally, a variety of interview schedules can be used to assess unawareness of cognitive deficit (Anderson & Tranel, 1989; Wagner & Cushman, 1994).

INTELLECTUAL ASSESSMENT Tests of intellectual ability generally are designed to measure individual differences in the constructive integration of multifaceted tasks that require multiple memory and control systems (Carroll, 1976; see also chapter 14). Intellectual assessment often is undertaken to better understand a patient's cognitive functioning as well as to help predict an individual's probability for success with educational and vocational tasks. Examples of commonly used intelligence tests include the *Wechsler Adult Intelligence Scale* (4th ed.) (WAIS-III; Wechsler, 2008), the *Wechsler Intelligence Scale for Children* (4th ed.) (WISC-IV; Wechsler, 2003) the *Stanford-Binet Intelligence Scales* (5th ed.) (SB5; Roid, 2003), the *Kaufman Assessment Battery for Children* (2nd ed.) (KABC-II; Kaufman & Kaufman, 2004), and the *Woodcock–Johnson III Tests of Cognitive Abilities* (WJIII COG; Woodcock, McGrew, & Mather, 2001).

Assessment of Global Psychosocial Functioning

An assessment of global psychosocial functioning examines how an individual forms and maintains reciprocal social interactions that facilitate the attainment of mutually desired goals. This requires evaluating the extent to which an individual understands that social behavior is meaningful and displays social behaviors that are age-appropriate and purposeful. Commonly used assessment methods include review of historical records, interviews, and behavioral observations. Moreover, a number of norm-referenced commercial rating scales are available. For example, the *Social Skills Rating System* (Gresham & Elliot, 1990) can be used to assess positive social behaviors (cooperation, empathy, assertion, self-control, and responsibility) as well as problem behaviors that hinder social functioning of children and youth. The *Childhood Autism Rating Scale* (Schopler, Reichler, & Renner, 1988) and the *Gilliam Asperger's Disorder Scale* (Gilliam, 2001) may be used to assist with assessment of an individual suspected of having an autistic spectrum disorder.

Adaptive behavior scales also measure socialization skills and can assist with assessing the social functioning of a wide array of individuals (e.g., people whose social functioning may be impaired due to disease or trauma). Examples of commonly used measures of adaptive behavior include the *Adaptive Behavior Assessment System* (2nd ed.) (Harrison & Oakland, 2003) and the *Vineland Adaptive Behavior Scales* (2nd ed.) (Sparrow, Cicchetti, & Balla, 2005; see also Chapter 15).

Assessment of Temperament and Personality

Temperament refers to a set of stylistic and relatively stable traits that subsume intrinsic tendencies to act and react in somewhat predictable ways to people, events, and other stimuli (Teglasi, 1998a, 1998b). Personality is a broader construct than temperament. Personality includes temperament as well as other characteristics such as values, self-concept, abilities, and dynamic motivations that help determine behavior (VandenBos, 2007). Although many methods used to assess temperament and personality also can be used to assess emotion, energy, and drive functions, the ICF distinguishes temperament and personality from emotion, energy, and drive functions (WHO, 2001).

Temperament and personality can be assessed using a variety of methods, including interviews, behavioral observations, projective techniques, and checklists (see chapter 18). A number of instruments can be used to assess global dispositions, including the *Revised NEO Personality Inventory* (Costa & McCrae, 1992) for adults, the *Myers–Briggs Type Indicator* (Myers, McCaulley, Quenk, & Hammer, 1998) for adolescents and adults, and the *Student Styles Questionnaire* (Oakland, Glutting, & Horton, 1996) for children and youth. Moreover, a number of omnibus personality measures assess global dispositions in addition to various behavioral characteristics. The *Minnesota Multiphasic Personality Inventory* (2nd ed.) (MMPI-2; Butcher, Dahlstrom, Graham, Tellegen, & Kaemmer, 1989) and the *Minnesota Multiphasic Personality Inventory–Adolescent* (MMPI-A; Butcher et al., 1992) are commonly used self-report measures designed to assess pathological symptoms for adults and adolescents, respectively. For children, co-normed omnibus measures can be used to gather information from a number of informants, including parents, teachers, and self (e.g., the *Behavior Assessment System for Children* (2nd ed.); Reynolds & Kamphaus, 2004).

ASSESSMENT OF ENERGY AND DRIVE A clinician often can acquire a general understanding of a patient's energy and drive from measures of temperament and personality, including the use of projective techniques in the hands of skilled and experienced clinicians. Although information on self-efficacy, resilience, and attitudes also may be helpful, they tends to examine relatively stable traits. Even though examination of stable traits typically provides rich information, complete understanding of a patient's energy and drive requires knowledge of the various and coexisting variables that influence human behavior. Although omniscience is not a reasonable assessment goal, assessment of dynamic motivational traits that may impact energy and drive may be fruitful.

Dynamic motivational traits refer to both instinctual goals and reactions to people, objects, or social institutions that cause behavior to fluctuate in response to the environment (Cattell & Kline, 1977). This information typically is gathered using interviews. However, some instruments assess motivation. For example, the *Academic Motivation Scale* (Vallerand et al., 1992) is designed to measure intrinsic and extrinsic sources of academic motivation in children and youth. However, research examining this test's structure suggests that construct validity is questionable (Fairchild, Horst, Finney, & Barron, 2005).

ASSESSMENT OF SLEEP   Sleep assessment may include interviews or tests designed to screen for sleep disorders. Examples include the *Sleep Disorders Inventory for Students* (Luginbuehl, 2003) and the *University of Toronto Sleep Assessment Questionnaire* (Cesta, Moldofsky, & Sammut, 1996). Individuals suspected of having a sleep disorder may be referred for a sleep study or polysomnogram. A polysomnogram is a multiple-component test that electronically transmits and records specific physical functions while the patient sleeps. Physical functions measured include brain wave activity, muscle activity, eye movements, heart activity, and respiration.

Assessment of Specific Mental Functions

Specific mental functions include but are not limited to attention, memory, psychomotor, emotional, perceptual, thought, higher-level cognitive, mental functions of language, calculations, mental functions of sequencing complex movements, and experience of self and time functions. With the exception of emotional functions and experience of self and time functions, these specific functions are defined within the Cattell–Horn–Carroll theory of cognitive abilities (McGrew, 2005). Thus, these abilities can be assessed using cognitive tests based on this theory (Alfonso, Flanagan, & Radwan, 2005).

Additionally, numerous neuropsychological tests (see Spreen & Strauss, 1998 for a compendium) can be used in an attempt to isolate specific mental functions. A traditional neuropsychological approach assumes complex behaviors can be divided into more specific behaviors, thus permitting clinicians to develop more precise hypotheses about performance deficits and strengths.

ASSESSMENT OF ATTENTION   Attention refers to "a state of awareness in which the senses are focused selectively on aspects of the environment and the central nervous system is in a state of readiness to respond to stimuli" (VandenBos, 2007, p. 82). Attention has limited capacity. Thus, people need a variety of attention functions to respond to environmental demands. Attention may be intentional (i.e., initiated by the frontal lobe) or reactive (i.e., unintentional direction of attention by qualities of stimuli in the environment, possibly including orienting response to avoid harm or escape pain).

Attention is easily compromised by trauma and disease that affect the central nervous system. Attention is integral to learning and memory and other higher cognitive functions. Thus, it frequently is assessed. Attention may be assessed using direct behavioral observation, diagnostic interviews, a variety of behavior rating scales such as the *Behavior Assessment System for Children* (2nd ed.; Reynolds & Kamphaus, 2004) or the *Conners' Rating Scale* (Conners, 1997), tasks that require rapid scanning and identification of targets (e.g., the Digit Symbol-Coding subtest from the *WAIS-III* [Wechsler, 1997]), and commercially available versions of the continuous performance test such as the *Conners' Continuous Performance Test* (Conners & Multi-Health Systems Staff, 1995).

ASSESSMENT OF MEMORY   Memory is the ability to retain information or representations of past experiences (VandenBos, 2007). Memory is pervasively important in daily living activities. Memory is a powerful indicator of the functional and physiological integrity of the brain. Memory loss or disturbance is a common complaint in persons who experience disorders that impact higher cognitive functioning (Baron, Fennell, & Voeller, 1995).

Interviews are useful for developing initial hypotheses about the etiology of memory problems. Behavioral observations are useful in determining the strategies a patient tends to use when performing tasks that require memory and may help identify other problems that may hinder performance with memory tasks, such as distractability and short attention span. There are a number of major test batteries for assessing memory such as the *Wechsler Memory Scale* (Wechsler, 1997), the *Children's Memory Scale* (Cohen, 1997), and the *Test of Memory and Learning* (Reynolds & Bigler, 1994).

ASSESSMENT OF LANGUAGE   Mental functions of language allow for the expression or communication of thoughts through speech sounds, sign language, or written symbols (VandenBos). A clinician may use one or more of the following measures when evaluating general language: *Clinical Evaluation of Language Fundamentals* (4th ed.) (Semel, Wiig, & Secord, 2003), *Oral and Written Language Scales* (Carrow-Woolfolk, 1996), or the *Test of Adolescent and Adult Language* (3rd ed.) (Hammill, Brown, Larsen, & Wiederholt, 1994). Clinicians interested in a quick assessment may use the *Peabody Picture Vocabulary Test* (3rd ed.) (Dunn & Dunn, 1997) or the *Test of Auditory Comprehension of Language* (3rd ed.) (Carrow-Woolfolk, 1999) for receptive language and the *Expressive One-Word Picture Vocabulary Test* (2000 ed.) (Gardner, 2000) or the *Expressive Vocabulary Test* (Williams, 1997) for expressive language. When assessing aphasia (i.e., inability to understand and produce speech resulting from brain injury or disease) in adults with acquired neurological disorders (e.g., stroke, head injury, dementia), clinicians may use the *Western Aphasia Battery* (Rev. ed.) (Kertesz, 2006). Additionally, assessment of language functions may involve measuring reading and written language with norm-referenced tests, criterion-referenced tests, or curriculum-based measures (i.e., brief, fluency-based measures designed to be sensitive to change over time).

ASSESSMENT OF EMOTIONAL FUNCTIONS   Emotional functions can be examined through record reviews, interviews, omnibus measures, and tests designed to measure specific emotions (e.g., anger and anxiety). Examples of tests that measure specific emotions include the *State-Trait Anxiety Inventory* (Spielberger 1983) and the *State-Trait Anger Expression Inventory* (Spielberger, 1996).

EXPERIENCE OF SELF AND TIME FUNCTIONS   The term *orientation* is used to describe the experience of self, outer reality, and time functions (VandenBos, 2007). Orientation may be assessed using individualized procedures or standardized tests such as the *Mini Mental State Exam* (Folstein, Folstein, & McHugh, 2001).

Body Structures

The term *body structures* refer to anatomical parts of one's body (e.g., organs, limbs, and their components; WHO, 2001). The primary goal of assessing body structures is to determine the presence or absence of anatomical abnormalities. Impairment of body structures is qualified in terms of severity, nature of change in body structure (i.e., no change, total absence, partial absence, additional part, aberrant dimensions, discontinuity, deviating position, qualitative changes including accumulation of fluid), and

location of impairment (i.e., multiple regions, right, left, both sides, front, back, proximal, distal).

Assessment of body structures often includes physical examination and imaging techniques. The use of imaging techniques is expanding rapidly in the diagnosis of pathologic anatomy (Schneck, 1998). Musculoskeletal, spine and spinal cord, and brain imaging occur somewhat frequently in rehabilitation settings.

Activity and Participation

Whereas the body (i.e., body function and body structure) component of the ICF reflects the importance of anatomy and physiology, the activity and participation component reflects the importance of the execution of tasks or actions that facilitate independent living as well as participation in society. Within the ICF, the term *activity* is defined as the execution of a task or action, and the term *participation* is defined as involvement in life situations (Peterson, 2005). These terms are operationalized in terms of capacity (i.e., to what extent *can* a patient execute a task or action successfully) and performance (i.e., what important life tasks or actions *does* an individual actually perform). Chapters in part 4 of this text address how to assess the activity and participation component.

Many of the methods discussed in the body function section of this chapter (e.g., interviews and behavioral observations) can be used to assess capacity and performance within activity and participation domains. Additionally, many rating scales can be used to measure some of these domains. For example, adaptive behavior scales (e.g., the *Adaptive Behavior Assessment System* [2nd ed.] [Harrison & Oakland, 2003] and the *Vineland Adaptive Behavior Scales* [2nd ed.] [Vineland-II; Sparrow, Cicchetti, & Balla, 2005]) can be used to assess activity and performance in most of these domains.

Functional assessments are used to examine functional capacity for the execution of meaningful tasks (Crewe & Dijkers, 1995). Rating scales such as the FIM™ (Uniform Data System for Medical Rehabilitation, 1997)[1] often are used to assist with functional assessments, although these measures reflect observed performance rather than capacity. Capacity is evaluated by determining if tasks or actions can be executed successfully either independently or with appropriate assistance or accommodations (see also chapters 11, 16, and 19 for examples).

---

[1] FIM used to be an acronym for Functional Independence, but is referred to only as the FIM™ by the current copyright holder (Wright, 2000).

The measurement of adaptive behavior is important in the assessment of performance. Adaptive behavior is needed to cope effectively with environmental demands, to function independently (e.g., with tasks such as preparing meals, eating, and maintaining personal hygiene), and to be socially integrated and productive in one's community (American Association on Mental Retardation, 1992). Patients may display both strengths and limitations in adaptive skills. Thus, because their adaptive skills may have situation specificity, information regarding adaptive behavior should be obtained from multiple sources on multiple occasions. Essential sources of information include but are not limited to family members, peers, teachers, educational records, employment history, and medical records.

Some recent measures have been developed to assess either activity (i.e., the performance of tasks) or participation (i.e., social integration and productivity in the community) based on the premise that one's ability to perform a task does not necessarily result in its use—its participation (Perenboom & Chorus, 2003). An efficient and precise measurement system based on the activity dimension of the ICF is available at http://icfmeasure.com/ (Velozo & Gray, 2004). Some instruments designed specifically to measure participation include the *Participation Scale* (Van Brakel et al., 2006) and the *Community Integration Measure* (McColl, Davies, Carlson, Johnston, & Minnes, 2001).

Quality of life measurement can be used to assess a combination of activity and participation (see chapter 27). Quality of life is defined as the extent to which a person derives happiness and satisfaction from life (VandenBos, 2007). Quality of life determinations largely are subjective and dependent on the degree to which personal needs and desires as well as societal expectations are met (Dijkers, 2003). Quality of life can be measured using qualitative interviews (e.g., Duggan & Dijkers, 1999) and rating scales such as the *SmithKline Beecham Quality of Life Index* (Dunbar, Stoker, Hodges, & Beaumont, 1992).

Environmental and Personal Factors

Both environmental and personal factors affect functioning. The ICF does not classify personal factors. Nevertheless, personal factors are important to understanding disability. Awareness of these factors contributes to an accurate interpretation of test scores and fairness of decisions derived from assessment data.

A patient's environment is likely to contain both facilitators and barriers that impact functioning. Thus,

assessment should involve examining policies, systems, and services to determine the extent to which they encourage or discourage participation and equal access. For example, a clinician may examine the extent to which the rehabilitation, home, and work or school environments implement public policy designed to eliminate physical barriers and facilitate access to buildings and services for individuals with disabilities. An environmental assessment also should evaluate the nature and suitability of accommodations made to support functioning within one's home, workplace, or school, including the use of assistive technology. Assessment of environmental factors also should examine attitudes held by and degrees of support expected from those who engage with the patient. The importance of animals to a patient's recovery should not be overlooked.

STRUCTURAL ASSESSMENT

Structural assessment involves examining parts (i.e., components of individuals, programs, or organizations) and their interaction (Donabedian, 1966; see also chapter 1). Structural information can be aggregated at the levels of individual patients (e.g., focus on their need for and capacity to benefit from health care), individual clinicians (e.g., their knowledge, skills, and ability to provide health care), and units within a health care organization (e.g., its physical and professional resources needed to meet prevalent community health care needs), or across units within an organization.

At programmatic and organizational levels, assessment involves examining components of an organization and how these components interact. The focus of this assessment is to evaluate components and determine capacity to provide health care. Capacity refers to the adequacy of programmatic and organization components (e.g., facilities, equipment, personnel, administration) as well as access to services (e.g., clinic appointment waiting time, average time in days between the scheduling date and the appointment date).

PROCESS ASSESSMENT

Assessments in rehabilitation and health settings may focus mainly on treatment outcomes and less on treatment planning and other processes associated with providing services (DeJong, Horn, Gassaway, Slavin, & Dijkers, 2004). Process assessment involves examining the sequence of operations (e.g., diagnosis, treatment planning, and treatment delivery) that leads to service delivery outcomes (Donabedian, 1966). Lack of information acquired through a process assessment limits knowledge of what actions and services improved outcomes.

Process assessment can focus on different service features, including the appropriateness of care (e.g. diagnosing, planning, and decision-making), treatment integrity, and patient dignity and involvement (e.g., empowerment of patient, communication, concern, and empathy). At times, agreed-upon rehabilitation plans and actual services differ. Thus, an evaluation should consider treatment fidelity: What plan was established, and what plan was implemented? Assessment of treatment implementation may involve the use of behavioral observation, interviews, or direct measures of treatment fidelity and objectives. This assessment would be *formative* (i.e., the collection and use of data to assist in on-going decision-making) and thus guide program development. Such assessment would involve specifying target variables for change, monitoring response to interventions or accommodations, and modifying treatments based on objective measures of progress as well as patient input. Specification of target variables and the measurement approach used to monitor patient input are dependant on the logical relatedness between rehabilitation interventions, psychometric or biometric soundness, and sensitivity to patient gain.

OUTCOME ASSESSMENT

Outcome assessment involves examining the extent to which service delivery achieves desired benefits (Commission on the Accreditation of Rehabilitation Facilities, 1995). Practitioners are expected to demonstrate the effectiveness of their services (Evidence-Based Medicine Working Group, 1992). Thus, outcome assessment has become essential to service provision in health and rehabilitation settings. Government and managed care organizations have increased accountability, quality, and outcomes demands on rehabilitation specialists and other professionals (Johnston, Maney, & Wilkerson, 1998). Although limitations associated with this greater emphasis on treatment outcomes are recognized (Posavac & Carey, 1992; Wilkerson & Johnston, 1997), evidence-based practice has become the standard in health and rehabilitation settings.

Evidence-based practice involves supplementing clinical expertise with evidence from systematic research when making decisions about the care of individual clients (Sackett, Rosenberg, Gray, Haynes, & Richardson, 1996). Although evidence-based practice has merit, the outcomes of such practice are still probabilistic. For example, a treatment protocol based on strong scientific support generally is developed to address the needs of most typical patients. The protocol may not be effective with some clients or when implemented in certain settings. Thus, outcome assessment is necessary to ensure quality service delivery. In contrast to the formative methods used for process assessment, outcome assessment uses *summative* methods (i.e., the collection and use of data to assess the extent to which program goals were attained or the program was successful in other ways).

Outcome measurement historically has focused on both specific target outcomes (e.g., range of motion, walking) and broad global outcomes of health and health related quality of life (Mermis, 2005). Functional measures have and continue to be the most prominent tools used for outcome assessment. The FIM™ (Uniform Data System for Medical Rehabilitation, 1997) remains the most widely used outcome measure (Mermis, 2005). Measures of adaptive behavior and quality of life also are used commonly. Myriad rating scales also exist for individuals with specific health issues. The National Quality Measures Clearinghouse maintains a database containing outcome measures that can be used across conditions and condition-specific outcome measures (http://www.qualitymeasures.arq.gov/).

Outcome data can be aggregated at the level of individual patients or units within a health care organization or across units within an organization (Heinemann, 2005). Outcome data can be used to evaluate quality of care, effectiveness of interventions, and efficiency (i.e., maximizing benefits while minimizing costs).

Some approaches evaluators may take to utilize outcome data include statistical significance testing (i.e., determining whether an effect occurred as the result of chance), effect size examination (i.e., examining the magnitude of the effect), benchmarking (i.e., identifying and defining an outcome, setting an outcome standard, measuring the outcome, and making comparisons between the standard and observed outcomes), and statistical projection (i.e., analyzing variance from a quantitative trajectory of progress, with this trajectory being derived from outcome data, and this outcome data being obtained from a representative sample of individuals who previously received the same intervention).

These approaches can be used to make intraorganizational and interorganizational comparisons to determine why some service recipients fare better than others and to identify performance gaps between an organization and its competitors. When these comparisons indicate that observed outcomes do not meet agreed-upon standards, action plans to improve performance may be needed, which in turn are followed by subsequent comparisons used to evaluate the results of the action plan (Heinemann, 2005).

Summary and Conclusion

Testing and assessment are integral to planning, implementing, and evaluating services in rehabilitation and health settings. Assessment is a more inclusive term than testing. Assessment refers to a comprehensive process used to gather information necessary for making decisions and accomplishing objectives related to promoting health, independent functioning, and well-being. Assessments can focus on determining rehabilitation and healthcare needs and capacity for beneficial outcomes (i.e., structural assessment), examining the sequence of operations used during implementation of services to identify variables that impact treatment outcomes (i.e., process assessment), and the extent to which service delivery achieves desired benefits (i.e., outcome assessment).

Rehabilitation and health practitioners rely on several assessment methods, including interviews, reviews of historical records, behavioral observation, and tests. The nature of assessment methods is likely to change as a function of technological advances. At present, the most obvious advances are in testing methodology. A plethora of tests has been developed to measure a wide array of phenomena, and thousands of new tests are developed annually.

Given the wide array of options available, the savvy practitioner must know how to identify well-constructed tests and assessment methods with adequate validity evidence to support an intended assessment purpose. To facilitate this task, this chapter contains descriptions of types of tests and assessments with adequate validity evidence to support their application to standard functions of rehabilitation and health assessment. Notably, these descriptions are intended to be illustrative rather than exhaustive, and some useful tests or assessment techniques may be excluded from this chapter. Finally, as an important caveat, practitioners are encouraged to consider technical properties of tests such as reliability and validity as well as legal, ethical, and practical issues when selecting tests and assessment methods.

Self-Check Questions

1. Discuss why a review of historical records is important when evaluating a patient's current functioning.
2. Identify tests and other methods used to assess (a) sensory functions and pain, (b) global and specific mental functions, (c) speech and voice functions, and (d) activity and participation. How are these similar or different in type?
3. Discuss some reasons for using multiple assessment methods.
4. Discuss situations in which quantifying behavior might be difficult.
5. Describe advantages and disadvantages of standardizing tests.
6. Distinguish between norm-referenced and criterion-referenced tests.
7. Discuss the implications of measuring only the duration of sleep for a person with a sleep disorder. What other characteristics of sleep behavior should be measured?
8. Examine the claim that both environmental and personal factors affect functioning. Discuss how both of these may facilitate or impede functioning.
9. Discuss how process assessment can improve treatment outcomes in settings with inadequate treatment outcomes.

Case Study—Assessment Use

1. James

James, a 21-year-old single male, was injured recently in an automobile accident. He was unconscious for several days following the accident and remains hospitalized. He was referred to you for assessment due to several concerns. Following the accident, he displayed difficulty remembering information, difficulty following directions, and frequent crying. Moreover, he made several sexually inappropriate comments to female staff. You are charged with assessing him and developing a treatment plan. Discuss possible types of assessment for this client. Justify your selection.

2. Mary

Mary, a 53-year-old female, recently suffered a left hemisphere stroke. Her motor skills generally appear to be unaffected and she speaks clearly and frequently. However, she displays difficulty comprehending verbal information and naming objects. These difficulties are negatively affecting her work performance. She is employed as a purchasing agent for a medical equipment company. Her primary responsibilities include purchasing medical equipment, furniture, computer equipment, and office supplies. You are charged with assessing her and developing a treatment plan. Discuss possible types of assessment for this client. Justify your selection.

References

Alfonso, V.C., Flanagan, D.P., & Radwan, S. (2005). The impact of the Cattell–Horn–Carroll theory on test development and interpretation of cognitive and academic abilities. In D. Flanagan & P. L. Harrison (Eds.), *Contemporary intellectual assessment: Theories, tests, and issues* (2nd ed., pp. 185–202). New York: Guilford.

American Association on Mental Retardation. (1992). *Definitions, classifications, and systems of supports* (9th ed.). Washington, DC: Author.

American Educational Research Association, American Psychological Association, and National Council of Measurement in Education (AERA/APA/NCME). (1999). *Standards for educational and psychological testing.* Washington, DC: American Psychological Association.

Anderson, S.W., & Tranel, D. (1989). Awareness of disease states following cerebral infarction, dementia, and head trauma: Standardized assessment. *The Clinical Neuropsychologist, 3,* 327–339.

Aronow, E., Reznikoff, M., & Moreland, K. (1994). *The Rorschach technique.* Needham Heights, MA: Allyn & Bacon.

Barkmeier, J. (2004). Disorders of voice and swallowing. In E. Plante & P. M. Beeson, *Communication and communication disorders: A clinical introduction* (2nd ed., pp. 126–148). Boston: Pearson Education, Inc.

Baron, I. S., Fennell, E. B., & Boeller, K. K. S. (1995). *Pediatric neuropsychology in the medical setting.* London: University Press.

Berg, R., Franzen, M., & Wedding, D. (1987). *Screening for brain impairment: A manual for mental health practice.* New York: Springer.

Berven, N. L. (2001). Assessment interviewing. In B. F. Bolton (Ed.), *Assessment and evaluation in rehabilitation* (3rd ed., pp. 197–213). Gaithersburg, MD: Aspen Publishers.

Butcher, J. N., Dahlstrom, W.G., Graham, J. R., Tellegen, A., & Kaemmer, B. (1989). *Minnesota Multiphasic Personality Inventory* (2nd ed.) (MMPI-2): *Manual for administration and scoring.* Minneapolis: University of Minnesota Press.

Butcher, J. N., Williams, C. L., Graham, J. R., Archer, R. P., Tellegen, A., Ben-Porath, Y. S., & Kaemmer, B. (1992). *Minnesota Multiphasic Personality Inventory–Adolescent (MMPI-A): Manual for administration and scoring.* Minneapolis: University of Minnesota Press.

Byrne, B. M., Shavelson, R. J., & Muthén, B. (1989). Testing for the equivalence of factor covariance and mean structures: The issue of partial measurement invariance. *Psychological Bulletin, 105,* 456–466.

Campbell, D. T., & Fiske, D. W. (1959). Convergent and discriminate validation by the multitrait–multimethod matrix. *Psychological Bulletin, 56,* 81–105.

Carroll, J. B. (1976). Psychometric tests as cognitive tasks: A new structure of intellect. In L. B. Resnick (Ed.), *The nature of intelligence* (pp. 27–56). Hillsdale, NJ: Erlbaum.

Carrow-Woolfolk, E. (1996). *Oral and Written Language Scales.* Circle Pines, MN: American Guidance Service.

Carrow-Woolfolk, E. (1999). *Test of Auditory Comprehension of Language* (3rd ed.). Austin, TX: Pro-Ed.

Cattell, R. B., & Kline, P. (1977). The scientific analysis of personality and motivation. In D. T. Lykken (Series Ed.), *Personality and psychopathology: A series of monographs, texts, and treatises.* New York: Academic Press.

Cesta, A., Moldofsky, H., & Sammut, C. (1996). The University of Toronto Sleep Assessment Questionnaire (SAQ). *Sleep Research, 25,* 486.

Cohen, J. (1988). *Statistical power analysis for the behavioral sciences* (2nd ed.). Hillsdale, NJ: Erlbaum.

Cohen, M. (1997). *Children's Memory Scale.* San Antonio, TX: Harcourt Assessment.

Commission on the Accreditation of Rehabilitation Facilities. (1995). *Employment and community services standards manual.* Commission on the Accreditation of Rehabilitation Facilities, Tucson: AZ.

Conners, C. K. (1997). *Conners' Rating Scale Manual* (Rev. ed.). North Towanda, NY: Multi-Health Systems.

Conners, C. K., & Multi-Health Systems Staff. (1995). *Conners' Continuous Performance Test.* Toronto: Multi-Health Systems.

Costa, P. T., & McCrae, R. R. (1992). *Revised NEO-PI Professional Manual.* Odessa, FL: Psychological Assessment Resources.

Crewe, N. M., & Dijkers, M. (1995). Functional assessment. In L. A. Cushman & M. J. Scherer (Eds.), *Psychological assessment in medical rehabilitation* (pp. 101–144). Washington, DC: American Psychological Association.

Critchley, M. (1953). *The Parietal Lobes.* London: Edward Arnold.

Crocker, L., & Algina, J. (1986). *Introduction to classical and modern test theory.* New York: Harcourt.

DeJong, G., Horn, S. D., Gassaway, J. A., Slavin, M. D., & Dijkers, M. P. (2004). Toward a taxonomy of rehabilitation interventions: Using an inductive approach to examine the "black box" of rehabilitation. *Archives of Physical Medicine and Rehabilitation, 85,* 678–686.

Dijkers, M. P. (2003). Individualization in quality of life measurement: Instrument and approaches. *Archives of Physical Medicine and Rehabilitation, 84,* S3–S14.

Donabedian, A. (1966). Evaluating the quality of medical care. *Milbank Memorial Fund Quarterly: Health and Society, 44,* 166–203.

Duggan, C., & Dijkers, M. (1999). Quality of life peaks and valleys: A qualitative study of the narratives of persons with spinal cord injury. *Canadian Rehabilitation Journal, 12,* 179–189.

Dunbar, G. C., Stoker, M. J., Hodges, T. C., & Beaumont, G. (1992). The development of SBQOL-a unique scale for measuring quality of life. *British Journal of Medical Economics, 2,* 65–74.

Dunn, L. M., & Dunn, L. M. (1997). *Peabody Picture Vocabulary Test* (3rd ed.). Circle Pines, MN: American Guidance Services.

Edelbrock, C. S., & Costello, A. J. (1988). Structured psychiatric interviews for children. In M. Rutter, A. H. Tuma, & I. Lann (Eds.), *Assessment diagnosis in child psychopathology* (pp. 87–112). New York: Guilford.

Erickson, R. P., & McPhee, M. C. (1998). Clinical evaluation. In J. A. DeLisa & B. M. Gans, (Eds.), *Rehabilitation medicine: Principles and practice* (3rd ed., pp. 61–108). Philadelphia: Lippincott-Raven Publishers.

Evidence-Based Medicine Working Group. (1992). Evidence-based medicine: A new approach to teaching the practice of medicine. *Journal of the American Medical Association, 268,* 2420–2425.

Exner, J. Jr. (1986). *The Rorschach: A comprehensive system. Vol. 1; Basic foundations* (2nd ed.). New York: Wiley.

Fairchild, A. J., Horst, S. J., Finney, S. J., & Barron, K. E. (2005). Evaluating existing and new validity evidence for the academic motivation scale. *Contemporary Educational Psychology, 30,* 331–358.

Fazio, R. H., & Olson, M. A. (2003). Implicit measures in social cognition research: Their meaning and use. *Annual Review of Psychology, 54,* 297–327.

Folstein, M. F., Folstein, S., & McHugh, P. R. (2001). *The Mini-Mental State Exam.* Lutz, FL: Psychological Assessment Resources.

Fudala, J. B. (2000). *Arizona Articulation Proficiency Scale* (3rd ed.). Los Angeles: Western Psychological Services.

Gardner, M. F. (2000). *Expressive One-Word Picture Vocabulary Test* (2000 ed.). Novato, CA: Academic Therapy Publications.

Gilliam J. (2001). *Gilliam Asperger's Disorder Scale.* Austin, TX: Pro-Ed.

Goldman, R., & Fristoe, M. (2000). *The Goldman-Fristoe Test of Articulation* (2nd ed.). Circle Pines, MN: American Guidance Services.

Goleman, D. (1995). *Emotional intelligence.* New York: Bantam Books.

Green, B. F., Jr. (1981). A primer of testing. *American Psychologist, 36,* 1001–1011.

Gresham, F. M., & Elliot, S. N. (1990). *Social Skills Rating System: Manual.* Circle Pines, MN: American Guidance Service.

Hammill, D. D., Brown, V. A., Larsen, S. C., & Wiederholt, J. L. (1994). *Test of Adolescent and Adult Language* (3rd ed.) Austin TX: PRO-ED.

Hanley, G. P., Iwata, B. A., & McCord, B. E. (2003). Functional analysis of problem behavior: A review. *Journal of Applied Behavior Analysis, 36,* 147–185.

Harrison, P. L., & Oakland, T. D. (2003). *Adaptive Behavior Assessment System* (2nd ed.). San Antonio, TX: The Psychological Corporation.

Hayden, D., & Square, P. (1999). *Verbal motor production assessment for children.* San Antonio, TX: The Psychological Corporation.

Heinemann, A. W. (2005). Putting outcome measurement in context: A rehabilitation psychology perspective. *Rehabilitation Psychology, 50,* 6–14.

Johnston, M. V., Maney, M., & Wilkerson, D. L. (1998). Systematically assuring and improving the quality and outcomes of medical rehabilitation programs. In J. A. DeLisa & B. M. Gans, (Eds.), *Rehabilitation medicine: Principles and practice* (3rd ed., pp. 287–320). Philadelphia: Lippincott-Raven Publishers.

Kaufman, A. S., & Kaufman, N. L. (2004). *Kaufman Assessment Battery for Children* (2nd ed.). Circle Pines, MN: American Guidance Service.

Kertesz, A. (2006). *Western Aphasia Battery* (Rev. ed.). San Antonio: Harcourt Assessment.

Khan, L. M., & Lewis, N. P. (2000). *Khan-Lewis Phonological Analysis* (2nd ed.). Minneapolis: Pearson Assessments.

Kiernan, R. J., Mueller, J., Langston, J. W., & Van Dyke, C. (1987). The neurobehavioral cognitive status examination: A brief but quantitative approach to cognitive assessment. *Annals of Internal Medicine, 107,* 481–485.

Lezak, M. D. (1995). *Neuropsychological assessment* (3rd ed.). New York: Oxford Press.

Luginbuehl, M. (2003). *Sleep Disorders Inventory for Students.* San Antonio, TX: Harcourt Assessment.

Matthews, G., Zeidner, M., Roberts, R. D. (2002). Emotional intelligence: Science and myth. Cambridge, MA: The MIT Press.

McColl, M. A., Davies, D., Carlson, P., Johnston, J., & Minnes, P. (2001). The community integration measure: Development and preliminary validation. *Archives of Physical Medicine and Rehabilitation, 82,* 429–434.

McDowell, I, & Newell, C. (2006). *Measuring health: A guide to rating scales and questionnaires* (3rd ed.). New York: Oxford University Press.

McGrew, K. S. (2005). The Cattell–Horn–Carroll theory of cognitive abilities: Past, present, and future. In D. Flanagan & P. L. Harrison (Eds.), *Contemporary intellectual assessment: Theories, tests, and issues* (2nd ed., pp. 136–181). New York: Guilford.

Mermis, B. J. (2005). Developing a taxonomy for rehabilitation outcome measurement. *Rehabilitation Psychology, 50,* 15–23.

Myers, I. B., McCaulley, M. H., Quenk, N. L., & Hammer, A. L. (1998). *MBTI manual: A guide to the development and use of the Myers–Briggs Type Indicator* (3rd ed.). Palo Alto, CA: Consulting Psychologists Press.

Nitko, A. J. (1984). Defining "criterion-referenced test." In R. A. Berk (Ed.), *A guide to criterion-referenced test construction* (pp. 8–28). Baltimore: Johns Hopkins University Press.

Nock, M. K., & Banaji, M. R. (2007). Prediction of suicide ideation and attempts among adolescents using a brief performance-based test. *Journal of Consulting and Clinical Psychology, 75,* 707–715.

Oakland, T., Glutting, J. J., & Horton, C. B. (1996). *Student Styles Questionnaire Manual.* San Antonio, TX: Psychological Corporation.

O'Neill, R., Horner, R., Albin, R., Sprague, J., Storey, K., & Newton, S. (1997). *Functional assessment and program development for problem behavior: A practical handbook.* Pacific Grove, CA: Brooks/Cole.

Paulson, G. W. (1977). The neurological examination in dementia. In C. E. Wells (Ed.), *Dementia* (2nd ed., pp. 169–188). Philadelphia: F. A. Davis.

Perenboom, R. J. M., & Chorus, A. M. J. (2003). Measuring participation according to the International Classification of Functioning, Disability and Health (ICF). *Disability and Rehabilitation, 25,* 577–587.

Peterson, D. B. (2005). International classification of functioning, disability and health: An introduction for rehabilitation psychologists. *Rehabilitation Psychology, 50,* 105–112.

Plante, E., & Beeson, P. M. (2004). *Communication and communication disorders: An introduction for rehabilitation psychologists.* Boston: Pearson Education, Inc.

Pokingborne, D. E., & Gribbons, B. C. (1999). Applications of qualitative research strategies to school psychology research problems. In C. R. Reynolds & T. B. Gutkin (Eds.), *The handbook of school psychology* (pp. 108–136). New York: John Wiley and Sons.

Posavac, E. J., & Carey, R. G. (1992). *Program evaluation: Methods and case studies* (4th ed.). Englewood Cliffs, NJ: Prentice Hall.

Reynolds, C. R. (1997). Postscripts on premorbid ability estimation: Conceptual addenda and a few words on alternative and conditional approaches. *Archives of Clinical Neuropsychology, 12,* 769–778.

Reynolds, C. R., & Bigler, E. D. (1994). *Test of memory and learning.* Austin, TX: Pro-Ed.

Reynolds, C. R., & Kamphaus, R. W. (2004). *Behavior Assessment System for Children* (2nd ed.). Circle Pines, MN: American Guidance Service.

Riley, G. D. (1994). *Stuttering Severity Instrument for Children and Adults* (3rd ed.). Circle Pines, MN: American Guidance Service.

Roid, G. (2003). *Stanford-Binet Intelligence Scale* (5th ed.). Chicago: Riverside.

Sackett, D. L., Rosenberg, W. M., Gray, J. A., Haynes, R. B., & Richardson, W. S. (1996). Evidence-based medicine: What it is and what it isn't. *British Medical Journal, 312,* 71–72.

Salvia, J., & Ysseldyke, J. E. (1998). *Assessment* (7th ed.). Boston: Houghton Mifflin.

Sameroff, A. J., & MacKenzie, M. J. (2003). Research strategies for capturing transactional models of development: The limits of the possible. *Development and Psychopathology, 15,* 613–640.

Sattler, J. M. (1998). *Clinical and forensic interviewing of children and families: Guidelines for the mental health, education, pediatric, and child maltreatment fields.* San Diego: Sattler.

Sattler, J. M. (2002). *Assessment of children: Behavioral and clinical applications* (4th ed.). San Diego: Sattler.

Schneck, S. A. (1998). Doctoring doctors and their families. *Journal of the American Medical Association, 23,* 2039–2042.

Schopler, E., Reichler, R. J., & Renner, B. R. (1988). *The Childhood Autism Rating Scale.* Los Angeles: Western Psychological Services.

Schulte, M. J., Ree, M. J., & Carretta, T. R. (2004). Emotional intelligence: Not much more than *g* and personality. *Personality and Individual Differences, 37,* 1059–1068.

Semel, E. M., Wiig, E. H., & Secord, W. A. (2003). *Clinical Evaluation of Language Fundamentals* (4th ed.). San Antonio, TX: Psych Corp/Harcourt.

Skinner, B. F. (1953). *Science and human behavior.* New York: Macmillan.

Sparrow, S, Cicchetti, D, & Balla, D. (2005). *Vineland Adaptive Behavior Scales* (2nd ed.). Circle Pines, MN: American Guidance Service.

Spielberger, C. D. (1983). *Manual for the State-Trait Anxiety Inventory (STAI).* Palo Alto, CA: Consulting Psychologists Press.

Spielberger, C. D. (1996). *State-Trait Anger Expression Inventory: STAXI professional manual.* Tampa, FL: Psychological Assessment Resources.

Spreen, O., & Strauss, E. (1998). *A compendium of neuropsychological tests: Administration, norms, and commentary* (2nd ed.). Oxford: Oxford University Press.

Stachtchenko, S., & Jenicek, M. (1990). Conceptual differences between prevention and health promotion: Research implications for community health programs. *Canadian Journal of Public Health, 81,* 53–59.

Sulzer-Azaroff, B., & Mayer, G. R. (1991). *Behavior analysis for lasting change.* Orlando, FL: Harcourt Brace Jovanovich.

Teglasi, H. (1998a). Introduction to mini-series: Implications of temperament for the practice of school psychology. *School Psychology Review, 27,* 475–478.

Teglasi, H. (1998b). Temperament constructs and measures. *School Psychology Review, 27,* 564–585.

Torgesen, J. K., & Bryant, B. R. (2004). *Test of Phonological Awareness* (2nd ed.) *Plus.* Austin, TX: PRO-ED.

Vallerand, R. J., Pelletier, L. G., Blais, M. R, Brière, N. M., Senécal, C., & Vallières, E. F. (1992). The academic motivation scale: a measure of intrinsic, extrinsic, and amotivation in education. *Educational and Psychological Measurement, 52,* 1003–1017.

Van Brakel, W. H., Anderson, A. M., Mutatkar, R. K., Bakirtzief, Z., Nicholls, P. G., Raju, M. S., & Das-Pattanayak, R. K. (2006). The Participation Scale: Measuring a key concept in public health. *Disability and Rehabilitation: An International Multidisciplinary Journal, 28,* 193–203.

VandenBos, G. R. (2007). *APA Dictionary of Psychology.* Washington, DC: American Psychological Association.

Velozo, C., & Gray, D. B. (2004). ICFmeasure.com–A web based computerized adaptive survey. Retrieved February 8, 2007, from http://www.icfmeasure.phhp.ufl.edu/.

Wagner, M. T., & Cushman, L. A. (1994). Neuroanatomic and neuropsychological predictors of unawareness of cognitive deficit in the vascular population. *Archives of Clinical Neuropsychology, 9,* 57– 69.

Wagner, M. T., Nayak, M., & Fink, C. (1995). Bedside screening of neurocognitive function. In L. A. Cushman & M. J. Scherer (Eds.), *Psychological Assessment in Medical Rehabilitation* (pp. 145–198). Washington, DC: American Psychological Association.

Wechsler, D. (1997). *Wechsler Memory Scale* (3rd ed.). San Antonio, TX: Harcourt Assessment.

Wechsler, D. (2003). *Wechsler Intelligence Scale for Children* (4th ed.). San Antonio, TX: Harcourt Assessment.

Wechsler, D. (2008). *Wechsler Adult Intelligence Scale* (4th ed.). San Antonio, TX: Harcourt Assessment.

Wilkerson, D. L., & Johnston, M. V. (1997). Outcomes research and clinical program monitoring systems: Current capability and future directions. In M. Fuhrer (Ed.), *Medical rehabilitation outcomes research* (pp. 275–305). Baltimore: Paul H. Brookes.

Williams, K. T. (1997). *Expressive Vocabulary Test.* Circle Pines, MN: American Guidance Service.

Witt, J. C., Heffer, R. W., & Pfeiffer, J. (1990). Structured rating scales: A review of self-report and informant rating processes, procedures, and issues. In C. R. Reynolds & R. W. Kamphaus (Eds.), *Handbook of psychological and educational assessment of children: Personality, behavior, and context.* New York: Guilford Press.

Woodcock, R. W., McGrew, K. S., & Mather, N., (2001). *Woodcock-Johnson III Tests of Cognitive Abilities.* Itasca, IL: Riverside Publishing.

World Health Organization. (2001). *International Classification of Functioning, Disability and Health.* Geneva, Switzerland: Author.

World Health Organization. (2006). *About WHO.* Retrieved on September 25, 2006, from http://www.who.int/about/en/.

Wright, J. (2000). The FIM(TM). *The Center for Outcome Measurement in Brain Injury.* http://www.tbims.org/combi/FIM (accessed February 9, 2007).

Statistical Concepts

JAMES M. FERRIN
Langston University, Tulsa

MALACHY BISHOP
University of Kentucky, Lexington

TIMOTHY N. TANSEY
Michigan State University, East Lansing

OVERVIEW

This chapter discusses statistical terms and concepts that are used in developing, scoring, and interpreting measures used in rehabilitation and health care. The chapter begins with a description of levels of measurement and thus provides a foundation for understanding whether a variable is categorized, ordered, ranked, or continuous. The chapter discusses the normal curve, frequency distribution, as well as measures of central tendency and variability. Methods to transform raw scores to standard or standardized scores so as to reflect an individual's comparative performance on a standardized scale also are discussed. The chapter addresses norm-referenced and criterion-referenced measures. The chapter concludes with a discussion of the standard error of measurement, confidence intervals, reliability of difference scores, and unstandardized and standardized effect sizes.

LEARNING OBJECTIVES

By the end of the chapter, readers should be able to:

- Name and describe the four basic levels of measurement
- Define a normal curve and a frequency distribution
- Name, describe, and apply to data sets the concepts of central tendency and variability
- Transform raw data into standard or standardized scores
- Differentiate between a standard error of measurement and a confidence interval
- Recognize and apply norm- and criterion-referenced group measures
- Explain effect sizes and their applications

INTRODUCTION

Measures used in rehabilitation and health care are described throughout this book. The breadth and scope of the topics presented in this book underscore the large number and variety of instruments that have been designed and developed for use in health care and rehabilitation assessment. The majority of instruments provide time-limited and content-specific samples of behavior or other personal qualities along with explicit rules for assigning numbers to the behaviors. The broad purpose of this process, in the context of rehabilitation and health care, is the description of behavior and interpretation and translation of these numbers into effective treatment, rehabilitation planning, or enhanced understanding of the individual or group being measured. An understanding of the rules and methods by which human characteristics are translated into numbers is required to achieve these goals.

The development of measures used in rehabilitation and health care is based on shared and commonly understood principles, methods, and techniques. Their interpretation into meaningful information and applications in practice also requires an understanding of these principles, methods, and techniques. The process of assigning numbers to human characteristics first requires one to identify the characteristic or constructs to be measured. A characteristic or construct that has been operationally defined can be measured by an instrument developed for this purpose. Test results first appear as raw scores. Statistical methods are used to transform raw scores into other scores to promote our understanding and inter- or intra-personal comparisons. Knowledge of basic statistical terms and concepts employed in the development and interpretation of measures used in rehabilitation and health care is essential to this work.

TESTS AND MEASURES

Measurement is a process of assigning numbers to human characteristics (Bolton & Brookings, 2001). Thus, the use of measures discussed in this book involves the assignment of numbers to human attributes or traits and psychological constructs.

Measures can be distinguished in various ways. Some are standardized or unstandardized. Some can be administered to groups and others only individually. Measures of maximum performance are designed to assess a person's best knowledge or abilities (e.g., intelligence, achievement, motor skills). In contrast, measures of typical performance are designed to measure qualities typically displayed (e.g., measurement of personality and attitudes).

The use of standardized tests promotes objectivity. Their scores are expressed in numbers on a common scale and thus provide quantification and specificity. The use of numbers and scales promotes shared meaning between test users and thus promotes communication. Unlike unstandardized tests, clinical judgments, observation, and unstructured interviewing, standardized tests have specific rules that govern how a test is administered and how the numbers are recorded and scored.

Norm-referenced tests use the performance of a norm (i.e., peer) group to interpret scores. The performance of every person who takes the test is compared with the people who took the test when it was being standardized. Thus, persons taking a test should be comparable to the qualities of the norm (i.e., standardization) group in terms of age, gender, and general personal experiences (Power, 2006).

Criterion-referenced tests use knowledge of one's attainment of specific criteria or skills to interpret test performance. Criterion-referenced tests determine "... what test takers can do and what they know, not how they compare to others" (Anastasi, 1988, p. 102). Thus, an individual's performance is measured against a set standard or criteria rather than compared to the performance of others who take the same test. Criterion-referenced tests use a specified content domain as the frame of reference for

---

DISCUSSION BOX 6.1

Let's assume you are a new director of an assessment center in which you are working with young adults with mental retardation. You discover that the assessment center's testing resources include both norm-referenced and criterion-referenced measures to use in assessing the client's academic and prevocational skills. Discuss under what conditions the client may be best served by the use of norm-referenced and criterion-referenced tests. Describe the potential assets and limitations when using them to better understand a client's levels of competence and for use in program planning.

interpreting results. For example, the test required to obtain a driver's license typically requires passing a multiple-choice test and successfully completing an on-the-road driving test. Everyone can pass the test if they know the driving rules and drive reasonably well.

MEASUREMENT SCALES

Variables, by definition, have more than one value. The values of a variable are measured with one of the following four scales: nominal, ordinal, interval, or ratio scales. Each type of scale informs us whether a variable is being named, ranked, ascribed with equal intervals, or contains measurement units and an absolute zero.

Nominal scales classify information (e.g., a car's license plate or a social security number). Numbers are assigned arbitrarily to characteristics as labels. They do not represent a mathematical value. Other frequently represented nominal scale variables include gender, marital status, and religious affiliation. For example, one may differentiate between males and females by designating males as belonging to Group 1 and females to Group 2. The assignment of a number is arbitrary and does not indicate that one group is better or worse, only different.

Ordinal scales provide a relative order to the variables. The variables are logically ordered, and numbers are assigned to represent that order. Ordinal scales typically rank variables from low to high. For example, patients may be asked to rate how much pain they experience by using a scale from 1 (no pain at all) to 10 (worst pain imaginable). Data on an ordinal scale allow us to determine whether the qualities are more than or less than others. However, we do not know how much more or less. That is, using the above example, although we know 8 means more pain than a 4, we do not know whether 8 reflects twice as much pain as a 4 or whether the difference between 1 and 2 is the same as the difference between 9 and 10. Ordinal scales lack a commonly understood equal unit of measurement.

Interval scales allow us to classify (as do nominal scales), rank order (as do ordinal scales), as well as provide equal intervals between scores. Thus, data on an interval scale can be expressed in terms of meaningful intervals. Scores on measures of ability typically are recorded on an interval scale. Temperature also is expressed on an interval scale. For example, 80° is 10 degrees warmer than 70°, and the distance between the two temperatures is the same as that between 20° and 10°. Interval scales do not have a meaningful or "true" zero. Thus, unlike measuring weight, scores or values on an interval scale do not represent an absolute magnitude of the characteristic or variable measured. For example,

60° is not twice as hot as 30°. Thus, a value of zero on an intelligence test or thermometer does not mean the absence of intelligence or the complete absence of heat.

Ratio scales have the characteristics of the scales discussed above (i.e., they categorize, rank order, have equal units) and have a true zero. Physical characteristics frequently are measured using a ratio scale (e.g., height, weight), when a meaningful absence of the characteristic is possible. Most psychological constructs are measured using ordinal or interval scales.

DESCRIBING DATA

After completing a test, professionals typically organize and transform test data to assist in describing behavior and drawing comparisons between the person tested and his or her peer group (e.g., using the test's norms). Raw scores must be transformed into other scores to obtain more meaningful information. The following discussion describes concepts associated with the distribution of data, score transformation, and the statistical concepts that are applied to data in order to understand and use them.

Normal Curve

A normal curve (see Figure 6.1), also called the Gaussian distribution, bell curve, or normal distribution, represents a symmetrical distribution of observations. If this symmetric distribution were divided at the mean, both halves would be identical. The normal curve represents a special case of symmetrical distribution in which *kurtosis*, the measure of the peak of a distribution, is zero.

Many qualities are distributed in a normal curve. The occurrence of normal distributions can be understood by the central limit theorem that states, if the sum of the observed variables has a finite variance, then those observations will be approximately normally distributed. Therefore, if a limited range of scores exists, then the scores will be distributed in a normal curve.

For example, if we conducted a study to measure the foot size of adult males living in the United States and rounded our measurements to the nearest inch, a normal distribution would likely occur after sampling a relatively small number of individuals. However, a skewed distribution can result when infinite variability exists in a measure. The probability of outliers (i.e., extreme scores) increases as the variability of a measure increases. Consequently, normal distributions are less likely to occur as the probability of outliers increases.

For example, when measuring foot size, imagine that we measure to the nearest one thousandth of an inch

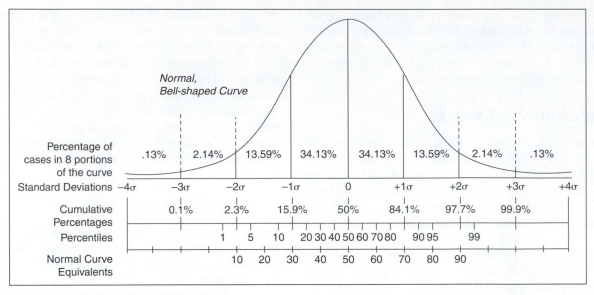

FIGURE 6.1 The Normal Distribution Curve

instead of to the nearest inch. Greater variability exists in this range, thus increasing the probability that non-normal distributions can occur.

The normal curve is used widely in evaluating performance and comparing an individual's scores to those of the population. Due to the mathematical precision of the normal curve, test developers can estimate the percent of cases that fall within a certain range with respect to the normative sample.

Skewness

A normal curve occurs when a distribution either is naturally distributed symmetrically or is adjusted statistically to be distributed symmetrically. However, a skewed distribution can result when finite variability does not exist. Skewness refers to the *asymmetry* of a distribution. An asymmetrical distribution is likely to occur when a test either is too difficult or too easy or when a disproportionate percent of people in a sample rate themselves as either below or above the mean. The latter situation occurs frequently when people are asked to rate their quality of life (e.g., most rate it above average). Thus, a skewed distribution occurs when the number of scores or observations on one end of the curve is more than on the other end. For example, if a classroom examination is too difficult, a greater number of observations are found in the left side of the distribution (see Figure 6.2). When this occurs, the distribution is said to be positively skewed. Alternatively, if the classroom test is too easy, a greater number of observations are found on the right side of the distribution (see Figure 6.2). This

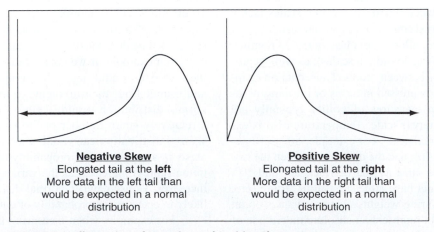

Negative Skew
Elongated tail at the **left**
More data in the left tail than would be expected in a normal distribution

Positive Skew
Elongated tail at the **right**
More data in the right tail than would be expected in a normal distribution

FIGURE 6.2 Illustration of Negative and Positive Skew

distribution is said to be negatively skewed. Classroom examination results that are skewed in either direction may not effectively discriminate ability or achievement levels of individuals taking the test.

FREQUENCY DISTRIBUTIONS

Percentiles and Percentile Ranks

Percentiles and percentile ranks commonly are used to classify an individual score in relation to raw scores in a population. A percentile marks the location of a score in a distribution of scores to reflect the percent of cases that have scored equal to or below that score. Percentiles range from 1 to 100. Higher percentile scores reflect high raw scores relative to the rest of the population. For example, if a student received a raw score of 95 on a math test and if 88% of the students taking this test received this score or a lower score, then the student's percentile rank would be 88 or at the 88th percentile.

Percentile scores are similar to percentile ranks in that they focus on the rank of a score and the score associated with that rank. For example, using the data set provided in Table 6.1, someone may want to know the rank of the observed score for an individual who scored in the 33rd percentile.

The first step in calculating a percentile is to rank order the observations. For example, reordering the above data, the table below categorizes each number by its rank in the distribution (See Table 6.2).

Next, enter the data into the formula for calculating percentiles where p is the percentile (33rd) and N (i.e., the number of test scores) is 20 to find the rank (R) of the score at that percentile.

$$R = \frac{P}{100} \times (N + 1) \qquad \text{Equation 1}$$

$$R = \frac{33}{100} \times (20 + 1) \rightarrow R$$
$$= .33 \times 21 \rightarrow R = 6.93$$

If R were a whole number, the percentile would be the score with that rank. However, since R is not a whole number, interpolation is required to find the specific score associated with the 33rd percentile (i.e., 6.93).

TABLE 6.2 Calculating the Percentile Rank

Score	Rank	Score	Rank
4	1	28	11
12	2	28	12
14	3	29	13
15	4	30	14
16	5	31	15
17	6	32	16
20	7	34	17
24	8	35	18
26	9	38	19
27	10	40	20

The first step is to find the ranks that surround the observed rank. The rank below the observed rank is labeled R_i while the one above the observed rank is labeled R_{i+1}. In this case, R_i is equal to 6 and R_{i+1} is equal to 7. The corresponding scores for these ranks are 17 and 20. To calculate the specific score associated with the percentile, the fractional portion of R (.93), labeled R_f must be interpolated between these two numbers. Interpolation is done by multiplying the fractional portion of R by the difference between R_i and R_{i+1} and adding R_i to the product. For example:

$$R_x = R_f \times (R_{i+1} - R_i) + R_i \qquad \text{Equation 2}$$

and using equation 2 and calculating:

$$R_{33} = .93 \times (20 - 17) + 17 \rightarrow R_{33}$$
$$= .93 \times 3 + 17 \rightarrow R_{33}$$
$$= 2.79 + 17 \rightarrow R_{33} = 19.79$$

Thus, a score of 19.79 is at the 33rd percentile.

Expressing raw scores as percentile scores is the most common form of score transformation. However, there are limitations in using percentiles in assessment. Percentile scores are arranged on an ordinal scale. Thus, the distance between scores is not equal. As a result, percentile scores may present an inaccurate representation of an individual's actual scores compared to others.

Percentile scores can misrepresent the distance between raw scores on an assessment. This misrepresentation is seen clearly at the tails of the distribution. For

TABLE 6.1 Sample Scores

12	28	17	35	40	26	4	20	29	31
34	27	24	16	38	32	14	28	30	15

$\sum X = 12 + 28 + 17 + 35 + 40 + 26 + 4 + 20 + 29 + 31 + 34 + 27 + 24 + 16 + 38 + 32 + 14 + 28 + 30 + 15 = 500$

example, as seen under the normal curve (Figure 6.1), the difference in raw scores between individuals at the 5th and 15th percentiles is greater than the difference in raw scores between individuals at the 50th and 60th percentiles. Using the data described above, the difference between scores at the 5th and 15th percentiles is 9.75 while the difference between the 50th and 60th percentile scores is only 1.1. Therefore, professionals using percentile scores should understand that their ordinal scale values have inherent limitation and guard against misinterpreting differences in scores.

In addition, because percentile scores are not on an equal-interval scale, they tend to cluster in the center of the normal curve rather than being distributed evenly throughout the normal curve. This limitation prevents percentile scores from being used in other statistical analyses. For example, because they are not evenly distributed, percentile scores should not be used when calculating gain scores (i.e., differences between prior and current scores) or difference scores in a pre- and posttest administration.

Normal Curve Equivalents

Although percentile scores have limited statistical utility, normal curve equivalents (NCE) are scores that can be used in a wide array of statistical procedures. NCEs are derived through a conversion of percentile ranks to standard scores. They range from 1 to 99 with a mean of 50. NCE is an equal-interval scale, thus allowing scores to be manipulated mathematically and analyzed statistically. For example, if an individual received an NCE score of 15 on one administration and 25 on a second administration, the individual's two scores can be averaged or used to show overall change in score during the period between the two administrations. In addition, since NCEs are equally distributed, they do not distort the underlying measurement scale used to provide raw scores; that is, even though there can be profound differences in scores represented by percentiles, differences in NCE scores better reflect the underlying measurement scale.

MEASURES OF CENTRAL TENDENCY

Measures of central tendency are used to describe the points on the normal curve where scores fall most frequently. The following three measures of central tendency are used most often: mean, median, and mode. Please refer to the scores in Table 6.1 to understand their differences.

Mean

The arithmetic mean, or average, of a set of scores is the sum of the scores divided by the total number of scores. The mean is the most widely used measure of central tendency. Obtain the mean (M) by dividing the sum of all the scores (ΣX) by the total number of scores (N) in the set. The formula is as follows:

$$M = \frac{\Sigma X}{N} \qquad \text{Equation 3}$$

Using the set of numbers provided in Table 6.1 and Equation 3 we calculate:

$$\begin{aligned} \Sigma X &= 12 + 28 + 17 + 35 + 40 + 26 + 4 \\ &\quad + 20 + 29 + 31 + 34 + 27 + 24 + 16 \\ &\quad + 38 + 32 + 14 + 28 + 30 + 15 \\ &= 500 \end{aligned}$$

In completing the formula for the mean for this sample of 20 scores (N = 20; see below):

$$M = \frac{500}{20} = 25$$

Therefore, the mean of the scores in this sample is 25.

Among the three measures of central tendency, the mean is the most influenced by scores in the tails (i.e., ends) of the distribution. Thus, in skewed distributions, the mean may not be representative of the center of the sample.

Median

The median is the middle point of a set of scores—the score that is the center value when the scores are arranged from lowest to highest. The median separates the top half from the bottom half of scores. When there is an even number of scores, the median is the arithmetic mean of the two scores in the middle of the distribution. Unlike the mean, the median is less affected by skewed distributions. Rather, it represents a central point of all scores regardless of the range of scores.

Using the sample of scores in Table 6.2, the median is found by ordering the scores from lowest to highest.

4 12 14 15 16 17 20 24 26 $\boxed{27}$ $\boxed{28}$ 28 29 30 31 32 34 35 38 40

Since there are 20 numbers, the median is found by determining the average of the two scores in the middle, 27 and 28. The mean of these two scores, and thus the median, is 27.5. If there had been an odd number of scores, the median would have been the middlemost score in the distribution. For example, if the score of 40 is dropped, the median of the remaining 19 scores would be 27 (data from Table 6.2):

4 12 14 15 16 17 20 24 26 |27| 28 28 29 30 31 32 34 35 38

Mode

The mode is the most frequently occurring score in a set of scores. The mode can be used as a meaningful measure of central tendency only when scores cluster close to the center of the score distribution. When multiple scores occur with the same frequency in a distribution (multimodal distribution), the mode may be less representative of the center of the distribution and more reflective of sample fluctuations. While the mode has limited mathematical utility, it is the only measure of central tendency appropriate for use in evaluating nominal data. Using the sample provided earlier (Table 6.2), the mode is found by counting the number of times a score appears in the sample:

12 |28| 17 35 40 26 4 20 29 31 34 27 24 16 38 32 14 |28| 30 15

In this sample, 28 is the only number that appears more than once. Therefore, 28 is the mode. As stated earlier, in a multimodal distribution, more than one score occurs with the largest frequency. For example, look at the sample below taken from Table 6.2 in which an additional number, 24, has been added:

12 |28| 17 35 40 |24| 4 26 29 31 34 27 |24| 16 38 32 14 |28| 30 2

M	M		M	M
1	2		2	1

This sample is bimodal. In it, both 24 and 28 appear two times and each score would be considered a mode. Bimodal distributions often occur when an external variable affects the distribution of scores. For example, females are more likely to live longer than males. A random sample of the lifespan of adults would most likely result in a bimodal distribution with females having a higher average lifespan than males.

MEASURES OF VARIABILITY

Measures of variability are used to understand the dispersion of scores in a distribution. Knowledge of the variation in scores is useful in understanding where individual scores fall within a distribution. Measures of variability assist in understanding an individual's score or position relative to the mean of the population when a distribution is skewed or has a kurtosis greater than zero. Identifying the comparative performance of individuals is relatively straightforward in a normal distribution. However, because of the limitations in measuring a specific trait or ability, random error or the lack of the test's precision can result in distributions that do not resemble a normal curve. A number of statistics commonly are used to describe the variability within a score distribution. Three are discussed below: range, standard deviation, and variance.

Range

The *range* is the simplest and possibly the least used measure of variability. The range is the difference between the highest score and lowest score found in a distribution. To calculate the range of scores (R), the lowest score in the distribution is subtracted from the highest score. For example, using the set of scores provided earlier:

$$R = \text{Highest Score} - \text{Lowest Score} \quad \text{Equation 4}$$
$$R = 40 - 4 \rightarrow R = 36$$

The range for the sample is 36. The range rarely is used because it provides little assistance when interpreting individual scores.

Quartiles and the Interquartile Range

The range of a group of scores can be subdivided into smaller sections called *quartiles*. Quartiles are used to further differentiate scores within the established range. Quartiles consist of the three values that divide the data into four equally sized groups. The first quartile (Q1) demarks the point at which 25% of the values are equal to or less than, and 75% of the values are more than this score. The second quartile (Q2) is the same as the median. Thus, 50% of the values are less and 50% are more than Q2. The third quartile (Q3) demarks the point at which 75% of the values are less than, and 25% of the values are equal to or more than this score.

The interquartile range also is a measure of variability within the range. The interquartile range of a set of scores is the difference between the upper (Q3) and lower (Q1) quartiles. Thus, the interquartile range encompasses the middle 50% of the scores in a distribution. The interquartile range tends to be a more stable statistic than the range because it is less sensitive to extreme scores.

Standard Deviation and Variance

The *standard deviation* and the *variance* are the average amount that each score in a distribution deviates from the mean. Although the range may be the simplest and least used measure of dispersion of a distribution, the standard deviation is the most common measure. The standard deviation, similar to the mean, is affected by skew in observations and outlying observations. The standard deviation increases as scores occur at greater distances from the mean. In contrast, the standard deviation and variance decrease in size as the scores cluster closely around the mean. If all scores are the same and thus equal to the mean, the standard deviation and variance of the score distribution are zero. The standard deviation is found using the following formula:

$$\sigma = \sqrt{\frac{\sum (X_i - M)^2}{N}} \quad \text{Equation 5}$$

To calculate the standard deviation, first find the difference of each observed score (X_i) from the mean (M). Using the data from Table 6.1 and the mean ($M = 25$), first calculate the deviations ($X_i - M$) and then square the deviations ($X_i - M)^2$ (See Table 6.3).

TABLE 6.3 Calculating the Variance and Standard Deviation

X_i	$X_i - M$	$(X_i - M)^2$
12	−13	169
28	3	9
17	−8	64
35	10	100
40	15	225
26	1	1
4	−21	441
20	−5	25
29	4	16
31	6	36
34	9	81
27	2	4
24	−1	1
16	−9	81
38	13	169
32	7	49
14	−11	121
28	3	9
30	5	25
15	−10	100

After calculating each of the squared deviations from the mean, then calculate the sum of the squared deviations $[\sum X_i - M)^2]$ as demonstrated below:

$$\begin{aligned}\sum (Xi - M)^2 &= 169 + 9 + 64 + 100 + 225 + 1 \\ &\quad + 441 + 25 + 16 + 36 + 81 \\ &\quad + 4 + 1 + 81 + 169 + 49 + 121 \\ &\quad + 9 + 25 + 100 \\ &= 1726\end{aligned}$$

Finally, using the sum of the squared deviations, the standard deviation can be calculated as follows:

$$\sigma = \sqrt{\frac{\sum (X_i - M)^2}{N}} \rightarrow \sigma = \sqrt{\frac{1726}{20}} \rightarrow \quad \text{Equation 6}$$

$$\sigma = \sqrt{86.3} \rightarrow \sigma \approx 9.29$$

Therefore, the standard deviation of the distribution is approximately 9.29. Thus, 68% of scores fall 9.29 points above and below the mean.

The variance is simply the square of the standard deviation or the result of the formula above before taking the square root. For clarification, the formula for the variance is provided below:

$$\sigma^2 = \frac{\sum (Xi - M)^2}{N} \quad \text{Equation 7}$$

Using the sample calculation of standard deviation, the variance can be determined as the square of 9.29. In reviewing the solution for the above formula, the variance already has been calculated. In this distribution, the variance is 86.3 or the number before the square root was applied in the formula for the standard deviation.

Standard Scores

Standard scores are scores that have been transformed from raw or other scores. A raw score reflects the performance of an individual whereas the *transformed standard score* reflects the individual's performance relative to a referenced norm group. The transformed score is interpreted along a sampling distribution line with a known mean and a known standard deviation. Standard scores reflect the measured distance on either side of the population mean, plus or minus (±) standard deviation units. Commonly used standard scores are described below.

A Z-score has a mean (M) of 0 and a standard deviation (SD) of 1. The Z-score is found using the following formula:

$$Z = \frac{x_i - \mu}{\sigma} \quad \text{Equation 8}$$

A *Z*-score equals the difference between an individual score and the population mean divided by the population standard deviation.

Other scores, such as a *Wechsler Adult Intelligence Scale–IV* (WAIS–IV) Full Scale intelligence quotient (IQ) also can be transformed into standard deviation units. If we consider the *Z*-score for an individual with a WAIS–IV Full Scale IQ of 105 and given the WAIS–IV mean of 100 and the standard deviation of 15, then using Equation 8:

$$Z = \frac{105 - 100}{15} = .33$$

Thus, the individual's IQ of 105 is .33 standard deviation units above the population mean.

A *T*-score is a standard score with a mean (*M*) of 50 and a standard deviation (*SD*) of 10:

$$T = \frac{10(X - M)}{SD} + 50 \qquad \text{Equation 9}$$

where *X* = the raw score to be transformed; or if the *Z*-score is known then:

$$T = 10z + 50 \qquad \text{Equation 10}$$

The vast majority of *T*-scores fall within the range of 20 to 80, or within three standard deviations of the mean. *T*-scores commonly are used in measures of personality and psychopathology on which *T*-scores of 80 or higher are clinically significant.

SAT and Graduate Record Exam (GRE) subtests have a mean of 500 and a standard deviation of 100. Thus, a GRE verbal standard score of 600 is one standard deviation above the mean.

Stanine (i.e., standard nines) scores, developed by the United States Air Force during World War II, have 9 units, a mean of 5, and a standard deviation of approximately 2. Sten (i.e., standard ten) scores, a variation of the stanine, has 10 units, with 5 units above and 5 units below the mean (5.5) and a standard deviation of 2. The scores that fall farther from the mean in either a high or low direction are considered more extreme. The 16 Personality Factor uses the sten scale for interpreting the 16 personality factors. For example, on a subtest measuring *warmth*, one extreme of the scale reflects a reserved, impersonal, or distant personality and at the opposite extreme, reflects a personality that is outgoing and attentive to others. A more extreme score reflects a more extreme personality type.

Standard Error of Measurement and Confidence Intervals

An individual's obtained test score may be assumed to represent his or her best effort on an administration of the test. However, a number of factors (e.g., boredom, weariness, unsuitable test-taking skills) may negatively influence the individual's test performance. In addition, an individual's test scores are likely to vary some because no test is completely reliable. If the test were administered again, the individual may do better (or worse) on the second administration. If the test were administered a number of times, the score that best represents the individual's capacity, or "true score" would lie somewhere among the scores resulting from these administrations. However, multiple administrations of the same test are not feasible or desirable. Alternatively, a statistical method exists to estimate the range around an observed score (i.e., a person's standard test score) within which the individual's true score falls. This estimate requires knowledge of the test's reliability and standard deviation. This range is represented as the standard error of measure (SE_M). The range of the true score can be estimated by:

$$SE_M = SD\sqrt{1 - r_{xx}} \qquad \text{Equation 11}$$

The SE_M equals the standard deviation (*SD*) times the square root of 1 minus the reliability coefficient (r_{xx}). The SE_M measures the amount an observed score is expected to fluctuate or deviate around the true score. The SE_M is expressed in standard deviation units and thus reflects the deviation of the measurement error in the distribution around the obtained score.

We can select the degree of confidence we want to establish that the individual's true score lies within the range of the SE_M. The size of the range of the SE_M increases as our need for confidence increases (e.g., to be 68% or 95% confident). Recognize too that, as the range of the SE_M increases, the scores are less precise.

Returning to the WAIS–IV Full Scale IQ of 105, the SE_M can be calculated as follows. We know from the WAIS–IV manual that the Full Scale IQ reliability coefficient is .98 and the standard deviation is 15. The standard error of measurement is calculated using Equation 11:

$$SE_M = 15\sqrt{1 - .98} = 2.12$$

When interpreted at the 68% confidence level (± 1 standard deviation), we estimate that, given an observed IQ of 105, the true IQ is between 103 and 107 (i.e., ± 2.12 standard errors from 105).

CONFIDENCE INTERVALS   We understand the potential for measurement error associated with the observed score and thus the use of the standard error of measurement to help account for this error. The above example allows us to estimate the range of the true score with 68% confidence. We may want to know, with 95% confidence, the interval that likely contains the individual's true score.

Using as our example again with the WAIS–IV Full Scale IQ of 105 and a SE_M measure of 2.12, we can calculate the lower and upper ranges of the potential true score within a 95% confidence interval in the following way:

$$105 \pm 1.96(2.12)$$
$$105 \pm 4.16$$
$$105 + 4.16 = 109.16$$
$$105 - 4.16 = 100.84$$

Thus, given the observed score of 105 and a SE_M of 2.12, we can be 95% confident that the true score is within the interval between 101 and 109.

Effect Size—Practical Significance

Let us assume a male practitioner is meeting for the first time with a female client who wants to stop smoking (Benowitz, Jacob, Kozolowksi, & Yu, 1986; David, Brown, & Papandonatos, 2007; West, McEwen, Boiling, & Owen, 2001). The clinician is considering whether to use a particular 12-week intervention program. He first examines research evidence on the smoking intervention program (e.g., Group 1 received the intervention and Group 2 served as a no-treatment control group) to determine the treatment's effect estimate. He then discusses this information with his client.

The effect estimate is determined by noting the difference in the mean number of cigarettes smoked after 12 weeks by participants in Groups 1 and 2. The practitioner and client then may decide whether the magnitude of the mean difference is sufficient to warrant further consideration of implementing this smoking cessation program.

The mean difference of cigarettes smoked after the treatment or without treatment is referred to as an unstandardized effect estimate (*UEE*):

$$UEE = M_{Group1} - MD_{Group2} \quad \text{Equation 12}$$

Before the intervention, both groups smoked an average of 20 cigarettes a day. After an intervention, those in Group1 averaged 10 cigarettes a day, and those in

Group 2 continued to average 20 cigarettes a day. The unstandardized effect size estimate is calculated between the two groups using Equation 12: $UEE = 10 - 20 = 10$. The practitioner and client conclude that the treatment that led to a 10-cigarette (i.e., 50%) reduction in daily smoking behavior for individuals engaged in the intervention may be beneficial for her. However, unknown is whether this 50% reduction is statistically significant.

Effect Size—Clinical Significance

The following example is used to describe effect size. Let's assume a practitioner working with a client with low self-esteem engages in a program designed to improve her self-esteem and assesses her self-esteem with a scale prior to and after the program (Baccus, Baldwin, & Packer, 2004). The client's scores were initially 27 and finally 44. The practitioner may derive a clinical index of change through the use of the reliable change index (*RCI*), thus helping to evaluate the degree to which the intervention was effective (Johnson, Dow, Lynch, & Hermann, 2006). The *Reliable Change Index* (RCI):

$$RCI = \frac{(x_2 - x_1)}{SE_{diff}} \quad \text{Equation 13}$$

where $(x_2 - x_1)$ represents the difference between the posttest and pretest of the self-esteem measure, SE_{diff} represents the standard error of the difference, and the RCI is a standardized clinical index of change. The RCI is used to determine whether the client clinically improved as a result of the self-esteem intervention.

The SE_{diff} describes the spread in the distribution of change scores expected if no actual change had occurred (Johnson et al., 2006). The SE_{diff} is derived from the standard error of measurement, a concept discussed above. The SE_M is calculated by using Equation 11 if it is unavailable in the test manual. We use an $r = .85$ and a $SD = 4.57$ for the present example to derive a SE_M of 1.77:

$$SE_M = 4.57\sqrt{1 - .85} = 1.77$$

We now calculate SE_{diff} with:

$$SE_{diff} = \sqrt{2(SE_M^2)} \quad \text{Equation 14}$$

We use Equation 14 and calculate:

$$SE_{diff} = \sqrt{2(1.77^2)} = 2.50$$

We now can calculate the reliable change index using the client's test scores of 27 and 44 and the SE_{diff} of 2.50 with Equation 14:

$$RCI = \frac{(44 - 27)}{2.50} = 6.8$$

The interpretation of a RCI score uses the following principles. If the RCI score is greater than the cut-off score, then the client showed improvement. If the RCI score is the same or less than the cut-off score, then the client respectively either stayed the same or declined in function from baseline (pretest). We calculate the cut-off score using a variation of Equation 15:

$$\pm Z\alpha(SE_{diff}) \qquad \text{Equation 15}$$

where a cut-off value (±) is calculated from the multiple of the $Z\alpha$ and the standard error of the difference (SE_{diff}). We use a $Z\alpha$ of 1.96 for an alpha (α) of .05 or 95% confidence interval and $SE_{diff} = 2.50$ to derive the RCI from Equation 15:

$$1.96(2.50) = 4.9$$

Using 4.9 as the positive cut-off score, we can conclude with 95% confidence that the client made a reliable clinical improvement in self-esteem based on a positive RCI score of 6.8—a score above the cut-off score of 4.9.

Reliability of Difference Scores

Reliability of difference scores also may be used to determine whether change from pretest to posttest scores is significant. Its use has been controversial (see chapter 7). The reliability of difference scores tends to be lower than the reliability of either the pretest or posttest scores. These change scores aggregate the test's measurement errors.

For example, if an individual's pretest score were 50 and the standard error of measurement were 5, then there would be a 68% probability that the individual's true score would fall between 45 and 55. If the individual's posttest score were 60 on the same test (e.g., a static change score of 10 points), then there would be a 68% probability that the individual's true score would fall between 55 and 65. The range of possible scores from pretest to posttest reveals that an individual may not have made any gains (if we use the upper limit of the first test and the lower limit of the second test: $55 - 55 = 0$) or may have had a sizable change in scores (i.e., if we use the lower limit of the first test and the upper limit of the second test: $65 - 45 = 20$). Thus, the static change score of 10 either may overstate or understate the true change of the individual. Thus, when attempting to reflect changes in an individual accurately, difference scores should be used only when the test is highly reliable.

Summary and Conclusion

The interpretation of assessment information requires an understanding of basic measurement and statistical concepts. The concepts discussed in this chapter build on one another. For example, all variables have levels of measurement (i.e., nominal, ordinal, interval, and ratio scales). These levels must be known in order to determine which measures of central tendency and variability to use. Some concepts are basic to test interpretations, such as understanding the difference between percentiles and percentages, the former providing an ordering or ranking of performance and the latter a ratio of performance.

The interpretation of test results requires knowledge of the transformation of raw data to standard scores. Transformed scores include Z-scores ($M = 0$, $SD = 1$), T-scores ($M = 50$, $SD = 10$); those used commonly with measures of cognitive ability ($M = 100$, $SD = 15$); and those used with the SAT and the Graduate Record Exam subtests ($M = 500$, $SD = 100$). The advantages and disadvantages of norm-referenced tests (e.g. the ability to compare an individual's score with a peer group) and criterion-referenced tests (e.g., the ability to compare an individual's scores against a predetermined criteria) should be understood.

The use of test data should consider the potential errors (e.g., standard error of measurement) of an observed score. The observed score is not necessarily the client's true score. Test interpretation is enhanced by establishing the desired confidence interval around the observed score. An interval is calculated from knowledge of the standard error of measurement and the desired confidence level (e.g. 68% or 95%).

Methods to calculate and interpret the effect size were discussed and may assist clinical practice. The interpretation of a clinical effect size is further enhanced from the calculation of a cut-off score. The cut-off score is a calculated value that is compared with the reliable change index (an estimate of the clinical effect size) and addresses the question whether the change is statistically significant.

Self-Check Questions

1. Describe and provide an example of each level of measurement.
2. Draw and describe a normal curve and a frequency distribution.
3. Determine the mean, median, mode, and standard deviation of the following sets:
   a. 8, 12, 27, 27, 34, 38, 39, 41, 41, 41, 50, 53, 53, 54, 55, 55, 58, 62, 67, 70, 72, 80, 95, 250, 300
   b. 56, 60, 64, 66, 68, 69, 72, 73, 74, 75, 78, 78, 79, 80, 82, 82, 83, 83, 84, 85, 85, 85, 85, 87, 87, 87, 90, 91, 92, 94, 95, 96, 97, 98, 98, 100
   c. 20, 22, 29, 30, 34, 38, 40, 43, 44, 45, 45, 50, 51, 53, 55, 58, 60, 63, 63, 66, 68, 70, 74, 75, 77, 80, 85, 90, 93, 96, 100
   d. 34, 35, 36, 40, 41, 50, 55, 59, 60, 61, 62, 94, 95, 96
4. Which of the above sets of data will have the largest standard deviation?
5. Which set of data will have the smallest standard deviation?

References

Anastasi, A. (1988). *Psychological testing* (6th ed.) New York: Macmillan.

Baccus, J. R., Baldwin, M. W., & Packer, D. J. (2004). Increasing implicit self-esteem through classical conditioning. *Psychological Science, 15*, 498–502.

Benowitz, N. L., Jacob, P., III, Kozlowski, L. T., & Yu, L. (1986). Influence of smoking fewer cigarettes on exposure to tar, nicotine, and carbon monoxide. *New England Journal of Medicine, 315*, 1310–1313.

Bolton, B.F., & Brookings, J. B. (2001). Scores and norms. In B. F. Bolton (Ed.), *Handbook of measurement and evaluation in rehabilitation* (3rd ed., pp. 3–28). Austin, TX: ProEd.

David, S. P., Brown, R. A., & Papandonatos, G. D. (2007). Pharmacogenetic clinical trial of sustained-released bupropion for smoking cessation. *Nicotine & Tobacco Research, 9*, 821–833.

Johnson, E. K., Dow, C., Lynch, R. T., & Hermann, B. P. (2006). Measuring clinical significance in rehabilitation research. *Rehabilitation Counseling Bulletin, 50*(1). 35–45.

Power, P. W. (2006). *A guide to vocational assessment* (4th ed.). Austin, Tx: ProEd.

Schneider, M., Dunton, G. F., & Cooper, D. M. (2008). Physical activity and physical self-concept among sedentary adolescent females: An intervention study. *Psychology of Sport and Exercise, 91*(1), 1–14.

West, R., McEwen, A., Boiling, K., & Owen, L. (2001). Smoking cessation and smoking patterns in the general population: A 1-year follow-up. *Addiction, 96*, 891–902.

7

Reliability and Validity of Assessment

HARRISON KANE
CHARLES PALMER
Mississippi State University

OVERVIEW

This chapter provides an introductory discussion of reliability and validity as they pertain to the provision of rehabilitation and health services. Although the issues are discussed in reference to test use, the concepts and principles are applicable for all forms of data used professionally, including observations and interviews. Keep in mind that reliability and validity are dynamic in nature, evolving with complexity of assessment techniques, the social implications of test data, and statistical advances. Therefore, this chapter offers a broad summary of concepts and techniques, the essentials that rehabilitative clinicians need to know in order to begin their program of study. Interested readers are encouraged to consult the specific professional literature pertaining to their own practice and interests as well as a number of works that are considered "classics" in the field of psychometrics (e.g., Betz & Weiss, 2001; Carroll, 1993; Cronbach, 1988; Cronbach & Meehl, 1955; Gustafsson, 2002; Messick, 1989; Spearman, 1904; Thorndike, 2001; Thurstone, 1925).

LEARNING OBJECTIVES

By the end of the chapter, readers should be able to:

- Identify four primary methods used to estimate reliability and give examples of each
- Describe (a) considerations in evaluating reliability estimates, (b) methods to improve reliability, and (c) the impact of floor and ceiling effects on reliability
- Describe four broad approaches used to support the validity of a test and give examples of each
- Distinguish between types of test validity and the evidence for those specific types
- Identify and explain the conditions affecting reliability
- Identify methods test developers may use to improve reliability
- Explain the relationship between validity and reliability

INTRODUCTION

Broadly defined, a *test* is any procedure or method used to examine or determine the presence of some factor or phenomenon (VandenBos, 2007). As used in this chapter, a test provides a standardized set of questions or other items designed to assess the knowledge, skills, interests, and other characteristics of an examinee. The value of these collected questions and items is that they are accompanied by definitive standardized procedures (e.g., administration guidelines, scoring criteria, and interpretative schemes) that enable all examiners to use a test in the same way to quantify, evaluate, and interpret an examinee's responses as reflecting individual characteristics and attributes (Kane, 2006). In simpler terms, tests are indirect and imperfect indicators of the examinee's particular characteristic that is really of interest. For example, the *Becker Work Adjustment Profile* (BWAP; Becker, 2005) is a 63-item test designed to identify work behavior deficits in persons with physical, mental, or emotional disabilities. In completing the BWAP, we are not directly measuring a client's work adjustment. In actuality, a direct measure of work adjustment would take days or weeks and involve numerous techniques and sources of information, including work products, interviews with the client and coworkers, and observations across an array of work and nonwork settings. The realities of practice demand that we sacrifice depth and thoroughness for conciseness and timeliness. Thus, instead of measuring work adjustment directly, we draw informed conclusions of the client's work adjustment from the obtained test scores.

RELIABILITY

Reliability theory begins with the fundamental assumption that an examinee's observed test score represents a random variable; that is, whenever an examinee's test performance is quantified as an obtained score, this score is only one observation from a larger hypothetical distribution of possible scores from that same examinee. Moreover, for any particular examinee, a test or other assessment procedure may yield different scores for any number of reasons.

Let us suppose that a neuropsychologist administers a test of memory (e.g., Rivermead Behavioral Memory Test-III; Wilson, Greenfield, et al., 2008) to an adolescent client with traumatic brain injury. If memory is assessed through anecdotal evidence of the examinee's observed everyday behaviors, ratings from the examinee and caregivers may differ. If the client is required to complete a series of increasingly difficult tasks related to memory (e.g., repeating a string of digits or recalling geometric patterns), test length may introduce the confounding effect of fatigue, thus impacting the accuracy of scores. Similarly, subtleties in the examiner's administration (e.g., rapport and appropriate queries) may impact the patient's responsiveness, persistence, and motivation. Further complicating the issue is the fact that literally hundreds of tasks may be used to assess memory, and different sets and constellations of items from this universe of tasks may yield different scores. For the examiner, any of these obtained scores (e.g., self-ratings, examinee responses, and behavioral observations) may serve the overall purpose of the assessment. However, the scores obtained under these different conditions are unlikely to be identical—that is, to be reliable.

Because an examinee's test performance may assume a range of values, there always is some degree of uncertainty for the test user that a single sample of elicited behavior (i.e., an observed test score from a single session) provides an optimal or even adequate portrait of the characteristic being measured. Therefore, well-informed interpretations require the clinician to have an idea of the extent to which an observed test score may depart from what might be considered the typical or average score, for both the individual patient and the population. All other things being equal, our conclusions and judgments are more accurate when based on results from tests that precisely measure the desired attribute.

Most dictionaries define *reliability* in terms of desirable traits possessed by individuals (e.g., dependability, consistency, and trustworthiness). These same descriptors apply to the context of measurement and assessment. Essentially, the overriding concern of reliability is to quantify the precision of test scores and procedures. Precise test scores lend themselves to dependable, consistent, and trustworthy interpretation.

Classical Test Theory

Classical test theory (also called *true-score theory*) provides the simplest and most elegant model for conceptualizing reliability theory. Classical test theory begins with the pragmatic assumption that error is inherent in all measurement (Crocker & Algina, 1986). Nothing can be measured with absolute accuracy, especially latent human traits and conditions. Accordingly, we may conceptualize an individual's *observed score* as consisting of the sum of two other scores: an individual's *true score* (i.e., the test score that would be obtained if there were no error in measurement) and the *residual error score* associated with a particular observed score. This conception can be represented simply:

$$X_{\text{Observed Score}} = T_{\text{True Score}} + E_{\text{Error}}$$

Importantly, both true score and the error associated with an observed score are mathematical abstractions; that is, these values are never truly known with absolute certainty. If it were possible to determine the exact amount of error associated with an examinee's observed score, then the client's true score of the attribute could be calculated by simply subtracting this value from the observed score. Instead, these values are always estimated.

Practically speaking, the intent of testing is to reveal as much of the examinee's true score as possible. Depending on the stability of the attributes being measured, an examinee's true score is expected to remain stable across test occasions. At other times, we may expect an individual's true score to change, as in the case of a client's response to intervention, maturation, learning, or accident (e.g., head injury). Under such circumstances, changes in true score are not distractions or disruptions, but actually the focus of our testing.

In a similar vein, residual error is the difference between an individual's true score and observed score. As measurement error increases, less true score is necessarily captured in the patient's observed score. With this loss of precision, the usefulness of the observed test score inevitably decreases. If an observed score were comprised entirely of error (i.e., the test is absolutely unreliable and offers no measure of true score), we could not form any meaningful interpretation from the data. Generally, residual error is considered random. After all, if the sources of error in test scores could be identified, then the examiner could account entirely for these sources in their interpretation of test results. Some examples of sources of error are identified in Table 7.1.

TABLE 7.1 Sources of Random Errors of Measurement

Internal Sources	External Sources
Client's physical state	Irregularities in test administration
Fatigue	Timing
Discomfort	Lighting/acoustics
Visual acuity	Acoustics
Auditory acuity	Interruptions/distractions
Illness	Examiner's skill/fluency with the test
Client's psychological or emotional state	Rapport
Anxiety	Recording errors
Attentiveness	Test characteristics
Memory	Item/content sampling
Engagement and motivation	Inter-rater reliability
Perceived importance of test	Mode of administration/response format
Other sources	Ease of administration/scoring/interpretation
Mistakes	Other sources
Speed over accuracy	Luck/chance/guessing
Carelessness	Appropriateness of test for the examinee/client
Guessing	Personal relationship/domestic tranquility/relationships
Misunderstanding/questions/directions	Examiner's perceived importance and use of scores
Clerical Errors	

Note: These examples of measurement error do not represent an exhaustive list of all possible sources of measurement error, nor does every one of these sources of measurement error actually apply in every instance of assessment. Every assessment is unique, and the sources of error impacting observed scores vary according to the situation.

Because true score and error are abstractions, an exact and absolute measure of reliability cannot be known. Just as error always is associated with an observed score, estimates of reliability always are imprecise. Reliability is estimated, not definitively known. Going one step further, the earlier concept of an observed score as comprised of true score and error ($X_{\text{Observed Score}} = T_{\text{True Score}} + E_{\text{Error}}$) can be extended to include the variance (i.e., score differences among individuals) associated with each of these terms. That is, the variation in observed performance (X_σ) is a cumulative summation of *true score variance* (T_σ) and *error score variance* (E_σ):

$$X_\sigma = T_\sigma + E_\sigma$$

Thus, observed score variance captures (1) some degree of the true score differences between examinees that are attributable to real and stable differences in the underlying abilities, knowledge, traits, or attitude that are measured by the testing procedure, plus (2) the random variance associated with the sources of error. Test data are more reliable when true score variance is associated with an observed score. Thus, the reliability of a test score may be conceptualized as the ratio of the true score variance to observed score variance. In notation form:

$$\text{Reliability} = T_\sigma / X_\sigma$$

Under this model, the reliability of test scores is defined as the proportion of the observed score that is due to true score differences (Crocker & Algina, 1986). Basically,

the more true score revealed by a test, the more reliable the procedure.

Because true score variation is considered an indication of an examinee's stable and enduring characteristics, observed test scores across different forms, examiners, and occasions will be similar to the extent that they measure the individual differences associated with true score. The *reliability coefficient* is considered the summary statistical representation of this proportion and ratio.

Reliability coefficients can be classified into four broad categories: (1) estimates obtained from the administration of a single test form on different occasions, (2) estimates based on the administration of different forms of the test to the same group of examinees, (3) estimates derived from the single administration of a test, and (4) the agreement between different examiners in scoring a test or sample of behavior. Each of these reliability estimates considers a different source of random error.

Therefore, reliability estimates may vary, depending on the method of estimation. For example, reliability estimates for the composite scores of the *Adaptive Behavior Assessment System* (2nd ed.) (ABAS-II; Harrison & Oakland, 2003) range from .82 to .99, depending on which aspect of reliability is targeted (e.g., internal consistency, stability of scores, or equivalence across raters and forms). The primary methods for estimating reliability are presented in Table 7.2 (Reynolds, Livingston, & Willson, 2006, p. 91). Each of these approaches yields a reliability coefficient that can be broadly interpreted as the amount of observed total score variation attributable to real differences in true score. For example, a reliability coefficient of .80 indicates

TABLE 7.2 Major Types of Reliability

Type of Reliability	Number of Test Forms	Number of Test Sessions	Summary
Test–Retest	One form	Two sessions	Administer the same test to the same group on two different occasions. Correlate scores.
Alternate forms	Two forms	Varies	Administer two forms of the same test to the same group of people. Administration may take place in one or more sessions. Correlate scores.
Split-half	One form	One session	Administer the test to a single group at one session. Divide the test into two equivalent halves. Correlate scores.
Coefficient alpha	One form	One session	Administer the test to a group one time. Apply appropriate statistical procedures.
Inter-rater	One form	One session	Administer the test to a group one time. Two or more raters complete the test independently.
			Correlate scores or apply appropriate statistical procedure.

that 80% of the variance in observed test scores is attributable to individual differences in true score. Conversely, this statistic also implies that 20% of individual differences in scores can be traced to random error. As a real world example, the reported reliability coefficients for the various subscales of the *Scales of Independent Behavior*, Revised (SIB-R; Bruininks, Woodcock, Weatherman, & Hill, 1996) generally are above .90. The implication for rehabilitation counselors and health service providers using this instrument is that approximately 90% of the variation they observe in their clients (i.e., why one person requires pervasive supports while another individual functions with absolute autonomy) is attributable to the abstract but real characteristics of the examinee that are measured by the items comprising the SIB-R (e.g., items that measure an individual's self-care, maladjustment, coping skills, and self-direction).

Test-Retest Reliability

The most direct method of estimating the reliability of test data is to administer the test to the same or an equivalent group of examinees on two different occasions. Scores from these successive testings then are correlated. The resulting *test–retest reliability coefficient* can be interpreted as the degree to which the test measures enduring examinee characteristics that are stable across occasions and time. Test–retest reliability is sensitive to time sampling, or the day-do-day fluctuations that constitute a source of random error. Almost always, the correlation will not be perfect (i.e., 1.00). Therefore, the length of time between the two test occasions is an important consideration to note when calculating and interpreting test–retest reliability. If the time interval is too short (e.g., a matter of hours), examinee fatigue may set in because of a lengthy test administration, or performance may reflect the immediate influence of practice. If the time interval is too long (e.g., weeks or months), the reliability coefficient can be lowered by real changes in the construct being measured. Longer time intervals tend to diminish the estimated reliability.

No established time interval is deemed optimal in calculating test–retest reliability. Therefore, the time interval is best determined by considering the client's characteristic under assessment. For example, a century of research suggests that an adult's intelligence can remain relatively stable over years, whereas anxiety and depression are more transient and influenced by particular situational factors (e.g., Carroll, 1993; Caspi,

Roberts, & Shriner, 2005). Therefore, we have reasonably higher expectations for the stability of scores from intelligence tests than for personality tests. Similarly, following a stroke, the immediate introduction of physical and speech therapy can produce remarkable and real changes in a patient's capabilities. In the case of individuals with attentional disorders, the administration of a stimulant such as Ritalin can change behavior (i.e., attention) in a matter of hours. An understanding of the temporal and developmental nature of the construct being measured is essential in obtaining an estimate of reliability that lends itself to reasoned interpretation.

In all cases, even in the assessment of stable traits and characteristics, observed performance may fluctuate from day to day simply as a result of random error. Professionals in rehabilitation are well aware that clients have "good days" and "bad days." However, the random nature of these deviations implies that they will average out in the long run.

In addition to the temporal nature of the construct being assessed, the intended use of the test also should be considered when estimating test–retest reliability. Stability is more of a concern in some situations than in others. For example, because the SAT (often taken first in the 11th grade) is expected to predict college achievement, the stability of these scores is a reasonable expectation. Conversely, the long-term stability of teacher-made classroom tests is less of an essential matter inasmuch as classroom performance is expected to change with exposure to daily instruction.

The confounding effects of practice or interventions impose natural limitations on test–retest methods of estimating reliability (Guttman, 1945). In ideal test–retest situations, the test content is the same across occasions; therefore, testing occasions are not independent. For some tests (e.g., memory, intelligence, and motor performance) the practice effect can be substantial because the examinee is cued to the content and has the luxury of time between administrations to rehearse, practice, and obtain information to improve their responses (Sattler, 2001). Even if the content of a test is entirely novel, the examinee is more testwise and poised on the second test administration. In either case, idiosyncrasies of the first administration carry over to the second administration, possibly changing the nature of the test (e.g., item difficulty) or examinee. As a result of this carryover, the amount of true score variance is diminished on the second test, and the interpretive value of these test scores is compromised due to *systematic nonrandom sources of error.*

Alternate or Parallel Forms Reliability

Because of the considerations noted previously (e.g., practice effects and familiarity with test format), attempts to administer the same test repeatedly generally are impractical. Thus, *alternate* or *parallel forms* of some tests have been developed. The terms *alternate or parallel* refer to two (or more) tests that have similar item content, format, item difficulty, norms, test specifications, identical observed score distributions, equal covariance among forms, as well as equal covariance with other measures—a tall order that few tests achieve.

The major psychometric issue associated with alternate form reliability methods is the degree to which the forms are equivalent. As in test–retest methods, parallel or alternate forms reliability assumes that variance associated with true score and error are independent and constant across forms. Thus, the correlation of observed scores between the two forms is equal to the ratio of true score variance to the observed score variance on either form. The more true score captured by each alternate form, the higher the correlation between the two forms. When different but alternate forms of a test are administered to the same individuals, the resulting correlation between their total scores is referred to as an *equivalence coefficient* (American Educational Research Association, American Psychological Association, National Council on Measurement in Education, 1999).

Alternate forms reliability based upon their simultaneous administration is primarily sensitive to measurement error related to content sampling (e.g., the test forms may have different item content and difficulty). Alternate forms reliability has a distinct advantage in reducing *practice effects*—a primary concern of using test–retest methods. However, when determining alternative form reliability, practice effects are not eliminated entirely. Simply exposing test takers to the format of a test may inform an examinee of helpful strategies during the first administration that can be used on the second administration (Nunnally & Bernstein, 1994).

Efforts to develop alternate forms of a test present formidable challenges for test authors and developers. The development of alternate forms or procedures that truly are equivalent in item content, format, and difficulty requires considerable effort. Obviously, few practitioners or test developers have the luxury and resources of time, manpower, money, and compliant examinees that are needed to develop alternate forms.

The combination of test–retest and alternate forms methods provides the most stringent and practical estimate of reliability insofar as it reflects how test data often are used in clinical settings. In this scenario, alternate forms of a test or procedure are administered within a suitable time interval to a single group of individuals. The resulting correlation in test scores is called a *coefficient of stability and equivalence.* This combined approach accounts for the examinee's responses to the particular test occasion (i.e., possible lack of stability) and test forms (i.e., possible lack of equivalence), and random error stemming from pure chance. As noted previously, the time interval between administrations should be sufficiently long to accommodate the random transient fluctuations in examinee performance yet not so long as to reveal lasting changes in the attributes measured that are attributable to intervention, maturation, and learning.

Reliability Estimates from a Single Administration

Although test–retest and alternate forms methods may be ideal for estimating reliability, they also are difficult to obtain and rarely used. Few tests offer alternate forms. Moreover, if alternative forms are available, their use is likely to be resisted due to the burdens of time, money, and effort imposed by repeated testings. Thus, there always is an abiding interest in realizing the advantages of parallel forms and test–retest estimates of reliability.

Reliability estimates obtained from a single administration examine the *internal consistency* of a test. Estimates of reliability obtained from a single test administration generally involve dividing the test into two or more constituent parts that are assumed to be equal in content and form and then calculating a correlation between the subtests. The resulting coefficient, an estimate of internal consistency, primarily reflects error variance related to the sampling of content and test behaviors.

A test may be subdivided in various ways, each of which creates shortened forms of a larger and longer test (Cronbach, Schonemann, & McKie, 1965). For example, items may be divided as even-numbered versus odd-numbered items. On other occasions, the format of the test as a whole suggests a logical division based upon items pertaining to a particular content area or common stimulus (e.g., clusters of items pertaining to a reading passage or a step-by-step procedure). A test also may be divided at the midpoint of its items. As a caution, this method usually is not appropriate for power tests (i.e., those tests on which a person is encouraged to do their very best, such as tests of motor skills and cognitive abilities), as item difficulty tends to increase as the test progresses, making the subtest comprised of the first half of items substantially easier than the second half.

As a general rule, reliability is increased as items are added to a test. The logic is straightforward. Because a test is considered a sample of behavior, the inclusion of more items provides a larger sample from the possible universe of behaviors in the domain being assessed. The more adequately and representatively a domain is sampled, the more true score variance is captured in the measurement. Accordingly, an estimate of internal consistency obtained from two shortened forms tends to underestimate the true reliability of the entire instrument. On such occasions, the *Spearman–Brown* formula is used to estimate the reliability of an entire test when a coefficient is determined using two split halves of one test:

$$\text{Reliability of Full Test} = 2\, r_{\text{half-test}}/1 + r_{\text{half-test}}$$

As an example, assume that a 100-item test is divided into halves using an even versus odd procedure to assign items to the two halves. Let's assume further that the correlation between the two halves is .75. Applying the Spearman–Brown formula, the reliability of the full test would be corrected to a much preferred and acceptable estimate of .85(1.50/1.75 = .85). The Spearman–Brown formula makes the stringent assumption of equal true score and error variances for the two forms. Although this assumption often is violated, the Spearman–Brown formula still renders a reasonable estimate of reliability for the test in its entirety.

By far, Cronbach's *coefficient alpha* (Cronbach, 1951) and the *Kuder–Richardson* formulas (Kuder & Richardson, 1937) are the most widely known and applied procedures to estimate *internal consistency* and *content heterogeneity* of items. Among the various formulas offered by Kuder–Richardson, the most widely used is the Kuder–Richardson formula 20 (*KR 20*). The *KR 20* is applicable when items are scored dichotomously (i.e., as right or wrong). The formula for calculating the *KR 20* is straightforward, requiring only the test length, the individual item difficulties (i.e., called the *p-values* or the proportion of correct responses), and the variance of number of correct scores:

$$KR20 = k/k - 1\frac{(SD^2 - \sum \rho_i \times q_i)}{SD^2}$$

Where

    k = number of test items
    SD^2 = variance of total test scores
    ρ = difficulty of item
    q = proportion of incorrect responses on item

The Kuder–Richardson 21 formula is a simplification of the KR 20 in which the proportion of correct responses on an item (i.e., *p*-value or item difficulty) is replaced with the mean score on the test. Thus, the KR 21 allows for the calculation of internal consistency using only the length of the test, mean score, and standard deviation. While the estimates offered by the KR 20 and KR 21 are close in practice, the use of KR 21 always yields a smaller value.

Cronbach's alpha may be calculated from items scored either dichotomously or with multiple responses (e.g., 0, 1, and 2). Because Cronbach's alpha can be applied to tests with items that produce multiple scores, it has more general applications than the Kudor–Richardson formulas and is the most widely used procedure to determine item heterogeneity (i.e. *internal consistency*). To calculate Cronbach's alpha, the number of items, variance of the individual items, and variance of the total scores are needed:

$$\text{Cronbach's alpha} = (k/k - 1)(1 - \sum SD_1{}^2/SD^2)$$

Where

    k = number of items
    $SD_1{}^2$ = variance of individual items
    SD^2 = variance of total test scores

Coefficient alpha is equal to the average of all possible split-half reliability coefficients, thereby controlling for the possible error associated with an arbitrary split of the test. However, like all methods of reliability estimation that are based on split-half procedures, the Kuder–Richardson and coefficient alpha formulas are sensitive to content sampling error.

Interestingly, despite its popularity, Cronbach, the inventor of the alpha statistic, asserted, "I no longer regard the formula (of Cronbach's alpha) as the most appropriate way to examine most data. Over the years, my associates and I developed the complex generalizability (*G*) theory" (Cronbach & Shavelson 2004, p. 403). *Generalizability theory* is an extension of classical test theory that applies *analysis of variance* (ANOVA) techniques to the simultaneous estimation of the combined effects of multiple sources of error on test scores (Urbina, 2004, p. 221). However, to apply *G* theory appropriately, it is necessary to obtain multiple measures of all possible hypothetical sources of error variance on a given test for a given individual. Thus, relatively few authors have applied these techniques to the development of new tests. The demands of reality favor Cronbach's alpha as a reasonable estimate of internal consistency.

The utility of split-half methods is limited because they cannot be used with speeded tests. For example, many standardized tests of intelligence, neuropsychology, and motor functioning include subtests that are intended to measure the speed and efficiency of information processing. For example, the Trials A and B require the patient to draw a line connecting circles and numbers according to a predetermined sequence. Additionally, many tests of cognitive ability include measures of fluency that require an examinee to complete simple academic problems quickly under timed conditions. Because these tests are designed to measure speed, not knowledge of content, reliability estimates obtained by methods such as split-half, KR 20 and Cronbach's alpha are inappropriate. As a result, the reliability of speeded tests is best estimated with test–retest procedures.

Importantly, estimates based on a single test administration may not shed light on sources of error that are illuminated only by repeated testings. "When behavioral observations are gathered in an hour or less, certain sources of error "stand still" for each examinee . . . and are not reflected in the estimate of test error variance. Artful manipulation of the data from single testing occasion cannot alter this basic fact" (Feldt & Brennan, 1989, p. 110). In other words, in estimating reliability from a single administration, error variance that is averaged from repeated testing may be misinterpreted as true score. For this reason, exclusive reliance on internal consistency tends to overestimate reliability.

Reliability of Ratings and Observations

Measurement of an examinee's characteristics may rely on subjective judgment. This often occurs in clinical settings. For example, two therapists may be asked to perform observations of a child referred for traumatic brain injury, or two parents may be asked to independently rate their child's adaptive behavior. In such cases, there is a need to determine the level of agreement when two or more examiners or respondents apply the same rating procedure to the recording or scoring of items or the evaluation of behavioral observations. Estimating *inter-rater* reliability (sometimes called *interobserver* agreement) is a straightforward matter. Each clinician or respondent independently records his or her data during a single observation. The items then are scored. The correlation between scores offers an *inter-rater coefficient*.

A simpler alternate procedure for estimating inter-rater reliability is to determine the percentage of times two raters assign the same score to an examinee's sample of behavior. For example, assume that two raters are expected to evaluate the work products of 30 individuals in an assisted living setting (e.g., cleaning the home). In judging the work products, ratings can range in value from 1 (poor) to 5 (excellent). Predictably, some projects are judged as poor while others receive exemplary ratings. If both raters assigned the same ratings for 25 of the 30 examinees, the interrater agreement is 25/30 = .83. Notably, inter-rater reliability does not reflect error due to content, fluctuations in examinee performance, or time sampling. Rather, it only indicates the degree of agreement between raters' judgments.

Occasionally, some situations and settings allow for more than two raters to record behaviors over a time period (e.g., several clinicians may record a client's behaviors as a means of monitoring progress). Increases in the number of raters or duration of observations serve the same purpose as increasing the number of items on a test. These efforts offer more opportunities to capture true score variance and produce the greatest benefit in reliability estimation.

The Spearman–Brown Prophecy Formula

The *length of a test* has a predictable impact on estimates of reliability. Generally speaking, longer tests are more reliable. However, at times, practicality dictates a test must be shortened (e.g., when used as a screening procedure). Therefore, a test user may want to determine how a test's reliability would be affected if it were lengthened or shortened. For example, consider a scenario in which the neurocognitive functioning of an elderly patient must be measured. The administration time of many commonly used instruments (e.g., Halstead–Reitan Neuropsychological Test Battery) is 60 to 90 minutes. Therefore, fatigue may be an issue. For this reason, a shortened or brief test form that reduces administration time may be preferred over the more traditional test.

Nevertheless, if reliability is compromised substantially, interpretations based on scores from the shortened form would be untenable. Under such situations, the *Spearman–Brown Prophecy Formula* is used to predict the impact on reliability if a test or procedure is shortened or lengthened:

$$r = \frac{n \times r_{xx}}{1 + (n - 1)r_{xx}}$$

Where

r = estimated reliability of test with added items
n = factor by which the test is lengthened what if it is
r_{xx} = reliability of original version of the test

Likewise, a publisher or author may have a desired target reliability in mind during test development and standardization. Thus, the Spearman–Brown Prophesy formula has equally important applications in test development, as when authors must balance the need for precision in test scores (i.e., to increasing test length to attain an acceptable level of reliability) with the realities of test length and administration time (i.e., inordinately lengthy tests are less likely to be used).

Reliability of Composite Scores

Many standardized psychological and educational tests are structured to yield scores from distinct traits or constructs that can be compiled to form a weighted *composite score*. For example, the *Adaptive Behavior Assessment System* (2nd ed.) (ABAS-II; Harrison & Oakland, 2003) measures 10 skills areas (i.e., has 10 subtests), the scores from which are combined to form three domains and a composite (i.e., total score) of adaptive behavior (chapter 15

of this volume provides a more complete discussion of this process). The component scores often lend themselves to ipsative comparisons, as when clinicians identify and interpret significant relative strengths and weaknesses after comparing subtest differences. As with subtest scores, composite scores are assumed to consist of true score and error score variances. Thus, many of the same statistical and conceptual considerations that apply to single tests also apply to composite scores. More information (e.g., having more items) generally leads to more true score variance being captured in the assessment. Thus, the reliability of the composite score always is higher than the reliabilities of the individual subtests that contribute to this composite score. The reliability of the composite score is influenced by the number of subtests, the correlation between subtests, and the reliabilities of the subtests. Stated differently, by combining several measures, we increase the sample size, the number of items on a test, and number of observations, and thus improve reliability.

DISCUSSION BOX 7.1

Summing Sources of Error

Urbina (2004, p. 139) notes that different sources of error may accumulate to drastically impact the reliability of a test. The most widely used individually administered standardized test of children's intelligence, the *Wechsler Intelligence Scale for Children* (4th ed.) (WISC-IV) was used to exemplify this idea. The WISC-IV contains 15 subtests that form four composites: verbal comprehension, perceptual reasoning, working memory, and processing speed. The five subtests that comprise the verbal comprehension (listed below) require the examiner to score the client's responses using a scale of 0, 1, or 2 points.

For each subtest, the total score is the sum of the points earned by the examinee on the attempted items. This total score then is converted to an age-based standard score, with a mean of 10 and standard deviation of 3.

The scores on these various subtests are susceptible to content sampling as well as the possibility of different ratings by examiners. A review of the *WISC-IV Technical and Interpretive Manual* (Wechsler, 2004) finds the following average reliability coefficients for various sources of error:

Subtest	Average Internal Consistency	Average Test-Retest Reliability	Average Interrater Reliability	Sum of Error Variance from Different Sources	Estimated True Score Variance (1.0 – error)
Similarities	.86	.86	.98	.14 + .14 + .02 = .30	.70
Vocabulary	.89	.92	.95	.11 + .08 + .05 = .24	.76
Comprehension	.81	.82	.95	.09 + .08 + .05 = .23	.77
Information	.86	.89	.96	.14 + .11 + .04 = .29	.71
Word Reasoning	.80	.82	.97	.20 + .18 + .03 = .41	.59

The preceding calculations emphasize that reliance on a single estimate of reliability may dramatically underestimate the actual influence of error. Multiple sources of error need to be considered to obtain a realistic estimate of an examinee's true score.

Questions

1. Identify scenarios in assessment where one source of error is more important than other sources of error.

Reliability of Change Scores

Rehabilitation and health service providers often track changes in characteristics of their patients in order to determine the client's response to their interventions. For example, physical therapists may monitor changes in a client's coordination and balance following an amputation. Speech pathologists may look for improvements in a patient's articulation following a stroke. These changes may be determined by examining differences between tests scores acquired prior to and after treatment. Thus, having test data prior to the onset of a condition against which to compare subsequent treatment-related data is ideal. However, this ideal rarely occurs.

Little support exists for the common practice of using the difference between the initial and later levels of performance to represent an individual's response to intervention (Cronbach & Furby, 1970). These *gain or change scores* are inexact because they necessarily include error associated with both the pretest and posttest. In addition, the higher the correlation between initial and final levels of performance (i.e., *pretest and posttest scores*), the lower the reliability of the gain score.

Conceptually, this issue is similar to the problems associated with multicollinearity in multiple regression. For example, let's suppose the reliabilities of a pretest and posttest are .90 and .80, respectively. If pretest and posttest data correlated at .80, which is entirely feasible in a clinical setting, the reliability of the gain scores would be .25. Since true score variance is needed to calculate the relationship between variables, reliability necessarily places a ceiling on estimates of predictive validity. Therefore, even in circumstances where clinicians are using reliable and established instruments, their findings and conclusions may be tenuous at best.

Considerations in Evaluating Reliability

A number of factors should be considered when evaluating a reliability coefficient. The acceptability of a reliability coefficient depends on the construct being measured, the methods used in test construction, the use of the test scores, the availability of time for data collection, and methods used in estimation (Cronbach, 1990).

CONSTRUCT   Some constructs are more difficult to measure than others. This is because the domain of items that hypothetically represent the construct may be difficult to sample adequately. For example, as a general rule, behaviors that reflect aspects of personality (e.g., openness and conscientiousness) are more difficult to sample than behaviors that reflect physical or cognitive functioning (e.g., tactile strength and quantitative reasoning). Therefore, estimates of reliability acceptable for measures of personality may be lower and thus deemed lacking and unacceptable compared to measures of physical and cognitive ability. In evaluating the adequacy of a reliability coefficient, a clinician should weigh and consider the nature of the construct and the difficulty in sampling pertinent behaviors.

METHOD OF TEST CONSTRUCTION   Distinctions often are made between informal and formal assessments. Some tests and procedures are constructed on an ad hoc basis as well as informally. For example, service providers often conduct a brief mental status exam during their discussions with a patient. Such exams that informally assess memory and orientation are based on the cohesiveness and accuracy of a client's speech, conversation, and responses to simple questions (e.g., the day of the week, one's city and state). Additionally, many countries do not have the economic resources to develop standardized tests that reflect the particular and unique demographic characteristics of their populations. Clinicians in these countries often rely on translations or adaptation of established tests from other countries, a practice that may be tenuous (see chapter 3).

Conversely, formal procedures involve standardized tests with established procedures for administration, scoring, and interpretation. The imposition of standardization during test development tends to increase the accuracy and precision of the resulting scores. Obviously, standardization is a costly endeavor. Thus, to be cost-effective and profitable, standardized tests are expected to be used for years. Whereas informal tests often have questionable or undetermined reliability, formal tests are expected to have reliability estimates that warrant their continued long-term use and acceptance (Linn, 1989).

USE OF THE TEST   At times, *high-stakes decisions* will be made based on test data. Thus, diagnostic and prognostic decisions stemming from test results may substantially impact the course of one's life. For example, the results drawn from an assessment of intelligence and adaptive behavior may lead to a diagnosis of mental retardation, a determination that can lead to restrictive, stigmatizing, and irreversible outcomes (Lauchlan & Boyle, 2007). Therefore, the reliability and accuracy of these tests and diagnostic procedures should be held to the highest (i.e., high-stakes) standards.

In contrast, rehabilitation counselors may use brief screening procedures to identify patients who seemingly need services (e.g., from a speech–language pathologist or occupational therapist). Patients who score above an established cutoff score (e.g., 90th percentile) are referred for more in-depth individualized testing. In this case, results of the screening procedure are not used to make permanent and irreversible decisions (i.e., they have a low-stakes impact). Therefore, a lower reliability coefficient may be acceptable.

High-stakes decisions should be made only with highly reliable and accurate information. As a general rule of thumb, if the decisions are important and irreversible, researchers recommend reliability coefficients of .90 or higher (Linn & Gronland, 1995). This high standard often is attained in individually administered standardized tests of intelligence, academic achievement, adaptive behavior, motor skills, neurocognitive functioning, and structured personality inventories. In the context of high-stakes assessment, tests with reliability estimates below .70 should be used with extreme caution, if at all. Remember, drawing upon classical test theory, a reliability coefficient of .70 indicates that 70% of the observed score variance is attributable to true score variation. The obvious corollary is that 30% of observed score variance is due to random error. Very few people would be willing to make a life altering decision if the odds of irreversible failure are about 1 out of 3.

TIME AVAILABILITY FOR TESTING Circumstances arise that may reduce the time available for testing. Clinicians often find their days to be structured and fragmented. As a result, brief assessment procedures tend to be less reliable, yet their use may be necessary. Clinicians must be cautious to achieve a balance between using tests that are sufficiently reliable yet reflect the practical parameters of the testing situation (e.g., time demands and situational distractions).

METHODS OF ESTIMATING RELIABILITY Reliability estimates vary according to their method of estimation. For example, split-half estimates that do not accommodate time sampling error often yield higher reliability coefficients than parallel forms or test–retest methods. Generally, reliability estimates that take into consideration multiple sources of error will be lower than those that consider fewer sources of error (Kane, 1996).

Improving Reliability

Reliability is improved when the observed score captures more true score variance and decreases the amount of variance associated with random error. The best insurance and assurance of strong reliability is to construct, develop, and retain test items that clearly and adequately represent the construct being measured. As mentioned previously, the easiest method to increase reliably is to add items to the test. As long as the additional items maintain the high psychometric qualities of the existing items, the reliability will increase as more relevant information contributes to the observed performance. Therefore, the items considered for inclusion on a test should be evaluated to determine their potential for improving reliability.

The statistical process of *item analysis* is intended to assist authors in the selection, development, and retention of items that possess desired measurement characteristics. For example, a common procedure in item analysis is to calculate *item discrimination*. Stated differently, the item is evaluated to determine whether it clearly samples individual differences that fall along the continuum of the construct being measured. Using the example of a test of gross motor performance, item discrimination would reveal if individuals whose total scores are high (i.e., those who display strong gross motor skills) displayed better performance on each question more often than individuals whose total scores are low (i.e., those who display diminished gross motor skills). In a clinical setting, item discrimination on a test of depression would indicate if individuals who are and are not depressed respond differently to items (e.g., Westen, Lohr, & Silk, 1990).

Additionally, reliability may be increased by imposing clear administration procedures, scoring criteria, and interpretive guidelines. Thus, reliability estimates tend to be higher for standardized tests than for informal assessments because the latter form of testing lacks these important features. Of course, there are circumstances when standardized administration may be abandoned in favor of obtaining information that is not readily available within the boundaries dictated by the test format. As an example, a speech–language pathologist may administer subtests of a battery out of the recommended order so as to maintain motivation or accommodate fatigue and frustration.

Case Study 7.1—Testing Accommodations

Isaac P., age 15, displays moderate symptoms of cerebral palsy. Cerebral palsy is one of a number of neurological disorders that appear in infancy or early childhood and permanently affect body movement and muscle coordination. In the case of Isaac, his cerebral palsy impacts his fine and gross motor skills. Articulation difficulties are noticeable in his speech, and he struggles with most tasks that involve writing. Your goal is to provide a comprehensive assessment of Isaac's current status. Along with observations and interviews, you select a number of standardized instruments designed to measure several dimensions of Isaac's abilities and aptitudes. Included in the test battery is the *Bruininks-Oseretsky Test of Motor Proficiency, Second Edition-II* (BOT-II) (Bruininks & Bruininks, 2006), a measure of gross and fine motor skills. The BOT-II is individually administered, providing standard scores that permit a comparison of Isaac's performance to his same-aged peers. Importantly, the BOT-II includes several items that require Isaac to

perform motoric tasks as quickly as possible, under timed conditions. You are aware that the major presenting difficulty in assessing a child with cerebral palsy is motoric. Likewise, you are aware that clinicians are encouraged to make reasonable accommodations in the assessment of individuals with disabilities. Therefore, you decide to disregard time limits in order to accommodate Isaac's impaired motor functioning.

QUESTION

What is the impact of your decision when interpreting Isaac's obtained scores?

High-stakes decisions should be based on assessment data obtained from *multiple sources and methods*. The use of two or more sources helps insure the data are accurate. The use of two or more measures to assess the same characteristic helps minimize measurement error, especially systematic error. The various measures are unlikely to share the same sources of systematic error. Moreover, the clinician may triangulate the test's results (i.e., compare the results from two or more different measures) to obtain a more accurate description of the behavior.

Although desirable, constructs often are not measured with the same precision across the spectrum of individual differences. Reliability estimates for scores in the middle of a distribution (e.g. average scores) may be higher than those at the ends of the distribution (e.g. either high or low scores). This is an important consideration for therapists inasmuch as their effort and concern often are directed toward atypical and unusual performance levels. Reliability estimates of scores near the center of a distribution tend to differ from those scores that are very high or low (Kane, 1996). Two factors contribute to this.

First, regardless of the construct being measured, fewer individuals obtain extreme scores. Consider scores obtained from individually administered tests of language disorders, such as the *Comprehensive Assessment of Spoken Language* (CASL; Carrow-Woolfolk, 1999). Recall that most human traits may be displayed with a normal bell-shaped distribution. Whereas 68% of individuals obtain scores in the average range (i.e., one standard deviation above and below the population mean), only 2% obtain scores in the aphasic or severely delayed ranges. Thus, there are fewer individuals who may contribute to a complete understanding of the construct being assessed.

Second, reliability is inferred from true score variance. True score variance can be measured only in light

of a full range of ability, even at the individual level. For example, an individual who misses all items on a test has not yet revealed his/her true score. An accurate assessment requires an examinee to both pass and fail some items. Thus, when completing a measure of expressive language, a conclusion that an individual who misses all items has no expressive language or an individual who passes all items has perfect expressive language would be inaccurate. In both instances, the true score has not yet been measured because the range of an individual's performance has not been observed. In practice, a test that does not measure the lowest extremes of a trait is said to have an insufficient *floor* while a test that does not measure the upper extremes of a trait possesses insufficient *ceiling*. Floor and ceiling effects diminish opportunities to capture true-score variance and in turn lower estimates of reliability (Bracken, 1988). Most tests are developed under the incorrect assumption that reliability is the same for high, average, and low scores. Thus, the examiner should exercise some caution in interpreting extreme scores.

The same caution holds for groups that are *restricted in range* in regard to the trait being measured. In such instances, the homogeneity of the examinees naturally reduces the observed individual differences in test scores. Recall that true score variance is central to conceptions of reliability. Consequently, in situations where true score variation is attenuated due to homogeneity in the traits being measured, the reliability may be underestimated. For example, the reliability estimates drawn from scores obtained from samples of persons with mental retardation or traumatic brain injury will be lower than estimates based on a sample comprised of individuals spanning the entire spectrum of cognitive ability. The use of a *correction for attenuation* is needed when reliability estimates are obtained from homogenous samples:

$$r_{xy,\ \text{corrected}} = r_{xy} = \frac{r_{xy}}{\sqrt{r_{xx}r_{yy}}}$$

Where

$r_{xy,\ \text{corrected}}$ = the corrected reliability coefficient
r_{xy} = the uncorrected coefficient
r_{xx} and r_{yy} = the reliability of measures (scales) x and y

Basically, the degree of variability in test performance impacts the reliability estimate. Groups with large variances (heterogeneous) display markedly higher reliability estimates than groups whose members are similar (homogeneous).

STANDARD ERROR OF MEASUREMENT

Let us assume an infinite number of equal and parallel forms of a test could be created and administered to the same individual with no carryover effects (e.g., practice, familiarity, or fatigue). This would result in a normal distribution of scores that represent every possible legitimate score the individual could obtain on the tests of the given trait. No two scores may be exactly the same because every observed score also includes random error variance. Even if each test administration measured the trait or construct equally well, the examinee is likely to obtain different scores due to random error. Sometimes error results in a person obtaining higher scores. For example, all of us have experienced the surprise of passing an exam for which we were unprepared. At other times, error would result in obtaining lower scores. A normal distribution of test scores occurs by assembling all the scores from these hypothetical administrations. The mean of this distribution would be the examinee's true score, whereas the standard deviation of this distribution is referred to as the *standard error of measurement* (SE_M). The error associated with each score contributes to the resulting normal distribution.

The SE_M holds particular implications for the interpretation of observed scores inasmuch as it is a direct function of the reliability of a test and provides an estimate of the error associated with an examinee's observed score. The calculation of the SE_M is a simple matter:

$$SE_M = SD\sqrt{1 - r_{xx}}$$

Where

SD = Standard deviation of the test
r_{xx} = reliability of the test

As the reliability (i.e., the true score variance associated with test scores) of a test increases, the SE_M (i.e., the error variance associated with test scores) decreases. Stated differently, the lower the SE_M, the more precisely a test assesses the underlying trait or traits. Thus, the lower the SE_M, the more confidence we have that the person's observed score is his or her true score on that test and accordingly the more confident the clinician can be in the results of the assessment.

For clinicians, the SE_M is especially useful in calculating *confidence intervals*—that is, the range of scores within which the examinee's true score likely falls. Recall that, if an individual could be tested repeatedly on a construct with no carryover or practice effects, the hypothetical distribution of an examinee's scores would be normally distributed, with the mean of the distribution being the examinee's true score and the standard deviation of this distribution being the error associated with each observed score. The SE_M is the standard deviation of the distribution of these intraindividual differences. Approximately 68% of the examinee's observed test scores will fall within one SE_M (i.e., the standard deviation) of his/her true score (i.e., the mean of the distribution). Approximately 95% of the examinee's observed scores will fall within 1.96 SE_M.

Let's assume we are evaluating a patient with chronic pain and we want to determine the impact of pain on daily activities. We use a rating scale developed in our hospital. Our hypothetical rating scale is completed by a caregiver and has a range of 0 (no pain) to 100 (intense debilitating chronic pain). If the test has a SE_M of 5, confidence intervals may be constructed around an observed score that indicate the likelihood that the patient's true score is measured. That is, if an examinee obtained an observed score of 78, we could bet with 68% confidence that his/her true score falls within an interval established by one SE_M (i.e., a range of 73 to 83—one standard error of measurement around the observed score of 78). Under this circumstance, we would be about 68% certain that this range of scores captures the patient's true score in pain response. The confidence interval may be expanded or diminished depending on the degree of certitude the examiner desires in the scores. The use of smaller confidence intervals provides a more exacting range of scores, albeit one that may not include the true score and thus may be less accurate. The use of larger confidence intervals provides less exacting scores, albeit ones that likely include the true score. As a cautionary note, a clinician should keep in mind that the use of large confidence intervals may offer results that are clinically meaningless. For example, the SE_M of many intelligence tests is on the order of 3 to 4 points. Suppose that a patient obtains an IQ of 80, in the low average range of intellectual ability and the $SE_M = 4$. At a 95% confidence interval (1.96 SE_M), the scores range from 72 to 88. A 99% confidence interval (2.58 SE_Ms) may offer a possible range of scores from 70 (possibly mentally handicapped) to 90 (average). The SE_M and associated confidence intervals serve to

remind practitioners that no test is perfectly accurate. One observed score is unlikely to portray fully an examinee's true abilities, skills, and traits precisely. Consequently, accepted practice dictates that examiners report scores in light of confidence intervals.

Case Study 7.2—Applying the SE$_M$

The scores below were drawn from a comprehensive assessment of Jennifer, a 14-year-old adolescent female hospitalized for suicidal ideation and chemical dependency. In order to obtain confidence intervals for Jennifer's observed score (X_0), we need to apply the SE_M for each of the subtests. Although all subtests have an identical mean (10) and standard deviation (3), each has a different reliability. Therefore, each subtest has a different associated SE_M. Recall that, for each subtest, the SE_M represents the standard deviation of a hypothetical distri-

bution of observed scores if Jennifer were to be tested an infinite number of items. The mean of this hypothetical distribution would be Jennifer's true score. Characteristics of the normal distribution dictate that approximately 68% of the scores fall within ± 1 SE_M from the mean, 95% fall within ± 1.96 SE_M, and 99% fall within ± 2.58 SE_M. Applying this logic to Jennifer's observed performance on the Similarities subtest, we can be 68% confident that Jennifer's true score likely falls in the interval of 7 ± 1.64; that is, between 5.36 and 8.64.

Subtest	Obtained Standard Score	Estimated Reliability Coefficient	Calculated SE$_M$	68% Confidence Interval	95% Confidence Interval
Word Reasoning	9	.60	1.90	7.10 to 10.90	5.28 to 12.72
Similarities	7	.70	1.64	5.36 to 8.64	3.79 to 10.21
Information	10	.71	1.62	8.38 to 11.62	6.83 to 13.17
Vocabulary	6	.76	1.46	4.54 to 7.46	3.14 to 8.86
Comprehension	8	.77	1.43	6.57 to 9.43	5.20 to 10.80

After reviewing the above table, a few conclusions are obvious. First, as reliability increases, the SE_M decreases. Therefore, the confidence intervals calculated from the SE_M also become smaller (i.e., we are more precise in our estimate of Jennifer's true score). Second, for tests with less than exceptionally high reliability, as we expand the confidence interval, the range of scores becomes large and thus sacrifices the clinical utility of our interpretations (e.g., see the Word Reasoning subtest). At

the 95% confidence interval, Jennifer's true score may range from the 7th to the 81st percentiles on this scale.

QUESTION

When should the SE_M be considered in making a diagnosis? For example, if the cutoff for a diagnosis of mental retardation is an IQ equal to or below 70, should the SE_M be a factor in making the diagnosis?

VALIDITY

Validity and Validation

The purpose of testing is to accurately describe an examinee's personal qualities. Ultimately, the challenge for the clinician is to interpret limited samples of behavior when drawing conclusions about the examinee's qualities. "*Validity* refers to the degree to which evidence and theory support the interpretation of test scores entailed

by proposed uses of the test. Validity is therefore the most fundamental consideration in developing and evaluating tests" (American Educational Research Association [AERA], et al., 1999, p. 9).

Validity theory addresses fundamental concerns about the meaning and uses of test scores. During the last century, different models of validity have been proposed, with each subsequent model reflecting advances in statistics and theory (Angoff, 1988). However, some researchers (e.g., Messick, 1989, 2000) have increasingly espoused that these different models actually represent different methods of collecting evidence to support the overall validity of a test. Therefore, models of validity have shifted toward a unitary concept that is supported by different types of evidence.

As described by Messick (1989), *evidence of validity* may be divided into distinct types: (a) criterion-related evidence involves a test's examination of the relationships between the test and external variables that are believed to be direct measures of the identified construct; (b) evidence based on item content examines the relevance and correspondence of the test content to the domain content; and (c) evidence of the test's internal structure and construct validity includes the integration of findings from research to infer the meaning or interpretation of a test's scores. Each of these forms of evidence is discussed below.

Evidence Based on Test Score Relations to Other Variables (Criterion-Related Validity)

Criterion validity may be defined as "the correlation between the actual test scores and the . . . criterion score (Cureton, 1951, p. 623). Support for validity often can be inferred by examining the relationship between test scores to other relevant variables, typically called a *criterion*. A criterion is an attribute or outcome of primary interest that is represented by a variable. For example, research indicates that a robust predictor of outcomes in the vocational rehabilitation of individuals with psychiatric disabilities is the continuing severity of symptoms, such as enduring withdrawal or blunt affect (Bolton, 2001a; Pickett, Cook, & Razanno, 1999). In this instance, these findings offer valid evidence that the patient's symptomology should be a consideration when determining expected outcomes of interventions.

The *criterion model* comes in two versions, concurrent and predictive validity (Anastasi & Urbina, 1997; Messick, 1989). *Concurrent validity* studies examine the correlation between a test and a criterion, with scores on each variable obtained at the same time. Using an example drawn from the vocational rehabilitation literature, increasing levels of acceptance from peers is positively related to a patient's sense of independence and treatment acceptability (Cook and Pickett, 1994). Evidence of *predictive validity* is demonstrated in the correlation between a test and a criterion, with scores on the criterion variable obtained at some later time. For example, a client's expectation of recovery is often predictive of treatment outcomes in physical rehabilitation,

including his/her willingness to return to work (Schultz, Crook, Berkowitz, Milner, & Meloche, 2005).

In each approach to criterion validity, scores are collected and then correlated, often while controlling for the influence of confounding variables (e.g., age, level of one's education, and social class). Criterion validity approaches offer a simple and intuitively appealing approach to establishing the validity of a test or procedure. Additionally, the use of the criterion model produces objectively obtained data—a *validity coefficient*. For this reason, criterion approaches remain the gold standard in determining the validity of placement (Cronbach & Gleser, 1965), treatment outcomes (Bolton, 2001b), admissions (Guion & Highhouse, 2006), and employment decisions (Schmidt & Hunter, 2004). Evidence of predictive validity is especially useful when making high-stakes selection decisions. For example, rather than leaving matters to chance, scores from the Armed Services Vocational Assessment Battery are the military's primary means of predicting successful completion of expensive and dangerous specialized training, such as flight school (Roberts, Markham, & Matthews, 2005).

However, criterion-related methods have limitations. The primary criticism stems from the acceptable definition and selection of the criterion (Cureton, Cronbach, & Meehl, 1996). In some cases, an attempt to identify and implement a criterion that is as good as or better than the test itself (e.g., job appraisals) may be difficult. In other instances, the criterion may be difficult to conceptualize. For example, a common goal of therapists who work with recovering elderly patients may be to increase their self-determination. In order for therapists to fully comprehend the myriad of factors that may impact their patients achieving this honorable objective, all parties must have a clear understanding of what is meant by "self-determination." Complicating the matter is the possibility that "self-determination" may be a different construct in non-Western societies that place less value on individualistic pursuits.

For a validity coefficient to be useful, both the predictor and the criterion must be reliable. Simply stated, if a particular characteristic of a patient cannot be measured with accuracy, there is no point using it as a predictor. Thus, *reliability is a prerequisite for validity*. On the other hand, *reliability does not necessarily ensure validity*. For example, both hair color and temperament can be measured reliably. However, hair color is not a valid predictor of an individual's level of introversion/extroversion. In determining a test's validity through criterion methods, the criterion must be the best possible measure of the construct under investigation. We must have a well-defined and stable target to serve as the criterion. Otherwise our efforts are simply "shots in the dark" at a constantly moving target.

Contamination is particularly troublesome when evaluating evidence of criterion validity. Contamination occurs when the criterion and the predictor are not independent and instead are related by a confounding variable. For example, a clinician may complete a rating scale designed to assess a patient's psychopathology. If the clinician is aware of the patient's history, the ratings may be biased in favor of a particular diagnosis. In this case, contamination introduced by prior knowledge spuriously inflates the resulting validity coefficient, suggesting a stronger relationship between the predictor and criterion than what actually exists.

INTERPRETING VALIDITY COEFFICIENTS   Correlation coefficients portray the relationship between two variables. A *validity coefficient* should be sufficiently large to indicate the predictor will be of value in predicting an examinee's performance on the criterion. To some extent this is a subjective judgment; that is, even if a test has a small validity coefficient, it may be useful in predicting criterion performance. As a result, test developers are reluctant to specify a minimum threshold for the value of a validity coefficient. For example, the validity coefficient describing the relationship between the SAT and college performance is about .30 (Kuncel, Credé, & Thomas, 2005). Although this coefficient may appear to be low, it actually provides unique information that complements the information offered by subjective and often inflated high school grades.

Convergent and Discriminant Evidence

Convergent evidence of a test's validity is found when there is a significant relationship between a test and other instruments intended to measure the same construct. For example, individuals with mental retardation are disproportionably afflicted with personality, psychiatric, and other mental disorders, with prevalence rates approaching three to four times those seen in the general population (Masi, 1998). The combination of mental retardation and another psychological disorder is known as a *dual diagnosis*. There is an increasing interest in this condition as individuals with mental retardation are incorporated into community settings. One instrument designed explicitly for the purpose of measuring psychopathology in this population is the Psychopathological Instrument for Mentally Retarded Adults (PIMRA; Matson, 1988). However, to be a reasonable alternative to other tests, such as the Thematic Apperception Test (TAT), the PIMRA also must measure the same constructs in roughly the same degree. In building convergent evidence of the validity of the PIMRA, the authors correlated scores with more established tests that reportedly measure the same constructs (e.g., anxiety, somatoform, and aggression). Generally, the relationships were in the expected direction and magnitude (positive and strong), thereby supplying evidence in favor of the PIMRA as a measure of psychopathology.

DISCUSSION BOX 7.2

Test Validation

Reliability and validity hold considerable importance for the use of tests. Additionally, stakeholders in the assessment process (e.g., examiners, therapists, and patients) need to keep in mind that these psychometric considerations are tied to, but not necessarily bound by, the context of the assessment. As an example, Bolton (1979) reported that the validity coefficients for the *Workshop Scale of Employability* (with 500 consumers of the Chicago Workshop; Bolton, 1982) were 0.23, 0.23, and 0.26 for the three criteria of early placement, long-term placement, and maintenance, respectively. He also reported the corresponding validity coefficients for a sample of 100 consumers of the Indianapolis Goodwill Workshop were 0.43, 0.43, and 0.31, respectively. Consequently, Bolton concluded correctly that placement in employment was clearly more predictable using the *Workshop Scale* in Indianapolis than in Chicago. The rehabilitation professional then must attempt to identify the factors that may have accounted for the difference, such as economic conditions or differences among the sample groups (Power, 2006). When tests are used to make decisions about individuals or groups, all the available evidence should be studied before any attempt is made to ascertain the validity of the scores.

Questions

1. Publishers of large scale standardized tests spend considerable time, money, and effort to ensure that the standardization sample is representative of the expected clientele. What demographic variables should be considered when developing tests, and why?

Discriminant validity is based on evidence of a predictable *lack of relationship* with irrelevant or unrelated variables. Physical therapists expect tests of motor dexterity to correlate strongly with each other. Mental health counselors expect tests designed to measure depression also to correlate strongly. However, because they are different constructs, we would expect a negligible relationship between measures of manual dexterity and depression.

Recognizing the complementary nature of convergent and discriminant evidence, Campbell and Fiske (1959) combined their use into the *multi-trait/multi-method technique*. Using this technique, two traits are examined using two or more measurement methods (e.g., self-report and teacher report). The researcher then compares the actual correlations obtained with those predicted a priori by theory and past research. In addition to providing information regarding the convergent and discriminant evidence about the constructs under examination, this technique also allows the researcher to identify and account for the confounding influence of common measurement method. That is, if two theoretically different constructs (e.g., self-efficacy and attention) are correlated, the multi-trait/multi-method approach permits the clinician to determine whether this correlation may be an indication of similar methods in measurement (e.g., self-report), not a genuine overlap of true score variance from the qualities being tested.

Related to contrasting methods and traits, validity evidence also may be supplied by examining the test performance of groups that are expected to display contrasting performance on the trait or construct. For example, in developing a measure of executive functioning, the test authors may expect significant differences in performance for those with and without traumatic brain injury. Similarly, cognitive abilities display marked developmental trajectories—both up and down. Older adults are more likely to demonstrate strengths when tested on their retention of previously acquired information (i.e., crystallized abilities) than on new and novel information (i.e., fluid abilities). Among older adults, their crystallized abilities generally remain relatively stable while the ability to process new information declines. If a new test of cognition displays these patterns of differences across contrasting groups (i.e., adolescents and elderly), the evidence converges to support the validity of the construct and thus the test.

Evidence Based on Test Content (Content Validity)

Test validity also is supported by establishing a rational link between the test content and the construct or domain the test is designed to measure. The *Standards for Educational and Psychological Testing* (AERA et al. 1999) define *content* as the "themes, wording, and format of the items, tasks, or questions on a test, as well as the guidelines regarding administration and scoring" (p. 11). Evidence of *content validity* is found when the particular sampling of behaviors (i.e., test items) used to measure a trait or characteristic "reflects performance or standing on the whole domain of behaviors that constitute that trait" (Betz & Weiss, 2001, p. 53). In doing so, the coverage of a test's content should closely resemble the construct being tested.

Content coverage typically is reviewed by experts knowledgeable of the domain being tested. The influence of bias and identifiable sources of error (e.g., content and time sampling) can be minimized when the domains are defined clearly, the selected items and tasks are found to be representative, and standardized procedures for scoring and interpretation are in place. The client's performance on the sampled behaviors indicates the level of skill acquisition and mastery.

The delineation of the domains from which skills, knowledge, and behaviors are sampled is especially important. Therefore, a *table of specifications* often is used to guide test development. The table of specifications serves as a blueprint that demarcates the domains and topics to be measured matched to their relative importance in defining the overall construct. For example, when composing a test to measure reading achievement, a panel of curricular experts is likely to identify the skill components that contribute to reading mastery, including decoding skills, word recognition, comprehension, fluency, and perhaps reading speed. The relative contribution of each of these skills would be determined, items developed, and items deleted or retained on the basis of their representation of the construct of reading. The examinee's developmental characteristics would be considered inasmuch as decoding skills are more important to emergent readers while comprehension and fluency are more important at later ages. The test is considered to display content validity to the extent that items directly match the specifications of the test blueprint in terms of content relevance and coverage.

Face Validity

Discussions of content validity often incorporate the term *face validity*. A test possesses face validity if it appears to the untrained eye to measure what it is believed to measure. Face validity is concerned with the appearance of content validity rather than what the test actually measures. For example, many personality tests (e.g., the house/tree/person technique and the Rorschach Inkblot test) lack face validity because, to an untrained examiner, they do not appear to measure personality. Content validity

---

DISCUSSION BOX 7.3

A Cautionary Tale

═══

Although some professionals may believe the concepts of reliability and validity are directly important only to statisticians and test developers, these concepts have important practical implications for practitioners and patients. Consider a classic and controversial study conducted by Rosenhan (1973). Rosenhan persuaded eight pseudo-patients (including three psychologists and a psychiatrist) to gain admission to psychiatric wards in five states. The pseudo-patients, very much like authentic psychiatric patients, entered the psychiatric hospital with no foreknowledge of when they would be discharged. Rosenhan challenged each pseudo-patient to gain his/her own discharge, essentially by convincing the hospital staff that he/she was sane. Upon admission, the pseudo-patients were highly motivated to behave as "normally" as they would in their everyday lives. As it turned out, the length

of stay in the psychiatric wards for the pseudo-patients varied from 7 to 52 days, with an average of 19 days. Moreover, test data collected during their hospitalizations (i.e., clinical notes and ratings) found that true psychiatric patients were more accurate than trained professionals in detecting signs of mental sanity. In fact, many patients accurately concluded that the pseudo-patients were conducting research.

Questions

1. How might our personal views impact the reliability and validity of test results?
2. What are some disadvantages of relying exclusively on test results? What are some disadvantages of relying exclusively on clinical judgment?

---

is determined through a systematic and technical evaluation of test items, whereas face validity is determined by a cursory inspection.

Technically speaking, face validity is not a form of validity, only one's subjective impression as to whether the test appears to be measuring the desired trait. Of course, face validity is not totally irrelevant or an undesirable characteristic of a test. Examinees are more engaged in a test and motivated to perform well when tests appear to be appropriate for their intended use (Chan, Schmitt, DeShon, Clause, & Delbridge, 1997). The general public as well as many inadequately trained professionals are not likely to view a test with poor face validity as meaningful even if the available technical and psychometric evidence support its use (Ebel, 1961).

Evidence Based on Internal Structure (Construct Validity)

Because of the availability of statistical software, the most accessible and common means of obtaining evidence of validity is to examine the *internal structure* of a test or battery of tests. The structure of a test is determined by examining whether the test items are consistent with the constructs the test is intended to measure. The structure of a test typically is revealed by means of *factor analysis*, an advanced multivariate statistical procedure (Gorsuch, 2003). Factor analysis offers a simplified portrait of the constructs measured by a test. Consider the example of the *Wechsler Intelligence Scale for Children* (4th ed.)

(WISC-IV; Wechsler, 2003), which has 15 different subtests divided into 10 core and 5 supplemental subtests. Undoubtedly, the WISC-IV is not measuring 15 different constructs. Some means are needed for determining the most concise and parsimonious explanation of the interrelationships among the variables. Factor analysis is a data reduction technique used to identify a smaller number of latent variables (i.e., factors) that can best account for the variation in test scores. In the case of the WISC-IV, the 15 different subtests as well as the dozens of different correlations between these subtests can be summarized adequately by 4 factors (Wechsler, 2003). For the clinician, these factors are defined as verbal comprehension, perceptual reasoning, working memory, and processing speed.

Factor analysis also may be used to postulate beforehand that certain observed variables will be related to certain latent variables. Optimally, these relationships are guided by theory. For example, the interpretive structure of the Wechsler scales suggests that observed individual differences in the vocabulary subtest contribute to latent differences in the verbal comprehension composite. In confirming these suggested relationships, the researcher examines the empirical goodness of fit between the observed data and the associated variables that are thought to be guided by theory. A good fit occurs when the empirical data adequately match the theoretical structure of the test. Because *confirmatory factor analysis* relies heavily on theory, the use of these statistical techniques provides an ideal method for establishing the *construct validity* of tests and the theory on which they rest.

RESEARCH BOX 7.1

Scale Development (Gard, Rivano, & Grahn, 2005)

Objective: The primary purpose of this study was to describe the development of the *Motivation for Change Questionnaire* (MCQ), a test intended to assist in the rehabilitation planning process. The MCQ was developed by an international team of rehabilitation therapists and is intended for use by counselors spanning a range of disciplines.

Method: The preliminary development of the MCQ occurred in the three stages: (1) based on an exhaustive literature review, researchers and practitioners from university, hospital, and community settings identified 10 motivating factors for change in the life and work of individuals receiving rehabilitation services; (2) a large pool of items were generated based on these identified factors; and (3) following an initial tryout, a factor analysis was conducted in order to identify items that strongly measured each construct. Items that were not robust indicators of their intended factors were eliminated from the scale (item reduction). This lead to a 48-item scale that measures 9 factors related to patient motivation. Using this abbreviated final scale, 44 patients receiving treatment in a Swedish hospital completed the MCQ on two occasions, separated by a 3-to 15-day interval.

Results: Internal consistency, as indicated by Cronbach's alpha, was fair to excellent, ranging from .54 (Job Satisfaction) to .90 (Social Support). Test–retest correlations were similar, on the order of .74 across the factors measured. Factor analysis supported the internal structure of the MCQ, with correlations between individual items and their respective factor generally above .40.

Conclusions: Despite a small sample size, the findings suggest that the MCQ can identify an individual's motivating factors for change as a basis for rehabilitation. Further research is needed with particular and well-defined clinical samples that vary according to age and disability (e.g., TBI and individuals with fibromyalgia), as well as different settings.

Question

What might explain why the test–retest reliability coefficient was not higher?

Integrating Sources of Evidence

The *Standard for Educational and Psychological Testing* (AERA et al. 1999) states that "validation can be viewed as developing a scientifically sound *validity argument* to support the intended interpretation of test scores and their relevance to the proposed use" (p. 9). The term *validity argument* refers to the integration of various lines of evidence into a coherent commentary and judgment on the adequacy of a particular test and procedure (Cronbach, 1988). Table 7.3 summarizes the sources of validity evidence that may be integrated to provide a basis for the interpretation of a test (Urbina, 2004, p. 162).

TABLE 7.3 Aspects of Construct Validity and the Related Sources of Evidence.

Aspect of Validity	Source of Evidence
Content-related	Representativeness and relevance of test content, format, and response processes.
Convergence and divergence	Correlation among tests and subtests that follow patterns predicted by theory.
Multitrait–Multimethod matrix	Score differences and correlations follow patterns expected by differences in constructs, response format, and response processes.
Exploratory factor analysis	Statistical analysis indicates the interrelationships among test variables follow those advanced by theory. The pattern of interrelationships offers insights into the latent traits/constructs being measured.
Confirmatory factor analysis	Statistical analysis indicates that the a priori factor structure/model is adequately represented by the empirical data. A good fit of the data to the factor model provides evidence of construct validity.
Criterion-related	Accuracy of educational, clinical, and occupational decisions based on concurrent validation (i.e., correlations between test scores and an existing criterion/outcome).
	Accuracy of educational, clinical, and occupational decisions based on predictive validation (i.e., correlations between test scores and a predicted criterion/outcome).

As data from various studies are integrated, researchers and practitioners must remain aware that judgments pertaining to a test's validity are influenced by one's values, necessarily requiring considerations of intended and unintended consequences of the test use (Messick, 1994, 2008). Ethical principles typically require professionals to consider possible ramifications of their work and, when possible, to maximize the benefit and prevent or minimize harm to individuals and society. When applied to test use, this principle requires professionals to select tests and other assessment procedures that display acceptable and suitable reliability and validity.

Summary and Conclusion

Efforts to establish a test's reliability and validity are the shared responsibility of test authors, test publishers, researchers, and clinicians. In judging the appropriateness of test results, each of these entities needs to weigh the evidence in light of their purposes, situations, and settings. The responsibility for test selection and use ultimately rests with clinicians in that their professional work most directly impacts the lives of patients.

Self-Check Questions

1. Describe reliability as conceptualized by Classical Test Theory.
2. What is the primary difference between predictive and concurrent approaches to validity evidence?
3. How do face and content validity differ?
4. What is the impact of standardization on reliability?
5. Why is the development of a test that is valid but not reliable impossible?

References

American Educational Research Association, American Psychological Association, & National Council on Measurement in Education (1999). *Standards for educational and psychological testing.* Washington, DC: American Educational Research Association.

Anastasi, A., & Urbina, S. (1997). *Psychological testing* (7th ed.). Englewood Cliffs, NJ: Prentice-Hall, Inc.

Angoff, W. H. (1988). Validity: An evolving concept. In H. Wainer & H. Braun (Eds.), *Test validity* (pp.19–32). Hillsdale, NJ: Erlbaum.

Becker, R. (2005). *Becker Work Adjustment Profile.* Lutz, FL: Pro Ed.

Betz, N. E. & Weiss, D. J. (2001). Validity. In B. Bolton (Ed.), *Handbook of measurement and evaluation in rehabilitation* (pp.49–76). Gaithersburg, MD: Aspen Publications.

Bolton, B. (1979). *Rehabilitation counseling research.* Baltimore: University Park Press.

Bolton, B. (1982). *Vocational adjustment of disabled persons.* Austin, TX: PRO-ED.

Bolton, B. F. (2001a). *Handbook of measurement and evaluation in rehabilitation* (3rd ed.). Gaithersburg, MD: Aspen Publications.

Bolton, B. F. (2001b). Measuring rehabilitation outcomes. *Rehabilitation Counseling Bulletin, 44,* 67–75.

Bracken, B.A. (1988). Ten psychometric reasons why similar tests produce dissimilar results. *Journal of School Psychology, 26,* 155–166.

Bruininks, B. D. & Bruininks, R. H. (2006). *Bruininks-Oseretsky Test of Motor Proficiency*, 2nd Edition. Bloomington, MN: Pearson.

Bruininks, R. H., Woodcock, R. H., Weatherman, R. F., & Hill, B. K. (1996). *Scales of Independent Behavior* (Rev. ed.). Itasca, IL: Riverside Publishing.

Campbell, D. T., Fiske, D. W. (1959). Convergent and discriminant validation by the multitrait–multimethod matrix. *Psychological Bulletin, 56,* 81–105.

Carroll, J. B. (1993). *Human cognitive abilities: A survey of factor-analytic studies.* New York: Cambridge University Press.

Carrow-Woolfolk, E. (1999). *Comprehensive Assessment of Spoken Language.* Bloomington, MN: Pearson.

Caspi, A., Roberts, B. W., & Shiner, R. L. (2005). Personality development: Stability and change. *Annual Review of Psychology, 56,* 453–484.

Chan, D., Schmitt, N., DeShon, R. P., Clause, C. S., & Delbridge, K. (1997). Reactions to cognitive ability tests: The relationships between race, test performance, face validity perceptions, and test-taking motivation. *Journal of Applied Psychology, 82,* 300–310.

Cook, J. A. & Pickett, S. A. (1994). Recent trends in vocational rehabilitation for people with psychiatric disabilities. *Journal of Vocational Rehabilitation, 1,* 21–28.

Crocker, L, & Algina, J. (1986). *Introduction to classical and modern test theory.* Fort Worth: Harcourt Brace Jovanovich College Publishers.

Cronbach, L. J. (1951). Coefficient alpha and the internal structure of tests. *Psychometrika, 16,* 297–334.

Cronbach, L. J. (1988). Five perspectives on the validity argument. In H. Wainer & H. I. Braun (Eds.), *Test validity* (pp. 3–17). Hillsdale, NJ: Erlbaum.

Cronbach, L. J. (1990). *Essentials of psychological testing* (5th Ed.) New York: Harper & Row.

Cronbach, L. J. & Furby, L. (1970). How we should measure "change": Or should we? *Psychological Bulletin, 74,* 68–80.

Cronbach, L. J., & Gleser, G. C. (1965). *Psychological tests and personnel decisions.* Oxford, England: University of Illinois Press.

Cronbach, L. J. & Meehl, P. E. (1955). Construct validity in psychological tests. *Psychological Bulletin, 52,* 281–302.

Cronbach, L. J., Schonemann, P., & McKie, D. (1965). Alpha coefficients for stratified-parallel tests. *Educational and Psychological Measurement, 25,* 291–312.

Cronbach, L. J., Shavelson, R. J. (2004). My current thoughts on coefficient alpha and successor procedures. *Educational and Psychological Measurement, 64,* 391–418.

Cureton, E. E. (1951). Validity. In E. F. Lindquist (Ed.), *Educational measurement* (pp. 621–694). New York: American Council on Education.

Cureton, E. E., Cronbach, L. J., & Meehl, P. E. (1996). Validity. In: A. Ward, H. W. Stoker, & M. Murray-Ward (Eds.), *Educational measurement: Origins, theories, and explications: Vol. 1: Basic concepts and theories.* (pp. 125–243) Lanham, MD: University Press of America.

Ebel, R. L. (1961). Must all tests be valid? *American Psychologist, 16,* 640–647.

Feldt, L. S., & Brennan, R. L. (1989). Reliability. In R. L. Linn (Ed.) *Educational measurement* (pp. 105–146). New York: Macmillan Publishing Co, Inc.

Feldt, L. S. & Qualls, A. L (1999). Variability in reliability coefficients and the standard error of measurement from school district to district. *Applied Measurement in Education, 12,* 367–381.

Gard, G., Rivano, M., & Grahn, B. (2005). Development and reliability of the Motivation for Change Questionnaire. *Disability and Rehabilitation, 27*(17), 967–976.

Gorsuch, R. L. (2003). Factor analysis. In J. A. Schinka & W. Velicer, (Eds.) *Handbook of psychology: Research methods in psychology.* (pp. 143–164) Hoboken, NJ: John Wiley & Sons.

Guion, R. M., & Highhouse, S. (2006). *Essentials of personnel assessment and selection.* Mahwah, NJ: Lawrence Erlbaum Associates Publishers.

Gustafsson, J. E. (2002). Measurement from a hierarchical point of view. In H. Braun, D. Jackson, & D. E. Wiley (Eds.) *The role of constructs in psychological and educational measurement* (pp. 73–95). Mahwah, NJ: Lawrence Erlbaum Associates Publishers.

Guttman, L. A. (1945). A basis for analyzing test–retest reliability. *Psychometrika, 10,* 255–282.

Harrison, P. & Oakland, T. D. (2003). *Adaptive Behavior Assessment System* (2nd ed.) San Antonio, TX: The Psychological Corporation.

Hausknecht, J. P., Halpert, J. A., Di Paolo, N. T. (2007). Retesting in selection: A Meta-analysis of coaching and practice effects for tests of cognitive ability. *Journal of Applied Psychology, 92,* 373–385.

Kane, M. (1996). The precision of measurements. *Applied Measurement in Education, 9,* 109–133.

Kane, M. (2006). Precision of measurements. *Applied Measurement in Education, 9,* 355–379.

Keeves, J. P. (1988). *Educational research, methodology, and measurement: An international handbook.* Elmsford, NY: Pergamon Press.

Kuder, G. & Richardson, M. (1937). The theory of estimation of test reliability. *Psychometrika, 2,* 151–160.

Kuncel, N. R., Credé, M., & Thomas, L. L. (2005). The validity of self-reported grade point averages, class ranks, and test scores: A meta-analysis and review of the literature. *Review of Educational Research, 75,* 63–82.

Lauchlan, F. & Boyle, C. (2007). Is the use of labels in special education helpful? *Support for Learning, 22,* 36–42.

Linn, R. L. (Ed.) (1989). *Educational Measurement: 3rd Edition,* New York: Macmilan Publishing Co.

Linn, R. L. & Gronlund, N. E. (1995). *Measurement and evaluation.* Upper Saddle River, NJ: Merrill.

Masi, G. (1998). Psychiatric illness in mentally retarded adolescents: Clinical features. *Adolescence, 33,* 425–434.

Matson, J. L. (1988). *The Psychopathology Instrument for Mentally Retarded Adults.* Orland Park, IL: International Diagnostic Systems.

Messick, S. (1989). Validity. In R. L. Linn (Ed.), *Educational measurement* (pp. 13–103). New York: American Council on Education.

Messick, S. (1994). Foundations of validity: Meaning and consequences in psychological assessment. *European Journal of Psychological Assessment, 10,* 1–9.

Messick, S. (1999). Psychological assessment. In D. Bersoff (Ed.) *Ethical conflicts in psychology* (pp. 283–337). Washington, DC: American Psychological Association.

Messick, S. (2000). Consequences of test interpretation and use: The fusion of validity and values in psychological assessment. In R. D. Goffin & E. Helmes (Eds.), *Problems and solutions in human assessment: Honoring Douglas N. Jackson at Seventy* (pp. 3-20.). New York: Plenum Publishers.

Messick, S. (2008). Test validity and the ethics of assessment. In D. N. Bersoff (Ed.), *Ethical conflict in psychology* (4th ed., pp. 273–275). Washington, DC: American Psychological Association.

Nunnally, J. & Bernstein, I. (1994) *Psychometric Theory*. New York: McGraw Hill,

Picket, S. A., Cook, J. A., & Razzano, L. (1999). Psychiatric rehabilitation services and outcomes: An overview. In A. Horwitz & T. L. Scheid (Eds.), *A handbook for the study of mental health: Social contexts, theories, and systems* (pp. 484–492). New York: Cambridge University Press.

Power, P. (2006). *A guide to vocational assessment*. Austin, TX: PRO-ED.

Reynolds, C. R., Livingston, R., & Willson, V. (2006). *Measurement and assessment in education*. New York: Pearson.

Roberts, R., Markham, P. M., & Matthews, G. (2005). Assessing intelligence: Past, present, and future. In O. Wilhelm & R.W. Engle (Eds.), *Handbook of understanding and measuring intelligence*. (pp. 333–360), Thousand Oaks, CA: Sage Publications, Inc.

Rosenhan, D. L. (1973). On being sane in insane places. *Science, 179,* 250–258.

Rosenthal, R., Jacobson, L. (1968). *Pygmalion in the classroom: Teacher expectation and pupils' intellectual development*. New York: Holt, Rinehart & Winston.

Sattler, J. (2001). *Assessment of children* (4th ed.). San Diego, CA: Author.

Schmidt, F. L., & Hunter, J. (2004). General mental ability in the world of work: Occupational attainment and job performance. *Journal of Personality and Social Psychology, 86,* 162–173.

Schultz, I. Z., Crook, J., Berkowitz, J., Milner, R., & Meloche, G. R. (2005). Predicting return to work after low back injury using the psychosocial risk for occupational disability instrument: A validation study. *Journal of Occupational Rehabilitation, 15*(3) 365–376.

Spearman, C. (1904). 'General intelligence,' objectively determined and measured. *American Journal of Psychology, 15,* 201–293.

Thorndike, R. L (1951). Reliability. In: E. F. Lindquist (Ed.) *Educational measurement.* (pp. 560–620). New York: American Council on Education.

Thorndike, R. M. (2001). Reliability. In: B. Bolton (Ed.), *Handbook of measurement and evaluation in rehabilitation* (pp. 29–48). Gaithersburg, MD: Aspen Publications.

Thurstone, L. L. (1925). *The fundamentals of statistics.* Oxford, England: Macmillan.

Urbina, S. (2004). *Essentials of psychological testing.* Hoboken, NJ: John Wiley & Sons.

VandenBos, G. R. (2007). *APA dictionary of psychology.* Washington, DC: APA.

Wechsler, D. (1997). *Wechsler Adult Intelligence Scale* (3rd ed.). San Antonio, TX: The Psychological Corporation.

Wechsler, D. (2003). *Wechsler Intelligence Scale for Children* (4th ed.). San Antonio, TX: The Psychological Corporation.

Wechsler, D. (2004). *WISC-IV integrated technical and interpretive manual.* San Antonio, TX: The Psychological Corporation.

Westen, D., Lohr, N., & Silk, K.R. (1990). Object relations and social cognition in borderlines, major depressives, and normals: A thematic apperception test analysis, *Psychological Assessment, 2,* 355–364.

Wilson, B., Cockburn, J. & Baddeley, A. (1986). *Rivermead Behavioral Memory Test.* San Antonio, TX: The Psychological Corporation.

Wilson, B. A., Greenfield, E., Clare, L, Baddeley, A., Cockburn, J., Watson, P., Tate, R., Sopena, S., & Nannary, R. (2008). *Rivermead Behavioural Memory Test*, 3rd Edition. Los Angeles, CA: Western Psychological Services.

Woodcock, R. W., McGrew, K. S., & Mather, N. (2001). *Examiner's manual. Woodcock-Johnson III Tests of Cognitive Ability.* Itasca, IL: Riverside Publishing.

Standards for Selecting Tests and Other Assessment Methods

MARY E. STAFFORD
University of Houston–Clear Lake

OVERVIEW

Standards for selecting tests and other assessment instruments for the purposes of documenting functional abilities in patients who have health needs are necessary to ensure that the instruments address referral issues and provide accurate and timely information. This chapter discusses standards for the selection of tests and other assessment methods, provides an historic perspective on the development of these standards as well as the systems of classification of disability and functioning, provides a checklist to help assessment specialists select appropriate assessment instruments, discusses cultural and professional issues that influence instrument selection, and summarizes national and international standards for assessment.

LEARNING OBJECTIVES
By the end of this chapter, readers should be able to:

- Identify specific standards related to assessment
- Discuss the history of sources of codes of testing standards
- Identify and explain cultural and professional issues related to standards for testing
- Define the following keywords: (a) code of ethics, (b) standards for test selection, (c) ethical principles, and (d) classification systems
- Relate selection of assessment instruments to goals, processes, and outcomes of assessment

INTRODUCTION

Professionals strive to provide services of the highest quality. Their quality can be determined, in part, by reviewing them in light of professional standards. All health care professions use tests. Thus, standards are needed to direct test selection and use, evaluate their effectiveness, and develop a common language that addresses these issues—thereby better serving the public good. Consider the following:

> Mr. P was brought by ambulance to the hospital emergency room. The doctors and nurses evaluated him and determined that he had suffered a stroke. He was stabilized over the next several days and his functional cognitive, language, and motor abilities began improving. After a week he was transferred for further therapy to a rehabilitation center at which you work. You receive a referral to evaluate Mr. P's functioning. How do you proceed with selecting assessments for intervention? This chapter discusses standards for selecting assessment instruments. The standards have been developed to establish best practices in assessment.

Assessment specialists working in rehabilitation settings use various measures to evaluate the patient's levels of functioning in multiple areas, to determine environmental and systemic factors that may facilitate or limit the patient's recovery, and to document progress toward functional goals. Professionals need confidence that data upon which they base their decisions address important issues in reliable and valid ways. This chapter focuses on issues important to assessment specialists as they strive to select tests that meet these broad and important goals.

Assessment in rehabilitation and health is critical in our efforts to provide beneficial interventions that enable patients to function to their fullest potential and to have as much independence as they are capable of handling safely when navigating their surroundings. We want to be confident that we have the best data upon which to base an intervention, and we want

to provide the greatest protection for the patient. Discussion in this chapter focuses on the definitions related to this topic and standards that currently exist for selection of tests and other assessment methods; relevant settings for which this discussion of standards for assessment apply; an historical perspective on the development of these standards, as well as the systems of classification of disability and functioning that drive the selection of tests and other assessment methods; a selection checklist for a step-by-step approach to help examiners in the process of selecting appropriate assessment instruments; cultural and professional issues that relate to the selection of assessment instruments; and national and international standards for assessment.

DEFINITIONS AND STANDARDS RELATED TO ASSESSMENT

A *test* is any procedure or method to examine or determine the presence of some factor or phenomenon; a standard set of questions or other items designed to assess knowledge, skills, interests, or other characteristics of an examinee; or a set of operations, usually statistical in nature, designed to determine the validity of a hypothesis (VandenBos, 2006; see also chapters 5 and 7). A test can be standardized and thus provide specific rules for its administration and scoring, and may provide suggestions that guide data interpretation. Most neuropsychological, intelligence, achievement, or personality tests are standardized and thus display these requirements.

Other tests are nonstandardized and thus are less likely to provide specific rules for their administration and scoring. Interviews, screening measures, bedside tests, and others used commonly by rehabilitation specialists display these qualities.

The term *assessment* refers to overall investigation into an individual's functional capacities and limitations. Some assessments are brief, perhaps using one measure. Others are comprehensive, utilizing information from interviews, observations, record reviews, and various standardized and informal tests.

Standards governing test use (American Educational Research Association [AERA], American Psychological Association [APA], & National Council on Measurement in Education [NCME], 1999), a topic broader than the one addressed in this chapter, emphasize the importance of acquiring information from various sources (e.g., the patient and others who know him or her), by using various assessment methods (e.g., interviews, observations, standardized tests) in order to examine various traits (e.g., adaptive behavior, cognition, language, motor, sensory perception, and acuity) displayed in various settings (e.g., home, work, school) over time (historically and currently).

Most professional organizations have *codes of ethics* that contain both principles and standards that govern acceptable practice. Their main goals are to inform the public as to professional standards they can expect and to inform professionals of deserved and often required conduct.

Ethical principles identify virtues to which practitioners strive. They may emphasize laudatory behaviors such as to do no harm and to show respect for the patient's dignity and worth. Although behaviors stated as standards in ethical standards are required to be displayed, ethical principles are desired and not required.

Ethical standards specify behaviors that members of the professional organization are expected to follow (Koocher & Keith-Spiegel, 2008). Standards related to assessment typically include those governing the selection, administration, and scoring of tests, reporting and interpreting test results, and informing the patient of the nature of the tests and their rights in the assessment process. The following assessment standards exemplify a comprehensive albeit general set from one organization (Joint Committee on Testing Practices, 2004, pp. 5–11):

- Test users should select tests that meet the intended purpose and that are appropriate for the intended test takers.
- Test users should administer and score tests correctly and fairly.
- Test users should report and interpret test results accurately and clearly.
- Test users should inform test takers about the nature of the test, test taker rights and responsibilities, the appropriate use of scores, and procedures for resolving challenges to scores.

More specific standards are written for each of these broad categories.

Although some may believe these standards apply only to the use of standardized measures, they also apply to nonstandardized and clinical assessment methods. This chapter focuses primarily on the application of the first standard (i.e., test users should select tests that meet the intended purpose and that are appropriate for the intended test takers).

PURPOSES OF ASSESSMENT

There are multiple purposes of assessment (Hinderer & Hinderer, 2005). Among these purposes are uses of tests to evaluate specific behaviors, traits, or functional skills in depth; to provide information for planning interventions; to monitor progress; and to examine the support systems that facilitate the patient's recovery. Thus, test data are used to derive a diagnosis and to develop and evaluate interventions. When forming a diagnosis, a professional aligns a patient's personal limitations with professionally established criteria. When developing appropriate interventions, assessment specialists gather test data about the patient's personal abilities as well as about the characteristics of the patient's environment that will facilitate or inhibit the patient's recovery (see chapter 4 for further discussion of this issue).

Professionals generally rely on a *classification system* when determining what symptoms fall into which diagnoses. These systems provide standards for determining what illness or disorder a patient is likely to display or, in a more recent classification system, a patient's general functioning. Classification systems typically are based on research evidence and developed by highly acclaimed experts on classification. For example, the requirements for a diagnosis of mental retardation (i.e., subaverage intellectual functioning along with concurrent deficits in adaptive functioning) are based on years of research together with public policy.

The focus of assessment on patients' functional abilities and limitations is more recent. This focus is consistent with the goal to implement medical, social, psychological, behavioral, or other forms of interventions in light of a patient's functional needs and desires. Interventions must be based on reliable and valid data, often acquired through the use of tests that indicate what a patient can and cannot do. Strengths and limitations are reviewed in light of the functional skills that a patient needs and/or desires. Accurate assessment is dependent on maintaining high standards for selecting tests and other assessment methods and administering and scoring those measures accurately.

Assessment specialists often begin their work by developing *hypotheses* about what may be wrong with the patient. The hypotheses represent the assessment specialist's best-informed judgment about the patient's functioning and what diagnosis the patient's symptoms are likely to suggest. Classification systems can provide the assessment specialist with information for developing hypotheses. The hypotheses are developed from the assessment specialist's understanding of the characteristics

DISCUSSION BOX 8.1

Taking your loved one to be admitted to a rehabilitation center

Your aunt has had a stroke and, following hospitalization, is transferred to a rehabilitation center. She is able to speak, but slurs her words and is not easily understood. Her left arm and leg are paralyzed, and she needs some assistance when eating.

Questions

1. What assessment information would you expect to follow her from the hospital to the rehabilitation center?

2. What functional abilities and needs should the rehabilitation center staff assess?

3. How much should you participate in the assessment process on behalf of your aunt?

4. What questions might you expect during the assessment about the sources of support and home environment in which your aunt lives?

and criteria that comprise the affected areas of functioning. The assessment specialist selects assessment methods based on this hypothesis to determine the level of the patient's functional ability and limitation.

APPLICABILITY OF ASSESSMENT STANDARDS

Virtually all professions use tests and other assessment tools. Thus, professions that use standards include but are not limited to the following: counselors, educators, nurses, occupational therapists, physicians, physical therapists, speech–language pathologists, psychologists, and others engaged in the rehabilitation process. The standards address standardized and nonstandardized measures, those used in settings throughout the rehabilitation process (e.g., emergency room, patient's hospital room, rehabilitation center, nursing care facility, educational institutions, and home or assisted living facility). The availability of a common set of standards for assessment benefits all professions by prescribing methods designed to protect patients while promoting effective service delivery systems (Johnston, Keith, & Hinderer, 1992).

The following section discusses the historical background of classification systems often used by rehabilitation specialists as well as standards designed to ensure that patients' needs are addressed and their rights and dignity respected.

HISTORY OF THE DEVELOPMENT OF STANDARDS FOR TESTING

Various classification systems have been developed to aid assessment specialists in diagnosing and developing interventions based on functioning and disability. A system for classifying diseases had its origins in the 1850s (World Health Organization [WHO], 2006a). The first edition, the *International List of Causes of Diseases*, was developed and, in 1893, was adopted by the International Statistical Institute. When WHO was formed in 1948, it assumed responsibility for this classification system with the publication of the 6th edition, now called the *International Statistical Classification of Diseases* [ICD]. The ICD has become the international standard diagnostic classification for epidemiology and health management (World Health Organization [WHO], 2006a). The current ICD-10 can be found at http://www3.who.int/icd/currentversion/fr-icd.htm (WHO, 2006b).

In 1952, the American Psychiatric Association developed its first *Diagnostic and Statistical Manual* (DSM-I) to provide criteria for classifying mental health disorders. The current DSM (4th ed.) (DSM-IV-TR) continued this tradition (American Psychiatric Association, 2000).

In 2001, WHO developed the *International Classification of Functioning, Disability and Health* (ICF) to focus on various domains of functional abilities. It provides a system for diagnosing disabilities and assessing the functional levels in both primary and secondary disabilities. For example, a patient may have a severe respiratory disability that requires the use of oxygen. Knowledge of how the patient functions in activities and what restrictions to activity are evident, together with an understanding of the effect of the respiratory disability on mental functions (e.g., on one's energy levels, drive, and memory) provide information necessary for the development of interventions for the patient.

The ICF classification system addresses body functions and structures, activities and participation, and environmental factors (WHO, 2001). Compared to previous classification systems that focus on either physical or mental disorders and deficits, the ICF addresses both disability and functioning throughout areas of the human body together with recognition of a person's engagement in his or her environment. The ICF also is unique by classifying both mental and physical functioning, not one or the other. This inclusion is important because·it acknowledges reciprocal relationships between physical and mental health.

Standards for assessment also have their history. These standards often are embedded in professional ethics codes. The Hippocratic Oath (400 B.C.E.) was the first example of a professional code of ethics, one for medicine (Leach & Oakland, 2007). Standards for assessment now are found in codes from various professional associations, principally from those whose members commonly use behavioral measures. These associations include those for counselors (American Counseling Association [ACA], 2005; American School Counselor Association [ASCA], 2004; Association for Assessment in Counseling [AAC], 2003b); psychologists (American Psychological Association [APA], 2002; International School Psychology Association [ISPA], 1991; National Association of School Psychologists [NASP], 2000); and speech therapists (American Speech–Language–Hearing Association [ASHA], 2003). Ethics codes of other professional organizations typically address assessment in a general way (e.g., the code of ethics for physical therapists; American Physical Therapy Association [APTA], 2004). Most codes have been developed by one professional association and only for its members. Codes typically are revised every 10 to 20 years to reflect changes in practices and issues impacting professional service.

Starting in the mid-1960s a new trend occurred, one in which standards for assessment were developed by three or more associations. For example, a joint commission comprised of three professional organizations (i.e., the American Educational Research Association [AERA], American Psychological Association [APA], and the National Council on Measurement in Education [NCME]) was formed specifically for the purpose of defining standards for test development and use (AERA, APA, & NCME, 1966). Its latest edition of the Standards was published in 1999 (AERA et al., 1999).

The Joint Committee on Testing Practices [JCTP] is another multiprofessional body, with expanded representation from the American Counseling Association, American Educational Research Association, American Psychological Association, American Speech–Language–Hearing Association, National Association of School

Psychologists, National Association of Test Directors, and National Council on Measurement in Education. Its *Code of Fair Testing Practices in Education* is intended to be consistent with relevant parts of the Standards discussed above (AERA et al., 1999). Its purpose is to advance the quality of testing practices (JCTP 2004).

Efforts are underway to develop measurement standards for use in interdisciplinary medical rehabilitation. A report from the American Congress of Rehabilitation Medicine's Task Force on Measurement and Evaluation (Johnston, Keith, & Hinderer, 1992) is an initial attempt to propose standards for assessment applicable to all professions that provide assessment services to patients in need of medical rehabilitation (e.g., speech therapy, occupational therapy, rehabilitation nursing, psychology, rehabilitation counseling, physiatry).

STANDARDS FOR SELECTING ASSESSMENT MEASURES

Both the *Code of Fair Testing Practices in Education* (JCTP 2004) and the *Measurement Standards for Interdisciplinary Medical Rehabilitation* (Johnston, Keith, & Hinderer, 1992) present standards that address standardized tests. Many of these standards also apply to nonstandardized clinical assessment methods. The standards from these documents were converted into questions and are presented in Table 8.1. This table lists important issues an assessment specialist should consider when selecting assessment tools: Define the purpose of testing, evaluate the availability of testing tools, select the best ones, provide accommodations if needed, and evaluate one's administrative skills.

Table 8.1 is structured in the following way. Two columns appear to the right of each question. One applies to standardized tests (*S*), and the other applies to nonstandardized assessment methods (*N*). Standards for best practices in assessment are met by answering *yes* to every question. When the cell to the right of the question under the *S* column is not shaded, the question relates to standardized tests; when the cell under the *N* column is not shaded, the question relates to nonstandardized clinical methods.

Defining the Purpose of Testing

The first step in selecting a test is to define the purpose for using it (JCTP 2004). The question in section A in the checklist (see Table 8.1) addresses this standard. An assessment is inadequate if it begins with poorly defined presenting problems that the assessment specialist is

TABLE 8.1 Checklist for Selecting Tests and Other Assessment Methods	S	N
Directions: Place a check in the blank boxes to the right, if the answer to the question is "Yes." To select an appropriate test for the assessment, you should be able to answer yes to each question.		
A. Defining the purpose of testing		
1. Have you fully defined in observable, measurable terms the primary purpose or complaint that the patient has and for which you will do the assessment?		
B. Evaluating available tests or other assessment methods		
1. Before selecting a test or other assessment method, have you evaluated a representative sample of test questions and/or practice tests, directions, answer sheets, manuals, and score reports?		
2. For the tests you consider using, did their manuals adequately describe the development of the instrument and its norming and scaling processes?		
3. Have you evaluated the test's technical qualities by reviewing information in the test manual, research articles, and test reviewers?		
Specifically, does the test:		
a) Provide evidence of good reliability for measuring the constructs to be assessed?		
b) Provide information about standard errors of measurement and confidence intervals?		
c) Provide evidence of adequate validity to address the reasons for using the test and in light of the patient's demographic qualities?		
d) Provide information about norms for the comparison group to which the patient belongs?		
4. Following your review, have you found the test procedures and materials to not be potentially offensive in content and language?		
C. Selecting the best test or other assessment method		
1. Have you selected a test or other assessment method that:		
a) Addresses the needs for the assessment in light of the test's content and skills?		
b) Is appropriate in light of the patient's age, gender, cultural/racial/ethnic, and developmental level?		
c) Has clear, accurate, and complete psychometric information?		
d) Has the potential of providing information relevant to the development or evaluation of intervention(s) for this patient?		
D. Providing accommodations for subgroups		
1. If the test taker has disabilities that require special accommodations, have you selected tests for which modified forms and/or administration procedures exist or can be developed?		
2. If the test takers are members of diverse subgroups, have you evaluated cultural learning factors relevant to test-taking behaviors and determined to the extent feasible which performance differences are likely to be caused by factors related to culture rather than skills being assessed?		
E. Evaluating your administration skills for the selected test		
1. Do you have the appropriate knowledge, skills, and training to properly administer the selected assessment method?		

Note: **S** = standard that applies to use of standardized instruments; **N** = standard that applies to nonstandardized assessment methods (e.g., bedside practices, informal interviews, etc.).

asked to address. Without a measurable understanding of the patient's problem, the results of the assessment are likely to lack meaning.

For example, if a patient, following an accident, presents with a complaint that he or she feels bad, the professional does not have sufficient information to know where to begin the assessment. Thus, in the beginning of the assessment, one first must obtain a clear understanding of all of the aspects of the complaint. On occasion, referrals received by assessment specialists from other rehabilitation specialists are too vague to guide the purposes of the requested testing and thus require clarification (see chapter 4 for a further discussion of this issue).

Let's assume you have received a referral from a neurologist of a 38-year-old woman who reported experiencing muscle weakness in her right hand and arm during the last month. She also reported that her hand and arm "go to sleep," and feeling is gone for some hours. This information adds to an understanding of potential areas of focus for assessment (e.g., evidence of stroke along motor pathways in brain, muscular strength in arms, infectious process in body, pinched nerves) and to a beginning definition of the chief complaint. Thus, the professional can narrow the possible areas that must be assessed. The assessment specialist now can focus on selecting the assessment instruments that will evaluate the woman's functioning in reference to the referral.

Evaluating Available Tests or Other Assessment Methods

Standards instruct assessment specialists to review the prospective test or tests, manuals, record forms, test questions, score reports, together with other supporting materials to determine whether the test content and coverage as well as skills tested are appropriate and their content and language are not offensive (JCTP, 2004). This includes evaluating the evidence for the technical quality of the test or other assessment method—that is, its reliability and validity.

Questions in section B of Table 8.1 address these standards. The review of the test should address the appropriateness of test content, skills tested, and content coverage for the intended purpose. Thus, the assessment specialist needs to determine whether the questions asked on the test or the skills the patient is asked to perform actually reflect the important qualities needing assessment. The content coverage refers to whether the test fully addresses every aspect of the purpose of the assessment.

Questions 3a through 3d address standards related to the test's reliability and validity. A test's manual reports information on its reliability and validity. However, this information together with other information found in research articles, books, and test reviews may need to be considered to form a clear understanding of the test's reliability and validity for your intended purposes. A test may have good estimates of reliability and validity for measuring one thing (for example, self-concept) and poor reliability and validity to measure something else (e.g., depression). This point may seem trivial yet is important. One must evaluate the reliability and validity of a test in light of evidence that it measures the qualities for which the test is being used.

RELIABILITY[1]   Reliability refers to the trustworthiness or the accuracy of a measure (AERA et al., 1999; Kurpius & Stafford, 2006). Thus, a test's reliability typically is *estimated* based on the *internal consistency* and *stability* of a test's scores. Internal consistency refers to the degree to which all parts of a test measure the same construct. The Cronbach's alpha test typically is used to estimate internal consistency. Stability refers to the degree to which a test measures the same quality at different times or in different situations. The term, *test–retest reliability*, refers to the consistency of scores obtained from the same persons when tested on two or more occasions. A test is considered to be reliable if the scores provide consistent information about the person, (see chapter 7 for additional details).

Greater diligence and higher standards are needed when making high-stakes than low-stakes decisions. Thus, estimates of internal consistency generally should be .90 or higher when data are being used to assist in making high-stakes decisions and .80 or higher when making low-stakes decisions (Wasserman & Bracken, 2002). On occasion, reliable estimates of tests used in making clinical decisions may not reach .90. Thus, clinicians may consider reliability estimates between .70 and .79 to be fair, and clinical decisions should be supportable by other strong evidence. Estimates between .80 and .90 are considered to be good, and those above .90 to be excellent (Cicchetti & Sparrow, 1990). Tests with internal reliability estimates below .70 generally are considered to be too unstable to be used with confidence.

Reliability coefficients rarely, if ever, reach +1.00 because every measure has some error. Every test score is composed of three scores: the score the person obtains on a test (called the observed score), a person's true score, and an error score. Because all tests have some error, a person's observed score never is the true score. Tests with lower reliability have more error. We have less assurance a person's observed score equals his or her true score when there is low reliability and thus considerable error. See chapters 6 and 7 for a discussion of standard error of measurement.

VALIDITY   According to the *Standards for Educational and Psychological Testing* (AERA et al., 1999), "the process of [test] validation involves accumulating evidence to provide a sound scientific basis for the proposed score interpretations" (p. 9). Evidence of validity

---

[1]See chapter 7 for a more thorough discussion of reliability and validity.

is accumulated through various studies that eventually will lead us to know the degree of support that exists for a test to be used in one or more ways. The assessment specialist makes a decision of the degree to which a test is valid based on its use over time as well as empirical evidence and other forms of scholarship.

As with reliability, standards exist for evaluating validity. Like reliability coefficients, test manuals and other sources report correlations or other measures that show relationships between test score and some other important behaviors. Tests with higher validity coefficients allow us to use a test with greater confidence. Validity coefficients also range from 0 to 1.00. The higher the coefficient, the higher the validity and thus the greater confidence we have in using a test's scores to make decisions.

Reliability and validity coefficients provide important psychometric information as to the confidence one has in the interpretation of test scores. These coefficients have specific meaning in measurement and, as discussed above, are expressed most often in quantitative terms. However, it is more difficult to determine the reliability and validity of informal tests or measures. If these methods have been used over time and have been shown to be consistent in giving accurate information, they can be seen as being reliable. If one can use the test results of the nonstandardized method to predict systematically the patient's future behavior, the test is likely to be valid. The issue for using both formal and informal methods of assessment centers on how much confidence one has that the results of the test yield a reliable (i.e., consistent, stable, accurate) result that can be used to describe current behavior or predict future behavior or circumstance (i.e., a valid result). Standards for selecting assessment tools suggest that these measures must have good reliability and validity estimates.

TEST NORMS During its development, a publisher typically administers a standardized test to a sample of persons representative of those with whom it is intended to be used in order to establish the test's norms. The norms provide information about the test's average and typical range of scores. Test norms are used to determine whether a patient's scores are higher, near, or lower than the average scores. Some tests also provide norms for males and females separately or for one or more subgroups (e.g., those with mental retardation, closed head injuries) to assist clinicians when interpreting scores from patients who display these conditions.

When selecting a test, consider the relevance of the norms in light of the test's use. When using tests to compare a client with the general population, look for test norms developed on the general population. When using tests to compare a client with others who also display specific disabilities or disorders, look for norms developed on them. Tests are more likely to have norms developed on a general population than on smaller clinical samples. When reviewing a test's norms, look for those that are larger rather than smaller, were acquired recently, and are representative of the general population, including persons from various racial/ethnic groups, socioeconomic levels (e.g., from various education levels) and with disabilities in proportion to their representation in the population.

The assessment specialist should review a test to ensure its content and language are not potentially offensive. This standard protects the relationship between the patient and assessment specialist and helps ensure the patient completes the test accurately. Thus, nonoffensive content or language enhances the accuracy of the assessment.

Selecting the Best Test or Other Assessment Method

After evaluating the available tests or other assessment methods, the assessment specialist must select the best test for the intended purpose. The questions in section C are similar to those in section B of Table 8.1 in that the evaluation of available assessment methods should lead to a conclusion that one or more tests best meet the standards. Thus, based on a review of the test's content, norms, reliability, and validity, its use is likely to provide the best information that addresses the referral issues. Although unstated, the assessment specialist also will consider practical issues such as the time required to administer and score the test, its cost, and availability.

Providing Accommodations for Subgroups

Standards for selecting tests instruct us to "select tests with appropriately modified forms or administration procedures for test takers with disabilities who need special accommodations," as well as to "evaluate the available evidence on the performance of test takers of diverse subgroups [and] determine to the extent feasible which performance differences may have been caused by factors unrelated to the skills being assessed" (JCTP, 2004, p. 5). Questions in section D of Table 8.1 address these standards.

A test's administrative procedures are designed to help ensure the test obtains either the patient's best performance or typical performance. Some tests measure a

RESEARCH BOX 8.1

Introduction: Farin, et al. (2004) present their research using the *Quality Profile* to measure the quality of rehabilitation centers in Germany. They measured the structural, process, and outcome quality of treatment in 26 cardiac and orthopedic rehabilitation centers. The *Quality Profile* is an indicator system comprised of (1) a structural quality measure to compare the quality of the center to previously defined basic criteria of structural quality; (2) a peer review of process quality; (3) the IRES questionnaire to measure outcome quality; (4) a physician's questionnaire to measure clinical parameters with admission, discharge, and goal values; (5) a patient satisfaction questionnaire; (6) an employee satisfaction questionnaire; and (7) a clinical audit involving inspection of the center by a clinical expert and quality management expert.

Objective: Farin et al. ask the following research questions:

1. What is the quality of in-patient rehabilitation centers in Germany?
2. Are in-patient rehabilitation centers in Germany similar in the quality of their care?
3. Does the *Quality Profile* indicator system adequately provide a comprehensive, comparative measurement of quality of in-patient rehabilitation centers?

Method: The researchers examined structural quality and employee satisfaction of all employees in all centers. To measure process quality, 20 randomly selected cases based on discharge reports and therapy plans were chosen in each of the 26 rehabilitation centers. To measure the medical outcome, a sample of 200 consecutively admitted patients were given the IRES questionnaire at three time points (admission, discharge, and 6-month follow-up); the physician's questionnaire provided the physician's perception of the effectiveness of treatment; and each patient completed a patient satisfaction questionnaire. Finally, a random sample of the centers participating in the program underwent a clinical audit.

Results: Farin et al. indicate that the overall level of quality of medical rehabilitation in the participating institutions was high. However, there were clear differences between centers on almost all quality dimensions, "which point to the usefulness of benchmarking analyses . . ."

Conclusion: The researchers state that the indicator system is a starting point for comprehensive, comparative measurement of the quality of in-patient rehabilitation centres.

Discussion: This article highlights a process for examining the quality of care in rehabilitation centers and reports the collection of data to assess multiple aspects of that quality. The methodological quality for the patient and employees has been assessed. However, information about the levels of reliability and validity for these or other instruments used for data collection is lacking.

Questions

1. What are the implications for understanding the results of quality assessment if the instruments used for data collection are not reliable and valid for use in rehabilitation centers?
2. What should rehabilitation centers consider when selecting instruments for assessing patient functioning and growth?

person's ability to perform tasks under ideal conditions. Examples include tests of sensory, motor, achievement, and intellectual abilities. They are administered in ways to obtain the person's best or optimal performance. In contrast, other tests measure a person's actual daily performance, not their best performance. Examples include tests of adaptive behavior, social and emotional qualities, and personality. They are administered in ways to obtain the person's typical performance.

When the goal of testing is to obtain maximum performance, methods used to administer the test must be suitable. For example, without making accommodations, test results are unlikely to yield one's best performance in patients who are acutely or chronically ill; display motor impairments, an uncorrected visual and auditory acuity disability, or diminished receptive or expressive language skills; or who lack adequate knowledge of English or another language used during the administration. For example, a test that requires visual skills, if administered to a person with visual impairment, is unlikely to yield the person's best performance. Thus, its results would be invalid.

Various accommodations may be used, including testing at certain times of the day and taking frequent breaks; the use of larger type or Braille; sound amplification or other auditory modifications; reading the test items; and the use of translators.

Test specialists should be guided by information in test manuals that discuss accommodations. However, test developers cannot anticipate the need for all forms of accommodation and thus may not discuss this issue fully in the manual. Thus, test specialists often must use their professional judgment when considering test modifications and use those that help ensure the patient's best performance without seriously jeopardizing the standardized manner in which the test typically is administered. Test specialists also may contact the test publisher or author to receive guidance on the use of accommodations. The types of accommodations used should be described in the test report.

The second standard in this section addresses issues related to diverse subgroups. The term *diverse subgroups* typically refers to persons with disabilities or disorders, of color, from low social and economic groups, and with limited English proficiency. When appropriate, test interpretations should be guided, in part, in light of the expectations and opportunities that characterize the person's environment. The assessment specialist should be alert to qualities that may have influenced the assessment significantly, including those that may have unintentionally inflated or depressed scores.

For example, optimum test performance requires a patient to be adequately motivated, cooperative, attentive, alert, and fully engaged in the tasks. Test results of persons who do not display these test-taking qualities are likely to be attenuated and thus may be invalid (Oakland, Glutting, & Watkins, 2005).

Evaluating Your Administration Skills for the Selected Test

This standard emphasizes the importance of gaining competence through training and experience to ensure test specialists administer, score, and interpret tests competently (American Counseling Association, 2005; American Psychological Association, 2002; American School Counselor Association, 2004; American Speech–Language–Hearing Association, 2003; Association for Assessment in Counseling, 2003a; International School Psychology Association, 1991; National Association of School Psychologists, 2000). The use of both standardized and nonstandardized assessment instruments requires assessment specialists to evaluate their competence to administer, score, and interpret them. Some believe this competence is most critical when using standardized tests because such tests require a specific order and exactness when using them. Deviations from standard practices may invalidate the test data. Others believe the use of nonstandardized methods require more competence in that their use requires test specialists to make informed professional

judgments on the best ways to administer, score, and interpret them. Thus, assessment specialists require training and experience in the use of a wide range of assessment tools.

CULTURAL AND PROFESSIONAL ISSUES RELATED TO SELECTION OF ASSESSMENT METHODS

Various standards exist for the provision of services to persons from diverse groups (APA), 1990; AAC, 2003b; Association for Multicultural Counseling and Development [AMCD], 1992). *Standards for Multicultural Assessment* (AAC, 2003b) provide the most inclusive set that relate to the selection of assessment methods for members of diverse groups. These standards include the issues that have been discussed previously. Some additional standards focus on test selection (see AAC, 2003b, p. 3), including the following four.

1. Select tests that are fair to all test takers.
2. Eliminate language, symbols, words, phrases, and content that generally are regarded as offensive by members of racial, ethnic, gender, or other groups, except when judged to be necessary for adequate representation of the domain.
3. Minimize the linguistic or reading demands of the test to a level necessary for the valid assessment when the level of linguistic or reading ability is critical to the assessment,
4. Describe linguistic modifications and a rational for the modifications in detail in the test manual.

Despite one's best intentions, everyone, including assessment specialists, has biases that favor or disfavor certain groups. These biases generally reflect one's cultural learning and other personal experiences. Information and guidance from family, teachers, religious groups, other community groups as well as the media help people understand their world and make judgments about the suitability of behaviors displayed by them and others.

Cultural groups may differ in their views of the world as well as the suitability of behaviors displayed by their members. Given their affiliation with one or more cultural groups, assessment specialists can be expected to have formed opinions as to behaviors that are and are not suitable. Accuracy in testing requires assessment specialists to be objective in their work. Thus, they need to be aware of their biases, work to reduce them when possible, and take steps that minimize biases that may impact

DISCUSSION BOX 8.2

Selecting tests to assess disability and functioning in stroke patients in Albania

A team of rehabilitation specialists consisting of an occupational therapist, a physical therapist, a rehabilitation nurse, and a medical doctor specializing in rehabilitative medicine from the United States have been asked by several medical doctors in Albania to assist in establishing a new clinic devoted specifically to the rehabilitation of stroke patients. One of the tasks for the visiting U.S. team is to identify assessment instruments to evaluate emotional functioning in patients, given that mental health problems, particularly depression, often are the result of diminished capacity following stroke. The U.S. team asks the Albanian doctors whether there are instruments available for evaluating a variety of mental health symptoms. They find that there are none that have been developed and normed in Albania. The U.S. team is aware of

instruments written and normed in the United States but they are concerned about the cultural relevance of those instruments for people in Albania. For example, do Albanian people manifest depressive symptoms in the same way that people in the United States do?

Questions

1. What other concerns are relevant to the discussion of appropriate tests for use with stroke victims in Albania?
2. What should the United States team recommend to the Albanian doctors regarding considerations they should make when selecting appropriate tests for use with this population?

their objectivity and thus the quality of their work. Test specialists should not engage in work that may be attenuated by their biases and instead ask others to perform it.

NATIONAL AND INTERNATIONAL STANDARDS FOR ASSESSMENT

The 2004 *Code of Fair Testing Practices in Education* was formed through the participation of American Counseling Association, American Educational Research Association, American Psychological Association, American Speech–Language–Hearing Association, National Association of School Psychologists, National Association of Test Directors, and National Council on Measurement in Education. This national effort by various associations provides strong support for the need across disciplines to develop common standards to enhance communication among those who use tests. A somewhat similar process is occurring among professions engaged in medical rehabilitation. The Task Force on Measurement and Evaluation commissioned by the American Congress of Rehabilitation Medicine has developed measurement standards for interdisciplinary medical rehabilitation (Johnston, Keith, & Hinderer (1992). This effort attempts to bring greater unity to the work of those engaged in medical rehabilitation, including physical therapy, occupational therapy, rehabilitation nursing, rehabilitation counseling, and psychiatry, among others.

Ethical standards governing assessment are found in ethics codes in at least 31 countries (Leach & Oakland, 2007). For example, those related to test selection are found in codes from 11 countries (Australia, Chile, China, Croatia, Israel, Italy, Latvia, New Zealand, Philippines, South Africa, and Turkey).

In 1991, the International Association of School Psychologists adopted an ethics code governing the delivery of school psychology services among its international membership. This code contains specific standards for assessment (Oakland, Goldman, & Bischoff, 1997).

In the 1990s, the International Test Commission (ITC) developed a set of guidelines to encourage best practice for psychological and educational testing in various linguistic and cultural contexts (International Test Commission, 2000, 2007). These guidelines were developed by a 25-member multinational council of the ITC and are recommended for use as guidelines against which national standards for assessment can be compared for coverage and international consistency throughout the world.

The American Psychological Association is working with the World Health Organization to develop international standards for applying the International Classification of Functioning (Reed et al., 2005). After being field tested, the guidelines are expected to provide a common cross-disciplinary language for discussing assessment results internationally (Stambor, 2006) and for assessing patients along the continuum of care.

Test use occurs in all professions that provide human services and in all countries. Thus, efforts to develop test standards have moved from single organizations at the national level to various organizations cooperating at the international level in developing standards for assessment. This change can be expected to create more uniform methods for test use internationally as well as to elevate standards in those countries in which test use is emerging.

Summary and Conclusion

Standards for selecting tests and other assessment methods for the purposes of documenting functional abilities in patients who have health crises are necessary to ensure that the assessment is accurate and the resulting interventions are potentially beneficial to the patient. Without standards governing their selection and use, confidence in test data and the relevance of its applications are questionable. Standards allow professionals to start with a common understanding, including language, for discussing test selection and use.

This chapter summarized standards for selecting tests and other assessment methods, including the need to define the purpose of testing; evaluate available tests or other assessment methods, including their psychometric properties; select the best test or tests; provide accommodations for subgroups; and evaluate the assessment specialist's administration skills in using tests. The brief description of relevant definitions and historic milestones in the development of test standards and systems of classification of disability and functioning was intended to promote understanding of issues that influence test selection and use, with particular emphasis on the ICF. The checklist for selecting tests and other assessment methods provides a step-by-step approach to help assessment specialists select appropriate instruments. Discussion of cultural and professional issues that influence selection of assessment instruments and national and international standards for assessment add to the understanding of standards for the selection of tests for use.

Self-Check Questions

1. What is the difference between ethical standards and ethical principles?
2. Which standards for assessment are suggested by the Joint Committee on Testing Practices (2004)?
3. Classification systems of disease and disability have existed for more than 100 years. More recently there has been a change in focus of assessment. Discuss this change in focus and how it has changed our understanding of patients' abilities and needs.
4. Why is it important to define the purpose of testing prior to selecting tests for the assessment?
5. Define reliability.
6. What are some ways to estimate the reliability of a test's scores?
7. What reliability estimate range is considered good? What is considered excellent?
8. What is the relationship between the reliability estimate, the standard error of measurement, and the confidence intervals around the observed score in a test?
9. Why are test norms important when assessing a patient's functioning?
10. Discuss reasons why it is important to evaluate your administration skills for a selected test before administrating that test.
11. Discuss the benefits and challenges of creating a common set of standards for assessment that will apply to countries around the globe.
12. Discuss the benefits and challenges of creating and enforcing a common set of standards for assessment that will apply to all fields of medical rehabilitation (e.g., physical therapy, occupational therapy, rehabilitation nursing, physiatry, rehabilitation counseling, etc.).
13. How might informal clinical questionnaires (e.g., the physician, without using a standardized test, asks the patient to describe her symptoms) become instruments that have reliability and validity estimates?

Case Study

This chapter began with Mr. P arriving by ambulance at the hospital emergency room. The doctors and nurses evaluated him and determined that he had suffered a stroke. He was stabilized over the next several days and his functional abilities began improving. After a week he was transferred to a rehabilitation center for further therapy. You work at this rehabilitation center, and when Mr. P arrives with his records, you prepare to conduct a formal assessment of his overall functional abilities. His records indicate that he has difficulty speaking, is paralyzed on his right side, and has difficulty dressing and feeding himself. You meet his wife and two adult children, all of whom appear to be concerned about Mr. P.

You have outlined a plan for the assessment, and now you must select standardized and/or nonstandardized tests to be used for gathering data on Mr. P's personal and environmental functioning. Given the standards for selection of tests and other assessment methods, what would you need to consider when selecting tests to use?

References

American Counseling Association [ACA]. (2005). *ACA code of ethics.* Alexandria, VA: Author. Retrieved September 28, 2006, from http://www.counseling.org/Resources/CodeOfEthics/TP/Home/CT2.aspx

American Educational Research Association (AERA), American Psychological Association (APA), & National Council on Measurement in Education (NCME). (1966). *Standards for educational and psychological testing.* Washington, DC: APA.

American Educational Research Association (AERA), American Psychological Association (APA), & National Council on Measurement in Education (NCME). (1999). *Standards for educational and psychological testing* (3rd ed.). Washington, DC: APA.

American Physical Therapy Association (APTA). (2004). *APTA Guide for Professional Conduct.* Alexandria, VA: Author. Retrieved September 29, 2006, from http://www.apta.org/AM/Template.cfm?Section=Home&TEMPLATE=/CM/ContentDisplay.cfm&CONTENTID=24781

American Psychiatric Association (APA). (2000). *Diagnostic and statistical manual of mental disorders* (DSM-IV-TR). Arlington, VA: Author.

American Psychological Association (APA). (1990). *APA guidelines for providers of psychological services to ethnic, linguistic, and culturally diverse populations.* Washington, DC: Author. Retrieved September 28, 2006, from http://www.apa.org/pi/guide.html

American Psychological Association (APA). (2002). Ethical principles of psychologists and code of conduct. *American Psychologist, 57,* 1060–1073.

American School Counselor Association (ASCA). (2004). *ASCA ethical standards for school counselors.* Alexandria, VA: Author. Retrieved September 28, 2006, from http://www.schoolcounselor.org/files/ethical%20standards.pdf

American School Counselor Association (ASCA), & Association for Assessment in Counseling (AAC). (1998). *Competencies in assessment and evaluation for school counselors.* Alexandria, VA: Author.

American Speech–Language–Hearing Association (ASHA). (2003). *ASHA Code of Ethics.* Rockville, MD: Author. Retrieved September 28, 2006, from http://www.asha.org/NR/rdonlyres/F51E46C5-3D87-44AF-BFDA-346D32F85C60/0/v1CodeOfEthics. pdf

Association for Assessment in Counseling [AAC]. (2003a). *Responsibilities of users of standardized tests* (3rd. ed.). Alexandria, VA: Author. Retrieved September 28, 2006, from http://aac.ncat.edu/Resources/documents/RUST2003%20v11%20Final. pdf

Association for Assessment in Counseling (AAC). (2003b). *Standards for multicultural assessment.* Alexandria, VA: Author. Retrieved September 28, 2006, from http://aac.ncat.edu/Resources/documents/STANDARDS%20FOR%20MULTICULTURAL%20ASSESSMENT%20FINAL.pdf

Association for Multicultural Counseling and Development (AMCD). (1992) *Multicultural counseling competencies and standards.* Alexandria, VA: American Counseling Association.

Cicchetti, D. V., & Sparrow, S. S. (1990). *Assessment of adaptive behavior in young psychology: A handbook* (pp. 173–196). New York: Pergamon Press.

Farin, E., Follert, P., Gerdes, N., Jackel, W. H., & Thalau, J. (2004). Quality assessment in rehabilitation centres: The indicator system 'Quality Profile.' *Disability and Rehabilitation, 26*(18), 1096–1104.

Geisinger, K. F. (1992). The metamorphosis of test validation. *Educational Psychologist, 27,* 197–222.

Hinderer S. R., & Hinderer K. A. (2005). Principles and applications of measurement methods. In J. A. DeLisa, B. M. Gans, & N. E. Walsh (Eds.), *Physical medicine & rehabilitation: principles and practice* (4th ed.) (chapter 53, pp. 1139–1157). Hagerstown, MD: Lippincott, Williams, & Wilkins.

Hippocrates. (400 B.C.E.). *The Hippocratic Oath.* Retrieved February 23, 2007, from http://classics.mit.edu/Hippocrates/hippooath.html

International School Psychology Association (ISPA). (1991). *ISPA Code of Ethics.* Copenhagen, Denmark: Author. Retrieved September 29, 2006, from http://www.ispaweb.org/Documents/ethics_fulldoc.html

International Test Commission (ITC). (2000). *International guidelines for test use.*

International Test Commission (ITC). (2007). *ITC guidelines.* Retrieved on February 25, 2007, from http://www.intestcom.org/itc_projects.htm

Johnston, M.V., Keith, R.A., & Hinderer, S.R. (1992). Measurement standards for interdisciplinary medical rehabilitation. *Archives of Physical Medicine and Rehabilitation, 73* (12-S), 3–23. Retrieved October 13, 2006, from http://www.medscape.com/medline/abstract/1463386?src=emed_ckb_ref_0[Medline].

Joint Committee on Testing Practices (JCTP). (2000). *Rights and responsibilities of test takers: Guidelines and expectations*. Washington, DC: Author.

Joint Committee on Testing Practices (JCTP). (2004). *Code of fair testing practices in education*. Washington, DC: Author.

Koocher, G. P., & Keith-Spiegel, P. (2008). *Ethics in psychology* (3rd ed.). New York: Oxford University Press.

Kurpius, S. E. R., & Stafford, M. E. (2006). *Testing and measurement: A user-friendly guide*. Thousand Oaks, CA: Sage.

Leach, M. M., & Oakland, T. (2007). Ethics standards impacting test development and use: A review of 31 ethics codes impacting practices in 35 countries. *International Journal of Testing. 7* (1). 71–88.

National Association of School Psychologists (NASP). (2000). *Professional conduct manual; Principles for professional ethics; Guidelines for the provision of school psychological services*. Bethesda, MD: Author.

Oakland, T. Glutting, J., & Watkins, M. (2005). Assessment of test behaviors with the WISC-IV. In A. Prifitera, D. Saklofske, & L. Weiss, (Eds.) *WISC-IV: Clinical use and interpretation* (pp. 417–434) New York: Elsevier Academic Press.

Oakland, T., Goldman, S. & Bischoff, H. (1997). Code of ethics of the International School Psychology Association. *School Psychology International, 18*, 291–298.

Reed, G. M., Lux, J. B., Bufka, L. F., Peterson, D. B., Threats, T. T., Trask, C., Stark, S., Jacobson, J. W., & Hawley, J. A. (2005). Operationalizing the international classification of functioning, disability and health in clinical settings. *Rehabilitation Psychology, 50*, 122–131.

Salvia, J., & Ysseldyke, J. (2003). *Assessment in special and inclusive education* (9th ed.). Boston, MA: Houghton Mifflin.

Stambor, Z. (2006, January). Changing health care's focus: A newly released APA draft manual aims to transform the way health professionals approach health care. *Monitor on Psychology*, 42–43.

VandenBos, G. R. (Ed.). (2006). *APA dictionary of psychology*. Washington, DC: American Psychological Association.

Wasserman, J. D., & Bracken, B. A. (2002). Selecting appropriate tests: Psychometric and pragmatic considerations. In J. F. Carlson & B. B. Waterman (Eds.), *Social and personality assessment of school-aged children: Developing interventions for educational and clinical use* (pp. 18–43). Boston, MA: Allyn & Bacon.

Waterman, B. B., & Carlson, J. F. (2002). Domains and contexts of social and personality assessment. In J. F. Carlson, & B. B. Waterman (Eds.), *Social and personality assessment of school-aged children: Developing interventions for educational and clinical use* (pp. 1–17). Boston, MA: Allyn & Bacon.

World Health Organization (WHO). (2001). *International classification of functioning, disability and health (ICF)*. Geneva, Switzerland: Author. Retrieved August 28, 2006, from http://www3.who.int/icf/onlinebrowser/icf.cfm

World Health Organization. (2006a). *International Statistical Classification of Diseases (ICD)*. Geneva, Switzerland: Author. Retrieved August 28, 2006, from http://www.who.int/classifications/icd/en/

World Health Organization. (2006b). *International Statistical Classification of Diseases and Related Health Problems* (10th ed.) [ICD-10]. Geneva, Switzerland: Author. Retrieved August 28, 2006, from http://www3.who.int/icd/currentversion/fr-icd. htm

9

Administering, Scoring, and Reporting Test Results

Oliver W. Edwards
University of Central Florida, Orlando

OVERVIEW

This chapter addresses issues important to test administration, scoring, and reporting results orally and in writing. A test's administrative procedures are designed to help ensure the test results represent either a person's best performance or typical performance (see also chapter 5). Some tests measure a person's ability to perform tasks under ideal conditions. Examples include tests of sensory, motor, academic, and intellectual abilities. They are administered in ways to obtain the person's best or optimal performance. In contrast, other tests measure a person's actual daily performance, not his or her best performance. Examples include tests of adaptive behavior, social and emotional qualities, and personality. They are administered in ways to obtain the person's typical performance. Test results can be used in formative and summative ways, including for diagnosis, and to plan interventions. Data from individually administered tests can have an enduring (e.g., high stakes) impact on patients' lives. Thus, clinicians must ensure that tests are administered and scored appropriately and that the results are conveyed clearly, comprehensively, and compassionately.

LEARNING OBJECTIVES

By the end of this chapter, readers should be able to:

- Describe the key phases of the assessment process
- Identify and explain important test administration competencies
- Outline core standards for test administration
- Explain the relevance of rapport building and maintenance skills
- Relate the importance of accurate scoring of tests
- Explain the significance of cogent and sensitive reporting of test results

INTRODUCTION

Tests are designed to assess patients' functioning using five basic approaches: norm referencing, criterion referencing, interviews and questionnaires, direct observations of behavior, and informal assessment techniques. The five basic approaches provide clinicians with scores that permit measurement of the magnitude of characteristics or attributes of persons. These approaches, described briefly here, are addressed more completely in chapter 5.

Tests are standard procedures used to measure one or more characteristics of a person. Clinicians administer tests to persons across the age spectrum to help determine their functioning (American Psychological Association [APA], 2006). More specifically, tests are used to describe well-being and illness, predict future behaviors, develop rehabilitation and health services, plan interventions and evaluate progress, screen for special needs, diagnose disabling disorders, help place persons in jobs or programs, and assist in determining whether persons should be credentialed, admitted/employed, retained, or promoted (Edwards, 2006)

Scores obtained from the appropriate administration, scoring, and interpretation of tests are important metrics that, when reported properly, can be used to determine a person's functioning, risk for health problems, treatments, and need for services to improve health outcomes (World Health Organization [WHO], 2001). Group assessment data obtained from targeted populations are used to design preventive programs to aid persons who display physical, social, or psychological disorders as well as to evaluate program effectiveness (Paulin, 2007).

TEST ADMINISTRATION

A comprehensive evaluation involves a process in which important information is obtained about a patient's functioning. Information is integrated, interpreted, and reported by a clinician or team of clinicians and used by them in other ways to help the patient experience success in the environment or to minimize the impact of adverse conditions (APA, 2006). Test administration is part of a comprehensive evaluation. It refers to a process in which trained clinicians carefully

observe and record the actual performance of persons under standard conditions. During testing, clinicians interact with patients, present test materials according to standardized procedures, and observe and record patients' performance (Kamphaus, 2001; Romero, 1999).

TEST RECORDING AND SCORING

Test recording and scoring involve the use of rubrics constructed by the test developers and included in the test manuals to appropriately record patients' behaviors, responses to tasks, and answers to questions. Clinicians score test items using precise rules as described in the test manual. Additionally, clinicians calculate test scores and complete the test record forms or protocols using a set format.

REPORTING RESULTS

Data obtained from comprehensive assessment must be organized, synthesized, and integrated in order to be communicated clearly to patients and other appropriate parties (Salvia & Ysseldyke, 1998). Assessment findings are communicated to the referral source, patient, parents, guardians, or other professionals individually or collectively. The typical method of conveying test findings is by oral and/or written reports. Quality assessment reports convey more than mere facts. They integrate data with interpretations of the findings seasoned with professional judgment (Edwards, 2007).

IMPLICATIONS OF TESTING

Test data acquired in the context of providing rehabilitation services almost certainly involve high-stakes decisions that are likely to have an enduring impact on a patient's life. Thus, efforts are needed to recognize and minimize possible errors inherent in the test as well as those in the administration, scoring, and reporting process. These efforts are necessary before data can be used confidently to provide needed services (Edwards & Oakland, 2006).

The ethical principal *to do no harm* is central to all practices of health care professionals. In keeping with this principal, clinicians exert considerable effort to ensure that the test administration and scoring facilitate rather than diminish patient well-being. Additionally, the test findings should be conveyed in a manner that enables consumers of this information to value and thus respect the patient as a person.

Furthermore, clinicians should not administer tests merely to determine program eligibility or whether a patient has a disorder or disability. Testing that is conducted primarily to determine diagnosis often results in confirmatory bias (Kamphaus & Frick, 2002; Sattler, 2001). *Confirmatory bias* is the tendency to notice and emphasize information that confirms an existing viewpoint and to discount or disregard information that contradicts the viewpoint. For example, the mere act of referring a patient due to suspected motor problems can lead to testing and subsequent placement in a treatment program to remediate motor problems without full consideration of other alternatives such as neurological difficulties. Clinicians mitigate confirmatory bias by asking themselves questions such as, "Could it be something else?" or "Are two problems co-occurring?" Moreover, testing conducted with the intent to describe a wide range of relevant behaviors, including strengths and limitations, is likely to benefit patients who do not meet diagnostic criteria (Radnitz, Bockian, & Moran, 2000).

EARLY EFFORTS AT TESTING, SCORING, AND REPORTING RESULTS

Test Use

Test use in China began around 2200 B.C.E. when measures of problem-solving, visual spatial perception, divergent thinking, creativity, and other characteristics that reflected important qualities were used somewhat commonly. Later, under the Sui dynasty (581–618), a civil service examination system consisting of three parts was initiated: classical cultural knowledge, an examination on planning and administrative features before the emperor, and finally martial arts (Wang, 1993). Subsequently, classical Greek philosophers such as Plato and Aristotle contemplated the importance of examining a person's cognitive skills to help determine his or her position in the Republic (Hergenhahn, 2005). Efforts to develop and use tests declined, only to be revived following scientific developments during and after the Middle Ages.

Scoring

Around 1510, English judge Sir Anthony Fitzherbert developed a test consisting of items that assessed counting, knowledge of one's own age, the ability to identify one's parents, and similar qualities to help differentiate those who did and did not display mental retardation (Drummond & Jones, 2006). Later, efforts in the late 19th century by Weber and Fechner in Germany and Wundt in London led to the development of various tests and resulting scoring systems, albeit for use largely in laboratory and research settings (Roback, 1961).

Reporting Results

Assessment findings historically were communicated and transmitted through oral and written reports. Telephone, computer-generated, video, and/or audio reports have been added to those employed to report assessment findings. Information typically is conveyed only to the patient and others who are ethically and legally permitted to receive the information.

DOMAINS OF ASSESSMENTS

Comprehensive evaluations often are essential due to the multifaceted conditions that may impact health, dysfunction, and resulting rehabilitation services. Functioning is shaped by interactions among specific personal factors (e.g., genes, body structure, and personality), interpersonal relationships, participation within particular environments, and contextual factors including specific injury.

Comprehensive assessments enhance the probability that all areas pertinent to diagnosis as well as treatment planning, implementation, and follow-up evaluation are assessed (Kamphaus & Frick, 2002). These areas pertinent to diagnosis, treatment planning, implementation, and evaluation include organ systems (e.g., vision and hearing) as well as assessment of mental functioning (e.g., cognitive ability); broader syndromes (e.g., emotional well-being); and overall health and quality of life (McDowell & Newell, 1996). In addition, clinicians need to consider the environment and context in which the behaviors are performed because they have implications for activity and participation.

Comprehensive assessments often use various assessment methods that draw upon information from several sources in order to assess relevant personal qualities that are displayed in different settings both previously and currently. This method may be referred to as multimethods, sources, traits, settings, and times.

Multimethod assessments typically rely on the five previously identified assessment methods: norm referencing, criterion referencing, interviews and questionnaires, direct observations of behavior, and informal assessment techniques. Assessments may include two or all five approaches depending on patient needs. *Multisetting assessments* often involve obtaining test information from the clinic, home, workplace, school, playground, and others, and help determine the effect of environment on functioning. *Multisource assessments* provide insight into a patient's functioning from differing perspectives and contexts. Important sources of assessment information include the patient, family members, employers, teachers, previous records, and evaluations, and other relevant sources. *Multitrait assessments* refer to the different abilities, skills, or other personal qualities that are assessed. Depending on need, these areas, as determined by *International Classification of Functioning, Disability, and Health* (ICF) guidelines, broadly include (a) body structure and function and (b) activity and participation (WHO, 2001). Finally, *multitimes assessments* provide information on the patient's functioning over several assessments. Multiple assessments are used to derive data regarding the patient's progress during ongoing treatment periods. Multiple assessments may be needed to determine whether different treatments or interventions are required or whether they need adjustment.

Methods of Test Administration

Tests are administered either individually or to groups. Tests can be administered directly by an examiner, a viewed performance (e.g., directly observing a patient while performing a skill and or other function), use of paper and pen tasks, and computers (Stein, Bentley, & Natz, 1999). Some tests lend themselves to self-administration (Drummond & Jones, 2006). Additionally, tests can be completed using rating scales or checklists. Table 9.1 describes the advantages and disadvantages of several methods of test administration.

PROCEDURES IN ADMINISTRATION, SCORING, AND REPORTING OF RESULTS

Specialists in assessment strive to administer and score tests using standard procedures outlined in the test manual. Exact adherence to the test directions allows clinicians to use test scores in the manner recommended in the test manual. Deviations in the directions stated by the test manual may result in inaccurate, unreliable, and invalid test data and thus faulty interpretation, ineffective treatment, and inadequate outcomes (Drummond & Jones, 2006).

Notwithstanding the aforementioned, clinicians are mindful that assessments are conducted with patients in light of functional lifestyles that are limited due to acute or chronic difficulties. Visual or hearing impairments may necessitate assessments that rely on verbal or nonverbal measures. In addition, clinicians may need to modify standardized procedures when assessing patients with language, physical, or other limitations. For example, some patients may be asked to utilize alternate means of communication such as pantomime. Modifications made to standard procedures need to be described clearly in reports, and results obtained from modified procedures are used cautiously during diagnosis and program planning.

Standards for Administering, Scoring, and Reporting Test Results

Test standards have been developed by professional associations. For example, *The Standards for Educational and Psychological Testing* (American Educational Research Association [AERA], American Psychological Association [APA], & National Council on Measurement in Education [NCME], 1999), the *International Guidelines for Test Use* (International Test Commission, 2000), and APA's *Ethical Principles of Psychologists and Code of Conduct* (APA, 2002a) constitute three important resources for test users. These resources provide ethical and other professional standards that impact the rights of patients and others as well as test development and use (e.g., proper test administration, scoring, interpretation, and communication procedures).

Adequate training followed by supervised professional experiences, together with knowledge of good testing practices, the constructs being assessed, factors which influence human behavior, and awareness of measurement concepts provide a foundation for suitable assessment practices (Drummond & Jones, 2006). Additionally, clinicians are expected to understand the purposes of the assessment and its probable consequences (AERA et al., 1999).

Most test publishers establish professional standards for those who should use their tests. Clinicians should respect these standards. These standards anticipate the level of training, experience, and other qualifications needed to administer, score, and interpret

TABLE 9.1 Common Methods of Administering Tests

Method	Procedure	Strengths	Limitations
Individually Administered	A clinician directly administers the test to one patient adhering to standard procedures described in the test manual.	Clinicians can gauge the motivation and mood of patients. Clinicians can encourage and prompt patients to ensure best or typical effort.	Time consuming and expensive. Requires extensive clinician training.
Viewed Performance or Direct Observation	A clinician observes a patient engaging in specific activities in the clinic, school, hospital, or natural environment.	Provides an objective method of assessing behavior, changes in behavior, and how the behavior is connected to responses and environmental stimuli.	Time consuming and requires extensive training. Patients may alter their behaviors in the presence of an observer.
Group-administered	Clinicians adhere to procedures in the test manual to administer the test to several patients at the same time.	Generally quite time- and cost-efficient. Clinicians also can compare the behavior and performance of individuals within the group.	Difficult to ensure patients understand the directions and are exerting their best effort. Cannot be used to assess many skills. Requires proctoring to prevent patients distracting each other or copying responses.
Self- or Respondent-report Measures	Patients administer the test to themselves adhering to directions on the test protocol. Persons who know the patient well complete questionnaires about patient functioning.	The presence of a clinician is unnecessary.	Difficult to determine whether respondents understand the directions and are exerting their best effort. Memory may be faulty and responses biased.
Computer Administration	The test and instructions are presented via the monitor. Testing, scoring, and report writing can be accomplished using computer software.	The presence of a clinician may not be required. This method allows for flexibility in scheduling and often provides patients with immediate feedback.	Certain patients are apprehensive about computers. This approach cannot be used to assess many skills and to evaluate persons with certain conditions.

each test. Many publishers require evidence of these qualifications before selling their tests. For example, Harcourt Assessment's Website (2007) notes the following regarding qualifications for purchasers:

> The tests listed in this catalog are carefully developed assessment instruments that require specialized training to ensure their appropriate professional use. Eligibility to purchase these tests, therefore, is restricted to individuals with specific training and experience in a relevant area of assessment. These standards are consistent with the *Standards for Educational and Psychological Testing* and with the professional and ethical standards of a variety of professional organizations. (Retrieved March 19, 2007, from http://harcourtassessment.com/haiweb/Cultures/en-S/Footer/Terms+and+Conditions+of+Sale.htm)

Although test publishers and test authors are responsible for developing tests that display suitable statistical and psychometric properties, clinicians are ultimately responsible for test selection and use (AERA et al., 1999).

Types of Test Scores

A patient's test performance may be quantified through the use of one or more of the following five sets of scores: raw, standard, percentile, age or grade-equivalent, and criterion-referenced scores (see also chapter 7). These scores provide information about a patient's performance or capacity as it relates to body functions, activities, and participation (Perenboom & Chorus, 2003). Scores are obtained in broad domains of functioning that include physical (e.g., pain, range of motion, gait speed, strength, mobility), psychological (e.g., cognition, emotional well-being.), social (e.g., relationships, quality of life), and participation or involvement in fulfilling life situations (Finch, Brooks, Stratford, & Mayo, 2002). Raw, standard, percentile, age or grade-equivalent, and criterion-referenced scores constitute different ways a patient's performance, capacity, or other personal qualities can be quantified. Assessment specialists need to be experts in their use.

Raw scores refer to a sum of the item scores and often offer little knowledge about the examinee's performance compared to peers. Raw scores typically are transformed to one of the other four types of scores. Standard scores are derived from raw scores and converted to a distribution with a designated mean and standard deviation. These scores are used frequently in norm-referenced tests. Standard scores provide data useful for making comparisons among persons and for determining the degree a patient's score deviates from the normative mean. These scores provide information about a person

and the person's test score in relation to other test scores. Figure 6.1 in chapter 6 shows a normal curve which identifies the location of scores among a distribution of scores.

Scores that reflect percentile ranks provide a person's position relative to others in the norm group (APA, 2006). Percentile ranks have a mean of 50. A patient whose score is at the 20th percentile performs the same as or better than 20% of persons in the norming sample.

Age-equivalent scores refer to the age in years and months at which a particular raw score is the mean score (APA, 2006). To illustrate these scores: A patient may obtain a standard score of 100 on a measure of adaptive functioning. A standard score of 100 is usually the overall mean score for many measures of adaptive behavior and is at the 50th percentile. A standard score at the overall mean likely results in an age-equivalent score identical to the patient's chronological age.

Age-equivalent scores for physical characteristics such as height are accepted widely. However, because age equivalents are on a rank-order scale, the distance between adjoining scores may not be equal. In addition, identical age equivalent scores on two different tests may provide different meanings. For example, although a patient may obtain the same age-equivalent score on two different tests of adaptive functioning, the tests may measure adaptive constructs differently and the scores will convey different meanings. Although age-equivalent scores from two tests of adaptive behavior may be the same (e.g., 15 years and 11 months) the patient may display different functional skills (e.g., is employed part-time or is a member of a competitive sports team). Due to this and other limitations, age equivalent scores, as well as grade equivalent scores, typically are not used when making diagnostic and programming decisions (Kamphaus & Frick, 2002; Salvia & Ysseldyke, 1998).

DISCUSSION BOX 9.1

Several assessment methodologies are available to clinicians who conduct comprehensive assessments. These methods include self-report and respondent report measures, diagnostic interviews, standardized tests, and direct observations. Many clinicians prefer one method to others. Some clinicians use an eclectic approach in which they may use a combination of methods. Each methodology has its advantages and disadvantages.

Experts may disagree or hold diverse views regarding which assessment methodology is most appropriate for their discipline. Some clinicians believe direct observation is most appropriate because it involves a variety of techniques and

strategies that help them directly determine the causes and functional severity of a person's limitations. Other clinicians prefer norm-referenced standardized assessment because it helps them determine differences from expected performance compared to a comparison group.

Questions

1. In reference to your discipline and based on available evidence, what are your views regarding the most appropriate assessment methods?
2. What are advantages and disadvantages associated with differing forms of assessment methods?

Criterion-referenced scores help determine whether a patient has reached a pre-established standard or threshold of desired or expected functioning (e.g., a desired level of strength, mobility, or sensory acuity). For example, a score of 80 may indicate adequate grip strength, a score of 70–79 may suggest the need for independent exercises, and a score below 69 may suggest a need for treatment from a clinician to strengthen the grip. Scores from well-designed criterion-referenced tests that have many items that assess a specific and narrow construct can be more sensitive to change (e.g., to measure treatment progress) than scores from tests that assess behaviors more narrowly. Unlike some scores, one cannot use criterion-referenced scores to make comparisons among persons or different tests.

Scoring Test Items

Scoring test items properly requires knowledge of the scoring rubric and criteria as presented in the test manual. For example, clinicians need to know whether a response to a test item receives full, partial, or no credit. Scoring of some test items is challenging as the scoring rubric may not be as explicit as desired. Clinicians utilize good professional judgment and consult with colleagues and supervisors when uncertain about how to score questionable responses. Test publishers also may have customer service personnel who can be contacted via telephone or email to assist with item scoring questions.

Scoring Tests

Tests commonly are scored either by hand or by computer methods. When scoring most norm-referenced tests by hand, clinicians must ensure that each test item is evaluated correctly, each item is assigned a correct number, these numbers are summed for the subtest on which these items appear, raw scores are transformed to scaled scores, and the scaled scores from the various subtests are summed to obtain the total test score. Errors may occur at one or more of these five steps. Clinicians or those involved in high-stakes decisions often double check their scoring to prevent scoring errors, especially when the scores do not match expectations. Inexperienced clinicians also may ask a colleague or mentor to review their scoring.

Computers have automated test scoring. A clinician or technician enters information on the person's age, sex, and other demographic information as well as the raw item data. A computer program performs other scoring functions and often provides tables that display the results, and may provide a report outline that can form part of a clinician's report. Clinicians increasingly use computer scoring options when they are available in order to improve the efficiency and accuracy of data entry, scoring, and reporting.

FACTORS AFFECTING ADMINISTRATION, SCORING, AND REPORTING

Test administration, scoring, and reporting are affected by qualities that should be considered as part of the assessment process. These qualities may be specific to the patient, the clinician, the tests, and the method in which the findings are conveyed. Understanding how the qualities contribute to the findings enhances opportunities for quality assessments.

Patient Factors

Obtaining reliable and valid information for use in diagnosis, program eligibility, and treatment planning and evaluation requires understanding important patient characteristics that can influence scores. Characteristics to consider before and during testing include patients' perception of the testing process and environment, their emotional well-being, their attitude toward the clinician, and their test-taking behaviors. Patients who have favorable perceptions of testing and the environment are likely to be motivated to exert good effort during testing. Patients who are emotionally content, feel positively about the clinician, and display positive test-taking behaviors generally are willing to comply with the demands of testing. Fatigued, unhappy, or irritated patients usually do not exert good effort during testing. In addition, patients who display low cognitive ability may have difficulty understanding directions, resisting distractions, and using strategies to function well during testing. Assessment specialists consider these characteristics prior to and while administering tests in an effort to eliminate or reduce extraneous variables that negatively affect scores (Edwards & Oakland, 2006).

Clinicians are responsible for selecting tests that are appropriate in light of the referral questions and the personal qualities of those being assessed. Thus, a patient's language competence and, if multilingual, language dominance, together with visual acuity, acute or chronic maladies (e.g., pain, trauma, medications that may have side effects), physical and emotional stamina, and other conditions that may attenuate test performance, should be screened prior to testing. In addition, some tests cannot provide accurate information about a patient because of the patient's physical limitations. Clinicians will need to be vigilant about how specific health conditions can be assessed best, and which assessments are least likely to provide biased results. (See chapter 3 for more extensive information about bias in testing.

Clinicians recognize that tests and other forms of assessments provide only a sample of a patient's behavior at a particular time and place. Thus, the data may not reflect the functioning of patients under typical conditions. A patient's performance may not represent how the person could have performed under more favorable conditions of comfort, motivation, lower test anxiety, or diminished family and personal stress (Sattler, 2001). Clinicians recognize that scores do not represent people and instead merely help describe a patient's functioning. Competent clinicians refrain from reifying or deifying a patient's obtained test scores.

Clinician Factors

Clinicians understand the importance of establishing collaborative relationships with patients. The first 5 to 10 minutes of their first meeting may set a tone that affects all subsequent interactions. The expression of the clinician's desire to form a collaborative relationship helps build trust and faith—the foundation for any professional relationship. Although clinicians remain in charge, they and their patients need to display a cooperative relationship throughout all stages of the assessment process. Testing involves the use of tests with, not on, the patient.

During the evaluation, clinicians are alert to behaviors that suggest the patient is inattentive, unmotivated, uncooperative, or is displaying other unsuitable test-taking behaviors. These and other qualities that adversely impact test-taking are examples of construct-irrelevant behaviors that contribute to test error (Anastasi & Urbina, 1996; Salvia & Ysseldyke, 1998).

Clinicians seek optimal patient outcomes by demonstrating genuineness, understanding, good judgment, keen observational skills, flexibility, and patience. They understand human behavior and how to obtain the best possible effort from patients, even from those who are uncooperative (Anastasi & Urbina, 1996; Cohen & Swerdlik, 2005; Kamphaus, 2001). Their verbal and nonverbal behaviors, warmth, and understanding as expressed through their personality, and level of preparedness can influence the testing situation and thus enhance or hinder patients' performance. For example, clinicians who appear frustrated or unhappy can reduce patients' motivation to complete the assessment. Clinicians who engagingly and efficiently administer test items can improve patients' motivation. Behaviors that are too formal or too casual may generate psychological barriers or cause uneasiness (Romero, 1999; Sattler, 2001).

Furthermore, a clinician's personal positive or negative biases toward a patient are likely to pejoratively affect their ability to remain objective and neutral during the entire assessment process. Clinicians carefully avoid the *halo effect*; that is, they do not judge patients in a favorable manner merely because the patients' possess positive personal characteristics. A temptation to be overly generous or overly critical when scoring test responses or interpreting tests must be avoided (Martin, 1988). Proficient test administering and scoring as well as reporting data from tests should be accomplished in a nonbiased manner. Capable clinicians recognize that, as they become more experienced, the testing process may become routine or automatic, resulting in taking shortcuts and deviating from other standard methods. Clinicians should periodically monitor their administration technique to ensure they are in accord with standard procedures (Kamphaus & Frick, 2002).

Health-related conditions may significantly impact a person's disposition and mood as well as create physical limitations that restrict their ability to take tests properly. Clinicians must be vigilant about how a client's health condition may be impacting these and other personal qualities, be aware of conditions that may distort or otherwise bias results, and plan how best to assess desired traits. Adhering to standardized practices may not be providing best practices.

Preparing for the Assessment Session

A test administration begins by ensuring the test environment is properly prepared for testing. Appropriate lighting, ventilation, suitable table and chair heights, arrangement of test materials, and patient positioning are necessary to ensure that the work is completed efficiently and that patients are comfortable and have an opportunity to demonstrate suitable efforts (Romero, 1999).

Efficient and well-organized assessment specialists prepare in advance of testing to prevent or minimize distractions, interruptions, and other situations that may reduce a patient's attention, interest, energy, and motivation. They understand test techniques and are very familiar with the tests to be used and their administrative sequence. For example, many patients enjoy taking tests that employ game-like activities or that require manipulatives or fine and gross motor skills. These types of tests that patients are likely to enjoy and find somewhat interesting often are administered first. Specialists know and respect the agency's schedule (e.g., lunch and other breaks) and the patient's schedule (e.g., treatments, other test sessions). Clinicians who are perceived as efficient and well organized improve the testing process and patient outcomes.

Introducing the Tests

Clinicians can begin the testing session by introducing themselves. Introductory comments may vary depending upon the type of test administered as well as the developmental level, cognitive understanding, and motivation of patients (Anastasi & Urbina, 1996; Sattler, 2001). Many test manuals offer guidelines regarding introducing the test to patients.

Tests measuring cognitive abilities may be introduced in the following fashion. "We will be using some tests that most people enjoy. Some of the items are easy. Others are difficult. I do not expect you to get all the items correct. However, I want you to do your very best. Will you? . . . Do you have any questions before we begin?"

Rapport Building

Establishing and maintaining rapport is central to the assessment process. The goal of rapport building is to establish a cordial, relaxed, mutually respectful relationship between the clinician and patient. Rapport improves opportunities to obtain a valid representation of the qualities assessed during the evaluation (Anastasi & Urbina, 1996; Cohen & Swerdlik, 2005). Patients often enter the assessment session fearing the testing process and the possible implications of the findings. Rapport building techniques reduce test anxiety through patient encouragement and support. Before beginning the testing, clinicians may allay patients' anxieties by conversing with them about their family, pets, daily events, or hobbies. Information on whether they ate that day, are upset due to prior events, have needed glasses or hearing aids, and have prepared for the testing in other ways allows the specialist to decide whether testing should proceed.

During this initial rapport building process, matters of informed consent and the legal rights of patients can be discussed if they have not been addressed previously. Chapter 2 addresses informed consent relative to the patient's legal rights. Informed consent also can be considered an important element of rapport building. A discussion of informed consent, confidentiality (albeit often limited), who will have access to the test scores, and how the test findings may be used may communicate the clinician's professionalism and respect for the patient (Kamphaus & Frick, 2002; Drummond & Jones, 2006). During this discussion, clinicians can address the Health Insurance Portability & Accountability Act (HIPPA) regarding how patients' health data and confidentiality are protected. Confidentiality generally is limited in cases when there is reasonable suspicion that a child examinee is exposed to abuse or neglect or when an examinee is believed to be in imminent danger of harming themselves or others. Clinicians generally are required to report these situations to the authorities.

Coping with Challenging Patients

Testing some patients may present a daunting challenge because of their attempts to exert control during the test session. These patients' behaviors may be an attempt to reduce test anxiety or stress. Additionally, hospital patients may be tired and unhappy about participating in what they may perceive as strenuous activities. Understanding human behavior and patients' goals as well as demonstrating respect and empathy for patients are helpful in responding to them.

A professional must be in control of assessment and other professional services. Clinicians maintain control of the assessment session by presenting themselves as caring and considerate professionals whose goal is to collaborate with the patient to enhance the patient's chances for favorable health outcomes. When working with unmotivated patients, clinicians articulate and emphasize this goal of improving the patient's functioning as a means of encouraging better effort. Taking breaks, changing to easier or less anxiety-provoking tasks may be necessary to improve patient motivation. In addition, patients may require extensive prompting, praise, and encouragement before they exhibit the necessary effort. Despite the aforementioned, on some occasions the testing session may need to be discontinued for the day when the clinician–patient relationship does not allow the patient to demonstrate appropriate effort or when the patient cannot be dissuaded from attempting to control the assessment (Romero, 1999). Although competant clinicians are cognizant of the need to complete test referrals in a timely manner, they are equally aware of the needs of patients and to acquire data that can be used in a valid manner. The focus of each assessment must be on the patient and not the test instruments, procedures, or how quickly testing can be completed (Kamphaus & Frick, 2002). Table 9.2 offers guidelines to enhance patients' effort and motivation during the testing.

USE OF TEST ACCOMMODATIONS

Tests may be biased against patients in light of their disabilities or chronic illnesses. Clinicians will need to be vigilant about how specific health conditions can be assessed

TABLE 9.2 Testing Tips to Enhance Clients' Effort and Motivation

1. Interact with the patient in an engaging yet professional manner to obtain the best effort from the client.
2. Involve the client in the assessment. Employ an appealing "bedside manner" (e.g., smile, laugh, converse with the client).
3. Make eye contact and observe the client's verbal and nonverbal behaviors. Your observations are very important in determining his or her affect, attitude, effort, strengths, and difficulties.
4. Encourage clients to be diligent and persistent. If a client gives up too easily, their scores may be inaccurate.
5. Although the administration of only the standard or core battery of an instrument is acceptable, the administering of additional tests in the battery may offer specific information relevant to the client's strengths and difficulties.
6. Carefully follow the test manual's directions regarding timing.
7. Do not place objects that would serve as barriers directly between you and the client; they often serve as impediments to rapport.
8. Note whether the client is using prescription glasses, hearing aids, etc.
9. Use behavior specific praise; offer ample praise and encouragement for effort and motivation (not for correctness of response!).
10. End the session by thanking the client for their cooperation and effort during the evaluation (Drummond & Jones, 2006; Sattler, 2001).

best and which assessments are least likely to provide unbiased results. In certain cases, clinicians make test accommodations or modify the test. Test accommodations are made to permit persons with disabilities to participate fully in the testing process. The accommodation changes standardized testing method so as to remove sources of measurement error caused by the disability (Fuchs & Fuchs, 2001). The goal of testing accommodations is to prevent a disability (e.g., hearing impairment) from speciously limiting test performance when the test is designed to measure a construct other than hearing-related abilities (e.g., fine motor skills). In this case, oral directions that are part of the test's standardized administration procedures may spuriously affect the patient's scores.

Scholars have diverse views regarding whether test accommodations differ from test modifications. Whereas some scholars consider these terms synonyms, others draw distinctions between them (Behuniak, 2002). The National Center on Educational Outcomes and the Parents Engaged in Education Reform Project (1997, p. 14) indicated, "[D]istinctions between the meanings of the terms are not worthy of discussion because they are used to mean the same thing as often as they are to mean different things." This chapter uses the terms *test accommodations* and *test modifications* synonymously.

Clinicians review the possible impact of a patient's disabilities or chronic illnesses to determine whether test accommodations are necessary to improve their access to tests and to provide a fair opportunity to complete test questions and tasks (Behuniak, 2002). An appropriate test accommodation increases an examinee's access to assessment, provides valid data, and preserves the meaningfulness or validity of scores. Numerous test accommodations are available. They vary as a function of the needs of the examinee and the specific test and the test modality. For example, extended time given beyond the standard time indicated in the test manual is a frequent accommodation (Fuchs & Fuchs, 2001). In addition, a test's standard procedures may require examinees to read the directions and instructions themselves. Reading the directions and instructions to examinees with reading disabilities is a potential accommodation. Directions also may be provided via pantomime and sign language. Examinees with fine or gross motor difficulties may be accommodated by allowing them to dictate their responses. Clinicians may make changes to the test stimuli. For example, changes in the size of pictures, letters, and forms may assist examinees with visual disabilities to be assessed. Some tests may be published in large print and others can be reprinted in larger print, or visual aids such as magnifying lenses can be used. Clinicians determine which accommodations are most appropriate based on the specific needs of the patient and the reasons for referral. Whenever possible, rather than making test accommodations, the use of alternate measures administered in a format that accommodates the special needs of patients with specific disabilities can reduce sources of measurement error (Behuniak, 2002).

REPORTING TEST FINDINGS

Evaluation findings may be reported to the referral source, one's colleagues, patient, family members, teachers, agency personal, and other professionals. The principal goals of reporting assessment results are to describe a patient's strengths, limitations, and current level of functioning. Good reports also answer the referral question(s). Patients and referral sources often are disappointed with reports if the noted goals are unmet (Kamphaus & Frick, 2002).

DISCUSSION BOX 9.2

Employing test accommodations is a controversial practice because researchers have not fully addressed the validity implications of such accommodations in light of the violation of norm-referenced standardization procedures. Employing test accommodations that limit spurious effects can result in changes in the meaning of test scores. Researchers suggest that test accommodations generally should not benefit all examinees, but should reduce the effects of the deficit manifested by persons with the disability (Zuriff, 2000). When persons with and without disabilities benefit similarly from a test accommodation, the accommodation is considered unfair (Fuchs & Fuchs, 2001). Proper test accommodations provide differentially large benefits (the "differential boost" hypothesis) to the test scores of persons with disabilities when compared to persons without disabilities (Lewandowski, Lovett, Parolin, Gordon, & Codding, 2007).

Questions

1. What are the validity implications of testing accommodations as a violation of norm referenced standardization procedures?
2. Do test accommodations differ from test modifications?
3. Are testing accommodations considered fair for persons both with and without disabilities?
4. How can examiners determine the conditions under which the differential boost hypothesis is true?
5. Why should persons with a disability benefit more from a specific accommodation than persons without a disability?
   - Is it because persons without disabilities generally function at their potential when standardized test administration procedures are used?
6. Since extended time on test is often used as a test accommodation, how can examiners determine which tests *should* measure speed?
7. How much of a test accommodation is enough?
   - For example, how much extended time is needed to ensure only persons with a disability experience a substantial benefit?
8. To resolve the test accommodation controversy, are test developers able to design tests that are fair (e.g., unlimited testing time, verbal and nonverbal directions) to all potential examinees, including those with disabilities?

Additionally, assessment reports serve as a legal document, particularly in light of the litigious climate in patient assessment and care. The reports may be used as evidence to support a claim of alleged clinician malpractice or negligence (Bradley-Johnson & Johnson, 2006). Although lengthy reports often are contraindicated, quality reports are sufficiently detailed to help prevent legal or ethical challenges to practice.

The report must communicate clearly and succinctly all of the *relevant* information. Clinicians may describe the patient's behaviors, body structure, and function. In addition, they may indicate whether the behaviors differentially influence the patient's activity and participation in areas of interest such as mobility, motor skills, self-care, communication, learning and applying knowledge, interpersonal interactions, community, and social and civic life (Finch et al., 2002). Reports discuss and provide a record of test results, furnish meaningful baseline information useful for progress monitoring, indicate applicable clinical impressions, and may offer treatment and other recommendations (Sattler, 2001; Schwean et al., 2006). Recommendations help professionals or others design and implement treatment or other interventions to improve patient functioning. Appropriate recommendations are specific to the needs of each patient.

Report Formats

Two different formats typically are used to convey evaluation findings: oral reports as well as written reports to both the patient and the professional staff. Both formats offer distinct advantages to better understand patients, intervene, and enhance their functioning.

ORAL REPORTS   Clinicians use oral reports in rehabilitation settings to convey findings of the assessment to the patient and/or the patient's family members as well as other professional colleagues. Oral reports allow clinicians to determine whether the information is understandable and to modify their statements to ensure listeners comprehend the information. Oral reports enable clinicians to rephrase and explain statements, engage in dialog, draw graphs and diagrams, and present the findings in ways to enhance comprehension (Schwean et al., 2006).

Clinicians begin their oral report by indicating the estimated length of their report presentation. Reports that are succinct and cogently convey relevant information regarding the patient's strengths, limitations, and functioning are meaningful and communicate efficiently. Effective oral reports include an introductory statement regarding the reason(s) for the assessment.

These reasons are to answer the referral question(s) and describe patients' strengths, limitations, and current level of functioning.

Clinicians inform others that they are able to ask questions anytime or that they should wait for the end of the report. Early in the oral presentation the specialist notes strengths or positive qualities of the patient to prevent listeners from perceiving the specialist as overly negative or biased. In addition, clinicians report findings that are valid for use in the patient care process. Findings that are invalidated (e.g., due to errors in assessment, administration, or selection of tests offered) are not reported (Kamphaus & Frick, 2002).

Oral reports do not provide a permanent record of the assessment and baseline data that can guide future treatment. Thus, although oral reports are used frequently as part of rehabilitation assessments, a written report may be required in many settings, including in forensic settings.

WRITTEN REPORTS   The process of writing reports can be daunting. The audiences of the report may differ, perhaps warranting different forms and information. The data may be extensive. Thus, attempts to summarize them both completely and meaningfully in a few pages are difficult. In addition, some nonprofessional readers may have difficulty understanding written reports and may make inaccurate judgments about the report or patient. As a result, it is often helpful to explain the findings verbally when providing relevant parties a copy of the report.

Written reports display the assessment specialist's keen attention to details and good judgment. Each report should describe the client, serve as a means of communication to the referral source and other relevant parties, provide a record of the evaluation, furnish meaningful baseline information to monitor the client's progress, and assist with program planning (Sattler, 2001). Reports commonly discuss the impact of the assessed behaviors on the patient's activity and participation in such areas as mobility, motor skills, and others as mentioned previously (Finch et al., 2002). Clinicians should note whether the behaviors are differentially affecting the client's ability to perform necessary life functions. Good reports refrain from using terminology known only to professionals, limit abbreviations and acronyms, and eliminate other features that reduce understanding.

Clinicians who excel and enhance patient outcomes do more than merely report scores. They must integrate test information obtained from multi-methods, sources, traits, settings, and times, and communicate this information in a cogent and organized manner to describe the patient's functioning. Thorough and reflective clinicians who learn to conceptualize test results and integrate and report results within the context specific to the individual patient will grow professionally and sustain that growth over the years.

Some reports are developed through the use of commercially available computer-assisted report writing programs. Their efficiency and standardized formats are attractive features. Some of these programs also generate standard scores from raw scores. Although these features are attractive, their use may limit the preparation of a personalized report that reflects a patient's strengths, limitations, and functioning. Thus, if used, the computer software should allow clinicians to easily modify computer-generated statements to ensure they are both accurate and provide a personalized account of the findings.

Test score reporting practices are influenced by procedures, policies, and practices of the individual organizations. Thus, practices in reporting vary across institutions and depend on precedent, best practices, and case law. Clinicians should consult their supervisors and colleagues regarding the specific practices of their organization. In addition, reading multiple written reports from different clinicians and listening to different oral reports from organizational colleagues can give new clinicians an impression as to what types of reports are expected and regarded highly within the organization. Tables 9.3 and 9.4 provide several tips for conveying assessment results.

Reporting Unpleasant Information

As noted elsewhere, the primary goal of assessment is to describe behavior accurately. Thus, assessment results need to be reported clearly and candidly in ways that promote understanding of a patient's functioning. Everyone enjoys reporting findings that indicate an absence of problems. The reporting of contrary findings may be difficult.

The readiness and willingness of patients, family members, and others to accept the results differ. The recency of an accident or illness and their acceptance of its long-term consequences, their receipt of unanticipated or negative assessment findings, and their interests in and attitudes toward the patient may affect their ability or willingness to comprehend or accept findings in the report (Drummond & Jones, 2006). Additionally, cultural and linguistic differences between the clinician and patient also may serve as obstacles. Either party may

TABLE 9.3 Some General Report Writing Comments

1. The goal of reports is to integrate the information and test findings to describe the client and not merely to report measurements, test scores, and clinical impressions.
2. Address how the client's body structure and functioning are affecting activity and participation.
3. Discuss the possible impact of the information on the client's immediate and future functioning.
4. It is acceptable to describe the tests, but only briefly.
5. As much as possible, use positive statements. Instead of writing that Jami was not afraid to work with the clinician and was not apprehensive, state that Jami seemed to enjoy the test and willingly began work. Negatively worded statements may be perceived as expecting or wanting these negative qualities to appear in the client.
6. Always include at least a few positive statements about the client's skills and functioning.
7. Provide examples of the client's behaviors and test scores to support statements and clinical impressions.
8. Write professionally by eliminating contractions and personal pronouns, jargon, and colloquialisms.
9. Try to use the same tense in each paragraph (i.e., past, present, future).
10. Edit assessment reports thoroughly to prevent errors that will limit readers' confidence in the clinician's credibility (see Bradley-Johnson & Johnson, 2006; Kamphaus & Frick, 2002)

misinterpret the other's communication and intent. Thus, clinicians must consider the recipients when providing oral and written reports. See chapter 3 for a discussion of cultural and linguistic issues that may impact the assessment process. Clinicians who are accepting of patient differences strive to administer tests and report findings in a manner that benefits patients. They are prepared to manage potential disagreement and conflict.

Establishing and maintaining positive relationships with the patient and other pertinent persons can serve to avert disagreements and conflicts. Demonstrating the validity of the results for diagnosis, highlighting the implications of the results for rehabilitation programs, conveying the integrated results clearly and compassionately, and focusing on the ultimate goal of improving patient outcomes and minimizing future problems can help prevent or diffuse confrontation (Drummond & Jones, 2006).

RESEARCH REGARDING GENERAL PERSONAL QUALITIES THAT IMPACT TEST PERFORMANCE

Reports typically include a section on test behavior. Patients often display important differences in behaviors that may impact their test performance. These behaviors include such general qualities as their receptive and expressive language, fine and gross motor coordination, motivation, temperament, cognitive limitations, and rapport with clinician. Knowing this, clinicians typically are alert to and assess these and other general qualities that may have a deleterious effect on patients' test performance formally or informally. Formal methods of assessing test session behaviors may more accurately determine their impact on test data.

When accommodations are used, clinicians may focus less on standard scores and more on patients' functional behaviors and needs by clearly describing what patients can and cannot do. Additionally, when test accommodations are employed, the clinician should ensure the constructs measured by the test are not altered in order to permit the valid use of the test scores (Fuchs & Fuchs, 2001). They also should describe the accommodations that were made. According to Standard 5.2 of the *Standards for Educational and Psychological Testing* (AERA et al., 1999): "Modifications or disruptions of standardized test administration procedures or scoring should be documented" (p. 63). This documentation permits readers to better interpret the test scores. On occasion, describing the test accommodations in a report may violate federal legislation. This is primarily a concern when admissions and employment tests are used. (Mehrens & Ekstrom, 2002). It is the clinician's responsibility to determine whether it is legally permissible to document accommodations in the report.

Specific Qualities That Impact Test Performance

On occasion, an examinee's scores may be influenced by the person's social identity (e. g., their age, gender, religion, culture, and ethnicity). Steele's research on stereotype threat (1992) suggests that the effect on examinees' scores may result from negative stereotypes regarding group members' typical performance. For example, when a person's social identify is associated with an ethnic group that is attached to a negative stereotype, the person may perform poorly in a manner consistent with the stereotype. Steele contends the poor performance is partly due to anxiety that the person will conform to the negative

---

TABLE 9.4 A Written Report Sample Format

The first page should be a cover sheet that indicates the information on the pages to follow is confidential and should be read only by authorized persons. Modify the following categories to reflect the person's age, gender, and other personal qualities.

- Identifying Information
- Typically presented in a list form at the top of the second page such as:

  ___ Name: Parents:

  ___ Age: Address:

  ___ Birth Date: Teacher:

  ___ School: Clinician:

  ___ Grade: Assessment Dates:

  ___ Gender: Report Date:

- Eliminate data on school, grade, and teacher when working with adults.
- Reason for referral
- Background information
- Assessment methods
- Behaviors observed

  ___ Behaviors conducive to learning

  ___ Behaviors that interfere with learning

- Results

  ___ Strengths

  ___ Difficulties

- Diagnoses
- Recommendations

---

stereotype (Steele & Aronson, 1995). The anxiety is represented by reticence to respond, difficulty sustaining attention, increased distractibility, and changes in body temperature. Moreover, these effects do not occur only among historically disadvantaged groups, because all persons are susceptible to stereotype threat in certain contexts (Jordan & Lovett, 2007). For example, women can perform poorly as a function of stereotypes regarding their abilities in math. However, Oakland & Emmer (1973) found little evidence that test scores from adolescents are influenced by their social identify.

RACE AND ETHNICITY Recent research that investigates the effects of examiner race or ethnicity on patient performance indicates that racial and ethnic differences between examiners and examinees generally do not, yet at times may, impact the test performance of examinees (see Sattler, 1988). Some examinees may experience higher anxiety when evaluated by an examiner from a different ethnic group, and the level of anxiety may depress their scores (Steele, 1992). In addition, some examiners may allow their own or their patients' subgroup membership based on age, gender, culture, or ethnicity to influence the scores their patients' obtain (Sattler, 2001). The belief that examinees and examiners should be from the same racial/ethnic group is unsupported. Furthermore, "the argument that standardized tests cannot accurately measure the cognitive ability of individuals from differing linguistic backgrounds is simply false" (Sattler, 2008, p 174).

Culturally competent clinicians limit sources of measurement error associated with these factors to ensure patients' test scores can be used in a valid manner. Culturally competent clinicians learn about their patients' culture and language, establish rapport, eliminate stereotypes they may have had, and take measures to prevent cultural differences from resulting in measurement error (Sattler, 2001).

RESEARCH BOX 9.1

Objective: Research (Steele & Aronson, 1995) was conducted to answer the following question: Will African American college-age examinees underperform relative to Caucasian examinees when informed a test reflects intellectual ability compared to a condition when informed the test does not reflect intellectual ability? The researchers hypothesized the African American examinees will underperform when they believe the test is a measure of their intellectual ability.

Method: African American and Caucasian college students participants in the study were administered a 30-minute test comprised of items from the verbal Graduate Record Examination (GRE). Ethnicity of the participants and description of the tests as diagnostic or nondiagnostic of intellectual ability were the independent variables. The main dependent variable was the examinees' scores on 30 verbal items, 27 of which were from GRE study guides. The number of items correct and the accuracy index of the number correct over the number attempted were analyzed.

Results: The results supported the researchers' hypotheses. When informed that the test was diagnostic of intellectual ability, African American examinees scored about 15 points lower than the Caucasian examinees. However, in the condition when participants were informed the test was not diagnostic of ability, the African American and Caucasian examinees performed similarly. The results suggest the situational consequence of an ethnic stereotype lowered African American examinees' test performance (Jordan & Lovett, 2007).

Conclusion: "Clearly the diagnostic instructions caused these participants to experience a strong apprehension, a distinct sense of stereotype threat" (Steele & Aronson, 1995, p. 805). Similar stereotype threat effects have been found in studies of test scores as a function of group membership based on age, gender, and culture (Jordan & Lovett, 2007). Culturally competent clinicians consider the potential effects of stereotype threat. They take steps to reduce or eliminate such threat.

Questions

1. What are various ways to reduce or eliminate stereotype threat during individual test administration?
2. What are various ways to reduce or eliminate stereotype threat prior to individual test administration?
3. How can rapport building influence stereotype threat?
4. In what areas of physical and rehabilitation assessment will stereotype threat appear most relevant?
5. Who is most vulnerable to stereotype threat among the patients with whom you will typically work?
6. What specific factors (e.g., distractibility, anxiety) are implicated in stereotype threat in your discipline?
7. Is it likely that there are different types of stereotype threat? For example, does stereotype threat differ as a function of whether one's self or one's group is threatened?

Culturally competent clinicians consistently, fairly, and accurately score and report test responses when evaluating patients from all subgroups. They continually assess whether they are overly lenient or rigorous in their scoring practices (Kamphaus & Frick, 2002). In addition, they frequently reflect on their test scoring practices when evaluating patients from diverse subgroups to maintain validity of test score use. Students and clinicians who have recently begun practicing can ask peers, colleagues, mentors, or supervisors to observe or monitor their scoring practices to ensure accuracy. Several professional associations have published guidelines for evaluating ethnically, linguistically, and culturally diverse populations (e.g., APA, 2002b; see Chapter 3). Culturally competent clinicians adhere to these guidelines. The guidelines usually are located on each association's Website.

PERSONAL FACTORS Test behaviors facilitate or impede the collection of valid test data. Three test-taking behaviors negatively influence children's test performance and can be expected to influence adult test performance: when examinees avoid test tasks and are fearful; are uncooperative, require excessive praise to continue, and do not adjust well; and are inattentive and display inadequate impulse-control (Oakland, Glutting, & Watkins, 2005). Persons who display these qualities obtain lower scores on measures of cognitive abilities. Thus, the validity of test data obtained from persons who display these behaviors is questionable.

Methods of Codifying Test Session Behavior

The use of individually administered tests permits the observation of patients' test session behavior to ascertain whether their test scores are valid for use in diagnosis and program planning. It also allows clinicians to compare the behaviors of a particular patient with other patients, providing an indicator of normal behavior (Glutting, Oakland, & Konold, 1994). However, to assure satisfactory reliability and validity, observations of the test session behavior of patients must not depend solely on the observational skills of the clinician. Some standardized method of codifying test session behavior should be utilized (Glutting et al., 1994).

Several systems have been developed to assess test behaviors (e.g., the Standford-Binet Observation Schedules, Thorndike, Hagen, & Sattler, 1986; and the Behavior and Attitude Checklist, Sattler, 1988). These systems have limited value because they do not provide norms to compare behavior among persons. Thus, clinicians are not able to determine whether the observed behaviors are normal (Glutting et al., 1994, McDermott, 1986). Norms help determine what behaviors are common and what behaviors are uncommon.

The *Guide to the Assessment of Test-Session Behavior* (GATSB, Glutting, & Oakland, 1993) addresses these limitations by providing a norm-referenced standardized system for recording and comparing test session behaviors (Frisby, 1999; Oakland et al., 2005). The GATSB was developed to examine the test session behavior of children during the administration of cognitive assessments. Research has supported the efficacy of utilizing the GATSB when evaluating children ages 6 through 17 (Frisby; Oakland et al.). Instruments such as the GATSB may be designed or modified to assist in evaluating the test session behavior of adult patients during rehabilitative and health evaluations.

COLLABORATIVE TEST ADMINISTRATION, SCORING, AND REPORTING RESULTS

The development of collaborative relationships among the different disciplines and agencies involved in comprehensive rehabilitation and health assessments is essential to enhance successful outcomes. Patients often present with multiple difficulties and require a wide array of services from various professionals to address their needs, including audiologists, educators, nurses, nutritionists, occupational therapists, physical therapists, physicians, psychologists, social workers, and speech–language therapists. Each professional may have direct expertise in different patient skills areas and may wish to conduct parts of the overall assessment (LaRoche & Kruger, 1999). For example, an audiologist, occupational therapist, physical therapist, and psychologist may evaluate a patient presenting

with cognitive, auditory, and motor difficulties. The multidisciplinary, interdisciplinary, and transdisciplinary models constitute three team organization approaches used most commonly in assessments involving multiple professionals.

Three Models of Team Organization

MULTIDISCIPLINARY MODEL   Professionals using a multidisciplinary model use assessment procedures and recommend treatments somewhat specific to each of their disciplines. Limited interaction occurs among the professionals, and test findings are reported separately to the patient or referral source. Patients may be responsible for integrating the information and forming and prioritizing recommendations provided by the different professionals. As a result, the process may be redundant and confusing, the findings may be conflicting, and the interventions may not be prioritized in reference to functional needs (McLean & Crais, 2006).

INTERDISCIPLINARY MODEL   The interdisciplinary model uses a more unified approach to assessment and treatment planning. In this model, professionals may work independently or in subgroups, yet engage in more communication and consultation across disciplines. Teams are likely to have formal avenues through which to communicate information, generate goals, share test findings, and develop treatment plans. However, this model does not use an integrated approach to comprehensive assessment and intervention. Communication problems may persist because team members may not accurately understand each member's training, terminology, and expertise (McLean & Crais, 2006). Resulting disagreements may lead to differences in diagnosis, recommendations, treatment planning, and report writing.

TRANSDISCIPLINARY MODEL   The transdisciplinary model attempts to optimize communication and collaboration among team members (McLean & Crais, 2006). In this model, one or two team members work directly with the patient while other team members observe these interactions. Professionals may engage in role release in which team members transfer certain portions of their normal roles to other team members to enhance efficiency and practicality (LaRoche & Kruger, 1999).

Rehabilitative and health clinicians administer tests that examine similar traits. For example, both physical and occupational therapists may have an interest in a patient's coordination, range of motion, and strength. Transdisciplinary (sometimes called arena) assessment involves simultaneous assessment of a patient by multiple clinicians from different disciplines. This type of assessment is said to minimize patient stress, reduce redundancy, and improve collaboration (LaRoche & Kruger, 1999). Arena assessment may be especially useful when assessing preschool children and patients in hospitals or acute care settings where they may be assessed by several clinicians in succession. Arena assessment methods may be inappropriate when patients experience difficulty working with more than one clinician simultaneously.

The transdiciplinary model is reported to facilitate collaborative decision-making and enhance patient outcomes (McLean & Crais, 2006). The model is time and labor intensive because of the simultaneous involvement of multiple clinicians (McGonigel, Woodruff, & Roszmann-Millican, 1994). Overall, using various combinations of these three models at different points during the assessment may be necessary due to an agency's resources, clinicians' skills, and patient's needs (LaRoche & Kruger, 1999).

Summary and Conclusion

Testing is a process in which trained examiners carefully observe and record the actual performance of persons under standardized conditions (APA, 2006). Data from individually administered tests are likely to have a high-stakes immediate impact on a patient's diagnoses, treatment plans, and other rehabilitation services and may have an enduring impact on his or her life. Clinicians who administer tests strive to create testing conditions that allow patients to demonstrate either their best performance or typical performance.

Data obtained from comprehensive assessments must be organized, synthesized, and integrated in order to be reported clearly to patients and other appropriate persons. Oral and written assessment reports serve as the vehicle through which clinicians describe a patient in ways that enhance others' understanding and lead to viable treatment plans. Reports integrate data and the interpretation of the findings in a manner intended to help improve patients' functioning, activity, and participation. Reports also provide evidence for needed services. As a result, clinicians ensure tests are suitably selected, administered, and scored, and the results conveyed clearly, comprehensively, and compassionately.

Self-Check Questions

Pair and Share Activities
1. Pair up with a classmate to generate some potential referral questions relevant to your discipline.
2. Pair up with a classmate to role-play introducing the test session as well as establishing and maintaining rapport. Each student should take a turn as clinician and as patient.
3. Pair up with a classmate to discuss how best to assess a patient with multiple disabilities as relevant to your discipline.

4. Pair up with a classmate to discuss specific clinician behaviors that reduce a patient's ability to perform well on tests.
5. Pair up with a classmate to discuss, compare, and contrast challenges associated with testing children and adults.

Case Study 9.1

You conducted a comprehensive evaluation of a 30-year-old male patient. Based on your assessment, you diagnosed the patient with a condition (e.g., fine or gross motor deficits—select a disorder specific to your discipline) that will continue to substantially affect the patient's body structures (e.g., joints) and functions (e.g., mobility), activity (e.g., writing, word processing), and participation (e.g., in his work, daily living, and sports environments). Reflect on, and role play, communicating the assessment information, diagnosis, prognosis, recommendations, and treatment plan orally to the patient and the patient's wife.

Case Study 9.2

A 60-year-old patient who recently emigrated from China is referred because of suspected lower extremity strength deficits (or other concern relevant to your discipline) to a first-year non-Asian clinician. The clinician has not previously evaluated Asian patients and has little experience relating to Asians. What preliminary information should the clinician obtain and in what activities should the clinician engage before beginning the evaluation?

References

American Educational Research Association (AERA), American Psychological Association (APA), & National Council on Measurement in Education (NCME). (1999). *Standards for educational and psychological testing.* Washington, DC: Author.

American Psychological Association (APA). (2002a). *Ethical principles of psychologists and code of conduct.* Retrieved October 16, 2006, from www.apa.org/ethics/code2002.pdf.

American Psychological Association. (2002b). *Guidelines on multicultural education, training, research, practice, and organizational change for psychologists.* Retrieved October 16, 2006, from http://www.apa.org/pi/multiculturalguide lines/guideline5.html.

American Psychological Association (2006). *American Psychological Association dictionary of psychology.* G. R. VandenBos (Ed.). Washington, DC: Author.

Anastasi, A., & Urbina, S. (1996). *Psychological testing.* New York: Prentice Hall.

Behuniak, P. (2002). Types of commonly requested accommodations. In R. B. Ekstrom, & D. K. Smith (Eds.), *Assessing individuals with disabilities in educational, employment, and counseling settings* (pp. 45–58). Washington, DC: American Psychological Association.

Bradley-Johnson, S. & Johnson, C. M. (2006). *A handbook for writing effective psychoeducational reports* (2nd ed.). Austin, Tx: Pro-Ed.

Cohen, R. J., & Swerdlik, M. E. (2005). *Psychological testing and assessment: An introduction to tests and measurement* (6th ed.). New York: McGraw Hill.

Drummond, R. J., & Jones, K. D. (2006). *Assessment procedures for counselors and helping professionals* (6th ed). Upper Saddle River, NJ: Pearson.

Edwards, O.W. (2006). Special education disproportionality and the influence of intelligence test selection. *Journal of Intellectual & Developmental Disability, 31,* 246–248.

Edwards, O.W. (2007). An analysis of the differential impact of IQ: Considering consequential validity and disporportionality. *Research in the Schools, 14,* 29–39.

Edwards, O.W. & Oakland, T. D. (2006). Factorial invariance of Woodcock-Johnson III scores for Caucasian Americans and African Americans. *Journal of Psychoeducational Assessment, 24,* 358–366.

Edwards, O.W., & Paulin, R. (2007). Referred students scores on the Reynolds Intellectual Assessment Scales and the Wechsler Intelligence Scale for Children-IV. *Journal of Psychoeducational Assessment, 27,* 334–340.

Finch, E., Brooks, D., Stratford, P. W., & Mayo, N. E. (2002). *Physical rehabilitation outcome measures* (2nd ed.). Hamilton, Ontario: Canadian Physiotherapy Association.

Frisby, C. L. (1999). Culture and test session behavior: Part I. *School Psychology Quarterly, 14,* 263–280.

Fuchs, L. S., & Fuchs, D. (2001). Helping teachers formulate sound testing accommodation decisions for students with learning disabilities. *Learning Disabilities Research and Practice, 16,* 174–181.

Glutting, J., & Oakland, T. (1993). *Guide to the assessment of test session behaviors for the WISC-III and WIAT.* San Antonio, TX: The Psychological Corporation.

Glutting, J., Oakland, T., & Konold, R. (1994). Criterion-related bias with the guide to the assessment of test-session behavior for the WISC-III and WIAT: Possible race, gender, and SES effects. *Journal of School Psychology, 32,* 355–369.

Harcourt Assessment Website (2007). Retrieved March 19, 2007, from http://harcourtassessment.com/haiweb/Cultures/en-S/Footer/Terms+and+Conditions+of+Sale.htm.

Hergenhahn, B. R. (2005). *An introduction to the history of psychology* (5th ed.). Belmont, CA: Thomson Learning.

International Test Commission. (2000). *International guidelines for test use.* Retrieved October 16, 2006, from http://www.intestcom.org/test_use.htm.

Jordan, A. H. & Lovett, B. J. (2007). Stereotype threat and test performance: A primer for school psychologists. *Journal of School Psychology, 45,* 45–59.

Kamphaus, R. W. (2001). *Clinical assessment of child and adolescent intelligence.* Needham Heights, MA: Allyn & Bacon.

Kamphaus, R. W., & Frick, P. J. (2002). *Clinical assessment of child and adolescent personality and behavior* (2nd ed.). Needham Heights, MA: Allyn & Bacon.

LaRoche, M., & Kruger, L. J. (1999). Implementing the results of preschool assessments: Transforming data and recommendations into action. In E. V. Nuttall, I. Romero, & J. Kalesnik (Eds.), *Assessing and screening preschoolers: Psychological and educational dimensions* (pp. 407–420). Needham Heights, MA: Allyn & Bacon.

Lewandowski, L., Codding, R., Kleinmann, A., & Tucker, K. (2003). Assessment of reading rate in postsecondary students. *Journal of Psychoeducational Assessment, 21,* 134–144.

Lewandowski, L., Lovett, B., Parolin, R., Gordon, M., & Codding, R. (2007). Extended time accommodations and the mathematics performance of students with and without ADHD. *Journal of Psychological Assessment, 25,* 17–28.

Martin, R. P. (1988). *Assessment of personality and behavior problems: Infancy through adolescence.* New York: Guilford.

McDermott, P. A. (1986). The observation and classification of exceptional child behavior. In R. T. Brown & C. R. Reynolds (Eds.), *Psychological perspectives on childhood and exceptionality: A handbook* (pp. 136–180). New York: Wiley Interscience.

McDowell, I., & Newell, C. (1996). *Measuring health: A guide to rating scales and questionnaires* (2nd ed.). New York: Oxford University.

McGonigel, M. J., Woodruff, G., & Roszmann-Millican, M. (1994). The transdisciplinary team: A model for family-centered early intervention. In L. J. Johnson, R. J. Gallagher, P. L. Hutinger, & M. B. Karnes (Eds.), *Meeting early intervention challenges: Issues from birth to three* (2nd ed., pp. 95–132). Baltimore: Paul H. Brookes.

McLean, M., & Crais, E. R. (2006). Procedural considerations in assessing infants and preschoolers with disabilities. In M. McLean, M. Wolery, & D. B. Bailey Jr. (Eds.), *Assessing infants and preschoolers with special needs* (3rd ed., pp. 45–70). Upper Saddle River, NJ: Pearson.

Mehrens, W. A., & Ekstrom, R. B. (2002). Score reporting issues in the assessment of people with disabilities: Policies and practices. In R. B. Ekstrom & D. Smith (eds.) *Assessing individuals with disabilities in education, employment, and counseling settings.* Washington DC: American Psychological Association, PP. 87–100.

National Center on Educational Outcomes and the Parents Engaged in Education Reform Project. (1997). *Opening the door to educational reform: Understanding educational assessment and accountability.* Boston: Author.

Oakland, T., & Emmer, E. (1973). Effects of knowledge of criterion group on actual and expected performance of Negro and Mexican American eighth graders. *Journal of Consulting and Clinical Psychology, 40,* 155–159.

Oakland, T., Glutting, J., Watkins, M. W. (2005). Assessment of test behaviors with the WISC-IV. In A. Prifitera, & D. Saklofske, L. G. Weiss (Eds.), *WISC-IV clinical use and interpretation: Scientist–practitioner perspectives* (pp. 435–463) San Diego, CA: Elsevier Academic.

Paulin, J., Kingi, V., and Mossman, S.E. (2008). The public defence service pilot evaluation: Third interim report, February 2008. Wellington: Legal Services Agency.

Perenboom, R. J. M., & Chorus, A. M. J. (2003). Measuring participation according to the international Classification of Functioning, Disability and Health (ICF). *Disability and Rehabilitation, 25,* 577–587.

Radnitz, C. L., Bockian, N., & Moran, A. I. (2000). Assessment of psychopathology and personality in people with physical diabilities. In R. G. Frank & T. R. Elliot (Eds.), *Handbook of rehabilitation psychology* (pp. 287–309).Washington, DC: American Psychological Association.

Roback, A. A. (1961). *History of psychology and psychiatry.* New York: Philosophical Library.

Romero, I. (1999). Individual assessment procedures with preschool children. In E. V. Nuttall, I. Romero & J. Kalesnik (Eds.), *Assessing and screening preschoolers: Psychological and educational dimensions* (pp. 59–71). Needham Heights, MA: Allyn & Bacon.

Salvia, J., & Ysseldyke, J. E. (1998). *Assessment* (7th ed.). Boston, MA: Houghton Mifflin.

Sattler, J. M. (1988). *Assessment of children* (3rd ed.). San Diego, CA: Author.

Sattler, J. M. (2001). *Assessment of children: Cognitive applications* (4th ed.). San Diego, CA: Author.

Sattler, J. M. (2008). *Assessment of children: Cognitive foundations* (5th ed.). San Diego, CA: Author.

Schwean, V., Oakland, T. Saklofske, D., Weiss, L., Holdnack, J., & Prifitera, A. (2006). Report writting: A child centered approach. In L. G. Weiss, A. Prifitera, D. Saklofske, & J. Holdnack (Eds.). *WISC-IV Advanced Clinical Interpretations.* New York: Academic Press, 371–420.

Steele, C.M. (1992, April). Race and the schooling of Black Americans. *The Atlantic Monthly,* 68–78.

Steele, C. M., & Aronson, J. (1995). Stereotype threat and the intellectual test performance of African Americans. *Journal of Personality and Social Psychology, 69,* 797–811.

Stein, F., Bentley, D. E., & Natz, M. (1999). Computerized assessments: The Stress Management Questionnaire. In B. J. Hemphill-Pearson (Ed.), *Assessments in occupational therapy mental health: An integrative approach* (pp. 322–337). Thorofare, NJ: Slack.

Thorndike, R. L., Hagen, E. P., & Sattler, J. M. (1986). *Guide for administering and scoring the Stanford-Binet Intelligence Scale* (4th ed.) Chicago: Riverside.

Wang, Z. M. (1993) Psychology in China: A review. *Annual Review of Psychology, 44,* 87–116.

World Health Organization (WHO) (2001). *Literature review on the role of environmental factors in functioning and disability.* Geneva, Switzerland: Author.

Zuriff, G.E. (2000). Extra examination time for students with learning disabilities: An examination of the maximum potential thesis. *Applied Measurement in Education, 13,* 99–117.

10

Clinical Interviews

NORMAN L. BERVEN
University of Wisconsin–Madison

OVERVIEW

This chapter provides a discussion of the clinical interview as a method of assessment in rehabilitation and health settings. Definitions of terms are provided along with a brief review of the history of the use of clinical interviews in professional practice. Different types of clinical interviews are identified—including degree of structure, which is an important factor on which clinical interviews can vary—and factors related to the reliability and validity of information and judgments provided through interviews are considered. In addition, interview techniques are briefly reviewed along with clinical judgment, which is an important component of both clinical interviews and assessment in general. Finally, research and professional training issues are considered. Empirical documentation to support the use of clinical interviews is limited. Nevertheless, it remains the most frequently used of all assessment procedures in rehabilitation and health settings.

LEARNING OBJECTIVES

By the end of the chapter, readers should be able to:

■ Understand the role of clinical interviews in rehabilitation and health settings in both initial and intake interviews and in screening and diagnostic interviews, as well as the importance of integrating clinical interviews with other assessment methods

■ Understand the advantages and disadvantages associated with different degrees of structure in the conduct of clinical interviews

■ Apply the measurement concepts of reliability and validity to clinical interviews and understand general approaches to studying and documenting the reliability and validity of information, impressions, and judgments achieved

■ Identify interview strategies and techniques that can facilitate open, honest, and in-depth exploration in clinical interviews, thus improving the reliability and validity of information, impressions, and judgments achieved, and recognizing that reliability and validity are highly dependent on the interviewing skills of individual practitioners, perhaps more than any other general approach to assessment

■ Recognize limitations in the reliability and validity associated with clinical interviews, particularly less structured interviews, resulting in a healthy degree of skepticism in processing and using information, impressions, and judgments achieved

INTRODUCTION

Assessment typically is conducted in health and rehabilitation settings to guide the provision of treatment and other services. More specifically, Berven (2004) suggests that the purpose of assessment is threefold: (1) to define and understand concerns, problems, and needs, including as many contributing factors as possible; (2) to establish goals and objectives to be accomplished through intervention; and (3) to identify treatment and other services indicated and to develop a comprehensive intervention plan. All information obtained directly from or about an individual to be served contributes to assessment, including information from referral sources; information from the individual through interviews; past records; examinations and evaluations conducted by other professionals; and provided by family, friends, and associates.

Standardized psychological, medical, and related tests commonly are used (see chapter 4 for a further discussion of this issue). Test data result from procedures that most often are identified with assessment in health and rehabilitation settings. However, clinical interviews also are important and widely used assessment procedures. Clinical interviews utilize direct interactions between practitioners and individuals with the goal to elicit information and impressions, including observations of the individual during the interview. Clinical interviews can vary dramatically in their degree of structure or standardization, and the results can be reported in a variety of ways, including diagnostic classifications that are consistent with information and observations obtained; treatment plans; and narrative histories or descriptions that are consistent with the specific purpose of the assessment. In some instances, clinical interviews may be the only formal assessment procedure used. In contrast, when standardized tests are used, they typically are combined with clinical interviews, thus providing a context in which to test hypotheses and to integrate all information obtained through tests and other sources (Craig, 2005; Groth-Marnat, 2003).

Clinical interviews probably are the most flexible of all assessment procedures. Their scope, focus, and depth of assessment are limited only by the skills and inclinations of the practitioner and time available to conduct them.

Although tests are available that provide standardized measures of many personal characteristics, many characteristics are unable to be assessed by standardized tests. In contrast, clinical interviews potentially can focus on virtually any characteristic of interest in rehabilitation and health. For example, in considering the different domains in body functions, body structures, activities and participation, and environmental factors that are operationalized in the World Health Organization's (WHO, 2001) *International Classification of Functioning, Disability and Health* (ICF), any of the domains potentially can be explored through clinical interviews by formulating lines of inquiry that focus on those specific domains.

Some clinical interviews are conducted solely for assessment purposes, with assessment results shared with the individual and referral sources, which, in turn, use the information to design intervention and service plans. At other times a clinician conducts and coordinates the assessment as a part of the overall treatment or services provided. In such instances, while clinical interviewing is more heavily concentrated in the initial stages, it often pervades the entire treatment or intervention process, resulting in revisions in treatment or service plans and guiding the moment-to-moment decisions and interactions that occur throughout the process. Thus, virtually all interactions that occur between professional practitioners and their clients, patients, or consumers may be conceptualized as clinical interviewing.

DEFINITIONS

The *APA Dictionary of Psychology* (VandenBos, 2007) defines a *clinical interview* as "a meeting between a patient or client and an interviewer, such as a clinical psychologist or psychiatrist, for the purpose of obtaining relevant information" (p. 179). *Clinical evidence* is cross-referenced, apparently to elaborate on the meaning of "relevant information," which is defined as "information about clients or patients that is relevant to clinical diagnosis and therapy" (p. 179). In other words, clinical interviews are interpersonal interactions between a professional (e.g., physician, psychologist, counselor, nurse, occupational or physical therapist, speech and language therapist, or other rehabilitation or health professional) and a patient or client, with

Case Study 10.1

Meyer et al. (2001) have suggested that the use of unstructured clinical interviews alone will provide an incomplete understanding of clinical needs; they further suggest that an optimal clinical understanding will come from multiple methods of assessment that are integrated in a sophisticated manner.

Assume that Jeffrey, a 27-year-old man, has been referred for a psychological assessment to facilitate treatment planning and to help chart a new direction for his life. He experienced a stroke, precipitated by an overdose of amphetamines, and he has experienced a resulting partial paralysis of his dominant (right) extremities in addition to other possible limitations. He has worked as a caddy on the Nationwide Tour, a developmental professional golf tour, and he had hoped to eventually move up to the regular Professional Golf Association Tour. Much to his distress, he will most likely be unable to resume his career, and he feels that his life dreams have been lost. His work has been

his source of income and even more importantly the primary source of his identify and social network.

Assume that Jeffrey has been referred for an assessment as a basis for identifying treatment needs and goals and to begin the process of charting a new course for his life. An assessment would typically begin with a clinical interview.

Questions

1. What topics would be important to pursue?
2. What interview strategies and techniques may be used to facilitate the assessment?
3. What other sources of information and assessment methods may be important to include?
4. How would the clinical interview serve to guide the use of other assessment methods and procedures?
5. How may the interview be integrated with these other methods?

---

the clinical purpose to obtain information that will assist in diagnosing illnesses or conditions, determining clinical needs, and planning interventions, treatments, or other services to address those needs. Alternative terms with a similar meaning are *assessment interview* (e.g., Berven, 2008; Groth-Marnot, 2003) and *diagnostic interview*, which is defined by VandenBos as exploring an individual's "presenting problem, current situation, and background, with the aim of formulating a diagnosis and prognosis, as well as developing a treatment program" (p. 278). Included under these broader terms are more specific types of clinical interviews, such as intake, initial, and case history interviews; mental status examinations; and diagnostic interviews to formulate a diagnosis based on the American Psychiatric Association (APA, 2000) *Diagnostic and Statistical Manual of Mental Disorders* (DSM).

The clinical interview is by far the most widely used of all assessment procedures in virtually all rehabilitation and health disciplines. The information, perceptions, and judgments obtained typically contribute substantially to an overall assessment, guiding the conceptualization of concerns and needs, goals and objectives, and intervention plans. Even in medicine, where relatively definitive diagnostic procedures and tests more often are available compared to those available in other disciplines, clinical interviews play a major role in diagnosis and treatment planning. According to Coulehan and Block (2006), medical students are taught that "the clinical history is the most important source of diagnostic information; in fact, perhaps 70% to 80% of all relevant data are derived from

the medical interview" (p. xv). In addition, clinical interviews provide a context for understanding other assessment information, whether from psychological or medical tests (Meyer et al., 2001; Shea, 1985).

HISTORY

Clinical interviews provided the earliest approach in psychology to obtaining information and determining the needs of individuals seeking assistance (Groth-Marnat, 2003). Initially these clinical interviews followed the question-and-answer style of physicians inquiring about medical problems, symptoms, and history. The evolution of clinical interviews followed the theoretical evolution of psychology in general and counseling and psychotherapy in particular (e.g., see Berven, Thomas, & Chan, 2004). The emergence of psychoanalysis in the late 1800s and early 1900s led to a more free-flowing approach to interviewing than typical history-taking in medicine. The emergence of the client-centered approach to counseling and psychotherapy beginning in the 1940s (Rogers, 1942, 1951) emphasized the therapeutic relationship and the importance of providing the therapeutic conditions of empathy, genuineness, and unconditional positive regard to facilitate open disclosure in interviews as well as positive therapeutic change. The behavioral approach, which became popular in the 1950s, also had a major influence, resulting in a greater focus on overt behavior as opposed to covert cognitions and affect, and conducting behavioral observation as a part of the clinical interview process.

The theoretical perspectives of practitioners conducting clinical interviews play an important role in the approaches, styles, emphases, and procedures followed in the interview process. There are hundreds of theoretical approaches to counseling and psychotherapy. In addition, surveys consistently have found that most clinicians identify their theoretical orientations as eclectic (Prochaska & Norcross, 1999), drawing from multiple theories and resulting in even greater diversity in approaches to clinical interviews.

The evolution of diagnostic interviewing, beginning in the early 1900s with the mental status examination pioneered by Adolph Meyer was another important historical development (Groth-Marnat, 2003, Rogers, 2001). Mental status examinations provided structured interview procedures to develop a comprehensive picture of an individual's "current functioning, such as general appearance, behavior, thought processes, thought content, memory, attention, speech, insight, and judgment" (Groth-Marnat, 2003, p. 70). Along with the development of more highly structured interviews, dissatisfaction with unstructured clinical interviews stimulated the development of standardized psychological testing to provide more reliable and valid information at lower cost, as compared to time-consuming face-to-face interviews. In addition to the many standardized psychological tests that have been developed in subsequent years, a number of standardized diagnostic interviews also have been developed, many of them providing standardized interview procedures to achieve DSM diagnoses.

With the advent of managed care, psychological testing has come into increasing disfavor (e.g., Eisman et al., 2000; Griffith, 1997; Wood, Garb, Lilienfeld, & Nezworski, 2002). Citing evidence from studies of both companies and practitioners, managed care companies have come to view clinical interviews as a cost-effective alternative to psychological tests and assessment batteries, and they often are disinclined to authorize and pay for psychological testing. Thus, the same perceived cost advantages that historically led to the development and increasing reliance on psychological testing are now leading back to a greater reliance on interviews.

METHODS

Degree of Structure in Clinical Interviews

Clinical interviews can range from structured to semistructured to unstructured (Beutler, 1995; Groth-Marnat, 2003). Structured interviews are similar to standardized tests in specifying the questions to be asked in the interview, the order in which they are asked, and the follow-up questioning to be used, thus providing little flexibility to the practitioner. In contrast, semistructured interviews provide a greater degree of flexibility, often specifying questions to be asked, yet allowing some discretion on the part of the practitioner in the order in which questions are asked and the extent and manner in which follow-up questioning may be pursued. According to Rogers (2001), semistructured interviews allow unstructured follow-up questions, while structured interviews use carefully specified optional probes for follow-up. In unstructured interviews, the practitioner has much greater freedom in all aspects of the interview, including content, direction, questions, follow-up questions, and other interview responses used.

The degree of structure in clinical interviews has a number of implications for the utility of interviews and the information obtained. Greater structure results in less variability between practitioners and increases the likelihood that different practitioners conducting an interview with the same person in the same clinical situation will obtain similar information and observations, and will reach similar conclusions. Because of the importance of reducing variability across practitioners, Beutler (1995) suggests that "it is desirable to impose at least a modest amount of standardization on an interview whenever circumstances will permit" (p. 98). In contrast, less structured interviews allow practitioners to exercise clinical judgment in tailoring interviews to the needs of specific clinical situations; thus interviews seem less mechanical, facilitating more open communication, and can result in more useful information. However, nonverbal and verbal facilitative communication skills of the practitioner that communicate warmth and caring can be more important than the degree of structure used in the interview, thus neutralizing some of the negative effects associated with more highly structured interviews (Whiston, 2005).

Types of Clinical Interviews

There are many specific types of clinical interviews (e.g., see Craig, 2005). Moreover, clinical interviewing can pervade the entire intervention process. However, there are two general categories of clinical interviews: (1) initial and intake interviews and (2) diagnostic and screening interviews.

INTAKE AND INITIAL INTERVIEWS Practitioners in rehabilitation and health settings, as in other human services, typically begin their clinical work with an intake or initial interview. Parker and Bolton (2005) provide a distinction between initial and intake interviews in rehabilitation settings, consistent with definitions in the *APA*

Dictionary of Psychology (VandenBos, 2007). *Intake* interviews focus on the elicitation of factual information from individuals to be served while also providing information about services available and procedures to be followed during the subsequent intervention process. In contrast, *initial* interviews focus on "relationship building, attending to client behaviors, and developing a beginning picture of the client's cultural context, circumstances, values, needs, aspirations, and goals" (p. 315). Intake interviews may be conducted by case service assistants or by professional practitioners, often with the elements of both intake and initial interviews combined. As a major part of intake and initial interviews, information and explanations are provided to individuals, and informed consent is obtained regarding treatment and other services to be provided, including the nature and duration of services, confidentiality provisions and limits on confidentiality, rights to appeal treatment decisions and to terminate service, logistical procedures (e.g., scheduling and changing appointments), emergency procedures, and fee arrangements (Shaw, 2004; Shaw & Tarvydas, 2001). The assessment information obtained through initial and intake interviews is limited only by the ability and willingness of individuals to provide the requested information, facts, perceptions, thoughts, and feelings, along with the skills of practitioners in eliciting information and observing behavior during the interview.

The information obtained can be useful in a number of determinations and decisions as service proceeds (Berven, 2004). One decision concerns selection for treatment or other services, which often is based in part on determinations regarding the potential of the individual to benefit from the services available in relation to the costs associated with providing those services, along with determinations regarding any eligibility criteria related to diagnosis of disability, presence of particular qualifying types of problems, and financial need and resources. Another type of determination concerns the formulation of career and other life goals that are consistent with the strengths, limitations, preferences, and needs of the individual, which then may be pursued with the aid of the practitioner. Another type of determination is the identification of interventions, treatment, or other services that may be most helpful to the individual. Thus, the major purpose of initial and intake interviews is to obtain information, observations, and judgments that will facilitate such determinations.

Initial and intake interviews vary considerably across specific rehabilitation and health programs due to differences between agencies or programs in services provided, resources available, and eligibility criteria. Many programs develop their own interview guides for the intake or initial interview to help insure that the required information will be obtained. In addition, a number of textbooks on assessment and interviewing provide general interview guides with topics identified that may be important to explore in initial interviews (e.g., Drummond & Jones, 2006; Farley & Rubin, 2006; Groth-Marnat, 2003; Power, 2006; Sommers-Flanagan & Sommers-Flanagan, 2009). As one example, Farley and Rubin identify a number of topics that may be important to address, along with possible interview questions, organized under the following categories: (1) physical factors, including those related directly to disability; (2) psychosocial factors, including adjustment, interpersonal relationships, and social networks; (3) educational–vocational factors, including education and work history; and (4) economic factors, including income, sources of support, debt, and insurance coverage. Such interview guides can serve as a basis for intake and initial interviews, tailoring the topics and subtopics identified to meet assessment needs in specific settings. Standardized intake questionnaires also have been developed, as exemplified by the Quick View Social History, comprised of 130 questions, with responses analyzed by computer to produce a narrative report (Giannetti, 1992). Intake guides and questionnaires can help focus practioners, attention on the presenting concerns and can help insure that important points are not missed during intake or initial interviews (Hood & Johnson, 2007).

DIAGNOSTIC AND SCREENING INTERVIEWS Diagnostic interviews focus specifically on formulating a diagnosis and prognosis and, like clinical interviews in general, facilitating treatment and service planning. Diagnostic interviews often are structured and thus follow a standardized interview protocol. Most diagnostic interviews are intended to achieve DSM diagnoses (Craig, 2005) as indicated by an analysis of literature citations on clinical interviews, which found that the overwhelming majority focused on the diagnosis of disorders according to DSM criteria (Craig, 2003). An example is the *Structured Clinical Interview for DSM-IV Axis I Disorders (SCID-I)-Clinician Version* (First, Spitzer, Gibbon, & Williams, 1997), which provides a series of interview questions that lead the interviewer through a decision tree, culminating in a DSM diagnosis.

Mental status examinations constitute another common type of diagnostic interview. Daniel and Crider (2003) point out that comprehensive mental status examinations are similar to physical examinations in medicine. They focus on the physical (appearance, behavior, and motor activity), emotional (attitude, mood and affect, thought and perception, and insight and judgment), and cognitive (orientation, attention and concentration, speech and language, memory, and intelligence and abstraction) domains. As with other types of diagnostic interviews, mental status examinations rely on responses to interview questions along with observations of behavior during the interview. A number of structured interview protocols are available, such as the *Mini-Mental State Exam*, comprised of 11 items that focus on orientation, registration, attention, calculation, and language (Folstein, Folstein, & McHugh, 1975).

Other diagnostic interview protocols focus on specific disorders, including anxiety disorders, mood disorders, schizophrenia, personality disorders, alcohol problems, drug abuse, sexual dysfunctions and deviations, eating disorders, psychophysiological disorders, and both combat and noncombat posttraumatic stress disorders (Hersen & Turner, 2003). In addition, diagnostic interviews focusing on vocational capacity and earning potential are used in many vocational and forensic rehabilitation settings to facilitate determinations and opinions for legal proceedings in personal injury (e.g., motor vehicle crashes, product liability, and medical malpractice) and worker's compensation cases (Choppa & Shafer, 1992; Lynch & Lynch, 1998). Vocational diagnostic interviews provide a primary tool, along with medical record reviews, physical capacity evaluations, and standardized tests, to determine capacity to meet the demands of different occupations and settings and the loss of earning potential associated with the onset of a disability (Toppino & Boyd, 1996). Structured interview protocols typically are used, including perceptions of the individual regarding the disability and treatment, strengths and limitations, employment goals, education and training, and work and social histories (Cutler & Ramm, 1992).

Finally, interview protocols and procedures also are available to screen for problems such as suicide risk, and alcohol and other drug use and abuse, by identifying indicators on which screening interviews and observations should focus. Examples of suicide risk assessment protocols include the SAD PERSONS Scale that provides a quick screening on 10 factors indicative of risk (Patterson, Dohn, Bird, & Patterson, 1983); the Suicide Assessment Checklist that includes 12 self-report items for clients and 9 items for the counselor–observer to assess risk (Rogers, Alexander, & Subich, 1994); and a decision tree approach to screening, based on the three risk factors of previous suicide attempts, suicide plans and preparation, and desire and suicidal ideation (Joiner, Walker, Rudd, & Jobes, 1999). An example of screening interviews for alcohol and other drug problems is the CAGE, a brief interview protocol that utilizes four questions indicative of problems associated with alcohol use, with the four letters in the name of the instrument representing key words in each of the four questions (Ewing, 1984; Kitchens, 1994). See Hood & Johnson (2007) for a review of other interview protocols used for diagnostic assessments

Psychometric Considerations

Clinical interviews are used for assessment and diagnostic determinations. Thus, they should be subjected to the same psychometric scrutiny as any other psychological test or assessment measure (Berven, 2008; Groth-Marnat, 2003). Although clinical interviews typically do not produce the types of numerical scores that are characteristic of most standardized tests, they do result in clinically-relevant information, perceptions, impressions, determinations, and judgments. Thus, their reliability and validity are important.

RELIABILITY Reliability refers to the extent to which information produced is "consistent over repeated applications of a measurement procedure" and "free from errors of measurement" (American Educational Research Association [AERA], American Psychological Association [APA], and National Council on Measurement in Education [NCME], 1999, p. 180). Information produced by clinical interviews would appear to be most vulnerable to two sources of error: time-sampling and the clinical interviewers (Berven, 2008; Rogers, 2001).

Time-sampling error refers to inconsistencies in information, perceptions, and judgments produced by clinical interviews that may be conducted with the same person on different occasions. On different occasions, the communications and interview behavior of the individual may fluctuate in random and haphazard ways along with elements of the situational context in which the interview occurs. The behavior displayed by the interviewer also may vary across occasions, thus influencing the behavior of those being interviewed. To the extent that clinical interviews are vulnerable to those variations, inconsistencies will occur across interview occasions in the information, perceptions, and judgments produced. Thus, the conclusions reached may differ substantially if the interview had been conducted on a different day or at a different time. Vulnerability to time-sampling error may be assessed through test–retest reliability estimates.

Error due to interviewers refers to inconsistencies in information, perceptions, and judgments produced by interviews that may be conducted by different practitioners with the same individual. Many variations may occur between interviewers. To the extent that unstructured or semistructured interviews are utilized, different interviewers may ask different questions, may organize the interview differently, may followup client statements in different ways and to different degrees, and may pursue very different directions of inquiry, thus producing different information and judgments. In addition, even where interviews are highly structured, differences between interviewers' characteristics (e.g., warmth, caring, and style and manner of communicating, even when the same words are used) can influence the communication and behavior of the client, resulting in differences in information and judgments obtained. Finally, interviewers may differ in the ways in which information provided by a client is perceived, remembered, and processed, which also would result in differences in the information and judgments produced. Error due to interviewers may be assessed through inter-rater or inter-interviewer reliability estimates.

In general, more highly structured clinical interviews are less vulnerable to both time-sampling and interviewer error, and thus elicit information and judgments that are more reliable or consistent (Garb, 1998, 2005; Groth-Marnat, 2003; Miller, 2003). However, both test–retest and inter-interviewer reliability estimates, at best, are modest even with more highly structured interviews. Higher reliability estimates are found for broader determinations, such as the presence or absence of psychosis, and lower for more specific diagnostic determinations. In his comprehensive reviews of the research literature, Garb concluded that consistency between practitioners tends to be relatively good in rating psychiatric symptoms, ranging from fair to excellent in rating probabilities of violent or suicidal behavior, and varying dramatically in judgments about specific personality traits.

To the extent that clinical interviews are vulnerable to time-sampling error, the information, perceptions, and judgments obtained through interviews will be dependent on the particular occasion on which the interview is conducted. Thus, interviewing the same person at different times may produce different information, perceptions, and judgments. When test–retest reliability is low, clinicians should consider spacing the interviews over multiple occasions, expanding the range of times sampled, and providing for the possibility of reconciling any differences across occasions. To the extent that clinical interviews are vulnerable to error due to interviewers, the conclusions drawn may be highly dependent on and specific to the practitioner conducting the interview, with very different results obtained if a different practitioner had conducted the interview. When inter-interviewer reliability is low, the use of two or more practitioners may be needed to conduct interviews with the same individual and to then reconcile differences in information and observations obtained and conclusions reached.

VALIDITY Validity is defined as the "degree to which accumulated evidence and theory support specific interpretations of test scores entailed by proposed uses of a test" (AERA et al.,1999, p. 184). Validity refers to the empirical support available for different types of determinations, predictions, and judgments that are formulated through clinical interviews or other forms of assessment. For example, how useful are determinations based on clinical interviews in diagnosing psychopathology? What evidence supports judgments based on clinical interviews for determining potential success in a particular type of living environment or occupation? What evidence supports the inferences drawn from clinical interviews in determining treatment needs and the potential utility of specific treatments and other services?

A number of factors can diminish the validity of information, perceptions, judgments, and determinations resulting from clinical interviews. Moreover, because reliability is basic to validity, measurement errors that decrease reliability also threaten validity. Different sources of systematic error or bias can diminish validity. Some sources of systematic error are based on the communication styles and other behaviors either of the individual interviewed or the practitioner. Individuals interviewed may intentionally alter their words and behavior in an interview in order to make a desired impression (e.g., attempting to appear more compliant or more or less pathological), thus influencing the determinations and judgments of the practitioner. In addition, individuals may not be particularly accurate in reporting information even when attempting to do so, perhaps due to faulty or incomplete memory of events. Retrospective reports often are erroneous in reporting psychosocial history, such as past emotional distress or family conflicts, and even in reporting historical facts such as work histories and other life events (Henry, Moffitt, Caspi, Langley, & Silva, 1994). In addition, the behavior of the practitioner can influence the words and behavior of the client (e.g., resulting in more or less openness in disclosing and reporting information, thoughts, and feelings), which in turn can influence the validity of determinations and judgments made.

Cognitive processes of practitioners also are important components of the clinical determinations and judgments formulated through clinical interviews. Three types of cognitive processes can influence the validity of clinical judgments: cognitive heuristics, cognitive biases, and knowledge structures (Garb, 1998, 2005). *Cognitive heuristics*, such as the availability and representativeness heuristics, are short-cuts used to simplify and improve the efficiency of clinical judgments. These also may increase error in judgment. As an example of the availability heuristic, a practitioner who recently completed a training program on alcoholism may be unduly influenced by that information, given its ready availability in memory, when concluding that the behaviors of an individual may likely indicate alcohol abuse.

A number of *cognitive biases* also can threaten the validity of clinical judgments. Confirmatory bias can lead practitioners to be more heavily influenced by words and behavior that support preconceived notions or hypotheses about an individual while tending to ignore or deemphasize the importance of words and behaviors that are inconsistent with those hypotheses (Haverkamp, 1993; Strohmer, Shivy, & Chiodo, 1990).

Knowledge structures refer to knowledge and theories held by practitioners that may influence their clinical judgments, including stereotypes. For example, stereotypes held about race and ethnicity can influence practitioner judgments about the existence of pathology (Lopez, 1989), and also can lead practitioners to underestimate educational and employment potential (Rosenthal & Berven, 1999).

EXISTING EMPIRICAL DOCUMENTATION With the exception of research on the reliability and validity of structured diagnostic interviews primarily based on DSM diagnostic criteria (see Rogers, 2001), extensive research has not been conducted regarding the validity of judgments and determinations formulated through clinical interviews. Given the many factors that can pose threats, validity limitations can be expected. In his extensive reviews of research, Garb (1998, 2005) concluded that validity tends to be fair to poor in identifying and rating clinical symptoms, and poor in the diagnosis of psychopathology when predicting future behavior as well as in formulating case-effective treatment plans. More highly structured clinical interviews tend to produce more reliable and valid determinations and judgments than less highly structured interviews. "The typical or 'unstructured' clinical interview is also among the least reliable and potentially the least valid measures used in psychological assessment" (Beutler 1995, p. 94).

Clinical Interview Strategies

The reliability and validity of the information, perceptions, determinations, and judgments achieved through clinical interviews depend on two factors: (1) the communications and observations of the individual being interviewed and (2) the perceptions, interpretations, and judgments formed by the practitioner in processing and understanding the communications and behaviors produced. Structured interviews remove much of the variability among practitioners in conducting interviews by specifying the questions and the sequence in which they are to be asked. This standardization typically results in greater reliability as compared to less highly structured interviews and, to the extent that the content of the structured interview is relevant to the determinations and judgments to be made, also results in greater validity. In contrast, the reliability and validity of semistructured and unstructured clinical interviews are more highly dependent on the skills and behaviors of the practitioner who conducts the interview and processes the information.

ELICITATION OF INFORMATION AND BEHAVIOR FROM THE CLIENT Entire textbooks have been devoted to theory and technique in conducting interviews (e.g., Chan,

DISCUSSION BOX 10.1

The unstructured clinical interview is the most frequently used assessment procedure in rehabilitation and health, as well as in other human service settings. Unstructured clinical interviews frequently are used in initial contacts with individuals to be served. In that assessment is a continuous process throughout the duration of treatment and service, they are typically a part of all clinical encounters that follow. As discussed in this chapter, unstructured interviews frequently have been criticized as a source of reliable and valid assessment information.

Questions
1. What are the major criticisms of unstructured clinical interviews?
2. What are some of the positive features of unstructured clinical interviews that may account for their widespread use?
3. What steps may be taken to improve the usefulness of unstructured interviews in various types of settings in order to minimize their limitations?

Berven, & Thomas, 2004; Cormier, Nurius, & Osborn, 2009; Ivey & Ivey, 2007), including some devoted entirely to clinical interviews (e.g., Sommers-Flanagan & Sommers-Flanagan, 2009). Three important interview components include: (1) the context surrounding the interview, including the physical and interpersonal environment; (2) the content of the interview; and (3) the behaviors and techniques of the practitioner in conducting the interview (Beutler, 1995).

The *physical and interpersonal environment* in which an interview is conducted can play an important role in an individual's comfort, openness, and willingness to disclose information in a clinical interview, qualities that are critical to valid determinations and practitioner judgments. The promotion of privacy is the most important aspect of the environment that facilitates open disclosure (Sommers-Flanagan & Sommers-Flanagan, 2009). Other aspects of the physical environment also can influence client behavior and disclosure, including office colors, space, furnishings, seating arrangements, lighting, items displayed on walls (e.g., licenses, diplomas, posters, art work), and books and other items displayed on shelves, tables, and desks (Cook & Zambrano, 2007). The grooming, dress, and demeanor of the practitioner and office staff also are important parts of the physical environment that can influence the attitudes and behaviors of individuals entering a clinical interview. For example, the friendliness of staff during the first telephone call or other contact to schedule the interview appointment and the greeting received upon arrival for the interview are influential. Cultural differences also can impact the ways in which different aspects of the environment influence individuals and their behavior in clinical interviews (e.g., see Cormier et al., 2009; Ivey & Ivey, 2007).

The *content* of a clinical interview is based on the types of determinations to be made and the types of information and judgments that are most relevant to those determinations. The content should be empirically documented as relevant. For example, clinical interviews designed to provide diagnostic determinations of depression or other psychiatric disorders typically use DSM diagnostic criteria as a basis for determining the content of the interview. Clinical interviews to determine employability focus interview content on factors that have been empirically determined to influence one's ability and desire to work. Finally, clinical interviews to facilitate treatment or other service planning focus on practitioner knowledge of factors that are likely to influence the efficacy of different treatment and service alternatives.

Structured interviews specify the content of clinical interviews, and interview guides and protocols can facilitate decisions about the content and focus of semistructured and unstructured clinical interviews. Information often is obtained in advance of the interview from referral sources, other professionals, and from questionnaires and intake forms completed by individuals prior to their interview that can facilitate the planning of content and directions for clinical interviews. The content on which interviews focus will greatly influence the validity of determinations formulated through those interviews. In structured and semistructured interviews, the content of interviews is specified in the interview protocol. In unstructured interviews, although a number of interview guides can help practitioners in making decisions about interview content and focus, considerable variability may occur across practitioners in the specific content that they choose to include in the interview.

Practitioner behaviors and techniques used in conducting clinical interviews also are critical to facilitating the breadth, depth, comprehensiveness, and accuracy of information elicited, which are basic to the validity of determinations and judgments that are ultimately achieved. Practitioner communication of the basic therapeutic conditions of empathic understanding, positive regard, and genuineness facilitate the building of a positive therapeutic relationship, open communication, and disclosure. Perceptions of a practitioner's expertness, attractiveness (particularly interpersonal attractiveness), and trustworthiness by individuals being interviewed can be facilitated by practitioner attentiveness, the use of insightful and thought-provoking responses, friendliness, openness, nondefensiveness, and honesty (Cormier et al., 2009; Goldstein & Higgenbotham, 1991; Rogers, Gendlin, Kiesler, & Truax, 1967; Strong,1968;).

Ivey and Ivey (2007) define the task of practitioners in clinical interviews as helping individuals "tell their stories" through the use of active listening responses. Ivey and Ivey identify a "basic listening sequence" in introducing a topic with an open-ended question and then following up the response with a series of encouragers, paraphrases, reflections of feeling, and follow-up questions to expand the detail and specificity of the story being told. One of the most important techniques is to follow up responses to a sufficient degree to provide a thorough understanding of the facts of situations as well as thoughts and feelings, particularly questions that ask for specific examples to show what individuals mean by statements made (Sommers-Flanagan & Sommers-Flanagan, 2009).

CLINICAL JUDGMENT Clinical judgment is important to the ultimate determinations reached through clinical interviews and to the moment-to-moment decisions that practitioners make in conducting clinical interviews. Practitioners must perceive the communications of the individual, including the nonverbal components of the communication; process, interpret, and understand the communication; and choose from the universe of responses that may be used in responding to the communication. Clinical judgment can influence each of these processes. Variations in clinical judgment among practitioners account for much of the variability in the moment-to-moment behavior of different practitioners. For example, one practitioner may assume that he or she knows what an individual is implying through a particular communication, even though it may not have been stated explicitly, while another may respond with follow-up questions to better understand what is meant by that communication. As a result, the two practitioners may elicit very different information, which then influences their subsequent interview responses and behavior.

As stated by Meyer et al. (2001), exclusive use of clinical interviews in assessment will lead to limited understanding. An integration of findings from a variety of assessment methods provides the most complete understanding. However, with the reluctance of managed care companies to authorize and pay for psychological testing to use in conjunction with clinical interviews, practitioners often rely on interview information and observations as the primary or even sole basis for clinical judgment and planning. Garb (1998, 2005) has made a number of recommendations for improving clinical judgments, which apply both to final determinations made in clinical interviews and to the judgments made in guiding the moment-to-moment conduct of interviews: (1) emphasize empirically supported interpretations rather than clinical experience in guiding interviews and formulating determinations; (2) maintain sensitivity to and attempt to counteract potential biases due to race, gender, income, disability, and other client characteristics; (3) focus on client strengths, not only on limitations and pathology; (4) remember the reliability and validity of clinical perceptions and judgments are limited; (5) emphasize systematic and comprehensive inquiry in conducting clinical interviews; (6) supplement clinical interviews with psychological tests and behavioral observations in order to enhance the reliability and validity of judgments; and (7) consider multiple alternatives in attempting to understand phenomena, interpret and integrate information, and formulate judgments.

RESEARCH AND PROFESSIONAL TRAINING NEEDS

Clinical interviews are the most widely used assessment procedure and technique by different disciplines in rehabilitation and health settings. Even in those instances when definitive tests are available in medicine to facilitate diagnosis and treatment decisions, clinical and history taking interviews are a standard component of diagnosis and treatment planning, both as a primary source of information and as a context for interpreting other assessment results (Coulehan & Block, 2006). Despite the extensive use of clinical interviews, research to understand and document the reliability and validity of determinations achieved through clinical interviews has not been extensive. In addition, training in clinical interviewing may be lacking, as professional education programs may provide more extensive and systematic training in the interpretation of standardized tests as opposed to clinical interviewing and clinical judgment in the integration of assessment information and findings.

Research is required to document the reliability and validity associated with clinical interviews. Most research on clinical interviews has focused on structured and semistructured diagnostic interviews (see Rogers, 2001). Empirical documentation typically is limited, even with diagnostic interviews, and often is based on older versions of diagnostic interviews and to a limited range of specific diagnostic categories (Miller, 2003).

Computer-administered interviews hold promise and are deserving of research and development efforts. They often are more comprehensive and reliable and less biased than other types of clinical interviews and evaluations (Emmelkamp, 2005; Garb, 2007; Kobak, et al., 1997; Plutchik & Karasu, 1991). Computers can administer structured interviews without any deviations whatsoever from standardized interview procedures, thus enhancing reliability and validity. In addition, the use of computer assisted interviews may promote greater openness and honesty in communication when compared to a live practitioner.

Relative to psychological tests and other types of assessment procedures, the reliability and validity of determinations and judgments from clinical interviews, particularly unstructured interviews, are more highly dependent on the skills of the practitioner, both in conducting the interviews and in processing and interpreting the findings. Training can improve interview skills (e.g., see a research review by Daniels, Rigazio-DiGilio, & Ivey, 1997). However, research is needed to link specific

RESEARCH BOX 10.1

Rosenthal and Berven (1999) provide an example of a study to better understand potential bias in clinical judgment and, more specifically, the influence of racial stereotypes on those judgments.

Objective: The objective of the study was to examine the possible effects of client race on clinical impressions of a client (general evaluation of the client and perceptions regarding the likelihood of psychopathology indicated) and estimates of educational and vocational potential.

Method: Participants were 110 white graduate students in rehabilitation counseling from nine different universities. Two sets of written case materials for a simulated client were developed that were identical, except that the client was portrayed as white in one set and African American in the other. The materials were divided into a minimal information component (a referral letter from a detoxification unit; an admission form from the detoxification unit; a report from an arrest for driving under the influence, including a photograph of the client; and an initial interview transcript) and a subsequent information component (an alcohol and other drug abuse assessment; documentation of participation in treatment for retention of his driver's license; letter from a veterans organization explaining his military discharge; a letter from the most recent employer; and a vocational evaluation report). The minimal information materials, similar to those that may be available at the earliest stages of treatment and service, were written so as to elicit impressions consistent with some of the common stereotypes that may influence perceptions of African Americans. The subsequent information materials were written so as to contradict some of the more negative impressions and judgments that may have been elicited initially. Participants were assigned randomly

to two different groups, one viewing the materials for the client portrayed as African American, and the other for the same client portrayed as White. Participants then rated the client on the measures of clinical impressions and on judgments about potential of the client, with ratings completed twice, once after reading the minimal information materials, and again after reading the subsequent information materials.

Results: Although there were no differences between groups on the measures of general evaluation and likelihood of psychopathology when the client was portrayed as African American, he was viewed as having less educational and vocational potential than when portrayed as White even though all information other than client race was identical in the two conditions. These differences were found after participants had reviewed the minimal client information. The differences persisted after they had reviewed the subsequent client information designed to counter any stereotypes that may have been elicited.

Conclusion: The generalizability of the results was limited due to the use of a case simulation rather than an actual clinical encounter; in addition, generalizability was limited by the use of graduate students as research participants as opposed to practitioners. However, because of random assignment of participants to conditions and the control of all variations between conditions, except for the independent variable of client race, the differences in clinical judgment regarding the educational and vocational potential of the client could be clearly attributed to the client's race. Thus, the results suggest the possibility that counselor judgment regarding client potential may be influenced by the client's race, which could influence career guidance and opportunities made available to clients by practitioners.

interview skills and clinical judgment skills to the reliability and validity of determinations and judgments achieved through clinical interviews and to document the effectiveness of training procedures to develop those

skills. Given the importance of skills in clinical interviewing, systematic instruction in developing those skills should be an important part of professional education in all rehabilitation and health disciplines.

Summary and Conclusion

Clinical interviews are the most frequently used assessment procedures in rehabilitation and health disciplines. Nearly all clinical work begins with an intake or initial interview. Structured diagnostic interviews also are used frequently. Standardized psychological, medical, and other tests do not assess all specific and important human

qualities and characteristics. In contrast, clinical interviews can be tailored to focus on virtually all characteristics of interest. The degree of structure for an interview can vary greatly, and thus its qualities should be considered carefully. Structured interviews have the advantage of greater reliability and validity of resulting information, judgments, and determinations. Unstructured interviews have the advantage of greater flexibility to adapt to different clinical situations. In addition, clinical interviews are highly dependent on clinical skills, with considerable variability among practitioners in the reliability and validity of determinations achieved through clinical interviews.

Finally, in addition to producing important assessment information in their own right, clinical interviews provide a context for understanding and interpreting information provided by standardized tests and other assessment procedures, thus contributing to their importance in rehabilitation and health practice and settings.

Self-Check Questions

1. What are some of the specific types of diagnostic and screening interviews and what roles may they play in different types of rehabilitation and health settings?
2. How may clinical interviews be integrated with tests and other assessment procedures to enhance the validity of overall assessments in rehabilitation and health settings?
3. What are some of the major threats to reliability and validity of information, impressions, and judgments achieved through clinical interviews?
4. The effectiveness of clinical interviews in producing valid information, impressions, and judgments is highly dependent on the behavior of the practitioner. What are some of the techniques and behaviors that a practitioner may use to enhance the effectiveness of interviews conducted?
5. What steps may practitioners take when obtaining and processing assessment information in order to enhance the validity of their clinical judgments?

References

American Educational Research Association (AERA), American Psychological Association (APA), & National Council on Measurement in Education (NCME). (1999). *Standards for educational and psychological testing*. Washington, DC: American Educational Research Association.

American Psychiatric Association. (2000). *Diagnostic and statistical manual of mental disorders* (4th ed., text rev.). Washington, DC: Author.

Berven, N. L. (2004). Assessment. In T. F. Riggar & D. R. Maki (Eds.), *Handbook of rehabilitation counseling* (pp. 199–217). New York: Springer.

Berven, N. L. (2008). Assessment interviewing. In B. F. Bolton & R. M. Parker (Eds.), *Handbook of measurement and evaluation in rehabilitation* (4th ed. pp. 241–261). Austin, TX: Pro-Ed.

Berven, N. L., Thomas, K. R., & Chan, F. (2004). An introduction to counseling for rehabilitation health professionals. In F. Chan, N. L. Berven, & K. R. Thomas (Eds.), *Counseling theories and techniques for rehabilitation health professionals* (pp. 3–16). New York: Springer.

Beutler, L. E. (1995). The clinical interview. In L. E. Beutler & M. R. Berren (Eds.), *Integrative assessment of adult personality* (pp. 94–120). New York: Guilford.

Chan, F., Berven, N. L., & Thomas, K. R. (Eds.). (2004). *Counseling theories and techniques for rehabilitation health professionals*. New York: Springer.

Choppa, A. J., & Shafer, K. (1992). Introduction to personal injury and expert witness work. In A. J. Choppa & J. M. Siefker (Ed.), *Vocational evaluation in private sector rehabilitation* (pp. 135–168). Menomonie: University of Wisconsin-Stout, Stout Vocational Rehabilitation Institute.

Cook, K., & Zambrano, E. (2007, March). *My office is speaking: Using elements of interior design to communicate to clients*. Paper presented at the meeting of the American Counseling Association, Detroit, MI.

Cormier, S., Nurius, P. S., & Osborn, C. J. (2009). *Interviewing and change strategies for helpers: Fundamental skills and cognitive behavior interventions* (6th ed.). Belmont, CA: Brooks/Cole.

Coulehan, J. L., & Block, M. L. (2006). *The medical interview: Mastering skills for clinical practice* (5th ed.). Philadelphia: F. A. Davis.

Craig, R. J. (2003). Assessing personality and psychopathology by interviews. In I. B. Weiner (Chief Ed.) & J. R. Graham & J. A. Naglieri (Vol. Eds.), *Handbook of psychology: Vol. 10. Assessment psychology* (pp. 487–508). Hoboken, NJ: Wiley.

Craig, R. J. (2005). The clinical process of interviewing. In R. J. Craig (Ed.), *Clinical and diagnostic interviewing* (2nd ed., pp. 21–41). Lanham, MD: Jason Aronson.

Cutler, F., & Ramm, A. (1992). Introduction to the basics of vocational evaluation. In J. M. Siefker (Ed.), *Vocational evaluation in private sector rehabilitation* (pp. 31–66). Menomonie: University of Wisconsin-Stout, Stout Vocational Rehabilitation Institute.

Daniel, M. S., & Crider, C. J. (2003). Mental status examination. In M. Hersen & S. M. Turner (Eds.), *Diagnostic interviewing* (3rd ed., pp. 21–46). New York: Kluwer Academic/Plenum.

Daniels, T., Rigazio-DiGilio, S., & Ivey, A. (1997). Microcounseling: A training and supervision paradigm. In E. Watkins (Ed.), *Handbook of psychotherapy supervision* (pp. 277–295). New York: Wiley.

Drummond, R. J., & Jones, K. D. (2006). *Assessment procedures for counselors and helping professionals* (6th ed.). Upper Saddle River, NJ: Pearson.

Eisman, E. J., Dies, R. R., Finn, S. E., Eyde, L. D., Kay, G. G., Kubiszyn, T. W., et al. (2000). Problems and limitations in using psychological assessment in the contemporary health care delivery system. *Professional Psychology: Research and Practice, 31,* 131–140.

Emmelkamp, P. M. G. (2005). Technological innovations in clinical assessment and psychotherapy. *Psychotherapy and Psychosomatics, 74,* 336–343.

Ewing, J. A. (1984). Detecting alcoholism: The CAGE Questionnaire. *Journal of the American Medical Association, 252,* 1905–1907.

Farley, R. C., & Rubin, S. E. (2006). The intake interview. In R. T. Roessler & S. E. Rubin (Eds.), *Case management and rehabilitation counseling: Procedures and techniques* (4th ed., pp. 51–74). Austin, TX: Pro-Ed.

First, M. B., Spitzer, R. L., Gibbon, M., & Williams, J. B. W. (1997). *Structured Clinical Interview for DSM-IV Axis I Disorders (SCID-I)-Clinician Version.* Washington, DC: American Psychiatric Press.

Folstein, M. F., Folstein, S. E., & McHugh, P. R. (1975). "Mini-Mental State": A practical method for grading the cognitive state of patients for the clinician. *Journal of Psychiatric Research, 12,* 189–198.

Garb, H. N. (1998). *Studying the clinician: Judgment research and psychological assessment.* Washington, DC: American Psychological Association.

Garb, H. N. (2005). Clinical judgment and decision making. *Annual Review of Clinical Psychology, 1,* 67–89.

Garb, H. N. (2007). Computer-administered interviews and rating scales. *Psychological Assessment, 19,* 4–13.

Giannetti, R. A. (1992). *User's guide for Quickview Social History–Clinical Version.* Minneapolis, MN: NCS Pearson.

Goldstein, A. P., & Higginbotham, H. N. (1991). Relationship-enhancement methods. In F. H. Kanfer & A. P. Goldstein (Eds.), *Helping people change: A textbook of methods* (4th ed.). New York: Pergamon.

Griffith, L. (1997). Surviving no-frills mental health care: The future of psychological assessment. *Journal of Practical Psychiatry and Behavioral Health, 3,* 255–258.

Groth-Marnat, G. (2003). *Handbook of psychological assessment* (4th ed.). New York: Wiley.

Haverkamp, B. E. (1993). Confirmatory bias in hypothesis testing for client-identified and counselor self-generated hypotheses. *Journal of Counseling Psychology, 40,* 303–315.

Henry, B., Moffitt, T. E., Caspi, A., Langley, J., & Silva, P. A. (1994). On the "remembrance of things past": A longitudinal evaluation of the retrospective method. *Psychological Assessment, 6,* 92–101.

Hersen, M., & Turner, S. M. (Eds.). (2003). *Diagnostic interviewing* (3rd ed.). New York: Kluwer Academic/Plenum.

Hood, A. B., & Johnson, R. W. (2007). *Assessment in counseling: A guide to the use of psychological assessment procedures* (4th ed.). Alexandria, VA: American Counseling Association.

Ivey, A. E., & Ivey, M. B. (2007). *Intentional interviewing and counseling: Facilitating client development in a multicultural society* (6th ed.). Pacific Grove, CA: Brooks/Cole.

Joiner, T. E., Walker, R. L., Rudd, M. D., & Jobes, D. A. (1999). Scientizing and routinizing the assessment of suicidality in outpatient practice. *Professional Psychology: Research and Practice, 30,* 447–453.

Kitchens, J. M. (1994). Does this patient have an alcohol problem? *Journal of the American Medical Association, 272,* 1782–1787.

Kobak, K. A., Taylor, L. vH., Dottl, S. L., Greist, J. H., Jefferson, J. W., Burroughs, D., Katzelnick, D. J., & Mandell, M. (1997). Computerized screening for psychiatric disorders in an outpatient community mental health clinic. *Psychiatric Services, 48,* 1048–1057.

Lopez, S. R. (1989). Patient variable biases in clinical judgment: Conceptual overview and methodological considerations. *Psychological Bulletin, 106,* 184–203.

Lynch, R. K., & Lynch, R. T. (1998). Rehabilitation counseling in the private sector. In R. M. Parker & E. M. Szymanski (Eds.), *Rehabilitation counseling: Basics and beyond* (3rd ed., pp. 71–105). Austin, TX: Pro-Ed.

Meyer, G. J., Finn, S. E., Eyde, L. D., Kay, G. G., Moreland, K. L., Dies, R. R., et al. (2001). Psychological testing and psychological assessment. *American Psychologist, 56,* 128–165.

Miller, C. (2003). Interviewing strategies. In M. Hersen & S. M. Turner (Eds.), *Diagnostic interviewing* (3rd ed., pp. 47–66). New York: Kluwer Academic/Plenum.

Parker, R. M., & Bolton, B. (2005). Psychological assessment in rehabilitation. In R. M. Parker, E. M. Szymanski, & J. B. Patterson (Eds.), *Rehabilitation counseling: Basics and beyond* (4th ed., pp. 307–334). Austin, TX: Pro-Ed.

Patterson, W. M., Dohn, H. H., Bird, J., & Patterson, G. A. (1983). Evaluation of suicidal patients: The SAD PERSONS Scale. *Psychosomatics, 24,* 343–349.

Plutchik, R., & Karasu, T. B. (1991). Computers in psychotherapy: An overview. *Computers in Human Behavior, 7,* 33–44.

Power, P. W. (2006). *A guide to vocational assessment* (4th ed.). Austin, TX: Pro-Ed.

Prochaska, J. O., & Norcross, J. C. (1999). *Systems of psychotherapy: A transtheoretical approach* (4th ed.). Pacific Grove, CA: Brooks/Cole.

Rogers, C. R. (1942). *Counseling and psychotherapy.* Boston: Houghton Mifflin.

Rogers, C. R. (1951). *Client-centered therapy.* Boston: Houghton Mifflin.

Rogers, C. R., Gendlin, E., Kiesler, D., & Truax, C. (1967). *The therapeutic relationship and its impact: A study of psychotherapy with schizophrenics.* Madison: University of Wisconsin Press.

Rogers, J. R., Alexander, R. A., & Subich, L. M. (1994). Development and psychometric analysis of the Suicide

Assessment Checklist. *Journal of Mental Health Counseling, 16,* 352–368.

Rogers, R. (2001). *Handbook of diagnostic and structured interviewing.* New York: Guilford.

Rosenthal, D. A., & Berven, N. L. (1999). Effects of client race on clinical judgment. *Rehabilitation Counseling Bulletin, 42,* 243–264.

Shaw, L. R. (2004). Risk management for rehabilitation counseling and related professions. In F. Chan, N. L. Berven, & K. R. Thomas (Eds.), *Counseling theories and techniques for rehabilitation health professionals* (pp. 423–443). New York: Springer.

Shaw, L. R., & Tarvydas, V. M. (2001). The use of professional disclosure in rehabilitation counseling. *Rehabilitation Counseling Bulletin, 45,* 40–47.

Shea, V. (1985). Overview of the assessment process. In C. S. Newmark (Ed.), *Major psychological assessment instruments* (pp. 1–10). Boston: Allyn & Bacon.

Sommers-Flanagan, J., & Sommers-Flanagan, R. (2009). *Clinical interviewing* (4th ed.). Hoboken, NJ: Wiley.

Strohmer, D. C., Shivy, V. A., & Chiodo, A. L. (1990). Information processing strategies in counselor hypothesis testing: The role of selective memory and expectancy. *Journal of Counseling Psychology, 37,* 465–472.

Strong, S. R. (1968). Counseling: An interpersonal influence process. *Journal of Counseling Psychology, 15,* 215–224.

Toppino, D., & Boyd, D. (1996). Wage loss analysis: Vocational expert foundation and methodology. *American Rehabilitation Economics Association Journal, 1,* 1–12.

VandenBos, G. R. (2007). *APA dictionary of psychology.* Washington, DC: American Psychological Association.

Whiston, S. C. (2005). *Principles and applications of assessment in counseling* (2nd ed.). Belmont, CA: Brooks/Cole.

Wood, J. W., Garb, H. N., Lilienfeld, S. O., & Nezworski, M. T. (2002). Clinical assessment. *Annual Review of Psychology, 53,* 519–543.

World Health Organization (WHO). (2001). *International classification of functioning, disability and health (ICF).* Geneva, Switzerland: Author.

11

Forensic Assessment

RALPH M. CRYSTAL
ALICE S. ERICKSON
University of Kentucky, Lexington

OVERVIEW

This chapter discusses forensic assessment in vocational settings. The history of proprietary rehabilitation practice as it is related to vocational assessment with work injury cases is reviewed. The chapter discusses vocational and employability assessment; roles and functions of forensic rehabilitation practitioners; research related to forensic rehabilitation practice; methods used to evaluate, assess, and determine health related to vocational and occupational functioning; and emerging roles for forensic rehabilitation practice. Although primary emphasis is on vocational aspects, several life span–life space issues are considered briefly, including life care planning, domestic aspects, and wrongful death.

LEARNING OBJECTIVES

By the end of the chapter, readers should be able to:

- Differentiate aspects of assessment in proprietary and public vocational assessment involving work injury cases
- Outline the history of forensic vocational assessment and its developmental influence on current vocational rehabilitation practices
- Describe the roles and functions of forensic rehabilitation and vocational practitioners
- Provide a survey of key research findings related to forensic vocational practice
- Evaluate methods used to assess and determine vocational potential and compensation with work injury
- Discuss emerging assessment roles of forensic rehabilitation practitioners

INTRODUCTION

Forensic rehabilitation is the specialization within *proprietary rehabilitation practice* that is involved in *private for profit vocational rehabilitation*. In contrast to *public vocational rehabilitation,* private for profit vocational rehabilitation typically provides services to clients who have had a work or personal injury or allege workplace discrimination. These disputes typically are resolved in a civil or administrative court. *Proprietary rehabilitation* typically is adversarial. The client's goal is to resolve the dispute and receive some monetary award from insurance programs (i.e., worker compensation, long-term disability, personal and automobile accident coverage). In contrast, *public rehabilitation* typically is nonadversarial. The client's (in some venues referred to as consumer's) goal is to achieve a positive employment outcome, not a monetary award, benefits, or remuneration for loss of potential earning power and revenue streams as a result of injury or death.

Forensic experts are found in all professions. Their goal is similar: to provide information that assists civil and administrative law judges, magistrates, juries, and other finders of fact to resolve legal disputes. The goal of forensic rehabilitation assessment is to acquire and provide information that estimates the impact of a person's injury on his or her ability to work and hold a job in light of physical and mental abilities.

This chapter reviews the evolution, nature, and scope of forensic rehabilitation practice. Assessment procedures and formats used by the private rehabilitation practitioner are emphasized. Clients (often through plaintiff and defendant attorneys or insurance companies) seek the services of forensic rehabilitation professionals to help resolve issues associated with worker compensation, long-term disability, social security disability, personal injury, employment discrimination, domestic relations (e.g., divorce), life care planning, and wrongful death lawsuits. A sequential return to work process, including assessment procedures, is described that is used by private rehabilitation professionals in an attempt to restore the client's preinjury status with the objective of making the client as functional as possible.

The role and definition of an *expert witness*, also called the *vocational expert*, are described. The O*NET and its precursor, the Dictionary of Occupational Titles, work life expectancy tables, and software packages are discussed in light of providing professional services that are objective and effective when attempting to determine a client's residual transferable skills and employment options. Ethical issues that emphasize the use of assessment tools and software as well as counselor–client and counselor–employer relationships are discussed.

WHAT IS FORENSIC REHABILITATION?

Proprietary rehabilitation practitioners provide various client services. These include vocational assessment, vocational counseling, and labor market analyses; job placement services, including resume writing, job search strategies, interviewing, and assistance with securing employment such as job development and job modification; and expert witness services.

As an expert witness, the proprietary rehabilitation practitioner provides forensic services. Forensic experts assist the legal system to resolve issues associated with a person's employability, earning capacity, and job availability (Maze, 1996). Their work compares the income an individual can reasonably be expected to earn in the future in light of his or her mental or physical injuries with the amount of income the individual would have earned prior to injury (Maze, p.79). The terms *forensic rehabilitation* and *proprietary rehabilitation* often are used interchangeably. Forensic practitioners usually work in the civil or administrative law court system and provide expert witness services. Proprietary rehabilitation practitioners may provide forensic expert testimony as well as actual vocational rehabilitation and job placement services. Issues resolved through forensic and proprietary rehabilitation typically occur in a courtroom, through mediation, or through mutual agreement prior to reaching an administrative or civil court.

Proprietary rehabilitation practitioners deal with definitions of disability, which differ depending on the source. For example, an individual may be determined totally disabled and unable to work under Social Security regulations while only partially disabled and able to perform some work under worker compensation regulations. The reason for this discrepancy is that Social Security regulations consider all aspects of the individual, including all disabling conditions as well as the age and education of the person. A person will be found totally disabled under Social Security regulations if he/she is unable to perform a significant number of jobs in the national economy. An administrative law judge determines what constitutes a significant number. A person can be found to be disabled under Social Security even though jobs exist that the person can perform. However, the individual is deemed disabled under the Social Security Act if those jobs do not exist in "significant" numbers.

In contrast, worker compensation regulations consider only the specific work injury condition. Additionally, a disability may or may not completely prevent the injured person from being able to engage in substantial gainful activity or work. Nevertheless, an accident or impairment may alter an individual's ability to work and earn money.

The ability to perform work under Social Security and worker compensation typically is based on how the job normally is performed without job modifications. Factors such as reasonable accommodation and undue hardship are not considered in determining a person's ability to work. A further complicating factor is that, under Social Security, the national economy is considered. In contrast, in worker compensation, work within a state or even a region within a state may be considered for employment purposes. No such standards of work exist in civil court cases, and the forensic expert is free to discuss employability based on job accommodations.

Forensic rehabilitation services are adversarial and litigious by definition. They involve the gathering of information, including test data, generally for three purposes: (1) to describe a person's current vocational and occupational status; (2) to guide predictions of future work life based on a systematic, objective, and scientific analysis of employability; and (3) to assist rehabilitation practitioners in their work to assist the injured or impaired employee to return to work. Civil personal injury cases consider a person's pre- and postinjury earning capacity. Decisions impacting monetary awards generally make this work adversarial.

A forensic rehabilitation expert conducts a comprehensive assessment of vocational-related qualities, including demographic information (e.g., age, sex, socioeconomic status) as well as information about the individual's work history and residual and transferable job skills for the purpose of drawing conclusions about employability and earning capacity as well as possible monetary awards. In civil and personal injury matters, the ability to work or the diminished capacity to work then is translated into a loss of capacity to earn money. When

employed by the plaintiff (e.g., the client), the role of the forensic expert is to provide information that highlights the impact of the injury in ways that lead to greater monetary awards. When employed by the defendant (e.g., an insurance company, Social Security Administration), the role of the forensic expert is to provide information that mitigates the injury's impact and thus minimizes monetary awards (Brodwin 2001; Dunn, 2001; Lynch & Lynch, 1998; Power, 2000; Siefker, 1992).

HISTORICAL PERSPECTIVES OF FORENSIC REHABILITATION

Forensic rehabilitation services often are a component of work provided by proprietary rehabilitation experts. As noted previously, forensic experts work in the court and administrative law systems, whereas proprietary rehabilitation practitioners provide actual rehabilitation services and also may provide forensic services. Many nonforensic proprietary rehabilitation practitioners may find themselves, in the course of their casework, faced with the prospects of presenting case assessments and defending their work and opinions in a civil or administrative court on a periodic but not regular basis.

The passage of the federal Social Security Disability Insurance Program, particularly the 1954 Social Security Act, has had a decided impact on forensic rehabilitation practice. This legislation and associated federal policies allow for the payment of monetary benefits to persons whose work or nonwork related disabilities prevent them from working (Shaw, 1995).

The former Social Security Disability Insurance Program, now the Office of Disability Adjudication and Review, is responsible for producing information regarding the employability of individuals with disabilities. In l962, the Social Security Administration established criteria for employing vocational experts to provide opinions on job availability that may be suitable for a claimant, including guidelines for determining work availability and the claimant's ability to perform jobs. Vocational rehabilitation experts are able to provide assessment data and labor market research needed by administrative law judges to make fair decisions regarding whether a person applying for Social Security disability benefits is able to perform a significant number of jobs in the national economy. Thus, these experts increasingly have been requested to present testimony in these cases. The federal courts have continued to require federal Social Security administrative law judges to obtain expert vocational testimony in order to make determinations whether an individual meets the criteria for disability under Social Security.

During the 1970s, proprietary rehabilitation services emerged from public sector vocational rehabilitation services due to two landmark events. First, the passage of the Rehabilitation Act of 1973 prioritized public sector vocational rehabilitation services to the clients with the most severe disabilities. Thus, an *order of selection* (Rehabilitation Act, 1973) was established: The most severely disabled applicants would be served before others with fewer barriers to employment. In addition, this legislation underscored the belief that all persons can work at some level and in some capacity (Siefker, 1992). Injured workers were served less often by public rehabilitation programs following passage of the Rehabilitation Act of 1973.

In 1972, the National Commission on State Workers' Compensation Laws encouraged states to make vocational rehabilitation services available to eligible injured workers within the framework of a state's worker compensation bureau (Siefker, 1992). This resulted in each state developing policy that lead to the delivery of rehabilitation services to eligible injured workers. This stimulated the development of the private rehabilitation services sector as a viable and important resource to insurance companies and their injured workers.

Proprietary rehabilitation practitioners receive referrals that may originate from state worker compensation agencies; companies providing disability insurance; and attorneys handling accident, product, third party liability, domestic relations matters, employment discrimination, wrongful death, and long-term disability litigation. The Social Security Office of Disability Adjudication and Review maintains its own roster of vocational experts who are called on a rotating basis. Many Social Security vocational experts also provide vocational expert testimony and/or vocational rehabilitation services in other venues. In general, the forensic vocational expert considers the impact of an injury and/or disability on an individual's future ability to work and earn money.

DIFFERENCES BETWEEN THE PRIVATE AND PUBLIC REHABILITATION SECTORS

Types of Clients in Private and Public Rehabilitation

Proprietary and public sector rehabilitation clients differ in two important ways. First, most proprietary sector clients have a prior work history, and many have extensive predisability work skills that may be used when implementing an appropriate return to work plan or when incorporated as transferable skills in a new job. Unlike public vocational rehabilitation providers, proprietary rehabilitation providers do not work with clients whose exclusive injury is birth-related. However, they may work with clients with disabilities that preexisted a current injury.

Thus, most proprietary rehabilitation referrals are persons with adult-onset disabilities due to being injured or disabled. Prior to their current injuries, many never have had chronic illness or been injured and instead enjoyed a normal lifestyle. The acquisition of an injury and disability often leads to acute emotional, psychological, and social adjustment issues that should be considered in the return to work plan. Rehabilitation specialists working in the private sector attempt to return the client to work as soon as possible, typically following a determination by a physician that the individual has reached maximum medical improvement.

The presence of soft tissue or musculoskeletal injuries is common in injured workers as well as in personal injury civil litigation cases. In worker compensation, about 50% of cases involve back injuries, 35% are upper extremity injuries, and the remaining 15% display other conditions (Siefker, 1992). A mental impairment may overlay a physical injury. Unless the injury is catastrophic or profound, such as brain injury or paralysis, most injured workers are expected to return to work with appropriate planning and assistance after rehabilitation services. Although the injured individual may have the capacity to return to work, many do not for various reasons (e.g., their advanced age, lack of transferable vocational skills, or potential lower earnings).

Public and proprietary rehabilitation clients often differ in their background, disability etiology, and their personal perspectives or attitudes. Clients seen by public rehabilitation specialists generally voluntarily seek services in order to be rehabilitated and receive assistance in order to return to work. However, clients seen by proprietary rehabilitation (i.e., forensic) specialists generally want to return to work only if they can resume their prior work; if unable to do so, they seek monetary benefits. Thus, forensic practice is frequently an adversarial process, and the individual is often an involuntary participant. This is especially true when a person is referred by a defendant for a vocational evaluation. Refusal to participate in the evaluation may lead to dismissal of the case by the judge. The client attempts to appear as disabled or limited as possible, often with the encouragement of family members and significant others. The length of time between injury and disability claim resolution also can impact outcome. Although a client's return to work is more difficult when out of work

DISCUSSION BOX 11.1

Predicting Return to Work

How should one best measure a person's ability to work and whether the individual will actually return to work? Many individuals say that early intervention and a good support system are the best predictors of returning an individual to productive employment. Others argue that disincentives such as potential disability payments, length of time to resolve a case, lack of education an advanced age, and lack of transferable job skills serve as disincentives to a return to productive employment. How can these be best investigated to determine how to best facilitate a return to employment?

for longer periods, this generally is unrelated to the ultimate forensic vocational question: whether the person can engage in competitive work.

A client's self-esteem, self-image, or self-concept often is associated with one's work. Thus, a client's self-worth may be diminished when out of work or if he or she returns to work that is demanding or personally or financially unrewarding. Issues associated with self-worth may impact their subsequent employment related decisions. For example, clients who consider either applying for Social Security disability or accepting a lesser paying job may decide to claim a total disability because this status may provide funds equivalent to what they could have earned in an alternate job. Moreover, a disabled status may allow the individual to maintain a sense of self-worth because having a disability may be viewed as more acceptable than performing a menial job. In addition, persons who experience pain or other physical discomfort may benefit by being at home on disability rather than at an alternate job earning about the same as the disability payment.

DIFFERENCES IN VOCATIONAL PLANNING IN PRIVATE AND PROPRIETARY REHABILITATION

Funds for public rehabilitation agencies generally come from federal and state sources while those for private sector rehabilitation come from fee-for-services, paid mainly by insurance companies and third party administrators (e.g., insurance companies and self-insured companies.)

Public and proprietary rehabilitation services generally have similar vocational goals and follow a somewhat standard protocol when working with persons who have incurred a disability (Rubin & Roessler, 2001; Siefker 1992; Wright, 1980). A proprietary vocational rehabilitation evaluation has three basic goals. First, restore the client to the same job that he or she had prior to

incurring a disability. Second, if previous skills cannot be restored or a disability accommodated, then enhance other skills as well as change the client's environment to such a degree that he or she can use compensatory methods and thus seek alternate work. Third, if the individual cannot return to prior or other work using existing vocational skills, accommodations, and compensatory methods, then attempt to develop alternative skills and/or select a different career path.

A goal of public rehabilitation generally is to assist a person with a disability to develop or regain his or her skills needed for successful employment. This often includes extensive retraining and may include additional education. Rehabilitation assessment and planning should consider the whole person, including injury or disability related issues, especially when serving persons with severe disabilities and those that are progressive with anticipated escalating functional limitations.

A goal of proprietary rehabilitation, especially when working with clients seeking worker compensation, is to assist persons to restore function or to mitigate the adverse impact of the current injury. Provisions impacting worker compensation rehabilitation generally do not consider the possibility of further dysfunction. When receiving services from proprietary rehabilitation, rehabilitation plans are unlikely to include provisions for preexisting conditions, especially plans authorized under worker compensation and possibly those plans related to personal injury. For example, assume a worker with preexisting diabetes and peripheral neuropathy incurs a back injury from an accident and is referred for vocational rehabilitation services. The worker's preexisting conditions would not be included in the private rehabilitation specialist's rehabilitation plan for the client.

The scope and planning of a return to work rehabilitation program differs for public and private rehabilitation specialists. Public rehabilitation counselors address all relevant issues and attendant conditions when

DISCUSSION BOX 11.2

Differences between Public and Proprietary Rehabilitation

Questions

1. Are their differences in the characteristics of individuals who go into public and private rehabilitation practice?

2. What factors predict success in public and proprietary rehabilitation and how can these be assessed?

conducting their assessment and developing rehabilitation plans. In contrast, proprietary rehabilitation specialists focus on the compensable injury when providing rehabilitation and return to work services. In some instances, public and proprietary practitioners may collaborate on a case.

For example, a person with a slip and fall injury may be assisted by a proprietary rehabilitation professional for the resulting back injury and by a public rehabilitation counselor for an underlying mental impairment. The person may be unable to return to past work. The proprietary counselor may be limited regarding the amount of funds available for retraining through worker compensation, while the public counselor may be able to pay for a four-year degree that is consistent with the individual's abilities and assures a substantial long-term job placement. Both the public and proprietary counselors contribute to the rehabilitation and return to work of the person with the disability.

SERVICE OPTIONS AND ASSESSMENT IN PRIVATE REHABILITATION

The goal of proprietary vocational rehabilitation is to return an individual to employment as soon as possible at a wage as close to preinjury as possible and in an occupation as similar as possible. This goal is especially important when working with worker compensation clients. However, clients often will not be released to return-to-work by their physician until reaching maximum medical improvement and in many instances will not seek return-to-work services until their case has been resolved by a civil or administrative court. The following seven-step hierarchy is frequently used in proprietary rehabilitation practice, especially worker compensation (Lynch & Lynch, 1998; Rubin & Roessler, 2001).

1. *Return the person to work at the same job held prior to the injury with the same employer.* Assessment often includes a comprehensive interview and review of medical and vocationally related services required to quickly return the employee to his or her former position. At Level 1, extensive evaluation and testing are not needed since the worker will be doing the exact same job. The involvement of a forensic specialist is unlikely in that, after the worker regains maximum medical improvement with some possible financial settlement for residual loss in wages, he or she will return to the former occupation.

2. *Return the person to work with the same employer with modified duties to accommodate the worker's functional limitations.* The assessment procedures are similar to those in Level 1 along with an evaluation of the client's functional physical capacities as well as work experience to determine the types and breadth of changes that may be needed to accommodate the employee on the same job. This procedure often is described as *job carving*. It involves an analysis of activities, removal or adaptation of some duties, and the addition of new duties to accommodate the injured worker's new limitations (Region IV, 2003). Propriety rehabilitation at Levels 1 and 2 generally has the highest success rate. Injured workers with fewer physical restrictions are most likely to resume job activities (Bose, Geist, Lam, Slaby & Arens, 1998; Lam, Bose & Geist, 1989). The presence of few physical restrictions along with knowledge that one's former employer has a job waiting also reduces postinjury anxiety about return to work. Other key determinants associated with one's early return to work, particularly for workers with back injuries, include age and education as well as level and extent of injury. A retrospective study of 227 injured workers found workers under age 50 with high school educations and with jobs requiring light to moderate lifting were more successful upon returning to work than injured workers over age 50 with less education and less potential to secure employment after injury (Blackwell, Leierer, Haupt, Kampitsis, & Wolfson, 2004).

3. *Return to work at a different job with the same employer.* Assessment at this level also is relatively uncomplicated. It may include a personal interview after the client's full physical recovery, an evaluation of the client's job-related skills, and an evaluation of the client's former work. This evaluation is intended to identify transferable skills needed for a new position that as closely as possible matches the worker's prior wage. A client's return to work in the same or similar environment requires less adjustment and increases the chances for a successful transition to employment (Dunn, 2001).

4. *Return to work at the same job, with or without modification, with a different employer.* Assessments used in Levels 1–3 also would be utilized here together with the provision of job–seeking skills training and a job placement plan. Clients who may be served in Level 3 may find Level 4 services more attractive by providing an opportunity to move to a new job. The client's age, years and types of experience, adaptability, and the availability of appropriate potential job openings in the local labor market are considered as a part of the rehabilitation plan.

5. *Return to work at the same job, with or without on-the-job training, with the same or different employer.* Assessments used in Levels 1–4 also may be utilized here, together with additional diagnostic testing to identify the level of a client's specific aptitudes required for the new position.

6. *Return to work after completing a training or educational program.* Shorter training programs are preferred over longer educational programs. When changing a client's job or occupation, the assessment focuses on the client's demographic characteristics, transferable skills, residual postinjury skills, job aptitudes and attitudes, and local labor market opportunities, along with the feasibility of staying out of the labor market for an extended period. One's success in returning to work diminishes the longer one is out of the labor market.

7. *Consider self-employment.* This option rarely is considered unless self-employment is likely to be successful. Otherwise limited labor market alternatives in the employee's geographical area may warrant a self-employment plan, particularly if small businesses and other cottage industries are profitable and self-sustaining in the client's geographic area. Self-employment may be viable when the client demonstrates specific skills and aptitudes, including self-motivation, and possibly prior experience as a business entrepreneur. Self-employment may be feasible for workers who have high employability potential yet have a low probability of placeability.

Employability refers to one's ability to display skills and attitudes needed to perform one or several occupations, possibly in the national economy. *Place ability* refers to the actual probability that one can secure and maintain a job (Sleister, 2000). A number of conditions impact an individual's hiring potential, including age, prior work history, educational level, and availability of job openings within the individual's proximal geographical area and, in larger cities, the greater metropolitan area.

The above model applies mainly to worker compensation cases. An individual typically is not compensated for loss of capacity to earn money. The services of a forensic rehabilitation expert may be obtained in personal injury cases when an individual has access only to jobs that pay substantially less money and provide little opportunity for advancement. An injured worker may feel inappropriately compensated when the wage, position, and opportunities for advancement are considerably less than those in his or her former occupation.

For example, assume a supervising registered nurse now walks only with the use of a cane or walker after undergoing back surgery following an injury sustained while lifting a heavy patient. Further physical improvement is not expected. The client's former employer offers an alternate position as a medical records clerk. The nurse and rehabilitation specialist weigh various issues, including accommodations that may allow the nurse to perform his or her former job. Note, too, that only 5% of workers with back injuries who remain out of the labor market for 2 or more years eventually return to work (Hopp, 2002).

Forensic vocational assessments conducted to investigate issues important to worker compensation or personal injury cases may include an evaluation of a client's functional abilities, academic aptitude, achievement, and personality together with a review of all pertinent reports and records. The forensic expert often summarizes these findings in a comprehensive report that describes the client's residual and transferable skills and abilities, physical capacity, attitudes toward work, together with estimated remaining work years and earning capacities. The report generally recommends whether the client is likely to be served better by returning to work (e.g., using the above example, as a medical records clerk) or by receiving additional training to be able to develop job skills that would allow the client access to jobs that pay at preinjury level wages.

DISCUSSION BOX 11.3

Predicting Rehabilitation Outcome for Supplemental Security Income and Social Security Disability Income Recipients

The United States government provides income replacement assistance for individuals with disabilities through two programs: Social Security Disability Income (SSDI) and Supplemental Security Income (SSI). To be considered disabled under either of these programs, the individual must have a severe disability that will result in death or an inability to perform substantial gainful activity for at least 12 months.

Although an identical definition of disability is used for the two programs, differences exist in qualifying for each. To be qualified for SSDI one must have worked and made contributions to Social Security. Conversely, only those individuals who have not made enough work contributions to qualify for SSDI and who meet income and resource limits are eligible for SSI (Wheeler, Kearney & Harrison, 2001/2002).

The number of individuals receiving SSDI and SSI dramatically increased during the 1990s. As a result, the Social Security Administration (SSA) is attempting to understand this trend and to find methods to help individuals with disabilities remain in the labor force or return to work

(Wheeler et al., 2001/2002). One method of assistance is through the provision of vocational rehabilitation services. Vocational rehabilitation services have been found to have a positive effect on return-to-work rates for people receiving disability benefits (Hennessey & Muller, 1995). However these services, appear to be underutilized.

Questions

1. How can vocational rehabilitation personnel effectively work to assist returning SSDI and SSI recipients to maintain employment?
2. What are some incentives and disincentives regarding returning to work?
3. What supports (e.g., medical insurance and a certain level of earnings) may be needed to enhance return-to-work options?
4. What incentives, such as monetary payments, are needed, and what type of program is needed to encourage rehabilitation professionals to work with SSDI and SSI recipients? How should they be structured?

VOCATIONAL ASSESSMENT IN FORENSIC REHABILITATION

Vocational assessment is the cornerstone of sound vocational planning in private and public rehabilitation (see also chapter 19). Subsequent services often include planning, treatment, and termination (Rubin & Roessler, 2001). Vocational adjustment may be influenced by many personal and treatment conditions. Thus, goals and methods used in vocational assessment often differ depending on the stage of a client's treatment program and degree of recovery. The assessment may occur once or may be recurring or continuous throughout the rehabilitation process. For example, the forensic expert preparing an evaluation report for court or for vocational planning may not see the client and instead conduct a review of existing records, including depositions and other legal documents (Weikel, 2003). The expert may assess the injured worker on one or more occasions. The forensic expert may or may not be a member of the rehabilitation team that assists an injured worker to return to work. In some situations, two rehabilitation experts are involved, one representing the plaintiff and another representing the defendant.

DIFFERENCES BETWEEN VOCATIONAL ASSESSMENT, VOCATIONAL EVALUATION, VOCATIONAL ANALYSIS, AND JOB ANALYSIS

Vocational Assessment

Vocational assessment refers to the process of gathering information about clients in order to make employment decisions. Vocational assessment is used by proprietary, public, and forensic rehabilitation specialists to describe, explain, and predict a client's psychological, social, and vocational behavior as well as to identify specific vocational goals for the client (Parker & Schaller, 1996). Needs assessment, along with environmental, geographic, economic, psychosocial, and medical information, comprise a somewhat comprehensive evaluation (Brodwin & Brodwin, 2002). These efforts require multidisciplinary collaboration among rehabilitation specialists, including physicians, psychologists, counselors, occupational therapists, and educators, together with family members (Bishop, Tschopp, & Mulvihill 2000).

DISCUSSION BOX 11.4

The Use of Vocational Tests

A number of forensic practitioners rely on vocational tests as a method to ascertain the academic abilities, aptitudes, and intellectual level of injured individuals. Other practitioners rely on the work and educational background as well as the statement of the injured individual regarding the functioning of the individual in these areas.

Questions

1. How reliable is an individual's past work and education to ascertain academic, aptitude, and intellectual functioning?

2. How can a child or a still-born child's potential be determined?

3. What effect does pain have on influencing vocational test results?

4. What effect does not being in an academic setting for many years have with regard to testing academic, intellectual, and aptitude functioning?

Vocational Evaluation

Vocational evaluation refers to the review and use of test data. Various types of tests may be used to evaluate vocational aptitudes and abilities, including standardized tests that assess maximum performance abilities such as intelligence, academic achievement, and job–specific aptitudes. Other tests assess typical performance and require people to express their opinions. Examples include measures of interests, values, attitudes, opinions, and personality. These tests are more qualitative in nature and have no right or wrong answers (Bolton, 2001). Measures of adaptive behavior or life skills assess functional behaviors displayed at home, school, work, and the community (see chapter 15). They often are used to determine the client's current level of behavioral functioning in various environments. Functional work behavior evaluations often are included in this category.

Vocational Analysis

Vocational analysis involves a review of a person's work history, examination of predisability work-related experiences, residual work skills, skills the client has and may not have used, types and length of jobs held, specific vocational preparation, education levels, transferable skills, and extensive local labor market and occupational research to determine types and numbers of jobs a client may be able to perform. A vocational analysis may predict worklife expectancy based upon the above variables, statistics provided by the United States Census Bureau, work descriptors from the *Dictionary of Occupational Titles*, the U. S. *Occupational Guides* (U.S. Department of Labor, 2006), and other government publications, as well as actuarial studies. "Worklife expectancy is a statistic used to define the probable number of years an individual is likely to be employed throughout the life expectancy" (Gamboa & Jones, 2006, p 33). Tables along with data published by the U.S. Census Bureau (e.g., the current population survey) and the survey of income and program participation are utilized in an effort to accurately estimate an individual's worklife expectancy based upon one's gender and age (Anderson & DeTurk, 2002).

Job Analysis

Job analysis involves an extensive review of the duties, activities, expected performance levels and standards, types of movement and duration, and environmental exposures in an occupation. A job analysis describes ". . . what a worker does; how the work is performed; the results of the work; the skills, knowledge, and abilities required to perform the work; and the context in which the work occurs in an organizational structure [USDOL]" (Johnson & Growick, 2003, p.35). It is a study of the work activity and focuses on the position, not the individual performing the work activity (United States Department of Labor, 1982).

FORENSIC EXPERT PREPARATION FOR COURT

When preparing for a court appearance, the forensic expert often first reviews all relevant and essential medical, psychological, physical rehabilitation, employer, and accident reports prior to the initial interview with the client. Careful consideration of these reports assists the forensic expert in determining the breadth and scope of the initial interview. Gaps in work history, contradictions in medical and other

DISCUSSION BOX 11.5

The Relationship between Education, Abilities, and Prior Employment of Persons with Work Injuries and Employment

In the following study, Crystal (2000) examined a database of injured manual laborers who were not working at the time but had previously performed semiskilled and skilled work. The investigator was attempting to determine the ability of these injured workers to return to their customary or other work following their workrelated injury. The ability of these individuals to work in the competitive labor market at some level was based in part on their residual physical and mental abilities. The data set included only individuals who had been employed successfully in their prior occupations. The employment held by these individuals primarily was in construction and equipment operation, jobs that typically are learned through on-the-job training and experience rather than a formal education and training program.

As part of the study, the injured workers were tested to determine their aptitudes, intelligence level, and academic abilities. Without considering any physical or mental impairment, it was determined that these injured workers would be unable to perform their past work (as the requirements for the work is described on the federal *Dictionary of Occupational Titles*) based on their academic, intellectual, and aptitude test results. The implications of this study are that persons in this data set who had successfully performed semiskilled and

skilled manual labor jobs would be unable to perform such work if the criteria to do the work are based only on matching the workers' standardized test scores with the published mental and academic requirements to perform this work.

Questions

1. What are the implications for career counseling for individuals entering the labor market with regard to performing semiskilled manual labor jobs?
2. How can a rehabilitation professional make recommendations for jobs with individuals who may have limited academic, intellectual, and aptitude abilities?
3. What does this study suggest about the validity of standardized tests in predicting future behaviors?
4. What other ways can be used to determine the ability of a person either entering the workforce or needing to identify an alternate job following an injury?
5. Why may these workers score at lower levels than the expected requirements for this work?
6. Should workers receive formal training prior to entering the job market or following a work injury or other job market displacement?
7. What additional studies are needed to address this issue?

information, as well as the client's work-related concerns, attitudes, feelings about the injury, and his or her subsequent limitations, together with attitudes toward reemployment can be clarified during an interview.

The initial interview is important in obtaining information that can facilitate the identification of additional needed test data. The forensic specialist identifies questions he or she has together with those likely to be raised by the defense and/or plaintiff attorneys. These questions guide the selection of tests that have the potential to provide needed information (Power, 2000). The forensic expert must anticipate a cross examination that often is adversarial. The forensic expert must be fully informed, prepared, and able to communicate clearly and succinctly.

Steps in Formulating a Comprehensive Forensic Assessment Report

A vocational rehabilitation assessment conducted prior to offering testimony has four components (Anchor, 1995). An interview allows the rehabilitation professional to

acquire information directly from the client in reference to various questions and to observe firsthand how the client communicates and how the client perceives the evaluation process, and to identify the client's expectations regarding the pending litigation process.

Second, the previously described testing segment occurs. A series of diagnostic tests are utilized to establish the client's aptitudes, skills, and functional abilities. A functional capacity assessment may be done in simulated or real job settings. This assessment allows the forensic professional to observe the client in actual work settings for several hours to determine strength, stamina, and agility. "In short, the functional evaluation translates physical abilities and tolerances into vocationally relevant terms" (Lynch & Lynch, 1998, p. 83). Tests used are expected to be standardized, to yield data that are reliable (i.e., consistent) and valid for the specific purposes for which they are used, as well as generally accepted by forensic and other vocational rehabilitation practitioners.

Testing materials must be selected carefully to ensure that their use, purpose, and results can be communicated clearly to tryers of fact, including juries. The Certified Rehabilitation Counselor Code of Ethics (Commission on Rehabilitation Counselor Certification, 2002), outlines the responsibilities of the rehabilitation counselor in the selection, administration, interpretation, and utilization and disclosure of test materials (Section F.6.- F.12—http://www.crccertification.com/pages/30code.html). Test data should describe and help predict numerous employability characteristics of the client, withstand cross examination and comparison to other instruments, be current, and be supported by research substantiating their goodness of choice by the forensic expert.

Supreme Court decisions in *Daubert v. Merrell Dow Pharmaceuticals, Inc.*, and *Kumho Tire Co. v. Carmichael* established the trial judge's responsibility to determine whether a person displays sufficient expertise to serve as an expert witness, the relevance and reliability of the testimony, and whether the evidence is based on scientific standard, including peer review. Test materials must satisfy the refined scrutiny at a number of levels of jurisprudence by using standardized methods for their administration and scoring, and yielding data and interpretations that are reliable and can be verified by science.

The third stage of assessment can use tests to determine the client's temperament as well as attitudes and interests relative to work and environment. Again, the instruments must be widely accepted in rehabilitation, have been peer reviewed in professional journals and publications, display acceptable standards of usage in the vocational evaluator's discipline, and be able to stand the litmus test of judicial scrutiny.

A fourth stage of assessment (one that not always is used) may examine a client's intellectual abilities by a psychologist, not an expert in rehabilitation. The client's attorney may request this testing and an associated report. These reports, together with information from other specialists, are reviewed by the forensic rehabilitation expert for inclusion in his or her comprehensive assessment.

The forensic rehabilitation expert then reviews background reports and physical functioning information to determine physical and mental work abilities. Based on the interview, vocational test results, and physical and mental functioning records reviewed, the forensic expert prepares a report describing the employability of the individual.

LEGAL SYSTEM ISSUES The legal system uses an adversarial model to arrive at truth (Weed & Field, 1990). Vocational experts are obligated by their ethics codes to acknowledge the limitations of their expertise and base

their testimony only on that expertise. When serving as a witness, the forensic vocational expert may serve at the request of the court, yet typically is retained and paid by either the plaintiff or the defendant. Irrespective of who pays, the expert is expected to testify in a truthful and objective way, without bias toward either side. An expert may be hired by the plaintiff's attorney on one case and by the defendant's attorney on another. Of course, two different vocational experts may be hired for the same trial, one by the plaintiff and the other by the defendant. An attorney with whom an expert is working typically interviews the expert prior to presenting testimony. If the attorney learns that the expert is likely to present evidence contrary to the best interests of the client, the attorney is likely to dismiss the expert and not call him or her to testify.

The plaintiff's attorney may attempt to prohibit the defendant's forensic expert from interviewing the client or to restrict the expert's access to desired evidence. However, the forensic expert should make all needed requests in writing and, if denied, document the refusal when presenting his or her findings (Field, 2006).

The plaintiff's attorney will utilize the conclusions of its vocational experts in an attempt to help prove that the scope and severity of the vocational impairment are greater than recognized by the defendant. Similarly, the defendant's attorney will rely on its vocational experts to mitigate the adverse effects of the plaintiff's injuries on future employment (Gries, 2002). Regardless of which argument prevails, the rules and procedures that must be followed are the same in formulating vocational opinions.

The role of the vocational expert is to "...review all pertinent information, assume that each physician's report is correct and determine the client's occupational loss or employability under those varying assumptions. The expert then must relate a series of opinions based upon the assumed correctness of each report, so that the judge, jury, or administrative law body can then decide.... Excellent databases are a must to back up your opinions" (Weikel, 2003, p 56).

SOCIAL SECURITY VOCATIONAL EXPERTS Practitioners who may want to pursue a career as a forensic expert, yet may be deterred by the adversarial nature of the judicial system, should consider serving as an expert witness for the Social Security Administration's Office of Disability Adjudication and Review. When testifying as to a person's employability and placeability, the vocational expert presents vocational and job information to an administrative court based on hypothetical questions posed by the administrative law judge who ultimately rules on the findings. The expert reviews the court record in the case but does not interview the claimant or prepare a report. The expert is expected to be present during the testimony at the hearing. Cross-examination by the claimant's representative typically is less adversarial than in worker compensation and personal injury cases.

A roster of vocational experts is maintained by the Office of Disability Adjudication and Review. Unlike other forms of forensic practice, experts are called on a rotating basis to appear at hearings. Generally, a master's degree in rehabilitation counseling or a related area and experience in job placement with persons with disabilities are criteria for being an expert in this system. However, this process is undergoing review, and changes in the expert witness program are anticipated.

Statutes Governing the Admissibility of Expert Testimony

Two key federal statutes, established since 1993, serve to determine the breadth and scope of requirements for the vocational expert. Prior to the 1993, Federal Rule 702 in the Federal Rules of Evidence (1973) set forth the standards that governed expert testimony in the federal court system. That rule follows:

> If scientific, technical, or other specialized knowledge will assist the trier of fact to understand the evidence or to determine a fact in issue, a witness qualified as an expert by skill, experience, training, or education may testify thereto in the form of opinion or otherwise (Sleister, 2000, p.120).

In its 1993 *Daubert v. Merrell Dow Pharmaceuticals, Inc.* decision, the Supreme Court overturned rulings of two lower federal courts. Those courts refused to allow expert testimony of a plaintiff based on the 70-year-old *Frye* decision that stated scientific evidence had to meet the standard of being *generally accepted* by the scientific community. Considerable testimony had been disallowed following the *Frye* ruling because it was not generally accepted by the scientific community (Valpar International Corporation, 2000). In *Daubert*, the Supreme Court was asked to decide whether the *Frye* test had been superceded by the adoption, in 1973, of the Federal Rules of Evidence (Nordberg, 2006). The Supreme Court stated that ". . . trial courts must serve as gatekeepers to insure that evidence presented by experts is relevant, reliable, and helpful to the jury, and conversely, to exclude expert testimony that is unreliable" (Gries, 2002, p. 54; *Daubert v.*

*Merrell Dow Pharmaceuticals,*1993). The Supreme Court then set forth several criteria for use by trial judges to determine whether expert testimony is reliable, based on a peer reviewed scientific standard, and therefore properly admissible. The criteria for admissibility includes

- Whether the theories and techniques employed by the scientific expert have been tested
- Whether they have been subjected to peer review and publication
- Whether the techniques employed by the expert have a known error rate
- Whether they are subject to standards governing their application
- Whether the theories and techniques employed by the expert enjoy widespread acceptance (Nordberg, 2006)

In *Kumho Tire Company v. Carmichael* (1999) the Supreme Court further clarified the position of expert testimony and the forensic expert as a presenter of opinions based upon principles and methodologies. The Court determined that experts first must establish a foundation of reliability before being allowed to testify about their observations and conclusions, and that publication, peer review, error rates, and acceptability in the relevant scientific community were helpful standards in determining the reliability of a particular theory or technique (Sleister, 2000).

Subsequently, the *Kumho* decision substantiated the *Daubert* decision as it relates to scientific, technical, or other specialized knowledge and reaffirmed the need for reliable, relevant standards of admissibility of an expert's testimony. Instead of making it harder for expert testimony to pass muster, the *Daubert* ruling made it easier (Valpar International Corporation, 2000). Trial judges serve as gatekeepers of standards applicable to providing evidence to help ensure that the expert's testimony rests on reliable evidence. The trial judge has considerable discretion when determining admissibility of evidence.

Examples of testimony offered by vocational experts include application of vocational testing, labor market statistics, job analyses, projected loss of earning capacity, life care planning, and transferable skills analysis (Gamboa & Jones, 2006). Testimony on these issues requires specialized knowledge and methodologies. Forensic experts use various tools and techniques, including software, to assist in their preparation of a comprehensive vocational assessment. *Daubert* and subsequent court decisions have encouraged vocational experts to scrutinize and elevate standards governing their evaluations and other professional practices used in evaluations.

DISCUSSION BOX 11.6

The Impact of Federal Rule 702 and the *Daubert* and *Kumho* Decisions

The *Daubert* and *Kumho* decisions require experts to base their opinions on peer reviewed and scientific evidence.

Questions

1. Since there are over 130 million jobs in the economy, how can an expert use scientific information to describe a person's past and potential future work?

2. The use of work life tables and government statistics on earnings has been controversial. How can experts know how long a person will work and earn?

3. How can experts best utilize objective medical information and a person's self report in determining employability?

THE FORENSIC EXPERT'S RESPONSE TO FEDERAL RULE 702, *DAUBERT*, AND *KUMHO* DECISIONS

Vocational forensic experts are acquiring a heightened awareness of the extent their testimony may be scrutinized in the courtroom (Field, Johnson, Schmidt, & Van de Bittner, 2006; Field, 2006; Gamboa & Jones 2006; McCroskey, 2003). A survey of more than 40 cases involving forensic rehabilitation consultants in federal courts were reviewed to determine how the courts were responding to rehabilitation (i.e., soft science) testimony (Field, 2006). Critical issues focused on an expert's credentials, generally accepted peer reviewed methodology, the proper use of foundational data and information, and the proper use of resources in the formulation of opinion related to the facts of the case. Standards set forth in *Daubert* were less problematic.

Testimony is most likely to withstand judicial scrutiny when it is complete, well laid out, considers all variables pertaining to an individual's potential employability, and is supported by data from tools and techniques that are accepted, peer reviewed, and has enjoyed longevity of use. Testimony that relies on only one or two of these factors is likely to be dismissed. Additionally, testimony that utilizes government tables and data such as those set forth in the *Dictionary of Occupational Titles* (United States Department of Labor, 1991a), its accompanying *Revised Handbook for Analyzing Jobs* (United Stated Department of Labor, 1991b), the *Guide to Occupational Exploration* (United Stated Department of Labor, 1993), and other actuarial resources proffered by the U.S. Census Bureau with annual updates are least likely to invite criticism during testimony.

Sixty-one tools, methods, and protocols used in forensic rehabilitation practice were reviewed in light of the two *Daubert* criteria (i.e., general acceptance and peer review) (Field, Johnson, Schmidt, & Van de Bittner, 2006). Nearly all items passed peer review, general acceptance, and publication standards, yet lacked sufficient statistical analysis of their validity. The authors concluded that, when deciding to use nonvalidated items, vocational experts should be aware of the literature surrounding each procedure, including peer-reviewed publications. Furthermore, vocational experts should be sufficiently familiar with the tools they use to explain the test's theory, issues of reliability and validity, and the appropriate use of the test (Butcher, 2002).

DISCUSSION BOX 11.7

Determining who is an Expert

What is the basis for determining who is an expert witness?

Questions

1. What should be the basis for determining the qualifications of an expert witness?

2. Should expertise be based on education, training, and experience or a combination of these factors? What would be the balance?

THE DICTIONARY OF OCCUPATIONAL TITLES, O*NET, TRANSFERABLE SKILLS ANALYSIS, AND WORKLIFE EXPECTANCY TABLES

Dictionary of Occupational Titles

The Dictionary of Occupational Titles (U. S. Dept. of Labor, 1991a) and its accompanying *Handbook for Analyzing Jobs* (U.S. Dept. of Labor, 1991b) have been fundamental resources for job descriptions and transferable skills analysis in the vocational community. Its replacement in 1991 by another database, O*NET (U.S. Department of Labor, 2000), has resulted in consternation and often confusion because of its inadequacy for use by forensic experts. Limitations in O*NET have been especially apparent when preparing for the Social Security Administration's Disability Determination process (Gustafson & Rose, 2003). O*NET, along with its accompanying vocational preparation guides for each occupation, has been an outstanding tool for career planning. However, forensic experts have found its job groupings and characteristics to be too general and thus of limited use in the assessment of transferable work skills required in comprehensive assessment for litigation.

Transferable Skills Analysis

Many vocational experts have engaged the cross-referenced feature of these resources between the O*NET and the Dictionary of Occupational Titles (DOT) in an attempt to be more explicit in their analyses (Field, 2002). Others (McCroskey, Hahn & Dennis, 2000; McCroskey, 2003) have augmented the DOT with software programs that have added to and expanded the parameters of the DOT for use with another software system, the McCroskey Vocational Quotient System, in an effort to maintain current, reliable, and valid methods to obtain transferable skills analysis (McCroskey & Hahn, 1998).

Worklife Expectancy Tables

McCroskey (2002) developed a vocational quotient to predict worker earning capacity. Gamboa and his associates (Gamboa, 1998; Gamboa, 2002; Gumboa & Jones, 2006) developed methods that can be used by the forensic expert to predict work life expectancy by gender, level of educational attainment, and level of work disability. These tools and others have been peer reviewed and have received mixed acceptance in the field of forensic vocational testimony. Each has enjoyed success and failure in the courtroom depending upon the forensic expert's presentation, the variability of each case, and the judge's views as to its reliability and relevancy (Field, 2006). Continual revisions of these tools that rely more on updated government generated data seem to be the trend (Gamboa & Jones 2006; Field, 2002, McCroskey, 2002). Attempts by McCroskey and Hahn and others to supplant the *Dictionary of Occupational Titles* have not been recognized by the Social Security Administration or the Department of Labor (Field, 2006).

CODES OF ETHICS FOR THE FORENSIC VOCATIONAL ANALYST

The American Board of Vocational Experts is a professional organization of vocational experts who work exclusively in forensic rehabilitation. This organization developed a code of conduct specific for the forensic experts (http://www.abve.net/certethics.htm).

Although the code acknowledges core values and beliefs shared by all human service professions, the code also recognizes that forensic practice "demands a differing set of behavioral constructs than rehabilitation counseling" (Curtis, Martin, Graham, & Sinsabaugh, 2006). The Canons and Rules of Professional Conduct are set forth with similarities to those in the Code of Ethics for Rehabilitation Counselors along with some distinctive changes in definition. For example, in the context of forensic vocational experts, the term *client* always means the *referral source* (Curtis et al.,). In contrast, using the Code of Ethics for Rehabilitation Counselors, the client always means the *person with the disability* (Sec. A.1.a.). Ethical decision making models for resolving ethical dilemmas generally are similar among the professions (Curtis et al.).

EXPANDED AREAS OF SERVICE IN FORENSIC REHABILITATION

In addition to their work in traditional fields discussed in this chapter (e.g., worker compensation, long-term disability, and civil litigation), the scope of work performed by vocational experts is expanding to include other issues. Some are discussed below.

Employment Discrimination

Cases involving employment discrimination in hiring or termination are likely to raise questions about vocational loss and monetary damages due to discrimination in hiring practices or in wrongful termination—issues that can be addressed by vocational forensic experts.

Vocational experts provide testimony in instances of alleged violation of Title VII of the Civil Rights Act of 1964, the Age Discrimination Act of 1967, The Rehabilitation Act of 1973, the Equal Pay Act of 1963, and the Americans with Disabilities Act of 1990. These statutes are united by two premises: Members of groups protected by these statutes are economically at a disadvantage, and discrimination practices of employers further contribute to their disadvantagement (Johnston & Growick, 2003). The relevance of work by forensic experts in age discrimination lawsuits is apparent. The relevance of their work in employment discrimination lawsuits is increasing.

Life Care Planning

Life care plans are utilized by injured persons, their families or guardians, insurance carriers, and the legal system to estimate and plan for the long-term needs and associated costs when caring for persons who have incurred catastrophic injuries. Life care planning has developed into a specialty, first within proprietary rehabilitation and later in forensic rehabilitation practice as private rehabilitation practitioners are asked to provide case management services associated with long-term living plans (Lynch & Lynch, 1998). Life care planning considers a client's need for therapy, surgery, medications, home health services, and home and vehicle modifications, together with case management recommendations. Planning requires the coordination and integration of services and resources with the goal of maintaining and enhancing a client's functioning and quality of life.

Rehabilitation practitioners often face various challenges when developing life care plans, including ways to fund expenses associated with medical, essential living, and rehabilitation care. Their work with each client often is protracted and involves teams of rehabilitation professionals, physicians, physiatrists, social workers, psychologists, and other health care providers. The potential for litigation heightens scrutiny and can lead to other important conditions that impact the formation and execution of life care plans (Shahnasarian, 2002).

Domestic Relations

Forensic vocational experts provide testimony in divorce cases when a spouse is requesting subsidy and/or maintenance for him or her and children. For example, women may allege that their ability to support themselves by means of substantial gainful employment has diminished as a result of years spent as a homemaker or otherwise outside of the competitive labor market. Longer periods of unemployment often create more complex problems, especially if one is old and has limited or no substantial work skills. Whether the grieving party can maintain his or her standard of life with or without additional education or training also may be considered. Comprehensive forensic assessment includes labor market surveys and predictions of work life expectancy.

Wrongful Death

Forensic vocational experts assess potential work life earnings of individuals who are killed in order to determine monetary payments to the survivors. In cases that involve the loss of a parent by a child, the earning capacity of the parent and the family's socioeconomic status are assessed by the forensic expert to estimate the deceased person's potential employment income.

Projections as to future earnings losses are more reliable when individuals have education and work histories. The wrongful death of a child poses challenges, given his or her limited education and no work history. In this event, rehabilitation practitioners rely upon the background (e.g., educational and employment) of biological family members, including parents and siblings who may be employed. Practitioners interview and test family members, knowing that their current education and work may underestimate their potential and thus the potential of the deceased child.

Summary and Conclusion

The practice of private vocational rehabilitation grew significantly during the last quarter of the 20th century. Forensic rehabilitation experts in particular have become highly sought in the judicial system because of their combined skills in vocational assessment, individualized vocational planning, estimating the effects of disability for the worker in the workplace, and predicting occupational life expectancy and earnings capacity. Assessment procedures have become more highly scrutinized due to precedent setting court cases such as *Daubert* and *Kumho Tire Co.* and the desire of professionals engaged in vocational rehabilitation to offer services based on scientific support. The variability that occurs naturally in human behavior poses formidable challenges. Rehabilitation experts strive to maintain high standards of professionalism without losing sight of the original intent of vocational rehabilitation—namely successful employment outcomes of people with disabilities. When this goal is unobtainable (e.g., due to catastrophic and/or profound injury), forensic experts predict what could have been a productive preinjury work life and assist in developing appropriate alternative quality of life plans.

Forensic vocational rehabilitation has developed several specialties. Each specialty area requires the same foundation knowledge in forensic assessment plus expertise in one or more areas of law. Forensic vocational and rehabilitation experts should be current in their knowledge of legislation, case law, as well as with federal and state government policy impacting their specialties along with current knowledge of labor market information and trends. High standards of ethics and objectivity are required in order to be successful. Forensic rehabilitation is emerging as a demanding and challenging occupation, one that has tremendous potential for those interested in pursuing this as a career.

Self-Check Questions

1. Discuss the difference between public and proprietary rehabilitation practice.
2. Describe the roles and functions of a forensic rehabilitation expert.
3. Discuss ethical issues related to proprietary rehabilitation practice and expert witness practice.
4. Discuss the impact of *Daubert* and *Kumho Tire* on expert witness practice.
5. Describe your understanding of vocational and employability assessment in forensic rehabilitation practice.
6. Indicate your understanding of the expertise needed to work as a forensic vocational expert.

Case Studies

Review the following two cases and answer the following questions:

1. What is your initial assessment of this case?
2. Can this person return to his/her past or other work? Elaborate.
3. Is additional information needed, and if so what would that be?
4. How do you resolve conflicts in medical information?
5. What vocational skills does the individual possess, and does the individual have transferable vocational skills?
6. How would you proceed with this case?
7. What jobs does the individual qualify for, or is the person totally disabled?
8. What are the barriers and facilitators regarding a return to productive employment for each case?

Case 1. Elmer Adams

Background Information

Mr. Adams is age 44.

Education: Mr. Adams graduated from high school. He does not have any formal vocational training. Mr. Adams reported the ability to read, write, and perform arithmetic. For example, he is able to read and understand a newspaper and general interest magazines. He can count change at a store and write a check. He can write a message, note, and a list. He passed the written driver's test.

Employment: At the time he was injured, he earned $57,000 annually plus benefits. Mr. Adams worked for a railroad. He started as a brakeman, then worked as trainman, and then as a hostler or yard engineer—moving trains and doing repair work in the rail yard, changing air hoses and air compressors. He prepared train manifests. Lifting entailed weights of 97 pounds.

Injury: Mr. Adams injured his lower back, neck, left leg, and shoulders when he tripped and fell. He has not had surgery. He reports having pain in his lower back, neck, left leg, and between his shoulder blades. He has difficulty turning his neck.

Physical and Psychological Functioning

1. William Combs M.D. stated Mr. Adams could stand and walk for 2 hours in 8 total hours. He could sit a

total of 6 hours in an 8-hour workday. He requires a sit and stand option at 15–20 minute intervals. Mr. Adams can occasionally lift 10 pounds or less. He should never bend, stoop, crouch, squat, or climb. He can never reach above shoulder level and cannot push or pull. He is unable to work at unprotected heights, operate moving machinery, or be on uneven terrain.

2. Major Williams M.D. stated that Mr. Adams has no objective findings. Dr. Williams stated that it was safe to allow Mr. Adams to return to his work activities.

3. Sam Johnson M.D. opined that Mr. Adams's condition is permanent. Mr. Adams' lifting restriction is 5 pounds frequently and 10 pounds on occasion.

4. Howard Roberts M.D. diagnosed Mr. Adams with a mood disorder. His GAF is 75. Dr. Roberts stated that Mr. Adams does not require psychiatric restrictions.

5. Neville Campbell M.D. diagnosed Mr. Adams with major depression. Mr. Adams has a GAF of 45–55.

Mr. Adams described pain in his lower back, neck, left leg, and between his shoulder blades. He has difficulty turning his neck in either direction and has urinary retention. He said that both of his hands hurt, with the right hand being worse.

The pain is mild to very severe even when he takes medication; activity is restricted to one position; and cold, wet, and humid weather increases the pain. The pain affects his ability to think, concentrate, and remember. Mr. Adams said that he could occasionally lift 10 pounds. He reported the ability to sit for 10 minutes, stand for 15 minutes, and walk about 100 feet.

Mr. Adams feels he has developed depression since being injured. He feels short-tempered, frustrated, and irritable. He said that people and noise bother him.

Mr. Adams had physical therapy, which he said did not help and caused him more pain. He has not had surgery. Mr. Adams takes medication for the pain. The medication helps ease the pain. He does not have any known side affects to the medication.

Mr. Adams does not feel he can perform any of his prior jobs or any other work because of the pain. He is not looking for work and feels that he is in too much pain to work. Mr. Adams has not thought about returning to school or obtaining additional training. Mr. Adams said that if he were employed he would need more than the usual rest breaks. He said that he would like to feel better physically so that he can return to work.

Mr. Adams said that his certifications have expired. He does not have the skills to perform clerical work or supervise employees.

Vocational Testing

The first test was an aptitude test battery. An aptitude is an ability to learn in a specific area. Mr. Adams' aptitude results indicate that he would do best in a job learned through a short-term or on-the-job training program.

Mr. Adams was administered two tests of hand dexterity. His results indicate that he would qualify for jobs related to assembly, machine operation, cutting and trimming, bench polishing and cleaning, inspection, weighing, measuring and checking, and sorting and packaging. He can use his hands and fingers for fine and gross bilateral dexterity work activities.

Mr. Adams was administered an interest inventory. He demonstrated high interests in jobs related to manual labor and sales work activities.

Mr. Adams was administered a standardized test of academic achievement. The results indicate that he can read, write, and perform arithmetic at a level which would allow him to perform a wide range of entry level jobs requiring academic abilities such as clerical, cashier, counter clerical, service, and administrative support occupations. He qualifies for jobs in these areas, which are typically learned through on-the-job training and experience. However, his academic levels are below the level necessary for entry into a formal education program at a college level.

Mr. Adams was administered a test of intellectual ability. The results indicate that his overall intelligence is in the average- to low-average range of mental functioning.

Case 2. Gail Jones

Background Information

Ms. Jones is age 27.

Education: Ms. Jones has a 12th grade education. She attended college for 2 years and left to go to work and get married. She was taking basic courses and was interested in becoming a school teacher. Ms. Jones said that she has the ability to read, write, and perform arithmetic. She can read and understand a newspaper and general interest magazines. She can write a message and a grocery list.

She can count change at a store, write a check, and can perform fractions, decimals, and percentages. She said that she passed the written driver's test.

Employment: At the time of the injury she was employed with a pharmaceutical company for several years. She also worked there after being injured. At the time she was last employed, Ms. Jones earned $1,960 per month plus benefits. Her job was to promote drugs and medications to physicians. Ms. Jones worked after her injury and said that she could structure her job and was not required to perform extensive physical work. Ms. Jones said that she had a flexible schedule and could take breaks as needed. After having surgery on her back she still had pain and was unable to work and has not worked since this time.

Prior to being injured and her work with the pharmaceutical company, Ms. Jones worked as a sales clerk in a department store. She said that she earned $9.00 per hour. She assisted customers and operated a cash register. She also has worked as a server in a restaurant and as a telemarketer.

Injury: Ms. Jones was injured in a slip and fall accident at a store. She now reports having pain in her neck, low back, and right arm. She drops items. She also has periodic headaches.

Physical and Psychological Functioning

1. Linda Montgomery M.D. stated that Ms. Jones is permanently disabled and will not be able to perform gainful employment.
2. Don Keller M.D. stated Ms. Jones can perform sedentary and light duty work.
3. Burt Dooley M.D. diagnosed an adjustment disorder with depressed and anxious features. Depression related to chronic pain. A GAF of 50–55 was assessed. Ms. Jones does not feel capable of returning to her prior job because of her physical condition.

Ms. Jones described pain in her neck, low back, and right arm. Her right hand and arm also tingle, and she drops items. Her left hand is not impaired. She is right hand dominant.

The pain is moderate to very severe. She said that medication makes the pain tolerable. Cold, wet, and humid weather increases the pain. The pain affects her ability to think and concentrate, and she is forgetful. Ms. Jones said that she could lift about 10 pounds using her left hand because this hand is not impaired. She uses her right hand as a helper. She can sit for about 10–25 minutes depending on the chair. Ms. Jones said that she could stand for about 5–15 minutes and then needs to sit down for pain relief. She can walk about 200 feet. She is unable to climb, balance, bend, or kneel without difficulty.

She feels that she developed depression because of the pain. She feels frustrated and aggravated, and has mood swings.

Ms. Jones said that she had physical therapy but this did not help. She has not worked since having surgery on her back. Ms. Jones takes medication for pain and depression. The medication makes the pain tolerable.

Ms. Jones said that she cannot perform her prior or other work because of the pain and resulting limitations. She is not looking for work and feels she has too much pain to work. Ms. Jones has not thought about returning to school but would like to finish school. However, she feels in too much pain to return to school at present.

Vocational Testing

The first test was an aptitude battery. An aptitude is an ability to learn in a specific area. Ms. Jones' aptitude results indicate that she would do best in a job related to a skilled occupation learned at a technical or community college.

Ms. Jones was administered a test of hand dexterity. Her results indicate that she would be a good candidate for keyboarding, writing, and activities involved with gross manipulative activities with her right hand and fine and gross manipulative activities with her left hand.

Ms. Jones was administered an interest inventory. Ms. Jones' SDS identifying code indicated interests in jobs related to working with people and problem-solving work activities.

Ms. Jones was administered a standardized test of academic achievement. The results indicate that she can read, write, and perform arithmetic at a level which would allow her to perform a wide range of jobs requiring academic abilities such as clerical, cashier, counter clerical, service, and administrative support occupations. Her academic levels are at the level necessary for entry into a formal education program at a college level.

Ms. Jones was administered a test of intellectual ability. The results indicate that her overall intelligence is in the average range of mental functioning.

References

American Board of Vocational Experts, (2006a). Code of conduct. *Journal of Forensic Vocational Analysis, 9,* 51–56.

American Board of Vocational Experts, (2006b). http://www.abve.net/certethics.htm.

Anchor, K. N. (1995). The vocational expert in forensic rehabilitation. In W. H. Burke (Ed.), *The Handbook of Forensic Rehabilitation* (pp.75–106). Houston, TX: HDI.

Anderson, R. N., & DeTurk, P. B. (2002). *National Vital Statistics Report, vol. 50 no. 6, United States Life Tables, 1999.* Hyattsville, MD: National Center for Health Statistics.

Bishop, M., Tschopp, M. K., & Mulvihill, M. (2000). Multiple Sclerosis and epilepsy: Vocational aspects and the best rehabilitation practices. *Journal of Rehabilitation, 66*(2), 50–56. Retrieved October 2005, from EBSCO-HOST database.

Blackwell, T. L., Leierer, S. J., Haupt, S. S., Kampitsis, A., & Wolfson, J. R. (2004). Prediction of vocational outcomes for workers' compensation claimants with back injury. *Journal of Applied Rehabilitation Counseling, 25*(2), 32–38.

Bolton, B. F. (2001). *Handbook of measurement and evaluation in rehabilitation* (3rd ed.). Gaithersburg, MD: Aspen Publishers, Inc.

Bose, J. L., Geist, G. O., Lam, C. S., Slaby, M., & Arens, M. (1998). Factors affecting job placement success in proprietary rehabilitation. *Journal of Applied Rehabilitation Counseling, 29*(3), 19–24.

Brodwin, M. G. (2001). Rehabilitation in the private-for-profit sector: Opportunities and challenges. In S. E. Rubin & R.T. Roessler (Eds.). *Foundations of the rehabilitation process* (5th ed., pp. 475–495). Austin, Texas: PRO-ED, Inc.

Brodwin, M. C. & Brodwin, S. K. (2002). Rehabilitation: A case study approach. In M. G. Brodwin, T. Tellez, & S. K. Brodwin (Eds.), *Medical, psychosocial and vocational aspects of disability* (pp. 1–13). Athens, GA: Elliott & Fitzgerald, Inc.

Butcher, J. N. (2002). Assessment in forensic practice. In B. Van Dorsten (Ed.), *Forensic psychology: From classroom to courtroom* (pp. 65–82). New York: Kluwer Academic/Plenum Publishers.

Commission on Rehabilitation Counselor Certification (2002). *Code of professional ethics for rehabilitation counselors.* Rolling Meadows, IL. Author.

Curtis, R. S., Martin, E. D. Jr., Graham, C. M., & Sinsabaugh, L. L. (2006). The vocational expert and ethics. *Journal of Forensic Vocational Analysis, 9,* 43–48.

Daubert v. Merrell Dow Pharmaceuticals (92–102), 509 U.S. 579 (1993)

Dennis, M. L., & Dennis, K. L. (1998). Job search software under *Daubert. Journal of Vocationology, 4* (1), 1–10.

Dunn, P. L. (2001). Trends and issues in proprietary rehabilitation. In P. D. Rumrill, Jr., J. L. Bellini & L. C. Koch (Eds.), Emerging issues in rehabilitation counseling: Perspectives on the new millennium (pp.171–199). Springfield, IL: Charles C. Thomas.

Federal Rules of Evidence (1973). In D. Nordberg, *The Daubert worldview.* Retrieved from October 10, 2006 from http://www.Daubertontheweblcom/chapter_2.htm

Field, T. (2002). Transferable skills analysis: A common sense approach. *Journal of Forensic Vocational Analysis, 5,* 29–39.

Field, T. (2006). Vocational expert testimony: What we have learned during the post-*Daubert* era. *Journal of Forensic Vocational Analysis, 9,* 7–18.

Field, T., Johnson, C., Schmidt, R., & Van de Bittner, G. (2006). *Methods and protocols: Meeting the criteria of general acceptance and peer review under Daubert and Kumho.* Athens, GA: Elliott & Fitzpatrick, Inc.

Gamboa, A. M. Jr. (1998). *The new worklife expectancy tables (revised).* Louisville, KY: Vocational Econometrics, Inc.

Gamboa, A. M. Jr., (2002). *The new work life expectancy tables (revised) 2002.* Louisville, KY: Vocational Econometrics, Inc.

Gamboa, A. M. Jr., & Jones, L. L. (2006). Understanding work life expectancy. *Journal of Vocational Forensic Analysis, 9,* 33–42.

Gries, A. R. (2002). A *Daubert* perspective on transferable skills analysis: A defense attorney's perspective. *Journal of Forensic Vocational Analysis, 5,* 53–57.

Gustafson, S. G., & Rose, A. M. (2003). Investigating O*NET's suitability for the Social Security Administration's disability determination process. *Journal of Forensic Vocational Analysis, 6* 3–16.

Hennessey, J. C. & Muller, L. S. (1995). The effect of vocational rehabilitation and work incentives on helping the disabled-worker beneficiary back to work. *Social Security Bulletin, 58*(1) 15–28.

Hopp, E. (2002). Back and neck pain in industrial injuries. In M. G. Brodwin, F. Tellez, & S. K. Brodwin (Eds.), *Medical, psychosocial and vocational aspects of disability* (pp. 252–264). Athens, GA: Elliott & Fitzgerald, Inc.

Johnson, C. S. & Growick, B. (2003). Utilizing vocational experts in employment discrimination cases. *Journal of Forensic Vocational Analysis, 6,* 27–40.

Koch, L. C., & Rumrill P. D. (2001). Vocational assessment in the Americans with Disabilities Act. In P. D. Rumrill., J. L. Bellini, & L. C. Koch (Eds.), *Emerging issues in rehabilitation counseling: Perspectives on the new millennium* (pp 88–122). Springfield, IL: Charles C. Thomas, Publisher, Inc.

Lam, C. S., Bose, J. L., & Geist, C. G. (1989). Employment outcomes of private rehabilitation clients. *Rehabilitation Counseling Bulletin, 32*(4), 300–311.

Lynch, R. K., & Lynch, R. T. (1998). Rehabilitation counseling in the private sector. In R. M. Parker, & E. M. Szymanski (Eds.), *Rehabilitation counseling: Basics and beyond* (pp.71–95). Austin, TX: Pro-Ed.

Maze, M. (1996). Career counselors as vocational experts Determining earning capacity. *Career Planning and Adult Development Journal, 12*(1), 79–89.

McCroskey, B. J. (2002). Frequently asked questions regarding the MVQS 2001 programs. *Journal of Forensic Vocationalogy, 7*(1), 10–13.

McCroskey, B. J. (2003). *Billy Joe McCroskey's most significant papers on vocational rehabilitation research.* Athens, GA: Elliott & Fitzgerald, Inc.

McCroskey, B. J. & Hahn, S. J. (1995). The validity of the Vocational Quotient as a predictor of calendar year (CY) 1994 starting wages in Minnesota: Study #1. *Journal of Vocationology, 1*(1), 6–8.

McCroskey, B. J. & Hahn, S. J. (1998). The McCroskey Vocational Quotient (VQ) as a predictor of earnings capacity: Criterion-referenced validity follow-up studies. [Abstract}], *Journal of Vocationology, 4*(1b). Retrieved October 2, 2006, from http://www.vocationology.com/abstracts4_1/abstract4_1_b.htm.

McCroskey, B. J., Hahn, S. J., & Dennis, K. L., (2000). MTSP 2000 VQ-QES wage estimation. *Journal of Vocationology, 6*(1), 107–135.

Nordberg, P. (2006). *Daubert* in a nutshell. In *The Daubert worldview* (chap.2). Retrieved September 19, 2006, from http://www.dauberontheweb.com

Osipow, S. H. (2005). Forensic vocational analysis as a specialty. *Journal of Forensic Vocational Analysis, 8,* 7–9.

Parker, R. M., & Schaller, J. L. (1996). Issues in vocational assessment & disability. In E. M. Szymanski & R. M. Parker (Eds.), (1996). *Work and disability: Issues and strategies in career development and job placement* (pp. 127–164). Austin, TX: Pro-Ed.

Power, P. W. (2000). *A guide to vocational assessment* (3rd ed.). Austin, TX: Pro-Ed.

The Region IV Employment Partner's Team (2003). *Effective employer relationships: A practical guide for Region IV.* Retrieved on October 19, 2006, from the National Clearinghouse of Rehabilitation Training Materials at http://ncrtm.org.ed.usu.edu

Rubin, S. E. & Roessler, R. T. (2001). *Foundations of the rehabilitation process* (5th ed.). Austin, TX: Pro-Ed.

Shahnasarian, M. (2002). The rehabilitation counselor as forensic expert, life care planner, and case manager in catastrophic disability: A case illustration. *Journal of Applied Rehabilitation Counseling, 33*(4) 5–9.

Shaw, L. R., (1995). Forensic rehabilitation: Historical and future perspectives. In W. H. Burke (Ed.), *The Handbook of Forensic Rehabilitation* (pp.1–17). Houston, TX: HDI.

Siefker, J. M. (1992). What is the difference between public and private sector rehabilitation? In J. M. Siefker (Ed.), *Vocational Evaluation in Private Sector Rehabilitation* (pp.1–30). Menomonie: University of Wisconsin-Stout.

Sleister, S. L. (2000). Separating the wheat from the chaff: The role of the vocational expert in forensic vocational rehabilitation. *Journal of vocational rehabilitation, 14,* 119–129.

Skoog, G. R., & Toppino, D. C. (1999). Disability and the new work life expectancy tables from vocational econometrics, 1998: A critical analysis. *Journal of Forensic Economics, 12*(3), 239–254.

Truthan, J. A. & Karman, S. E. (2003). Transferable skills analysis and vocational information during a time of transition. *Journal of Forensic Vocational Analysis, 6,* 17–26.

U.S. Department of Labor, Employment and Training Administration (1991a). *Dictionary of occupational titles,* (4th ed.). Washington, DC: U.S. Government Printing Office.

U.S. Department of Labor, Employment and Training Administration (1991b). *Handbook for analyzing jobs.* Washington, DC: U.S. Government Printing Office.

U.S. Department of Labor, Employment and Training Administration (2006). *Occupational guides.* Washington, DC: U.S. Government Printing Office.

U.S. Department of Labor, Employment and Training Administration (1993). *Guide to occupational exploration.* Washington, DC: U.S. Government Printing Office.

U.S. Department of Labor (2000). *O*NET: Occupational information network*, Washington, DC. Retrieved October 1, 2006, from http://www.onetcenter.org.

Valpar International Corporation (2002). *On Daubert, Daubertization, and being Daubertized.* Retrieved on March 11, 2002, from http://www.valparint.com/daubert.htm

Weed, R. O. & Field, T. F. (1990). *Rehabilitation consultant's handbook.* Athens, GA: Elliott & Fitzpatrick, Inc.

Weikel, W. J. (2003). Forensic rehabilitation counseling. In W. J. Weikel (Ed.). *Days in the lives of counselors* (pp. 55–58). Boston: Allyn and Bacon.

Wheeler, P. M., Kearney, J. R., & Harrison, C. A. (2001/2002). The U.S. study of work incapacity and reintegration. *Social Security Bulletin, 64*(1), 32.

Wright, G. N. (1980). *Total rehabilitation.* Boston, Little, Brown and Co.

12

Assessment of Disability
Social Security Disability Evaluation

Neuropsychology & Rehabilitation Consultants, P.C. Chapel Hill, NC

ALAN L. GOLDBERG
Sole Practitioner Tucson, AZ

OVERVIEW

This chapter discusses Social Security disability evaluations with reference to psychological constructs and eligibility criteria for Social Security based on one's mental function status. The process for Social Security disability determination based on a person's physical status is somewhat independent from an evaluation of a person's mental function status, is not a process in which psychologists participate, and thus is not discussed in this chapter. Therefore, readers should be aware that, although the assessment of mental function status and physical status may overlap, the psychologist's role is limited to that of obtaining an understanding of psychological/mental function status as it relates to Social Security.

LEARNING OBJECTIVES

By the end of the chapter, readers should be able to:

- State the Social Security Administration definition of (a) disability for adults and children; (b) a medically determinable physical or mental impairment, and those mental impairments that qualify claimants for disability; and (c) consultative examination

- Describe the 5-step sequential process used in the determination of disability (by the Social Security Administration)

- Outline similarities and differences between own-occupation disability policies and Social Security disability

- Examine issues in the determination of credibility, and validity of provided information

- Discuss ethical issues for professionals that are unique to the Social Security Administration disability determination process

INTRODUCTION

The concept of *disability* is used in various circumstances and ways, with not all definitions being the same. Therefore, misunderstandings about the definition of disability may be common. The belief that disability is a clinically defined status also is somewhat common. However, when used in determining disability under Social Security or for other insurance policy contracts, the term *disability* is defined contractually. Personnel involved in Social Security disability determination, including its administrative personnel, professional healthcare providers, lawyers, and judges, use the following definition.

The Social Security Administration regulations indicate the following (Social Security Administration, 2006):

FOR ADULTS

"The law defines disability as the inability to engage in any substantial gainful activity by reason of any medically determinable physical or mental impairment(s) which can be expected to result in death or which has lasted or can be expected to last for a continuous period of not less than 12 months (p. 2)."

FOR CHILDREN

A disabled child must be under age 18 and have a medically determinable physical or mental impairment or combination of impairments that cause marked or severe functional limitations, and can be expected to cause death or last for a continuous period of at least 12 months.

These definitions refer to various constructs. A person must have a physical or mental impairment that can be *medically determinable*. Due to that impairment, a person must be unable to engage in any *substantial gainful activity* (or in children *have marked or severe functional limitations*). In addition, the condition must meet *duration of impairment* standards: either it is expected to result in death, or to last for a continuous period of not less than one year. Therefore, under this definition, disability can be understood to be the interaction of a medically determinable impairment that lasts for a sufficiently long period of time so as to preclude the individual's ability to engage in substantial gainful activity (or, if a child, has marked or severe functional limitations).

EXPLANATION OF TERMS

An understanding the concepts of *impairment*, *disability*, and *handicap* as they relate to functional status is important. These terms have various meanings when discussing a person's functional capabilities.

Definition of Impairment

An *impairment* is an abnormality in body structure or function. According to the American Medical Association (AMA), "An impairment is a deviation from normal in a body part or organ system and its functioning"(AMA, 1995, p. 1). The World Health Organization (WHO) defined impairment as ". . . any loss or abnormality of psychological, physiological, or anatomical structure or function" (WHO, 1980.) In its more recent writings on the International Classification of Functioning, Disability and Health (ICF), the WHO stated "Impairments are manifestations of dysfunction in the body structures or functions, differentiated from the underlying pathology itself" (Peterson, 2005, p.106).

The Social Security Administration reports "a medically determinable physical or mental impairment is an impairment that results from anatomical, physiological, or psychological abnormalities which can be shown by medically acceptable clinical and laboratory diagnostic techniques. A physical or mental impairment must be established by medical evidence consisting of signs, symptoms, and laboratory findings—not only by the individual's statement of symptoms"(Social Security Administration, 2006).

Definition of Disability

The AMA (1995, p. 2) defines a *disability* as: ". . . an alteration of an individual's capacity to meet personal, social, or occupational demands, or statutory or regulatory requirements, because of an impairment. Disability refers to an activity or task the individual cannot accomplish. A disability arises out of the interaction between impairment and external requirements, especially those of a person's occupation. Disability may be thought of as the gap between what a person *can* do and what the person *needs* or *wants* to do."

The WHO's ICF views a disability as impairments, limitations on activity, or restrictions of participation that result from the interaction between a person's health condition and personal status and personal existing external factors (Peterson, 2005, p. 106).

Thus, definitions of disability commonly characterize disability as the dynamic interaction between an individual and his or her environment, not as a static condition.

Definition of Handicap

The AMA (1995, p.2) defined *handicap* as a condition in which an individual with an impairment experiences ". . . obstacles to accomplishing life's basic activities that can be overcome only by compensating in some way for the effects of the impairment." When making a disability determination, a decision as to whether a person displays a handicap is considered in light of the use of compensatory strategies, devices, and other aids that may result in a person being able to perform tasks that otherwise he or she could not accomplish without the use of compensatory aids. The use of compensatory aids that reduce problems associated with interacting with the environment may preclude an impairment from reaching the level of disability.

DIFFERING TYPES OF DISABILITY INSURANCE

Various insurance products and contracts are available to the general public. A general understanding of the differences in prevalent products and contracts promotes understanding of how policy and contract law interact with health and functional status to determine disability.

Own-Occupation Policies

An *own-occupation* disability insurance policy is designed to protect an individual from disability that prevents that individual from continuing to engage in the individual's specific occupation. For example, a professional football player and/or the team on which he plays may carry an own-occupation disability insurance policy that would provide compensation in the event that a broken hand would prevent the athlete from continuing to play professional football. Although a broken hand may prevent playing football professionally, the individual may be able to engage in various other occupations despite having a broken hand. In this situation, the policyholder may receive the benefits from the own-occupation policy while continuing to be engaged in full-time active and gainful employment in another occupation. Thus, an *own-occupation* policy provides benefits in reference to a person's *specific* occupation. The standards that apply

to own-occupation policies and Social Security differ considerably.

Two Social Security Disability Programs

Social Security has two disability programs, namely Title II Social Security Disability Insurance (SSDI) for those who contribute Social Security taxes, and Title XVI Supplemental Security Income (SSI) for those who meet separate income and resource limits. In general, eligibility determination is consistent between these two programs.

Eligibility for Social Security disability benefits requires an adult to be unable to engage in *any* occupational activity. In children, the impairment must cause marked or extreme functional limitations. Returning to the above example, the football player may receive policy benefits from his own-occupation policy yet would not be eligible for benefits under Social Security disability.

When trying to understand whether one is eligible for benefits, differences between own-occupation and Social Security disability may not be well understood. The former provides benefits for being unable to perform one's typical occupation while permitting other forms of employment. In contrast, the latter provides benefits only for those unable to perform *any* occupation.

CONSTRUCTS IMPORTANT IN SOCIAL SECURITY DISABILITY DETERMINATION

Medically Determinable Impairment

The Social Security Administration requires an impairment to be determinable by medical techniques. A decision that an individual displays an impairment requires more than a professional report that alleges an impairment.

When evaluating mental impairments, an individual typically is interviewed by a psychologist or psychiatrist and may be administered standardized tests that assess general intellectual ability, memory, and other cognitive functioning—together with measures of personality as well as adaptive behavior. This information is pertinent to decisions as to whether a person displays a medically determinable impairment.

Eligible Diagnoses

The Social Security Administration defines specific diagnoses that are eligible for consideration under the disability program. Diagnoses used for disability determination for adults and children differ. Aside from an occasional rare exception, only specific diagnoses are eligible for

Social Security benefits. Unless otherwise indicated, the following diagnoses apply to both adults and children: anxiety-related disorders; affective disorders (mood disorders in children); attention deficit hyperactivity disorder (this category is *only* for children); autistic disorder and other pervasive developmental disorders; developmental and emotional disorders of newborn and younger infants; mental retardation; organic mental disorders; personality disorders; schizophrenic, paranoid and other psychotic disorders (also schizoaffective disorder in children); somatoform disorders (also eating disorders and tic disorders in children); and substance addiction disorders (psychoactive substance dependence disorders in children).

Persons who display these disorders exhibit a spectrum of signs and symptoms that inform professionals when concluding they have one or more specific disorders. The criteria used by the Social Security Administration parallels the *Diagnostic and Statistical Manual-IV* (American Psychiatric Association, 2000), criteria with which all mental health professionals are familiar.

Severity of Impairment

Determination of eligibility requires evidence of an impairment, its severity, and its functional impact on a person's life. The severity of an impairment and its effect on a person's functional status may range from no or little interference with occupational or functional activities to full and complete interference. For example, although a person may experience mild depression, he or she may continue to be meaningfully engaged in occupational and other functional daily activities. Although the depression is troubling, it does not reach the level that prevents the individual from engaging in work-like activities (see also the following paragraph on functional limitations in children).

Substantial Gainful Activity in Adults

The concept of *substantial gainful activity* relates to work. Substantial gainful activity refers to one's ability to engage in occupational activity that results in financial remuneration in excess of an amount defined in Social Security policy. The specific dollar amount pertinent to determining substantial gainful activity changes periodically. At the time of this writing, the amount is roughly $10,000 per year.

An individual able to earn through work at least the yearly income included in the current definition of substantial gainful activity is unlikely to be eligible for

Social Security disability benefits. Additionally, the degree to which one is able to work at a suitable pace and with persistence without significant interruption due to psychological or mental conditions also may be evaluated and considered when determining eligibility.

Functional Limitations in Children

A child must demonstrate a set of medical findings that lead to a professional judgment of being disabled as well as a set of impairment-related functional limitations to be classified as disabled. Thus, two criteria must be met: a medical finding of disability and an impairment-related functional limitation. Children also may display *functionally equal* listings. This term refers to a *marked limitation* as determined either by at least 2 of the 6 evaluated domains or an extreme limitation in 1 domain. The 6 domains are acquiring and using information, attending and completing tasks, interacting and relating with others, moving about and manipulating objects, caring for yourself, and maintaining health and physical well-being.

The Social Security Administration defines a *marked limitation* as follows. The impairment(s) interferes seriously with the person's ability to independently initiate, sustain, or complete domain-related activities. A marked impairment exists when a child's functioning, as measured by a valid standardized test, results in scores at least 2 but less than 3 standard deviations below the mean together with supporting evidence that the child's daily functioning in domain-related activities is consistent with this score. For ages 0 through 3, the infant's functioning must be between one-half to two-thirds of the level of functioning displayed by the infant's chronological age peers.

An *extreme limitation* interferes very seriously with the child's ability to independently initiate, sustain, or complete domain-related activities. An extreme limitation is more severe than a marked limitation. An extreme limitation exists when a child's functioning, as measured by a valid standardized test, results in scores at least 3 standard deviations below the mean, together with supporting evidence that the child's daily functioning in domain-related activities is consistent with this score. For ages 0 through 3, the infant's functioning must be less than one-half of the level of functioning displayed by the infant's chronological age peers.

A child's functioning is compared to those of same-age children who are representative of the national population. The combined effects of multiple impairments and the interactive and cumulative effects of an impairment(s)

DISCUSSION BOX 12.1

Eligibility for Social Security disability program benefits requires specified diagnoses. The U.S. Supreme Court has ruled that a person's decision not to take medications that may minimize the adverse impact of an impairment could prevent that person from being disabled under certain policy language and thus not receive benefits. For example, a person with hypertension who decides not to take antihypertensive medication may not be disabled or eligible for work accommodations otherwise thought to be due to this medical disorder. Persons with mental disorders who elect to discontinue medication deemed helpful to their condition may not be displaying noncompliant behaviors because not taking medication may be part of the symptoms of the disorder.

Questions

1. Is the situation involving a mental disorder and treatment noncompliance different from that of high blood pressure? Why or why not?
2. How might a psychologist try to determine whether a person is not taking medication due to the effects of the mental disorder?

---

on the child's activities must be considered. Additionally, the nature and degree of special help needed, adaptations, need for structured and supportive settings, the child's functions in unique, not only routine, settings, their need for early and special education programs, the effects of such interventions, and the impact of chronic illness are considered when documenting impairment and its degree.

Duration of Disability

The duration of a disability must meet criteria established by the Social Security Administration. Social Security disability benefits are intended to provide coverage for long-term or chronic, not short-term disability, which may be provided by other insurance policies. For example, an individual with an impairment that results in a disability to engage in occupational activity for 6 months, after which the individual would be able to resume occupational activity, is not covered. Eligibility for children and adults requires the duration of disability to be during the previous 12 months, is expected to persist for at least the next 12 months, or is expected to result in death.

Psychiatric Review Technique Form

Determination of eligibility is based on evidence of the existence of an eligible mental disorder. The Psychiatric Review Technique form is used internally by Social Security employees to review determination of eligibility of all adults based on diagnostic categories and level of severity of impairment. This form may be used jointly with a Mental Residual Functional Capacity form (see following section) to determine eligibility. When an applicant is rated as either mild/not severe or at the opposite extreme, very severe, the Psychiatric Review Technique form may be sufficient for internal reviewers, and the use of the Mental Residual Functional Capacity may not be needed.

Mental Residual Functional Capacity

An individual's mental impairment may not be sufficiently severe to meet criteria for one of the mental health listings. However, if the impairment is more than mild, then the Mental Residual Functional Capacity (MRFC) form may be used to document and rate the degree of impairment in one or more of the following functional domains: understanding and memory, sustained concentration and persistence, social interaction, and adaptation. Each of these 4 domains is subdivided further, resulting in a total of 20 categories. Ratings in these categories then are used to determine if the individual has the capacity for work.

Childhood Disability Evaluation Form (CDEF or Form 538)

This is the only form used in the adjudication of childhood disability applications. The form provides space for "meets listings" and for "functionally equals" the listings—the latter based on marked or extreme limitations in one or more of the 6 domain areas previously listed under *Functional Limitations in Children.*

APPLICATION PROCESS SUMMARY

An application for Social Security disability benefits may be filed with the Social Security Administration either at one of its offices (i.e. the Office of Disability Adjudication and Review), with a call to a toll free number, or online. Once filed, an initial interview is held, at which time demographic and nonmedical eligibility issues are discussed and clarified, including age, marital status, employment status (including the number of calendar quarters of earnings), citizenship status, income, and financial resources.

For children, Title XVI demographic and nonmedical eligibility issues consider parent's household income, the number of individuals in the household, along with resource limits (currently $3,000 for the parents and $2,000 for the child). The claimants provide information on alleged impairment(s), onset date, and medical treating sources, and sign releases. After assembling this initial information, the case is transferred to a state disability determination services office. These agencies are funded by the federal government.

The case then is assigned to a disability examiner who is responsible for further developments. The disability examiner attempts to obtain all relevant medical and school records as well as other pertinent information. The disability examiner sends an age-appropriate Functional Activity Form to the claimant and/or third party for completion.

After their return, the disability examiner assembles and reviews all information to determine if evidence is sufficient to warrant a medical review. If the information is insufficient, a consultative examination will be purchased (see the 5 steps following for a brief discussion of commonly utilized consultative examination assessment techniques).

After the evidence is sufficient, an adjudicative team composed of the disability examiner and medical reviewer completes the adjudication. This internal review is the key step in determining whether the evidence supports a finding of a disability. The process consists of 5 steps for adult claimants. The process can end with a determination of disability at any of the steps.

Step 1 in the sequential evaluation is to determine if the claimant is working. For calendar year 2007, if the claimant earned more than $900/month, the claimant will not be considered disabled (note that there is a higher earning threshold for individuals with blindness). If the individual is not working, or if s/he makes less than $900/month, then the process continues to Step 2.

Step 2 involves a determination of severity of the condition and whether it interferes with basic work-related activities. If the condition is not severe enough to interfere with basic work-related activities, then the claimant will not be considered to be disabled. If the condition does interfere with basic work-related functions, then the process continues to step 3.

Step 3 involves a determination of whether the condition of the claimant is found in the Social Security list of disabling conditions. Some conditions are considered so severe that having one of these conditions automatically leads to a determination of disability. If the claimant's condition is not on the list, a determination will be made as to whether the condition is of equal severity to a condition on the list. If it does not, then the claim will be denied. If it does, then the process will continue to step 4.

Step 4 involves a decision whether the claimant still can do work that was previously done. If the claimant's condition is severe yet it does not interfere with the ability to do the work that was done previously, then the claim will be denied. If the condition does interfere with the ability to do prior work, then the process continues to step 5.

Step 5 involves a determination of whether the claimant is able to do other work. Diagnosis, age, education, prior work experience, and transferable skills are all considered at this step. If the claimant cannot adjust to other work, the claim will be approved. For further information concerning the 5 step process as well as "special situations" go to http://www.ssa.gov/dibplan/dqualify.htm.

After completing the adjudication, the case is returned to the Social Security Administration Office of Disability Adjudication and Review for appropriate action.

A claimant who disagrees with the determination may file an appeal for reconsideration. This process involves the assignment of the case to a different disability examiner and medical reviewer. If new evidence is provided, it is collected prior to this review. A claimant who continues to disagree with findings may lodge an appeal through the Office of Hearings and Appeals. The appeal will be heard and ruled on by an administrative law judge.

ROLE(S) FOR PSYCHOLOGISTS IN THE SOCIAL SECURITY DISABILITY DETERMINATION PROCESS

Psychologists may play a number of roles within the Social Security disability determination process. For example, a psychologist who has been providing services to the applicant may submit records, if requested. If evidence in the client's file is insufficient, then a psychologist (it may be other than the treating psychologist) may be asked to provide a consultative examination involving examination of the claimant and review of relevant records. This examination is conducted solely for the purpose(s) of determining whether a disability exits and is expected to address issues necessary to make such a determination. Psychologists may participate in cases of alleged mental impairment by reviewing medical and psychological evidence of impairment/disability and participating in determining eligibility for benefits. Psychologists also may be qualified and serve as medical experts if called by the administrative law judge to testify on complex issues.

RESEARCH BOX 12.1

Objective: To determine if a person can "fake" a disability such as cognitive impairment.

Method: Neuropsychologists have studied individuals suspected of malingering and/or healthy subjects instructed to feign impairment.

Results: Many studies have found that the incidence of symptom exaggeration or "malingering" may be much higher than one might suspect, likely due to the financial incentives often involved (Larrabee, 2005; Reynolds, 1998; Duddleston et al., 2002; Allen et al., 1997) These and other studies indicate that symptom exaggeration may interfere with examination results in determining disability.

Conclusion: Appropriate evaluation of disability should include methods for assessing symptom exaggeration.

Questions

1. Discuss ways in which symptom exaggeration may be detected.
2. Review the neuropsychological literature in the area of malingering of brain injury. Write a brief description of the strengths and weaknesses inherent in various methods that may detect symptom exaggeration.

RELATIONSHIP OF SOCIAL SECURITY DISABILITY DETERMINATION TO APPLICABLE INTERNATIONAL CLASSIFICATION FUNCTIONING AND HEALTH ASPECTS

The constructs currently used under the Social Security Administration disability determination programs are an attempt to provide an understanding of one's functional capabilities in light of one's level of impairment. The MRFC may be conceptualized as an approximation of the type of rating that may be provided more completely by use of the International Classification of Functioning, Disability and Health (ICF). The ICF provides a structure within which many of the above concepts and constructs can be applied to understand disability. It provides for the interaction of physical and psychological functioning, activities, participation level, capacity, and performance constructs in an effort to understand how an individual engages with the environment. At present, the Social Security disability determination process does not utilize the ICF; however, the ICF may prove quite useful in the future as a means of understanding disability, perhaps to the point of effecting public policy (Peterson, 2005).

HISTORY OF RESEARCH IN SOCIAL SECURITY DISABILITY DETERMINATION

Attorneys and advocates can play a role in the disability determination process. Although disability examiners (DE) send record requests and follow up requests, they are not required to follow up extensively to ensure that records are obtained. Advocates can help claimants

by doing more extensive records searches than can be accomplished by the DEs. Attorneys sometimes use their own expert psychologists to conduct examinations that will be used during the adjudication process. Dow and Boaz (1994) found that persons who were applying for Social Security disability benefits and had assistance in filing appropriate forms and records were twice as likely to secure the benefits as those who did not have such assistance. Burkhauser, Butler, & Weathers (2001–2002) found that social and environmental factors such as workplace accommodations can significantly affect decisions to apply for Social Security disability benefits. These authors also found that, in states with higher acceptance rates (granting of disability benefits), persons were more likely to apply for benefits sooner after an impairment began to be troublesome than in states with lower acceptance rates. Symptom exaggeration and depression have been reported to impact an individual's perception of disability (Duddleston, Blackston, Bouldin, & Brown 2002). The authors of this chapter have found that there are differences in quality assurance programs between districts. Some states or regions have internal quality assurance teams and mandates that are more stringent than other states or regions.

CURRENT ASSESSMENT METHODS IN SOCIAL SECURITY DISABILITY DETERMINATION

Diagnostic information from a licensed doctoral level source *must* be in every file with the following exception. When the claimant is a child, a nondoctoral level school psychologist and/or speech–language pathologist may provide some types of evidence. The doctoral level individual can be a treating source or a consultative examination vendor. Psychiatric nurse practitioners and physician assistants are not approved sources of information for purposes of disability determination.

Subjective or Nonpsychometric Approaches

The psychiatric interview is one subjective approach that can be used by mental health professionals in disability determination. A formally structured psychiatric interview rarely is used (e.g., Schedule for Affective Disorders and Schizophrenia—Lifetime version [Endicott & Spitzer, 1978], Research Diagnostic Criteria [Spitzer, Endicott, & Robins, 1975] Mini-Mental Status Examination [Folstein, Folstein, & McHugh, 1975]. Psychiatric interviews typically focus little on clinician observations and instead contain a claimants' subjective self-reports about their conditions. Therefore, the information they provide has limited utility during the disability determination process.

Objective or Psychometric/Quantitative Approaches

Standardized testing frequently is used. Testing may be done by treating psychologists, consultative examination vendors, or experts specifically retained to provide information for use in disability determination. They often are employed by attorneys retained by claimants.

Medical chart reviewers are delighted to find detailed neuropsychological examinations done by treating psychologists in files. These reports tend to provide rich quantitative data and qualitative descriptive information. Individuals with insufficient file information may be referred to a Consultative Examiner for testing, the services for which are paid by the Social Security Administration. Those evaluations often are more limited in scope than are those provided by professionals interested in issues that extend beyond disability determination (e.g., treatment planning). For example, a consultative examination for an individual alleging a brain injury may consist of measures of mental status, intelligence, and memory. Use of standardized tests is helpful during the adjudication process due to being norm referenced, thus comparing a claimant with one's peers in the population. Examples of such tests include the Wechsler Adult Intelligence Scale (3rd ed.) (Wechsler, 1997a) and the Wechsler Memory Scale (3rd ed.) (Wechsler, 1997b). The self-report Minnesota Multiphasic Personality Inventory (2nd ed.) (Hathaway and McKinley, 1989) frequently is used to evaluate psychopathology. Although response bias or symptom validity (e.g, through the

Computerized Assessment of Response Bias; Allen, Conder & Cox, 1997) may help in indicating the validity of the results obtained from testing, they rarely are included in these examinations.

Writing a Psychological Report Following a Disability Determination Evaluation

A report is submitted that contains needed information in sufficient detail to address issues important to a Social Security disability determination. The report's focus should highlight one's functional status and capacity as opposed to emotional experience. Reports that respond to a referral question as to an individual's ability to engage in work or work-like activities are most useful, especially when they include objective data and behavioral descriptors.

Consultative examination vendors and treating psychologists may attempt to be helpful by using in their reports terminology used on Social Security disability forms. These attempts can be problematic when the report writer is not thoroughly knowledgeable about the precise use of terminology during the disability determination process. Therefore, psychologists are encouraged to refrain from such attempts.

Psychologists often attempt to understand a client's experience, including the psychological and physical aspects of the client's condition. Thus, they often evaluate a person's status in the context of that person's general environment. Although psychologists are unlikely to conduct a physical examination, the applicant's physical status generally is considered when evaluating his or her life conditions.

Thus, most psychologists are prepared to evaluate a person's response to physical limitations, environmental and psychosocial factors, and their interactions. The biopsychosocial assessment model generally is accepted within mainstream psychology when attempting to understand an individual.

However, under certain circumstances, psychologists should weigh the importance of one's personal qualities when conducting an evaluation. Evaluations that address a specific referral question may be limited to those qualities and thus ignore others. For example, a referral requesting evaluation of a child who may meet policy guidelines for special services in a school system may warrant the use of measures of intelligence and achievement and attend little to the etiology of underlying conditions. The purpose of that examination may be to determine whether the child meets public policy standards. A differential diagnosis may not be needed.

DISCUSSION BOX 12.2

Pain may be an exaggerated symptom in a person's presentation. Case Example: Ms. Smith presents complaining of chronic pain, depression, and memory problems. She indicates that she also is experiencing marital difficulty. She states that this all began after she slipped and fell at work, resulting in a back strain that has left her feeling too unwell to return to work.

Questions

1. Discuss the difficulties inherent when attempting to evaluate pain and its impact on a person's functional status.

2. How can a psychologist determine if a person's report of pain is valid?

3. How may a psychologist evaluate disability due to pain? For example, consider the effects of mood and pain on thinking skills. Remember to avoid including physical status in the psychological evaluation and conclusions as they fall within the domain of the physicians.

Similarly, evaluations conducted for disability determination may request the psychologist to focus on specific aspects of an individual's experience and status and specifically request other aspects of behavior not be evaluated. For example, Social Security regulations ask the psychologists to evaluate emotional and cognitive factors and specifically require physical factors be deferred to an examining physician. Although physical pain may be troubling, it alone is not considered in disability determination. Physical pain is difficult to measure, is highly susceptible to self-report bias, and may or may not impact daily activity.

CRITICAL ISSUES IN DISABILITY DETERMINATION ASSESSMENT

The Role of Effort and Secondary Gain in Presentation (Response Bias Testing)

Challenges to the credibility and validity of data need to be anticipated and at times are difficult to address. When conducting assessments that will be reviewed by private insurers or prepared for use in forensic settings, best practice guidelines emphasize the use of tests that assess the examinee's effort and tendency to malinger. However, vendors who report to Social Security rarely include such testing. Although the Social Security Administration wants reports to address issues of the tests' validity, psychologists are not compensated for assessing effort, malingering, response bias, or symptom validity. Despite not being compensated for this work, some psychologists continue to test these qualities given their belief that these results are critical to their work.

However, this is not the norm. Instead, responsibility for identifying unusual patterns in performance (e.g, failing easy items, and inconsistencies between results and home/community function reports) typically rests on the work of the file reviewer. When data warrant, a fraud investigation may be requested. It may include surveillance as well as interviews of neighbors and others.

Legal and Professional Issues for the Psychologist

DECIDING WHO IS THE CLIENT   When a psychologist performs a consultative examination, the client and employer are one: the Social Security Administration, *not*

DISCUSSION BOX 12.3

Ethical Issues with Symptom Exaggeration

Discuss ethical issues involved in evaluating symptom exaggeration. Include in your discussion possible ethics and legal issues that may be involved in interviewing others, conducting surveillance, and engaging in other needed activities. Consider the financial impact of paying for testing of symptom exaggeration. Discuss other means of detecting fraud versus the cost involved in paying disability to people who may not be disabled. Attempt to consider both sides of this issue.

Consider using the following scenario: Mr. Rogers struck his head on a cabinet as he rose from his chair at work. He continued working that day and for several days following. The next Monday, he called in sick and indicated that he was experiencing significant neck pain and headache. A coworker, however, has indicated that he subsequently saw Mr. Rogers doing yard work, cutting the lawn and trimming a tree.

the person being examined (i.e., the claimant). The records belong to the Social Security Administration. Thus, most Disability Determination Services offices request that the psychologist *not* keep a copy of the records—a condition that may be inconsistent with the psychologist's ethics code as well as best practice guidelines. The consultative examination (CE) vendor may be forbidden to release reports to claimants. Instead, if desired by them, claimants must contact the Social Security Administration for the records. Claimants have the right to inspect records under the Federal Freedom of Information Act and the Privacy Act. The Social Security Administration screens a claimant's request to review his or her medical records, including the report, to ensure that release of evidence will not adversely impact the claimant. If a determination is made that it may have an adverse impact, then the report will be released only to an authorized representative designated by the claimant.

CLINICAL EVALUATION V. RECORD REVIEW The work of psychologists who work as consultative evaluation vendors is *clinical* in nature. In contrast, their work as medical reviewer is *administrative* in nature. The latter work may require ordering tests for use in administrative decision-making. This may create liability issues because the medical reviewer is not a treating source and may obtain information about clinical diagnoses that are unknown to claimants or members of their medical teams. In part, as a result of liability concerns, some Disability Determination Services offices have hired medical reviewers as staff rather than as consultants. As state employees, these medical reviewers are covered under state liability policies and are less apt to be charged with ethical or legal violations.

HIPAA ISSUES (HEALTH INSURANCE PORTABILITY & ACCOUNTABILITY ACT) The Health Insurance Portability & Accountability Act was designed to protect Americans from losing health insurance when they changed jobs or residences, to streamline the health care system through adoption of consistent standards for transmitting uniform electronic health care claims, and to adopt standards for record storage and protection of an individual's privacy. The actual HIPAA may be read on the Internet at http://aspe.hhs.gov/admnsimp/pl104191.htm). An understanding of HIPAA's various definitions aid practitioners in their various professional roles. Important definitions are reviewed below.

Health Information This includes any information, whether oral or recorded in any form, created or used by health care professionals or health care entities.

Individually Identifiable Health Information This information comprises a subset of health information that either identifies the individual or can be used to identify the individual.

Protected Health Information Individually identifiable health information becomes protected health information when it is transmitted or maintained in any form or medium. Protected health information includes past, present, or future physical or mental health conditions of an individual; the provision of health care to an individual; or the past, present, or future payment for the provision of health care to an individual; and that identifies the individual or could reasonably be used to identify the individual.

In the context of administrative proceedings and forensic work, the psychologist must recognize who the client is and be mindful of any specific issues that relate to the release of information. Informed consent is vital. When conducting Social Security disability consultative examinations, informed consent forms should indicate that information will be presented to and maintained by the Social Security Administration (the client). Although the Centers for Medicare & Medicaid Services have indicated that Social Security disability evaluations are not a HIPAA–covered activity, opinions differ on this. Thus, consultation with malpractice insurance carriers and attorneys is recommended to understand whether HIPAA applies to Social Security disability examinations. One should consult the appropriate professional code of ethics; for example, psychologists should refer to *Ethical Principles of Psychologists and Code of Conduct* (American Psychological Association, 2002; http://www.apa.org/ethics/code2002.html).

For psychologists, the following ethical standards may apply in situations involving Social Security disability evaluations.

3.06 Conflict of interest: This may apply when a treating source is asked to do a consultative examination for the Social Security Administration.

3.07 Third party requests for services: Clarification of the nature of the relationship and the role of the psychologist with the examinee and the Social Security Administration from the outset is vital.

3.09 Cooperation with other professionals: Practitioners who provide client services and do not respond to requests for records from Social Security may be a violation of 3.09.

3.10 Informed consent: See above under HIPAA.

DISCUSSION BOX 12.4

Ethics Code Review

Read the ethics code as published by the American Psychological Association (2002) (http://www.apa.org). Discuss each area of the document as it might relate to disability determination work.

Consider the various roles that a psychologist may have in the disability determination process. Is any particular role more or less prone to ethical dilemmas? Why or why not?

3.11 Psychological Services delivered to organizations: This section of the Code defines exactly what areas should be addressed in the informed consent forms used for Social Security consultative examinations.

4.01 Maintaining confidentiality, 4.02 Discussing the limits of confidentiality, and 4.05 Disclosures: These issues need to be addressed with the contracting agency and through informed consent with examinees.

6 Record keeping & fees: This standard applies only when records are under a psychologist's control. According to Social Security policy, the records are its property. Fee agreements are standard between the Disability Determination Service of the state and the psychologists who conduct examinations for the agency or provide medical evidence as treating sources.

9 Assessment: Every standard in this section of the Code is relevant to the work performed by psychologists for the Social Security Administration through the state Disability Determination Service agencies.

Summary and Conclusion

The determination of disability involves the application of clinical information to policy language that leads to an administrative decision. A person with an impairment may or may not meet the definition of disability as defined under specific contractual language in a given insurance policy.

In order to meet Social Security disability eligibility requirements, the impairment must be present, must have already lasted 12 months, or be expected to last for at least 12 months, or be anticipated to lead to death. Any substantial gainful activity (employment) must be precluded due to the impairment. A person's income from work may be little, yet still exceed the amount permitted under substantial gainful activity standards. Children applying for Social Security under the Title XVI program must display a set of medical findings determined to be disabling as well as a set of impairment-related functional limitations at marked or extreme levels.

Individuals may be more likely to be granted benefits if they have had assistance in applying and gathering the appropriate records and information (Dow & Boaz, 1994). Social environmental factors influence when people apply for disability benefits as opposed to continuing to try to work with accommodations. Conditions such as symptom exaggeration and depression can affect an individual's presentation and should be attended to by examining professionals (Duddleston, et al., 2002).

Psychologists play a role in the Social Security disability determination process in a number of ways. They may be treating providers, may be contracted by Social Security to conduct consultative examinations, may serve as medical/psychological records reviewers, and/or may serve as consultative experts to administrative law judges. Each role has a unique place in the disability determination process.

Examinations conducted for the purpose of disability determination generally include subjective information gleaned from an interview and other data collection methods as well as objective information obtained through standardized tests. These test data can be particularly helpful due to their quantitative nature and the availability of normative comparisons. The report should include a statement regarding the validity of information. Formal assessment of response bias and malingering, although quite helpful, often is not obtained and constitutes an area for future attention in the disability determination process.

A number of ethical issues may arise during disability examinations. Thus, psychologists should consider applicable ethics standards. When conducting disability examinations, the client or customer being served is the Social Security Administration, not the person being evaluated. This role impacts legal issues, including the release of data and HIPAA provisions.

Self-Check Questions

1. What are the principle differences between clinical and administrative decision making?
2. Why do insurance companies have differing definitions of disability? Is there a best definition? Why doesn't everyone use the Social Security definition?
3. Compare and contrast SSDI and SSI programs for disability.
4. Describe the Social Security 5-step process for disability determination.
5. Is the application process for Social Security Disability programs accessible to individuals with disabilities? Discuss issues of accessibility as they relate to the application process.
6. What is the mechanism for appeals when a claimant is turned down for Social Security disability benefits?
7. Do claimants have a better chance of success in the disability determination process if they have outside assistance with the process? If so, why is this true?
8. Why is the concept of symptom validity testing (sometimes also known as effort testing) important in disability determination work?
9. Why would an insurance company want to have its claimants apply for Social Security Disability?
10. Discuss ethical issues of importance for mental health providers who interface with the Social Security Disability programs.

Case Studies

Case 1

Eric, a 31-year-old male, was diagnosed with schizophrenia. He has applied for SSDI benefits because he has been unable to hold a job. He worked last as a part-time stocker at a grocery store, but was let go due to his sporadic attendance. Eric is under the care of a psychiatrist who has prescribed antipsychotic medication. Eric's compliance with the medication is not the best. He tends to stop taking it when he "feels better" and then decompensates under stress, resulting in his poor work history. He also has a tendency to use marijuana frequently, apparently in an attempt to self-medicate his symptoms.

Eric was approved for SSDI benefits. Despite his substance abuse history, his presentation was deemed to meet the criteria established for schizophrenia. The marijuana use was considered a part of, or secondary to, his illness and therefore not a causative factor for his inability to maintain employment. His intermittent compliance with medication was deemed related to his schizophrenia, not to a volitional decision not to engage in appropriate therapy.

Case 2

Irene always had a tough time getting herself going. She worked as a clerk in a law office, but seemed to lack initiative and frequently saw the negative in situations. Her marriage was stressful to her in that she and her husband did not communicate well. She complained of being depressed. She reported that she always has been unhappy. She could take care of herself, engage in routine daily activities, and maintain work, but eventually applied for SSDI benefits after quitting her job due to "not being able to handle the stress." She was not in any mental health treatment and was sent for a consultative evaluation as part of the SSDI process. The report indicated a diagnosis of Dysthymic Disorder, and Personality Disorder NOS with dependent traits. Her application was not approved. Her symptoms did not reach the level of a Major Depression or other diagnosis that would establish eligibility. Moreover, she had demonstrated the ability to work in the recent past, and her ability to engage in sustained gainful activity over the years was well documented. Although she presented with complaints of depression and perhaps would benefit from treatment, she was not in treatment.

Discussion Issues

Discuss each case with reference to the issues presented. Also discuss what specifics in the cases may change the determination of eligibility for benefits and why. Be sure to include areas such as engagement in and compliance with treatment, substance abuse issues, possible symptom exaggeration, and ability to sustain and maintain routine work-like activities.

References

Allen, L. M., Conder, R. L. & Cox, D. R. (1997). *CARB '97: Computerized Assessment of Response Bias. Test & Manual.* Durham, NC: Cognisyst, Inc.

American Medical Association. (1995). *Guides to the Evaluation of Permanent Impairment:* (4th ed.). Chicago: American Medical Association.

American Psychiatric Association. (2000). *Diagnostic and Statistical Manual of Mental Disorders* (4th ed., etxt rev.). Arlington, VA: American Psychiatric Association.

American Psychological Association (2002). Ethical principles of psychologists and code of conduct. *American Psychologist, 57,* 1060–1073.

Burkhauser, R. V., Butler, J. S. & Weathers, R. R. (2001–2002). How policy variables influence the timing of applications for Social Security Disability Insurance. *Social Security Bulletin, 64*(1), 52–83.

Dow, M. G. & Boaz, T. L. (1994). Assisting clients of community mental health centers to secure SSI benefits: a controlled evaluation. *Community Mental Health Journal, 30*(5), 429–440.

Duddleston, D. N., Blackston, J. W., Bouldin, M. J. & Brown, C. A. (2002). Disability examinations: A look at the Social Security Disability Income System. *American Journal of Medical Science, 324*(4), 220–226.

Endicott J., & Spitzer, R. (1978). A diagnostic interview: The schedule for affective disorders and schizophrenia. *Archives of General Psychiatry, 35,* 837–844.

Folstein, M., Folstein, S., & McHugh, P. (1975). Mini-Mental State: A practical method for grading the cognitive state of patients for the clinician. *Journal of Psychiatric Research, 12,* 189–198.

Hathaway, S. R. & McKinley, J. C. (1989). *The Minnesota Multiphasic Personality Inventory.* Minneapolis: University of Minnesota Press.

Larrabee, G. J. (2005) Forensic Neuropsychology: A scientific approach. New York: Oxford University Press.

Peterson, D. B. (2005). International Classification of Functioning, Disability and Health: An introduction for rehabilitation psychologists. *Rehabilitation Psychology, 50,* 105–112.

Reynolds, C. R. (1998). *Detection of malingering during head injury litigation.* New York: Plenum Press.

Social Security Administration. (2006). Disability Evaluation Under Social Security–June 2006. (Note: The Social Security Website for disability determination may be found at: http://www.ssa.gov/disability/professionals/bluebook/)

Spitzer, R., Endicott, J., & Robins, E. (1975). *Research diagnostic criteria for a select group of functional disorders* (2nd ed.). New York: New York State Psychiatric Institute. Biometrics Research.

Wechsler, D. (1997a). Wechsler Adult Intelligence Scale (3rd ed.) Administration and Scoring Manual. San Antonio, TX: The Psychological Corporation.

Wechsler, David. (1997b). Wechsler Memory Scale (3rd ed.): Administration and Scoring Manual. San Antonio, TX: The Psychological Corporation.

World Health Organization. (1980). International Classification of Impairments, Disabilities, and Handicaps. Geneva, Switzerland: World Health Organization.

13

Assessment for Workplace Accommodations

CARRIE BRUCE
JON A. SANFORD
Georgia Institute of Technology, Atlanta

OVERVIEW

This chapter provides an overview of the importance and process of assessment for workplace accommodations. The legislative evolution of workplace accommodations is traced, pointing out the lack of conventional guidelines for performing workplace assessments. A brief history of the science and practice behind workplace accommodation assessment demonstrates the interdisciplinary nature of this specialized field. Research on workplace accommodation assessments is discussed and a theoretical framework for understanding the components of assessment instruments is introduced.

LEARNING OBJECTIVES

By the end of the chapter, readers should be able to:

- Describe the limitations of existing legislation related to guiding the assessment process
- Explain the influence of Person–Environment fit theory on the workplace accommodation assessment process
- Describe and explain the key components in the workplace accommodation assessment process
- Provide a rationale for selecting appropriate assessment instrument for a particular work accommodation situation

INTRODUCTION

Workplace accommodations enable individuals with disabilities to gain and maintain employment (Gamble, Dowler, & Orslene, 2006; Inge, Wehman, Strobel, Powell, & Todd, 1998) and enable employers to retain productive and qualified employees (Blanck, 1994; Unger & Kregel, 2003). The use of accommodations helps support the inclusion of workers with disabilities and older adults and promotes a more diverse workforce. Their use also can reduce the risk of injury (Zwerling et al., 2003) and can be utilized by coworkers without disabilities to improve their job performance (Unger & Kregel, 2003).

Workplace accommodations are broadly defined as "any change in the work environment or in the way things are customarily done that enables an individual with a disability to enjoy equal employment opportunities" (Equal Employment Opportunity Commission [EEOC], 1992). More specifically, workplace accommodations refer to modifications or adjustments (a) to a job application process to permit an individual with a disability to be considered for a job (e.g., providing application forms in alternative formats like large print or Braille); (b) necessary to enable a qualified individual with a disability to perform the essential functions of the job (e.g., providing sign language interpreters); and (c) that enable employees with disabilities to enjoy equal benefits and privileges of employment (e.g., removing physical barriers in an office cafeteria).

Considerable evidence supports the belief that the provision of accommodations can improve job opportunities for people with disabilities. Despite this evidence, their provision has not occurred on a wide scale. This limited use is due, in part, to inadequate accommodation selection strategies and assessment methodologies (Bat-Chava, Deignan, & Martin, 2002; Gamble et al., 2006; Scherer & Craddock, 2002). Moreover, a systematic assessment process may improve the perceived effectiveness of accommodations and reduce accommodation costs (Gamble et al., 2006).

IMPORTANCE OF WORKPLACE ACCOMMODATIONS TO REHABILITATION AND HEALTH

The Role of Workplace Accommodations as a Rehabilitation Strategy

Work is an essential life activity. It provides the means for achieving status and recognition, acquiring income, and developing relationships (Ginzberg, 1983). In fact, outside of sleep, work is the activity that consumes the largest amount of time in an individual's life (Bernspang & Fisher, 1995; Sandqvist & Henriksson, 2004). Thus, participation in the workforce is crucial to the health of working age adults.

Despite its importance, almost two–thirds (21.3 million) of the 33 million working age adults with disabilities in the United States live with conditions that restrict their ability to work and to participate in the workforce. Moreover, the number of people with work-related disabilities is expected to rise dramatically as the U.S. workforce continues to age (Zwerling et al., 2003).

The number of jobs in the United States is projected to increase by almost 19 million between 2004 and 2014 (Hecker, 2005), resulting in a shortage of workers to fill them. As a result, employers must adopt new strategies that will enable them to draw on untapped sources of labor, including people with disabilities. Workplace accommodations constitute an important rehabilitation strategy that can effectively reduce work-related disabilities. Thus, the general use of workplace accommodations by employers can be expected to increase in order to cope with market forces and demographic changes in the workforce.

The use of workplace accommodations by employers must be consistent with federal legislation enacted to promote participation of people with disabilities in the workforce. For example, Title I of the Americans with Disabilities Act of 1990 (ADA) prohibits employers with 15 or more employees from discriminating against a qualified applicant or worker who has a physical or mental impairment that substantially limits a major life activity. The roots of this legislation are found in Section 501, which prohibits federal executive branch agencies from discriminating against qualified individuals with disabilities, and Section 504 of the Rehabilitation Act of 1973, which prohibits exclusion of people with disabilities from any program or activity that either receives federal financial assistance or is conducted by any executive agency or the United States Postal Service (U.S. Department of Justice, *A Guide to Disability Rights Laws*, 2005). The ADA and Sections 501 and 504 express the requirement that an

RESEARCH BOX 13.1

Background: As individuals get older, they experience changes in body structure and function that affect vision, hearing, upper and lower extremity use, and cognition. These age-related changes can result in difficulty performing job tasks. This section discusses research undertaken to understand the types of workplace accommodations that are commonly used by workers in various age groups and with different types of functional limitations (Williams, Sabata, & Zolna, 2006).

Objective: To understand the needs of aging workers with functional limitations and the types of workplace accommodations commonly used.

Method: Survey responses from 510 individuals with self-reported functional limitations who were employed or had been employed in the past were used. Participants responded to survey questions through online, telephone, or paper formats. The survey primarily focused on: 1) demographics, including age, gender, income, and education of people working with disabilities; 2) functional limitations and how they have affected employment; 3) prevalence of disabilities that affect workers' abilities and difficulties created by such disabilities; and 4) accommodations received in response to these difficulties.

Results: Respondents included individuals in the *preretirement age* group (55 to 64 years of age, N = 123) and the *retirement age* group (65 years of age or older, N = 49). More than two–thirds of the respondents (67%) reported that their disability had at times prevented performance of job duties. Survey results indicated that a variety of functional limitations were reported, including vision and hearing issues. Thirty-two percent of individuals aged 55 to 64 experienced problems performing visual tasks, whereas 18% reported difficulties in the aged 65 and older group. Seventeen percent of the individuals in the preretirement group and 50% of the retired group reported that they did not have accommodations for their vision difficulties. Hearing problems were reported by 42% of individuals aged 55 to 64 and by 49% of individuals over age 65. Only 88% of those in the preretirement group and 83% in the retired group received accommodations for hearing impairments.

Conclusions: Older people often do not have workplace accommodations to address their needs. Most notable are the 50% of older adults who reported no accommodations for visual impairments.

Questions

1. What does this research indicate regarding aging workers and their workplace accommodation needs?
2. Despite the potential for age-related work disability, the Americans with Disabilities Act of 1990 does not consider aging to be a disability. Why do you think aging is not covered under the ADA?
3. What are some specific considerations that should be acknowledged in an assessment for an aging worker?

individual must be able to perform the essential functions or fundamental job duties on his/her own or with the help of a *reasonable accommodation*.

Section 508 of the Rehabilitation Act of 1973, the Workforce Investment Act of 1998 (WIA), and the New Freedom Initiative (1999) also were designed to promote inclusion of people with disabilities in the workplace.

Section 508 requires that commonly used electronic and information technology (e.g., phones, copiers, fax machines) used by the federal government be accessible to people with disabilities. Although this legislation is applicable only to the federal government, it has had far reaching impact, setting the precedent, if not the standard, for all electronic and information technology developed in the past three decades.

The Workforce Investment Act of 1998 established One-Stop Centers that provide various services to help individuals meet employment and training needs and assist local employers in meeting their needs for qualified personnel. Finally, Executive Order 13217 (2001) enacted President Bush's New Freedom Initiative (1999), which established various loan programs and tax incentives designed to promote increased access to workplace accommodations by people with disabilities.

The Need for Assessment

A workplace accommodation, similar to other rehabilitation strategies, must be customized to the person, work setting, work tasks, and task performance. In recognition of the personalized nature of rehabilitation, Title I of the ADA merely mandates the provision of accommodation. This broad and generic approach differs from the Title III accessibility guidelines that provide specific standards for accessibility in public facilities. Whereas an assessment is not needed to apply Title III guidelines for the general public, the provision of workplace accommodations mandated by Title I requires an individualized assessment to tailor accommodations to the needs of each employee.

In response to workforce needs and legislative mandates for workplace accommodations, information about the accommodation process and types of accommodations is available from multiple sources. However, professionals performing assessments have little guidance on what to assess or how to use assessment information to provide accommodations. This lack of guidance has led to the use of various assessment methods, resulting in variability in the appropriateness of accommodations for employees.

For example, the Job Accommodation Network (JAN) has developed the Searchable Online Accommodation Resource to provide users with accommodation ideas based on categories of health conditions and functional limitations. Accommodation suggestions in the Searchable Online Accommodation Resource are nonspecific to an individual, his/her job tasks, and work environment. In contrast, AbleLink Technologies' VRXpert software program goes one step further by combining an individual's functional limitations with a standard set of job tasks from the O*NET[1] job categories to identify potential accommodations. However, VRXpert is limited by its inability to include nonstandard job tasks (i.e., not found in O*NET) and its lack of consideration of environmental influences on job performance.

In practice, assessment is used primarily at the beginning of the employment process to determine the basic and immediate accommodations needed to get an individual into a job. Assessment as a comprehensive and continuing process to identify long-term needs and changes over time is less frequent. As a result, workers with disabilities may not have access to the full set or even the most appropriate accommodations needed to maintain employment or to advance in the workplace. Equally important, accommodations based on initial cursory assessments may be less effective over time (Unger & Kregel, 2003).

Assessments are frequently conducted by an employer's own internal managerial resources (e.g., human resources department), which often has an inadequate understanding of the Americans with Disabilities Act requirements, disability, and accommodations (Unger & Kregel, 2003). In fact, human resource professionals generally acknowledge their limited understanding and experience in supporting employees with disabilities (Casper, 1993; Curry, 1996; Pitt-Catsouphes &

Butterworth, 1995; Unger & Kregel, 2003), thus suggesting a need for a more structured assessment process.

In recognition of the need for employers to establish procedures for improving the provision of accommodations, the federal government established the Computer/Electronic Accommodations Program (CAP) in 1990 and the Technology Accessible Resources Gives Employment Today (TARGET) Center in 1992 to improve the provision of accommodations. These programs offer assessment services and systematically approach the provision of accommodations by requiring employees and managers to go through a request process for purchasing assistive technology. Both programs focus primarily on computer, electronic, and ergonomic adaptations. As a result, they do not provide assessments that cover the full range of accommodation possibilities (e.g., environmental modifications and adaptive strategies).

Foundations of Workplace Assessment

Assessments for workplace accommodations are conducted by various professionals, including rehabilitation engineers, assistive technology practitioners, occupational therapists, ergonomists, and human resources personnel. As a result, the conceptual foundations and theoretical models guiding assessment differ. Many assessment models have been influenced by Lawton and Nahemow's Environmental Press Model, which features the importance, of the interaction between the individual and his/her environment as the outcome of the transaction between the person's competencies (or abilities) and the environmental demands, or press (Lawton & Nahemow, 1973). The Environmental Press Model was the first to recognize the importance of the fit between person and environment. However, its focus is narrow in that it does not account for the contributions of the activity itself. As a result, other ecological models emerged that directly addressed an individual's capacities and performance of activities in the workplace (Christiansen, 1991; Christiansen & Baum, 1997; Dunn, Brown, & McGuigan, 1994; Durand, Loisel, Hong, & Charpentier, 2002; Hagedorn, 1995, 2000; Ivancevich, Matteson, & Preston, 1982; Kielhofner, 1995; Kristof, 1996; Law et al., 1996; NCMRR, 1993; Vagg & Spielberger, 1999; World Health Organization, 2001). Perhaps the most influential models come from occupational therapy (e.g., PEO model), where performance has been treated as a dynamic association between an individual, the activities, and the surrounding environment (Baum & Christiansen, 2005; Baum & Law, 1997; Christiansen, 1991; Christiansen & Baum, 1997; Sandqvist & Henriksson, 2004).

---

[1] The O*NET database contains information on hundreds of standardized and occupation-specific descriptors. For more information, see http://www.onetcenter.org/

The International Classification of Functioning, Disability and Health (ICF), which was developed by the World Health Organization (World Health Organization, 2001), has been used primarily for health information systems evaluation (Ewert et al., 2004; Grill, Quittan, Huber, Boldt, & Stucki, 2005; Kuijer et al., 2006); design of medical records systems (Doolan, Bates, & James, 2003); and development of surveys for research (Bruyere, VanLooy, & Peterson, 2005; Swanson, Carrothers, & Mulhorn, 2003). However, it offers a new framework that has the potential to guide the assessment and accommodation process.

The ICF's taxonomy identifies a number of constructs that represent the essential components of workplace assessment. These include body structure, body function, activities and participation, environmental factors, and personal factors. Work concepts are clearly incorporated into activities and participation through specific references in the domain of *major life areas*: work and employment (d840–d859); and environmental factors in the domain of *products and technology*: products and technology for employment (e1350–e1359). However, some aspect of workplace assessment can be found in every domain under environmental factors due to the various activities associated with the plethora of job tasks, capacities required to perform job tasks, and environments within which job tasks are performed.

Work concepts also are found in the domains of *communication* (d300–399) and *support and relationships* (e300–399) under activity and participation. The first domain includes general and specific features of communicating, including carrying on conversations, receiving and producing messages, and using communication devices and techniques. The second domain includes the people or animals that provide support, nurturing, protection, assistance, and relationships to other persons at home, work, school, play or in other aspects of their daily activities. Finally, although the construct of "personal factors" has not yet been classified, it is very likely to be pertinent to work as it captures an individual's habits, coping styles, motivations, and experiences.

HISTORY OF RESEARCH AND PRACTICE IN WORKPLACE ACCOMMODATIONS ASSESSMENT

Although research evidence provides some general foundation for work performance, the field of workplace accommodations is relatively immature and thus practice-dominated due to need. The assessment processes and instruments used in its practice generally have been created by and adapted to the needs of the individual practitioner or organization. Although accommodations typically are individualized for each employee, the selection and use of assessment measures to address similar situations across individuals are dependent on the expertise and experience of the person conducting the assessment.

Additional evidence-based practice may alter and could formalize the process used to perform workplace accommodation assessments. However, the breadth of resources needed to accomplish this important objective is lacking. Not surprisingly, much of the evidence base for accommodation assessment is practice-based. The aggregate knowledge base is dominated by anecdotal case studies that describe specific accommodations made for specific individuals.

A review of research on workplace accommodations found 19 of the 30 articles were single subject case studies (Butterfield & Ramseur, 2004). Few studies have described and compared the types of accommodations used by people within and across user groups (e.g., people with similar and different needs). Moreover, few studies have focused on identifying barriers and solutions in a systematic manner, and even fewer have investigated assessment processes or instruments. As a result, workplace assessment and accommodations have been practice driven. Thus, the field is best described as driven by practice-based evidence rather than evidence-based practice (Sanford & Milchus, 2006).

Workplace accommodations can be traced back to early practice in the occupational medicine profession in the late 17th century. However, workplace accommodation research and application truly began to take shape during the mid-19th century through the early 1920s. During this time, efforts to identify strategies that supported productivity, efficiency, and competitiveness were examined first. These efforts mainly concentrated on workers as a whole group, with the design of tools and machinery to increase output and thus company profits. Various disciplines (e.g., ergonomics, occupational therapy, vocational rehabilitation, industrial psychology, and rehabilitation engineering) emerged during this period and began to focus attention on individual workers with an eye toward improving or adapting work tools and strategies in order to reduce the likelihood of work-related injury and to compensate for injury or impairment. Although most of these professions focused primarily on workers without functional limitations, their research and practice can be applied equally to all workers regardless of ability.

Occupational Medicine

Bernardino Ramazzini (1633–1714) is considered to be the father of occupational medicine (Franco & Franco, 2001). The earliest documented recognition of the interactions among the individual, work environment, and health typically is attributed to him. Ramazzini published information on workers' health problems and descriptions about diseases associated with specific work activities in his *De Morbis Artificum Diatriba* (Diseases of Workers). This work provided accounts of workplaces, typical job tasks, how tasks were performed, and frequent suggestions for improving the work environment. This pioneering work led to the field of occupational medicine and a focus on the prevention and management of occupational and environmental injury, illness, and disability (American College of Occupational and Environmental Medicine, 1996).

Ergonomics

Ergonomics, first defined in 1857 as *the study of work* (Jastrzebowski, 1857a, 1857b, 1857c, 1857d) by the Polish scientist, Wojciech Jastrzebowski, now is recognized as "the scientific discipline concerned with the understanding of interactions among humans and other elements of a system (e.g., work activities and tasks), and the profession that applies theory, principles, data and methods to design in order to optimize human well-being and overall system performance" (International Ergonomics Association, 2000).

Research from the early 1900s on work study (Gilbreth & Gilbreth, 1973), scientific management (Taylor, 1911), and later, during World War II, on human–machine interaction, laid the foundation for modern ergonomics and accommodation. Specifically, work study and scientific management principles were used to investigate human motion during tasks, employing task analysis in order to determine the individual steps, body movements, and time involved in completion of a task. Task analysis methodology has been widely adopted and adapted in workplace assessment to understand the tasks required to complete a job, the components of the environment (e.g., machines and products) with which a worker must interface, and a possible misfit between the two that results in breakdowns or inefficiencies.

Occupational Therapy

The profession of occupational therapy (OT) can be traced to the founding of the National Society for the Promotion of Occupational Therapy in 1917. Based on the belief that meaningful activity or *occupations* were an important therapeutic tool in the recovery and revitalization of people with health conditions and disabilities, occupational therapy was a response to a growing population of individuals with long-term residual disability (e.g. veterans returning from World War I and people injured in industrial and automotive accidents) who had few resources for reconstructing lives.

Occupational therapy has recognized the importance of relationships between the person and environment in assessment through development of several occupational therapy-specific models. Six contemporary models share similar person, environment, and occupation factors (Baum & Christiansen, 2005), yet each has unique characteristics that generate distinct information. They include the Person–Environment–Occupation–Performance Model (Christiansen, 1991; Christiansen & Baum, 1997); Ecology of Human Performance Model (Dunn et al., 1994); Model of Human Occupation (Kielhofner, 1995); Person–Environment–Occupation Model (Law et al., 1996); Canadian Model of Occupational Performance (Canadian Association of Occupational Therapists, 1997); and Occupational Performance Model: Australia (Chapparo & Ranka, 1997).

Rehabilitation Counseling

The profession of vocational rehabilitation also began shortly after World War I in response to the needs of soldiers returning from the war. Vocational guidance, training, occupational adjustment, and job placement services were provided to individuals with disabilities following the passage of legislation designed to respond to the needs of veterans and civilians. By the 1950s, specialized educational programs for rehabilitation counselors began preparing professionals in vocational rehabilitation. Rehabilitation counseling has gone through many changes over the years as various disability rights movements have steered the profession toward person-centered planning that supports individuals through employment-related activities such as job training, placement, and accommodations.

Rehabilitation Engineering

The profession of rehabilitation engineering began in the mid-20th century in response to the need for better artificial limbs for veterans returning from World War II. Originally promoted by the Veterans Administration's prosthetic programs, rehabilitation engineering grew into a specialty field in the 1960s. This was due in part to further support the growing needs of vocational rehabilitation as it applied technologies, engineering methodologies, and scientific principles to meet the needs of

DISCUSSION BOX 13.1

Although the Americans with Disabilities Act of 1990 mandates that individuals with disabilities must be provided with reasonable accommodations, there are no regulations as to how the accommodations should be identified. Thus, identification of accommodations can be affected by the assessment instrument as well as by the individual who is performing the assessment. This chapter discusses problems related to a lack of guidance for assessment instruments and provides a framework for evaluating assessments to determine whether they meet situational needs. The chapter does not examine the issues surrounding the qualifications of individuals performing workplace accommodation assessment because this is a highly debatable topic. Currently, there is no formal certification or education requirement defined in legislation for performing a workplace accommodation assessment. In fact, workplace accommodation assessments are performed by many different individuals, including the employee with a disability. In some cases, insurance companies, employers, or vocational rehabilitation may require that a workplace accommodation be performed by a licensed health-care professional. However, even professional licenses do not guarantee that individuals are experienced and knowledgeable in workplace accommodations.

Questions

1. Given the importance of accurately identifying accommodations in order to meet the needs of individuals with disabilities, what are the pros and cons of not requiring certain qualifications for a person performing a workplace accommodation assessment?

2. Is one certain profession better prepared than others to perform and more knowledgeable about workplace accommodation assessments?

and address the barriers confronted by people with disabilities at work and in the community (Childress, 2002; Maki & Riggar, 1997; Reswick, 2002).

CURRENT PRACTICES IN WORKPLACE ACCOMMODATION ASSESSMENT

Assessment provides a practical means of systematically acquiring information; organizing, analyzing, and translating that information into appropriate recommendations for decision-making; and evaluating those decisions as a method of outcome measures. Systematic acquisition of information provides a structured framework for organizing the multiple, diverse factors that are involved in an assessment as well as helps to ensure that all relevant issues are included and accumulated before making intervention decisions. Assessments also promote an objective analysis of data, not merely their applications. As such, workplace accommodations decisions rely on evidence rather than assumptions, biases, or personal experience alone. Finally, assessment information provides preintervention, data-driven, baseline information against which the effectiveness of current and subsequent accommodations can be evaluated.

Assessment Process and Instruments

The workplace accommodation *assessment process* involves the collection and analysis of information necessary for understanding how to create a suitable work situation for an individual. The process identifies and characterizes problems that occur in the conduct of work activities, and then utilizes this information to make decisions about accommodation strategies and solutions intended to improve the fit between the person, environment, and work activities/tasks. An *assessment instrument* is the structured guide used in the accommodation process for identifying, acquiring, and generating relevant information.

Assessment instruments constitute the heart of the accommodation process. Thus, their use must lead to valid and reliable information that can be readily interpreted and used to develop appropriate interventions. Despite one's prior knowledge about potential accommodations, if the pertinent information is not identified from the start, determining best-fit solutions will be more guesswork than informed decision-making. As a result, the selection of suitable instruments to use during the assessment process is crucial.

A large number of readily available assessment instruments used in workplace accommodations have been obtained and analyzed. As expected, the assessment instruments differed considerably in their design, content, scientific soundness (i.e., psychometric qualities), and their use. While these differences have implications for the interpretation of information and the determination of interventions, some assessment instruments go well beyond traditional investigative data gathering by applying various levels of expert analysis, translation, and synthesis to help guide decision-making about workplace accommodations. Other instruments go even further and actually provide guidance on accommodation recommendations.

Based on the analysis of existing instruments, a conceptual framework was developed (Table 13.1). The

TABLE 13.1 Conceptual Framework of Assessment Activities

Type of Info P–E Factors		Assessment Activities							
		Investigation			Interpretation			Intervention	
		Characteristics of P–E Conditions	P–E Transaction Influences	Attributions of P–E Misfit	Performance Requirements	Prescriptive Requirements	Alternative Solutions	Trial Outcomes	Best Fit Solutions
Person	Individual								
	Physical								
Press	Social								
	Organizational								
	External								
	Task								
Performance									

*P–E = Person–Environment

framework identifies three distinct activities (investigation, interpretation, and intervention) that may be incorporated into an assessment as well as three key factors (person, performance, and press) that may be included in any of these activities.

The concept of *person* incorporates ICF constructs of *body structure*, *body function*, and their associated *capacities* (i.e., what an individual is capable of doing). In contrast, information about *performance* represents *engagement in activities and participation in society* as measured by what an individual actually does. *Press* is comprised of the contextual factors that place demands on the individual and contribute to differences between capacity and actual performance. These factors include ICF constructs of *individual factors* (e.g., preferences, cultural or spiritual beliefs, values, financial limitations); *environmental factors,* including physical factors (e.g., characteristics of workstation, ambient conditions, equipment); social factors (e.g., coworkers' attitudes and abilities); and organizational factors (e.g., policies, employer support); and *external factors* (e.g., legal restrictions, cost, and availability of assistive technologies) that lie outside the control of the individual, practitioner, or employer. Press also can be attributed to *task factors*, including the speed at which the work has to be completed or the quantity of work that has to be done.

Assessment Activities

The workplace accommodation assessment process can serve one or more of the following three general purposes: characterization (achieved through *investigation* activities), analysis (achieved through *interpretation* activities), and/or management of problems (achieved through *intervention* activities) to make the person more independent in the workplace. Successful assessment activities must address their intended purpose(s).

Investigation is common to and the primary activity of all assessments. Although the individual displaying difficulty, his/her employer, or other people associated with the situation can dictate the identification of problems and goals, investigation constitutes that phase of the assessment activity that provides critical information from which decisions are made. The failure to acquire adequate, valid, reliable, and relevant information will result in work accommodations that risk failing to meet the activity goals of a particular individual. Common investigative methods used in assessment include searches of archival records, subjective reporting, systematic observation, and direct measurement. Each of these four is described below.

1. *Searches of archival records.* A review of information from case files, local building codes, accessibility codes, trade journals, product literature, and research may be important for acquiring an understanding of mediating factors, intervention strategies, and solutions.

2. *Subjective reporting.* Questionnaires and interviews are valuable for obtaining information about preferences, tastes, priorities, and the individual's perception about the situation. Activity logs and diaries are useful for tracking performance over time (e.g., time spent at various activities). However, self-report data tend to be less reliable than other data because both the questions and responses are open to interpretations as well as influenced by the personal biases of those conducting and undergoing the assessment.

3. *Systematic observation.* Systematic observations of task performance, physical traces of past performance, and documentation of characteristics of the person and environment help overcome individual biases by permitting the evaluator to witness performance while being exposed to the full range of verbal and nonverbal behaviors and sights, sounds, and activity. Performance evaluations can occur in the workplace or be videotaped for later analysis (i.e., allows for repeated viewing) or both. Physical traces permit serendipitous observation of activity to gauge performance (e.g., scuffs on walls or gouged doorframes from a wheelchair, use or disuse of certain items).

4. *Direct measurement.* This includes anthropometric measurements of the individual and his/her abilities (e.g., reach, stature, grasp) as well as the workplace, including measurements (e.g., door width, shelf height) and photographic documentation (e.g., location of objects and spaces, colors, and styles).

Investigation is characterized by the *acquisition* of information related to three qualities: the characteristics of person–environment conditions, person–environment transaction influences, and attributions of person–environment misfit either by direct observation or self-report methods. Each of these three is discussed below.

CHARACTERISTICS OF PERSON-ENVIRONMENT CONDITIONS These independent measures describe existing conditions of the individual, workplace, and task performance that contribute to problems with completing work activities (Figure 13.1). These person–environment conditions are described through physical measures, observation, archival and/or self-report data, and depict the actual state of person, press, and performance factors at the time of the assessment. By itself, this information can be used by experts to identify

---

Characteristics of Person-Environment Conditions describe *what*

Person Factors: Statements of health status, including health condition (e.g., arthritis, multiple sclerosis), body structures (anatomical parts of the body), and body functions (physiological functions of the body systems). For example, does the person have use of hands, fingers, and arms? Function may also be measured in terms of an individual's capacity to execute an action or task (the highest probable level of function at a given moment without any assistance and presuming a standardized environment). For example, what is the individual's grip strength?

Press Factors: Quantitative and qualitative descriptions of individual attributes (e.g., preferences, tastes); task requirements (e.g., amount of weight to be lifted or pulled, reach requirements); and environmental attributes, including physical attributes (e.g., height, width, length, color, surface, type of handle) of workspaces, products, and technologies and social attributes (e.g., availability and attitudes of coworkers toward providing assistance); organizational attributes (e.g., descriptions of accommodation policies); and external attributes (e.g., technical requirements mandated by codes and standards). For example, what type of mouse or cursor control device is used?

Performance Factors: Describe what activities/tasks are performed and how they are performed. For example how does the person use and access the mouse?

FIGURE 13.1 Characteristics of Person–Environment Conditions

potential or anticipated barriers to task performance. Alternatively, taken in conjunction with person-–environment transaction influences, actual barriers and intervention needs can be defined.

PERSON-ENVIRONMENT TRANSACTION INFLUENCES (EFFECTS OF CHARACTERISTICS)   These dependent outcome measures describe the degree of fit between person and press factors (Figure 13.2). This degree of fit can be based on actual transactions (e.g. observed or self-reported outcomes) or predictions of performance, activity limitation, or participation restriction (e.g., based on individual, environmental, or task characteristics).

Whereas the ICF focuses solely on level of difficulty, other common outcome measures include the following six dependent outcomes: ease/difficulty, success/failure, independence/dependence, degree of safety, degree of pain, and competence.

ATTRIBUTIONS OF PERSON-ENVIRONMENT MISFIT   Attributions of person–environment misfit are judgments about causal relationships between performance deficits and existing conditions (Figure 13.3). Attribution information generally refers to the individual being assessed and is characterized by adverbs/adjectives of degree or intensity, such as *too much or little*, *not enough*, or *requires*

Person–Environment Transaction Influences describe *how well*

Person Factors: A subjective measure that describes an individual's capability to execute an action or task (e.g., success/failure, ease/difficulty, safe/unsafe, independently/dependently). For example, does the individual have difficulty gripping objects?

Press Factors: Outcomes of person–environment transactions that are associated with environmental conditions, individual preferences or experiences, or task requirements. Grammatically, environmental, individual or task demands, rather than one's impairment or ability, are presented as the object of the statement or question. For example, is the computer mouse or other cursor control device difficult to use?

Performance Factors: Outcomes of person–environment transactions that are expressed in levels of performance (e.g., success/failure, ease/difficulty, safe/unsafe, independently/dependency) For example, does the individual have difficulty using the mouse or cursor control device?

FIGURE 13.2 Person–Environment Transaction Influences

Attributions of Person–Environment Misfit are used to explain *why*

Person Factors: Judgments about the impact of body function and structure on capacity. For example, is the grip strong enough or does gripping cause too much pain?

Press Factors: Judgments about why individual, task, and/or environmental characteristics cause activity limitations. For example, is the mouse too big or too small to grip?

Performance Factors: Judgments about why person or press factors result in activity limitations or diminished task performance. For example, is the individual gripping or holding the mouse tightly enough to control the mouse?

FIGURE 13.3 Attributions of Person–Environment Misfit

more. Intervention needs based on judgments could be strengthened by the support of person–environment conditions or transaction information. However, assessments that rely on judgments typically do not collect other information.

Interpretation is the process of translating investigative information into worker needs and intervention strategies. Interpretation is not inherent in any assessment instrument and is often omitted in favor of practitioners applying their own clinical reasoning to the investigative information. However, when interpretation is included in an instrument, investigation information is used to inform usability requirements for potential interventions. These requirements can be either *prescriptive* (i.e., specific characteristics or qualities of an intervention) or *performance* (i.e., goals which the intervention must attain) based. Performance requirements permit more flexibility in the types and range of solutions that can be used to meet intervention. However, unlike prescriptive requirements (Figure 13.4), performance requirements do not identify

Prescriptive requirements for workplace accommodations identify (i.e., prescribe) specific goals or strategies for modifications that are related to how to use something, placement, product type, or dimensions:

Person Factors: Structure or function changes that improve capacity. For example, individual should use two hands to improve grip.

Press Factors: Characteristics of workplace accommodations or technical specifications to which the accommodations should adhere. For example, replace a standard mouse with an alternative device that can be used via head movement.

Performance Factors: Change how the individual performs the task or activity. For example, the individual should grip the mouse tightly with two hands to move the cursor.

Performance requirements provide nonspecific goals or strategies for modifications that are related to how something operates or how it will be used to improve the person's abilities:

Person Factors: Structure or function changes that improve capacity. For example, individual should grip mouse differently.

Press Factors: Operational characteristics of workplace accommodations. For example, provide a different way to move the cursor.

Performance Factors: Change how the individual performs the task, or activity. For example, use multiple methods for moving the cursor.

FIGURE 13.4 Prescriptive and Performance Requirements

Alternative solutions are the translation of usability criteria into strategies or specific accommodations that will potentially create desired conditions or "best fit". These can be very closely related to performance or prescriptive requirements (or in some cases, exactly the same), but typically mention particular products or strategies.

Person Factors: These potential solutions are related to function and structure that cause a change in capacity. For example, use two hands in a hand-over-hand or side-by-side strategy for improving grip strength.

Press Factors: Suggestions for additions or changes to environmental, individual, or task/activity factors. For example, try XYZ Infrared or ABC Camera-Based head tracking systems to move the cursor.

Performance Factors: Modifications to how something is done that improves performance and enhances participation. For example, the individual should try moving the cursor at varying rates of speed, with periodic rest breaks.

Trial outcomes are the result of evaluating alternative solutions for usability. Trials with equipment or strategies can help prevent costly mistakes and may save time in the long run. In the absence of actual use trials, analysis of technical specifications and other archival data may be used to determine best-fit.

Best-Fit solutions for any situation are those interventions that meet the usability strategies or technical requirements and will produce the best functional outcomes within the context of application.

FIGURE 13.5 Alternative Solutions, Trial Outcomes, and Best Fit Solutions

specific characteristics that make it easy to target potential interventions.

Intervention is the last type of assessment activity. In this activity, information is gathered on alternative solutions, trials are completed with potential solutions, and best-fit solutions are recommended. Like interpretation activities (i.e., performance and prescriptive requirements), many assessment instruments may not include intervention activities. However, some newer assessment instruments use electronic databases to assist in interpretation and intervention activities. These instruments rely on the collection of relevant investigative information to feed into the database in order to generate performance and prescriptive requirements as well as alternative solutions (see Figure 13.5).

Disciplinary Perspectives in Selecting an Assessment Instrument

Assessments for workplace accommodations typically are conducted either by rehabilitation service providers (e.g., therapists, rehabilitation engineers and technologists, and rehabilitation counselors), or employer personnel (e.g., human resource professionals, ADA managers,

and supervisors). Professionals in each of these two groups have their own disciplinary perspectives that influence their knowledge of person, press, and performance issues. In addition, the degree of one's experience with workplace accommodations impacts one's knowledge of accommodations, which then impacts the methods and strategies used to perform an assessment. Additionally, organizations that pay for accommodations will require assessments that adhere to their guidelines. Therefore, assessments typically are biased by one's discipline, experience, and system factors.

DISCIPLINARY BIAS   Disciplinary bias tends to affect the key factors (i.e., person, press, and performance) that are included in an assessment. In general, disciplinary bias places primary emphasis on collecting information applicable to the types of interventions that are within the evaluator's training to recommend. Therefore, instruments developed for/by therapists typically focus more on task/activity, performance and person factors. In contrast, tools used by rehabilitation engineers, rehabilitation technologists, and ergonomists focus primarily on physical environment demands and performance factors. Instruments used by employers (e.g., human resource personnel, supervisors) mainly focus on task/activity factors, organizational environmental demands, and external factors.

EXPERIENCE BIAS Experience bias is more likely to impact the type of information that is collected. Instruments developed for use by professionals with limited experience with workplace accommodations tend to focus on information that requires less analysis and thus less expertise. As a result, these instruments are primarily comprised of attribution and prescriptive requirements. These instruments place less emphasis on detailed characteristics of person–environment conditions, person–environment transaction influences, performance requirements, and intervention alternatives—qualities that require substantial clinical reasoning to use effectively. In contrast, instruments used by experienced professionals presume that information will be used for problem management. These instruments focus more on investigative details that drive intervention solutions.

SYSTEM BIAS System bias impacts the scope or purpose of the assessment. System bias is the influence of funding or policy issues of the organization that are contributing to the accommodation. This type of bias usually places limitations on the type information that is gathered via assessment activities, although system bias also may result in an assessment that is overly comprehensive. For example, in some worker compensation cases, the instrument may cover only investigation activities that characterize a problem for documentation and future planning, thus eliminating the immediate need to gather information through interpretation and intervention activities.

Biases should be kept in mind when selecting an instrument because they affect the types of information collected and person–environment fit factors measured. Selection of an assessment instrument also should consider the nature of the referral, purpose of the assessment, and whether the selected instrument will acquire the appropriate information. Therefore, the suitability, relevancy, and comprehensiveness of the assessment instrument should be evaluated.

The best instrument for the situation will collect information that satisfies the purpose of the assessment (suitability), applies directly to the situation (relevance), and meets information quantity and quality needs (comprehensiveness). An evaluator trying to determine whether an instrument meets the needs of the situation should answer the following questions: (1) Does the instrument include measures that address the purpose

of the assessment? (2) Does the instrument provide information that is applicable to the situation? (3) Does the instrument provide sufficient depth and breadth to recommend best fit solutions? Each of these is discussed below.

SUITABILITY Proper selection of an assessment instrument for a particular situation starts by considering whether the information to be acquired and generated through the assessment activities (i.e., investigation, interpretation, and intervention) is likely to achieve the purposes of the assessment. The purposes may be established by the individual, funding entity, employer, or evaluator, and may involve one, two, or all three assessment activities.

Suitability refers to the degree to which an instrument measures its intended constructs. Assessments intended to characterize problems should be performed using an assessment instrument that includes information collected through investigation activities. Assessments intended to understand and manage problems should gather information via interpretation and intervention activities, respectively. Suitability occurs when there is a match between assessment purpose and the three major columns in the conceptual framework (i.e., investigation, interpretation, and intervention).

RELEVANCE Information that meets the situational needs related to the person, press, or performance factors also must be included. For example, the need to use a mouse might be achieved by obtaining relevant measures about the person, (e.g., upper extremity capacity), press (e.g., configuration of work station and person–environment transactions that involve the computer), and performance (e.g., movement of the cursor during a work task) through investigative activities, analyzing the results of the person–environment fit or misfit related to computer use, and identifying potential interventions that will support mouse use.

COMPREHENSIVENESS Comprehensiveness refers to the quantity of information that is included in an assessment instrument. Comprehensiveness can be gauged both in terms of the assessment instrument's diversity (i.e., breadth) and intensity (i.e., depth).

• *Breadth of Information.* Breadth of information is signified by the number of cells (the intersections of rows and columns) in the conceptual framework represented by assessment information. However, as stated earlier, because investigation is the primary assessment activity, an instrument should adequately address the characteristics of the person–environment conditions, person–environment transaction, and attributions of person–environment misfit for as many of the key person–environment factors as possible to represent adequate breadth, including person, press (physical, social, organizational, individual, external, and task/activity), and performance. Additional cells covered in interpretation and intervention improve breadth yet may not be needed by experienced evaluators.

• *Depth of Information.*   Depth of information is signified by the amount and specificity of information in each cell. To be useful, information acquired by a particular assessment must have sufficient richness to facilitate informed and accurate decisions about workplace accommodations. Richness of information is reflected in the number of questions related to a specific factor (e.g., capacity, environmental feature, task/activity demand), information acquisition methods, and recording techniques used.

Each method used influences reliability. The use of a combination of methods provides greater depth by capitalizing on the strengths of each method and compensating for weaknesses in others (e.g., comparing data from self-report with that from observations). In addition, data can be recorded in various ways, such as checklists, measurements, pictures, fill-ins, and open-ended descriptions. The more structured or closed-ended recording technique usually has less depth yet provides more assistance to the inexperienced evaluator. In contrast, more unstructured or open-ended recording techniques warrant the need for an experienced evaluator and often provide richer information.

No one assessment instrument can be used in every situation for workplace accommodations. The framework presented in this chapter enables readers to select instruments that portray the most inclusive representation of the barriers and facilitators to participation and guides the identification of the most effective strategies for enhancing independence. Additionally, this framework can be used to develop assessment instruments.

MAJOR ISSUES THAT NEED ATTENTION IN WORKPLACE ACCOMMODATION ASSESSMENT

Assessments related to work and disability vary significantly, including their purpose, comprehensiveness, and intended user. There are more than 800 formalized processes and instruments (Matheson, Kaskutas, McGowan, Shaw, & Webb, 2001), and probably an equal or greater number of idiosyncratic protocols and "seat-of-the-pants" procedures used by individuals. Despite their diversity and number, guidelines for the development and use of assessment instruments associated with current legislative mandates for workplace accommodations do not exist. Moreover, no one specific profession or field of practice is responsible for performing workplace accommodation assessments or developing instruments for them.

Thus, assessment instruments designed to assess key person, press, and performance factors often are not standardized. Due to this limitation, consistent or sufficient data may not be collected (Schwanke & Smith, 2005), and questions about the suitability, relevance, and comprehensiveness of the instruments may not be raised. Among those instruments that are standardized, some require specialized training or certification to use, and few are suitable for use when determining workplace accommodations. Due to a limited number of standardized workplace accommodation assessments, various protocols biased by discipline, expertise of the user, and requirements of funding agencies have been developed. Their use raises important questions about their effectiveness in actually meeting the accommodation needs of the client.

Finally, lacking adequate standardization, estimates of the reliability and validity of workplace accommodation assessment instruments typically are unknown. Assessment instruments should measure what they are intending to objectively measure (validity) and be designed to be used by various disciplines, resulting in the same or similar accommodations regardless of the evaluator's perspective (thus ensuring their reliability).

Summary and Conclusion

Employment is an essential component of life for individuals with disabilities. However, many persons cannot participate in the workforce without appropriate accommodations. Our nation's workforce is growing and changing, resulting in a need for accessible work settings as well as a need for assessments that properly identify the accommodation needs of workers with disabilities.

However, within existing legislation and the rehabilitation disciplines, guidance on the structure of the assessment or the specific information to collect in an accommodation assessment has not been consistent.

Accommodation assessment has roots in several fields of practice, incorporating perspectives from engineering, medical, and vocational models. These disciplines and their professions emphasize the importance of determining a suitable person–environment fit—a model essential to understanding the accommodation process.

Although the number of instruments used to perform accommodation assessments is abundant, there is a dearth of instruments that adequately address key person, press, and performance factors. Instruments vary significantly in the information that is collected, who collects it, and how it is analyzed. This chapter discussed a model useful for the selection of assessment instruments that meet the needs of the situation. The model also can be used in the development of instruments that are suitable, relevant, comprehensive, and that potentially demonstrate validity and reliability.

Assessment instruments inform decisions about workplace accommodations that ideally meet the needs of workers with disabilities. Based on the person–environment fit models, an assessment should provide a holistic view of person, press, and performance factors. Further, inclusion of these factors should be relatively balanced to ensure that interventions, including changes to the individual, the workplace, and the way tasks are carried out, will meet the needs of the individual and the workplace.

Self-Check Questions

1. Discuss why it is important for individuals with disabilities to be employed and the benefits that accommodations can provide.
2. Describe the difference between the assessment process and an assessment instrument.
3. Identify and describe the different types of biases that can affect the design of an assessment instrument.
4. Define what person, press, and performance factors are and discuss their importance to the assessment process.
5. Discuss the major problems that result from a lack of standardization in assessment instruments.
6. Briefly describe investigation, interpretation, and intervention activities. Which of these activities helps to characterize or define the problem?

Case Study

Molly, a 43-year-old woman, had a stroke about 4 months ago that affected her speech and movement on her right side. She went through rehabilitation and is able to walk with a slight limp, but has some difficulty using her right hand. Her speech is slightly slurred, and she is unable to talk above a whisper. She recently returned to her job as a supervisor of a cleaning crew in a large office building and has become frustrated by not being able to do things the way she used to. As part of her insurance program, she can request a workplace accommodation assessment and reluctantly agreed to pursue one. You have been asked to perform the assessment, but do not feel comfortable doing it alone. Think of your strengths and weaknesses in collecting certain types of information. What other professionals would you ask to assist and why?

References

American College of Occupational and Environmental Medicine. (1996). OEM Vision. Retrieved September 25, 2006, from http://www.acoem.org/general/vision.asp

Bat-Chava, Y., Deignan, E., & Martin, D. (2002). Rehabilitation counselors' knowledge of hearing loss and assistive technology. *Journal of Rehabilitation, 68*, 33–41.

Baum, C., & Christiansen, C. (2005). Person–environment–occupation–performance: An occupation-based framework for practice. In C. Christiansen, C. Baum & J. Bass-Haugen (Eds.), *Occupational therapy: Performance, participation, and well-being,* (3rd ed.). Thorofare, NJ: SLACK, Inc.

Baum, C. M., & Law, M. (1997). Occupational therapy practice: Focusing on occupational performance. *The American Journal of Occupational Therapy, 51*, 277–288.

Bernspang, B., & Fisher, A. G. (1995). Differences between persons with right or left cerebral vascular accident on the assessment of motor and process skills. *Archives of Physical Medicine and Rehabilitation, 76*(12), 1144–1151.

Blanck, P.D. (1994). *Communicating the Americans with Disabilities Act, transcending compliance: A case report on Sears, Roebuck and C.* Iowa City: Annenburg Washington Program. http://www.annenburg.nwu.edu/pubs/sears.

Bruyere, S., VanLooy, S., & Peterson, D. (2005). The International Classification of Functioning, Disability and Health: Contemporary literature overview. *Rehabilitation Psychology, 50*(2), 113–121.

Butterfield, T., & Ramseur, H. (2004). Research and case study findings in the area of workplace accommodations including provisions for assistive technology: A literature review. *Technology and Disability, 16*(4), 201–210.

Canadian Association of Occupational Therapists. (1997). *Enabling occupation: An occupational therapy perspective.* Ottawa, ON: CAOT Publications.

Casper, M. W. (1993). Seasons of change—The Americans with Disabilities Act: Implementation in the workplace. *Journal of Rehabilitation Administration,* 123–126.

Chapparo, C., & Ranka, J. (1997). *Occupational performance model (Australia), Monograph 1.* Unpublished manuscript, Sydney.

Childress, D. S. (2002). Development of rehabilitation engineering over the years: As I see it. *Journal of Rehabilitation Research and Development, 39* (6), 1–10 Supplement.

Christiansen, C. (1991). Occupational therapy: Intervention for life performance. In C. Christiansen & C. M. Baum (Eds.), *Occupational therapy—overcoming human performance deficits.* Thorofare, NJ: Slack, Inc.

Christiansen, C., & Baum, C. (1997). *Occupational therapy: Enabling function and well-being* (2nd ed.). Thorofare, NJ: Slack, Inc.

Curry, D. A. (1996). Employers' perceptions of the Americans with Disabilities Act and its effects on vertical mobility in the business world (Doctoral dissertation, University of Rochester, 1996). *Dissertation Abstracts International, 57-05A*(2185).

Disability Status 2000—Census 2000 Brief. 2003. Washington, DC: U.S. Census Bureau. http://www.census.gov/prod/2003pubs/c2kbr-17.pdf

Doolan, D. F., Bates, D. W., & James, B. C. (2003). The use of computers for clinical care: A case series of advanced U.S. sites. *Journal of the American Medical Informatics Association, 10*(1), 94–107.

Dunn, W., Brown, C., & McGuigan, A. (1994). The ecology of human performance: A framework for considering the effect of context. *American Journal of Occupational Therapy, 48*(7), 595–607.

Durand, M., Loisel, P., Hong, Q., & Charpentier, N. (2002). Helping clinicians in work disability prevention: The work disability diagnosis interview. *Journal of Occupational Rehabilitation, 12*(3), 191–204.

Equal Employment Opportunity Commission. (1992). *Employment provisions (Title I) technical assistance manual.* Retrieved September 24, 2006 from http://www.adata.org/adaportal/Employment/Browse_TAM_I/Browse_TOC.html.

Ewert, T., Fuessl, M., Cieza, A., Andersen, C., Chatterji, S., Kostanjsek, N., & Stucki, G. (2004). Identification of the most common patient problems in patients with chronic conditions using the ICF checklist. *Journal of Rehabilitation Medicine*(4), 22–29.

Franco, G., & Franco, F. (2001). Bernardino Ramazzini: The father of occupational medicine. *American Journal of Public Health, 91*(9), 1382.

Gamble, M., Dowler, D., & Orslene, L. (2006). Assistive technology: Choosing the right tool for the right job. *Journal of Vocational Rehabilitation, 24*(2), 73–80.

Gilbreth, F. B., & Gilbreth, L. M. (1973). *Applied motion study: A collection of papers on the efficient method to industrial preparedness.* Easton, PA: Hive.

Ginzberg, E. (1983). Life without work: Does it make sense? In H. S. Parnes (Ed.), *Policy issues in work and retirement* (pp. 29–38). Kalamazoo, MI: W. E. Upjohn Institute for Employment Research.

Grill, E., Quittan, M., Huber, E., Boldt, C., & Stucki, G. (2005). Identification of relevant ICF categories by health professionals in the acute hospital. *Disability & Rehabilitation, 27*(7–8), 437–445.

A Guide to Disability Rights Laws. (2005). Retrieved April 2, 2008 from http://scholar.google.com/scholar?q=A+guide+to+disability+rights+laws.+(2005)&hl=en&lr=&client=firefox-a.

Hagedorn, R. (1995). *Occupational therapy: Perspectives and processes.* Edinburgh, UK: Churchill Livingstone.

Hagedorn, R. (2000). *Tools for practice in occupational therapy: A structured approach to core skills and processes.* Edinburgh, UK: Churchill Livingstone.

Hecker, D. E. (2005). Occupational employment projections to 2014. *Monthly Labor Review, 128*(11), 70–101.

Inge, K., Wehman, P., Strobel, W., Powell, D., & Todd, J. (1998). Supported employment and assistive technology for persons with spinal cord injury: Three illustrations of successful work supports. *Journal of Vocational Rehabilitation, 10,* 141–152.

International Ergonomics Association. (2000). An official definition of ergonomics. Retrieved September 25, 2006, from http://www.iea.cc/ergonomics/

Ivancevich, J. M., Matteson, M., & Preston, C. (1982). Occupational stress, Type A behavior, and physical well being. *Academy of Management Journal, 25*(2), 373–391.

Jastrzebowski, W. (1857a). An outline of ergonomics, or the science of work based upon the truths drawn from the science of nature, Part I. *Nature and Industry, 29,* 227–231.

Jastrzebowski, W. (1857b). An outline of ergonomics, or the science of work based upon the truths drawn from the science of nature, Part II. *Nature and Industry, 29,* 236–244.

Jastrzebowski, W. (1857c). An outline of ergonomics, or the science of work based upon the truths drawn from the science of nature, Part III. *Nature and Industry, 29,* 244–251.

Jastrzebowski, W. (1857d). An outline of ergonomics, or the science of work based upon the truths drawn from the science of nature, Part IV. *Nature and Industry, 29,* 253–258.

Kielhofner, G. (1995). *A model of human occupation: Therapy and application* (2nd ed.). Baltimore, MD: Williams & Wilkins.

Kristof, A. (1996). Person-organization fit: An integrative review of its conceptualizations, measurement, and implications. *Personnel Psychology, 49*(1), 1–49.

Kuijer, W., Brouwer, S., Preuper, H. R. S., Groothoff, J. W. J., Geertzen, H. B., & Dijkstra, P. U. (2006). Work status and chronic low back pain: Exploring the international classification of functioning, disability and health. *Disability & Rehabilitation, 28*(6), 379–388

Law, M., Cooper, B., Strong, S., Stewart, D., Rigby, P., & Letts, L. (1996). The person–environment–occupation model: A transactive approach to occupational performance. *Canadian Journal of Occupational Therapy, 63*(1), 9–23.

Lawton, M. P., & Nahemow, L. (1973). Ecology and the aging process. In C. Eisdorfer & M. P. Lawton (Eds.), *Psychology of Adult Development and Aging* (pp. 619–674). Washington, DC: American Psychological Association.

Maki, D., & Riggar, T. (1997). Role of technology: Engineering and computers. In *Rehabilitation counseling: Profession and practice*. New York: Springer Publishing Company.

Matheson, L., Kaskutas, V., McGowan, S., Shaw, H., & Webb, C. (2001). Development of a database of functional assessment measures related to work disability. *Journal of Occupational Rehabilitation, 11*(3), 177–199.

NCMRR. (1993). *Research Plan*: National Center for Medical Rehabilitation Research.

Pitt-Catsouphes, M., & Butterworth, J. (1995). *Different perspectives: Workplace experience with the employment of individuals with disabilities*. 1995. Rehabilitation Research and Training Center: Promoting the employment of individuals with disabilities. Institute for Community Inclusion at Children's Hospital. Center on Work and Family at Boston University. http://www.communityinclusion.org/employer/index.php?page=whyhire

Reswick, J. B. (2002). How and when did the rehabilitation engineering center program come into being? *Journal of Rehabilitation Research and Development, 39*(6), 11–16 Supplement.

Sandqvist, J., & Henriksson, C. (2004). Work functioning: A conceptual framework. *Work, 23*, 147–157.

Sanford, J. A., & Milchus, K. L. (2006). Evidence-based practice in workplace accommodations. *Work, 27*(4), 329–332.

Scherer, M., J., , & Craddock, G. (2002). Matching Person and Technology (MPT) assessment process. *Technology and Disability, 14*(3), 125–131.

Schwanke, T., & Smith, R. (2005). Assistive technology outcomes in work settings. *Work, 24*, 195–204.

Swanson, G., Carrothers, L., & Mulhorn, K. A. (2003). Comparing disability survey questions in five countries: a study using ICF to guide comparisons. *Disability & Rehabilitation, 25*(11/12), 665–675.

Taylor, F. W. (1911). *The principles of scientific management*. New York: Harper and Brothers.

Unger, D., & Kregel, J. (2003). Employers' knowledge and utilization of accommodations. *Work, 21*(1), 5–15.

U.S. Department of Justice (2005). *A Guide to Disability Rights Laws*. Retrieved September 15, 2006, from http://www.ada.gov/cguide.htm.

Vagg, P. R., & Spielberger, C. D. (1999). Occupational stress: Measuring job pressure and organizational support in the workplace. *Journal of Occupational Health Psychology, 4*(3), 288–292.

Williams, M., Sabata, D., & Zolna, J. (2006). User needs evaluation of workplace accommodations. *Work, 27*(4), 355–370.

World Health Organization. (2001). *International Classification of Functioning, Disability and Health*. Geneva Switzerland: Author.

Zwerling, C., Whitten, P. S., Sprince, N., Davis, C. S., Wallace, R., Blanck, P. D., & Heeringa, S. G. (2003). Workplace accommodations for people with disabilities: National Health Interview Survey Disability Supplement, 1994–5. *Journal of Occupational and Environmental Medicine, 24*, 24–38.

Measures of Development and Adjustment

14

Intelligence

JACK A. NAGLIERI
George Mason University, Fairfax, VA

SAM GOLDSTEIN
University of Utah, Salt Lake City

CARA CONWAY
George Mason University, Fairfax, VA

JOY JANSEN
George Mason University, Fairfax, VA

OVERVIEW

General measures of intellectual ability provide a valuable way to measure global intellectual ability. However, many of these measures of intelligence have shown little change since the early 1900s. Recently there has been an evolution toward tests that measure basic psychological processes that have implications for interventions. Some have expressed the belief that cognitive processing should be considered as a modern conceptualization of intelligence. As the concept of intelligence is evolving toward cognitive processing, researchers have begun to see the utility of these new methods, especially for individuals who may have learning and behavioral disabilities as well as those being addressed through rehabilitation, particularly when the goal is to guide the acquisition or reacquisition of vocational skills, plan interventions, and set reasonable thresholds for progress.

LEARNING OBJECTIVES
By the end of the chapter, readers should be able to:

- Understand differences between a general ability and processing approaches to intelligence
- Be more informed about the utility of tests of cognitive processing for fair assessment
- Understand the historical evolution of intelligence tests

INTRODUCTION

INTERNATIONAL CLASSIFICATION OF FUNCTIONING (ICF)

The World Health Organization's *International Classification of Functioning, Disability and Health* (ICF; World Health Organization [WHO], 1999) provides a framework for viewing behaviors from three broad and different perspectives (see Figure 14.1): body functions and structures (e.g., possible *impairment* in physiologic, physical, and psychological functions); activities (e.g., whether a person displays *limitations* in their engagement in functional life activities); and participation (e.g., possible restrictions in their participation in social settings). Both environmental and personal factors impact all three.

Body functions typically focus on physical, physiological, and psychological functions, including mental, sensory, respiratory, digestive, reproductive, and neuromusculoskeletal functions. *Body structures* typically focus on the anatomy, including the nervous system (with obvious relationships with mental abilities), movement, and voice and speech. *Activities* focus on the execution of a skill, task, or action. *Participation* focuses on one's involvement in life activities. Examples of activities and participation include learning and applying knowledge, communication,

movement, and adaptive behavior. Environmental factors focus on a person's physical, social, and attitudinal qualities that can serve either as facilitators or barriers. Personal factors include one's age, socioeconomic status, race, gender, and other personal qualities that may influence functioning and disability.

Thus, an understanding of a client's health requires knowledge of the dynamic nature among body functions and structures, activities, participation, as well as environmental and personal factors. Each influences the others. The use of measures of intelligence and other cognitive abilities is critical in helping to understand possible deficits related to the body structure, (e.g., the brain), body functions (e.g. memory, attention), as well as activities and participation (e.g., the ability to act purposefully, think rationally, and deal effectively within one's environment). Thus, information from measures of intelligence discussed in this chapter may be critical to efforts by rehabilitation specialists to describe a patient's behaviors, plan and carry out interventions, and evaluate their impact.

In the eyes of the public and professionals, the concept of intelligence has become synonymous with general ability—measured using verbal, quantitative, and nonverbal questions. Intelligence tests, used widely in clinical practice

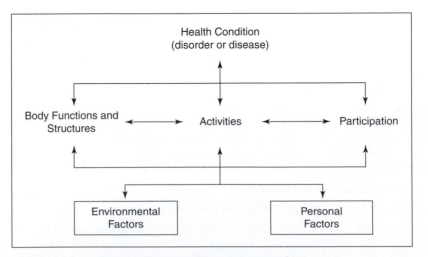

FIGURE 14.1 Interactions between the Components of ICE

Note: From *The International Classification of Functioning, Disability and Health* (p. 18), by the World Health Organization, 2001, Geneva, Switzerland.

and to determine eligibility for educational programming, are among the most advanced methods by which cognitive ability is judged. Although revisions of popular intellectual measures are refined and statistically much better constructed than those of years ago, they continue to be designed primarily to provide estimates of general cognitive ability. Although these tests have improved their statistical and psychometric qualities, some question their utility beyond assisting in diagnosis, particularly their value in guiding interventions.

This chapter defines and discusses intelligence tests associated with general cognitive ability and describes a new concept that goes beyond general ability for the measurement of intellectual processes. We suggest that a cognitive processing approach to conceptualizing and measuring intelligence represents a second and significant development in intelligence testing. Cognitive processes provide a valid and reliable assessment of intellectual functions that more strongly predicts academic, behavioral, and vocational outcomes. This new cognitive processing perspective provides valuable information that helps us understand the reasons individuals with disabilities may struggle and the best means of helping them in various situations and settings, and, importantly, that assists professionals in understanding the assets needed for these individuals to function effectively.

The chapter provides a brief overview of the history and definitions of intelligence, discusses some widely used measures of intelligence, examines the overlap between intelligence and achievement, and concludes with a discussion of three case studies. The importance of understanding how intelligence is conceptualized and measured by different authors and the implications this has for assessment of individuals who vary on cultural and linguistic characteristics within the ICF context is stressed.

HISTORY AND DEFINITIONS OF INTELLIGENCE: PAST AND PRESENT

Alfred Binet and David Wechsler solidified the view that intelligence could be measured using verbal, nonverbal, and quantitative questions. Most professionals in psychology, rehabilitation, and other health professions consider intelligence tests to represent a gold standard for the definition and assessment of intelligence (Matarazzo, 1992). Measures that assess the broad and important qualities that comprise intelligence and yield a total score (i.e., an IQ) significantly predict performance in academic and vocational settings (Lobinsky, 2000; Watkins, Glutting & Lei, 2007) and provide information that allows clinicians to better understand various other personal qualities. The predictive power of data from these measures in reference to a client's aptitudes for academic attainment, vocational development, and daily functioning makes them especially valuable to rehabilitation specialists in their treatment planning.

Traditional tests of intelligence had their beginning in 1905 with the publication of the Stanford-Binet (Binet & Simon, 1905), and were further solidified in the late 1930s with the publication of the Wechsler-Bellevue Scales (Wechsler, 1939). These tests made a substantial contribution to our society, shaping how we define intelligence and assisting professionals in making hundreds of important practical decisions (Anastasi & Urbina, 1997). Results from these tests have influenced the lives of countless children and adults in the United States and around the world. While intelligence tests represent one of the most influential contributions made by psychology to society in general, they also have become embedded in our views as *the* way to measure ability.

The Binet and Wechsler scales have measured intelligence using tests of similar content since the early part of the last century. Wechsler's tests were based on Binet's work (Kaufman & Lichtenberger, 2000) and methods used by the U.S. military in the early 1900s (Yoakum & Yerkes, 1920). Wechsler included verbal and performance (also called nonverbal) tests. However, their inclusion does not mean he intended to measure two different forms of intelligence: verbal and nonverbal intelligences (Wechsler & Naglieri, 2006b). Nonverbal tests were included to ". . . minimize the over-diagnosing of feeble-mindedness that was, he believed, caused by intelligence tests that were too verbal [academic] in content. . . . [In fact] he viewed verbal and performance tests as equally valid measures of intelligence and criticized the labeling of performance (nonverbal) tests as measures of special abilities" (Boake, 2002, p. 396).

This is similar to the approach described by Yoakum and Yerkes (1920) in the *Army Mental Tests*. During World War I, the U.S. military developed two intelligence tests, the Army Alpha to assess literate draftees and the Army Beta to assess illiterate draftees. The Beta tests were used because persons with limited

DISCUSSION BOX 14.1

Intelligence traditionally was measured using tests that have verbal and quantitative test questions as well as those that are described as nonverbal or performance. Some authors have argued (Naglieri & Ford, 2003) that these verbal and quantitative tests are very similar to those found in measures of achievement. Considering that many children from low-income families have low achievement, the use of achievement-like verbal and quantitative tests in a measure of ability may make traditional intelligence tests problematic for minorities.

Questions

1. What differences should there be between tests of intelligence and achievement?

2. How can this distinction help practitioners more accurately evaluate the ability of persons who have limited educational backgrounds?

3. Do you agree that verbal intelligence is a real concept and, if so, what evidence is that based on?

4. Do studies that examine the correlation between verbal intelligence and achievement tests suffer from criterion contamination?

educational training, especially low reading and writing skills in English, could fail the Alpha tests due to these limitations rather than limited intelligence. These persons then were tested with the nonverbal tests to avoid "injustice by reason of relative unfamiliarity with English" (Yoakum & Yerkes, 1920, p. 19). Thus, the goal was not to measure two different forms of intelligence—verbal intelligence and nonverbal intelligence—but rather to use verbal and nonverbal methods to assess one common construct: intelligence. These methods reflected a practical need that existed 100 years ago and one that remains relevant today (Naglieri & Ford, 2003).

There is considerable empirical support for the concept of general intelligence as measured by tests such as those developed by Binet and Wechsler (see Jensen, 1998, for a review). The fact that their scores are a good, although not necessarily the best, predictor of school achievement constitutes one of the most important sources of validity evidence for traditional intelligence tests (Naglieri & Bornstein, 2003; Ramsey & Reynolds, 2004). However, at this point in the evolution of the concept of intelligence and its measurement, much research is needed to better understand how changing the way the construct is measured might influence the utility of ability tests, especially across national boundaries. For example, some have argued that, although traditional tests of intelligence have withstood the test of time, there are several reasons why ability should be conceptualized and measured using tests that evaluate basic psychological processes (Das, 2002; Fagan, 2000; Naglieri, 2002). First, processing tests avoid the knowledge base required to answer verbal and quantitative questions found on most traditional tests of intelligence (Suzuki & Valencia,

1997). Second, a processing approach could provide early detection of disabilities that often lead to academic failure, could have better diagnostic utility, and could help professionals better understand children's disabilities (Ceci, 2000). Third, because a processing approach does not rely on test items with language and mathematics content, it is considered more appropriate for assessment for culturally and linguistically diverse populations (Fagan, 2000; Suzuki & Valencia, 1997). Fourth, a cognitive approach to intelligence could have more relevance to instruction and help tailor interventions (Das, Naglieri & Kirby, 1994; Naglieri, 2002; 2003). Fifth, a multidimensional theory of cognitive processing could provide a more comprehensive view of ability (Naglieri, 2002; Sternberg, 1988). All these possibilities warrant careful experimental examination.

SELECTED ASSESSMENT METHODS

The World Health Organization uses data from measures of intelligence for a wide variety of policy and position statements. The concept of intelligence provides a means of calibrating a vital dimension of people within the *International Classification of Functioning, Disability and Health* (ICF) system. For example, our understanding of the effects of chemical exposure, breastfeeding, social competence, fitness, malnutrition, and diseases often is examined using tests of intelligence. Given the important role an intelligence test has for the generation of knowledge in so many areas of concern, there are several important considerations that should be taken into account. First, if the concept of intelligence is to be used as a description of intelligence, researchers must realize that not all tests of intelligence are the same. Consequently, different tests of intelligence may lead to varying results because they conceptualize and measure intelligence differently. For example, a traditional test of intelligence designed to measure general ability using verbal, quantitative, and nonverbal test questions will likely yield different results for some groups than an entirely nonverbal test of general ability. Second, traditional tests of intelligence measure ability differently than more modern tests designed to measure basic psychological processes. These issues are more fully described in the section on current assessment practices that follows.

CURRENT ASSESSMENT PRACTICES

Several commonly used intelligence tests are described here. These tests were chosen to illustrate the range of approaches rather than to provide an exhaustive listing. There are 15 or more tests of intelligence from which to choose. Our goal is to help the reader recognize each instrument's basic psychometric and practical qualities such as reliability, validity, and diagnostic utility. These tests represent traditional measures of general ability and include the *Wechsler Intelligence Scale for Children* (WISC-IV, Wechsler, 2003a), the *Wechsler Adult Intelligence Scale* (3rd ed.) (WAIS-III; Wechsler, 1997b), the *Wechsler Nonverbal Scale of Ability* (WNV; Wechsler & Naglieri, 2006a), and the *Universal Nonverbal Intelligence Test* (UNIT: Bracken & McCallum, 1998a). Nontraditional measures of cognitive processes include the *Kaufman Assessment Battery for Children* (2nd ed.) (KABC-II; Kaufman & Kaufman, 2004a) and the *Cognitive Assessment System* (CAS; Naglieri & Das, 1997a). Case studies also will be presented that illustrate various interpretive and use dimensions.

Wechsler Adult Intelligence Scale (3rd ed.) (WAIS-III)

The Wechsler Adult Intelligence Scale (3rd ed.) (WAIS-III; Wechsler, 1997a) is an individually administered measure of general intellectual ability used commonly with adults ages 16 to 89. The test is composed of 11 subtests that yield a Full Scale Intelligence Quotient (FSIQ) and four index scaled scores: Verbal Comprehension, Perceptual Organization, Working Memory, and Processing Speed. The configuration of subtests to scales is shown in Table 14.1. The FSIQ and the index scores are reported as a standard score with a mean of 100 and a standard deviation of 15. The WAIS-III was standardized on a large sample of adults (N = 2,500) who represented the U.S. population on a number of important demographic variables. This intelligence test, like all the

other Wechsler tests, is very well standardized and illustrates a high standard of psychometric excellence (Wechsler, 1997b).

The WAIS-III has strong psychometric properties. The overall internal reliability consistency coefficient for the Full Scale score is high (.98) (Wechsler, 1997b). The *WAIS-III Technical Manual* (Wechsler, 1997b) reported evidence in support of the validity of the test such as intercorrelation, factor analytic, and special clinical group studies as well as correlations with other variables including intellectual ability, achievement, language, attention, and memory. More comprehensive information about reliability and validity associated with use of WAIS-III scores can be found in its *Technical Manual* (Wechsler, 1997b).

Wechsler Intelligence Scale for Children (4th ed.) (WISC-IV)

The Wechsler Intelligence Scale for Children (4th ed.) (WISC-IV; Wechsler, 2003a) is a multisubtest and multiscale measure of general intellectual ability that is used to assess children ages 6 through 16. The WISC-IV has 15 subtests that include 10 core-battery subtests and five supplemental subtests. The following four composite scores can be derived to represent a child's intellectual functioning: Verbal Comprehension Index, Perceptual Reasoning Index, Working Memory Index, and Processing Speed Index. All composite scores yield a standard score with a mean of 100 and a standard deviation of 15 (Wechsler, 2003b). The sample used to standardize the WISC-IV was composed of 2,200 children representative of the U.S. population based on the demographic variables of age, gender, geographic region, ethnicity, and socioeconomic status (Flanagan & Kaufman, 2004).

The FSIQ represents the child's overall general intelligence while the four additional composite scores are indexes that contribute to the FSIQ and represent more specific areas of the child's general intellectual functioning (Wechsler, 2003b). According to the test manual, the Verbal Comprehension Index is comprised of subtests that involve verbal reasoning, comprehension, and expression. The Perceptual Reasoning Index contains subtests that involve perceptual reasoning and organization sometimes described as fluid reasoning. The Working Memory Index involves attention, concentration, and working memory. The Processing Speed Index subtests require mental and graphomotor speed (Wechsler, 2003b). An abbreviated general intellectual ability score, the General Ability Index (GAI), also can be derived from the WISC-IV based on scores from the Verbal Comprehension Index and Perceptual Reasoning Index when a clinician determines

TABLE 14.1 Subtests and Scales Included in the WAIS-III, WISC-IV, and Wechsler Nonverbal Scale of Ability

	WAIS-III	WISC-IV	WNV
Verbal Comprehension			
Vocabulary	x	x	—
Similarities	x	x	—
Information	x	(x)	—
Comprehension	—	x	—
Word Reasoning	—	(x)	—
Perceptual Organization			
Picture Completion	x	(x)	—
Block Design	x	x	—
Matrix Reasoning	x	x	x
Picture Concepts	—	x	—
Object Assembly	—	—	x
Recognition	—	—	x
Picture Arrangement	—	—	x
Working Memory			
Arithmetic	x	(x)	—
Digit Span	x	x	—
Letter–Number Sequencing	x	x	—
Spatial Span	—	—	x
Processing Speed			
Digit Symbol—Coding	x	x	x
Symbol Search	x	x	—
Cancellation	—	(x)	—

Note: x = regular subtest; (x) = supplemental subtest

the FSIQ is not interpretable based on significant variation among the four index scores (Flanagan & Kaufman, 2004).

Evidence of reliability and validity is provided in the *WISC-IV Technical and Interpretive Manual* (Wechsler, 2003b) as well as in other sources (e.g., Flanagan & Kaufman, 2004). The WISC-IV has strong psychometric properties. The validity of the WISC-IV was supported by studies of the test's internal structure (e.g., intercorrelations and factor analysis), special clinical group studies, and by correlations with other measures of intellectual ability, achievement, and memory.

Wechsler Nonverbal Scale of Ability (WNV)

The WNV (Wechsler & Naglieri, 2006a) is the newest in the Wechsler series and differs from the other Wechsler tests in that it was designed to measure general ability nonverbally. This test was standardized on a large representative sample of children ages 4 through 21 who closely represented the U.S. population on a number of important demographic variables. The WNV also was

standardized on a large representative sample of Canadian children ages 4 through 21 who closely represented the characteristics of that country (for more details see Wechsler & Naglieri, 2006b). The test yields a Full Scale standard score (mean of 100 and standard deviation of 15) based on the combination of either two or four subtests that are scaled using a T-score metric (mean of 50 and standard deviation of 10).

The WNV is comprised of subtests that were either adapted from other Wechsler tests, are new, or are modeled after the Naglieri Nonverbal Ability tests (NNAT; Naglieri, 1997; Naglieri, 2003). The WNV consists of six subtests carefully selected to take into consideration developmental differences between the ages of 4:0–21:11. For this reason, the age range was divided into two age bands, ages 4:0–7:11 and ages 8:0–21:11, with each age band having different combinations of subtests.

The WNV was designed to be appropriate for examinees who come from a wide range of cultural and linguistic backgrounds as well as those with special needs for whom a traditional verbal and language loaded

DISCUSSION BOX 14.2

Many traditional intelligence tests have been organized according to the content of the tests and yield IQs for verbal, quantitative, and nonverbal scales. These scores imply that different types of intelligences are being measured. Authors of nonverbal tests (Bracken & McCallum, 1998a) believe that general ability can be measured regardless of the content of the tests and that these distinctions are misunderstood. That is, verbal and nonverbal describe the content of the tests, not the type of thinking.

Questions

1. What is the difference between a nonverbal test of general ability and a traditional measure of general ability?
2. How can we determine if a nonverbal test is as good as one that has varying content?
3. What are the advantages and disadvantages of using a nonverbal test of general ability?

measure of intelligence may be problematic. The WNV was built so that administration is accomplished using a unique combination of nonverbal and minimal verbal directions. The WNV uses pictorial directions to inform the examinee of the demands of the test. Pictorial directions are included for all subtests and are designed to provide a nonverbal and engaging method to communicate the task requirements to the examinee. Pictorial directions are supplemented by simple verbal directions provided in English, French, Spanish, Chinese, German, and Dutch. The translated verbal directions are used only as needed and by professionals who are able to perform the testing in the examinee's preferred language. *See* Figure 14.2.

The WNV, like other Wechsler tests, uses subtests that vary in content and specific requirements. However, it differs from other Wechsler tests because it was designed to measure general ability using tests that do not have verbal content. The advantage of using nonverbal tasks to measure general ability is that it minimizes the need for language skills and eliminates the influence of language and mathematic skills on the examinee's test performance. Although nonverbal tests on the WNV do not require language or arithmetic skills, they differ in their specific requirements. This multidimensionality of task requirements distinguishes the WNV from nonverbal tests that use one type of task requirement, such as a progressive matrix format.

The WNV, like the other Wechsler Scales, has strong psychometric properties. The internal consistency for the FSIQ is high for the four subtest administration (.91) and two subtest administration (.91) (Wechsler & Naglieri, 2006b). As described in the *WNV Technical and Interpretive Manual* (Wechsler & Naglieri, 2006b), the validity of the test was supported by intercorrelation studies, factor analytic studies, and special clinical group studies, and by correlations with external variables including additional measures of cognitive ability, including achievement. One goal of the WNV is to provide an instrument that is fair for children and youth from different cultural and linguistic backgrounds as well as those who are deaf or hard of hearing. The WNV manual provides the results of studies that examine ethnicity, language, and hearing limitations. The results of these studies provide strong support for the use of the WNV as an effective measure of ability for these diverse populations.

FIGURE 14.2 Wechsler Non Verbal Scale of Ability Pictorial Directions
Wechsler Nonverbal Scale of Ability (WNV). Copyright 2006 by NCS Pearson, Inc. Reproduced with permission. All rights reserved.

"Wechsler Nonverbal Scale of Ability" and "WNV" are trademarks, in the U.S. and/or other countries, of Pearson Education, Inc. or its affiliate(s).

DISCUSSION BOX 14.3

Many professionals have been influenced by the structure of the Wechsler scales when they think about what intelligence is.

Questions

1. Did David Wechsler believe that his scales measure different *types* of intelligence or that they were different *ways* to measure intelligence?

2. Does it make sense to derive a theory of intelligence based on data from one test?

3. Should the theory come before the development of the test?

Some General Features of the Wechsler Scales

The WAIS-III, WISC-IV (Wechsler, 2003a) and WNV (Wechsler & Naglieri, 2006a) are based on Wechsler's (1939) view that "intelligence is the aggregate or global capacity of the individual to act purposefully, to think rationally and to deal effectively with his environment (p. 7)." The composition of these Wechsler scales reflects the recognition of the value of general ability measured using tests that vary in content and specific requirements. For example, some WAIS-III and WISC-IV subtests require knowledge of words and comprehension of verbal relationships; others involve memory of the sequence of numbers; and others require reasoning with arithmetic and spatial stimuli. This diversity is important in these tests because, as Wechsler (1975) noted, ". . . the attributes and factors of intelligence, like the elementary particles in physics, have at once collective and individual properties (p. 138)." That is, despite the individual demands of any specific subtest, each combines with the others to form a cohesive whole, which is expressed by the test's Full Scale score and reflects the overall concept of general ability.

Universal Nonverbal Intelligence Test (UNIT)

The Universal Nonverbal Intelligence Test (UNIT; Bracken & McCallum, 1998a) is a completely nonverbal, individually administered test that measures general intelligence for children ages 5 through 17. The UNIT is designed to be appropriate for children who would be at a disadvantage if given traditional measures of intelligence that have verbal questions. Such children include those who have speech, language, or hearing impairments, who are verbally uncommunicative, or who have different cultural or language backgrounds. The UNIT is administered through the use of gestures and without any spoken language (Bracken & McCallum, 1998a).

The UNIT is conceptually based on a combination of theories. These theories are Spearman's (1927) theory on general ability (*g*), Jenson's (1980) dichotomy between associative ability (memory) and cognitive ability (reasoning), and Sternberg and Powell's (1982) conceptualization of procedure classifications according to processing demands such as symbolic and nonsymbolic processing. These theories provide the foundations for the four UNIT scales: Memory Quotient, Reasoning Quotient, Symbolic Quotient, and Nonsymbolic Quotient (Bracken & McCallum, 1998b). These scales are comprised of overlapping subtest configurations and, like the UNIT Full Scale IQ, are expressed as standard scores with a mean of 100 and a standard deviation of 15. The sample used to norm the test was composed of 2,100 children who closely matched the U.S. population on important demographic variables (Bracken & McCallum, 1998b).

The UNIT has six subtests (see Table 14.2). Clinicians can use three different administration options based on their own and a child's needs. The administration options are the Abbreviated Battery, Standard Battery, and Extended Battery. Among its six subtests,

TABLE 14.2 Subtests and Scales Included in the UNIT

	Memory	Reasoning
Symbolic	Symbolic Memory	Anagogic Reasoning
	Object Memory	—
Nonsymbolic	Spatial Memory	Cube Design
	—	Mazes

two are included in the Abbreviated Battery and can be used as a screener of intellectual functioning. The Standard Battery consists of the first four subtests and is intended to be the most frequently used administration option that is appropriate for educational placement evaluations. The Extended Battery includes all six subtests and is useful when a more in-depth assessment is necessary (Bracken & McCallum, 1998b). These batteries have strong psychometric properties of reliability, including high internal consistency coefficients for the Abbreviated Battery (.96), the Standard Battery (.98), and the Extended Battery (.98). The manual also provides information on exploratory and confirmatory factor analysis and a number of additional important validity studies. Further details of these and other psychometric properties can be found in the UNIT's examiner's manual (Bracken & McCallum, 1998b).

The purpose of the UNIT was to create an intelligence test that optimized fairness for individuals who differ on various traits including age, race, ethnicity, and language. Additionally, the UNIT was created to be a fair assessment tool for children with different disabilities, deficiencies, and impairments. The UNIT's manual summarizes the results of comparative studies based on gender, race, ethnicity, and language. In general, the results of these studies provide support for the use of the UNIT as an effective measure of intellectual ability.

Kaufman Assessment Battery for Children (2nd ed.) (KABC-II)

The Kaufman Assessment Battery for Children (2nd ed.) (KABC-II; Kaufman & Kaufman, 2004a) is an individually administered measure of processing and cognitive abilities that is used for children ages 3 through 18. It is grounded in two models: the Cattell–Horn–Carrol psychometric model of broad and narrow abilities and Luria's processing model (Kaufman & Kaufman, 2004b). The KABC-II yields two global scores: the Mental Processing Index and the Fluid-Crystallized Index. The Mental

Processing Index is the global score based on the Luria model, and the Fluid-Crystallized Index is the global score based on the Cattell–Horn–Carrol model. Both global scores yield a standard score that has a mean of 100 and a standard deviation of 15. In addition to the Fluid-Crystallized Index and Mental Processing Index, the KABC-II has a Nonverbal Scale that contains subtests that can be administered in pantomime and responded to motorically. The Nonverbal Index is particularly useful when assessing individuals who have limited English proficiency, impaired hearing, moderate to severe language or speech impairments, or other disabilities that make the core battery inappropriate (Kaufman, Lichtenberger, Fletcher-Janzen, & Kaufman, 2004). The KABC-II was normed on a large and representative sample (N = 3,025) of children ages 3 through 18 who closely represented the U.S. population on a number of important demographic variables (Kaufman & Kaufman, 2004b).

The dual theoretical perspective of the KABC-II gives clinicians the choice of which model to use based on each child's background and reasons for referral. In addition, process-oriented interpretations may be derived from either model (Kaufman, Lichtenberger, Fletcher-Janzen & Kaufman, 2004). See Table 14.3 for a comparison of the theoretical foundations.

The Cattell–Horn–Carrol model provides a psychometrically supported spectrum of broad cognitive abilities. In contrast, Luria's theory has a clinical and neuropsychological framework that leads to the recognition of three functional systems that represent the brain's basic functions: to maintain arousal, to code and store information, and to plan and organize behavior. This theory also is supported by psychometric research. However, the KABC-II differs from the Cattell–Horn–Carrol model in that it deemphasizes acquired knowledge. A more detailed summary of both of these theories is presented in the KABC-II manual (Kaufman & Kaufman, 2004b) and Naglieri (1999).

The KABC-II has five scales. Based on the Cattell–Horn–Carrol perspective, the KABC-II measures

TABLE 14.3 Theoretical Foundation of the KABC-II Scales and Global Scales

KABC-II Scales	Luria Perspective	CHC Perspective
Sequential/Gsm	Sequential Processing	Short-Term Memory (Gsm)
Simultaneous/Gv	Simultaneous Processing	Visual Processing (Gv)
Learning/Glr	Learning Ability	Long-Term Storage and Retrieval (Glr)
Planning/Gf	Planning Ability	Fluid Reasoning (Gf)
Knowledge/Gc		Crystallized Ability (Gc)

crystallized ability, fluid reasoning, visual processing, short-term memory, and long-term storage and retrieval. Based on Luria's theory, the KABC-II scales assess learning ability, sequential processing, simultaneous processing, and planning ability. The KABC-II's scales' names include both the Luria process and the Cattell–Horn–Carrol Broad Ability. These scales are learning/long-term storage and retrieval, sequential/short-term memory, simultaneous/visual processing, and planning/fluid reasoning. There are 18 subtests in the KABC-II that are separated into two types: those that assess core qualities (i.e., they should be administered) and those that assess supplementary qualities (i.e., those that may be used to augment assessment).

The KABC-II has strong psychometric properties. For example, the average internal consistency coefficients for the five scales generally are in the .90s. The validity of the KABC-II is supported by factor analytic studies, correlational data, and by special clinical group studies. Additional information on reliability and validity is available in the KABC-II Manual (Kaufman & Kaufman, 2004b), as well as other sources (Kaufman, Lichtenberger, Fletcher-Janzen, & Kaufman, 2004).

Cognitive Assessment System (CAS)

The Cognitive Assessment System (CAS; Naglieri & Das, 1997a) is a multidimensional measure of intelligence based on a cognitive processing theory called Planning, Attention, Simultaneous, and Successive (PASS) (Naglieri, 1999, 2005). Each of these four cognitive processing scales and the Full Scale score yields a standard score with a mean of 100 and standard deviation of 15. The scales are described in Table 14.4 (for further explanation, see Naglieri, 1999). This test was normed on a large sample of children ages 5 through 17 (N = 2,200) who closely represented the U.S. population on a number of important demographic variables (Naglieri & Das, 1997b).

The CAS is designed to measure four basic psychological processes that are described in the PASS theory of intelligence (Naglieri, 1999; Naglieri & Das, 2005). These processes provide a means of operationalizing the basic psychological processes in the definition of a specific learning disability provided in federal legislation (Individuals with Disabilities Education Act 2004) (see Naglieri, 2005). These four PASS constructs are based on a strong empirical research foundation and reflect the result of a merger of cognitive and neuropsychological constructs that include executive function (planning), selective attention (attention), visual–spatial ability (simultaneous), and the serial nature of language and memory

TABLE 14.4 Structure of the Cognitive Assessment System

CAS Full Scale
  Planning Scale
    Matching Numbers
    Planned Codes
    Planned Connections
  Attention Scale
    Expressive Attention
    Number Detection
    Receptive Attention
  Simultaneous Scale
    Nonverbal Matrices
    Verbal Spatial Relations
    Figure Memory
  Successive Scale
    Word Series
    Sentence Repetition
    Sentence Questions

(successive). The four PASS processes are described in the following discussion (Naglieri & Das, 2005).

Planning involves mental activities that provide cognitive control; use of processes, knowledge, and skills; intentionality; organization; and self-regulation. This includes self-monitoring and impulse control as well as generation, evaluation, and execution of a plan. Planning processing provides the means to solve problems and may involve control of attention, simultaneous and successive processes, as well as acquisition of knowledge and skills. The essence of the construct of planning and tests to measure it is that they provide a novel problem-solving situation for which children do not have a previously acquired strategy.

Attention involves mental activities that provide focused, selective cognitive activity over time and resistance to distraction. This process is involved when a person must demonstrate focused, selective, sustained, and effortful activity. Focused attention involves directed concentration toward a particular activity. Selective attention is important for the inhibition of responses to distracting stimuli. Sustained attention refers to the variation of performance over time, which can be influenced by the different amount of effort required to solve the test.

Simultaneous processing involves mental activities by which a person integrates stimuli into interrelated groups or a whole. Simultaneous processing tests typically have strong spatial demands, but the process can be measured with tests that have nonverbal as well as verbal content as long as the cognitive demand of the task requires the integration of information.

Successive processing involves mental activities by which the person works with stimuli in a specific serial order that form a chain-like progression. Successive processing involves both the perception of stimuli in sequence and the formation of sounds and movements in order. For this reason, successive processing is involved with recall of information in order as well as phonological analysis and the syntax of language.

Evidence of reliability and validity of the CAS is strong (Naglieri & Das, 1997b). The reliability for the Full Scale Score is high (.96). The validity findings include correlations with achievement, special clinical group studies (e.g., learning disabled, attention deficit, mentally retarded), factor analytic results, and relationships between constructs and strategy use. The theory-based scale structure of the CAS also was supported by more recent research (Blaha, 2003). The CAS correlates strongly with achievement and other measures of intelligence (Naglieri & Rojahn, 2004; Naglieri & Bornstein, 2003). Moreover, PASS scores are sensitive to instructional interventions. Additionally, the CAS yields similar scores for groups of whites and blacks (Naglieri, Rojahn, Matto, & Aquilino, 2005) as well as whites and Hispanics (Naglieri, Rojahn, & Matto, 2007). Summaries of the test's validity, especially race and ethnic differences as well as relevance to intervention, can be found in Naglieri (2001, 2005).

ILLUSTRATIVE CASE STUDIES

The following three case studies illustrate the use of some of these tests—one with a child, another with an adolescent, and then an adult. Susan, a first grader, demonstrates strong general intellectual ability along with weaknesses in intellectual processes. Michael, a sixteen-year-old tenth grader, demonstrates weak intellectual ability and an interesting pattern of intellectual processes. Finally, George, a middle-aged, professionally accomplished adult, has a history of severe traumatic

RESEARCH BOX 14.1

Naglieri, J. A., Rojahn, J. & Matto, H. (2007). Hispanic and Non-Hispanic Children's Performance on PASS Cognitive Processes and Achievement. *Intelligence, 35,* 568–579.

Background: Current research in assessment of Hispanic children has been conducted using tests of cognitive processing. Hispanics are now the largest minority group in the United States. Importantly, the children in Hispanic families come largely from working class homes with parents who have limited education and English language skills. This presents a challenge to those who assess Hispanic children using traditional measures of intelligence that contain verbal and quantitative tests.

Objective: The objective of the study was to determine how Hispanic children perform on tests of cognitive processing and if different ways of measuring ability results in reduced differences between Hispanic and non-Hispanic children. Three complementary sampling methodologies and data analysis strategies were chosen to compare the ethnic groups. Sample size was maximized using nationally representative groups, and demographic group differences were minimized using smaller matched samples.

Method: The scores of Hispanic (N = 244) and White (N = 1,956) children on the four PASS processes were obtained and the respective correlations between PASS and achievement compared.

Results: Small differences between Hispanic and non-Hispanic children were found when ability was measured with tests of basic PASS processes. In addition, correlations between the PASS constructs and achievement were substantial for both Hispanic and non-Hispanic children and were not significantly different between the groups.

Conclusions: Measures of basic psychological processes may be useful for measuring cognitive ability in Hispanic children and adolescents because such ability can be measured without requiring verbal expression and comprehension. Importantly, because PASS processes have been shown to have relevance for diagnosis and intervention, these processes may have utility for providing, understanding and promoting treatment options for those served by rehabilitation specialists.

Questions

1. Why do the results from ethnic studies differ when a traditional intelligence test is used as opposed to a test of cognitive processing?
2. Do nonverbal tests of general ability such as the UNIT or Wechsler Nonverbal also yield smaller differences between White and Black as well as White and Hispanic groups?
3. What role do verbal tests have in the measurement of ability, particularly for Hispanic children?

DISCUSSION BOX 14.4

Some researchers have argued (e.g., Naglieri & Das, 2005) that traditional intelligence tests should be replaced by tests of basic psychological processes. These tests are thought to represent an evolution in thinking about intelligence and approach the construct from a different perspective.

Questions

1. How does the content of a cognitive processing measure of intelligence differ from a general intelligence test?
2. Do tests of cognitive processing have as much validity as those built on traditional notions of intelligence?

3. What advantages do cognitive processing tests have over those that contain verbal and quantitative test questions?

Some authors have argued that traditional tests of intelligence have little relevance to instruction and intervention while tests of cognitive processing do.

Questions

1. What research literature is there that would support this statement?
2. What are the advantages of a cognitive processing approach to rehabilitation services?

---

brain injury. George's case demonstrates the utility of general intellectual ability and processing–based measures of intelligence for predicting and understanding functional behavior and impairment.

The Case of Susan

Seven-year-old Susan was referred for evaluation due to problems with reading and achievement in general. Despite academic tutoring, Susan continued to struggle in school. Although her developmental history appeared unremarkable, her parents reported that she experienced some problems mastering sequential tasks such as memorizing the alphabet, her address, and her phone number. In class, Susan was described as pleasant and cooperative. She got along well with her peers, teachers, and parents. Even in the face of classroom challenges, Susan persevered. Susan's teacher reported that, in conversation, Susan appears to be bright and capable.

Susan's academic achievement was evaluated with the third edition of the Woodcock Johnson Tests of Achievement (see Table 14.5). On this instrument, Susan demonstrated average mathematic skills; well below average regular and pseudo word (e.g., *vib, koz*) reading skills (Word Attack and Letter/Word identification standard scores were 85 and 87, respectively); and difficulty with passage comprehension (standard score of 66). Despite these low academic scores, Susan's WIC-IV scores were variable, with most in the average range or higher. However, her Working Memory was low.

Her cognitive processing problems become more apparent on the CAS on which Susan scored in the average range for planning and simultaneous processing, and below average on attention (standard score = 82), and especially successive (standard score = 78) processing

scales. Susan's strong general intellectual ability and her average scores on planning and simultaneous processes suggested that her abilities are variable. Her low processing abilities are likely to help account for her specific academic difficulties.

Whereas differences between one's WISC-IV Full scale and achievement scores traditionally have been used as evidence of a specific learning disability, greater insight into the reasons why Susan was struggling was better understood with knowledge of her underlying cognitive processes. Knowledge of Susan's problem with attention and successive processing, in contrast to her average planning and simultaneous processing abilities, provides insight and appreciation of the reasons Susan struggled to master reading and continued to struggle despite support and intervention. Additionally, an appreciation of these weaknesses, particularly Susan's problems with successive processing, provides foundational information from which to begin the necessary skill building to accelerate her rate of reading development. For example, phonic-based methods that emphasize sequences of sounds and letters and their correspondence will likely be less effective than whole language methods that deemphasize the blending of separate sounds. Additionally, methods that help Susan work with information, such as mnemonic devices (see Mastropieri & Scruggs, 2007) and chunking (see Naglieri & Pickering, 2003), should be utilized (see Naglieri 2005 for more instructional suggestions).

THE CASE OF MICHAEL

Sixteen-year-old Michael was referred for evaluation due to concerns about depression and low school achievement. His history included chronic difficulty with unfinished school work (at the time of the evaluation he was

TABLE 14.5 Test Results for the Case of Susan

	Standard Score
WJ-III Achievement Test Scores	
Letter/Word Identification	87
Word Attack	85
Calculation	103
Spelling	98
Passage Comprehension	66
Applied Problems	95
Academic Skills	93
WISC-IV	
Full Scale IQ	109
Verbal Comprehension	128
Perceptual Reasoning	100
Working Memory	86
Processing Speed	109
CAS	
Full Scale	82
Planning	91
Simultaneous	97
Attention	82
Successive	78

Note: All standard scores have a normative mean of 100 and SD of 15.

failing three classes), disorganization, and inattention. His current symptoms are consistent with a diagnosis of attention deficit hyperactivity disorder. In addition, Michael reported symptoms consistent with depression, including feelings of helplessness, hopelessness, and problems with sleep. Michael's family has a history of mood and anxiety disorders. Throughout his childhood he often had symptoms of adverse mood and anxiety for which, as an 8-year-old, he was briefly prescribed a medication for anxiety.

Michael's total score of 93 on the third edition of the Woodcock Johnson Tests of Achievement suggested overall average performance. However, he displayed academic problems especially in math calculation (standard score of 82) and math concepts (standard score of 89). Screening for memory problems using the Wide Range Assessment of Memory and Learning yielded average general performance yet very low complex verbal memory (standard score of 75). His WAIS-III Full Scale IQ of 90 similarly suggested average ability. However, his separate scores varied from 88 (perceptual organization index) to 103 (processing speed index). Michael also earned a low score 85 on the simultaneous processing

scale of the CAS. His remaining scores were in the average (attention and successive processing) and above average (planning) ranges (see Figure 14.3).

The results of this evaluation suggest an important pattern. Both his perceptual organization and simultaneous processing abilities are low and consistent with his academic problems in math. These findings imply that he has considerable difficulty working with information that must be interrelated to be understood, regardless of whether the information is academic (math) or nonacademic (perceptual organization on the WAIS-III or simultaneous on CAS). Importantly, his problems remembering a story are related to his difficulty with what can be described as spatial tasks found on the WAIS-III perceptual organization and CAS simultaneous scales because he has difficulty remembering and forming the information into an organized coherent whole. Finally, self-reported measures of depression and anxiety were elevated and suggestive of symptom complaints consistent with both conditions.

Michael's PASS profile is not like most children who have ADHD and low planning ability as measured by the CAS (Naglieri & Goldstein, 2006). His strong ability to plan and organize suggests that he does not

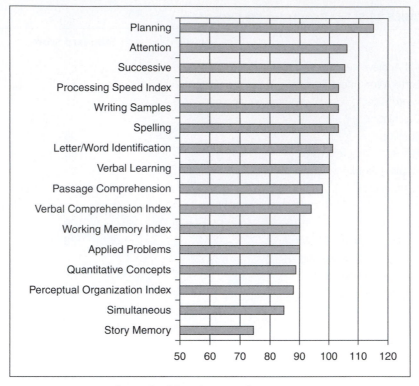

FIGURE 14.3 Scores for Michael (aged 16 years)

have the cognitive impairment seen in research on children with ADHD (Naglieri, 2005). This suggests that his academic problems are more likely related to his low simultaneous processing, a quality also apparent in his history of ADHD symptoms (e.g., disorganization). His cognitive weakness in simultaneous processing (which also is seen in his performance on the WISC-IV perceptional organization scale) is consistent with his academic problems together with his difficulties recalling information, and suggests that interventions that help him develop and use relationships among ideas should be considered (see Naglieri & Pickering, 2003). That is, despite having average general intellectual ability as demonstrated by the WISC-IV and CAS Full Scale scores, Michael's weakness with simultaneous processing is likely to contribute significantly to his school-based problems and difficulty with complex verbal memory. The use of story maps and webbing should be employed to help Michael better meet the demands of these types of tasks. See Mastropieri and Scruggs (2007) and Naglieri and Pickering (2003) for further details.

THE CASE OF GEORGE

George held a number of important positions at a state college at the time an automobile accident caused a severe traumatic brain injury. He had nearly completed his doctoral degree and had a strong academic history. The unfortunate accident lead to a long period of rehabilitation and recovery. At discharge from a rehabilitation program, George demonstrated marked deficits in processing speed, attention, and problem-solving. George did not recognize the impact of these deficits in his ability to perform complex tasks. George was unable to return to work due, in part, to problems with concentration, memory, learning new information, and regulating emotions.

George obtained a verbal IQ of 114, performance IQ of 81 and full scale IQ of 99 on the WAIS-III. Importantly, his verbal comprehension index was 134, a working memory index of 95, a perceptual organization index of 84, and processing speed index of 81. On the third edition of the Wechsler Memory Scale, George's memory generally was in the average range. His basic academic skills also were in the average range, well below estimates of George's preaccident functioning based upon his academic and vocational accomplishments. Despite the fact that George still possessed good general intellectual ability and very strong verbal comprehension postaccident, his cognitive efficiency and executive processes (similar to Planning and Attention components from the PASS theory) were below the 5th percentile. His injury had considerable negative impact on his ability to organize, strategize, and solve novel problems. Individuals with planning problems can be taught to better utilize strategies when doing academic work, resulting in improved academic performance (see Naglieri [2005] for a summary and Naglieri & Pickering [2003] for instructional materials).

Summary and Conclusion

Since their introduction in the early 1900s, measures of general intellectual ability have provided a valuable way to measure global ability However, they had limited utility for diagnosis and intervention for persons with learning and other neurocognitive disorders commonly seen by rehabilitation specialists. In recent years, additional tests that measure basic psychological processes have been developed. Some scholars believe cognitive processing should be considered a modern conceptualization of intelligence. As the concept of intelligence is evolving toward cognitive processing, researchers have begun to see the utility of these new methods, especially for individuals who display cognitive and behavioral problems, particularly when the goal of rehabilitation is the reacquisition of academic and vocational skills through planned interventions with reasonable goals to mark improvement. This chapter reviewed various types of intelligence tests. Measures of basic psychological processes offer multiple advantages by providing a more differentiated cognitive perspective and one that measures the ability fairly for diverse populations.

Case Studies

Case 1

Consider the case of Susan (p. 236). Answer the following questions regarding that case.

QUESTIONS

1. How would problems with successive processing impact a person's daily living skills?
2. How would problems with attention interfere with Susan's interpersonal behavior?
3. What methods could be used to help Susan reduce the impairment that might result because of her cognitive weaknesses?
4. How could Susan's strengths in planning and simultaneous processing be used to help her function better?

Case 2

Consider the case of George (pp. 238–239). Answer the following questions in regard to that case.

QUESTIONS

1. How would problems with perceptual organization likely impact George's behavior on a day-to-day basis?
2. Would difficulty with processing speed influence George in some specific areas of functioning?
3. How could George's strong verbal IQ be used to help him mitigate the effects of his cognitive weaknesses?

References

Anastasi, A., & Urbina, S. (1997). *Psychological testing.* Upper Saddle River, NJ: Prentice Hall.

Binet, A., & Simon, T. (1905). New methods for the diagnosis of the intellectual level of subnormals. *L'Ann'e Psychologique*, 11, 191–244.

Blaha, J. (2003). *What does the CAS really measure: An exploratory hierarchical factor analysis of the Cognitive Assessment System.* Paper presented at the National Association of School Psychologists Convention. Chicago, IL.

Boake, C. (2002). From the Binet-Simon to the Wechsler-Bellevue: Tracing the history of intelligence testing. *Journal of Clinical & Experimental Neuropsychology, 24,* 383–405.

Bracken, B. A., & McCallum, R. S. (1998a). *Universal Nonverbal Intelligence Test.* Itasca, IL: Riverside Publishing Company.

Bracken, B.A., & McCallum, R.S. (1998b). *Universal Nonverbal Intelligence Test: Examiner's manual.* Itasca, IL: Riverside Publishing Company.

Bracken, B.A., & Naglieri, J.A. (2003). Assessing diverse populations with nonverbal tests of general intelligence. In C. R. Reynolds & R. W. Kamphaus (Eds.) *Handbook of psychological and educational assessment of children* (2nd ed., pp. 243–273). New York: Guilford.

Ceci, S. J. (2000). So near and yet so far: Lingering questions about the use of measures of general intelligence for college admission and employment screening. *Psychology, Public Policy, and Law, 6,* 233–252.

Das, J.P. (2002). A better look at intelligence. *Current Directions in Psychology, 11,* 28–32.

Das, J. P., Naglieri, J. A., & Kirby, J. R. (1994). *The assessment of cognitive processes: The PASS theory of intelligence.* Boston: Allyn & Bacon.

Fagan, J. R. (2000). A theory of intelligence as processing: Implications for society. *Psychology, Public Policy, and Law, 6, 168–179.*

Flanagan, D. P., & Kaufman, A. S. (2004). *Essentials of WISC-IV assessment.* New York: Wiley.

Jensen, A. R. (1980). *Bias in mental testing.* New York: Free Press.

Jensen, A.R. (1998). *The 'g' factor: The science of mental ability.* Westport, CT: Praeger Publishers.

Kaufman, A. S., & Kaufman, N. L. (2004a). *Kaufman Assessment Battery for Children* (2nd ed.). Circle Pines, MN: AGS Publishing.

Kaufman, A.S., & Kaufman, N.L. (2004b). *Kaufman Assessment Battery for Children Second Edition Manual.* Circle Pines, MN: AGS Publishing.

Kaufman, A. S., & Lichtenberger, E. O. (1999). *Essentials of WAIS-III assessment.* New York: Wiley.

Kaufman, A. S, & Lichtenberger, E. O. (2000). *Essentials of WISC-III and WPPSI-R assessment.* New York: Wiley

Kaufman, A. S., Lichtenberger, E. O., Fletcher -Janzen, E. & Kaufman, N. L. (2004). *Essentials of KABC-II assessment.* Hoboken, NJ: Wiley.

Lobinsky, D. (2000). Scientific and social significance of assessing individual differences: Sinking shafts at a few critical points. *Annual Review of Psychology, 51,* 405–444.

Lohman, D., & Hagen, E. (2001). Cognitive Abilities Test. Itasca: Riverside Publishing Company.

Mastropieri, M. A. & Scruggs, T. E. (2007). *The inclusive classroom: Strategies for effective instruction* (3rd ed.). New York: Prentice Hall.

Matarazzo, J. (1992). Psychological testing and assessment in the 21st century. *American Psychologist, 47,* 1007–1018.

Naglieri, J. A. (1985). *Matrix Analogies Test—Expanded Form.* San Antonio: The Psychological Corporation.

Naglieri, J. A. (1997). *Naglieri Nonverbal Ability Test.* San Antonio: The Psychological Corporation.

Naglieri, J. A. (1999). *Essentials of CAS assessment.* New York: Wiley.

Naglieri, J. A. (2001). Cognitive Assessment System: A test built from the PASS theory. In A. S. Kaufman & N. L. Kaufman (Eds), *Learning disabilities: Psychological assessment and evaluation* (pp. 141–177), Cambridge, UK: Cambridge University Press.

Naglieri, J. A. (2002). Best practices in interventions for school psychologists: A cognitive approach to problem solving. In A. Thomas & J. Grimes (Eds.). *Best Practices in School Psychology* (4th ed., pp. 1373–1392). Bethesda, MD: National Association of School Psychologists.

Naglieri, J. A. (2003). Current advances in assessment and intervention for children with learning disabilities. In T. E. Scruggs & M. A. Mastropieri (Eds.) *Advances in learning and behavioral disabilities Volume 16: Identification and assessment* (pp. 163–190). New York: Reed Elsevier.

Naglieri, J. A., (2005). The Cognitive Assessment System. In D. P. Flanagan & P. L. Harrison (Eds.) *Contemporary Intellectual Assessment*: (2nd ed.) (pp. 441–460). New York: Guilford.

Naglieri, J. A., & Bornstein, B. T. (2003). Intelligence and achievement: Just how correlated are they? *Journal of Psychoeducational Assessment, 21,* 244–260

Naglieri, J. A., & Das, J. P. (1997a). *Cognitive Assessment System.* Itasca: Riverside Publishing Company.

Naglieri, J. A., & Das, J. P. (1997b). *Cognitive Assessment System interpretive handbook.* Chicago: Riverside Publishing Company.

Naglieri, J. A., & Das, J. P. (2005). Planning, attention, simultaneous, successive (PASS) theory: A revision of the concept of intelligence. In D. P. Flanagan & P. L. Harrison (Eds.) *Contemporary Intellectual Assessment* (2nd ed.) (pp. 136–182). New York: Guilford.

Naglieri, J., & Ford, D. Y. (2003). Addressing under-representation of gifted minority children using the Naglieri Nonverbal Ability Test (NNAT). *Gifted Child Quarterly, 47,* 155–160.

Naglieri, J. A., & Goldstein, S. (2006). The role of intellectual processes in the DSM-V diagnosis of ADHD. *Journal of Attention Disorders, 10,* 3–8.

Naglieri, J. A., & Pickering, E. (2003). *Helping children learn: Instructional handouts for use in school and at home.* Baltimore: Brookes.

Naglieri, J. A., & Rojahn, J. R. (2004). Validity of the PASS Theory and CAS: Correlations with achievement. *Journal of Educational Psychology, 96,* 174–181.

Naglieri, J. A., Rojahn, J., & Matto, H. (2007). Hispanic and Non-Hispanic Children's Performance on PASS Cognitive Processes and Achievement. *Intelligence, 35,* 568–579.

Naglieri, J. A., Rojahn, J. R., Matto, H. C., & Aquilino, S. A. (2005). Black white differences in intelligence: A study of the PASS theory and Cognitive Assessment System. *Journal of Psychoeducational Assessment, 23,* 146–160.

Ramirez, R. R., & de la Cruz G. P. (2002) The hispanic population in the United States: March 2002. *Current Population Reports,* (pp. 20–545). Washington DC: U.S. Census Bureau.

Ramsey, M. C., & Reynolds, C. R. (2004). Relations between intelligence and achievement tests. In G. Goldstein & S. Beers (Eds.) *Comprehensive handbook of psychological assessment* (pp. 25–50). New York: John Wiley Inc.

Roid, G. (2003). *Stanford-Binet* (5th ed). Itasca, IL: Riverside.

Spearman, C. (1927) *The abilities of man, their nature and measurement.* New York: Macmillan and Company.

Sternberg, R. J. (1988). *The triarchic mind: A new theory of human intelligence.* New York: Viking.

Sternberg, R. J., & Powell, J. S. (1982). Theories of intelligence. In R. J. Sternberg (Ed.) *Handbook of intelligence* (pp. 975–1006) New York: Cambridge University Press.

Suzuki, L. A., & Valencia, R. R. (1997). Race-ethnicity and measured intelligence. *American Psychologist, 52,* 1103–1114.

Watkins, M. W., Glutting, J. J., & Lei, P. W. (2007). Validity of the full scale I.Q. when there is significant variability among WISC-III and WISC-IV factor scores. *Applied Neuropsychology, 14,* 13–20.

Wechsler, D. (1939) *Wechsler-Bellevue Intelligence Scale.* New York: Psychological Corporation.

Wechsler, D. (1975) *Intelligence defined and undefined: A relativistic appraisal. American Psychologist, 30,* 135–139.

Wechsler, D. (1997a). *Wechsler Adult Intelligence Scale* (3rd ed.). San Antonio, TX: The Psychological Corporation.

Wechsler, D. (1997b). *Wechsler Adult Intelligence Scale - Third Edition Technical Manual* . San Antonio, TX: The Psychological Corporation.

Wechsler, D. (1991). *Wechsler Intelligence Scale for Children* (3rd ed.). San Antonio, TX: The Psychological Corporation.

Wechsler, D. (2001). *Wechsler Individual Achievement Test* (2nd ed.). San Antonio, TX: The Psychological Corporation.

Wechsler, D. (2003a). *Wechsler Intelligence Scale for Children* (4th ed.). San Antonio, TX: The Psychological Corporation.

Wechsler, D. (2003b). *Wechsler Intelligence Scale for Children - Fourth Edition : Technical and Interpretive Manual.* San Antonio, TX: The Psychological Corporation.

Wechsler, D. & Naglieri, J. A. (2006a). *Wechsler Nonverbal Scale of Ability.* San Antonio, TX: Harcourt Assessment.

Wechsler, D. & Naglieri, J. A. (2006b). *Wechsler Nonverbal Scale of Ability. Technical and Interpretive Manual.* San Antonio, TX: Harcourt Assessment.

Woodcock, R. W., McGrew, K. S., & Mather, N. (2001a). *Woodcock Johnson III Test of Achievement.* Ithasca, IL: Riverside Publishing Company.

Woodcock, R. W., McGrew, K.S., & Mather, N.(2001b). *Woodcock-Johnson III Tests of Cognitive Abilities.* Ithasca, IL: Riverside Publishing Company.

World Heath Organization. (1999). *International Classification of Functioning and Disability.* Geneva, Switzerland: Author.

Yoakum, C. S., & Yerkes, R. M. (1920). *Army mental tests.* New York: Henry Holt & Company.

15

Adaptive Behavior

JEFFREY DITTERLINE
THOMAS OAKLAND, PH.D., ABPP, ABPN
University of Florida, Gainesville

OVERVIEW

Adaptive behavior generally refers to the ways in which individuals meet their daily personal needs as well as deal with the natural and social demands in their environment. Thus, adaptive behavior has a pervasive impact on one's quality of life, including the ability to function independently at school, work, home, and the community. This chapter reviews four commonly used scales of adaptive behavior, reviews diagnoses for which adaptive behavior information is required, identifies federal legislation and policy for which adaptive behavior data are important (e.g., for Individuals with Disabilities Education Improvement Act, Supplemental Security Income, Medicaid, and Social Security programs), and discusses ways this information aids professionals in developing, monitoring, and ameliorating individual and family services, education, transition, and rehabilitation plans for people with various disabilities.

LEARNING OBJECTIVES

By the end of this chapter, readers should be able to:

■ Define adaptive behavior and explain its importance in rehabilitative health

■ Provide a comprehensive account on the legal and professional issues surrounding the assessment of adaptive behavior

■ Differentiate among the methods and structures of current measures used to assess adaptive behavior

■ Interpret results from measures of adaptive behavior to determine the skill deficits displayed by individuals who are treated by rehabilitation specialists

■ Understand the importance of adaptive behavior within the World Health Organization's International Classification of Functioning, Disability, and Health model and guidelines

INTRODUCTION

Adaptive behavior generally refers to personal qualities associated with the ways in which individuals meet their daily personal needs as well as deal with the natural and social demands in their environment (Nihira, Leland, & Lambert, 1993). Adaptive behavior is related to age as well as self-expectations and the expectations of others, is malleable, and is defined by a person's typical performance.

Adaptive behavior includes a constellation of skills that are important in everyone's daily lives. Skills include those needed to care for one's personal health and safety needs, dress and bathe, clean one's home, communicate, display suitable social and academic skills, function effectively in one's community, and engage in leisure and work. For most people, these skills begin to develop early in life and remain important until death. Their importance is underscored by the belief of early Greek scholars who thought that a person's adaptive behaviors and skills reliably reflected intelligence and maturity (Clarke, Clarke, & Berg, 1985). Persons displaying adaptive behaviors similar to others in the community were thought to have normal intelligence. Those displaying lower adaptive behaviors were thought to be of lower intelligence.

Grossman (1973) was among the first modern scholars to provide a viable definition of adaptive behavior. He described it as "the effectiveness and degree to which the individual meets the standard of personal independence and social responsibility expected for his and her cultural group" (p. 11). Grossman (1983) later suggested that adaptive behavior is what an individual does to take care of him or herself and to relate to others when engaged in daily living.

IMPORTANCE OF ADAPTIVE BEHAVIOR TO REHABILITATION AND HEALTH

The assessment of adaptive behavior and skills is useful for diagnosis, classification, planning, and treatment evaluation (American Association on Mental Retardation, 2002). The use of information from measures of adaptive behavior has a long history when diagnosing clients with mental retardation and providing services for them. Thus, there is considerable value in using measures of adaptive behavior when working with clients who display mental

retardation. Policies and practices established by the American Association on Intellectual and Developmental Disabilities (AAIDD; formerly the American Association on Mental Retardation) and the American Psychiatric Association (APA) emphasize the importance of evaluating adaptive skills to aid in the diagnosis of mental retardation. Eligibility considerations for individuals with mental disabilities typically are based on the combined results from measures of intelligence and adaptive behavior. "Mental retardation is a disability characterized by significant limitations both in intellectual functioning and in adaptive behavior as expressed in conceptual, social, and practical adaptive skills. This disability originates before age 18" (American Association on Mental Retardation, 2002, p. 13).

Although the assessment of adaptive behavior and skills traditionally has been associated with mental retardation, there is increasing recognition that their assessment should be routine for individuals who display other difficulties and disorders that may interfere with daily functioning (Harrison, 1990; Reschly, 1990). For example, individuals with the following diagnoses may display problems in daily living: attention disorders, auditory and visual acuity impairments, autism spectrum disorders, behavioral and emotional disorders, brain injuries, dementia, developmental disorders, learning disabilities, psychotic disorders, stroke, and substance-related disorders.

Definitions of Adaptive Behavior

The AAIDD defines adaptive behavior as ". . . the collection of conceptual, social, and practical skills that have been learned by people in order to function in their everyday lives" (p. 73, American Association on Mental Retardation, 2002). Conceptual skills include receptive and expressive language, reading and writing, and self-direction (see Table 15.1). Social skills include responsibility, obeying rules and laws, naiveté, and competence in interpersonal interactions. Practical skills include personal and instrumental self-care activities such as toileting, taking medication, dressing, preparing meals, eating, using the telephone, managing money, and using transportation, as well as occupational skills and maintaining a safe environment (American Association on Mental Retardation, 2002).

Importantly, adaptive behavior and skills are influenced by age, environmental opportunities and expectations, and sociocultural background. Adaptive behaviors and skills generally improve between birth and the mid-20s, then plateau, and then decline during one's later years. For example, most children ages 4 to 6 are taught

TABLE 15.1 American Association on Intellectual and Developmental Disabilities' (2002) Ten Adaptive Skills and Three Domains

	Adaptive Skills
Communication	Speech, language, and listening skills needed for communication with other people, including vocabulary, responding to questions, and conversation skills
Community Use	Skills needed for functioning in the community, including use of community resources, shopping skills, and getting around in the community
Functional Academics	Basic reading, writing, mathematics, and other academic skills needed for daily, independent functioning, including telling time, measurement, as well as writing notes and letters
Home Living	Skills needed for basic care of a home or living setting, including cleaning, straightening, property maintenance and repairs, as well as food preparation and performing chores
Health and Safety	Skills needed for protection of health and to respond to illness and injury, including following safety rules, using medicines, and showing caution
Leisure	Skills needed for engaging in and planning leisure and recreational activities, including playing with others, engaging in recreation at home, and following rules in games
Self-Care	Skills needed for personal care including eating, dressing, bathing, toileting, grooming, and hygiene
Self-Direction	Skills needed for independence, responsibility, and self-control, including starting and completing tasks, keeping a schedule, following time limits, following directions, and making choices
Social	Skills needed to interact socially and get along with other people, including having friends, showing and recognizing emotions, assisting others, and using manners
Work	Skills needed for successful functioning and holding a part-time or full-time job in a work setting, including completing work tasks, working with supervisors, and following a work schedule
Motor Skills*	Basic fine and gross motor skills needed for locomotion, manipulation of the environment, and the development of more complex activities such as sports, including sitting, pulling up to a standing position, walking, fine motor control, and kicking
	Three Domains and Associated Skills
Conceptual	Includes communication, functional academics, self-direction, and health and safety skills
Practical	Includes social skills and leisure skills
Social	Includes self-care, home/school living, community use, health and safety, and work skills

* Although fine and gross motor development is not included as one of the ten skills identified by the American Association on Intellectual and Developmental Disabilities, it is included in some scales of adaptive behavior.

and then expected to place their dirty clothes in a clothesbasket, wipe up spills, and put things in their proper place. Later, they will be expected to continue to perform these tasks as well as to wash their clothes and perform household repairs. Persons at much older ages may be unable to perform tasks expected of younger persons.

Adaptive behavior also is influenced by environmental opportunities and individuals' expectations (Dykens et al., 1996). For example, although most children ages 4 to 6 can and do perform the household tasks described above, some children are not taught or expected to acquire and display these behaviors. Some are able, yet refuse to perform them. Others may not be able to perform these tasks due to physical or mental limitations.

The International Classification of Functioning, Disability, and Health model, discussed in the following paragraphs, underscores the importance of knowing if desired behaviors may not be present due to biological and individual conditions, as well as social situations, which may include others' expectations.

The display of adaptive behavior and skills also differs due to cultural differences. For example, in some cultures, parents may not encourage or even allow males to cook or clean, whereas in other cultures they may be expected to assume these duties at an early age. Additionally, some parents may not encourage or even allow girls to acquire an education or socialize with nonfamily members, while others strongly encourage these qualities.

Children raised in urban communities may have more access to community resources and media than those raised in rural areas.

An evaluation of one's adaptive behavior and skills should consider opportunities and expectations from one's sociocultural background. Social and cultural groups differ in promoting personal independence or interdependence, leading to possible differences in what persons are expected to do. Thus, an evaluation of adaptive behavior and skills should consider age, environmental opportunities, expectations, and sociocultural background.

Applicable International Classification of Functioning, Disability, and Health Aspects

The assessment of a client's adaptive behavior and skills is essential to the implementation of the World Health Organization's International Classification of Functioning, Disability and Health (ICF; World Health Organization [WHO], 2001). The ICF outlines a useful model that enables rehabilitation health care providers to classify health and disability. Specifically, the activities and the participation components address the execution of a task or action by an individual and involvement in a life situation (WHO, 2001).

The activities and participation framework includes many variables common to the assessment of adaptive behavior. The term *activities* refers to skills, tasks, or actions a client is able to perform. Examples for older children and adults include writing, talking, and calculating. The term *participation* (or *performance*) refers to activities that become integrated into one's life. Examples for adults include regularly exchanging written correspondence, conversing with family and friends, and balancing one's checkbook.

A client may have an activity *skill deficit* and thus a *performance deficit* or may have merely a performance deficit. For example, a client who does not have the capacity to feed himself displays a skills deficit and thus a performance deficit by not feeding himself regularly. In contrast, a client who has the capacity to feed himself and does not do so regularly is described as having only a performance deficit.

Activities and participation include the following nine domains (with examples of corresponding adaptive skills in parentheses): learning and applying knowledge (e.g., functional academics); general tasks and demands (e.g., work); communication (e.g., communication); mobility (e.g., fine and gross motor skills); self-care (e.g., self-care); domestic life (e.g., school and home living); interpersonal interactions and relationships (e.g., social skills); major life areas (e.g., health and safety,

leisure skills); and community, social, and civic life (e.g., community use).

The skills noted in parentheses are those identified by the American Association on Intellectual and Developmental Disabilities (American Association on Mental Retardation, 2002) and the Diagnostic and Statistical Manual of Mental Disorders (DSM-IV; American Psychiatric Association, 2000) as important components of adaptive behavior. There is considerable agreement among the World Health Organization, American Association on Intellectual and Developmental Disabilities, and the American Psychiatric Association as to the importance of these skills when assessing adaptive behavior. Therefore, the assessment of adaptive behavior is directly applicable to the utilization of the ICF and can assist in better understanding, describing, and classifying a client's functioning, disability, and health under this model.

Diagnoses in the medical sciences often suggest preferred intervention protocols. In contrast, diagnoses in the behavioral sciences rarely suggest preferred intervention protocols. A client's diagnosis in the behavioral sciences, although important, generally provides little information as to the client's needs for services, the specific nature of these services, levels of support, prognosis, length of services, receipt of disability benefits, school and work performance, and eventual social integration. Knowledge of a client's functional status in the hands of experienced professionals is likely to provide information that assists professionals in addressing these issues (Peterson, 2005). Knowledge of one's functional status better predicts health system use than knowledge of one's diagnosis. Thus, the ICF emphasizes the importance of acquiring information about a client's functional status through knowledge of the skills a client displays and the need for these skills in daily life. Measures of adaptive behavior provide this information.

When diagnosing disorders, the ICF can be used as a companion to the World Health Organization's *International Statistical Classification of Diseases and Related Health Problems* (10th ed.) (ICD-10; WHO, 1992). The ICD-10 provides a system for classifying and diagnosing health conditions, including diseases, disorders, and injuries based on etiology. In contrast to the ICD-10, the ICF emphasizes a client's full and accurate description, not diagnosis, based on medical and social models of disability through biological, individual, and social perspectives of health. Once deficits in adaptive behavior and skills have been identified and an individual has been found to be in need of rehabilitative services, the ICF aids in describing the disability in terms of an interaction between impairment, functioning, and the environment. Strength or weakness may be identified, including the adequacy of one's adaptive skills, in light of environmental needs. When a diagnosis is needed to obtain benefits, the ICD-10 may be used to classify a client's disability. The combined use of the ICF and ICD-10 provides for more comprehensive descriptions, program planning, and diagnostic related rehabilitative services than the use of either alone.

In employing the ICF and ICD-10, a search for possible conditions that impact activities and performance deficits is essential. An understanding of a client's health requires knowledge of the dynamic nature body functions, body structures, activities as well as participation, and environmental factors. Each influences the others. Thus, an understanding of a client's activities and performance requires knowledge of personal, social, and environmental conditions that may impact them.

For example, a client's communication skill deficits may be adversely influenced by his or her body functions (e.g., mental, sensory, and neuromusculoskeletal functions) and structures (e.g., nervous, cardiovascular, and metabolic systems). Additionally, his or her environment may not provide needed opportunities to acquire skills or may not support and reward their use. Thus, knowledge of a client's adaptive behavior and skills in conjunction with body functions, structures, and environment is important to diagnosis and is essential to the design, delivery, and monitoring of rehabilitation services intended to have an instrumental and functional impact on a client's life.

CURRENT ASSESSMENT METHODS IN ADAPTIVE BEHAVIOR

Widely used measures of adaptive behavior, such as those reviewed in this chapter, typically are normed on a representative sample of a country's population. Thus, clinicians can compare the scores from a client with others of the same age and gender on whom the test was normed. The measures also are standardized. That is, the directions specify the ways in which the test is to be administered and scored; suggestions for its interpretation also may be provided. Examples of professionals who may administer these scales include community service and outreach workers, counselors, educators, nurses, occupational therapists, physical therapists, psychologists, residential aides, speech/language pathologists, teachers, vocational trainers, and others who are properly educated and trained in their use.

Data from measures of adaptive behavior may be used for several purposes, including clinical assessment for individual evaluation, assisting in differential diagnosis, establishing eligibility for special services (e.g., early childhood, school, family, Medicaid, and Social Security support), informing program planning, monitoring change, and conducting research.

A major use of adaptive behavior measures is to aid in the diagnosis of individuals with mental retardation, developmental disabilities, or other disorders. Many adaptive behavior scales align with requirements specified by state and local agencies as well as federal legislation and policies that mandate the assessment of adaptive behavior when evaluating the education needs of students and determining eligibility for special services. Professionals may use the results of measures of adaptive behavior in conjunction with results from intelligence tests in order to qualify individuals for placement in special programs for those with mental retardation or developmental disabilities. Also, the data may provide evidence of coexisting or separate emotional or behavior disorders and aid in program planning for treatment and management for clients with any disabilities that interfere with daily independent functioning. Information from these measures can identify individuals' strengths and weaknesses, thus aiding professionals in developing, monitoring, and ameliorating individual and family service plans as well as education, program, transition, and rehabilitation plans for people with various disabilities. This information also can help in developing interventions for those entering prevocational training or vocational activities. This information may be especially helpful when determining the degree of support needed by the elderly, including their need for assisted living facilities.

General Issues Associated with the Use of Adaptive Behavior Scales

Almost all measures of adaptive behavior can be administered using an interview format. Some require an interview, whereas others do not. Clinicians who decide to use a measure that requires an interview also may want to engage in another broader interview, one typically called a clinical interview.

A clinical interview is an important and common form of evaluation that is additional to and complements the assessment (Sattler, 1998; Watkins, Campbell, Nieberding, & Hallmark, 1995). An interview commonly is a formally arranged conference between two or more persons, the interviewer (i.e., a professional) and one or more respondents (i.e., persons answering the questions). The interviewer's goal is to obtain critical information about a client from the respondent. Additionally, the interviewer also uses this opportunity to establish or build rapport and to convey the importance of working together to achieve common goals (see chapter 10 for a discussion of clinical interviews).

Some measures of adaptive behavior require the clinician also to use an interview to acquire needed test data. The clinician must acquire information on all items included on the measure. Most measures of adaptive behavior do not require an interview. For example, when using the *Adaptive Behavior Assessment System* (2nd ed., Harrison & Oakland, 2003a), an examiner may decide a respondent is able to complete the scale by reading the items without assistance from others. Under this arrangement, the examiner first informs the respondent why this information is important and how to complete the scale. The examiner answers any questions the respondent may have after reading the test's directions and later, before the respondent leaves the clinical setting, reviews the respondent's answers and acquires information about items that were not completed or were guessed. The decision to administer an adaptive behavior measure using an interview format or to have the respondent complete it independently should be made after considering the ability of the respondent to read and answer the items correctly. Issues pertaining to time also are important. Self-administered scales require only a portion of the time required by an interview format.

Using Rating Scales to Assess Adaptive Behavior

When using rating scales, respondents typically record their answers by circling numbers that represent how frequently a behavior is displayed when needed. For example, on the *Adaptive Behavior Assessment System* (2nd ed., Harrison & Oakland, 2003a), respondents rate behaviors by circling 0 if the person is not able to perform the behavior (i.e., has an activity or skill deficit); 1 if the person has the ability to perform the behavior but never or almost never does (i.e., has a performance deficit); 2 if the person performs the behavior sometimes when needed; or 3 if the person performs the behavior always or almost always when needed.

Rating Scale Advantages

Rating scales used to assess adaptive behavior and skills allow for a comprehensive yet quick assessment of a large number of important and naturally occurring behaviors. The scales provide information about what a client actually does and how often he or she does it when needed in home, school, community, and work settings.

By providing norms, the data for one client can be compared with his or her peers. The use of such scales facilitates the involvement of various respondents, thus providing an opportunity to acquire information from two or more respondents and therefore view adaptive skills from multiple perspectives (self, parents, supervisors, teachers) displayed in various environments (e.g., home, work, school). In brief, rating scales of adaptive behavior generally are considered to provide a reliable, valid, practical, and efficient method for assessing adaptive skills.

Limitations in Using Rating Scales

Rating scales that assist in assessing adaptive behavior and skills also have limitations. Ratings reflect the respondent's perceptions of behaviors and skills and his/her honesty in communicating these perceptions. For example, some persons do not have opportunities to observe all behaviors assessed by the scale. In addition, at times, persons who complete adaptive behavior scales intentionally provide invalid information. Some may underreport adaptive skills in an attempt to qualify a client for some benefit (e.g., Social Security or workman's compensation). Others may overreport scores in an attempt to characterize a client as being normal when, in fact, the client displays significant skill deficits. In addition, ratings for individual items reflect a summary of the relative frequency, not the exact frequency, a client displays each skill. Thus, rating scales do not allow us to know how many times a behavior is performed each day or week. In addition, ratings reflect respondent's standards for skills. Respondents may be influenced by their personal feelings about the client and not report behaviors accurately. These standards may differ from respondent to respondent and from setting to setting. Respondent's ratings also may be influenced by a response bias (e.g., a tendency to respond in a particular way to test items). Persons displaying a response bias tend to rate many or all items either too high or too low.

Clinician's Responsibilities When Using Adaptive Behavior Scales

When using adaptive behavior scales, professional personnel are responsible for ensuring the data are acquired from respondents who are reliable, know the client well, and complete the scale accurately. Thus, professional personnel select both the measure to be used and the respondents, coordinate the completion of questionnaire booklets by respondents, and score and interpret results. Professional personnel should be knowledgeable of basic principles of assessment and test interpretation, the strengths and limitations of tests, and the use of assessment in data-based

---

DISCUSSION BOX 15.1

In *Atkins v. Virginia*, 536 U.S. 304 (2002), the U.S. Supreme Court ruled that persons who are mentally retarded cannot be executed. A diagnosis of mental retardation typically requires evidence that a person younger than age 19 displays subaverage mental abilities and adaptive behavior.

Let's assume you have been asked by the court to conduct an evaluation of a 55-year-old death-row inmate to determine whether he is mentally retarded. The court reported there are no school or other records of the person's intelligence and adaptive behavior at age 18. Although his mother is deceased, he has two living siblings.

Discuss ways you would proceed to obtain information needed to offer your professional opinion as to the person's intelligence and adaptive behavior as of age 18. Identify the strengths and limitations of your methods.

---

decision-making. Although they may ask other service providers (e.g., paraprofessionals, aides) to assist in the administration and scoring of these measures, professional personnel ultimately are responsible for the test's use.

Selection of Respondents

The validity of data provided by adaptive behavior scales is highly dependent on the ability of the respondents to provide current and accurate information about the client's display of important adaptive skills. Respondents should have frequent and recent contacts with the client (e.g., almost daily). The contacts should be sufficiently long (e.g., several hours for each contact) so as to provide an understanding of the display of various skills.

When assessing preschool children, information should be obtained from parents and other primary careproviders who live with or have daily responsibility for the care of the preschool children and thus are familiar with their daily activities. When assessing school-aged children, information should be obtained from parents, teachers, and other persons who are familiar with the children's adaptive skills displayed in both structured (e.g., classrooms, mealtimes, at home) and less structured (e.g., lunchrooms, playing in the neighborhood) settings and are responsible for the children's daily care. When assessing adults, possible respondents include parents, other family members, guardians, care workers, job supervisors, and others familiar with the daily activities of the client. When assessing higher functioning adult clients, the respondent may be the client himself or herself.

Quantitative Methods

The more widely used norm-referenced measures of adaptive behavior and skills are described in the following discussion. Although this review is not exhaustive, it includes instruments that are comprehensive, commercially available, and provide extensive data concerning psychometric properties. The following measures are intended to assist in identifying strengths and weaknesses, diagnosing disorders, determining eligibility for special programs, developing individual education plans, as well as documenting and monitoring progress. Knowledge of each measure will assist practitioners in selecting the best test and thus providing relevant services to their clients.

A brief review of measurement concepts often used with measures of adaptive behavior may be helpful in understanding the information that follows. When scoring measures of adaptive behavior, one first must add the scores for all items (i.e., 0s, 1s, 2s, 3s) on one skill subtest (e.g., communication) to obtain a total raw score for that subtest. Raw scores for each subtest are converted to derived scores or age equivalent scores using norms tables. Age equivalent scores express a person's performance as being equivalent to the average performance for a particular age (Salvia & Ysseldyke, 2001). For example, an age equivalent score of 5 years, 7 months (5-07) indicates the person's score is similar to that received by the average person at age 5 years, 7 months.

Examples of derived scores include scores of relative standing such as percentile ranks (the percentage of people whose scores are at or below a given raw score) and standard scores (scores that have been transformed to produce a distribution with a predetermined mean and standard deviation; Salvia & Ysseldyke, 2001). Standard scores allow us to determine the relative standing of an individual's raw score compared to raw scores received by others of a similar age. For example, standard scores allow us to know if an individual's scores are above average, average, or below average. These scores allow us to compare the performances of different people, even when they differ in age or the test that was administered (see chapter 6 for additional details).

Knowledge of a test's *standardization sample*, often called the *norm group* or *normative sample*, also is important. These three terms typically are synonymous and refer to the group of individuals of known characteristics (e.g., age, gender) who were carefully selected to first take the test (Salvia & Ysseldyke, 2001). Their data become the standard against which the scores of later test-takers are compared.

Knowledge of the terms *reliability* and *validity* also is important (see chapter 7 for additional details on reliability and validity). *Reliability* refers to consistency. Test consumers typically are interested in three forms of consistency: the degree to which test items consistently measure the tested quality (i.e., a test's internal consistency), the degree to which two or more respondents are consistent when rating a person (inter-rater reliability), and the degree to which the test scores remain consistent over time (test–retest reliability).

The term *validity* refers to the extent to which accumulated evidence and theory support specific interpretations of test scores. Professionals may interpret data from measures of adaptive behavior in various ways. Each interpretation should be supported by evidence and theory. A test should measure a well-defined construct or trait (with evidence provided, in part, by factor analysis data), and scores on two or more tests that measure the same quality (e.g., communication skills) should be similar for the same person (i.e., concurrent validity, with evidence provided, in part, by correlation data).

American Association on Mental Retardation Adaptive Behavior Scale

The American Association on Mental Retardation Adaptive Behavior Scale 2nd ed. (ABS: 2; Lambert, Nihira, & Leland, 1993; Nihira, Leland, & Lambert, 1993) has two forms—the Residential and Community (ABS-RC: 2) and School (ABS-S: 2) forms (see Table 15.2). The Residential and Community form is designed for individuals from age 18 through 79. The Residential and Community form was standardized on 4,103 examinees with developmental disabilities who were representative of the national population of adults with mental retardation. Thus, this scale is intended to be used only with adults with developmental disabilities. The absence of norm data on the general adult population limits the scale's applicability (Carey & Harrison, 1998).

The School form is an abbreviated version of the Residential and Community form. It was normed on individuals ages 3 through 21, including 2,074 with mental retardation (ages 3 through 21) and 1,254 students without mental retardation (ages 3 through 18).

The sample was representative of demographic variables of the national population. The date the norms were acquired is not provided. Thus, the norms may need to be updated.

The School form measures two components of adaptive behavior: personal independence and social behavior. Part one, concerned with personal independence, comprises nine behavior domains and 18 subdomains: independent functioning (including eating, toilet use, cleanliness, appearance, care of clothing, dressing and undressing, travel, and other independent functioning); physical development (including sensory development and motor development); economic activity (including money handling and budgeting, and shopping skills); language development (including expression, verbal comprehension, and social language development); numbers and time; prevocational/vocational activity; self-direction (including initiative, perseverance, and leisure time); responsibility; and socialization. Part two, concerned with social behaviors, comprises seven domains: social behavior, conformity, trustworthiness, stereotyped and hyperactive behavior, self-abusive behavior, social engagement, and disturbing interpersonal behavior. The Residential and Community form adds domestic activity (cleaning, kitchen, and other domestic duties) and sexual behavior domains; they are not part of the school form (see Table 15.2).

Scores from both forms of the ABS: 2 are reported for domains as well as for specific areas. The specific areas for personal independence are personal self-sufficiency, community self-sufficiency, and personal–social responsibility. The specific areas for responsibility in daily living are social adjustment and personal adjustment.

The School as well as Residential and Community forms display high internal consistency, with correlations in the .90s. The test–retest and inter-rater reliabilities among professionals trained in assessment also are high, generally in the high .80s to .90s. The ABS: 2 demonstrates strong criterion– and construct validity.

A review of the scale noted that, at the time of publication in the early 1990s, the psychometric qualities were good and the ABS: 2 was one of the best available scales for assessing adaptive behavior of persons with mental retardation. Also, it was thought that the ABS: 2 made a contribution to the field because it was more comprehensive than other measures in that it assessed adaptive and maladaptive behaviors (Harrington & Stinnett, 1998).

TABLE 15.2 Descriptions of Current Assessment Methods in Adaptive Behavior

Title and Date of Publication/Development	Authors	Forms and Ages	Approximate Administration Time	Behavior Domains and Skills Measured
American Association on Mental Retardation Adaptive Behavior Scale – Second Edition (1993)	Nihira, K., Lambert, N., & Leland, H.	Residential and Community (3 years-79 years) & School (3 years-21 years)		**Domains:** Independent Functioning, Physical Development, Economic Activity, Language Development, Numbers and Time, Prevocational/Vocational Activity, Self-Direction, Responsibility, Socialization, Social Behavior, Conformity, Trustworthiness, Stereotyped and Hyperactive Behavior, Self-Abusive Behavior, Social Engagement, Disturbing Interpersonal Behavior. ABS-RC: 2 adds Domestic Activity and Sexual Behavior. **Skills:** Eating, Toilet Use, Cleanliness, Appearance, Care of Clothing, Dressing & Undressing, Travel, and Other Independent Functioning; Sensory Development and Motor Development; Money Handling & Budgeting and Shopping Skills; Expression, Verbal Comprehension, and Social Language Development; Initiative, Perseverance, and Leisure Time. ABS-RC: 2 adds Cleaning, Kitchen, and Domestic Duties
Adaptive Behavior Assessment System–Second Edition (2003)	Harrison, P. & Oakland, T.	Parent/Primary Caregiver Form (ages 0-5 years); Teacher/Day Care Provider Form (ages 2-5 years); Parent Form (ages 5-21 years); Teacher Form (ages 5-21 years); & Adult Form (ages 16-89)	15 minutes, plus 10 minutes to score	**Domains:** General Adaptive Composite, Conceptual, Social, Practical. **Skills:** Communication, Community Use, Functional Academics, Health & Safety, Leisure, Motor, Self-Care, Self-Direction, School/Home Living, and Social.

(continued)

TABLE 15.2 *(continued)*

Title and Date of Publication/ Development	Authors	Forms and Ages	Approximate Administration Time	Behavior Domains and Skills Measured
Scales of Independent Behavior–Revised (1999)	Bruininks, R., Woodcock, R., Weatherman, R., & Hill, B.	Full Scale (ages 3 months-80 years); Short Form (ages 3 months-80 years); & Early Development Form (Infancy to 6 years of age or to older individuals with developmental ages ≤ 8 years)	15–20 minutes for the Short and Early Development Forms	**Domains:** Motor; Social Interaction and Communication; Personal Living; Community Living; Broad Independence; Internalized Maladaptive Behavior; Asocial Maladaptive Behavior; Externalized Maladaptive Behavior; Problem Behaviors (General). **Skills:** Gross-Motor and Fine-Motor; Social Interaction, Language Comprehension, and Language Expression; Eating & Meal Preparation, Toileting, Dressing, Personal Self-Care, and Domestic Skills; Time & Punctuality, Money & Value, Work Skills, and Home/Community Orientation; Hurtful to Self, Unusual or Repetitive Habits, and Withdrawal or Inattentive Behavior; Socially Offensive & Uncooperative, Hurtful to Others, Destructive to Property, and Disruptive Behavior.
Vineland Adaptive Behavior Scales - Second Edition (2005)	Sparrow, S., Cicchetti, D., & Balla, D.	Survey Interview Form (birth-90 years); Expanded Interview Form (birth-90 years, recommended for younger ages or low functioning individuals); Parent/Caregiver Form; & Teacher Rating Form (3-21 years)		**Domains:** Adaptive Behavior Composite, Communication, Daily Living, Socialization, Motor, Maladaptive Behaviors. **Skills:** Receptive, Expressive, and Written Skills; Personal, Domestic, and Community skills; Interpersonal Relationships, Play & Leisure Time, and Coping Skills; Gross and Fine Motor; Internalizing and Externalizing Behaviors.

Adaptive Behavior Assessment System

The Adaptive Behavior Assessment System (2nd ed.; ABAS-II; Harrison & Oakland, 2003a) provides an assessment of adaptive behavior and skills for persons from birth through age 89. Five forms are provided: Parent/Primary Caregiver form (for ages 0–5); Teacher/Day Care Provider form (for ages 2–5); Parent form (for ages 5–21); Teacher form (for ages 5–21); and an Adult form (for ages 16–89) (see Table 15.2). Its standardization sample is representative of United States data from 1999–2000 in reference to gender, race/ethnicity, parental education, and proportion of individuals with disabilities (Harrison & Oakland, 2003b). Parent forms are available in Spanish, and all five forms are available in French–Canadian.

The ABAS-II is consistent with the model advocated by the American Association on Mental Retardation (2002). Scaled scores in 11 adaptive skill areas are summarized in Table 15.3, below. Ten skill area scores combine to produce standard scores in their respective domains: conceptual (communication, functional academics, and self-direction); social (social skills and leisure); and practical (self-care, home or school living, community use, health and safety, and work) (see Table 15.2). A general adaptive composite score is derived from all skill scores.

The ABAS-II demonstrates suitable psychometric qualities. Internal consistency is high, with reliability coefficients of .85 to .99 for the general adaptive composite, three adaptive behavior domains, and skill areas. Test–retest reliability coefficients are in the .80s and .90s for the general adaptive composite, three domains, and skill areas (Harrison & Oakland, 2003a). Inter-rater reliability coefficients (e.g., between teachers, daycare providers, and parents) range from the .60s to the .80s for the skill areas and are in the .90s for the general adaptive composite.

Its construct validity is strong as displayed through factor analyses. Its concurrent validity with the Vineland Adaptive Behavior Scales–Classroom Edition's Adaptive Behavior Composite is .82 (Harrison & Oakland, 2003b). Clinical validity also is highly evident.

A review of the ABAS-II noted several advantages over other measures (Meikamp & Suppa, 2005). The behavior domains align with the newest AAIDD recommendations. The scale allows for multiple respondents from multiple settings and an adult self-report. The ABAS-II allows one to guess about behaviors—and to be verified through other sources. The scale provides respondents the opportunity to answer each question without a trained interviewer present. In a separate review, Burns (2005) noted that the ABAS-II is based on sound theory and empirical methodology, the norm group is sufficiently representative and large, scores from the general adaptive composite are adequate for eligibility and entitlement decisions, while domain scores are useful for clinical and intervention utility.

Reviewers Rust and Wallace (2004) note that the items, manual, and record forms are easy to use. The ABAS-II sufficiently conforms to revised AAIDD domain guidelines and as such provides an important addition to the assessment of adaptive behavior. The ABAS-II strengthens the comprehensive assessment of adaptive behavior for mental retardation and is technically superior to its competitors (Burns, 2005). Thus, the ABAS-II is viewed as being technically sound and valuable when providing a complete assessment of an individual's adaptive functioning pursuant to planning for effective rehabilitation and other services.

Scales of Independent Behavior

The Scales of Independent Behavior (Rev. ed.; SIB-R; Bruininks, Woodcock, Weatherman, & Hill, 1996) offers three forms: a short form, an early development form, and the full scale form. The short form is used as a screener for all ages. It contains items from the 14 subscales that comprise the full scale form. The early development form is to be used with children from infancy to age 6, or with older individuals with severe disabilities that place their functioning at developmental levels below age 8 (see Table 15.2).

The SIB-R was normed on 2,182 individuals ages 3 months through 80 (see Table 15.2). The norm group reflects the demographic characteristics of the United States in the 1990 census in reference to gender, race/ethnicity, occupational status and level, geographic regions, and type of community. Many individuals also were administered Woodcock–Johnson Tests of Cognitive Ability to obtain a concurrent measure of intellectual functioning.

The SIB-R measures adaptive behavior in four broad categories that include 14 different skill areas: motor skills (including gross-motor skills and fine-motor skills); social interaction and communication skills (including social interaction, language comprehension, and language expression); personal living skills (including eating and meal preparation, toileting, dressing, personal self-care, and domestic skills); and community living skills (including time and punctuality, money and value, work skills, and home/community orientation).

A broad independence score is derived from scores in these areas (see Table 15.2).

A problem behavior scale also is provided. This form assesses problem behavior in three domains and eight problem areas: internalized maladaptive behavior (including hurtful to self, unusual or repetitive habits, and withdrawal or inattentive behavior); asocial maladaptive behavior (including socially offensive and uncooperative behaviors); and externalized maladaptive behavior (including hurtful to others, destructive to property, and disruptive behavior). A general problem behaviors score is derived from scores in these areas.

The SIB-R demonstrates high internal consistency, with most correlations in the high .80s and .90s. Inter-rater reliability also is high, generally in the .80s and .90s. Test-retest reliability is high (above .95) for most forms. However, coefficients for the maladaptive behavior scale are lower and generally range from .74 to .92. The reliability coefficients of the short form and early development form also are low (Maccow & Zlomke, 2001).

The SIB-R demonstrates acceptable concurrent validity through high correlations (mostly in the .90s) with the original version of the Scales of Independent Behavior. Also, correlations between the SIB-R early development form and the early screening self-help and social profiles (from the Vineland Adaptive Behavior Scales) range from .77 to .90. Thus, there is evidence of validity in the measurement of adaptive behavior using the SIB-R.

A critical review of the scale noted various positive features. The SIB-R is easy to administer and score. The SIB-R provides information about problem behaviors that may interfere with independent functioning (Maccow & Zlomke, 2001). In addition, training objectives are provided at the end of each subscale to determine which of an individual's skills need the most improvement. This may help professionals determine the curriculum area or performance level to which an individual should be assigned upon entering programs to promote homeliving or vocational skills.

Vineland Adaptive Behavior Scales

The Vineland Adaptive Behavior Scales (2nd ed.; VABS-II; Sparrow, Cicchetti, & Balla, 2005) is the second edition of a popular norm-referenced assessment of adaptive behavior. The VABS-II has four forms: a survey interview form (for birth through age 90); expanded interview form (for birth through age 90, recommended for younger ages or low functioning individuals); parent/caregiver form (age ranges not provided); and

teacher rating form (for ages 3 through 21) (see Table 15.2). The survey and expanded interview forms are administered by a professional using a semistructured interview format. The parent/caregiver form uses a checklist procedure to assess the same content as the survey interview form and may be used when an interview is not possible or for progress monitoring purposes. The teacher rating form may be completed independently by a respondent.

The VABS-II was normed on 3,695 individuals from birth through age 90 (see Table 15.2). Its standardization is based on a nationally representative norm group consistent with the U.S. population in 2001, including age, sex, race/ethnicity, socioeconomic status, geographic region, and educational placement.

The VABS-II provides scores at different levels. The adaptive behavior composite score is derived from scores on four domains: communication (including receptive, expressive, and written skills); daily living skills (including personal, domestic, and community); socialization (including interpersonal relationships, play and leisure time, and coping skills); and motor skills (including gross and fine motor). The VABS-II also provides a measure of maladaptive behaviors, including internalizing and externalizing behaviors (see Table 15.2).

The VABS-II has suitable reliability. Internal consistency is high, generally ranging from .84 to .97 for the adaptive behavior composite, domains, and subdomains. Test–retest reliability generally is in the .80s to .90s. Inter-interviewer and inter-rater reliability also are high, generally in the .70s and above. Concurrent and construct validity are evident. Correlations between the domain and adaptive behavior composite scores from the first edition and second edition of the VABS are in the .80 to .95 range. Factor analytic data provide additional support for the validity of the VABS-II.

RESEARCH CRITICAL TO ISSUES IN ADAPTIVE BEHAVIOR ASSESSMENT

Much of the research on adaptive behavior has been conducted using two scales: the Adaptive Behavior Assessment System (2nd ed.) and the Vineland Adaptive Behavior Scales (2nd ed.). The findings of research using the standardization samples of these two scales are summarized in Table 15.3 and are discussed in the following section.

The Adaptive Behavior Assessment System (2nd ed.) shows sensitivity between clinical and nonclinical

Case Study

Lewis, a 46-month-old male, lives with his mother, stepfather, 14-year old sister, and a 65-year old maternal grandmother. His father is employed in the construction industry and his mother remains at home, largely to care for Lewis.

As an infant, Lewis displayed delayed oral and sensory motor development following a normal pregnancy and birth. He currently displays no serious injuries, illnesses, allergies, or acuity deficiencies. His diet is restricted to foods he willingly eats. He smells his food prior to eating and eats with his hands.

Lewis displays no fears and minimal awareness of danger. He tantrums, bangs his head, twirls, and kicks when reprimanded. His mother is very concerned about her inability to control his behaviors. Professionals have not advised her about methods commonly used with children who display these behaviors.

Lewis does not interact with family members and has no neighborhood friends. He goes to bed at 8 p.m. and sleeps through the night. He takes Zoloft 100 mg twice daily to improve his concentration and attention.

Lewis began attending school daily from 9 a.m. to 3 p.m. about 6 months ago. He is in a class with children who display similar behaviors and who either are diagnosed as having a developmental delay or autism. His teacher's use of applied behavioral management principles at school has lead to an improvement in his school-related behaviors.

Lewis was referred for an evaluation. His cognitive development, as measured by the Bayley Scales of Infant and Toddler Development-III, is at the 1st percentile, with a standard score of less than 50. His language skills, as measured by the Clinical Evaluation of Language Fundamentals Preschool (2nd ed.), are similar to children between 16 and 20 months (i.e., less than half his chronological age), with standard scores of 38 for receptive language, 47 for expressive language, and 43 for total language. Lewis' autism was confirmed, in part, through the results of the Gilliam Autism Rating Scale (2nd ed.).

Lewis' mother and teacher completed the Adaptive Behavior Assessment System-II (ABAS-II). Lewis' general adaptive behavior at both home and school is at the 1st percentile. Many of Lewis' adaptive skills do not differ significantly at home and school (i.e., home/school living, health and safety, self-care, self-direction, social, and motor). His functional academic skills constitute his highest skills, a pattern commonly found in children with autism.

His adaptive skills show some signs of being slightly better developed at school than at home. His teacher attributes this to the positive impact applied behavior management principles seemingly are having on his development there.

Parent	Teacher	Skill Areas
1	4	Communication
1	-	Community Use
7	10	Functional Academics
1	2	Home/School Living
1	3	Health and Safety
1	4	Leisure
1	3	Self Care
3	3	Self Direction
2	1	Social
6	7	Motor
57	72	Conceptual Domain
50	55	Social Domain
43	56	Practical Domain
49	61	General Adaptive Composite

After the mother observed Lewis' classroom, a parent–teacher conference was held to discuss these findings and their implications. The mother was impressed with the effectiveness of applied behavior management principles at school and requested training and supervision for their use at home. The school's curriculum seemingly is having a desired impact on Lewis' beginning functional academic skills and will be maintained.

A review of ABAS-II data underscored the need to develop a joint school–home program designed to promote his communication, social, and health and safety skills. The presence of communication and social skill deficits is common in children with autism. Given the critical importance to health and safety skills, efforts to develop them always are warranted when they are low. The teacher and parent agreed to meet the following week with specialists in curriculum and special education to help design and implement these programs. They also agreed that the ABAS-II should be used again in 6 months to help evaluate changes in these three desired skills.

groups as well as different profiles displayed with children, adolescents, and adults who have been diagnosed with various disabilities, including mental retardation, developmental delays, autism, physical impairments, attention deficit/hyperactivity disorder, emotional/behavioral disorders, learning disabilities, and deaf or hard of hearing (see Table 15.3; Harrison & Oakland, 2003a).

The mean General Adaptive Composite for individuals with mental retardation generally is two or more standard deviations below the population mean. Thus, their general ability to independently display important adaptive skills is diminished. Persons with mental retardation tend to display the greatest deficits in the conceptual domain (i.e., communication, functional academics, self-direction). Low scores also were evident in the social and practical domains.

Children with developmental delays generally displayed mean general adaptive composite scores that were one or more standard deviations below the mean (see Table 15.3). Mean conceptual, practical, and social domain scores also were low. Thus, children with developmental delays generally express difficulty with many daily living tasks when compared to peers. However, the children with developmental delays did not show significant deficits in all adaptive skills. These children may display patterns of strength and weakness in different skill areas depending on their individual development and personal profiles.

Children with autism displayed general adaptive composite scores that were two or more standard deviations below the mean (see Table 15.3). Large deficits were displayed in communication and social skills as well as in health and safety.

Children with motor and physical impairments usually displayed deficits in their general adaptive behavior. Their fine and gross motor skill development was significantly delayed as seen in low scores on motor skills. Deficits in motor skills may contribute to lower practical adaptive domain scores, including self-care skills. Thus, individuals with motor and physical impairments may display deficiencies in other skill areas that require dexterity, strength, or physical mobility.

Children with an attention deficit/hyperactivity disorder (ADHD) displayed deficits in adaptive skills (see Table 15.3). The greatest deficits were found in the self direction skill area, confirming that they often have difficulty with self-motivation and self-direction, including starting and completing tasks. These behaviors are especially problematic in an educational setting where older individuals are required to be organized and thorough as well as responsible for their own work. Ratings from parents and teachers often differ for children with ADHD. In contrast to their adaptive skills displayed in their homes, these children generally display more ADHD-type behaviors in structured classroom settings in which attention to precise academic tasks, rule-governed behaviors, and self control are required. Thus, ratings on adaptive behavior and skills of children with ADHD tend to be higher for parents than for teachers.

Children with behavioral disorders and emotional disturbance often display profiles that are similar to those displayed by children with ADHD. Their lowest performance tends to be in self-direction. Social skill deficiencies also were evident, confirming that individuals with behavioral and emotional disturbances generally display problems when interacting with others.

Children with learning disabilities generally obtained below average general adaptive composite scores (see Table 15.3). They tend to perform most poorly on the communication, functional academics, and self-direction skill areas. Thus, although their academic problems may be most apparent, they also display deficiencies in other adaptive skill areas.

Individuals who are deaf or hard of hearing did not display deficits in general adaptive composite scores (see Table 15.3). As expected, their communication skills displayed the largest deficit.

The Vineland Adaptive Behavior Scales (2nd ed.) also distinguishes clinical from nonclinical groups, including those with mental retardation, autism spectrum disorder, learning disability, emotional/behavioral disturbance, attention deficit/hyperactivity disorder, visual impairment, and hearing impairment (VABS-II; Sparrow, Cicchetti, & Balla, 2005).

Individuals with mental retardation displayed significant deficits in the adaptive behavior composite as well as the four behavior domains: communication, daily living skills, socialization, and motor skills (see Table 15.3).

Individuals with autism displayed an adaptive behavior composite that is two or more standard deviations below the mean (see Table 15.3). Deficiencies also were evident in the socialization domain, as well as the expressiveness, interpersonal relationships, and play and leisure time subdomains. Adaptive behavior deficits in socialization and language expression can be expected for persons with this disorder.

Those diagnosed with attention deficit/hyperactivity disorder (ADHD) showed deficits in the communication and socialization domains. Individuals with ADHD also displayed elevated maladaptive behavior index scores.

TABLE 15.3 Research with Clinical Samples

Adaptive Behavior Composites, Domains, and Skill Areas Scores that Fall Greater than Two Standard Deviations Below the Mean for each Disability (Harrison and Oakland, 2003a; Sparrow et al., 2005)*

Disability	ABAS-II	VABS-II
Mild Mental Retardation	GAC**; Social, Practical, and Conceptual domains; Communication, Functional Academics, School/Home Living, Health & Safety, Leisure, Self-Care, Social Skills	ABC***, Communication, Daily Living Skills, Socialization, Written, Community, Play & Leisure Time
Moderate MR		ABC***, Communication, Daily Living Skills, Socialization, Receptive, Expressive, Written, Personal, Community, Interpersonal Relationships, Play & Leisure Time
Severe MR		ABC***, Communication, Daily Living Skills, Socialization, Receptive, Expressive, Written, Personal, Domestic, Community, Interpersonal Relationships, Play & Leisure Time, Coping Skills
Dev. Delay	Communication	
Motor Impairments	School/Home Living, Health & Safety, Self-Care, Motor Skills	
Physical Impairments	GAC**; Practical, Conceptual domains; Communication, Community Use, Functional Academics, School/Home Living, Health & Safety, Leisure, Self-Care, Self Direction, Social Skills	
Pervasive Developmental Disorder	GAC**; Practical and Communication domains; Community Use, School/Home Living, Health & Safety, Leisure, Self-Care, Self Direction, Social Skills, Motor Skills	
Autism	GAC**; Social, Practical, and Conceptual domains; Communication, Community Use, Functional Academics, School/Home Living, Health & Safety, Leisure, Self-Care, Self Direction, Social Skills (ages 5-18 years)	Autism Verbal: ABC***, Communication, Daily Living Skills, Socialization, Expressive, Personal, Community, Interpersonal Relationships, Play & Leisure Time, Autism; Nonverbal: same as above plus Motor Skills, Receptive, Written, Domestic, Coping Skills, Fine Motor Skills
ADHD	Communication, Community Use, Functional Academics, School/Home Living, Health & Safety, Leisure, Self-Care, Self Direction, Social Skills (ages 5-9 years)	
Behavior Disorders	Communication, Community Use, Functional Academics, School/Home Living, Health & Safety, Leisure, Self-Care, Self Direction, Social Skills	
Emotional Disorders	Communication, Community Use, Functional Academics, School/Home Living, Health & Safety, Leisure, Self-Care, Self Direction, Social Skills	
Learning Disabilities	Communication, Community Use, Functional Academics, and Self-Direction	

*From the standardization samples of the Adaptive Behavior Assessment System-Second Edition (ABAS-II; Harrison and Oakland, 2003a) and the Vineland Adaptive Behavior Scales-Second Edition (VABS-II; Sparrow et al., 2005).

**GAC = General Adaptive Composite

***ABC = Adaptive Behavior Composite

DISCUSSION BOX 15.2

The assessment of adaptive behavior traditionally has been used to diagnose mental retardation. However, there is increasing recognition that individuals diagnosed with various disabilities may display adaptive behavior deficits (Harrison, 1990; Reschly, 1990). Individuals with attention disorders, autism spectrum disorders, behavioral and emotional disorders, brain injuries, dementia, developmental disorders, hearing and visual impairments, learning disabilities, psychotic disorders, stroke, and substance-related disorders may display problems in adaptive functioning. Thus, adaptive behavior assessment may become routine for individuals who display difficulties beyond those associated with mental retardation.

Questions

1. How can the assessment of adaptive behavior and skills be useful in planning treatments and rehabilitation for individuals with disabilities other than mental retardation?
2. Why is the assessment of adaptive behavior helpful for evaluating treatments and programming decisions?
3. Under what conditions, if any, can adaptive behavior scales developed for use in Western cultures be used with recent immigrants from non-Western cultures?

Individuals with emotional/behavioral disturbances exhibited adaptive behavior composites that averaged one standard deviation below the population mean. They displayed significantly lower scores in the socialization domain, receptive and written subdomains, and daily living skills, as well as elevated internalizing and externalizing behaviors.

Individuals with learning disabilities exhibited deficits in the communication domain and the written subdomain.

Individuals with visual impairment displayed a mean adaptive behavior composite that was one standard deviation below the mean of the nonclinical group. Deficiencies in the socialization domain and daily living skills also were evident. Individuals who are deaf or hard of hearing displayed below average behaviors in communication and daily living skills domains.

PROFESSIONAL ISSUES THAT IMPACT THE ASSESSMENT OF ADAPTIVE BEHAVIOR

The American Association on Intellectual and Developmental Disabilities (AAIDD) has assumed national leadership for defining the concept of adaptive behavior and its related skills. This leadership is consistent with the AAIDD's efforts to help ensure the suitable diagnosis of mental retardation and the provision of care for those with mental retardation.

AAIDD's first concept of adaptive behavior was broad and referred to an individuals' daily performance in coping with environmental demands through taking care of themselves and relating to others (Lambert, Nihira, & Leland, 1993). During the last two decades, the AAIDD

has revised and sharpened its concept of adaptive behavior, first to devote greater attention to 10 important adaptive skills (American Association on Mental Retardation, 1992) and more recently to reaffirm the importance of these 10 skills in light of three domains (see Table 15.1; American Association on Mental Retardation, 2002).

The importance of adaptive skills, not merely adaptive behavior, is found in AAIDD's 1992 definition of mental retardation. "Mental retardation refers to substantial limitations in present functioning. It is characterized by significantly subaverage intellectual functioning, existing concurrently with related limitations in two or more of the following applicable adaptive skill areas: communication, self-care, home living, social skills, community use, self-direction, health and safety, functional academics, leisure, and work. Mental retardation manifests before age 18" (American Association on Mental Retardation, 1992, p. 5).

The AAIDD (1992, p. 15) cited two reasons for movement away from the broader concept of adaptive behavior to one that emphasizes the more narrow adaptive skills: Evaluation of adaptive skills confirms that a person has functional limitations and, more importantly, identification of functional adaptive skill limitations can be linked to a person's needs for interventions and other services. The AAIDD's recognition of the importance of a person's needs for interventions and other services is reflected in the deletion of the four levels of severity of mental retardation (i.e., mild, moderate, severe, and profound) from its prior definition of mental retardation. Instead, the 1992 American Association on Mental Retardation manual identifies four intensities of supports individuals with mental retardation may need: intermittent, limited, extensive, and pervasive.

Professional Standards from the American Psychiatric Association's *Diagnostic and Statistical Manual of Mental Disorders*

The Diagnostic and Statistical Manual of Mental Disorders (4th ed.), Text Revision (DSM-IV) also emphasizes the importance of adaptive behavior in its definition of mental retardation: "A. Significantly subaverage general intellectual functioning. . . [along with] B. Concurrent deficits or impairments in present adaptive functioning (i.e., the person's effectiveness in meeting the standards expected for his or her age by his or her cultural group) in at least two of the following skill areas: communication, self-care, home living, social/interpersonal skills, use of community resources, self-direction, functional academics, work, leisure, health and safety. C. The onset is before age 18 years" (American Psychiatric Association, 2000, p.39). Thus, this definition reflects the essential features of AAIDD's 1992 definition of mental retardation.

The DSM-IV also acknowledges the importance of adaptive behavior in its description of learning disorders. For example, reading, mathematics, or written language disorders may be diagnosed when one or more of these disorders significantly interferes with academic achievement or activities of daily living that require reading, mathematics, or writing skills (American Psychiatric Association, 2000, p. 49).

NATIONAL/STATE PRACTICES IN ADAPTIVE BEHAVIOR ASSESSMENT

Special education legislation, including the 1975 Education for All Handicapped Children Act (Ninety-fourth Congress of the United States, 1975) and later the 1991 Individuals with Disabilities Education Act (IDEA) and its 1997 (U.S. Department of Education, 1999) and 2006 (U.S. Department of Education, 2006) amendments emphasize the importance of adaptive behavior when assessing developmental delays in young children and mental retardation in school age children. According to IDEA, "Mental retardation means significantly subaverage general intellectual functioning, existing concurrently with deficits in adaptive behavior and manifested during the developmental period, that adversely affects a child's educational performance" (U.S. Department of Education, 1999, p. 12422). The 2004 Individuals with Disabilities Education Improvement Act (IDEIA; One-hundred eighth Congress of the United States, 2004) and other legislation, policies, and programs such as Medicaid, Social Security, and Supplemental Security income also require the assessment of adaptive behavior.

IDEIA calls for early intervention services to address the learning and behavioral needs of young children in order to reduce their later need for services. The adaptive behavior and skills of young children ages 3 through 6 should be screened routinely to identify those who need a more comprehensive evaluation. Following this universal screening, interventions can be implemented that promote adaptive skills. Examples include social skills for young children with emotional or behavioral disorders or communication and social skills for children with autism. Under IDEIA, students who no longer are eligible for special education services because of their graduation or age limits must receive a summary of their academic achievement and functional performance, including recommendations on how to meet postsecondary goals. An assessment of adaptive behavior and skills is likely to provide useful information about a student's daily living skills, including his or her strengths and limitations to function independently, and thus aid in developing postsecondary school interventions.

Further, Section 504 of the Rehabilitation Act of 1973 (United States Code Service, 2006) prohibits discrimination against individuals, including students, by schools receiving federal funding. Students ages 3 through 21 with disabilities have a right to suitable educational aids and opportunities, comparable to peers who are nondisabled. Examples of disabilities covered under Section 504 include asthma, allergies, attention deficit/hyperactivity disorder, Tourette's Syndrome, cancer, diabetes, Human Immunodeficiency Virus/Acquired Immunodeficiency Syndrome (HIV/AIDS), tuberculosis, epilepsy, and heart disease (Wright & Wright, 2006). Students who are covered by Section 504 must have a physical or mental impairment that substantially limits one or more major life activities (Matthews Media, LLC, 2005). Major life activities are basic activities that an average person in the general population can perform with little or no difficulty. Examples include working, speaking, and caring for one's self. Measures of adaptive behavior are useful for gathering data from a variety of sources regarding major life activities for use by committees responsible for making decisions regarding physical, organizational, instructional, evaluation, or behavioral accommodations.

Qualification for services under other federal programs (e.g., Supplemental Security Income, Medicaid, and Social Security) may be based on a combination of functional (e.g., adaptive skills) assessment as well as state and local administration plans. Eligibility decisions for Medicaid and Social Security often consider information from adaptive skills assessments, especially information that identifies daily functional limitations. Those applying for Medicaid services may be required to provide a copy of

RESEARCH BOX 15.1

Background: Information on adaptive behavior increasingly is being used for comprehensive assessment, treatment planning, intervention, and program evaluation for individuals with various disorders. This section discusses research of the adaptive behavior profiles of children eligible for special education services due to diagnoses of specific learning disability, emotional disturbance, specific learning disability in combination with emotional disturbance, and autism disorders (Ditterline, Banner, Oakland, & Becton, 2008).

Objective: Determine strengths and weaknesses in the adaptive behavior and skills of children eligible for special education services due to different diagnoses.

Method: Data were obtained from 98 students, ages 4 through 14, who attend 4 elementary schools in a large southeastern suburban school district. The students met eligibility criteria for special education services based on the following disorders: specific learning disability, emotional disturbance, coexisting specific learning disability and emotional disturbance, and autism disorders. Data from the Teacher/Day Care Provider (ages 2–5) and Teacher (ages 5–21) forms of the Adaptive Behavior Assessment System (2nd ed.; Harrison & Oakland, 2003a) assessed the adaptive behavior and related skills of students.

Results: Compared to students in the general population, students in the 4 disability groups demonstrated deficiencies in their adaptive behaviors and skills. Additionally, those with more severe disabilities (e.g., autism) or multiple diagnoses (e.g., specific learning disability in combination with severe emotional disorders) displayed lower adaptive behavior and skills.

Conclusion: Measures of adaptive behavior may be useful as screening instruments for students suspected of displaying various disabilities. Further, the use of data from adaptive behavior scales may promote understanding of individuals with different disabilities and improve intervention planning.

Questions

1. What do results imply regarding the importance of adaptive behavior assessment?
2. In clinical assessment and intervention, how are data from adaptive behavior measures useful for informing treatment planning and evaluation?
3. Describe possible research designs that may be used to examine the stability of the adaptive behavior and skills of children with different disabilities who do and do not receive behavioral interventions.
4. Describe other research methods that may help identify the impact of disabilities on other family members.

their adaptive behavior evaluation. Diagnoses such as developmental delay and mental retardation cannot be based solely on a medical evaluation and must be demonstrated through the use of standardized scales of adaptive behavior and skills so as to highlight functional limitations. For example, to qualify for Supplemental Security Income, individuals with physical impairments or mental disorders must demonstrate severe functional limitations for at least 12 months. Limitations may exist in areas such as interacting with others, caring for oneself, and maintaining one's physical well-being. Adaptive behavior measures that directly evaluate areas such as social skills, self-care, and health and safety may be integral to establishing stable functional limitations and thus eligibility for services.

Summary and Conclusion

Adaptive behavior refers to personal qualities associated with the abilities and skills used to meet personal needs and social demands in daily living activities. Information from the assessment of adaptive behavior has a long history when diagnosing and providing services for clients with mental retardation. The American Association on Intellectual and Developmental Disabilities and the American Psychiatric Association recognize that mental retardation is characterized by significant limitations in intellectual functioning and adaptive behavior.

The assessment of adaptive behavior is becoming increasingly important for the diagnosis, classification, planning, treatment, and evaluation of individuals with various disabilities. Adaptive skills may be routinely assessed for any individuals who have difficulties that interfere with daily functioning. Specifically, individuals with attention disorders, autism spectrum disorders, brain injuries, behavior disorders, developmental disabilities, dementia, including Alzheimer's type, motor impairments, learning disabilities, psychotic disorders, sensory impairments, stroke, or substance-related disorders may experience deficits in daily living skills. The assessment of adaptive behavior provides important information useful for diagnosis, functional assessment, and treatment planning and evaluation for these and other individuals.

The World Health Organization's International Classification of Functioning, Disability, and Health (ICF) provides a framework that rehabilitation specialists may find useful for gathering information about clients' functional status. Measures of adaptive behavior help provide this information. The activities and participation portions of the ICF emphasize the acquisition of knowledge about the skills clients use in daily life, allowing professionals to provide a more comprehensive description of clients' situations.

Moreover, qualification for services under federal programs and statutes often requires information from measures of adaptive behavior. The Individuals with Disabilities Education Improvement Act, Supplemental Security Income, Medicaid, and Social Security programs often consider information from adaptive skills assessments. This information may be required to establish

stable daily functional limitations, information often necessary for the receipt of services. Thus, information from adaptive behavior assessments aids professionals in developing, monitoring, and ameliorating individual and family service, education, program, transition, and rehabilitation plans for people with various disabilities. The information is helpful in the creation of programs for those entering prevocational training or vocational activities. These data also are useful in the evaluation of the needs of the elderly for assisted living and other forms of support.

Professionals can choose from several reliable and valid norm referenced measures of adaptive behavior. Four scales were reviewed in this chapter. This information is intended to help professionals select one or more measures that best meet their needs. Rehabilitation specialists and others may discover that measures of adaptive behavior are valuable because results provide data useful for clinical assessment for individual evaluation, assisting in differential diagnosis, establishing eligibility for special services, informing program planning, and identifying changes over time in the skills used by individuals to effectively function in their daily lives.

Self-Check Questions

1. A client with traumatic brain injury (TBI) seeks rehabilitative health services. How can the daily living activities of this client, including the conceptual, practical, and social skills that comprise adaptive behavior, be impacted by TBI?

2. As a rehabilitative specialist, you advise a client on returning to work as well as eligibility for Supplemental Security

Income, Medicaid, and Social Security disability benefits. How can an assessment of adaptive behavior inform this consultation?

3. Consider the rehabilitation needs of individuals with stroke and mental illness. List differences in adaptive skill deficits they may experience, and describe the use of adaptive behavior assessments to plan interventions in these cases.

References

American Association on Mental Retardation. (1992). *Definitions, classifications, and systems of supports* (9th ed.). Washington, DC: Author.

American Association on Mental Retardation. (2002). *Mental retardation: Definition, classification, and systems of support* (10th ed.). Washington, DC: Author.

American Association on Mental Retardation. (2005). Retrieved April 14, 2006, from http://www.aamr.org/Policies/faq_mental_retardation.shtml.

American Psychiatric Association. (1994). *Diagnostic and statistical manual of mental disorders* (4th ed.). Washington, DC: Author.

American Psychiatric Association. (2000). *Diagnostic and statistical manual of mental disorders* (4th ed., text revision). Washington, DC: Author.

Bruininks, R., Woodcock, R., Weatherman, R., & Hill, B. (1999). *Scales of Independent Behavior* (Rev. ed.). Chicago: Riverside Publishing.

Burns, M. K. (2005). Review of the Adaptive Behavior Assessment System – Second Edition. In R. Spies & B. Plake (Eds.), *The sixteenth mental measurements yearbook*. Lincoln, NE: Buros Institute of Mental Measurements.

Carey, K. & Harrison, P. (1998). Review of the Adaptive Behavior Scale – Residential and Community, 2nd Ed. In J. Impara &

B. Plake (Eds.), *The thirteenth mental measurements yearbook.* Lincoln, NE: Buros Institute of Mental Measurements.

Clarke, A. M., Clarke, A. D. B., & Berg, J. M. (1985). *Mental deficiency: The changing outlook.* New York: Free Press.

Ditterline, J., Banner, D., Oakland, T., & Becton, D. (2008). Adaptive behavior profiles of students with disabilities. *Journal of Applied School Psychology, 24,* 191–208.

Dykens, E., Ort, S., Cohen, I., Finucane, B., Spiridigliozzi, G., Lachiewicz, A., Reiss, A., Freund, L., Hagerman, R., & O'Conner, R. (1996). Trajectories and profiles of adaptive behavior in males with Fragile X Syndrome: Multicenter studies. *Journal of Autism and Developmental Disorders, 26*(3), 287–301.

Grossman, H. J. (Ed.). (1973). *A manual on terminology and classification in mental retardation* (Rev. ed.). Washington, DC: American Association on Mental Deficiency.

Grossman, H. J. (Ed.). (1983). *Classification in mental retardation* (Rev. ed.). Washington, DC: American Association on Mental Deficiency.

Harrington, R. & Stinnett, T. (1998). Review of the Adaptive Behavior Scale—School, (2nd ed.). In J. Impara & B. Plake (Eds.), *The thirteenth mental measurements yearbook.* Lincoln, NE: Buros Institute of Mental Measurements.

Harrison, P. (1990). Mental retardation, adaptive behavior assessment, and giftedness. In A. S. Kaufman (Ed.), *Assessing adolescent and adult intelligence* (pp. 533–585). Boston: Allyn and Bacon.

Harrison, P. & Oakland, T. (2003a). *Adaptive Behavior Assessment System* (2nd ed.). San Antonio, TX: Harcourt Assessment.

Harrison, P. & Oakland, T. (2003b). *Technical report: Adaptive Behavior Assessment System* (2nd ed.). San Antonio, TX: The Psychological Corporation.

Lambert, N., Nihira, K., & Leland, H. (1993). *AAMR Adaptive Behavior Scale—School* (2nd ed.). Austin, TX: PRO-ED.

Maccow, G. & Zlomke, L. (2001). Review of the Scales of Independent Behavior—Revised. In B. Plake & J. Impara (Eds.), *The fourteenth mental measurements yearbook.* Lincoln, NE: Buros Institute of Mental Measurements.

Matthews Media, LLC. (2005). Section 504 & the ADA articles & resources. Retrieved September 10, 2006, from http://www.reedmartin.com/section504articlesandresources.htm.

McConaughy, S. H. (2005). *Clinical interviews for children and adolescents.* New York: Guilford.

Meikamp, J., & Suppa, C. H. (2005). Review of the Adaptive Behavior Assessment System – Second Edition. In R. Spies & B. Plake (Eds.), *The sixteenth mental measurements yearbook.* Lincoln, NE: Buros Institute of Mental Measurements.

Nihira, K., Leland, H., & Lambert, N. (1993). *AAMR Adaptive Behavior Scale-Residential and Community* (2nd ed.). Austin, TX: PRO-ED.

Ninety-fourth Congress of the United States. (1975). Public laws 91-696, 93-650, 93-651 and the laws and concurrent resolutions enacted during the first session of the 94th congress of the United States of America 1975 and proclamations. United States Statutes at Large, 89(48). Washington, DC: U.S. Government Printing Office.

One-hundred eighth Congress of the United States. (2004). Public Law 108-446, Individuals with Disabilities Education Improvement Act of 2004. Washington, DC: U.S. Government Printing Office.

Peterson, D. (2005). International classification of functioning, disability, and health: An introduction for rehabilitation psychologists. *Rehabilitation Psychology, 50*(2), 105–112.

Reschly, D. J. (1990). Best practices in adaptive behavior. In A. Thomas & J. Grimes (Eds.), *Best practices in school psychology* (2nd ed.) (pp.29–42). Washington, DC: National Association of School Psychologists.

Rust, J. O. & Wallace, M. A. (2004). Test review: Adaptive Behavior Assessment System. *Journal of Psychoeducational Assessment, 22,* 367–373.

Salvia, J. & Ysseldyke, J. (2001). *Assessment.* Boston: Houghton Mifflin.

Sattler, J. (1998). *Clinical and forensic interviewing of children and families: Guidelines for the mental health, education, pediatric, and child maltreatment fields.* San Diego, CA: Author.

Sparrow, S., Cicchetti, D., & Balla, D. (2005). *Vineland Adaptive Behavior Scales* (2nd ed.). Circle Pines, MN: AGS Publishing.

U.S. Department of Education. (March 12, 1999). Assistance to States for the Education of Children with Disabilities and the Early Intervention Program for Infants and Toddlers with Disabilities; Final Regulations, 34 CFR Parts 300 and 303. Federal Register, Vol. 64, No. 48, Washington, DC: U.S Government Printing Office.

U.S. Department of Education. (2006). *IDEA regulations.* Washington, DC: Author.

United States Code Service. (2006). 29 USCS Section 794. *LexisNexis.*

Watkins, C., Campbell, V., Nieberding, R., & Hallmark, R. (1995). Contemporary practice of psychological assessment by clinical psychologists. *Professional Psychology Research and Practice, 26,* 54–60.

World Health Organization (1992). *International statistical classification of diseases and related health problems* (10th rev.) (ICD-10). Geneva, Switzerland, Author.

World Health Organization (2001). *International classification of functioning, disability and health* (ICF). Geneva, Switzerland: Author.

Wright, P. W. D., & Wright, P. D. (2006). Section 504. Retrieved September 10, 2006, from http://www.wrightslaw.com/info/sec504.index.htm.

16

Neuropsychological Assessment

JEANNE M. LeBLANC
Private Practice, Vancouver, BC

OVERVIEW

Clinical neuropsychology is a specialized field of psychology that is concerned with the behavioral aspects of brain functioning (Lezak, Howieson, & Loring, 2004). Clinical neuropsychologists provide assessment, diagnosis, treatment, and/or rehabilitation of individuals who experience changes of brain function due to neurological, medical, developmental, and/or psychiatric conditions. Multiple data sources (including psychological, cognitive, behavioral, physiological, and neurological concepts, as well as medical information) are utilized to evaluate an individual's thinking skills and behavioral and emotional strengths and weaknesses as well as their relationship to brain functioning (Barth, 2003).

This chapter explores neuropsychological assessment in the context of the World Health Organization's (2001) *International Classification of Functioning, Disability, and Health (ICF)*. This chapter also discusses the role of neuropsychological assessment in rehabilitation and the historical development of neuropsychology, quantitative and qualitative approaches to testing, current research of critical issues, and relevant cultural, legislative, and professional topics. The role of neuropsychological data in a multidisciplinary rehabilitation setting is described, with an emphasis on holistic rehabilitation.

LEARNING OBJECTIVES

By the end of the chapter, readers should be able to:

- Explain the history behind neuropsychological assessment in rehabilitation and health settings
- Differentiate between quantitative and qualitative approaches to neuropsychological assessment and understand the pros and cons of each
- Identify factors that may influence test performance and/or alter the basic interpretation of findings
- Discuss International Classification of Functioning's applications to neuropsychological assessments in rehabilitation and health settings
- Understand the impact of culture in critical areas of neuropsychological assessment

INTRODUCTION

IMPORTANCE OF NEUROPSYCHOLOGICAL ASSESSMENT TO REHABILITATION AND HEALTH

As Benson indicates in "Types of Tests and Assessments" (chapter 5, this text), *tests* are designed to measure a behavior or ability. In the context of neuropsychology, *assessment* refers to using clinical judgment to integrate test data with historical information, observations, medical records, and an individual's everyday functioning and psychosocial involvement.

Neuropsychological assessment provides a comprehensive overview of cognitive abilities that can be pertinent to all health-related professions (e.g., medicine, nursing, social work, physical therapy, speech–language therapy, occupational therapy, recreational therapy, and psychology). Individuals of all ages may be assessed to answer questions in respect to (1) differential diagnosis, (2) research, (3) forensic issues, (4) medical care and planning, (5) treatment planning and remediation, and/or (6) evaluation of treatment efficacy (Lezak et al., 2004).

Definitions and Theories of Neuropsychological Assessment

Rehabilitation and health teams utilize neuropsychological assessments diagnostically in various ways. For example, assessments may differentiate between dementia and depression, screen for the presence or absence of cognitive symptoms after a mild head injury, establish an individual's stage of cognitive recovery following a coma or severe injury, or reveal the presence of disorders that are difficult to define with medical imaging, such as toxic encephalopathy.

In health-related research, neuropsychological assessment is utilized to investigate the behavioral components of neurophysiology. Testing frequently is used to understand the behavioral aspects of neuroanatomical findings from imaging techniques, such as functional Magnetic Resonance Imaging (fMRI; see Official Position paper of APA Division 40, 2004). Forensic uses for neuropsychological assessment include establishing competency of self-care and/or ability to perform complex activities of daily living (e.g., independence with personal finances),

existence and sequelae of a brain injury for the purpose of civil litigation, or cognitive capacity to participate in criminal proceedings.

Applicable International Classification Functioning and Health Aspects

With respect to neuropsychological assessment in the rehabilitation setting, the ICF framework has clear applications for all aspects of care, planning, treatment, and evaluation of treatment efficacy. A neuropsychological evaluation using this framework will assess degree deficits related to body structures (e.g., the brain) and body functions (e.g., attention, memory, higher level cognitive functions—planning, organization, cognitive flexibility), as well as identify limitations and abilities in activities and participation (e.g., learning and applying knowledge, communication, and ability to perform in major life areas such as work and education). A thorough neuropsychological assessment also will consider environmental factors that impact the individual's functioning, such as the availability of assistive devices, attitudes of the social support network, and aspects of the natural environment (e.g., rural home versus urban high-rise; Bilbao, et al., 2003). The neuropsychologist also will note strengths and suggest strategies or compensatory techniques for minimizing impairment and disability in an effort to promote personal independence.

HISTORICAL DEVELOPMENT OF NEUROPSYCHOLOGICAL ASSESSMENT

Records indicating relationships between areas of the brain and basic behavioral functioning have been found on ancient Egyptian papyrus. During the late 17th century and early 18th century, investigators sought to locate the area of the brain responsible for the mind or soul. René Descartes (1596–1650) believed the pineal gland was the source of the soul and thought its location in the brain enabled it to respond to and implement changes in the "spirits" contained within the brain's ventricles. Later, scholars sought to divide various mental abilities into specialized aspects of functioning using physical indicators of these skills (Walsh, 1987).

Franz Josef Gall (1758–1828) and Johan Casper Spurzheim's (1776–1832) phrenology was the first global theory of the brain's workings, and integrated physical aspects with behavior (Kolb & Wishaw, 1996). Based on observations (e.g., noticing that students with good memories had large, protruding eyes), Gall believed the skull's bumps and depressions would indicate the brain's neuroanatomical features, which could be correlated with behavioral traits such as wit, inquiry, agreeableness, self-esteem, and destructiveness. A bump suggested greater brain development and ability in a certain domain while a depressed area reflected lesser development and weaker skills.

Pierre Flourens (1794–1867) opposed phrenology and developed the holistic theory that the whole brain—rather than specific parts (or indentations)—is responsible for mental functions. Flourens removed or lesioned parts of the cerebral cortex of animals and studied their behavior afterwards; he observed that an initial loss of abilities often was followed by recovery to the point of appearing normal. Furthermore, the magnitude of functional loss was correlated with the *amount* of cortical damage (i.e., the more cortex that was damaged, the greater the impairment—regardless of lesion site). He also believed that undamaged portions of the cortex could recover postinjury brain functioning (Kolb & Wishaw, 1996; Walsh, 1987).

The discovery of specific areas of localization of behavioral functioning within the brain led to questions about Flourens's generalized emphasis on brain functioning. Paul Broca (1824–1880) found that a lesion in a specific part of the frontal lobes led to a loss of fluent speech (aphasia) despite intact vocal mechanisms. Carl Wernicke (1848–1904) observed that patients with confused and nonsensical speech as well as decreased comprehension had a lesion in the left temporal lobe

(Kolb & Wishaw, 1996; Walsh, 1987). Such work established the use of behavioral components for diagnosing specific neurological lesion sites.

Modern Neuropsychology

These theoretical, anatomical, and philosophical concepts paved the way for modern neuropsychology's use of neurological and psychological knowledge to aid in understanding brain–behavior relationships. Neuropsychology further benefited from the intellectual and academic tools developed by educational and clinical psychologists, which emphasize reliable measurement techniques based upon standardized approaches and normative data.

As with the development of intelligence testing (see chapter 14 "Intelligence"), the fairly rapid growth and development of neuropsychological tests can be partially attributed to demands of war. Intelligence testing was developed partly to assess a person's capabilities following enlistment. Neuropsychological assessment, on the other hand, expanded in response to an increased need for screening, diagnosis, and rehabilitation of brain injury (and behavioral disturbance) in servicemen returning from World War I (Lezak et al., 2004).

Neuropsychological insights into brain–behavior relationships and functioning continue to change rapidly due to results from neuroanatomical research. This is a benefit and a challenge to neuropsychology. As Lezak et al. (2004) note, "In this complex and expanding field, few facets or principles can be taken for granted, few techniques would not benefit from modifications, and few procedures will not be bent or broken as knowledge and experience accumulate (pg. 4)."

DISCUSSION BOX 16.1

Flourens's theory of potential for functional recovery after cortex loss is partially supported by recent neuroplasticity research (see R. Moucha's [2006] review of plasticity in rehabilitation for more information on this topic). Interestingly, Flourens's work continues to impact the public's view of brain functioning. More specifically, a commonly accepted yet incorrect Flourensian hypothesis is that most people do not use more than 10% of their brains (Kolb & Wishaw, 1996). However, imaging studies (such as PET scans and functional MRIs) disprove this theory. Flourens worked largely with pigeons and chickens—animals without a great deal of cerebral cortex. Thus, he drew his conclusions based upon observations

of basic behaviors and abilities—rather than the higher-level thinking skills present in humans who have considerably more cerebral cortex. See http://www.snopes.com/science/stats/10percent.asp for theories about how this myth is encouraged by some of those who believe in psychic abilities.

Questions

1. Discuss the pros and cons of using animal models when establishing theories of human brain functioning.
2. What areas of research most warrant the use of animal models? Why?

DISCUSSION BOX 16.2

Military needs are still a driving force behind the development of neuropsychological services. Many service personnel who are now surviving extensive injuries as a result of improved body armor are experiencing brain injury due to blast (including shock waves) projectiles and/or strikes to the head. Overall statistics of injury reflect approximately five times more brain injuries than amputations (Warden, 2006). It is not surprising that brain injury has been deemed the "signature wound" of the U.S. war in Iraq.

Questions

1. How might the increased chance of brain injury during military service impact the environment to which service personnel return with respect to support and attitudes?

2. What is the likelihood that this may become a stereotyped disorder of Iraq veterans, much as post-traumatic stress disorder has become a stereotyped disorder of Vietnam veterans?

3. How may these environmental features impact the individual's functioning upon return from service (with or without a brain injury)?

4. Would these issues encourage or discourage a client's willingness to admit symptoms or obtain assistance?

NEUROPSYCHOLOGICAL ASSESSMENT METHODS IN REHABILITATION AND HEALTH

Neuropsychological assessment emphasizes identifying and measuring cognitive and behavioral deficits as well as describing intact abilities through various (typically standardized) tests. A typical neuropsychological evaluation will provide information related to such cognitive areas as (1) orientation; (2) intelligence; (3) attention/concentration; (4) memory—visual and verbal; (5) learning; (6) sensory perception (visual, tactile, auditory, and perhaps olfactory); (7) executive functioning (i.e., the skills needed for complex tasks such as initiation, planning, productive action, and adaptation to novel demands); (8) concept formation and reasoning; (9) language; (10) constructional skills; (11) academics; (12) personality/psychological status; and (13) level of effort. Neuropsychologists also perform an extensive clinical interview and observe behavior throughout to further their understanding of the client.

As indicated earlier, neuropsychological assessment has been linked closely to a medical, neurological model of health. Initially, testing was utilized primarily to assist in diagnosis and localization of a possible lesion site in the brain—particularly before imaging technology had advanced. In ICF terminology, neuropsychological assessment has been directed toward defining deficits related to body structures and functions. As a result, the needs of the health care community have driven the development and use of quantitative and standardized measures administered in a structured and standardized environment (i.e., a quiet office with no distractions and one-to-one interactions with the examiner), designed to provide a numerical indicator of ability (similar to a laboratory test providing data) to aid in diagnosis.

However, as medical science has benefited from improved imaging, the need for localization and diagnosis based on neuropsychological testing has decreased. Currently more individuals with neurological conditions are living longer lives, and their rehabilitation teams increasingly look to neuropsychological assessments to provide qualitative (or descriptive) data for intervention and planning. In respect to everyday functioning, the results often are most useful for the client, her/his support system, and the interdisciplinary rehabilitation team as they attempt to understand the person's ability for self-care, independence in activities of daily living, and future potential for meaningful and productive participation in life. Therefore, neuropsychological measures are considered increasingly in terms of their *ecological validity* (i.e., ability to predict real-world behaviors) and their ability to promote qualitative observations to assist with interpreting results (Rabin, Burton, & Barr, 2007).

When performing a neuropsychological assessment, the time since onset of the condition (e.g., a stroke or brain injury) is considered because the assessment will answer different questions for the individual at varying stages of recovery (Lezak et al., 2004). In the earlier stages of recovery, simple examinations elucidate the individual's capacity to understand and follow commands, her or his competency to make decisions about personal care, or her or his ability to participate in a more complex rehabilitative program. Because the brain may be recovering and capabilities (and thus test results) may be changing considerably during these initial postinjury days, full formal assessment often is not conducted during the first 6 to 12 weeks.

For example, three to six months after the illness' onset, the first comprehensive exam may determine whether (or how) the individual may resume pre-illness activities and the client's cognitive strengths and weaknesses for the purpose of additional rehabilitation. One to two years post-illness, assessment typically is sought to understand the person's long-term ability to participate in training, education, or work and to establish the hypothesized long-term level of cognitive functioning. The information also is used to illuminate present and future therapeutic needs, including community assistance, cognitive rehabilitation, and/or counselling (Lezak et al., 2004). For progressive conditions (e.g., brain tumor or dementia), neuropsychological testing can provide a baseline of abilities against which future results can be compared. This information can facilitate treatment planning, gathering of community resources, and issues related to competence as the condition progresses.

Regardless of the approach to or timing of neuropsychological testing, an individual's performance should be compared with a normative standard of the population (e.g., average score for the client's age and gender peers) to determine whether it reflects a lack of expected ability or a particular strength for that person. Because factors such as age, gender, culture, socioeconomic status, and education level can influence many test results, the findings obtained for one individual should be compared to the appropriate peer group when determining whether they are within normal range or deviate from the average.

Hundreds of tests have been developed to help neuropsychologists meet their need to provide information about an individual's cognitive abilities. An examination of all measures is far beyond the scope of this chapter. The reader is referred to Lezak, Howieson, and Loring's (2004) and Strauss, Sherman and Spreen's (2006) seminal texts of neuropsychological tests for more in-depth reviews. This chapter introduces some of the more widely used measures that provide quantitative and qualitative data used in neuropsychological evaluations.

Quantitative and Qualitative Approaches to Neuropsychological Testing

Quantitative measures provide numerically represented data about certain neuropsychological abilities for interpretation and comparison. The scores are derived from the standardized test administration (i.e., the test is administered as closely as possible in the same manner to everyone), and the data provide actuarial (numerical) information. The scores are categorized on a continuum from below average, average, to above average. See chapter 6 for a more details on score distributions.

Quantitative measures often provide standardized scores (i.e., scores transformed to reflect the distance from average), allowing a professional to compare various tested abilities. Some believe the actuarial approach is more accurate in diagnosing impairment than qualitative testing (Dawes, Faust, & Meehl, 1989); others believe this is too simplistic (Lezak et al., 2004).

A *qualitative* approach to neuropsychological testing entails directly observing the test-taker's behaviors (e.g, mood, approach to testing, response to failure, appearance). Qualitative tests commonly are not standardized. Thus, a test may be altered to assess the individual's capabilities and to understand his or her approach to problem-solving. Because they are not standardized, qualitative approaches tend to have lower reliability (i.e., the degree the test is free from measurement error or random influences), and standardization can be questionable due to differences in clinical interpretation. Furthermore, reliance on qualitative results to ascertain degrees of impairment in the context of what is most typical is difficult.

In summary, quantitative test data can be meaningless to the individual if not placed in the context of the person being assessed. On the other hand, qualitative findings, when not placed in the context of normal or expected performance, often do not inform diagnosis or the relative degree of the client's impairment (Lezak et al., 2004). Thus, most neuropsychologists strive to integrate both quantative and qualitative data for the highest level of insight into the abilities of the client (Ogden-Epker & Cullum, 2001). As Goldstein (1948) states in reference to brain injury in World War II veterans:

> The usual scoring method, based on a scale of difficulty which has been standardized on a statistical basis, offers no adequate instrument for determining the nature or the degree of the patient's impairment. Unless one takes into account the entire procedures, the specific reasons for the difficulty the patient encounters, one cannot simply read from a score which task represents a greater difficulty and which is lesser. Any statistical evaluation must be based upon a qualitative analysis of test results that must precede statistical analysis. It must first be determined what kind of qualitative difficulty a given task represents in relation to the performance capacity of the patient; thereupon a quantitative inference as to the degree of impairment, etc., can be made (pp. 94–95).

Case Study 16.1

Consider the pros and cons of utilizing quantitative versus qualitative tests in the following scenario. Mr. Angove, a logger hurt on the job in rural Canada, scored in the moderately impaired range on a measure of memory for information read to him. During the assessment, he tended to have difficulty communicating with Dr. Reid. He frequently looked away from her and seemed to have problems focusing on what she was saying. His recall of the given information was poor when questioned a few minutes later. This behavior is consistent with the problems reported by his family members.

QUESTIONS

1. Based on this information, does it appear that Mr. Angove's test score may be a good representation of his cognitive capabilities in respect to memory? Why or why not?
2. What would you conclude about his memory?

Consider the following. At one point, Mr. Angove turned away from Dr. Reid while in his seat for a full one to two minutes, staring at the wall. Later, during a break from testing, Dr. Reid observed Mr. Angove behaving in a similar manner while alone in the waiting room. When she called his name, she was surprised to see tears in his eyes. Mr. Angove turned quickly away once again with a loud sigh. In a strained voice, he reported that he has been experiencing severe back pain since his accident, but that he didn't want anyone else to know. "Everyone is already too wrapped up in this . . . I don't want to add more to it, and I know this should just go away." Upon query, Dr. Reid ascertained that Mr. Angove's pain had been preventing him from participating in conversations with his family, assisting his wife with domestic chores, and attending his son's hockey games. A later physical exam found that he had experienced a hairline fracture of his vertebrae and an impingement of his nerve.

QUESTIONS

1. How might the quantitative result be interpreted differently now that additional qualitative (as well as individual information about his activities/participation and environment) data have been provided?

Thus, if neuropsychological assessments are used to hypothesize which ICF-related body functions and body structures are affected (i.e., to assist with diagnosis), features of the individual (including activity/participation and environmental factors in the context of test performance) must be considered when interpreting test results.

Commonly Utilized Neuropsychological Tests

As indicated in the previous discussion, neuropsychological assessment has many purposes. In this section, each basic area of a full neuropsychological test battery will be considered, with a sample of widely used measures.

CLINICAL INTERVIEW   The clinical interview is conducted by the neuropsychologist with the client, usually during the initial meeting. (See "Clinical Interview," chapter 10.) History-taking generally includes (1) basic demographic information; (2) a description of medical condition; (3) medical/substance/psychological history; (4) developmental history (including prenatal alcohol); (5) educational history (e.g., grades, level obtained, presence of a learning disability); (6) vocational history; (7) family history (e.g., medical and psychological); and (8) review of the symptoms and functional impact of the condition in question (e.g., sleep, appetite, energy level, psychological symptoms, communication skills, sensory abilities—including hearing and vision, as well as memory, and problem-solving). Available medical, psychological, educational, and/or vocational records are reviewed.

Although the individual may have difficulty answering questions, the clinician attempts to discover what that person does recall. Those who have known the person prior to the illness or injury also may participate in the clinical interview. A discrepancy between the individual's recollection versus records or what collaborative informants recall provides an important source of information about the client's insight into her or his cognitive status.

ORIENTATION   Individuals with severe brain injury or neurological illness may have decreased awareness of basic information such as where they are, what date or day it is, and/or why they are in a health care setting. Typically, the more severe or persistent the disorientation, the more significant the illness or injury (Lezak et al., 2004). Measures of orientation are utilized most during

RESEARCH BOX 16.1

The Galveston Orientation and Amnesia Test (GOAT) is a quantitative measure that may provide a straightforward measure of orientation after head injury. However, the open-ended questions on this measure require the test-taker to display a certain degree of communication ability.

Objective: To determine how well the GOAT reflects amnesia in individuals with aphasia (decreased ability to express themselves verbally) following brain injury.

Method: Jain, Layton, & Murray (2000) assessed 22 patients with aphasia and 22 patients without aphasia, first with the GOAT and then with an amended version (AGOAT)—one with a multiple-choice format.

Results: Of the 15 individuals with aphasia classified with amnesia on the GOAT, 8 met normal criteria with respect to orientation on the AGOAT.

Conclusion: This study illustrates the importance of considering activity/participation characteristics of the individual—in this case, speaking ability—when interpreting even somewhat simple questionnaires of basic abilities.

Questions

1. What may be the consequences of misclassifying an individual as amnesic when, in fact, he or she is fully aware of who he or she is, where he or she is, what happened, and the date?
2. Consider allocation of treatment resources, potential discharge plans, and level of involvement the person may have in his own treatment.

---

acute care (i.e., inpatient hospital), in the acute rehabilitation setting soon after the onset of illness, and during the course of a progressive disease (e.g., dementia).

The Galveston Orientation and Amnesia Test (GOAT; Levin, O'Donnell, & Grossman, 1979) is a ten-question verbal (or written) examination designed to assess an individual's orientation to person, place, and time (e.g., "What is your name?" "Where are you now?"). Memories before the occurrence of brain injury are queried to assess for amnesia of events preceding the injury (i.e., retrograde amnesia) as well as a recall of events immediately following the incident (i.e., posttraumatic amnesia). Levin et al. (2004) recommend that full formal testing of cognition be delayed until GOAT scores are normal. Performance on the GOAT has been shown to be a strong indicator of functional recovery level following neurorehabilitation; the greater the duration of below normal scores, the more the functional impairment at time of discharge from rehabilitation (Zafonte, 1997).

INTELLIGENCE Neuropsychologists generally consider intelligence measures as indicators of general cognitive abilities. Aspects of intelligence testing are less likely to decline following a brain injury or neurological condition. Thus, results acquired after an injury may indicate premorbid intellectual abilities (in combination with demographic data such as education level and age).

Thus, general estimates of intelligence can provide a standard against which to compare other cognitive scores. For instance, memory and executive functioning skills generally are expected to be within the same range as intellectual abilities. Thus, a marked difference between these scores may suggest a loss in skill. As a result, individuals performing in the moderate mental retardation range of intellectual ability throughout their lives are unlikely to perform in the average range on measures of memory or problem-solving. In contrast, a deficit may be suspected when individuals in the superior range of intelligence obtain average scores on neuropsychological tests.

ATTENTION/CONCENTRATION Attention includes ". . . processes that enable an individual to engage in certain cognitive operations while ignoring others. . . . Attention also refers to the ability to focus and maintain interest for a given task or activity (pg. 24)" (*International Neuropsychological Society [INS] Dictionary of Neuropsychology*, 1999). An individual must attend to learn and recall information. Difficulties with attention may be misattributed to memory problems. Neuropsychologists consider many aspects of attention, including attention for visual and verbal information, attention in simple situations (i.e., in a quiet setting–one demand at a time), span of attention (i.e., sustained attention), and attention for multiple demands (i.e., divided attention).

Simple attention may be assessed by the *Wechsler Adult Intelligence Scale*-III's (WAIS-III; Wechsler, 1997a) subtest, Digit Span, Forward, whereas Digit Span, Backwards can indicate divided attention. Digit Span involves repeating random sequences of numbers read aloud, first with forward repetition and then backward repetitions of given number items. Sentence Repetition assesses attention span. (Benton, Hamsher, & Sivan, 1994) with repetition of increasingly longer stated sentences. This is considered a naturalistic test and represents functions such as comprehending and following conversations (Lezak et al., 2004).

Although Digit Span commonly is used to indicate functional attention skills, its ecological validity is questionable (Groth-Marnat, 2003). The Test of Everyday Attention (Robertson, Ward, Ridgeway, & Nimmo-Smith 1994) provides a naturalistic measure of attention. This test is presented as a mock trip to Philadelphia (in the version for the United States) that requires tasks such as using a map or a telephone book—with and without distractions. The test's ceiling effects may limit its use. *Ceiling effects* occur when a test is unable to measure or discriminate above a certain level, usually because the items are not sufficiently difficult.

LEARNING, VISUAL, AND VERBAL MEMORY Memory is considered to be the capacity to retain information that can be used in day-to-day activities, often involving utilization of learning skills. The *INS Dictionary of Neuropsychology* lists 24 definitions of different aspects of memory. This chapter will discuss information regarding tests of memory for what is spoken or read and recall of nonverbal or visual items.

The *Wechsler Memory Scale* (3rd ed.) (WMS-III, Wechsler, 1997b) battery of tests is designed to measure both visual and verbal memory.

Nonverbal or *visual memory* refers to the ability to learn and recall data that have been observed visually. Pure visual memory abilities can be difficult to assess given the natural tendency for individuals to verbalize (or think through verbally) visual information for later recall (i.e., recalling where you left your car by thinking to yourself, "I parked my car next to the large tree"). Thus, abstract measures of memory sometimes are considered to be better indicators of pure visual recall.

The Rey-Osterrieth Complex Figure Test (ROCF; Meyers & Meyers, 1995) assesses recall of an abstract and detailed figure, which is first copied. Thus, when using drawings to assess visual memory, one also is assessing planning and organizational skills, thus confounding an assessment of only visual memory. Recall

on this measure has been shown to have a moderate relationship to functional memory skills (Ostrosky-Solis, Jaine, & Ardila, 1998). The WMS-III subtest Family Pictures was designed to measure everyday visual memory by showing a family in a number of scenes (e.g., participating in outdoor activities, shopping). Information about specific details is queried immediately and after a delay. Performance on Family Pictures can be influenced by one's verbal abilities due to a tendency to verbalize what is seen to assist in later recall.

Verbal memory involves learning and retaining rote items (e.g., lists, telephone numbers, instructions) as well as information that is placed into context and is more personally meaningful—as in conversations. The *California Verbal Learning Test*-II (CVLT-II; Delis, Kramer, Kaplan, & Ober, 2000), a measure of rote verbal recall, provides information about learning strategies, ability to retain information after delays, and efficacy of recall when given cues. The Logical Memory subtest of the WMS-III consists of orally reading brief stories to the client who then is asked questions about the story content. This measures the ability to recall conversational or more meaningful verbal information about people, objects, places, and events.

The *Rivermead Behavioral Memory Test* (2nd ed.; RBMT-II, Wilson, Cockburn, Baddeley, & Hiorns, 2003) measures both verbal and visual aspects of memory. The RBMT was developed to measure everyday memory impairment by imitating the demands on memory found in daily tasks. It includes remembering names, an item's location, an appointment, a story, faces, a new route, and the date. *Prospective memory* (i.e., memory to perform a task in the future) also is assessed. This measure is sensitive to various neurological impairments and correlates with ratings of deficits by patients and relatives. Persons with mild impairments may not show deficits due to the test's low ceiling (Strauss et al., 2006).

Sensory Perception

Brain injury, disease, and nonneurological events can alter sensory abilities (i.e.,visual, auditory, tactile, and olfactory perception). An understanding of an individual's sensory skills is important when interpreting assessment results so as to make the best possible hypothesis regarding a client's abilities. For example, someone who has partial sensorineural hearing loss may perform poorly on verbally administered measures, such as memory testing, or may not follow directions. Without awareness of the hearing impairment, one could erroneously conclude that memory or attention deficits are the primary issues.

Tests for visual–perceptual skills, such as visual neglect, may include cancellation tasks such as Letter Cancellation (Diller et al., 1974). It requires a person to cross out a particular letter each time it is located. The Bell's Test (Gauthier et al., 1989) provides a nonverbal (and less structured) measure of visual neglect. It requires a person to mark all the bells on a page of randomly placed pictures. Functional observations include whether the individual overlooks all items in a certain area (often the left side) or whether she or he evidences inattention and decreased executive functioning by utilizing a very haphazard or random approach to task completion.

Auditory perceptual difficulties may include conduction, a sensorineural hearing loss, and difficulty in discriminating between similar sounds. The Phoneme Discrimination test (Benton, Sivan, & Hamsher, 1994) requires one to discriminate between same and different speech sounds. The clinician will benefit from observing whether the person tends to turn her or his head the same direction when given information or if she or he has difficulty comprehending directions if facing away.

EXECUTIVE FUNCTIONING AND PROBLEM-SOLVING

This area of functioning includes the ability to formulate an appropriate plan of action; initiate, execute, and stop the activity once completed; self-monitor and be self-aware; change actions based upon feedback; have time-sharing/cognitive flexibility; and adapt a response strategy when the task demands are varied. *Problem-solving* refers to the ability to derive a solution to an immediate issue. *Executive functioning* refers to higher level cognitive processes that organize and order behavior, including but not limited to logic and reasoning, abstract thinking, problem-solving, planning, and carrying out or terminating goal-directed behaviors. Thus, measures of executive functioning assess a client's ability to plan, implement, follow through, and alter a response when needed.

Deficits in executive functioning have been linked to diminished social, vocational, and educational outcomes. However, neuropsychological tests of executive functioning generally do not predict real-world skills (LeBlanc, Hayden, & Paulman, 2000). This limitation is likely due to the acquisition of neuropsychological data in structured and controlled testing situations, conditions that differ considerably from real-life situations—given common distractions, frequent changes, and lack of structure. These latter qualities are not embedded in the testing situation.

Obtaining observational information about executive functioning during assessment as well as in a real-life setting is highly recommended in rehabilitation or health care settings. During testing, behaviors indicative of executive dysfunction include impairments in initiating, planning, organizing, inhibiting; shifting thoughts or approaches; decreased working memory; inflexibility; perseveration (i.e., getting "stuck" on a certain approach); impaired (or inconsistent) cognitive strategies; and problems with self-correcting or using feedback to alter response.

Although observational information may be most useful when assessing executive functioning, formal measures of executive functioning may elicit samples of executive dysfunction to the keen observer and allow standardized scores to be obtained for comparison. The *Delis-Kaplan Executive Function System* (D-KEFS, Delis, Kaplan, & Kramer, 2001) utilizes tests of nine different aspects of verbal and nonverbal executive functioning. It is a compilation of versions of previously established measures, such as Trail Making Test, Verbal Fluency, and Design Fluency.

Observational information from collaborative sources of information (e.g., family members, friends) can be helpful in providing information about an individual's executive functioning in daily life. The Behavior Rating Inventory of Executive Function–Adult Version (BRIEF–A; Roth, Isquith, & Gioia, 2005) utilizes a questionnaire format that allows the individual being assessed and/or someone who knows them well to provide information about their behavioral regulation and metacognition. The measure's validity scales provide information that enables a clinician to identify consistent or atypical responses.

LANGUAGE   (See chapter 25, "Measures of Speech and Communication.") Some of the most obvious forms of language impairment include the aphasias (which include naming, fluency, comprehension, repetition deficits, and deficits of reading and writing) and impaired articulation (dysarthrias). Not surprisingly, education, intelligence, ethnicity, and acculturation can impact performance. A speech–language pathologist (SLP) often is involved in a health care setting, in part, to assess language skills. Nevertheless, neuropsychologists also should consider language issues as SLP services may not have been provided or available.

The *Boston Naming Test* (2nd ed.) (Kaplan, Goodglass, & Weintraub, 2001) assesses an individual's ability to locate in her or his word repertoire and say the correct words to identify a number of black-and-white drawings. Word-finding deficits are a common complaint following changes to the brain (particularly after a traumatic brain injury). The *Multilingual Aphasia Examination* (Benton, Hamsher, Rey, & Sivan, 1994) assesses most common areas of language abilities impacted by aphasia. These include oral expression (e.g., naming, repetition, and fluency); comprehending and following basic commands; written comprehension; and spelling. The clinician also can observe naming deficits through a tendency to "talk around" specific subjects, use of a number of nonspecific terms (e.g., "things" or "them" when describing information), or a tendency to slur or mumble while speaking.

CONSTRUCTIONAL SKILLS   Constructional skills (e.g., building, drawing, and assembling) are dependent on other skills, including visual perception, spatial awareness, motor functioning, and executive functioning. Deficits in this area have been associated with functional tasks, including impaired meal planning and driving (Lezak et al., 2004).

The previously described Rey-Osterrieth Complex Figure assesses one's ability to copy information by requiring an individual to draw an abstract and detailed figure. Difficulties with spatial judgment, planning, and organization can be evident by the process by which the individual approaches the task. Block Design, a WAIS-III subtest, commonly is used to assess assembly skills. It involves using blocks to build replicas of pictures or figures. A nonstandardized version, used to "test the limits" of an individual's capabilities, involves asking the person to verbalize as he works or allowing as much time as needed to attempt to complete the demand, after the initial completion of the subtest. As with the ROCF, observations of the approach used (i.e., piecemeal, impulsive, etc.) can be informative.

ACADEMIC ATTAINMENT   A person's academic skills can provide information about: (1) preinjury functioning levels, (2) existence of a preinjury learning disability, and (3) data related to reading comprehension level, which can guide the use of questionnaires and written instructions. When the latter issue is overlooked, invalid performance on measures involving reading cannot be interpreted as a purposeful decision to not comply with testing. (See chapter 17, "Achievement.")

PERSONALITY   Data on an individual's personality and emotional functioning are relevant to a neuropsychological evaluation. Emotional distress (e.g. depression, psychosis, or anxiety) can negatively impact results on tests of memory and attention and on tasks requiring quick motoric reactions. When interpreting personality tests, clinicians needs to be aware of common and genuine symptoms associated with neurological disorders that can elevate scales associated with psychopathology in those with no neurological concerns. For example, most questions on the Minnesota Multiphasic Personality Inventory–II (MMPI-2) that pertain to neurologic symptoms load on a scale designed to reflect a psychotic disorder or one often associated with neurosis (Lezak et al, 2004). (See chapter 18, "Personality.")

LEVEL OF EFFORT   The increased use of neuropsychology in forensic settings and the growing awareness of factors that contribute to a lack of effort during testing have emphasized the importance of formally assessing level of effort as standard protocol for most neuropsychological evaluations. Assessment of very severely impaired individuals, such as those only capable of participating in measures of orientation, and young children are exceptions to this rule. Determining incomplete effort is a complex task that involves (1) evidence of inconsistency in the history or examination; (2) the likelihood that the set of symptoms and neuropsychological test profile (including validity measures) makes medical sense (e.g., is a known disease pattern); (3) an understanding of the individual's present situation, personal/social history, and emotional functioning; and (4) emotional reactions to these symptoms and complaints (Lezak et al., 2004).

Effort can be impaired due to (1) a lack of desire to participate in testing; (2) medication that creates significant cognitive fatigue (e.g., high levels of pain medications); (3) medical concerns such as significant physical pain or lack of sleep; (4) personality disorder (e.g., antisocial, histrionic); (5) preoccupation with events outside of the testing situation (e.g., a very recent death of a loved one); (6) psychological issues (e.g., depression, anxiety); and (7) a volitional attempt to appear more impaired for secondary gain (e.g., malingering or fictitious disorder). A comprehensive understanding of the individual's current and past abilities is essential for understanding the reasons behind insufficient effort.

Authors of some validity measures request that their test not be reported as a specific measure of effort due to a concern that individuals (primarily in a forensic setting) may be coached on which tests to respond to genuinely versus which they can exaggerate (Green, 2003). For the purpose of this chapter, the student is advised that formal measures of effort may come in the form of verbal or nonverbal memory, problem-solving tasks, and self-report measures, to name a few. Additionally, standard tests (e.g., the WAIS-III and WMS-III) have methods for analyzing results to determine level of effort, and many other measures have incorporated validity measures in their scales.

RESEARCH CRITICAL TO NEUROPSYCHOLOGICAL ASSESSMENT

The term *ecological validity* refers to the *functional* meaning a test score has for the individual's day-to-day life. In rehabilitation, functional issues frequently include level of independence for work, home, community and/or leisure activities. Research supports using neuropsychological assessment to provide predictive data for many specific areas of functioning. For example, assessed visual scanning is associated with safety and number of falls (Diller & Weinberg, 1970). Rote memory ability is associated with bill paying (Hoskin, Jackson, & Crowe, 2005).

However, the formal setting in which neuropsychological testing occurs may underestimate the scope of difficulties an individual with brain injury may display when in unstructured natural settings—particularly in the area of executive functioning (Spector, 1995). The test environment is structured, quiet, and controlled. Although tests may require cognitive flexibility or other executive skills, administration does not occur with additional common distracters such as a telephone ringing,

a noisy television, or a request from a family member. As a result, an individual may appear to be more capable in the structured test environment than when performing everyday tasks or vocational behaviors (Hoskin et al., 2005; LeBlanc et al., 2000).

Approximately one third of practicing neuropsychologists surveyed reported they regularly utilized test instruments specifically designed to predict functional behaviors (Rabin et al., 2007). Although ecologically valid measures appear to be good measures of a specific capability (i.e., they have face validity), the less-standardized approach to their administration may impact psychometric properties (Hoskin et al., 2005) such as test–retest reliability (see chapter 8 regarding test selection for discussion of the importance of psychometrics). Thus, continued validation and design of ecologically valid measures are needed for the purposes of rehabilitation and health care.

Measures of adaptive behaviour can assist the clinician in developing a broader understanding of an individual's functional behaviors at home, the workplace, and community. However, the direct assessment of adaptive functioning based on current observations within a hospital is likely to be invalid due to the lack of opportunity for a person to display behaviors in a normal setting. (See chapter 15 for a discussion of adaptive behavior assessment.)

Case Study 16.2

Shea, a professional motorcycle racer, was injured after a box fell on his head and knocked him unconscious while he worked at a seasonal job in a post office. He always considered himself to be "bullet-proof" and found this injury to be an embarrassment—after all, he wasn't racing or engaging in risky behavior when it happened. Results from formal testing indicated his memory generally was normal, problem-solving appeared to be intact, and only mild inefficiencies were shown on measures of executive functioning in respect to sequencing and use of feedback. However, on his first day back to work, Shea was using the copy machine located in the middle of a busy and noisy office when it jammed. After one attempt to clear it, he was at a loss for what to do next and did not want to admit he needed help on "such a simple task." As his anxiety level rose, his ability to assess what needed to be done declined further, and he felt more overwhelmed. His frustration and embarrassment grew, and he left work without informing

his supervisor, got in his car, and drove one mile home. When his girlfriend asked him why he was home, he angrily replied, "I don't know," and locked himself in his room.

QUESTIONS

1. What cognitive skills might be used when operating a copy machine?
2. Was Shea's attention, memory, and/or his executive functioning impaired? Why (or why not)?
3. What environmental aspects of his job site were different from the environment of the formal test situation?
4. What aspects of his activity and/or participation are limited or restricted in the job setting but don't appear to be in the testing milieu?
5. What are pertinent personal variables? How did they contribute to the outcome?

LEGISLATIVE AND PROFESSIONAL ISSUES IMPACTING NEUROPSYCHOLOGICAL ASSESSMENT

Neuropsychological assessments can be complex and lengthy undertakings. For a full battery of testing, the person being assessed can expect to spend one to two days in the neuropsychologist's office, often with six to twelve hours of assessment (depending upon the individual and his or her needs). As a result, a neuropsychological assessment can cost thousands of dollars (with forensic cases typically being at the higher end of the spectrum). Most individuals find it difficult to fund this evaluation themselves, particularly those who have experienced a change in health status and vocational ability due to neurological impairment.

The instances of medical insurance automatically paying for these evaluations appear to be quite limited—at least in the United States. In contrast, persons living in British Columbia may have a number of funding sources, including worker's compensation, the provincial health care system while in a hospital or as an outpatient, and provincially-funded organizations designed to maximize vocational/leisure independence in those with functional limitations. Thus, a neuropsychologist in the United States must consider what should be done for the individual who needs neuropsychological testing if funding has been denied by third-party payors. "These realities may force clinicians to limit or eliminate psychological testing, ask clients to pay out of pocket for needed testing, or provide testing with little or no financial compensation. . . ." (Turchik, Karpenko, Hammers, & McNamara, 2007, page 158). In response, scholarship is needed that identifies the cost:benefits of neuropsychological assessment for rehabilitative diagnosis and outcomes, thus assisting in the lobbying of governments, insurance companies, and other third-party sources for suitable funding. These evidence-based data can help the assessment be approved as medically pertinent for the individual.

MULTIDISCIPLINARY OR INTERDISCIPLINARY APPROACHES

Within the treatment team, rehabilitation neuropsychologists provide an overview or "big-picture" approach to the client. They assist team members in understanding how the client's neurocognitive features contribute to his

---

RESEARCH BOX 16.2

The following summarizes representative research that examines the efficacy of neuropsychological (NP) assessment for the diagnostic or treatment needs of individuals in the health system.

Coleman et al., 2002: Objective: Determine if NP testing predicted resumption of driving in those with moderate to severe traumatic brain injuries, one year postinjury.

Results: NP assessment was the best predictor of actual driving record postinjury.

Desmond et al., 1998: Objective: Determine if NP testing predicted death and/or recurrent stroke over a median time of 56 months in 244 patients examined 3 months poststroke.

Results: NP testing-based diagnosis of dementia was a better predictor than Mini-Mental Status Exam or clinical judgment in predicting mortality.

Miller and Donders, 2003: Objective: To evaluate NP test scores with respect to special education placement following a child's brain injury.

Results: NP test scores explain a significant amount of variance in educational outcome after brain injury—more than if demographic and medical variables are considered alone.

Questions

Lack of funding from providers for neuropsychological assessment is partly responsible for a greater emphasis on using evidenced-based interventions for health care. Difficulty securing funding creates a number of issues that can be detrimental to the person needing assessment (e.g. overly abbreviated test battery, cash-only payment for testing). However, this also has encouraged increased research pertaining to the efficacy of neuropsychological assessment to aid in diagnosis and treatment.

1. If you were to design an optimal health care system, what information would you require in order to approve neuropsychological testing?

2. As an individual considering participating in a 12-hour assessment, what would you want to know about what you are doing in order to feel that it is time well spent?

or her ability to perform a variety of tasks. They also facilitate increased understanding of how emotional or psychological aspects of the client and/or the client's support system may impact treatment and recovery. The psychologist also is alert to team dynamics and potential biases that may impede the course of treatment, and provides guidance to the team when needed.

Working with treatment teams can be both challenging and rewarding for rehabilitation neuropsychologists. They can offer a broad range of knowledge to the team and may be able to assist participation in all areas of treatment. For example, a physical therapist may be encouraged to try to treat an agitated client in a less noisy environment than the gym. The occupational therapist may discover her or his client (who has significant executive dysfunction) would be safer in the kitchen if provided with a checklist or structure. The speech therapist may find that, although worksheets seem to indicate improved word finding, the client's ability to initiate conversation at a social gathering is abysmal due to problems with selective attention and memory, leading to feelings of anxiety and depression that further impede social skills.

Rehabilitation neuropsychologists also should recognize that the team offers key insights into the injured individual's functional capabilities that are likely to go unseen in a formal neuropsychological assessment. When team members offer views that differ or are at odds with what is found on neuropsychological assessment, the rehabilitation neuropsychologist is responsible for finding out why the person is performing differently in two or more settings. Since the ecological validity of neuropsychological assessment is debatable for some behaviors, the psychologist is cautioned against standing behind formal test results to the exclusion of real-world observations.

Successful work within a treatment team requires that the rehabilitation neuropsychologist and others not become egocentric—believing their word is the best word. They and other team members have much to learn from one another. Neuropsychologists should consider requesting opportunities to observe the work of other therapists with clients and learn successful approaches from them. Suggestions should be couched in collegial language, such as: "Mr. Smith is really having problems with depression and not feeling like he is capable of anything. Maybe we could experiment with using compliments to reinforce each step he accomplishes in occupational therapy today. Let me know how it turns out . . . and if he is still noncompliant, let's work together and try something else."

In summary, the rehabilitation neuropsychologist provides a broad overview of an individual's neuropsychological strengths and weaknesses to the treatment team, while the team augments the neuropsychologist's understanding of the individual's abilities in an array of demands and settings. The optimal treatment team listens and learns from each other, resulting in a holistic approach toward rehabilitation.

NATIONAL AND INTERNATIONAL PRACTICES IN NEUROPSYCHOLOGICAL ASSESSMENT

Cultural issues are a concern with respect to neuropsychological assessment, both in the United States and in other countries that use neuropsychological measures developed on a largely Caucasian, Westernized culture. Some concerns are discussed below.

There are numerous issues to consider when interpreting neuropsychological assessments of individuals who are non-English speaking (Poreh, 2002). Four examples follow.

1. Illiteracy negatively affects the validity of tests.
2. The normative group used to compare test scores may be unsuitable even with translated tests.
3. Education level is associated with test performance in many domains. Educational processes differ among countries, thus calling into question the similarities in opportunities to acquire cognitive skills.
4. The amount of research on the effect of bilingualism on testing is meager. Other concerns include cultural differences in the expression of symptoms, level of acculturation even among English-speaking persons, and cultural aspects in the expectations the individual may have about the delivery of assessment services.

Aspects of neuropsychological assessment differ in other areas of the world. For example, in Japan, grammatical and written differences between Japanese and commonly used European languages have direct implications for evaluating speech and language skills (Murai, Hadano, & Hamanaka, 2002). Hispanics reportedly place more emphasis on good rapport and comfort with the examiner and see speed of task completion to be less important than accuracy (Ardila, Rodriguez-Menendez, Rosselli, 2002). This latter issue has clear implications for performance on the many tests that have time limits for completion.

Case Study 16.3

Normative data (i.e., test norms) have been developed to assist in determining whether an individual's test scores are considered to be normal in comparison to others. There are two basic approaches to test interpretation: (1) comparing test scores to those of the general population as a whole or (2) evaluating test scores in light of what is normal for the individual's particular subgroup. Consider the following scenario.

Ms. Gonzalez, a 34-year-old woman who immigrated to the United States from Honduras ten years ago, was assessed following a mild head injury she sustained while at work. She was given intellectual testing (in English) and found to be below average. Those with below average intelligence often perform at a similarly low level on memory testing. Thus, her below average scores on memory tests that also were administered in English were considered to reflect essentially no change in her (hypothesized) previously below average abilities. Her impaired memory was viewed by the neuropsychologist as perhaps reflecting a psychological condition, such

as a Somatoform Disorder, or a desire to magnify symptoms in light of a potential lawsuit. This led him to doubt the source of difficulties on the rest of his test results as well. He reported his conclusions to the payor source—worker's compensation.

QUESTIONS

1. What may be the consequences of this testing for Ms. Gonzalez? Consider how this may impact her activities/participation and environmental factors in her life from the perspective of psychological, economic, and/or functional issues.
2. Suppose that you were working in a country with different languages and customs (i.e., rural Asia or Africa) and sustained a brain injury. How would you want to be assessed? Would you want to be compared to others from that country or those from your home country? What would be your major concerns about an assessment?

Neuropsychological assessments of litigants in the United States and South Africa, following a motor vehicle accident, can have completely different approaches. For example, in the United States, forensic assessment is driven by the systematic use of tests that have established reliability and validity. In contrast, a case study of an assessment of a rural South African woman with severe brain injury and spinal fracture, a 5th grade education, and living in a communal setting describes a different approach (Lazarus & Lazarus, 2007). Rather than administer paper-and-pencil measures of functioning, the clinician observed

and measured the individual's ability to perform her previous job of selling snack-type foods, seeking out potential points of sales, scheduling time for sales, reconciling finances, managing home finances, participating in raising her family, as well as fulfilling communal obligations and participating in ritual cultural activities. The clinicians reported that the court would not allow use of Western formal test instruments due to their lack of validity for a woman with this background. Instead, the court was quite receptive to the professional relying on his or her observations to report her loss of function as a result of injury.

Summary and Conclusion

Neuropsychological assessment in rehabilitation and other health-related settings provides information for various needs, including diagnosis, treatment planning and intervention, and establishment of competencies. Many aspects of ICF classification are pertinent for neuropsychological assessment, as obtained data are meaningful only in a person's holistic context.

Historically, neuropsychology is built upon the fields of philosophy, neurology, medicine, and psychology. Since World War I, military need has been and still is a catalyst for the development of neuropsychological tests

to assist in diagnosis and rehabilitation. Dominant theories that link brain and behavior have varied from reductionistic to generalized, and both schools of thought remain in vogue. Regardless of one's theoretical approach, professionals need to be responsive to new scholarship. Thus, the only constant in the field of neuropsychology appears to be additional knowledge and resulting change.

Methods of neuropsychological assessment in rehabilitation and health encompass a wide variety of tests—both in the domains assessed and in the types of tests utilized (i.e., qualitative and/or quantitative). In addition to assessing intelligence, personality, and achievement, the neuropsychologist may assess orientation, attention/concentration, visual and verbal memory, learning, sensory perception, executive functioning, concept formation and reasoning, language, constructional skills, and level of effort. The extent of the assessment will vary according to factors such as severity of injury/illness, time since onset, and purpose of evaluation. The assessment's usefulness will depend largely upon the neuropsychologist's ability to integrate her or his knowledge of brain–behavior relationships and test data along with a comprehensive understanding of the person's life and culture.

Research regarding neuropsychological assessment's ecological validity, or its meaningfulness in predicting everyday functional skills, is pertinent to rehabilitation and other health care settings. Although assessment has been shown to be a useful predictor for somewhat circumscribed abilities, the research does not yet fully support utilizing traditional neuropsychological assessment measures to predict with considerable accuracy an individual's general level of executive functioning or ability to perform skills in domains such as vocational functioning. Although more ecologically valid instruments have been developed, their use has not been fully supported in the literature due to their psychometric limitations.

Prominent legislative and professional issues impacting neuropsychological assessment include the cost of assessment and the implications of increased difficulty in obtaining funding by third-party payors in the United States. This has both negative and positive consequences. For example, a patient may be unable to attempt to obtain a full neuropsychological battery because it is not covered by insurance. Neuropsychologists run the risk of not being compensated for their work. However, on the positive side, the need to lobby for better coverage has increased evidenced-based research in an effort to establish the need for assessment in a health setting, thus providing pertinent information to both the clinician and consumer.

Within health care, neuropsychologists are able to provide the multidisciplinary treatment team with a holistic overview of an individual's cognitive strengths and weaknesses and other psychological issues that may impact the response to rehabilitation. Given the weaknesses in formally assessing executive functioning through standardized methods, reliance on observations of the treatment team may supplant information obtained by the neuropsychologist as to the client's functional abilities related to activity/participation and environment. Finally, issues that typically impact the selection, use, and interpretation of tests and other assessment methods in neuropsychology when working with those from English-speaking and/or westernized countries may be inappropriate when such assessments are provided to those from different cultures and traditions. Their use may lead to invalid results and interpretations.

Self-Check Questions

Problem 1

When a functional MRI (fMRI) is used, the individual lies in a high magnetic field that allows magnetic fields associated with processes like blood flow to be measured. Some believe that brain functioning (such as use of working memory) and neural activity can be monitored as they occur, thus providing information about localization of function. However, criticisms include:

- The signal used for measuring response indirectly measures neural activity and can be impacted by other physiological events.
- The mathematical model used for understanding the signals does not account for variance in blood-flow reactions among different areas of the brain.

- fMRI has a poor temporal relationship between blood flow and the electrical neural responses.

Additionally, the fMRI environment is very different from real-life demands because the individual being evaluated is asked to lie perfectly still for approximately 30 minutes while performing tasks purportedly involving cognitive skills such as working memory, language functioning, executive functioning, and others. (All of these cognitive tasks are conducted while lying still in the fMRI machine; this often includes pressing a button in response to visual or auditory stimuli.)

Miller et al. (2007) report, "the fact that fMRI is strikingly primitive is commonly overlooked in the popular press" (p. 62).

Questions

1. Compare and contrast historical movements in the development and understanding of neuropsychological aspects of cognition (e.g., phrenology) with the current fMRI literature.
2. Look up and read at least three journal articles under the search "neuropsychological assessment" and "functional MRI," with special attention to the methods used to measure the neuropsychological construct.
3. How well does the method mirror real-life demands?
4. Do you think it will be helpful to individuals you may be working with, or is it more hypothetical at this stage?
5. Consider how fMRI data may be interpreted by a researcher 50 years from now.

Problem 2

Baxendale (2004) reports that Dory, a blue tropical fish in the movie *Finding Nemo* (2003), is one of the most accurate depictions of an amnesic syndrome from a neuropsychological standpoint. The author notes, "Dory is a fish with profound memory disturbance. The aetiology is unclear, but her difficulties in learning and retaining any new information, recalling names, and knowing where she is going or why are an accurate portrayal of the considerable memory difficulties faced daily by people with profound amnesic syndromes. The frustration of the other fish around her with constant repetition also accurately reflects the feelings of people who live with amnesic patients. Although her condition is often played for laughs during the film, poignant aspects of her memory loss are also portrayed when she is alone, lost, and profoundly confused."

Questions

1. Watch the movie, *Finding Nemo*. Identify the limitations and restrictions of Dory with respect to activities and participation using ICF classification.
2. Define the environmental factors in which she experiences barriers.

The ICF checklist may be obtained at the ICF homepage or at http://www.who.int/classifications/icf/site/icftemplate.cfm?myurl=checklist.html&mytitle=ICF%20Checklist.

Problem 3

In your own words, describe the difference between quantitative and qualitative neuropsychological assessment measures. Consider the simple measure Mini Mental State Exam. Describe the quantitative information obtained from this measure as well as qualitative data that could be obtained.

Problem 4

1. List five personal factors that could negatively impact neuropsychological test performance, potentially resulting in a false indication of cognitive impairment.
2. How may the examiner adjust his or her battery to accommodate these issues?

Problem 5

Consider the case study presented in reference to the woman in South Africa (p. 275). Westernized measures were not utilized with her. Reverse the situation, and imagine if you—as a non-African—were suddenly placed into her unfamiliar role of cooking and selling snacks, participating in community rituals, and raising a family—as a measure of your neuropsychological functioning.

Questions

1. What possible neuropsychological conclusions could be drawn from your performance?
2. How would this situation be similar to the South African woman being assessed by Westernized measures?
3. Would use of an interpreter, alone, remedy the situation? Why or why not?

Problem 6
Questions

1. Explain the term *ecological validity*.
2. What are the limitations of paper and pencil measures in respect to measuring behavior?
3. What are the positive aspects of using standardized and reliable test instruments

Problem 7

Search the terms *evidence-based practice* and *neuropsychological assessment* to identify at least two studies that provide evidence-based data of the benefit of neuropsychological assessment in the health care setting.

Questions

1. How do these studies differ from research that is not evidence-based?
2. Is evidence-based practice equally effective for individuals and groups? Why or why not?
3. Use the information you obtained as justification to an insurance company for performing a neuropsychological examination.

References

Ardila, A., Rodriguez-Menendez, G., Rosselli, M. (2002) Current issues in neuropsychological assessment with Hispanics/Latinos. In Lisse, The Netherlands Swets and Zeitlinger. *Minority and cross-cultural aspects of neuropsychological assessment.* F. R. Ferraro (Ed.), (pp. 161–179).

Barth, J. T. (2003). Introduction to the NAN 2001 definition of a clinical neuropsychologist. NAN Policy and Planning Committee. *Archives of Clinical Neuropsychology, 18*(5), 551–555.

Baxendale S. (2004). Memories aren't made of this: Amnesia at the movies. *British Medical Journal, 18–25,* 329.

Benton, A.L., Hamsher, K. deS., & Sivan, A.B. (1994). *Multilingual Aphasia Examination.* San Antonio, TX. Psychological Corporation.

Benton, A. L., Sivan, A., Hamsher, K. deS. (1994). *Contributions to neuropsychological assessment. A clinical manual* (2nd ed.). *New York: Oxford University Press.*

Bilbao, A., Kennedy, C., Chatterji, S., Ustun, B., Barquero, J. L., & Barth, J. T. (2003). The ICF: Applications of the WHO model of functioning, disability and health to brain injury rehabilitation. *NeuroRehabilitation. 18,* 239–250.

Coleman, R. D., Rapport, L. J., Ergh, T. C., Hanks, R. A., Ricker, J. H., & Millis, S. R. (2002). Predictors of driving outcome after traumatic brain injury. *Archives of Physical Medicine & Rehabilitation, 83*(10), 1415–22.

Dawes, R. M., Faust, D., & Meehl., P. E. (1989). Clinical versus actuarial judgment. *Science, 243,* 1668–1674.

Delis, D., Kaplan, E., & Kramer, J. (2001). *Delis–Kaplan Executive Function System.* San Antonio, TX: The Psychological Corporation.

Delis, D. C., Kramer, J. H., Kaplan, E., & Ober, B. A. (2000). *The California Verbal Learning Test.* (2nd ed., Adult Version). San Antonio, TX: The Psychological Corporation.

Desmond D. W., Moroney, J. T., Bagiella, E., Sano, M., & Stern, Y. (1998). Dementia as a predictor of adverse outcomes following stroke: An evaluation of diagnostic methods. *Stroke; A Journal of Cerebral Circulation, 29*(1), 69–74.

Diller, L., Ben Yishay, Y., Gerstman, L., Goodkin, R., Gordon, W., and Weinberg, J. (1974). *Studies in Cognition and Rehabilitation in Hemiplegia* (Rehabilitation Monograph, No. 50). New York: New York University Medical Center Institute of Rehabilitation Medicine.

Diller, L. & Weinberg, J. (1970). Evidence for accident-prone behavior in hemiplegic patients. *Archives of Physical Medicine and Rehabilitation.* June, 358–363.

Ferraro, F. R. (Ed.). (2002) *Minority and cross-cultural aspects of neuropsychological assessment.* Lisse, The Netherlands: Swets and Zeitlinger.

Gauthier, L., DeHaut, F., & Joanette, Y. (1989). The Bells Test: A quantitative and qualitative test for visual neglect. *International Journal of Clinical Neuropsychology,* 11, 49–54.

Goldstein, K. (1948). *Aftereffects of brain injuries in war.* New York: Grune and Stratton.

Green, P. (2003). *Green's Word Memory Test for Microsoft Windows.* Edmonton, Alberta: Green's Publishing Inc.

Green, P. (2005). *Green's Word Memory Test. User's manual.* Edmonton, AB: Green's Publishing, Inc.

Groth-Marnat G. (2003). Digit Span as a measure of everyday attention: A study of ecological validity. *Perceptual and Motor Skills, 97*(3 Pt 2), 1209–1218.

Hoskin, K. M., Jackson, M., & Crowe, S. F. (2005). Money management after acquired brain dysfunction: The validity of neuropsychological assessment. *Rehabilitation Psychology, 50*(4), 355–365.

INS Dictionary of Neuropsychology. (1999). D. Loring (Ed.). New York: Oxford University Press.

Jain, N.; Layton, B. S.; Murray, P. K. (2000) Are aphasic patients who fail the GOAT in PTA? A modified Galveston Orientation and Amnesia Test for persons with aphasia. *Clinical Neuropsychologist, 14*(1), 13–17.

Kaplan, E., Goodglass, H., & Weintraub, S. (2001). *The Boston Naming Test* (2nd ed.). Philadelphia: Lippincott Williams and Wilkins.

Kolb, B., & Wishaw, I. (1996). *Fundamentals of human neuropsychology. 4th ed.* W.H. Freeman and Company.

Lazarus, G. T., & Lazarus, T. (2007) Neuropsychological assessment of rural South African motor vehicle accident litigants: A case study. Presented at National Academy of Neuropsychology Annual Conference.

LeBlanc, J. M., Hayden, M. E., & Paulman, R. G. (2000). A comparison of neuropsychological and situational assessment for predicting employability after closed head injury. *Journal of Head Trauma Rehabilitation, 15*(4), 1022–1040.

Levin, H. S., O'Donnell, V. M., & Grossman, R. G. (1979). The Galveston Orientation and Amnesia Test: A practical scale to assess cognition after head injury. *Journal of Nervous and Mental Disease, 167,* 675–684.

Lezak, M., Howieson, D., & Loring, D. (2004). *Neuropsychological assessment* (4th ed.) New York: Oxford University Press.

Meyers, J., & Meyers, K. (1995). *The Meyers Scoring System for the Rey Complex Figure and Recognition Trial: Professional manual.* Odessa, FL: Psychological Assessment Resources.

Miller, G., Elbert, T., Sutton, B., & Heller, W. (2007). Innovative clinical assessment technologies: Challenges and opportunities in neuroimaging. *Psychological Assessment, 19*(1), 58–73.

Miller, L. J., & Donders, J. (2003). Prediction of educational outcome after pediatric traumatic brain injury. *Rehabilitation Psychology, 48*(4), 237–241.

Moucha, R. (2006). Cortical plasticity and rehabilitation. *Progress in Brain Research, 157,* 111–122.

Murai, T., Hadano, K., & Hamanaka, T. (2002). Current issues in neuropsychological assessment in Japan. In F. R. Ferraro (Ed.), *Minority and cross-cultural aspects of neuropsychological assessment* (pp. 100–127). Lisse, The Netherlands: Swets and Zeitlinger.

Official Position of the Division of Clinical Neuropsychology (APA Division 40) on the Role of Neuropsychologists in Clinical Use of fMRI: Approved by the Division 40 Executive Committee July 28, 2004. *Clinical Neuropsychologist, 18*(3), 349–351.

Ogden-Epker, M., & Cullum, C. M. (2001). Quantitative and qualitative interpretation of neuropsychological data in the assessment of temporal lobectomy candidates. *The Clinical Neuropsychologist*, 15, 183–195.

Ostrosky-Solis, F., Jaine, R. M., and Ardila, A. (1998). Memory abilities during normal aging. *International Journal of Neuroscience, 93*, 151–162.

Poreh, A. (2002). Neuropsychological and psychological issues associated with cross-cultural and minority assessment. *Minority and cross-cultural aspects of neuropsychological assessment* (pp. 329–343). Lisse, Netherlands: Swets & Zeitlinger Publishers.

Rabin, L. A., Burton, L. A., Barr, W. B. (2007). Utilization rates of ecologically oriented instruments among clinical neuropsychologists. *The Clinical Neuropsychologist, 21*(5), 727–743.

Robertson, I. H., Ward, T., Ridgeway, V., & Nimmo-Smith, I. (1994). *The test of everyday attention*. Bury St. Edmunds, England: Thames Valley Test Company.

Roth, R., Isquith, P., & Gioia, G. (2005). *BRIEF-A Behavior Rating Inventory of Executive Function—Adult Version. Professional Manual.* Lutz, F. L.: Psychological Assessment Resources.

Spector, J. (1995). Integrating cognitive and clinical neuropsychology. In R. Mapou & J. Spector (Eds.), *Clinical neuropsychological assessment: A cognitive assessment* pp. 339–354. New York: Plenum Press.

Strauss, E., Sherman, E., & Spreen. O. (2006) *A compendium of neuropsychological tests. Administration, norms, and commentary* (3rd ed.) New York: Oxford University Press.

Turchik, J. A., Karpenko, V., Hammers, D., & McNamara, J. R. (2007). Practical and ethical assessment issues in rural, impoverished, and managed care settings. *Professional Psychology: Research and Practice, 38*(2), 158–168.

Walsh, K. (1987). *Neuropsychology. A clinical approach* (2nd ed). New York: Churchill Livingstone.

Warden, D. (2006). Military TBI during the Iraq and Afghanistan Wars. *Journal of Head Trauma Rehabilitation, 21*(5), 398–402.

Wechsler, D. (1997a). *Wechsler Adult Intelligence Scale* (3rd ed.). San Antonio, TX: The Psychological Corporation.

Wechsler, D. (1997b) Wechsler Memory Scale—Third Edition. The Psychological Corporation. Harcourt Brace & Company. San Antonio, TX.

Wechsler, D. (1997c). *WMS-III Administration and Scoring Manual.* San Antonio, Texas: The Psychological Corporation.

Wilson, B., Cockburn, J., Baddeley, A. & Hiorns, R. (2003). *The Rivermead Behavioral Memory Test-II Supplement Two*. Bury St. Edmunds, England: Thames Valley Test Company.

World Health Organization. (2001). *International Classification of Functioning, Disability and Health*, Geneva: World Health Organization. http//www.who.int/icf

Zafonte, R. D. (1997). Posttraumatic amnesia: Its relation to functional outcome. *Archives of Physical Medicine & Rehabilitation, 78*(10), 1103–1106.

17

Academic Achievement Measures in Rehabilitation

SCOTT L. DECKER
Georgia State University, Atlanta

DAVID E. MCINTOSH
Ball State University, Muncie, IN

OVERVIEW

This chapter provides an overview of assessment of academic skills and functions and provides information critical to rehabilitation activity and participation deficits in educational and social contexts. Assessment of academic skills facilitates the exploration of strengths and weaknesses that may be the focus of rehabilitative efforts. A clearer understanding of an individual's academic deficits improves a clinician's ability to develop targeted interventions and assists researchers in determining interactions among factors that influence success and failure in activities and participations that involve academic functions. We consider classifications important in understanding the use of achievement measures in rehabilitation and health settings. Most academic classification systems lack functional specifications, thus presenting problems in their use in rehabilitation and health settings. Three specific measures of academic functioning will be discussed. Measurement characteristics of these instruments will be reviewed as well as the correspondence between each instrument and the International Classification of Functioning, Disability and Health (ICF) classification system. Finally, a case study will be presented to demonstrate the use of achievement measures in academic rehabilitation.

LEARNING OBJECTIVES

By the end of this chapter, readers should be able to:

- Demonstrate how classification systems are important for understanding the usefulness of academic measures in rehabilitation and compare how different classification systems use different criteria for classifying and determining academic deficits

- Compare the International Classification of Functioning, Disability and Health (ICF) system to other systems of classifying academic problems

- Explain both benefits and limitations of using the ICF or alternative classifications systems for achievement measures

- Describe the major measures of achievement used in rehabilitation and health settings and evaluate the evidence for their use

- Apply some general guidelines in interpreting results from achievement measures

INTRODUCTION

Academic skills are critical for adapting to the complex demands of society. They constitute the basis for acquiring and enriching an individual's fund of knowledge needed in many life activities. Thus, they often are an important component in rehabilitation. Academic content areas generally are described in reference to math, reading, and writing. Each of these areas may be subdivided into more differentiated skills.

Efforts to rehabilitate academic skills have been facilitated by several conditions. A theoretical understanding of the nature and components of academic skills has improved understanding of how academic skills develop. The measurement of academic skills has improved substantially through the use of modern psychometric techniques. These techniques include normative-based metrics as well as interval-level measures that are ideally suited for measuring intervention effects. The linking of theory and measurement has led to comprehensive batteries of achievement measures that assess both content knowledge and processing skills involved in applying academic knowledge. This integration of theory and measurement has resulted in clinicians taking a more functional perspective when assessing individuals with academic difficulties (Dean, Woodcock, Decker, & Schrank, 2003).

Notably absent from typical applications of achievement measures is a classification system to describe categories of learning disorders that also specifies underlying functional deficits contributing to learning disorders. For example, stating that an individual has a math disorder does not specify the origin of this problem. Therefore, linking the ICF classification system with theory-based measures of achievement can assist in determining the underlying causes of a learning disorder and assist in developing functional interventions.

ACADEMIC CLASSIFICATION SYSTEMS

Numerous classification systems include disorders characterized by deficits in academic skills or learning (Oakland, Mpofu, Gregoire, & Faulkner, 2007). However, in general, classification systems that describe academic functions and disorders are inconsistent and demonstrate significant heterogeneity. Professionals ascribing to different systems of classification use different nomenclature that limit clear communication (McIntosh & Decker, 2005). Additionally, most classification systems do not specify functional abilities comprehensively or explicitly.

Diagnostic and Statistical Manual for Mental Disorders

The *Diagnostic and Statistical Manual for Mental Disorders* (4th ed.) provides specific diagnostic categories for Learning Disorders with Reading, Math, and Written Expression. A diagnosis is made when achievement performance, as measured by a standardized test, is *substantially below* expectations for chronological age, intelligence, and educational opportunity (American Psychiatric Association, 2000). Underlying functions and specific dimensions of academic areas (e.g., math application, math calculation) are not specified. Thus, this categorical system does not always inform clinical reality (Jablensky, 1999).

Individuals with Disabilities Education Act

Federal government-supported categorical diagnostic systems also are frequent used. For example, special educational funding for services provided to students with various disabilities is based on federal guidelines that specify the nature of the disability and, in some instances,

---

DISCUSSION BOX 17.1

Measures of achievement may assess academic constructs that do not match federal guidelines (e.g., phonological awareness). In some cases, the differences are a matter of semantics. In other cases, there can be a clear semantic match, but the content or construct is vastly different. This creates a disagreement in the measurement scope of academic achievement measures in how they are aligned with classification systems.

Question

1. Describe the consequences or benefits of obtaining consensus in describing academic disorders among professionals on both a national and international level.

criteria for diagnosing the disability. The passage of Public Law 94-142 in 1975 provided the greatest impetus to operationally define achievement skills for the purpose of identifying and remedying academic problems. The 1997 Individuals with Disabilities Educational Act (IDEA, Public Law 105-17) specified particular academic areas and defined learning disabilities as underachievement within these domains. The academic areas specified by IDEA are: oral expression, listening comprehension, written expression, basic reading skill, reading comprehension, mathematics calculation, and mathematics reasoning (IDEA; Sec. 300.541).

Learning disabilities constitute the largest special education category for students receiving services in schools. The diagnosis of learning disabilities using federal guidelines for special education has been controversial. Although most agree that the category for learning disability is useful, the controversy primarily centers on how to operationally define the criteria used to diagnose the condition (Dehn, 2006). Students often are diagnosed based on definitions that require rigid applications of a discrepancy between scores on tests of achievement and intelligence (e.g., achievement test scores must be lower than intelligence test scores by one or one and one-half standard deviations). This procedure has some appeal because it uses a simple mathematical formula to discern a learning disability, which gives the sense of objectivity and requires little clinical competence and judgment (Simpson & Buckhalt, 1990). The professional preparation of personnel who assess many school-related disabilities (e.g., school psychologists, speech–language pathologists, occupational therapists) often is somewhat brief and when making a diagnosis test administration rather than clinical judgment is emphasized.

These issues have led some to suggest a movement toward noncategorical classification with less emphasis on psychometric testing and more emphasis on functional analyses of behavior (Reschly & Ysseldyke, 2002). Although some professionals believe problems with diagnosis can be overcome by not using test data, others believe tests are not at fault and instead that efforts are needed to improve the operational definition of academic disorders and that the use of tests provide functional applications.

10th Revision of the International Classification of Diseases and Related Health Problems (ICD-10)

The 10th revision of the International Classification of Diseases and Related Health Problems (ICD-10) also contains diagnostic categories concerning academic functioning. The category Disorders of Psychological Development (F80-F90) includes Specific Developmental Disorders of Scholastic Skills. Reading, spelling, arithmetic, mixed, other, and unspecified academic skills are believed to not develop normally due to a cognitive processing disorder rather than a lack of opportunity or acquired trauma. According to the ICF, impairment reflects a deviation from a certain generally accepted population standard and does not necessarily imply a disorder or disease. Impairment in activities that involve math, writing, spelling, or reading may limit an individual's participation in numerous cultural functions. The ICD-10 also provides a category for Specific Developmental Disorders of Speech and Language (F80), Motor Functions (F82), and Mixed Specific Developmental Disorder, Pervasive (F83). These also may impact academic functioning.

International Classification of Functioning, Disability, and Health (ICF)

The *International Classification of Functioning, Disability, and Health* (ICF; World Health Organization [WHO], 2001; see also chapter 1) provides a comprehensive model to describe health and health-related states for the purpose of conceptualizing functioning and disability that complements the ICD-10 (WHO, 2001). Additionally, it provides a coding system for the constructs Body Functions (b), Body Structure (s), Activity & Participation (d), and Environmental Factors (e). The letter associated with each construct is used with a numeric label for particular diagnostic descriptions. For

---

DISCUSSION BOX 17.2

Some mental health professionals believe we should not use any classification system, in part, because its use labels a person, perhaps resulting in stigmatizing connotations. Thus, a professional should understand the merits and limitations of a classification system.

Question

1. Discuss the merits and limitations of using the International Classification of Functioning, including how its use may be less stigmatizing than other classification systems.

example, b175.3 refers to a severe impairment in specific language functions, which is classified under Body Functions as indicated with the letter "b." The ICF describes academic problems in a comprehensive framework that includes domains of mental functions, activities and participation, and environmental factors.

The ICF classifies mental functions as global or specific. Difficulties with academic activities typically are directly connected to specific mental functions of language and calculation. Functional deficits may result from any combination of mental or physical (e.g., fine motor) problems.

Mental functions of language broadly include activities involving the use of signs and symbols. ICF language functions are divided into the categories of receptive, expressive, integrative, other, and unspecified. Reception of language uses subcategories of spoken, written, and sign. Expression of language similarly uses subcategories of spoken, written, and sign language.

Functions involving mathematical symbols form a separate category. Calculation functions include simple (b1720) and complex calculations (b1721). Simple calculation functions include addition, subtraction, multiplication, and division. Complex functions involve multistep calculations. The diagnostic code begins with the letter "b" to indicate this function, and defined in Body Functions under the label 1720.

The ICF defines activities as the execution of a task or action and participation as involvement in a life situation. Activities and participation contain a section for learning and applying knowledge that includes several categories relevant to academic knowledge. The Basic Learning category (d130–d159) includes specific categories for problems learning to read (d140), write (d145), and calculate (d150). The Applying Knowledge category (d160–d179) includes specific categories for executing or performing activities involved in reading (d166), writing (d170), and calculating (d172). Notice, the letter "d" is used to specifically indicate the description for each of these categories classified under the construct of Activity & Participation.

The ICF also provides coding conventions to designate contextual and environmental qualities relevant to academic learning. These contextual and environmental aspects include qualities for educational institutes (e5850), training systems (e5851), and educational training policies (e5852). These areas include aspects of administrative control, monitoring mechanisms, and policies governing the delivery of educational programs. Additionally, the code includes the letter "e" to indicate classification under Environmental Factors.

IMPORTANCE OF ICF TO ACHIEVEMENT CLASSIFICATIONS

The ICF system has the potential of becoming the dominant classification system in mental health. The ways in which the ICF system specifies academic functions is similar to or surpasses that found in other classification systems. Essentially, the ICF provides a systems-based comprehensive model of functioning that extends beyond academic areas to encompass multiple aspects of psychological and health-related domains. This ICF feature is important for rehabilitative efforts in conceptualizing the interaction of individual functioning and disability with contextual factors.

Other models that merely provide diagnostic categories deemphasize attention to underlying deficits that are causing a disorder. Moreover, other models do not link diagnostic and intervention processes. That is, protocols do not exist that link specific interventions to a diagnosis. Considerably more information than a diagnosis is needed to plan and carry out a successful patient-centered intervention.

Given the importance of academic attainment to education, methods to classify academic disorders are especially needed in educational settings. ICF terminology is consistent with academic categories specified under the Individuals with Disabilities Educational Improvement Act. They include oral expression, listening comprehension, written expression, basic reading skill, reading comprehension, mathematics calculation, and mathematic reasoning. Additionally by including functional domains, ICF has significant value over other categorical systems. The ICF model could potentially be implemented in school districts nationally and help resolve many of the issues regarding categorical assessment of disability classification.

Table 17.1 illustrates the correspondence between ICF and educational categories described under the Individuals with Disabilities Educational Improvement Act (IDEA).

Educational classification categories under ICF and IDEA correspond closely, differing only on reading. Although the ICF provides one global category for reading, IDEA divides reading into two areas: basic reading and reading comprehension.

A number of widely used tests are available to operationally measure these functional qualities (see Tables 17.1 and 17.2). Some test batteries measure them more comprehensively than others. Therefore, it is theoretically possible the ICF system could be used and implemented throughout U.S. schools to determine educational functioning.

TABLE 17.1 Comparison of ICF and IDEA Guidelines with Corresponding Test Measures

Classification System		Achievement Measure and Subtests		
ICF	Federal	WJ-III	WIAT-II	WRAT-4
Reception of Spoken Language	Listening Comprehension	Understanding Directions	Listening Comprehension	
Reception of Written Language	Reading Comprehension	Passage Comprehension	Reading Comprehension	Reading Comprehension
	Basic Reading Skills	Letter-Word ID Reading Fluency	Pseudoword Decoding Word Reading	Word Reading
Expression of Spoken Language	Oral Expression	Story Recall	Oral Language	
Expression of Written Language	Written Expression	Spelling Writing Fluency Writing Samples	Written Expression Spelling	Spelling
Calculation Function: Simple Calculation	Mathematic Calculation	Calculations Math Fluency	Numerical Operations	Arithmetic
Calculation Function: Complex Calculation	Mathematic Reasoning	Applied Problems	Mathematics Reasoning	

Diagnostic models and accompanying assessment practices increasingly need to demonstrate their relevance, utility, and functional relationship to important life skills and adaptive behavior. The ICF demonstrates these qualities. The ICF's diagnostic utility is found in the comprehensiveness of its system and its correspondence with the ICD-10. Whereas other classification systems end by providing classification definitions, the ICF theoretically provides the capability to further define specific psychological processes that help clarify and determine the severity of the functional impairment.

For example, let's assume an assessment specialist receives a referral to investigate possible reading problems in a child who is obese. The use of standardized measures of reading confirmed problems in word recognition and comprehension. Various attributes may cause a reading disorder, including low motivation, phonological processing deficits, and diminished mental abilities. Let's assume motivation is found to be a contributing attribute. Using the ICF, Activities and Participation reading performance (d166) as well as the mental function of motivation (b1301) could be noted. Other notations could be used to acknowledge the adverse impact of phonological processing deficits or diminished mental abilities on reading. The added sophistication of the ICF classification enables clinicians to identify and communicate specific functional deficits (e.g., poor processing speed) and the underlying cause (e.g., neurological impairment) of the deficit. Additionally, the added sophistication enables researchers to document and code specific and different interacting aspects of disorders and thus better reflects clinical reality.

This added sophistication also enables them to investigate the simultaneous influences of personal attributes and treatment effects, research that may lead to treatment options based on both personal qualities as well as the nature and severity of a particular disability.

ACADEMIC CONTENT AREAS

Vocational evaluations may occur prior to planning one's rehabilitation program. Comprehensive vocational evaluations should include an assessment of receptive language, both spoken and written, expressive language, both spoken and written, and math calculation abilities. More in-depth vocational evaluations may include more specific functional assessment (e.g., memory, speed of information processing, and fine motor manipulation) using more specific functional measures (e.g., Wechsler Memory Scale, 3rd ed., 1997), depending on the focus of the evaluation. Table 17.2 provides an overview of some commonly used measures of achievement and the academic areas each assesses. When selecting a measure, the professional must consider the nature of the referral, age of the individual being assessed, the individual's level of cognitive functioning, the goals and objectives of the evaluation, and recommendations that will be needed based upon the results.

Reading Decoding and Comprehension

The ICF system describes reading as a mental function involved in the reception of written language. Reading involves two different and related skills: decoding and

TABLE 17.2 Academic Areas Assessed by Different Achievement Measures

Measure	Decoding Reading	Reading Comprehension	Mathematic Computation	Mathematic Application	Written Language	Expressive Language	Receptive Language
Woodcock–Johnson							
Tests of Achievement (3rd ed. ages 2–90)	X	X	X	X	X	X	X
Kaufman Test of Educational Achievement (2nd ed. ages 4.5–25)	X	X	X	X	X	X	X
Wechsler Individual Achievement Test (2nd ed.) (ages 4–85)	X	X	X	X	X	X	X
Peabody Individual Achievement Test-Revised (ages 5–18)	X	X	X		X		
Wide Range Achievement Test (4th ed.) (ages 5–94)	X	X	X				
Academic Competence Evaluation Scales (ages 5–21)	X	X	X	X	X	X	
Diagnostic Achievement Test for Adolescents (2nd ed.) (12–18)	X	X	X	X	X	X	X
Basic Achievement Skills Inventory (ages 8–80)	X	X	X	X	X		
Norris Educational Achievement Test (ages 4–17)	X	X	X	X	X		

comprehension. Decoding involves the process of accurately identifying or phonetically decoding graphic symbols; for example, correctly pronouncing the beginning, middle, and ending of a word. An assessment of word identification is one method to measure decoding skills where an examinee reads a list of words that are arranged in order of difficulty, from easy to difficult.

Reading comprehension refers to the ability to construct and project meaning onto graphic symbols (Brown, Hammill, & Wiederhold, 1995). Standardized measures assess reading comprehension in a variety of ways. Some tests use the cloze technique. It requires an examinee to read one or several sentences in which a word is missing and to provide the missing word (e.g., *The boy _____ on the horse*.). Other measures require an individual to read a short passage and answer questions. Some measures enable an examiner to analyze the types of errors made (e.g., those associated with details, sequencing, or inference).

Mathematic Calculation and Application

Math calculation is synonymous with "simple calculation" as used by the ICF system. Calculation primarily involves the use of numerical operators of addition, subtraction, multiplication, and division. Math calculation typically is assessed by having an individual complete a paper-and-pencil math task. The math problems are graded in difficulty. Some tests limit the time one has to complete the task.

Math applications involve the use of math calculation skills in a context. For example, problem-centered stories may be read either to or by the examinee who then applies his or her knowledge of math to solve them. Most math application measures allow the examinee to use paper and pencil to assist in solving problems.

Written Language and Spelling

The ICF system defines writing as a mental function of language necessary to produce meaningful written messages. Written language is assessed using various methods that range in complexity from spelling words to writing compositions. For example, an examinee may be asked to write words and sentences or, at a more complex level, to write a paragraph. Some measures penalize an examinee for punctuation, capitalization, and spelling errors.

Expressive Language

The ICF defines expressive language as a specific mental function to produce spoken, written, signed, or other forms of messages. Expressive language refers to a broad set of qualities. Thus, its measurement is not specific to one language process. For example, examinees may be asked to repeat stories told to them. Thus, both receptive language and short-term memory are measured. Examinees also may be asked to explain orally how they would clean a kitchen or to give directions from their house to the grocery store.

Receptive Language

The ICF defines receptive language broadly to include the ability to decode messages in spoken or written forms to obtain their meaning. Receptive language has two forms: written and oral. Receptive written language is assessed by tests that assess reading. Receptive oral language is assessed by tests that assess one's ability to listen and respond meaningfully to what one hears. Reception of spoken language can be measured in various ways. For example, on some measures, an examinee may be asked to listen to and then follow directions that increase in complexity. As noted in the previous section, others may ask an examinee to repeat stories. A receptive vocabulary task followed by a sentence comprehension task may be used on other measures of receptive language.

CURRENT PRACTICES IN USE OF ACHIEVEMENT MEASURES

One of the primary objectives of a comprehensive vocational assessment is to identify and assess the academic functioning of an individual with the goal of helping that individual achieve success in a specific employment setting (Levinson, 2002). Therefore, academic functioning in receptive/expressive language, written language, reading, and mathematics is assessed to the extent these skills are critical to one's job performance. Data from these measures are important when developing vocational components of rehabilitation plans. Unfortunately, the importance of academic achievement test data to vocational planning may be underestimated. These skills often directly influence an individual's ability to make good decisions and maintain successful employment (Levinson, 2002).

In general, achievement measures assess a person's proficiency to perform academic tasks. Proficiency in performance is related directly to acquired knowledge and the ability to display it. The process of acquiring knowledge requires the use of many personal qualities together with the richness of one's environment. Deficits in academic performance may result from numerous causes beyond that of knowledge acquisition. For example, poor motivation, cultural deprivation, and lack of family support can adversely influence the acquisition or display of achievement. Deficiencies in academic skills may be attributed to environmental factors (e.g., opportunity) or impairment in one or more psychological functions (e.g., memory, depression, anxiety), which may result in restrictions and limitations in various activities.

Tests of academic achievement differ in their scope, the skills measured, and the degree measures are aggregated to form composite scores. Some measures have a narrow scope and assess a single academic function whereas others are broader and assess multiple skills. Some tests go beyond the measurement of academic skills by also assessing important processes associated with the development of those skills. For example, in addition to assessing reading decoding and comprehension, some tests also assess phonological processing, reading fluency, and reading rate—qualities that impact one's acquisition and display of reading skills.

Functional assessment is possible due to the use of modern techniques of test development. For example, a test assessing math calculation consists of a series of items ordered by difficulty. The item order represents the order in which the quality or skill develops (e.g., addition is learned before multiplication, which is learned before geometry). An examinee's ability is calibrated in response

DISCUSSION BOX 17.3

Standardized achievement measures provide information on how a particular student compares to a normative group. Generally, achievement measures use a large, nationally-based representative sample of age-matched individuals as a means of gaining a fair and valid comparison of skill development. Curriculum based measurement (CBM) has become a popular form of achievement assessment that does not rely on norms. Rather, CBM's focus on particular skills uses achievement measures developed from a student's curriculum material to monitor progress toward a particular academic goal. Controversy exists as to whether such measures contain sufficient reliability and validity.

Questions

1. What is the benefit in using standardized achievement measures?
2. For what purposes would using a standardized versus an unstandardized measure be useful?

to whether the examinee passes or fails a set of test items. Easier items are administered first and more difficult items later. Items are administered continually until establishing a consistent pattern of item failure attributed to the level of difficulty of the items given at the person's ability (see also chapter 8).

Ability level is a direct indicator of the individual's level of functioning. An individual's level of functioning can be estimated through the use of both quantitative data (e.g., test scores) and qualitative methods. Quantitative measurement provides information as to the likelihood an individual is proficient on the measured skill.

However, the practical significance of proficiency depends on an understanding of the measurement dimension because most achievement measures consist of numerous skills arranged in a developmental order. For example, math calculation skills first measure number identification followed by addition, subtraction, multiplication, and so on. Understanding how proficient an individual is in math calculation requires an interpretation of what the person can and cannot do along this continuum, which is not easily captured by a raw or standard score. Other qualities, including experience as well as needed and desired levels of proficiency, should be considered before determining whether the functional level suggests a disability. For example, many first-grade children will perform at a functionally lower level, as would be expected, when compared to fourth graders on tasks that require phonological decoding. For example, children may hear the word *cat* without the /a/ sound (e.g., k_t) and be asked to complete the word. First graders are expected to perform lower than fourth graders on this test because they have not developed the phonological skills at the same level that would be expected of fourth graders. However, children in the fourth grade are expected to display phonological decoding skills similar to other fourth graders. Therefore, a fourth grader who scores significantly lower than the average

fourth grader may display a functional deficit on this quality. Normative information is crucial in this regard. Measurable deficits in reading concurrent with deficits in phonological decoding may be suggestive of a disability as long as other factors (e.g., learning opportunity, cultural background) are also considered. The aforementioned example would be true whether it were phonological decoding, reading comprehension, written language, or other skills.

There are numerous comprehensive achievement measures commercially available. Three of the most frequently used measures in the United States are the Woodcock-Johnson Tests of Achievement (3rd ed.; WJ-III), Wechsler Individualized Achievement Test (2nd ed.; WIAT-II), and the Wide Range Achievement Test (4th ed.; WRAT-4). Of these measures, the WJ-III is perhaps the most frequently used. The WJ-III was nationally standardized and can be used for individuals between the ages of 2 and 90+. The WJ-III comprehensively measures important areas of academic functioning including broad areas of reading, writing, and mathematics through a variety of tests. Additionally, certain processing measures are included such as the Word Attack subtest, which measures phonological decoding. Users may choose scoring information based on age or grade. Standard scores and percentile ranks provide a normative comparison for score interpretation. It is co-normed with the WJ-III Tests of Cognitive Abilities. As co-normed instruments, elaborate profile and discrepancy procedures are available. Intraindividual comparisons involve a statistical analysis that determines if a particular achievement area is significantly better or worse than the other achievement areas. This type of discrepancy provides information on a person's particular academic strengths and weaknesses.

The WIAT-II is also a comprehensive measure of academic skills frequently used in the United States. Norms for the WIAT-II were based on a nationally representative sample. It is appropriate for a broad age range (4 to 85 years of age) and includes both age and grade composite scores. The WIAT-II includes composite measures of reading, math, written language, and oral language. A screener composite also is included that consists of spelling, word reading, and numeric operations subtests. Percentile ranks, normal curve equivalent, and age and grade equivalent scores can be obtained for both composites and subtests. Although not co-normed, it is empirically linked to the WISC-IV and WAIS-III. Discrepancies between achievement composites and intelligence composites can be obtained. Composites and subtests of the WIAT-II have adequate to superior reliability.

The WRAT-4, although less comprehensive, is used frequently due to its ease of use and rapid administration. It may be used appropriately for individuals 5 to 94 years of age. The WRAT-4 follows in line with previous editions of focusing on the areas of reading, spelling, and arithmetic. Whereas previous editions contained only three tests, one for each area, the WRAT-4 has added several new tests to measure academic functions more comprehensively (e.g., sentence comprehension). Grade and age-based norms are available. Normative scores available include standard scores, percentile ranks, grade equivalent, normal curve equivalent, and stanines. Statistical comparisons between subtests can be made to determine individual strengths and weaknesses.

Quantitative Interpretation

During vocational planning, various methods facilitate the use of data from standardized tests of achievement (see also chapters 19 and 20). For example, standardized tests summarize a person's performance through standard scores, grade equivalent scores, and percentile ranks, which are quantitative metric standard scores; percentile ranks are used to compare an individual's performance to a specific norm group (e.g., same-aged peers). Each of these normative scores can be found on the WJ-III, WIAT-II, and the WRAT-4. The primary quantitative metric used in each of these tests is the standard score. The standard score is based on a mean of 100 and a standard deviation of 15. For example, the WJ-III Broad Reading standard score for the case study at the end of this chapter was 82 with a percentile of 12. This indicates the person's score was a little more than 1 standard deviation below the mean. Furthermore the percentile rank indicates the person scored no better than 12% of the standardization sample. This would indicate the person's ability is in the Low Average range. Similar

interpretations can be made for each of the other achievement areas on the WJ-III as well as the WIAT-II and the WRAT-4.

Practitioners often find the use of grade equivalent scores to be more useful for educational programming and in developing vocational accommodations. Several measures (e.g., Woodcock-Johnson Tests of Achievement, 3rd ed.) provide an estimate of an individual's independence, instructional, and frustration levels when learning and applying academic skills. This information is quite useful when conducting situational assessments, arranging job shadowing, and analyzing performance tests and work samples.

Alternative Assessments

The use of situational assessments helps evaluate an individual's interests, aptitudes, and work habits in actual or simulated work situations (Levinson, 2002). Job shadowing allows an individual to follow or observe a worker (e.g., plumber, cook, painter) with the goal of determining whether requirements of the job are consistent with his or her interests and abilities. Performance tests require individuals to carry out specific nonverbal tasks designed to evaluate their ability to perform comparable tasks in actual work settings. Tests that require a person to perform work samples in an actual working setting may provide a more authentic assessment of an individuals' abilities and skills.

When conducting the aforementioned assessments, the academic functioning of the individual and the academic skills needed to perform jobs successfully must be considered. Most jobs require some degree of reading, math, and written language. Therefore, if a specific job requires reading (e.g., cooks need to read orders or computers, truck drivers need to read directions), the level of reading needed to be successful for that job must be known and, in job applicants, must be assessed. Thus, successful rehabilitation efforts require knowledge of the academic requirements of jobs and an individual's ability to demonstrate job-related skills. An applicant's abilities must match job requirements. When significant disparity exists, the rehabilitation plan considers efforts to promote needed academic skills, applications of suitable accommodations, or modifications in job requirements.

Qualitative Interpretation

Some assessment specialists rely solely on standard scores when interpreting tests. Others go beyond the standard scores and conduct analysis of the items (also see chapter 9). For example, an analysis of the types of errors may reveal a pattern that can facilitate recommendations. For example, the WJ-III, WIAT-II, and WRAT-4 require individuals to read printed words. When reading orally, an examinee may have difficulty pronouncing sounds at the end of words but easily pronounce sounds at the beginning of words. This information may assist in designing visual prompts to assist with job tasks. Similarly, the WJ-III, WIAT-II, and WRAT-4 assess math calculations. When an examinee is asked to calculate numbers, the examiner may recognize that, when completing double digit subtraction, errors occur due to problems related to spatial relations (e.g., difficulty keeping columns straight) but not when adding or subtracting. This error can be addressed readily with the appropriate accommodations. Finally, items are ordered based on item difficulty, which corresponds to level of skill. For example, the Letter–Word Identification subtest of the WJ-III begins with identifying letters, then simple words, then more complex words. Similarly, math calculations begin with number identification, addition, subtraction, multiplication, division, and so on. The quantitative score obtained does not indicate what the individual can or cannot do. A qualitative review of which items an individual answered correctly and which incorrectly provides such information and also provides guidance for focusing rehabilitation efforts.

Some assessment specialists readminister standardized measures using accommodation methods. This method commonly is called *testing the limits*. Information from this process can help determine how well an individual can perform academic-related tasks with accommodations. For example, after administering a measure of math calculation using standardized procedures, the specialist may allow the examinee to retake the failed items while using a calculator. Scores from standardized measures that have been modified in these and other ways cannot be used to make a diagnosis (Cohen & Swerdlik, 1999). Modifications in standardized test administration methods have the goal to determine how the examinee's performance can be enhanced with accommodations, not to report higher scores.

Achievement tests come in two administrative forms: those designed to be given to groups or those intended for individual use. The use of group tests decreases costs. The major advantage of individually administered measures is that they provide an opportunity for the examiner to observe the examinee working and solving problems (Salvia, Bolt, & Ysseldyke, 2006).

The assessment specialist can record various personal qualities, including how an examinee performs tasks, as well as their motivation, frustration tolerance, and coping skills. This qualitative information is considered when developing accommodations and proposing job selection.

In summary, the utility of standardized measures does not have to stop after they are administered, scored, and interpreted. A close analysis of the test item and testing the limits through the use of accommodations may reveal details important to rehabilitation planning. The need to compare the academic requirements of a job to the level of academic functioning of the individual is important to underscore. An illustration of these principles is seen in the case study at the end of this chapter.

Research on the use of achievement measures in rehabilitation and health settings using standardized instruments is scarce because achievement measures typically are one part of a comprehensive assessment. However, measures of academic achievement frequently are used in rehabilitation. Efforts to rehabilitate academic skills have been facilitated by several conditions. A theoretical understanding of the nature and components of academic skills has improved understanding of how academic skills develop. The measurement of academic skills has improved substantially through the use of modern psychometric techniques. These techniques include normative-based metrics as well as interval level measures that are ideally suited for measuring intervention effects. The linking of theory and measurement has led to comprehensive batteries of achievement measures that assess both content knowledge and processing skills involved in applying academic knowledge.

This integration of theory and measurement has resulted in clinicians taking a more functional perspective when assessing individuals with academic difficulties (Dean et al., 2003). One example of such a study used select subtests of the Woodcock-Johnson achievement to measure the effectiveness of phonological interventions for children with reading disabilities. Not only did children improve in reading, but there was a measured correspondence between reading improvement and brain activation in the occipitotemporal area of the brain, the dysfunctional area hypothesized to contribute to visual–sound relationships (Shaywitz et al., 2004).

It is anticipated that future studies will similarly investigate the cognitive processes behind other academic functions, such as mathematics and writing.

RESEARCH BOX 17.1

Development of left occipitotemporal systems for skilled reading in children after a phonologically based intervention. Shaywitz, B. A., Shaywitz, S. E., Blachman, B. A., Pugh, Fulbrigh, R. K., Skudlarski, P., Mencl, W. E., Constable, R. T., Holahan, J. M., Marchione, K. E., Fletcher, J. M., Lyon, G. R., & Gore, J. C. (2004). *Biological Psychiatry, 55i*, 926–933.

Objective: This study examined the effectiveness of a phonological-based intervention in improving reading.

Method: A phonological intervention was given to an individual with known reading problems over a period of 8 months. A series of academic measures were administered, including subtests from the Woodcock-Johnson Tests of Achievement. Additionally, brain scans showing activation differences between normal readers and dyslexic readers were completed. Both academic measures and brain scans were repeated after the 8-month period as a postintervention measurement.

Results: An ANOVA of the gain in reading was statistically significant. Interestingly, initial differences in the temporal–occipital areas, a brain area known to be important for reading, was reduced. That is, as children with reading disabilities got phonological training in reading, their brain activation patterns looked more like normal readers.

Conclusion: This was one of the first comprehensive studies to demonstrate the utility of academic measures not only in identifying children with reading problems, but also in measuring intervention outcomes. Such measures are essential for determining what works in remediating academic deficits, and for understanding the corresponding changes in brain activation.

Questions

1. What is the role of understanding the role of the brain in academic achievement?
2. What role do academic achievement measures play in neurologically focused interventions?

Summary and Conclusion

The assessment of academic functions, including the documentation of academic deficits or disabilities, comprises important components of the rehabilitation process. The manner in which academic deficits or disabilities are determined is influenced by the specific nomenclature used. The most frequently used systems include federal and state department of education policies as well as the Diagnostic and Statistical Manual of Mental Disorders (4th ed., text revision) based guidelines. Their use limits a professional's ability to specify and conceptualize academic measurement for rehabilitation purposes.

In contrast, the International Classification of Functioning provides a viable alternative for conceptualizing the measurement of academic deficits and disabilities. Its benefits include a focus on person–environment interactions and its specification of deficit areas that provide functional descriptions of what behaviors are limiting activities or participation outcomes. A person's academic deficits may be due to conditions in addition to his or her knowledge of academic content (e.g., physical disability, motor impairment). The ICF provides a more comprehensive system to describe academic difficulties by allowing greater specification that more holistically captures the problems and circumstances of a given individual. Other classification systems do not.

The WJ-III, WIAT-2, and WRAT-4 are frequently used in practice to measure academic functions. This chapter reviewed similarities as well as differences in these measurement instruments. Additionally, the correspondence between these measures and the ICF system was explored.

The International Classification of Functioning is merely a classification system. A diagnosis may not be ultimately sought-after benefit of rehabilitation services. As with all classification systems, use of the ICF system does not establish a regimen that, when followed, is guaranteed to result in desired improvements. Although the ICF improves the coding of behavioral and environment–person interactions, it does not specify how to change behaviors or currently undesirable person–environmental relationships. Only thoughtful, knowledgeable, and experienced clinicians make such decisions.

Self-Check Questions

1. What value do academic achievement measures have when using classification systems?
2. How can academic achievement measures be used with classification systems to improve rehabilitative outcomes?
3. How does the International Classification of Functioning, Disability and Health (ICF) system compare to other systems when classifying academic problems?
4. Describe how the results from an academic achievement measure can be interpreted quantitatively or qualitatively.
5. When would a more comprehensive measure of achievement be preferred to a less comprehensive measure? When would a less comprehensive measure be preferred to a more comprehensive measure?

Case Study—The Case of Stephen

Stephen, aged 47, is a Caucasian male living with his wife and two children in a rural location in Indiana. Stephen always worked in the construction trades since dropping out of school following his eighth grade year. However, a fall six years earlier left his right shoulder severely injured, which greatly diminished his ability to work. After four years of multiple surgeries and increasingly larger doses of pain medication, Stephen no longer was able to return to work. His limited work experience, limited academic background, and poor self-image left him wondering if there was anything he could do vocationally. Stephen was referred to a clinic for a psychoeducational evaluation at the request of his lawyer who believed Stephen's limited intellectual abilities and low academic skills may qualify him to receive vocational rehabilitation and other services.

As an adult, Stephen described ongoing difficulties in reading, writing, and mathematics. He was unable to look up words in the dictionary or locate names in the phone book. He could read the newspaper but not comprehend the articles. He could not write cursively or spell simple words. He was unable to help his children read simple books. Even his math skills were very limited, which was ironic given his past vocation as a carpenter. For example, Stephen expressed dismay that he was never able to measure within 1/8th of an inch or read architectural plans.

Stephen was administered the Wechsler Adult Intelligence Scale (3rd ed.; WAIS-III) and the Woodcock-Johnson Tests of Achievement (3rd ed.; WJIII-ACH). Both are reliable and valid measures of intellectual functioning or academic achievement. Average standard scores on both measures fall between 90 and 110. Stephen's scores are presented in the following tables.

Wechsler Adult Intelligence Scale - Third Edition (WAIS-III)			
(Mean = 100, Standard Deviation = 15)			
Scale	**Standard Score**	**Percentile**	**95% Confidence Interval**
Full Scale IQ	72	3	68-77
Verbal IQ	67	1	63-73
Performance IQ	81	10	75-89
Index Scores			
Verbal Comprehension	72	3	67-79
Perceptual Organization	89	23	83-97
Processing Speed	88	21	80-98
Verbal Subtests	**Scaled Score**	**Percentile**	
Vocabulary	4	2	
Similarities	7	16	
Arithmetic	4	2	
Digit Span	3	1	
Information	4	2	
Comprehension	5	5	

(continued)

Performance Subtests

Picture Completion	11	63
Digit Symbol-Coding	6	9
Block Design	4	2
Matrix Reasoning	10	50
Picture Arrangement	5	5
Symbol Search	10	50

Woodcock-Johnson III-Tests of Achievement-Form A (WJIII-ACH-B)
(Mean = 100, Standard Deviation = 15)

Composite	SS	PR	95% Confidence Interval	Grade Equivalent Easy	Difficult
Total Achievement	81	10	80–82	2.8	4.6
Broad Reading	82	12	81–84	3.2	4.6
Broad Math	76	6	73–80	3.0	5.1
Broad Written Lang.	81	10	78–84	2.1	4.0
Math Calc. Skills	72	3	67–77	2.5	4.8
Written Expression	83	12	78–87	1.9	4.1
Academic Skills	76	5	73–78	2.8	3.9
Academic Fluency	81	10	79–83	3.4	5.5
Academic Applic'n	81	10	77–84	2.4	4.5

Subtests	SS	PR	95% Confidence Interval	Grade Equivalent Easy	Difficult
Letter–Word Ident.	80	9	77–83	3.2	4.2
Reading Fluency	87	19	85–89	4.4	6.1
Calculation	68	2	60–76	2.4	3.7
Math Fluency	81	10	78–84	3.0	7.9
Spelling	78	8	74–83	2.4	3.9
Writing Fluency	83	13	78–88	2.3	3.9
Passage Comp.	80	9	76–85	2.1	3.3
Applied Problems	81	11	77–86	3.7	5.5
Writing Samples	80	9	71–89	1.6	4.6

Intelligence and Achievement Test Results

STOP: Do not read any further until you complete this exercise. As a learning exercise, review the table of scores carefully. Use the information in the chapter about what each score metric (standard score, percentile rank, etc.) means and write down some interpretive statements about these scores. Are the scores generally high, low, or average? Are there any specific strengths or weaknesses? What types of rehabilitation recommendations would you make? Compare your recommendations to those made below.

Summary

Stephen's weakness in processing verbal information and thinking with words will considerably hinder him in solving problems that primarily are language-based. His academic achievement is in the low average range and commensurate with his general intellectual functioning as measured by his non-verbal skills. Stephen will not perform as well as his same aged peers in attaining and applying knowledge and problem-solving behaviors. His memory skills range from low average to borderline and indicate Stephen will experience more difficulty than his peers learning and retrieving new information. His low working memory contributes to his difficulty analyzing, mentally manipulating, and responding to both verbal and visual information. Stephen is experiencing moderate levels of depression due to chronic pain, lack of meaningful employment, hopelessness, and low self-esteem.

Recommendations/Accommodations

1. Due to difficulty in dealing with stressors of everyday life and general concern, Stephen may benefit from individual counseling services. In counseling,

the therapist should address his expressed concerns, help him develop appropriate coping skills and normalize his reactions to stressors, and explore causes or antecedents of his depression. Stephen may benefit from a directive, problem-solving type of therapy. The counseling also should include career and vocational counseling.

2. Stephen will need accommodations in all areas of achievement. Math accommodations will be needed if he is to return to work that requires math skills. Regarding Stephen's difficulty with basic mathematical skills, he should carry a small calculator to assist him in daily activities requiring math. Its utilization will reinforce his basic number facts and properties in the four operations, help him develop understanding of selected algorithms by using repeated operations, and help him solve problems that normally are too time-consuming to be computed by hand.

3. Instructions should be written at his grade level to help with understanding and comprehension. Visual representation of instructions and steps also should be considered.

4. Stephen has the motivation to pursue and maintain work. He lacks skills needed to complete job applications and follow-up during the interview process. Cards that contain the essential information of job applications should be developed to assist Stephen when completing such applications. When applying for work, if possible, he should take applications home and have another person check his responses prior to submitting them. He should request two applications—one to complete as a draft and another to complete and return.

5. His written language skills are at the independent level—around the middle first grade level. He will need considerable assistance in this area. Directions should be given to him orally. Instructions could be recorded so he can listen to them repeatedly, if needed.

6. Due to Stephen's physical problems, he should consider working with an occupational therapist (see chapter 28 in this book). According to the American Occupational Therapy Association (www.aota.org), services typically include:

   (a) Customized treatment programs to improve an individual's ability to perform daily activities
   (b) Comprehensive home and job site evaluations with adaptation recommendations
   (c) Performance skills assessments and treatment
   (d) Adaptive equipment recommendations and usage training
   (e) Guidance to family members and caregivers.

7. These results are seen as an accurate description of Stephen's cognitive abilities and limitations. He should convey these results to his attorney and apply for support from the Social Security Administration (see chapter 12 in this book).

8. Stephen takes walks to help reduce stress and clarify his thinking. He should incorporate walking into his daily routine. Stephen should consider inviting his family to walk with him occasionally.

9. Stephen indicated he enjoyed reading the paper, but frequently failed to comprehend what he read. His reading comprehension skills may be further developed by setting aside time each week to read newspaper articles out loud with his wife. After reading an article Stephen and his wife could discuss its content.

References

American Psychiatric Association. (1994). *Diagnostic and Statistical Manual of Mental Disorders* (4th ed.). Washington, DC: American Psychiatric Association.

American Psychiatric Association. (2000). *Diagnostic and Statistical Manual of Mental Disorders* (4th ed. text rev ed.). Washington, DC: American Psychiatric Association.

Brown, V. L., Hammill, D. D., & Wiederhold, J. L. (1995). *Test of Reading Comprehension* (3rd ed.). Austin, TX: PRO-ED.

Carroll, J. B. (1993). *Human cognitive abilities: A survey of factor-analytic studies*. Cambridge, England: Cambridge University Press.

Cohen, R. J., & Swerdlik, M. E. (1999). *Psychological testing and assessment: An introduction to tests and measurement* (4th ed.). Mountain View, CA: Mayfield.

Dean, R. S., Woodcock, R. W., Decker, S. L., & Schrank, F. A. (2003). A cognitive neuropsychological assessment system. In F. L. Schrank & D. P. Flanagan (Eds.), *WJ III Clinical use and interpretation*. San Diego: Elsevier Science.

Dehn, M. J. (2006). *Essentials of processing assessment*. Hoboken, NJ: John Wiley & Sons, Inc.

Flanagan, D. P., Ortiz, S. O., Alfonso, V. C., & Mascolo, J. T. (2002). *The achievement test desk reference (ATDR): Comprehensive assessment and learning disabilities*. Boston: Allyn & Bacon.

Horn, J. L. (1988). Thinking about human abilities. In J. R. Nesselroade & R. B. Cattell (Eds.), *Handbook of multivariate psychology* (pp. 645–685). New York: Academic Press.

Jablensky, A. (1999). The nature of psychiatric classification: Issues beyond ICD-10 and DSM-IV. *Australian and New Zealand Journal of Psychiatry, 33*, 137–144.

Levinson, E. M. (2002). Best practices in school-based vocational assessment. In A. Thomas & J. Grimes (Eds.), *Best practices in school psychology IV: Volume 2* (pp. 1569–1584). Bethesda, MD: National Association of School Psychologists.

McIntosh, D. E., & Decker, S. L. (2005). Understanding and evaluating special education, IDEA, ADA, NCLB, and Section 504 in school neuropsychology. In R. C. D'Amato, E. Fletcher-Janzen, & C. R. Reynolds (Eds.), *Handbook of School Neuropsychology*. Hoboken, NJ: John Wiley & Sons.

Oakland, T., Mpofu, E., Gregoire, G., & Faulkner, M. (2007). An exploration of learning disabilities in four countries: Implications for test development and use in developing countries. *International Journal of Testing, 7*(1), 53–69.

Reschly, D. J., & Ysseldyke, J. E. (2002). Paradigm shift: The past is not the future. In A. Thomas & J. Grimes (Eds.), *Best practices in school psychology* (3rd ed., pp. 3–36). Washington DC: NASP.

Salvia, J., Bolt, S., & Ysseldyke, J. E. (2006). *Assessment: In special and inclusive education* (10th ed.). Boston: Houghton Mifflin.

Shaywitz, B. A., Shaywitz, S. E., Blachman, B. A., Pugh, K. R., Fulbright, R. K., Skudlarski, P., et al. (2004). Development of occipitotemporal systems for skilled reading in children after a phonologically-based intervention. *Biological Psychiatry, 55,* 926–933.

Simpson, R. G., & Buckhalt, J. A. (1990). A non-formula discrepancy model to identify learning disabilities. *School Psychology International 11*, 273–279.

Wechsler, D. (1997). *Wechsler Memory Scale* (3rd ed.). San Antonio, TX: The Pyschological Corporation.

Wechler, D. (2002). *Wechler Individual Achievement Test* (2nd ed.). San Antonio, TX: The Psychological Corporation.

Wilkinson, G. S., & Robertson, G. J. (2006). *Wide Range Achievement Test* (4th ed.). San Antonio, TX: Psychological Corporation.

Woodcock, W. R., McGrew, K. S., & Mather, N. (2001). *Woodcock-Johnson-III Test of Cognitive Abilities*. Itasca, IL: Riverside Publishing.

World Health Organization (WHO). (2001). *International classification of functioning, disability and health (ICF)*. Geneva, Switzerland: Author.

18

Personality

DIANA JOYCE
*University of Florida,
Gainesville*

ERIC ROSSEN
*Prince George's County Public Schools
Chesapeake ADHD Center of Maryland*

OVERVIEW

This chapter begins by defining personality and ways in which assessment data may inform rehabilitation treatment. Personality assessment may be helpful at several stages in the rehabilitation process, from early diagnostic procedures to the measurement of final goal attainment. Next, a history of personality assessment is presented with reference to how theoretical constructs have evolved over time. Contemporary personality instruments are reviewed, including projective measures, adult rating scales, and specialized assessments designed for children and adolescents. Finally, critical issues related to multicultural perspectives in evaluation procedures, representativeness of norming samples, appropriate testing accommodations, and rater bias also are discussed.

LEARNING OBJECTIVES

By the end of the chapter, readers should be able to:

- Describe the role of personality assessment within the context of rehabilitation
- Name and describe the major personality assessment instruments and their uses
- Explain the application of personality assessment data in rehabilitation intervention
- Evaluate personality assessment as applied to rehabilitation and health interventions

INTRODUCTION

Rehabilitation is intended to improve an individual's functioning and enable that person to perform normal daily activities. This includes community integration at three levels: physical, social, and psychological (Heinemann, 2005). When considering functioning within these broad domains, many personality characteristics can serve to facilitate or hinder an individual's coping strategies; therefore, the assessment of personality is important to effective treatment planning.

This chapter begins by defining personality and ways in which assessment data may inform rehabilitation treatment. Next, a history of personality assessment is presented with reference to how theoretical constructs have evolved over time. Contemporary personality measures are reviewed including projective measures, adult rating scales, and specialized instruments designed for children and adolescents. Finally, critical issues related to multicultural perspectives in evaluation procedures, representativeness of norming samples, appropriate testing accommodations, and rater bias also are reviewed.

DEFINITION OF PERSONALITY

Personality may be defined as a complex pattern of characteristics that are relatively stable over time and that uniquely distinguish the emotional reactions and behaviors of one individual from others. Characteristics include temperament, attitudes, interests, disposition, self-regulation ability, and motivations (Joyce, 2007). These characteristics are thought to result from genetic predisposition, environmental influences, and personal choices (Cole & Cole, 1996). Some characteristics can be observed from birth as evidenced by differences in the interaction patterns, activity levels, and disposition of infants (Thomas & Chess, 1989).

Rehabilitation assessment and evaluation may serve several important roles as summarized by the National Institute on Disability and Rehabilitation Research (NIDRR). Those roles include determining eligibility for benefits or services, assessing current functioning levels, designing appropriate treatment, and estimating the potential for recovery (NIDRR, 1992). Questions arise within each of these roles that personality data can answer. When determining eligibility for services, personality assessment can help measure mood states such as anxiety or depression as well as interpersonal skills. When associated with trauma, these characteristics may change from mild to a clinically significant level that requires a combination of both physical therapy and rehabilitative counseling support services. For example, symptoms of pervasive foreboding and avoidance of social environments associated with a traumatic event such as severe injury can indicate a post-traumatic stress disorder (PTSD). Attempts to integrate a client back into her/his community and social life may require a multifaceted treatment approach that specifically addresses the influence of PTSD on recovery. Some measures also can identify malingering, a quality that may preclude justification for services.

Personality assessment measures can provide information regarding current functioning levels through evaluation of interpersonal skills, attitudes toward one's own self-efficacy (i.e., locus of control), and decision-making styles. Treatment planning may include personality information that addresses the patient's intrinsic motivation, temperament, and social affect. The same behavior may have different underlying causes. Thus, identifying problematic symptoms in patients alone may not provide all the information practitioners require to best design therapeutic interventions. For example, aggressiveness may be associated with expected frustration during rehabilitation or with more willful and predatory behavior found in conduct disorders or criminality. Personality assessment that distinguishes between patient anger that is impulsive and intermittent rather than deliberate and chronic can inform the type and duration of therapy required as well as the prognosis for adapting.

Through the process of identifying stable personality characteristics, clinicians can determine both strengths and weaknesses that estimate the potential for recovery and treatment compliance (Krug, 2001; Walls & Tseng, 1987). Strengths can be particularly important in making vocational choices that are likely to bring long-term satisfaction for clients. For example, occupational adjustment for a highly extroverted person may require substantially better social interaction capabilities than that required by an introverted person (Myers, McCaulley, Quenk, & Hammer, 1998).

Several studies have demonstrated links between personality and the effectiveness of rehabilitative interventions among individuals with disabilities. Therefore, an in-depth understanding of an individual's personality traits can add valuable insight to treatment planning. For example, traits that reflect maladaptive personality disorders have been found to impact treatment

RESEARCH BOX 18.1

Hopwood, C. J., Creech, S. K., Clark, T. S., Meagher, M. W., & Morey, L. C. (2007). The convergence and predictive validity of the multidimensional pain inventory and the personality assessment inventory among individuals with chronic pain. *Rehabilitation Psychology, 52*(4), 443–450.

Objectives: This study examined converging factors when administering both the Multidimensional Pain Inventory (MPI) and the Personality Assessment Inventory (PAI) to predictive treatment outcomes for clients. The Multidimensional Pain Inventory is one of the most widely utilized measures for evaluation of patients experiencing chronic pain (e.g., arthritis). Prior research has established the validity of the MPI in predicting several pain-related outcomes (e.g., sick leave, pain acceptance). However, some researchers argue that, when administering instruments such as the MPI, the addition of other measures designed to understand a broad range of psychological factors may enhance patient evaluation for treatment planning. The PAI was chosen for this study as it also is a well-established measure and has not been studied previously in conjunction with the MPI for redundant and convergent factors.

Method: The sample included 235 patients referred to an outpatient treatment program as a result of treatment-resistant chronic pain. The mean client age was 49 with an average of 9 years of persistent pain, and 73% were females. Ethnicity included 86% European American, 10% African American, and 4% Hispanic. The patients had a variety of diagnoses including fibromyalgia, cervical pain,

and lumbar spine radicular symptoms. Baseline data were acquired for the original 235 patients who began treatment. The baseline measures included the Beck Depression Inventory, Beck Anxiety Inventory, Rand 12-Item Short-Form Health Survey, the Oswestry Disability Questionnaire, and a clinician rating of the patient's ability to stand and carry. Only 187 patients completed the 20-day treatment program. Thus, data analyses were limited to those 187 clients. Analyses methods included scale-level intercorrelations, conjoint analysis of the MPI and PAI, and orthogonal rotation.

Results: Analyses indicated that some (e.g., Life Control) but not all of the MPI scales (e.g., General Activity Level, Pain Severity) correlated with the PAI. Five factors (i.e., Negative Affect, Support, Externalizing, Physical Dysfunction, and Impulsivity) accounted for 59% of the variance between the MPI and PAI. An unexpected finding of the study indicated some MPI and PAI variables predicted overall mental health.

Conclusion: The findings of this study suggest that utilizing the MPI and PAI jointly adds some predictive validity to rehabilitation assessment of patients with chronic pain.

Questions

1. What implications do these findings have for including personality measures when planning comprehensive rehabilitation assessments?
2. Would there be better predictive validity for treatment planning if multiple measures of personality were included?

---

outcomes in rehabilitation negatively (Paolucci et al., 1999; Tyrer, Merson, Onyett, & Johnson, 1994). Also, distress has been associated with longer rehabilitation periods and fewer self-care behaviors (Malec & Neimeyer, 1983). In contrast, positive personality characteristics such as extraversion, positive self-esteem, and adaptive coping ability may facilitate rehabilitation as well as vocational adaptation outcomes (Radnitz, Bockian, & Moran, 2000; Richter, Brown, & Mott, 1991). In addition, personality measures can provide information that may guide how caregivers interact with patients so as to maximize intervention efficacy (Radnitz et al., 2000). Some researchers suggest therapists may facilitate patient satisfaction with treatment by considering both stable traits and temporary states of thought.

INTERNATIONAL CLASSIFICATION OF FUNCTIONING (ICF) APPLICATIONS

The International Classification of Functioning (ICF) delineates two interactive components (i.e., Functioning/Disability and Contextual Factors), each with two domains of client functioning that can facilitate or inhibit rehabilitation. The two areas within Functioning and Disability are Body Functions/Structures and Activities/Participation. Environmental Factors and Personal Factors are domains within Contextual Factors. Data from personality tests are most applicable to the Personal Factors domain. It consists of internal influences on functioning and disability and the impact of attributes on the individuals. These may include personality traits such as optimism, extroversion, and attribution

DISCUSSION BOX 18.1

Distinguishing Traits and States

In addition to traditional personality characteristics and rehabilitation needs, other variables intrinsic to the individual can influence treatment outcomes. Patients may begin treatment with a wide range of preconceived ideas about the treatment process, the therapist, their own treatment needs, and expectations for recovery. Some researchers argue these personal notions are the result of enduring personality traits, whereas others believe they are more transient states of thought. The specific outcome may be less important in determining patient satisfaction with the treatment than the alignment of initial expectations and the final outcome. A range of outcomes are perceived as acceptable if they align well with the patient's initial perceptions and thus do not disappoint the patient. *States* are defined as temporary characteristics or moods created by situations that are frequently changing and short in duration. *States* are considered more easily remediable, often by discussion or removal from the event, than personality traits.

Several studies investigated pretreatment counseling that provided the patients with information regarding therapy procedures, treatment demands, and realistic expectations.

The premise was that brief educational information could easily realign preconceived thoughts if they were indeed dependent on temporary states rather than personality traits. The results indicated increased positive outcomes and patient satisfaction with treatments for those who received pretreatment explanations (Beutler, 1983; Lorian & Felner, 1986).

Considering that some patient variables may be states rather than enduring traits suggests therapists may easily influence change in state-related areas. Information on states can be obtained simply by asking the client. Preconceived ideas may be changed easily by providing accurate information. The caveat in considering states is that, precisely because they are dynamic and dependent on immediate circumstances, they can emerge quickly and frequently.

Questions

1. Do you agree with the researchers that some personality variables are temporary states?
2. Does the research described definitively answer the question?

---

systems. More detailed descriptions of specific personality constructs are noted in the review of individual instruments later in this chapter.

HISTORY OF RESEARCH AND PRACTICE IN PERSONALITY ASSESSMENT

Intellectual curiosity regarding patterns of human behavior has existed for ages. Early Greek philosophers such as Hippocrates, Galen, and Aristotle described behavioral clusters observed in individuals that corresponded to long-term positive or negative outcomes (Galen, trans. 1916; trans. 1992). Although their conceptualizations were erroneously attributed to bodily functions, many attributes they described remain clearly identifiable. Those attributes include melancholy, variable moods, irritability, apathy, sadness, and unwarranted somatic complaints. As recently as 200 years ago, a shift occurred from philosophical explanations of personality characteristics to more empirical approaches. The first scientific inquiry methods were applied systematically to the study of psychology, and the first laboratory emphasizing measurement was established in 1879 by Wundt (Hergenhahn, 1997).

Personality theory, like many disciplines, has integrated a variety of historical perspectives into current practice. The influences of the following major paradigms are apparent in many personality measures today. The psychoanalytic perspective of personality theory, based on the early work of Freud and others, emphasizes early childhood experiences as possible determinants of later behaviors. Conscious, unconscious, and preconscious drives and impulses, as well as defense mechanisms are explored in an effort to provide insight into client behaviors (Fadiman & Frager, 2005). Current practices from this perspective include a long-standing tradition of psychoanalysis, projective measures, and clinical judgment based on expertise acquired through clinical practice. Projective instruments such as the Rorschach and the Thematic Apperception Test are based on the psychoanalytic perspective.

In the early 1900s, with the advent of behaviorism, Pavlov, Watson, Skinner, and others became known for human behavioral studies that explored responses to stimuli and the ability to reshape these responses through manipulation of stimuli and reinforcers (Hergenhahn, 1997). Formal measurement of behaviors became more popular in the 1960s and now often is assessed through clinical interview (chapter 13), anecdotal records, and observations. Observations determine the frequency, duration, and rate of particular target behaviors. Recording antecedents and consequences of those incidents provides clues to successfully modifying the behaviors (Kaplan, 1995). These procedures often are described as a functional behavioral assessment. Treatment strategies from these measures may include behavioral modification through operant conditioning, reinforcement, counterconditioning, systematic desensitization, and extinction plans.

The cognitive–behavioral perspective measures attributions as well as rational and irrational thought patterns that may sustain maladaptive behaviors. Treatment strategies include self-instruction, self-talk, cognitive restructuring, problem-solving, verbal mediation, self-calming techniques for stress, and anger management training. These treatments may be aided by biofeedback that assists in monitoring patient physiological responsiveness to internal dialogue strategies, such as self-affirming statements. Cognitive behavioral therapy often requires a therapist to help the patient identify self-defeating thought patterns (e.g., "I'm never going to get better"), and replace them with more productive thought patterns (e.g., "If I keep trying, I can improve"). Identification of internal dialogue themes can be acquired by review of patient diaries that they use to record their own thoughts each day. Some personality measures also provide scales that identify the patient's locus-of-control and attribution patterns. Ellis's (1984) rational–emotive therapy and Beck's (1976) cognitive therapy are examples of cognitive–behavioral approaches. Within personality assessment and evaluation there remain tenets of many early theories. A more comprehensive understanding of individual rehabilitation needs can be obtained by including a variety of methods and measured constructs.

From the 1920s through the 1980s, modern theorists, such as Jung, Myers, and Briggs referenced the early work of Galen and provided more sophisticated models of temperament-based personality characteristics (Jung 1921/1971; Myers & Myers, 1980). Their distinguishing qualities include the constructs of introversion and extroversion, decision-making preferences based on either thinking or feeling, learning preferences for intuition or direct experience (i.e., sensing), and daily lifestyle preferences for organized (i.e., judging) or spontaneous (i.e., perceiving) events. Temperament research has documented differences in limbic site activity (Kagan & Snidman, 1991), hypertension (Shelton, 1996), and cortical arousal (Wilson & Languis, 1990)

based on self-reported temperament qualities. For example, extroverts have lower activity in each of these areas, which could explain their propensity to seek out more interaction with others and more environmental stimuli when compared to introverts. Understanding these differences can aid therapists in deciding whether patients are more likely to benefit from group and/or individualized services.

Throughout the 1960s and 1970s several prominent theories defining core personality factors emerged. Eysenck's (1976) theory proposed neuroticism, extroversion and psychoticism constructs of personality. Cattell's (1986) theory postulated as many as 35 different personality variables. The advent of easy-to-use factor analysis methods in the 1980s allowed us to better define broad and narrow characteristics within personality theory. More recently, theory has endorsed a five-factor model of personality that includes extroversion, agreeableness, conscientiousness, emotional stability, and intellect. This model is based on the five-factor theory that forms the basis for the NEO Personality Inventory, the Hogan Personality Inventory, and the Sixteen Personality Factor Questionnaire (Krug, 2001).

Emotional intelligence is an emerging and highly controversial theory that may impact personality assessment. Emotional intelligence can be defined as the ability to use emotions in reasoning and problem-solving to enhance thought. Definitions of emotional intelligence combine aspects of general cognitive ability demonstrated by higher-order reasoning skills including problem-solving and executive functioning associated with planning and self-control. When problem-solving and executive functioning skills are well-developed, they facilitate goal-oriented behaviors that serve to increase positive outcomes (Barkley, 1997; Hanks, Rapport, Millis, & Deshpande, 1999). However, as often occurs when new constructs emerge, different definitions for emotional intelligence can be found within the literature. Thus, the nature of the emotional intelligence construct and how it should be operationally defined for measurement are being debated (Van Rooy & Viswesvaran, 2004).

CURRENT PERSONALITY ASSESSMENT METHODS

Contemporary psychologists can assess personality with various measures that provide a holistic understanding of the individual. A comprehensive listing of instruments and technical properties can be obtained through the *Mental Measurements Yearbooks* (Geisinger, Spies,

---

DISCUSSION BOX 18.2

Does Emotional Intelligence Exist?

Cognitive abilities assessed by intelligence tests best predict success in many educational outcomes. Nevertheless, approximately 50% to 75% of the variance associated with success in schools and life-time achievement can be attributed to other traits and characteristics. As a result, researchers have looked for alternative constructs to supplement or replace data from intelligence tests to improve prediction. Some claim emotional intelligence (EI) measures can substantially improve prediction. However, the validity of existing EI measures is inconclusive, in part due to the relative novelty of EI and subsequent limited empirical research. In addition, researchers struggle with how to define the construct of EI operationally (Van Rooy & Viswesvaran, 2004). Mayer, Salovey, & Caruso (2000) believe most definitions of EI fall within one of two groups of EI theoretical models: mixed models and ability model.

Mixed Models of Emotional Intelligence

In mixed models, EI is seen as a mixture of abilities and other personality traits that generally are assessed using self-report questionnaires (Mayer, Salovey, & Caruso, 2000; 2002). Authors of mixed model EI measures claim that they predict success and other important outcomes fairly well, including happiness, alcohol use, and one's ability to benefit from

rehabilitation programs (Austin, Saklofske, & Egan, 2005; Bar-On, 1997; Furnham & Petrides, 2003; Goleman, 1998; Spence, Oades, & Caputi, 2004). Therefore, one could argue that mixed model measures of EI are multidimensional indicators of personality.

Ability Model

To establish EI as a unique ability, Mayer and Salovey (1997) proposed a hierarchical model of EI that separates it from well-known personality traits. They define emotional intelligence as consisting of the ability to: (a) accurately perceive emotions, (b) use emotions to facilitate thinking, (c) understand emotional meanings, and (d) manage emotions.

Questions

1. Do you believe the constructs of emotional intelligence as noted in the discussion are unique from personality characteristics?
2. What potential does a measurement of EI that emphaszees self-management of one's emotions have for screening and treatment in rehabilitation?
3. What more do we need to know about measuring emotional intelligence before it can be used confidently in rehabilitation services?

Carlson, & Plake, 2007). This section reviews only some of the more widely used measures of personality and behavior and the type of personality information each instrument can provide.

Personality assessment techniques may include bedside structured and semistructured interviews that document the patient's history, goals, and apprehensions. Measures also may include projective instruments that use ambiguous visual stimuli and open-ended questions to elicit unguarded or less-censored responses. Among the most popular measures are empirically based rating scales that provide norms referenced to the general population. Omnibus rating scales may sample behavior among a number of constructs. Some omnibus measures include subscales for adaptive skills required for independent living; however, adaptive subscales on personality measures typically consist of a brief set of items. More comprehensive information on adaptive behavior and skills should be obtained with measures designed specifically to assess them (see chapter 15). If an omnibus scale suggests pathology, single construct

measures (e.g., Beck's Depression Inventory) as well as additional interviews or observations may be used to examine the behaviors more closely and thus to confirm a hypothesis or diagnosis.

The purpose of personality assessment in rehabilitation often is to establish traits that may enhance or prohibit optimal adaptation during the rehabilitation process. Personality characteristics typically are considered to be relatively stable over time and to exist within the person rather than the situation (Butcher, 1995). However, there are circumstances that may result in brief or temporary changes in personality characteristics (e.g., elevated anxiety) among rehabilitative patients. These changes may be the result of environmental stressors or cognitive impairments. More transient changes can indicate states of functioning rather than traits. Thus, therapists should consider whether observed behaviors reflect contextual states or stable traits of personality when determining appropriate short-term and long-term rehabilitation interventions. Although not common, some patients requiring rehabilitation also may have chronic clinically significant personality disorders (Radnitz et al., 2000). In the United States, 17,000 cases of personality disorder have been reported as a cause of activity limitation (LaPlante & Carlson, 1996).

Projective Methods

RORSCHACH The Rorschach is a projective measure that presents clients with ten inkblots. Their answers are scored based on their responses in reference to location, determinants, and content. Frequency data determine ratio, percentage, and derivative interpretations of several sections: core, ideation, affect, mediation, processing, interpersonal, and self-perception. In addition, six special indices can be obtained: schizophrenia, depression, coping deficit, suicide constellation, hypervigilance, and obsessive style. Cognitive structures and themes are identified, given the premise that the way a respondent structures her/his answers to ambiguous stimuli is the way she or he will respond to other ambiguous situations in the environment (Groth-Marnat, 1997). Several complex scoring systems have been developed for the Rorschach. However, the Exner Comprehensive System is utilized most often because it is based on extensive research (Groth-Marnat, 1997; Krishnamurthy & Archer, 2003).

THEMATIC APPERCEPTION TEST (TAT) The TAT consists of 20 picture stimulus cards. Examinees are shown one or more cards and instructed to create a story for each picture. Both quantitative and qualitative scoring techniques are available. Verbal responses are reviewed for main themes, hero/heroine, concept of the environment, conflicts, anxieties, fears, ego adequacy, and ego integration. Interpretation relies on familiarity with a complex scoring system, an understanding of psychopathology, and clinical judgment (Groth-Marnat, 1997).

Rating Scales

ACHENBACH SYSTEM OF EMPIRICALLY BASED ASSESSMENT (ASEBA) The ASEBA, a measure of psychopathology, may be particularly well-suited for monitoring chronic or long-term rehabilitation needs as it spans ages 1½–90. The system includes self-report (for ages 11 and above) as well as caregiver rating forms. The ASEBA assesses four areas of positive competencies, six areas of adaptive functioning, eight syndrome constructs, six DSM-IV oriented scales, and internalizing,

externalizing, and total problems (Achenbach & Rescorla, 2000, 2001, 2003).

The inclusion of positive competencies as well as negative personality traits is important, given the need to assess an individual's strengths as well as weaknesses that may facilitate or impede rehabilitation. For example, the social and activities competency scales may indicate the level of physical activity that may be incorporated initially into rehabilitative interventions. Further, the working hard adaptive functioning scale also may indicate the length interventions realistically can be expected to be sustained. Conversely, the presence of conduct problems or anxiety problems may impede rehabilitation and require unique intervention strategies.

CALIFORNIA PSYCHOLOGICAL INVENTORY (CPI) The CPI can be administered in groups or individually for ages 12–70. Items are written at a fourth-grade reading level. Approximately 40% of the test items were selected from the Minnesota Multiphasic Personality Inventory. The measure provides 20 scales including interactional (e.g., social presence), internal attributes (e.g., self-control), and personal functioning (e.g., flexibility, intellect) domains. Validity scales assess the tendency to fake good, fake bad, and to provide popular responses. Research within the rehabilitation community includes a number of studies that have utilized the CPI to explore personality characteristics associated with substance abuse, addiction, and coronary heart disease (Groth-Marnat, 1997; Krug, 2001).

MILLON CLINICAL MULTIAXIAL INVENTORY (3RD ED.) (MCMI-III) The MCMI-III is designed for adults, at least 18 years of age, with an eighth-grade reading level. There are 28 scales in five categories: modifying indices, clinical personality patterns, severe personality pathology, clinical syndromes, and severe syndromes. The scales are based on the *Diagnostic and Statistical Manual of Mental Disorders* (4th ed.) (DSM-IV) criteria and are particularly well-suited for diagnosis of psychiatric disorders. The instrument includes scales to identify criminality and antisocial characteristics including sadistic aggression. Among the 28 scales, several may be particularly applicable to rehabilitation counseling, including self-defeating, negativistic, drug dependence, alcohol dependence, and post-traumatic stress disorder. Administration of the test can be as brief as 20 minutes, which is helpful in limiting fatigue. The test is available in written, audiotape, and Spanish forms. In addition, Millon has developed a measure of coping and prognosis

(Millon Behavioral Health Inventory) for patients with physical illness (Groth-Marnat, 1997; Krug, 2001; Millon, 1997).

Two Millon instruments are designed specifically for adolescents. The *Millon Adolescent Personality Inventory* (MAPI) is designed for ages 13–18, written on a sixth-grade level, and assesses normal adolescent behavior. The measure yields scores in three core areas: personality styles, expressed concern, and behavioral adjustment. The personality styles scales include introversive, inhibited, cooperative, sociable, confident, forceful, respectful, and sensitive. The expressed scales include self-concept, personal esteem, sexual acceptance, peer security, social tolerance, family rapport, and academic competence. The aspects of behavioral adjustment scales include impulse control, attendance consistency, societal conformity, and scholastic achievement (Hoge, 1999; Millon, Green, & Meagher, 1982; Millon, 1993).

The *Millon Adolescent Clinical Inventory* (MACI), an adaptation of the MAPI is designed to assess maladaptive personality characteristics of teenagers 13–19. It measures similar dimensions as the MAPI, although it maintains a clinical focus, that emphasizes assessment of psychological disturbances including depression, anxiety, and substance abuse potential (McCann, 1997). Scores provide indicators for personality disorders defined in the DSM-IV (Hoge, 1999; Millon, 1993; Millon, Green, & Meagher, 1982).

MINNESOTA MULTIPHASIC PERSONALITY INVENTORY (2ND ED.) (MMPI-2) The MMPI-2 includes ten clinical scales: hypochondriasis, depression, hysteria, psychopathic deviate, masculinity-femininity, paranoia, psychasthenia, schizophrenia, mania, and social introversion. There are four validity scales; cannot say, lie, infrequency, and correction. The MMPI is primarily interpreted based on profiles of scores across scales rather than just single scales. In addition, there are several supplemental scales that measure particular symptoms or personality characteristics (e.g., anxiety, repression, ego strength, alcoholism). The instrument often is used to identify pathology, maladaptive behaviors, and psychiatric diagnosis. The MMPI scores are based on a national norming sample that includes minority representation. The instrument can be administered in groups, individually, by audiotape, computer, and in videotaped American Sign Language. The MMPI-2 has been translated into more than 150 languages. In rehabilitative therapy, the MMPI has been utilized to collect both pre- and postintervention data to measure treatment outcomes for patients including persons with spinal cord injuries, head injuries, and psychiatric disturbances. However, like many personality measures, the instrument is designed primarily to measure pathology. Thus, there are few MMPI studies specifically for persons with disabilities who do not exhibit maladaptive personality characteristics or pathology (Elliott & Umlauf, 1995; Krug, 2001).

The *Minnesota Multiphasic Personality Inventory–Adolescents* (MMPI-A) is an adapted version of the MMPI, for adolescents ages 14–18. It provides 7 validity scales, 10 basic profile scales, and 21 content as well as supplementary scales. The validity scales assess various types of response bias (e.g., faking good). The basic profile scales measure dimensions of pathology such as depression and paranoia. The content and supplementary scales assess aspects of personality dysfunction, including anger, anxiety, and family problems (Butcher et al., 1992). Several studies have examined the MMPI-A among clinical populations, including anxiety disorders (James, Reynolds, & Dunbar, 1994), depression (Figuered, 2002), eating disorders (Cumella, Wall, & Kerr-Almeida, 1999), psychiatric inpatients (Hilts & Moore, 2003), suicidal adolescents (Kopper, Osman, Osman, & Hoffman, 1998), and substance abusing adolescents (Ingersoll, 2003). However, there are little data on the MMPI-A with adolescents who have physical disabilities (Hoge, 1999).

NEUROTICISM, EXTROVERSION, AND OPENNESS PERSONALITY INVENTORY (NEO-OI) The NEO-PI is based on the five-factor model of personality: extroversion, neuroticism, openness to experience, conscientiousness, and agreeableness. The scales include measures of negative affect, vulnerability, maladaptive coping, motivation toward goals, and unrealistic ideas—qualities that may be helpful in rehabilitative counseling and treatment planning. Items addressing interpersonal interaction, intellectual curiosity, and openness to experience may inform estimates of the patient's readiness for reintegrating into the community. Although items have face validity, few studies have investigated the test's utility in rehabilitative therapy (Elliot & Umlauf, 1995).

SIXTEEN PERSONALITY FACTOR QUESTIONNAIRE (16PF) The 16PF measures 16 primary scales, five global factors, and three response style indicators. The primary scales are warmth, reasoning, emotional stability, dominance, liveliness, rule consciousness, social boldness, sensitivity, vigilance, abstractedness, privateness, apprehension, openness to change, self-reliance, perfectionism, and tension. The global factors include extroversion, anxiety, tough-mindedness, independence, and self-control. Response styles are impression management, infrequency, and acquiescence. Rehabilitative assessment specialists may find the 16PF's Form F useful. Items are written at third- to fourth-grade reading levels, and the use of the scale is supported by item validity studies for persons with disabilities. The norming sample included persons with vision and hearing impairments, those receiving rehabilitation services, and those who are incarcerated (Krug, 2001).

Other Pediatric and Juvenile Measures

ADOLESCENT PSYCHOPATHOLOGY SCALE (APS) The APS is a self-report measure of psychopathology, personality, and social–emotional problems designed for use by individuals ages 12–19. This instrument measures psychological problems and behaviors that may interfere with an adolescent's psychosocial functioning, including substance abuse, suicidal ideation, excessive anger and aggression, and introversion (Reynolds, 1998).

BEHAVIOR ASSESSMENT SYSTEM FOR CHILDREN-2 (BASC-2) The BASC-2 includes five parallel forms: for teachers, self, and parents, an observation form, and a developmental history survey for ages 2–21. Positive characteristics assessed include self-esteem, self-reliance, adaptability, and functional communication—qualities that may contribute to how an individual responds to intervention and his/her ability to maintain positive self-care habits. In addition, computer scoring software yields content scales that may be directly relevant to treatment. Treatment planning may be influenced by scores on the resiliency or executive function scales, which measure the ability to control behavior by planning, anticipating, inhibiting, or maintaining goal-directed activity, and by reacting appropriately to feedback in a purposeful way (Reynolds & Kamphaus, 2004). Pathology scales measured by the BASC-2 include externalizing and internalizing problems as well as several clinical subscales (e.g., aggression, anxiety, attention problems, atypicality, conduct problems, depression, learning problems, somatization, and withdrawal). The BASC-2 also provides negative content scales that may be relevant to rehabilitation, such as negative emotionality, which measures the tendency to overreact to any changes in everyday activities or routines.

CHILDREN'S PERSONALITY QUESTIONNAIRE (CPQ) The CPQ was constructed based on the 16PF and contains items designed to measure 14 personality traits within the domains of personal, social, and academic development. The measure is designed for children ages 8–12. Items are written at a third-grade reading level. The scale may be read or explained to patients (Porter & Cattell, 1992).

EARLY SCHOOL PERSONALITY QUESTIONNAIRE (ESPQ) The ESPQ was designed for young children ages 6–8. This instrument yields 13 scales: reserved versus warmhearted, dull versus bright, affected by feelings versus emotionally stable, undemonstrative versus excitable, obedient versus dominant, sober versus enthusiastic, disregards rules versus conscientious, shy versus venturesome, tough-minded versus tender-minded, vigorous versus doubting, forthright versus shrewd, self-assured versus guilt-prone, and relaxed versus tense. Similar to the CPQ, the ESPQ's theoretical structure was derived from the 16PF. The ESPQ's 13 scales also summarize to provide information on four secondary factors similar to the CPQ: extraversion, anxiety, tough poise, and independence (Coan & Cattell, 1976).

HIGH SCHOOL PERSONALITY QUESTIONNAIRE (HSPQ) The HSPQ is designed for adolescents ages 12–18 who read at least at a sixth-grade level or above. Its structure parallels that of the 16PF and thus is based on Cattell's trait-view theory of personality (Hoge, 1999). As such, 14 dimensions of normal personality are assessed yielding four secondary factors: extraversion, anxiety, tough poise, and independence (Cattell & Cattell, 1975).

PERSONALITY INVENTORY FOR CHILDREN (2ND ED.) The *Personality Inventory for Children* (2nd ed., PIC-2) is a widely used personality instrument designed to be completed by a parent or other knowledgeable individual to assess characteristics of children ages 5–19. The instrument includes 22 subscales that combine to yield nine adjustment scales: cognitive impairment, family dysfunction, psychological discomfort, impulsivity and distractibility, reality distortion, social withdrawal, delinquency, somatic concerns, and social skills deficits. The PIC-2 also contains three response validity scales; inconsistency, dissimulation, and defensiveness (Lachar & Gruber, 2000). The PIC-2 offers computer-based actuarial test interpretations, which enable a clinician to translate scaled scores into specific predictions for the patient. For example, a T-score between 80 and 89 on the delinquency scale translates to a 10% probability that the individual will be involved with the police and a 42% probability they will drop out of school (Hoge, 1999).

PERSONALITY INVENTORY FOR YOUTH (PIY) The PIY is a self-report measure of personality for individuals ages 9–18. Although it was designed to compliment the parent-completed PIC-2, it may be used as an independent source of information from children and adolescents. The nine scales are aligned with those of the PIC-2 and are derived from 24 clinical subscales. It has a third-grade reading level (Lachar & Gruber, 1995).

PIER'S HARRIS CHILDREN'S SELF-CONCEPT SCALE (2ND EED.; PHCSCS-2) The PHCSCS-2 is designed to assess the self-concept of youths ages 7–18. Scores include those from six self-concept subscales: behavioral adjustment, freedom from anxiety, happiness and satisfaction, intellectual and school status, physical appearance and attributes, and popularity. A global self-esteem score also is provided. Additional validity scales assess response bias. Items are written at a third-grade level. Although this instrument should not be considered a multidimensional assessment tool per se, self-concept and self-esteem are strongly associated with disability acceptance and maintenance of behavior change (Heinemann & Schontz, 1982; Malec & Lemsky, 1995; Piers, Harris, & Herzberg, 2002).

RESEARCH AND CRITICAL ISSUES IN PERSONALITY ASSESSMENT

Multicultural Perspectives in Personality Assessment

According to the 2000 Census, the prevalence of disability (sensory, physical, mental, self-care, employment, or difficulty going outside the home) among persons from minority groups was greater than that found for the overall population (U.S. Census Bureau, 2003). For example, approximately 18% of working-age adults with a disability are African American, although African Americans comprise only 12% of the population in the United States (Belgrave & Jarama, 2000). Additionally, compared to whites, minority group members seek treatment at a lower rate than do whites (Scogin & Crowther, 2003) and are less likely to obtain employment following a disability (Elliott & Umlauf, 1995). This may be due, in part, to differences in socioeconomic status, to a willingness to seek and accept professional services, or to biases in assessment practices, as some instruments do not adequately sample minority populations in their norms. In addition, potential cultural barriers to seeking assessment and treatment in rehabilitation settings may exist. Thus, the need to inform members of minority groups of the potential value of personality assessment to rehabilitation services is evident.

Personality instruments administered to individuals of varied cultures, races, and ethnicities should demonstrate evidence of cultural validity prior to use in rehabilitation settings (see also chapter 3). Cultural validity is contingent on three conditions: conceptual, linguistic, and metric equivalence (Kwan & Aldarondo, 2001). Conceptual equivalence refers to whether a test has the same psychological meaning for different racial/ethnic groups. Dana (1993, 1998) noted that most personality instruments are etic in nature and thus apply a single universal standard across all cultural groups. This may be problematic. For example, the meaning of anxiety or depression may differ across cultural groups. Thus, Dana (1993) suggests use of an emic approach, one that evaluates behavior within the context of specific cultures.

Linguistic equivalence refers to test bias due to differences in response style and issues of language proficiency and familiarity of item content (Kwan & Aldarondo, 2001). Test developers often attempt to minimize cultural and verbal components while testing, as even subtle language nuances can result in differences among various linguistic groups.

Metric equivalence refers to whether normative samples contain an adequate representation of minority groups. Norms typically reflect the percent that racial/ethnic groups comprise in the population. Thus when norming a personality test, 13% may be Black, 14% may be Hispanic, and 4% may be Asian (U.S. Census Bureau, 2005). The members of minority groups in normative samples may not sufficiently account for culture and social class differences. Thus, some argue that norms reflecting acculturation status would increase cultural validity, whereas racial/ethnic-specific norms may be invalid due to high levels of within-group homogeneity (Dana, 2001).

Examiner/clinician characteristics also may impact the outcomes of assessment. For example, confirmatory bias may result when a therapist conducts an assessment with preconceived expectations for performance prior to assessment, which may affect the type of data collected and how they are interpreted (Ortiz, 2002; Rabin & Schrag, 1999; Sandoval, 1998). Similarly, examiner/clinician biases also may result from stereotypes, prejudice, or minimizing the differences within groups and exaggerating the differences between groups. Thus, it is ethically mandatory for all professional preparation programs to train students in multicultural awareness and sensitivity (Dana, 2001).

Disability Representation in Norming Samples

Most personality measurement instruments are normed on persons without significant physical or cognitive disabilities. If we believe all persons being tested should have had an opportunity to have been included in the tests' norms, then the interpretation of data from tests that excluded persons with disabilities may have some limitations. Rehabilitative therapy patients may have cognitive limitations that may impede general intellectual functioning, reading ability, and concentration—personal qualities that may limit attempts to acquire valid personality information. In addition, self-report measures of personality can require introspection and high levels of self-awareness when accurately describing attitudes and feelings. Because introspection requires sophisticated cognitive recollections and understanding of one's own behavior and emotions, temporary memory problems may hamper the level of self-awareness. Therefore, in these cases, personality assessment data should be interpreted with caution. The data may be supplemented with broader neuropsychological assessment to better determine effects of brain injuries, lesions, and disease of specific anatomical structures (Lezak, 1995).

Testing Accommodations

Self-report rating scales often require patients to read and respond to more than 100 items. Therefore, their use must be carefully considered in light of a patient's physical limitations. These limitations often dictate the need for brief measures or adaptations in administration within the rehabilitation setting (Elliot & Umlauf, 1995).

Test manuals may discuss possible changes in administration including reading questions to patients, administering surveys in multiple sessions, or utilizing Braille formats as best suited for some types of disabilities. Accommodations also may require changes in the testing environment such as lighting, furniture, or the provision of assistive devices. The possible effects of medication and time-of-day for administration also are important considerations (Ekstrom & Smith, 2002).

Rater Bias

Data from rating scales may have one or more of the following forms of bias: inconsistency, response sets, and response style patterns. Inconsistency can occur when clients are answering randomly or untruthfully. They are detected by comparing two responses on very similar items. Additionally, response sets may occur, reflecting excessively negative or excessively positive answers on many items. Excessively negative answers could indicate malingering (i.e., faking bad) and overly positive answers may suggest an attempt at socially acceptable answers (i.e., faking good). Response style patterns can include a client's tendency to answer all questions in a similar manner regardless of the content. Examples include answering all questions in a neutral manner (e.g., middle score on a Likert scale), an acquiescence style that endeavors to agree with items, or a deviance style that strives to answer in unusual ways. Each of these forms of bias poses threats to validity of the scores. Some measures provide validity indices to determine if patients are exhibiting these forms of bias. However, many measures do not, and this determination relies on the examiner's clinical judgment (Sattler & Hoge, 2006).

Summary and Conclusion

Information provided by measures of personality can provide significant insight into a patient's personal characteristics. These attributes influence both emotional responses and behaviors that can serve to facilitate or hinder the rehabilitative process. Objective measurement of some maladaptive personality traits can help establish diagnoses, need for services, projected length of hospitalization or out-patient treatment, and readiness for independent living.

Methods for assessing personality include interviews, observations, projective assessments, and rating scales. When used in the hands of a skilled assessment specialist, each form of assessment has the potential to contribute to a professional's understanding of the patient. Ratings scales typically provide information on a patient's interpersonal skills, attributions, affect, coping strategies, adaptive skills, and symptoms of personality disorders or substance abuse. Newer instruments include validity scales to detect inconsistency in responses, informant attempts to fake good or bad answers, and possible malingering. Several revised tests of personality have increased their norming samples to better reflect the U.S. population in reference to race/ethnicity, social class, and disability categories. The need for testing accommodations for some patients is apparent. The impact on treatment efficacy will become increasingly important as the constructs and measurement of personality continue to advance.

Self-Check Questions

Self-Check Matching Exercise

Match the following testing accommodations with corresponding disabilities:

1. reading questions to patients _____
2. computer administration of test _____
3. frequent breaks during administration _____
4. multiple shorter sessions for test _____
5. assistive technology devices _____
6. Braille format _____
7. Audiotaped administration _____
8. Sign language administration _____
9. Alternate language version _____

a. limited wrist movement
b. non-English dominant speaker
c. visually impaired
d. speech impairment
e. chronic fatigue
f. limited hearing ability
g. limited attention and concentration
h. recent immigrant
i. difficulty sitting

Questions

1. In the accommodations matching exercise, did you find that more than one disability may apply to particular testing modification?
2. Which of the measures discussed in the chapter have sufficient age ranges to be used as a long-term repeated outcome measurement from ages 20 through 40?
3. Write a definition of personality. Did you include the same components mentioned in the chapter?
4. Within the International Classification of Functioning model, what environmental and personal factors information can be obtained from personality evaluations?
5. What are the critical issues and possible limitations of personality measures?

Case Study

Wanda, a 19-year-old Caucasian female, was born and has always resided in the United States. Her only spoken language is English. She has an intellectual disability with diagnosed mental retardation in the moderate range. Wanda lives with her elderly parents and attends a day program for adults with mental retardation. With parental assistance, Wanda displays a clean and neat appearance. She understands simple directions and typically complies with requests. Her vision and hearing are within normal limits. Parental interviews indicate Wanda is shy and withdrawn. Day program personnel would like to increase her social interaction to prepare her to live in a supervised group home.

QUESTIONS

1. Among the various types of instruments available to assess personality, which may be most helpful in further identifying Wanda's personal qualities and needs?
2. What are the advantages of selecting an instrument such as the *Personality Inventory for Children* when assessing personality characteristics for adolescents like Wanda?
3. What are the limitations of the *Personality Inventory for Children* with adolescents like Wanda?

References

Achenbach, T. M., & Rescorla, L. A. (2000). *Manual for ASEBA Preschool Forms & Profiles*. Burlington: University of Vermont, Research Center for Children, Youth, and Families.

Achenbach, T. M., & Rescorla, L. A. (2001). *Manual for ASEBA School-Age Forms & Profiles*. Burlington: University of Vermont, Research Center for Children, Youth, and Families.

Achenbach, T. M., & Rescorla, L. A. (2003). *Manual for ASEBA Adult Forms & Profiles*. Burlington: University of Vermont, Research Center for Children, Youth, and Families.

Austin, E. J., Saklofske, D. H., & Egan, V. (2005). Personality, well-being and health correlates of trait emotional intelligence. *Personality and Individual Differences, 38*, 547–558.

Barkley, R. A. (1997). Behavioral inhibition, sustained attention, and executive functions: Constructing a unifying theory of ADHD. *Psychological Bulletin, 121,* 65–94.

Bar-On, R. (1997). *The Bar-On Emotional Quotient Inventory (EQ-i): Technical manual.* Toronto, ON, Canada: Multi-Health Systems.

Beck, A. T. (1976). *Cognitive therapy and the emotional disorders.* New York: International Universities Press.

Belgrave, F. Z., & Jarama, S. L. (2000). Culture and the disability and rehabilitation experience: An African-American example. In R. G. Frank & T. R. Elliot (Eds.), *Handbook of rehabilitation psychology* (pp. 585–600). Washington, DC: American Psychological Association.

Beutler, L. E. (1983). *Eclectic psychotherapy: A systematic approach.* Elmsford, NY: Pergamon.

Butcher, J. N. (1995). *Clinical personality assessment: Practical approaches.* New York: Oxford.

Butcher, J. N., Williams, C. L., Graham, J. R., Archer, R. P., Tellegen, R. P., Ben-Porath, Y. S., & Kaemmer, B. (1992). *MMPI-A: Manual for administration, scoring, and interpretation.* Minneapolis: University of Minnesota Press.

Cattell, R. B. (1986). The 16PF personality structure and R. Eysenck. *Journal of Social Behavior and Personality,* 1, 153–160.

Cattell, R. B., & Cattell, M. D. (1975). *Handbook for the Jr.-Sr. High School Personality Questionnaire.* Champaign, IL: Institute for Personality and Ability Testing.

Coan, R. A., & Cattell, R. B. (1976). Early School Personality Questionnaire. Champaign, Ill.: Institute for Personality and Ability Testing.

Cole, M., & Cole, S. R. (1996). *The development of children* (3rd ed.). New York: W. H. Freeman.

Cumella, E. J., Wall, D. A., & Kerr-Almeida, N. (1999). MMPI-A in the inpatient assessment of adolescents with eating disorders. *Journal of Personality Assessment, 73,* 31–44.

Dana, R. H. (1993). *Multicultural assessment perspective in professional psychology.* Boston: Allyn & Bacon.

Dana, R. H. (1998). Cultural identity assessment of culturally diverse groups: 1997. *Journal of Personality Assessment, 70,* 1–16.

Dana, R. H. (2001). Multicultural issues in assessment. In B. F. Bolton (Ed.), *Handbook of measurement and evaluation in rehabilitation* (pp. 449–470). Gaithersburg, MD: Aspen.

Ekstrom, R. B., & Smith, D. K. (2002). *Assessing individuals with disabilities: In educational, employment and counseling settings.* Washington, DC: American Psychological Association.

Elliott, T. R., & Umlauf, R. L. (1995). Measurement of personality and psychopathology following acquired physical disability. In L. A. Cushman & M. J. Scherer (Eds.), *Psychological assessment in medical rehabilitation* (pp. 325–358). Washington DC: American Psychological Association.

Ellis, A. (1984). Rational-emotive therapy. In R. J. Corsini (Ed.), *Current psychotherapies* (3rd ed.). Itasca, IL: Peacock Press.

Eysenck, H. J. (1976). *The measurement of personality.* Lanchaster, England: MTP Press.

Fadiman, J., & Frager, R. (2005). *Personality and personal growth* (6th ed.). Upper Saddle River, NJ: Prentice Hall.

Figuered, B. V. (2002). The concurrent validity of the Minnesota Multiphasic Personality Inventory-Adolescent in the assessment of depression. *Dissertation Abstracts International: Section B: the Sciences & Engineering, 62*(10-B), 4782. US: University Microfilms International.

Furnham, A., & Petrides, K. V. (2003). Trait emotional intelligence and happiness. *Social Behavior and Personality, 31,* 815–824.

Galen (1916). *Galen on the natural forces.* (A. J. Brook, Trans.). Cambridge, MA: Harvard University Press. (Original work published date unknown)

Galen (1992). *The art of cure—Extracts from Galen: Maimonides' medical writings.* (U. S. Barzel, Trans.). Haifa, Israel: Maimonides Research Institute. (Original work published date unknown)

Geisinger, K. F., Spies, R. A., Carlson, J. F., & Plake, B. S. (Eds.) (2007). *Seventeenth mental measurments yearbook.* NE: Buros Institute of Mental Measurments.

Goleman, D. (1998). *Working with emotional intelligence.* New York: Bantam Books.

Groth-Marnat, G. (1997). *Handbook of psychological assessment.* New York: John Wiley and Sons.

Hanks, R. A., Rapport, L. J., Millis, S. R., & Deshpande, S. A. (1999). Measures of executive functioning as predictors of functional ability and social integration in a rehabilitation sample. *Archives of Physical Medicine and Rehabilitation, 80,* 1030–1037.

Heinemann, A. W. (2005). Putting outcome measurement in context: A rehabilitation psychology perspective. *Rehabilitation Psychology, 50,* 6–14.

Heinemann, A. W., & Schontz, F. (1982). Acceptance of disability, self-esteem and sex role identify in deaf adolescents. *Rehabilitation Counseling Bulletin, 25,* 197–203.

Hergenhahn, B. R. (1997). *An introduction to the history of psychology* (3rd ed.). New York: Brooks/Cole Publishing.

Hilts, D., & Moore, J. M. (2003). Normal range MMPI-A profiles among psychiatric inpatients. *Assessment, 10,* 266–272.

Hoge, R. D. (1999). *Assessing adolescents in educational, counseling, and other settings.* Mahwah, NJ: Lawrence Erlbaum Associates.

Ingersoll, J. B. (2003). Predicting the underreporting of substance abuse symptoms in adolescent males in an outpatient substance abuse treatment program. *Dissertation Abstracts International: Section B: The Sciences & Engineering, 63*(10-B), 4906. US: University Microfilms International.

James, E. M., Reynolds, C. R., & Dunbar, J. (1994). Self-report instruments. In T. H. Ollendick & N. J. King (Eds.), *International handbook of phobic and anxiety disorders in children and adolescents* (pp. 317–329). New York: Plenum Press.

Joyce, D. (2007). Personality assessment. In C. R. Reynolds & E. Fletcher-Janzen (Eds.), *Encyclopedia of special education, a reference for the education of children, adolescents, and adults with disabilities and other exceptional individuals* (3rd ed.). (pp. 1544–1545). Hoboken, NJ: John Wiley & Sons.

Jung, C. G. (1971). *Psychological types*. (R. F. C. Hull, Revision of Trans. By H. G. Baynes). Princeton, NJ: Princeton University Press. (Original work published 1921)

Kagan, J., & Snidman, N. (1991). Infant predictors of inhibited and uninhibited profiles. *Psychological Science, 2*(1), 40–43.

Kaplan, J. S. (1995). *Beyond behavior modification: A cognitive-behavioral approach to behavior management in the school.* Austin, TX: Pro-ed.

Kopper, B. A., Osman, A., Osman, J. R., & Hoffman, J. (1998). Clinical utility of the MMPI-A content scales and Harris-Lingoes subscales in the assessment of suicidal risk factors in psychiatric adolescents. *Journal of Clinical Psychology, 54*, 191–200.

Krishnamurthy, R., & Archer, R. P. (2003). The Rorschach. In L. E. Beuthler & G. Groth-Marnat (Eds.), *Integrative assessment of adult personality* (2nd ed., pp. 262–314). New York: Guilford Publications, Inc.

Krug, S. E. (2001). Assessment of personality. In B. Bolton (Ed.), *Handbook of measurement and evaluation in rehabilitation* (3rd ed., pp. 125–143). Baltimore: Paul Brookes.

Kwan, K-L, & Aldarondo, F. (2001). Use of 16PF and CPI with U.S. racial and ethnic minorities: Issues of cultural application and validity. In L. A. Suzuki, J. G. Ponterotto, & P. J. Meller (Eds.), *Handbook of multicultural assessment: Clinical, psychological and educational applications* (2nd ed., pp. 253–278). San Francisco: Jossey-Bass.

Lachar, D., & Gruber, C. P. (1995). *Personality Inventory for Youth (PIY) manual: Administration and interpretation guide. Technical guide.* Los Angeles: Western Psychological Services.

Lachar, D., & Gruber, C. P. (2000) *Personality Inventory for Children Second Edition (PIC–2) manual.* Los Angeles: Western Psychological Services.

LaPlante, M., & Carlson, D. (1996). *Disability in the United States: Prevalence and Causes, 1992. Disability Statistics Report (7).* Washington, DC: U.S. Department of Education, National Institute on Disability and Rehabilitation Research.

Lezak, M. D. (1995). *Neuropsychological assessment* (3rd ed.). New York: Oxford University Press.

Lorian, R. P., & Felner, R. D. (1986). Research on psychotherapy with the disadvantaged. In S. L. Garfield & A. E. Bergin (Eds.), *Handbook of psychotherapy and behavior change* (3rd ed., pp. 739–776). New York: John Wiley and Sons.

Malec, J. F., & Lemsky, C. (1995). Behavioral assessment in medical rehabilitation: Traditional and consensual approaches. In L. A. Cushman & M. J. Scherer (Eds.), *Psychological assessment in medical rehabilitation* (pp. 199–236). Washington DC: American Psychological Association.

Malec, J., & Neimeyer, R. (1983). Psychological prediction of duration of inpatient spinal cord injury rehabilitation and performance of self-care. *Archives of Physical Medicine and Rehabilitation, 64,* 359–363.

Mayer, J. D., & Salovey, P. (1997). What is emotional intelligence? In P. Salovey & D. Sluyter (Eds.), *Emotional development and emotional intelligence: Implications for educators* (pp. 3–31). New York: Basic Books.

Mayer, J. D., Salovey, P., & Caruso, D. (2000). Emotional intelligence as zeitgeist, as personality, and as a standard intelligence. In R. Bar-On & J. D. A. Parker (Eds.), *Handbook of emotional intelligence* (pp. 92–117). New York: Jossey-Bass.

Mayer, J. D., Salovey, P., & Caruso, D. (2002). *Mayer-Salovey-Caruso Emotional Intelligence Test (MSCEIT).* Toronto, ON, Canada: Multi-Health Systems.

McCann, J. T. (1997). The MACI: Composition and clinical applications. In T. Millon (Ed.), *The Millon Inventories: Clinical and Personality Assessment* (pp. 363–388). New York: The Guilford Press.

Millon, T. (1993). *Millon Adolescent Clinical Inventory manual.* Minneapolis, MN: National Computer Systems.

Millon, T. (1997). *The Millon inventories: Clinical and personality assessment.* New York: Guilford Press.

Millon, T., Green, C. J., & Meagher, R. B. (1982). *Millon Adolescent Personality Inventory manual.* Minneapolis, MN: National Computer Systems.

Myers, I. B., McCaulley, M. H., Quenk, N. L., & Hammer, A. L. (1998). *MBTI Manual: A guide to the development and use of the Myers-Briggs Type Indicator* (3rd ed.). Palo Alto, CA: Consulting Psychologists Press.

Myers, I. B., & Myers, P. B. (1980). *Gifts differing.* Palo Alto, CA: Consulting Psychological Press.

National Institute on Disability and Rehabilitation Research (NIDRR). (1992). Human measurement in rehabilitation. *Rehab Brief.* Washington, DC: Author.

Ortiz, S. O. (2002). Best practices in nondiscriminatory assessment. In A. Thomas & J. Grimes (Eds.), *Best practices in school psychology IV* (pp. 1321–1336). Washington, DC: National Association of School Psychologists.

Paolucci, S., Antonucci, G., Pratesi, L., Traballesi, M,, Grasso, M. G., & Lubich, S. (1999). Poststroke depression and its role in rehabilitation of inpatients. *Archives of Physical Medicine and Rehabilitation, 80,* 985–990.

Piers, E. V., Harris, D. B., & Herzberg, D. S. (2002). *Manual for the Piers-Harris Children's Self Concept Scale* (2nd ed.; Piers-Harris 2). Los Angeles: Western Psychological Services.

Porter, R. B., & Cattell, R. B. (1992). *Children's Personality Questionnaire (CPQ).* Champaign, IL: Institute for Personality and Ability Testing.

Rabin, M., & Schrag, J. L. (1999). First impressions matter: A model of confirmatory bias. *The Quarterly Journal of Economics, 114,* 37–82.

Radnitz, C., Bockian, N., & Moran, A. (2000). Assessment of psychopathology and personality in people with physical disabilities. In R. G. Frank & T. R. Elliott (Eds.), *Handbook of rehabilitation psychology* (pp. 287–310). Washington, DC: American Psychological Association.

Reynolds, C. R., & Kamphaus, R. W. (2004). *Behavior Assessment System for Children* (2nd ed; BASC-2). Circle Pines, MN: American Guidance Service.

Reynolds, W. M. (1998). *Adolescent Psychopathology Scale.* Odessa, FL: Psychological Assessment Resources.

Richter, S. S., Brown, S. A., & Mott, M. A. (1991). The impact of social support and self-esteem on adolescent substance abuse treatment outcome. *Journal of Substance Abuse, 3,* 371–385.

Sandoval, J. (1998). Critical thinking in test interpretation. In J. Sandoval, C. L. Frisby, K. F. Geisinger, J. D. Scheuneman, & J. R. Grenier (Eds.), *Test interpretation and diversity: Achieving equity in assessment* (pp. 31–50). Washington, DC: American Psychological Association.

Sattler, J. M., & Hoge, R. D. (2006). *Assessment of children: Behavioral, social, and clinical foundations* (5th ed.). San Diego, CA: Jerome M. Sattler Publishing.

Scogin, F., & Crowther, M. R. (2003). Integrative personality assessment with older adults and ethnic minorities. In L. E. Beutler & G. Groth-Marnat (Eds.), *Integrative assessment of adult personality* (2nd. ed.) (pp. 338–355). New York: Guilford.

Shelton, J. (1996). Health, stress, and coping. In A. L. Hammer (Ed.), *MBTI applications: A decade of research on the Myers-Briggs Type Indicator* (pp. 197–215). Palo Alto, CA: Consulting Psychologists Press.

Spence, G., Oades, L. G., & Caputi, P. (2004). Trait emotional intelligence and goal self-integration: Important predictors of emotional well-being? *Personality and Individual Differences, 37,* 449–461.

Thomas, A., & Chess, S. (1989). Temperament and personality. In G. A. Kohnstamm, J. E. Bates, & M.K. Rothbart (Eds.), *Temperament in childhood.* New York: John Wiley & Sons Ltd.

Tyrer, P., Merson, S., Onyett, S., & Johnson, T. (1994). The effect of personality disorder on clinical outcome, social networks and adjustment: A controlled clinical trial of psychiatric emergencies. *Psychological Medicine, 24,* 731–740.

U.S. Census Bureau. (2003). *Disability status: 2000.* Retrieved on February 20, 2007, from http://www.census.gov/prod/2003pubs/c2kbr-17.pdf

U.S. Census Bureau. (2005). *USA QuickFacts.* Retrieved on February 1, 2007, from http://ask.census.gov

Van Rooy, D. L., & Viswesvaran, C. (2004). Emotional intelligence: A meta-analytic investigation of predictive validity and nomological net. *Journal of Vocational Behavior, 65,* 71–95.

Walls, R. T., & Tseng, M. S. (1987). Measurement of client outcomes in rehabilitation. In B. Bolton (Ed.), *Handbook of measurement and evaluation in rehabilitation* (2nd ed., pp. 183–201). Baltimore: Paul Brookes.

Wilson, M. A., & Languis, M. L. (1990). A topographic study of difference in the P300 between introverts and extraverts. *Brain Topography, 2*(4), 369–274.

19

Vocational Interest and Aptitudes

GARY W. PETERSON

ELIZABETH RUFF
Florida State University, Tallahassee, FL

OVERVIEW

Work is a significant aspect of most individual's lives. Almost everyone is involved in some form of work, whether it be part-time, full-time, paid or unpaid (Lacey, 1988). In our society, a job means much more than a source of income. There is a uniquely American tradition of equating job with personal value. For instance, employment in a highly prestigious occupation symbolizes respect, power, and social status (Lacey). For many, holding a job means being able to provide financial support and protection for families. Not only that, adults who have been in the working world for an extended period begin to shape their lives around their work. Jobs often determine where we live, who our friends are, how we dress, and even our sleep schedule. Therefore, the choice of an occupation to pursue is exceedingly important; perceptions of a person's interests and aptitudes are a vital part of the decision-making process.

This chapter is organized according to four major sections: (1) The first section provides important definitions, (2) the second presents a career decision-making process incorporating the use of interest and aptitude measures in making decisions, (3) the third describes commonly used interest and aptitude measures in career counseling, and (4) the fourth presents issues pertaining to how these measures are administered and how scores are interpreted to clients.

LEARNING OBJECTIVES

By the end of the chapter, readers should be able to:

- Define interest and aptitude assessments
- Consider disability as a factor in each of the phases of the career problem-solving and decision-making process using the Cognitive Information Processing (CIP) framework
- Describe examples of common interest and aptitude appraisals used in helping individuals make appropriate career choices
- Describe special considerations in using interest and aptitude measures in career choice with individuals with disabilities
- State important considerations in administering, scoring, and interpreting scores of commonly used measures of interests and aptitude measures with individuals with disabilities

INTRODUCTION

DEFINITIONS OF APTITUDES AND INTERESTS

Let us begin by determining what constitutes the terms aptitudes and interests. *Aptitudes* are commonly considered as an individual's " capacity for learning " (Mish, 1993, p. 58). *Aptitude tests* measure a person's present performance on selected tasks to provide information that can be used to estimate how the person will perform at some time in the future or in a somewhat different situation (Thorndike, 2005, p.238). You are probably familiar with some aptitude tests (see Salvia & Ysseldyke, 1978), and you may have even taken a few yourself. The Scholastic Assessment Test (SAT) and the Graduate Record Examination (GRE) are both examples of aptitude tests. The SAT, for instance, measures your verbal, mathematical, and writing aptitudes, which are intended to predict future academic performance at the college level.

Often the terms *aptitude* and *achievement* are inappropriately used interchangeably. *Achievement* is defined as "a result gained by effort" (Mish, 1993, p. 9). *Achievement tests* typically are given to find out how much individuals have learned from instruction or to determine their acquired level of knowledge or skill. The use of midterm and final examinations are examples of achievement tests because they measure how well students have mastered course objectives. However, *aptitude tests* are meant to predict future performance in education, training, or job environment (Cohen & Swerdlik, 2005). Think of it as a difference of function over content in that both types of tests may be comprised of the same assessment methods, such as multiple-choice test items, essays, or performances, but scores from aptitude and achievement tests are used for different purposes.

For the purpose of this chapter, consider that the term *interest* refers to "a feeling that accompanies or causes special attention to an object or class of objects" (Mish, 1993, p. 610). We often consider interests as those things which we like. However, dislikes can be beneficial to assess as well. *Interest inventories* are designed to "provide information about an individual's general pattern of likes and dislikes" (Thorndike, 2005, p.327). We use the term *inventory* rather than test because there are no right/wrong answers to the questions.

You may wonder why someone would take an interest inventory in the first place. Does what you like and do not like seem obvious? Do you enjoy building things with your hands? Do you like working as part of a team on a common goal? Would you rather decorate a room or discuss a philosophical issue with a group? Answering questions like these may come very naturally to some people. Some individuals may not perceive their interests as clearly as do others (Fouad, 2007). In either case, being able to transfer our knowledge of our interests into future career options can become somewhat challenging. The interest inventories reviewed in this chapter demonstrate how one might use interest measures to clarify perceptions of their interests as well as to match personal preferences to potentially satisfying occupations (Holland, 1997).

This chapter, explores examples of commonly used measures of interests and aptitudes inventories as they relate to career problem-solving and decision-making. As professionals, we must be able to help people measure aspects of themselves, as well as to understand how this information is vitally important in the career decision-making process. So, in order to grasp the significance of interest and aptitude assessment, we first describe a theoretical construct for understanding the roles of these personality attributes in a decision-making process.

A CAREER DECISION PROCESS

The Cognitive Information Processing (CIP) theory (Niles & Harris-Bowlsbey, 2005; Peterson, Sampson, & Reardon, 1991; Sampson, Reardon, Peterson, & Lenz, 2004) is built on two core constructs: (1) The Pyramid of Information Processing Domains (see Figure 19.1), and the Communication, Analysis, Synthesis, Valuing, and Execution (CASVE) cycle (see Figure 19.2). One of the cornerstones of the CIP Pyramid is self-knowledge. In order to derive appropriate potential career options, individuals first must possess clear perception of their interests and aptitudes (i.e., self-knowledge), and second they must understand how this information is combined with occupational knowledge to make satisfying and meaningful career choices.

The CIP Decision Model

Measuring and acquiring a clear appraisal of one's interests and aptitudes is only a first step. A person must learn how to apply this information to arrive ultimately at a career choice. The CASVE Cycle (*Communication, Analysis,*

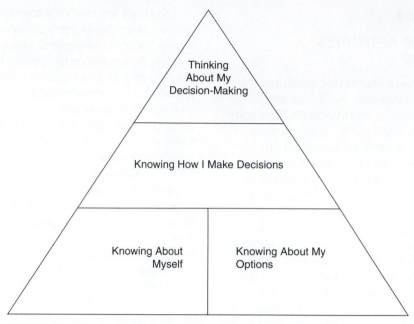

FIGURE 19.1 The Pyramid of Information Processing Domains

Source: From "A cognitive approach to career services: Translating concepts into practice," by J. P. Sampson Jr., G. W. Peterson, J. G. Lenz, and R. C. Reardon. *Career Development Quarterly, 41,* 67–74. © 1992, National Career Development Association.

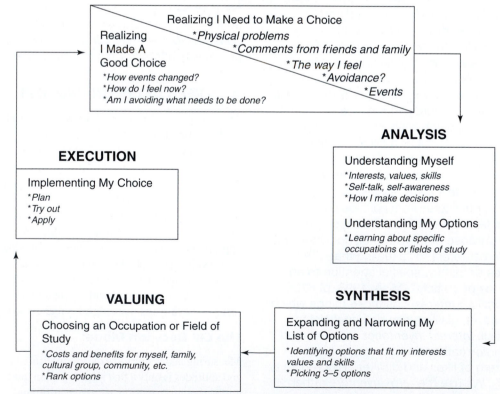

FIGURE 19.2 Communication, Analysis, Synthesis, Valuing, and Execution (CASVE) Cycle

Source: From "A cognitive approach to career services: Translating concepts into practice," by J. P. Sampson Jr., G. W. Peterson, J. G. Lenz, and R. C. Reardon. *Career Development Quarterly, 41,* 67–74. © 1992, National Career Development Association.

Synthesis, *V*aluing, and *E*xecution) can be thought of as a five-phase process in which individuals incorporate elements of self- knowledge and occupational knowledge to formulate a set of viable career options, prioritize them, and then implement a first choice (Reardon, Lenz, Sampson, & Peterson 2006). The aspect of disability is considered throughout this five-phase decision sequence. Let's look now to the CASVE cycle as it is used to integrate the element of disability into the decision-making process.

COMMUNICATION (C) *REALIZING I NEED TO MAKE A CHOICE* During the Communication phase, individuals are in a state of indecision and are attuned to internal and external cues encouraging them to engage in the decision-making process (Reardon et al., 2006). This state may entail dissatisfaction with a major field or job events that have happened in the near or distant past such as an accident or having to leave one's current work because of a disability. During the Communication phase, individuals also become very aware of what they are thinking and feeling as well as messages other people are sending to them (Sampson et al., 2004). This type of communication, whether verbal or nonverbal, may influence their feelings about themselves and the decision at hand. Individuals also become increasingly in touch with their own feelings about the complexity of their life circumstances. In order to proceed with the career problem-solving process, individuals must become fully aware of the thoughts and feelings about their career choice and their life context, including a disability. The key question at this phase is, "What am I thinking and feeling about my life and career choice at this moment?"

ANALYSIS (A) *UNDERSTANDING MYSELF AND MY OPTIONS* During the Analysis phase, individuals focus on developing a mental model of the problem at hand (Reardon et al., 2006). First, they explore their interests and aptitudes as well as other components of self-knowledge including values, abilities, and skills. At this point, all elements of self-knowledge are considered as a whole, being mindful to not overemphasize any one particular area such as a disability. Second, the Analysis phase includes acquiring an understanding of the world of work and how occupations are organized within it. Third, individuals should become attuned to their self-talk and self-awareness as career decision-makers (Sampson et al., 2004). The key question is, "What are the reasons for my present state of indecision? Could it be lack of self-knowledge? Lack of occupational knowledge? Or negative self-talk or discouragement?"

SYNTHESIS (S) *EXPANDING AND NARROWING MY LIST OF OPTIONS* This is the phase in which self-knowledge and occupational knowledge is combined to form viable career options (Reardon et al., 2006). Two processes occur within the Synthesis phase: (1) elaboration followed by (2) crystallization (Reardon et al.). During *elaboration*, individuals are encouraged to derive and explore potential options without inhibition or restraint.

They begin obtaining ideas of occupations through research based on the exploration of self-knowledge and occupational knowledge during Analysis. The objective is to generate as many options as possible even though some may seem unlikely at first. Following elaboration, *crystallization* entails narrowing the list of potentials through the further consideration of interests, aptitudes, values, abilities, and skills in light of job requirements and tasks of the selected occupations. Although disabilities may be a factor to consider while obtaining new information about occupations, it never should be the sole point of elimination of any option. The key question is, "What are viable career options that could effectively remove the state of indecision?" The outcome of this phase is identification of three to five occupations that have a high prospect of attaining occupational satisfaction and success (Sampson et al., 2004).

VALUING (V) *CHOOSING AN OCCUPATION OR FIELD OF STUDY* At this point in the decision-making process individuals begin to weigh the costs and benefits of each occupation identified during Synthesis with respect to themselves, family, cultural group, community, and any additional areas in which individuals derive meaning and fulfillment from work (Reardon et al., 2006). These are important considerations beyond the matching process involved in Synthesis. Again, the emphasis for individuals is not on limiting options but exploring how abilities, values, and special needs help to shape the quality of their work and personal lives. Individuals may be encouraged to consider how their decisions could be a point of inspiration or encouragement to others. They also may consider the extent to which they need financial assistance or socioemotional support from significant others. At this phase they rank-order options thereby arriving at a first choice of occupation with at least one viable alternative (Sampson et al., 2004). The key question is, "What is the best choice of occupation from among three to five viable options that will lead to success and fulfillment?"

EXECUTION (E) *IMPLEMENTING MY CHOICE* During the Execution phase, individuals develop and implement a plan of action to obtain employment in their chosen occupation identified in the Valuing phase. They may find that, in order to secure employment, they need to examine their aptitudes further for additional education or training. During the Execution phase, individuals are encouraged to consider how their specific interests, aptitudes, and needs will play into obtaining employment in their chosen occupation (Reardon et al., 2006). Issues pertaining to the employer's role in this consideration will be explored later in this chapter. During the job application process, candidates should be able to easily verbalize what their specific disability is, how it will or will not affect their ability to perform certain duties on the job, and possibly educate employers on types of accommodations that can be made to fit their special needs. The key question is, "How can I transfer my first choice into an action plan to secure employment and to set the plan into motion?"

COMMUNICATION (C) *REALIZING I MADE A GOOD CHOICE* The CASVE cycle does not end with Execution. After implementing a choice, individuals return to the Communication phase where they evaluate the success of their decision (Reardon et al., 2006). They may consider whether they are satisfied with their choice and if they are deriving the satisfaction on the job they anticipated. If they find that they are not satisfied with their current employment situation, or as their decisions bring up new challenges or issues, they simply move through the CASVE cycle again (Sampson et al., 2004). The key question, "Have I made a satisfying choice?"

Trends in Research and Public Policy Development

The CASVE cycle is representative of new trends in theory and research of the role of disabilities in decision-making. In terms of interest, there has been a shift from the philosophy of exclusion to one of inclusion (Kosciulek, 2004). We are encouraged to not look at individuals in terms of limitations but rather in terms of capabilities or competencies. The way we view aptitudes has also changed. This shift has been largely fostered by the Americans with Disabilities Act (ADA) of 1990. Under this Act, individuals are given greater opportunities to demonstrate their aptitudes for education and work since the institution of accommodations, such as extended time and allowable assistance in taking tests (ADA, 1990). This Act and other legislation will be explored in greater depth later in the chapter.

REPRESENTATIVE INTEREST AND APTITUDE MEASURES

Interest Measures

Development and measurement of interests have been on the forefront of career development experts' agendas since the earliest days of occupational counseling. Modern theorists (e.g., E. K. Strong, Ann Roe, and John Holland) have created a variety of instruments useful in the measurement, interpretation, and application of interests to career choice. Two prominent measures of interest used in career counseling are presented here as examples of interest assessment, each with its own characteristics, strengths, limitations, and utility. Nevertheless, both can be used to assist individuals in identifying strong and weak areas of interest, formulating educational and occupational goals, selecting college majors, or identifying plausible occupations in which they may find success and satisfaction.

SELF DIRECTED SEARCH (SDS) John Holland's *Self-Directed Search (SDS)* (Holland, Powell, & Fritzche 1994) assumes that: (1) people can be categorized as one of six different types juxtaposed in the form of a hexagon (see Figure 19.3); (2) environments, including work, education, and leisure can be similarly categorized; (3) persons are drawn toward those environments that complement their interest type; and (4) behavior is a result of interaction between individuals and their environment (Holland, 1997). Holland's RIASEC Theory will be referenced in interest measures discussed in the following paragraphs. After reading this section, it may be helpful to consider Case Study 19.1 at the end of this chapter. The corresponding group discussion questions are presented to further your understanding of this case study.

The Self-Directed Search (SDS) is a widely used interest assessment. It is intended for use with high school, college, and adult populations. It was designed based on the RIASEC hexagonal model (Figure 19.3), which examines how interests in different areas of a person's life interact and how these interests can be combined to match with occupations and leisure activities. According to the theory, proximal interest types on the hexagon have more in common than more distant or opposite interest types. Available in hand-written and computer versions, the SDS is considered an easy-to-use, self-administered inventory consisting of 228 items related to a person's likes and dislikes of activities and self-estimates of abilities. In general, administration takes about 30-40 minutes and should be accompanied

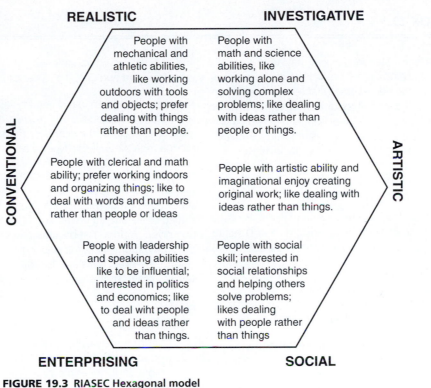

FIGURE 19.3 RIASEC Hexagonal model

Source: Reproduced by special permission of the publisher, Psychological Assessment Resources, Inc., 16204 North Florida Avenue, Lutz, FL 33549, from *Making Vocational Choices*, Third Edition, Copyright 1973, 1985, 1992, 1997 by Psychological Assessment Resources, Inc. All rights reserved.

by a counselor–client interpretation (Kapes & Whitfield, 2001). Results include an individual's two-or three-letter interest code as well as a list of matching occupations, areas of education and leisure activities. When used with *The Occupations Finder* (Holland, et al., 1994), a list of plausible occupations can be derived that match one's two- or three-letter code. An individual's combination of interests (the Holland Code) facilitates the linking of self-knowledge to occupational knowledge in the formulation of occupational alternatives as discussed previously in the Analysis and Synthesis phases of the CASVE cycle. (See Table 19.1 for a summary of the SDS.)

TABLE 19.1 Summary of Characteristics of *Self-Directed Search* (4th ed.; SDS-R)

Target Population	High school students, college students, and adults
Statement of Purpose	Assists individuals in finding occupations, education areas, and leisure activities that best suit their interests and self-rated skills
Titles of Subtests, Scales, and Scores Provided	Holland Code: Realistic, Investigative, Artistic, Social, Enterprising, Conventional; numerical scores in each of the 6 categories, Aspiration codes
Language Availability	English, English–Canadian, French–Canadian, Spanish, and 20 other languages
Test Time	30–45 minutes
Norm Groups	Working adults, universities and community colleges, high school; 17–65 years of age; males and females; Caucasian, African Americans, Hispanics, Asian Americans, and other ethnic backgrounds
Available Versions	Paper and pencil, computer, Braille, other languages

RESEARCH BOX 19.1

A current global trend is an increase in the use of technology. Assessments are no exception. A host of issues arises when an assessment becomes available online. Human services providers should not assume that scores on one version of a test may be used interchangeably with an online version unless there is sufficient supporting evidence to do so. As the use of technology rapidly increases, it is imperative that professionals remain current on research related to online versions of assessments. The following describes a portion of a recent article related to this topic.

Title: A Comparison Study of the Paper-and-Pencil, Personal Computer, and Internet Versions of Holland's Self-Directed Search (Lumsden, Sampson, Reardon, Lenz & Peterson, 2004)

Objective: To determine the extent to which score results from paper-and-pencil, personal computer, and internet versions of the SDS may be considered equivalent and how students react to each of these versions.

Method: Ninety-three undergraduate students were administered the SDS. Each student took two versions, either paper-and-pencil, personal computer, or online. The order of the administrations was counterbalanced. The independent variable was the method of administration,

and the dependant variable was how similar their results were from the two different types of administrations.

Results: Researchers ran several types of statistical analyses. Results indicated that there were no statistically significant differences in the scores or the subscales of the SDS Form R regardless of the type of administration.

Conclusion: Type of administration does not appear to affect scores. However, there are other differences that should be noted. For example, some sections are not included or are altered depending on the type of administration given. Administration time and cost varies. Access to the type of administration depends on the resources available to the user. The need for interpretation by a human services provider also varies by the type of administration.

Questions

1. Why is it important to stay up-to-date on current trends and availability of assessments?
2. What are the implications of assessments becoming more easily available to individuals without the assistance of a human services provider to interpret the results?

Potential use with special populations: The SDS is available in multiple languages including English, English–Canadian, French–Canadian, Spanish, and over 20 others. It was normed with females and males ranging from 17–65 years of age in high schools, community colleges, universities, and a variety of other settings (Niles & Harris-Bowlsbey, 2005). Norm groups include samples of Caucasians, African Americans, Hispanics, Asian Americans, Native Americans, and other backgrounds. An audiotape version for individuals with reading limitations, and a Braille version for individuals with visual impairments is available. A *Self-Directed Search-E* (4th ed.; SDS-E) is also available for adults and older adolescents with lower education levels or limited reading skills. The SDS-E contains 198 items and is written at the sixth-grade reading level with directions at the fourth-grade reading level. Audiotape is available with this version as well as a booklet with larger print size for persons who may be visually impaired.

Strengths and limitations: Conceptually, the SDS, modeled after the world of work in the form a hexagon, is very compelling and easily understood by clients of a wide range of abilities and interests. It is very easy to administer, score, and interpret the scores. Most clients

have little difficulty in self-scoring the instrument. The SDS-E is only available in English, English–Canadian, and Spanish and does not offer machine scoring.

STRONG INTEREST INVENTORY   The purpose of the Strong Interest Inventory (SII; Strong, Hansen, & Campbell, 1985) is to assess for patterns of interests, assuming that these patterns match persons who are successfully employed in certain occupations. For example, the assumption is made that a chemist would possess a different pattern of interests than an actor. Matching an individual to occupations with similar patterns is assumed to predict the likelihood of satisfaction and tenure within a particular occupation. Information provided is based on the same occupational themes used in the SDS (See Figure 19.3; Niles & Harris-Bowlsbey, 2005). A profile of the extent to which an individual's interests align with a series of occupations is also provided (i.e., the Occupational Scales). The SII consists of 282 items, with an additional 60 items comprising the Skills Confidence Inventory (SCI). The SCI was recently added to assist college students and adults who already have some work experience (Kapes & Whitfield, 2001). It measures self-perceived abilities related to occupational themes. (See Table 19.2.)

TABLE 19.2 Summary of Characteristics of the Strong Interest Inventory (SII)

Target Population	14 years and older
Statement of Purpose	Measure interests in a broad range of occupations, work activities, leisure activities, and school subjects
Titles of Subtests, Scales, and Scores Provided	General Occupational Themes based on Holland Codes (See SDS), Basic Interest Scales, Occupational Scales, and Personal Style Scales
Language Availability	English, French, French–Canadian, Italian, and Anglicsized adaptations
Test Time	35–40 minutes
Norm Groups	National sample based on U.S. census data
Available Versions	Paper and pencil, computer, other languages

Potential use with special populations: The SII is available in an online version. Individual responses are secured in such a way that users may save their answers and return to complete the instrument at another time. This feature may prove helpful in cases where an individual may require more time than is typical to complete the inventory.

Strengths and limitations: Since the SII is available online, it comes with additional helpful features such as technical online support and an online user's guide. The SII occupational norm groups have almost entirely achieved at least a high school diploma, and the majority have 4 or more years of higher education. Thus, the instrument may be biased toward individuals with higher levels of educational attainment (Kapes & Whitfield, 2001). The conceptual base of the SII also is easily understood and compelling to clients. Although it is easy to administer and interpret, it cannot be self-scored (Kapes & Whitfield 2001).

Aptitude Measures

As mentioned previously, self-knowledge is one of the cornerstones to enabling the identification of viable occupational options (Reardon et al., 2006). We have considered interest assessment, and now we will explore aptitude assessment. The sequence in formulating potential career alternatives begins with "What would I like to do," followed by "What can I do?" Before delving further into aptitude assessment, please be mindful that *interests* point to *what one would like or prefer doing*, whereas *aptitudes predict the likelihood of success* in educational or training programs or in the work of occupations.

Often, aptitude assessments are used to select qualified individuals from an applicant pool. Typically, the higher the score on the chosen aptitude measure, the higher the probability of being admitted to an educational or training program or being selected for a job from among a pool of applicants.

The aptitude assessments we have chosen to include in this chapter are ones that often are used for personnel selection in business and industry, government service, and in the military (Cohen & Swerdlik, 2005). Looking at scores, organizations may determine the extent to which candidates are prepared to enter training or jobs. In some cases, scores are used in a *norm-referenced* manner in which applicants in an applicant pool are compared to one another, and other times in a *criterion-referenced* manner in which applicants are compared to a minimum standard for entry into training or hiring for a job.

Before applying to educational programs or for job openings, individuals should become familiar with how aptitude assessments are used in the process of selection. For example, prior to entering graduate school, you most likely participated in an aptitude assessment utilized by most universities by taking the Graduate Record Examination (GRE). You may have noticed during your search of potential graduate schools to attend that, although the assessment tool remained constant, the criteria for admission varied. The minimum GRE score for admission to one school may have been set at one level, such as a total score of 1,000, while others may be set higher or lower. Beyond aptitude scores, other measurements are used, such as grade point average (GPA) and class rank. Further, given the importance of aptitude test scores in admission to education and training programs and in personnel selection in hiring, persons with disabilities are entitled to accommodations in aptitude testing (ADA, 1990). At times, individuals may be provided with readers, extended time, special norms, and other forms of accommodations (Cohen & Swerdlik, 2005). While reading about the following assessments, please consider the characteristics that may have particular relevance in terms of clients or persons with disabilities.

As with interests, aptitudes should be considered throughout the CASVE decision-making cycle. For example, during the Analysis phase, individuals consider, among their self-knowledge attributes, their higher and lower aptitudes (Sampson et al., 2004). During the Synthesis phase in which the individual is formulating and evaluating career options, the question here is, "Do I have the aptitudes to perform the work of a given occupation?" In Valuing, focus goes beyond interest to, "Given my aptitudes, what are the implications for training for the work and possible impact on my family in terms of time and financial resources?" Finally, during the Execution phase, one considers issues such as, "What are the admissions criteria for education and training programs leading to employment in my chosen occupation? Do I submit an application? If I am applying for certain jobs, what are their screening criteria?"

Described in the following section are two commonly used aptitude measures for personnel selection in business, industry, government, and military occupations whose subtests are representative of a wide variety of aptitude assessments available through psychological testing firms.

TEST OF ADULT BASIC EDUCATION (TABE)   The *Test of Adult and Basic Education (TABE)* is designed to assess the literacy and basic skills of adults (CTB/McGraw-Hill, 1994; Kapes & Whitfield, 2001). This test can be used both as an achievement test and an aptitude test. As an achievement test, the TABE can be used to determine the level of achievement an individual attains in an adult education program based on subtests measuring reading, language, mathematics, and (optional) spelling. As an aptitude test, it can be used as an entry level assessment for selection to a given training program to ascertain whether an individual is prepared to master the knowledge and skills taught in the program. TABE 7&8 Survey, the shortened version, and TABE Work-Related Foundation Skills also are available as supplemental or alternative measures. The latter is based on basic tasks common to most occupations. Used as an achievement test, scores are reported in grade equivalents; when used as an aptitude test, scores are reported as percentiles. Criterion-referenced information is provided in the form of minimum mastery level requirements for admission to training programs or entry to occupations. (See Table 19.3 for a summary of TABE.)

Potential use with special populations: The subtests used in the TABE are available at varying skill levels. A counselor may use a 50-item locator test to determine an appropriate ability level before using the entire test battery. There also is a literacy assessment that focuses on measuring pre- and beginning reading skills.

TABLE 19.3 Summary of Characteristics of the Test of Adult Basic Education

Target Population	Adult students including literacy and Adult Basic Education (ABE) instruction groups and General Educational Development (GED), Workforce Development, Vocational/Technical programs, and School-to-Work programs. Intended for ages 14.5 and older; can be administered to individuals or groups.
Statement of Purpose	Series of norm-referenced tests designed to measure achievement of basic skills commonly found in basic adult basic education curricula and taught in instructional programs. New additional measures can also assess skills in contexts that are of high interest to adults, e.g., life skills, work, and education. Scores can be used to evaluate individuals' abilities and to plan for specific educational and training needs.
Titles of Subtests, Scales, and Scores Provided	Complete Battery: reading, mathematics computation, applied mathematics, language, and spelling. Survey: A shortened version of the Complete Battery. Work-Related Foundation Skills: reading, language, and math. Work-Related Problem Solving: An assessment of problem-solving skills in work-related contexts. Problem-Solving Competencies: Define a problem, Examine a problem, Suggest solutions, and Evaluate solutions.
Language Availability	English and Spanish
Test Time	Times vary by subtests ranging from 10–50 minutes.
Norm Groups	High school juniors
Available Versions	Different forms are available: TABE 7&8: L-Literacy, E-Easy, M-Medium, D-Difficult, and A-Advanced; TABE-WF: D-Difficult, Health, Trade/Technical, Business/Office, and General.

TABLE 19.4 Summary of Characteristics of the Wonderlic Basic Skills Test (WBST)

Target Population	High school students and adults
Statement of Purpose	A measure of adult language and math skills required for entry to training programs or to employment.
Titles of Subtests, Scales, and Scores Provided	Subtests: verbal and quantitative skills; test of verbal skills includes word knowledge, sentence construction, information retrieval; test of quantitative skills includes explicit problem solving, applied problem solving, and interpretative problem solving.
Language Availability	English only.
Test Time	20 minutes for each subtest.
Norm Groups	High school, junior college, vocational schools and adults in work settings (manufacturing, financial services, fast food services, oil drilling, truck assembly, and highway construction).
Available Versions	Paper and pencil with machine scoring, and computer software.

A shorter survey version is available as an alternative or supplement, which may be more appropriate for some users. The layout of the survey version is easy to read with a clear large font.

Strengths and limitations: The choices of potential modifications for administering the TABE may be very useful for persons with disabilities.

WONDERLIC BASIC SKILLS TEST (WBST) The *Wonderlic Basic Skills Test (WBST)* is a 95-item test consisting of a 50-item Verbal Skills section and a 45-item Quantitative Skills section (Long, Artese, & Clonts, 2005; Kapes & Whitfield, 2001). It is designed for late adolescents and adults to determine the level of mastery of skills required for entry-level employment as established by the six-level General Educational Development (GED) scales set forth by the U.S. Department of Labor (DOL). Scores for each of the sections are reported in terms of DOL Levels 1, 2, and 3. Scores are compared to the skill-level required for specific occupations in order to assist individuals in estimating the potential for success in particular occupations. These skills were obtained from the *Dictionary of Occupational Titles* (DOT) (DOL, 2003). This test also is widely used in business and industry for applicant screening and selection in employee hiring as well. (See Table 19.4 for a Summary.)

Potential use with special populations: Shorter assessments such as this test may increase ease of use for some types of disabilities.

Strengths and limitations: This assessment is not available in other languages, which would increase the difficulty of administering this instrument to non-English-speaking clients or to applicants for training programs or employment.

USES OF INTEREST AND APTITUDE MEASURES IN CAREER COUNSELING

Interest Assessment Administration

Considering the lifespan development of individuals, the development and clarification of interests begin in childhood and continue into early adulthood and even longer (Super, 1990). However, the organization and policies of our educational systems and human services agencies often play a key role in setting the grades and ages in which the administration of interest inventories take place. Some school systems may begin interest assessments as early as late elementary or beginning middle school. Thus, in the administration of interest assessments, counselors and teachers, as well as human services providers should be aware of a student's or client's stage in the development of interests when interpreting the results.

Pipelines exist for certain occupations. For example, Widnall (1988) described a pipeline for science, technology, engineering, math, and medicine, known as the STEMM careers, that begins as early as elementary school. The term "pipeline" refers to individuals being eliminated from certain potential educational or occupational options based on educational choices or lack of preparation. For example, occupations in the STEMM careers are available only after completing necessary math, science, college major, and field requirements. Assessing for interests as early as middle school may encourage individuals to begin tracking on certain educational opportunities and requirements so that educational choices are made in a timely manner to remain in the pipeline.

Let us look at this from your future client's perspective. In a study consisting of 2,000 males and 2,000

DISCUSSION BOX 19.1

Policy is often a hot topic when it comes to education. Legislation is moving toward requiring middle school students to declare a major field of emphasis. This choice is a basis for selection of courses and extracurricular experiences.

Questions

1. What are the advantages in requiring students to declare a major field of emphasis so early in their academic career? What might be some disadvantages?

2. Consider the implications of this from several points of view (individual, guidance counselor or human services provider, school, university).

3. What are the implications of this type of policy for students with disabilities?

females, Widnall (1988) showed that by 9th grade, only 50% of males and 50% of females will have sufficient mathematic skills to remain in the pipeline for STEMM occupations. By the end of high school, only 14% of males and 11% of females could pursue STEMM technical careers. Further, by the end of college, only 2% of males and 1% of females will have completed intended math, science or engineering degrees at the B.S. level, meaning only .25% of the original male and .05% of the original females remained in the pipeline to attain a Ph.D. degree in science or engineering.

Widnall's (1988) study demonstrates how becoming involved in activities in our areas of interest too late may well exclude individuals from certain occupations consistent with their areas of interests. However, one must consider the implications of assessing interests at such an early age. For example, consider Case Study 19.2, Stephanie, at the end of this chapter to examine the potential effect of assessing interests and abilities early in one's psychosocial development. Please be mindful that interests continue to develop and evolve through the lifespan (Super, 1990). Moreover, when considering the additional element of aptitudes, they do not always align with interests, or they may place limits on the level of eventual educational and occupational attainment within an area of interest. Thus, interest and aptitude development should be systematically monitored throughout the adolescent and early adult years.

Interest and Aptitude Assessment Administration

The administration of interest and aptitude assessments should take into account standard conditions of administration as specified in the test manuals. Most often, the testing environment, the directions given to test takers, and the amount of time allotted to sections of the test are provided for test administrators in the

test manuals available from publishers of interest and aptitude measures. On maximum performance tests, special accommodations sometimes are warranted due to the Americans with Disabilities Act (ADA, 1990). Accommodations may include extended time in the case of documented learning disabilities and use of readers for the visually impaired.

Interpretation of Interest and Aptitude Scores to Clients in Career Choice

The first level of interpretation employs three forms of interpretation in reporting scores to clients: (1) norm-referenced interpretation, (2) criterion-referenced interpretation, and (3) idiographic interpretation. Norm-referenced interpretation entails informing clients how their interest or aptitude scores compared (i.e., high, medium, and low) to the distribution of scores of a norm group, typically published in the test manual (Salvia & Ysseldyke, 1978). Criterion-referenced interpretation involves comparing clients' scores with an external standard, such as minimum scores on certain aptitude tests to qualify for entry to an educational or training program (Salvia & Ysseldyke, 1978). Finally, idiographic interpretation entails comparing interest or aptitude scores to one another as earned by an individual (Cohen & Swerdlik, 2005). Here, clients inspect the results of testing in terms of relative strength and weakness of scores and ask, "What are my higher and lower interests?" and "What are my stronger and weaker aptitudes?"

The second level of interpretation concerns the relationship of scores to the respective phases of the CASVE Cycle in career problem-solving and decision-making. In the Communication phase, clients come in touch with the career problem and ask whether interests and aptitudes are components of the problem. At the Analysis phase, clients ask themselves what are their strong and weak interests and aptitudes, with an eye toward clarifying self-knowledge on which to base a decision. At the Synthesis phase, clients identify plausible occupational alternatives based on matching interests and aptitudes. In the Valuing phase, clients connect with significant others in discussing plausible educational and occupational alternatives in terms of strengths of interests and aptitudes and securing support for a given option and arrive at a first choice. Finally, at the Executive phase, clients inquire about minimum qualifications for educational and training programs or occupational placement. One can see that, in order to help clients use scores from interest inventories and aptitude tests, counselors must become familiar with their psychometric properties (e.g. validity, reliability, norms), and become knowledgeable in the use of test information at the respective phases of the decision cycle.

Employer Perspective as It Relates to Clients

Clients often can find it helpful to understand how interest and aptitude assessments may be used by prospective employers. As previously mentioned, employers may use assessments for a number of reasons, such as placement in training programs and selection for positions. Clients may ask how assessments will be used in the hiring or selection process. Thus, counselors should become familiar with the ways in which employees may or may not use results. For example, the TABE and the Armed Services Vocational Aptitude Battery Career Exploration Program (ASVAB) are used in schools and in walk-in career centers to measure a persons "interests, abilities, and personal preferences in relation to career opportunities in military, government, and civilian settings" (Cohen & Swerdlik, 2005, p. 292). The Wonderlic often is used by profit-making enterprises in personnel selection and advancement. As a practitioner, knowledge of how to explain clients' rights in terms of fair testing and how to explain needs to employers would be helpful. Also, become very familiar with the ADA of 1990 and the Uniform Guidelines on Employee Selection Procedures, 1978 regulations (U.S. Dept. of Justice, 1978). The use of this type of information may help clients in the Synthesis crystallization and Execution phases in career decision-making.

Summary and Conclusion

This chapter has defined the terms *interests*, *aptitudes*, and *achievement* and demonstrated the differences among them. Examples of commonly used interest and aptitude assessments have been provided, including their characteristics and special considerations for use with individuals with disabilities. This chapter also has discussed administering, scoring, and interpreting test results. The CIP theoretical framework has been used in case studies to demonstrate how human services providers may use assessment results within a career decision-making context. Finally, how these forms of assessments may be used for various purposes such as admission to educational or training programs, or in hiring for employment in workplace settings have been discussed.

Self-Check Exercises

1. Make a list of the different aptitude and interest assessments you have taken and/or heard of prior to reading this chapter.
2. Think about your interests and aptitudes. Create a list of things you like to do and things you are good at.
3. In your own words, compare and contrast the terms *aptitude, achievement*, and *interest*. Next, consider how you would describe differences among these to a client by pairing up and practicing with another student.

(a) Why is it important that the client and you understand the terminology?
(b) What types of questions are generated?
4. Why should clients know why they're being assessed? Why may they want to know how employers use assessments?
5. What are the two common uses of aptitude assessments?
6. State some of the important considerations in administering, scoring, and interpreting common measures of interests and aptitude measures with individuals with disabilities.

Case Study 19.1

Annie, a 19-year-old college freshman, is having difficulty deciding on a major. (Communication) She has been feeling very anxious recently. Her parents have been pressuring her to declare a major, and she recently received a letter from the Academic Advisory Office stating that she must declare a major by next semester. Annie is concerned because she does not know what type of occupations are out there and would like to get a sense of what she may want to do after college in order to pick a related major. (Analysis) Annie knows that she has done well in most of her math classes and prefers math to most other subjects. Because of a reading disability, Annie has not done well in reading and writing in the past but is working with a tutor to improve those skills. Beyond that, Annie has very little insight into her interests. While answering questions about herself on the SDS, Annie realizes that she prefers working alone to working in groups. Because of her disability, Annie has found it helpful to be in a very structured, organized environment although she does enjoy participating in creative activities such as drawing and creating original works of art. (Synthesis) According to Annie's SDS, her three highest scores are in *Investigative*, *Conventional*, and *Artistic types*. Annie reads the description of each of these types and feels they

best describe her. Next, she refers to occupations that fall within any combination of her code according to the Holland *Occupational Finder* (eg. ICA, IAC, AIC, ACI, CIA, CAI). Annie creates a list of all the occupations that look interesting or that she would like to know more about. As she researches these occupations, she will consider how they fit with her interests, strengths, and weaknesses. For example, she may rule out occupations that primarily require a lot of social interaction or significant amounts of writing. Eventually, Annie will narrow the list down to 3–5 occupations and determine what majors and possible minors may be most appropriate to help her prepare for those occupations.

QUESTIONS

1. Now that Annie has narrowed down (crystallized) her options, what should she do next? What phase will she be in? Given what you know about Valuing, who might Annie consider when ranking her options?
2. If you were working with Annie, how may you use information about her from her assessments and what she tells you to assist her?

Case Study 19.2

Stephanie was a high-achieving student throughout school. She took dance lessons, played soccer, and was a cheerleader for a football team. The oldest of four siblings, Stephanie often babysat for her parents and neighbors. During the summer, she helped out at her mother's daycare center. In eighth grade, Stephanie's class took the Strong Interest Inventory. She scored high in several occupations on the Strong Interest Scales and Basic Interest Scales, and her Holland Code was ISA with each letter being very close to each other (see Figure 19.3 for descriptions of these letters). Stephanie's list included Psychiatrist, Medical Technologist, and Nurse Practitioner. Stephanie showed the results to her parents. They were very excited and said it looked like she could be a doctor if she wanted. Since then, her family nicknamed her Dr. Steph. She was pleased with her parent's approval and enjoyed being able to tell other people that she planned to be a doctor. In high school, she joined the science club.

She did fairly well in most of her classes, but did not enjoy her higher-level math classes. She started working as a candy striper at the local hospital and really enjoyed working with the patients. She liked the feeling of helping others. When Stephanie entered college, she registered for premed classes but found that she had difficulty keeping up. Now her grade point average is suffering and she feels as though the information is not coming as easily to her as her peers. Stephanie is beginning to doubt her ability to become a doctor and now doesn't know what to do.

QUESTIONS

1. What are some of the external cues telling Stephanie that it may be time to make a decision?
2. In what ways may the pipeline have influenced Stephanie's motivation to explore options?
3. Where is Stephanie now in the CASVE cycle?

References

Americans with Disabilities Act of 1990, 42 U.S.C.A. 12101.

Cohen, R. J., & Swerdlik, M. E. (2005). *Psychological testing and assessment: An introduction to tests and measurement* (6th ed.). New York: McGraw Hill.

CTB/McGraw-Hill. (1994). *Test of Adult Basic Education (TABE)*. Monterey, CA.

Fouad, N. (2007). Work and vocational psychology: Theory, research, and applications. *Annual Review of Psychology (58)*, 5.1–5.22.

Holland, J. (1997). *Making vocational choices: A theory of vocational personalities and work environments.* (3rd ed.). Odessa, FL: Psychological Assessment Resources, Inc.

Holland, J. L. (2000). *The Occupations Finder.* Odessa, FL: Psychological Assessment Resources, Inc.

Holland, J. L., Powell, A.B. & Fritzche, B. A. (1994). *Self-Directed Search Professional Guide.* Odessa, FL: Psychological Assessment Resources, Ind.

Kapes, J. T., & Whitfield, E. A. (Eds.) (2001). *A counselor's guide to career assessment and instruments* (4th ed.). Columbus: Central Ohio Graphics.

Kosciulek, J. F. (2004). Empowering people with disabilities through vocational rehabilitation counseling. *American Rehabilitation* (Autumn).

Lacey, D. (1988). *The paycheck disruption: Finding success in the workplace of the '90s.* New York: Hippocrene Books, Inc.

Long, E. R., Artese, V. S., & Clonts, W. L. (2005). *Wonderlic Basic Skills Test (WBST).* Libertyville, IL: Wonderlic, Inc.

Lumsden, J., Sampson, J., Reardon, R., Lenz, J. & Peterson, G. (2004). A comparison study of the paper-and-pencil, personal computer, and internet versions of Holland's Self-Directed Search. *Measurement and Evaluation in Counseling and Development (37)*2, 85–94.

Mish, F. C. (Ed.). (1993). *Merriam Webster's collegiate dictionary* (10th ed.). Springfield, MA: Merriam-Webster, Inc.

Niles, S. G., & Harris-Bowlsbey, J. H. (2005). *Career development interventions in the 21st century* (2nd ed.). Columus, OH: Pearson Merrill Prentice Hall.

Peterson, G., Sampson, J., & Reardon, R. (1991). *Career development and services: A cognitive approach.* Pacific Grove, CA: Brooks/Cole.

Reardon, R. C., & Lenz, J. G. (1998). *The Self-Directed Search and related Holland career materials: A practioner's guide.* Odessa, FL: Psychological Assessment Resources, Inc.

Reardon, R. C., Lenz, J. G., Sampson, J. P., & Peterson, G. W. (2006). *Career development and planning: A comprehensive approach* (2nd ed.). Mason, OH: Thomson.

Salvia, J., & Ysseldyke, J. (1978). *Assessment in special and remedial education.* Boston: Houghton Mifflin Company.

Sampson, J. P., Jr., Reardon, R. C., Peterson, G. W., & Lenz, J. L. (2004). *Career counseling and services: A cognitive information processing approach.* Pacific Grove, CA: Wadsworth-Brooks/Cole.

Strong, E. K., Jr., Hansen, J. C., & Campbell, D. C. (1985). *Strong Vocational Interest Blank. Revised edition of Form T325, Strong-Campbell Interest Inventory.* Stanford, CA: Stanford University.

Super, D. (1990). A life-span, life-space approach to career development. In D. Brown & L. Brooks (Eds.), *Career choice and development* 2nd ed., pp. 197–261). San Francisco: Jossey-Bass.

Thorndike, R. M. (2005). *Measurement and evaluation in psychology and education* (7th ed.). Upper Saddle River, NJ: Pearson Merrill Prentice Hall.

U.S. Department of Justice. (1978). *Uniform guidelines on employee selection procedures. Federal Register,* 43, 38290–38309.

U.S. Department of Labor (2003). *Dictionary of Occupational Titles* (5th Ed.). Baton Rouge, LA: Claitor's Publishing Division.

Widnall, S. E. (1988). AAA presidential lecture: Voices from the pipeline. *Science (241)*4874, 1740–1745.

20

Assessment of Vocational and Work Adjustment

VIVIAN M. LARKIN
University of Wisconsin, Madison

SUZANNE TEW-WASHBURN
Troy University
Phenix City AL

OVERVIEW

The Rehabilitation Act mandated employment as the goal of service delivery in the rehabilitation of individuals with disabilities; thus, vocational assessment was used to identify vocational potential and possible job opportunities (Fourteenth Institute on Rehabilitation Issues, 1987). Work adjustment services evolved as a natural progression of vocational services. The Act serves to promote overall adjustment to work and other positive work related behaviors (Wright, 1980). Vocational assessment and work adjustment services are a central part of the vocational rehabilitation process.

Vocational assessment provides a basis for evaluating functional capacities. These assessments determine if an individual's capabilities can be enhanced by vocational training or compensated by the use of assistive devices or adaptations to the job. The integration of vocational, educational, psychological, medical, cultural, and socioeconomic factors come together to maximize vocational adjustment. When exploring a person's capabilities, the helping professional seeks information on client characteristics such as work interest, general intelligence, values, needs, transferable skills, physical capacities, work tolerance, and aptitudes. Vocational assessment is a comprehensive process designed to assist consumers and rehabilitation professionals in identifying and exploring levels of vocational functioning and employment readiness skills. This process should be holistic and humanistic in nature and should encompass all issues relevant to the consumer (i.e., family, environment, and the diverse nature of their existence).

This chapter provides an overview of vocational assessment and work adjustment services and discusses how the two components work together to encourage empowerment, informed choice, and independence in the development of vocational opportunities for consumers with disabilities. Theories of work adjustment are discussed, and the history of practices in assessment and work adjustment are explored. Also covered in this chapter is a description of the methods, models, and practices used in the field. Critical research related to roles, functions, and competencies are discussed followed by a discussion of legislative, professional, and cultural issues. To complete the chapter, a review of multidisciplinary and interdisciplinary approaches is given, and current issues driving change in the profession are addressed.

LEARNING OBJECTIVES

By the end of the chapter, readers should be able to:

- Outline the history and evolution of vocational assessment as a profession
- Identify best practices in vocational assessment and the standards of service guiding the profession
- Evaluate the methods of assessment and the associated instruments used to evaluate specific skills and traits
- Apply work adjustment theories in assessment and work adjustment practices

INTRODUCTION

Vocational assessment and work adjustment services are very important components of the rehabilitation process for individuals with disabilities. These two processes serve distinct purposes in the overall rehabilitation process. For individuals with disabilities, vocational assessment and work adjustment services come together to achieve successful transition to employment as well as full integration into the community. Vocational assessment is a process designed to evaluate work potential and predict work behavior. Vocational assessment and work adjustment services are used to identify and address barriers to successful employment. Recommendations from vocational assessments take into consideration the need for work adjustment services and specify the types of services needed. Some typical components in a work adjustment plan include measures to increase or improve an individual's work tolerance, interpersonal relations, punctuality, attendance, as well as other work behaviors and traits. Real or simulated work is used as the primary work adjustment training mechanism. Both vocational assessment and work adjustment are critical elements in the development of vocational goals for the consumer, in the job development process, and in establishing meaningful vocational outcomes.

KEY DEFINITIONS AND THEORIES

Presented in the following list are key terms, concepts, and definitions in vocational assessment and work adjustment services. Understanding these constructs helps to appreciate their application to the vocational assessment and work adjustment process.

Assistive Technology. Assistive technology refers to any item, piece of equipment, or product system, whether acquired commercially or off-the-shelf, modified or customized, that increases, maintains, or improves functional capacities of individuals with disabilities (Tech-Related Assistance of Individuals with Disabilities Act, 1988). These devices are a necessary component of the vocational assessment and work adjustment process.

Vocational Assessment. Vocational assessment utilizes a "systematic appraisal process to identify an individual's vocational potential" (Smith, Lombard, Neubert, Leconte, Rothenbacher, & Sitlington, 1995, p. 110). The vocational assessment process combines essential information regarding a consumer's history, including vocational, educational, psychological, medical, cultural, and socioeconomic factors.

Vocational Evaluator. A vocational evaluator explores a person's abilities, aptitudes, interests, general intelligence, transferable skills, physical capacity, and work tolerances. In order to assure a highly individualized and holistic process, an evaluator must include information germane to family dynamics, community inclusion, sociopolitical influences, and the diverse milieu of the consumer's life experiences. The consumer's full participation in the assessment process is imperative to achieving positive vocational outcomes.

Work Adjustment Training. Work adjustment training is designed to promote the development of self-confidence, self-control, work tolerances, interpersonal skills, and other positive worker attitudes and behaviors (Wright, 1980). Work adjustment plans typically are guided by the results of a vocational assessment and the recommendations made in the vocational evaluator's report.

Work Adjustment Specialist. A work adjustment specialist uses referral data, background information gathered from interviews, and recommendations from vocational assessment reports to develop individualized work adjustment plans (Williams & Faubion, 2002). The consumer's full participation in the development of the work adjustment plan and in all aspects of the work adjustment program is imperative.

THEORIES OF WORK ADJUSTMENT

According to Wright (1980), "work adjustment helps individuals develop self-confidence, self-control, work tolerances, skill at interpersonal relations, an understanding of the work world and worker attitude …" (p. 282). Work adjustment theories are readily translated into practice through the evaluation of "client needs, vocational problems, aspirations, personal history, and various ability levels" (Osipow & Fitzgerald, 1996, p. 184).

Educators and practitioners have invested little energy in developing theories specific to the rehabilitation profession (Lustig, Lam, & Leahy, 1985). However, theoretical approaches, such as career development theories (e.g., Ginzberg, Ginzburg, Axelrod, & Herma, 1959; Holland, 1959; Roe, 1957; Super, 1953) and work adjustment theories (Hershenson, 1981; Lofquist & Dawis, 1969), have greatly influenced the rehabilitation field. Work adjustment and career development are related concepts in the preparation of individuals for employment. In acknowledging the absence of the concept of ability in other career development theories, Savickas (1994) and Osipow (1994) identified work adjustment theory as a foundational career development theory. "Career development is, for most people, a lifelong process of getting ready to choose, choosing, and typically continuing to make choices from among the many occupations available in our society" (Brown & Brooks, 1984, p. ix). Work adjustment theory refers to the development of three domains: work personality, work competencies, and work goals (Hershenson, 1981). Hershenson's Work Adjustment Theory provides a conceptual framework of career development from birth through adult life. In this model, work personality develops during the preschool years, work competencies develop in the school years, and work goals develop during the later school years and continue to develop in adulthood (Szymanski, Hershenson, & Power, 1988).

The Minnesota Theory of Work Adjustment

The Minnesota Theory of Work Adjustment, which was developed based on research in the field of vocational psychology, is particularly relevant to vocational rehabilitation. The research, followed by the theory, resulted in the creation of many monographs, materials, and instruments needed in the assessment and work adjustment processes. For example, the Minnesota Importance Questionnaire is based upon the work adjustment theory and includes such values as achievement, comfort (self-expression), status, altruism, safety, and autonomy (Sharf, 1997). The Minnesota Theory of Work Adjustment is basically a matching model that emphasizes mutual correspondence (person and environment) and dynamic interaction (mutual responsiveness) (Brown et al., 1996). Work adjustment is the process of achieving and maintaining correspondence. Two key assumptions underlying the theory of work adjustment are known as "satisfaction" (of the individual with the work environment) and "satisfactoriness" (satisfaction of the work environment with the individual) (Osipow & Fitzgerald, 1996, p. 182). Satisfaction and satisfactoriness result in tenure (job retention), the primary indicator of work adjustment. The

importance of work and social adjustment in the workplace was underscored by Lenard in 1960. He found that the inability to maintain employment was attributable to lack of work skill and to defective social interaction with other workers.

The Minnesota Theory of Work Adjustment may not always predict satisfaction, satisfactoriness, and tenure accurately. Entry into jobs sometimes is due to chance or opportunity rather than the interests or preferences of the individual worker (Osipow & Fitzgerald, 1996). Also, prediction is compromised further by cultural variables because gender and minority group status are not considered to be major variables in the theories of work adjustment (Brown et al., 1996).

The International Classification of Functioning Framework

The International Classification of Functioning, Disability and Health (Homa & Peterson, 2005) provides new and promising model designed to better understand health and health-related conditions. Developed by the World Health Organization, the International Classification of Functioning (ICF) and its multidimensional approach offers a systematic method for better understanding disability and health-related conditions. Homa (2007) suggests that the ICF model has exceptional application in rehabilitation client assessment. This innovative model uses an ecological, systems-based approach to job placement (Homa), and is considered to be a brilliant tool for measuring functioning in society. In direct contrast to the Minnesota Theory of Work Adjustment, the ICF is broad in scope and takes into consideration factors such as age, race, culture, gender, and social status. Homa believes the ICF framework is compatible with environmental, systems-based approaches to career placement and holds promise as a functional instrument in job placement. According to Homa, this approach can assist vocational rehabilitation professionals in identifying needed interventions, implementing effective placement strategies, and assessing employment outcomes.

Recently revised, the theoretical framework of the ICF is now considered a multidimensional classification system for human functioning and disability (Hwang & Nochajski, 2003). This newly conceptualized framework offers a change from negative descriptions of impairments, disabilities, and handicaps to more unbiased imagery of body configuration and function, activities, and participation. It also recognizes the important role of environmental factors in facilitating functioning or creating barriers to employment for people with disabilities.

HISTORY OF PRACTICES IN VOCATIONAL ASSESSMENT AND WORK ADJUSTMENT

Vocational assessment is the cornerstone of the rehabilitation process. From a historical perspective, the development and growth of vocational assessment as a professional discipline can be traced back to (1) the expanding field of vocational rehabilitation, (2) federal legislation, and (3) the development of assessment technology. In the early half of the 20th century, vocational assessment instruments were developed primarily for use with veterans from World War I and World War II (Nadolsky, 1971a). The second half of the 20th century witnessed a notable shift in consumers receiving vocational assessment services. Between the 1950s and 1970s, assessment services offered through vocational rehabilitation services were primarily designated for persons diagnosed with developmental disabilities (Wesolek & McFarlane, 1992). The mid-20th century also witnessed a demand within the field of vocational rehabilitation for more appropriate assessment measures that did not discriminate against individuals with disabilities (Hamilton & Shumate, 2005), particularly those with the most severe disabilities. This era also included the "rehabilitation facility movement," which led to the rapid growth of rehabilitation facilities, the expansion of assessment services, and an increased number of highly qualified vocational evaluators. Before long, the vocational assessment process was declared the panacea for overcoming limitations of standardized psychological tests (Larkin, 1996). Because vocational assessment utilizes work, either real or simulated, as the focal point, this new profession was able to distinguish itself from other professions using standardized testing measures. The development of the Vocational Evaluation and Work Adjustment Association (VEWAA) and the advent of assessment technology in the 1960s further established vocational assessment as a separate discipline. The role of the vocational evaluator continues to evolve in response to legislative mandates, advances in technology, a shift in populations served (more diverse), and the involvement of consumers as full partners in the rehabilitation process. Work adjustment training was initiated in response to the rehabilitation facility movement in the 1960s and 1970s.

In the 1980s, community-integrated employment and training strategies emerged as an alternative to the traditional rehabilitation facility approach to placement (Szymanski, Handley-Maxwell, Hansen, & Myers, 1988). Whitehead (1987) reported as many as two thirds of rehabilitation facilities were incorporating community integrated strategies in their programs. Community-based services in the least restrictive environment appeared as a solid value that would be long-lasting (Couch, 1994; Mank, Rhodes, & Bellamy, 1986; Rusch, 1986; Wehman, 1986). Community-based work adjustment, transitional employment, and supported employment comprise three common applications of the community-integrated service model.

Work adjustment services, which typically had been provided in facilities, expanded to include enclaves within industries and job coaching in community work settings (Menchetti, 1992). Couch, May, Fadely, and Pell (1991) predicted that the future of work adjustment services would be "on the job in community settings" (p. 31). In a comparison of work adjustment services and the supported employment model, Couch and Pell (1991) concluded that there was significant overlap in the processes and professional practices of these two employment training approaches. For example, both approaches rely upon realistic job-based training in order for individuals with disabilities to obtain employment in the community and to live independently.

METHODS, MODELS, AND PRACTICES IN ASSESSMENT AND WORK ADJUSTMENT

Methods and Models of Assessment

Pioneer studies in the early 1970s resulted in two respected models of vocational assessment: Nadolsky's model for the vocational evaluation of the disadvantaged, and Leconte's model, the vocational assessment appraisal of the whole individual. Leconte and Roebuck revised the vocational assessment appraisal of the whole individual model in 1984. The revised model offers a more inclusive approach and therefore is widely used within the profession of vocational assessment.

Nadolsky (1971a) noted that the common practices of most vocational evaluation programs included individual assessment followed by job matching to the real work environment. Nadolsky's model of vocational evaluation takes into account the reality that, although people are capable of many types of jobs, they also lack ability in some areas. Nadolsky's model is "based upon a logical narrowing of vocational choice by and for each client through the elimination of occupations which are outside the realm of possible attainment." (p. 43). A pyramid (see Figure 20.1) demonstrates how the process encompasses all vocational goals as real possibilities initially and then systematically eliminates options that are not truly feasible in order to find the optimum

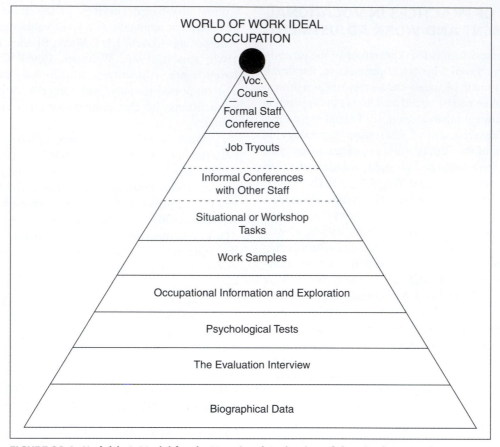

FIGURE 20.1 Nadolsky's Model for the Vocational Evaluation of the Disadvantaged.
Reprinted with permission from Julian Nadolsky.

occupation for the consumer. Nadolsky's categories and the applications of the model are in Table 20.1.

Leconte and Roebuck's (1984) model, the vocational assessment appraisal of the whole individual, is comprehensive in scope and looks at the consumer from all aspects of his or her life. The inner core of this model focuses on the individual's self-concept and self-esteem. The two outer cores focus on individual values and behaviors. Figure 20.2 presents a diagram of the model. Table 20.2 describes the career assessment process leading to a consumer's career profile (i.e., identifying strengths, needs, capabilities, and potential). The outcome of the career profile results in consumer empowerment, collaboration, implementation of recommendations, support services, and job placement.

In summary, these models played a major role in establishing a foundation for meaningful vocational assessment. Each demonstrates the importance of providing individualized assessments, establishing partnerships with consumers, and building collaborative networks with professionals and programs that provide support for people with disabilities. One of the strengths of Nadolsky's model is the midpoint staff evaluation which serves to incorporate appropriate feedback from key team members to help guide the remaining components of the assessment process.

Leconte and Roebuck's more recent model, which is holistic in its approach, places considerable emphasis on consumer empowerment and consumer choice. The model recognizes the impact of cultural variables in the lives of individuals with disabilities, and therefore considers the importance of culture in understanding the consumer's history. Other key components of Leconte and Roebuck's model are the inclusion of individual learning styles in the assessment process and the recognition that

TABLE 20.1 Description of Nadolsky's Model

1. **Biographical Data:** The acquisition of various types of biographical data is designed to identify the individual in his or her present situation by discovering the events and experiences in his history that have served to create and mold his or her individuality.

2. **Evaluation Interview:** The evaluation interview is used to enhance the evaluator's understanding of the client through the verification of biographical data, clarification of biographical data, or acquisition of supplemental information.

3. **Psychological Tests:** Psychological tests are used in vocational evaluation to heighten the evaluator's understanding of the client's general vocational assets and limitations.

4. **Occupational Information and Exploration:** With the provision of occupational information and the utilization of occupational exploration procedures, emphasis is placed upon the client gaining an understanding of that portion of the world of work that is within the realm of possible attainment. The client is confronted with the realities of appropriate occupations, and is provided with the opportunity to explore these occupations and gain first-hand knowledge of their specific nature and demands.

5. **Work Samples:** The work sample is a highly structured technique that provides a vehicle for confrontation. The work sample is a structured evaluation technique that allows the client to participate fully in the evaluation process as an active partner.

6. **Situational or Workshop Tasks:** Situational tasks are used in vocational evaluation primarily to observe client work behavior in a realistic, semistructured, controlled work environment.

7. **Informal Conferences with Other Staff:** When both the client and the evaluator have gained a clear understanding of the client's work behavior and vocational potential, this information should be discussed with other professionals who have worked with the client and who will be involved in the implementation of vocational recommendations.

8. **Job Tryouts:** Job tryouts are employed to assess the level of skill that a client displays in an actual and specific job situation.

9. **Formal Staff Conferences:** The formal staff conference is the most common vehicle for the discussion of vocational evaluation results and for the planning of service implementation. In short, the formal staff conference is designed to provide the evaluator with conclusive evidence about the overall feasibility of his tentative recommendations. By using the information gained during the formal staff conference, the evaluator is able to eliminate certain occupations from consideration and formulate formal vocational recommendations.

10. **Vocational Counseling:** Vocational counseling is designed to assist the client in deciding upon realistic vocational goals. It also enables the client to arrive at an understanding of the processes that may be followed for goal attainment. Through vocational counseling the client acquires a functional understanding of his or her vocational potential and of the methods that can lead to its fulfillment. Vocational counseling also provides the evaluator with an opportunity to understand his or her results as they relate to the client's future aspirations.

11. **Ideal Occupation:** The ultimate goal of vocational evaluation is to determine the ideal occupation for each client evaluated. Although vocational evaluation programs should strive to attain an ideal objective, the amorphous and unstable nature of the "ideal" concept must be recognized.

Nadolsky (1971a, pp. 40–47 adapted with permission).

many of the barriers confronting individuals with disabilities are environmental. Both models recognize the importance of applying multiple assessment techniques and instruments (see Appendix A at the end of this chapter) that can be applied in diverse settings.

Methods and Practices in Work Adjustment

Work adjustment services are recommended for individuals who have substandard or problematic work behaviors. Programs providing work adjustment services are designed to respond to recommendations or questions

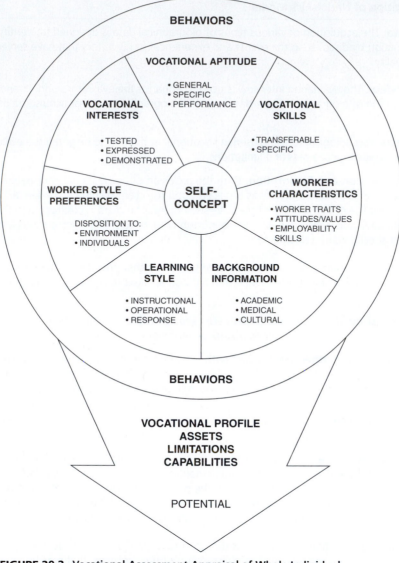

FIGURE 20.2   Vocational Assessment Appraisal of Whole Individual

Source: Reprinted with permission from UW–Stout Vocational Rehabilitation Institute, University of Wisconsin–Stout, and Pamela Leconte.

generated by vocational assessments. Work adjustment specialists make use of referral data, interviews with the consumer, as well as vocational assessment reports to develop treatment plans and the methods needed to improve work behaviors (Williams & Faubion, 2002).

Historically, staff of rehabilitation facility and work adjustment programs usually trained individuals for a period of time and then tried to place them successfully in a community job. On the other hand, community-integrated services (i.e., supported employment) required

practitioners to find the placement first and then provide the training.

The traditional approach, often referred to as train–place, requires the consumer to make improvements in his or her work behaviors and skills prior to being recommended for competitive employment (Szymanski, Handley-Maxwell, Hansen, & Myers, 1988). The train–place model is based on the assumption that most people with disabilities have similar needs and require job-readiness training (Botterbusch, 1988).

TABLE 20.2 Integrative Appraisal of the Individual Dimension

The following categories describe typical attributes of an individual that must be assessed to assist in vocational planning and career decision-making. All information collected about these attributes should be vocationally *relevant, valid and current.* These also form the components that make up the content of an individual's vocational assessment.

1. **Self-Concept:** represents the core of any individual. This core equates one's ideas about who he or she is. Self-image, one's inner mirror, comprises the way one sees and thinks about one's self (Roebuck, L., 1991). Self-image often is indistinguishably bound to self-concept, *which is reflected via behaviors and performances that emanate through the remaining attributes.* By observing self-concept, one's self-esteem can be defined better, meaning the feelings, both positive and negative, one holds about who he or she is (Roebuck, L., 1991).

2. **Behaviors:** manifestations of how the person presents him or herself to the world. Observations of behaviors can lead to true indications of one's abilities, interests, unique talents, and needs.

3. **Vocational or Career Interests:** comprise what one wants to do, would be happy doing, and/or dreams of doing in regard to careers, occupations, and jobs.

4. **Worker Style Preferences or Temperaments:** refer to personal traits that reflect one's disposition or responses and choices toward environments and other individuals. Preferences for working with people, data, or things are tied to a person's temperament.

5. **Learning Preferences and Styles:** entails how one *prefers* to receive, organize, and use information. Often learning modalities, such as auditory, visual, kinesthetic, and variations of these are associated with learning styles. Other characteristics of learning preferences include environmental (light, sound, temperature), emotional (motivation, persistence) and physical (time of day, mobility) considerations as well as sociological ones that may involve other people (working with peers or authority figures) (Dunn & Dunn, 1978).

6. **Developmental Background:** often referred to as background information, does not refer to a comprehensive case history but includes information that is pertinent to one's performances and future regarding vocational development. Background information can include previous work history or avocational activities, academic performances, or vocational implications of disabilities.

7. **Worker Characteristics:** include personal traits, values, attitudes, employability skills and work related behaviors, such as work habits, social skills, job-seeking skills.

8. **Vocational/Occupational Skills:** refers to specific technical, industrial/business or other types of skills that are required in actual occupations or jobs. Sometimes these are categorized as occupationally specific, avocational, and transferable.

9. **Vocational Aptitudes:** can be defined as one's ability to learn something or one's potential to learn. More specifically, it represents a person's capacity and capability to acquire proficiency within a given amount of time with formal and/or informal training.

10. **Functional/Life Skills:** encompasses those skills that an individual needs to succeed in personal life and in the realms of community and independent living (Rothenbacher & Leconte, 1990). Examples of such life skills include financial management, use of transportation, decision-making, and problem-solving.

Information from each of these categories is analyzed, synthesized, and interpreted into an individual vocational profile that emphasizes vocational strengths, needs, and recommendations for implementation within the overall career development process.

Adapted from Leconte and Roebuck, 1984

Traditional work adjustment training was intended to prepare individuals to meet the general demands of work in areas such as attendance, punctuality, and quality of work (Wuenschel & Brady, 1959). Use of this model requires the consumer to be able to generalize job skills and transfer them from one work setting to another. (Szymanski et al.). Another assumption of the train–place model is that people with disabilities are happier and better adjusted when they live in exclusion from society in general. The results of numerous research studies on the train–place model suggest that, due to its exclusive nature, the model has failed to provide individuals with disabilities meaningful employment opportunities (Bellamy, Rhodes, & Albin, 1986; Horner, Meyer, & Fredericks, 1986; Noble & Conley, 1987; Whitehead, 1987). The place–train model, a community integration approach to placement, often is used as a synonym for community-based work adjustment. Because the place–train approach recognizes the value of inclusiveness and the benefits of "on-the-job" training, it results in significantly superior employment outcomes for people with disabilities. Both traditional and community-based approaches provide goal-oriented, individualized treatment programs designed to maximize a consumer's employability. Real or simulated work activities are increased on a graduated basis to improve overall physical tolerance, productivity, and work behavior (California VEWAA, 1992).

RESEARCH CRITICAL TO ASSESSMENT AND WORK ADJUSTMENT PRACTICES

Two areas have been the focus of research interest: roles, functions, and competencies for vocational evaluators as well as the use of interdisciplinary approaches. Each of these areas is considered in the following discussions.

Roles, Functions, and Competencies of Vocational Evaluators

The primary responsibilities of vocational evaluators are to work in partnership with consumers to assess their employment potential, to recommend rehabilitation services leading to increased vocational opportunities, and to establish job and career options based on the consumer's interests and abilities (Fourteenth Institute on Rehabilitation Issues, 1987). The roles, functions, and competencies of vocational assessment personnel are multifaceted. As a result, the evaluator is required

to be knowledgeable, versatile, and to possess a set of specialized skills. They must be proficient interviewers, have a keen understanding of human behavior and disability, and possess an appreciation of cultural differences. In addition to having a working knowledge of assistive technology, vocational evaluators must be able to analyze the job market, identify the essential functions of the job, and evaluate the work culture. Another function fundamental to the role of the vocational evaluator is the selection, administration, and interpretation of assessment techniques. According to Thomas (2000), in addition to these roles and functions, the vocational evaluator also must assume the responsibilities of an educator. In this role, the vocational evaluator informs others about disability, employment, and the value of vocational assessments. As a result of this advocacy role, the vocational evaluator is able to increase the public's overall awareness of the vocational assessment profession.

A recent study identifying the importance of function and knowledge domains required for effective vocational assessment practice was completed by Hamilton and Shumate (2005). Participants in this study were professionals from around the country who received their certification from the Commission on Certification of Work Adjustment and Vocational Evaluation Specialist (CCWAVES). Findings revealed six major knowledge domains: foundations of vocational assessment, standardized assessment, occupational information, implications of disability, communication, professional networking. Six major job functions also were identified: clinical skills to analyze and synthesize assessment data, behavioral observation/evaluation techniques, case management, occupational analysis/information, vocational counseling, and professionalism. Hamilton and Shumate's results were consistent with Leahy and Wright's (1988) findings that also identified competencies important to evaluators.

INTERDISCIPLINARY PRACTICES. Rehabilitation personnel other than vocational evaluators may provide abbreviated vocational assessment services; however, professional vocational evaluators are required to meet highly specialized standards of practice. The Interdisciplinary Council on Vocational Evaluation and Assessment strongly recommends that all individuals providing vocational assessment services demonstrate the following competencies (Smith, Lombard, Neubert, Leconte, Rothernbacher, & Sitlington, 1995) (see Table 20.3).

TABLE 20.3 Competencies Recommended by the Interdisciplinary Council on Vocational Evaluation and Assessment

Competency

1. The ability to select, adopt, and/or develop methods and approaches that are used in determining an individual's attributes, abilities, and needs.

2. The ability to utilize alternative methods and approaches that can be used to cross validate information generated from other assessment sources.

3. The ability to conduct formal and/or informal behavioral observation strategies that can be integrated in a variety of settings.

4. The ability to collect and interpret ongoing data that can be utilized to promote successful transition through critical junctures of the individual's career development.

5. The ability to interpret assessment data in a manner that contributes to the total service delivery system. Vocational assessment team members must be capable of synthesizing and reporting formal and informal data in a manner that promotes appropriate planning, appropriate goal setting, and coordination of needed support services.

6. The ability to function as an effective participant on an interdisciplinary team.

7. The ability to select, implement, and integrate assessment approaches that are current, valid, reliable, and grounded in career, vocational, and work contexts.

DISCUSSION BOX 20.1

Some professionals believe that traditional methods of vocational assessment, when practiced by experienced evaluators, can be effective with almost all individuals regardless of disability. Other practitioners, however, make the argument that traditional assessment is not appropriate for some individuals, particularly those with the most severe disabilities. They contend that many people with disabilities have a host of skills that can be acknowledged and addressed only by an assessment done in the community.

Questions

1. According to the Interdisciplinary Council on Vocational Evaluation and Assessment, all evaluators providing vocational assessment services should demonstrate seven important competencies. Which of these seven competencies seem most relevant to vocational evaluators who do assessments in the community?

2. In practice, community-based assessments commonly done are in an informal manner by staff persons who have little, if any, training and experience in the field. Give your opinion about this practice. Specifically, do you think assessment done in this manner represents a threat to the profession? Ideally, all assessment should be done by highly qualified personnel; however, when there are not well-trained vocational evaluators available in the community, what should be done to adequately serve individuals with severe disabilities?

LEGISLATIVE, PROFESSIONAL, AND CULTURAL ISSUES THAT IMPACT ASSESSMENT AND WORK ADJUSTMENT

Legislation in Rehabilitation Services

Federal legislation has a major influence on the development and growth of rehabilitation services. The 1954 Rehabilitation Act Amendments mandated the provision of vocational evaluation and work adjustment services to individuals with disabilities. This Act also allocated federal funds for the development of graduate-level training in rehabilitation and the establishment of rehabilitation facilities. The 1965 Rehabilitation Act Amendments provided a platform for the emergence of vocational assessment as a professional discipline (Wright, 1980).

The disability consumer movement of the 1970s played a significant role in the pursuit of equality for individuals with disabilities and related legislation reform (Rubin & Roessler, 2001). One of the first laws in response to this consumer-driven movement was the Rehabilitation Act of 1973. This law made it mandatory for state vocational rehabilitation agencies to give priority to serving individuals with the most severe disabilities, and to expand and improve services to this population. Vocational assessment was viewed as a continuum of tools necessary to help consumers reach their goals of independence, community integration, and meaningful employment.

Public law 94-142, also known as The Education for all Handicapped Children Act of 1975, mandated educational services for all students with disabilities. Individualized educational program planning, education in the least restrictive environment, and involvement of the student and the parents in the planning process were vital components of this law. Subsequently, vocational assessment also was identified as a key service needed to implement effective planning for students. In addition to setting the stage for more comprehensive assessments and career planning for students with special needs, adult consumers with disabilities also benefited. Following the implementation of P.L. 94-142, state vocational rehabilitation agencies began to receive an increased number of school referrals, parent involvement in planning educational goals for their children increased, and advocacy became an accepted role for individuals with disabilities and their supporters. This shift in the educational system influenced all services provided to people with disabilities (Fourteenth Institute on Rehabilitation Issues, 1987).

The Rehabilitation Act of 1978 further emphasized the provision of priority services to individuals with severe disabilities by establishing independent living programs. As a result, the independent living movement set into motion new paradigms that endorsed the concepts of consumer empowerment and consumer choice. Thus, vocational assessment was viewed as an important tool to provide consumers and their counselors the information by which they could make informed decisions. The Carl Perkins Act of 1984 and the Rehabilitation Act Amendments of 1986 expanded the consumer populations being served by vocational evaluators and work adjustment specialists. The Carl Perkins Act mandated that all students enrolled in vocational education programs be provided vocational assessment services. The 1986

Amendments to the Rehabilitation Act established supported employment programs as a service for individuals with disabilities, thereby increasing the need for community-based programs, including work adjustment services outside the confines of a facility. This change represented yet another shift in society's attitude toward individuals with disabilities by advocating for people with severe disabilities to have the support they need for competitive and inclusive employment.

The purpose of Title I of the 1990 Americans with Disabilities Act is to increase employment opportunities for individuals with disabilities. The Act recognized the high rates of unemployment and employment inequalities among this population. Vocational assessment and work adjustment services provided an important step in the identification and enhancement of employment potential.

The Amendments to the Rehabilitation Act of 1992 (P.L. 102-569) reemphasized the foundation laid by the 1973 Rehabilitation Act by extending vocational rehabilitation services to individuals with the most severe disabilities (Giordano & D'Alonzo, 1995). The 1992 Amendments also accentuated the rights of individuals receiving services to participate in the planning of their own programs, identified the need for assistive teams to involve a diverse group of professionals, provided for the development of interagency programs, and mandated priority of services for individuals from underrepresented groups and members of other populations that had traditionally been underserved. As a result of the Act, evaluators were encouraged to meet the needs of a broader population by individualizing assessments and using a more holistic approach in the assessment process.

Title IV of the Workforce Investment Act (P.L. 105-220) contains the 1998 Amendments to the Rehabilitation Act of 1973. The 1998 Amendments allowed individuals a greater role in shaping their individual plans for employment, renamed the Individual Written Rehabilitation Plan (IWRP) the Individual Plan for Employment (IPE), increased language emphasizing informed choice, and supported self-employment and telecommuting as appropriate employment outcomes (Thomas, 1999). The Act modified the definition of "employment outcomes" to allow individuals working in supported employment below the minimum wage to continue to receive services as long as they are working toward competitive work. Also included in this Act was the presumption that a person could benefit from services, thereby requiring the vocational rehabilitation agencies to provide "clear and convincing evidence" (i.e., exploring the individuals' abilities, capabilities, and capacity to perform in work situations through the use of trial work experiences) that an individual is incapable of benefiting in terms of an employment outcome from services due to the severity of the disability. A significant component of this law, which impacts the provision of rehabilitation services, is the requirement that vocational assessments include real work (i.e., community-based evaluations). Rehabilitation legislation led to significant advances in the availability of services to a diverse population. More realistic and comprehensive methods were established to facilitate consumer vocational potential. The utilization of simulated or real work in the assessment process provided a realistic basis for evaluating consumer potential, career options, and successful adjustment to employment.

For many years, the terms *vocational assessment* and *vocational evaluation* have been used interchangeably. In the 1980s and 1990s, some professionals also promoted *vocational appraisal* as an umbrella term that included both vocational assessment and vocational evaluation. In fact, there have been many lively debates about which term is broader and encompasses various types of assessment techniques and methods. The Interdisciplinary Council on Vocational Evaluation and Assessment (a national coalition founded in 1992) combines the terms *vocational evaluation* and *assessment* to describe the profession and the methods, tools, and approaches used within the profession. Arguably, vocational assessment now is accepted as the umbrella term in most professional arenas.

MULTIDISCIPLINARY AND INTERDISCIPLINARY APPROACHES IN ASSESSMENT AND WORK ADJUSTMENT

The team approach, a recommended practice for use in comprehensive assessment and work adjustment training, brings together professionals from multiple disciplines to collaborate on providing services to assist the consumer in the career acquisition process (VEWAA, 1975.) A vocational evaluator, as a facilitator of these meetings, presents findings on the consumer, asks pertinent questions, and solicits relevant comments and suggestions (Nadolsky, 1971b). The all-inclusive comments and suggestions are very helpful in making recommendations for work adjustment training and other services, as applicable. A major improvement in contemporary staffing practices is the inclusion of the consumer as a full partner in the process.

The Interdisciplinary Council on Vocational Evaluation and Assessment offers the following set of guidelines that identify and establish best practices in vocational assessment (Smith et al., 1995) (see Table 20.4).

DISCUSSION BOX 20.2

Changing trends in vocational evaluation are driven by many factors. These include labor market changes, shifts in consumer populations, advances in health care, and innovations in technology. Thus, the roles, functions, and competencies of the vocational evaluator are multifaceted. As a result, the evaluator is required to possess a specialized set of skills. Over the years several studies have attempted to identify the primary job competencies of the evaluator. The most widely accepted professional competencies were identified by the Interdisciplinary Council on Vocational Evaluation and Assessment (see Table 20.4).

Questions
1. Identify four key components of behavior observation as recommended by the Interdisciplinary Council on Vocational Evaluation and Assessment.

2. Discuss the pros and cons of using different methods, tools, and approaches to verify assessment information.
3. Discuss the importance of using vocational assessments as the basis for planning needed services, resources, and support for people with disabilities.
4. In your opinion, what is the significance of using a collaborative approach in data collection and decision-making in the assessment process?

TABLE 20.4 Guiding Principles of the Interdisciplinary Council on Vocational Evaluation and Assessment

Guiding Principles

1. A variety of methods, tools, and approaches should be used to provide accurate vocational assessments. A broad range of questions must be posed to determine what makes an individual as well as his/her abilities and needs unique. Separating an individual's attributes into categories, such as interest, aptitude, or learning-style preferences, helps organize assessment.

2. Vocational assessment information should be verified by using different methods, tools, and approaches. Using alternative methods or approaches to validate findings usually can be achieved by (a) observing an individual's demonstrated or manifested behaviors, such as performances on actual work; (b) using an individual's self-report or expressed statements; and/or (c) administering some type of survey, inventory, structured interview, or test.

3. Behavior observation is essential in any vocational assessment process. Behavioral observation (e.g., observing physical performance, social characteristics, interaction with people and other aspects of the environment) occurs throughout the assessment process. The observation process can be (a) informal or formal, (b) occur in a variety of environments, (c) made by a variety of people, and (d) should be documented and presented in an objective, nonbiased manner.

4. Vocational assessment may be an on-going and developmental process in career development. However, individuals, especially those with disabilities, may need assessments of varying degrees given at different junctures over their career life-span.

5. Vocational assessment should be an integral part of larger service delivery systems. Vocational assessment should be the basis for planning needed services, resources, and support; therefore, it can be an integral part of the total service delivery system. Vocational assessment information should be interpreted and conveyed to the consumer as well as to others within the system.

6. Vocational assessment requires a collaborative approach to data collection and decision-making. Vocational assessment requires the collection of input from a variety of individuals and requires an understanding of how to use the results of the assessment process. An interdisciplinary team approach allows for the effective use of information that can be translated into effective planning, implementation activities (e.g., placements, support services, counseling), and fulfilled vocational development for consumers.

7. Vocational assessment should be current, valid, and relevant. Vocational assessment is grounded in career, vocational, and work contexts.

ISSUES INFLUENCING CHANGES IN ASSESSMENT AND WORK ADJUSTMENT

Critical issues influencing changes in assessment and work adjustment practices include continued high rates of unemployment of people with disabilities and inequitable access to technology. Unfortunately, persons with disabilities continue to face discrimination in the workplace. An estimated 50,000,000 (one in five) Americans have disabilities (Census Bureau, 2000), and persons with disabilities comprise nearly 20% of the working age population (Harris & Associates, 2000). Research identifies a consistent discrepancy between the unemployment rates of people with disabilities as compared to individuals without disabilities. Although people without disabilities have a 21% unemployment rate

(Harris & Associates, 1998), both the 1986 and 2003 Harris Polls reported that nearly two thirds of people with disabilities are unemployed.

In order to address the work crisis of people with disabilities, the 1998 Rehabilitation Amendments mandated community-based assessments, trial work experiences, consumer empowerment, and a greater focus on career development. According to Zahn (2005), these Amendments appear to have influenced changes in the vocational assessment process. For example, the evaluators responding to Zahn's survey reported serving increased numbers of consumers with severe disabilities, as well as placing greater emphasis on providing assessments in the community. Further research is needed to determine if these changes in services will translate into increased rates of employment and career opportunities.

DISCUSSION BOX 20.3

A person living with HIV or AIDS (PLWHA) is protected as a person with a disability by the Americans with Disabilities Act (ADA). With the increase of PLWHAs, there are understandably a large number of persons seeking employment and needing vocational services. Some rehabilitation professionals believe this new area of responsibility is radically different from the services they have traditionally provided. They see the need for HIV/AIDS rehabilitation specialists with intensive in-service training on rehabilitation of these new consumers. Other professionals acknowledge the need for training but do not see the necessity for rehabilitation practitioners to specialize. They believe that, since rehabilitation personnel are competent in working with a broad range of individuals, they can make use of their existing policies and practices to effectively rehabilitate PLWHAs.

Questions

1. Discuss the pros and cons of developing a rehabilitation specialist position. Include in your discussion the perceived financial and social costs, as well as the benefits.

2. Discuss the pros and cons of including persons living with HIV/AIDS in general caseloads. Include in your discussion the perceived financial and social costs, as well as the benefits.

3. In your opinion, which approach should be taken? What is your rationale for making this decision?

4. What can rehabilitation professionals do to effectively advocate for persons living with HIV and AIDS? Be specific.

Evaluators traditionally completed the majority of a vocational assessment prior to involving the services of an assistive technology specialist. However, an evaluation of a consumer's technology needs should be done in the initial stages to facilitate a barrier-free assessment process. The consumer's ability to access technology is an issue that also needs attention. Individuals from traditionally underrepresented populations with culturally diverse backgrounds (i.e., Native Americans, African Americans, Latinos, and Asian Americans) are faced with multiple barriers in accessing the technology needed to assist in securing and maintaining employment. Carey, DelSordo, and Goldman (2004) recognize these barriers as including, a lack of access not only to assistive technology (AT) devices, and to AT services and AT funding, The authors recommend several strategies implemented by an outreach program ("AT for All") designed to increase access to AT:

1. *Create a network of leader organizations and volunteer information centers using organizations, based within, directed by, and serving each community.*

2. *Create partnerships with minority-owned banks and lending institutions.*

3. *Increase the capacity…to provide effective, culturally competent services to persons with disabilities from these diverse communities.*

4. *Create options that make loans more affordable to individuals with disabilities…through minority banks.*

(CAREY, DELSORDO, & GOLDMAN, 2004, P. 2000)

Summary and Conclusion

Vocational assessment and work adjustment services are critical components in the rehabilitation process. They serve key roles in the implementation of the consumer's career development. In order for vocational assessment and work adjustment to have a meaningful impact on career planning, they must be holistic in scope, utilize a variety of assessment tools, and consider factors such as culture, learning styles, assistive technology needs, and environmental influences.

Obtaining a thorough and accurate history (background) of an individual is critical throughout the assessment process, including preparation for work adjustment services. Rapport between the vocational evaluator and the consumer must be established in the initial interview in order for effective communication to take place. The initial interview and subsequent contacts provide opportunities for the consumer to make decisions based on informed choices. Opportunities also are provided the vocational evaluator and/or work adjustment specialist to assess communication skills, mental status, interpersonal skills, self-concept, and aspirations (Watson, 2006).

An understanding of technology and occupational information is important for vocational evaluators and work adjustment specialists. Fortunately, a great deal of valuable information on technology and occupational information is easily accessible on the Internet. For example, the Rehabilitation Engineering and Assistive Technology Society of North America (RESNA) hosts a Website (www.resna.org) that provides data on credentialing programs, assistive technology suppliers, and information on engineering technologists. The O*NET database, the primary source of occupational information (http://online.onetcenter.org), contains detailed descriptions of hundreds of occupations, career exploration tools, and assessment instruments.

Inclusion of the consumer throughout the assessment process promotes empowerment and informed choice in career planning and placement. Key to the rehabilitation process is having trained vocational evaluators who utilize validated tools, provide services that are highly individualized, and are respectful of cultural differences. Applications of these principles will permit the fullest possible vocational integration of people with disabilities into the world of work.

RESEARCH BOX 20.1

Kosciulek, J., Prozonic, L., & Bell, D., (1995). On the congruence of evaluation, training, and placement. *Journal of Rehabilitation*, 20–23.

Objective: This study investigated the congruence among vocational evaluation job recommendations, vocational skills training, and jobs obtained by vocational rehabilitation consumers.

Methods: The sample in this study consisted of 78 successfully rehabilitated (ie., closed cases) consumers who previously received services from a state/federal rehabilitation agency in the Southeastern United States. The sample was majority White; the average age was 30.4 years, and the average education level was 11.5 years. Thirty-five percent had orthopedic disabilities, 22% had been diagnosed with developmental disabilities, and 17% were diagnosed with some type of mental illness. The disability types for the remaining subjects included neurological impairments, visual impairments, hearing impairments, chronic medical conditions, and substance abuse.

Results: The results indicated a low to moderate (40%) congruence rate across vocational evaluation job recommendations, vocational skills training, and jobs obtained by vocational rehabilitation consumers. In fact, fewer than half of the subjects obtained jobs that had been recommended as a result of the evaluation process.

Conclusion: Vocational evaluation recommendations were implemented approximately 50% of the time and only one half of the subjects obtained jobs consistent with their training. More community-based assessments were recommended to increase the congruence levels among vocational evaluation job recommendations, vocational skills training, and jobs obtained by vocational rehabilitation consumers.

Question

1. What are some factors that affect congruence in the rehabilitation process?
2. Discuss how you would implement a qualitative follow-up study to identify factors affecting congruence among vocational evaluation job recommendations, vocational skills training, and jobs obtained by vocational rehabilitation consumers.

Self-Check Questions

1. Compare and contrast the work adjustment theories of Hershenson and Dawis.
2. Discuss the importance of Super's career development theory.
4. Identify trends or patterns that emerged in rehabilitation legislation over the years. Are these trends or patterns evident in more recent legislation such as the American with Disabilities Act of 1990 and the Rehabilitation Act Amendments of 1998?

5. Rehabilitation legislation mandates important societal changes, and societal changes encourage the passage of legislation. What can you identify in U.S. history in the 1940s that would have supported services being extended to persons with mental illness and mental retardation in 1943?
6. The Interdisciplinary Council on Vocational Evaluation and Assessment recommends that all vocational evaluators providing vocational assessment services should demonstrate

seven important competencies. What are the seven job competencies an evaluator should possess and why?

7. Explain the differences between the train–place approach and the place–train approach. Community-based work adjustment and supported employment represent which approach?

Case Study—Vocational Assessment of Functional Capabilities—The Case of Victoria Harper

Victoria Harper, a 39-year-old female, was referred to Lake Shore Vocational Evaluation Program in Atlanta by her rehabilitation counselor, William Moore, for an assessment of her current vocational interests, academic achievement, aptitudes, and abilities. As a result of an automobile accident, Ms. Harper suffered an injury to her back, right shoulder, and neck, resulting in loss of strength and limited range of motion. According to the rehabilitation counselor, she is unable to perform her work-related duties as a distribution clerk, and therefore requires alternative employment.

During the evaluation process, Ms. Harper completed a battery of tests (e.g., interest, academic achievement, aptitude, and work sample assessments). The assessment process took place over a 3-day period during which she was punctual and engaged in the process. She was dressed appropriately and presented herself in a manner favorable for employment. In addition, she willingly attempted all tasks presented her, attended to each task through completion, and appeared to work to the best of her ability. Further, she was "coach-able" and responded positively to corrective directions. Overall, her work performance met competitive standards for a sedentary (deskbound) position.

Throughout the assessment process, Ms. Harper exhibited the ability to work up to an 8-hour workday, in a sedentary position as defined by the Dictionary of Occupational Titles (DOT). The primary assessment process consisted of the administration of paper and pencil tests and eight work sample activities. Ms. Harper did not report or exhibit pain at any time during the evaluation process. However, when discussing her ability to perform prolonged keyboarding activities, she revealed problems with her right shoulder becoming fatigued during certain activities. A referral was made to an assistive technology specialist for an ergonomic evaluation to determine appropriate assistive technology devices that could remediate these symptoms.

Results from the Gordon Occupational Checklist II and Self-Directed Search (SDS) suggest that Ms. Harper's vocational interest's are in bookkeeping and office management. These results are in keeping with Ms. Harper's expressed interest. Academic testing using the Wide Range Achievement Test and the Tests of Adult Basic Education reveal Ms. Harper is currently functioning within the 9th–10th-grade levels in language comprehension and usage and within the 8th–10th-grade levels in math. In addition, the results of a measure of general abstract reasoning were within the average to above average range and paralleled her achievement scores. Further, Ms. Harper's scores suggest she would perform best in office management positions, and that she may experience some difficulty in high-stress level people management and decision-making positions.

The results of bookkeeping and office management aptitude tests and work samples suggest Ms. Harper is capable of learning and carrying out the requirements for a variety of semiskilled and skilled office-related occupations. This was evident based on the results of the Minnesota Clerical Test, which indicated her ability to learn data entry, word processing, and bookkeeping techniques. She also demonstrated an ability to learn computerized bookkeeping tasks as indicated by her perfect scores on the bookkeeping subtests of the Valpar Clerical Comprehension and Aptitude Work Sample. Moreover, she demonstrated the ability to calculate complicated figures, and to work in situations that did not follow the norm. Other batteries administered (e.g. Job-seeking Skills Assessment and the Tennessee Self Concept) suggest that Ms. Harper possesses appropriate job-seeking and interviewing skills. Overall, Ms. Harper does demonstrate the ability to learn and execute the requirements for those positions for which she expressed an interest.

QUESTIONS

1. Using Appendix A in this chapter, identify what category the following assessment instruments are listed under (e.g. Aptitude, Interest, etc.):

   (a) Gordon Occupational Checklist II
   (b) Self-Directed Search (SDS)
   (c) Wide Range Achievement Test
   (d) Tests of Adult Basic Education

2. Based on what you know about Ms. Harper's skills, strengths, weaknesses, interests, and so on, what job(s) do you feel would be appropriate for her? Using the Dictionary of Occupational Titles (DOT), identify possible jobs and list the major job tasks performed in these jobs.

3. Next go to O*NET to determine if the identified jobs/positions are actually available in her area. Also, locate salary ranges for the jobs you choose for the consumer.

Case Study—Returning to Work After Vision Was Lost: The Case of Jane Cup

Jane Cup, age 43 recently lost her vision following an automobile accident. She had worked as a bookkeeper in her local bank for more than 20 years and would like to return to work in this area. Jane is the mother of 12-year-old Kelly, who is active in the school newspaper, science, and debate clubs. Jane is the primary caregiver for Kelly and would like to keep Kelly involved in school activities. Jane says she cannot rely on her ex-husband to get Kelly to her after school activities, and she needs to work to keep her home and provide for her daughter. Although the consumer's mother and father are usually unavailable to help Jane, because they work long hours, they are nonetheless supportive of Jane's need to be independent.

Jane's rehabilitation counselor, Barbara Clark, is planning to contact the human resources officer of a local financial institution. Although she can easily present Jane as an experienced and responsible worker, Barbara doesn't fully understand Jane's current ability to perform the essential functions of a bookkeeper's job in this particular bank. Jane's responsibilities as a mother and her transportation needs have not been discussed. Barbara wisely decides to defer the job search until after a comprehensive vocational assessment is done.

QUESTIONS

1. What specific questions should Barbara ask in her vocational assessment referral?
2. What service(s) can be requested to assist Barbara in making recommendations regarding reasonable accommodations?
3. The information given in the case study indicates Barbara may have neglected to fully include Jane's perspective in all aspects of her rehabilitation program. Identify legislation discussed in the chapter that would mandate Jane be allowed to fully participate in the process.
4. How can Barbara best include the consumer in the assessment process? Should she also enlist input from Jane's family members and the potential employer?

References

Bellamy, G. T., Rhodes, L. E., & Albin, J. M. (1986). Supported employment. In W. Kiernan, & J. Stark (Eds.), *Pathways to employment for adults with developmental disability* (pp. 129–138). Baltimore: Paul H. Brookes Publishing Co.

Bellamy, G. T., Rhodes, L. E., Bourbeau, P. E., & Mank, D.M. (1986). Mental retardation services in sheltered workshops and day activity programs: Consumer outcomes and policy alternatives. In F. Rusch (Ed.), *Competitive employment issues and strategies* (pp. 257–271). Baltimore: Paul H. Brookes.

Botterbusch, K. F. (1988). A survey of needs in six rehabilitation services administration priority areas in vocational rehabilitation facilities. *Vocational Evaluation and Work Adjustment Bulletin, 21*(1), 15–24.

Brown, D., & Brooks, L. (1984). Preface. In D. Brown, L. Brooks, & Associates, *Career choice and development: Applying contemporary theories to practice.* San Francisco: Jossey-Bass.

Brown, S. D., Ryan, N. E., & McPartland, E. B. (1996). Why are so many people happy and what do we do for those who aren't? In S. D. Brown & R. W. Lent (Eds.), *Career development and counseling: Putting theory and research to work* (pp. 525–550). New York: Wiley.

California VEWAA. (1992). California Standards for provisions of vocational evaluation, assessment and work adjustment services, Redwood City, CA: Author.

Carey, A.C., DelSordo, V., & Goldman, A. (2004). Assistive technology for all: Access to alternative financing for minority populations. *Journal of Disability Policy Studies, 14*(4), 194–203.

Census Bureau (2000). Available online at www.census.gov/main/wwwcen2000.html.

Couch, R. H. (1994). Yesterday, today, and tomorrow: The history of adjustment services in America. *Vocational Evaluation and Work Adjustment Bulletin, 27*(1), 5–13.

Couch, R. H., May, V. R., Fadely, D. C., & Pell, K. L. (1991). Adjustment in the 90's: Coming of age. In R. Fry (Ed.), *The issues papers: Fifth national forum on issues in vocational assessment* (pp. 25–33). Menomonie, WI: Materials Development Center, Stout Vocational Rehabilitation Institute, University of Wisconsin-Stout.

Couch, R. H., & Pell, K. (1991). Adjustment in supported employment. In R. Fry (Ed.), *The issues papers: Fifth national forum on issues in vocational assessment* (pp. 35–42). Menomonie, WI: Materials Development Center, Stout Vocational Rehabilitation Institute, University of Wisconsin-Stout.

Dawis, R. V., & Lofquist, L. H. (1984). *A psychological theory of work adjustment: An individual-differences model and its application.* Minneapolis: University of Minnesota Press.

Dunn, R., & Dunn, K. (1978). Teaching students through their individual learning styles: A practical approach. Reston, VA: Reston Publishing.

Fourteenth Institute on Rehabilitation Issues: The Use of Vocational Evaluation in VR. (1987). Menomonie, WI: Research and Training Center, University of Wisconsin-Stout.

Ginzberg, E., Ginzburg, S. W., Axelrod, S., & Herma, J. L. (1959). *Occupational choice: An approach to a general theory.* New York: Columbia University Press.

Giordano, G., & D'Alonzo, B. J. (1995, Autumn-Winter). Challenge and progress in Rehabilitation: A review of the past 25 years and a preview of the future. *American Rehabilitation*, 14–21.

Hamilton, M., & Shumate, S. (2005). The role and function of certified vocational evaluation specialists. *The Journal of Rehabilitation, 71*(1), 5–19.

Harris, L. & Associates (1986). *The NOD/Harris Survey on Employment of People with Disabilities.* New York: Author.

Harris, L. & Associates (1998). *The NOD/Harris Survey on Employment of People with Disabilities.* New York: Author.

Harris, L. & Associates (2000). *The NOD/Harris Survey on Employment of People with Disabilities.* New York: Author.

Harris, L. & Associates (2003). *The NOD/Harris Survey on Employment of People with Disabilities.* New York: Author.

Hershenson, D. B. (1981). Work adjustment, disability and the three R's of vocational rehabilitation: A concept model. *Rehabilitation Counseling Bulletin, 25,* 91–97.

Hershenson, D. B. (1996a). A systems reformulation of a developmental model of work adjustment. *Rehabilitation Counseling Bulletin, 40,* 2–10.

Hershenson, D. B. (1996b). Work adjustment: A neglected area in career counseling. *Journal of Counseling & Development, 74,* 442–446.

Holland, J. L. (1959). A theory of vocational choice. *Journal of Counseling Psychology, 6,* 35–45.

Homa, D. (2007). Using the International Classification of Functioning, Disability and Health (ICF) in job placement. *Workplace Issues and Placement, 29,* (4), 277–286.

Homa, D. & Peterson, D., (2005). Using the International Classification of Functioning, Disability and Health (ICF) in teaching Rehabilitation Client Assessment. Rehabilitation Education, 19(2&3), 119–128.

Horner, R. H., Meyer, L. H., & Fredericks, H. D. (Eds.). (1986). *Education of learners with severe handicaps.* Baltimore: Paul Brookes.

Hwang, J., & S. Nochajski, (2003). The International Classification of Function, Disablity and Health (ICF) and its application with AIDS. *Journal of Rehabilitation, 69*(4).

Kosciulek, J., Prozonic, L., Bell, D., (1995). On the congruence of evaluation, training, and placement. *Journal of Rehabilitation,* 20–23.

Larkin, V. (1996). Evaluating essential characteristics of Apticom, a computer-assisted vocational evaluation tool. Unpublished doctoral dissertation, Auburn, AL.

Leahy, M. J., & Wright, G. N. (1988). Professional competencies of the vocational evaluator. *Vocational Evaluation and Work Adjustment Bulletin, 21*(4), 127–132.

Leconte, P. J. (1989). Statement on rehabilitation training and education needs and priorities to the Rehabilitation Services Administration. *Vocational Evaluation and Work Adjustment Bulletin, 22*(2), 47–50.

Leconte, P. J. (1991). In support of training in rehabilitation. *Vocational Evaluation and Work Adjustment Bulletin, 22*(2), 151–156.

Leconte, P. & Roebuck, L. (1984). Integrative vocational appraisal: Assessing the total individual. Unpublished manuscript. Washington, DC: The George Washington University.

Leconte, P. & Roebuck, L. (1984). Vocational assessment appraisal of whole individual. In the Fourteenth Institute on Rehabilitation Issues: *The Use of Vocational Evaluation in VR.* (1987). Menomonie, WI: Research and Training Center, University of Wisconsin-Stout.

Lenard, H. M. (1960). Supportive placement for the mentally retarded. *Journal of Rehabilitation,* 16–17.

Lofquist, L. H., & Dawis, R.B. (1969). *Adjustment to work: A psychological view of man's problems in a work oriented society.* New York: Appleton-Century-Crofts.

Lustig, P., Lam, C., & Leahy, M. (1985). A conceptual approach to job placement with psychiatric and mentally retarded clients. *Journal of Applied Rehabilitation Counseling, 17*(1), 20–23.

Mank, D., Rhodes, L., & Bellamy, G. T. (1986). Four supported employment alternatives. In W. E. Kiernan & J. A. Stark (Eds.), *Pathways to employment for adults with developmental disabilities* (pp. 139–155). Baltimore: Brookes.

Menchetti, B. M. (1992). From work adjustment to community adjustment. *Vocational Evaluation and Work Adjustment Bulletin/ Richard J. Baker Memorial Monograph.*

Nadolsky, J. (1971a). *Development of a model for vocational evaluation of the disadvantaged.* Research Grant No. 12-P-55140/4-01. Washington, DC: Social and Rehabilitation Services, Department of Health, Education and Welfare.

Nadolsky, J. (1971b). Patterns of consistency among vocational evaluators. *Vocational Evaluation and Work Adjustment Bulletin, 4*(4), 13–25.

Noble, J. H., & Conley, R. W. (1987). Accumulating evidence on the benefits and costs of supported and transitional employment for persons with severe disabilities. *Journal of the Association for Persons with Severe Handicaps, 12*(3), 163–174.

Nunnaly, J. (1978). *Psychometric theory*. New York: McGraw Hill.

Osipow, S. H. (1983). *Theories of career development* (3rd ed.). Englewood Cliffs, NJ: Prentice-Hall.

Osipow, S. H. (1994). Moving career theory into the twenty-first century. In M. Savickas & R. Lent (Eds.), *Convergence in career development theories: Implications for science and practice* (pp. 217–224). Palo Alto, CA: Consulting Psychologists Press.

Osipow, S. H., & Fitzgerald, L. (1996). *Theory of career development* (4th ed.). Toronto, ON, Canada: Allyn and Bacon.

Peterson, D. & Rosenthal, D., (2005) The International Classification of Functioning, Disability and Health (ICF) as an allegory for history and systems in rehabilitation education. *Rehabilitation Education*, 19, 95–104.

Power, P. (2000). *A guide to vocational assessment* (3rd ed.). Austin, TX: Pro-Ed.

Roe, A. (1957). Early determinants of vocational choice. *Journal of Counseling Psychology, 4*, 212–217.

Roebuck, L. (April 1991). Self-concept, self-esteem, self-image and locus of control. Presented in graduate class: Introduction to Vocational Assessment of Individuals with Disabilities. Washington, DC: George Washington University.

Rothenbacher, C., & Leconte, P. (1990). Vocational Assessment: A Guide for Parents and Professionals (NICHCY Transition Summary No. 6). Washington DC: National Information Center for Children and Youth with Disabilities.

Rubin, S. E., & Roessler, R. T. (2001). *Foundations of the vocational rehabilitation process* (4th ed.). Austin TX: Pro-Ed.

Rusch, F. R. (1986). *Competitive Employment Issues and Strategies*. Baltimore: Paul H. Brookes.

Savickas, M. (1994). Convergence prompts theory renovation, research unification, and practice coherence. In M. Savickas & R. Lent (Eds.), *Convergence in career development theories: Implications for science and practice* (pp. 235–257). Palo Alto, CA: Consulting Psychologists Press.

Sharf, R. S. (1997). *Applying career development theory to counseling*. Pacific Grove, CA: Brooks/Cole Publishing Company.

Smith, F., Lombard, R., Neubert, D., Leconte, P., Rothenbacher, C., & Sitlington, P. (1995). The position statement of the interdisciplinary Council on Vocational Evaluation and Assessment. *Career Development for Exceptional Individuals, 18*(2), 109–112.

Super, D. E. (1953). A theory of vocational development. *American Psychologist, 8,* 85–190.

Szymanski, E. M., Hershenson, D. B., & Power, P. W. (1988). Enabling the family in supporting transition from school to work. In P. W. Power, A. Dell Orto, & M. B. Gibbons (Eds.), *Family interventions throughout chronic illness and disability* (pp. 216–233). New York: Springer.

Szymanski, E.M., Handley-Maxwell, C., Hansen, G.M., & Myers, W.A. (1988). Work adjustment training, supported employment, and time-limited transitional employment programs: Context and common principles. *Vocational Evaluation and Work Adjustment Bulletin, 21*(2), 41–45.

Tech-Related Assistance of Individuals with Disabilities Act (1988), P.L. 100-407.

Thomas (Library of Congress site) (1999). *The Workforce Investment Act* (Conference Report No. 105-659) (Available from: http://www.Thomas.loc.gov.)

Thomas, S. (2000). Emerging roles of the vocational evaluator. *VEWAA Newsletter, 3*(27), 2–5.

Thomas, S., (1996). A position paper supporting the continued funding of vocational evaluation training by the Rehabilitation Services Administration. *Vocational Evaluation and Work Adjustment Bulletin, 29*(1), 4–8.

U.S. Department of Labor. (2001). Dictionary of occupational titles (DOT). Indianapolis, IN: JIST Works, Inc.) http://www.occupationalinfo.org/

Vocational Evaluation and Work Adjustment Bulletin. (1975). Vol. 8, Special Edition: Vocational Evaluation Project Final Report Part 3 (p. 70). Menomonie: University of Wisconsin–Stout,

Vocational Evaluation and Work Adjustment Bulletin (VEWAA) Standards. (1977, 1978). Vocational development standards—A joint VEWAA-CARF Report.

Watson, D. (2006). Presentation at Region VII Conference on Issues in Deafness & Deaf Blindness. Kansas City: University of Missouri RCEP.

Wehman, P. (1986). Supported competitive employment for persons with severe disabilities. *Journal of Applied Rehabilitation Counseling, 17*(4), 24–29.

Wesolek, J., & McFarlane, F. (1992). Vocational assessment and evaluation: Some observations from the past and anticipation for the Future. *Vocational Evaluation and Work Adjustment Bulletin, 25*, 51–54.

Whitehead, C.W. (1987). Supported employment: Challenge and opportunity for sheltered workshops. *Journal of Rehabilitation, 53*(3), 23–28.

Williams, C. A., & Faubion, C. W. (2002). Careers and professions: Employment settings for rehabilitation practitioners. In J. D. Andrew & C.W. Faubion (Eds.), *Rehabilitation services: An introduction for the human services professional*. Osage Beach, MO: Aspen Professional Services.

Wright, G. (1980). *Total rehabilitation*. Boston: Little, Brown and Company.

Wuenschel, R. J., & Brady, J. E. (1959). Principles and techniques of placement. *Journal of Rehabilitation*, 16–18.

Zahn, K. (2005). Vocational evaluation in the 21st century: Populations being served, types of evaluations being conducted, and the impact of the 1998 Rehabilitation Act

Appendix A

Amendments. *Vocational Evaluation and Career Assessment Professionals Journal, 2*(1), 62–76.

Assessment Instruments

ACHIEVEMENT

    KTEA

    PIAT

    Slossan O. Reading Test

    WRAT-2

    WRAT-3

    WoodCock Johnson

    ABLE 1-2-3

    TABE 4-5-6-7-8

    California Qualification Test

    College Qualification Test

    Gray Oral Reading Test

    California's Achievement Test

    WIAT

    Adult Basic Learning Examination

    SRA Arithmetic Index

    SRA Reading Index

    Wide Range Achievement Test–Revised

APTITUDE

    Career Ability Placement Survey (CAPS)

    Detroit Tests of Learning Aptitude (DTLA)

    Differential Aptitude Test (DAT)

    Occupational Aptitude Survey (OAS)

    Computer Operator Aptitude Battery (COAB)

    Computer Programmer Aptitude Battery (CPAB)

    SRA Clerical Aptitudes

    Short Tests of Clerical Ability

    Flanagan Aptitude Classification Tests

    Florida Inst. Diag. Presc. Voc. Comp. Profile

    Minnesota Clerical Test

    Computer Aptitude Literary and Interest

    Career Scope

    Bennet Mechanical Test

BASIC SKILLS

    SPIB

    SSSQ

    Vineland Maturity Scale

    Skills for Everyday Living

    Basic Skills Test Battery

    Behavioral Problem Checklist

    A Behaviors–S & G

    Time Appreciation Test

DEXTERITY

    Bennett Hand Tools

    Crawford Small Parts

    Minnesota Rate of Manipulation (MRMT)

    Pennsylvania Bi-Manual

    Purdue Pegboard

    General Clerical Test

INTELLIGENCE

    Beta III Examination

    Raven Progressive Matrices

    Slossan Intelligence Test

    Stanford-Binet Intelligence Test

    WAIS-R 3-4

    Wide Range Intelligence Personality Test

    Kaufman Brief Intelligence Test

    Otis Quick Scoring Intelligence Test

    Culture Fair Intelligence Test

    California Psychological Inventory

    Peabody Picture Vocabulary Test (PPVT)

    Shipley Institute of Living

    Wonderlic Personnel Test (WPT)

INTEREST

    C.O.P.S

Geist Picture Interest Inventory

Gordon Occupational Checklist

CHOICES

Campbell Interest and Skill Survey

Becker Reading Free Interest Inventory (BRFVII)

OASIS

Holland Self-Directed Search (SDS)

Harrington O'Shea (CDM)

Ohio Vocational

Jackson Vocational Interest Inventory

Career Assessment Inventory

Wide Range Interest and Option Test (WRIOT)

United States Employment Service Interest Inventory (USESII)

LEARNING STYLES

Center for Innovative Teaching Experience (CITE)

PMT

Vocational Learning Style Assessment

Learning Efficiency Test

LET—Learning Style Assessment

Murdock Learning Styles Assessment

MULTI-BATTERY

Apticom A5

McCarron Dial (MDWES)

MESA

Valpar 2000

Skills Assessment Module

Multi Dimensional Aptitude Battery

Wide Range Employability Sample Test

S.A.G.E.

MicroTower

PERSONALITY

Edwards Personality Profile

Person Personality Factor (16PF)

Tennessee Self Concept

Taylor Johnson Temperament

Myers Briggs Type Indicator (MBTI)

WORK SAMPLES

Work Samples — VALPAR (Mechanical)

1-Small Tools

2-Size Discrimination

3-Number Sorting

4-Upper Body Range of Motion

5-Clerical Comprehension & Aptitude

6-Problem Solving

7-Multi-Level Sorting

8-Assembly

9-Whole Body Range of Motion

10-Tri-Level Measurement

11-Eye Hand Foot Coordination

12-Electron Soldering & Inspection

15-Electron Circuitry & Print Reading

16-Drafting

17-Pre-Vocational Readiness Battery

JEVS-Payroll and Adding Machine

OTHER

Job-Seeking Skills Assessments

Occupational Access System (OASYS)

Social and Pre-Vocational Information Battery

Substance Abuse Subtle Screening Instrument (SASSI)

21

Assessment in Rehabilitation and Health

Transition Outcomes

Darlene D. Unger
De Paul University, Chicago

Amy J. Armstrong
Virginia Commonwealth University, Richmond

OVERVIEW

This chapter discusses assessment as it pertains to youth receiving special education services and their transition from school to postschool environments. The initial sections of the chapter provide rehabilitation and health professionals with information related to the need for comprehensive transition planning and programming for youth with disabilities as well as the historical and legal foundations for transition assessment. The remaining sections of the chapter present key transition domains and relevant assessments, as well as challenges to effective transition assessment and implementation.

LEARNING OBJECTIVES

By the end of the chapter, readers should be able to:

- Discuss evidence related to the postschool outcomes of youth with disabilities
- Identify the legal requirements related to transition assessment
- Identify potential roles for rehabilitation and health professionals in the transition assessment process for youth with disabilities
- Describe transition-focused assessment instruments relevant to transition-outcome domains
- Discuss challenges to rehabilitation and health professionals' participation in the transition assessment process.

INTRODUCTION

One area of assessment relevant to rehabilitation and health professionals often overlooked or absent from practice involves participation in the assessment of young adults with disabilities transitioning from publicly-funded special education entitlement programs to eligibility-based adult services, employment, and educational programs. According to Clark and Patton (1997) the purpose of conducting transition assessment is to produce information that results in the development of a comprehensive transition plan. This process, if done correctly, may ultimately result in successful transition outcomes for young adults with disabilities. Given the emphasis on standards-based assessment and "high-stakes" testing that is pervasive in our publicly-funded education system, how well are educators, rehabilitation, and health professionals doing in implementing effective transition assessment that drives students' education and transition programming?

TRANSITION OUTCOMES OF YOUTH WITH DISABILITIES

For the most recent reporting period, approximately 7 million students ages 3–21 receive publicly-funded special education services in our nation's schools, with slightly more than one third (33.74%) of the students representing transition age students, those who are aged 14–21 (U.S. Department of Education, 2007). Approximately 10% of transition-age students exit school annually (U.S. Department of Education, 2007). Although the majority of special education students represents individuals with mild-to-moderate support needs, all students could potentially benefit from a systematic transition planning and assessment process to facilitate the identification of individual interests, abilities, supports, and desired long-term goals.

Despite much emphasis on improving the postschool outcomes for youth exiting K–12 educational programs and recent public policy initiatives directed toward transition assessments, young adults with disabilities report less favorable postschool outcomes when compared to their nondisabled peers (Blackorby & Wagner, 1996; Phelps & Hanley-Maxwell, 1997; President's Commission on Excellence in Special Education, 2002; Wagner, Newman, Cameto, Garza, & Levine, 2005). For youth with significant disabilities, findings indicate that fewer than 1 out of 10 will attain integrated employment, 5 out of 10 will experience indefinitely long waits for postschool employment services, and most of these individuals will earn less than $2.40/hour in sheltered employment settings (LaPlante, Kennedy, Kaye, & Wenger, 1996). In addition, as the number of functional domains affected by a youth's disability increases, the likelihood of employment decreases (Cameto, 2005).

In an effort to address the poor postschool outcomes of youth with disabilities, the United States Congress included several new provisions within the reauthorization of the Individuals with Disabilities Education Act (IDEA) in 2004. Many of these provisions were directed at improving student assessment and the relationship between data gleaned from assessments, and educational and transition programming for youth with disabilities.

The increased focus on the transition assessment and programming process presents unique opportunities for occupational and speech therapists, rehabilitation counselors, psychologists, and other health professionals to increase their involvement in the transition assessment process. Expertise in their discipline, combined with applications related to career and vocational assessments, self-determination, workplace accommodations, adaptive behavior, and other areas influencing successful transitions for youth with disabilities, should significantly enhance the quality and relevancy of transition-related assessments and programming.

TRANSITION-OUTCOME MEASURES AND THE INTERNATIONAL CLASSIFICATION OF FUNCTIONING, DISABILITY, AND HEALTH (ICF)

The significance of transition measures, as they relate to the ICF, is reflected in the idea that many of the student or environmental factors assessed in preparation for transition planning and programming for youth with disabilities are well-represented within the ICF. Assessment related to transition seeks to identify students' present levels of functioning, postschool goals, and then the services and supports that students will need to access in order to progress in postschool environments. Unlike many of the diagnostic instruments or procedures used in the education, rehabilitation, and health fields, transition assessment does not result in a classification or diagnosis leading to a prescribed educational or training program designed for individuals with the same classification or label.

Instead, transition planning and assessment seeks to identify individual interests, abilities, and supports that might be needed in order to address potential barriers to accessing and participating in postschool community, employment, or educational environments. This premise—that the situation of the person being evaluated is described in relation to a variety of health or health-related domains while considering the context of environmental and personal factors—is consistent with the application of the ICF (Bruyère, Van Looy, & Peterson, 2005; Peterson, 2005)

Assessment data corresponding to the ICF core structure domains (functioning and disability and contextual factors) could be readily ascertained from students' transition assessment measures and educational programming. For instance, information within a student's educational records indicates that the student has challenges with memory and attending to task (impairment). During the student's educational programming, the student exhibits challenges in focusing on assigned seat work that requires sustained attention and oftentimes fails to complete the activity in the time allotted by the teacher (capacity limitation). The same behavior is also observed of the student in the work setting, where the student has difficulties in completing specific tasks within a job, attributed to the student's ability to stay focused on a specific task through completion (capacity limitation). While participating in the regular classroom environment or the employment setting, the student falls behind in independent class work and work requirements because he cannot focus on a required task for longer than 10 minutes (performance problems in the domain of sustaining attention). Thus, the student's involvement and success in the general education classroom and the workplace is jeopardized because of teacher and employer expectations of the ability of students or employees to sustain their attention through the completion of required tasks.

For transition-age youth with disabilities, especially individuals with more significant disabilities, the ICF represents a useful and much needed tool in which professionals engaged in the transition process, as well as stakeholders in human service agencies, employment support organizations, and medical and rehabilitation facilities, can accurately communicate and have a shared understanding of the student's functioning and support needs as his/her needs are assessed specific to the context of postschool environments and services. Despite utilizing assessment measures and procedures that produce data that could be codified in accordance with the ICF, Individualized Education Program (IEP) teams or

transition planning teams have little practice in translating evidence gathered from these assessments into the ICF framework. Within the activities and participation classification, several of the domains reflect areas that are often the focal point of transition outcome measures, such as subclassifications under the major life areas of vocational training, higher education, as well as the broader domain of work and employment.

For many educators or professionals that facilitate transition planning or programming for youth with disabilities, the ICF represents unfamiliar territory. Thus, rehabilitation and health professionals serve an increasingly important role in the transition planning and programming process. The purpose of this chapter is to describe the historical and legal foundation for transition assessment, describe essential transition outcome domains and relevant assessments, and present challenges related to implementing transition assessments. Within each of these areas, evidence supporting the need for more active involvement of rehabilitation and health professionals in the transition assessment process for young adults with disabilities will also be reviewed.

HISTORICAL AND LEGAL FOUNDATIONS FOR TRANSITION ASSESSMENT

Since the mid-1970s, federal law has mandated that students with disabilities are entitled to a free and appropriate education (FAPE) in the least restrictive environment, and that for each student found eligible for special education services, an Individualized Education Program (IEP) would be developed based on the child's current level of academic performance, strengths, and challenges. During the past 3 decades, we have witnessed a series of amendments to the law, now titled The Individuals with Disabilities Education Improvement Act (IDEA) 2004, in response to changing societal values toward individuals with disabilities and improved educational, medical, and rehabilitative interventions. Yet, the requirements for FAPE and IEPs have consistently framed educational services for children and youth with disabilities with assessment, representing a defining and evolving aspect of special education service delivery.

Indeed, there has been much discussion on the purpose, uses, and practices of assessment and its impact on the quality of life of people with disabilities (Sitlington, Neubert, Begun, Lombard & Leconte, 2007; Snell, 1993). The results of assessment procedures can be used to: (a) include or exclude students from opportunities of integration and community participation; (b) determine the existence and extent of a disability (screening); (c) make major life decisions concerning students with disabilities and the services and supports they receive (diagnosis, placement); and (d) assist in the identification and development of skills and goals (evaluation and curriculum development).

Although assessment has been a pivotal aspect of special education programming since the law's inception, the mandate for the provision of transition services did not appear until the amendments in 1990. These amendments established responsibilities for educational agencies regarding planning and coordinating transition-focused education services and programming based on students' long-term goals; although, at the time, the regulations provided little guidance related to the transition assessment process.

Since 1990, there have been a number of changes to the law, such as the age that transition services should commence (currently, prior to a student's 16th birthday), but the mandate for transition services has remained relatively constant until the reauthorization of the law in 2004. IDEA 2004 defines transition services as "a coordinated set of activities for a child with a disability that:

(a) are designed to be within a results-oriented process, that is focused on improving the academic and functional achievement of the child with a disability to facilitate the child's movement from school to postschool activities, including postsecondary education, vocational education, integrated employment (including supported employment), continuing and adult education, adult services, independent living, or community participation; [602(34)(A)]

(b) are based on the individual child's needs, taking into account the child's strengths, preferences, and interests; [602(34)(B)] and

(c) includes instruction, related services, community experiences, the development of employment and other postschool adult living objectives, and when appropriate, acquisition of daily living skills and functional vocational evaluation (Section 602 (34), H.R. 1350).

Within section (a), the law provides guidance as to the specific postschool domains that educators and rehabilitation and health professionals should address through their assessment efforts, although not all students will require assessment information reflecting performance and support needs in all domains. The current definition reflects a change in language, from *outcome-oriented*, appearing in the 1997 amendments, to *results-oriented*—meaning that

school districts are responsible for providing, and are being held accountable for implementing, educational services that produce evidence of students' academic and functional achievements as well as progress toward accomplishing their transition goals.

The 2004 amendments have placed increased accountability on educational agencies to design and deliver effective teaching and learning experiences that result in favorable educational and postschool outcomes for young adults with disabilities. The current law now states that, beginning not later than the first IEP to be in effect when the child turns 16 and then updated annually thereafter, the IEP must include "appropriate measurable postsecondary goals based upon age-appropriate transition assessments related to training, education, employment, and where appropriate, independent living skills." §300.320(b)(1). Yet, the law had previously provided little direction as to specific assessment responsibilities related to transition planning and programming. Specific language regarding required elements of students' IEPs emphasized the importance of transition assessment. These requirements include:

- Measurable postsecondary and annual goals;
- A description of how the student's progress toward meeting annual goals will be measured and reported;
- A statement providing for individually appropriate accommodations to measure academic achievement and functional performance on state and district assessments;
- For all students eligible to graduate from high school with a regular diploma, or those exceeding the age of eligibility for services under the IDEA, a summary statement of the student's academic and functional performance, which shall include recommendations on how to assist the student in meeting postsecondary goals (Authority: 20 U.S.C. § 1414 *et seq.*).

For rehabilitation and health professionals working with transition-age youth, the idea of a summary statement of the student's academic and functional performance is of critical importance. In addition to containing evidence related to academic achievement and functional performance, the document will also include the student's postsecondary goals and recommendations to facilitate the student's achievement of the goals. The Summary of Performance (SOP) requirement, with the accompanying documentation, presents a unique opportunity for rehabilitation and health professionals to work with representatives from local education agencies and transition-age youth to identify assessments that produce evidence that is most useful to representatives who assist the student in the transition process.

For instance, the information required for the SOP is necessary under Section 504 of the Rehabilitation Act and the Americans with Disabilities Act to help establish a student's eligibility for reasonable accommodations and supports in postsecondary settings. For those individuals who pursue postsecondary education, information contained within the SOP regarding the student's current level of functioning should assist representatives from postsecondary institutions and student disability services offices in considering student accommodations for access to academic programs. It is also valuable for young adults who may potentially access the federal/state vocational rehabilitation program because the SOP will be most useful during the Vocational Rehabilitation Comprehensive Assessment process. However, the evidence in the SOP will only be as good as the assessments utilized to generate the information, so careful analysis and selection of appropriate assessments is warranted. The SOP represents an important tool to assist students in the transition from high school to vocational training, employment, and higher education.

The conceptual framework for transition assessment addresses the linkages among curricula and instruction, services and supports, and postschool goals and outcomes while drawing on the collective expertise of educators, rehabilitation and health professionals, and the student and his or her parents. The student, supported by his or her IEP team, identifies long-term goals. These goals are developed based on the student's interests, preferences, and abilities, which are facilitated by a continuous and comprehensive assessment process that reflects key domains related to postschool environments, such as employment, postsecondary education and training, and community living. Information gathered from the assessments is also used to identify the student's present level of performance related to his or her long-term goals as well as the student's needs related to closing the gap between the student's current level of performance and the knowledge, skills, and abilities needed for the individual to achieve his or her postschool goals. Once these transition services needs are identified, the IEP team works to design and deliver transition-focused education services. Yet, the process is not static, with assessments completed at various developmental markers or stages in the student's education. Instead, there is a longitudinal process of assessment and programming that evolves as the student's knowledge, skills, interests, and support needs progress during his or her educational experiences.

DISCUSSION BOX 21.1

Summary of Performance (SOP) and Transition-Age Youth: Challenges or Opportunities for Rehabilitation and Health Professionals?

The 2004 reauthorization of IDEA requires that each student receiving special education services receive a Summary of Performance prior to the individual exiting school. This policy change has implications for rehabilitation counselors and other health professionals working with transition-age youth with disabilities. Information contained within a SOP reflects the young adult's academic, behavioral, social, and vocational strengths and support needs, and these data can be used to determine eligibility for services. Section 504 of the Rehabilitation Act of 1973 requires young adults to self-identify their disability and provide documentation of their disability in consideration of eligibility for services. The required documentation often includes one or more of the following: (a) the date and diagnosis of the disability, (b) how the diagnosis was determined, (c) the credentials of the professional, (d) how the disability affects a major life activity, and (e) academic and functional limitations that are caused by the disability.

Yet, the law is vague because it does not identify who is responsible for developing the SOP or the specific information required. Thus, the local education agency can identify an individual (e.g., psychologist, school counselor) or group of individuals responsible for developing the SOP (e.g., IEP team). In order to determine eligibility for services, many adult service providers and vocational rehabilitation agencies will consider whether the SOP provides them with a diagnosis signed by a credentialed professional and enough current information about how one's disability affects major life activities.

Questions

1. Will the Summary of Performance requirement within IDEA strengthen or limit the involvement of rehabilitation and other health professionals in the transition process?

2. How can rehabilitation and other health professionals contribute to the development of student SOPs that reflect the evidence needed to determine eligibility for services as well as identify appropriate supports and interventions to assist the individual in achieving his or her postschool goals?

Although the assessment process is student-centered, the focus of the assessment is not solely the student, as the process also encompasses an analysis of desired or anticipated environments in order to identify supports needed for the student to participate in different residential, employment, and educational environments.

TRANSITION OUTCOMES AND ASSESSMENT METHODS

Conducting Transition-Focused Assessments

Special and general educators as well as family members and the student should constitute the core of any IEP team. Ideally, the IEP and the transition process should be student-driven or centered, as the student is the central figure in determining the direction of his or her transition from school to adult life. IDEA 2004

mandates that the student must be invited to the IEP meeting when issues related to transition are to be discussed. Increasingly, students are leading or taking more active roles in their IEP meetings following participation in instruction and training related to developing self-determination skills. Evidence indicates that teaching students with disabilities a self-regulated problem-solving process enables them to self-direct their learning and to achieve educationally relevant goals, including transition related goals (Agran, Blanchard, & Wehmeyer, 2000; Palmer, Wehmeyer, Gipson, & Agran, 2004; Wehmeyer, Palmer, Agran, Mithaug, & Martin, 2000). The student and/or family members should also be asked who they would like to include as their team members.

The results of an assessment can drive the selection of needed team members. For example, perhaps residential options and supports have been identified as a need for the student. In this instance, an obvious team member might be an adult service professional who has

---

RESEARCH BOX 21.1

Zhang, D. (2001). The effect of *Next S.T.E.P.* instruction on the self-determination skills of high school students with learning disabilities. *Career Development for Exceptional Individuals, 24*, 121–131.

Objectives: The purpose of this study was to examine the effect of the *Next S.T.E.P* curriculum on self-determination skills of high school students with learning disabilities. The *Next S.T.E.P* curriculum was designed to teach students the following skills: (a) self-evaluation of important skills needed for the transition; (b) choosing goals and activities in four important transition areas, including personal life, education and training, jobs and living on one's own; (c) taking charge of their IEP meeting related to transition; and (d) following through on choices and keeping track of progress.

Method: The investigation used an untreated control group design with pretest and posttest. The sample consisted of 71 9th-grade students with learning disabilities (52 male, 19 female) attending 9th-grade within two school districts in Louisiana. The participants ages ranged from 14 to 19 years (M = 15.7 years), and in terms of racial status, 40 (56%) were African Americans, and 31 (44%) were Caucasians. The *Arc's Self-Determination Scale (Adolescent Version)* (Wehmeyer & Kelchner, 1995), a self-report measure of self-determination, was used to produce the dependent variable of self-determination. Self-determination instruction using the

Next S.T.E.P curriculum represented the independent variable.

Results: The *Next S.T.E.P.* instruction significantly improved participants' self-determination skills as measured by the *Arc's Self-Determination Scale* (Wehmeyer & Kelchner, 1995). The *Next S.T.E.P.* instruction improved the performance of students in the treatment group, and this improvement was not likely caused by other factors.

Conclusion: The practical implications for educators and professionals involved in the transition process include the idea that instructional activities in the *Next S.T.E.P.* curriculum can improve transition-age youth's general abilities in self-evaluation, goal setting and achievement, and planning for the future.

Questions

1. Are self-determination skills needed by students representing various disability labels?
2. In what instance might it be necessary for young adults with disabilities to exercise self-determination skills when participating in postsecondary education or employment environments?
3. How can rehabilitation and health professionals assess self-determination skills?
4. How can student participation in the IEP process and educational decision-making process build self-determination skills?

experience in housing, such as someone from Housing and Urban Development, or a representative from the local Center for Independent Living. The goals and support needs of students should assist with the identification of key participants in the transition process. Their experiences and expertise should contribute to the identification of appropriate assessment procedures as well as the successful attainment of goals and objectives. However, the lack of information and knowledge of resources related to transition services and supports available through rehabilitation and health professionals and organizations they may represent is well-documented (Wittenburg & Maag, 2002).

The areas of expertise represented by rehabilitation and health professionals, such as vocational interests and aptitude, orientation and mobility, or measures of independent living, can assist special educators in arranging assessments of student skills and needs relating to these areas impacting transition outcomes. Health professionals, such as occupational therapists or rehabilitation professionals and including vocational rehabilitation counselors or service coordinators working for mental retardation and developmental disabilities agencies, may be able to assist the team in establishing instructional, learning, and performance goals as well as identifying areas where comprehensive supports or interventions might be warranted.

The majority of students with disabilities receiving special education or support services have mild to moderate support needs, and a much smaller percentage experience health limitations or chronic illnesses. However, in many instances rehabilitation and health professionals are not involved in the development of transition goals or programming (American Occupational Therapy Association [AOTA], 2000; Arnold, 2000; Michaels & Orentlicher, 2004; Spencer, Emery, & Schneck, 2003). Indeed many students with physical, sensory, or mental health disabilities may benefit from more active involvement of rehabilitation and health professionals in the development of transition programming.

In instances when occupational therapists or employment specialists are involved in conducting transition-related assessment, it qualifies them or an individual who can interpret data gathered from their assessments as a required IEP team member. Oftentimes, assessment information is gathered prior to the identification of team members, and school districts are required by federal and state law to provide copies of assessments and other educational records to the family and/or student before the IEP meeting (20 U.S.C. §1414(b)(4); 34 C.F.R. §300.562). It is important to note that the assessment process should be developed and implemented in such a way that students with disabilities and/or their families are active participants in the assessment team (Sitlington et. al., 2007).

Transition Domains

With the reauthorization of IDEA in 1990, departments of education in several states issued guidelines for local school districts in developing and implementing transition

---

DISCUSSION BOX 21.2

What services and supports can rehabilitation and other health professionals provide to facilitate successful transition outcomes for youth with disabilities?

The American Occupational Therapy Association (AOTA) identifies "Transition Services" as one of the eight Standards of Practice for Occupational Therapy (see Standard VII, AOTA, 2000) emphasizing the provision of supports in major life areas. AOTA also describes areas of occupation using language that is similar to that of IDEA 2004. The definition of transition services within the Rehabilitation Act Amendments of 1992 coincides with the definition of transition services within the IDEA, and more so than ever before, vocational rehabilitation counselors are participating in the IEP planning process. Evidence also exists that documents the important roles that other health professionals, such as a speech and language pathologists, can play in documenting the nature and type of communication services needed by youth with challenges in communicating (Cascella & McNamara, 2004). Yet, we know that many young adults with disabilities could benefit from more active involvement by professionals involved in rehabilitation services much sooner in their educational careers.

Questions

1. What are potential barriers and facilitators to participation by rehabilitation and other health professionals in the transition assessment and planning process?

2. In what instances might active participation by professionals in these areas be warranted?

3. Who is responsible for encouraging participation in the transition assessment and planning process, and how are these services funded?

services and often identified domains related to employment, postsecondary education, and independent living. Data from 17 state guidelines indicated the number of transition planning areas ranged from 4 to 23, with differences in the domains attributed more to organization and clustering rather than to content (Clark & Patton, 1997). There appeared to be general agreement that planning for postsecondary education, employment, community participation, and other adult-related outcomes were the essence of transition services planning (Clark & Patton, 1997).

Other findings suggest that states vary in the domains used to determine transition supports and services and that employment and continued education typically have been addressed in transition planning to the exclusion of other life areas (Sitlington et al., 1996). Despite the somewhat inconsistent findings, it is evident that transition planning must include several areas of life to ensure a successful transition to adulthood and community participation. In addition to employment and postsecondary education or training, other areas of life, or domains, may include but are not limited to the following:

- Community access and participation, including safety, social, recreational, and leisure
- Financial literacy, including benefits planning
- Orientation and mobility including transportation
- Residential
- Health, wellness, and medical
- Service and support coordination
- Self-determination, advocacy, and legal

Interestingly, many transition domains or transition-outcome areas identified within the special education literature are consistent with several of the World Health Organization's International Classification of Functioning, Disability, and Health (ICF) activities and participation component.

For example, the ICF activities and participation domains that directly relate to or encompass many of the transition-outcome areas include such areas as mobility, self-care, domestic life, interpersonal interactions and relations, major life areas, and community, social, and civic life. The significance of this is that health and rehabilitation professionals involved in the transition process have the opportunity to provide comprehensive assessments related to many of the ICFs domains over an extended period (e.g., 7 or more years) versus the much more episodic or time-limited nature of health care and rehabilitation service delivery systems.

Increasingly, many special educators and IEP teams are beginning to work with students, using person-centered

practices to develop comprehensive transition planning and programming to assess and address students' needs related to several of the transition outcome domains (Cross, Cooke, Wood, & Test, 1999; Everson, 1996; Flannery et al., 2000). Special educators often rely on the expertise of representatives from adult service providers, including medical and rehabilitation professionals, benefits counselors, and representatives from the local office of mental retardation and developmental disabilities to suggest avenues for assessment and support. However, it is an unfortunate reality that far too many special education students and their families leave the public school system not knowing about the potential services and supports that are available to provide guidance or training encompassed by many of these transition-outcome domains. An effective transition assessment process that facilitates the identification of student needs relying on the collaborative expertise of representatives from rehabilitation and adult service providers should go a long way toward improving the transition outcomes for youth with disabilities.

Transition-Outcomes Assessment Methods

There is a plethora of formal and informal assessments available to educators and health and rehabilitation professionals working with transition-age youth with disabilities. The challenge rests in identifying an appropriate combination of instruments and practices that will provide for a comprehensive transition assessment for students representing a variety of disability labels and abilities. Unfortunately, many schools and IEP teams utilize a transition assessment process that is based on an existing protocol designed by the district and derived from a commercially available product (Cohen & Spenciner, 2007). In educational assessment, a recurring question for educators is, "What qualifies as a good and meaningful evaluation procedure?" (Brown & Snell, 1993). Assessment must be meaningful and student-centered if it is to lead to the development of an appropriate educational program that facilitates successful transition outcomes. A basic theoretical assumption is that good, comprehensive transition assessment leads to good, comprehensive transition planning and, in general, one does not usually exist in the absence of the other (Clark, 2007).

Therefore, IEP team members must be familiar with and select the assessments and procedures that will yield accurate information to guide transition programming as well as produce evidence that will assist youth with disabilities in making informed choices about their futures. The following section identifies standardized and nonstandardized assessment tools and strategies related to transition domains.

Descriptions of assessment instruments related to transition planning and implementation are well-documented in the professional literature (e.g., Clark, 2007; Clark, Patton, & Moulton, 2000; Cohen, et al., 2003; Repetto, 2001; Rojewski & Black, 2002). Repetto (2001) and Cohen et al. (2003) provide a comprehensive review of published instruments related to the following domains: work-related behaviors, skills, and aptitudes; vocational interests; adaptive behavior and life skills; work samples; curriculum-based vocational assessment; and performance-based assessment. Perhaps the most complete review of practices and instruments related to transition identifies over 23 areas to target for transition assessment as well as instruments and strategies for conducting assessments related to these areas (Clark, 2007). Not surprisingly, the vast majority of the assessment instruments and processes related to transition involve assessing the individual and not one's future or current environments. Clark (2007) provides a comprehensive discussion and review of various assessment practices and instruments for transition planning, including standardized and informal assessments.

Standardized Assessment Instruments Related to Transition Outcomes

There are several types of formal assessments that target many of the transition-outcome domains. For instance, aptitude tests may identify one's ability to perform certain tasks or occupational skills, and evidence resulting from an aptitude test may help the student and the IEP team in making informed decisions regarding vocational training or employment. Yet, data resulting from an aptitude test may not be as useful in developing transition goals related to community living or financial literacy. In fact, very few formal or standardized assessments are comprehensive in terms of addressing the majority of the transition-outcome areas within a single assessment or series of assessments. Examples of types of widely used formal assessments that are specific to a limited number of the transition-outcome domains follow:

- *Interest inventories* attempt to quantify interests by providing a score to describe what a person likes and dislikes.
- *Aptitude tests* identify an ability or characteristic (i.e., mental or physical, native, or acquired) that is believed or known to indicate a person's capacity

or potential for learning a particular skill or acquiring certain knowledge.
- *Achievement tests* are designed to provide an evaluation of specific information that individuals have learned from their education and/or life experiences.
- *Domain-referenced achievement tests* target achievement within the primary domains of transition planning.
- *Intelligence tests* represent another standard measure used in the assessment of youth with disabilities.

Increasingly, educators working in pupil personnel services, special education, and school psychology are broadening their collection of standardized assessment procedures to include tests or commercially available products that align more closely with several transition domains, such as the *Transition Planning Inventory–Updated Version* (TPI-UV; Clark & Patton, 2006) or the *Quality of Student Life Questionnaire* (QSL.Q; Keith & Schalock, 1995), and that also include students with disabilities in their standardization samples. Descriptions of several of the more commonly used assessments follow.

TRANSITION PLANNING INVENTORY–UPDATED VERSION (TPI-UV) Perhaps one of the most comprehensive standardized transition assessment instruments, the *Transition Planning Inventory–Updated Version* (TPI-UV; Clark & Patton, 2006), utilizes data gathered from multiple sources including the student, the student's parents, guardians, and professionals at school to develop a profile and further assessment recommendations for the student. Data reflecting the student's knowledge, skills, or behaviors across nine transition areas is collected from all respondents independently, using forms targeted for each type of respondent (i.e., student, parents/guardian, or school personnel). The nine transition areas include: employment, further education/training, daily living, leisure, community participation, health, self-determination, communication, and interpersonal relationships.

The TPI-UV consists of 46 transition planning statements, organized according to the nine transition areas. Each statement is evaluated in consideration of the present level of performance or current level of functioning that the student consistently displays in each transition area with respondents rating each statement along a scale of 0 to 5 (0 = strongly disagree; 5 = strongly agree). The TPI-UV Student and Home Forms also request preferences and interests in likely postschool settings and responses are used to supplement the data on present level of functioning to help the IEP team to focus planning on the student's preferences and interests as well as his or her strengths and needs.

The TPI-UV is suitable for all disability populations and for students between the ages of 14–25. The TPI-UV may be self-administered, guided, or administered orally, and the home form is available in Spanish, Chinese, Korean, and Japanese. The availability of a computer version of the *Transition Planning Inventory– Computer Version* (TPI-UV; Clark & Patton, 2004) represents an alternate format to the print version and assists in making the instrument accessible for respondents with reading and vocabulary difficulties. Supplements to the TPI-UV provide for interpretation of results and additional assessments in transition domains where there may be a lack of information or consensus among the raters.

QUALITY OF LIFE QUESTIONNAIRE (QOL.Q) The QOL.Q (Schalock & Keith, 1993) was designed to assess quality of life as an outcome measure for persons with developmental disabilities, but the authors claim that it may be used with any disability population and is targeted for individuals who are 18 or older. Five subscales address satisfaction, competence/productivity, empowerment/independence, and social belonging/community integration, all of which are areas of concern for assessing independent living and self-determination. Each item is rated on a three-point scale, forced-choice response format. Results are presented as a total score and there are separate percentile scores for each of the five subscales. The QOL.Q is administered in an interview format, and the estimated time for completion is 20 minutes.

QUALITY OF STUDENT LIFE QUESTIONNAIRE (QSL.Q) The *Quality of Student Life Questionnaire* (QSL.Q; Keith & Schalock, 1995) is designed for use with secondary and postsecondary students with disabilities for the purpose of assessing the psychological and social indicators that represent subjective student reactions to and perceptions of life experiences while in school. The scale has 40 items measuring four factors: satisfaction, well-being, social belonging, and empowerment/control, all of which are areas of interest in assessing certain features of self-determination (Clark, 2007).

The QSL.Q may be administered to students who have sufficient receptive and expressive language (natural or augmented) to understand and to respond to the questions through either an interview or a written questionnaire format. Estimated time for administration is 15 minutes. A total score can be obtained through hand scoring or through the QSL.Q scoring software. Percentile ranks can be estimated for hand-scored scales or can be calculated automatically through the software scoring program. Norms are based on secondary and postsecondary student populations. The QSL.Q has been used to assess individual social and educational needs, to evaluate program outcomes, and as a dependent measure in research on a variety of social and educational issues related to student quality of life.

RESPONSIBILITY AND INDEPENDENCE SCALE FOR ADOLESCENTS (RISA) The *Responsibility and Independence Scale for Adolescents* (RISA; Salvia, Neisworth, & Schmidt, 1990) is a norm-referenced, individually administered instrument specifically designed to measure adolescents' adaptive behavior in terms of responsibility and independence. It is similar to adaptive behavior scales, but RISA targets more complex skills and behaviors and may be better suited for young adults with mild disabilities or juvenile offenders, whereas most measures of adaptive behavior target low-level skills and are designed for students with developmental disabilities.

The nine subscales are consistent with the transition domains referenced in the literature including: domestic skills, money management, citizenship, personal planning, transportation skills, career development, self-management, social maturity, and social communication. Administration time for RISA is approximately 30–45 minutes. RISA was standardized nationally on 2,400 subjects and is appropriate for individuals aged 12-0 through 19-11. Scale scores and percentile ranks are norm-referenced indicators. Internal consistency and test–retest reliabilities for RISA were reported in the 90s. Studies have shown this assessment to correlate well with the Scales of Independent Behavior and the Vineland Adaptive Behavior Scales.

LIFE-CENTERED CAREER EDUCATION (LCCE) COMPETENCY ASSESSMENT KNOWLEDGE BATTERIES *Life-Centered Career Education* (LCCE) *Competency Assessment Knowledge Batteries* is a curriculum-based assessment instrument that assesses the career education knowledge and skills of students with disabilities in grades 7–12. The battery is a standardized, criterion-referenced set of 200 multiple-choice questions spread across the three domains of the LCCE model: awareness, exploration, and occupational guidance. This assessment is designed to be used with the *Life Centered Career Education (LCCE) Competency Assessment Performance Batteries* (Brolin, 1992) as part of the LCCE curriculum program (Brolin, 1992).

Limitations of Standardized Instruments

Depending on the needs and abilities of an individual, a student may participate in a variety of formal assessments. The advantages and limitations of standardized assessments were delineated within chapter 7 and are also well-documented in the special education literature (Hammill, 1987; McLoughlin & Lewis, 2004; Salvia & Ysseldyke, 2007; Taylor, 2006). Standardized assessment instruments related to transition often tend to target only one or two of the primary transition domains; for example, postsecondary education or training and employment (Clark, 2007). For many young adults with disabilities, this may be appropriate given that the majority of students receiving special education services have mild to moderate disabilities.

Additionally, assessment during a student's education is heavily weighted toward achievement testing. Thus, for students who spend the vast majority of their school day in academic environments, it becomes increasingly difficult to implement assessments related to functional achievement, notwithstanding the fact that all young adults could benefit from career and vocational assessments. In addition, the use of standardized assessment instruments is somewhat removed from tasks or processes required in employment and adult living (Sitlington et al., 2007).

Standardized assessment instruments may serve as useful starting points from which to develop a comprehensive transition assessment plan that will guide instructional programming and transition service delivery. Information resulting from standardized assessments will be useful in determining a student's knowledge level relating to many aspects of transition programming such as community living skills or specific occupations. However, information resulting from these assessments informs the transition team less well about how students' apply the knowledge or perform in real-life contexts.

Challenges with using standardized assessment instruments rest with fact that many of the readily available assessment instruments, such as interest inventories or aptitude tests, do not include young adults with disabilities in their standardization samples. Though these assessments may be useful or appropriate for youth with disabilities, the results should be interpreted with caution and never presented as the sole source of assessment data.

Similar to other diagnostic and evaluation instruments, the selection of appropriate, nonbiased transition assessment instruments must be made with the characteristics of the individual in mind. Age, developmental level, reading ability, primary language, and cultural background of a student must all be taken into account when identifying a student-centered transition assessment process. Despite commonality in special education disability labels, there is little evidence that a general, one-size-fits-all approach to transition assessment is the most effective means for capturing valid and reliable assessment data from a diverse group of students representing various abilities, learning styles, and demographic characteristics.

Furthermore, many young adults with disabilities will require some type of accommodation to complete an assessment. Examples include accommodations related to the environment (e.g., administering the test in an individual session, allowing the student to take the test in a place where he or she feels most comfortable); time (e.g., allowing additional time to complete a test, spacing testing over a period of days); or format (e.g., providing an enlarged copy of the test, using sign language).

Nonstandardized or Informal Assessment

Increasing emphasis is being placed on skill identification and training needs through informal techniques, particularly for those students with more significant disabilities (Parent, Unger, & Inge, 1997; Targett, Ferguson, & McLaughlin, 1998). The growing popularity of informal methods strongly suggests the importance for transition team members, including rehabilitation and health professionals, to become familiar with such techniques.

The usefulness of the data obtained from nonstandardized assessment tools depends on the face validity of the instrument. *Face validity* is a subjective appraisal of what a test seems to measure (Power, 2000). It is the extent to which items on a test appear to be meaningful and relevant. For example, a test that measures independent living skills should have items that look like they measure independent living skills. This very crude technique is needed to ensure that a test is acceptable to potential users. If a test is used to predict ability to perform a job, and the assessment has no relationship to the job, it would be void of face validity.

Nonstandardized procedures provide a variety of options for obtaining valuable information for transition planning. Most informal assessments are developed in-house or are adapted versions of tools obtained from other transition service providers (Clark & Patton, 1997). Some examples of informal assessment approaches follow:

• *Group planning or Person-Centered Planning Meetings:* A meeting of the important individuals in the student's life is held to explore the student's life experiences, desires, and abilities. The process draws on the knowledge and contributions of the student's network of friends, family, and support people. Strategies include lifestyle or futures planning (O'Brien, 1987); the McGill Action Planning System (MAPS) (Vandercook, York, & Forest, 1989); PATH (Pearpoint, O'Brien & Forest, 1993); and the Circle of Friends (Mount & Zwernick, 1988). Hagner and DiLeo (1993) indicate that this type of approach is particularly useful when a student has difficulty expressing him or herself, or when an array of supports will probably be needed to implement a plan. This type of assessment is based upon the skills, strengths, preferences, and dreams of the individual. This process requires a long-term commitment and results in the development of a plan of action.

• *Curriculum-based assessment:* During curriculum-based assessment, skills are assessed and taught according to a predetermined curriculum. This approach has its advantages and disadvantages. First, it is easy to use. Teachers can easily pick up the tool and begin to use it immediately. Students are assessed in relation to their performance of various examples of skills embedded in the targeted curriculum. The primary disadvantage is that teachers cannot consider "real world" environments and may assess students on skills that are not relevant to them. For example, the curriculum may assess the ability to use public transportation; however, if the student has no access to this option either now or in the future, instruction in this area would be useless.

• *Portfolios:* Portfolios, as an assessment tool, have gained in popularity within school systems as educators seek to acquire an accurate portrayal of a student's abilities. Sitlington and Clark (2006) delineate the primary steps in portfolios development to include: curricular area, overall goals of the portfolio, the portfolio format and type of materials to include, procedures for evaluating materials to be included, and how the portfolio will be summarized. Portfolios can include a collection of the student's work, teacher evaluations, and a student's self-reflections, results of interest inventories, samples of projects, and more (Lankes, 1995; Sitlington et. al., 2007). A portfolio represents the progress and achievements of the student and is performance based.

• *Observations in natural environments:* In this approach the teacher does not simulate materials or cues; instead, observations are made in the setting where the behavior naturally occurs (Browder, 1993). For example, information about a student's ability to wash clothes would be gathered where the family does laundry—in his or her home or perhaps at a laundromat. The student is given the opportunity to demonstrate his or her competencies in a natural or "criterion" environment. To obtain data that

more accurately reflects the student's abilities, observations should sample all appropriate settings and take place over several days.

• *Vocational situational assessments:* Students are observed performing "real" work tasks at a community-based employment site (Parent, Unger, & Inge, 1997; Targett, Ferguson, & McLaughlin, 1998). Data is collected on current skills, and ideas on future vocational skill development are provided.

• *Adaptive, behavior, or functional skill inventories:* These tools often come in the form of a checklist and are usually developed in-house to meet the needs of a specific student or group of students. Often, they are variations of informal instruments developed by other professionals in the field (Clark & Patton, 1997).

• *Environmental assessment strategies:* Environmental assessment strategies, like criterion-referenced tests, examine the environment to determine the skills students need. However, instead of commercially prepared instruments, select strategies are used to assess the environments that are relevant to a specific student. Brown and Snell state that, "the purposes of environmental assessments are to identify functional routines and activities across relevant settings, such as home, school, work and community, and to measure or estimate a student's performance on specific routines and activities found within those settings." The curriculum domains selected should represent major life areas, lead to the selection of practical skills, and emphasize the functional goals of self-sufficiency. Brown and Snell warn teachers that this does not mean that communication, motor, or social skills are ignored. Instead, those skills are taught within the context of each domain.

Challenges to Implementing Transition Assessments

When one considers the potential for transition assessments as they relate to potential postschool environments as well as the requirement for state- and district-wide assessments, it can be quite overwhelming. One of the challenges that professionals involved in transition assessment encounter is how to implement a process that meets the needs of all students, that can be implemented in a timely manner, and for which there are adequate resources for implementation. At a minimum, the transition assessment process must comply with the legal mandates of IDEA or risk a due process hearing or lawsuit.

Another challenge involves identifying appropriate personnel to implement the transition assessment process. Decisions surrounding whether a designated professional within the school will be responsible for overseeing the processing and taking the responsibility for compiling the Summary of Performance or whether these responsibilities will fall to the special education teachers must be addressed. In addition, processes for involving nonschool personnel, such as rehabilitation counselors or occupational therapists, in assessments and identifying arrangements for services, fee structures, and reimbursements all need to be addressed.

Summary and Conclusion

The successful transition from school to adult community life depends on comprehensive transition planning and programming. Such planning, in turn, depends on the accurate assessment of students with disabilities. Because no two students are alike, and all will enter diverse work, social, and residential environments upon leaving school, an individualized assessment of each student's strengths and support needs within the environment in which he or she functions or is expected to function is critical.

Self-Check Questions

1. Recall your transition from secondary education to post-secondary education or employment. How did you identify what you wanted to do after you graduated or exited high school? What role did educators and nonschool personnel play in your transition? What barriers or facilitators did you encounter in your transition? How might your experiences compare or contrast to those experienced by young adults with disabilities?

2. Define transition as it relates to youth with disabilities exiting special education programs.

3. Identify transition domains that were presented within the Individuals with Disabilities Education Improvement Act, and discuss why these domains are important to youth with disabilities.

4. Discuss the role of nonschool personnel in the transition assessment process and whether participation from non-school personnel is mandated by law or voluntary.

5. Describe the requirements for Summary of Performance. What might be some of the challenges in developing a Summary of Performance?

6. Compare and contrast formal and informal transition-related assessment instruments and processes.

7. Identify and describe transition-related assessments that are relevant to independent living, employment, or self-determination.

8. Why might it be important to conducted student assessments as well as assessments of the student's desired postschool environments?

9. In your role as a rehabilitation and health professional, what are some of the potential contributions you can make to the transition assessment process for youth with disabilities?

Case Study

Martha is an 18-year-old student with severe physical disabilities due to cerebral palsy and moderate mental retardation. She has right-side hemiplegia, ataxia, and a seizure disorder. Martha uses a motorized wheelchair, which she can maneuver independently. During this past school year, she has been attending regular classes at the high school. Her communication abilities include the use of natural gestures (e.g., leading, pointing, showing), facial expressions, body orientation, and behavioral responses. Martha speaks in phrases of one to five words that are intelligible to familiar listeners.

Martha's educational records provide evidence of a history of participation in educational assessments, including those directed at identifying her current knowledge and performance, as well as services and support needs. Records in her file indicate a variety of informal and formal assessments related to the following areas: adaptive skills; cognitive development and performance; motor skills, including orientation and mobility; and speech, language, and communication skills. As many of her needs related to communication and mobility were addressed early in her educational career, Martha demonstrated progress toward her IEP goals. However, services and supports from the school district's speech and language pathologist, contracted services from a local physical therapist, and an orientation and mobility trainer from the local board of mental retardation and developmental disabilities waned as she advanced from elementary to middle school.

When Martha was 14, school personnel began to conduct a variety of assessments with her across multiple environments. Ongoing informal assessments conducted by school personnel and her parents, such as ecological assessments in community environments, have demonstrated that Martha has interests in learning more about how to navigate her community through public, nonspecialized transportation as well as potential jobs in places that she frequents with her family and friends. These businesses include book or multimedia stores, libraries, and financial institutions. School personnel observed Martha during the school day and during her work experiences within the school and then, a few years later, at local businesses. Her work experiences included working as a library aide in her local library, where she was responsible for retrieving library materials from the three return drops and using a scan to input a record of the return and then place the materials on the appropriate cart for reshelving. The vast majority data derived from these assessments were gathered by educators and paraprofessionals as well as Martha's parents, supervisors, and coworkers at the employment sites.

Martha's special education teacher began to identify potential avenues for nonschool-based support and guidance as to how to best analyze the future environments that Martha desired to participate in and to identify the supports or accommodations that Martha would need to access and be successful in those environments. The special

educator quickly realized that many of the professionals that played a critically important role in Martha's educational experiences early in her career were now needed to assist in identifying effective teaching and learning goals and strategies as well as supports to facilitate access to and participation in community and workplace environments.

QUESTIONS

1. Identify rehabilitation and health professionals that the special educator, Martha, or Martha's parents may want to involve in the transition-planning process. Describe the role that the professionals you have identified would serve in the transition-planning and assessment process.

2. Based on your knowledge of the ICF and the information presented in the case study, identify the classifications within the ICF that would provide the most useful information in determining potential barriers to access and participation in the following transition domains: a) mobility and transportation training; b) employment; c) social relationships; d) postsecondary education or training; and e) independent living.

3. Describe some challenges that rehabilitation and health professionals would encounter in working with transition-age youth with disabilities. Think in terms of communicating with members of the IEP team, cost, and provision of services (e.g., who pays for the involvement of rehabilitation and health professionals).

References

Agran, M., Blanchard, C., & Wehmeyer, M. L. (2000). Promoting transition goals and self-determination through student self-directed learning: The Self-Determined Learning Model of Instruction. *Education and Training in Mental Retardation and Developmental Disabilities, 35(4)*, 351–364.

AOTA (American Occupational Therapy Association) (2000) *AOTA 2000 Member Compensation Survey*. Bethesda, MD: Author.

Arnold K (2000). *The occupational therapist's role in the high school*. Durham: University of New Hampshire.

Blackorby, J., & Wagner, M. (1996). Longitudinal postschool outcomes of youth with disabilities: Findings from the National Longitudinal Transition Study. *Exceptional Children, 62(5)*, 399–413.

Brolin, D. E. (1992). *Life Centered Career Education: Competency assessment batteries*. Reston, VA: Council for Exceptional Children.

Brolin, D. E., & Loyd, R. J. (2004). *Career development and transition services: A functional approach* (4th ed.). Upper Saddle River, NJ: Merrill-Prentice Hall.

Browder, D. M. (1993). *Assessment of individuals with severe disabilities* (2nd ed.). Baltimore: Brookes.

Brown, F., & Snell, M. (1993). Meaningful assessment. In M. Snell & F. Brown (eds.), *Instruction of students with severe disabilities*. Upper Saddle River, NJ: Prentice-Hall.

Bruyère , S., VanLooy, S., & Peterson, D. (2005). The international classification of functioning, disability and health (ICF): Contemporary literature overview. *Rehabilitation Psychology, 50(2)*.

Cameto, R. (2005). Employment of youth with disabilities after high school. In *After high school: A first look at the postschool experiences of youth with disabilities*. Office of Special Education Programs. Accessed October 10, 2007 at http://www.nlts2.org/reports/2005_04/nlts2_report_2005_04_complete.pdf

Cascella, P.W., & McNamara, K.M. (2004). Practical communication services for high school students with severe disabilities: Collaboration during the transition to adult services. *The ASHA Leader, 9*(9), 6–7, 18–19.

Chandler J, O'Brien P. Weinstein L. (1996). The role of occupational therapy in transition from school to work for adolescents with disabilities. *Work 6*, 53–59.

Clark, G. M. (2007). *Assessment for transitions planning* (2nd ed.). Austin, TX: PRO-ED.

Clark, G. M. & Patton, J. R. (1997). *Transition Planning Inventory*. Austin, TX: PRO-ED.

Clark, G. M. & Patton, J. R. (2004). Transition planning inventory: Computer version: Manual. Austin, TX: PRO-ED.

Clark, G. M., & Patton, J. R. (2006). *Transition Planning Inventory–Updated*. Austin, TX: PRO-ED.

Clark, G. M., Patton, J. R., & Moulton, L. R. (2000). *Information assessments for transition planning*. Austin, TX: PRO-ED.

Cohen, L. G., & Spenciner, L. J. (2007). *Assessment of children and youth with special needs* (3rd ed.). Boston: Allyn and Bacon.

Cohen, L. G., Spenciner, L. J., & Twitchell, D. (2003). Youth in transition. In L. G. Cohen & L. J. Spenciner (Eds.), *Assessment of children and youth with special needs* (2nd ed., pp. 459–479). Boston: Pearson Education.

Cross, T., Cooke, N. L., Wood W. M., & Test, D. W. (1999). *Comparison of the effects of MAPS and ChoiceMaker on students' self-determination skills*. Education and Training in Mental Retardation and Developmental Disabilities, 34, 499–510.

Everson, J. M. (1996) Assessing the transition needs of young adults with dual sensory and multiple impairments. Assessment Guidelines, V 3. Accessed October 15, 2007 at: http://eric.ed.gov/ERICDocs/data/ericdocs2sql/content_storage_01/0000019b/80/16/13/8b.pdf

Flannery, B., Newton, S., Horner, R., Slovic, R., Blumberg, R., & Ard, W. K. (2000). The impact of person centered planning on the content and organization of individual supports. *Career Development for Exceptional Individuals, 23*, 123–137.

German, S. L., Martin, J. E., Huber-Marshall, L., & Sale, R. P. (2000). Promoting self-determination: Using *Take Action* to teach goal attainment. *Career Development for Exceptional Individuals, 23*, 27–37.

Hagner, D. C., & DiLeo, D. (1993). *Working together: Workplace culture, supported employment, and persons with disabilities*. Cambridge, MA: Brookline Books.

Hammill, D. D. (1987). Assessing students in the schools. In J. L. Wiederholt & B. R. Bryant (Eds), *Assessing the reading abilities and instructional needs of students* (pp. 1–32). Austin, TX: PRO-ED.

Individuals with Disabilities Education Improvement Act of 2004, 20 U.S.C. § 1400 *et seq.* (2004) (reauthorization of IDEA 1990).

Keith, K. D., & Schalock, R. L. (1995). *Quality of student life questionnaire*. Worthington, OH: IDS Publishing Corporation.

Lankes, A. M. D. (1995). *Electronic portfolios: A new idea in assessment*. Syracuse, NY: ERIC Clearinghouse on Information & Technology. (ERIC Document Reproduction Service No. ED3903777).

LaPlante, M. P., Kennedy, J., Kaye, H. S., & Wenger, B. L. (1996). *Disability and employment, disability statistics abstract #11*. Disability Statistics Rehabilitation Research and Training Center. Washington, DC: National Institute on Disability and Rehabilitation Research.

Martin, J. E., Van Dycke, J. L., Greene, B. A., Gardner, J. E., Christensen, W. R., Woods, L. L., & Lovett, D. L. (2006). Direct observation of teacher-directed IEP meetings: Establishing the need for student IEP meetings instruction. *Exceptional Children, 72*(2), 187–200.

Mason, C., Field, S., & Sawilowsky, S. (2004) Implementation of self-determination activities and student participation in IEPs. *Exceptional Children, 70*(4), 441–451.

McLoughlin, J. A., & Lewis, R. B. (2004). *Assessing special students* (7th ed.). New York: Merrill.

Michaels, C. A., & Orentlicher, M. L. (2004). The role of occupational therapy in providing person-centered transition services: Implications for school-based practice. *Occupational Therapy International, 11*(4), 209–228.

Mount, B. & Zwernick, K. (1988). *It's never too early, it's never too late: An overview on personal futures planning*. St. Paul, MN: Governor's Council on Developmental Disabilities.

Nuehring, M. L., & Sitlington, P. L. (2003). Transition as a vehicle: Moving from high school to adult vocational service provider. *Journal of Disability Policy Studies, 14*(1).

O'Brien, J. (1987). A guide to lifestyle planning. In B. Wilcox & T. Bellamy (Eds.), *A comprehensive guide to the activities catalog*. Baltimore: Paul Brookes.

Palmer, S. B., Wehmeyer, M. L., Gipson, K., & Agran, M. (2004). Promoting access to the general curriculum by teaching self-determination skills. *Exceptional Children, 70*, 427–439.

Parent, W., Unger, D., & Inge, K. (1997). Customer profile. In V. Brooke, K. J. Inge, A. J. Armstrong, & P. Wehman, (Eds.), *Supported employment handbook: A customer-driven approach for persons with significant disabilities*. Richmond, VA: Virginia Commonwealth University, Rehabilitation Research and Training Center on Supported Employment.

Pearpoint, J., O'Brien, J., & Forest, M. (1993). *PATH*. Toronto, ON, Canada: Inclusion Press.

Peterson, D. B. (2005). International classification of functioning, disability, and health: An introduction for rehabilitation psychologists. *Rehabilitation Psychology, 50*, 105–112

Phelps, L. A., & Hanley-Maxwell, C. (1997). School-to-work transitions for youth with disabilities: A review of outcomes and practices. *Review of Educational Research, 67*(2), 197–226.

Power, P.W. (2000).*A guide to vocational assessment* (3rd ed). Austin, TX: PRO-ED.

President's Commission on Excellence in Special Education (2002). *Source: A New Era: Revitalizing Special Education for Children and Their Families, July 2002.*

Repetto, J. B. (2001). Assessment for transition. In McLoughlin, J. & Lewis, R. (Eds.). *Assessing students with special needs* (5th ed.). Columbus, OH: Merrill-Prentice Hall.

Rojewski, J.W. & Black, R. S. (Eds.) (2002). *Assessments that support the transition from school to work for adolescents with disabilities.* Reston, VA: Council for Exceptional Children.

Salvia, J., Neisworth, J., & Schmidt, M. (1990). *Examiner's manual: Responsibility and independence scale for adolescents.* Allen, TX: DLM.

Salvia, J., & Ysseldyke, J. E. (2007). *Assessment in special and inclusive education* (10th ed.). Boston: Houghton Mifflin.

Schalock, R. L. & Keith, K. D. (1993). *Quality of life questionnaire.* Worthington, OH: IDS Publishing Corporation.

Shertzer, B. & Linden, J. O. (1979). *Fundamentals of individual appraisal: Assessment techniques for counselors.* Boston: Houghton Mifflin.

Sitlington, P. L., and Clark, G. M. (2006). *Transition education and services for students with disabilities* (4th ed). Boston: Allyn & Bacon.

Sitlington, P. L., Neubert, D. A., Begun, W., Lombard, R. C., & Leconte, P. J. (1996). *Assess for success: Handbook on transition assessment.* Reston, VA: Council for Exceptional Children, Division of Career Development and Transition.

Sitlington, P. L., Neubert, D. A., Begun, W. H., Lombard, R. C., Leconte, P. J. (2007). *Assess for success: A practitioner's handbook on transition assessment* (2nd Ed). Thousand Oaks, CA: SAGE.

Snell, M. (1993). *Systematic instruction for individuals with severe disabilities* (4th ed.) New York: Merrill.

Spencer, J. E., Emery, L. J., Schneck, C. M. (2003). Occupational therapy in transitioning adolescents to postsecondary activities. *American Journal of Occupational Therapy,* 57, 435–41.

Targett, P. S., Ferguson, S. S., & McLaughlin, J. (1998). Consumer involvement in vocational evaluation. In P. Wehman & J. Kregel (Eds.), *More than a job* (pp. 95–117). Baltimore: Brookes.

Taylor, R. (2006). *Assessment of exceptional students: Educational and psychological procedures.* Upper Saddle River, NJ: Prentice Hall.

Test, D.W., & Neale, M. (2004). Using *The Self-Advocacy Strategy* to increase middle graders' IEP participation. *Journal of Behavioral Education,* 13(2), 135–145.

U.S. Department of Education, Office of Special Education Programs. (2007). *Individuals with Disabilities Education Act, child count.* https://www.ideadata.org/AnnualTables.asp11/21/07.

U.S. Department of Education, President's Commission on Excellence in Special Education, (2002). *Reforming the Individuals with Disabilities Education Act.* Washington, DC: Author.

U.S. General Accounting Office (GAO). (2001). *Improving return to work efforts.* GAO-01-153, 1/12/2001.

Vandercook, T., York, J., & Forest, M. (1989). The McGill Action Planning System (MAPS): A strategy for building the vision. *Journal of the Association for Persons with Severe Handicaps,* 14(3), 205–215.

Wagner, M., Newman, L., Cameto, R., Garza, N. & Levine, P. (2005). *After high school: A first look at the postschool experiences of youth with disabilities. A report from the National Longitudinal Transition Study-2 (NLTS2).* Menlo Park, CA: SRI International.

Wehmeyer, M. L., & Kelchner, K. (1995). *The Arc's self-determination scale.* Arlington, TX: The Arc.

Wehmeyer, M. L., Palmer, S. B., Agran, M., Mithaug, D. E., & Martin, J. E. (2000). Promoting casual agency: The Self-Determined Learning Model of Instruction. *Exceptional Children,* 66(4), 439–453.

Whitney-Thomas, J., Shaw, D., Honey, K., & Butterworth, J. (1998). Building a future: A study of student participation in person-centered planning. *Journal of the Association of the Severely Handicapped,* 23, 119–133.

Wittenburg, D. C., & Maag, E. (2002). School to where: A literature review on economic outcomes of youth with disabilities. *Journal of Vocational Rehabilitation,* 17(4), 265–280.

World Health Organization (2001). International Classification of Functioning, Disability and Health. Resolution WHA 54.21. Accessed October, 3, 2007 at: http://www.who.int/classifications/icf/en/.

22

Assessment of Disability-Related Attitudes

STEVEN R. PRUETT
The Ohio State University, Columbus

FRANK J. LANE
Illinois Institute of Technology, Chicago

OVERVIEW

This chapter explores issues related to the assessment of attitudes with particular attention to persons with disabilities. Definitions of attitude and attitude measurement are defined and related to the International Classification of Functioning, Disability, and Health. The history of attitude assessment is explored with discussion of the function of attitudes, the relationship between attitude and behavior, attitude change, and attitudes toward persons with disabilities. The discussion on attitude measurement includes specific approaches such as explicit and implicit measures. Specific instruments such as the Attitude towards Disabled Persons Scale (ATDP), the Interaction with Disabled Persons Scale (IDP) and the Issues in Disabilities Scale (IDS), to name a few, are explored in depth. Cultural, legislative, and professional issues that impact attitude measurement are reviewed. Finally, multicultural and interdisciplinary approaches to attitude measurement are discussed.

LEARNING OBJECTIVES

By the end of the chapter, readers should be able to:

- Define attitude and concepts related to attitudes towards persons with disabilities and attitude measurement
- Describe the functional aspect of attitudes and the theories that attempt to explain the relationship between attitudes and behavior
- Describe and discuss the attitude measures covered in the chapter
- Discuss the research on the assessment of attitudes across different cultures and discipline contexts
- Describe and discuss the cultural, legislative and professional factors that impact attitude assessment
- Distinguish between an explicit and an implicit measure of attitude

INTRODUCTION

The role of attitudes in everyday life is pervasive. For example, Wright (1988) observed that there is a "fundamental negative bias" toward persons with disabilities. This negative bias in itself is difficult to observe. Attitudes are frequently subtle. However, there are consequences of these attitudes. According to the American Community Survey Profile 2005 by the U.S. Census Bureau, approximately 12.1% of individuals aged 16–64 (roughly 22,753,000) have a disability (U.S. Census Bureau, 2006). These working-aged individuals are frequently subject to many social disparities such as higher incidences of unemployment (U.S. Census Bureau; Taylor, October 7, 2000); workplace discrimination (Chan, McMahon, Cheing, Rosenthal, & Bezyak, 2005); reduced access to health care (Fouts, Andresen, & Hagglund, 2000; Shigaki, Hagglund, Clark, & Conforti (2002); and overall social stigma (Link & Phelan, 2001). Likewise, there is a substantial amount of research in special education concerning attempts to modify the negative attitudes both of fellow students (Milsom, 2006; Slininger, Sherill, & Jankowski, 2000) and of educators (Beattie, Anderson, & Antonak, 1997).

In an attempt to understand why attitudes exist at all, some attitude psychologists cite an overarching function of attitudes as facilitating an individual's environmental adaptation and promotion of well-being (Eagly & Chaiken, 1998). Katz (1960) identified four specific functions of attitudes. The first function is the *instrumental* or *utilitarian* function, which implies that people develop favorable attitudes toward things that aid or reward them and develop negative attitudes toward things that penalize. The next function is *ego-defensiveness*, which focuses on attitudes as a protection from, or deflection of, the harshness of reality. Third, there is a *value-expressive* function of attitudes, which purports that attitudes help establish social identity and self-concept. Finally, Katz identifies the *knowledge* function, where attitudes provide a structure for an individual to make meaning and clarity of his or her environment.

IMPORTANCE OF ATTITUDES TO REHABILITATION AND HEALTH

Definitions and Theories of Attitudes

According to the Oxford English Dictionary (Simpson & Weiner, 1989), the etymology of the term *attitude* (as well as *aptitude*) derives from the Latin word *aptus*, which means fit. Attitude was originally used in the fine arts to describe the posture or disposition of a figure. The construct of a mental attitude was first used by early psychologists in the mid- to late-1800s (see Spencer, 1862 and Bain, 1868) and was used as describing a means of guiding beliefs and evaluations. Allport (1968) regarded attitude to be "the most distinctive and indispensable concept in contemporary American social psychology" (p. 59).

As can be seen, the definition of attitude has evolved over the course of the time. There have been numerous attempts to define the construct of attitude. In 1980, Ajzen and Fishbein reported that more than 500 definitions of attitude had been offered. Thurstone (1931) offered an early emotion-oriented definition of attitude as "affect for or against a psychological object" (p. 261). Allport (1935) provided a comprehensive definition by asserting that it is "a mental and neural state of readiness, organized through experience, exerting a directive or dynamic influence upon the individual's response to all objects and situations with which it is related" (p. 810). Katz (1960) defined attitude as "the predisposition of the individual to evaluate some symbol or object or aspect of his world in a favorable or unfavorable manner" (p. 168). English and English (1958) offered a decidedly behaviorally-oriented definition of attitude as an "enduring learned predisposition to behave in a consistent way toward a given class of objects" (p. 50).

During the middle of the 20th century, the categories of cognition and behavior as well as affect were accepted by a consensus of scholarly community. This became known as the *tripartite* definition of attitudes. According to the tripartite definition, attitudes are comprised of three or four facets: cognitive, affective and cognitive/behavioral, with each of these facets having some sort of bearing on an evaluation (Breckler, 1984; Breckler & Wiggins, 1989; Katz & Stotland, 1959; Rosenberg & Hovland, 1960).

The tripartite model of attitudes was found to be lacking due to concerns about the validity of the behavioral component (Greenwald, 1989; Wicker, 1969; Zanna & Rempel, 1988). According to current literature, the tripartite model of attitudes is no longer being used by most attitude researchers (Ajzen & Fishbein, 2000; Petty, Wegener, & Fabrigar, 1997), and it has been supplanted by the understanding that attitude has to do with the extent of favorableness or unfavorableness that someone has toward a psychological object (Ajzen, 2001; Greenwald et al., 2002; Petty, Priester, & Wegener, 1994). However, the tripartite definition of attitudes continues to reside in social psychology textbooks (c.f., Aronson, Wilson, & Akert, 1997). The most current definitions assert that an attitude is first and foremost an evaluation (Ajzen, 2001). Affect has a strong effect on evaluation, but the term generally implies mood states that exist without an object of reference (e.g., happiness versus sadness) (Ajzen & Fishbien, 2000). Albarracín, Zanna, Johnson, and Kumkale (2005) assert that although affect, beliefs, and behaviors interact with attitudes, they are not components of attitudes. This definition of attitudes allows for an incongruence of behavior and attitudes.

Attempts to improve the understanding of attitudes and behaviors led to Ajzen and Fishbein's (1980) theory of reasoned action. This theory assumes that "human beings are usually quite rational and make systematic use of the information available to them…We argue that people consider the implications of their actions before they decide to engage or not engage in a given behavior" (5). A theory of planned behavior (Ajzen 1988, 1991) succeeded the theory of reasoned action. This variant purports that when someone has to make a decision on a course of behavior, he or she most likely will take into consideration the consequences of all the alternatives and consider the expectations of other important relationships (individuals or groups), as well as taking into account the needed resources and/or obstacles. This process then assists in the formation of an attitude toward the planned behavior and perception of behavioral control (Ajzen, 1996).

Greenwald (1990) argued that when people do not consciously attend to their attitudes, there is a strong effect of attitude on behavior. He lists several examples of this type of attitude–behavior congruency, such as the "halo" effect, which involves the development of a new positive or negative evaluation of an individual when a positive or negative attitude toward that individual already preexists. Greenwald concluded that many attitudes exist on a similar level as implicit cognition or memory. He suggested that in order to determine if an attitude would have an effect on behavior, a researcher would need to use indirect measures of attitude versus direct, because bringing awareness of the attitude to the

subject would inhibit the corresponding behavior. Later, Greenwald and Banaji (1995) proposed that there exists an "indirect, unconscious, or implicit mode of operation for attitudes and stereotypes" (p. 4). They defined these implicit attitudes as "introspectively unidentified (or inaccurately identified) traces of past experiences that mediate favorable or unfavorable feeling, thought, or action toward social objects" (p. 8). This understanding of implicit attitude development is consistent with the research into the automatic activation of attitudes by Fazio, Sambonmatsu, Powell, and Kardes (1986) and Devine (1989). It was suggested that many of the findings in psychoanalytic, behaviorist, and cognitive treatments can be reinterpreted into the construct of implicit cognition (Greenwald & Banaji, 1995).

Because attitude is an evaluation and is related to other psychological constructs such as memory, beliefs, personality, motivation, and affect, there may be many parts of the brain that are related to attitudes. Recent advances in neural imaging (e.g., functional Magnetic Resonance Imaging: fMRI, and Positron Emission Tomography: PET scans) have allowed for the study of neurological processes that are involved in affective processing. For example, Phelps et al. (2000) used fMRI imaging and found a relationship between amygdala activation and racial evaluations, and O'Doherty et al. (2003) found neuronal activity in the medial orbiofrontal cortex in response to presentation of attractive faces.

Attitude may also have relations with physical health. Leventhal, Hansell, Diefenbach, Leventhal, and Glass (1996) found that negative affective states were associated with an acute illness and more chronic somatic complaints among older adults. Thus, there is some evidence that feeling physically poor can have a negative influence on attitudes. Waller, Kojetin, Bouchard, Lykken, and Tellegen (1990) found greater similar religious interests, attitudes, and values among monozygotic twins than dizygotic twins. This suggests that there is some evidence that attitudes are, at least partially, genetically influenced.

Applicable International Classification of Functioning, Disability, and Health Aspects

The inclusion of attitudes into the *International Classification of Functioning, Disability, and Health* (ICF) in 2001 by the World Health Organization (WHO) is significant. It represents a paradigm shift in how society conceptualizes disability. The model provides a framework whereby disability is viewed, in part, as a function of attitudes and not solely on the functional ability of the individual (WHO, 2001).

The WHO views attitudes as being driven by personal values and beliefs that influence individual behavior, affecting the ability of the individual with the health condition to participate fully in society (WHO, 2001). Although driven by personal values and beliefs, an attitude requires an evaluative component. It is the evaluation by factors external to the individual with the health condition that is believed to qualitatively and quantitatively limit the activity and restrict the participation of the individual. The attitudes of immediate family members, friends, personal care attendants, and health professionals, societal attitudes, and social norms, practices, and ideologies are important to health outcomes.

The WHO model is considered to be an environmental model of disability (Smart, 2000). Let's consider, for example, an individual with a high-level spinal cord injury who ambulates with a power chair, who wants to explore available job openings in a particular area. The individual drives to the local one-stop career center, and is able to access the building because of accessible parking spaces, curb cuts, and electronic door openers. However, once in the career center, the receptionist possesses the attitude that individuals who ambulate in a wheelchair can't perform the jobs listed at the career center and sends the individual home. It is not the individual's disease or disorder creating the disability; it is the attitude of the receptionist.

The Short-Form ICF Checklist, designed for use by clinicians, is designed to assess impairment of body structures and body functions, degree of limitation of activities and restriction of participation, and environmental factors (WHO, 2001). The environmental factor section includes the assessment of attitudes. The attitude component is first determined to function as a *barrier* or *facilitator*, and the degree is rated on a 5-point Likert-type scale where 0 = no barrier/facilitator, 1 = mild barrier/facilitator, 2 = moderate barrier/facilitator, 3 = severe barrier/facilitator, and 4 = complete barrier/facilitator. The Short-Form ICF should be regarded by practitioners as a tool to screen for attitudes within a larger environmental context.

HISTORY OF RESEARCH AND PRACTICE IN THE ASSESSMENT OF ATTITUDES

The detrimental effect of negative bias toward individuals with disabilities on their integration into society has been documented repeatedly in rehabilitation literature (Brodwin & Orange, 2002; Cook, 1998; Frank & Elliott, 2002; Livneh & Antonak, 1997; Siller, 1976; Smart,

2000). The influence of society's attitudes toward people with disabilities has direct and indirect bearing on their life experiences; social, educational, and vocational opportunities; and help-seeking behaviors. Since negative attitudes toward persons with disabilities have so many ramifications, they are perceived as an "invisible barrier" to successful rehabilitation (Chubon, 1982). Thus, the study of attitudes toward people with disabilities persists as a critical area of research in rehabilitation counseling and rehabilitation psychology.

Because rehabilitation health professionals have considerable control over disability-related services and information (Benham, 1988; Brodwin & Orange, 2002; Estes, Deyer, Hansen, & Russell, 1991), the attitudes of rehabilitation professionals and students toward people with disabilities have drawn particular interest. Negative disability-related attitudes held by rehabilitation professionals can translate into restricted opportunities or poor quality of services for their clients (Altman, 1981; Benham, 1988; Brodwin & Orange, 2002; Paris, 1993), and thereby may have an adverse effect on rehabilitation outcomes such as integration, independence, and employment of people with disabilities (Antonak & Livneh, 1988).

Measurement of Attitudes

Because an attitude is a psychological construct, it cannot be easily measured like a physical object or a behavior. Over the course of the 20th century, many social scientists attempted to devise techniques to measure people's attitudes. Following the understanding of explicit attitudes as primarily controlled and belief-oriented in nature, and implicit attitudes as automatic and visceral, this section will first address explicit instruments or techniques, then discuss indirect and disguised measures, and will finally focus on instruments and techniques designed to measure implicit attitudes.

EXPLICIT MEASURES OF ATTITUDES   Most explicit measures are developed from one or a series of direct queries of participants' feelings, beliefs, or opinions regarding an attitudinal object, or from inferences drawn from the participants' evaluations and responses. The easiest way to find out someone's attitude is to ask them for their evaluation of a given topic. The development of sound psychometric techniques or instruments, however, is not that simple. Frequently, attitude surveys use a single item such as, "Do you approve or disapprove of gay marriages?" Respondents may then be asked to assign a numerical value (e.g., ranging from one to five) that corresponds with the anchors of "strongly agree" to "strongly disagree." On the whole, these measures can be very useful and reliable when the attitudes are well-established and thought out (c.f., Robins, Hendin, & Trzesniewski, 2001, Study 1). However, single-item scales are susceptible to leading phraseology and contamination by previous questions. Likewise, threats to reliability and construct validity of single-item scales can occur when the topic is complex and multidimensional (Ajzen, 2002).

The first psychological technique specifically devised to measure attitudes was developed by Thurstone (1928). Thurstone used a paired comparison methodology with a panel of at least 25 "judges." A set of attitude statements are generated. Following this, each judge is required to read every possible pair of statements and make a determination as to which statement is more favorable to the topic at hand. A precise score can then be calculated for each item. Items are then selected that have equal intervals and have the smallest interquartile range. Respondents are then asked whether they agree or disagree with the selected items. A mean score for each respondent is then calculated. This technique is rather cumbersome; thus, it has fallen from favor by social scientists.

The most popular methods used in explicit attitude measurement are the evaluative semantic differential (Osgood, Suci, & Tannenbaum, 1957) and the Likert-type scale (Likert, 1932). Osgood and his associates used bipolar adjectives such as *good–bad, pleasant–unpleasant,* and *useful–useless* as anchors on 7-point scales. This technique allows researchers to gather affective attitudinal information by documenting the evaluative connotations of given psychological object (Osgood et al.).

The Likert method of attitude measurement consists of a summated rating technique that is associated with a large number of belief-based statements that are pertinent to the attitudinal object (Likert, 1932). A common attitudinal theme is then inferred from the respondents' belief-based answers (see Fishbein & Ajzen, 1975). Generally, Likert scales instruct respondents to state how much they agree or disagree with each item on a 5-point scale (e.g., strongly agree, agree, neither agree nor disagree, disagree, strongly disagree) although 7-and 9-point scales are not uncommon. Even-numbered scales have been used to omit the "undecided" choice, thus forcing respondents to provide an evaluative opinion. When a significant number of issues related to the attitudinal object are addressed, it is possible to tease out the multiple dimensions that constitute the topic at hand, thus allowing for greater detail

than is possible with evaluative semantic differential and other direct measures. Because this technique can involve numerous items it can take some time to administer and may not be suitable for quick surveys or batteries with multiple instruments.

Another explicit technique that has been used in the measurement of attitudes is the scalogram technique (Guttman, 1944, 1947, 1950). This technique has been used in various unidimensional measurements, but is no longer a popular method (Ajzen, 2002). Other methods that have been used in the measurement of attitudes over the years include the Q-methodology (Stephenson, 1953), adjective check list (Gough, 1960), and the unfolding technique (Coombs, 1964).

DISGUISED MEASURES.   One of the major problems with explicit measures of attitudes lies in the obvious purpose of the instrument and the possible unwillingness of a respondent to provide his or her true beliefs or feelings concerning the attitudinal object (Ajzen, 2002; Antonak & Livneh, 1988, 1995, 2000; Edwards, 1953; Lenski & Leggett, 1960; Livneh & Antonak, 1994). Social desirability has been identified as one of the most serious biases affecting explicit measures (Paulhus, 1991). The likelihood of social desirability-biased responses becomes greater when the attitude object is controversial or socially sensitive, such as prejudice based on race (Sigall & Page, 1971), sexual standards (Knudson, Pope & Irish, 1967), or disability (Feinberg, 1967; Sigall & Page). In an attempt to control for this type of response bias, a respondent may initially be deceived by the researcher as to the intent of the investigation (Ajzen, 2002) or his or her ability to control the responses (Jones & Sigall, 1971). When planned deception is used by a researcher in the structured collection of attitudinally relevant data, the method is considered a disguised procedure (Antonak & Livneh, 1988). The problem with social desirability response bias may be partly addressed by updating explicit instruments so that they do not contain flagrant socially incorrect phrases or words that make the intent of the instrument blatantly obvious in the current society (Ajzen, 2002). An example of this approach to control for social desirability bias is the Modern Racism Scale (McConahay, Hardee, & Batts, 1981), probably the most popular explicit instrument in measuring attitudes toward African Americans. It has toned down obviously charged words and phrases and instead focuses on racial ambivalence versus outright hostility. However, the Modern Racism Scale is still rather transparent and therefore remains susceptible to social desirability response bias.

Methods that use deception to ascertain attitudes are not as common as the direct techniques previously discussed. Some techniques that have been devised include the error–choice method (Hammond, 1948), randomized response technique (RRT; Greenberg, Abdula, Simmons, & Horvitz, 1969; Warner, 1965), and conjoint analysis (American Marketing Association [AMA] 1992).

The error–choice method (Hammond, 1948) uses very detailed fact-related questions concerning the attitude object. These questions are mixed into a larger group of difficult general questions in an attempt to hide the true intention of the researchers. It is likely that no one would actually know the correct answer to the relevant questions, but whether a respondent systematically answers on the favorable side or unfavorable side of the actual answer is considered reflective of a respondent's attitude. Participants are generally deceived into believing that the test is measuring knowledge of a given topic. Weschler (1950a, 1950b, 1950c) validated the error–choice method by correctly identifying groups that were known to have differing attitudes on management and labor. Subsequently the method has been used only sporadically, predominantly because of Weschler's (1951) concern over the ethics involved in the deception required by the error–choice method.

The RRT was originally developed by Warner (1965) and was subsequently refined by Greenberg et al. (1969). In the RRT, two questions are posed to the respondent, each with the same type of response, usually yes and no. One question is the question of interest while the other is a question for which the distribution of the responses for the population is known. The interviewer uses a coin toss or another randomizing device to choose which question to ask. The respondent is not informed of the result of the random selection. The respondent answers "yes" or "no" to the question. Further validation of the RRT, using a national probability sample of 2,084 adults, demonstrated its usefulness in securing stigma sensitive information on marijuana usage (Zdep, Rhodes, Schwartz, & Kilkenny, 1979).

Conjoint analysis (AMA, 1992; Louviere, 1988) was developed by business researchers to answer questions such as the following: "Which product attributes are important or unimportant to the consumer?" "What levels of product attributes are the most or least desirable ones in the consumer's mind?" "What is the market share of preference for leading competitors' products versus our company's existing or proposed product?" Respondents are asked to make choices by trading off features, one against another (AMA, 1992). As a

RESEARCH BOX 22.1

Rosenthal, D. A., Chan, F. & Livneh, H. (2006). Rehabilitation students' attitudes towards persons with disabilities in high and low stakes social contexts: A conjoint analysis. *Disability and Rehabilitation, 28,* 1517–1527.

Objectives: This article sought to examine factors that influence the disability-related attitudes of undergraduate rehabilitation services students in two social contexts.

Method: The sample consisted of 99 student participants (23 male, 76 female) taking undergraduate courses in rehabilitation services. The participants' ages ranged from 18 to 61 years (M = 23.77 years, SD = 6.94). Participants sorted 55 stimulus cards in each of two groups, a high-stakes context group and a low-stakes context group. The high-stakes context consisted of a rehabilitation administrator hiring a counselor, and the low-stakes context consisted of preference for an individual as a mentor or companion.

Results: In the low-stakes group, age and disability type were the most influential in attitude preference. The youngest age group was more preferred than the oldest

age group. Also, disabilities regarded as more stable or predictable (e.g., orthopedic) were ranked higher than those regarded as uncertain such as HIV/AIDS. In the high-stakes group, performance and work experience contributed the most in terms of predicting participant attitudes.

Conclusion: Conjoint analysis can be used to explore factors that influence attitude preferences for persons with disabilities in different social contexts. This awareness, in turn, can be used to assist in developing interventions designed to change attitudes.

Questions

1. Given the results of this study, what other type of assessment intervention would you recommend for addressing the influence of age and disability type in low-stakes social contexts?

2. How would you account for the finding that only performance and work experience influenced participant attitudes in a high-stakes context and from an assessment perspective?

measurement technique, it provides an enhanced portrayal of the decision-making process of groups and of individuals, thus taking into account the balancing and weighing of combinations and interactions that exist among multiple factors. Respondents are usually told that the conjoint analysis is an attempt to understand their preferences concerning a given topic. The stimuli are presented in card format. Respondents then sort the cards according to their personal preference. The researchers then document the sequence of the sorted cards and can thereby infer the attitudes of the respondents toward the object.

Conjoint analysis as an attitude measure has been gradually leaving the realm of business. Researchers have used conjoint analysis in determining respondents' decision-making processes in public opinion (Shamir & Shamir, 1995) as well as fertility decisions (Nickerson & McClelland, 1988).

The bogus pipeline (Jones & Sigall, 1971) is different from the other disguised measures because respondents are told that their attitudes are being measured. However, respondents are told that they are being connected to a very sophisticated lie detector, whereas, the device, in fact, measures nothing. Thus, the respondents feel that they are compelled to communicate their actual attitudes toward a psychological object or they will otherwise be seen as untruthful. There is evidence that the bogus-pipeline can reduce social desirability bias (Quigley-Fernandez & Tedeschi, 1978).

IMPLICIT MEASURES OF ATTITUDE Like the bogus pipeline, implicit attitude instruments do not deceive the respondent concerning the purpose of the test. Rather, implicit attitude instruments measure attitude-related behaviors or reactions over which the respondent has little to no control. Although there have been a variety of implicit techniques developed, the most commonly used are generally physiological in nature or use a priming or response-latency approach (Ajzen, 2002, Fazio & Olson, 2003).

Physiological approaches such as heart rate, blood pressure, galvanic skin conductance, and pupil constriction (Petty & Cacioppo, 1983) are thought to measure a respondent's automatic physiological responses to attitude relevant stimuli. Unfortunately these instruments have demonstrated low reliability and validity for attitude measure because they primarily measure arousal, whether it is positive, negative, or otherwise (Ajzen & Fishbein, 2005). One of the more promising physiological techniques is the use of facial electromylography (EMG) (Ajzen, 2002). This measures the minute contractions of muscles in the respondent's face when he or she is provided with attitude pertinent stimuli, thus revealing the changes in affective state of the respondent (Petty & Cacioppo, 1983). A recent study involving identification of implicit racial attitudes toward African Americans has used facial EMG (Vanman, Paul, Ito, & Miller, 1997).

Another physiological method that is gaining interest in attitude measurement is the measure of respondent's startle eyeblink modulation when introduced to salient stimuli (see Bradley, Cuthbert, & Lang, 1999). This technique has been utilized as a measure of automatic attitude activation. Startle eyeblink modulation has been found to be related to lower scores on a self-report scale measuring motivation to respond without prejudice (Amodio, Harmon-Jones, & Devine, 2003).

With advances in medical technology, studies using neurological tests such as event-related potentials (Ito & Urland, 2003) and functional magnetic resonance imaging (Cunningham, Johnson, Gatenby, Gore, & Banaji, 2003; Hart et al., 2000; Phelps et al., 2000) to measure attitudinally relevant constructs are establishing a new line of neurosocial psychological research. However, the administration of any of these physiological tests is involved and takes considerable training, time, and money; thus, they are not practical for large-scale studies and are useful only in laboratory situations (Ajzen, 2002).

The bona-fide pipeline (Fazio, Jackson, Dunton, & Willliams, 1995) method uses deception and an unobtrusive priming by means of a computer task to measure automatically activated racial attitudes. In the original study, researchers reported evidence of automatically activated racial attitudes that were predictive of an African American target's ratings of the quality of interactions with each respondent. Respondents who had received negative racial priming behaved less friendly than those who did not receive the negative racial priming (Fazio et al, 1995).

The most popular method used to measure implicit attitudes is the Implicit Association Test (IAT: Greenwald, McGhee, & Schwartz, 1998). Like the title implies, the IAT measures the association of two target concepts (e.g., race, as represented by photos of European American faces and African American faces, and pleasantness, as represented by positively and negatively valenced words). The primary assumption behind the IAT is "...if two concepts are highly associated, the IAT's sorting tasks will be easier when the two associated concepts share the same response than when they require different responses" (Greenwald & Nosek, 2001,

p. 85). The most popular variant of this test is administered by computer. Respondents are required to make alternate associations between the concepts (e.g., African American + unpleasant and European American + pleasant followed by African American + pleasant and European American + unpleasant) and record their responses as quickly as possible by correctly pressing the appropriate computer key assigned to that particular association. The response-latency for each association is recorded. Differences in times between forced associations are then used as a measure of implicit attitude. For example, if it took longer for European American respondents to associate incongruent associations (positively valenced words with African American faces and negatively valenced words with European American faces) than congruent associations (negatively valenced words with African American faces and positively valenced words with European American faces), this would reflect a negative implicit bias against African Americans (see Greenwald et al.).

The computer IAT has been used to measure implicit bias among a variety of topics. Besides implicit racial attitudes as documented by Greenwald et al. (1998), the IAT has been used with a variety of social attitudes. For example, Rudman, Greenwald, Mellott, and Schwartz (1999) found evidence of underlying implicit prejudice based on religious ethnicity (Christian vs. Jewish), age (young vs. old), and nationality (American vs. Soviet). Participants were able to make more rapid responses associating favorable attributes with their specific ingroups and associating unfavorable attributes to the corresponding outgroup versus the complimentary associations.

Greenwald and Nosek (2001) reported that within 3 years of its introduction, the IAT had been used in over 30 published and in-press articles. Research into the convergent validity between the IAT and other indirect methods has generally found weak correlations (Cunningham, Preacher, & Banaji, 2001; Greenwald & Nosek). It has been suggested that the measurement error of various indirect methods is a strong confound to this type of research (Cunningham et al.; Yuker, 1994).

Although not as commonly used, a paper version of the IAT also exists. The basic format is similar to the computer-based IAT in that it still requires the respondents to associate two concepts; however, instead of measuring the response latency for each item, the paper version measures how many items can be correctly categorized within a specific length of time (usually 20 seconds). This paper IAT approach has been used to measure implicit attitudes concerning race (Lemm,

Sattler, Khan, Mitchell, & Dahl, 2002; Lowery, Hardin, & Sinclair, 2001), sexual orientation (Lemm 2000), and obesity (Teachman & Brownell, 2001; Teachman, Gapinski, Brownell, Rawlins, & Jeyaram, 2003).

SELF-REPORT INSTRUMENTS MEASURING ATTITUDES TOWARD PEOPLE WITH DISABILITIES There are many instruments that have been developed to measure attitudes toward people with disabilities. Antonak and Livneh (1988) provided excellent psychometric information on many instruments that measure disability-related attitudes. However, that text is nearly 20 years old, and has become quite dated. Sadly, it has not been updated. The following paragraphs provide a quick description of several instruments that measure attitudes toward people with disabilities that are still being used or were not included in the Antonak and Livneh text.

ATTITUDES TOWARD DISABLED PERSONS SCALE
The Attitudes Toward Disabled Persons (ATDP) scale is undoubtedly the most popular scale in measuring disability-related attitudes. It has a large body of research reflecting its reliability and validity (e.g., Yuker, Block & Campbell, 1960; Yuker, Block & Younng, 1966; Yuker & Block, 1986). The ATDP is a unidimensional, self-report scale that comes in three different forms: O, A, and B. Form O is the oldest and consists of 20 items, whereas Forms A and B were generated a few years later and consist of 30 items (Yuker & Block). It has been a popular scale among rehabilitation researchers. Yuker and Block documented over 200 studies that had used the ATDP. The instrument continues to be used in research, although the wording of the ATDP has been modified to person-first language in some recent studies (e.g., Pruett & Chan, 2006).

The ATDP uses a 6-point Likert-type scale to indicate individuals' agreement or disagreement with each item. The scale ranges from –3 ("I disagree very much") to +3 ("I agree very much."). Test-retest reliability of the ATDP form A has been reported to range from .68–.91 (interval of 5 months or less) with a median estimate of .79. The internal consistency of the ATDP form A has been considered acceptable, given reported Cronbach alphas ranging from .83 – .85 (Yuker & Block, 1986).

INTERACTIONS WITH DISABLED PERSONS SCALE
The Interactions with Disabled Person Scale (IDP; Gething, 1991, 1994) was developed in Australia. It was designed to measure social discomfort pertaining to interactions with persons who have a disability. It consists

of 20 items and uses a 6-point scale that is anchored by "agree very much" and "disagree very much." Like the ATDP, there is no neutral point. Gething (1991) reported significant correlations between the IDP and other scales of attitudes toward people with disabilities. Gething (1994) reported six factors in the scale: discomfort in social interaction, coping/succumbing framework, perceived level of information, vulnerability, and coping. There have been additional studies attempting to replicate these factors. MacLean and Gannon (1995) failed to find evidence of all six factors and proposed that only the first two factors be used. Forlin, Fogarty, and Carroll (1999) were able to replicate the six factors by means of a large subject pool from Australia and South Africa and confirmatory factor analysis. Loo (2001), however, was unable to replicate either the two- or the six-factor model of the IDP; whereas Thomas, Palmer, Coker-Juneau, & Williams (2003) found three factors using exploratory and confirmatory factor analysis.

ISSUES IN DISABILITY SCALE The Issues in Disability Scale (IDS; Makas, Finnerty-Fried, Sigafoos, & Reiss, 1988) was developed as a multidimensional self-report attitude scale, and was designed to assess attitudes across multiple situations and social distances (e.g., intimate social, nonintimate social, legal, educational). It consists of 55 items and uses a 7-point scale anchored by "strongly disagree" and "strongly agree." It does contain a neutral midpoint. Unfortunately this scale has not received much psychometric attention and has been used on only two peer-reviewed articles since it is publication nearly 20 years ago (Garske 1996, 2000; Garske & Thomas, 1990).

MODIFIED ISSUES IN DISABILITY SCALE The Modified Issues in Disability Scale (MIDS; Makas, 1985) is closely related to the IDS in that they share several items; however, it differs from the IDS in that a nonrandom group of people with disabilities selected the items that went into the development of the scale (Makas, 1991). Another difference is the MIDS was constructed as a unidimensional scale. It uses the same rating scale as the IDS. However, instead of 55 items, the original MIDS was comprised of 37 items. A group of people with disabilities modified the MIDS in 1994 when it underwent another review (Makas, 1994). Several items were totally removed, and some new items were inserted into this updated version. The number of items in the scale dropped from 37 to 33. Like the IDS, only a handful of peer-reviewed publications have used

the MIDS (Gibson, 2001; Granello & Wheaton, 2001; Pheiffer, Sam, Guinan, Ratliffe, Robinson, & Stodden, 2004), and none have used the revised version.

RELATIONSHIPS WITH DISABLED PERSONS SCALE The Relationships with Disabled Persons Scale (RDPS; Satcher & Gamble, 2002) was developed to measure affective responses to persons with disabilities. Respondents are instructed to write down the first type of disability that comes to their mind when the word "disability" is spoken. With this particular disability in mind, respondents are asked to rate their level of comfort using a 6-point scale pertaining to five different interpersonal situations with persons with disabilities. These situations increase in level of intimacy from casual to marriage.

MULTIDIMENSIONAL ATTITUDES SCALE TOWARD PERSONS WITH DISABILITIES Recently the Multidimensional Attitudes Scale Toward Persons with Disabilities (MAS; Findler, Vilchinsky, & Werner, 2007) was developed. The dimensions of the scale follow the tripartite model of attitudes: affect, cognition, and behavior. Participants are presented with a vignette and then are asked to respond to 34 items using a 5-point degree of likelihood scale with anchors of "not at all" and "very much."

FRAGEBOGEN ZUR EISTELLUNG GEGNÜBER KÖRPERBEHINDERTEN When researchers wish to measure attitudes of non-English speaking respondents, they frequently translate an English language scale into the different languages. However, there are scales to measure attitudes toward people with disabilities that have been developed in other languages. One example of this is the Fragebogen zur Eistellung gegnüber Körperbehinderten (EKB; "Questionnaire about Attitudes toward the Physically Disabled") by Seifert and Bergmann (1983). It contains 38 negatively valenced statements concerning people with disabilities. Respondents use a 7-point Likert-type scale anchored by "totally disagree" to "totally agree." The EKB is multidimensional and addresses feelings of unease and uncertainty in interactions with people who have a physical disability; reduced competency and functioning; poor social adaptability and emotional instability; and also reports a rejection of integration of people with disabilities (supporting segregation) in society.

We have attempted to discuss some of the most recent instruments as well as the venerable ATDP scale.

Please note that there are many other self-report instruments, such as the Disability Factors Scale (DFS; Siller, Ferguson, Vann, & Holland, 1967), Disability Social Distance Scale (DSDS; Tringo, 1970), and Scale of Attitudes Toward Disabled Persons (SADP; Antonak 1981, 1982), which have been developed over the years. For more information concerning these older scales (and others) see Antonak and Livneh (1988).

Indirect, Implicit, or Disguised Methods of Measuring Attitudes Toward People with Disabilities

One of the major difficulties with self-report instruments is that respondents may not wish to share their opinions or feelings. The subject matter may be too sensitive or politically heated for someone to provide an honest answer. It is for these reasons social scientists have developed indirect or disguised methods to measure attitudes. Indirect measures of attitudes generally avoid a self-report technique. Instead, they employ a variety of data collection techniques such as unobtrusive behavioral observations or nonreactive measures (Webb, Campbell, Schwartz, & Sechrest, 1966; Webb, Campbell, Schwartz, Sechrest, & Grove, 1981). For example, Kleck, Ono, and Hastorf (1966) used an experimental design that consisted of an undergraduate student being greeted by one of two confederates—either a person using a wheelchair or a person without an obvious disability. They found participants generally spent less time with the person with a disability and behaved in a more stereotypical manner than with the confederate without a disability. Other indirect methods of measuring attitudes have included projective methods (e.g., the Rorschach); disguised methods (e.g., error—choice); and physiological data (Antonak & Livneh, 1995, 2000; Livneh & Antonak, 1994).

There has been very limited research into the measurement of automatic, unconscious attitudes toward people with disabilities. Most of this research has used physiological methodology and has suggested that there are some different results than those found with direct self-report instruments (Antonak & Livneh, 1988). The galvanic skin response (GSR) measures the amount of electrical conductance in the skin. Increased sympathetic nervous system activity results in sweat gland activity, thus promoting the level of electrical conductance of the skin (Fuller, 1977). GSR has been considered as a measure of attitudes for many years (e.g., Abel, 1930) and has been found to be useful in measuring racial prejudicial attitudes (Cooper, 1959). Zych and Bolton (1972) used GSR in conjunction with the ATDP form B. They found

no difference between skin conductance and ATDP scores when individuals were viewing a photograph of an individual with no disability, but did find significant differences in skin conductance between high ATDP and low ATDP groups when respondents were viewing the photo of a person with a disability. Wesolowski and Deichmann (1980) used GSR and heart rate to measure respondents' reactions to three different photographic scenes (people with no disability, people with a visible disability, and neutral scenery). They were able to use the physiological measures to discriminate between photographic scenes. Heart rate has also been used to measure state anxiety of respondents' interactions with people with a visible disability and was found to correlate with Disability Factors Scale – Cosmetic scores (Marinelli & Kelz, 1973). Voice modulations as measured by a psychological stress evaluator (PSE) have also been used to ascertain respondents' level of stress when interacting with people with disabilities (Vander Kolk, 1976). Increased stress among respondents was identified when interacting with people with disabilities. Additionally, a discrepancy was found between respondents' desirability of disability rankings and the PSE scores. These techniques have been useful in bypassing the response bias validity threat, but have been criticized for a lack of reliability and psychometric validation (Yuker, 1994).

There have been a series of studies using error–choice methodology (e.g., Antonak, 1994; Antonak & Livneh, 1995; Byon, 2000; Clarke & Crewe, 2000), and conjoint analysis (e.g., Tsang, Chan, & Chan, 2004; Wang, Thomas, Chan, & Cheing, 2003; Wong et al., 2004) to measure various disability-related attitudes.

Recently Pruett and Chan (2006) developed a paper and pencil IAT that measures implicit attitudes of rehabilitation counseling students toward persons with disabilities. They found rehabilitation counseling students more easily associated negatively valenced words than positively valenced words with images of persons with physical disabilities.

RESEARCH CRITICAL TO ISSUES IN ATTITUDES ASSESSMENT

There are several issues that are important in assessment of attitudes toward persons with disabilities. First, it is important to obtain a true attitude in an applied environment. Attitudes do not exist in a vacuum. They exist in the context of time, relationship, and place. Measuring the true feelings and beliefs of people in the world in which they live is critical to understanding how attitudes toward persons with disabilities develop and change. Secondly, it is important to understand how people with disabilities understand how they are being perceived in society and in certain situations. How do they perceive negative attitudes, and how do these attitudes affect their lives? Another area of interest is the relationship of positive psychology constructs, such as hope and gratitude, to attitudes toward persons with disabilities.

There have been great strides in the development of theory of attitudes by social psychologists over the past several decades. The new understandings of automatic activation of attitudes, implicit attitudes, and theories relating attitudes to behaviors are truly exciting. The study of disability-related attitudes needs to embrace these theories and develop psychometrically sound instruments using modern test theory, as well as conduct social experiments to gain greater understanding about strength and malleability of attitudes toward persons with disabilities in the societies of the present day.

It would behoove rehabilitation and health care researchers to adopt a model of functioning that includes individual and societal attitudes such as the *International Classification of Functioning* (World Health Organization, 2001). This would allow for greater understanding of environmental factors on individual's functioning and changes in functioning.

CULTURAL, LEGISLATIVE, AND PROFESSIONAL ISSUES THAT IMPACT SPECIFIC COUNSELING ASPECTS OR PROCEDURES

There have been many studies examining attitudes toward people with disabilities from various cultures (e.g., Byon; 2000; Chan, Lee, Yuen, & Chan, 2002; Chen, Brodwin, Cardoso, & Chan, 2002; Horner-Johnson et al., 2002; Lau & Cheung, 1999; Wang, 1998). The study of differences among cultures is a popular topic in studies of attitudes toward people with disabilities. For example Wang, Thomas, Chan, and Cheing (2003) conducted an attitude study using participants in the United States and in Taiwan. He found that younger and more highly educated females with milder disabilities were preferred by the male and female Taiwanese groups as well as the female American group. Additionally individuals with physical disabilities were preferred by the male and female Taiwanese groups, whereas persons with developmental disabilities were preferred by the female American group.

Similarly Peltzer, Cherian, and Cherian (2001) studied the attitudes of South African and Indian university students toward people with disabilities. They found that the South African students had a more favorable attitude toward people with disabilities than the Indian students. Additionally they found more positive attitudes toward individuals with physical disabilities over psychiatric disabilities.

Policy and Legislative Issues

While the U.S. Government cannot legislate how people think, it has passed legislation to promote equity for people with disabilities. The most sweeping law involving people with disabilities is the Americans with Disabilities Act of 1990. This law required the federal government and public entities to make their facilities accessible and prohibited employment discrimination based on disability. Likewise, the Health Insurance Portability and Accountability Act of 1996 requires all health care providers and insurance carriers to protect the privacy of patients' medical and personal information. Although the federal government has not passed a patients bill of rights law, the Association of American Physicians and Surgeons adopted a patient's bill of rights in 1995. This bill of rights provides patients with several assurances; among them are that they will be treated with confidentiality, be informed about choices in medical treatment as well as be allowed to refuse treatment (Association of American Physicians and Surgeons, 1995). The Hate Crime Statistics Act included disability as a protected class in 1996. The act requires the federal government to collect data on crimes where the victim was chosen because of his/her membership in one of the following groups: race, ethnicity, sexual orientation, religion, and now disability (McMahon, West, Lewis, Armstrong, & Conway, 2004). The inclusion of disability in 1996 over other groups lobbying for inclusion such as gender and the elderly is further recognition of the inequality of persons with disabilities and the need to affirm their basic civil rights when necessary.

Ethical Codes

Most all professional ethical codes of conduct include a clause not to discriminate against a client or patient for many reasons such as gender, ethnic origin, sexual orientation as well as disability. Some codes such as those for the Certified Rehabilitation Counselors (Commission on Rehabilitation Counselor Certification, 2001) and Certified Psychiatric Rehabilitation Practitioners (International Association of Psychosocial Rehabilitation Services, 2001) include a clause for advocacy.

MULTICULTURAL OR INTERDISCIPLINARY APPROACHES

Measurement of Professionals' Disability-Related Attitudes

Studies of attitudes of health professional students and related health professionals toward persons who have a disability have produced contradictory results, some finding favorable attitudes and others reporting unfavorable attitudes (Brodwin & Orange, 2002; Chubon, 1982; Cook, 1998). Positive attitudes of beginning rehabilitation counseling students were reported by Garske and Thomas (1990). The students' mean scores on the Issues in Disability Scale were similar to the mean positive scores reported by Makas et al. (1988) in the standardization of the instrument. Estes et al. (1991) found that occupational therapy students reflected a more positive attitude toward people with disabilities than medical technology students, as reflected by ATDP scores. In another study using the ATDP, rehabilitation service majors were found to have more positive attitudes toward people with disabilities than business majors (Hunt & Hunt, 2000). However, research has also shown little to no difference in disability-related attitudes between a health professional group and a nonhealth professional group as reported by Lyons (1991). In this study, occupational therapy students' attitudes, as measured by the ATDP, did not differ from business students. In another study of attitudes between Chinese occupational therapy and business students, Chan et al. (2002) found that both first-year occupational therapy and business students had similar attitudes, but noted differences in trends of attitudinal change. Occupational therapy students at the end of the first year of studies had significantly more positive disability-related attitudes, whereas the business students grew more negative. It was concluded that the positive attitudinal change in the occupational therapy students was a result of the academic studies in a clinical program. Rehabilitation counselors have been found to possess more negative perceptions concerning the employability of individuals with mental retardation than employers (Byrd, Byrd, & Emener, 1977). A comprehensive review of the rehabilitation research literature by Cook (1998) concluded that rehabilitation professionals have similar dispositions toward prejudiced bias as the population at large. He postulated that detrimental factors such ineffectiveness, fears, and negative experiences on the part of the counselor may contribute to these attitudes. Wong, Chan, Cardoso, Lam, and Miller (2004) used a conjoint analysis technique to examine the factors that contribute to the attitudes and the formation of attitudes toward people with disabilities of rehabilitation counseling students. The type of disability, education, age, and ethnicity of people with disabilities were all found to contribute to attitude formation and preference of rehabilitation counseling students despite various social contexts (Wong et al.).

Besides disability-related attitudes, research has examined the negative attitudes toward other groups. Kaplan and Thomas (1981) found evidence among rehabilitation counseling students of an antifat bias when assessing clients. More current research by Teachman and colleagues (Teachman et al., 2003; Teachman & Brownell, 2001), has identified implicit negative attitudes toward people who are obese among health care professionals. Rosenthal and Berven (1999) documented a racial bias among European American rehabilitation counseling students by means of an analog study.

DISCUSSION BOX 22.1

Research on the disability-related attitudes of health professionals has yielded contradictory results. Some studies have found that rehabilitation professionals possess negative attitudes similar to nonhealth professionals, such as business students; whereas, other studies report more positive attitudes. Other studies found no difference between health and nonhealth professionals, but noted a difference in the trend of attitude change with occupational therapy students forming more positive attitudes over time. Studies of practicing rehabilitation professionals have shown they may have a negative bias similar to the general population and, in some instances, may have more negative attitudes toward the employment of persons with disabilities than employers. Think about your profession and the organizational culture where you work or intend to work.

Questions

1. What factors in that environment could facilitate forming negative or positive attitudes toward clients?
2. How best may those attitudes be measured?
3. How can you account for the contradictory findings in studies on disability-related attitudes among professionals?

Two groups of white students examined two hypothetical rehabilitation cases that were identical with the sole exception of the race of the client. The African American client was perceived to have a higher degree of mental illness with lower potential for education and employment than did the European American client. Because all of the case information was the same, with the notable exception of race, the differences between groups of respondents were concluded to be a result of racial bias.

Summary and Conclusion

Allport regarded attitudes to be distinct and indispensable to social psychology. Over 500 definitions of attitude have been reported in the literature since its conception in the 1800s. However varied the definitions are, the common thread to them all is the belief that an attitude is an evaluation and the evaluation is strongly influenced by emotion. In addition to emotion, cognition and behavior were common components of attitude definitions. Moreover, the belief that individual attitudes dictate behavior was accepted by early attitude scientists as axiomatic.

The function of attitudes and the mechanism for attitude change has been and will probably continue to be the focus of attitude researchers for some time. Although the earlier definitions of attitude, including behavior, were criticized and regarded as inaccurate, researchers have continued to explore the relationship between the two. Although the predictive power of attitudes is not strong, research has shown that awareness of one's own attitude, the setting of a personal goal to not respond with prejudice, and the motivation to engage in a rational evaluation of alternatives is predictive of behavior. Attitude change has also received much attention in the literature. Research has shown that individuals who have a high internal motivation coupled with a low external motivation respond without prejudice; recollection, recall or pertinent information, comparison of previously held attitudes, and interpersonal contact between groups can change attitudes.

Instruments that measure attitudes are as complex and varied as the constructs they measure. Scales that measure attitudes are categorized as explicit measures, disguised measures, and implicit measures. Explicit measures query participants' feelings, beliefs, or opinions regarding an attitudinal object and operate from the belief that the easiest way to discover an individual's evaluation of an object or topic is to ask them directly. Disguised measures employ the use of deception in order to control for response bias such as social desirability. Implicit measures employ attitude-related behaviors or reactions over which the respondent has little to no control to discover an individual's evaluation.

The measurement of attitudes is critical to understanding the environment in which people with disabilities live. Moreover, attitude measures help us understand how people with disabilities react to the attitude-laden environment. The importantce of this research was realized and prolific through the 1970s and 1980s. However, recent advancements in the theory of attitudes by social psychologists since that time has created an opportunity to modernize the tools used to measure attitudes toward people with disabilities and, as the ultimate goal is to change attitudes in a positive direction, updated instruments function to measure attitude change.

Self-Check Questions

1. What is the history of research and practice in the assessment of attitudes?
2. What is the International Classification of Functioning, Disability and Health? What role do societal attitudes play and how is attitude measured?
3. What is the difference between implicit and explicit attitude measures?
4. Create a table with at least two columns, one for implicit measures and the other for explicit measures. Then list the different measures, describe how each is performed, and provide benefits and disadvantages for each measure.
5. What are the benefits and limitations of implicit and explicit attitude measures?
6. Create a table and list the self-report attitude measures in the chapter. Then, create columns for important information such as number of items, research on the scale, alternate forms, reliability and validity data, and scale type, to name a few.
7. What are the weaknesses and strengths of physiological approaches to measure attitudes? Explain the circumstances when a practitioner would choose to use a physiological approach.
8. Describe and discuss the research on the assessment of attitudes across different cultures and disciplines.
9. Describe two pieces of public policy and/or legislation. How can its impact on attitude be measured?

Case Study

Marcus is a 19-year-old male who sustained a moderate-to-severe traumatic brain injury secondary to a motor vehicle accident. Marcus was intoxicated at the time of the accident, although he has not been charged with the accident. He currently receives outpatient speech therapy, occupational therapy, and physical therapy at the local rehabilitation hospital 5 days a week. In addition, he is working with vocational rehabilitation, which is waiting for him to complete his therapy before ordering a Vocational Work Evaluation to establish a vocational goal.

At the time of the accident, Marcus was unemployed and living at home with his parents. He has worked at a number of fast-food restaurants, but is typically released before the end of the probationary period for excessive absenteeism. The speech and language pathologist (SLP) has been working with Marcus for about 2 weeks. She is working with him to develop compensatory strategies for deficits in attention/concentration, information processing, and memory.

Marcus ambulates independently. He has never missed an appointment and has expressed motivation to excel in his therapy so he can participate in vocational rehabilitation. His expressed desire, in therapy, is to attend a local community college and study to become an electrician. Marcus's parents are anxious about the peers with whom he is friendly. Otherwise, they are very supportive and are happy that Marcus appears motivated to participate in therapy and vocational rehabilitation.

After two weeks of therapy, Yvonne, the SLP, decided to terminate Marcus's therapy, stating that he had failed to make progress in his sessions and alluded to some noncompliance issues. The supervisor checked with the OT and PT and learned he was progressing well in his other therapies. Further exploration showed discrepancies in cognitive functioning between the SLP and consulting psychologist reports. The supervisor met with Yvonne to discuss his lack of progress, and then met with Marcus to evaluate his acquisition of compensatory strategies. The supervisor concluded that Marcus had made progress in his therapy, but it appeared he was

avoiding Yvonne because he sensed that she didn't like him. The supervisor transferred Marcus to another SLP. The supervisor noted this was the third case where Yvonne had moved to discharge a patient because of lack of progress when the client was making progress in his/her treatment. The supervisor reviewed the case files and observed that in each of the three cases, the patient was intoxicated at the time of the accident.

The supervisor met with Yvonne and discussed her findings. Moreover, she encouraged Yvonne to take a disability-related attitude survey to determine the cause of her denying some patients access to SLP care. After an interview and attitude survey, it was determined that Yvonne did have a negative attitude toward individuals who consumed alcohol and operated a motor vehicle under the influence. Moreover, Yvonne's brother was killed by a drunk driver 5 years ago. The supervisor told Yvonne that she must develop a plan for addressing her negative attitude and present it to her in 2 days.

Yvonne recalled that some of her co-workers had confronted her on the possibility of this a few months previous to the incident with Marcus. She apparently feels bad about the incident with Marcus and the other patients. Yvonne develops an intervention for addressing her negative attitudes and the apparent influence they have had on her behavior. She approaches you as her co-worker to help her identify a way to measure the impact the intervention has had on her attitudes.

QUESTIONS

How would you recommend to Yvonne that she measure her attitude? Support your answer with information on whichever measure you choose. Consider the type of technique you are recommending in terms of strengths and weaknesses. Also consider the reliability and validity statistics of the instrument(s) you choose. Also consider available resources and personnel to assist with your recommendation.

References

Abel, T. M. (1930). Attitudes and the galvanic skin reflex. *Journal of Experimental Psychology, 13*, 47–60.

Ajzen, I. (1988). *Attitudes, personality, and behavior.* Chicago: Dorsey Press.

Ajzen, I. (1991). The theory of planned behavior. *Organizational Behavior and Human Decision Processes, 50*, 179–211.

Ajzen, I. (1996). The directive influence of attitudes on behavior. In P. M. Gollwitzer & J. A. Bargh (Eds.), *The psychology of action: Linking cognition and motivation to behavior* (pp. 385–403). New York: Guilford.

Ajzen, I. (2001). Nature and operation of attitudes. *Annual Review of Psychology, 52*, 27–58.

Ajzen, I. (2002). Attitudes. In R. Fernandez Ballestereos (Ed.), *Encyclopedia of psychological assessment* (Vol. 1, pp. 110–115). London: Sage.

Ajzen, I., & Fishbein, M. (1980). *Understanding attitudes and predicting social behavior.* Englewood Cliffs, NJ: Prentice-Hall.

Ajzen, I., & Fishbein, M. (2000). Attitudes and the attitude-behavior relation: Reasoned and automatic processes. In W. Stroebe & M. Hewstone (Eds.), *European Review of Social Psychology* (pp. 1–33). New York: John Wiley & Sons.

Ajzen, I., & Fishbein, M. (2005). The influence of attitudes on behavior. In D. Albarracín, B. T. Johnson, & M. P. Zanna (Eds.), *Handbook of attitudes and attitude change: Basic principles* (pp. 173–221). Mahwah, NJ: Erlbaum.

Albarracín, D., Zanna, M. P., Johnson, B. T., & Kumkale, G. T. (2005). Attitudes: Introduction and scope. In D. Albarracín, B.T. Johnson, & M. P. Zanna (Eds.). *The Handbook of Attitudes* (pp. 3–19). Mahway, NJ: Erlbaum.

Allport, G. W. (1935). Attitudes. In C. Murchison (Ed.), *Handbook of social psychology* (pp. 798–884). Worcester, MA: Clark University Press.

Allport, G. W. (1968). The historical background of modern social psychology. In G. Lindzey & E. Aronson (Eds.), *Handbook of social psychology* (Vol. 1, pp. 1–80). Reading, MA: Addison-Wesley.

Altman, B. M. (1981). Studies of attitudes toward the handicapped: The need for a new direction. *Social Problems, 28*, 321–337.

American Marketing Association (1992). *Conjoint analysis: A guide for designing and interpreting conjoint studies.* Chicago: American Marketing Association.

Americans With Disabilities Act of 1990, 42 U.S.C.A. § 12101 et seq. (West 1993).

Amodio, D. M., Harmon-Jones, E. & Devine, P. G. (2003). Individual differences in the activation and control of affective race bias as assessed by startle eyeblink response and self-report. *Journal of Personality and Social Psychology, 84,* 738–753.

Antonak R. F. (1981) *Development and psychometric analysis of the Scale of Attitudes Toward Disabled Persons* (Technical Report No. 1). Durham: University of New Hampshire, Education Department.

Antonak, R.F. (1982). Development and psychometric analysis of the Scale of Attitudes Toward Disabled Persons. *Journal of Applied Rehabilitation Counseling, 13*(2), 22–29.

Antonak, R. F. (1994). Development and psychometric analysis of an indirect measure of attitudes towards individuals with mental retardation using the error-choice method. *Mental Retardation, 32*, 347–355.

Antonak, R. F., & Livneh, H. (1988). *The measurement of attitudes toward people with disabilities: Methods, psychometrics and scales.* Springfield, IL: Charles C. Thomas.

Antonak, R. F., & Livneh, H. (1995). Direct and indirect methods to measure attitudes toward persons with disabilities, with an exegesis of the Error-Choice test method. *Rehabilitation Psychology, 40*, 3–24.

Antonak, R. F., & Livneh, H. (2000). Measurement of attitudes toward persons with disabilities. *Disability and Rehabilitation, 22*, 211–224.

Aronson, E., Wilson, T. D., & Akert, R. M. (1997). *Social psychology* (2nd ed.). New York: Addison Wesley Longman.

Association of American Physicians and Surgeons (1995). *Patient's Bill of Rights.* Tucson, AZ: Author.

Bain, A. (1868). *Mental science.* New York: Appleton.

Beattie, J. F., Anderson, R. J., & Antonak, R. F. (1997). Modifying attitudes of prospective educators toward students with disabilities and their integration into regular classrooms. *Journal of Psychology, 131*, 245–259.

Benham, P. K. (1988). Attitudes of occupational therapy personnel toward persons with disabilities. *American Journal of Occupational Therapy, 42*, 305–311.

Bradley, M. M., Cuthbert, B. N., & Lang, P. J. (1999). Affect and the startle reflex. In M. E. Dawson, A. M. Schell, & A. H. Böhmelt (Eds.), *Startle modification: Implications for neuroscience, cognitive science and clinical science* (pp. 157–183). New York: Cambridge University Press.

Breckler, S. J. (1984). Empirical validation of affect, behavior, and cognition as distinct components of attitude. *Journal of Personality and Social Psychology, 47*, 1191–1205.

Breckler, S. J., & Wiggins, E. C. (1989). Affect versus evaluation in the structure of attitudes. *Journal of Experimental Social Psychology, 25*, 253–271.

Brodwin, M. G., & Orange, L. M. (2002). Attitudes toward disability. In J. D. Andrew & C. W. Faubion (Eds.), *Rehabilitation services: An introduction for the human service professional* (pp. 174–197). Osage Beach, MO: Aspen Professional Services.

Byon, K. H. (2000). A psychometric validation of direct and indirect attitude measurements toward people with mental retardation in Korea. *Dissertation Abstracts International, 61* (08), 3117 (UMI No. 9983734).

Byrd, E. K., Byrd, P. D., & Emener, W. G. (1977). Students, counselors, and employer perceptions of severely retarded. *Rehabilitation Literature, 38*, 43–44.

Chan, C. C. H., Lee, T. M. C., Yuen, H. K., & Chan, F. (2002). Attitudes toward people with disabilities between Chinese Rehabilitation and Business Students – An implication for practice. *Rehabilitation Psychology, 47*, 324–338.

Chan, F., McMahon, B.T., Cheing, G., Rosenthal, D. A., & Bezyak, J. (2005). Drivers of workplace discrimination against people with disabilities: The utility of Attribution Theory. *Work, 25*, 77–88.

Chan, F., Wang, M. H., Thomas, K. R., Wong, D., Chan, C. C. H., Lee, G., & Lui, K. (2002). Conjoint analysis in rehabilitation counseling research. *Rehabilitation Education, 16*, 179–195.

Chen, R. K., Brodwin, M. G., Cardoso, E., & Chan, F. (2002). Attitudes toward people with disabilities in the social context of dating and marriage: A comparison of American, Taiwanese, and Singaporean college students. *Journal of Rehabilitation, 68*(4), 5–11.

Chubon, R. A. (1982). An analysis of research dealing with attitudes of professionals toward disability. *Journal of Rehabilitation, 48*(1), 25–30.

Clarke, N. E., & Crewe, N. M. (2000). Stakeholder attitudes toward ADA Title I: Development of an indirect measurement method. *Rehabilitation Counseling Bulletin, 43,* 58–65.

Commission on Rehabilitation Counselor Certification (2001). *Code of Professional Ethics for Rehabilitation Counselors.* Rolling Meadows, IL: Author.

Cook, D. (1998). Psychosocial impact of disability. In R. M. Parker & E. M. Szymanski (Eds.), *Rehabilitation counseling: Basics and beyond* (3rd ed., pp. 303–326). Austin, TX: PRO-ED.

Coombs, C. H. (1964). *A theory of data.* New York: John Wiley and Sons.

Cooper, J. B. (1959). Emotions in prejudice. *Science, 130,* 314–318.

Cunningham, W. A., Johnson, M. K., Gatenby, J. C., Gore, J. C., & Banaji, M. R. (2003). Neural components of social evaluation. *Journal of Personality and Social Psychology*, 85, 639–649.

Cunningham, W. A., Preacher, K. J., & Banaji, M. R. (2001). Implicit attitude measures: Consistency, stability, and convergent validity. *Psychological Science, 12,* 163–170.

Devine, P. G. (1989). Stereotype and prejudice: Their automatic and controlled components. *Journal of Personality and Social Psychology, 56,* 5–18.

Eagly, A. H., & Chaiken, S. (1998). Attitude structure and function. In D. T. Gilbert & S. K. Fiske (Eds.), *The Handbook of Social Psychology* (4th ed., Vol. 2, pp. 269–322). Boston: McGraw-Hill.

Edwards, A. L. (1953). The relationship between the judged desirability of a trait and the probability that the trait will be endorsed. *Journal of Applied Psychology, 37,* 90–93.

English, H. B., & English, A. C. (1958). *A comprehensive dictionary of psychological and psychoanalytic terms: A guide to usage.* New York: McKay.

Estes, J., Deyer, C. A., Hansen, R. A., & Russell, J. C. (1991). Influence of occupational therapy curricula on students' attitudes toward persons with disabilities. *The American Journal of Occupational Therapy, 45*(2), 156–158.

Fazio, R. H., Jackson, J. R., Dunton, B. C., & Williams, C. J. (1995). Variability in automatic activation as an unobtrusive measure of racial attitudes: A bona fide pipeline? *Journal of Personality and Social Psychology, 69,* 1013–1027.

Fazio, R. H., & Olson (2003). Implicit measures in social cognition research: Their meaning and uses. A*nnual Review of Psychology, 54,* 297–327.

Fazio, R. H., Sambonmatsu, D. M., Powell, M. C., & Kardes, F. R. (1986). On the automatic activation of attitudes. *Journal of Personality and Social Psychology, 50,* 229–238.

Feinberg, L. B. (1967). Social desirability and attitudes toward the disabled. *Personnel and Guidance Journal, 46,* 375–381.

Findler, L., Vilchinsky, N., & Werner, S. (2007). The Multidimensional Attitudes Scale Toward Persons with Disabilities (MAS): Construct and validation. *Rehabilitation Counseling Bulletin, 50,* 166–176.

Fishbein, M., & Ajzen, I. (1975). *Belief, attitude, intention and behavior: An introduction to theory and research.* Reading, MA: Addison-Wesley.

Forlin, C., Fogarty, G., & Carroll, A. (1999). Validation of the factor structure of the Interaction with Disabled Person Scale. *Australian Journal of Psychology, 51,* 50–55.

Fouts, B. S., Andresen, E., & Hagglund, K. (2000). Disabilty and satisifaction with access to health care. *Journal of Epidemiology & Community Health, 54,* 770–771.

Frank, R., & Elliott, T. (2002). *Handbook of rehabilitation psychology.* Washington, DC: American Psychological Association.

Fuller, G. D. (1977). *Biofeedback: Methods and procedures in clinical practice.* San Francisco: Biofeedback Institution.

Garske, G. G. (1996). The relationship of self-esteem to attitudes of personal attendants toward persons with disabilities. *Journal of Applied Rehabilitation Counseling, 27*(1), 3–6.

Garske, G. G. (2000). The significance of rehabilitation counselor job satisfaction. *Journal of Applied Rehabilitation Counseling, 31*(3), 10–13.

Garske, G. G., & Thomas, K. R. (1990). The relationship of self-esteem and contact to attitudes of students in rehabilitation counseling toward people with disabilities. *Rehabilitation Counseling Bulletin, 34,* 67–71.

Gething, L. (1991). *Interaction with Disabled Persons Scale: Manual and kit.* Sydney, Australia: University of Sydney.

Gething, L. (1994). The interaction with disabled persons scale. *Journal of Social Behavior and Personality, 9*(5), 23–42.

Gibson, B. (2001). Long-term ventilation for patients with Duchenne Muscular Dystrophy: Physicians' beliefs and practices. *Chest, 119,* 940–946.

Gough, H. G. (1960). The Adjective Check List as a personality assessment research scale. *Psychological Reports, 6,* 107–122.

Granello, D. H., & Wheaton, J. E. (2001). Attitudes of undergraduate students toward persons with physical disabilities and mental illnesses. *Journal of Applied Rehabilitation Counseling, 32*(3), 9–16.

Greenberg, B. C., Abdula, A. L., Simmons, W. L., & Horvitz, D. G. (1969). The unrelated question in randomized response model, theoretical framework. *Journal of the American Statistical Association, 64,* 520–539.

Greenwald, A. G. (1989). Why are attitudes important? In A. R. Pratkanis, S. J. Breckler, & A. G. Greenwald (Eds.). *Attitude structure and function* (pp. 1–10). Hillsdale, NJ: Erlbaum.

Greenwald, A. G. (1990). What cognitive representations underlie social attitudes? *Bulletin of the Psychonomic Society, 28*, 254–260.

Greenwald, A. G., & Banaji, M. R. (1995). Implicit social cognition: Attitudes, self-esteem, and stereotypes. *Psychological Review, 102*, 4–27.

Greenwald, A. G., Banaji, M. R., Rudman, L. A., Farnham, S. D., Nosek, B. A., & Mellott, D. S. (2002). A unified theory of implicit attitudes, stereotypes, self-esteem, and self-concept. *Psychological Review, 109*, 3–25.

Greenwald, A. G., McGhee, D. E., & Schwartz, J. L. K. (1998). Measuring individual differences in implicit cognition: The implicit association test. *Journal of Personality and Social Psychology, 74*, 1464–1480.

Greenwald, A. G., & Nosek, B. A. (2001). Health of the Implicit Association Test at age 3. *Zeitschrift für Experimentelle Psychologie, 48*, 85–93.

Guttman, L. (1944). A basis for scaling qualitative data. *American Sociological Review, 9*, 139–150.

Guttman, L. (1947). The Cornell technique of scale and intensity analysis. *Educational and Psychological Measurement, 7*, 247–280.

Guttman, L. (1950). The basis for scalogram analysis. In S. A. Stouffer, L. Guttman, E. A. Suchman, P. F. Lazarsfeld, S. A. Star, & J. A. Clausen (Eds.), *Measurement and prediction* (pp. 60–90). New York: John Wiley and Sons.

Hammond, K. R. (1948). Measuring attitudes by error choice: An indirect method. *Journal of Abnormal and Social Psychology, 43*, 38–48.

Hart, A. J., Whalen, P. J., Shin, L. M., McInerney, S. C., Fisher, H. & Rausch, S. L. (2000). Differential response in the human amygdala to racial outgroup vs ingroup face stimuli. *Neuroreport, 11*, 2351–2355.

Health Insurance Portability and Accountability Act of 1996, Public Law No. 104–191, 110 Statute 1936 (1996).

Horner-Johnson, W., Keys, C., Henry, D., Yamaki, K., Oi, F., Watanabe, K, Shimada, H., & Fugimura, I. (2002). Attitudes of Japanese students toward people with intellectual disability. *Journal of Intellectual Disability Research, 46*, 365–378.

Hunt, B., & Hunt, C. S. (2000). Attitudes toward people with disabilities: A comparison of undergraduate rehabilitation and business major. *Rehabilitation Education, 14*, 269–283.

International Association of Psychosocial Rehabilitation Services (2001). *Code of ethics for psychiatric rehabilitation professionals*. Linthicum, MD: Author.

Ito, T. A., & Urland, G. R. (2003). Race and gender on the brain: Electrocortical measures of attention to the race and gender of multiply categorizable individuals. *Journal of Personality and Social Psychology, 85*, 616–626.

Jones, E. E., & Sigall, H. (1971). The bogus pipeline: A new paradigm for measuring affect and attitude. *Psychological Bulletin, 76*, 349–364.

Kaplan, S. P., & Thomas, K. R. (1981). Rehabilitation counseling student perceptions of obese clients. *Rehabilitation Counseling Bulletin, 25*, 106–109.

Katz, D. (1960). The functional approach to the study of attitudes. *Public Opinion Quarterly, 24*, 163–205.

Katz, D., & Stotland, E. (1959). A preliminary statement to a theory of attitude structure and change. In S. Koch (Ed.), *Psychology: A Study of a Science* (Vol. 3, pp. 423–475). New York: McGraw-Hill.

Kleck, R., Ono, H., & Hastorf, A. H. (1966). The effects of physical deviance upon face-to-face interactions, *Human Relations, 19*, 425–436.

Knudson, D. D., Pope, H., & Irish, D. P. (1967). Response differences to questions on sexual standards. *Public Opinion Quarterly, 31*, 290–297.

Lau, J., T-f., & Cheung, C-k. (1999). Discriminatory attitudes to people with intellectual disability or mental health difficulty. *International Social Work, 42*, 431–444.

Lemm, K. (2000). *Personal and social motivation to respond without prejudice: Implications for implicit and explicit attitude and behavior.* Unpublished doctoral dissertation, Yale University, New Haven, CT.

Lemm, K, Sattler, D. N., Khan, S., Mitchell, R. A., & Dahl, J. (2002). Reliability and validity of a paper-based implicit association test. Poster presented at the 2002 conference for the Society of Personality and Social Psychology. Savannah, GA. February 2, 2002.

Lenski, G. E., & Leggett, J. C. (1960). Caste, class and deference in the research interview. *American Journal of Sociology, 65*, 463–467.

Leventhal, E. A., Hansell, S., Diefenbach, M., Leventhal, H., & Glass, D. C. (1996). Negative affect and self-report of physical symptoms: Two longitudinal studies of older adults. *Health Psychology, 15*, 193–199.

Likert, R. (1932). A technique for the measurement of attitudes. *Archives of Psychology, 140*, 5–53.

Link, B. G., & Phelan, J. C. (2001). Conceptualizing stigma. *Annual Review of Sociology, 27*, 363–385.

Livneh, H., & Antonak. R. (1994). Indirect methods to measure attitudes toward people with disabilities. *Rehabilitation Education, 8*, 103–137.

Livneh, H., & Antonak, R. F. (1997). *Psychosocial adaptation to chronic illness and disability*. Gaithersburg, MD: Aspen.

Loo, R. (2001). A psychometric re-analysis of the interaction with disabled persons scale. *Canadian Journal of Behavioural Science, 33*, 245–250.

Louviere, J. J. (1988). *Analyzing decision making: Metric conjoint analysis: Series quantitative applications in the social sciences.* Thousand Oaks, CA: SAGE.

Lowery, B. S., Hardin, C. D., & Sinclair, S. (2001). Social influence effects on automatic racial prejudice. *Journal of Personality and Social Psychology, 81*, 842–855.

Lyons, M. (1991). Enabling or disabling? Students' attitudes toward persons with disabilities. *The American Journal of Occupational Therapy, 45*(4), 311–316.

MacLean, D., & Gannon, P. M. (1995). Measuring attitudes toward disability: The Interaction with Disabled Persons Scale revisited. *Journal of Social Behavior and Personality, 10*, 791–806.

Makas, E. (1985). *The MIDS (Modified Issues in Disability Scale)*. Washington DC: The George Washington University.

Makas, E. (1991). In the MIDST: Modified Issues in Disability Scale testing. In G. Kriger & S. Hey (Eds.), *The Social Organization of Disability Experiences* (pp. 109–114). Salem, OR: The Society for Disability Studies and Williamette University.

Makas, E. (1994). MIDS-life changes: The updating of the Modified Issues in Disabilities Scale. In E. Makas & L Schlesinger (Eds.), *Insights & Outlooks: Current Trends in Disability Studies* (pp 129–136) Portland, ME: The Society for Disability Studies and Edmund S. Muskie Institute for Public Affairs.

Makas, E., Finnerty-Fried, P., Sigafoos, A., & Reiss, D. (1988). The Issues in Disability Scale: A new cognitive and affective measure of attitudes toward people with physical disabilities. *Journal of Applied Rehabilitation Counseling, 19*(1), 21–29.

Marinelli, R. P., & Kelz, J. W. (1973). Anxiety and attitudes toward visibly disabled persons. *Rehabilitation Counseling Bulletin, 16*, 198–205.

McConahay, J. B., Hardee, B. B., & Batts, V. (1981). Has racism declined in America: It depends on who is asking and what is asked. *Journal of Conflict Resolution, 25*, 563–579.

McMahon, B.T., West, S. L., Lewis, A. N., Armstrong, A. J., & Conway, J. P. (2004). Hate crimes and disability in America. *Rehabilitation Counseling Bulletin, 47*(2), 66–75.

Milsom, A. (2006). Creating positive school experiences for students with disabilities. *Professional School Counseling, 10*, 66–72.

Nickerson, C. A. E., & McClelland, G. H. (1988). Extended axiomatic conjoint measurement: A solution to a methodological problem in studying fertility-related behaviors. *Applied Psychological Measurement, 12*, 129–153.

O'Doherty, J. Winston, J., Critchley, H., Perrett, D., Burt, D. M., & Dolan, R. J. (2003). Beauty in a smile: The role of medial orbitofrontal cortex in facial attractiveness. *Neuropsycholgica. Special Issue: The cognitive neuroscience of social behavior, 41*, 147–155.

Osgood, C., Suci, G., & Tannebaum, P. (1957). *The measurement of meaning*. Urbana: University of Illinois Press.

Paris, M. J. (1993). Attitudes of medical students and healthcare professionals toward people with disabilities. *Archives of Physical Medicine and Rehabilitation, 74*, 818–825.

Paulhus, D. L. (1991). Measurement and control of response bias. In J. P. Robinson, P.R. Shaver, & L. S. Wrightsman (Eds.), *Measures of personality and social psychology attitudes* (pp. 17–59). San Diego, CA: Academic Press.

Peltzer, K., Cherian, L, & Cherian, V. I. (2001). Attitudes toward handicaps in South African and Indian university students. *Psychological Reports, 89*, 216.

Petty, R. E., & Cacioppo, J. T. (1983). The role of bodily responses in attitude measurement and change. In J .T. Cacioppo & R. E. Petty (Eds.), *Social psychophysiology: A sourcebook* (pp. 51–101). New York: Guilford.

Petty, R. E., Priester, J. R., & Wegener, D. T. (1994). Cognitive processes in attitude change. In R. S. Wyer & T. R. Srull (Eds.), *Handbook of social cognition* (Vol. 1, 2nd ed., pp. 69–142). Hillsdale, NJ: Erlbaum.

Petty, R. E., Wegener, D. T., & Fabrigar, L. R. (1997). Attitudes and attitude change. *Annual Review of Psychology, 48*, 609–647.

Pheiffer, D., Sam, A. A., Guinan, M., Ratliffe, K. T., Robinson, N. B., & Stodden, N. J. (2004). Ethnic and religious perspectives on disability and the helping professions. *Social Science Journal, 41*, 683–687.

Phelps, E. A., O'Connor, K. J., Cunningham, W. A., Funayama, E. S., Gatenby, J. C., Gore, J. C., & Banaji, M. R. (2000). Performance on indirect measures of race evaluation predicts amygdala activation. *Journal of Cognitive Neuroscience, 12*, 729–738.

Pruett, S. R., & Chan, F. (2006). The development and psychometric validation of the Disability Attitudes Implicit Association Test. *Rehabilitation Psychology, 51*, 202–213.

Quigley-Fernandez, B., & Tedeschi, J. T. (1978). The bogus pipeline as lie detector: Two validity studies. *Journal of Personality and Social Psychology, 36*, 247–256.

Robins, R. W., Hendin, H. M., & Trzesniewski, K. H. (2001). Measuring global self-esteem: Construct validation of a single-item measure and the Rosenberg Self-Esteem Scale. *Personality and Social Psychology Bulletin, 27*, 151–161.

Rosenberg, M. J., & Hovland, C. I. (1960). Cognitive, affective and behavioral components of attitudes. In C. I. Hovland, & M. J. Rosenberg (Eds.), *Attitude organization and change: An analysis of consistency among attitude components* (pp. 1–14). New Haven, CT: Yale University Press.

Rosenthal, D. A., & Berven, N. L. (1999). Effects of client race on clinical judgment. *Rehabilitation Counseling Bulletin, 42*, 243–265.

Rudman, L. A., Greenwald, A. G., Mellott, D. S., & Schwartz, J. L. K. (1999). Measuring the automatic components of prejudice: Flexibility and generality of the implicit association test. *Social Cognition, 17*, 437–465.

Satcher, J. & Gamble, D. (2002). Attitudes of law students toward persons with disabilities. *Journal of Applied Rehabilitation Counseling, 33*(2), 13–16.

Seifert, K. H., & Bergmann, C. (1983). Entwicklung eines Fragebogens zur Messung der Einstellungen gegenüber Köperbehinderten. [Development of a questionnaire to measure attitudes toward the physically disabled]. *Heilpädagogische Forschung, 10, 290–320.

Shamir, M., & Shamir, J. (1995). Competing values in public opinion: A conjoint analysis. *Political Behavior, 17*, 107–133.

Shigaki, S. L., Hagglund, K. J., Clark, M., & Conforti, K. (2002). Access to health care among people with rehabilitation needs receiving Medicaid. *Rehabilitation Psychology, 47*, 204–218.

Sigall, H., & Page, R. (1971). Current stereotypes: A little fading, a little faking. *Journal of Personality and Social Psychology, 18*, 247–255.

Siller, J. (1976). Attitudes toward disability. In H. Rusalem & D. Malikin (Eds.), *Contemporary vocational rehabilitation* (pp. 67–79). New York: New York University Press.

Siller, J., Ferguson, L. T., Vann, D. H., & Holland, B. (1967). *Attitudes of the non-disabled toward the physically disabled: The Disability Factors Scales – Amputation, Blindness, Cosmetic Conditions.* Studies in reactions to disabilities: XII. New York: New York University School of Education.

Simpson, J. A., & Weiner, E.S.C. (Eds.) (1989). *Oxford English Dictionary* (2nd ed.). New York: Oxford University Press.

Slininger, D., Sherrill, C., & Jankowski, C. M. (2000). Children's attitudes toward peers with severe disabilities: Revisiting contact theory. *Adapted Physical Activities Quarterly, 17,* 176–196.

Smart, J. (2000). *Disability, society, and the individual.* Austin, TX: PRO-Ed.

Spencer, H. (1862). *First principles* (Reprinted from 5th London ed.). New York: Burt.

Stephenson, W. (1953). *The study of behavior: Q-technique and its methodology.* Chicago: University of Chicago Press.

Taylor, H. (October 7, 2000). Conflicting trends in employment of people with disabilities 1986–2000. *The Harris Poll* #59. Available on-line at http://www.harrisinteractive.com/harris_poll Retrieved January 14, 2004.

Teachman, B. A., & Brownell, K. D. (2001). Implicit anti-fat bias among health professionals: Is anyone immune? *International Journal of Obesity, 25,* 1525–1531.

Teachman, B. A., Gapinski, K. D., Brownell, K. D., Rawlins, M., & Jeyaram, S. (2003). Demonstrations of implicit anti-fat bias: The impact of providing causal information and evoking empathy. *Heath Psychology, 22,* 68–78

Thomas, A., Palmer, J. K., Coker-Juneau, C. J., & Williams, D. J. (2003). Factor structure and construct validity of the Interaction with Disabled Persons Scale. *Educational and Psychological Measurement, 63,* 465–483.

Thurstone, L. L. (1928). Attitudes can be measured. *American Journal of Sociology, 33,* 529–554.

Thurstone, L. L. (1931). The measurement of social attitudes. *Journal of Abnormal and Social Psychology, 26,* 249–269.

Tringo, J. L. (1970). The hierarchy of preference toward disability groups. *Journal of Special Education, 4,* 295–306.

Tsang, H. W .H., Chan, F., & Chan, C. H. H. (2004). Factors influencing occupational therapy student's attitudes toward people with disabilities: A conjoint analysis. *American Journal of Occupational Therapy, 58,* 426–434.

U.S. Census Bureau American Fact Finder (2006). 2005 American Community Survey, S1801 Disability Characteristics. Retrieved May 25, 2007, from http://factfinder.census.gov/servlet/STTable?_bm=y&-geo_id=01000US&-qr_name=ACS_2005_EST_G00_S1801&-ds_name=ACS_2005_EST_G00_

Vander Kolk, C. J. (1976). Physiological and self-report reactions to the disabled and deviant. *Rehabilitation Psychology, 23,* 77–83.

Vanman, E. J., Paul, B. Y., Ito, T. A., & Miller, N. (1997). The modern face of prejudice and structural features that moderate the effect of cooperation on affect. *Journal of Personality and Social Psychology, 73,* 941–959.

Waller, N. G., Kojetin, B. A., Bouchard, T. J., Lykken, D. T., & Tellegen, A. (1990). Genetic and environmental influences on religious interests, attitudes, and values: A study of twins reared apart and together. *Psychological Science, 1,* 138–142.

Wang, M. H. (1998). *Factors influencing preferences for persons with disabilities: A conjoint analysis and cross-cultural comparison.* Unpublished doctoral dissertation, University of Wisconsin, Madison.

Wang, M. H., Thomas, K. R., Chan, F., & Cheing, G. (2003). A conjoint analysis of factors influencing American and Taiwanese college students' preferences for people with disabilities. *Rehabilitation Psychology, 48,* 195–201.

Warner, S. L. (1965). Randomized response: A survey technique for eliminating evasive answer bias. *Journal of the American Statistical Association, 60,* 63–69.

Webb, E. J., Campbell, D. T., Schwartz, R. D., & Sechest, L. (1966). *Nonreactive measures in the social sciences.* Boston: Houghton Mifflin.

Webb, E. J., Campbell, D. T., Schwartz, R. D., Sechrest, L., & Grove, J. B., (1981). *Nonreactive measures in the social sciences* (2nd ed.). Boston: Houghton Mifflin.

Weschler, I. R. (1950a). An investigation of attitudes toward labor and management by means of the error-choice method: I. *The Journal of Social Psychology, 32,* 51–62.

Weschler, I. R. (1950b). A follow-up study on the measurement of attitudes toward labor and management by means of the error-choice method: II. *The Journal of Social Psychology, 32,* 63–69.

Weschler, I. R. (1950c). The personal factor in labor mediation. *Personnel Psychology, 3,* 113–133.

Weschler, I. R. (1951). Problems in the use of indirect methods of attitude measurements. *Public Opinion Quarterly, 15,* 133–138.

Wesolowski, M. D., & Deichmann, J. (1980). Physiological activity and attitudes toward disabled persons. *Rehabilitation Counseling Bulletin, 23,* 218–226.

Wicker, A. W. (1969). Attitudes vs. actions: The relationship of verbal and overt behavioral responses to attitude objects. *Journal of Social Issues, 25,* 41–78.

Wong, D. W., Chan, F., Cardoso, E. D., Lam, C. S., & Miller, S. M. (2004). Rehabilitation counseling students' attitudes toward people with disabilities in three social contexts: A conjoint analysis. *Rehabilitation Counseling Bulletin, 47,* 194–204.

World Health Organization (WHO) (2001). *International classification of functioning, disability and health.* Author: Geneva, Switzerland.

Wright, B. A. (1988). Attitudes and the fundamental negative bias: Conditions and corrections. In H. E. Yuker (Ed.), *Attitudes toward people with disabilities* (pp. 3–21). New York: Springer.

Yuker, H. E. (1994). Variables that influence attitudes toward people with disabilities: Conclusions from the data. *Journal of Social Behavior and Personality, 9*(5), 3–22.

Yuker, H. E., & Block, J. R. (1986). *Research with the Attitude Toward Disabled Persons scales (ATDP): 1960–1985.* Hempstead, NY: Hofstra University.

Yuker, H. E., Block, J. R., & Campbell, W. J. (1960). *A scale to measure attitudes toward disabled persons* (Human Resources Study No. 5). Albertson, NY: Human Resources Center.

Yuker, H. E., Block, J. R., & Younng, J. H. (1966). *The measurement of attitudes toward disabled persons.* (Human Resources Study No. 7). Albertson, NY: Human Resources Center.

Zanna, M. P., & Rempel, J. K. (1988). Attitudes: A new look at an old concept. In D. Bar-Tal & A. W. Kruglanski (Eds.). *The social psychology of knowledge* (pp. 315–334). New York: Cambridge University Press.

Zdep S. M., Rhodes I. N., Schwarz R. M., & Kilkenny M. J. (1979). The validity of the Randomized Response Technique. *Public Opinion Quarterly, 43*, 544–549.

Zych, K., & Bolton, B. (1972). Galvanic skin responses and cognitive attitudes toward disabled persons. *Rehabilitation Psychology, 19*, 172–173.

PART

IV

Measures of Participation

381

23

Measures of Physical and Functional Performance

CHRISTINE CHAPPARO
EV INNES
JUDY RANKA
ANNE HILLMAN
MICHELLE DONELLY
LYNDA R. MATTHEWS
KATE O'LOUGHLIN
ROB HEARD
University of Sydney
Sydney, Australia

OVERVIEW

This chapter presents an overview of the methods used to assess physical aspects of functional performance across a hierarchy that includes measurement of body structure and function, personal care activities and routines and mobility, and the physical aspects of roles. Definitions relevant to functional performance are provided and historical developments in the assessment of functional performance examined. Current assessment methods related to physical participation, personal care routines and tasks, mobility, and body structure and function are detailed. A number of vital issues relevant to accurate assessment of functional performance, such as understanding the purpose of an assessment or assessment approach, the context in which assessment occurs, and the paradigmatic framework adopted, are examined, and the implications of these aspects for conducting accurate assessments are discussed.

LEARNING OBJECTIVES

By the end of the chapter, readers should be able to:

- Describe the nature of physical and functional assessments and their role in rehabilitation and health
- Identify and outline factors that comprise physical and functional performance and major assumptions underlying research and practice in rehabilitation of physical ability and function
- Evaluate current assessment methods of physical aspects of functional performance, especially body structure and function, personal care activities and routines, and the physical aspects of roles
- Discuss the advantages and limitations of assessments of physical and functional performance in relation to purpose, approach, and context

INTRODUCTION

The ability to physically engage in the performance of everyday roles, routines, and tasks depends on some degree of physical ability and capacity. Physical function involves a hierarchical organization that assumes that lower-level bodily structure and functions, such as strength and endurance, are related to a higher-level physical ability to carry out activities that everyday life demands (Trombly Latham, 2008). A primary aim of rehabilitation is to enable people with disabilities to achieve the highest level of physical and functional performance possible to support their participation in everyday life. Physical aspects of functional performance are a vital part of human development and the lived experience of people (Law, 2002). This chapter presents selected examples of methods used to assess physical aspects of functional performance across a hierarchy that includes measurement of body structure and function, personal care activities and routines, and the physical aspects of roles.

IMPORTANCE OF PHYSICAL AND FUNCTIONAL PERFORMANCE TO REHABILITATION AND HEALTH

Definitions of Physical and Functional Performance

There are many conceptual models that illustrate the proposed links between physical and functional abilities of people. The definitions outlined in this section are guided by those found in the *International Classification of Functioning* (ICF), which classifies health by examining the interaction between people with health conditions and the environments in which they live (World Health Organization [WHO] 2001, 2002). *Functional performance* refers to a person's ability to carry out needed or desired everyday activities and routines, such as the ability to dress, to buy food, to care for children, or to carry out work tasks. Although there are many universal similarities in the way people carry out functional activities and routines, what people choose or need to do and how they go about doing it is highly idiosyncratic and influenced by age, gender, culture, and personal preference. The physical performance of daily activities and routines is one way people achieve satisfaction in day-to-day life. It is also a vehicle through which people

can express their personal identities. The degree to which people are physically able to carry out daily activities contributes to their ability to participate in life roles and situations within the wider community as individuals and in concert with others.

One early and significant component of many rehabilitation programs is the remediation of limitations in the functional performance domains known as self-care and mobility. *Self-care* refers to the ability to care for oneself, to wash and dry oneself, to care for one's body and body parts, to dress oneself, to eat and drink by oneself, and to look after one's health and mobility (WHO, 2001, p.149). *Mobility* refers to the ability to move oneself by changing body position or location or by transferring from one place to another (WHO, 2001, p.138). Assessments of personal care generally focus on identifying the capacity of a person to perform key personal care activities, which may include being able to get to a location or to transfer one's body from one surface to another. Typically, assessment of these activities is administered under clinical conditions and focuses on how a person performs an activity with or without the use of assistive devices. Often, these same assessments are used in home and community contexts or other real-world situations. Many contemporary functional assessments contain predetermined items rather than the needs of the person or the relevant social network. Questions have been raised about the degree to which these types of assessments yield a valid picture of real-world performance (Law, Baptiste, Carswell, McColl, Polatajko & Pollock, 1998).

Limitations refers to an inability to carry out everyday activities and routines, and can result from impairments in physical functioning, cognitive functioning, or psychosocial functioning, as well as contextual constraints such as physical or social barriers. One common cause of functional performance limitations most typically observed in rehabilitation is impairment in the physical functioning of the body. *Physical performance* refers to the integrity and function of body structures that support and enable performance of the functional activities and routines of daily life. These include the structures and functions that give people the ability to move and to use extremities against resistance for an extended period (Flinn, Trombly Latham & Podolski, 2008, p.92). Often these functions are assessed in clinical situations under specific test conditions to gain a perspective of a person's physical functioning and impairment. There are few standardized assessments of a person's physical functioning during the performance of needed or desired functional activities

TABLE 23.1 ICF Perspective on Factors to Consider when Assessing Physical and Functional Performance of Personal Care.

Personal Factors

Collection of information about a person's individual preferences regarding personal care and the needs of others in that person's social context, including: age, gender, social network, customs, cultural practices, as well as the value and meaning a person places on personal care and the satisfaction gained from performance.

Contextual Factors

Collection of information about a person's contexts and factors that impact on personal care performance, including: the physical, sensory, social, political, and economic dimensions of present and future contexts, and specifically what the context requires of a person in terms of personal care.

Participation

Assessments of a person's ability to carry out personal care activities and routines under real world conditions using available supports and the level of satisfaction a person and his or her social networks gain from that level of participation.

Personal Care Activity Assessments

Assessments of the capacity of a person to care for himself or herself, including: washing and drying self, caring for body parts, toileting, dressing, eating, drinking, looking after health in terms of physical comfort, diet and fitness, and healthy living practices. These may or may not include assessments of the ability to get himself or herself to places where personal care activities are carried out, and of the ability to transfer the body from one supporting surface to another.

Body Function Assessments

Assessments of neuromusculoskeletal and movement-related functions, including: functions of mobility of joints, stability of joints, mobility of bones, muscle power, muscle tone, muscle endurance, motor reflexes, involuntary movements, gait patterns, and sensations related to muscles and movement functions.

Body Structure Assessments

Assessments of structures related to movement, including: structures of the head and neck region, shoulder region, upper extremity, pelvic region, lower extremity, trunk and other musculoskeletal structures related to movement.

and routines in contexts where those activities and routines typically occur.

The domain of physical and functional performance contains many complex elements. Assessments of physical and functional performance typically fall within the body structure and function component of the ICF classification or within the activities component. As discussed above, performance of personal care activities and participation in real-world contexts requires consideration of more than these two components. Table 23.1 presents a framework for the factors that are considered important to assess during physical and functional performance using the ICF nomenclature. The table provides a framework for the remainder of this chapter.

Typically, in rehabilitation, assessments of physical and functional performance begin with an examination of body structure and function, as appear at the bottom of Table 23.1. Personal care activities are then assessed to gain a perspective on a person's capacity to use physical functions in a daily life activity, and this is followed by a consideration of the remaining factors in

Table 23.1. In this chapter, the idea will be presented that this strategy should be reversed. It will be posed that in order to focus rehabilitation on achieving the aim of enabling optimum participation in life, assessments should begin with the collection of information about the person, the person's life context, and the unique needs and desires of that person and others in that person's social context. This information is then used to determine which critical personal care needs should be assessed, and in turn, what body structure and functional assessments will yield information of most use in planning interventions.

HISTORY OF RESEARCH AND PRACTICE IN THE ASSESSMENT OF PHYSICAL FUNCTIONING

Contemporary practice in the assessment of physical functioning developed largely within the rehabilitation field. The origins of the word rehabilitation mean "to make fit again," and, although the concept has been around for centuries, it was sometime after World War II that rehabilitation and its associated assessment practices became formalized in the developed world. The focus was predominantly on physical restoration and compensation. For example, Rusk (1958), one of the early promoters of rehabilitation in the United States, stated that its objectives were to eliminate physical disability, if possible; to alleviate the disability to the greatest extent possible; and to retrain people with residual physical disability to live and work to their maximum capabilities.

A major assumption underlying the research and practice in rehabilitation of physical ability and function is that performance of everyday roles, tasks, and activities is closely aligned to a person's physical abilities. For example, Nagi's (1969, 1991) model of disablement poses causative links among disease (physical signs and symptoms), impairments (musculoskeletal, neuromuscular, cardiovascular), functional limitations (physical, psychological, social), and disability (role). It has been particularly influential in explaining health status and the relationship between physical and other variables that describe health status in the rehabilitation literature (Guccione & Scalzitti, 2007). Early research in physical rehabilitation focused on investigation of the link between physical ability and functional outcome. Assessment practice in the mid-to late-20th century mirrored this focus with the development of a plethora of standard clinical assessment tools to measure various physical dimensions of performance. Many of these are still in use today (Guccione & Scalzitti; Radomski & Trombly Latham, 2008). In the last decade, the evidence-based practice movement has prompted research to improve the reliability of these clinical measures (O'Sullivan, 2007a; Ottenbacher, Tickle-Degnen, & Hasselkus, 2002; Sackett, Richardson, Rosenberg, & Hayes, 1997). At the same time, the disability movement questioned the usefulness of such individual measures of physical ability, asserting that the overwhelming cause of handicap for people with reduced physical function is lack of contextual opportunities and supports for them to physically engage in meaningful life activity (Hagner, 2000; Leake, James, & Stodden, 1995).

The concept of a physical/function hierarchy finds tentative support in research (Dijkers, 1997, 1999; Geertzen et al., 1998; Sveen, Bautz-Holter, Sodring, Wyller, & Laake, 1999), which shows that only part of a person's overall functioning has been accounted for by physical ability (Trombly Latham, 2008). Research suggests that where a strong relationship exists within this hierarchy, it is between two adjacent variables (e.g., musculoskeletal impairment and self-care), rather than two nonadjacent variables (e.g., musculoskeletal impairment and role performance or participation). For example, Dijkers (1999) found a significant relationship between life satisfaction and roles, but not between physical impairments and life satisfaction in persons with spinal cord injury. He concluded that these relationships indicated a "causal chain" (1999, p. 874) with a step-wise progression from physical ability to other higher-order variables (Table 23.1), rather than a direct impact of physical impairment on handicap and participation. Other contemporary researchers are in agreement with this position (Dagfinrud, Kjeken, O'Sullivan & Schmitz 2007; Rogers & Holm, 1994; Rondinelli, et al., 1997; Mowinckel Hagen, Kvien 2005; Trombly Latham). While early assessment practice in rehabilitation focused on measurement of physical parameters of human performance to explain functional limitation, contemporary assessment practice supports the need for using an assessment approach that includes sampling of variables through the physical/function hierarchy.

CURRENT METHODS OF ASSESSING PHYSICAL FUNCTIONING

Assessment Methods Related to Physical Participation: Roles

The word *role* has been widely used in professional and popular literature. The dictionary defines role as "proper or customary function" (Delbridge, Bernard, Blair, Ramson, & Butler, 1981). In everyday language, *role* is used to denote the links between particular contexts and expected ways of behaving in them (Toal-Sullivan & Henderson, 2004). When people refer to roles, they acknowledge the assumption that behavior, including physical behavior inherent in that role, might change according to a particular context. From the perspective of physical function, the word role is often used by people to express *ideas* about what motor behavior needs to happen in particular situations, the *rules* for motor behavior, and *judgments* about the extent to which people's motor behaviors fit with expected roles.

Researchers have shown that role behavior is complex (Lemay, 1999). This may be because roles are content specific and tied to the social situations in which they are embedded (Schultz-Krohn, 2005). In any one day, people are expected to adopt a number of roles that become functionally interlocked. People behave in the role of *friend* when talking to others with whom they have a close relationship; *worker* when working on tasks that are directed by the job; *player* when engaging in leisure pursuits and having fun; *self-carer* during personal care; and *community member* when traveling on transport or helping others. Each role has its own repertoire of motor behaviors that support it. People may have difficulty generating motor behaviors that are associated with particular roles, or they may have difficulty making the behavioral transition between different roles. For example, someone with Parkinson's disease and excessive rigidity may find it difficult to relax enough to assist a caregiver with transfers at bedtime in order to rest. Someone who uses crutches for all daily mobility may find it difficult to maintain the level of upper limb endurance required for activities at the end of the day, thereby losing independent function.

Roles have been described as having two dimensions. One is governed by expectations or demands placed upon us by our environment, and the other dimension is governed by our personal choice (Burns, 1991; Landis, 1995). Expectations of roles are sometimes seen as formal agreements that are shared among people (Lemay, 1999). A large part of expected role behavior concerns expectations that people are able to generate and calibrate motor behaviors to *fit* different social situations. For example, when people live together in a family, there is some agreement about how much responsibility individual group members adopt for their own dressing, eating, and mobility (self-care role). People agree among themselves about physical and other behaviors that will make up particular leisure pursuits (leisure role). Expectations of physical ability become *behavioral rules* when they are used as a model of how the role "should be" performed. These expectations can be overt, clearly stated as expectations of people's motor behavior in the home or community, or covert, when the expected role behavior is made known through more complex and subtle communications.

Throughout life, roles are modified by age, ability, experience, circumstance, and time. People are workers, players, community members, and friends at various times during the day, with each role assigned its own particular constellation of tasks, motivations, and expectations. They are a means by which people can exercise personal control in a range of social contexts (Krause & Shaw, 2000; Lawton, 1982). Roles establish identity and social fit (Krause & Shaw, 2000), and they relate strongly to the *participation* component of the ICF classification. Assessment of roles can be carried out by means of standardized or nonstandardized instruments, each with its own strengths and weaknesses depending upon its purpose.

STANDARDIZED ROLE ASSESSMENT Researchers have developed lists of roles that are believed to be commonly held and have used these for assessment purposes (e.g. Jackoway, Rogers, & Snow, 1987; Krause & Shaw, 2000; Toal-Sullivan & Henderson, 2004). For example, the Role Checklist (Oakley, Kielhofner, Barris, & Reichler, 1986) is a two-part self report assessment that measures valued participation in ten major life roles: student, worker, volunteer, caregiver, home maintainer, friend, family member, religious participant, hobbyist, participant in organization. It has acceptable test–retest reliability and is used widely both in research and by clinicians (e.g. Bränholm & Fugl-Meyer, 1992; Dickerson & Oakley, 1995; Elliott & Barris, 1987). Although standardized role assessments are useful where there are a large number of culturally homogeneous participants being studied (Fasoli, 2008), they are unrepresentative of the range of roles held by a single person with a physical disability (Hillman & Chapparo, 1995). Standardized lists are, by their nature, socially and culturally bound and do not reflect the choices people make about how they function or wish to function in specific roles.

NONSTANDARDIZED ROLE ASSESSMENT There is an alternate approach to role assessment. Viewing people as experts about their own abilities to engage in role behavior is thought to provide information that is more accurate and relevant for clinical purposes than standardized checklists. Using an interview format without prescriptive role behaviors and typologies is consistent with the ICF classification of participation. Few role assessments seek the account of the individual about his or her role performance. A protocol developed by Hillman and Chapparo (Hillman 2006, 2007; Hillman & Chapparo, 1995) uses the idea of *knowing, doing*, and *being* as an important part of the conceptualization of role. The physical aspects of role performance (*doing*) are informed by the knowledge held by the individual about the role (*knowing*), while the motivation for performance is influenced by the experience of doing, from which people derive a sense of *being*.

A role assessment interview using this approach begins with a broad question such as: "Tell me about the roles you have at the moment," or, "Tell me something about your life at present." The interviewer and interviewee work together to develop a confirmed list of salient roles. The interviewee is asked to order the roles so that the most highly valued role is at the top. The top three roles are selected. Further questioning and discussion reveals what the person actually does in each role.

Examples of *doing* questions are: "What sort of things do you do in relation to this role?"; "How often do you do something in this role?"; and "Who else is involved in doing things in this role?" Each individual's reasoning in relation to acknowledged role incumbency and participation is important in order to develop an understanding of the specific ways in which roles are performed. To provide a temporal context, questions are asked about what the person used to do in a given role and what they hope to be able to do in the future. The person's important role partners are interviewed in a similar fashion to deepen information about social context and to identify potential conflicts. These interviews provide specific information about physical aspects of role performance in highly valued roles. It is not culturally or socially bound because the person is able to talk as an expert about his or her own life.

Assessment Methods Related to Personal Care Routines and Tasks

When considering the assessment of functional performance with regard to the routines and tasks associated with self-care or activities of daily living (ADL), the following areas are usually included: eating, dressing, bathing, grooming, toileting, and mobility; management of medication and communication may also be included (Anderson, 2000). There are standardized and nonstandardized approaches to assessment in this area. Both approaches are primarily based on clinical observation of an individual's performance when engaged in self-care activities. There are also self-report measures that attempt to gain an appreciation of the person's view of his or her ability.

There is a vast range of instruments as well as nonstandardized methods of determining functional performance in ADL; however, it is beyond the scope of this chapter to review all the instruments available. Clinicians need to consider the purpose of assessing this area of function: Is it to determine outcomes, or is it to assist in designing appropriate interventions? Is it necessary to understand performance in all areas of ADL, or only those that the client identifies as important and necessary? How much detail is required (e.g., dressing in general, or ability to put on a singlet, a T-shirt, a front-buttoning shirt, a jacket, etc.)? Although it is necessary to consider the functional abilities that a person has, is it necessary to use a disease-specific instrument?

Assessing ADL in unfamiliar settings can have a significant impact on performance (Fasoli, 2008), and therefore it "has been recommended that assessment of self-care activities be performed in the environment in which the client would ordinarily carry out those activities" (Law, 1997, p.423). Contextual observation also enables identification of the need for assistive devices, environmental modifications, and/or cueing (physical and/or verbal prompts) (Anderson, 2000). Variations in performance across different environments, however, have not been incorporated into standardized ADL assessments (Letts & Bosch, 2005).

Assessment of functional performance in ADL often begins with an interview with the client and the family, and can be used to screen for the need for more detailed performance-based assessments (Foti & Kanazawa, 2006). Checklists are often used to guide the interview to ensure that no areas are overlooked. However, the use of self-report measures or those that

---

DISCUSSION BOX 23.1

How does context impact on physical and functional performance?

Research has demonstrated that functional performance is affected by the context in which it occurs (Rogers, et al., 2003). Standardized functional assessments of personal care usually occur in clinical settings unfamiliar to the person being assessed. The environment chosen for assessment may have little relevance to the place in which the routines and tasks are usually performed by this person. Contextual differences may include the physical layout of the environment, type and availability of equipment and devices, time constraints, and variation to usual daily routines. Clinic-based assessments may indicate significant limitations in a person's personal care performance. These

findings are used to make decisions about future care needs. However, in the person's own environment some of these limitations may have little or no impact on functional performance.

Questions

1. What other information would you require in order to make appropriate recommendations regarding this person's future care needs for personal care?
2. How would you ensure that the results of the assessments conducted in a clinical setting are relevant to the person you are assessing?

rely on interviewing clients and/or their families/caregivers as a substitute for clinical observation of self-care performance can be controversial (Law, 1997). A study examined variation in disability status determined by self-report, proxy report, clinical judgment based on impairment measures, and performance testing in an occupational therapy clinic, and compared them with the criterion standard of performance testing in participants' homes (Rogers et al., 2003). Results showed that disability estimates based on these methods were not interchangeable with in-home task performance, although the inclusion of self-reports with in-home performance testing was encouraged (Rogers et al.).

The standardized instruments commonly in use have been developed for use in western, industrialized, and developed nations, although this is often not acknowledged. This means that some items may not be culturally relevant or appropriate (e.g., put on/take off mittens/gloves), or relevant items may not be included (e.g., eating with chopsticks).

Examples of commonly used standardized instruments are presented with a brief overview. More extensive reviews of a wider range of ADL instruments have been published and can be examined for further detail (e.g. Asher, 1996; Finch, Brooks, Stratford & Mayo, 2002; Gitlin, 2006; Law, 1997; Letts & Bosch, 2005).

ADL Instruments: Client-Centered Approaches

CANADIAN OCCUPATIONAL PERFORMANCE MEASURE (COPM) The COPM (Law et al., 1998) is suitable for all ages and is focused on the person's perception of performance and satisfaction in self-care, productivity, and leisure. It is a semistructured interview that can be used to set goals with the client and also as an outcome measure to determine change over time. Identified problems are individualized and reflect the client's own importance ratings (Finch, et al., 2002; Gitlin, 2006; Law, 1997). Test–retest reliability is good to excellent; content validity is adequate; and other aspects of validity have been examined (Finch, et al.; Gitlin; Law).

PATIENT-SPECIFIC FUNCTIONAL SCALE (PSFS) The PSFS uses an interview format with specific wording to elicit up to five important activities that the client is having difficulty performing or is unable to perform. Difficulty is then rated on a 0–10 scale. The PSFS can be used with all age groups and conditions, although most studies have used reasonably healthy subjects with orthopedic conditions (Finch, et al., 2002; Letts & Bosch,

2005). Test–retest reliability and internal consistency are high, and content and construct validity are acceptable (Finch, et al.; Letts & Bosch).

ADL Instruments: Outcome Measures

BARTHEL INDEX The Barthel Index is one of the early measures of ADL performance and was developed in the mid-1960s. The original version covered ten items (feeding, bathing, dressing, grooming, bowel and bladder control, toilet and chair/bed transfers, ambulation, and stair climbing) (Letts & Bosch, 2005). Its purpose is to evaluate independence before, during, and after inpatient rehabilitation (Gitlin, 2006; Letts & Bosch). Information can be obtained through observation of performance or through interview (Finch, et al., 2002). There have been various modifications to items and scoring over time, so users need to be aware of this (Letts & Bosch). All aspects of reliability are good to excellent (Asher, 1996; Finch, et al., 2002; Gitlin; Letts & Bosch). Various validity studies have been conducted examining convergent and construct validity. It has been compared to other commonly accepted measures of ADL (e.g., Katz, FIM, and others), and correlations are generally good (Letts & Bosch). It is also responsive to change, although there are potential floor and ceiling effects for people living in the community (Letts & Bosch).

FUNCTIONAL INDEPENDENCE MEASURE (FIM™) The FIM™ is an indicator of the level of disability and changes in the level of disability over time and is also used to evaluate outcomes of rehabilitation (Gitlin, 2006; Letts & Bosch, 2005). It is also considered to be an indicator of caregiver burden (Finch, et al., 2002; Gitlin). It is probably the most extensively used and researched measure of ADL and is used worldwide. There have been many studies examining all aspects of reliability and validity, giving strong support for its use. Training is required to conduct the FIM, and sites using the measure must be licensed (Letts & Bosch). It should be noted, however, that the measure is most appropriate to classify the level of care required by individuals (Finch, et al.), and "therapists should be cautioned not to use the FIM for evaluation of change in individual clients, as it is less responsive in this situation" (Law, 1997, p.426).

KATZ INDEX OF ACTIVITIES OF DAILY LIVING The Katz Index of ADL is a quick and simple assessment of self-care designed for use in institutions to identify problems in six broad areas of self-care (feeding, bathing, dressing, toileting, transfers, and continence) and to determine the need for attendant care (Guccione & Scalzitti, 2007; Law, 1997). It uses direct observation and client report over a recommended 2-week period, which is considered unrealistic for many settings (Letts & Bosch, 2005). It is considered less useful for intervention planning due to the difficulty in identifying specific areas of need (Letts & Bosch). Internal consistency, inter-rater reliability, and content and construct validity have been examined (Letts & Bosch).

ADL Instruments: Activity Specific for Program Planning

KLEIN–BELL ACTIVITIES OF DAILY LIVING SCALE   The Klein–Bell ADL Scale contains 170 items in six areas (dressing, eating, bathing/hygiene, elimination, mobility, and emergency telephone communication) and is used to determine a person's current level of functioning, to document progress in rehabilitation, and to develop specific and comprehensive treatment plans (Asher, 1996; Gitlin, 2006). It is also used to communicate with families regarding the specific areas of difficulty a person may have. "This allows for targeting of help for discrete components of a task and enabling a person to remain independent in other components" (Gitlin, p.159). It is based on direct observation of task performance and was developed to be sensitive to small changes in function over time (Law, 1997). The use of assistive devices and equipment is not marked down or penalized when scoring the Klein–Bell. This is different from many other instruments. Test–retest reliability is high, and predictive validity regarding Klein–Bell scores on discharge and need for personal care assistance were strongly negatively correlated (Asher, 1996; Gitlin; Law). Scores were also responsive to change, and parent and therapist reports of children's function had high agreement (Asher; Gitlin; Law).

Assessment Methods Related to Body Structure and Physical Function

Assessment of physical function is a multifaceted process that requires a number of different and specific tests and measures. The overall purpose of assessment of body structure and function is to identify the cause of impairment. As with other levels within the impairment/participation hierarchy, assessment modes can be either qualitative, using observations of performance in situ, or quantitative. Experienced practitioners are more efficient in making decisions based on observation than are novices (Riolo, 1996). The following clusters of assessment methods are just a sample of the many standardized and nonstandardized measures that have evolved and are used for specific purposes within each rehabilitation discipline.

JOINT RANGE OF MOTION   Trauma or injury affects joint structures and the surrounding tissue and can reduce the amount of motion available at joints. This limitation in body structure is thought to have an impact on higher-level functioning, particularly where multiple joints are involved. Assessment of joint range may be done actively or passively. *Passive range of motion* is the amount of motion at any given joint when it is moved through a maximum range by an outside force and generates information about structural impediments that prevent physical activity. *Active range of motion* is the amount of range people can demonstrate at a joint using their own muscle strength and is used as a supplement to manual muscle strength assessment (Flinn, Trombly Latham, & Podolski, 2008). A goniometer is used for measuring joint motion (either manual or electronic), and when standard measurement procedures are used, intra-rater reliability is high (Awan, Smith & Boon, 2002). Active motion measurements are more reliable than passive, and the position of the client during assessment affects the consistency of measures taken (Flinn, et al., 2008).

MUSCLE TONE AND ASSOCIATED FACTORS   *Muscle tone* is the resistance of a muscle to passive elongation or stretching (Shumway-Cook & Woollacott, 2001). Muscle tone is measured by observing the response of a group of muscles to passive stretch. This is a highly unreliable test, as muscle tonus can change from day to day in the same person. Reliability is also affected by effort, emotional stress, temperature, fatigue, changes in health (e.g., infection, virus), and head position (Mathiowetz & Bass-Haugen, 2008). Authors suggest that rigid standardization is required if results are not to be misleading (Burridge et al., 2005). The *Modified Ashworth Scale* is a qualitative and quantitative scale that is most commonly used and has modest reliability (Ashworth, 1964).

STRENGTH   *Strength* refers to the degree of muscle power (Jacobs & Jacobs, 2004). *Weakness* is a reduction in muscle power that has the potential to limit a person's functioning. The assumption underlying assessment of strength is that determination of the degree and distribution of weakness assists with the development of a rehabilitation plan for remediation or compensation (Flinn, et al., 2008). Manual muscle testing is a valid and reliable clinical procedure to measure muscle strength when a standard method of testing is used (Medical Research Council, 1976).

ENDURANCE   Strength and endurance are closely related physical capacities. *Endurance* of a muscle or muscle group is its ability to sustain intensive activity. Limitations in endurance are signaled by symptoms of muscle fatigue (cramping, burning, tremor), and reduced ability to hold a muscle contraction. As muscles gain strength, endurance for functional activity is also assumed to increase (Mathiowetz & Bass-Haugen, 2008). Dynamic assessment of endurance includes the number of repetitions per unit of time or the percentage of maximal heart rate generated exercise (Metabolic Equivalent Level). Static assessment is assessed by the amount of time muscle can remain in a contracted state (American College of Sports Medicine, 2000). The choice of dynamic or static evaluation of endurance should be determined by the purpose of the assessment. The *Borg's Rate of Perceived Exertion Scale* (Borg, 1985) is one example of a standardized dynamic assessment of endurance. If a person is expected to engage in daily function that requires mostly isotonic activity, dynamic endurance is measured. If a person is expected to engage in a significant amount of daily activity involving isometric activity, then methods of static endurance assessment are more appropriate.

COORDINATION   An examination of coordination provides practitioners with information about the underlying origins of impairments. Several standardized tests are available to examine arm–hand and eye–hand coordination as well as fine motor dexterity. Many of these measures were originally used to predict success in manual employment and include normative data relative to age, gender, performance time, and hand dominance. Although they are useful in providing objective measures of client progress, the link to overall functional ability is tenuous. Examples include the *Jebsen–Taylor Hand Function Test* (Samons Preston Roylan); the *Minnesota Manual Dexterity Test* (Lafayette Instrument Co.); the *Purdue Pegboard* (Lafayette Instrument Co.); and the *Crawford Small Parts Dexterity Test* (Harcourt Assessment).

MOBILITY   To most people, loss of mobility is perhaps the one physical function on which they place the most emphasis (Chiou & Burnett, 1985). Poor mobility is the most common single disability seen to affect community living (Wade, 1992) because it is commonly impaired by pathology or injury. The following measures have been chosen as examples of the range of mobility assessments because they are in current use and have been examined for reliability and validity (Schmitz, 2007). The *Functional Ambulation Profile* is designed to examine gait skills on a continuum from assisted standing to independent ambulation (Nelson, 1974). A more recent version has added five environmental challenges, giving practitioners the opportunity to observe the client's ability to walk on different floor coverings, sit to stand, and to walk negotiating an obstacle course and stairs (Wolf, Catlin & Gage, 1999). The *Iowa Level of Assistance Scale* examines four mobility tasks: getting out of bed, walking, walking up steps, and walking down steps, and is rated according to seven levels of assistance required (Schmitz). The *Modified Gait Abnormality Rating Scale and Modifications* was designed to identify people living in nursing homes who were at risk of falling. The total score represents a rank ordering for risk of falling based on the number of abnormalities identified and is a good predictor for persons at risk for falls (Van Swearingen, 1996). Kinematic and kinetic analyses of gait have become popular in clinical as well as research settings over the last 2 decades. Technological advances now offer the potential for practitioners to gather data about higher levels of function by assessing abnormalities in gait within real-world contexts (Schmitz).

MOTOR CONTROL AND MOTOR LEARNING   The ability to generate controlled physical movement to obtain a functional goal involves more than simply physical parameters. Motor control is generated by a system of control that is distributed among many systems that include musculoskeletal, sensory, and cognitive abilities. Control emerges from the interaction of these systems. There is no strict order of command, and the information that is processed for movement changes with task requirements (Mathiowetz & Bass-Haugen, 2008). These contemporary views of physical function have altered the focus of physical assessment in the last 2 decades (Mathiowetz & Bass-Haugen; O'Sullivan & Schmitz, 2007). Less emphasis is placed on assessment using measures of individual body structure and function, and there is increased focus on the ability of people to generate motor patterns that 'fit' the task at hand. This has been referred to as a *task oriented approach* to the assessment of physical function (Mathiowetz & Bass-Haugen). Contemporary task-focused assessments that are currently used include the *Motor Assessment Scale* (Carr & Shepherd, 1987).

RESEARCH BOX 23.1

Brooks, D., Davis, A.M., & Naglie, G. (2006). Validity of 3 physical performance measures in inpatient geriatric rehabilitation. *Archives of Physical Medicine and Rehabilitation, 87*, 105–110.

Objectives: This study sought to evaluate the construct validity and responsiveness of three physical performance measures with respect to their ability to reflect functional and ambulatory status and their responsiveness in frail older persons in an inpatient geriatric setting.

Method: Subjects were 52 (33% male) patients aged 80 ± 8 years admitted to one of three inpatient geriatric rehabilitation programs with similar admission criteria, goals for mobility and functional improvement, and program characteristics. A pre–post design with measures at admission and discharge was used to test hypotheses. Performance was measured using the Timed Up & Go (TUG), the 2-minute walk test (2MWT), and functional reach. Functional status was measured using the FIM instrument and Modified Barthel Index (MBI). Tests were conducted on admission and during the last week of rehabilitation, and were performed in a randomized order, with adequate rest periods between tests and at the same time of day. Ambulation status (i.e., use of an aid) was recorded at admission and discharge.

Results: TUG and 2MWT scores differed significantly ($p = .006$) across the levels of ambulation, indicating the ability to discriminate between the use of aid or no aid

during ambulation. Moderate to strong correlations were found between TUG and FIM and between 2MWT and FIM at admission and discharge. In contrast, no significant differences were found in functional reach and levels of ambulation, indicating an inability to discriminate between levels of ambulation. Further, functional reach had weak nonsignificant correlations with the FIM ($p < .09$). The TUG showed the highest responsiveness to rehabilitation interventions between admission and discharge as determined by standardized response means (1.1 for TUG, 0.7 for 2MWT, and 0.5 for functional reach).

Conclusion: Results indicate that the TUG and 2MWT are valid and responsive outcome measures in frail older persons participating in rehabilitation. Functional reach however did not consistently reflect ambulatory or functional status but was a moderately responsive outcome measure.

Question: The results of this study suggest that the relationship between physical performance measures and functional status was moderate; that is that physical performance and functional measures provide different information.

- What are the clinical implications of these results for health care professionals working in inpatient geriatric rehabilitation settings?

This brief assessment includes eight items ranging from total body physical abilities such as lying-to-sitting, to fine motor abilities such as advanced hand activities. Reliability for the total score is reported as high. The *Arm Motor Ability* (Kopp et al, 1997) and the *Wolf Motor Function Test* (Wolf et al., 2001) are examples of tests of motor control in the upper limbs that are used to measure increases in motor function.

CULTURAL, LEGISLATIVE, AND PROFESSIONAL ISSUES THAT IMPACT PHYSICAL AND FUNCTIONAL ASSESSMENT PRACTICES

Understanding the purpose of an assessment or assessment approach is an important consideration in evaluating assessment relevance, accuracy, and the utility of measures of physical functioning (Fawcett, 2007). The purposes of physical and functional assessment can be

diverse, as outlined previously in this chapter. Four categories of assessment purposes identified by Law (1993) are descriptive, discriminative, predictive, and evaluative purposes. In addition to these assessment purposes, assessment of physical function occurs within a clinical, community, and/or policy context. For example, assessments of physical and functional need are constrained by financial considerations (Priestly, 1999). The policy context in which assessment is conducted influences the function of an assessment, sometimes paradoxically. Assessment also informs policy (Lollar & Crews, 2003). Some of the functions of an assessment in a policy context include the allocation and rationing of scarce resources and the identification and management of the political impact of need, now and in the future (See Table 23.2).

The clinical, community, and policy contexts also have implications for the paradigmatic framework adopted in the conduct of functional assessment. For example, in order to distance decision-makers from

TABLE 23.2 Examples of Purposes and Functions of Physical and Functional Assessment

Type	Purpose	Use
Descriptive	Describes the person's current function and needs (Fawcett, 2007)	To determine to whom resources and supports will be allocated
Discriminative	Distinguishes between individuals and groups on an underlying dimension (Law, 2002)	To determine eligibility for resources and supports
Predictive	Determines future abilities or needs	To determine future demands on resources
Evaluative	Detects change in function (Fawcett, 2007)	To determine the cost effectiveness and opportunity cost of resources allocated

politically sensitive efforts to restrict, ration, or limit access to services, policy may mandate the use of assessment tools that utilize a positivist framework. Assessment mechanisms are defended for their *objectivity* at the same time as privileging the roles of professionals in assessment decisions and outcomes. Assessment practices that are used to describe physical and functional performance are particularly vulnerable to financial and policy interventions. For example, quantitative assessments of physical impairment using objective measurement are increasingly being required by the health care system and third party payers to support the need for and the effectiveness of services (O'Sullivan, 2007b) despite questions about their relevance to individual client situations.

In contrast to this approach and consistent with the principles of a participatory paradigm, people being assessed would collaborate in important assessment decisions and processes with professionals and other key stakeholders (Priestly, 1999), including decisions about the purpose and use of the assessment and its interpretation and implications. A participatory approach could make clearer the balance of power and control in the assessment process, particularly the power of definition and identity (Liggett, 1988). A participatory approach does not assume that the cultural context in which the assessment was developed and applied is the same as the cultural background, values, priorities, and experience of the person being assessed. The contrasting features of participatory and positivist approaches are outlined in Table 23.3.

The core concepts that have influenced statute and policy changes in disability (Turnbull, Wilcox, Stowe, & Umbarger, 2001), such as the development of individualized and collaborative services and participatory decision-making, have influenced the functional assessment context. This has included mandates for the use of individual service/program/education/care plans and individual and family-focused assessment and intervention. Service development initiatives to address core policy concepts such as empowerment, capacity-based focus, capacity building, and culturally responsive services (Turnbull, et al., 2001) are still in progress. In order to ensure that any of these core concepts are effective and sustained beyond a tokenistic level, further research and redevelopment would be necessary, including the implications of these concepts for functional assessment. It is unclear how this policy context will be articulated with the influence of neoconservative economics and scientism on functional assessment, as supported by

TABLE 23.3 Basic Beliefs of Alternative Inquiry Paradigms

Paradigm	Ontology	Epistemology	Methodology
Positivism	Naïve realism 'real' reality but can be apprehended	Dualist/ objectivist; findings true	Experimental/manipulative; verification of hypotheses; chiefly quantitative methods
Participatory	Participative reality Subject-objective reality co-created	Critical subjectivity in participatory transaction, propositional and practical knowing	Political participation in collaborative action inquiry; use of language grounded in shared experiential context

(Excerpted and adapted from: Lincoln, Y.S., & Guba, E.G. (2000). Paradigmatic controversies, contradictions and emerging confluences in N. K. Denzin & Y. S. Lincoln (Eds). *Handbook of qualitative research* (2nd ed., p. 69). Thousand Oaks: Sage.

evidence-based practice initiatives and the globalization of care. This includes for example, the privatization of disability services where funding contracts typically prescribe assessment processes and outcomes and the reliance on the international recruitment of a range of professionals and support workers.

MULTIDISCIPLINARY AND INTERDISCIPLINARY PRACTICE IN PHYSICAL AND FUNCTIONAL ASSESSMENT

Managing one's self-care and the physical ability to engage in it is critical for engagement in a wider range of roles (e.g., worker, player, community activity participant). Many health professionals, therefore, will have an interest in a person's ability to successfully and adequately function in this area because of the impact it will have on engagement in all areas of a person's life. If a person requires assistance to complete self-care activities, then the involvement of another is required, and so the role of carer for others is also considered when health professionals work with their clients.

Although all health professionals may be interested in a person's level of independence with regard to self-care and physical performance, the assessment of self-care activities has traditionally been associated with occupational therapists and nurses. These health professionals consider self-care (assessment and rehabilitation) as an integral aspect of their professional roles. Physiotherapists and occupational therapists have tended to be involved in assessment of physical function. Other health professionals, however, may also assess aspects of physical function or at least use the assessment information provided by others.

It is necessary, therefore, for all health professionals to be at least informed consumers of the information provided by assessments of self-care and physical function. Some assessments of self-care have been developed from a specific professional perspective and are designed for use by these professionals (e.g., COPM developed for use by occupational therapists), while others have specific training requirements (e.g., FIM).

Due to the major influence that limitations in self-care function can have on individuals and the people with whom they have close and daily contact, assessment of this area is also more likely to include family members, other caregivers, and role partners. Therefore, assessment of self-care and physical function is the concern of the individual, family members, caregivers, role partners, and a wide range of health professionals.

CRITICAL ISSUES IN PHYSICAL AND FUNCTIONAL ASSESSMENT PRACTICE AND RESEARCH

Evidence-based practice, together with a push to improve the quality of rehabilitation outcomes, has evolved with the need to generate better methods to measure functional and physical outcomes. Assessment of functional outcomes in physical rehabilitation continues to reflect the struggle between the need for comprehensive and sensitive outcome measures and the demand for assessment strategies that have high clinical utility in a variety of rehabilitation settings. Internationally, rehabilitation services are faced with pressure to justify the intervention provided and to demonstrate not only positive outcomes, but also their efficiency and feasibility (Jette & Hayley, 2005). As a result, hundreds of instruments have been developed to measure functional and physical outcomes in populations of persons with chronic disease who need or receive rehabilitation (McHorney, 1997). However, few functional and physical outcome measures have been considered "gold standard," and there are major challenges to be overcome to create effective assessment for use in the future.

First, the scope of available measures remains extremely narrow. In response to social change and clinical advances, physical rehabilitation is now facing new measurement challenges (McHorney, 1997). With changing professional, consumer, and societal expectations, new means of assessments need to reflect broader rehabilitation goals including community integration and physical aspects of social participation. A study of assessment focus in stroke rehabilitation publications over a 30-year period, for example, indicated that participation assessments accounted for less than 6% of all measurement citations (Salter, Foley, Jufai, & Teasall 2007). Around 56.8% of studies reported multicomponent assessment. Of these, 25% included assessment at the level of ICF participation. The researchers concluded that despite increasing awareness of the significance of participation issues in physical and functional assessment, few studies have used assessment measures that link function to social participation.

Second, there is little interface between the plethora of existing assessment methods. This makes it impossible to track relevant functional outcomes across different care settings, across programs, or even across an entire rehabilitation episode (Jette & Hayley, 2005). Third, traditional assessment models do not suit the heterogeneous population of clients who will require rehabilitation in a predicted aging future. The length and complexity of many fixed-form outcome measures have become increasingly burdensome to practitioners and rehabilitation organizations and are being discarded. Contemporary functional outcome instruments based on the ICF framework are currently being developed and tested by rehabilitation researchers worldwide (Jette & Hayley). The goal is to develop quantitative and qualitative functional outcome instruments that will replace earlier generations of limited functional outcome instruments that continue to be the norm.

Summary and Conclusion

In summary, this chapter outlined selected examples of methods used to assess physical aspects of functional performance across a hierarchy that includes measurement of body structure and function, personal care activities and routines, and the physical aspects of roles. Three major areas of assessment that were aligned with the International Classification of Function were described. These included the assessment of the physical aspects of role performance (participation); the assessment of routine and task performance (focusing on personal care); and the assessment of body structure and function. It was suggested that effective assessment is tailored to the needs of the client and contains elements of both standardized (positivist) and observational (naturalistic) approaches. Practitioners should consider the range of assessment methods across the hierarchy of physical functioning from participation (roles) to body structure and function to obtain the best data to assist with interventions and to measure outcomes.

Self-Check Questions

1. What factors need to be considered when assessing physical and functional performance? Are some factors more important than others when gaining information to inform an assessment for rehabilitation that is aimed at enabling optimal participation in life?
2. List the types of physical and functional assessments, their purposes and use. Discuss how each of these can influence individuals' participation.
3. Over the last decade there have been changes in the focus of physical and functional assessments. What are they, and what implications do they have for contemporary assessment practice?
4. Discuss the differences in standardized and nonstandardized methods of assessment. What considerations need to be made when deciding on the type of assessment measure to use?
5. What is your understanding of the potential influence of physical and functional performance assessments on policy interventions? Provide examples of how this can both promote and limit access to services.

Case Study

Andrew is 68 years old and lives with his wife Sarah in their own home. Role assessment identified that Andrew's most valued roles are husband, father, and nature lover. His marriage is very important to him, and he has always tried his best to look after Sarah and his children. He used to work as a ranger for the National Parks and Wildlife Board, retiring 3 years ago. Until recently, Andrew worked as a volunteer on a bush regeneration program in his local bush reserve, but has been unable to attend for several months because of his arthritis. He enjoys bushwalking, playing bridge, and gardening.

Andrew has osteoarthritis (OA) (onset at 55 years) and has had rheumatoid arthritis (RA) for the last 5 years. His condition has deteriorated over the last year. He has noticed increasing pain and stiffness in his wrists, hands, knees, and shoulders. This is now restricting his performance in personal care and other everyday routines and tasks related to his most valued roles.

Due to pain in his joints, Andrew finds it hard to get enough sleep; however, he tries to rest during the day. He has periods of malaise and fever when his RA is active and this lowers his energy levels.

When interviewed, Andrew identified problems in various areas of personal care. He required Sarah's help with feeding and dressing, and this reliance on Sarah constituted a role reversal that concerned him greatly. This was investigated in more detail through the use of the COPM, where Andrew indicated that he had difficulty feeding himself, toileting, dressing, bathing, and grooming. He then rated his performance and satisfaction with these routines. Further discussion with Andrew and Sarah indicated environmental aspects that affected his performance. A home visit was arranged to assess this in more detail. Some environmental modifications were recommended for the bathroom and toilet.

Observational assessment of Andrew's personal care performance was undertaken, and the Klein–Bell ADL Scale was used to identify specific aspects of problematic task performance. This allowed the identification of alternative techniques and assistive devices that Andrew could use to maintain independence in personal care routines.

Assessment of Andrew's active range of motion and functional muscle strength indicated that he had restrictions in his knees (making it difficult to get on/off a low toilet, and in/out of the shower recess) and his upper limbs (making it difficult to reach his feet, his back, and up to his head; hold small items such as eating utensils, soap, and dentures; lift moderately heavy items such as a full mug of coffee; grasp and adjust items such as clothing). Assessment of Andrew's endurance showed that it was poor (e.g., having a shower required him to rest for up to an hour afterwards). His assessed upper limb function indicated poor coordination and manual dexterity (e.g., difficulty cutting his nails, doing up shoelaces, and manipulating buttons and zips).

Environmental modifications were made to Andrew and Sarah's home. Andrew was provided with assistive devices and practiced using them. Both Andrew and Sarah identified that they would like to know more about energy conservation, joint protection, alternative techniques, and safe equipment use to enable Andrew to regain his independence in personal care. The COPM and Klein–Bell ADL Scale were used following all these interventions as outcome measures.

References

American College of Sports Medicine. (2000). *Guidelines for exercise testing and prescription.* (6th ed.). Baltimore: Lippincott Williams & Wilkins.

Anderson, D. S. (2000). Functional assessment. In S. Kumar (Ed.), *Multidisciplinary approach to rehabilitation* (pp. 209–241). Boston: Butterworth-Heinemann.

Asher, I. E. (1996). *Occupational therapy assessment tools: An annotated index* (2nd ed.). Bethesda, MD: American Occupational Therapy Association.

Ashworth, B. (1964). Preliminary trial of carisoprodol in multiple sclerosis. *Practitioner, 192,* 540–542.

Awan, R., Smith, J., & Boon, A. J. (2002). Measuring shoulder internal rotation range of motion: A comparison of 3 techniques. *Archives of Physical Medicine and Rehabilitation, 83,* 1229–1234.

Borg, G. A. (1985). *An introduction to Borg's RPE-Scale.* New York: Mouvement.

Bränholm, I.-B., & Fugl-Meyer, A. R. (1992). Occupational role preferences and life satisfaction. *Occupational Therapy Journal of Research, 12*(3), 159–171.

Brooks, D., Davis, A. M., & Naglie, G. (2006). Validity of 3 physical performance measures in inpatient geriatric rehabilitation. *Archives of Physical Medicine and Rehabilitation, 87,* 105–110.

Burns, R. B. (1991). *Essential psychology* (2nd ed.). Dordrecht, Netherlands: Kluwer Academic Publishers.

Burridge, J. H., Wood, D. E., Hermens, H. J., Voerman, G. E., Johnson, G. R., van Wijck, F., Platz, T., Gregoric, M., Hitchcock, R., & Pandyan, A. (2005). Theoretical and methodological considerations in the measurement of spasticity. *Disability and Rehabilitation, 27,* 69–80.

Carr, J., & Shepherd, R. B. (1987). *Neurological rehabilitation.* Oxford: Butterworth Heinemann.

Chiou, I. L., & Burnett, C. N. (1985). Values of activities of daily living: A survey of stroke patients and their home therapists. *Archives of Physical Medicine and Rehabilitation, 65,* 901–906.

Dagfinrud, H., Kjeken, I., Mowindkel, P., Hagen, K. B., & Kvien, T. K. (2005). Impact of functional impairment in ankylosing spondylitis: Impairment, activity limitation, and participation restrictions. *Journal of Rheumatology, 32,* 516–523.

Delbridge, A., Bernard, J. R. L., Blair, D., Ramson, W. S., & Butler, S. (Eds.). (1981). *The Macquarie Dictionary.* St. Leonards, NSW: Macquarie Library Pty. Ltd.

Dickerson, A. E., & Oakley, F. (1995). Comparing the roles of community-living persons and patient populations. *American Journal of Occupational Therapy, 49*(3), 221–228.

Dijkers, M. P. (1997). Quality of life after spinal cord injury: A meta-analysis of the effects of disablement components. *Spinal Cord, 35,* 829–840.

Dijkers, M. P. (1999). Correlates of life satisfaction among persons with spinal cord injury. *Archives of Physical Medicine and Rehabilitation, 80,* 867–876.

Elliott, M. S., & Barris, R. (1987). Occupational role performance and life satisfaction in elderly persons. *Occupational Therapy Journal of Research, 7*(4), 215–224.

Fasoli, S. E. (2008). Assessing roles and competence. In M. Vining Radomski & C. A. Trombly Latham (Eds.), *Occupational therapy for physical dysfunction* (6th ed., pp. 65–90). Baltimore: Lippincott Williams & Wilkins.

Fawcett, A.L. (2007). *Principles of assessment and outcome measurement for occupational therapists and physiotherapists: Theory, skills and application.* Chichester: John Wiley and Sons.

Finch, E., Brooks, D., Stratford, P. W., & Mayo, N. E. (2002). *Physical rehabilitation outcome measures: A guide to enhanced clinical decision making* (2nd ed.). Baltimore: Lippincott Williams & Wilkins.

Flinn, N. A., Trombly Latham, C. A., & Podolski, C. R. (2008). Assessing abilities and capacities: Range of motion, strength, and endurance. In M. V. Radomski & C. A. Trombly Latham (Eds.), *Occupational therapy for physical dysfunction* (6th ed., pp. 91–185). Philadelphia: Wolters Kluwer, Lippincott Williams & Wilkins.

Foti, D., & Kanazawa, L. M. (2006). Activities of daily living. In H. McHugh Pendleton & W. Schultz-Krohn (Eds.), *Pedretti's occupational therapy: Practice skills for physical dysfunction* (6th ed., pp. 146–194). St. Louis, MO: Mosby Elsevier.

Geertzen, J. H., Dijkstra, P. U., van Sonderen, E. L., Groothoff, J. W., Duis, H. J., & Eisma, W. H. (1998). Relationship between impairments, disability and handicap in reflex sympathetic dystrophy patients: A long-term follow-up study. *Clinical Rehabilitation, 12,* 402–412.

Gitlin, L. N. (2006). *Physical function in older adults: A comprehensive guide to its meaning and measurement.* Austin, TX: PRO-ED.

Guccione, A. A., & Scalzitti, D. A. (2007). Examination of functional status and activity level. In S. B. O'Sullivan & T. J. Schmitz (Eds.), *Physical rehabilitation* (pp. 373–400). Philadelphia: F. A. Davis Co.

Hagner, D. (2000). Supporting people as part of the community: Possibilities and prospects for change. In J. Nisbet & D. Hagner (Eds.), *Part of the community: Strategies for including everyone* (pp. 15–42). Baltimore: Paul H. Brookes Publishing Co.

Hillman, A. M. (2006). *Perceived control in the everyday occupational roles of people with Parkinson's disease and their partners.* Retrieved October 24, 2007, from http://hdl.handle.net/2123/1621.

Hillman, A. M. (2007). *Occupational role performance in the presence of disability.* Berlin: VDM Verlag Dr. Müller.

Hillman, A. M., & Chapparo, C. J. (1995). An investigation of occupational role performance in men over 60 who have had a stroke. *Occupational Science: Australia, 2*(3), 88–99.

Jackoway, I. S., Rogers, J. C., & Snow, T. L. (1987). The Role Change Assessment: An interview tool for evaluating older adults. *Occupational Therapy in Mental Health, 7*(1), 17–37.

Jacobs, K., & Jacobs, L. (Eds.). (2004). *Quick reference dictionary for occupational therapy.* (4th ed.). Thorofare, NJ: Slack.

Jette, A. M., & Hayley, S. M. (2005). Contemporary measurement techniques for rehabilitation outcomes assessment. *Journal of Rehabilitation Medicine, 37,* 339–345.

Johnston M. (1997). Representations of disability. In K. Petric & J. A. Weinman (Eds.), *Perceptions of health and illness.* (pp. 189–212). New York: Hardwood Academic Publishers.

Kopp, B., Kunkel, A., Flor, H., Platz, T., Rose, U., Mauritz, K. H., Gersser, K., McCulloch, K. L., & Taub, E. (1997). The Arm Motor Ability Test: Reliability, validity, and sensitivity to change of an instrument for assessing disabilities in activities of daily living. *Archives of Physical Medicine and Rehabilitation, 80,* 624–628.

Krause, N., & Shaw, B. A. (2000). Role-specific feelings of control and mortality [electronic version]. *Psychology and Aging, 15*(4), 617–626.

Landis, J. R. (Ed.) (1995). *Sociology: Concepts and characteristics* (9th ed.). Belmont, CA: Wadsworth.

Law, M. (1993). Evaluating activities of daily living: Directions for the future. *American Journal of Occupational Therapy, 47,* 3, 233–237.

Law, M. (1997). Self-care. In J. van Duesen & D. Brunt (Eds.), *Assessment in occupational therapy and physical therapy* (pp. 421–433). Philadelphia: W.B. Saunders Co.

Law, M. (2002). Participation in the occupations of everyday life. *American Journal of Occupational Therapy, 56,* 640–649.

Law, M., Baptiste, S., Carswell, A., McColl, M., Polatajko, H., & Pollock, N. (1998). *Canadian occupational performance measure* (3rd ed.). Toronto, On, Canada: CAOT Publications *Journal of Occupational Therapy, 47,* 3, 233–237.

Lawton, M. P. (1982). Competence, environmental press, and the adaptation of older people. In M. P. Lawton, P. G. Windley, & T. O. Byerts (Eds.), *Aging and the environment: Theoretical approaches* (pp. 33–59). New York: Springer.

Leake, D., James, R., & Stodden, R. (1995). Shifting paradigms to natural supports: A practical response to a crisis. In O. Karan & S. Greenspan (Eds.), *Community rehabilitation services for people with disabilities* (pp. 20–37). Boston: Butterworth-Heinemann.

Lemay, R.A. (1999). Role, identities and expectancies: Positive contributions to normalization and social role valourization. In R.J. Flynn & R. A. Lemay (Eds.), *A quarter of a century of Normalization and Social Role Valourization: Evolution and Impact.* Ottawa, ON, Canada: University of Ottawa Press.

Letts, L., & Bosch, J. (2005). Measuring occupational performance in basic activities of daily living. In M. Law, C. Baum, & W. Dunn (Eds.), *Measuring occupational performance: Supporting best practice in occupational therapy* (2nd ed., pp. 179–225). Thorofare, NJ: Slack.

Liggett, H. (1988). Stars are not born: An interpretive approach to the politics of disability. *Disability, Handicap & Society, 3,* 263–275.

Lincoln, Y. S. & Guba, E. G. (2000). Paradigmatic controversies, contradictions and emerging confluences in N. K. Denzin & Y. S. Lincoln (Eds.), *Handbook of qualitative research* (2nd ed.). Thousand Oaks, CA: Sage.

Lollar, D. J. & Crews, J. E. (2003). Redefining the role of public health in disability. *Annual Review of Public Health in Disability, 24,* 195–208.

Mathiowetz, V., & Bass-Haugen, J. (2008). Assessing abilities and capacities: Motor behavior. In M.V. Radomski & C. A.

Trombly Latham (Eds.), *Occupational therapy for physical dysfunction.* (6th ed.) (pp.186–211). Philadelphia: Lippincott Williams & Wilkins.

McHorney C. (1997). Generic health measurement: Past accomplishments and a measurement paradigm for the 21st century. *Annals of Internal Medicine, 127,* 743–750.

Medical Research Council. (1976). *Aids to the examination of the peripheral nervous system.* London: Her Majesty's Stationary Office.

Nagi, S. (1969). *Disability and rehabilitation.* Columbus: Ohio State University Press.

Nagi, S. (1991). Disability concepts revisited. In A. M. Pope & A. R. Tarlov (Eds.), *Disability in America: Toward a national agenda for prevention.* (p. 100). Washington D.C: National Academy Press.

Nelson, A. J. (1974). Functional ambulation profile. *Physical Therapy, 54,* 1059.

Oakley, F., Kielhofner, G., Barris, R., & Reichler, R. K. (1986). The Role Checklist: Development and empirical assessment of reliability. *Occupational Therapy Journal of Research, 6*(3), 157–170.

O'Sullivan, S. B. (2007a). Clinical decision making. In S. B. O'Sullivan & T. J. Schmitz (Eds.), *Physical Rehabilitation.* (5th ed.) (pp. 4–24). Philadelphia: F. A. Davis Company.

O'Sullivan, S. B. (2007b). Examination of motor function: Motor control and motor learning. In S. B. O'Sullivan & T. J. Schmitz (Eds.), *Physical Rehabilitation.* (5th ed.) (pp. 228–271). Philadelphia: F. A. Davis Company.

O'Sullivan, S. B., & Schmitz, T. J. (Eds.). (2007). *Physical Rehabilitation* (5th ed.). Philadelphia: F. A. Davis Company.

Ottenbacher, K., Tickle-Degnen, L., & Hasselkus, B.R. (2002). Therapists awake! The challenge of evidence-based occupational therapy. *American Journal of Occupational Therapy, 56,* 247–249.

Priestley, M. (1999). *Disability politics and community care.* London: Jessica Kingsley.

Radomski, M. V., & Trombly Latham, C.A. (Eds.). (2008). *Occupational therapy for physical dysfunction.* (6th ed.). Baltimore: Lippincott Williams & Wilkins.

Riolo, L. (1996). Skill differences in novice and expert clinicians in neurologic physical therapy. *Neurology Report,* 20–60.

Rogers, J. C., & Holm, M. B. (1994). Accepting the challenge of outcome research: Examining the effectiveness of occupational therapy practice. *American Journal of Occupational Therapy, 48,* 871–876.

Rogers, J. C., Holm, M. B., Beach, S., Schultz, R., Cipriani, J., Fox, A., et al. (2003). Concordance of four methods of disability assessment using performance in the home as the criterion method. *Arthritis & Rheumatism (Arthritis Care & Research), 49*(5), 640–647.

Rondinelli, R. D., Dunn, W., Hassanein, K. M., Keesling, C. A., Meredith, S. C., Schultz, T. L., & Lawrence, N. J. (1997). A simulation of hand impairments: Effects on upper extremity function and implications toward medical impairment rating and disability determination. *Archives of Physical Medicine and Rehabilitation, 78,* 1358–1363.

Rusk, H. (1958). *Rehabilitation medicine: A textbook on physical medicine and rehabilitation.* St. Louis, MO: Mosby.

Sackett, D. L., Richardson, W. S., Rosenberg, W., & Hayes, R.B. (1997). *Evidence-based medicine.* New York: Churchill Livingstone.

Salter, K. L., Foley, N.C., Jufai, J.W., & Teasall, R.B. (2007). Assessment of participation outcomes in randomized controlled trials of stroke rehabilitation interventions. *International Journal of Rehabilitation Research, 30,* 339–342.

Schmitz, T. J. (2007). Examination of coordination. In S. B. O'Sullivan & T. J.Schmitz. (Eds.). *Physical Rehabilitation.* (5th ed.) (pp. 193–226). Philadelphia: F. A. Davis Company.

Schultz-Krohn, W. (2005). Culture and development. In A. Cronin & M. Mandich (Eds.), *Human development and performance throughout the lifespan.* (pp. 55–70). Clifton Park, NY: Thomson Delmar Learning.

Shumway-Cook, A., & Woollacott, M. (2001). *Motor control: Theory and practical applications* (2nd ed.). Philadelphia: Lippincott Williams & Wilkins.

Sveen, U., Bautz-Holter, E., Sodring, K. M., Wyller, T. B., & Laake, K. (1999). Association between impairments, self-care ability and social activities 1 year after stroke. *Disability and Rehabilitation, 21,* 372–377.

Toal-Sullivan, D., & Henderson, P. R. (2004). Client-oriented role evaluation (CORE): The development of a clinical rehabilitation instrument to assess role change associated with disability. *American Journal of Occupational Therapy, 58*(2), 211–220.

Trombly Latham, C. A. (2008). Conceptual foundations for practice. In M. V. Radomski & C. A. Trombly Latham (Eds.), *Occupational therapy for physical dysfunction.* (6th ed.). (pp. 1–20). Baltimore: Lippincott Williams & Wilkins.

Turnbull, H. R., Wilcox, B. L., Stowe, M. J., & Umbarger, G. T. (2001). Matrix of federal statutes and deferral and state court decisions reflecting the core concepts of disability policy. *Journal of Disability Policy Studies, 12*(3), 144–176.

Van Swearingen, J. M. (1996). The Modified Gait Abnormality Rating Scale for recognizing the risk of recurrent falls in community dwelling elderly adults. *Physical Therapy, 77,* 812.

Wade, D. (1992). *Measurement in neurological rehabilitation.* Oxford, UK: Oxford University Press.

Wolf, S. L., Catlin, P. A., Ellis, M., Archer, A. L., Morgan, B., & Piacentino, A. (2001). Assessing Wolf Motor Function Test as outcome measure for research in patients after stroke. *Stroke, 32,* 1635–1639.

Wolf, S. L., Catlin, P. A., & Gage, K. (1999). Establishing the reliability and validity of measurements of walking using the Emory Functional Ambulation Profile. *Physical Therapy, 79,* 1122.

World Health Organization (WHO) (2001). *International Classification of Functioning, Disability and Health (ICF).* Geneva, Switzerland: Author.

World Health Organization (WHO). (2002). *Towards a common language for functioning, disability and health ICF.* Retrieved June 13, 2007, from www.who.icf/

Measures of Independent Living

DEBRA A. HARLEY
University of Kentucky

DIANE L. SMITH
REGINALD J. ALSTON
University of Illinois

OVERVIEW

Individuals with disabilities include persons with physical, mental, emotional, and cognitive impairments, which limit, impede, or disrupt quality of life functions and independent living. Many of these impediments are attitudinal whereas others are functional and medically determined. *Independent living* (IL) refers to the acquisition and application of skills required to function in social, political, economic, cultural, and technological segments of society The notion of independent living is strongly connected to the idea of community integration, implying that people should not be institutionalized if it is not necessary (Institute for Prospective Technological Studies, 2006). Thus, the effect of disability on independent living is a function of the interaction of the individual and the environment (National Institute on Disability and Rehabilitation Research [NIDRR], 2006). In addition, independent living means having both the capacity and opportunity to make decisions that affects one's own life, and being active in the mainstream of community. This chapter seeks to advance an understanding of the effectiveness of independent living that involves assessment of strengths and needs/skills building across various categories: education, career plans, employment skills, family supports, peer interaction and supports, financial management, health care, residential living, community service, community supports, interaction skills and processes, and transportation.

LEARNING OBJECTIVES

By the end of the chapter, readers should be able to:

- Identify pertinent research in the assessment of independent living
- Identify current research methods in independent living
- Understand cultural, legislative, and professional issues impacting specific counseling aspects or procedures
- Recognize multiple approaches to independent living
- Discuss national and international practices in independent living assessment
- Identify and project future needs in independent living assessment

INTRODUCTION

The assessment of independent living includes the items previously mentioned. It also covers an individual's capacity to perform or complete a variety of activities of daily living, broadly construed to include cooking and nutrition, advocacy, socialization, grooming and hygiene, health care, homemaking, sexuality, recreation/leisure, citizenship and civic literacy, and disability rights (Independent Living Assessment, 2001).Community integration and social participation may depend on the customs and practices of the community itself.Daily living assessment and community integration need to be assessed from several perspectives: diverse family systems, culturally diverse populations, and quality of life in the context of culture (Suzuki, Ponterotto, & Meller, 2001).

The purpose of this chapter is to present information on measures of independent living and community involvement in the United States. Information is presented on independent living in rehabilitation and health services; the history of independent living; assessment methods in independent living; critical research; cultural, legislative, and professional issues; multidisciplinary approaches; and national and international practices in independent living assessment. In addition, major issues in independent living that need to be addressed are discussed. The intent is to integrate theory and practice.

IMPORTANCE OF INDEPENDENT LIVING TO REHABILITATION AND HEALTH SERVICES

Human beings are social beings; they live, work, play, and relax together. However, many individuals with disabilities experience loneliness, anxiety, and frustration in community and social situations. The goals of quality of life and social competence, which include community living, presence and procedures, and social inclusion of individuals with disabilities are now firmly established because of normalization and deinstitutionalization programs (Riches, 1996). The essential goal of independent living should be to achieve a sense of community connectedness, rather than being concerned with functioning alone (Cummins & Lau, 2003).

Implicit in the philosophy and practice of independent living is the belief that individuals with disabilities have a right to define themselves with respect to promoting a sense of belonging in a community and to promote independence and interdependence as natural supports (Institute for Prospective Technological Studies, 2006). "The duties and obligations of the active citizen are to contribute to their own individual welfare because, only in this way, can the welfare of all be maximized" (Oliver, 1996, p. 50).

Independent living centers have had profound effects on rehabilitation and health services because, underpinning the establishment of IL centers, was the attempt of people with disabilities to leave residential care and live independently in the community (Dublin CIL, 2005). People with disabilities started the process of liberating themselves from the medical profession, which has constrained them for centuries. "Doctors and paramedics colonized disability, and turned disabled people into material for research and experimentation" (Baird, 1992, p. 5). Not until the social change movement of the 1960s were major services for people with disabilities seriously considered by federal legislation. Although the Social Security system provided benefits to those who had become disabled, there was no attempt to broaden the base of services for them beyond the vocational rehabilitation approach. The IL movement marked the first time in U.S. history in which consumers, advocates, and service providers began an intensive examination of the human service delivery system to decide what was missing. As a result, community-based programs for people with disabilities began growing all over the nation in an attempt to fill the gaps left by these missing services (Shreve, 1982).

As with many emerging and continuing trends, the list of solutions and approaches that are available to measure independent living and quality of life is substantial. Personal outcome measures include the following: (a) identity (e.g., people choose personal goals, where and with whom they live, and where they work; have intimate relationships, are satisfied with services, and are satisfied with their personal life situation); (b) autonomy (e.g., people choose their daily routine, have time, space, and opportunity for privacy, decide when to share personal information, and use their environment); (c) affiliation (e.g., people live in integrated environments, participate in the life of the community, interact with other members of the community, perform different social roles, have friends, and are respected); (d) attainment (e.g., people choose services and realize personal goals); (e) safeguards (e.g., people are connected to natural support networks and are safe); (f) rights (e.g., people exercise rights and are treated fairly; and (g) health and wellness (e.g., people have the best possible health, are free from abuse and neglect, and experience continuity and security) (Community Living Campbellford/Brighton, 2006).

In 1974, 4 independent living programs existed in the United States. By 2006, there were more than 600 independent living programs (Frieden, Widmer, & Richards, 1983). Likewise, IL programs saw an increase in funding, as well as an increase in the number of individuals with disabilities being served. An independent living program is defined as a community-based program having substantial consumer involvement that provides directly, or coordinates indirectly through referral, those services necessary to assist individuals with severe disabilities to increase self-determination and to maximize unnecessary dependence on others. The IL program has three major characteristics: It is community-based, it has consumer involvement, and it provides specific services. Independent living programs include three types of programs: independent living center, independent living residential program, and independent living transitional living program.

Internationally, the focus of disability perspectives suggests that new rehabilitation approaches will simultaneously focus on improving individual capacity and removing environmental barriers. However, in the United States, a strong reliance exists on a medical or impairment-related approach. Unfortunately, this view has resulted in a persistent prescription of services based on an impairment or individual definition of disability, rather than a social or environmental one (Fabian, McInerney, & Santos Rodrigues, 2005). However, the international paradigm shift in assessing disability, as reflected in the International Classification Functioning, Disability and Health (ICF),

represents a comprehensive, coherent, and cohesive viewpoint that disability rights advocates around the world endorse (Hurst, 2003). In fact, Ustan, Chatterju, Brickenbach, Kostanjesk, and Schneider (2003) referred to the ICF as a "tool" for understanding disability and health.

As for evaluation standards, they are becoming increasingly international in the sense of being more indigenous, more global, and more transnational (Chelimsky & Shadish, 1997; Russon & Russon, 2005). For people with disabilities working to achieve community integration, the ICF specifically classifies functioning at the level of body as body part, whole person, and whole person in social context. The concept of independent living falls within the activity and participation domain of the ICF. According to the ICF, activity is defined as the execution of a task or action by an individual. Participation is involvement in a life situation. The domains for the activities and participation component are given in a single list that covers the full range of life areas, from basic learning and watching, to composite areas such as social tasks. The two qualifiers for the activities and participation component are the performance qualifiers and the capacity qualifiers. The performance qualifier describes what an individual does in his or her current environment. The capacity qualifier describes an individual's ability to execute a task or an action. Examples of activities and participation include general tasks and demands, mobility, self-care and domestic life (World Health Organization, 2001). This domain is appropriate for independent living because measurement of these components is essential to determine potential for independent living. See more on the World Health Organization's Website at http://www3.who.int/icf/ictemplate.cfm. There is also additional information in chapter 12.

DISCUSSION BOX 24.1

Natural Disasters

The occurrence of natural disasters is disruptive to the lives and employment of individuals. This is more so for those with disabilities, especially as they seek to return to independent living status. Many issues become more urgent than before: housing, transportation, employment, social networks, and health care.

Questions

1. How are individuals with disabilities affected by natural disasters?

2. What is the role of IL centers in assisting displaced consumers with disabilities for short-term and long-term recovery?

3. What role does assessment play in recovery efforts after natural disaster?

HISTORY OF RESEARCH AND PRACTICE IN THE ASSESSMENT OF INDEPENDENT LIVING

Five social movements of the 1960s and 70s contributed to the creation of the necessary atmosphere for the current activities of the disability rights movement and the development of centers for independent living: (1) civil rights movement, (2) consumerism, (3) self-help, (4) de-medicalization, and (5) de-institutionalization (DeJong, 1979a; McDonald & Oxford, 2006; Shreve, 1982). The significance of the *civil rights movement* for people with disabilities focused on them being denied access to basic services and opportunities such as employment, housing, transportation, education, and so forth. *Consumerism* gave people with disabilities the autonomy or power over the services and products they would use. In essence, they became consumers first and "patients" last. The *self-help* approach reinforced the concept that people with disabilities know best how to serve others who have the same or similar disabilities. *Demedicalization* removed the involvement of medical professionals from the daily lives of people with disabilities because they are not "sick" and do not need to depend upon medical professionals for everyday needs. *Deinstitutionalization* began in response to the institutionalization and hospitalization of those with mental illness and developmental disabilities, who are only disabled by some permanent type of condition. Since these individuals are not ill, placement in institutions is inappropriate and far more costly than community-based services (McDonald & Oxford; Shreve). According to Shreve, "the disability rights and independent living movement is a complication of all five social movements as they pertain to and are defined by people who have disabilities" (p. 3).

According to Dejong (1979b), it is difficult to pinpoint the time when or where the IL movement began. In 1962, the program for students with disabilities at the University of Illinois at Champaign Urbana was among the first to facilitate community living for persons with severe physical disabilities. In the 1960s, Justin Dart, Jr., initiated a program through his company, Japan Tupperware, to offer employment and independent living skills training to institutionalized Japanese with physical disabilities (Nosek, 1992). However, the birth of the IL movement has been attributed to a group of students with disabilities at the University of California (UC) at Berkeley who were enrolled between 1962 and 1969. This program has served as a model for a network of over 200 IL centers that have since developed with the assistance of federal and state funding (Nosek). Students at UC–Berkeley drew on their experience to develop a philosophy of IL. These principles included: (a) those who know best the needs of people with disabilities and how to meet those needs are the people with disabilities themselves; (b) the needs of people with disabilities can be met most effectively by comprehensive programs that advocate for the rights and needs of people with disabilities and provide a variety of supportive services; and (c) people with disabilities should be integrated as fully as possible into their community (California Department of Rehabilitation, 2006). The first center for independent living (CIL) was established in Berkeley, California, in 1972 (Dublin CIL, 2005: Nosek, 1992). Additional historical information on IL is available at the following Websites: Center for Independent Living History at http://www.centerforindependence.org/il_history/index.htm, Cornell University ILR School, Employment and Disability Institute at http://www.ilr.cornell.edI, the World Institute on Disability at http://www.wid.org, and Independent Living Research Utilization at TIRR at http://www.ilru.org.

Over 2 decades ago, DeJong and Hughes (1982) indicated that a vexing issue in disability research and practice is the specification and measurement of long-term outcome measures relevant to the evaluation of IL programs and services. This issue is as prevalent today. A response to this issue is the ranking and weighting methodology that can take into account the value judgments implicit in the development of long-term outcome measures for IL and medical rehabilitation programs (DeJong & Hughes; Myers, Ager, Kerr, & Myles, 1998).

CURRENT ASSESSMENT METHODS IN INDEPENDENT LIVING

Methods of assessing independent living are varied and each has its own advantages and disadvantages. Typically, assessment methods have been aimed at capturing information from the opinions and perceptions of family members and significant others or from direct observation of activities of daily living, social performance, and work adjustment (Institute for Prospective Technological Studies, 2006). Methods include standardized and nonstandardized assessment tools, objective checklists, rating scales completed by peers, adults who know the individual well, self-rating scales, sociometric observation, social validation procedures, and ecological inventories (Riches, 1996). For example, early studies published through the 1950s relied almost exclusively on archival data (Stumpf, 1990). Other methods of assessment include qualitative, case study, quantitative, and single subject research.

Many issues need to be addressed when assessing for a consumer's ability to return to home and live independently. Historically, assessment of self-care has meant establishing the degree to which an individual was dependent in those tasks related to activities of daily living (Cummins & Lau, 2003). Assessment of the consumer included evaluating ambulation ability (either by walking or using some type of assistive device such as a cane, walker or wheelchair), visual perceptual skills, cognitive skills, endurance, safety, and use of adaptive equipment. Assessment must also be made of the consumer's home environment (Steinfeld, 2005). The home should also be evaluated with regard to accessibility and safety. The following are common assessments used to evaluate consumers and their home/environmental factors.

Assessment of Consumers

Historically, assessment of self-care has meant establishing the degree to which an individual was independent in those tasks related to the activities of daily living (ADL), transferring, and mobility (see chapter on measures of physical functioning). Below we present select instruments that measure consumers' levels of performance (see chapter 23 on types of test and assessments for other instruments).

KLEIN–BELL ADL SCALE This scale is based on critical categories of self-care, which are easily observable components of behaviors that are necessary for independent functioning. The scale includes 170 items that relate to ADL and emergency communication. Each item on the scale is scored as either "achieved" or "failed," depending upon whether the person needs either physical or verbal assistance in order to perform the task. Successful performance or achievement of an item yields the total number of points possible for that item, and unsuccessful performance results in a score of zero. The points achieved within each ADL area are totaled and combined to yield an overall ADL independence score. Score totals are designed to measure change in an individual's raw performance (Christiansen, 1991). A high degree of correlation was found between scores on the scale and the number of hours per week a person required assistance during a 5–10 month period after discharge (Klein & Bell, 1982). A study by Smith et al. (1986) found that use of the Klein–Bell Scale within a clinical setting improved documentation and communication of the self-care needs

of patients, and thereby enhanced the effectiveness of the rehabilitation team.

KOHLMAN EVALUATION OF LIVING SKILLS *The Kohlman Evaluation of Living Skills* (KELS) is an evaluation of basic living skills, which combines interview and task performance (McGourty, 1988). The KELS assesses 18 living skills grouped within five major categories of self-care, safety and health, money management, transportation and telephone, and work and leisure in which the individual is able to perform without the assistance of others (McGourty, 1979). For reliability and validity of the KELS, see studies by Ilika and Hoffman (1981), Kaufman (1982), and Tateichi (1984).

ASSESSMENT OF MOTOR AND PROCESS SKILLS *The Assessment of Motor and Process Skills* (AMPS) is an occupational therapy-specific ADL assessment. An AMPS observation begins with the trained rater interviewing a participant to determine the types of tasks he or she performs on a daily basis (Fisher, 2003a,b). Three to six of the 83 standardized ADL task options that offer the individual an appropriate challenge level are identified. In turn, the consumer chooses at least two tasks to perform in which he or she is scored using a 4-point ordinal scale (4 = competent, 3 = questionable, 2 = ineffective, and 1 = markedly deficient). Finally, AMPS raters analyze the consumer's raw score using the AMPS computer-scoring program, a specialized application of many-faceted Rasch (MFR) analysis, to convert raw ADL skill item scores into linear ADL ability measures. This MFR analysis adjusts the final ADL ability estimates to account for task challenges, ADL skill item difficulty, and the severity of score used by the rater (Hayase et al., 2004). Numerous studies have been conducted on the test–retest reliability as well as validity of the AMPS ability measures across age, gender, ethnic group, and world region (Bernspang, 1999; Dickerson & Fisher, 1993; Duran & Fisher, 1996; Fisher, 2003a; Merrit & Fisher, 2003; Stauffer, Fisher & Duran, 2000).

FUNCTIONAL ASSESSMENT INVENTORY AND LIFE FUNCTIONING INDEX. The *Functional Assessment Inventory* (FAI) (Crewe & Athelstan, 1979, 1984) is a comprehensive scale of functional limitation and a checklist of ten special strength areas, designed specifically to help those involved in vocational rehabilitation to effectively organize and use information about problems of consumers with severe disabilities. The index consists of 30 behavioral scales of functional limitation. The FAI also includes a checklist of special strengths and provisions for identifying areas of expected change. The scales are intended to apply to all disability groups and are completed by the evaluator based upon interview data, medical charts, and diagnostic evaluations without requiring the consumer to be present (Christiansen, 1991). Reliability estimates of the FAI were conducted by Crewe and Athelstan (1981), Crewe, Athelstan, and Meadows (1975), and Crewe and Turner (1984).

THE LIFE FUNCTIONING INDEX   The *Life Functioning Index* (LFI) (Crewe & Turner, 1984) was developed to assess significant change in life status as part of a project in 1980 to develop a state/federal management information system for vocational rehabilitation programs (Christiansen, 1991). This instrument measures change in vocational areas and relevant areas of adjustment related to vocational success. The LFI is designed to complement the FAI, and measures six categories of life function: vocation, education, self-care, residence, mobility, and communication. Validity of the LFI were similar to that of the FAI, which demonstrated correlations between the instrument and vocational counselor's ratings of the severity of disability and likelihood of employability (Christiansen, 1991).

SCALES OF INDEPENDENT BEHAVIOR—REVISED
The *Scales of Independent Behavior* (Rev. ed.) measures both adaptive functioning and functional independence in various environments including the home, school, workplace, and other community settings. It serves as a tool or guide to plan education, training, and support interventions, along with providing a measure to evaluate a consumer's progress. It has three different forms: (1) the early development form (ages below 6 years and older adults with severe developmental disabilities); (2) the short form (all ages); and (3) the full scale (divided into four adaptive behavior clusters: motor skills, social interaction and communication skills, personal living skills, community living skills). The SIB-R also includes a short form for people with visual disabilities and a problem behavior scale. The instrument is shown to have good reliability. The SIB-R can provide professionals with an understanding of various behaviors a consumer performs, thus providing a measure of which training and intervention programs would be valuable in enhancing different independent living skills. It also provides an option to measure problematic behaviors that can interfere with independent and community-based living. The SIB-R can be administered together with the Woodcock Johnson Psychoeducational battery (Woodcock & Johnson, 1977) for a more comprehensive analysis.

CHECKLIST OF ADAPTIVE LIVING SKILLS.   The *Checklist of Adaptive Living Skills* (CALS) is a criterion-referenced instrument developed to measure functioning in various aspects of daily living, such as self-care and personal independence, along with adaptive behaviors in different environments, such as community and residential settings and places of work and leisure. The CALS can be administered to individuals from the ages of infancy up to 40+ years and is applicable to people with and without disabilities. The main objective behind the development of CALS is to provide a measure of adaptive behavioral functioning that can directly inform training and instructional programs. The CALS basically aims to be a tool to aid professionals in developing interventions by allowing them to assess specific skills and then develop focused training goals. It can be used in residential, work, community, and leisure settings (Bachelor, 1995).

ASSESSMENT OF LIVING SKILLS AND RESOURCES
The *Assessment of Living Skills and Resources* (ALSAR) evaluates 11 tasks of Instrumental Activities of Daily Living (IADL) (see Camp, 1998). It measures both skills levels and the ability to perform certain tasks. Originally designed for older adults living in community settings, the ALSAR can be used to assess IADL tasks for people with disabilities as well. The ALSAR provides a good template to measure the represented 11 IADL tasks. Rehabilitation professionals and IL professionals can use the instrument to design targeted interventions, assess needs for support and resources, and measure the progress of IADL skills. However, there is a lack of published studies indicating the use and effectiveness of this instrument.

Measures of Accessibility

There is a dearth of standardized scales assessing the home environment for architectural accessibility and safety. Before a client is discharged to home, it is important that the home environment be assessed for accessibility, potential use of adaptive equipment, and safety. One of the most reliable and valid assessment instruments for the home is the *Housing Enabler* developed by Prof. Edward Steinfeld. Prof. Steinfeld researched issues of accessibility, gradually leading to the housing standards of the American National Standards Institute (ANSI). The original publication was published in 1979 (Iwarsson & Isacsson, 1996).

The *Housing Enabler* begins with a descriptive part concerning individual or group data and housing standards. There are three steps: (1) An interview is conducted in combination with observation, with the aim of assessing the individual's functional limitations; (2) the environment is assessed, with items concerning the home and its immediate vicinity; and (3) predefined points for the various assessment items in the environmental assessment are used to calculate a total score predicting the degree of accessibility problems in a particular case.

Another important aspect of the measure of accessibility is that of universal design. The challenge is to change the way society thinks about design of all products and environments. Universal design is different from accessible design. Accessible design refers to products and buildings that are accessible and usable by people with disabilities. Universal design refers to products and buildings that are accessible and usable by everyone, including people with disabilities. Universal design provides one solution that can accommodate people with disabilities as well as the rest of the population. Moreover, universal design means giving attention to the needs of individuals who are older as well as young, women as well as men, and left-handed as well as right-handed (Steinfeld, 2005). According to Steinfeld, the creation and production of universal products can improve competitiveness in the world market, and the development of a public infrastructure and cultural and recreational sites that are usable by all can improve tourism and contribute to general economic welfare. The major step in operationalizing the universal design philosophy is designing for a broader range of people.

Both assessment and success of universal design are dependent on it having a high standard of aesthetics. In fact, the most successful universal designs often express the usability features of the product or environment as strong aesthetic qualities, and they are successful precisely because they are beautiful as well as useful for people with disabilities. Four principles are helpful to assure that this goal will be achieved: (1) insuring a wide range of anthropometric fit, (2) reducing energy expenditure, (3) clarifying the environment, and (4) using the systems approach (Steinfeld, 2005). In the final analysis, universal design is effective because it promotes full integration in every way and it symbolizes that integration. It acknowledges the social trends that are changing our societies, and it acknowledges differences as a part of everyday life.

RESEARCH CRITICAL TO ISSUES IN INDEPENDENT LIVING ASSESSMENT

Many of these evaluations have been tested in clinic sites and need to be tested in the future in home sites to determine whether the skills learned in the rehabilitation setting are transferable to the home setting. For example, arranging a house for independent living and safety is more than shifting furniture and observing someone perform activities of daily living in a supervised setting. It also means shifting mental gears and making changes in perception (Research Information on Independent Living, 2007a). For example, in the home setting, a wheelchair user should be evaluated on his or her response to an unexpected incident (e.g., knocking over a lamp, which ignites sparks). In such a real life situation, the individual is evaluated on his or her ability to respond under stress. In addition, many of these evaluations have been tested and standardized on a number of particular demographics, including age, impairment, or disability. For example, in Germany, researchers held training sessions for elderly individuals in an accessible "smart house" that had technologies such as an emergency call system and adaptable cupboards. Before program entry, an individual had to move independently in a wheelchair, transfer independently, eat without the help of another person, have enough endurance to take part in the program, and be motivated to succeed. To assist in transition, the researchers devised IL training in three phases: (1) an assessment; (2) weekly documentation and final assessment at the end of on-site training; and (3) home adaptation, follow-up visits, and documentation (Research Information on Independent Living, 2007b). Further research needs to evaluate these assessments on other consumer populations, as well as internationally. For example, evaluations that have been standardized on consumers with mental retardation should be restandardized before use on consumers with cognitive deficits experienced from a head injury or stroke because of differences in needs, interests, abilities, and self-determination (Research Information on Independent Living, 2007c).

Finally, more standardized tests need to be developed to assess the home environment with regard to accessibility and safety. As the baby-boomer generation continues to age, homes will need to be evaluated and adapted to allow these persons to live at home and avoid institutionalization. Evaluations that only consider the abilities of the consumer without evaluation of the home environment may not provide an effective evaluation of independent living skills and may compromise the success of the consumer.

Another important issue in IL assessment is the use of virtual reality (VR). In virtual reality, advanced technologies are used to produce simulated, interactive and multidimensional environments in which therapy and training can be provided within a functional, purposeful, and motivating context (Sveistrup, 2004).

With VR visual interfaces, including desktop monitors and head-mounted displays, haptic interfaces and real-time motion-tracking devices are used to create environments that allow users to interact with images and virtual objects in real-time through multiple sensory modalities. A key feature of all VR applications is interaction. According to Sveistrup, central to the issues of virtual environments (VE) as a training medium, is the question, does task improvement or does learning transfer reliably from VE to a real environment? Research reveals demonstrated improvements of specific motor function (e.g., balance and posture, locomotion, upper and lower extremity function, exercise, and pain tolerance), cognitive impairment, and visual disabilities with specific populations (Kizony, Katz, & Weiss, 2003; McComas & Sveistrup, 2002; Schultheis & Mourant, 2001; Yano, Kasai, Saitou, & Iwata, 2003).

In the future, research on assessment of independent living should address participatory research as well as classical and contemporary test theory. Likewise, measures of independent living for individuals with disabilities should include both traditional and contemporary test theory. A number of studies have sought to examine the question of the feasibility of independent living deployment readiness and community competence from various dimensions.

As stated earlier, the early studies published through the 1950s relied almost exclusively on archival data, with the reporting of descriptive statistics. Presently, quasiexperimental designs, permitting the use of powerful statistical analyses on data, dominate the literature. Techniques that have been used to analyze the data have varied widely, including multivariate analysis, multiple regression, discriminate function analysis and simple t-test, nonparametric statistics, and qualitative techniques (Huck & Cormier, 1996; Stumpf, 1990). Additional information on research and resource centers is available in the research boxes 24.1, 24.2, and 24.3.

CULTURAL, LEGISLATIVE, AND PROFESSIONAL ISSUES IMPACTING MEASURES OF INDEPENDENT LIVING

Identifying and assessing disability is related to the variation in how it is understood in different cultures. For example, the term *disability* does not exist across cultures. Although non-Western cultures may have terms for specific impairments, the idea of including all in an umbrella term may be missing (Fabian et al., 2005). What appears to be more important is the need to create "a social and physical environment in which the independence, prosperity, and equality of every person will be a natural result of the process of culture" (Nosek, 1992, p. 129).

Various pieces of legislation support the independent living movement and the rights of people with disabilities, nationally and internationally. In the United States the "bible" of civil rights for people with disabilities is the Rehabilitation Act of 1973 (McDonald & Oxford, 2006). The groundwork for federally funded centers of independent living was laid by the passage of such legislation as the Civil Rights Act (1964), Architectural Barriers Act (1968), Urban Mass Transit

---

RESEARCH BOX 24.1

Objective: A study by Burr, Mutchler, and Warren (2005) examines the impact of state variation in commitment to the provision of home and community-based services on living arrangement outcomes of older unmarried females with functional limitations.

Method: The authors combined data from the 1990 U.S. Census of Population (PUMS) with state-level information on long-term care, home and community-based service expenditures, nursing home bed availability, and Medicaid nursing home costs from a special report that compares state variation in long-term care systems. Multilevel logistic regression modeling techniques were used.

Results: Results found the risk of institutionalization compared to community living arrangements is reduced as spending for home and community-based services at the state level is increased.

Conclusion: Independent living and community-based living are cost effective arrangements.

Questions

1. What are some special concerns with regard to this population and independent living?
2. What are the implications of this study to independent living?
3. How might assessment be used?

RESEARCH BOX 24.2

Objective: Dunkoh, Underhill, and Montgomery (2006) conducted a study to assess the effectiveness of independent living programs for young people leaving care systems.

Method: A search of electronic databases was conducted to look at studies comparing independent living programs and traditional care systems.

Results: No study was found that met inclusion criteria for the review. Eighteen studies using nonrandomized or noncomparative designs were found that generally reported favorable outcomes for independent living participants.

Conclusion: Reliable inferences could not be drawn due to weak methodology.

Questions

1. What type of methodology might have been more appropriate for this study?
2. What is the importance of this study to independent living?
3. How could assessments have assisted in this process?

RESEARCH BOX 24.3

Objective: Moore, Steinman, Giesen, and Frank (2006) surveyed a national sample of elders served by the Independent Living Program for Older Individuals.

Method: The authors used national representative data to address six main areas of inquiry that pertained to functional outcomes and/or satisfaction with services among the participants. Among the ten survey items, three were specifically designed to assess the participants' satisfaction with their independent living program.

Results: Results showed that overall they were highly satisfied with the quality and timeliness of services and help in achieving independent living goals.

Conclusion: A slight improvement was found in their perceptions of functional outcomes from 1999 to 2004.

Questions

1. What implication does this study have for independent living?
2. What questions might you ask on a survey of this type?

Act (1970), Education of All Handicapped Children Act (PL 94-142) (1975), Air Carrier Access Act (1988), Fair Housing Amendments Act (1988), and Americans with Disabilities Act (1990). (See Table 24.1 for additional chronological listings and brief descriptions.)

More recent legislation includes the Workforce Investment Act (1998), The Ticket to Work and Work Incentives Improvement Act (1999), and the Help America Vote Act (2002) (Kilbury, Stotlar, & Eckert, 2005). More information on advancing independent living and the rights of individuals with disabilities through consumer-driven advocacy is available at http://www.ncil.org. Legislation and court cases that have specific implications for independent living include, but are not limited to, the Medicaid Community Attendant Services and Support Act (MiCASSA) (S 971 and HR 2032), the New Freedom Initiative, and the Olmstead case. Each of these is discussed below.

MiCASSA sets up a national program of community-based attendant services and supports for people with disabilities, regardless of age or disability type. This legislation, which changes Title XIX of the Social Security Act (Medicaid), permits those eligible for *Nursing Facility Services of Intermediate Care Facility Services* who are mentally retarded to choose to get services in their community instead of a nursing home or other institution. In addition, funds also provide payment for essentials needed when coming out of nursing homes (e.g., recent deposit, house supplies). MiCASSA is an individualized system that addresses each individual's needs. The money follows the individual instead of a facility receiving money to offer care. Specifically, provisions of MiCASSA include the following:

- Includes hands-on assistance to accomplish daily activities

TABLE 24.1 List and Description of Key Federal Laws

1964–Civil Rights Act: prohibits discrimination on the basis of race, religion, ethnicity, national origin, and creed—later, gender was added as a protected class.

1968–Architectural Barriers Act: prohibits architectural barriers in all federally owned or leased buildings.

1970–Urban Mass Transit Act: requires that all new mass transit vehicles be equipped with wheelchair lifts.

1973–Rehabilitation Act: particularly Title V, Sections 501, 503, ad 504, prohibits discrimination in federal programs and services and all other programs or services receiving federal funding.

1975–Developmental Disabilities Bill of Rights Act: among other things, established Protection and Advocacy (P&A).

1975–Education of All Handicapped Children Act (PL 94-142): requires free, appropriate public education in the least restrictive environment possible for children with disabilities. This law is now called the Individuals with Disabilities Education Act (IDEA).

1978–Rehabilitation Act Amendments: provides for consumer-controlled centers for independent living.

1983–Rehabilitation Act Amendments: provides for the Client Assistance Program (CAP), an advocacy program for consumers of rehabilitation and independent living services.

1985–Mental Illness Bill of Rights Act: requires protection and advocacy services (P&A) for people with mental illness.

1986–Rehabilitation Act Amendments: grants consumer control for Title VII, Part B center boards; supported work programs created and funded.

1988–Civil Rights Restoration Act: counteracts bad case law by clarifying Congress' original intention that, under the Rehabilitation Act, discrimination in ANY program or service that is a part of an entity receiving federal funding–not just the part that actually and directly receives funding–is illegal.

1988–Air Carrier Access Act: prohibits discrimination on the basis of disability in air travel and provides for equal access to air transportation services.

1988–Fair Housing Act Amendments: prohibits discrimination in housing against people with disabilities and families with children. Also provides for architectural accessibility of certain new housing units, renovation of existing units, and accessibility modifications at the renter's expense.

1990–Americans with Disabilities Act: provides comprehensive civil rights protection for people with disabilities; closely modeled after the Civil Rights Act and Section 504 of Title V of the Rehabilitation Act and its regulations.

1992–Rehabilitation Act Amendments: emphasizes priority of services to people with disabilities of underrepresented groups; encourages access to disability support services; most significant in terms of choice or consumer control over vocational outcome.

1994- Technology-Related Assistance Act for Individuals with Disabilities Amendments: provides access to assistive technology service and devices for individuals with disabilities of all ages.

1999–Olmstead Decision (although not an Act, it is significant): upholds the ADA's Integration mandate that affirms the right for people with disabilities to live equally in their community.

2006–The Money Follows the Person Act (MFP): requires that a percentage of state monetary funds that would normally only be given to nursing homes or institutions will follow an individual out into the community and into community-based service.

- Requires that services be provided in the most integrated setting possible
- Provides services based on need, rather than diagnosis or age
- Has backup and emergency attendant services
- Lets service users select, manage, and control services
- Allows service users to chose from vouchers, cash payments, fiscal agents, and agency providers for payment options
- Allows people who are not licensed by state laws to perform services
- Covers expenses that occur when someone moves out of a nursing home such as rent deposits, bedding, etc.
- Establishes quality check programs for services provided
- Is available to people who have incomes above the current institutional income limitation, if the state chooses to allow this to increase the person's employment options

- Allows matches of up to 90% of federal funds for people whose costs exceed 150% of average nursing home costs (Research Information on Independent Living, 2007d).

The New Freedom Initiative was announced by President George W. Bush on February 1, 2001. The purpose of the initiative is to remove community living barriers for people with disabilities. It is a comprehensive plan to make sure that all Americans have the opportunity to learn and develop skills to do productive work, to make choices about their daily lives, and to participate fully in community life. The goals of the New Freedom Initiative are to:

- Increase access to assistive and universally designed technologies
- Expand educational opportunities
- Promote home ownership
- Integrate Americans with disabilities into the workforce
- Expand transportation options
- Promote full access to community life

The President issued Executive Order 13217, "Community-Based Alternatives for Individuals with Disabilities," on June 18, 2001. This order was inspired, in part, by the July 1999 *Olmstead* Supreme Court decision (discussed in the following paragraph), which challenges governments at all levels to develop more community services for individuals with disabilities. In addition, the order requires the Departments of Justice, Health and Human Services, Education, Labor, and Housing and Urban Development, and the Social Security Administration to evaluate their policies and programs to improve the availability of community-based services for people with disabilities. Part of the plan is putting into place the Ticket to Work and Work Incentives Improvement Act of 1999 (Research Information on Independent Living, 2007e).

The *Olmstead* court decision (*Olmstead v. L.C.*, 527 U.S. 581, [1999]) promotes personal assistance services even though it does not explicitly say states must provide home and community services. The case was filed on behalf of Lois Curtis and Elaine Wilson, two women patients with both mental retardation and psychiatric disorders in an Atlanta, Georgia, state hospital. This is one of the most significant ADA cases to define states' care obligations because it was the first to disregard costs and resulted in active state planning to move eligible people out of institutions into the community. The court ruled that states are required to offer a choice of community settings rather than only institutions when community placement is appropriate, the individual does not oppose the transfer from institutional care to a less restrictive setting, and the placement can be reasonably accommodated. In addition, the court ruled that states (a) must have comprehensive plans to move more people with disabilities out of institutions and into the community, (b) move at a reasonable pace to provide community-based alternatives, and (c) maintain a range of care facilities, including institutions for those who need them. Although the *Olmstead* decision does not change the Medicaid program, individual benefits, or state obligations, states have begun to focus strongly on their Medicaid policies and program choices regarding long-term care because states use a significant portion of their Medicaid money on long-term care (Research Information on Independent Living, 2007f).

Several ethical issues surface in the case of provider- rather than consumer-led independent living interventions. First, in the case of cognitive impairment, there is a fundamental concern about who makes decisions. The question is raised of how self-determination and autonomy can best be fulfilled when an individual's information processing and decision-making power is deteriorating. Second, information sharing and exchange of what is very detailed data about personal matters comes with serious concerns about infringing on the privacy of the users. Third, bringing technology with monitoring functions into a person's home may create possible conflicts with principles of dignity, independence, and privacy. Fourth, an ethical challenge is to avoid the perception that the use of technology replaces human care and precipitates the erosion of social interactions. Finally, if the personal autonomy of the individual is to be fully respected, he or she must have the right to decline intervention (Institute for Prospective Technological Studies, 2006; Research Information on Independent Living, 2007g).

Professional issues impacting specific counseling aspects or procedures of independent living assessment include the holistic/comprehensive nature of IL programs, peer counseling, advocacy, and important differences between centers and service providers. Overwhelmingly, IL programs, particularly IL centers, are far more comprehensive in scope than other types of human service organizations providing IL services to individuals with disabilities. In fact, IL programs are much more likely to be able to facilitate independent living by individuals with disabilities than are more narrowly focused vocational and medical rehabilitation programs.

In addition to self-advocacy, the government will play an increasing role to ensure individuals with disabilities are properly integrated into the community. For example, policy, regulatory agencies, and research organizations such as the Food and Drug Administration (FDA), Health Insurance Portability and Accountability Act (HIPAA), NIDRR, National Center for Medical Rehabilitation Research (NCMRR), and the World Health Organization (WHO) will increasingly mandate that mechanisms be in place to ensure any solution and infrastructure minimize risks to public health, promote independence and social integration, and enhance empowerment and participatory initiatives.

MULTIDISCIPLINARY OR INTERDISCIPLINARY APPROACHES

Assessment of independent living for consumers requires the expertise of many rehabilitation professionals. According to the Institute for Perspective Technological Studies (2006), there is a need for integration of all health and social services and closer cooperation among the various services to make the IL assessment as effective as possible. In fact, the emerging paradigm of *shared care* or *integrated care*, presents a promising reference for organizing health services and assessment for independent living. Therefore, a multidisciplinary approach is the preferred method of evaluation of a consumer. For example, in the case of rehabilitation for patients following stroke, a multidisciplinary team approach for assessment would include a rehabilitation counselor, technologist, physical therapist, occupational therapist, doctor/neurologist, home care providers, and employment specialist. Each member of the team is designated to work with clients across several domains involving range of motion, speed of movement, cognitive processing, home adaptation and technology, self-care, and employment.

Researchers may seek to establish multidisciplinary units that encourage collaboration between departments as well as institutions (e.g., law, public health, sociology, social work, rehabilitation). In addition, federal and private research sponsors should encourage the conduct of research in a variety of settings (e.g., inner city, rural, community health centers), and should encourage participation of researchers from ethnic and racial minority groups and individuals with disabilities (Smedley, Stith, & Nelson, 2003). Perspectives of vocational and rehabilitation counselors, occupational and physical therapists, nurses, social workers, and medical doctors, as well as the consumer and his or her family, are all useful for supplying the most comprehensive information

that can be used to provide the client with the best outcome. Many of these evaluations require training in order to preserve reliability and validity.

A multidisciplinary approach can provide information on mobility, motor skills, visual–perceptual skills, cognitive skills, vision, endurance, safety, and the use of adaptive equipment, as well as information about the home environment. By providing this information, and in an integrated manner, all aspects of independent living can be addressed. Settings in which multidisciplinary/interdisciplinary assessments may occur include rehabilitation hospitals (with the advantage of simulated activities and the disadvantage of real-life evaluation), centers for independent living (with the advantage of self-advocacy, individual advocacy, systems advocacy), and in-home (with the advantage of hands-on practice).

NATIONAL, STATE, AND FEDERAL/ INTERNATIONAL PRACTICES IN INDEPENDENT LIVING ASSESSMENT

One international approach that has developed simultaneously in the United States and other parts of the world is community-based rehabilitation in which services are offered within a defined organizational structure (Fabian et al., 2005). Most IL programs in the United States assess independence primarily in terms of functional capacities or environmental circumstances, and almost all subscribe to a definition of independence focusing on psychological and social factors developed by Frieden, Richards, Cole, and Bailey (1979) and adopted into the National Policy for Persons with Disabilities (National Council on Disability, 1983).

Independent living paradigms differ from those of vocational rehabilitation across six domains. The first domain is the definition of the problem in which dependence is on professionals, relatives, and so forth. Second, is the locus of the problem, which is in the environment and the rehabilitation process. The third is that the solution to the problem is with peer counseling, advocacy, self-help, consumer control, and removal of barriers. Next is that the social responsibility is with the consumer. Fifth, the consumer is in control. Finally, the desired outcome is independent living. Conversely, vocational rehabilitation defines the problem in terms of impairment and lack of vocational skills, the locus of the problem being in the individual, the solution resting with professional intervention, the client being in the social role, the professional being in control, and the desired outcomes being maximum ADL and gainful employment. Elements of the state–federal process include agency identification, procedures for determining eligibility for services, hierarchy of authority, and methods for statewide studies of needs of individuals with disabilities, and expansion and improvement of services. Both IL programs and the rehabilitation process offer a planned, orderly sequence of services related to the total needs of the individual.

The philosophical assertions of independent living are solid while the state–federal rehabilitation program continues to evolve through the influence of rehabilitation philosophy and legislation (Nosek, 1992; Research Information on Independent Living, 2007g). Independent living and rehabilitation continue to strive to identify and develop "best practices" for service delivery. However, a distinguishing feature of the state–federal rehabilitation system is its emphasis on the final outcome—the placement of the consumer in appropriate employment. On the other hand, IL's emphasis is on helping individuals with disabilities to have self-determination. In the final analysis, IL and rehabilitation seek to help individuals with disabilities to be productive and contributing citizens.

MAJOR ISSUES THAT NEED ATTENTION IN INDEPENDENT LIVING ASSESSMENT

Issues related to assessment in independent living include both contemporary and persistent problems or concerns. For example, contemporary issues include cultural diversity and immigrant groups, and the graying of America and the increase in the number of aging and older adults with disabilities. For each of these groups, language, stamina, and fatigue are important factors to consider in the assessment process. Understanding and being able to communicate with others is a key function

in independent living. In addition, an individual's physical stamina during assessment provides a good picture of his or her ability to perform the tasks of IL. In fact, aging is recognized as a major research agenda for the 21st century due to changing family structures, intergenerational transfer systems, and emergent patterns of family and institutional dynamics (Harley, Donnell, & Rainey, 2003; Research Agenda on Aging for the 21st Century, 2004). For IL assessment, aging is a relevant issue with regard to employment, competence, mobility, and self-care skills. Persistent issues include meeting the needs of people with disabilities in rural areas (Harley, Bishop, & Wilson, 2002), and sexuality, gender, and cultural issues. For each of these issues, the goal is to develop and implement unique techniques that address need, and develop appropriate assessment of IL competencies that are culturally, geographically, and psychosocially sensitive. Although current social provision has improved considerably since 1964, the existence of unequal opportunities and outcomes remain for many people with disabilities. Kilbury et al. (2005) predicted "while CILs operate in order to make themselves obsolete, the slow progress toward equal participation for Americans with disabilities will apparently be needed well into the twenty-first century" (p. 313).

One of the areas in which continual attention is needed in IL assessment is technological assistance. This need may be greater in rural areas (in the United States and other countries) because of availability and accessibility issues. In general, rural residents have more physical and mental health problems than individuals living in urban areas. Furthermore, residents in rural areas must contend with limited community resources, educational attainment, and employment opportunities (Congressional Rural Caucus, 2001; Harley, Savage, & Kaplan, 2005).

As far as research methodologies are concerned, future research needs to expand the use of mixed methods (i.e., qualitative and quantitative). Researchers have suggested that the implicit association between prediction and quantitative approaches to understanding community adaptation have yielded little understanding (Berg, 2007; Stumpf, 1990). In addition, many quantitative methods comprise inadequate approaches to the phenomenon of IL because they presume that success and failure are fixed and static outcomes (Denzin & Lincoln, 2005). Instead of isolating variables, which may or may not predict a person's ability to live independently, a more practical approach may be the description of interpersonal relationships, internal locus of control, external locus of control, life experiences, and the individual's own understanding of successful independent living (Berg, 2007; Institute for Prospective Technological Studies, 2006; Stumpf, 1990). The reader can find additional information on qualitative research at http://www.qual.auckland.ac.nz/. Several other areas in need of attention in IL assessment include health status and health maintenance practices that are critical in the individual's ability to live independently, relevant instruction in independent living in public schools and all postsecondary programs with a disability focus, longitudinal curriculum, and characteristics of responsive change.

Summary and Conclusion

Independent living assessment differs greatly. One assessment approach may be successful in meeting the needs of people with disabilities, whereas another approach may not. In addition, the research methodology used for assessment may produce different outcomes. The nature of the assessments themselves and the responsiveness of consumers involved determine, to a large extent, their effect on the lives of people with disabilities. Many issues have to be considered to determine a consumer's readiness for independent living. The person must be evaluated regarding physical abilities and endurance; psychosocial, cognitive, and perceptual skills; and ability to perform basic and instrumental activities of daily living. In addition, the home environment should be assessed for safety and architectural accessibility to provide the consumer with a supportive environment.

The future of IL assessment research requires expanded and comprehensive methodologies. Collaboration across disciplines will need to expand, not only to evaluate success, but also to increase opportunities for individuals with disabilities. Of all of the uncertainties in life, one thing is certain—rehabilitation counselors, human service professionals, and medical personnel must leave service potential and opportunities for individuals with disabilities "more vital and vibrant than when we began" (McFarlane, Dew, Enriquez, & Schroder, 2003, p. 80).

Self-Check Questions

1. Why is the ICF domain of activities and participation appropriate for IL?
2. What issues existed that led to the development of the IL movement? What system failures exacerbated this development?
3. What were the five social movements that contributed to the creation of the disability rights movement and development of CILs?
4. What are the major areas of assessment for independent living?
5. Name two areas of research that need to be conducted regarding independent living assessment.
6. What was the most influential piece of legislation affecting the establishment of CILs?
7. Why is a multidisciplinary approach the preferred method of evaluation of a consumer?
8. What are the major differences between a vocational rehabilitation approach and an independent living approach?
9. What are some persistent issues facing independent living assessment?

Case Studies

For each of the case studies presented below, what assessment related questions might you ask to determine their ability to live independently?

1. *Spinal cord injury*

Sean was in a multivehicle accident approximately 3 weeks ago and sustained a C4-C5 injury. This injury has resulted in quadriplegia with some shoulder and bicep movement, but no control of the wrist or hand. He also needs a ventilator from time to time to help him breathe. Sean is 45 years old and unmarried. He worked in the city as a construction worker and lives in an apartment on the third floor. His closest family member is his sister who lives 150 miles away in a small town, is married, and has two young children. Sean has received physical and occupational therapy at the rehabilitation center located within the hospital.

QUESTIONS

1. What type of assessment does Sean need to determine his functional capacity for activities of daily living?
2. What vocational assessments will benefit Sean?
3. What psychosocial needs does Sean need to address?

2. *Cerebal palsy*

Sandi is an 18-year-old woman with spastic cerebral palsy. Sandi currently ambulates with forearm crutches and an electric wheelchair. Her intelligence level is normal, but she has difficulty with speech and vision. She has completed high school and was mainstreamed throughout. Sandi would like to go to college approximately 50 miles away from home. Currently, she lives in a ranch-style home with her parents.

QUESTIONS

1. What technology needs does Sandi have?
2. What environmental barriers need to be considered for Sandi to live in college housing?
3. What type of assessment does Sandi need to determine social adjustment and integration?

3. *Stroke*

George is a 70-year-old man who recently experienced a stroke on the left side of his brain, which has resulted in paralysis of his right side (hemiplegia). He is having physical therapy and can walk with a walker and someone to assist him. He has no movement in his right arm. His occupational therapist is teaching him how to do his ADLs with his left (nondominant) hand, and he is able to complete basic hygiene and feed himself, but is unable to dress or bathe himself independently. He also has difficulty with speech (expressive aphasia). George lives with his wife, Laura, who has been diagnosed with rheumatoid arthritis, causing her to experience weakness and pain in her joints. George is retired but enjoys playing golf and gardening.

QUESTIONS

1. What consideration must be give to George's age when selecting appropriate assessment instruments?
2. Should an evaluation be done for both George and his wife? Why or why not?
3. In what areas should George be assessed?

References

Bachelor, P. A. (1995). Review of the Checklist of Adaptive Living Skills. In J. C. Conoley & J. C. Impara (Eds.), *The twelfth mental measurement yearbook* (pp. 172–173). Lincoln, NE: Buros Institute of Mental Measurements.

Baird, V. (1992). Difference or defiance. *New Internationalist*, 293, 3–9.

Berg, B. L. (2007). *Qualitative research methods for the social sciences* (6th ed.). Boston: Pearson.

Bernspang, B. (1999). Rater calibration stability for the Assessment of Motor and Process Skills. *Scandanavian Journal of Occupational Therapy*, 6, 101–109. Burr, Mutchler, & Warren, (2005).

Burr, J. A., Mutchler, J., & Warren, J. (2005). State commitment to home and community based services: Effects on independent living for older unmarried women. *Journal of Aging and Social Policy*, 17, 1–18.

California Department of Rehabilitation. (2006). *Independent living history*. Retrieved October 16, 2006 from http://www.dor.ca.gov/is/ilhist.html.

Camp, C. J. (1998). Review of the Assessment of Living Skills and Resources. In J. C. Impara & B. S. Plake (Eds.), *The thirteenth mental measurements yearbook* (pp. 64–65). Lincoln, NE: Buros Institute of Mental Measurements.

Chelimsky, E., & Shadish, W. (1997). Preface. In E. Chelimsky & W. Shadish (Eds.), *Evaluation for the twenty-first century*. Thousand Oaks, CA: Sage.

Christiansen, C. (1991). Occupational performance assessment. In C. Christiansen & C. Baum (Eds.), *Occupational therapy: Overcoming human performance deficits* (pp. 375–424). Thorofare, NJ: SLACK, Inc.

Community Living Campbellford and Brighton. (2006). *Personal outcome measures*. Retrieved September 16, 2005 from http://www.communitylivingcampbellford.com/personal_outcome_m....

Congressional Rural Caucus. (2001). Fast facts. Retrieved January 16, 2003, from http://www.house.gov/emerson/crc/overview/faq.html.

Crewe, N. M., & Athelstan, G. T. (1979). Functional assessment in vocational rehabilitation. *International Journal of Rehabilitation Research, 2*, 535–536.

Crewe, N. M., & Athelstan, G. T. (1981). Functional assessment in vocational rehabilitation: A systematic approach to diagnosis and goal setting. *Archives in Physical Medicine and Rehabilitation, 62*, 299–305.

Crewe, N. M., & Athelstan, G. T. (1984). *Functional Assessment Inventory Manual*. Menomenie: Materials Development Center, University of Wisconsin Stout.

Crewe, N. M., Athelstan, G. T., & Meadows, G. (1975). Vocational diagnosis through assessment of functional limitations. *Archives of Physical Medicine and Rehabilitation, 56*, 513–516.

Crewe, N. M., & Turner, R. R. (1984). A functional assessment system for vocational rehabilitation. In A. S. Halpern & M. D. Fuhrer (Eds.), *Functional assessment in rehabilitation* (pp. 223–238). Baltimore: Paul H. Brookes.

Cummins, R. A., & Lau, A. L. D. (2003). Community integration or community exposure? A review and discussion in relation to people with an intellectual disability. *Journal of Applied Research in Intellectual Disabilities,16*, 145–157

Dejong, G. (1979a). *The movement for independent living: Origins, ideology, and implications for disability research* (Occasional Paper No. 2). East Lansing: University Center for International Rehabilitation, Michigan State University.

Dejong, G. (1979b). Independent living: From social movement to analytic paradigm. *Archives of Physical Medicine and Rehabilitation, 60*, 435–446.

DeJong, G., & Hughes, J. (1982). Independent living: Methodology for measuring long-term outcomes. *Archives of Physical Medicine and Rehabilitation,62*, 68–73.

Denzin, N., & Lincoln, Y. S. (2005). *The Sage handbook of qualitative research* (3rd ed.). Thousand Oaks, CA: Sage.

Dickerson, A. E., & Fisher, A. G. (1993). Age differences in functional performance. *American Journal of Occupational Therapy, 47*, 686–692.

Dublin CIL. (2005). *Historical perspective*. Retrieved October 10, 2006 from http://ww.dublincil.org/aboutus/historu.html.

Dunkoh, C., Underhill, K., & Montgomery, P. (2006). Independent living for improving outcomes for young people leaving the care system. *Cochrane Database of Systematic Reviews* (Issue 3, No. CD005558, DOI).

Duran, L., & Fisher, A. G. (1996). Male and female performance on the Assessment of Motor and Processing Skills. *Archives of Physical Medicine and Rehabilitation, 77*, 1019–1024.

Fabian, E.S. McInerney, M., & Santos Rodrigues, P. (2005). International education in rehabilitation: A collaborative approach. *Rehabilitation Education, 19*, 15–24.

Fisher, A. G. (2003a). *Assessment of Motor and Processing Skills: Development, Standardization, and Administration Manual* (5th ed.). Fort Collins, CO: Three Star Press.

Fisher, A. G. (2003b). *Assessment of Motor and Processing Skills: User Manual* (5th ed.). Fort Collins, CO: Three Star Press.

Frieden, L., Richards, L., Cole, J., & Bailey, D. (1979). *ILRU sourcebook: A technical assistance manual on independent living*. Houston: Institute for Rehabilitation and Research.

Frieden, L., Widmer, M. L., & Richards, L. (1983). The independent living program movement. In R. A. Lassiter, M. H. Lassiter, R. E. Hardy, Underwood, J. W., & Cull, J. C. (Eds.), *Vocational evaluation, work adjustment, and independent living for severely disabled people* (pp. 253–262). Springfield, IL: Charles C. Thomas Publisher.

Granger, C. V., Hamilton, B. B., Keith, R. A., Zielezny, M., & Sherwin, F. S. (1986). Advances in functional assessment for medical rehabilitation. *Topics in Geriatric Rehabilitation, 1*, 59–74.

Harley, D. A., Bishop, M., & Wilson, K. B. (2002). Rural rehabilitation: Old problems in a new day. *Journal of Rehabilitation Administration, 26*, 5–13.

Harley, D. A., Donnell, C., & Rainey, J. A. (2003). Interagency collaboration: Reinforcing professional bridges to serve aging populations with multiple service needs. *Journal of Rehabilitation, 69*, 32–37.

Harley, D. A., Savage, T. A., & Kaplan, L. E. (2005). Racial and ethnic minorities in rural areas: Use of indigenous influence in the practice of social work. In L. H. Ginsberg (Ed.), *Social work in rural communities* (4th ed., pp. 367–385). Alexandria, VA: Council on Social Work Education.

Hayase, D., Mosenteen, D., Thimmaiah, D., Zemke, S., Atler, K., & Fisher, A. G. (2004). Age-related changes in activities of daily living ability. *Australian Occupational Therapy Journal, 51*, 192–198.

Huck, S. W., & Cormier, W. H. (1996). *Reading statistics and research*. New York: Harper Collins.

Hurst, R. (2003). The international disability rights movement and the ICF. *Disability and Rehabilitation, 25*, 572–576.

Ilika, J., & Hoffman, N. G. (1981). Reliability study on Kohlman Evaluation of Living Skills. Reported in L. K. McGourty (1987). Kohlman Evaluation of Living Skills (pp. 133–146). In B. J. Hemphill (Ed.). (1987). *Mental health assessment in occupational therapy.* Thorofare, NJ: SLACK, Inc.

Independent Living Assessment. (2001, August). Retrieved October 10, 2006 from http://www.independentliving.org.

Institute for Prospective Technological Studies. (2006). *User needs in ICT research for independent living, with a focus on health aspects: Report on a Joint JRC/IPTS-DG INFSO Workshop.* Seville, Spain: IPTS, Edificio Expo-WTC.

Iwarsson, S., & Isacsson, A. (1996). Developing a novel instrument for occupational therapy of assessment of the physical environment in the home – A methodological study on "The Enabler." *Occupational Therapy Journal of Research, 16*, 227–244.

Kaufman, L. (1982). *Concurrent validity study on the Kohlman Evaluation Living Skills and the Global Assessment Scale.* Unpublished master's thesis. Gainesville, FL: University of Florida.

Kilbury, R. F., Stotlar, B. J., & Eckert, J. M. (2005). Centers for independent living. In W. Crimando & T. F. Riggar (Eds.*), Community resources: A guide for human service workers* (2nd ed, pp. 304–314). Long Grove, IL: Waveland Pres.

Kizony, R., Katz, N., Weiss, & P. L. (2003). Adapting an immersive virtual reality system for rehabilitation. *The Journal of Visualization and Computer Animation, 14*, 261–268.

Klein, R. M., & Bell, B. (1982). Self-care skills: Behavioral measurement with the Klein Bell ADL Scale. *Archives of Physical Medicine and Rehabilitation, 63*, 335–338.

McComas, J., & Sveistrup, H. (2002). Virtual reality application for prevention, disability awareness, and physical therapy rehabilitation in neurology: Our recent work. *Neurology Report, 26*, 55–61.

McDonald, G., & Oxford, M. (2006). *History of independent living.* Retrieved October 10, 2006 from http://www.acils.com'acil/ilhistory.html.

McFarlane, F. R., Dew, D. W., Enriquez, M., & Schroder, F. (2003). Rehabilitation leaders: The challenge to build tomorrow's organizations. *Journal of Rehabilitation Administration, 27*, 71–81.

McGourty, L. K. (1979). *Kohlman Evaluation of Living Skills.* Seattle, WA: KELS Research.

McGourty, K. L. (1988). Kohlman Evaluation of Living Skills. In B. J. Hemphill (Ed.), *Mental health assessment in occupational therapy* (pp. 133–146). Thorofare, NJ: SLACK, Inc.

Merritt, B. K., & Fisher, A. G. (2003). Differences between men and women in ADL performance. *Archives of Physical Medicine and Rehabilitation, 84*, 1872–1877.

Moore, J. E., Steinman, B. A., Giesen, J., & Frank, J. J. (2006). Functional outcomes and consumer satisfaction in the older blind independent living program. *Journal of Visual Impairment and Blindness, 100*, 289–294.

Myers, F., Ager, A., Kerr, P., & Myles, S. (1998). Outside looking in? Studies of the community integration of people with learning disabilities. *Disability & Society, 13*, 389–413.

National Council on Disability. (1983). *National policy for persons with disabilities.* Washington, DC: Author.

National Institute on Disability and Rehabilitation Research. (2006). *Proposed long-range plan for fiscal year 1999–2004.* Available at http://www.accessiblesociety.org. Washington, DC: Author.

Nosek, M. A. (1992). Independent living. In R. M. Parker & E. M. Szymanski (Eds.), *Rehabilitation counseling* (2nd ed., 103–133). Austin, TX: Pro ed.

Oliver, M. (1996). *Understanding disability: From theory to practice.* New York: St. Martin's Press.

Research Agenda on Aging for the 21ˢᵗ Century. (2004). *A joint project of the United Nations Office on Aging and the International Association of Gerontology.* Retrieved October 10, 2006 from http://www.valenciaforum.com/ raa.html

Research Information on Independent Living. (2007a). *Physically accessible housing* (Volume 1, Issue 9). Retrieved May 9, 2007, from http://www.getriil.org/briefs/housing.html.

Research Information on Independent Living. (2007b). *Elderly care options* (Volume 1, Issue 8). Retrieved May 9, 2007, from http://www.getriil.org/briefs/elder.html.

Research Information on Independent Living. (2007c). *Self-determination assistance* (Volume 1, Issue 1). Retrieved May 9, 2007, from http://www.getriil.org/briefs/SelfDetermination,html.

Research Information on Independent Living. (2007d). *MiCASSA* (Volume 2, Issue 11). Retrieved May 9, 2007, from http://www.getriil.org/briefs/micassa.html.

Research Information on Independent Living. (2007e). *New Freedom Initiative* (Volume 2, Issue 9). Retrieved May 9, 2007, from http://www.getriil.org/briefs/freedom.html.

Research Information on Independent living (2007f). *Olmstead & state plan* (Volume 2, Issue 8). retrieved May 9, 2007, from http://www.getriil.org/briefs/olmstead_state. html.

Research Information on Independent Living. (2007g). *Independent living concept* (Volume 1, issue 6). retrieved May 9, 2007, from http://www.getriil.org/briefs/independent. html.

Riches, V. (1996). *Everyday social interactions: A program for people with disabilities.* Baltimore: Paul H. Brookes Publishing.

Russon, C., & Russon, G. (2005). *International perspectives on evaluation standards.* American Evaluation Association: Jossey-Bass.

Schultheis, M. T., & Mourant, T. (2001). Virtual Reality and driving: The road to better assessment for cognitively impaired populations. *Presence: Teleoperators & Virtual Environments, 14*, 119–146.

Shreve, M. (1982). *The movement for independent living: A brief history.* Retrieved October 10, 2006 from http://www.ilusa.com/articles/mshreve_article_ilc.html.

Smedley, B. D., Stith, A. Y., & Nelson, A. R. (Eds.). (2003). *Unequal treatment: Confronting racial and ethnic disparities in health care.* Washington, DC: The National Academic Press.

Smith, R.O., Morrow, M. E., Heitman, J. K., Rardin, W. J., Powelson, J. L., & Von, T. (1986). The effects of introducing the Klein-Bell ADL scale in rehabilitation service. *American Journal of Occupational Therapy, 40,* 420–426.

Stauffer, L. M., Fisher, A. G., & Duran, L. (2000). ADL performance of black and white Americans on the Assessment of Motor and Processing Skills. *American Journal of Occupational Therapy, 54,* 607–613.

Steinfeld, E. (2005). *The concept of universal design.* Buffalo, NY: Center for Inclusive Design and Environmental Access.

Stumpf, S. H. (1990). *Pathways to success: Training for independent living.* Washington, DC: American Association on mental Retardation.

Suzuki, L. A., Ponterotto, J. G., & Meller, P. J. (Eds.). (2001). *Handbook of multicultural assessment: Clinical, psychological, and educational applications.* San Francisco: Jossey-Bass.

Sveistrup, H. (2004). Motor rehabilitation using virtual reality. *Journal of NeuroEngineering and Rehabilitation,* 1(10).

Retrieved May 9, 2007, from http://jneuroengrehab.com/content/1/1/10.

Tateichi, S. (1984). *A concurrent validity study of the Kohlman Evaluation of Living Skills.* Master's thesis. Seattle: University of Washington.

Ustan, T. B., Chatterju, S., Brickenbach, J., Kostanjsek, N., & Schneider, M. (2003). The International Classification of Functioning, Disability and Health: A new tool for understanding disability and health. *Disability and Rehabilitation, 25,* 565–571.

Woodcock, R. W., & Johnson, M. B. (1977). *Woodcock-Johnson Psycho-Educational Battery.* Allen, TX: DLM Teaching resources.

World Health Organization. (2001). *Using the Assessment of Quality of Life instrument.* (Version 1.0). Centre for Health Program Evaluation. Monash University. University of Melbourne.

Yano, H., Kasai, K., Saitou, H., & Iwata, H. (2003). Development of a gait rehabilitation system using a locomotion interface. *The Journal of Visualization and Computer Animation, 14,* 243–252.

Communication Functioning and Disability

Travis T. Threats
Saint Louis University

OVERVIEW

This chapter presents an overview of the broad categories of communication disorders and general information concerning the assessment of communication disorders. Specifically, this chapter addresses the issues surrounding assessment of communication disorders including historical and current trends in assessment; research challenges for improving the assessment process; and future issues. The increasing influence of the World Health Organization's *International Classification of Functioning, Disability, and Health* (ICF) on the assessment of persons with communication disabilities is addressed in this chapter.

LEARNING OBJECTIVES

By the end of the chapter, readers should be able to:

- Describe the importance of communication as an essential component of functional health
- Explain the relationship of the World Health Organization's *International Classification of Functioning, Disability and Health* (ICF) as it relates to communication and swallowing disorders
- Demonstrate a broad appreciation of the different types of communication disorders
- Discuss the challenges of incorporating evidence-based practice and the ICF into the assessment process, including outcome assessment
- Outline the challenges of practice faced by speech–language pathologists when it comes to cultural sensitivity and ethical issues in the field
- Examine speech-language pathology's relationship to other health professions in the assessment process

INTRODUCTION

Communication in humans is unique among the animal kingdom. Whereas all animals have some form of communication, it is hard-wired and stereotypical. Humans use communication for forming society, enjoyment, expression of emotion, fellowship, employment, and also for our inner thought processes.

When there is difficulty with communication, it can have wide ranging effects on persons' functioning and quality of life. The professions that evaluate and treat persons with communication disorders are speech–language pathologists and audiologists. How these professions provide assessment and intervention is evolving with an increased emphasis on life participation, quality of life issues, and evidence-based practice.

IMPORTANCE OF COMMUNICATION AND SWALLOWING DISORDERS TO REHABILITATION AND HEALTH

The capacity for communication is part of the standard neurological structure and functioning for human brains, and, for most people, it is so effortless that it is taken for granted, and thus its true complexity is not appreciated. That complexity is often only realized when a person has a communication disorder. Speech–language pathologists work with persons with a wide range of known and unknown etiologies in order to improve their ability to communicate and thus improve their quality of life. Speech–language pathologists also provide evaluation and treatment of persons with oral and pharyngeal dysphagia (swallowing disorder).

The World Health Organization (WHO) defines health as "the complete physical, mental, and social well-being of a person or a population and not merely the absence of disease or infirmity." (WHO, 1948). Disorders of communication can isolate people socially, which can lead to poor mental well-being. Communication is also important for maintaining physical health, such as when a person cannot express that he or she is feeling pain or has difficulty reading prescription bottle instructions. Persons with communication disorders can also be limited in getting help with mental health needs such as depression. Sometimes the etiology of a communication disorder is known, such as aphasia secondary to a stroke. However, many times, there is no such known physical reason for the communication disorders, such as in stuttering or delayed language acquisition in children.

Dysphagia (swallowing disorders) can lead to illness or even death via dehydration, malnutrition, choking, or aspiration (food entering the lungs). In addition to its direct medical consequences, dysphagia is also a significant functional health limitation. Mealtime is an important social event, and thus, difficulty eating can cause retreating from this activity. Self-esteem and quality of life are also affected by having a swallowing disorder.

Areas of Impaired Communication

There are six main areas of possible impaired communication: (1) voice, (2) articulation, (3) language, (4) cognitive-communication, (5) fluency (e.g. stuttering), and (6) hearing. In addition, the field of speech–language pathology also covers persons with oral or pharyngeal swallowing problems. Some persons have difficulties or limitations with only one of these aspects of communication whereas others may have difficulty with more than one. Each type of disorder will be discussed briefly.

Voice, articulation, and fluency disorders are disorders of production of speech. *Voice disorders* are those that interfere with the production or quality of voicing. Voice disorders have a wide variety of etiologies, including vocal nodules and contact ulcers brought on by vocal abuse, and neurological disorders such as spasmodic dysphonia. Voice disorders include disorders of resonance such as when a person has velopharyngeal insufficiency resulting in sound going out of the nasal cavity instead of the mouth. A laryngectomy, surgical removal of the larynx due to cancer, results in a complete inability to produce voice.

Articulation is the production of sounds of a language. This complex and necessarily precise movement is considered the most complex of human movements. The difference between any two sounds in production is extremely small and this difference is usually only appreciated when trying to learn the sound system of a different language. In addition to being precise, these movements must be made very rapidly. Thus, any neurological or structural damage to oral and nasal cavities can produce noticeable differences in speech production.

Part of the physical production of speech is the ability to produce it smoothly and with coordination. It is possible to be able to produce the sounds of a language perfectly well, yet still have trouble connecting them in smooth fluent discourse. *Stuttering* is a disorder of fluency characterized by extensive dysfluencies that are markedly apparent to the listener. In addition to the disruptions in the fluency of speech, persons who stutter also may exhibit associated motor behaviors such as facial grimaces, head and hand movements, eye blinks, and excessive jaw and face tension while speaking. These associated motor behaviors can potentially be as or more disruptive to the communication than the dysfluencies themselves. Stuttering starts in childhood and can extend into adulthood.

Language is the currency of human communication exchange. It is a symbolic system whereby we all agree on what a given arbitrary series of sounds will mean. For example, the sounds "c-a-r" put together will mean a motorized vehicle operated to get around on land. Or more abstractly, the sounds "l-i-b-e-r-t-y" represents something so important that people are willing to die in its cause. The arbitrary nature of language is demonstrated by the thousands of languages on the planet. There is no "natural" name for anything—just what a given group of people agree to call something.

All languages have, however, the same components, namely phonology, morphology, semantics, and syntax.

Language disorders acquired in adulthood are primarily due to neurological disorders affecting the left hemisphere, usually involving the frontal and temporal lobes. The most common type of acquired neurologic communication disorder is aphasia, which is caused by damage to the left hemisphere of the brain. Aphasia is a language disorder that impairs, at some level, all modalities of communication, including comprehension, speaking, reading, and writing, but does not affect persons' cognitive or intellectual abilities.

Communication also includes nonlinguistic and nonliteral aspects of a language. Many of these nonlinguistic aspects of language are controlled by the right hemisphere. These nonlinguistic aspects include reception and expression of intonation, facial expression, body language, pragmatics of language, and figurative language. Intonation, facial expression and body language all contribute to communication. In fact, if these three behaviors conflict with the literal utterance of the speaker, the listener is more likely to believe these nonverbal behaviors as in when someone is obviously lying. Pragmatics of language involve knowing the appropriate use of language, such as how an individual talks to his or her boss as opposed to his or her children, or when it is or is not appropriate to tell a possibly offensive joke. Figurative language is nonliteral such as the expression, "Don't count your chickens before they're hatched." Thus, neurological disorders of the right hemisphere can lead to impairments to the above aspects of communication.

Cognitive-communication disorders are a group of disorders ranging widely in etiology, including traumatic brain injury, brain tumors, neurotoxicity, and dementia. In order to communicate, a person must first have an intent to convey a thought. These thoughts must be organized, and the characteristics of the listener taken into account. Thus, cognitive disorders of attention, memory, judgment, and pragmatic skills can all cause impairments in the ability to communicate. Patients with traumatic brain injury secondary to car accidents often use inappropriate implusive language and have difficulty putting together a coherent narrative. Such patients may also forget the topic of conversation when talking with others, which would obviously limit their effectiveness as a conversational partner. When these cognitive underpinnings of communication are disrupted, the person has a cognitive communication disorder.

In communication, humans use hearing both to monitor their own speech and to hear the auditory speech of others. The ear is not just a passive receiver of the speech signal, but, in fact, an active part of the process of oral communication. Although our speech mechanism is quite remarkable, it does not make every sound the same each time, and some sounds in running

---

DISCUSSION BOX 25.1

The spouse of a person with moderate stuttering wants you to try a new technique using electrical probes of the muscles of speech to determine the type of stuttering and thus which treatment would be best. You think that there is not evidence that this evaluation procedure and its subsequent intervention works and thus do not want to switch to it. You tell the spouse your views and she demands to know the proof that you have that your evaluation method is more valid. You feel that you are correct but have no research articles to back your approach.

Questions

1. Should you try this technique just because asked? What if you fear this assessment could cause physical harm to the client?

2. What aspect other than research can you use in the spirit of evidence-based practice to back up your position?

3. What would be your response to this spouse?

4. What is the relationship between the ethics of autonomy that are suspect in this case?

speech are barely produced at all. Human hearing makes up for these variations so efficiently that persons do not even notice the fluctuation in the speakers' sound productions. Hearing is the ultimate "smart" system largely due to the fact that the brain knows the patterns of speech and can predict sentences before they are even finished. Thus, if the signal is not fully there, which occurs often when listening to speech in a noisy environment, the ear can literally fill in the blanks.

Hearing disorders can be congenital or can be acquired in childhood or adulthood. Hearing loss is often complex; that is, it is not as simple as just needing sounds to be louder to be understood. Presbyscusis, for example, often affects the higher frequencies of sound more than the lower frequencies. This difference in hearing acuity at different frequencies results in the listener hearing the speaker, but being unable to fully understand him or her because the speech sounds of higher frequencies are not heard. Persons with such a hearing loss often complain that speakers are mumbling. Some persons hear with minimum difficulty in quiet environments and yet have difficulty in noise. Audiologists use sophisticated equipment to determine the specifics of a person's hearing, with an emphasis on the hearing needed to understand speech. Speech-language pathologists work with audiologists with this population.

International Classification of Functioning, Disability, and Health

The ICF (WHO, 2001) is highly useful in understanding communication disorders and guiding the assessment process. It is especially significant that within the ICF communication disorders are given parity with physical impairments, such as inability to walk. The ICF has been recognized by the field as an essential organizing principle in speech–language pathology and audiology, by using the ICF as the framework for the field in cardinal American Speech–Language–Hearing Association (ASHA) documents including the *Scope of Practice for Speech–Language Pathology* (ASHA, 2007), the *Scope of Practice for Audiology* (ASHA, 2003), and the *Preferred Practice Patterns for the Profession of Speech–Language Pathology* (ASHA, 2004).

Communication and swallowing disorders can all be assessed via the components of the ICF: body structure, body function, activity/participation, and environmental factors. The descriptions given of the various communication and swallowing disorders in the previous section are mostly descriptions of the ICF's body structure and body function impairments. This is common among textbooks concerning both the assessment and treatment of these disorders. However, as reflected in ASHA's revised cardinal documents, there is increasing recognition that the functional life consequences of communication and swallowing disorders need to be noted, assessed, and addressed in intervention.

Common to all communication and swallowing disorders are possible activity/participation limitations. In fact, two disorders that are very different in terms of their body function impairments, such as voice disorders and aphasia, can have similar activity/participation limitations. For example, a voice disorder can cause disruption of the ability of the speaker to engage in meaningful conversation with others, just as aphasia can. Different severities and types of communication and swallowing disorders can in some cases, however, predict activity/participation restrictions.

Activity/participation issues often cannot be clearly separated from the corresponding environmental factors. A person with traumatic brain injury with a moderate cognitive-communication disorder might function perfectly well with a knowledgeable and facilitative spouse. On the other hand, a person with a "mild" voice disorder from a body function viewpoint might work in a noisy environment, which renders their weaker voice production a serious limitation on their ability to function at their job.

Environmental factors are crucial to the success of someone with a communication or swallowing disorder. Although a person with a physical limitation needs physical access to fully engage in their environment, the single most important facilitator for a person with a communication disorder is having someone willing to and capable of talking with that person. For swallowing disorders, the availability of the appropriate food and liquid consistencies and/or feeding assistance are needed.

Personal factors interact with body function, activity/participation, and environmental factors to influence how persons with communication and swallowing disorders will function in their lives. Personal factors include both demographic characteristics, such as race or socioeconomic level, and personality characteristics, such as coping skills. Culture influences how different communication and swallowing disorders are viewed by persons themselves, as well as how they are viewed by others. For example, stuttering may be less of a social stigma in a work culture of furniture makers than in a work culture of attorneys. Socioeconomic and race factors may influence the ability of persons with communication and swallowing disorders to access needed rehabilitation services or other resources necessary to fully carry out their functional and personal needs and desires.

As with other disorders, how a person responds to a disorder will affect their ultimate disposition. Although aphasia is considered a more significant disorder than a lisp, the person with aphasia might mix freely with others, whereas the person with a lisp may avoid verbal contact with all but close family and friends.

HISTORY OF RESEARCH AND PRACTICE IN ASSESSMENT OF COMMUNICATION DISORDERS

Traditional Assessment Practices

Traditional assessment consisted of breaking down communication and swallowing into their components and testing each separately. For example, for a language disorder, the areas of syntax and semantics, both receptive and expressive, would be tested separately. This assessment approach focused primarily on the body function and body structure levels, and, in fact, testing is carried out on more finite and narrow categories than captured in the ICF body function codes. This approach was influenced by the fact that these traits are most amenable to testing in a clinical setting, and thus, more normative data exists for these specific body function level aspects of communication. Consequently, this type of evaluation is viewed as the most objective data that speech–language pathologists can obtain. The overall purposes of this traditional view of assessment was then to use this information to make a diagnosis, determine severity, and make a prognosis for improvement (Ross & Wertz, 2005)

Emerging Assessment Practices

More recent assessment practices place a greater focus on what are the functional needs for the clients, including looking at activity/participation and environmental factors. Assessment then becomes more linked to what is going to be done in therapy, as it is with outcome assessment. For example, digit span is a classic test of memory and is a useful diagnostic test. However, speech–language pathologists would not consider working directly on increasing digit-span memory as an appropriate goal of intervention.

An example of a paradigm shift in the approach to a broader view of assessment comes from the Life Participation Approach to Aphasia (LPAA) (Chapey et al., 2001), which states that it is a "consumer driven, service delivery approach that supports individuals with aphasia and others affected by it in achieving their immediate and longer term life goals....LPAA calls for broadening and refocusing of clinical practice and research on the consequences of aphasia... It focuses on re-engagement in life..." (p. 235). Concerning personal and environmental factors, the LPAA states, "Intervention consists of constantly assessing, weighing, and prioritizing which personal and environmental factors should be the targets of intervention and how best to provide freer, easier, and more autonomous access to activities and social connections of choice" (p. 237).

CURRENT ASSESSMENT METHODS IN COMMUNICATION DISORDERS

Specific assessments exist for the many different types of communication and swallowing disorders. However, there are several overriding principles that are coming into acceptance in thinking about assessment in communication disorders. One of the most significant changes in recent years has been the application of the ICF framework, as evident in the *Preferred Practice Patterns for the Profession of Speech–Language Pathology* (ASHA, 2004). The following excerpts from

---

DISCUSSION BOX 25.2

An adult who has had multiple strokes is evaluated by the speech-language pathologist and is found to have both language and significant cognitive difficulties. The insurance will pay only for aphasia therapy. People with aphasia have only language problems but not significant cognitive difficulties so you resist giving the communication diagnosis of aphasia.

Questions

1. Should the diagnosis be changed so the person can have therapy reimbursed?

2. If the insurance says it does not pay for people with cognitive disorders because research has not shown that people with this diagnosis get better, what would be your response?

3. How might the ICF be used to justify therapy for this person?

4. If approved, how might the ICF framework be used to best assess and evaluate the outcomes for this person?

this document's preamble demonstrate the most current view of general assessment guidelines:

Comprehensive assessment, intervention, and support address the following components within the World Health Organization's *International Classification of Functioning, Disability, and Health* (2001) framework.

— Body structures and functions:

Identify and optimize underlying anatomic and physiologic strengths and weaknesses related to communication and swallowing effectiveness. This includes mental functions such as attention as well as components of communication such as articulatory proficiency, fluency, and syntax.

—Activities and participation, including capacity (under ideal circumstances) and performance (in everyday environments);

—Assess the communication and swallowing-related demands of activities in the individual's life (contextually based assessment);

—Identify and optimize the individual's ability to perform relevant/desired social, academic, and vocational activities despite possible ongoing communication and related impairments;

—Identify and optimize ways to facilitate social, academic, and vocational participation associated with the impairment.

—Contextual factors, including personal factors (e.g., age, race, gender, education, lifestyle, and coping skills) and environmental factors (e.g., physical, technological, social, and attitudinal);

—Identify and optimize personal and environmental factors that are barriers to or facilitators of successful communication (including the communication competencies and support behaviors of everyday people in the environment).

Assessment may be static (i.e., using procedures designed to describe structures, functions, and environmental demands and supports in relevant domains at a given point in time) or

dynamic (i.e., using hypothesis testing procedures to identify potential for change and elements of successful interventions and supports).

As stated previously, the most developed guidelines are in the areas of body function and body structure. Because communication is an overt act, many specific aspects of it, such as the production of a given sound, the frequency of voice, or the complexity of grammatical structures used, can be measured and compared to nominative data. For body structures, these also can be measured and their adequacy described. For both body function and body structure assessment, quantitative measures can be used.

However with activity/participation, environmental factors, and personal factors, such quantitative measures may not be sufficient. Damico and Simmons-Mackie (2003) have argued that qualitative measures must be used more frequently and become more respected in the speech-language pathology to address those important aspects of communication that cannot be simply counted and compared numerically to a norm.

Ross and Wertz (2005) examined the current methods and procedures for assessment of persons with aphasia to determine which, if any, could be placed within the ICF framework. They concluded that the most used tests in both clinical assessment and research were body function level tests with such items as the semantic recognition of single spoken words.

Ross and Wertz (2005) reported less success in locating appropriate activity/participation measures for aphasia. The measures found tend to focus on the capacity qualifier of how a person completes a naturalistic communication act in a clinical setting interacting with the speech–language pathologist. Concerning aphasia, they state that performance level measures of persons' functioning and success in actual life situations have yet to be developed. Similarly, they found, in surveying assessment instruments for aphasia, that there have been no developed measures or adopted standard protocols for evaluating environmental or personal factors despite the fact that much has been written about their importance by prominent aphasiologists for many years.

Eadie and colleagues (2006) looked at six self-report instruments in speech–language pathology to ascertain how adequately they evaluated communication participation. Prominent self-report measures were chosen because, theoretically, they should allow for an insider's view of how a communication disorder has affected persons' lives and thus be important for planning intervention. The authors defined communicative participation as "taking part in life situations where knowledge, information, ideas, or feelings are exchanged. It may take the form of speaking, listening, reading, writing, or nonverbal means of communication. Communicative participation may occur in multiple life situations or domains and includes, but is not limited to, personal care, household management, leisure, learning, employment, and community life" (p. 309). Of the six self-report instruments evaluated in this study, four were for persons with voice disorders, and two for persons with acquired neurologically caused communication disorders.

Eadie et al. (2006) found that 34, or 26%, of the total of 132 items on the studied measures met their definition of communicative participation. After an analysis of the psychometric properties and their content, they concluded that none of the six instruments were fully adequate for measuring communicative participation. They then state that this work demonstrates the need to develop new instruments that measure communication in social contexts. To develop these more socially valid measures, the authors state, "There are three trends that lend support toward the selection or development of appropriate outcomes for measuring communicative participation: a) the stabilization of terminology and the conceptual framework related to health, functioning, and disability; b) the growing appreciation of client-centered decision-making; and c) advances in psychometric methods and instrument development" (p. 314).

RESEARCH CRITICAL TO ISSUES IN COMMUNICATION DISORDERS ASSESSMENT

Evidence-based practice is having a significant effect on the clinical fields in terms of both assessment and intervention. The American Speech–Language-Hearing Association (ASHA) uses the Sackett, Straus, Richardson, Rosenberg, and Haynes (2000) definition of evidence-based practice when it states, "The term *evidence based practice* refers to an approach in which current, high-quality research evidence is integrated with practitioner expertise and client preferences and values into the process of making clinical decisions" (ASHA 2004).

Fratalli (2000) defines outcomes as "the result of an intervention." Outcome measures involve ongoing assessment of one's intervention, but a result can only be ascertained via an assessment measure. If assessment procedures do not measure relevant factors in a reliable and valid manner, then it becomes impossible to determine the efficacy, effectiveness, or efficiency of a given intervention. Conversely, intervention that is not successful cannot be exposed as such without appropriate assessment tools. Thus, interventions have to have a semantic relationship to the assessment measure. A paramount reason for the role of research in development of assessment tools is for better outcomes research.

The challenges of evidence-based practice and the use of the ICF present a challenge to research in communication disorders. In the definition of evidence-based practice and in the ICF, client preferences and values are emphasized. Thus, to put it simply, the person receiving intervention should think that they have improved. If this concept is part of the evidence, then assessments must reflect this aspect of what is success in a therapeutic intervention. Part of what determines whether a person feels that they have improved is the effects on his or her real life functioning, which is what the ICF attempts to classify.

To say that the client's views should be systematically and formally assessed does not mean that all of our other measures are for naught. Threats (2002) states that using the ICF to guide evidence-based research in communication disorders can help elucidate the pressing

---

DISCUSSION BOX 25.3

A person is admitted to the hospital with a series of neurological difficulties including swallowing and communication. The physicians see some abnormalities with neuroimaging but not enough to explain his difficulties or to provide a definitive diagnosis. Your team is brought in to evaluate.

Questions

1. How could the team use the ICF to organize assessment of this patient?

2. Should the focus of the evaluation be to help the physician make a diagnosis? If yes or no, what other purposes would the assessment have?

3. How would the therapists determine if this patient is getting better or not?

4. Can evidence-based practice be used even when a medical diagnosis is not available?

research needs in the field. These areas include (1) the relationship between body function/body structure and activity/participation behaviors; (2) the reliable and valid assessment of activity/participation constructs; (3) the reliable and valid assessment of relevant environmental factors; (4) increased attention to the assessment of personal factors as they affect communication and swallowing disabilities; and (5) the relationship between ICF construct measurements and quality of life measurements.

The integration of research, systematic and thoughtful clinical expertise, and use of patient preferences in assessment as well as in intervention is demonstrated in this quote from Sackett, Rosenberg, Gray, Haynes, and Richardson (1996):

> Evidence based medicine is not "cookbook" medicine. Because it requires a bottom up approach that integrates the best external evidence with individual clinical expertise and patient's choice, it cannot result in slavish, cookbook approaches to individual clinical expertise. External clinical evidence can inform, but can never replace, individual clinical expertise, and it is this expertise that decides whether the external evidence applies to the individual patient at all, and, if so, how it should be integrated into a clinical decision. (p. 72)

CULTURAL, LEGISLATIVE, AND PROFESSIONAL ISSUES THAT IMPACT UPON COMMUNICATION DISORDERS AND THEIR ASSESSMENT

Cultural Issues

The principles embodied in evidence-based practice and the ICF include respect for individuals' preferences and needs in the assessment process. These preferences and needs will be influenced by their cultures. Culture influences but does not determine individual behavior. Similarly, communication styles, level and type of vocabulary, and even what is considered a communication disorder are influenced by culture, but the individual person sitting in front of the therapist must be evaluated. Some aspects of the ICF personal factors such as upbringing and views toward illness and disability may be more strongly influenced by culture. However, other aspects of personal factors, such as coping skills, and personality traits, may be less influenced by culture.

Assessment must thus not only be broadly culturally sensitive in assessment of communication, but also sensitive to the individual differences that exist within all cultures.

Legislative Issues

Most therapeutic services provided by speech-language pathologists are directly or indirectly paid for or have their payment influenced by governments. In school settings, therapists work directly for the local government. In medical settings, payment for services often comes from Medicare and Medicaid. Even with private insurance, what they pay for and how much they pay is influenced by Medicare or Medicaid policies and guidelines. Thus legislative actions can have both positively and negatively significant effects on the field of communication disorders. As third-party payers look at the services they pay for, a crucial issue to them is documentation of effectiveness and efficiency of therapeutic intervention. As stated previously, effectiveness can only be determined by appropriate and sound assessment measures.

Professional Issues

The ethical issues facing the field are similar to all health professions. Annex 6 of the ICF discusses the ethical issues of confidentiality, ethical clinical use, and social use of ICF information. In all three sections, specific themes are repeated. First, the ICF should always be used in a way that respects the inherent value of all persons and not as a label. Second, the ICF ratings should always be done with full explicit acknowledgement of the persons, or their advocates, whose behavior is being rated. Third, persons or their advocates should be participants in the assignments of codes and thus have the right to challenge or agree on the appropriateness of such codes. A fourth theme is that the ICF should be used to help empower persons to lead the lives they wish to live. The principal challenge in communication disorders with honoring the above ethical guidelines of the ICF is that some clients have significant cognitive and/or communication impairments that can complicate judgments of their autonomy and ability to make informed decisions about their rehabilitation.

MULTIDISCIPLINARY OR INTERDISCIPLINARY APPROACHES

Communication and eating occur in many contexts, including as part of family get-togethers, religious ceremonies, school, work, leisure, and community activities.

RESEARCH BOX 25.1

Issue: How should testing be appropriately used by agencies to determine if a person is "disabled enough" to receive services? An article discussing one aspect of the eligibility criterion in communication disorders is supplied in the following reference.

Spaulding, T., Plante, E., & Farinella, K. (2006). Eligibility criteria for language impairment: Is the low end of normal always appropriate? *Language, Speech, and Hearing Services in Schools, 37*, 61–72.

Objective: This study sought to examine a crucial aspect of the process of determining whether a child should qualify for speech–language services in school settings. School districts rely heavily, although not always exclusively, upon standardized testing to prove eligibility for services and vary between saying that a child must be 1.5 *SD* (Standard deviation) below the mean to more than 2 *SD* below the mean. In addition, research on children with communication impairment often uses standardized testing to classify children.

The objective of this study was to determine if widely used standardized tests for determination of language impairment in children had sufficient data within their clinical manuals to support that children with language impairments are likely to obtain low scores relative to their typically developing peers.

Method: Forty-three commercially available norm-referenced standardized tests were identified that stated that they could be used for children from 3–18 years old specifically for looking at language impairments. The tests were evaluated on two main aspects. One aspect was an examination of the magnitude of differences between the language-impaired and control groups or assumed normative mean, with the second aspect being the frequency that manuals for the standardized tests provided information on the sensitivity and specificity of the measures, including the cut-off score used to derive these data.

Results: Concerning the first aspect involving magnitude of differences between language-impaired and control groups, none of the test manuals indicated mean group differences between the language-impaired and typically developing or normative sample. However, 33 of the 43 tests contained sufficient information for the authors to calculate the mean group and standardized deviations of such. Only 10 of the 33 tests reported score differences greater than 1.5 *SD*, with 9 of the 33 actually having group mean differences within 1 *SD* of each other.

Concerning the second aspect involving sensitivity and specificity, only 9 of the 43 tests provided this information. Of these, only 5 reported acceptable identification accuracy according to the authors' criterion.

Conclusion: The authors state, "Our review suggests that the practice of applying an arbitrary low cutoff score for diagnosing language impairments is frequently unsupported by the evidence that is available to clinicians in test manuals" (p. 66). The article ends with the following statements, "This consideration of both the interpretation of test data and the confidence in that interpretation reflects the probabilistic nature of diagnostics. Test results can only indicate the likelihood, rather than the certainty, that an impairment is present. A simple review of the currently available evidence can greatly improve the clinician's certainty in this clinical determination" (p.70).

Questions

1. How often do government bodies or other third-party payers use cut-off scores not to insure that all get help, but instead possibly to limit the number of people who officially need help? In this article, it is shown that different states use cut-off criteria that are not proven by the tests used; that is, a given test that has many language-impaired children scoring within 1.5 *SD* of the control group in its sample could be used in a given school district that states that the child must score below 1.5 *SD* to receive services. By setting a low bar for services, a government agency or third-party payer could state that it is providing help for "all that show sufficient need" while in fact denying services to those who should receive services.

2. How does the fact that only the ICF Body Function level functions are evaluated by the standardized tests examined in this study reflect a bias toward impairment and away from activity/participation measures? How could that be improved?

3. How does the fact that environmental and personal factors are not used to determine "severity" or need for services affect how eligibility criterion are established?

4. What is the relationship between standardized scores on tests and health related quality of life measures, and why is this relationship important?

5. How does the use of standardized measures reflect the spirit of federal laws such as the U.S. Individuals with Disability Education Act (IDEA) or the Americans With Disabilities Act (ADA)? If routine criterion measures are not in the spirit of federal disability laws, what are the roadblocks, or "barriers" to implementing a broader based system for determining disability?

Thus, it is paramount that speech–language pathologists work with other professionals to help clients achieve their global goals. Clients do not come to an assessment wanting to know what percentile or severity rating they obtain on a given component of communication. Rather they come with difficulties in life situations that they want improved. The first step of this improvement is an accurate and comprehensive assessment of their functioning. Furthermore, third-party payers and grant-giving agencies want to have more "bang for their buck" and thus want to determine if overall programs, such as traumatic brain injury rehabilitation teams, produce real-life tangible results.

A model program for using the ICF to coordinate client-centered interdisciplinary assessment was described by speech–language pathologist Hancock (2003) in the following passage:

> Our Living Well program was developed as part of our hospital-based, 26-bed inpatient acute rehabilitation program. The caseload is composed of 50% orthopedic, 30% neurologic, and 20% other diagnoses including: deconditioning, cardiopulmonary, oncology, and amputee. Our rehabilitation team utilizes the ICF model as the framework for our interdisciplinary, person-centered practice. Discipline-specific evaluation of underlying impairments and limitations in basic body structures and/or functions is complemented by a team assessment of potential activity/participation restrictions. Our team's interdisciplinary approach lends itself to addressing the physical, psychosocial and/or cognitive-communicative issues that may undermine a person's ability to participate in life activities. This is accomplished via close collaboration between physical therapy, occupational therapy, speech language pathology, nursing, and social work.

Hancock collected outcome data on this on 240 patients who completed surveys concerning participation in this program over a 10-month period. The patients rated the activities worked on via this approach as "meaningful" with average of 85% to 98% in the five group protocols used. She concluded that the intervention based on an ICF assessment framework was effective in physical, psychosocial, and communicative gains in meaningful areas of their lives.

NATIONAL/STATE AND FEDERAL OR INTERNATIONAL PRACTICES IN COMMUNICATION DISORDERS ASSESSMENT

As previously stated, in the United States the ICF is used as the framework for communication disorders assessment in the cardinal documents of the American Speech-Language-Hearing Association (ASHA). In a report commissioned by ASHA, the ICF is also cited as a possible guiding agent for evidence-based practice research (Robey, et al., 2004).

Threats (2006) discusses the use of the ICF by speech–language pathologists in the United States, Australia, England, Ireland, Brazil, Chile, Japan, New Zealand, Canada, England, Germany, Greece, Finland, Denmark, South Africa, Sweden, China, and India. Use of the ICF in the literature in communication disorders is growing (Bornman, 2004; Brobeck, 2004; Brush, Threats, & Calkins, 2003; Davidson, Worrall, & Hickson, 2003; Donaldson, Worrall, & Hickson, 2004; Eadie, 2003, Feeney & Ylvisaker, 2003; Fey, Long, & Finestack, 2003; Hammerton, 2004; Hickson & Worrall, 2001; Hopper, 2004; Howe, Worrall, & Hickson, 2004; Isaki & Turkstra, 2002; John, 2002; John, Hughes & Enderby, 2002; Kagan, Elman & Simmons-Mackie, 2002; Larkins, Worrall, & Hickson, 2004; Law, 2004; Ma, 2003; Ma & Yiu, 2001; Marshall, 2004; McCooey, O'Halloran, Worrall & Hickson, 2004; McLeod, 2004; McLeod, 2006; O'Halloran, Worrall, Code, Toffolo & Hickson, 2004; Paul et al., 2004; Pimentel, Englebret, & Murphy, 2004; Ross & Wertz, 2005; Simmons-Mackie, 2004a; Simmons-Mackie, Threats, & Kagan, 2005; Threats, 2004; Vickers, 2004; Worrall & Hickson, 2003; Worrall, McCooey, Davidson, Larkins, & Hickson, 2002; Yaruss & Quesal, 2004; Ylvisaker, Hanks & Johnson-Greene, 2002).

Much of the ICF research is being done collaboratively by persons from different countries. The sharing of a common framework across countries should improve international cooperation among countries, despite their differences in health care administration and cultures. Using the same framework for assessment and outcome measures will improve the reasonably comparable databases needed for evidence-based practice.

Recently, two internationally respected journals in communication disorders had issues dedicated to the use of the ICF. Between the two journals, authors from the United States, Canada, South Africa, United Kingdom, Australia, Hong Kong, and New Zealand were included. In a 2007 issue of the journal *Seminars in Speech and*

Language, the use of the ICF with specific communication disorders was addressed and included articles pertaining to aphasia (Simmons-Mackie & Kagan, 2007), child articulation/phonological disorders (McLeod & McCormack, 2007), child language disorders (Westby, 2007), dementia (Hopper, 2007), acquired hearing disorders (Hickson & Scarinci, 2007), laryngectomy (Eadie, 2007), motor speech disorders (Dykstra, Hakel & Adams, 2007), fluency disorders (Yaruss, 2007), dysphagia (Threats, 2007b), cognitive communication disorders (Larkins, 2007), and voice disorders (Ma, Yiu, & Verdolini-Abbott, 2007). In 2008, the *International Journal in Speech-Language Pathology* published a special double issue that addressed the various components and applications of the ICF in relationship to communication disorders, which discussed the following: body functions/structures (McCormack & Worrall, 2008), activities and participation (O'Halloran & Larkins, 2008), contextual factors (Howe, 2008), quality of life (Cruice, 2008), clinical practice (Threats, 2008), research (Worrall & Hickson, 2008), teaching (Doyle & Skarakis-Doyle, 2008), professional policy (Brown & Hasselkus, 2008), epidemiology (Mulhorn & Threats, 2008), and the *ICF for Children and Youth* (McLeod & Threats,

2008) These two journal issues represent a broad survey of the state of the art of the use of the ICF in the field of communication disorders.

MAJOR ISSUES THAT NEED ATTENTION IN COMMUNICATION DISORDERS ASSESSMENT

The two main issues facing the field of communication disorders regarding assessment are evidence-based practice and implementation of the ICF by clinicians and researchers. There are ASHA documents and literature concerning the importance of both, but that has yet to effect the widespread changes needed in the field. As stated previously in this chapter, reliable and valid assessments must be used to determine whether a given intervention is effective, taking into account all aspects of what it means for a client to get "better." In this day of increased accountability by third-party payers and consumers themselves, speech-language pathologists must have assessment methods and corresponding interventions that address the real-life functioning of clients.

Summary and Conclusion

Communication disorders comprise a wide range of disorders that affect the ability of persons to interact with others, including conversation and nonverbal communication. When a person has a communication disorder, it can lead to depression or social isolation or to the person not reaching his or her full potential to contribute to life satisfaction or to society. Speech-language pathologists also work with persons with oral/pharyngeal swallowing disorders and these too can lead to social as well as medical difficulties. Communication and swallowing disorders are health concerns that fit with the WHO's definition of health because they affect the physical, mental, and social well-being of persons. The World Health Organization's *International Classification of Functioning, Disability, and Health (ICF)* can be used to describe the different aspects of decreased functioning and possible environmental and personal factors that can occur with persons with communication and/or swallowing disorders.

Historically, assessment has had as its primary focuses making a diagnosis, determining severity, and producing a prognosis for improvement. These assessments also have tended to focus primarily on the body function and body structure components of the ICF. More recently, the view of assessment in light of how it can inform intervention has come into the forefront. There are deficiencies in current assessment across all communication and swallowing disorders in evaluation of the activity/participation, environmental factors, and personal factors components of the ICF. There has been increased attention drawn to these limitations recently in the communication disorders literature.

The American Speech–Language–Hearing Association (ASHA), along with several leading scholars in communication and swallowing disorders, has been leading the push to use the ICF as the guideline for assessments in the field. However, reliable and valid measures have yet to be developed to address this challenge.

Evidence-based practice is beginning to influence researchers' views of assessment. In outcomes assessment, assessment must demonstrate improvement, not just provide a diagnosis and severity level. ASHA has also published a position paper on evidence-based practice recently that emphasizes the need to integrate high- quality research with clinician expertise and client values. The integration of both the ICF framework and the tenants of evidence-based practice needs to be the guide for developing these more functionally based and clinically meaningful assessments.

The practice of speech–language pathology does not, as with all clinical fields, exist in a vacuum. Cultural and legislative issues influence how clients are treated by the world and what resources speech-language pathologists have to provide intervention for them. Ethical issues in rehabilitation are coming to the foreground as the clinical fields address issues of client autonomy more seriously.

If speech–language pathology is to become more client-centered, then the field must consider more interdisciplinary integrated approaches to assist clients. If each field is only concerned about proving its own effectiveness, what is the overall best for the client may be missed. This chapter provided an example of an inpatient rehabilitation unit that used the ICF to help guide this integrated approach.

The ICF is being used internationally to help link speech–language pathologists in both research and clinical practice. These collaborations should result in increased success in helping clients. In addition, by looking across languages and cultures, the profession can glean insights into the bases of human communication.

The two major issues facing the field are use of evidence-based practice and the ICF. There has been positive movement in regard to both in ASHA practice documents and the literature, but there is not yet enough widespread use of these two necessary pillars to clinical practice. The future of the field depends upon this successful implementation of evidence-based practice and the ICF.

Self-Check Questions

1. Discuss how communication functioning should be considered health. Is not being able to communicate as much a disability as not being able to walk?
2. What are six broad categories of types of communication disorders?
3. What swallowing disorders do speech–language pathologists treat?
4. Looking at the six categories of communication disorders, pick three and explain how they might be described using the ICF's components of body function, body structure, activity/participation, environmental factors. In addition, how could these three disorders be manifested differently depending upon personal factors of individuals?

5. How has the profession of speech–language pathology integrated the use of the ICF in the United States? Is there international work in the field using the ICF?
6. What are the possible benefits of using the tenets of both the ICF and evidence-based practice in improving research in communication disorders?
7. What are some of the issues concerning working with persons of varying cultures for the field of communication disorders? Is it simply a matter of learning lists of the main characteristics of given racial or cultural groups?
8. Why do speech-language pathologists interact with other health professionals?

Case Studies

Case Study 1

A teenager who has been in and out of juvenile detention centers since age 12 is now 17 and has been involved in an automobile accident that has left him with traumatic brain injury resulting in mild to moderate cognitive impairments. At the time of the accident, he had already dropped out of school with one of the reasons given that he never became a proficient reader. He has been discharged from the hospital and is now in an inpatient rehabilitation hospital. How should the rehabilitation approach assessment of this individual in terms of the following: (1) standardized test scores, (2) possible pre-morbid cognitive and/or language difficulties, (3) using the ICF approach as the framework for assessment, (4) use of evidence-based practice to help determine appropriate evaluations for this population, and (5) appropriate method for determining outcome assessment for this boy.

Case Study 2

A formerly very physical and socially active 65-year-old woman from an aristocratic wealthy family in the South is admitted to a nursing home by her daughter because she is in the middle stage of Alzheimer's disease. Because the daughter lives in New York City, she has her transferred to a nursing facility near her Manhattan home. The mother is assessed by the rehabilitation team her first week. They conclude that she is (1) a dangerous wanderer because she keeps trying to go outside; (2) will not eat the food prepared for her and is thus at risk for malnutrition and dehydration, and they suspect must have an underlying swallowing disorder; (3) is a theft risk because she keeps walking into other residents' rooms and taking their possessions; (4) must have severe cognitive impairments because she refuses to answer orientation questions from the therapy staff or even cooperate with evaluation; (5) is belligerent because she frequently yells and even tries to hit nurses and others attempting to assist or direct her; and (6) is non-communicative in the current affairs discussion group. As a result of the group assessment, it is determined that she should be put on a g-tube for feeding and sedated on medication to keep her from being such a risk to others and herself. In addition, she is declared sufficiently cognitively compromised that she is not allowed to make any decisions for herself in the nursing home.

QUESTIONS

1. Identify whether you believe their assessment of this case is correct.
2. How could using the principals of the ICF better determine an evaluation for this resident and how could this assessment result in a different course of intervention?
3. What ethical issues are involved in this case?
4. What method of outcome assessment should be utilized with this resident?

References

American Speech–Language–Hearing Association (2003). *Scope of practice for audiology*. Rockville, MD: Author.

American Speech-Language-Hearing Association (2004). *Preferred practice patterns for the profession of speech-language pathology*. Rockville, MD: Author.

American Speech-Language-Hearing Association (ASHA, 2007). *Scope of practice for speech-language pathology*. Rockville, MD: Author.

Boles, L. (2004). The ICF language of numeric adjectives. *Advances in Speech-Language Pathology, 6*(1), 71–73.

Bornman, J. (2004). The World Health Organization's terminology and classification: Application to severe disability. *Disability and Rehabilitation, 26*(3), 182–188.

Brobeck, T. (2004). Strategies for enhancing the body of evidence in clinical decision making. *Perspectives on Neurophysiology and Neurogenic Speech and Language Disorders, 14*(1), 11–14.

Brown, J., & Hasselkus, A. (2008). Professional associations' role in advancing the ICF in speech-language pathology. *International Journal of Speech-Language Pathology, 10*(1,2), 78–82.

Brush, J., Threats, T., & Calkins, M. (2003). Influences on perceived function for a nursing home resident. *Journal of Communication Disorders, 36*, 379–393.

Chapey, R., Duchan, J., Elman, R., Garcia, L., Kagan, A., Lyon, J., & Simmons-Mackie, N. (2001). Assessment in aphasia. In R. Chapey (ED.) *Language Intervention Strategies in Aphasia and Related Neurogenic Communication Disorders- Fourth edition*, Baltimore, MD: Lippincott, Williams, & Wilkins.

Cruice, M. (2008). The contribution and impact of the International Classification of Functioning, Disability and Health on quality of life in communication disorders. *International Journal of Speech-Language Pathology, 10*(1,2), 38–49.

Cruice, M., Worrall, L., Hickson, L., & Murison, R. (2003). Finding a focus for quality of life with aphasia: Social and emotional health and psychological well-being. *Aphasiology, 17*(4), 333–353.

Damico, J. & Simmons-Mackie, N. (2003). Qualitative research and speech-language pathology: A tutorial for the clinical realm. *American Journal of Speech–Language Pathology,12*, 131–143.

Davidson, B., Worrall, L., & Hickson, L. (2003) Identifying the communication activities of older people with aphasia: Evidence from naturalistic observation. *Aphasiology, 17*(3), 243–264.

Donaldson, N., Worrall, L., and Hickson, L. (2004) Older people with hearing impairment: A literature review of the spouses' perspective. *The Australian and New Zealand Journal of Audiology, 26* (1) 30–39.

Doyle, P., & Skarakis-Doyle, E. (2008). The ICF as a framework for interdisciplinary doctoral education in rehabilitation: Implications for speech–language pathology. *International Journal of Speech–Language Pathology, 10*(1,2), 83–91.

Duchan, J. (2004). Where is the person in the ICF? *Advances in Speech–Language Pathology, 6*(1), 67–70.

Dykstra, A., Hakel, M., & Adams, S. (2007). Application of the ICF in reduced speech intelligibility in dysarthria. *Seminars in Speech and Language, 28*(4), 301–311.

Eadie, T. (2003). A proposed framework for comprehensive rehabilitation of individuals who use alaryngeal speech. *American Journal of Speech–Language Pathology, 12*(2), 189–197.

Eadie, T. (2007). Application of the ICF in communication after total laryngectomy. *Seminars in Speech and Language, 28*(4), 291–300.

Eadie, T., Yorkston, K., Klasner, E., Dudgeon, B., Deitz, J., Baylor, C., Miller, R., & Antmann, D. (2006). Measuring communication participation: A review of self-report instruments in speech-language pathology. *American Journal of Speech-Language Pathology, 15*, 307–320.

Feeney, T., & Ylvisaker, M. (2003). Context-sensitive behavioral supports for young children with TBI. *Journal of Head Trauma Rehabilitation, 18*(1), 33–51.

Fey, M., Long, S., & Finestack, L. (2003). Ten principles of grammar facilitation for children with specific language impairments. *American Journal of Speech-Language Pathology, 12*(1), 3–15.

Frattali, C. (1998). Outcomes measurement: Definitions, dimensions, and perspectives. In C. Frattali (Ed.) *Measuring outcomes in speech-language pathology.* New York: Thieme.

Frattali, C. (2000). Health-care restructuring in the United States. In L. Worrall, & C. Frattali (Eds.), *Neurogenic communication disorders: A functional approach.* New York: Thieme.

Garcia, L., Laroche, C., & Barrette, J. (2002). Work integration issues go beyond the nature of the communication disorder. *Journal of Communication Disorders, 35,* 187–211.

Hammerton, J. (2004). An investigation into the influence of age on recovery from stroke with community rehabilitation. Unpublished doctoral dissertation. University of Sheffield, Sheffield, UK.

Hancock, H. (2003) Rehabilitation for enhanced life participation: A living well program. *Speech Pathology Online* at http://www.speechpathology.com/

Hickson, L. & Scarinci, N. (2007). Older adults with acquired impairment: Applying the ICF in rehabilitation. *Seminars in Speech and Language, 28*(4), 283–290.

Hickson, L., & Worrall, L. (2001). Older people with hearing impairment: Application of the new World Health Organization International Classification of Functioning and Disability. *Asia Pacific Journal of Speech Language and Hearing, 6*(2), 129–133.

Hopper, T. (2004). Long-term care residents with dementia: Assessment and intervention. *The ASHA Leader, 24,* 10–11.

Hopper, T. (2007). The ICF and dementia. *Seminars in Speech and Language, 28*(4), 273–282.

Howe, T. (2008). The ICF contextual factors related to speech-language pathology. *International Journal of Speech-Language Pathology, 10*(1,2), 27–37.

Howe, T., Worrall, L., & Hickson, L. (2004) What is an aphasia-friendly environment? A review. *Aphasiology, 18*(11) 1015–1037.

Isaki, E., & Turkstra, L. (2002). Communication abilities and work re-entry following traumatic brain injury. *Brain Injury, 14*(5), 441–453.

John, A. (2002) Therapy outcome measures for benchmarking in speech and language therapy. Unpublished doctoral dissertation. University of Sheffield, Sheffield, UK.

John, A., Hughes, A, & Enderby, P. (2002) Establishing clinician reliability using the therapy outcome measure for the purpose of benchmarking services. *Advances in Speech-Language Pathology, 4*(2), 79–87.

Kagan, A., Elman, R., & Simmons-Mackie, N. (2002). *Usefulness of ICF in evaluating participation-based outcomes in aphasia.* Seminar presented at annual ASHA convention.

Larkins, B. (2007). Application of the ICF in cognitive communication disorders following traumatic brain injuries. *Seminars in Speech and Language, 28*(4), 334–342.

Larkins, B., Worrall, L., & Hickson, L. (2004). Stakeholder opinion of functional communication activities following traumatic brain injury. *Brain Injury, 18*(7), 691–706

Law, I. (2004) Functional communication following laryngectomy. Unpublished masters thesis. University of Hong Kong, Hong Kong, China.

League of Community-Based Speech–Language–Hearing Therapists (2004). *Conversation partners for people with aphasia: Let's talk with people with aphasia.* Tokyo: Chuohoki Shuppan (in Japanese).

Lubker, B. (1997). Epidemiology: an essential science for speech–language pathology and audiology. *Journal of Communication Disorders, 30,* 251–267.

Ma, E. (2003). Impairment, activity limitation and participation restriction issues in assessing dysphonia. Doctor of Philosphy thesis. Hong Kong: The University of Hong Kong.

Ma, E., & Yiu, E. (2001). Voice Activity and Participation Profile: Assessing the impact of voice disorders on daily activities. *Journal of Speech, Language and Hearing Research, 44,* 511–524.

Ma, E., Yiu, E., & Verdolini-Abbott, K. (2007). Application of the ICF in voice disorders. *Seminars in Speech and Language, 28*(4), 343–350.

Marshall, M. (2004) *A study to elicit the core components of stroke rehabilitation and the subsequent development of a taxonomy of the therapy process*. Unpublished doctoral dissertation. University of Sheffield, Sheffield, UK.

McCooey-O'Halloran, R., Worrall, L., & Hickson, L. (2004) Evaluating the role of speech-language pathology with patients with communication disability in the acute hospital setting, using the ICF. *Journal of Medical Speech Language Pathology, 12*(2), 49–58.

McCormack, J., & Worrall (2008). The ICF Body Functions and Structures related to speech-language pathology. *International Journal of Speech-Language Pathology, 10*(1,2), 9–17.

McLeod, S. (2004). Speech pathologists' application of the ICF to children with speech impairment. *Advances in Speech-Language Pathology, 6*(1) 75–81.

McLeod, S. (2006). The holistic view of a child with unintelligible speech: Insights from the ICF and ICF-CY. *Advances in Speech-Language Pathology, 8*(3), 293–315.

McLeod, S., & McCormack (2007). Application of the ICF and the ICF-Children and Youth in children with speech impairment. *Seminars in Speech and Language, 28*(4), 254–264.

McLeod, S., & Threats, T. (2008). Application of the ICF-CY to children with communication disabilities. *International Journal of Speech-Language pathology, 10*(1,2), 92–109.

Mulhorn, K., & Threats, T. (2008). Speech, hearing, and communication across five national disability surveys: Results of a DISTAB study using the ICF to compare prevalence patterns. *International Journal of Speech-Language Pathology, 10*(1,2), 61–71.

O'Halloran, R., & Larkins, B. (2008). The ICF Activities and Participation related to speech-language pathology. *International Journal of Speech-Language Pathology, 10*(1,2), 18–26.

O'Halloran, R., Worrall, L., Code, C., Toffolo, D., & Hickson, L. (2004). *The Inpatient Functional Communication Interview*. Oxon, UK: Speechmark.

Paul, D., Frattali, C., Holland, A, Thompson, C., Caperton, C., & Slater, S. (2004). *Quality of Communication Life Scale*. Rockville, MD: ASHA.

Pimentel, J., Englebret, E., & Murphy, C. (2004). Evidence-based practice application: Intensive case examinations—A non-thesis option. Seminar presented at annual ASHA convention.

Ripich, D., & Horner, J. (2004). The neurodegenerative dementias: Diagnosis and interventions. *The ASHA Leader*, 4–5.

Robey, R., Apel, K, Dollaghan, C., Elmo, W., Hall, N., Helfer, T., Moeller. M., Threats, T., Hooper, C, & Kent, R. (2004). *A report of the joint committee of evidence based practice*. Rockville, MD: ASHA.

Ross, K., & Wertz, R. (2005). Advancing appraisal: Aphasia and the WHO. *Aphasiology, 19*(9), 860–870.

Sackett, D., Rosenberg, W., Gray, J., Haynes, R., & Richardson, W. (1996). Evidence based medicine: what it is and what it isn't. *British Medical Journal, 312*, 71–72.

Sackett, D., Straus, S., Richardson, W., Rosenberg,W., & Haynes, R. (2000). *Evidence-based medicine: How to practice and teach EBM*. Edinburgh: Churchill Livingstone.

Simmons-Mackie, N. (2004a). Cautiously embracing the ICF. *Advances in Speech-Language Pathology, 6*(1), 67–70.

Simmons-Mackie, N. (2004b). Using the ICF framework to define outcomes. *Perspectives on Neurophysiology and Neurogenic Speech and Language Disorders, 14*(1), 9–11.

Simmons-Mackie, N., & Kagan, A. (2007). Application of the ICF in aphasia. *Seminars in Speech and Language, 28*(4), 244–253.

Simmons-Mackie, N, Threats, T., & Kagan, A. (2005). Outcome assessment in aphasia: A survey. *Journal of Communication Disorders, 38*, 1–27

Threats, T. (2001). New classification will aid assessment and intervention. *The ASHA Leader, 6*(18), 12–13.

Threats, T. (2002). Evidence based practice research using the WHO framework. *Journal of Medical Speech-Language Pathology, 10*(3), xvii–xxiv.

Threats, T. (2004). The use of ICF in intervention for persons with neurogenic communication disorders. *Perspectives on Neurophysiology and Neurogenic Speech and Language Disorders, 14*(1), 4–8

Threats, T. (2006). Towards an international framework for communication disorders: Use of the ICF. *Journal of Communication Disorders, 39*, 251–265.

Threats, T. (2007a). Access for persons with neurogenic communication disorders: Influences of Personal and Environmental Factors of the ICF. *Aphasiology, 21*(1), 67–80.

Threats, T. (2007b). Use of the ICF in dysphagia management. *Seminars in Speech and Language, 28*(4), 323–333.

Threats, T. (2008). Use of the ICF for clinical practice in speech–language pathology. *International Journal of Speech–Language Pathology, 10*(1,2), 50–60

Threats, T., Shadden, B., and Vickers, C. (2003, November). *Assessment & intervention of older adults using the ICF framework*. Short course presented at ASHA convention, Chicago, IL.

Threats, T. & Worrall, L. (2004a). Classifying communication disability using the ICF. *Advances in Speech-Language Pathology, 6*(1), 53–62.

Threats, T. & Worrall, L. (2004b). ICF is all about the person, and more: A response to Duchan, Simmons-Mackie, Boles, and McLeod. *Advances in Speech–Language Pathology, 6*(1), 83–87.

Vickers, C. (2004). Communicating in groups: One stop on the road to improved participation for persons with aphasia. *Perspectives on Neurophysiology and Neurogenic Speech and Language Disorders, 14*(1), 16–20.

Worrall, L. (2001). The social approach: another new fashion in speech–language pathology? *Advances in Speech–Language Pathology, 3*(1), 51–54.

Worrall, L., & Frattali, C. (Eds) (2000) *Neurogenic Communication Disorders: A Functional Approach*. New York: Thieme Medical Publishers.

Worrall, L., & Hickson, L. (2003) *Communication disability in aging: From prevention to intervention.* Clifton Park, NY: Thomson-Delmar Publishers.

Worrall, L., & Hickson, L. (2008). The use of the ICF in speech-language pathology research: Towards a research agenda. *International Journal of Speech–Language Pathology, 10*(10–2), 72–77.

Worrall, L., McCooey, R., Davidson, B., Larkins, B., & Hickson, L. (2002). The validity of functional assessments of communication and the activity/participation components of the ICIDH-2: Do they reflect what really happens in real-life? *Journal of Communication Disorders, 35*(2), 107–137

Worrall, L., & Yiu, E. (2000). Effectiveness of functional communication therapy by volunteers for people with aphasia following stroke. *Aphasiology, 14*, 911–924.

Yaruss, J. (2007). Application of the ICF in fluency disorders. *Seminars in Speech and Language, 28*(4), 312–322.

Yaruss, J., & Quesal, R. (2004). Stuttering and the International Classification of Functioning, Disability, and Health (ICF): An update. *Journal of Communication Disorders, 37*(1), 35–52.

Yiu, E. M-L., & Ma, E. (2002) Voice activity limitation and participation restriction in the teaching profession: The need for preventive voice care. *Journal of Medical Speech-Language Pathology , 10*(1), 51–60.

Ylvisaker, M., Hanks, R., & Johnson-Greene, D. (2002). Perspectives on rehabilitation of individuals with cognitive impairment after brain injury: Rationale for reconsideration of theoretical paradigms. *Journal of Head Trauma Rehabilitation, 17*(3), 191–209

Westby, C. (2007). Application of the ICF in children with language impairments. *Seminars in Speech and Language , 28*(4), 265–272.

World Health Organization (1948). World Health Organization constitution. Geneva, Switzerland. Retrieved from http://www.searo.who.int/EN/Section898/Section1441.htm

World Health Organization. (2001). *International Classification of Functioning, Disability, and Health.* Geneva, Switzerland: Author.

Assessment in Vision Rehabilitation

RICHARD G. LONG
Western Michigan University, Kalamazoo

JOHN E. CREWS
Centers for Disease Control and Prevention Atlanta, Georgia

OVERVIEW

This chapter explores issues related to the assessment of individuals with visual impairments. It offers a description of the components of the clinical assessment process for service planning, and discusses the substantial progress made during the past ten years regarding outcomes assessment. The chapter also provides a framework for assessment that is grounded in the International Classification of Functioning, Disability, and Health (ICF), and provides information on the ways that assessment can be strengthened by attending to the ICF conceptual model. The chapter concludes with a brief discussion of research needs in assessment of individuals with visual impairments.

LEARNING OBJECTIVES

By the end of the chapter, readers should be able to:

- Describe the prevalence of visual impairment in general and among subpopulations, such as older individuals
- Briefly describe the service delivery system in vision rehabilitation
- Describe assessment practices for eligibility determination, program planning, and outcomes measurement
- Relate assessment in vision rehabilitation to the ICF
- Briefly describe the Learning Media Assessment and the Distance Visual Recognition Assessment
- Describe research needs for assessment in vision rehabilitation

INTRODUCTION

DEFINITIONS AND THEORIES OF VISION REHABILITATION

The term *visual impairment* often is used collectively to describe individuals who have no vision at all and individuals who, while impaired, retain some ability to see. The term *blind* (contrasted with *legally blind*) usually refers to individuals who do not have usable vision, and the term *low vision* describes individuals who have some vision (Corn & Koenig, 1996, provide additional information on issues pertaining to the definition of various vision-related terms). Although population estimates vary because of differing case definitions, there are about 3.3 million people age 40 and over in the United States (Eye Diseases Prevalence Research Group, 2004) who have impaired vision. Prevalence estimates vary depending upon the definition of vision loss used (e.g., blindness or inability to read newspaper print) and the constraints of the methods employed (e.g., telephone surveys, face-to-face surveys, and clinical examination). The World Health Organization defines blindness as a visual acuity of less than 20/400, whereas by U.S. law, the definition of blindness is 20/200 or less in the better eye, corrected, or a peripheral visual field of no greater than 20 degrees (Eye Diseases Prevalence Research Group, 2004). (Low vision is defined as less than 20/40 in the better seeing eye, excluding those who are blind using the U.S. legal definition.) The designation of 20/20 means that a person located 20 feet from a target sees what a person with normal vision sees at 20 feet; therefore, 20/200 means that a person with that vision impairment located 20 feet from a target sees what a person with normal vision sees at 200 feet.

The U.S. legal definition of blindness is often used in determining eligibility for income transfer and rehabilitation programs (e.g., Medicare, Medicaid, Supplemental Security Income, Social Security Disability Income, and eligibility for services under the various state/federal vocational rehabilitation programs). However, service providers and researchers interested in assessment for program planning and outcomes measurement often find that assessment of the impact of visual acuity loss on function is more useful than the acuity data itself. For example, a functionally-based assessment might address whether life activities, such as moving about in one's community or taking care of personal needs, are significantly affected by visual loss. One reason for the focus on function rather than on acuity scores is that medical and rehabilitation providers working with individuals with visual impairments recognize that two individuals with similar etiology of visual loss and similar clinical function (e.g., acuity, visual field, contrast sensitivity) may function very differently as a result of experience and prior training, environmental and psychosocial factors, and other reasons.

A recent study by the Eye Diseases Prevalence Research Group (2004) estimated the prevalence of vision impairment ranged from .31/100 for those aged 40–49 to 23.73/100 for those aged 80+ (see Table 26.1). Prevalence of vision impairment is higher among women, blacks, and Hispanics.

Several recent studies have helped to refine our knowledge of the prevalence and incidence issues related to visual impairments. Lee, Gomez-Martin, Lam, Zheng, & Jane (2004) examining the National Health Interview Survey (NHIS) noted that trends in vision impairment showed no significant change in prevalence during the period 1986–1995. An investigation by Crews, Jones, and Kim (2006) examined 7 years of the NHIS Sample Adult file (1997–2004) to identify the prevalence of comorbid conditions and the effects of comorbid conditions in conjunction with vision loss among people aged 65 and over. Among the nine chronic conditions studied (including heart disease, hypertension, mild/moderate and severe depression, and stroke), people reporting vision loss were more likely to report these coexisting conditions than those who did not report vision loss. For example, 57.2% of people with vision loss report mild or moderate depression, whereas 43.5% of people without vision loss report depression. Similarly, 53.2% of people with vision loss report hearing impairment, whereas 38.9% of people without vision loss report problems with hearing. The clinical implications of these findings suggest that people with vision impairments are more likely to experience comorbid conditions that, in many cases, complicate rehabilitation interventions or require that comorbid conditions be addressed as part of an intervention. Some

TABLE 26.1 Estimated Prevalence of Vision Impairment in the United States, by Age and Race/Ethnicity, 2000.

Age	Number of person (in thousands) 95% Confidence Interval (CI)			No of persons (in thousands)	Prevalence for 100 individuals (95% CI)
	White	Black	Hispanic		
40–49	99	11	13	131 (108–153)	0.31 (0.25–0.36)
50–54	48	9	8	71 (64–77)	0.40 (0.36–0.44)
55–59	49	12	10	76 (69–83)	0.56 (0.51–0.61)
60–64	59	17	12	95 (87–104)	0.88 (0.80–0.96)
65–69	89	26	15	140 (128–152)	1.47 (1.34–1.60)
70–74	159	37	21	231 (211–250)	2.60 (2.38–2.83)
75–79	288	45	24	374 (340–407)	5.03 (4.58–5.49)
≥ 80	1961	110	65	2180 (1850–2509)	23.73 (20.14–27.32)
Total	2752	267	168	3298 (2963–3629)	2.76 (2.48–3.04)

Adapted from Eye Diseases Prevalence Research Group, 2004.

conditions, like depression—that is largely ignored among older people anyway—should reasonably be addressed before and during rehabilitation.

The leading causes of vision loss in the United States are cataract, diabetic retinopathy, macular degeneration, glaucoma, and retinitis pigmentosa. All vision disorders among people aged 40 years or older with vision impairments in the United States are estimated to cost $35.4 billion; this estimate includes the direct cost of medical care, institutional care, reduced productivity and labor force participation, as well as government-funded income transfer programs (Rein et al., 2006).

A broad range of medical and rehabilitative services is available to visually impaired youths who are transitioning from education to work, and to working and older adults with visual impairments. The majority of persons receiving vision rehabilitation services in the United States have low vision, and low vision services are offered by some optometrists and ophthalmologists and by certified low-vision therapists. These providers offer specialized clinical and functional visual assessments tailored to the needs of individuals with low vision, and they prescribe optical and nonoptical aids and devices and offer training in their use. Low-vision devices include hand-held magnifiers to enhance near vision, telescopes to enhance distance vision, and specialized devices such as closed circuit television systems and lighting systems designed for persons with low

vision. Many low-vision providers work in dedicated low-vision clinics affiliated with private or government-funded rehabilitation services, and in a few cases, low-vision medical care is offered as part of a general eyecare practice.

Instruction in orientation and mobility, low-vision device use, and various activities of daily living (including daily living skills using adaptive technologies and Braille instruction) is provided, respectively, by certified orientation and mobility specialists (COMS), certified low-vision therapists (CLVT), and vision rehabilitation therapists (CVRT). These professionals are certified by the Academy for Certification in Vision Rehabilitation and Education Professionals (ACVREP).

Reimbursement for vision rehabilitation services under Medicare and by third-party payers is limited. Most professionals providing vision rehabilitation services in 2006 under Medicare were occupational therapists (although as noted in the following discussion, Medicare reimbursement likely will be opened to ACVREP-certified vision rehabilitation professionals in the future). Currently, there is a pilot program to expand Medicare reimbursement to providers who are certified by ACVREP in orientation and mobility, vision rehabilitation therapy, and low-vision therapy.

All states offer rehabilitation services to adults with visual impairments under their respective federal–state vocational rehabilitation programs. These programs assist working-aged people to obtain competitive employment (the outcome is work), and programs supported by the federally funded Older Blind Program provide services that promote independence. Vocational rehabilitation services include medical diagnosis and treatment, psychological services, social services, vocational assessment, training and placement services, and personal adjustment training. In addition to the federal–state program of rehabilitative services for persons with visual impairments, there is a network of private, not-for-profit agencies throughout the United States that provide rehabilitation services. These programs often serve infants and children, working-age adults, and older adults. Also, the United States Department of Veterans Affairs operates a system of rehabilitation centers and clinics for eligible veterans with visual impairments and blindness. Many of the individuals served by the Department of Veterans Affairs are older adults, and they receive personal adjustment, medical, social, and other services. Some persons with visual impairment receive services in residential rehabilitation centers, and others are served by vision rehabilitation professionals in their homes and communities.

Despite the range of services available to persons with visual impairments, relatively few individuals who are eligible for vision rehabilitation services actually receive them. One reason for this is the dearth of certified personnel in vision rehabilitation, and increasing the supply is a concern to university programs and others who are involved in personnel preparation. Another issue in service delivery is the type of services clients can access. Some agencies that provide services in residential settings still require clients to participate in a relatively standardized "package" of services, and there is a need for developing service delivery options that make clients aware of the variety of services, but that allow greater choice about the services actually received.

APPLICABLE INTERNATIONAL CLASSIFICATION FUNCTIONING AND HEALTH ASPECTS

The aim of the ICF is to organize components of the rehabilitation intervention to achieve desired outcomes. The *b* codes in the ICF are related to body functions;

impairments are problems with body functions. Chapter 2 of the ICF addresses sensory functions and pain; seeing functions are found in b210. Code b2100 refers to visual acuity, and code b 2101 refers to visual field; these codes are used to determine eligibility for income transfer and vocational rehabilitation programs. Activity and activity limitations have to do with task performance by the individual, and participation and participation restrictions have to do with life situations. Activities and participation were combined in the final revision of the ICF, and both are given d codes. Activity and participation are captured in nine chapters, including 1) learning and applying knowledge; 2) general tasks and demands; 3) communication; 4) mobility; 5) self-care; 6) domestic life; 7) interpersonal interactions and relationships; 8) major life areas; and 9) community, social and civic life. Codes d320–d329 in chapter 3, "Communication," for example, capture reading newspaper print, and code d3601 includes "using writing machines," including computer and Braille writers. Chapter 4, "Mobility," (codes d450–d469) characterizes walking and moving around, and code d470 includes moving around using transportation. Chapter 5, "Self Care," deals with identifying clothing; chapter 6, "Domestic Life," deals with shopping, preparing meals, and doing housework. These discrete items look remarkably similar to the primary domains of vision rehabilitation: mobility, communication, and daily living. Chapter 7 addresses relationships, including family, friends, and intimate relationships; chapter 8 addresses the major life areas of education, work, and economic life. In vocational rehabilitation, education (codes d820–d839) may be viewed as an intervention that leads to employment. The aim of vocational rehabilitation is to obtain remunerative employment (d850)—roughly equivalent to a Status 26 closure—that hopefully allows for economic self-sufficiency (d870).

Clinical rehabilitation assessments and interventions used in vision rehabilitation may not match to the specificity of the ICF codes, but in aggregate, both clinical assessments and the ICF can characterize changes—gains or losses at various levels of measurement. Thus, it is productive to conceptually map the complex experience of vision loss to the domains of the ICF. For example, having a disease like macular degeneration, classified by the *International Classification of Diseases* (WHO, 2007), leads to changes in the structure and function of the macula (measured by visual acuity). Depending upon the severity of the visual impairment, one may have difficulty reading or driving a car (activity limitations) and thus may not be able to get together with friends and family or go to work (participation restrictions). Modifications to the environment—using large print and driving familiar routes in daylight—may allow individuals to continue to participate in desired social roles. Instruction in the various strategies for safe and efficient nonvisual travel may also impact social role fulfillment of persons with low vision and blindness. Although some items in the ICF activity and activities restrictions arena may seem beyond the scope of vision rehabilitation, many of the items could be easily mapped to existing assessment instruments. Hendershot, Placek, and Goodman (2006) backcoded vision questions in the National Health Interview Survey to the ICF, describing how each of the questions tap different levels within the ICF model. That exercise informs how one might go about backcoding activities and participation-related data in order to see the effectiveness of vision rehabilitation interventions in an ICF framework; but to date, no one has done so.

The ICF model is powerful in regard to visual impairment and rehabilitation because it helps to portray the multidimensional experience of vision loss, and it is useful for describing the characteristics and circumstances of people with vision impairments—at the person, group, or population levels. Moreover, the ICF enriches our understanding of the impact of interventions on broad, socially desirable rehabilitative outcomes, and, in that regard, the model informs disability policy. Applying the ICF to intervention in vision rehabilitation illustrates the utility of this conceptual framework and its language to link policy, clinical measures, and services to desired outcomes. For example, in the eligibility arena, Hendershot, Placek, and Goodman (2006) examined the 2002 National Health Interview Survey Vision Supplement and estimated that only 1.5 per 1,000 people with vision impairments currently receive vision rehabilitation services. (This estimate is based on a positive response to the question, "Do you use any vision rehabilitation services, such as job training, counseling, or training in daily living skills and mobility?") The presence of vision rehabilitation services represents resources in the environment, and the NHIS data would suggest that the use of vision rehabilitation as an environmental facilitator to enhance function at the various levels described in the ICF is, unfortunately, fairly rare. It may be prudent to invest resources in ensuring that availability of services is improved.

Beyond the availability of rehabilitation services, elements of the ICF correlate with decisions to be considered eligible for services and to obtain services, as well as relate to the nature of interventions sought or received and the outcomes that accrue from receiving services. An individual, for example, may not be able to successfully and safely cross a street prior to mobility instruction. After completing mobility training, however, that person may have sufficient skills to confidently, safely, and efficiently make a street crossing. However, crossing a street (an activity) is of little value unless a person has somewhere to go. Thus, in ICF terms, the sum of activity performance can be conceptualized as increased (or at least having the potential for increased) social participation. Many rehabilitation providers assume that increased skills (i.e., activity performance) logically translate to increased social participation; that is, a client is better able to conduct his or her life and participate more fully in social and civic roles—getting together with friends and relatives, socializing, attending church—as a result of services. Improvement in the environment—better lighting, larger print size, better signage, safer street crossings—presumably contribute, along with skills acquisition, to social participation. This application of the ICF to vision rehabilitation reveals the mixed conceptual frameworks employed in making decisions to address the needs of people with vision loss. Function is used to determine eligibility, and employment status is also considered. In this case, one cannot be working to obtain services. Eligibility is not determined by structure or disease, and eligibility is not determined by activity limitations. Outcomes for vocational rehabilitation are measured in terms of participation—work. The dilemma often faced by vocational rehabilitation organizations is that their clients make substantial gains in terms of activities. People learn travel skills, increased communication skills, and are often better able to manage daily living tasks. In addition, they may achieve success in education. But a variety of factors may prevent an individual from getting a job. Many of the factors that discourage employment are in the environment; that is, public transportation systems may be inadequate, employers may be biased against hiring people with visual impairment, or employers may not be willing to make accommodations for people with disabilities.

The result of this conceptual confusion is that some people make great strides in many areas but cannot achieve the primary goal of vocational rehabilitation—employment. The factors that prevent employment may be beyond the perceived responsibilities of rehab organizations; that is, rehabilitation programs may not view reforming the public transportation system as within their purview.

By contrast, an evaluation of the effectiveness of the federally funded Older Blind Program (chapter 2 of the Vocational Rehabilitation Act) (Moore, Giesen, Weber, & Crews, 2001) measured self-reported gains in activities ("I am better able to prepare meals by myself." [d6300, d6301] "I am better able to enjoy reading materials (such as books, newspapers)." [d325]) and gains in participation ("I am better able to participate in the life of my family, friends or community." [d750, d751]). This national program promotes independence among older people experiencing vision loss. The nine items measured in the survey can be backcoded to the ICF. Activities and participation were measured independently, and positive gains were reported in each domain. Because the success of this program did not rely upon uncontrollable events like the employment marketplace, it could measure more directly the effectiveness of the intervention.

HISTORY OF RESEARCH AND PRACTICE IN VISION REHABILITATION ASSESSMENT

Many of the assessment instruments in vision rehabilitation are informal tools developed by clinicians, and thus reliability, validity, and normative data for these instruments often are not available. The scarcity of valid and reliable tools is due in part to the evolution of the field from its "charity" origins, its relative youth when compared to other allied health professions, and the fragmentation of the service delivery systems in vision rehabilitation. The absence of third-party payers that would likely have stimulated the development of more rigorous requirements for assessment also probably plays a role in the current state of assessment in the field. (Several of the chapters in Moore, Graves and Patterson, 1997, provide additional information about these and other issues pertaining to the development and characteristics of the service delivery system in blindness and low-vision rehabilitation).

CURRENT ASSESSMENT METHODS

Eligibility

There are several purposes for assessment in vision rehabilitation. First, assessment serves to establish eligibility for services. Eligibility criteria often differ across programs. For example, eligibility for services under the state–federal vocational rehabilitation system typically requires not only that individuals meet the acuity requirements noted earlier, but also that a vocational goal be determined and that the services provided are likely to support attainment of that vocational goal. For older adults, the presence of a visual impairment that results in limitations in completing tasks of daily living is typically used as the criterion for service eligibility rather than acuity cutoff scores.

Program or Service Planning

To provide services that meet the needs of clients and that conserve the limited resources of the agencies and professionals who provide them, clients in vision rehabilitation programs must receive assessments that identify their existing skills and knowledge related to performance of activities that they value, and that aid in identifying the nature and extent of services they need. Assessments conducted for purposes of service or program planning also focus on the psychological, social, family, fiscal, and other resources that are available or can be made available to support the rehabilitation service plan. Assessments for program planning are ideally conducted by vision rehabilitation professionals working in partnership with clients and other professionals in transdisciplinary teams. These teams carry out the assessment, service planning, service delivery, and evaluation activities that will aid the client in reaching his or her rehabilitative goals. Via assessment, each member of the transdisciplinary team (particularly the client) participates in determining and prioritizing the goals and objectives for services. Assessment information is gathered not only from clients, but also from family members and from medical personnel, teachers, social workers, and others. For example, an individual who has diabetes should receive a comprehensive medical and social assessment of the impact of their diabetes on their participation in a rehabilitation program, and the vision rehabilitation service provider must incorporate this information into the rehabilitation assessment and program plan. One important role of the vision rehabilitation clinician is to support the work of other professionals involved in assessing clients with visual impairments. For example, vision rehabilitation therapists are skilled at adapting written assessments to ensure that they are in a format that is accessible to clients. Adaptations may include producing assessments in Braille, in large print, or in electronic formats, and may also include the production of tactile materials, such as tactile maps. Vision rehabilitation professionals also play an important role in assisting occupational and physical therapists in interpreting the findings of assessments in these disciplines. For example, individuals with low vision may have developed compensatory motor and postural strategies that aid them in using their vision most efficiently. The combined effort of therapists with a variety of backgrounds may be useful in evaluating these strategies and their implications for program planning.

Assessment for program planning typically involves a three-pronged approach, involving case file review, client interview, and performance assessment (Ponchillia & Ponchillia, 1996). The three approaches yield unique information and also are complementary, as findings from one approach often can confirm or disconfirm the findings from other assessment approaches. For example, clients may report proficiency in travel-related skills, but may be thinking only of travel in very familiar areas. When performance assessment is conducted in both familiar and unfamiliar travel environments, the professional may determine that clients have relatively good skills in familiar environments, but are significantly limited in their ability to self-familiarize to new places and to learn travel routes without instruction. It also is important to recognize that good rapport between client and professional is essential to obtaining assessment outcomes that are beneficial for program planning.

Vision rehabilitation professionals often begin the assessment process by reviewing case files to determine what services have been provided previously and what the outcome of those services was. Medical (both general and vision-specific) and psychological assessment information; social and family history; and vocational history compiled by social workers, case managers, and rehabilitation counselors can provide background information for a program planning assessment. It should be noted, however, that assessment information in case files is often outdated and sometimes biased, incomplete, very general, or in error, and thus should be considered secondary to the data gathered via interview and performance assessment.

The results of evaluations done by ophthalmologists, optometrists, other physicians, and allied health professionals should be included in the case file review completed by the vision rehabilitation professional. The vision-related medical information often includes the results of the clinical eye examination, including information about the etiology of visual impairment. It describes the client's visual acuity, visual fields, contrast sensitivity, ocular motility, previous medical treatment, and his or her clinical/functional vision at near, intermediate, and far distances. The impact of illumination level (including nighttime functioning) or the functional issues that can arise from variations some individuals experience in vi-

sual abilities from day to day may also be described. Clinical vision reports describe the optical and nonoptical aids and devices currently used, used previously, or recommended for trial by the client. The amount and type of low-vision training a client has received also should be documented in the case file. Low-vision evaluation and training, conducted by an optometrist or rehabilitation professional certified in vision rehabilitation, aids individuals in performing near and distance visual tasks such as reading with low vision, locating objects at a distance, using eccentric viewing techniques, managing the impact of severely reduced visual fields, and dealing with variations in illumination and glare on visual function. Counseling also is often effective in helping individuals to manage the psychological stresses that can accompany living with low vision.

The second aspect of a comprehensive assessment is the client interview. Interviews with clients and their family members are useful in learning about previous services and experiences in work, daily living, orientation and mobility, and one's use of visual and nonvisual information for task performance in these areas. Interviews aid in determining a client's perceived strengths and weaknesses, habits and interests, and their priorities for instruction, and for building the rapport that is essential for successful service delivery. They also are useful in identifying vocational interests and in gaining perspective on cultural, social, intellectual, and behavioral factors that may affect the rehabilitation process, and the client's perspective on his or her support system. Question sets are usually developed by the professional in advance of the interview, and open-ended questions are usually preferred when interviewing clients. They typically elicit more complete responses than closed-ended questions, and they tend to lead naturally to other questions. Clients should be viewed as team members in the rehabilitation process, and the interview portion of the assessment is an opportunity to ensure that the desires, needs, and concerns of the client are considered as the rehabilitation planning process unfolds. Many clients with low vision and blindness come to rehabilitation with little or no information about the potential impact of services on their everyday lives, and with little perspective on the possibilities for vocational, educational, and personal goal achievement despite their visual impairment. For example, clients may assume that persons who are blind do not travel independently because they have never known an individual with blindness who did and because they are not familiar with the strategies and techniques that support independent travel. Interviews offer rehabilitation providers the opportunity to begin to provide information about the services that vision

DISCUSSION BOX 26.1

In preparation for tackling a discussion of these topics, students are encouraged to conduct a literature search on "outcomes" and "blindness" and "rehabilitation," and read several articles on this topic. The introduction section to the various articles on this topic that have been published in the past ten years or so will provide much information for framing your discussion.

Questions

1. Most individuals who meet the legal definition of blindness have low vision. How would the process of assessment for purposes of program planning differ for individuals with low vision compared to individuals who are totally blind?

2. How would the assessment of individuals in these two groups be similar? Consider in your discussion the role of environmental factors, physical factors, and social and psychological factors in assessment of task performance.

3. Regarding environmental factors, for example, how might different levels and types of lighting affect the functioning of individuals with low vision? Think about indoor and outdoor settings and time of day in your discussion.

4. How would auditory, tactile, and visual information likely interplay when completing tasks like walking along a sidewalk, locating an object, and identifying the route number of an approaching bus?

5. How do clinicians evaluate whether they are using the perceptual information that is optimal, given the specific demands of a daily living or mobility-related task?

6. Would you expect that familiarity with a task and familiarity with the setting in which it is performed would affect task performance for people with low vision and blindness?

7. How long does it take people who are blind to become familiar with a particular task in a particular setting, such as crossing the street at a particular place? Does training in one setting (say one intersection) tend to generalize to other settings? What might we do to facilitate generalization?

8. Regarding physical factors, discuss, how might hearing disability concomitant with visual disability affect the everyday lives of individuals?

9. How might the lives of people who are deaf–blind differ from those with deafness only or blindness only?

10. Regarding social and psychological factors, individuals with low vision, particularly school-age individuals, often are reluctant to use the long cane or to use other technologies to aid in daily living tasks. This often is due to the reluctance to be identified as a person who is blind. How might this tendency on the part of some individuals to conceal their impairment and its effect on function affect the way you approach the assessment process and affect the services you may suggest to the client?

11. What impact does an individual's inclination for risk taking and competence in social settings have on the assessment and program planning process?

12. What services might be useful in helping individuals who are blind improve their social abilities and deal effectively with well-meaning sighted people who often have very negative stereotypes about the abilities of individuals who are blind?

rehabilitation professionals provide and to begin to educate clients about possibilities, via training, technologies, and other efforts, that can help them to improve the quality of their lives.

Although the client's stated and observed abilities and needs are a critical component of comprehensive assessment, there also is a need for the vision rehabilitation professional to consider the client's situation from the point of view of family members and others who are close to the client. When the client returns home following rehabilitation, family members can have a major influence on whether or not clients use the knowledge and skills they have acquired during their rehabilitation program. It is thus necessary to include social and family concerns in a comprehensive assessment of rehabilitation needs, and interviews with these individuals who are important in the lives of

persons with visual impairments should be included in a comprehensive assessment.

The third aspect of comprehensive assessment for program planning involves observing the client as he or she completes various tasks. There are few norm-referenced tools available to the vision rehabilitation clinician, and thus most observational assessments of task performance are guided by informal, instructor-developed, criterion-referenced checklists. Items on these checklists are categorized into various skill domains and tasks. Clients are rated on dimensions such as whether tasks were successfully completed or not and the apparent ease or difficulty of task completion. Many of these performance assessments involve highly specialized knowledge, such as knowledge of the Braille code, knowledge of specialized computer programs that convert text to speech, or knowledge of street crossing strategies used by individuals who are blind. Few professionals outside the vision rehabilitation realm have the knowledge or skills to adequately conduct these assessments.

Examples of domains include:

(a) Orientation and Mobility – the ability to move about independently, safely, and efficiently in familiar and unfamiliar environments and under varying illumination conditions

(b) Communication – reading and writing, including the production and use of Braille and large print (including technologies to assist with these tasks), and the use of technologies for computer access

(c) Daily living skills – managing home care and personal care needs, including cooking, grocery shopping, personal hygiene, clothing care, personal and home safety, and other needs

(d) Social skills – including skills for enhancing personal, family, and community relationships

(e) Vocational skills – the abilities and interests of the client in relation to various types of employment. Vocational assessment includes such areas as cognitive ability, academic ability and achievement, social skills as they relate to work, and sensory, physical, and motor abilities. Prior work history is a key component of vocational assessment.

Skills assessment typically follows the case file review and the interview, and good rapport between professional and client is needed to ensure a successful skills assessment. To conduct a skills assessment, rehabilitation professionals ask clients to accomplish a series of activities in the domains that were explored in the file review and interview portions of the assessment, which are noted in the preceding list. Professionals note not only the ability of individuals to complete activities; they also document (usually in narrative form, but sometimes by using checklists) their fluency and efficiency in activity performance, their apparent level of frustration, if any, and the perceptual information and problem-solving strategies they bring to bear when completing common activities of daily living. Attention should be given to the environment where assessment takes place. Clients are likely to demonstrate different abilities and limitations when assessed in their homes than when assessment takes place in the more unfamiliar rehabilitation center setting. The goal of skills instruction is to enable clients to generalize what they learn across settings, including generalization from the rehabilitation center to their home setting. Vision rehabilitation professionals must ensure that their clients can use the skills they learn in a variety of settings and that they have the ability to learn to adapt as the environment in which skills are used changes. Skills assessment, like interview-based assessment, provides an opportunity for the clinician to convey information to a client about the abilities of persons with visual impairments and the gains an individual may expect as a result of participation in rehabilitation services.

The characteristics of an individual physical environment also play a role in assessment. When conducting an orientation and mobility assessment, for example, instructors often ask the client to negotiate residential, small business, and urban environments in the daytime and at night, to ensure that a range of illumination conditions is considered. They may ask clients to demonstrate task performance in familiar environments, such as their neighborhood, or they may assess skills in unfamiliar places. Assessing clients in unfamiliar areas allows the clinician to determine how well clients are able to apply existing knowledge and strategies to new situations. Care must be taken to challenge the client in order to determine the limits of his or her abilities, but not to place them in situations where a lack of knowledge and skill about how to perform an activity results in a dangerous situation or results in unacceptable levels of frustration on the part of the client. Orientation and mobility specialists, for example, often encounter this situation when evaluating street crossing abilities of their clients. They must balance their need to test the limits of client abilities with the safety issues inherent in orientation and mobility (O&M) evaluation and the fact that clients may have had little experience crossing streets independently.

Most clients served by vision rehabilitation professionals have low vision, and thus the use of low vision should be a fundamental aspect of any assessment procedure. Clients with low vision often do not spontaneously use their remaining vision optimally, but can be taught skills to do so by low-vision therapists and other vision rehabilitation providers. Erin and Paul (1996) provide an excellent overview of the components of functional vision assessment for children and youth, and they describe in detail the linkage between functional assessment and program planning.

Assessment Instruments for Service Planning in Vision Rehabilitation: Two Examples

DISTANCE VISUAL RECOGNITION ASSESSMENT One assessment instrument, called Distance Visual Recognition Assessment or DVRA (Ludt & Goodrich, 2002), was developed at the Western Blind Rehabilitation Center of the Palo Alto Veterans Affairs Medical Center. The DVRA is part of a broader assessment and training protocol called Dynamic Visual Assessment and Training (DVAT) therapy. According to the authors, DVAT therapy "can be defined as therapy that incorporates clinical measures of visual function (visual acuity, diagnosis, visual field, and contrast sensitivity) and uses low-vision O&M assessments that take place in ecologically relevant (real-world) environments" (p. 8). As a component of DVAT, DVRA provides clinicians with a means to quantify the distance at which individuals with low vision can identify potential hazards ahead of them as they walk, such as obstacles on the footpath, changes in elevation such as curbs, and overhanging obstacles. The procedure also allows quantification (using a measure of distance) of the potential for an individual to increase his or her visual functioning in these areas, and of their actual gains following training. Training involves helping individuals to identify and use visual–perceptual cues that will aid in identifying objects at distance, and may also involve glare remediation efforts.

The DVRA validation study reported by Ludt and Goodrich (2002) involved 65 individuals with low vision who received services at the Western Blind Rehabilitation Center (WBRC), Palo Alto, California. Average age was 72 years, and all but two individuals were male. After receiving a comprehensive clinical visual examination, participants were interviewed as to their travel goals and then independently walked a route outdoors of approximately 250 feet. The route had naturally occurring drop-offs and one "planted" obstacle and overhang. Participants were asked to stop walking and to point to each of the three "hazards" when they first saw it. Gaze patterns were observed by the O&M specialist accompanying the client, and clients were asked what visual cues they used to locate the obstacles. Clients were then guided along an equivalent route, following instructions in vertical eye (not head) scanning, a technique dubbed "dynamic scanning method" or DSM. They were prompted to look at eye level, at street level, and at drop-off level, pausing briefly at each level. As with the first route, detection distances were noted. Clients then began O&M instruction at WBRC and were posttested on the same recognition distance task after about 10–15 hours of instruction. Posttraining visual detection distances for each of the three types of hazards increased significantly from the pretraining assessments, although the differences in predicted and posttraining distances were not significant for obstacles and overhangs. This indicates that the predicted distance recognition data were in good agreement with the posttraining values for these two obstacles. The authors report an effect size that appears to indicate that the differences obtained before and after training are clinically significant. Visual acuity and contrast sensitivity were found to have little predictive value for detection distance, leading to the conclusion that the DSM and other aspects of the training individuals received likely played an important role in the outcome of this study. As the authors point out, there was no control group in this study; thus the conclusions of this study are tentative. Also, reliability and validity studies have not been completed for the DVRA.

DVRA is important because it offers a model for developing and implementing objective assessment tools that can be used in vision rehabilitation settings. The tool appears to differentiate between those clients who may benefit from training and those who likely will not, either because they have adequate vision for distance identification without training or because their vision is impaired to the extent that training is not likely to impact their visual recognition distance abilities. This ability to discriminate between clients likely to benefit from services and those who likely will not has the potential to save agencies money by allowing them to focus resources more appropriately. Also, the authors note that one advantage of the DVRA assessment is that it provides objective data that is useful in situations where clients are reluctant to use devices, such as the long cane, by providing evidence to an individual that he or she cannot detect drop-offs or obstacles on the travel path with adequate time to react (the long cane has no impact on detection of overhangs). Clients may be more likely to accept use of a mobility device if they can be shown objective evidence of the need for it.

THE LEARNING MEDIA ASSESSMENT   According to Heinze (2000), the "learning media assessment determines the student's preferred and most efficient learning style, approaches, materials, and literacy media (such as Braille and print) and modifications (like enlarged print or pictures, tactile displays, and the use of low-vision devices) for use in additional areas requiring assessment" (p. 43). The Learning Media Assessment was developed by Koenig and Holbrook (1995). In this assessment, the senses of touch, vision, and hearing are assessed as they relate to the literacy-related needs of service recipients. As noted in Koenig, Holbrook, Corn, DePriest, Erin and Presley (2000), Learning Media Assessment includes an evaluation of a learner's reading and writing skills and needs, and an evaluation of appropriate media, often with a focus on whether an individual should rely primarily on Braille or on print reading. Certified vision rehabilitation therapists (CVRTs) evaluate the use of

RESEARCH BOX 26.1

Goodrich, G. L., Kirby, J., Wood, J., Peters, L. (2006). The reading behavior inventory: An outcomes assessment tool. *Journal of Visual Impairment and Blindness, 100,* 164–168.

Objectives: This study reported the development of the Reading Behavior Inventory (RBI), a measurement tool designed to measure changes in reading-related behaviors among individuals with visual impairments, including the types of materials that participants read, their reading speed, their satisfaction with reading, reported difficulty reading, and reported duration of reading. Reading speed was conceptualized as an outcomes effectiveness measure, while other items probed the reading behaviors and perceptions.

Method: The participants in this study were 64 individuals 48–89 years of age, with an average age of 74 years. They were 97% male. Participants were admitted into the visual skills program of the Western Blind Rehabilitation Center, a facility run by the U.S. Department of Veterans Affairs. All participants were legally blind (mean acuity of 20/250 aided), had the ability to read 1 M print, and had the manual dexterity needed to use a low-vision device. Data were collected before and after training and during a 2-month follow-up telephone interview. Forty of the 64 participants completed the follow-up.

Results: Reading speed from the "before" to "after" training assessment increased significantly (average increase of 34 words per minute). Participants read more and read a wider diversity of material after training, and the increases appeared to continue at follow-up. The RBI results for the participants' satisfaction and difficulty with reading, time spent reading, and reported difficulty reading significantly improved pre- to post-training and were maintained at the follow-up. Perceptions of reading abilities improved slightly from post training to follow-up, suggesting that the participants had solidified the training gains and learned to extend them even more on their own.

Conclusion: The authors conclude that the instrument they developed is useful for measuring the effectiveness of low-vision training as it relates to reading and an individual's assessing perceptions of reading rehabilitation.

Questions

1. Is the assessment of reading comprehensive?
2. What other reading-related behaviors might the instrument developers have included in their assessment?
3. How could the reliability and validity of this assessment be documented?
4. In what types of clinical applications other than the rehabilitation center setting could this assessment be used?
5. What are the limitations of this study?

a learner's various perceptual abilities, select an initial medium for use in reading and writing, and then conduct ongoing assessments to determine whether the initial choice continues to be appropriate as literacy skills improve and as other compensatory skills improve as a result of rehabilitation training. Visual functioning, tactile perception, reading efficiency, writing skills, and the use of technology are all considered in a comprehensive learning media assessment. The assessment typically permits clinicians and clients to determine optimal reading and writing modes for various literacy tasks, given the client's unique perceptual and cognitive abilities and literacy-related goals.

Outcomes

Although there has been limited development and use of assessment tools for program planning, the field of vision rehabilitation has enjoyed significant activity in the area of outcomes assessment. These outcomes research studies follow studies conducted in the '70s and '80s regarding outcomes assessment in general medical rehabilitation. Massof and Rubin (2001) provide an overview of the development and validation of various instruments to assess outcomes in vision rehabilitation, and they describe the methodological challenges faced by researchers who seek to develop and implement reliable and valid outcomes assessment.

Crews and Long (1997) illustrated how the ICF could be employed as a conceptual framework for outcomes measurement. The results of their outcomes assessment study in vision rehabilitation was published in a special issue of the *Journal of Visual Impairment and Blindness* in 2000, which was devoted to outcomes research (Long, Crews, & Mancil, 2000). Outcomes assessment in vision rehabilitation focuses at the activity level in ICF terms. Typically, these assessments involve the use of brief self-report questionnaires about various aspects of activity performance, although at least one assessment (Head, Babcock, Goodrich & Boyless, 2000) uses clinician ratings instead of self-report ratings of performance. De l'Aune, Williams, Watson, Schuckers, and Ventimiglia (2004) provide an example of this type of research. Several iterations of instrument development from 2000–2004 yielded an instrument the authors entitled the VA-13, a self-report measure of frequency, independence, and satisfaction with performance on 13 tasks. Approximately 5,000 individuals who completed inpatient rehabilitation center programs administered by the Department of Veterans Affairs rated their performance of these 13 tasks on a 1–5 scale after they completed a program of inpatient vision rehabilitation sponsored by the Department of Veterans Affairs. They also were asked to retrospectively rate how well they could perform the tasks prior to entering rehabilitation. Pre-to-post change scores for the 13 items overall and for questions pertaining to each of four subsets of items were computed, and each of the five paired t-tests indicated that significant

improvement in task performance occurred, presumably as a result of the services the veterans received. The subsets of items were labeled "low vision," "living skills," "manual skills," and "orientation and mobility" (O&M) skills. Another outcomes study, reported by Head, et. al., (2000), was conducted with veterans at single inpatient rehabilitation. In this study, clinicians rated the ability of veterans to perform tasks at the beginning and at the end of their rehabilitation service program, and found that ratings of task performance were significantly higher after training than before training. Although studies such as these document the self-reported gains as a result of receiving rehabilitation services, they do not reveal whether gains at the activity level (in ICF terms) are related to gains in participation (such as increased rates of employment or engagement in family or social activities). There is no study that we are aware of that links activity gain to participation outcomes, and such studies would be a fruitful line of research for individuals interested in outcomes assessment.

DISCUSSION BOX 26.2

The measurement of outcomes of health care is critical to improving our health care system. In rehabilitation, outcomes focus on effectively remediating the physical, social, functional, and psychological limitations that result from disability (with emphasis on improving function and reducing dependence on others in performing activities of daily living). Another key aspect of outcome measurement is efficiency of services, which relates to the cost of services relative to the outcomes achieved. Physical medicine and rehabilitation service programs have a long history of research about outcome measures, and these programs have systems in place to gather and analyze outcomes measurement data. Clinicians (usually therapists or nurses) record observations and self-report data from service recipients at entry to the various stages of rehabilitation and again at exit from a particular program. Service providers and payers examine these outcomes data for the magnitude of change within various diagnostic groupings, such as patients in stroke rehabilitation or those with orthopedic and cardiac challenges. They also examine what mix of services has the greatest possibility of yielding the best possible outcomes.

Questions

1. How have the concepts and tools of outcomes measurement that first developed in physical rehabilitation been applied in vision rehabilitation?

2. Should outcomes for vision rehabilitation be linked to functional, social, psychological, and physical status, as they are in physical rehabilitation?
3. How do differences in the approaches, goals, and values of vision rehabilitation and physical rehabilitation translate to differences in the ways we think about outcomes measurement?
4. What methodological and practical issues do outcomes measurement researchers face in vision rehabilitation? For example, physical rehabilitation often focuses on reduction in dependence on others in functional tasks. Does this strategy "work" in the vision rehabilitation realm?
5. How does the relatively low incidence of blindness and low vision, the lack of universally accepted standards of treatment, and variations in service settings (e.g., itinerant and center-based services) affect the way outcomes measurement in blindness and low vision is conceptualized?
6. Is it appropriate to use self-report measures of abilities to perform tasks prior to and after services as a measure of service outcomes, or should we rely on performance-based measures alone?
7. What if individuals learn to improve their performance on tasks, but place little value on their ability to perform those tasks in everyday life?
8. How might client values affect the design of outcomes measurement?

RESEARCH CRITICAL TO ISSUES IN ASSESSMENT IN VISION REHABILITATION

The National Eye Institute (NEI), in a strategic planning document entitled "Report of the Visual Impairment and Its Rehabilitation Panel," suggested several research areas that are critical to assessment in vision rehabilitation. The panel that developed this document noted the need for research that focuses not only on the impact of visual function on task performance but also includes a focus on cognitive, motor, and sensory components of task performance and the interrelationships of these components. The panel also noted the need for research regarding the "basic psychosocial processes and dynamics that address the motivational factors underlying rehabilitation and the desire for personal independence." Research in this area is particularly important given the key role that family and friends play in an individual's decision to participate in rehabilitation services and the way that skills are applied in the home and community setting following training.

In regard to program outcomes, the NEI planning document notes that studies of the effectiveness of rehabilitation services also are needed. Although outcomes research has received considerable attention from researchers in recent years, there is an ongoing need for multisite clinical trials that measure effectiveness of services and for smaller scale intervention evaluation studies that focus on measurement development or focused questions within the broad domain of outcomes measurement. The goal of outcomes research is to continue to improve the quality and efficiency of services provided for individuals with blindness and low vision. The NEI-Visual Functioning Questionnaire (NEI-VFQ; Mangione, Lee, Gutierrez, Spritzer, Berry, & Hays, 2001) has been developed and shown to be reliable and valid, but use of this outcomes instrument has been primarily targeted to patients with active disease processes rather than persons with untreatable visual impairment who have entered or completed rehabilitation services. More widespread use of the NEI-VFQ and the VF-13 described earlier is warranted, given the importance of outcomes assessment.

CULTURAL, LEGISLATIVE, AND PROFESSIONAL ISSUES THAT IMPACT ASSESSMENT IN VISION REHABILITATION

Individuals who assess persons with visual impairments often work with people who come from cultural backgrounds different from their own, and the cultural diversity in the United States appears to be increasing. Cultural diversity creates many professional challenges, including the challenge of establishing rapport with the service recipient and his or her family and community; determining the scope of assessment, particularly in regard to functional task performance in the home and community; and determining whether performance limitations are due to perceptual, motor, or cognitive impairment or due to the lack of experience or motivation. In addition, as noted in Table 26.1, and as elaborated in Kirchner and Peterson (1988), prevalence rates for visual impairments are higher among non-whites than among whites. Diabetes, for example, occurs much more often among Native American populations than for the general U.S. population (Rogers, Schmitt, & Scholl, 1997). Ponchillia (1993) offers guidance regarding culturally sensitive issues to vision rehabilitation professionals who serve Native Americans. Effective communication with clients with non-Eurocentric worldviews requires that counselors take into consideration the views of the service recipient toward disability and toward the ideas of independence and success.

Similar to issues of serving individuals from non-Eurocentric cultures are issues related to serving older persons with visual impairments. Visual impairment is associated with aging, and thus many of the individuals being referred for rehabilitation services are older. As is the case when serving any individual, clinicians must assess performance relative to individual goals, cultural, community, and family norms, and clients' beliefs about themselves and their rehabilitation potential. When assessing older individuals, it is important to consider the impact of other sensory impairments on overall function, as well as the contributions of cognitive impairment and psychological difficulties, such as depression and anxiety. This is because the client is likely to have other impairments that will impact overall function, and sorting out the relative contribution of visual and nonvisual impairment can be challenging. As with younger persons, the rehabilitation needs of older individuals may be addressed via training, technologies to improve task performance, or some combination of the two approaches. However, caution is necessary to ensure that the remedies for rehabilitation concerns fit the clients' perceptions about their problems and solutions. Problems that are addressed via adaptive technologies among younger clients may warrant other approaches for older persons.

In regard to legislative issues affecting vision rehabilitation professionals, perhaps the most significant change in service delivery to occur in many years is the move to expand Medicare reimbursement to providers who are certified in orientation and mobility, vision rehabilitation therapy, and low-vision therapy. Details on this multifaceted initiative can be found at www.lowvisionproject.org.

MULTIDISCIPLINARY/INTERDISCIPLINARY APPROACHES

The multiple origins of vision rehabilitation (charity-based services and vocational rehabilitation), as well as the fragmented system of service delivery (private agencies, state and federal agencies), create limitations as well as opportunities for collaborations and interdisciplinary approaches to assessment. The fragmentation of vision rehabilitation, as well as the inconsistent notions of what constitutes "rehabilitation," in large part, has led to the insularity of vision rehabilitation's efforts to collaborate with others. That may be changing. There are at least two areas where vision rehabilitation and its assessment strategies present distinct opportunities for collaborations: public health and aging.

Public Health

About the last thing people in vision rehabilitation think about is public health. There are no particular events that would naturally bring these two communities together. Because public health is about promoting health by encouraging good health practices (weight management, exercise) and avoiding poor practices (smoking, drinking, and risk taking), it is reasonable to consider how health promotion might be integrated into vision rehabilitation programs. The lack of health promotion begins with a failure in assessment. Generally health and health behaviors are marginal concerns for vision rehabilitation organizations. Health may be viewed as an indicator of someone's capacity to participate in a rehabilitation program, but improved heath is not viewed as within the purview of rehabilitation programs.

Public health has begun to address the positive design of communities that promote walking. The designs that promote walking for the general population are particularly useful for people with vision loss—for example, better sidewalks and walkable destinations. Moreover, other environmental changes, including larger print on medicine containers and improved lighting, have the effect of reducing medical error and avoiding injury—concerns of public health (Crews, 2003; Crews, Kirchner, & Lollar, 2006).

Public health surveillance programs, especially the Behavioral Risk Factors Surveillance System (BRFSS), estimates the magnitude of the problem and health disparities at the state and community level. The Centers for Disease Control and Prevention has overall responsibility for administering the BRFSS in the states, and a vision module is now available as part of the BRFSS to determine near, and distance function, as well as causes of vision loss (http://www. cdc. gov/brfss/ questionnaires/questionnaires.htm). This module will allow states to estimate the population of people who experience vision loss at the state level, and will provide valuable information for planning, policy, and services for people with vision impairment.

Moreover, public health provides an infrastructure that allows for problems to be addressed at the national, state, and community level. Therefore, it is possible to support health promotion activities for people with vision loss throughout the public health system, thus making health materials more accessible for people with vision impairment.

Aging

Perhaps aging serves as a more logical opportunity for collaboration with the vision rehabilitation community (Crews, 2000). Given the very high prevalence of vision loss among older people—5/100 for those aged 75–79 and 24/100 for those aged 80 and over—the aging community should "own" those who experience vision loss; it is a common problem. Like the public health system, aging provides a national, state, regional, and community structure that allows for assessment, aggregation of information, refinements of policy, and dissemination of services and information. Perhaps the gap in this system arises from incomplete assessment of the problem. Measures of the needs of older people in the community may not include sensitive measures of vision loss, and therefore, the aging network may not be entirely aware of the magnitude of the problem. The BRFSS cited above, however, may fill this gap. Efforts to support people in the community and assure their well-being and integration all have vision components. Therefore, by attending to environmental concerns—lighting, signage, and transportation—there are opportunities to promote greater independence, participation in the community, and quality of life.

At the state and regional level, better assessment allows for a more dimensional understanding of the problems of older people with vision impairments. These findings can be translated to community organization to assure that they have a capacity to include older people with vision loss in community-based programs. Some enhancements, like transportation, may be common to older people. Others, like lighting, print size, and signage, may not be so common, but generally these features create a more welcoming and comfortable environment even if vision loss is not severe.

MAJOR ISSUES THAT NEED ATTENTION IN ASSESSMENT IN VISION REHABILITATION

There are several major issues related to assessment in vision rehabilitation. First is the need for more assessment instruments with documented reliability and validity, and with demonstrated usefulness for program planning and for outcomes measurement. While some progress has been made in instrument development for outcomes measurement purposes, there is a critical need for more psychometrically sound tools for evaluating individuals' strengths and needs for program planning purposes. A related issue is that the field of blindness and low-vision rehabilitation is very small, and there is a need to train more clinician–researchers who can take on this very important instrument development role, and other leadership roles in the field.

A second major issue is the potentially significant change in vision rehabilitation that may occur as a result of the Medicare Vision Rehabiliation Services Act of 2001 (H.R. 2484/S.1967). This legislation provides for the implementation of a demonstration project conducted by the Centers for Medicare & Medicaid Services (CMS). The demonstration project will evaluate the effectiveness and efficiency of providing vision rehabilitation services that are reimbursed by CMS. Under this plan, vision rehabilitation services can be provided by therapists who have been certified by the Academy for the Certification of Vision Rehabilitation and Education Professionals (ACVREP) and who work under the supervision of a doctor. This demonstration began in 2006 with plans to continue through 2011.

Throughout the course of the Medicare Vision Rehabilitation demonstration, there is the potential for many changes to occur in the field of vision rehabilitation.

For example, services and training provided through the demonstration project will begin to operate more on a medical service delivery model rather than a social welfare model. As a result, services will be planned and provided based on the number and type of client contacts that are allowed under the current Medicare billing regulations. Also, the addition of Medicare reimbursement may create challenges in personnel preparation in vision rehabilitation. As more people with visual impairments and their doctors become aware of the benefits that vision rehabilitation professionals can add to their multidisciplinary service team, presumably the need for more service providers will grow, and the need for preservice and inservice educational opportunities will increase. The research literature in vision rehabilitation also should benefit from the expansion of services and personnel preparation because the expansion of services likely will stimulate more research. Finally, it remains to be seen how vision rehabilitation providers might partner successfully with other allied health providers to improve the quality and availability of services. As the baby boomer population ages and the incidence of age-related visual impairments increases, the demand for vision rehabilitation services is likely to skyrocket. It is vital that mechanisms be put in place now to ensure that services are available and accessible to those who need them.

A final significant issue in vision rehabilitation is the need to document the effectiveness of services. As noted above, outcomes measurement efforts in this field are relatively new. Some useful measures have been developed, and some rehabilitation providers have begun to track outcomes over time (the Department of Veterans Affairs has been a leader in this area). As outcomes data continue to be collected routinely, and as systems are put in place to mine outcomes data efficiently and apply the findings to program modifications, it should be possible to target particular groups of consumers with specific patterns of service that are most likely to yield positive rehabilitative outcomes. The challenge of keeping the outcomes research agenda moving ahead is both formidable and important for the continued development of the field.

Summary and Conclusion

This chapter has provided definitions of various terms used to describe individuals with vision impairment and has offered a brief overview of the incidence and prevalence of this impairment among adults in the United States. It also

described the service delivery system and the providers that aid individuals in adapting to vision impairment. The relationship of the ICF to the vision rehabilitation process was described, as was assessment for determining eligibil-

ity, planning rehabilitation programs, and measuring rehabilitation outcomes. Two assessment protocols then were
explained to illustrate the types of assessments that have
been used in vision rehabilitation. The chapter concluded
with a summary of some of the critical research issues that
need to be addressed to improve assessments in vision rehabilitation and the cultural, legislative, and professional
issues that impact service delivery.

Self-Check Questions

1. Imagine you are the executive director of a small, private,
   not-for-profit agency serving persons with visual impairments. Your board has asked that you present them with a
   set of strategies for documenting the benefit to your clientele of the services you provide. How would you respond?
2. How do people who are blind move about safely and independently?
3. What conclusions can you draw about the differences in
   the rehabilitative needs of individuals who are blind from
   birth as contrasted with those who lose their vision in
   adulthood?
4. What vocational barriers exist for persons with visual impairments and how might those barriers be overcome via
   training and technology?

Case Study

Joseph is a 67-year-old man who began losing his vision
at age 64 due to "dry" macular degeneration at age 60.
His visual acuity is 20/400. His vision loss is greater in
his right eye than in his left eye. He reports that he can
no longer see images on a television screen, nor can he
read any print smaller than 24 point (or about the size of
the headline in a newspaper article). He has no reported
or apparent disabilities other than vision disability. He
no longer travels or walks outside his home and yard un-
accompanied, and is dependent on his daughter, who
lives nearby, for transportation and personal needs. He
lives alone and receives Meals on Wheels assistance, but
he can prepare convenience foods and do some household chores. He reports that he is bored and depressed,
and wonders how he will manage as his vision continues
to decline. When asked what he does during the day, he
reports that he listens to baseball on television, but that
he has few outlets for recreation or socialization beyond
attending worship services on Sunday.

QUESTIONS

1. How would you begin to assist the individual in
   the case study in prioritizing his needs, and what
   options can you think of that might address his
   needs?
2. What information is available on the Web regarding
   the two primary forms of macular degeneration?

References

Corn, A.L., & Koenig, A.J. (1996). Perspectives in low vision.
In A. L. Corn & A. J. Koenig (Eds.), *Foundations of low
vision: Clinical and functional perspectives* (pp. 3–25).
New York: AFB Press.

Crews, J. E. (2000), The evolution of public policies and services to older people who are visually impaired. In B.
Silverstone, M. A. Lang, B. P. Rosenthal, & E. E. Faye
(Eds.), *Lighthouse handbook of vision impairment and
vision rehabilitation* (Vol. 2), New York: Oxford.

Crews, J. E. (2003). The role of public health in addressing
aging and sensory loss. *Generations*, 27, 83–90.

Crews, J. E., Jones, G. C., & Kim, J. H. (2006). Double jeop-
ardy: The effects of comorbid conditions among older people with vision loss. *Journal of Visual Impairment and
Blindness, 100*, 824–848.

Crews, J. E., Kirchner, C., & Lollar, D. J. (2006). The view
from the crossroads of public health and vision (re)habilita-
tion. *Journal of Visual Impairment and Blindness*, 100,
773–779.

Crews, J. E., & Long, R. G. (1997). Conceptual and methodological issues in rehabilitation outcomes for adults who
are visually impaired. *Journal of Visual Impairment and
Blindness, 91*, 117–130.

De l'Aune, W., Williams, M., Watson, G., Schuckers, &
Ventimiglia, G. (2004), Clinical application of a self-report.
Functional independence outcomes measure in the DVA's
Blind Rehabilitation Service. *Journal of Visual Impairment
and Blindness*, 98, 281–291.

Erin, J. N., & Paul B. (1996). Functional vision assessment and
instruction of children and youths in academic programs. In

A. L. Corn & A. J. Koenig (Eds.), *Foundations of low vision: Clinical and functional perspectives* (pp. 185–220). New York: AFB Press

Eye Diseases Prevalence Research Group, (2004). Causes and prevalence of visual impairment among adults in the United States. *Archives of Ophthalmology, 122,* 477–485.

Head, D. N., Babcock, J. L., Goodrich, G. L., & Boyless, J. A. (2000) A geriatric assessment of functional status in vision rehabilitation. *Journal of Visual Impairment and Blindness, 94,* 357–371.

Heinze, T. (2000). Comprehensive assessment. In A. J. Koenig & M. C. Holbrook (Eds.), *Foundations of education: Volume II, Instructional strategies for teaching children and youths with visual impairments* (pp. 27–60). New York: AFB Press.

Hendershot, G. E., Placek, P. J., & Goodman, N (2006). Taming the beast: Measuring vision-related disability using the International Classification of Functioning. *Journal of Visual Impairment and Blindness, 100,* 806–823.

Kirchner, C., & Peterson, R. (1988). Estimates of race-ethnic groups in the U.S., visually impaired population: Data on blindness and visual impairment in the U.S. In C. Kirchner (Ed.), *A resource manual on characteristics, education, employment and service delivery* (2nd ed., pp 81–89). New York: American Foundation for the Blind.

Koenig, A. J., & Holbrook, M. C. (1995). *Learning media assessment of students with visual impairments: A resource guide for teachers* (2nd ed.). Austin, TX: Texas School for the Blind and Visually Impaired

Koenig, A. J., Holbrook, M. C., Corn, A. L., DePriest, L. B., Erin & Presley, I. T. (2000). Specialized assessments for students with visual impairments. In A. J. Koenig & M. C. Holbrook (Eds.), *Foundations of education: Volume II, Instructional strategies for teaching children and youths with visual impairments* (pp. 103–172). New York: AFB Press.

Lee, D. J., Gomez-Martin, O., Lam, B. L., Zheng, D., & Jane, D. M. (2004). Trends in visual acuity impairment in US adults: The 1986–1995 National Health Interview Survey. *Archives of Ophthalmology, 122,* 506–509

Long, R. G., Crews, J. E., & Mancil, R. (2000). Creating measures of rehabilitation outcomes for people who are visually impaired; the FIMBA project. *Journal of Visual Impairment and Blindness, 94,* 292–306.

Ludt, R., & Goodrich, G. L. (2002). Change in visual perceptual detection distances for low vision travelers as a result of dynamic visual assessment and training. *Journal of Visual Impairment and Blindness, 96,* 7–21.

Mangione, C. M., Lee, P. P., Gutierrez, P. R., Spritzer, K., Berry, S., & Hays, R. D. (2001). Development of the 25-item National Eye Institute Visual Function Questionnaire (VFQ-25). *Archives of Ophthalmology, 119,* 1050–1058.

Massof, R.W. & Rubin, G. S. (2001). Visual function assessment questionnaires. *Survey of Ophthalmology, 45,* 531–548.

Moore, J. E., Giesen, J. M., Weber, J. M, & Crews, J. E. (2001). Functional outcomes reported by consumers of the independent living program for older individuals who are blind. *Journal of Visual Impairment and Blindness, 95,* 403–417.

Moore, J. E. Graves, W. H., & Patterson, J. B. (1997). *Foundations of rehabilitation counseling with persons who are blind and visually impaired.* New York: American Foundation for the Blind.

National Eye Institute (1997). *Report on visual impairment and its rehabilitation: A report of the National Eye Advisory Council.* Bethesda, MD: Author.

Ponchillia, S. (1993). The effect of cultural beliefs on the treatment of Native peoples with diabetes and visual impairments. *Journal of Visual Impairment and Blindness, 87,* 335–341.

Ponchillia, P. E., & Ponchillia, S.V. (1996). *Foundations of rehabilitation teaching with persons who are blind or visually impaired.* New York: AFB Press.

Rein, D. B., Zhang, P., Wirth, K. E., Lee, P. P., Hoeger, T. J., McCall. N., et al., (2006). The economic burden of major adult visual disorders in the United States, *Archives of Ophthalmology, 124,* 1754–1760.

Rogers, P. A., Schmitt, S. A., & Scholl, G. T. (1997). Demographic and cultural considerations in rehabilitation. In J. E. Moore, W. H. Graves, & J. B. Patterson (Eds.), *Foundations of rehabilitation counseling with persons who are blind and visually impaired* (pp. 150–178). New York: American Foundation for the Blind.

World Health Organization (1980). *International classification of impairments, disabilities and handicaps: A manual of classification relating to the consequence of disease.* Geneva: author.

World Health Organization (2001). *International classification of functioning, disability and health.* Geneva: author.

World Health Organization (2007). *International Statistical Classification of Diseases and Related Health Problems, 10th Revision.* Geneva: Author.

27

Health-Related Quality of Life

MALACHY BISHOP
University of Kentucky, Lexington

GLORIA K. LEE
University at Buffalo–the State University of New York

OVERVIEW

This chapter discusses the concept of health-related quality of life (HRQOL) within the context of health care and rehabilitation. The chapter begins with a discussion of historical perspectives and the evolution of HRQOL and quality of life in relation to the significant changes in health care during the past 30 years. The relationship between HRQOL and international classifications of functioning, disability, and health (ICIDH) definitions of disability and function also are noted. The definition of HRQOL and the distinctions and relationships between HRQOL and other related terms (e.g., health status) are discussed. Measurement issues, psychometric properties of existing scales, examples of general health-related quality of life measures, and considerations for clinical and research selection and utilization of HRQOL instruments are discussed. The chapter concludes with a discussion on the direction of health-related quality of life from an international perspective.

LEARNING OBJECTIVES

By the end of the chapter, readers should be able to:

- Outline the historical development of quality of life
- Define and differentiate among the concepts of quality of life, health-related quality of life, and health status
- Evaluate selected examples of health-related quality of life measures
- Discuss the clinical implications of rater perspective, psychometric adequacy, and instrument selection of the measure of health-related quality of life

INTRODUCTION

This chapter provides an overview of health-related quality of life (HRQOL), which has become one of the most important and frequently measured outcomes in health care and rehabilitation. Assessment of HRQOL occurs at the confluence of two dynamic and rapidly changing fields: health care and quality of life (QOL). Health-related QOL may be said to be concerned with the proper and most useful methods of measuring, describing, and valuing both health and QOL. The history of HRQOL has been characterized by rapid development and expansion. The broad scope of the HRQOL literature, plethora of assessment instruments, and numerous definitions of HRQOL and related concepts may seem overwhelming and confusing to those first approaching the topic. This chapter provides an introduction to the concept of HRQOL; explores its role in health care and rehabilitation; and reviews its definition, history, and application in practice.

THE ROLE AND IMPORTANCE OF HEALTH-RELATED QUALITY OF LIFE ASSESSMENT IN HEALTH CARE AND REHABILITATION

Health-related quality of life assessment has been identified as having multiple uses in health and rehabilitation outcomes assessment, treatment planning, and research. Some of these include the following: to supplement objective clinical or biological measures of disease, to assess the quality of service and the effectiveness of interventions, to develop baseline data to measure the effectiveness of subsequent interventions, to draw the clinician's attention to areas in which the patient is having difficulty, to help the clinician understand the patient's perspective, to prioritize treatment interventions, and to guide patient education and self-management programs (Beulow, 2001; Carr & Higginson, 2001; Hopkins, 1992).

The rapid expansion of the HRQOL construct in research and clinical practice is evident in its increased presence in the professional literature and its growing use across health care and rehabilitation settings. A search of the major medical, health, and rehabilitation literature databases reveals that, during the last 30 years, several thousand articles have featured the term *health-related*

quality of life in their titles, with a notable increase in the number of such articles with each succeeding decade. Several professional journals and texts are dedicated to QOL research, as are several comprehensive texts (e.g., Baker & Jacoby, 2000; Bowling, 2004; Fayers & Machin, 2000; Spilker, 1996). In addition, during the last several years, assessment of HRQOL has become a required component in many pharmaceutical clinical trials as pharmaceutical companies have recognized the need to expand the definition of benefits to include patient-reported outcomes (Chen, Li, & Kochen, 2005, Mason, Skevington, & Osborn, 2004). This rapid growth and expansion can be seen as resulting from, or at least occurring simultaneously with, several significant changes in the health care field. These changes are described in the following discussion.

Changing Perspectives on Health Care and Outcomes

The ways people seek, use, and evaluate health care services have changed considerably in the last 30 years. The nature of these combined changes has led to the recognition of HRQOL as a uniquely appropriate and effective component of outcome assessment. These changes have been influenced by rapid advances in medicine and technology, escalating health care costs, applications of managed care and related management models to health care delivery, shifting population demographics, and the emergence and dramatic expansion of the Internet and the World Wide Web. Patients and consumers of health care services are much better informed about, and more involved in, decisions about their health care. A growing consumerism and perception of choice in health care providers and services, along with the increased consumer access to health care information made possible through the Internet, have significantly altered the use and delivery of health care.

There have also been fundamental shifts in how health is defined, with a corresponding reevaluation of the meaning and value of health services and their outcomes. Outcome assessment in health care traditionally has been concerned primarily with such factors as symptom reduction or amelioration, morbidity and the length of time one survives with an illness, treatment cost and cost-effectiveness, and functional ability (Bowling, 2001; O'Boyle, 1997). Although reducing symptoms and enhancing functional capacity remain major goals of health care and rehabilitation efforts, changing definitions of health have led to an expansion in the scope and purposes of outcomes assessment beyond these traditional goals.

The World Health Organization's (WHO) 1947 definition of health as a state of physical, mental, and social well-being, not merely the absence of disease and infirmity, has been recognized as a key development in the incorporation of HRQOL as a critical component of outcomes assessment (Bowling, 2001). This comprehensive view of health, further developed in subsequent WHO statements (e.g., WHO, 1980, 1984), introduced the idea that health is more than an absence of illness, and implicitly identified the importance of including the (previously absent) perspective of the recipient of health care services in evaluating the success of a health care outcome. Because of its focus on the subjective perspective of the individual, typically across a range of life domains, the HRQOL paradigm fits well with this expanded view of health and health outcomes.

Another factor influencing the increased use of HRQOL measurement in health care and rehabilitation is the significant increase over the last 5 decades in the prevalence of individuals with chronic illnesses and disabilities in the United States (Dijkers, 1997). This increase is associated with a number of factors, but results primarily from the combination of the aging of a large sector of the population and advances in medicine and the allied health fields. Advances in medical treatment and acute care have expanded the capacity to save the lives of many patients who in the past could not have been saved, and to add years to the lives of individuals with chronic conditions illnesses and disabilities. Because chronic illness represents, by definition, a permanently altered health state caused by a nonreversible pathological condition (Miller, 1992), health care and rehabilitation professionals have increasingly focused research and clinical attention on enhancing the lives of persons living with chronic conditions (Jacoby, 1992), or "adding life to years" (Van Den Bos & Triemstra, 1999, p. 247). With this change in focus has come the need for new approaches to assessment of the patient's perspective in their interaction with health care and other aspects of their lives.

HEALTH-RELATED QUALITY OF LIFE AND THE INTERNATIONAL CLASSIFICATION OF FUNCTIONING, DISABILITY, AND HEALTH

The concept and measurement of HRQOL, which is predicated on a psychosocial well-being model, rather than a medical or disease-based model, is highly consistent and closely aligned with the focus and concepts of the *International Classification of Functioning, Disability and Health* (ICF) of the World Health Organization. Both HRQOL and the ICF have developed partly in response to a shift in the focus of health care from acute to chronic illnesses. The approach of the medical model, with its progression from etiology, to pathology, to diagnosis, to cure is not useful in describing outcomes for persons whose conditions persist over long periods of time. Thus, a model was needed that describes the experiences of persons with chronic conditions (Gray & Hendershot, 2000).

An important goal of the ICF is to provide a scientific basis for understanding the impact of health conditions on life situations (Gray & Hendershot, 2000). Similarly, HRQOL can be described as having been developed to foster a better understanding of the scientific basis for health care. The ICF, with its multidimensional approach to describing and assessing body functions and structures, activities, participation, and contextual factors, mirrors the approach of HRQOL assessment. Like HRQOL, the ICF classifies health and health-related domains that describe body functions and structures, activities and participation (WHO, 2007).

Definitions of Health-Related Quality of Life

Nearly all scholars who have reviewed the QOL literature have decried the lack of a uniform or consistently applied definition of QOL. For example, Campbell, Converse, and Rogers (1976) suggested, "quality of life is a vague and ethereal entity, something that many people talk about, but which nobody very clearly knows what to do about" (p. 87). Feinstein (1987) suggested that QOL represents "a kind of umbrella under which are placed many different indexes dealing with whatever the user wants to focus on" (p. 635). Although HRQOL represents one specific facet of the broader QOL construct, considerable definitional ambiguity about HRQOL exists as well. Two reasons may account for this ambiguity. First, HRQOL is closely aligned with, and therefore frequently confused with, a number of related constructs such as health status and functional capacity. Second, HRQOL assessment is used for different purposes and in different ways across health and rehabilitation contexts and settings.

The absence of a consensus about the definition of HRQOL, in both the professional literature and in instrument development, has been frequently noted. In their frequently cited review of the QOL literature, Gill and Feinstein (1994) found that, among the 75 study articles they reviewed, researchers defined what they meant by the term "quality of life" only 11 times (15%), and none of the articles distinguished between QOL and HRQOL. As O'Boyle (1997) observed, the meaning of HRQOL appears to depend on the user and the context in which the term is used. However, despite the fact that the definition of HRQOL is still debated frequently and remains unsettled, there is consensus about some of the fundamental elements of this construct. The following discussion presents several contexts for exploring the various points of definitional divergence and consensus.

Health-Related and General Quality of Life

The distinction between QOL and HRQOL has been the subject of considerable debate (Jacoby, 2000) and gets to the crux of one of the main definitional controversies: Which of the various aspects of life that contribute to one's QOL should be the focus in defining and assessing HRQOL? On one hand, some argue that among the broad range of human experiences that comprise QOL, HRQOL has as its focus only those areas of life that are affected by illness and are amenable to health care interventions. This idea forms the basis of the majority of HRQOL definitions. For example, Fletcher, Hunt, & Bulpitt (1987) defined HRQOL as the dimensions of QOL that are affected by a disease and its treatment, and that have the potential to be changed by the therapeutic situation. Patrick and Erickson suggested that HRQOL is "the value assigned to duration of life as modified by the impairments, functional states, perceptions, and social opportunities that are influenced by disease, injury, treatment or policy" (1993, p. 22). Similarly, Heinemann (2000) defined HRQOL as expounding "on those aspects of life that may be affected by health; these characteristics typically include functional status, energy level, pain, participation in social and daily activities, and ability to leave one's home" (p. 262).

Although most definitions of HRQOL share this focus on health and illness-related domains, some argue that separating out those domains of life that are affected by illness or its treatments from those that are not is an impossible (and, some suggest, misguided) task (Jacoby, 2000). Proponents of this latter perspective propose that broader definitions of HRQOL are necessary. For example, Bowling (2001, p. 33) suggested that HRQOL may be defined as "optimum levels of mental, physical, role (e.g., work, parent, career, etc.), and social functioning, including relationships and perceptions of health, fitness, life satisfaction, and well-being. It should also include some assessment of the patient's level of satisfaction with treatment, outcome and health status and with future prospects." Although this view leads to a more inclusive definition of HRQOL, Bowling distinguishes HRQOL from QOL by suggesting that general QOL also would include a focus on adequacy of housing, income, and perceptions of the immediate environment.

HRQOL as a Multidimensional Construct

Although disagreement exists about the domains of life that should be included in HRQOL assessment, there is consensus that HRQOL is most appropriately measured multidimensionally; that it includes more than one aspect of experience or functioning (e.g., Bowling, 1995; Cummins, 1997a; Fayers & Machin, 2000; Frisch, 1999). Support for this idea emerged from studies in which researchers, using a variety of approaches including literature reviews, large-scale surveys, and interviews, sought to discover what people considered important to their QOL. Scholars engaged in this research increasingly noted the consistency with which a relatively small set of life domains were identified as contributing to QOL (Bishop & Allen, 2003; George & Bearon, 1980; Hughes, Hwang, Kim, Eisenman, & Killian, 1995; Jalowiec, 1990; Padilla, Grant, & Ferrell, 1992). Among the most frequently and consistently identified domains are physical health, psychological or emotional health, social support, employment, and economic or material well-being. The consistency with which these domains were identified led Anderson and Burckhardt to remark that "it seems that quality of life has the same basic constituents for all people, although the relative importance of individual dimensions may vary over the life span or during illness episodes." (1999, p. 301).

That people place different levels of importance on life domains based on their health was empirically supported in Bowling's (1995) large-scale survey of people in Great Britain. Participants in the study were asked to identify and rank the importance of different life domains. Bowling reported that the priorities were different between persons who did and did not have chronic illnesses and disabilities. Persons who had a chronic illness or disability gave higher priority to functional and health-related aspects of their lives than people who did not have an illness or disability.

Although the domains used to assess HRQOL vary across individuals and from study to study, domains typically included in HRQOL assessment include general health, physical functioning, social functioning, physical symptoms and toxicity, pain, emotional functioning, sexual functioning, and existential issues (Fayers & Machin,

2000). For example, the Medical Outcome Study Short Form-36 (SF-36; Ware & Sherbourne, 1992), one of the most frequently used HRQOL instruments, assesses the following eight domains: physical functioning, social functioning, role limitations due to physical problems, role limitations due to emotional problems, mental health, energy/fatigue, bodily pain, general health perception, and general perception of health over the past year.

Subjective and Objective Perspectives on HRQOL

There is a growing consensus that HRQOL measurement should incorporate assessment of both objective and subjective components of experience (Cummins, 1997a). The objective component addresses norm-referenced measures of function or well-being, and the subjective components address the individual's unique personal perspective of his or her well-being. A purely objective measure would include only such indicators as physical function or symptoms that could be assessed by an external observer. Measures of this sort are more likely to be considered measures of health status or functional status. In contrast, a purely subjective measure assesses only the individual's perspective or opinion about his or her experience or circumstances. Although this latter perspective may be very important clinically, its assessment does not provide the level of sensitivity necessary in clinical studies. Generally, HRQOL measures include both perspectives, and this combined approach is preferable to using either perspective in isolation.

THE HISTORY OF HEALTH-RELATED QUALITY OF LIFE PRACTICE AND RESEARCH

The search for understanding the components and features of a good, happy, or satisfying life has concerned philosophers for centuries (Diener & Suh, 1997). However, the applications of science associated with QOL and well-being in the social and health sciences has a relatively recent history. For example, based on its debut as a search topic in *Index Medicus* in 1966, QOL has assumed importance in general medicine only during the last half century (McSweeny & Creer, 1995). The development of the current concept of HRQOL has occurred even more recently, having emerged in the professional literature during the late 1970s and 1980s (Fitzpatrick, 1996). The following discussion briefly reviews this history.

During the post-World War II era, a number of national and international surveys that examined population well-being or quality of life were conducted based on measures called social indicators. Social indicators are objectively measurable, group-based population statistics, characteristics, or variables (e.g., gross national product, wages, cost of housing, and rate of unemployment) (Cummins, 1997a). The main purpose of these early population-based surveys of life quality was to create concise and comprehensive understanding of their status (Cummins, 1997a) for use in guiding the development of public policy.

During the 1960s, the focus of QOL assessment shifted from one based on population statistics to an assessment based on personal perspectives (Cummins, 1997a), resulting in increased recognition that an individual's perspective about his or her life comprises an important component of general QOL. Recognition that objectively measurable social indicators accounted for a relatively small percentage of the individual's overall QOL was partly responsible for this shift in focus from group-based objective assessment to individual-based subjective indicators (Bowling, 2001; Day & Jankey, 1996). For example, objective indicators measured by social scientists at the time reportedly accounted for only 15% of the variance in an individual's QOL (Day & Jankey). Alternately, subjective perception of their circumstances appeared to explain much more of the variance in general QOL, thus leading to the recognition that one's subjective feelings of independence, control, autonomy, and satisfaction deserved greater recognition (Bowling, 2001; Cummins, 1997a).

During the 1960s, the importance of health as an objective in public policy received greater recognition (Kaplan, 1990; Sirgy et al., 2006). Several measures of health and functional status were developed to assess health by means of objective indicators. Early instruments developed to assess health status were designed for clinical use by health care staff and clinicians (Fayers & Machin, 2000). Examples include the Barthel Index (Mahoney & Barthel, 1965) and the Karnofsky Performance Scale (Karnofsky & Burchenal, 1949).

During the 1970s, a number of highly influential studies (e.g., Andrews & Withey, 1976; Campbell, Converse, & Rogers, 1976; Flanagan, 1978) stimulated further growth of QOL research. These studies explored the nature, dynamics, and components of QOL, life satisfaction, and well-being. Significant findings in these studies initiated interest in issues that continue to be addressed. These include the idea that subjective indicators could be reliably measured, that a group of domains important to QOL could be identified, and that the composite influence of these domains on the individual's QOL was both subjective and variable over time (Bishop, Chapin, & Miller, 2008).

During the 1970s and 1980s, the next generation of health status scales was developed to focus on physical functioning, physical symptoms, psychological symptoms, and the perceived impact of or distress from illness. Examples include the Sickness Impact Profile (SIP; Bergner, Bobbitt, Pollard, Martin, & Gilson, 1976) and the Nottingham Health Profile (Hunt, McKenna, McEwan, Williams, & Papp, 1981). These scales frequently were referred to as, but were not intended to be, HRQOL measures (Fayers & Machin, 2000).

The steady increase in QOL research activity continued into the 1990s, leading to significant advances in theory development. The potential applications of QOL concepts for policy development, clinical practice, and outcome assessment received increasing recognition among health care and rehabilitation professionals. As foreshadowed by Schalock, Keith, Hoffman and Karan (1989), QOL became for these fields "the issue for the 1990s" (p. 25), and helped create continued and sustained momentum.

Thousands of assessment instruments have been designed to assess QOL and HRQOL (Chen, Li, & Kochen, 2005; Taillefer, Dupuis, Roberge, & LeMay, 2003) and the number is increasing, particularly disease-specific instruments. Unfortunately, many instruments have paid little attention to psychometric standards (Taillefer et al.). Also, due to their narrowly focused content or assessment of only objectively measured characteristics, many instruments used as measures of HRQOL would better be described as measures of health status. Therefore, careful consideration is necessary in the selection and use of instruments for HRQOL measurement. Issues important to the development, selection, and use of HRQOL instruments are discussed in the following section.

RESEARCH BOX 27.1

Efficace, F., Bottomley, A., Osoba, D., Gotay, C., Flechtner, H., D'haese, S., & Zurlo, A. (2003). Beyond the development of health-related quality-of-life (HRQOL) measures: A checklist for evaluating HRQOL outcomes in cancer clinical trials—does HRQOL evaluation in prostate cancer research inform clinical decision making? *Journal of Clinical Oncology, 21*(18), 3502–3511.

Objectives: The purpose of this study was to evaluate whether the inclusion of health-related quality of life (HRQOL), as a part of the trial design in a randomized controlled trial (RCT) setting, supports clinical decision-making when planning future medical treatments for patients with prostate cancer.

Method: A minimum standard checklist for evaluating HRQOL outcomes in cancer clinical trials was devised to assess the quality of the HRQOL reporting and to classify the studies based on their robustness. It comprises 11 key HRQOL issues grouped into four broader sections: conceptual, measurement, methodology, and interpretation. Relevant studies were identified in a number of databases, including MEDLINE and the Cochrane Controlled Trials Register. Both their HRQOL and traditional clinical reported outcomes were analyzed to evaluate their consistency and their relevance for supporting clinical decision-making.

Results: Seventeen percent of the studies showed a difference in general survival; 74% of the studies showed some difference in terms of HRQOL outcomes. One third of the RCTs provided a comprehensive picture of the whole treatment including HRQOL outcomes to support their conclusions.

Conclusion: A minimum set of criteria for assessing the reported outcomes in cancer clinical trials is necessary to make informed decisions about clinical practice. Using a checklist developed for this study, HRQOL was found to be a valuable source of information in RCTs of treatment in metastatic prostate cancer.

Questions

This article raises an important issue about the use of HRQOL measures in clinical trials. Although the use of HRQOL instruments in clinical trials has increased significantly during the last decade, several researchers have suggested that the resulting information has not been used effectively to inform clinical decision-making.

1. With many treatment options available for various chronic mental and physical conditions, what role should HRQOL play in clinical decision-making?
2. What role might HRQOL play in helping people to make informed decisions about treatment?

ASSESSMENT METHODS FOR HEALTH-RELATED QUALITY OF LIFE

The process of selecting and effectively using a measure of HRQOL requires one to consider who will use the measure, its intended purpose, the appropriate domains to be assessed, and the measure's question and response format.

Generic and Disease-Specific Measures

HRQOL measures may be either general or disease-specific. The more common disease-specific measures are designed for use with persons with a specific condition or illness (Guyatt, Feeny, & Patrick, 1993). Disease-specific instruments are used to evaluate the impact of a specific disease or condition (e.g., diabetes, breast cancer, multiple sclerosis) on an individual's health and HRQOL, or to study the effectiveness of a treatment approach. General measures may be used to assess the general health of an individual. General measures are also used to evaluate health policy decisions, or to evaluate population health (Peterson & Bredow, 2004). The Short-Form 36-item Health Survey (SF-36; Ware, & Sherbourne, 1992) is currently the most commonly used general instrument (Sirgy et al, 2006). The WHOQOL-100 and WHOQOL-BREF are also general instruments, and their use has increased significantly in the last decade. Several hundred disease-specific instruments are available, and their numbers are increasing. Examples include the Quality of Life in Epilepsy Inventory (QOLIE-89; Devinsky et al., 1995), the Functional Assessment of Cancer-General (FACT-G; Cella et al., 1993), and the Diabetes Quality of Life Questionnaire (Jacobson, Barofsky, Cleary, & Rand, 1988).

There are different reasons that clinicians and researchers use either a general or a disease-specific instrument. General measures may provide more comprehensive assessment of domains not included in a disease-specific instrument, and these measures also allow comparisons across conditions—qualities that may be important when conducting comparative research. Alternately, disease-specific instruments may be more informative about an individual's experience with specific symptoms and more sensitive to changes in domains that are a specific focus of treatment or intervention. The use of disease-specific measures is readily understandable, for example, when one considers the unique impact of diabetes as compared to that of breast cancer or multiple sclerosis. However, the use of more narrowly focused domain-specific instruments may underestimate the impact of a disease on one's quality of life (Van den Bos & Triemstra, 1999). Thus, generic and disease-specific measures frequently are administered together to provide a more comprehensive assessment of the individual's experience.

Content and Format

In selecting a HRQOL measure, it is important to consider the type and amount of information that is being sought. As discussed earlier in this chapter, some HRQOL instruments provide a broad perspective on the individual's life and health experience, assessing physical, emotional, and social domains, and community participation, whereas others are more narrowly focused on physical health and functional status.

Instrument selection should be guided by a careful review of the domains assessed and their appropriateness for the individual or population being evaluated (Hyland, 1999). If the instrument was developed for use by persons with a specific condition or disability, then the domains assessed may not be appropriate for, or similarly meaningful to, persons with other conditions. Similarly, measures developed for persons in a specific age range (e.g., children, adolescents, or the elderly) may not be effective with persons outside that range. The response format should also be considered. The individual completing the instrument must be able to comprehend the question and the response format in order to accurately represent his or her experience. Increasingly, test developers are experimenting with nonnumeric (e.g., picture) scales, and other variations of response formats to enhance comprehension and usability.

Some recent HRQOL assessment methodologies offer a highly individualized approach to HRQOL assessment. These include methods designed to address the inherent limitations in instruments that have been developed based on predefined ideas of HRQOL and its relevant domains. As Bowling (2001) and others (e.g., Cohen, 1982) have pointed out, trying to identify the domains that are relevant to an individual's QOL is problematic because both the domains and their importance to the individual vary considerably across individuals and contexts. Instruments have been designed therefore that allow the respondent to identify domains that are personally important and to then rate their experience within the domain. Examples include the Schedule for the Evaluation of Individual QOL (SEIQOL; O'Boyle, McGee, Hickey, O'Malley, & Joyce, 1992; McGee, O'Boyle, Hickey, O'Malley, & Joyce, 1991; Browne,

O'Boyle, McGee, McDonald, & Joyce, 1997) and the Patient Generated Index of Quality of Life (PGI; Ruta, Garratt, Leng, Russell, & Macdonald, 1994). These instruments also allow the individual to indicate the relative importance of the domains.

Several other HRQOL and QOL instruments also incorporate domain weighting, allowing the respondent to identify which domains are more and less important. Examples include the Quality of Life Inventory (QOLI; Frisch, 1994), the Quality of Life Index (QLI; Ferrans & Powers, 1985), and the Comprehensive Quality of Life Scale (ComQol; Cummins, 1997b).

Psychometric Adequacy

The psychometric properties of HRQOL instruments must be considered. Important criteria to consider include their validity (i.e., the accuracy with which an instrument measures or reflects what it purports to measure), reliability (i.e., to measure an attribute consistently), sensitivity (i.e., to detect clinically important changes), and precision (i.e., to accurately measure and reflect true change) (Jacoby, 2000).

The process of developing an instrument is complex and lengthy (Fava, 1990). Despite the recent development of many HRQOL instruments and the availability of some well-constructed and psychometrically sound measures, the psychometric quality of many instruments is substandard (Kinney, 1995; Taillefer et al., 2003). Some who develop these measures lack sufficient skills in psychometrics. Others feel the need to develop their own measures quickly and without due regard for their psychometric quality (Taillefer et al.).

An instrument's psychometric qualities affect the quality of the information it provides and thus the quality of the decisions made from the data. Thus, professionals should examine the instrument's psychometric qualities carefully. Information about the psychometric qualities of HRQOL instruments is generally available from the instrument publishers or developers, or in research articles related to the instrument's development.

Instrument Selection

In summary, the selection of an appropriate instrument for use in clinical practice or research should be guided by a number of considerations. Researchers and clinicians should review instruments to insure that their content and assessment methods are suitable for the intended purposes. The instrument's psychometric qualities (e.g., whether the reliability and validity statistics reported for the instrument are adequate both generally and in relation to the specific population being assessed) and whether the instrument has been developed or used with populations similar to the intended group should be considered (Anderson & Burkhardt, 1999). Floor and ceiling effects (i.e., the ability of the instrument to measure HRQOL at both very low and high levels) also should be considered (Higginson & Carr, 2001).

Review the instrument's format and length in light of the population being assessed. Measures that are brief have the advantage of being used quickly yet may not provide sufficiently detailed information. Others that are longer are likely to provide more sufficient coverage yet may be daunting, leading to a reduced response rate and an overabundance of extraneous information. The language and reading level required are also important considerations and generally should be no higher than a fifth-grade reading level.

RESEARCH CRITICAL TO ISSUES IN HEALTH-RELATED QUALITY OF LIFE ASSESSMENT

Assessment of HRQOL occurs at the confluence of two dynamic and rapidly changing fields: health care and QOL. The expanding role of HRQOL as a component in clinical practices, including decisions on treatments as well as access to and allocation of health services, has enlivened critical considerations about the nature and scope of HRQOL assessment.

ISSUES CONCERNING DEFINITION AND PERSPECTIVE

Dramatic medical advances during the last 3 decades have spawned complex moral and ethical questions about the value and quality of life, as well as how they should be measured. In this context, decisions as to the definition of HRQOL involve more than an academic debate. Treatment access and clinical care decisions increasingly are being based on judgments about the resulting quality of life. Thus, the means by which HRQOL is defined and measured, together with knowledge of the respondent, can impact decisions instrumentally.

Originally, health status measures were developed to be completed by clinicians based on objectively measurable observations. More recently, as the importance and clinical value of the subjective perspective of the patient has been recognized, HRQOL measures have been developed to incorporate this perspective. However, this reliance on subjective, or "soft" data has been criticized (Jacoby, 2000). The question of which perspective is more important, objective or subjective, in the context of health care decisions is fundamental to HRQOL assessment (see Bowling, 2001; Carr & Higginson, 2001; Jacoby, 2000 for discussions).

Proxy Ratings

The perspective of the person rating HRQOL also has received considerable research attention. If the purpose of HRQOL assessment is to assess the impact of health and health care interventions on QOL, then the patient generally will be the most accurate respondent. However, under some circumstances, HRQOL assessments may be made for or about a person by a proxy, or representative, who may be a health professional, family member, a caregiver, or another who knows the patient well.

Ratings of health care providers and those from patients about a patient's HRQOL frequently differ (e.g., Gerhart, Koziol-McLain, Lowenstein, & Whiteneck, 1994; Mohide, Archibald, Tew, Young, & Haines, 1992). Ratings from health care providers may either be higher or lower than patients' ratings. This discrepancy may occur because physicians tend to over-emphasize medical criteria in judging their patients' life quality, whereas patients use health perceptions, interpersonal relationships, and other considerations in making QOL judgments (Anderson & Burckhardt, 1999). Discrepancies also exist among different health professionals (e.g., Slevin, Plant, Lynch, Drinkwater, & Gregory, 1988).

Ratings among patients, caregivers, and parents also may be discrepant. For example, patients with various forms of cancer frequently rate their QOL better than their caregivers (e.g., Deschler, Walsh, Friedman, & Hayden, 1999; Forjaz & Guarnaccia, 1999). Similarly, discrepant ratings also may exist for persons with other chronic conditions (Sprangers & Aaronson, 1992), as well as between parent and child (e.g., Ennett et al., 1991; Harding, 2001; Vogels et al., 1998). Ratings between patients and proxies have been more congruent when more objective and observable QOL qualities are rated and less congruent when more subjective qualities are rated (Jacoby, 2000).

International HRQOL Assessment

Growth in HRQOL assessment internationally has been significant. This growth is due to several conditions, including the rising rates of chronic illness, the broadened conception of health to include qualities other than the absence of disease, an increase in the elderly population, and a desire to measure the impact of health and rehabilitation interventions comprehensively, in part to help allocate resources (Bowden & Fox-Rushby, 2003; Nilsson, Parker, & Nahar Kabir, 2004).

Most HRQOL instruments have been developed in English. As a result, professionals in non-English-speaking countries have either developed new measures or have translated or adapted existing ones (Chen et al., 2005; Bowden & Fox-Rushby, 2003). Both approaches have been utilized, with a growing number of non-English instruments being developed. Although the validity and cultural appropriateness of translated or adapted instruments is of concern (Bowden & Fox-Rushby, 2003), many of the better-established U.S. measures have been translated for cross-cultural use (see Bowden & Fox-Rushby, 2003, for a comprehensive discussion). Discussion Box 27.1 describes the results of the World Health Organization's efforts at ameliorating these issues in the form of the WHOQOL instruments, which have demonstrated significant potential for cross-cultural and international HRQOL assessment.

The WHOQOL-100 and WHOQOL BREF

In 1991, the WHOQOL Group, through the World Health Organization, began a project designed to resolve some of the problems inherent in cross-cultural measurement of HRQOL (Skevington, 2002). An extensive development process that included recommendations from health experts from many countries, focus groups (e.g., from patients, caregivers, health personnel, and members of the general public), and pilot testing in multicultural field sites culminated in the development of the WHOQOL-100 (a 100-item QOL assessment instrument) and the WHOQOL BREF (a 26-item instrument based on the domains of the longer scale—WHOQOL-100) (Saxena & Van Ommeren, 2005). The WHOQOL was intended to provide an evidence-based instrument for use in multinational clinical trials, for the assessment of other population differences in health, and for the creation of a subjective self-report assessment for group and individual use (Skevington). "The WHOQOL collaboration pooled information throughout the project, and this procedure not only permits a high level of semantic and conceptual equivalence to be achieved between language versions but also creates a 'fast track' to the rapid establishment of multi-lingual instruments" (Skevington, Lotfy, & O'Connell, 2004).

The WHOQOL BREF has been used as an assessment of QOL with a growing number of chronic physical

DISCUSSION BOX 27.1

The International use of HRQOL assessment methods has grown rapidly during the last 2 decades. This increased use is due to several qualities, including the development or adaptation of larger numbers of HRQOL instruments and the recognition of the importance, efficiency, and usefulness of HRQOL assessment in measuring the impact of health and rehabilitation interventions comprehensively. Whether HRQOL and its component elements have the same meaning in diverse cultures is an important issue. Illness, disability, and health may be culturally determined concepts.

Questions

1. When the meaning of concepts differ cross-culturally, does their impact on or relationship to the various roles and domains of life also vary?

2. Further, although some domains of quality of life are shared across cultures, to what extent may the meaning of these domains and their importance to the individual and society differ?

3. The value placed on the quality of life may be high in some countries and cultures and different in others. In the face of such questions, to what extent can there be an internationally shared and common understanding of a single construct of HRQOL?

and mental conditions, including alcoholism (Da Silva Lima, Fleck, Pechansky, de Boni, & Sukop, 2005); HIV (Hsiung, Fang, Chang, Chen, & Wang, 2005; Fang, Hsiung, Yu, Chen, & Wang, 2002), Generalized Anxiety Disorder (Zhang, Li, & Wu, 2005), spinal cord injury (Chapin, Miller, Ferrin, Chan, & Rubin, 2004), and depression (Naumann & Byrne, 2004).

The WHOQOL–BREF has been evaluated in many nations and cultures (e.g., Hanestad, Rustøen, Knudsen, Lerdal, & Wahl, 2004; Jaracz, Kalfoss, Gorna, & Baczyk, 2006; Huang, Wu, & Frangakis, 2006; Izutsu et al., 2005;

Min et al., 2002; Noerholm et al., 2004; Trompenaars, Masthoff, Van Heck, Hodiamont, & De Vries, 2005; Tsutsumi et al., 2006; Wang, Yao, Tsai, Wang, & Hsieh, 2006) and generally has sound psychometric quality and cross-cultural validity. For example, Skevington and associates (2004) investigated the psychometric properties of the WHOQOL BREF in 23 countries (N = 11,830), including persons from both the general population and those in health care facilities (e.g., rehabilitation centers, hospitals). The WHOQOL BREF was found to have excellent psychometric properties and valid use of QOL cross-culturally.

Summary and Conclusion

Several significant changes during the last 3 decades (e.g., advances in medical care, changes in health care systems and their focus, shifts in perspectives on the meaning of health itself, and an increase in consumerism and patients' awareness about their health) have dramatically altered the assessment of health care outcomes. In health care and rehabilitation, the individual's personal perspective on HRQOL "complements the increasing emphasis on patient autonomy and informed consent" (O'Boyle, 1997, p. 1877). The assessment of HRQOL provides a person-centered and professionally useful approach to health care decision-making and outcomes measurement. The construct of HRQOL and its assessment focus are being revised.

International research on disparities in health between the developed and developing countries increasingly are merging quality of life with health (Sirgy et al., 2006). Health-related QOL assessments that are cross-culturally valid will play an important role in enhancing our understanding of health differences and disparities and the impact of health interventions on QOL.

The qualities that led to the emergence of HRQOL as a focus of outcomes assessment in the medical, health, rehabilitation, and related professions continue to evolve. A continuing international political agenda for HRQOL research, coupled with the development of methodological and technical advances in HRQOL assessment, suggest that the growth and evolvement of HRQOL will continue.

Self-Check Questions

1. Define HRQOL using your own terminology. Consider in your definition the issues of perspective, dimensions, and purpose discussed in the chapter.
2. Considering individual and cultural perspectives on health-related quality of life, list four or five qualities first you and then your parents may consider necessary for having a good quality of life. Compare your responses with another person who is culturally different (e.g., different gender, age, socioeconomic status, ethnicity). How are your perspectives similar and different?
3. Interview two persons, one who is well and another with a chronic disease, about their views toward quality of life. How are their perspectives similar and different, and what may account for their similarities and differences?
4. Consider subjective and objective perspectives on health-related quality of life. This chapter discussed the importance of including both the patients' subjective perspectives, including their personal, internal reactions to their experiences, and their objective perspectives, including those aspects of function that can be measured by an observer. What are the problems or limitations associated with using only one of these perspectives to assess HRQOL?
5. The distinction between quality of life and health-related quality of life has been described in this chapter as a point of debate. Discuss whether one can distinguish those aspects of life that are and are not affected by illness or chronic conditions.

Case Study

Mei-Wah, a 52-year-old Chinese female, immigrated to the United States from China 1 year ago. She was referred to the Workers Compensation Rehabilitation Clinic because she fell from a ladder in a factory where she worked 10 hours weekly as an inventory stock manager of office supplies. Her job involved counting the inventories of incoming stocks as well as moving the boxes and stacking them in a storage area. As a result of the fall, she strained her lower back muscles and she fractured her right elbow.

Mei-Wah and her husband have been married since they were in their 20s. While in China, her husband worked as a clerk in a local store part-time while the couple also maintained a farm. They had been living in this lifestyle for 30 years. They saved money and partially supported their only son, who also received a scholarship to study engineering in the United States. The son obtained a job in the United States after graduation, and he sponsored both parents to immigrate to Buffalo, NY, after he obtained a job. As a result of a promotion, the son has moved to a different state to work as a senior engineer while the couple remained in Buffalo.

Because Mei-Wah's job required minimal communication, she felt comfortable working. Her husband worked as a gardener for his neighborhood and was introduced to this job by one of his Chinese neighbors. He worked about 25 hours per week. Aside from their work, neither Mei-Wah nor her husband had many social activities other than occasional visits to two Chinese families. Her son provided some financial support on a monthly basis.

Mei-Wah was seen by a physician at a rehabilitation clinic because of her persistent pain. She was prescribed a muscle relaxant and was asked to keep her elbow in a sling for two weeks while focusing on a vocational rehabilitation program intended to return/improve her physical condition to be ready for the same job.

Mei-Wah appeared to be extremely anxious and nervous. She did not understand why the doctors did not provide pain medications to cure her pain and why she should be asked to bed rest because of her injury. She was anxious about having to take the time off for rehabilitation because she was afraid her employer would fire her because she was slacking off. She also worried that she was not contributing to the financial income of the family. She was unable to perform her housekeeping role as a wife. She was afraid that she would never be healed. She had nobody to talk to. She and her husband did not want to bother their son and thus always told him that they were doing fine. Mei-Wah had a hard time sleeping because of the worries, and her pain increased. She became restless, tired and teary. She was finally referred to see a psychologist. She appeared to attribute all the problems to herself and her injury. She wanted the pain to go away and to return to work as soon as possible. She was given permission to return to work for 2 hours per week after the first week of rehabilitation and instead worked 8 hours that week. Her pain increased further. In addition, she fell again on a slippery floor. She informed the psychologist that her problems were ten times more severe. She felt helpless and could not understand why the doctors did not give her pain medications to heal her injury and why she was encouraged to return to work too early.

QUESTIONS

1. How do you think Mei-Wah's injury and subsequent treatment and rehabilitation changed her perception of her quality of life?

2. Given her cultural perception about injury, especially pain, how would you conceptualize the different psychosocial qualities that may have contributed to her decreased quality of life? Psychosocial qualities taken into consider could include but are not limited to her lack of understanding of the medical and psychological aspects of the injury/pain, her emotional response (catastrophizing and helplessness), her role as a wife and as a financial contributor to the family, her attribution of her fault to the employer who would consider her to be lazy, her lack of social support, as well as her challenges in communicating her needs to the doctors and the rehabilitation professionals.

3. To follow up with question #2, what priorities would you set if you were working to improve Mei-Wah's quality of life?

References

Anderson, K. L., & Burckhardt, C.S. (1999). Conceptualization and measurement of quality of life as an outcome variable for health care intervention and research. *Journal of Advanced Nursing Research, 29*, 298–306.

Andrews, F., & Withey, S. (1976). Developing measures of perceived life quality: Results from several national surveys. *Social Indicators Research, 1*, 1–26.

Avis, N. E., & Smith, K.W. (1994). Conceptual and methodological issues in selecting and developing quality of life measures. In R. Fitzpatrick (Ed.), *Advances in medical sociology.* (pp. 255–280). London: JAI Press Inc.

Baker, G., & Jacoby, A. (2000). *Quality of life in epilepsy: Beyond seizure counts in assessment and treatment.* Amsterdam: Harwood Academic Publishers.

Barry, M. M., & Crosby, C. (1996) Quality of life as an evaluative measure in assessing the impact of community care on people with long-term psychiatric disorders. *British Journal of Psychiatry, 168*, 210–216.

Bergner, M., Bobbitt, R. A., Pollard, W. E., Martin, D. P., & Gilson, B. S. (1976). The sickness impact profile: Validation of a health status measure. *Medical Care, 14*(1), 57–67.

Beulow, J. M. (2001). Epilepsy management issues and techniques. *Journal of Neuroscience Nursing, 33*, 260–269.

Bishop, M., & Allen, C. A. (2003). Epilepsy's impact on quality of life: A qualitative analysis. *Epilepsy & Behavior, 4*, 226–233.

Bishop, M., Chapin, M., & Miller, S. (2008). Quality of life assessment in the measurement of rehabilitation outcomes. *Journal of Rehabilitation: Special Issue on Rehabilitation Outcomes, 74*(2), 45–55.

Bowden, A., & Fox-Rushby, J. A. (2003). A systematic and critical review of the process of translation and adaptation of generic health-related quality of life measures in Africa, Asia, Eastern Europe, the Middle East and South America. *Social Science and Medicine, 57*(7), 1289–1306.

Bowling, A. (1995). What things are important in people's lives? A survey of the public's judgments to inform scales of health related quality of life. *Social Science and Medicine, 41*, 1447–1462.

Bowling, A. (2001). Measuring disease (2nd ed.). Buckingham: Open University Press.

Bowling, A. (2004) *Measuring Health: A review of quality of life measurement scales* (3rd ed.). Buckingham, Eng.: Open University Press.

Browne, J. P., O'Boyle, C. A., McGee, H. M., McDonald, N. J., & Joyce, C. R. B. (1997). Development of a direct weighting procedure for quality of life domains. *Quality of Life Research, 6*, 301–309.

Campbell, A., Converse, P. E., & Rogers, W. L. (1976). *The quality of American life: Perceptions, evaluations, and satisfaction.* New York: Russell Sage.

Carr, A. J., & Higginson, I. J. (2001) Measuring quality of life: Are quality of life measures patient centred? *BMJ, 322* (7298), 1357–1360.

Cella, D. F., Tulsky, D. S., Gray, G., Sarafian, B., Linn, E., Bonomi, A., Silberman, M., Yellen, S.B., Winicour, P., and Brannon, J. (1993). The Functional Assessment of Cancer Therapy Scale: Development and validation of the general measure. *Journal of Clinical Oncology, 11*, 570–579.

Chapin, M., H., Miller,, S. M., Ferrin, J. M., Chan, F., Rubin, S. E. (2004). Psychometric validation of a subjective well-being measure for people with spinal cord injuries. *Disability and Rehabilitation: An International Multidisciplinary Journal, 26*(16), 1135–1142.

Chen, T. H., Li, L., & Kochen, M. M. (2005). (A systematic review: How to choose appropriate health-related quality of life (HRQOL) measures in routine general practice? *Journal of Zhejiang University Science, 6*(9), 936–940.

Chubon, R. A. (1995). *Manual for the Life Situation Survey* (1995 rev.). Columbia, SC: University of South Carolina, School of Medicine, Department of Neuropsychiatry and Behavioral Medicine, Rehabilitation Counseling Program.

Cieza, A., & Stucki, G. (2005). Content comparison of health-related quality of life (HRQOL) instruments based on the international classification of functioning, disability and health (ICF). *Quality of Life Research: An International Journal of Quality of Life Aspects of Treatment, Care and Rehabilitation, 14*(5), 1225–1237.

Cohen, C. (1982). On the quality of life—some philosophical reflections. *Circulation, 66*, 29–33.

Cookson, M. S., Dutta, S. C., Chang, S. S., Clark, T., Smith, J. A., Jr., & Wells, N. (2003). Health related quality of life in patients treated with radical cystectomy and urinary diversion for urothelial carcinoma of the bladder: Development and validation of a new disease specific questionnaire. *Journal of Urology, 170*(5), 1926–1930.

Cummins, R. A. (1997a). Assessing quality of life. In R. J. Brown (Ed.), Assessing quality of life for people with disabilities (pp. 116–150). Cheltenham, England: Stanley Thornes.

Cummins, R. A. (1997b). *Comprehensive Quality of Life Scale-Adult.* (5th ed.; ComQol-A-5) Melbourne, Australia: Deakin University School of Psychology.

Da Silva Lima, A. F. B., Fleck, M., Pechansky, F., de Boni, R., & Sukop, P. (2005). Psychometric properties of the World Health Organization Quality of Life instrument (WHOQOL BREF) in alcoholic males: A pilot study. *Quality of Life Research: An International Journal of Quality of Life Aspects of Treatment, Care and Rehabilitation, 14*(20), 473–478.

Day, H., & Jankey, S. G. (1996). Lessons from the literature: Toward a holistic model of quality of life. In R. Renwick, I. Brown, & M. Nagler (Eds.), *Quality of life in health promotion and rehabilitation* (pp. 39–62). Thousand Oaks, CA: Sage.

Deschler, D. G., Walsh, K. A., Friedman, S., & Hayden, R. E. (1999). Quality of life assessment in patients undergoing head and neck surgery as evaluated by lay caregivers. *Laryngoscope, 109*, 42–46.

Devinsky, O., Vickrey, B. G., Cramer, J., Perraine, K., Hermann, B., Meador, K., et al. (1995). Development of the Quality of Life in Epilepsy (QOLIE) Inventory. *Epilepsia, 36*, 1089–1104.

Diener, E., & Suh, E. (1997). Measuring quality of life: Economic, social, and subjective indicators. *Social Indicators Research, 40*, 189–216.

Dijkers, M. (1997). Measuring quality of life. In M. J. Fuhrer (Ed.) *Assessing medical rehabilitation practices: The promise of outcomes research* (pp. 153–180). Baltimore, MD: Paul H. Brooks Publishing Co.

Elliott, T. E., Renier, C. M., & Palcher, J. A. (2003). Chronic pain, depression, and quality of life: Correlations and predictive value of the SF-36. *Pain Medicine, 4,* 331–339.

Ennett, S., Devellis, B. M., Earp, J. A., Kredich, D., Warren, R. W., Wilhelm, C. L. (1991). Disease experience and psychosocial adjustment in children with juvenile rheumatoid arthritis: Children's versus mothers' reports. *Journal of Pediatric Psychology, 16*, 557–568.

Fallowfield, L. (1990). *Quality of life: The missing measurement in health care.* London: Souvenir Press.

Fang, C. T., Hsiung, P. C., Yu, C. F., Chen, M. Y., & Wang, J. D. (2002). Validation of the World Health Organization quality of life instrument in patients with HIV infection. *Quality of Life Research: An International Journal of Quality of Life Aspects of Treatment, Care and Rehabilitation, 11*(8), 753–762.

Farquhar, M. (1995). Elderly people's definitions of quality of life. *Social Science & Medicine, 41*, 1439–1446.

Fava, G. A. (1990). Methodological and conceptual issues in research on quality of life. *Psychotherapy & Psychosomatics, 54,* 70–76

Fayers, P. M., & Machin, D. (2000). *Quality of life: Assessment, analysis, and interpretation.* West Sussex, UK: John Wiley & Sons.

Feinstein, A. R. (1987). Clinimetric perspectives. *Journal of Chronic Diseases, 40,* 635–640.

Ferrans, C. E., & Powers, M. J. (1985). Quality of life index: Development and psychometric properties. *Advances in Nursing Science, 8*(1), 15–24.

Fitzpatrick, R. (1996). Alternative approaches to the assessment of health-related quality of life. In A. Offer (Ed.), *Pursuit of the Quality of Life* (pp. 140–162). Oxford: Oxford University Press.

Flanagan, J. C. (1978). A research approach to improving our quality of life. *American Psychologist, 33*, 138–147.

Fletcher, A. E., Hunt, B. M., Bulpitt, C. J. (1987). Evaluation of quality of life in clinical trials of cardiovascular disease. *Journal of Chronic Disease, 40*, 557–569

Forjaz, M. J., & Guarnaccia, C. A. (1999). Hematological cancer patients' quality of life: Self versus intimate or non-intimate confidant reports. *Psycho-Oncology, 8*, 546–552.

Frank-Stromberg, M. (1988). *Instruments for clinical nursing research.* Norwalk, CT: Appleton & Lange.

Frisch, M. B. (1994). *QOLI or Quality of Life Inventory.* Minneapolis, MN: Pearson Assessments.

Frisch, M. B. (1999) Quality of life assessment/intervention and the Quality of Life Inventory (QOLI). In M. R. Maruish (Ed.), *The use of psychological testing for treatment planning and outcome assessment* (2nd ed., pp. 1227–1331). Hillsdale, NJ: Lawrence Erlbaum.

George, L., & Bearon, L. (1980). *Quality of life in older persons.* New York: Human Sciences Press.

Gerhart, K. A., Koziol-McLain, J., Lowenstein S. R., & Whiteneck, G. G. (1994). Quality of life following spinal cord injury: Knowledge and attitudes of emergency care providers. *Annals of Emergency Medicine, 23*, 807–812

Gill, T. M., & Feinstein, A. R. (1994). A critical appraisal of the quality of quality-of-life measurements. *JAMA, 272,* 619–626.

Gray, D. B., & Hendershot, G. E. (2000). The ICIDH-2: Developments for a new era of outcomes research. *Archives of Physical Medicine and Rehabilitation, 81* (Suppl 2), S10–S14.

Guyatt, G. H., Feeny, D. H., & Patrick, D. L. (1993). Measuring health-related quality of life. *Annals of Internal Medicine, 118*, 622–629.

Haas, B. K. (1999). Clarification of similar quality of life concepts. *Image: Journal of Nursing Scholarship*, 31, 215–220.

Hanestad, B. R., Rustøen, T., Knudsen, O. Jr., Lerdal, A., & Wahl, A. K. (2004). Psychometric properties of the WHO-QOL questionnaire for the Norwegian general population. *Journal of Nursing Measurement, 12*(2), 147–159.

Hao, Y. T., Fang, J. Q., & Power, M. J. (2006). The equivalence of WHOQOL BREF among 13 culture versions. *Chinese Mental Health Journal, 20*(2), 71–75.

Harding, L. (2001). Children's quality of life assessments: A review of generic and health related quality of life measures completed by children and adolescents. *Clinical Psychology and Psychotherapy, 8*, 79–96.

Heinemann, A. W. (2000). Functional status and quality-of-life measures. In R. G. Frank & T. R. Elliott (Eds.), *Handbook of rehabilitation psychology* (pp. 261–286). Washington, D.C.: American Psychological Association.

Higginson, I. J., & Carr, A. J. (2001) Measuring the quality of life: Using quality of life measures in clinical settings. *British Medical Journal, 322*, 1297–1300.

Hopkins, A. (1992). *Measures of the quality of life, and the uses to which such measures may be put*. London: Royal College of Physicians.

Hsiung, P. C., Fang, C. T., Chang, Y. Y., Chen, M. Y., & Wang, J. D. (2005). Comparison of WHOQOL BREF and SF 36 in patients with HIV infection. *Quality of Life Research: An International Journal of Quality of Life Aspects of Treatment, Care and Rehabilitation, 14*(1), 141–150.

Huang, I. C., Wu, A. W., & Frangakis, C. (2006). Do the SF-36 and WHOQOL BREF measure the same constructs? Evidence from the Taiwan population. *Quality of Life Research: An International Journal of Quality of Life Aspects of Treatment, Care and Rehabilitation, 15*(1), 15–24.

Hughes, C., Hwang, B., Kim, J., Eisenman, L. T., & Killian, D. J. (1995). Quality of life in applied research: A review and analysis of empirical measures. *American Journal on Mental Retardation, 99*, 623–636.

Hunt, S. M., McKenna, S. P., McEwan, J., Williams, J. & Papp, E. (1981). The Nottingham Health Profile: Subjective health status and medical consultations. *Social Science Medicine, 15*(A), 221–229.

Hyland ME. (1999). A reformulation of quality of life for medical science. In: Joyce, C. R. B., McGee, H., O'Boyle, C. A., (Eds), *Individual quality of life. Approaches to conceptualisation and assessment*. Amsterdam, Harwood Academic Publishers.

Izutsu, T., Tsutsumi, A., Islam, M. A., Matsuo, Y., Yamada, H. S., Kurita, H., & Wakai, S. (2005). Validity and reliability of the Bangla version of WHOQOL BREF on an adolescent population in Bangladesh. *Quality of Life Research: An International Journal of Quality of Life Aspects of Treatment, Care and Rehabilitation, 14*(7), 1783–1789.

Jacobson, A., Barofsky, I., Cleary, P., & Rand, L. (1988) Reliability and validity of a diabetes quality-of-life measure for the diabetes control and complications trial (DCCT). *Diabetes Care 11*, 725–732.

Jacoby, A. (1992). Epilepsy and the quality of everyday life: Findings from a study of people with well-controlled epilepsy. *Social Science and Medicine, 34*, 657–666.

Jacoby, A. (2000). Theoretical and methodological issues in measuring quality of life. In: G.A. Baker and A. Jacoby (Eds.), *Quality of life in epilepsy: Beyond seizure counts in assessment and treatment* (pp. 43–64). London: Harwood Academic Publishers.

Jalowiec, A. (1990). Issues in using multiple measures of quality of life. *Seminars in Oncology Nursing, 6*, 271–277.

Jaracz, K., Kalfoss, M., Gorna, K., & Baczyk, G. (2006). Quality of life in Polish respondents: Psychometric properties of the Polish WHOQOL BREF. *Scandinavian Journal of Caring Sciences, 20*(3), 251–260.

Jenkins, C. D. (1992). Assessment of outcomes of health intervention. *Social Science and Medicine, 35*, 367–375.

Johnson, K. L., Amtmann, D., Yorkston, K., Klasner, E. R., & Kuehn, C. M. (2004). Medical, psychological, social, and programmatic barriers to employment for people with multiple sclerosis. *Journal of Rehabilitation, 70*, 38–49.

Kaplan, R. (1990). Behavior as the central outcome in health care. *American Psychologist, 45,* 1211–1221.

Kaplan, R. M., & Bush, J. W. (1982). Health-related quality of life measurement for evaluation research and policy analysis. *Health Psychology, 1*, 621–680.

Karnofsky, D. A., & Burchenal, J. H. (1949). The clinical evaluation of chemotherapeutic agents in cancer. In C. M. MacLeod (Ed.), *Evaluation of chemotherapeutic agents.* Columbia University Press.

Kazdin, A. E. (1993). Evaluation in clinical practice: Clinically sensitive and systematic methods of treatment delivery. *Behavior Therapy, 24*, 11–45.

Kinney, M. R. (1995). Quality of life research: Rigor or rigor mortis? *Cardiovascular Nursing, 31*, 25–28.

Leplege, A., & Ecosse, E. (2000). Methodological issues in using the Rasch model to select cross culturally equivalent items in order to develop a quality of life index: The analysis of four WHOQOL-100 data sets (Argentina, France, Hong Kong, United Kingdom). *Journal of Applied Measurement, 1*(4), 372–392.

Mahoney, F. I., & Barthel, D. (1965). Functional evaluation: The Barthel Index. *Maryland State Medical Journal, 14*, 56–61.

Mason, V. L., Skevington, S. M., & Osborn, M. (2004). Development of a pain and discomfort module for use with the WHOQOL-100, *Quality of Life Research, 13*, 1139–1152.

Matheson, L., Kaskutas, V., McCowan, S., Shaw, H., & Webb, C. (2001). Development of a database of functional assessment measures related to work disability. *Journal of Occupational Rehabilitation, 11*, 177–199.

McGee, H., O'Boyle, C.A., Hickey, A., O'Malley, K., & Joyce, C. R. B. (1991). Assessing the quality of life of the individual: The SEIQoL in a healthy and gastroenterology unit population. *Psychological Medicine, 21,* 749–759.

McSweeny, A. J., & Creer, T. L. (1995). Health related quality of life assessment in medical care. *Disease-a-Month, 41*(1), 1–72.

Michalos A. C., & Zumbo B. D. (2003). Leisure activities, health and the quality of life. In A.C. Michalos, (Ed.) *Essays on the Quality of Life* (Vol. 19, pp. 217–238). Boston, MA: Kluwer Academic Publishers.

Miller, J. F. (1992). *Coping with chronic illness: Overcoming powerlessness* (2nd ed.). Philadelphia: FA Davis.

Min, S. K., Kim, K. I., Lee, C. I., Jung, Y. G., Suh, S. Y., & Kim, D. K. (2002). Development of the Korean versions of WHO Quality of Life scale and WHOQOL BREF. *Quality of Life Research: An International Journal of Quality of Life Aspects of Treatment, Care and Rehabilitation, 11*(6), 593–600.

Mohide E. A., Archibald S. D., Tew M., Young J. E., & Haines T. (1992) Post-laryngectomy quality-of-life dimensions identified by patients and health care professionals. *American Journal of Surgery 164*, 619–622.

Naumann, V. J., & Byrne, G. J. A. (2004). WHOQOL BREF as a measure of quality of life in older patients with depression. *International Psychogeriatrics, 16*(2), 159–173.

Nilsson, J., Parker, M. G., & Nahar Kabir, Z. (2004). Assessing health-related quality of life among older people in rural Bangladesh. *Journal of Transcultural Nursing, 15*(4), 298–307.

Noerholm, V., Groenvold, M., Watt, T., Bjorner, J. B., Rasmussen, M. A., & Bech, P. (2004). Quality of life in the Danish general population – Normative data and validity of WHOQOL BREF using Rasch and item response theory models. *Quality of Life Research: An International Journal of Quality of Life Aspects of Treatment, Care and Rehabilitation, 13*(2), 531–540.

Noerholm, V., & Bech, P. (2001). The WHO Quality of Life (WHOQOL) questionnaire: Danish validation study. *Nordic Journal of Psychiatry, 55*(4), 229–235.

O'Boyle, C.A. (1997). *Measuring the quality of later life. Philosophical Transactions: Biological Sciences, 352,* 1871–1879.

O'Boyle, C. A., McGee, H., Hickey, A., O'Malley, K., Joyce, C. R. B. (1992). Individual quality of life in patients undergoing hip replacement. *The Lancet, 339,* 1088–1091.

O'Carroll, R. E., Smith, K., Couston, M., Cossar, J. A., & Hayes, P. C. (2000). A comparison of the WHOQOL-100 and the WHOQOL BREF in detecting change in quality of life following liver transplantation. *Quality of Life Research: An International Journal of Quality of Life Aspects of Treatment, Care and Rehabilitation, 9*(1), 121–124.

Padilla, G. V., Grant, M. M., & Ferrell, B. (1992). Nursing research into quality of life. *Quality of Life Research, 1,* 341–348.

Parker, R. M., & Bolton, B. (2005). Psychological assessment in rehabilitation practice. In R. M. Parker, E. M. Szymanski, & J. B. Patterson (Eds.), *Rehabilitation counseling: Basics and beyond* (4th ed., pp. 307–334). Austin, TX: PRO-ED.

Patrick, D. L., & Erickson, P. (1993). *Health status and health policy: Quality of life in health care evaluation and resource allocation.* New York: Oxford University Press.

Pearlman R. A., & Uhlmann R. F. (1988) Quality of life in chronic diseases: perceptions of elderly patients. *Journal of Gerontology 43*, M25–M30.

Petersen, C., Schmidt, S., Power, M., & Bullinger, M. (2005). Development and pilot-testing of a health-related quality of life chronic generic module for children and adolescents with chronic health conditions: A European perspective. *Quality of Life Research, 14*(4),1065–1077.

Peterson, S., & Bredow, T. S. (2004). *Middle range theories: Application to nursing research.* Baltimore: Lippincott, Williams, & Wilkins.

Power, M., Quinn, K., & Schmidt, S. (2005). Development of the WHOQOL old module. *Quality of Life Research: An International Journal of Quality of Life Aspects of Treatment, Care and Rehabilitation, 14*(10), 2197–2214.

Ruggeri, M., Bisoffi, G., Fontecedro, L., & Warner, R. (2001). Subjective and objective dimensions of quality of life in psychiatric patients: A factor analytical approach. *The British Journal of Psychiatry, 178*, 268–275.

Ruta, D. A., Garratt, A. M., Leng, M., Russell, T., & Macdonald, L. M. (1994). A new approach to the measurement of quality of life: the Patient Generated Index. *Medical Care, 32*, 1109–1126.

Saxena, S., & Van Ommeren, M. (2005). World Health Organization instruments for quality of life measurement in health settings. In K. Kempf-Leonard (Ed.), *Encyclopedia of social measurement* (Vol. 3, pp. 975–980). San Diego: Academic Press.

Schalock, R., Keith, K., Hoffman, K., & Karan, O. (1989). Quality of life: Its measurement and use. *Mental Retardation, 27*, 25–31.

Schipper, H., Clinch, J. J., & Olweny, C. L. M. (1996). Quality of life studies: Definitions and conceptual issues. In B. Spilker (Ed.), *Quality of life and pharmacoeconomics in clinical trials*, (2nd ed., pp. 11–23). New York: Lippincott-Raven.

Sirgy, M. J., Michalos, A. C., Ferriss, A. L., Easterlin, R. A., Patrick, D., & Pavot, W. (2006). The quality of life (QOL) research movement: Past, present, and future. *Social Indicators Research, 76*, 343–466.

Skevington, S. M. (2002). Advancing cross-cultural research on quality of life: Observations drawn from the WHOQOL development. *Quality of Life Research, 11*, 135–144.

Skevington, S. M., Lotfy, M., & O'Connell, K. A. (2004). The World Health Organization's WHOQOL BREF quality of life assessment: Psychometric properties and results of the international field trial. A report from the WHOQOL group. *Quality of Life Research: An International Journal of Quality of Life Aspects of Treatment, Care and Rehabilitation, 13*(2), 299–310.

Slevin M. L., Plant H., Lynch D., Drinkwater J., & Gregory W. M. (1988). Who should measure quality of life, the doctor or the patient? *British Journal of Cancer, 57*, 109–112.

Spilker, B. (1996). Introduction. In B. Spilker (Ed.), *Quality of life and pharmacoeconomics in clinical trials* (2nd ed., pp. 1–10). New York: Lippincott-Raven.

Sprangers, M. A. G., and Aaronson, N. K. (1992). The role of health care providers and significant others in evaluating the quality of life of patients with chronic disease: A review. *Journal of Clinical Epidemiology, 45*, 743–760.

Taillefer, M. C., Dupuis, G., Roberge, M. A., & LeMay, S. (2003). Health-related quality of life models: Systematic review of the literature. *Social Indicators Research, 64*, 293–323.

Taylor, W. J., Myers, J., Simpson, R., McPherson, K. M., & Wwatherall, M. (2004). Quality of life of people with rheumatoid arthritis as measured by the World Health Organization Quality of Life instrument, short form (WHOQOL BREF): Score distributions and psychometric properties. *Arthritis & Rheumatism: Arthritis Care & Research, 51*(3), 350–357.

Thunedborg, K., Allerup, P., Bech, P., & Joyce, C. R. B. (1993). Development of the repertory grid for measurement of individual quality of life in clinical trials. *International Journal of Methods in Psychiatric Research, 3*, 45–56.

Torrance, G. W. (1987). Utility approach to measuring health-related quality of life. *Journal of Chronic Diseases, 40*, 593–603.

Trompenaars, F. J., Masthoff, E. D., Van Heck, G. L., Hodiamont, P. P., & De Vries, J. (2005). Content validity, construct validity, and reliability of the WHOQOL BREF in a population of Dutch adult psychiatric outpatients. *Quality of Life Research: An International Journal of Quality of Life Aspects of Treatment, Care and Rehabilitation, 14*(1), 151–160.

Tsutsumi, A., Izutsu, T., Kato, S., Islam, M. A., Yamada, H. S., & Hiroshi, W. S. (2006). Reliability and validity of the Bangla version of the WHOQOL BREF in an adult population in Dhaka, Bangladesh. *Psychiatry and Clinical Neurosciences, 60*(4), 493–498.

Van den Bos, G. A. M., & Triemstra, A. H. M. (1999). Quality of life as an instrument for need assessment and outcome assessment of health care in chronic patients. *Quality in Health Care, 8*, 247–252.

Vogels, T., Verrips, G. H., Verloove-Vanhorick. S. P., Fekkes, M., Kamphuis, R. P., Koopman, H. M., Theunissen, N. C., & Wit, J. M. (1998). Measuring health-related quality of life in children: The development of the TACQOL parent form. *Quality of Life Research, 7*, 457–465.

Von Steinburchel, N., Lischetzke, T., Gurny, M., & Eid, M. (2006). Assessing quality of life in older people: Psychometric properties of the WHOQOL BREF. *European Journal of Ageing, 3*(2), 116–122.

Wang, W. C., Yao, G., Tsai, Y. J., Wang, J. D., & Hsieh, C. L. (2006). Validating, improving reliability, and estimating correlation of the four subscales in the WHOQOL BREF using multidimensional Rasch analysis. *Quality of Life Research: An International Journal of Quality of Life Aspects of Treatment, Care and Rehabilitation, 15*(4), 607–620.

Ware, J. E., Jr., & Sherbourne, C. D. (1992). The MOS 36-Item-Short Form Health Survey (SF-36). 1. Conceptual framework and item selection. *Medical Care, 30*, 473–483.

Warner, R. (1999) The emics and etics of quality of life assessment. *Social Psychiatry and Psychiatric Epidemiology , 34*, 117–121

WHOQOL Group (1993). Study protocol for the World Health Organization project to develop a Quality of Life assessment instrument (the WHOQOL). *Quality of Life Research 2*, 153–159.

WHOQOL Group (1994). The development of the WHO quality of life assessment instruments (the WHOQOL) (pp. 41–57). In J. Orley & W. Kuyken (Eds.), *Quality of life assessment: International perspectives*. Berlin: Springer-Verlag.

WHOQOL Group (1998). Development of the World Health Organization WHOQOL-BREF Quality of Life assessment. *Psychological Medicine 28*, 551–558.

Winkler, I., Matschinger, H., & Angermeyer, M. C. (2006). The WHOQOL OLD: A questionnaire for intellectual measuring of quality of life in the eldery. *Psychotherapie Psychchosomatik Medizinische Psychologie, 56*(2), 63–69.

World Health Organization. (1947). *Constitution of the World Health Organization*. New York: Author.

World Health Organization. (1980) *International classification of impairments, disabilities and handicaps*. Geneva: Author.

World Health Organization. (1984). *Uses of epidemiology in aging: Report of a scientific group, 1983*. Technical Report Series, no. 706. Geneva: Author.

World Health Organization. (2007). Retrieved December 15, 2007, from http://www.who.int/classifications/icf/site/icftemplate

Yao, G., & Wu, C. H. (2005). Factorial invariance of the WHOQOL BREF among disease groups. *Quality of Life Research: An International Journal of Quality of Life Aspects of Treatment, Care and Rehabilitation, 14*(8), 1881–1888.

Zhang, S. Y., Li, C. B., & Wu, W. Y. (2005). Reliability and validity of the WHOQOL BREF in patients with generalized anxiety disorder. *Chinese Journal of Clinical Psychology, 13*(1), 37–39.

Assessment of Occupational Functioning

Ev Innes
Lynda R. Matthews
University of Sydney

Kurt L. Johnson
University of Washington, Seattle

OVERVIEW

This chapter presents an overview of the types of evaluations used to assess occupational functioning in adults. Definitions and models relevant to occupational functioning are provided, and the hierarchical nature of the assessments is presented. Historical developments in the assessment of occupational functioning are explored, and specific examples of functional capacity evaluations and situational assessments are provided. A number of critical issues relevant to the accurate assessment of occupational functioning (e.g., lack of published research on reliability and validity) are examined along with the implications for conducting accurate assessments.

LEARNING OBJECTIVES
By the end of the chapter, readers should be able to:

■ Explain the value and contribution of an assessment of occupational performance to quality rehabilitation and health outcomes

■ Distinguish among the definitions of, and models related to, occupational performance and work functioning

■ Analyze the different types of assessments that comprise standardized and nonstandardized work-related assessments

■ Evaluate the major assessment measures used to assess occupational functioning and their advantages and limitations

INTRODUCTION

If people are unable to work as the result of an injury, illness, or disease, the impact on individuals, their families, employers, coworkers, and society can be profound. One example of this impact is the high cost of workers' compensation and occupational rehabilitation/disability management in industrialized countries. This increased focus on disability management has stimulated efforts to develop appropriate and effective assessment and rehabilitation approaches in order to facilitate a safe, speedy, and durable return to work for affected individuals.

Quality outcomes in occupational or vocational rehabilitation/disability management rely on the accurate and reliable assessment of a person's occupational functioning. Assessment is an essential part of a comprehensive approach to occupational rehabilitation (Innes & Straker, 1998a). Assessment results are used to help determine the need for rehabilitation services and program objectives, assist in return-to-work initiatives, assess the work environment, and to match it with an individual's abilities and limitations for work (National Occupational Health & Safety Commission, 1995).

IMPORTANCE OF OCCUPATIONAL FUNCTIONING TO REHABILITATION AND HEALTH

Definitions and Theories of Occupational Functioning

The term *occupational functioning* refers to one's ability to perform in a work context at an acceptable level. Work may be paid or unpaid. The level of expected performance is dependent on multiple factors, including societal expectations, environmental conditions and constraints, specific job and productivity requirements, and individual capacity. If a person sustains an injury or illness, or has a congenital or preexisting condition, then his/her occupational functioning may be compromised, and vocational or occupational rehabilitation may be required to assist the individual in achieving a high quality vocational outcome.

An accurate and reliable assessment of a person's occupational functioning is vital to a successful rehabilitation outcome. In most vocational and occupation-al rehabilitation systems, a successful rehabilitation outcome is benchmarked as a durable return to work. The social, psychological, physical, and economic advantages of a successful rehabilitation outcome for both individual and society cannot be understated because there is a strong relationship between work and health. Work provides a way for people to acquire income, define themselves, and improve their quality of life (Martella & Maass, 2000). Longitudinal studies have shown that people who work have lower levels of chronic illness and disability (Arber, 1996). They have lower mortality rates than average, especially for deaths from cardiovascular disease, lung cancer, accidents, and suicide in all social classes (Moser, Goldblatt, Fox, & Jones, 1987). People who work also experience better psychological health than those who are not working, including less anxiety and depression (Mathers & Schofield, 1998; Matthews & Hawkins, 1995). For people with mental illness, work is seen as part of their personal sense of recovery (Provencher, Gregg, Mead, & Mueser, 2002). Work promotes self-esteem and self-confidence (Jin, Shah, & Svoboda, 1997), reduces social isolation and poverty, and contributes to ongoing financial security (Marrone & Golowka, 1999).

Despite the overall benefits to health, work also can be hazardous to workers' health. In the United States, approximately 4,214,200 workplace injuries and illnesses occurred in private industry in 2005, resulting in 1,234,700 days away from work (U.S. Department of Labor, 2005). A number of different working conditions are associated with poor health, including job insecurity, underemployment, unsafe working conditions, job pace, control, and stress (Brunner, Chandola, & Marmot, 2007; Kinnunen, Feldt, Kinnunen, Kaprio, & Pulkkinen, 2006).

Therefore, credible and dependable assessments of occupational functioning facilitate earlier return-to-work (Gross & Battié, 2005; Gross, Battié, & Asante, 2006) and determine a worker's individual ability to fulfill a particular proposed job or worker role and to adapt to the work conditions that accompany it (Oesch, Kool, Bachmann, & Devereux, 2006). Comprehensive interdisciplinary assessments help ensure that all aspects of an individual's work-related potential are evaluated (see Table 28.1). Assessment of some of these qualities is reviewed in this chapter and others in this text.

The need for comprehensive assessments stems from the specific purposes and expected outputs of

TABLE 28.1 Factors to be Considered in an Assessment of Occupational Function

Factors	Description
Physical demands of the job	A careful analysis of the physical demands of the specific job or class of jobs targeted must be performed. It is important to identify critical but infrequent requirements.
Skill demands of the job	The skills requirements of the job must be carefully analyzed. This will include cognitive as well as manipulative skills and may often require direct observation and interviews with workers and supervisors.
Psychosocial demands of the job/workplace	The psychosocial demands in the workplace include the variables such as working alone or on a team, level of supervision, normative cultural expectations with respect to socializing on and off the job, etc.
Physical capacity of the worker	The physical capacity of the worker is evaluated as described in this chapter using a variety of techniques. This includes the capacity not only for lifting, stooping, reaching, etc., but also for exertion in general with consideration of patterns of fatigue. It is also important to predict potential improvement or deterioration in physical capacity.
Psychosocial functioning of the worker	Psychosocial functioning includes attention to personal style, tolerance for feedback and supervision, tolerance for varied stimulus conditions, features related to anxiety, depression, or posttraumatic stress that may have an impact on cognition or other performance and/or may require accommodation.
Cognitive functioning of the worker	A careful review of the cognitive status of the worker with respect to working memory, attention, divided attention, learning, audio processing, etc. is critical if there is any indication of cognitive compromise. This may also be useful if there is historical evidence of learning difficulties that were adequately compensated before the current disability that may become barriers in combination with the current condition.
Environmental facilitators/barriers to employment	These include a range of factors from interior and exterior temperature; weather conditions such as persistent heavy rain, snow, or ice; natural terrain such as straight on or lateral grades; and the built environment.
Systems facilitators/barriers to employment	Systems issues that facilitate or serve as barriers may include the presence or lack of health care coverage for the injured worker that is not contingent on disability status; predictability of wage replacements; the support the worker perceives for his or her efforts from the occupational rehabilitation/worker's compensation system; the qualifications or lack of qualifications of providers; and labor market variables.
Requirements for reconditioning	It will be useful to provide an assessment of the time and course of reconditioning necessary. Reconditioning is not "work hardening," but rather is a systematic process of improving fitness and is often done in a mainstream setting such as a gym or health club under the supervision of a health care professional familiar with the particular disability.
Requirements for vocational rehabilitation	The synthesis of the variables described above along with conclusions with respect to the conditions necessary for successful transition to employment should be formulated. These may include the kinds of accommodations necessary to permit the worker to participate in employment.

work-related assessments (Innes & Straker, 1998a), which include:

1. Diagnosing, determining the need for intervention and treatment, and planning treatment (e.g. return-to-work programs)
2. Determining an individual's ability to perform the roles, activities, tasks, and physical demands required for work
3. Determining sincerity and consistency of effort during assessment
4. Documenting outcome, achievement of goals and progress, and/or evaluating the intervention program,
5. Determining the level of impairment or disability
6. Developing and improving treatment resources for service provision and research

There are a number of different types of assessments used to achieve these goals. The following terms and definitions of work-related assessments can be considered as hierarchical, with the each term encompassing those following it.

VOCATIONAL ASSESSMENT   A vocational assessment uses "… multiple measures to determine an individual's ability to fulfill the worker role and identify the most appropriate occupational category, through an examination of physical, cognitive, and psychosocial abilities. It is usually a compilation of information provided by a multidisciplinary team, which may include an occupational therapist, physiotherapist, psychologist, and/or rehabilitation counselor. The measures used may include work-related assessments as well as psychometric tests and interest inventories" (Innes & Straker, 1998b, p.195). Further information about vocational assessments, vocational interests and aptitudes, and work adjustments can be found in chapters 19 and 20 of this edition and therefore will not be addressed in this chapter.

WORK-RELATED ASSESSMENT   A work-related assessment uses "… multiple measures to determine an individual's ability to perform the work requirements of specific job tasks or activities, an entire job, group of jobs (i.e., occupational category or group), or broadly defined work demands (e.g., sedentary, light, medium, heavy, very heavy)" (Innes & Straker, 1998b, p.195).

FUNCTIONAL CAPACITY EVALUATION (FCE)   An FCE is "… a one-time evaluation, using measures to determine maximal performance of physical demands and skills, including sitting, standing and walking tolerances, lifting, carrying, pushing, pulling, kneeling, stooping/bending, crouching/squatting, crawling, climbing, reaching, and manual dexterity" (Innes & Straker, 1998b, pp.194–195). Some FCEs may incorporate assessments of cognitive and/or psychosocial functioning. FCEs can be considered to have two distinct forms. These are described as follows.

FUNCTIONAL CAPACITY EVALUATION (NO JOB) (FCENJ)   Assessments of this type are "focused on an individual worker performing physical demands related to work in general rather than to a specific job or duties. Results [are] considered generalisable to general work demands or occupational categories, but not to specific jobs. … [FCENJs are] performed to determine the worker's ability to safely perform general physical demands and skills related to work, rather than a specific job …

[FCENJs are] also used to identify further rehabilitation, training and/or education options for the worker" (Innes & Straker, 2002b, pp.56–57).

FUNCTIONAL CAPACITY EVALUATION (JOB) (FCEJ)   Assessments of this type are "focused on an individual worker performing specific tasks within a specific workplace with an identified employer. Results [are] considered not generalisable to other tasks or workplaces …. [FCEJs are] primarily conducted to determine the worker's suitability to return to work and develop an appropriate rehabilitation plan, either in the form of a Return to Work (RTW) plan or a clinic-based work conditioning/hardening program" (Innes & Straker, 2002b, p.57).

Applicable International Classification of Functioning, Disability, and Health Aspects

Although occupational functioning can be affected by difficulties in any area, the World Health Organization's *International Classification of Functioning* (WHO ICF), places particular emphasis on activity limitations that may result in participation restrictions and on the impact that the environment and personal factors have on function. For example, personal factors, such as educational level, age, gender, self-efficacy, coping style, and self-esteem have an impact on occupational functioning for people with chronic low back pain (Kuijer et al., 2006; Slebus, Sluiter, Kuijer, Willems, & Frings-Dresen, 2007). Cognitive factors, such as poor insight regarding illness, short-term memory deficits, and poor time management, may limit employment for people with severe and persistent stress and mental health conditions (Lysaker, Bryson, & Bell, 2002; Matthews, 2005). Environmental factors, such as workplace design and layout, and equipment used, can facilitate or impair participation at work. Workplace culture also can be critical to participation, with poor organizational structure (e.g., lack of clear expectations about job tasks or policies and inadequate performance feedback) found to significantly predict work potential in people with persistent posttraumatic stress (Matthews, 2006). For these and other reasons, assessing the workplace environment and the actual job to be performed are considered essential before any return-to-work programs are designed and implemented. The degree of match between an individual's capacity for work and the actual workplace and job demands also should be assessed (Gibson, Allen, & Strong, 2002; Innes, 1997b).

Assessments of occupational functioning usually focus on a person's capacity to perform a range of work-related demands, with particular emphasis on activity

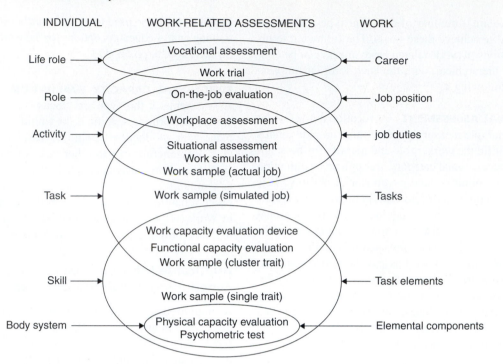

FIGURE 28.1 Work-related assessments relevant to individual performance and work levels

Source: From "Understanding Work in Society" by D. O'Halloran and E. Innes (2005) in G. Whiteford and V. Wright-St. Clair (Eds.) *Occupation and Practice in Context* (pp. 299–316). © 2005, Sydney: Elsevier.

limitations (Gibson & Strong, 2003). However, physicians specializing in treating injured workers tend to consider the ICF's "body function and structures" and "participation" components more frequently than other components (Slebus et al., 2007). Occupational functioning needs to consider all ICF components. The instruments used will vary depending on the purpose of the assessment.

Figure 28.1 illustrates the hierarchical nature of the various types of assessments used to determine occupational functioning (Innes & Straker, 1998b). They are also related to the individual level of functioning and the job level. This can be associated with the ICF levels of body structure and function, activity (incorporates activity/job duties, task/task, and skill/task elements levels) and participation (role/job position).

Another assessment hierarchy has been proposed (Gaudino, Matheson, & Mael, 2001; Matheson, Gaudino, Mael, & Hesse, 2000) and similarly considers body structure impairments, activity limitations, and participation restrictions with regard to work (Table 28.2). Both hierarchies reflect the need to consider the various components of the ICF when assessing occupational functioning.

HISTORY OF RESEARCH AND PRACTICE IN THE ASSESSMENT OF OCCUPATIONAL FUNCTIONING

Work-related assessments have been around in varying forms for more than 60 years. Standardized screening tests for employment were developed during the late 1800s and early 1900s. Hugo Munsterberg developed the first work sample, a simulated trolley car, to select potential conductors (Brolin, 1984). Various other screening tests and work samples were developed in the 1930s (e.g., Testing Orientation and Work Evaluation in Rehabilitation (TOWER); Minnesota Rate of Manipulation Test, Drussell, 1959) and continued into the 1940s (e.g., Purdue Pegboard) and 1950s (e.g., Crawford Small Parts Dexterity Test, Crawford & Crawford, 1956; Hand-Tool Dexterity Test). Valpar Component Work Samples were developed in the 1970s. Many of these screening tests and work samples continue to be used. They now often are incorporated into functional capacity evaluation systems or used as stand-alone assessments in rehabilitation to estimate people's capacity to work or return to work following injury or illness. Other tests (e.g., Jamar dynamometer for grip

TABLE 28.2 Units of Analysis Hierarchy (Gaudino et al., 2001)

Functional Assessment Unit of Analysis	Usual Effect on Person	Case Example
Component Structure—Integrity of person structures	Structural impairment	Lumbar disc herniation with nerve impingement
Component Function—Integrity of person functions	Functional impairment	Trunk strength; lower extremity stability
Actions—Ability to perform observable behaviors that are recognizable	Functional limitation	Sitting; standing; changing body position; stooping, kneeling and crouching; ambulating; climbing
Simple Tasks—Ability to perform combinations of actions sharing a common purpose recognized by the performer		Lifting and lowering objects; manipulating objects; carrying objects
Vocational Complex Tasks—Ability to perform combinations of tasks sharing a common purpose recognized by all employers	Vocational nonfeasibility	Attending daily and on time; remaining at the work station for the work day; adhering to safety rules
Occupational Complex Tasks—Ability to perform combinations of tasks sharing a common purpose recognized by the worker	Occupational disability	Repairing and maintaining mechanical equipment; operating vehicles, mechanized devices, or equipment; inspecting equipment, structures, or materials

strength, Bechtol, 1954) also are used extensively to determine injured workers' capacities to return to or enter work.

One of the earliest functional capacity evaluations (FCEs), the Physical Capacities Evaluation, was developed at Woodrow Wilson Rehabilitation Center (Reuss, Rawe, & Sundquist, 1958). Since then, a range of commercially available and/or published FCEs used to estimate a person's capacity to perform the physical demands of work have been developed. Most are based on the U.S. Department of Labor's (1991) historic classification of jobs with respect to various characteristics required of workers, including physical demands. There were significant concerns about the accuracy of these classifications and the U.S. Department of Labor has not maintained this job classification for many years. Many FCEs were developed and commercialized in the 1980s. Some continue to be used, others have been further developed and renamed, and some have fallen out of favor. New FCEs continue to be made commercially available indicating no one perfect or "gold standard" system meets the requirements of all users.

Assessments that focus solely on physical work demands are problematic because there is no evidence that work performance is predicted by physical performance alone (Innes & Straker, 1998b). Clinical symptoms and cognitive deficits associated with traumatic stress, anxiety, depression, and other mental health conditions can significantly influence a number of aspects of work performance including work habits and work quality (Drake, Becker, & Bond, 2003; Matthews, 1999; Matthews & Chinnery, 2005). In large scale prospective studies, such as Bigos et al. (1991), functional capacity, preemployment imaging, and other physical factors did not predict back pain disability. Rather, the best predictor of back pain was whether the worker felt valued in the workplace. Therefore, work performance assessments need to include personal and interpersonal factors (Kielhofner et al., 1999), and psychosocial, cognitive, and environmental demands in addition to physical requirements (Travis, 2002). A number of studies have identified the attributes (qualitative and quantitative) and criteria (established rules or principles) required for selecting and evaluating work-related assessments (Innes & Straker, 2002a, 2002b, 2003a, 2003b).

CURRENT ASSESSMENT METHODS IN OCCUPATIONAL FUNCTIONING

Current approaches to determining people's capacity for work use various work-related assessments. Depending on the context and regulatory requirements, assessments are workplace or clinic based. In either location, clinicians can use a decision-making process to determine the most appropriate tools. This process has been developed from research that examined the practices and attitudes of clinicians who administer work-related assessments (Innes & Straker, 2002a, 2002b, 2003a, 2003b)

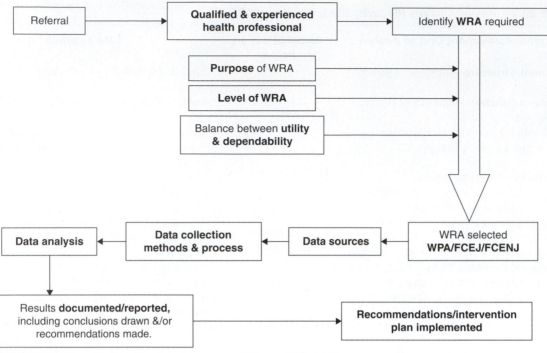

FIGURE 28.2 Process of work-related assessment (Innes, 2001, p.33).

Innes, E. *Factors influencing the excellence of work-related assessments in Australia.* Unpublished doctoral thesis, Curtin University, of Technology, 2001, Perth, W.A. Australia.

(Figure 28.2). Both standardized and non-standardized assessment approaches are used, depending on the purpose and context of the assessment.

Nonstandardized Assessments

Situational assessments and work simulations assess occupational functioning at the activity/duty and task levels (see Figure 28.1). These approaches involve the systematic observation of an individual's work behavior, cognitive and psychosocial responses to work demands, as well as physical capacity in a controlled, usually artificial, work environment (Innes, 1997a). In contrast to workplace-based assessments, situational assessments and work simulations allow for variables to be systematically altered. For example, when used as part of the evaluation for people with acquired brain injuries, persistent mental health conditions, or intellectual disabilities, a situational assessment often occurs within the context of the natural work environment because of concerns about lack of generalization from artificial environments. In some countries this is referred to as a work trial.

Work simulations allow for the assessment of specific work tasks and are used in conjunction with more formal or standardized assessments. Work simulation is relevant when determining a person's capacity to return to a specific job. If possible, the actual tools and materials required for the job task are used. However, similar equipment may be used, especially if modifications are required. For example, a computer workstation and office chair may be modified or adjusted to determine if these contribute to a person's work tolerance.

Nonstandardized assessments, such as work simulations, rely on the observation skills of the clinician conducting the assessment. These types of assessments may have more credibility for the person being evaluated because the activities are designed to assess specific work demands. Therefore, they are particularly suited to determining a person's capacity to return to a specific job with well-defined duties and tasks as occurs in a functional capacity evaluation (job) (FCEJ).

Standardized Assessments

Most commercially available or published work-related assessments are functional capacity evaluations, work capacity evaluation devices, and work samples. These assessment types commonly evaluate performance at the task and/or skill/task element levels. Occasionally actual and simulated job work samples assess at the activity/duty level.

FUNCTIONAL CAPACITY EVALUATIONS (FCES). The physical demands for work described by the U.S. Department of Labor (1991) form the basis of almost all FCE systems. As noted earlier, there were significant limitations in the U.S. Department of Labor analyses of the physical demands of work and the Department has not updated this database. Each system has protocols and subtests for determining (a) working positions (e.g. sitting, standing); (b) manual handling/exertion (e.g., lifting, carrying, pushing, pulling); (c) mobility (e.g., walking, climbing, crawling); (d) other work postures and nonmaterials handling (e.g., stooping/bending, crouching, kneeling, balancing); and (e) upper limb/ hand function and manipulation (e.g., reaching, handling, fingering, feeling). Tests of upper limb and hand function usually use preexisting tests (e.g., Crawford Small Parts Dexterity Test, Hand Tool Test, Minnesota Rate of Manipulation Test/Minnesota Dexterity Test, Purdue Pegboard, and/or Jamar Grip Strength Dynamometer). Other demands (e.g., seeing, hearing, and speaking) are commented on only if difficulties are evident during testing.

Each FCE has its own unique method for estimating a person's capacity for performing this range of physical demands. Therefore, while the components are similar, the results are not interchangeable or comparable. Various studies have demonstrated low correlations between different FCEs that appear to measure the same physical demand (Ijmker, Gerrits, & Reneman, 2003; Rustenburg, Kuijer, & Frings-Dresen, 2004; Schenk, Klipstein, Spillmann, Strøyer, & Laubli, 2006).

Most FCEs also incorporate several self-report measures that allow respondents to report their perceived level of activity limitations and participation restrictions. These vary depending on the person's injury or disability. A wide range of instruments may be used, including the Spinal Function Sort, Hand Function Sort, Disabilities of the Arm Shoulder and Hand, Oswestry Disability Questionnaire, Pain Disability Index, and Roland-Morris Disability Questionnaire.

While many FCEs are available commercially, only a few have evidence of reliability and validity published in peer-reviewed publications. Even for these few, FCEs have been validated only against gross criteria such as "disability/no disability," or, "employed/not employed," or "number of weeks on compensation." None have been effectively validated against criteria such as

predicting successful return to specific jobs. This is not to suggest that those systems that lack published evidence are unreliable or invalid. However, under these conditions, clinicians and researchers lack needed evidence in order to make informed decisions regarding which instruments are most appropriate. The following FCEs are those that currently have published information regarding their reliability and/or validity, or have been used as outcome measures in studies of treatment efficacy.

ERGO-KIT FCE. The Ergo-Kit FCE was developed relatively recently in the Netherlands. It incorporates 55 standardized work-related tasks, including lifting, carrying, and simulation of work-related tasks. The Physical Agility Tester (PAT), a component of the Ergo-Kit FCE, is used to test work postures and movements, handling, and dexterity.

Lifting tests generally have moderate to good test–retest reliability. However, the manipulation tests generally have low reliability (Gouttebarge, Wind, Kuijer, Sluiter, & Frings-Dresen, 2005). Inter-rater reliability generally is moderate to good. Studies of construct and concurrent validity indicate that results are not interchangeable between the Ergo-Kit and other FCEs, and self-reports of lifting capacity should not replace actual testing of lifting capacity (Ijmker et al., 2003; Kuijer, Gerrits, & Reneman, 2004; Rustenburg et al., 2004).

ERGOSCIENCE PHYSICAL WORK PERFORMANCE EVALUATION (PWPE) The Physical Work Performance Evaluation (PWPE) consists of 36 standardized tasks covering six areas: dynamic strength, position tolerance, mobility, balance, endurance, and coordination and fine motor skills (Durand et al., 2004). The PWPE is used in Australia, Canada, Israel, and the United States (Cotton, Schonstein, & Adams, 2006; James, Mackenzie, & Capra, 2006; Lysaght, 2004; Ratzon, Jarus, & Catz, 2007). Test–retest reliability varies for the six assessments, with acceptable levels of reliability for the dynamic strength and position tolerance tests and moderate to low reliability for the mobility tests (Tuckwell, Straker, & Barrett, 2002). This was also the case for inter-rater reliability across the six domains of the PWPE (Durand et al., 2004). The PWPE has been examined for some aspects of concurrent validity, with a moderate correlation between the overall work level recommended and the level of work currently performed (Lechner, Jackson, Roth, & Straaton, 1994).

ISERNHAGEN WORK SYSTEMS (IWS) FCE. The Isernhagen Work Systems (IWS) FCE consists of

20 work-related tests covering weighted tasks, flexibility and positional tasks, static work, ambulation/mobility tasks, and upper limb coordination (Isernhagen, 1988). This test is used widely in Australia, Canada, Europe and the United states (Cotton et al., 2006; Gouttebarge, Wind, Kuijer, & Frings-Dresen, 2004; James et al., 2006; Kaiser, Kersting, Schian, Jacobs, & Kasprowski, 2000; Lysaght, 2004; Reneman et al., 2006). During 2006, the IWS FCE changed its name to the WorkWell FCE v.2. This system places a high importance on the clinician's skill and ability to determine the endpoint of the assessment. The determination is based on biomechanical and physiological signs of effort to determine safe and maximum performance levels, termed a kinesiophysical approach by its developer (Gross & Battié, 2003; Isernhagen, 1995).

The IWS FCE is the most extensively researched FCE. It has well-established test–retest reliability for those with and without back pain, especially the lifting sub-tests (Brouwer et al., 2003; Reneman et al., 2004; Reneman, Bults, Engbers, Mulders, & Göeken, 2001). Intra-rater reliability is also good (Gardener & McKenna, 1999; Gross & Battié, 2002; Reneman, Fokkens, Dijkstra, Geertzen, & Groothoff, 2005; Reneman, Jaegers, Westmaas, & Göeken, 2002). Although originally developed as a 2-day assessment, its use during 1 day is adequate and does not affect reliability adversely (Reneman, Dijkstra, Westmaas, & Göeken, 2002).

The test's validity also has been extensively studied, and the data were found to be weakly linked to a greater likelihood and speedier return to work (Gross & Battié, 2005; Gross, Battié, & Cassidy, 2004; Matheson, Isernhagen, & Hart, 2002). It did not predict recurrence of back injury (Gross & Battié, 2004, 2005). Similar to the findings of other studies, comparison of the IWS FCE with other FCEs indicated that results were not interchangeable (Ijmker et al., 2003; Schenk et al., 2006).

Lifting Assessments

EPIC LIFT CAPACITY TEST.   The EPIC Lift Capacity (ELC) Test (Matheson, Mooney, Grant et al., 1995; Matheson, Mooney, Holmes et al., 1995) has superseded the WEST Standard Evaluation (Matheson, 1986; Ogden-Niemeyer, 1991) as a test of lifting. It tests occasional lifting (1 lift/cycle) and frequent lifting (4 lifts/cycle) over three ranges (waist-to-shoulder, floor-to-waist, floor-to-shoulder), and uses multiple measures to determine safe endpoints for the lifts (biomechanical, psychophysical, and aerobic). Normative data are available for males and females aged 18–60 years. The ELC has good to excellent test–retest and inter-rater reliability (Alpert, Matheson, Beam, & Mooney, 1991; Matheson, Mooney, Grant et al., 1995) and the data are sensitive to treatment effects (Matheson, Mooney, Holmes et al., 1995).

The ELC is incorporated into some broader FCE systems. The California Functional Capacity Protocol (Cal-FCP) incorporates the ELC to determine lifting capacity as well as the Spinal and Hand Function Sorts to determine perceived disability (Matheson, Mooney, Grant, Leggett, & Kenny, 1996; Mooney & Matheson, 1994). The BTE ER incorporates a computerized version of the ELC in its protocol.

PROGRESSIVE ISOINERTIAL LIFTING EVALUATION (PILE).   The PILE (Mayer, Barnes, Kishino et al., 1988; Mayer, Barnes, Nichols et al., 1988; Mayer, Gatchel, Barnes, Mayer, & Mooney, 1990) assesses lifting through two ranges, the lumbar test from floor-to-waist (0 to 76 cm/30 inches) and the cervical test from waist-to-shoulder (76 cm/30 inches to 137 cm/54 inches). The PILE uses endpoints based on psychophysical, aerobic, and safety criteria. Normative data are available for males and females (Mayer, Barnes, Kishino et al., 1988).

The PILE has good to excellent test–retest and inter-rater reliability both for uninjured populations and for those with back and neck pain (Hazard, Reeves, Fenwick, Fleming, & Pope, 1993; Horneij, Holmström, Hemborg, Isberg, & Ekdahl, 2002; Ljungquist, Harms-Ringdahl, Nygren, & Jensen, 1999; Lygren, Dragesund, Joensen, Ask, & Moe-Nilssen, 2005; Mayer, Barnes, Kishino et al., 1988). The sensitivity of the PILE to change in lifting ability following intervention has been demonstrated in a number of studies (Curtis, Mayer, & Gatchel, 1994; Hazard et al., 1989; Ljungquist, Fransson, Harms-Ringdahl, Björnham, & Nygren, 1999; Mayer et al., 1989; Yílmaz et al., 2003).

Work Capacity Evaluation Devices

These devices are computer-linked and capture assessment information. They also can be programmed for work hardening programs where these devices are used to improve conditioning. Work capacity evaluation devices tend to assess at the task and task element levels.

BTE TECHNOLOGIES.   Baltimore Therapeutic Equipment (BTE) has three work capacity evaluation devices—the BTE Work Simulator II, BTE Primus, and BTE ER Functional Testing System.

RESEARCH BOX 28.1

Oesch, P. R., Kool, J. P., Bachmann, S., & Devereux, J. (2006). The influence of a Functional Capacity Evaluation on fitness for work certificates in patients with non-specific chronic low back pain. *Work: A Journal of Prevention, Assessment and Rehabilitation, 26*, 259–271.

Objectives: This study sought to examine the influence of functional testing on decision-making by physicians concerning assessments of medical fitness for work. The authors hypothesized that additional information from the Functional Capacity Evaluation (FCE) would improve the quality of Fitness for Work Certificates (FWC) issued.

Method: Subjects were patients with nonacute nonspecific low back pain ages 20–55 who had used at least 6 weeks of sick leave during the previous 6 months. Patients with any comorbidity were excluded. A randomized controlled trial study design was used in which subjects were randomly assigned to two groups: One received function-centered treatment (FCT); the other received pain-centered treatment (PCT). FCEs for all subjects were performed by a research assistant blinded to groupings. Physicians were not assigned to groups but to hospital wards and were therefore responsible for FWCs for subjects from both groups. The physicians' determination of fitness for work was based on the FCE and medical findings for the FCT group and on medical findings alone for the PCT group.

Results: At baseline, both groups were comparable on a number of work-related variables. Subjects in each group were evenly distributed among the physicians, and ratings of the issued FWCs proved reliable. Quality of the FWCs was significantly better in the FCT group. Information regarding working capacity in previous work differed significantly between the two groups, with the FCT group having significantly more subjects considered fit for previous work either with or without modification.

Conclusion: FCE results improved the quality and information of medical FWCs in patients with chronic low back pain, including the determination of working capacity in relation to the previous work.

Questions

1. Discuss this study's findings in relation to its impact on decision-making regarding disability allowances.
2. What are the legal implications of a fitness for work certificate that does not reflect working capacity?
3. What additional differences to the FWCs do you think a workplace analysis that used direct observation would have made?

The BTE Work Simulator II was the first developed and has static and dynamic modes. A wide range of movements associated with various functional tasks can be simulated using various attachments. It was developed primarily for upper limb assessment and intervention (Curtis & Engalitcheff, 1981). Test–retest reliability for a range of attachments is good to excellent, with the static mode more reliable and accurate than the dynamic mode (Cetinok, Renfro, & Coleman, 1995; Coleman et al., 1996; Fess, 1993a, 1993b; Innes & Straker, 1999a; Kennedy & Bhambhani, 1991; McClure & Flowers, 1992; Trossman & Li, 1989; Trossman, Suleski, & Li, 1990). The results of validity studies vary depending on the attachment used, the population examined, and the comparisons made with the BTE Work Simulator (BTE WS) results (Beaton, Dumont, Mackay, & Richards, 1995; Beaton, O'Driscoll, & Richards, 1995; Bhambhani, Esmail, & Britnell, 1994; Esmail, Bhambhani, & Britnell, 1995; Fraulin, Louie, Zorrilla, & Tilley, 1995; Goldner et al., 1990; Innes & Straker, 1999b; Kennedy & Bhambhani, 1991; Rondinelli et al., 1997; Wilke, Sheldahl, Dougherty, Levandoski, & Tristani, 1993).

The BTE Primus also simulates various movements associated with functional tasks using different attachments. It has isotonic, isometric, and isokinetic modes and has applications for the upper and lower limbs and trunk. As for the BTE WS, the BTE Primus' static testing mode has better test–retest reliability than its dynamic mode (Lee, Chan, & Hui-Chan, 2001a; Shechtman, MacKinnon, & Locklear, 2001).

The BTE ER Functional Testing System, formerly known as the Hanoun Medical Functional Occupational Capacity Unbiased System (FOCUS), incorporates a computerized version of the EPIC Lift Capacity Test and the Functional Range of Motion (FROM) Assembly Test as part of its overall FCE. Very few studies have been published using this device. One study reports good test–retest reliability for the FROM Assembly Test (Matheson, Rogers, Kaskutas, & Dakos, 2002). Research using the EPIC Lift Capacity Test also is relevant to the BTE ER, as a computerized version of the ELC is incorporated into it.

ERGOS WORK SIMULATOR. The ERGOS Work Simulator consists of five test panels that use simulated work tasks to assess strength, body mechanics, cardio-vascular endurance, movement speed, and accuracy. Results are criterion-referenced and use methods–time–measurement industrial standards to interpret a person's performance.

Published reliability studies have examined only panels 1 (lifting—static and dynamic; reliability of computer versus human instructions) (Matheson, Danner, Grant, & Mooney, 1993) and 5 (seated work tolerances and upper limb/hand function) (Boadella, Sluiter, & Frings-Dresen, 2003). Concurrent validity of the ERGOS with other FCE approaches was not demonstrated (Dusik, Menard, Cooke, Fairburn, & Beach, 1993; Rustenburg et al., 2004), indicating that the various systems measure different qualities.

Work Samples

Work samples have four basic types that vary according their degree of correspondence with actual jobs (Jacobs, 1991, 1993). *Actual job samples* have been taken in their entirety from an employment setting and standardized for a testing environment. Their purpose is to evaluate an individual's aptitude while performing that specific job. *Simulated job samples* assess the common critical factors or segments of a job. However, not all salient factors from the job are replicated. *Cluster trait* and *Single trait samples* assess one or more traits inherent to a job or group of jobs (e.g., strength, endurance, range of motion, speed, and dexterity).

Due to their level of job specificity in actual and simulated job samples, they rarely are used in current practice. Cluster trait samples are able to cover a wider range of job types and, therefore, can be used with more people, making them more cost-effective. The advantages of work samples are that they have reasonably high face validity and provide an opportunity to observe work behaviors and physical functioning required in a variety of jobs. Compared to the equipment required for situational assessments and work simulations, work samples often are smaller and more compact. They also tend to have fewer language, cultural, and educational barriers than traditional pen and paper tests because administration can accommodate demonstration and practice.

VALPAR COMPONENT WORK SAMPLES (VCWS) are the most commonly used range of work samples. The more than 20 VCWS use generalized work-like tasks associated with industrial jobs. They are administered in a standardized manner and physical exertion requirements are categorized using the U.S. Department of Labor

criteria (U.S. Department of Labor Employment & Training, 1991). For example, VCWS 19 (Physical Dynamic Capacity) can assess sedentary to very heavy work. All VCWS are criterion-referenced tests using methods–time–measurement to compare performance with industrial standards. However, there is no evidence that these standards represent the level of performance necessary to succeed in everyday jobs. Although the work samples have been used to improve conditioning in the past, their use is rare in current practice. The work samples cited most frequently in the literature are VCWS 4 (Upper Extremity Range of Motion), 8 (Simulated Assembly), 9 (Whole Body Range of Motion), 11 (Eye–Hand–Foot Coordination), 19 (Dynamic Physical Capacities), and 204 (Fine Finger Dexterity).

The original (1974) administration manuals for Valpar Component Work Samples reported test–retest reliability for each work sample; however, these data no longer are included in the revised manuals (Botterbusch, 1987; Christopherson, 1992). Other than information reported by Valpar on their Website regarding data used to establish learning curves for the work samples (Valpar International Corp., 2003), there are no peer-reviewed studies published on reliability for these work samples. Good test–retest (VCWS 4, 9, and 19) and inter-rater reliability (VCWS 19) have been reported in conference proceedings and research theses (Ang, 1999; Barrett, Browne, Lamers, & Steding, 1997; Trevitt, 1997). The test's validity to differentiate between groups (e.g., those who are and are not sick-listed; formwork carpenters versus office workers) has been demonstrated (VCWS 8, 19, 204) (Lee, Chan, & Hui-Chan, 2001b; Schult, Söderback, & Jacobs, 1995, 2000; Söderback & Jacobs, 2000).

RESEARCH CRITICAL TO ISSUES IN ASSESSMENT OF OCCUPATIONAL FUNCTIONING

Published research on the reliability and validity of occupational functioning, particularly FCE systems, generally is meager. This problem is gradually being addressed by researchers and developers. However, many systems continue to be marketed with minimal or no published research supporting their usefulness and dependability. This should be a major concern for those who purchase and use these systems, and there are potential medico-legal implications for their use in legal contexts. There is no evidence to support the use of any FCE systems to predict successful return to work in specific jobs or even job clusters.

Results from various sources (e.g. self-report, clinical observations, measures of performance) can be used to triangulate data to compare for consistency or discrepancy. However, extreme caution should be taken when drawing conclusions about apparent discrepancies between self-reports and actual performance. Self-reports are likley to correspond more closely with workplace performance. Self-reports and functional testing of performance can differ significantly both in healthy individuals and in those with low back pain (Bootes, 2005; Brouwer et al., 2005; Innes & Hardwick, 2006).

Relationships are meager between FCE results and reports of pain and pain-related fear (Hart, Kirk, Howar, & Mongeon, 2007; Reneman, Preuper, Kleen, Geertzen, & Dijkstra, 2007), as well as between FCE results and self-reported lifting capacity and clinical examination by a physician (Brouwer et al., 2005; Kuijer et al., 2004). This suggests that assessing actual physical abilities through an FCE may be necessary to gain an accurate picture of a worker's performance. However, persons with higher functional self-efficacy beliefs have better FCE performance. Thus, strategies for altering these belief systems should also be considered (Asante, Brintnell, & Gross, 2007). The availability of FCE results have also been found to postively influence the quality of fitness for work certificates by physicians for people with chronic low back pain (Oesch et al., 2006) (see Research Box 28.1).

MULTIDISCIPLINARY OR INTERDISCIPLINARY APPROACHES

Work-related assessments use multiple data sources and data collection methods to determine an injured worker's abilities and limitations in relation to work-related criteria (Innes & Straker, 2002b; Travis, 2002). From this definition, the very nature of assessment requires evaluations from a number of work-related areas. It is widespread practice for rehabilitation and health professionals from several disciplines (e.g., medicine, occupational therapy, physiotherapy, psychology, rehabilitation counseling, social work, and speech therapy) to often use a number of models of practice to assess work function and disability (Matheson, Isernhagen, & Hart, 1998). These health professionals contribute their particular knowledge base and skills to work-related assessments and are involved in the provision of specialist rehabilitation case management services to injured individuals (O'Halloran, 2002). Although a number of professionals may contribute to an assessment, some assessment systems require practitioner accreditation or certification, thus requiring appropriate training in the system. For example, in Australia, the regulating workers' compensation body in New South Wales has developed cross-disciplinary competency standards to ensure quality in assessments (Travis, 2002). The standards provide set expectations for professional workplace training, professional education programs, assessing competence of rehabilitation professionals, measuring service quality, and a framework for evidence-based practice (Travis).

In addition to the multidisciplinary nature of work-related assessments, a number of stakeholders also are involved in workplace injury or disability management work. Typical stakeholders include the range of health professionals who use a series of work-related assessments to determine a person's capacity to work or return to work, injured workers, and their employers (Friesen, Yassi, & Cooper, 2001). The quality of communication

---

DISCUSSION BOX 28.1

Assessment of Pain and Work-Related Disability: Three Assessments, Three Different Results?

Information on occupational functioning can be gained from a range of perspectives, such as client self-reports (client perception), clinician observations (clinical perception), and standardized assessment tools (actual performance). These may produce evaluation findings that are inconsistent with each other. For example, when assessing pain-related disability, some researchers suggest that self-report methods overestimate the level of limitation in a person's functioning as a way a client can validate their pain and their need for treatment or time off from work. Many agree that results from clinical examinations, which are based on a professional perspective, personal experiences, and comparisons of the person with others, often underestimate the level of limitations. Others would suggest that standardized assessments such as FCEs are also affected by pain behaviors that result in underestimation of abilities. Self-reports, clinical observations, and standardized assessments are frequently used by clinicians despite the differing results from these types of assessments. Assume you had results from all three types of assessment that were inconsistent with each other. Discuss the aspects of each of the assessments that you would consider in your effort to resolve the differences. On which assessment(s) would you place most emphasis and why?

among stakeholders is critical to successful return-to-work outcomes (Gard & Larsson, 2003; Muenchberger, Kendall, & Mills, 2006). Effective collaborations with and positive influences from rehabilitation and health professionals involved in the rehabilitation process generally leads to better outcomes and greater satisfaction among injured workers (Beaumont, 2003). For this reason, effective communication and collaboration among all rehabilitation and health professionals involved in the provision of work-related assessments should be promoted to minimize the possible negative impact of work-related disability on the individual (Franche, Baril, Shaw, Nicholas, & Loisel, 2005).

NATIONAL/STATE/FEDERAL OR INTERNATIONAL PRACTICES IN THE ASSESSMENT OF OCCUPATIONAL FUNCTIONING

Occupational functioning is best assessed in the actual workplace, if possible. Although workplace assessment is relevant and useful for those who are returning to work or have a specific job or workplace to enter, it is not always possible or practical. For this reason, many clinic-based FCEs and other work-related assessments have been developed. For example, the current practice in Australia is for assessments to occur in the workplace, with subsequent return-to-work programs developed based on these findings. In fact, it is possible to get approval for the implementation of a return-to-work plan only if a workplace assessment has been conducted.

The interaction between the rehabilitation of injured workers and the context within which that rehabilitation occurs may complicate the assessment of functional capacity. Differences in policy and practice both between and within countries may be enormous. For example, Australia offers universal health care. People who are unemployed due to injury or illness are eligible for financial subsidy, thus providing a safety net independent of the status of their rehabilitation. In contrast, within the United States, depending on the individual's health insurance status, the only health coverage available may be for the work-related injury paid by the worker's compensation carrier. Since there is no generally available subsidy, the only available financial support is through wage replacement from workers' compensation benefits. The dependence of the injured worker on the workers' compensation insurance system for financial subsidy and health care may influence the efficacy of early interventions, and the relationship with providers may become adversarial when injured workers are fearful of their financial and health security and/or distrustful of a rehabilitation system.

Summary and Conclusion

Accurate assessments that offer reliable information about an individual's ability to work are central to successful rehabilitation outcomes. They provide a comprehensive picture of an individual's ability to perform the roles, activities, tasks, and physical demands required for work, and inform rehabilitation planning, interventions, and treatments. A number of personal and environmental factors may restrict the participation in and performance of a range of work-related activities. Various types of assessments have been developed that relate to the individual and job levels of functioning. Assessment hierarchies such as those proposed by Gaudino et al. (2001), Innes and Straker (1998b), and Matheson et al. (2000), provide a way to consider occupational assessment in the context of the WHO-ICF framework, that is, limitations to body structure and function, activity and participation.

Contemporary work-related evaluations are either workplace or clinic-based and incorporate both standardized and nonstandardized approaches (e.g., situational assessments, work simulations, FCEs, and work samples). However, where possible, assessments are best undertaken in the workplace. Some assessment systems require professional accreditation or certification by users. Regulations in some countries set standards to ensure consistency and quality in assessments. Substantial differences that exist in policy and practice from country to country may have implications for the way injured workers interact with their rehabilitation environment. Health care professionals are advised to be informed about legal and professional standards that impact their work. Further, the lack of published research on the reliability and validity of some forms of assessment is an issue that rehabilitation and health professionals need to consider when making informed decisions regarding selection of work-related assessments.

Self-Check Questions

1. Define occupational functioning. Explain the ways that an accurate and reliable assessment of a person's occupational functioning contributes to a successful and sustainable rehabilitation outcome.

2. What factors need to be evaluated when assessing occupational functioning? Recall a time when you had an injury or illness that limited your participation in any activity. Which factors were affected, and what changes in the factors would have been required to enable you to participate?

3. List and briefly describe the type of assessments that form the occupational functioning assessment hierarchy.

4. Discuss the advantages of using a combination of nonstandardized and standardized assessments over the use of only one of these in the assessment of occupational functioning.

5. What are the specific purposes of work-related assessments? How do these relate to the wider rehabilitation goals of an individual?

Case Study

Part A

John, age 42, sustained a crush injury while at work. John was repairing a machine at work when another employee inadvertently turned the machine on not knowing that John was working on it. The machine began operating and crushed John's hand. He sustained a crush injury to (R) dominant hand with subsequent amputation of (R) index and middle fingers proximal to the proximal interphalangeal joints and (R) thumb between the metacarpal–phalangeal and interphalangeal joints. Amputated fingers had full thickness burns and were severely crushed. Area of remaining stumps and over the dorsum of the hand received partial thickness burns. The wounds have healed. However, John has hypersensitivity associated with the stumps of his fingers and thumb.

John is a maintenance fitter for a pharmaceutical company. He worked for this company for 7 years. He qualified as a fitter and turner 23 years ago. He is considered to be a good worker, and his employer is keen for him to return. As part of his rehabilitation, John was required to undergo a work-related assessment to determine his ability to return to work. The work tolerances required for a maintenance fitter include (1) using a variety of hand tools, including spanners, pliers, screwdrivers, wrenches, and others for up to 2 hours without a break; (2) lifting up to 15 kilograms unilaterally from floor-to-waist height (e.g., weight of toolbox); (3) using vibrating tools and machinery (e.g., power drill, angle grinder); and (4) working in a variety of positions (e.g., sitting, standing, crouching, kneeling, overhead, and crawling).

QUESTIONS FOR PART A

1. You have received a referral to assess whether John is able to return to his preinjury job as a maintenance fitter. Work through the Process of Work-Related Assessment (Figure 28.2) and determine the following:
   a. What is the purpose of the assessment?
   b. What level(s) of work-related assessments need to be addressed (see Figure 28.1)? Why?
   c. What type(s) of assessment will you select? Why?
   d. What data sources will you need to access?
   e. What data collection methods will you use?

Part B

A workplace assessment was organized to determine John's actual job demands and to assess the work environment. However, while in the workplace, John was visibly anxious and repeatedly stated he was worried that the accident would happen again. Although his level of anxiety was such that he was not able to continue the workplace assessment to evaluate his work capacity, the job requirements and work environment were assessed. This was achieved through observation of coworkers performing the same or similar tasks to John's job; interviewing John, his supervisor and coworkers regarding job requirements; observing the work environment; and obtaining a range of measurements of distances, dimensions, weights, tolerances, and repetitions related to the work environment, tools and equipment used, and job requirements.

Due to John's anxiety, clinic-based standardized and nonstandardized assessments were organized to assess John's capacity to perform the actual tasks and task elements of his job. The assessment components formed an FCEJ that enabled a consideration of John's ability to return to a specific job. Standardized assessments of John's lifting and hand function were conducted. These included the EPIC Lift Capacity Test, VCWS 4 (Upper Extremity Range of Motion), the Hand-Tool Test, and Crawford Small Parts Dexterity Test. Nonstandardized assessments included an assessment of unilateral lifting of his toolbox with varying weights and use of various hand tools on machine components obtained from John's employer. Use of power tools, such as a drill, was also attempted.

These assessments revealed that John was very slow in using hand tools. He attempted to change hand dominance and to use tools in his unaffected nondominant hand. John was very hesitant about using electrical tools. Nondominant hand function was very good and exceeded the industrial standards for the tasks attempted. Hypersensitivity resulted in pain and avoiding the use of a strong gross grip required in some tasks. Bilateral and unilateral lifting capacity was below his preinjury levels yet sufficient for his job requirements.

The assessments undertaken in John's rehabilitation identified that he needed a number of interventions and treatments to assist his return to work: (1) referral to psychologist to help him address his accident-related stress and anxiety, (2) a desensitization program, (3) strengthening and hand function program with particular emphasis on work simulation activities requiring the use of hand tools, and (4) a return-to-work program consisting of alternate duties in the office and store areas initially (i.e., work that does not require the use of hand tools or moving machinery). This program gradually would be upgraded to introduce preinjury duties as John responded to the other intervention strategies.

QUESTIONS FOR PART B

2. How will the information obtained from the Workplace Assessment assist in determining what you will assess and how in the clinic-based assessment component?
3. Explain what each of the standardized and non-standardized components will assess. Why are these aspects relevant and necessary?
4. Explain how the assessment results assisted in determining the focus for treatment and intervention.

References

Alpert, J., Matheson, L., Beam, W., & Mooney, V. (1991). The reliability and validity of two new tests of maximum lifting capacity. *Journal of Occupational Rehabilitation, 1*(1), 13–29.

Ang, N. (1999). *Study on the test-retest reliability of the Valpar Component Work Sample 9 (Whole Body Range of Motion).* Unpublished honours thesis, University of Sydney, Sydney, Australia.

Arber, S. (1996). Integrating nonemployment into research on health inequalities. *International Journal of Health Services, 26*(3), 445–481.

Asante, A. K., Brintnell, E. S., & Gross, D. P. (2007). Functional Self-Efficacy Beliefs Influence Functional Capacity Evaluation. *Journal of Occupational Rehabilitation, 17*(1), 73–82.

Barrett, T., Browne, D., Lamers, M., & Steding, E. (1997). Reliability and validity testing of Valpar 19. In AAOT (Ed.), *Proceedings of the 19th National Conference of the Australian Association of Occupational Therapists* (Vol. 2, pp. 179–183). Perth, WA: AAOT.

Beaton, D. E., Dumont, A., Mackay, M. B., & Richards, R. R. (1995). Steindler and pectoralis major flexorplasty: A comparative analysis. *Journal of Hand Surgery, 20A*(5), 747–756.

Beaton, D. E., O'Driscoll, S. W., & Richards, R. (1995). Grip strength testing using the BTE work simulator and the Jamar dynamometer: A comparative study. *Journal of Hand Surgery, 20A*(2), 293–298.

Beaumont, D. G. (2003). The interaction between general practitioners and occupational health professionals in relation to rehabilitation for work: A Delphi study. *Occupational Medicine, 53,* 249–253.

Bechtol, C. O. (1954). The use of a dynamometer with adjustable handle spacings. *Journal of Bone & Joint Surgery, 36A*(4), 820–824, 832.

Bennett, G.K. (1965). *Bennett Hand-Tool Dexterity Test* (rev. ed.). San Antonio, TX: The Psychological Corporation.

Bhambhani, Y., Esmail, S., & Britnell, S. (1994). The Baltimore Therapeutic Equipment Work Simulator: Biomechanical and physiological norms for three attachments in healthy men. *American Journal of Occupational Therapy, 48*(1), 19–25.

Bigos, S. J., Battié, M. C., Spengler, D. M., Fisher, L. D., Fordyce, W. E., Hansson, T. H., et al. (1991). A prospective study of work perceptions and psychosocial factors affecting the report of back injury. *Spine, 16*(1), 1–6.

Boadella, J. M., Sluiter, J. K., & Frings-Dresen, M. H. W. (2003). Reliability of upper extremity tests measured by the Ergos™ Work Simulator: A pilot study. *Journal of Occupational Rehabilitation, 13*(4), 219–232.

Bootes, M. (2005). *Lifting capacity: A comparison of self-report measures and functional capacity evaluation in healthy young adult males.* Unpublished honours thesis, School of Occupation & Leisure Sciences, Faculty of Health Sciences, University of Sydney, Sydney.

Botterbusch, K. F. (1987). *Vocational assessment and evaluation systems: A comparison.* Menomonie: Materials Development Center, Stout Vocational Rehabilitation Institute, University of Wisconsin–Stout.

Brolin, D. E. (1984). Vocational Assessment. In J. L. Sheppard (Ed.), *Rehabilitation Counselling: Profession and Practice* (pp. 127–169). Lidcombe Australia: Cumberland College of Health Sciences.

Brouwer, S., Dijkstra, P. U., Stewart, R. E., Göeken, L. N. H., Groothoff, J. W., & Geertzen, J. H. B. (2005). Comparing self-report, clinical examination and functional testing in the assessment of work-related limitations in patients with chronic low back pain. *Disability and Rehabilitation, 27*(17), 999–1005.

Brouwer, S., Reneman, M. F., Dijkstra, P. U., Groothoff, J. W., Schellekens, J. M. H., & Göeken, L. N. H. (2003). Test-retest reliability of the Isernhagen Work Systems Functional Capacity Evaluation in patients with chronic low back pain. *Journal of Occupational Rehabilitation, 13*(4), 207–218.

Brunner, E. J., Chandola, T., & Marmot, M. G. (2007). Prospective effect of job strain on general and central obesity in the Whitehall II Study. *American Journal of Epidemiology, 165*(7), 828–837.

Cetinok, E. M., Renfro, R. R., & Coleman, E. F. (1995). A pilot study of the reliability of the dynamic mode of one BTE work simulator. *Journal of Hand Therapy, 8*(3), 199–205.

Christopherson, B. B. (1992). Revisions to Valpar Component Work Sample manuals. *Valpar International Technical Bulletin, 2* (March), 1–8.

Coleman, E. F., Renfro, R. R., Cetinok, E. M., Fess, E. E., Shaar, C. J., & Dunipace, K. R. (1996). Reliability of the manual dynamic mode of the Baltimore Therapeutic Equipment Work Simulator. *Journal of Hand Therapy, 9*(3), 223–237.

Cotton, A., Schonstein, E., & Adams, R. (2006). Use of functional capacity evaluations by rehabilitation providers in NSW. *WORK, 26*(3), 287–295.

Crawford, J. E., & Crawford, D. E. (1956). *Crawford small parts dexterity test* (Rev. ed.). New York: The Psychological Corporation.

Curtis, L., Mayer, T. G., & Gatchel, R. J. (1994). Physical progress and residual impairment quantification after functional restoration. Part III: Isokinetic and isoinertial lifting capacity. *Spine, 19*(4), 401–405.

Curtis, R. M., & Engalitcheff, J. J. (1981). A work simulator for rehabilitating the upper extremity—Preliminary report. *Journal of Hand Surgery, 6A*(5), 499–501.

Drake, R. E., Becker, D. R., & Bond, G. R. (2003). Recent research on vocational rehabilitation for persons with severe mental illness. *Current Opinion in Psychiatry, 16*, 451–455.

Drussell, R. D. (1959). Relationship of Minnesota Rate of Manipulation Test with the industrial work performance of the adult cerebral palsied. *American Journal of Occupational Therapy, 13*(2), 93–96, 105.

Durand, M., Loisel, P., Poitras, S., Mercier, R., Stock, S., & Lemaire, J. (2004). The interrater reliability of a functional capacity evaluation: The Physical Work Performance Evaluation. *Journal of Occupational Rehabilitation, 14*(2), 119–129.

Dusik, L. A., Menard, M. R., Cooke, C., Fairburn, S. M., & Beach, G. N. (1993). Concurrent validity of the ERGOS work simulator versus conventional functional capacity evaluation techniques in a workers' compensation population. *Journal of Occupational Medicine, 35*(8), 759–767.

Esmail, S., Bhambhani, Y., & Britnell, S. (1995). Gender differences in work performance on the Baltimore Therapeutic Equipment Work Simulator. *American Journal of Occupational Therapy, 49*(5), 405–411.

Fess, E. E. (1993a). Correction: Instrument reliability of the BTE Work Simulator: A preliminary study. *Journal of Hand Therapy, 6*(2), 82.

Fess, E. E. (1993b). Instrument reliability of the BTE Work Simulator: A preliminary study [Abstract]. *Journal of Hand Therapy, 6*(1), 59–60.

Franche, R. L., Baril, R., Shaw, W., Nicholas, M., & Loisel, P. (2005). Workplace-based return-to-work interventions: Optimizing the role of stakeholders in implementation and research. *Journal of Occupational Rehabilitation, 15*, 525–542.

Fraulin, F. O., Louie, G., Zorrilla, L., & Tilley, W. (1995). Functional evaluation of the shoulder following latissimus dorsi muscle transfer. *Annals of Plastic Surgery, 35*(4), 349–355.

Friesen, M. N., Yassi, A., & Cooper, J. (2001). Return-to-work: The importance of human interactions and organizational structures. *WORK, 17*(1), 11–22.

Gard, G., & Larsson, A. (2003). Focus on motivation in the work rehabilitation planning process: A qualitative study from the employer's perspective. *Journal of Occupational Rehabilitation, 13*(5), 159–167.

Gardener, L., & McKenna, K. (1999). Reliability of occupational therapists in determining safe, maximal lifting capacity. *Australian Occupational Therapy Journal, 46*(3), 110–119.

Gaudino, E. A., Matheson, L. N., & Mael, F. (2001). Development of the functional assessment taxonomy. *Journal of Occupational Rehabilitation, 11*(3), 155–175.

Gibson, L., Allen, S., & Strong, J. (2002). Re-integration into work. In J. Strong, A. M. Unruh, A. Wright, & G. D. Baxter (Eds.), *Pain: A textbook for therapists* (pp. 267–287). Sydney, Australia: Churchill Livingstone.

Gibson, L., & Strong, J. (2003). A conceptual framework of functional capacity evaluation for occupational therapy in work rehabilitation. *Australian Occupational Therapy Journal, 50*(2), 64–71.

Goldner, R. D., Howson, M. P., Nunley, J. A., Fitch, R. D., Belding, N. R., & Urbaniak, J. R. (1990). One hundred eleven thumb amputations: Replantation vs revision. *Microsurgery, 11*(3), 243–250.

Gouttebarge, V., Wind, H., Kuijer, P. P. F. M., & Frings-Dresen, M. H. W. (2004). Reliability and validity of functional capacity evaluation methods: a systematic review with reference to Blankenship System, Ergos Work Simulation, Ergo-Kit and Isernhagen Work System. *International Archives of Occupational & Environmental Health, 77*, 527–537.

Gouttebarge, V., Wind, H., Kuijer, P. P., Sluiter, J. K., & Frings-Dresen, M. H. (2005). Intra- and interrater reliability of the Ergo-Kit Functional Capacity Evaluation method in adults without musculoskeletal complaints. *Archives of Physical Medicine & Rehabilitation, 86*, 2354–2360.

Gross, D. P., & Battié, M. C. (2002). Reliability of safe maximum lifting determinations of a functional capacity evaluation. *Physical Therapy, 82*(4), 364–371.

Gross, D. P., & Battié, M. C. (2003). Construct validity of a kinesiophysical functional capacity evaluation administered within a worker's compensation environment. *Journal of Occupational Rehabilitation, 13*(4), 287–295.

Gross, D. P., & Battié, M. C. (2004). The prognostic value of functional capacity evaluation in patients with chronic low back pain: Part 2—Sustained recovery. *Spine, 29*(8), 920–924.

Gross, D. P., & Battié, M. C. (2005). Functional capacity evaluation performance does not predict sustained return to work in claimants with chronic back pain. *Journal of Occupational Rehabilitation, 15*(3), 285–294.

Gross, D. P., Battié, M. C., & Asante, A. (2006). Development and validation of a short-form functional capacity evaluation for use in claimants with low back disorders. *Journal of Occupational Rehabilitation, 16*(1), 50–59.

Gross, D. P., Battié, M. C., & Cassidy, J. D. (2004). The prognostic value of functional capacity evaluation in patients with chronic low back pain: Part 1—Timely return to work. *Spine, 29*(8), 914–919.

Hart, D. L., Kirk, M., Howar, J., & Mongeon, S. (2007). Association between clinician-assessed lifting ability and workplace tolerance and patient self-reported pain and disability following work conditioning. *WORK, 28*(2), 111–119.

Hazard, R. G., Fenwick, J. W., Kalisch, S. M., Redmond, J., Reeves, V., Reid, S., et al. (1989). Functional restoration with behavioral support: A one-year prospective study of patients with chronic low-back pain. *Spine, 14*(2), 157–161.

Hazard, R. G., Reeves, V., Fenwick, J. W., Fleming, B. C., & Pope, M. H. (1993). Test–retest variation in lifting capacity and indices of subject effort. *Clinical Biomechanics, 8*, 20–24.

Horneij, E., Holmström, E., Hemborg, B., Isberg, P., & Ekdahl, C. (2002). Inter-rater reliability and between-days repeatability of eight physical performance tests. *Advances in Physiotherapy, 4*(4), 146–160.

Ijmker, S., Gerrits, E. H. J., & Reneman, M. F. (2003). Upper lifting performance of healthy young adults in functional capacity evaluations: A comparison of two protocols. *Journal of Occupational Rehabilitation, 13*(4), 297–305.

Innes, E. (1997a). Work assessment options and the selection of suitable duties: An Australian perspective. *New Zealand Journal of Occupational Therapy, 48*(1), 14–20.

Innes, E. (1997b). Work programmes to enhance motor and neuromusculoskeletal performance components. In J. Pratt & K. Jacobs (Eds.), *Work practice: International perspectives* (pp. 224–244). Oxford, U.K.: Butterworth-Heinemann.

Innes, E. (2001). *Factors influencing the excellence of work-related assessments in Australia.* Unpublished doctoral thesis, Curtin University of Technology, Perth, WA, Australia

Innes, E., & Hardwick, M. (2006, 8–11 October). *Actual versus perceived physical capacity: Implications for disability management and injury prevention.* Paper presented at the third International Forum on Disability Management, Brisbane, QLD, Australia.

Innes, E., & Straker, L. (1998a). A clinician's guide to work-related assessments: 1 - Purposes and problems. *Work, 11*(2), 183–189.

Innes, E., & Straker, L. (1998b). A clinician's guide to work-related assessments: 2 - Design problems. *Work, 11*(2), 191–206.

Innes, E., & Straker, L. (1999a). Reliability of work-related assessments. *Work, 13*(2), 107–124.

Innes, E., & Straker, L. (1999b). Validity of work-related assessments. *Work, 13*(2), 125–152.

Innes, E., & Straker, L. (2002a). Strategies used when conducting work-related assessments. *Work, 19*(2), 149–165.

Innes, E., & Straker, L. (2002b). Workplace assessments and functional capacity evaluations: Current practices of therapists in Australia. *Work, 18*(1), 51–66.

Innes, E., & Straker, L. (2003a). Attributes of excellence in work-related assessments. *Work, 20*(1), 63–76.

Innes, E., & Straker, L. (2003b). Workplace assessments and functional capacity evaluations: Current beliefs of therapists in Australia. *Work, 20*(3), 225–236.

Isernhagen, S. J. (1988). Functional capacity evaluation. In S. J. Isernhagen (Ed.), *Work injury: Management and prevention* (pp. 139–180). Gaithersburg, MD: Aspen.

Isernhagen, S. J. (1995). Contemporary issues in functional capacity evaluation. In S. J. Isernhagen (Ed.), *The comprehensive guide to work injury management* (pp. 410–429). Gaithersburg, MD: Aspen.

Jacobs, K. (1991). *Occupational therapy: Work-related programs and assessments* (2nd ed.). Boston: Little, Brown & Co.

Jacobs, K. (1993). Work assessments and programming. In H. L. Hopkins & H. D. Smith (Eds.), *Willard and Spackman's occupational therapy* (8th ed., pp. 226–248). Philadelphia: J. B. Lippincott.

James, C., Mackenzie, L., & Capra, M. (2006). *Health professionals' attitudes and practices in relation to functional capacity evaluations [Poster].* Paper presented at the 14th World Federation of Occupational Therapists' Congress, Sydney, Australia.

Jin, R. L., Shah, C. P., & Svoboda, T. J. (1997). The impact of unemployment on health: A review of the evidence. *Journal of Public Health Policy, 18*, 275–301.

Kaiser, H., Kersting, M., Schian, H. M., Jacobs, A., & Kasprowski, D. (2000). Value of the Susan Isernhagen Evaluation of Functional Capacity Scale in medical and occupational rehabilitation [Der Stellenwert des EFL-Verfahrens nach Susan Isernhagen in der medizinischen und beruflichen rehabilitation]. *Die Rehabilitation, 39*(5), 297–306.

Kennedy, L. E., & Bhambhani, Y. N. (1991). The Baltimore Therapeutic Equipment Work Simulator: Reliability and validity at three work intensities. *Archives of Physical Medicine & Rehabilitation, 72*, 511–516.

Kielhofner, G., Braveman, B., Baron, K., Fisher, G., Hammel, J., & Littleton, M. (1999). The model of human occupation, understanding the worker who is injured or disabled. *WORK, 12*(1), 3–11.

Kinnunen, M., Feldt, T., Kinnunen, U., Kaprio, J., & Pulkkinen, L. (2006). Association between long-term job strain and metabolic syndrome factor across sex and occupation. *Journal of Individual Differences, 27*(3), 151–161.

Kuijer, W., Brouwer, S., Preuper, H. R. S., Groothoff, J. W., Geertzen, J. H. B., & Dijkstra, P. U. (2006). Work status and chronic low back pain: exploring the International Classification of Functioning, Disability and Health. *Disability and Rehabilitation, 28*(6), 379–388.

Kuijer, W., Gerrits, E. H. J., & Reneman, M. F. (2004). Measuring physical performance via self-report in healthy young adults. *Journal of Occupational Rehabilitation, 14*(1), 77–87.

Lafayette Instrument Company. (1986). *Instructions and normative data for model 32030 Purdue Pegboard.* Layfayette, IN: Lafayette Instrument Company.

Lechner, D. E., Jackson, J. R., Roth, D. L., & Straaton, K. V. (1994). Reliability and validity of a newly developed test of physical work performance. *Journal of Occupational Medicine, 36*(9), 997–1004.

Lee, G. K. L., Chan, C. C. H., & Hui-Chan, C. W. Y. (2001a). Consistency of performance on the functional capacity assessment: Static strength and dynamic endurance. *American Journal of Physical Medicine & Rehabilitation, 80*(3), 189–195.

Lee, G. K. L., Chan, C. C. H., & Hui-Chan, C. W. Y. (2001b). Work profile and functional capacity of formwork carpenters at construction sites. *Disability & Rehabilitation, 23*(1), 9–14.

Ljungquist, T., Fransson, B., Harms-Ringdahl, K., Björnham, Å., & Nygren, Å. (1999). A physiotherapy test package for assessing back and neck dysfunction: Discriminative ability for patients versus healthy control subjects. *Physiotherapy Research International, 4*(2), 123–140.

Ljungquist, T., Harms-Ringdahl, K., Nygren, Å., & Jensen, I. (1999). Intra- and inter-rater reliability of an 11-test package for assessing dysfunction due to back or neck pain. *Physiotherapy Research International, 4*(3), 214–232.

Lygren, H., Dragesund, T., Joensen, J., Ask, T., & Moe-Nilssen, R. (2005). Test–retest reliability of the Progressive Isoinertial Lifting Evaluation (PILE). *Spine, 30*(9), 1070–1074.

Lysaght, R. M. (2004). Approaches to worker rehabilitation by occupational and physical therapists in the United States: Factors impacting practice. *WORK, 23*(2), 139–146.

Lysaker, P. H., Bryson, G., & Bell, M. D. (2002). Insight and work performance in schizophrenia. *Journal of Nervous and Mental Disease, 190*, 142–146.

Marrone, J., & Golowka, E. (1999). If work makes people with mental illness sick, what do unemployment, poverty, and social isolation cause? *Psychiatric Rehabilitation Journal, 23*(2), 187–193.

Martella, D., & Maass, A. (2000). Unemployment and life satisfaction: The moderating role of time structure and collectivism. *Journal of Applied Social Psychology, 30*(5), 1095–1108.

Mathers, C. D., & Schofield, D. J. (1998). The health consequences of unemployment: The evidence. *Medical Journal of Australia, 169*(3), 178–182.

Matheson, L., Isernhagen, S., & Hart, D. (1998). Functional capacity evaluation as a facilitator of social security disability program reform. *WORK: A Journal of Prevention Assessment and Rehabilitation, 10*, 77–84.

Matheson, L. N. (1986). Evaluation of lifting and lowering capacity. *Vocational Evaluation & Work Adjustment Bulletin, 19*(3), 107–111.

Matheson, L. N., Danner, R., Grant, J., & Mooney, V. (1993). Effect of computerised instructions on measurement of lift capacity: Safety, reliability, and validity. *Journal of Occupational Rehabilitation, 3*(2), 65–81.

Matheson, L. N., Gaudino, E. A., Mael, F., & Hesse, B. W. (2000). Improving the validity of the impairment evaluation process: A proposed theoretical framework. *Journal of Occupational Rehabilitation, 10*(4), 311–320.

Matheson, L. N., Isernhagen, S. J., & Hart, D. L. (2002). Relationships among lifting ability, grip force, and return to work. *Physical Therapy, 82*(3), 249–256.

Matheson, L. N., Mooney, V., Grant, J. E., Affleck, M., Hall, H., Melles, T., et al. (1995). A test to measure lift capacity of physically impaired adults. Part 1 - Development and reliability testing. *Spine, 20*(19), 2119–2129.

Matheson, L. N., Mooney, V., Grant, J. E., Leggett, S., & Kenny, K. (1996). Standardized evaluation of work capacity. *Journal of Back & Musculoskeletal Rehabilitation, 6*, 249–264.

Matheson, L. N., Mooney, V., Holmes, D., Leggett, S., Grant, J. E., Negri, S., et al. (1995). A test to measure lift capacity of physically impaired adults. Part 2 - Reactivity in a patient sample. *Spine, 20*(19), 2130–2134.

Matheson, L. N., Rogers, L. C., Kaskutas, V., & Dakos, M. (2002). Reliability and reactivity of three new functional assessment measures. *Work, 18*(1), 41–50.

Matthews, L. R. (1999). Road trauma, PTSD and occupational functioning: Implications for policy development, intervention and rehabilitation. *Australian & New Zealand Journal of Public Health, 23*, 325–327.

Matthews, L. R. (2005). Work potential of road accident survivors with posttraumatic stress disorder. *Behaviour Research and Therapy, 43*, 475–483.

Matthews, L. R. (2006). Post-trauma employability of people with symptoms of PTSD and the contribution of work environments. *International Journal on Disability Management Research 1*, 87–96.

Matthews, L. R., & Chinnery, D. L. (2005). Prediction of work functioning following accidental injury: The contribution of PTSD severity and other established risk factors. *International Journal of Psychology, 40*, 339–438.

Matthews, L. R., & Hawkins, T. (1995). Long term unemployment and rehabilitation counselling: Problems faced and competencies required. *Australian Journal of Rehabilitation Counselling, 1*, 118–129.

Mayer, T. G., Barnes, D., Kishino, N. D., Nichols, G., Gatchel, R. J., Mayer, H., et al. (1988). Progressive isoinertial lifting evaluation I: A standardized protocol and normative database. *Spine, 13*(9), 993–997.

Mayer, T. G., Barnes, D., Nichols, G., Kishino, N. D., Coval, K., Piel, B., et al. (1988). Progressive isoinertial lifting evaluation II: A comparison with isokinetic lifting in a disabled chronic low-back pain industrial population. *Spine, 13*(9), 998–1002.

Mayer, T. G., Gatchel, R., Barnes, D., Mayer, H., & Mooney, V. (1990). Progressive isoinertial lifting evaluation: Erratum notice. *Spine, 15*(1), 5.

Mayer, T. G., Mooney, V., Gatchel, R. J., Barnes, D., Terry, A., Smith, S., et al. (1989). Quantifying postoperative deficits of physical function following spinal surgery. *Clinical Orthopaedics & Related Research, 244*, 147–157.

McClure, P. W., & Flowers, K. R. (1992). The reliability of BTE Work Simulator measurements for selected shoulder and wrist tasks. *Journal of Hand Therapy, 5*(1), 25–28.

Mooney, V., & Matheson, L. N. (1994). Objective measurement of soft tissue injury feasibility study: Examiner's manual [CD-ROM]. Los Angeles: Industrial Medical Council, State of California.

Moser, K. A., Goldblatt, P. O., Fox, A. J., & Jones, D. R. (1987). Unemployment and mortality: Comparison of the 1971 and 1981 longitudinal study census samples. *British Medical Journal (Clinical Research Education), 294*(6564), 86–90.

Muenchberger, H., Kendall, E., & Mills, E. (2006). Creating successful rehabilitation partnerships between health professionals and employers. *International Journal of Disability Management Research, 1*, 10–20.

National Occupational Health & Safety Commission. (1995). *Guidance note for best practice rehabilitation management of occupational injuries and disease [NOHSC:3021(1995)].* Canberra, ACT: Australian Government Publishing Service.

Oesch, P. R., Kool, J. P., Bachmann, S., & Devereux, J. (2006). The influence of a Functional Capacity Evaluation on fitness for work certificates in patients with non-specific chronic low back pain. *WORK, 26*(3), 259–271.

Ogden-Niemeyer, L. (1991). *Procedure guidelines for the WEST Standard Evaluation: "Assessment of range of motion under load"* (Rev. ed.). Long Beach, CA: Work Evaluations Systems Technology.

O'Halloran, D. (2002). An historical overview of Australia's largest and oldest provider of vocational rehabilitation—CRS Australia. *WORK, 19*(3), 211–218.

O'Halloran, D., & Innes, E. (2005). Understanding work in society. In G. Whiteford & V. Wright-St Clair (Eds.), *Occupation and practice in context* (pp. 299–316). Sydney, NSW, Australia: Elsevier.

Provencher, H. L., Gregg, R., Mead, S., & Mueser, K. T. (2002). The role of work in the recovery of persons with psychiatric disabilities. *Psychiatric Rehabilitation Journal, 26*, 132–144.

Ratzon, N. Z., Jarus, T., & Catz, A. (2007). The relationship between work function and low back pain history in occupationally active individuals. *Disability and Rehabilitation, 29*(10), 791–796.

Reneman, M. F., Brouwer, S., Meinema, A., Dijkstra, P. U., Geertzen, J. H. B., & Groothoff, J. W. (2004). Test–retest reliability of the Isernhagen Work Systems Functional Capacity Evaluation in healthy adults. *Journal of Occupational Rehabilitation, 14*(4), 295–305.

Reneman, M. F., Bults, M. M. W. E., Engbers, L. H., Mulders, K. K. G., & Göeken, L. N. H. (2001). Measuring maximum holding times and perception of static elevated work and forward bending in healthy young adults. *Journal of Occupational Rehabilitation, 11*(2), 87–97.

Reneman, M. F., Dijkstra, P. U., Westmaas, M., & Göeken, L. N. H. (2002). Test–retest reliability of lifting and carrying in a 2-day functional capacity evaluation. *Journal of Occupational Rehabilitation, 12*(4), 269–275.

Reneman, M. F., Fokkens, A. S., Dijkstra, P. U., Geertzen, J. H. B., & Groothoff, J. W. (2005). Testing lifting capacity: Validity of determining effort level by means of observation. *Spine, 30*(2), E40–E46.

Reneman, M. F., Jaegers, S. M. H. J., Westmaas, M., & Göeken, L. N. H. (2002). The reliability of determining effort level of lifting and carrying in a functional capacity evaluation. *Work, 18*(1), 23–27.

Reneman, M. F., Kool, J., Oesch, P., Geertzen, J. H. B., Battié, M. C., & Gross, D. P. (2006). Material handling performance of patients with chronic low back pain during Functional Capacity Evaluation: A comparison between three countries. *Disability and Rehabilitation, 28*(18), 1143–1149.

Reneman, M. F., Preuper, H. R. S., Kleen, M., Geertzen, J. H. B., & Dijkstra, P. U. (2007). Are pain intensity and pain-related fear related to functional capacity evaluation performances of patients with chronic low back pain? *Journal of Occupational Rehabilitation, 17*(2), 247–258.

Reuss, E. E., Rawe, D. E., & Sundquist, A. E. (1958). Development of a physical capacities evaluation. *American Journal of Occupational Therapy, 12*(1), 1–8, 14.

Rondinelli, R. D., Dunn, W., Hassanein, K. M., Keesling, C. A., Meredith, S. C., Schulz, T. L., et al. (1997). A simulation of hand impairments: Effects on upper extremity function and implications toward medical impairment rating and disability determination. *Archives of Physical Medicine & Rehabilitation, 78*(12), 1358–1363.

Rustenburg, G., Kuijer, P. P. F. M., & Frings-Dresen, M. H. W. (2004). The concurrent validity of the ERGOS™ Work Simulator and the Ergo-Kit ® with respect to maximum lifting capacity. *Journal of Occupational Rehabilitation, 14*(2), 107–118.

Shechtman, O., MacKinnon, L., & Locklear, C. (2001). Using the BTE Primus to measure grip and wrist flexion strength in physically active wheelchair users: An exploratory study. *American Journal of Occupational Therapy, 55*(4), 393–400.

Schenk, P., Klipstein, A., Spillmann, S., Strøyer, J., & Laubli, T. (2006). The role of back muscle endurance, maximum force, balance and trunk rotation control regarding lifting capacity. *European Journal of Applied Physiology, 96*, 146–156.

Schult, M., Söderback, I., & Jacobs, K. (1995). Swedish use and validation of Valpar work samples for patients with musculoskeletal neck and shoulder pain. *Work, 5*(3), 223–233.

Schult, M., Söderback, I., & Jacobs, K. (2000). Multidimensional aspects of work capability: a comparison between individuals who are working or not working because of chronic pain. *WORK, 15*(1), 41–53.

Slebus, F. G., Sluiter, J. K., Kuijer, P. F. M., Willems, J. H. B. M., & Frings-Dresen, M. H. W. (2007). Work-ability evaluation: A piece of cake or a hard nut to crack?, *Disability and Rehabilitation* (Vol. i-First, pp. 1–6).

Söderback, I., & Jacobs, K. (2000). A study of well-being among a population of Swedish workers using a job-related criterion-referenced multidimensional vocational assessment. *WORK, 14*(2), 83–107.

Travis, J. (2002). Cross-disciplinary competency standards for work-related assessments: Communicating the requirements for effective professional practice. *WORK, 19*(3), 269–280.

Trevitt, N. (1997). *A test–retest reliability study on the Valpar Component Work Sample 4.* Unpublished honours thesis, School of Occupational Therapy, Faculty of Health Sciences, University of Sydney, Sydney, NSW, Australia.

Trossman, P. B., & Li, P.-W. (1989). The effect of the duration of intertrial rest periods on isometric grip strength performance in young adults. *Occupational Therapy Journal of Research, 9*(6), 362–378.

Trossman, P. B., Suleski, K. B., & Li, P.-W. (1990). Test–retest reliability and day-to-day variability on an isometric grip strength test using the work simulator. *Occupational Therapy Journal of Research, 10*(5), 266–279.

Tuckwell, N. L., Straker, L., & Barrett, T. E. (2002). Test-retest reliability on nine tasks of the Physical Work Performance Evaluation. *WORK, 19*(3), 243–253.

U.S. Department of Labor Employment & Training. (1991). *The revised handbook for analyzing jobs.* Indianapolis, IN: JIST Works.

U.S. Department of Labor. (2005). *Injury statistics.* Retrieved May 19, 2007, from http://www.bls.gov/iif/#tables

Valpar International Corp. (2003). *Temporal reliability of selected Valpar Component Work Samples: Learning curve studies.* Retrieved Sept. 22, 2003, from http://www.valparint.com/wsstudy.htm

Wilke, N. A., Sheldahl, L. M., Dougherty, S. M., Levandoski, S. G., & Tristani, F. E. (1993). Baltimore Therapeutic Equipment Work Simulator: Energy expenditure of work activities in cardiac patients. *Archives of Physical Medicine & Rehabilitation, 74*(4), 419–424.

Yílmaz, F., Yílmaz, A., Merdol, F., Parlar, D., Sahin, F., & Kuran, B. (2003). Efficacy of dynamic lumbar stabilization exercise in lumbar microdiscectomy. *Journal of Rehabilitation Medicine, 35*(4), 163–167.

Family Functioning Assessment in Rehabilitation and Health

CHRISTINE E. RYAN
GABOR I. KEITNER
The Warren Alpert Medical School of Brown University, Providence, RI

OVERVIEW

There is a growing interest in assessing a family's functioning and in relating that functioning to a patient's course of illness, including paths to rehabilitation and/or adjustments to an illness condition. The idea of taking a broad view of illness and health care derives from following a biopsychosocial model of treating illness rather than the more limiting, but more widely used, biomedical model. As early as the 1970s, Engel proposed using a biopsychosocial model in the belief that use of the medical model only resulted in a neglect of important social, psychological, and behavioral dimensions of illness (Engel, 1977; Ryan, 2002). This chapter discusses family functioning as a health antecedent, process, and outcome.

LEARNING OBJECTIVES

By the end of the chapter, readers should be able to:

- Demonstrate an appreciation of the patient as part of a wider social context in rehabilitation and health
- Explain the value of a family assessment
- Discuss the religious, ethnic, and cultural diversity of families as they influence health outcomes
- Outline basic theoretical and methodological issues of family assessment
- Evaluate the importance of the clinical-research link when using family assessment

INTRODUCTION

With the advent of new pharmacological agents and devices, particularly from the mid-1980s through the mid-1990s, treatments and interests in the family were overshadowed as a new generation of drugs and drug therapy became the focus of treatment for many illnesses. By the late 1990s, however, clinicians and researchers were beginning to understand that a patient's course of illness and illness outcome were not solely the reduction or elimination of a patient's symptoms (Ryan, 2002; Keitner, Ryan, & Solomon, 2006). Patients may have gained some relief of their symptoms by medications, but how they functioned became a more recognized factor in their assessment. Although broadening the definition of a patient's outcome was, in part, due to limitations of medications in providing symptom relief, new demands of a changing health care system, including reimbursement for desired services (Fenderson, 1984), also helped to reinforce the inadequacy of a definition based solely on patient symptomatology (WHO, 2002; Üstün et al., 2003; Keitner, Ryan, & Solomon, 2006).

Once the focus shifted to include a patient's functioning, it quickly became apparent that functioning could be examined in a variety of contexts such as physical, work/school, social, and family (Peterson, 2005). Fortunately, even while pharmacological developments were in progress and featured most prominently in the medical field, work in family therapy and family assessments had continued to develop. Furthermore, innovations in computer software programs and advances in statistical applications became available to ease the use of assessments for clinical care and for use in large-scale, longitudinal research studies. During the same time period the development of the *International Classification of Functioning* (ICF) provided the conceptual framework to integrate medical and social perspectives with models of disability by linking a person's functioning and disability with their health condition and personal and environmental factors (Kearney & Pryor, 2004; Peterson, 2005; Reed et al., 2005).

RELATIONSHIP OF FAMILY ASSESSMENT TO REHABILITATION AND HEALTH

A major function of the family unit is to provide a setting for the social, psychological, and biological development and maintenance of family members (Epstein, Keitner, Bishop, & Miller, 1988; Ryan, Epstein, Keitner, Miller, & Bishop, 2005). Even though the composition of a family changes over time, the family unit—or alternative intimate living group—attempts to meet the basic living needs of family members. In the process of doing so, the family provides support and shares stresses as members deal with a variety of tasks and problems (Anderson, 2000; Falloon, 2003; Walsh, 2003). Family functioning is used to describe how the family works together as a unit to meet their basic needs. Some of the tasks that families confront include dealing with normal life processes (e.g., developmental life stages) that may be viewed either positively or negatively, depending on particular circumstances and viewpoints of family members. Examples of events that may elicit positive and/or negative feelings and actions in families include childbirth, retirement, beginning a new job or school, or a family vacation. The family adapts to each of these events and, depending on how the family functions, may do so effectively or ineffectively. The definition of functioning, then, can imply ability to fulfill a function (Walsh, 2003), ability to adapt (Beavers, 2003), or ability to carry out typical daily activities (McDowell & Newell, 1996).

A systems approach is a useful model to use when assessing a family's functioning because it assumes many levels of functioning (e.g., biological, personal, family, institutional, cultural), each of which influences the other (Beavers, 2003). A major tenet of systems theory posits that the behavior and actions of one family member affect all family members. Just as a patient's illness may affect family members and the family's functioning, the family environment may have an effect on the patient's illness (Epstein, Bishop, & Levin, 1978; Epstein, Ryan, Bishop, Miller, & Keitner, 2003; Keitner & Miller, 1990; Lewis, Beavers, Gossett, & Phillips 1976; Ryan et al., 2005). When viewed in the context of a family member's health and illness, a family's functioning is relevant across a wide variety of illnesses and throughout the course of a patient's illness, whether the illness is at an acute stage, rehabilitation phase, maintenance, or follow-up phase, and whether or not the nature of the illness is short-term, chronic, remitting and relapsing, or a deteriorating condition. When a family member develops a disabling disorder of any kind, the illness or disability can affect the family's functioning, and the family's functioning, in turn, can affect adjustment to the illness (Doherty & Baird, 1987; McCubbin, Joy, & Cabule, 1980; McDowell & Newell, 1996; Scherer & Cushman, 1997). Often the family's functioning will go through a variety of stages. For example, an accident or acute event may lead to a chronic illness and/or a prolonged rehabilitation period, all of which

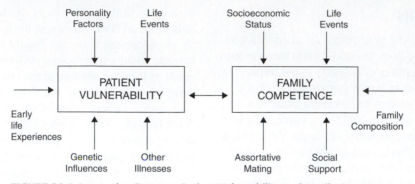

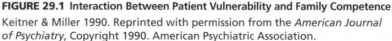

FIGURE 29.1 Interaction Between Patient Vulnerability and Family Competence

Keitner & Miller 1990. Reprinted with permission from the *American Journal of Psychiatry*, Copyright 1990. American Psychiatric Association.

can influence and be influenced by the functioning of the family (Barth, 1996; Schlote, Richter, Frank, & Wallesch, 2006)

Families can have both negative and positive impacts on a patient and other family members (see Figure 29.1). The physical, emotional, social, and financial strains that may result from diagnosis and treatment of a medical or psychiatric illness may exacerbate family and marital stress, particularly issues dealing with intimacy, communication, parenting, and role changes. Medical complications, lack of energy, and social withdrawal can result in increased morbidity, extended days absent from work, poorer social functioning, and poor self-perception on the part of the patient. The family may directly or indirectly pressure a patient if the illness causes a financial burden by time away from work, a lengthy hospital stay, or a prolonged convalescence. Resentment toward the patient may arise as family members take on added responsibilities (Ryan, 2002; Keitner, 2005). Critical, hostile, or overinvolved attitudes by family members may be directed toward a patient (Butzlaff & Hooley, 1998); fear and anxiety on the part of a family member may exacerbate a patient's unease.

On the other hand, a family may positively affect a patient's illness. The family may serve as the patient's ally by helping him/her with medication and treatment compliance. Family members can serve as caregivers, aid with logistic problems such as transportation and appointments, help monitor the illness by keeping track of residual symptoms and medication side effects, and encourage proper diets and exercise programs as feasible. Families can help patients stay positive, deal with illness conditions, and develop and strengthen channels of communication (Ryan, 2002).

Evidence for the reciprocal and dynamic nature of family functioning cuts across many diseases and has been measured as an outcome of the illness or a target of rehabilitation, treatment, or intervention (Doherty & Baird, 1987; Brockaw, Cieza, et al., 2004; Keitner, Ryan, & Solomon, 2006). For example, Mengel (1988) found that family functioning affected a patient's diabetic regulation, including treatment compliance and weight control. Family ties and social support were strong predictors of functional recovery in patients poststroke (Glass et al., 2004), and of rehabilitation outcome for patients enrolled in a traumatic brain injury (TBI) rehabilitation program (Sander et al., 2003). Male coronary patients who received spousal support reported less use of pain medication, lower length of hospital stay, and more rapid discharge from intensive care. In contrast, Stancin et al. (2001) found that families with a member who had a pediatric fracture had poor family functioning up to 6 months postinjury; Anderson and colleagues (Anderson, Catroppa, Haritou, Morse, & Rosenfeld, 2005) reported significant family burden 30 months after a child suffered a TBI; and Degotardi, Revenson, and Ilowite (1999) noted how juvenile rheumatoid arthritis in a family member can disrupt a family's functioning. Our own work on family functioning and mood disorders (e.g., major depression, bipolar illness) suggests a clear link between the family functioning of a patient and his or her likelihood of recovery from an illness episode (Keitner, Archambault, & Ryan, 2003; Keitner, Ryan, Miller & Norman, 1992; Miller et al., 2005; Ryan et al., 2005). Also, a series of studies done on caring for patients with

RESEARCH BOX 29.1

Krawetz P, Fleisher W, Neelan P, Staley D, Arnett J & Maher J. (2001). Family functioning in subjects with pseudo-seizures and epilepsy. *Journal of Nervous and Mental Disease, 189*, 38–43.

Objective: The purpose of the study was to compare family functioning in families of patients with pseudoseizures versus families of patients with epilepsy.

Method: Patients with pseudoseizures (N = 31) or epilepsy (N=31) and their family members (Total N of family members = 207) were recruited over a 4-year period and asked to complete measures of family functioning, depression and anxiety, seizure inventory, quality of life, and demographic information.

Results: Family functioning for the pseudoseizure group reached pathological levels in several areas of family functioning. Statistical differences between the pseudoseizure group and the epilepsy group was evident in the areas of affective involvement, communication, conflict, and general functioning. Patients found communication as a particularly problematic area of family functioning while family members rated role functioning as difficult.

Conclusion: This study provides evidence that both individuals and family members view difficulties in their family's functioning and suggests including patients and their family members in treatment interventions for patients with pseudoseizures.

Because of the emphasis on remission of symptoms, family/psychosocial functioning is a neglected outcome measure.

Questions

1. Discuss the rationale for including the assessment of family functioning as a routine part of clinical care.
2. It is not uncommon for patients and family members to view their functioning differently; can you suggest how and why their perspectives might differ?
3. One reason for assessing family functioning is because family functioning is amenable to change. How would you use a family assessment to improve a family's functioning?

dementia and caring for patients with chronic mood disorders was able to show a significant relationship between poor family functioning and increased stress, burden, and/or depression on the part of the caregiver/family member (Heru & Ryan, 2002; Heru, Ryan, & Iqbal, 2004; Heru, Ryan, & Vlastos, 2004).

Given the importance of the family and how a family's functioning can affect and be affected by an illness in the family, family assessment can be an important contribution to a patient's care by: (1) identifying a patient's needs and resources; (2) assessing a family's strengths and conflicts to guide appropriate interventions; (3) choosing suitable interventions; (4) monitoring response to treatment; (5) evaluating patient outcomes; and (6) identifying at-risk families (Clark, Shields, Aycock, & Wolf, 2003; Fenderson, 1984; Ryan et al., 2005). Family intervention may be one area of adjunctive therapy that may improve the odds of recovery, increase quality of life, or help patients and family members deal with a chronic, recurring, or deteriorating illness. If family therapy is not an option, at least assessing a family's functioning may provide information to the clinician that could be valuable in his/her recommendations for further treatment.

HISTORY AND PRACTICE

To shift from a medical model to a biopsychosocial model requires an understanding and acceptance of the effect of the environment and family on an individual's health and functioning (Hurst, 2003). If illness or disability were seen as a medical issue only, then the emphasis would have remained on the individual (Kearney & Pryor, 2004). But an expanded approach to functional assessment was related to an expanded philosophy in the field of rehabilitation, which originally had focused on impairment rather than on ability to function (Dittmar, 1997). Changes in concepts of assessments reflect changes in theoretical approaches to health and well-being (Dittmar, 1997; Frey, 1984; Halpern & Fuhrer, 1984. For example, in 1947, the World Health Organization (WHO) suggested that health status was not merely the absence of disease, but was a comprehensive state of physical, mental, and social well-being (Dittmar, 1997). Once put in the public forum, a variety of areas in which a person functions can be delineated, which include specific categories of health, intelligence, psychological, social, emotional, work, and family (Lawton, 1971).

As the relationship between family functioning and medical/psychiatric illness or rehabilitation gained acceptance, there was a perceived need to measure a family's functioning. As noted, work on family assessment in the mental health field had been ongoing throughout the 1980s and 1990s, approximately the same time that the International Classification of Impairments, Disabilities, and Handicaps (ICIDH) and the ICF were being conceptualized, delineated, and refined (Bruyere, Van Looy, & Peterson, 2005; Kearney & Pryor, 2004; Peterson, 2005). During this period, the emphasis of the ICF changed from a focus on the consequences of disease to a composite of healthy and unhealthy functioning as related to illness conditions (Kearney & Pryor, 2004; Peterson, 2005). The ICF framework provides a structure within which to report and classify functioning across a wide range of illness areas and conditions (Bruyere, et al., 2005; Kearney & Pryor, 2004; Peterson, 2005).

Family assessment easily fits into the ICF model as it provides a comprehensive picture of the family's strengths and weaknesses and, as described in the previous section, can affect or be affected by a family member's course of illness (Cohen & Anthony, 1984; Epstein et al., 1988; Keitner & Miller, 1990). Family assessments are derived from family therapy models that, in turn, are usually drawn from different theoretical perspectives. Because there are several models of family therapy, it should not be surprising that there are several ways to measure a family's functioning. Depending on the focus and assumptions of the model, some family constructs will be emphasized more than others, some models will view "normality" in different ways, and some concepts will be more easily measured than others. The family models that developed in the 1970s were a synthesis of communication theories, family theories, child and individual development theories, and cross-cultural comparisons that had become prominent a decade earlier. Theories originating with Parsons, Bateson, Erikson, and Maslow were guides to family models and, later, to the family assessments of Beavers, Moos, Epstein, and Olson (Browning & Green, 2003; McDowell & Newell, 1996; Ryan et al., 2005; Scherer & Cushman, 1997; Sholevar, 2003; Walsh, 2003). Detailed reviews are available that summarize different theoretical approaches to family therapy and family assessment. Some of the more prominent current family therapy models include systems, problem-centered, structural, narrative, postmodern, expressed emotion, Milan, cognitive–behavioral, psychodynamic, interpersonal, psychoeducational, and experiential models (Walsh, 2003; Keitner, 2005).

Many of the early models of family therapy focused on pathology within the family, resulting in assessments that were skewed toward measuring family deficits or conflicts (Walsh, 2003). The early emphasis on impairment or impaired functioning in the field of rehabilitation was linked to an evaluation of functioning and service delivery. An assessment of functioning before, during, and after rehabilitation programs was used to see if problems were addressed and corrective measures had taken effect (Dittmar, 1997). In the mental health field, the negative emphasis may have been the result of several factors. First, families were unlikely to consult the medical professionals when there were no problems. By the 1950s, child psychiatrists had recognized that the role of the mother was related to the behavior of the child and then assumed, wrongly, that families caused psychopathology in individual members. Second, many of the early family studies grew out of helping families deal with a member who was schizophrenic. Family psychoeducational approaches were developed that included methods for correcting a negative influence or decreasing stress in the family environment. Third, systems theories and cognitive–behavioral therapies emphasized communication, problem-solving, reframing, and behavior modification as mechanisms for dealing with troubling interactions within the family environment (Walsh, 2003; Ryan et al. 2005). Fourth, Minuchin and others challenged the belief that "normal" families lived in constant harmony. In order to question this last tenet, and to provide corrective behavior for troubling issues within the family, it was not surprising that clinicians and researchers concentrated on difficulties and problem areas within families.

Clinicians working with families grew to realize that families showed strengths as well as limitations in their functioning and that the family strengths could be recognized and harnessed to help deal with problem issues, including the illness of one or more family members (Epstein et al., 1988; Keitner, Ryan, & Epstein, 2006). Over time it became clear that families could have the same level of functioning (e.g., healthy or effective) even if their family members had different illnesses or even different severity levels of the same illness condition. On the other hand, the same illness and illness severity could affect a family's functioning in different ways (McDowell & Newell, 1996). What this suggested to clinicians and researchers was that there was no prototypical family type that was representative of poor family functioning associated with any given disorder (Ryan et al., 2005). The clinical implication of these findings suggested that family functioning is dynamic, that family functioning is likely a composite of both strengths and problematic areas, and that assessment of each family was warranted in order to develop a comprehensive understanding of the patient and his or her family environment.

A corollary of these findings and probably the most critical issue for both clinicians and researchers was the realization that: (1) a family's functioning was amenable to change and (2) family functioning was related to the course of an illness (Keitner et al., 1992). The focus of changing the family's functioning and the mechanism used to initiate the change are two areas that differentiate family treatment models. Family assessments, in turn, reflect the treatment model from which they are drawn (Ryan et al., 2005).

MEASURING FAMILY FUNCTIONING

Family functioning is related to health, rehabilitation, and illness conditions. In addition, family functioning is both changeable and measurable and is the crux of family assessment (Epstein et al., 1988; Keitner, Ryan, & Epstein, 2006). This section deals with the goals of conducting a family assessment, the variety of methods used to assess a family's functioning, what specific concepts are measured, who participates in the assessment, and when an assessment is undertaken. One question should be asked continuously when choosing the method, the participants, the timing, and whether or not to request a family assessment: What is the purpose of the assessment?

Why Conduct a Family Assessment

Family functioning has sparked interest in the medical field because of growing evidence suggesting that family functioning can affect a patient's course of illness. The purpose of the assessment could be an evaluation of the patient's environment or resources, a needs assessment, a guide for prevention or intervention strategy, a screen for at-risk populations—or all of the above (Bishop & Evans, 1990; Brockaw, Wohlfahrt, et al., 2004; Keitner, 2005; Ryan et al., 2005). Assessing the family's functioning can be seen as an outcome of the disease process, a target of rehabilitation, prevention, or intervention, or a quality assurance measure (McCubbin, McCubbin & Thompson, 1987; Stucki & Kroeling, 2000). Because a patient's functioning has been linked to the family's functioning, changes in family functioning over time can be used as another piece of data to help explain a patient's improvement, deterioration, or stabilization.

On a more general level, family assessment may be used for clinical purposes, research purposes, or both. If the driving force behind the assessment is clear, then choosing the methods, participants, concepts, and timing will be easier. One cautionary note when assessing families is that the correlation between a family's functioning and the course of a patient's illness or progress in rehabilitation does not imply causality. A patient's deteriorating course of illness is not necessarily a product of a poorly functioning family. The poorly functioning family may be a barrier to the patient's improvement and one factor that exacerbates the patient's condition. It may also reflect the distress in dealing with a family member's illness, a circumstance that would still suggest an appropriate intervention (Keitner & Miller, 1990; Keitner, 2005).

What to Measure in a Family Assessment

Family functioning is a measure of how a family typically appraises, operates, and behaves (McCubbin, McCubbin & Thompson, 1987; McCubbin & Thompson, 1991). Not

---

DISCUSSION BOX 29.1

Cause and Effect

How do we know if a family problem relates to a family member's illness? Perhaps it is the illness that creates a problem for the family. Should the family be involved in the treatment at all times and, if so, at what level? Most health professionals do not feel the need to ask information of family members beyond a cursory report on verification of medication(s) taken or the proximate reason for the health care visit.

Is there any reason to talk to the spouse of a patient who has high blood pressure? What about a family member of somebody who is depressed? An elderly woman who undergoes heart surgery? Is there any value in attributing a family's functioning as a cause or an effect to a specific condition?

Whether the family situation exacerbates an ongoing condition or positively influences its course, the relevance to a health care professional may be more in understanding the issues involved in a family's functioning and the implications for treatment than in trying to determine the specific cause and effect of an illness and the family's functioning.

TABLE 29.1 Well-Known Scales for Assessing Families

Model	Objective Measure	Subjective Measure	Key Constructs	References
Beavers Systems Model of Family Functioning	Beavers Interactional Styles Scales	Self-Report Family Inventory (SFI)	Family competence, Family style	Beavers, 1981; Beavers & Hampson, 1990; Beavers & Hampson, 2000
Circumplex Model of Marital and Family Systems	Clinical Rating Scale (CRS)	Family Adaptability and Cohesion Evaluation Scales (FACES)	Cohesion, Adaptability	Olson, Russell, & Sprenkle, 1989; Olson, 2000; Olson & Gorall, 2003
Expressed Emotion Model	Camberwell Family Interview (CFI)	Perceived Criticism Scale (PCS)	Expressed emotion, Perceived criticism	Brown & Rutter, 1966; Leff & Vaughn, 1985; Hooley & Teasdale, 1989; Van Humbeeck et al, 2002
Family and Extrafamily Resources	—	Family Environment Scale (FES)	Family conflict, Family cohesion & organization, Independence	Moos & Moos, 1981; Moos & Moos, 1994; Moos, Cronkite, & Moos, 1998
McMaster Model of Family Functioning	Clinical Rating Scale (CRS)	Family Assessment Device (FAD)	Problem-solving, Communication, Roles, Affective involvement	Epstein et al, 1988; Ryan et al, 2005

all models of family therapy or family assessment will cover all aspects of functioning. Models will focus on family dimensions that seem particularly relevant and have a major impact on the emotional and physical health or problems of family members. Dimensions of interest vary by theoretical orientation and may focus on problem-solving, expressed emotion, adaptability, resilience, communication, or competence, to name just a few. The choice of which dimensions to focus on and which model to follow will be guided by the clinical or research question(s) being addressed, which, in turn, will likely reflect the population being served.

Not surprisingly, there is a degree of overlap in some of the most widely used models of family assessments. The McMaster Model of Family Functioning identifies six dimensions that make up a family's functioning: the family's problem-solving ability; their communication style; the roles of each family member; the affective involvement and affective responsiveness of family members; and the rules and behavior patterns of the family (Epstein et al., 1988; Ryan et al., 2005). An overall rating of a family's functioning can also be assessed. Two major constructs in the Beavers Systems Model are identified as a family's competence and a family's style. This model explores how effective a family is in accomplishing tasks, how adults negotiate and

resolve conflicts, and how intergenerational boundaries are established, and it gauges the family style of relating (Beavers & Hampson, 2003). In Olson's Circumplex Model of Marital and Family Systems three dimensions are seen as particularly relevant: family cohesion, flexibility, and communication (Olson, Russell, & Sprenkle, 1989; Olson & Gorall, 2003). Moos and associates (Moos & Moos, 1981; Moos, Cronkite, & Moos, 1998) developed a model that measures 10 areas of family interactions to gauge the emphasis that families put on various family behaviors. Some key dimensions in their model include cohesion, expressiveness, conflict, organization, and control. (See Table 29.1 for a comparison of models.)

Several other constructs have received attention in family assessments. First developed several decades ago by Brown and associates, expressed emotion is an index of emotions, attitudes, and behaviors often centered on critical remarks made by family members (Brown, Monck, Carstairs, & Wing, 1962; Brown & Rutter, 1966; Vaughn & Leff, 1976; Jenkins & Karno, 1992; Van Humbeeck, Van Audenhove, De Hert, Pieters, & Storms 2002). McCubbin, McCubbin, and Thompson (1987; 1991) stressed problem-solving ability, adaptability, and cohesion, Mengel (1988) looked at family dynamics, and Degotardi, Revenson, and Ilowite et al (1999) focused on types of family-level coping strategies, including appraisal, problem-focused, and emotion-focused. Miklowitz and Clarkin (2003) evaluate an overall level of functioning and level of pathology by looking at problem-solving, family organization, and emotional climate. More recent models may draw on older theories to delve into specific constructs such as family conflict (Clark et al. 2003), resilience/adaptability, or coping methods.

How to Choose the Method of Family Assessment

Deciding on the reason for a family assessment, whether the assessment is oriented toward clinical care, research studies, or both, and what particular model to follow—will help to guide the method of obtaining the data. There are many options from which to choose. Being clear about the purpose of the assessment will help to clarify choices.

A major dichotomy in assessing families is the objective versus subjective perspective. Alternative strategies for assessing families are available within each perspective. An objective rating of a family's functioning may include an interview by the treating clinician, a structured or semistructured interview during a family meeting, observing the family via a two-way mirror, videotaping or audiotaping a family interaction, inclusion of the clinician within the family system, or a combination of these techniques. Whether or not a model is explicitly stated, each of these methods for assessing families is guided by a theoretical perspective.

Questions asked from a formal interview or a structured instrument probably reflect a model most directly (see Table 29.3). A trained interviewer can ask a series of questions in a systematic way that will address all components of a specific model. The interview can take one-half hour to three hours and may be completed in one or more sessions. The end result will be a family assessment using one or more scales and measuring one or more components of the family's functioning. When families are observed or videotaped, the coding that results from the taped session also is a function of a specific model. The kind of taping will actually suggest particular viewpoints. Some family assessments are done by asking family members to discuss a recent problem that occurred within the family. The interviewer may or may not provide specific questions to address: Was the problem resolved; if not, why not; if resolved, how did they do it; what options were available. The interviewer leaves the room for 10 minutes and videotapes the session. On returning, he/she may discuss the interactions within the family or provide feedback. Others may

assess a family's functioning by videotaping a family having a meal together (in the family home), observing the families in a play setting, or asking the family to complete a task (in a lab setting).

Arguably, the most positive aspect of a clinician assessing a family's functioning is the ability to obtain a comprehensive picture of the many factors that contribute to a patient's illness state. Understanding the psychosocial context of the illness may help the treating clinician maximize his/her therapeutic effectiveness and treatment recommendations (Epstein et al. 1988; Keitner, Miller, & Ryan, 1993, 1994). Other positive aspects of measuring family functioning objectively include the neutrality of the interviewer, the ability to observe the family interact as a unit, the use of different settings to observe the family, and the ability to review audiotapes or videotapes at a later period—for comparisons over time, to check an assumption, to amend an interpretation, to reexamine an interaction. For some schools of thought, the immediacy of conducting an assessment might also involve the ability to correct a misunderstanding or provide information about a misinterpretation of the illness, treatment, or rehabilitation program. It is very important to keep in mind, however, that the purpose of the interview is to obtain a family assessment. Therefore corrective information (e.g., about the nature of the illness) given during the interview process should be very brief, addressed to a specific point, and rare. At the conclusion of the family assessment, one recommendation may be that the patient/family member(s) be given supplemental reading materials or an in-depth educational session about the illness or disability.

The downside of using objective techniques is the prerequisite training, including the training needed to conduct a family interview and to administer a particular assessment model. Depending on the complexity of the model, training can take a few weeks to several months. On one hand, learning interviewing skills and treatment models are often already included in formal training programs in the field of health care and are not unique to family assessment training. Thus, applying a particular model for family assessment can be folded into training, much like developing expertise in a new specialty. On the other hand, formal training in conducting a comprehensive assessment of a family's functioning is often the first step in the treatment process for those enrolled in family therapy programs.

For some types of family assessments (e.g., videotaping family interactions, assessing emotional involvement), a certain amount of training is needed to learn the coding strategy. Of course, if the family assessment is part of a research study, then obtaining the appropriate information, accurate coding, and reliability with other interviewers and coders becomes even more important (Gottman, 1999). Additional negative aspects of using some of these objective methods include the expense or lack of available equipment needed to videotape, audio-tape, or use two-way mirrors; the complications of transporting equipment to a family's home; the time and cost of training interviewers and coders and the ability to retain trained personnel; having available space to accommodate all family members at once, and having appropriate equipment available in a lab.

The most common technique used to obtain a subjective assessment of a family's functioning is the paper-and-pencil approach—or a computer touch screen, the modern variant. Like the objective approaches discussed above, questions used in this type of assessment will also reflect the model associated with it. Paper-and-pencil assessments can take less than 5 minutes to complete or more than 1 hour, depending on the number of questions asked and scales used. For example, one global question "On a scale of 1 to 10 (with 1 being poor and 10 being good) how would you rate your family's functioning?" would take seconds to complete. Such an item may be very useful to assess risk or provide a screen or snapshot of a family's functioning, but it clearly would not be adequate for obtaining in-depth information on specific areas of a family's functioning.

Positive aspects of measuring family assessments using the subjective method are many. They are relatively easy to use, economical, tend to be brief, do not require any training or manuals to complete, can be easily trans-ported to a variety of settings, can be compared over time, and do not require trained personnel to administer. Further, these assessments can be used for both clinical and research purposes at a relatively low cost. Guidelines for constructing sound self-report family assessment scales are similar to those used in developing any self-report instrument. As with many self-report assessments, it is important to keep in mind the readability of the scale, length of the questionnaire, time for completion, cost of the instrument, and ease of scoring (Sawin & Harrigan, 1995). Developing a valid instrument and establishing satisfactory psychometric properties are time-consuming and require expertise in scale development. Whether used for clinical or research purposes, the data collected from multiple family members need to be collapsed into usable units. Timeliness in obtaining a family assessment score may be more of an issue when used clinically, but solutions are feasible (e.g., arrive a few minutes earlier for an appointment, mail completed forms before coming to the clinic, provide direct computer entry and scoring).

There are downsides to using the subjective perspective to assess family functioning. Paper-and-pencil tests cannot give a complete picture of a family's functioning (Scherer & Cushman, 1997). Observable family behavior is not captured when family members are completing questionnaires; therefore, family interactions cannot be rated objectively. If a patient or family member shows signs of cognitive distortion, results of an assessment may be skewed and distort the total family assessment (Epstein et al., 1988). Also, a large amount of data can be acquired in a fairly short time if every family member completes family assessments at regular

---

TABLE 29.3 Sample Questions of Family Functioning Assessment: *Problem Solving, Affective Involvement, Roles, and Communication*

Problem Solving:	What problems do you have as a family?
	Do you discuss the problems?
	Do you take action about the problem?
	Do you resolve the problem?
Affective Involvement:	What is important to you?
	Who pays attention to you?
	Are other family members interested in you?
Roles:	Who does what in the family?
	Is anyone overburdened with tasks/responsibilities?
	Discuss any major change(s) in the family.
Communication:	How many hours/day do you spend talking to and with each other?
	Do you talk about your feelings?
	Do family members understand what you are talking about?

Adapted from Ryan et al, 2005.

intervals. Coding, scoring, and data reduction methods need to be completed in a timely manner, particularly if the assessment is used clinically. Instruments need to be validated and reliable; too often scales are hastily put together and distributed despite a lack of rigorous testing. Finally, different scales will emphasize different aspects of family functioning, or measure the same concept differently, depending on the model from which they derive. For example, communication is a common construct that is measured by listening skills, speaking skills, self-disclosure, and clarity in one model (Olson & Gorall, 2003) and direct/indirect and clear/masked dichotomy in another model (Epstein & Bishop, 1981; Ryan et al., 2005). These differences are not limited to paper-and-pencil tests or to subjective ratings of family functioning. It is mentioned here because of the growing number of instruments being developed and the use or misuse of poorly defined yet commonly used concepts.

Whom to Include When Assessing the Family

When measuring a family's functioning, it is important to keep in mind that the assessment is not made up of a series of dyads or triads. While information may be obtained through individual family members, the purpose of the family assessment is to obtain a total family picture—not a series of individual problems. This applies whether the information is obtained through objective or subjective techniques as described earlier. Also, although one family member (the patient) may have been the reason for initiating a family assessment, the focus still remains on the family dynamics and the family's functioning. This is true whether the patient has a sudden catastrophic event (accident, head trauma), a relapsing and remitting illness (bipolar disorder), a deteriorating condition (multiple sclerosis, Alzheimer's disease), a chronic medical condition (hypertension,), or a severe yet recoverable event (heart attack, some cancers). As noted earlier, one purpose of the assessment is to discover how the family affects the patient's condition and how the patient's condition may affect family members.

Thus, the general rule is to have all salient family members participate if they are willing and if it is feasible. Some families will be able to discuss changes within the family's functioning as a result of the illness, adjust roles within the family and, ultimately, help in the patient's recovery or adaptation to a new condition. Other families will have great difficulty in adjusting to new circumstances within the family, or even fail to see the need for adjusting to a new condition, and inadvertently have a negative effect on the patient's recovery process.

Although it may be important to get each member's input into the family's functioning, it may be clinically impossible to do so. Patients with stroke, dementia, head trauma, or psychosis may not be able to communicate or to provide accurate information. If the family consists of a couple, one of whom is incapacitated, the informant may be restricted to one family member. Also, some children and adults may be unable to participate because of their reading ability. In the case of a single-parent family, the parent may be the sole family member providing information about the family's functioning. If an in-person assessment is conducted, very small children may stay in the interview room, while older children may be excused during some portions of the interview.

When to Conduct the Family Assessment

Once again, the timing of the assessment depends on the purpose of the assessment. Some family assessments are given to large populations in order to screen at-risk families. More likely, clinicians and researchers will make use of a family assessment when a patient or family member enters the health care system to address a specific problem. Baseline assessments should be completed as part of a comprehensive intake packet, particularly if part of the patient's care includes rehabilitation services. A family assessment can help determine how a family functions, as well as what family resources are available, to help inform treatment recommendations. More important, since a family's functioning is dynamic, it makes sense to conduct a family assessment at regular intervals, particularly if a family intervention is part of the treatment plan. Family therapists regularly conduct assessments to gauge whether or not the therapy is working. In a structured program, assessments may be done pre- and post-treatment, every 6 months, annually, or whatever time period seems appropriate given the family circumstances, the reason for the assessment, and the medical condition(s) facing the family. If the program is on-going, it may be wise to ask the family periodically about any changes in the family's composition. The health care provider can then use the information to decide whether or not any adjustments need to be made in the treatment plan.

CRITICAL ISSUES IN FAMILY FUNCTIONING ASSESSMENT

There are several points to keep in mind when assessing a family's functioning. First, there is no prototypical family functioning that can describe a uniform reaction to a family member's illness (Ryan et al., 2005). Two families in which a family member is diagnosed with the same illness or disability can differ in their level of family functioning just as two families with a member having completely different illnesses can, nonetheless, share a similar level of family functioning. Families that have similar patterns of functioning may have very different health conditions, and families that are deemed equally healthy may have very different levels of functioning (McDowell & Newell, 1996; Peterson, 2005; WHO, 2002). Thus, one issue to be cognizant of when assessing a family's functioning is to remain open-minded and not assume a level of a family's functioning based on a family member's illness or disability. A second and related point is to be aware of a variety of mediators that impact—or may reflect—a family's functioning. For example, the family composition; its social/economic circumstances; developmental stage when an assessment is completed; the ethnic, cultural, or religious make-up or practice of family members—all can influence a family's functioning (Beavers, 2003). In addition to how these variables might reflect various styles of family functioning, the level of disability or impairment may also affect, and be affected, by these factors.

Third, family functioning is dynamic and may change over time as a result of the progression of the illness, the family's adjustment to the illness condition, the coping or noncoping ability of the ill member as well as the family, and both the strengths and the limitations of family members (Ryan et al., 2005; Scherer & Cushman, 1997; Thoits, 1982; 1995). Progression of an illness is not always unidirectional or steady; neither is the family's ability to cope or to function. Families, like patients, may need to adjust in many areas at once, particularly in cases of sudden onset or crisis situations (Dittmar, 1997). In addition, just as some patients adjust quickly and function with greater independence than would be expected from their impairment, some families adapt and function better or worse than expected (Reed et al., 2005).

A fourth point dealing with family assessment falls under the rubric of methodology and covers a number of design issues. That is, for each of the topics addressed in the previous section, another series of questions can be generated. For example, the advantages and disadvantages of using objective and subjective measures of family functioning were discussed from a clinical perspective and from a practical, logistic perspective. Debates over which approach is preferable continue, but may be resolved by using some combination of the two. There is still no uniform agreement about which key concepts should be used to assess families and their functioning (Forman, Aronson, & Combs, 2003). The clinician or researcher should keep in mind the dimensions of interest needed to answer his/her question. Not every key concept will be assessed in every family functioning instrument, but there certainly should be some overlap as suggested earlier. Communication is a common construct that may, however, be measured in a variety of ways. Family functioning assessment methods and instruments will vary in their focus of interest and reflect the theoretical bent of the developer. Finally, instruments will differ in their scoring, psychometric properties, development, and generalizability. Users should carefully consider what particular aspect(s) of family functioning they are interested in measuring as a guide to choosing the most appropriate method of assessment.

There are commonalities between the issues touched upon regarding assessment of family functioning and some of the issues that the ICF has dealt with, or continues to struggle with, in the classification of functioning. In the ICF, there is an emphasis on direct measurement of skills and abilities needed to help patients adapt to their medical condition (Frey, 1984) just as there is an emphasis on how to measure family functioning. The emphasis on measurement may differ from an earlier focus on aptitudes and general abilities, but be in line with an effort to quantify scientific constructs. Also, the focus is on measuring functioning in the here-and-now.

To help understand family functioning, researchers have shied away from the use of the term *normal* and moved toward more meaningful and less value laden terms such as *functional/nonfunctional* or *healthy/unhealthy* with clearly defined anchor points that suggest a range of functioning within families. The ICF has also struggled to find suitable language that would apply to a variety of conditions over a variety of cultures.

Case Study—Problems Encountered When a Family Is Not Assessed

A therapist worked with a 72-year-old woman who had recently had a stroke leading to left-sided weakness and difficulties in ambulating and carrying out self-care. The patient had trouble participating with her physical therapy exercises. She was very anxious about managing her disabilities and gave up easily. She could not articulate her concerns. A meeting was held with the patient's retired 74-year-old husband, 44-year-old daughter, and 46-year-old son-in-law. The husband was noted to be supportive, but rigid and angry with his wife for not making a greater effort to help herself. He sympathized with her illness, but felt overwhelmed by having to help her with all of her daily functions. They had always been very proud of their independence, and he had a great deal of difficulty asking for and accepting help at home. His frustration led him to be irritable and critical of his wife—which discouraged her from sustaining her efforts at rehabilitation. The daughter and son-in-law were not aware of how much the patient and her husband were struggling. They were busy with their own lives and preferred to believe that steady progress was being made.

The family assessment allowed the family members to become more aware of the problems they were all having adjusting to the impact of the stroke. The therapist was also in a better position to recommend appropriate home services. The husband felt better once his sense of burden was validated. This allowed him to ask for and accept visiting nurses at home and the help of his daughter. As the husband felt less overwhelmed, he became more supportive and less critical of his wife. This in turn led to the patient becoming more relaxed and more able to focus on and persist with her rehabilitation program.

CULTURAL, PROFESSIONAL, AND LEGAL ISSUES RELATED TO ASSESSING FAMILY FUNCTIONING

We have already discussed the influence of ethnicity and culture on the assessment of family functioning and how the clinician/researcher needs to be mindful of and sensitive to the cultural context when assessing families. For some questions, it may be important to obtain assessments of families with and without the condition under study across different cultural contexts to help determine the range of "normal" functioning within a particular culture. The use of a control sample is even more important when comparing family functioning across cultures. Otherwise differences in family functioning across cultures may be attributed to an illness condition when, in fact, the difference is due to cultural differences or perceptions in functioning. There is a huge literature to draw on when conducting cross-cultural

research (Jenkins & Karno, 1992; Kleinman & Good, 1985). The reader is encouraged to review some of the literature on cross-cultural studies, as it is beyond the scope of this chapter to do so.

Whether the goal of rehabilitation services is restoration or enhancement of functioning (Fenderson, 1984), or change in functioning toward more independence and better quality of life (Granger, 1997), resources needed to provide rehabilitation services will likely be funded by government programs. Involvement by government initiatives then brings program accountability and program evaluations. Economic costs and concerns become more articulated, and patient assessments are more important to identify needs, monitor progress, and evaluate outcomes (Halpern & Fuhrer, 1984). Comprehensive evaluations now include physical, emotional, social, and vocational assessments of patients. A more complete evaluation will also include

---

DISCUSSION BOX 29.2
Cross-Cultural Issues in Family Functioning

A number of researchers translate assessment instrument(s) in order to understand family functioning in different ethnic/cultural groups. Another body of researchers argues that it is not possible or valid to use an instrument developed for one group by merely translating the words—the translated instrument could not possibly capture the identical nuances of different languages or cultures.

Questions

1. Is it possible to develop a meaningful measure of family functioning that cross-cuts ethnic groups/cultures? If, as many believe, the answer is a resounding "no," then how will researchers ever be able to compare family functioning in different cultural settings? One way

is to acknowledge cultural variation in family composition, family identity, emphasis on family dimensions, and how family goals are expressed or fulfilled.

2. Can you think of 5–10 concepts that span ages, family situations, development stages, cultures—but would be relevant in assessing family functioning? Once the concepts are agreed upon, then questions can be formulated. See if a group/class can agree on 1) a set of concepts; and 2) develop a set of questions to address/measure the concept.

3. Use the key constructs listed in the family models table Table 29.2: Well-Known Scales for Assessing Families) to start the discussion and generate some questions that could be used in different cultures.

family assessment because the time and effort needed to evaluate a family's functioning may provide critical information on how the patient and family affect each other positively and negatively, knowledge that may inform treatment recommendations (Keitner, Ryan, & Epstein, 2006).

INTERDISCIPLINARY USES OF FAMILY ASSESSMENT

Throughout this chapter, we have provided information on assessing a family's functioning, with specific reasons why it is important to obtain an assessment and who might find it of use. To reiterate, the focus of rehabilitation outcome has less to do with the underlying disease process and more to do with providing services to address disability/disease management, ameliorate the course of illness, and enhance the patient's quality of life and sense of well-being (Scherer & Cushman, 1997; Reed et al., 2005). Because an individual does not exist in a vacuum, but is usually part of a family system, the family's functioning is particularly relevant throughout the lifespan as well as across a wide range of illnesses, traumas, injuries, and disabilities (Keitner, Ryan, & Epstein, 2006).

Knowing a family's functioning, including its strengths and weaknesses, can be useful to rehabilitation therapists, primary care physicians, nurses, social workers, mental health workers, child development specialists, pastoral counselors, occupational therapists, pediatricians, school and physical health therapists, psychiatrists, and psychologists. Information obtained in a comprehensive evaluation can be applicable in a variety of health care settings and with a variety of presenting problems.

FUTURE ISSUES RELATING TO FAMILY ASSESSMENT

Over 20 years ago, Frey (1984) argued that, due to advances in science and technology, many acute illnesses may become controllable (e.g., diabetes, heart disease, arthritis) though not necessarily curable. Since then, his observation may be more relevant as advances in technology also result in patients surviving traumatic injuries, albeit with severe compromise to their functioning. While the underlying condition of these illnesses and injuries remains intact (Frey, 1984), refocusing the problem to effectively cope with long-term consequences of disease and/or injury has become more prominent. As clinicians and researchers have begun to understand the impact that family members have on each other, they are also beginning to understand how families can help or hinder a patient's progress and how a patient's distress or improvement can be reflected in his/her family. Also, as rehabilitation costs climb, there is an increased burden on health care facilities—and patients' families—regardless of the type of illness or disability (Halpern & Fuhrer, 1984; Heru & Ryan, 2002). Thus, many clinicians and researchers recognize the importance of including the family in a family member's rehabilitation as early in the process as possible (Sander et al., 2002; Sander et al., 2003; Ryan et al. 2005; Keitner, Ryan, & Epstein, 2006). At the least, a comprehensive patient assessment should include some evaluation of a family's functioning. As noted in this chapter, there are a variety of family assessments that have been tested and used for several years. Researchers will continue to refine concepts, particularly regarding the rehabilitative process, so that a comprehensive evaluation can inform an optimal treatment plan which may, in turn, lead to a more successful intervention and outcome.

DISCUSSION BOX 29.3

Pick an actual case—or create a fictitious case—based on your experience with your agency's clients or caseload.

Questions

1. Why would you conduct a family assessment with this family?
2. What additional information would you expect to obtain from the family that you could not obtain from an intake form, case report, or medical chart?
3. Who would you include in the family assessment?
4. What form/method of family assessment would you choose?
5. When would you conduct/administer the assessment? Why?
6. How would you use the results?
7. Compare/contrast your responses with others' responses for the same case and for different cases.

Summary and Conclusion

In this chapter, we tried to show how to integrate a complex topic—family assessment—into a complex field: rehabilitation and health. We argued the importance of viewing the patient within a wider social context and trying to gain a biopsychosocial perspective to a patient's health condition, rehabilitation, and course of illness. In our view, this perspective includes the patient's family and how it functions. Even though no family assessment purports to encompass every facet of a family's functioning, we provided an overview of different theoretical orientations, several methodologies for evaluating a family's functioning, and the plusses and minuses in using each method. We suggested how an assessment could be used by a variety of different health care professionals, and we listed particular issues to be aware of, including cultural sensitivity, awareness of one's own assumptions, and the ongoing, dynamic nature of family functioning. Finally, we suggested the growing attention that family functioning and its assessment will achieve in the future, particularly as clinicians and researchers learn to accept the limitations to treatment and the untapped resources that family members often provide.

Self-Check Questions

1. What kinds of outcomes are important to consider besides the patient's symptomology?
2. What is family functioning, and why is it important?
3. Provide three positive & three negative examples of how a sudden illness/accident could impact:
   (a) a family with 2 school-age children?
   (b) a retired couple?
   (c) a single parent family?
4. Provide three positive & three negative examples of how a chronic medical/psychiatric illness could impact:
   (a) a newly married couple?
   (b) a multigeneration family household?
5. Name three different ways to assess a family and cite the advantages and disadvantages of each.

References

Anderson, C. (2000). Views: Retrospective and prospective. *Family Process, 39*(1), 1–2.

Anderson, V. A., Catroppa, C., Haritou, F., Morse, S., & Rosenfeld, J. V. (2005). Identifying factors contributing to child and family outcome 30 months after traumatic brain injury in children. *Journal of Neurol Neurosurgical Psychiatry, 76*(3), 401–408.

Barth, J. C. (1996). Chronic illness and the family. In F. W. Kaslow. (Ed.). *Handbook of Relational Diagnosis and Dysfunctional Family Patterns.* New York: John Wiley & Sons, Inc.

Beavers, W. R. (1981). A system model of family for family therapists. *Journal of Marital and Family Therapy*, July, 299–307.

Beavers, W. R. (2003). Functional and dysfunctional families. In G. P. Sholevar and L. D. Schwoeri (Eds.), *Textbook of family and couples therapy* (pp. 317–340). Washington, DC: American Psychiatric Publishing, Inc.

Beavers, W. R., & Hampson, R. B. (1990). *Successful families: Assessment and intervention.* New York: Norton.

Beavers, W. R., & Hampson, R. B. (2000). The Beavers Systems model of family functioning *Journal of Family Therapy, 22*(2), 128–143.

Beavers, W. R. and Hampson R. B. (2003). Measuring family competence: The Beavers Systems model. In F. Walsh (Ed.), *Normal family processes growing diversity and complexity*, 3rd Ed. (pp. 549–580). New York/London: The Guilford Press.

Bishop, D. S., & Evans, R. L. (1990). Family functioning assessment techniques in stroke. *Stroke 21* (Suppl II), 50–51.

Brockaw, T., Cieza, A., Kuhlow, H., Sigl, T., Franke, T., Harder, M., & Stucki, G. (2004). Identifying the concepts contained in outcome measures of clinical trials on musculoskeletal disorders and chronic widespread pain using the International Classification of Functioning, Disability and Health as a reference. *Journal of Rehabilitation Medicine* (Suppl. 44), 30–36.

Brockaw, T. T., Wohlfahrt, K., Hillert, A., Geyh, S., Weigl, M., Franke, T., Resch, K. L., & Cieza, A. (2004). Identifying the concepts contained in outcome measures of clinical trials on depressive disorders using the international classification of functioning, disability and health as a reference. *Journal of Rehabilitative Medicine (Suppl. 44)*, 49–55.

Brown, G. W., Monck, E. M., Carstairs, G. M., & Wing, J. K. (1962). Influence of family life on the course of schizophrenic illness. *British Journal of Preventive and Social Medicine, 68*, 55–68.

Brown, G. W., & Rutter, M. (1966). The measurement of family activities and relationships: A methodological study. *Human Relations, 19,* 241–263.

Browning, S., & Green, R. (2003). Constructing therapy from strategic, to systemic, to narrative models. In G. P. Sholevar & L. D. Schwoeri (Eds.), *Textbook of family and couples therapy* Washington, American Psychiatric Publishing, Inc.: (pp 55–76).

Bruyere, S. M., Van Looy, S. A., & Peterson, D. B. (2005). The International Classification of Functioning, Disability and Health (ICF): Contemporary literature overview. *Rehabilitaion Psychology, 50*(2), 1–22.

Butzlaff, R. I., & Hooley, J. M. (1998). Expressed emotion and psychiatric relapse. *Archives of General Psychiatry, 55,* 547–552.

Clark, P. C., Shields, C. G., Aycock, D., & Wolf S. L. (2003). Preliminary reliability and validity of a family caregiver conflict scale for stroke. *Progress in Cardiovascular Nursing, 18*(2), 77–82, 92.

Cohen, B. F., & Anthony, W. A. (1984). Functional assessment in psychiatric rehabilitation. In A. S. Halpern & M. J. Fuhrer (Eds.), *Functional assessment in rehabilitation.* Baltimore, Paul H. Brookes Publishing Co.

Degotardi, P. J., Revenson, T. A., & Ilowite, N. T. (1999). Family-level coping in juvenile rheumatoid arthritis: Assessing the utility of a quantitative family interview. *Arthritis Care and Research, 12*(5), 314–324.

Dittmar, S. S. (1997). Overview: A functional approach to measurement of rehabilitation outcomes. In Dittmar S. S. & Gresham G. E. (Eds.), *Functional assessment and outcome measures for the rehabilitation health professional,* (pp. 1–10). Gaithersburg, MD: Aspen Publishers, Inc.

Doherty, W. J. & Baird, M. A. (1987). *Family-centered medical care: A clinical casebook.* New York: Guilford.

Engel, G. L. (1977). The need for a new medical model: A challenge for biomedicine. *Science, 196,* 129–136.

Epstein, N. B., & Bishop, D. S. (1981). Problem centered systems therapy of the family. *Journal of Marital and Family Therapy, 7*(1), 23–31.

Epstein, N. B., Bishop, D. S., & Levin, S. (1978). The McMaster Model of Family Functioning. *Journal of Marriage and Family Counseling, 4,* 19–31.

Epstein, N. B., Keitner, G. I., Bishop, D. S., & Miller, I. W. (1988). Combined use of pharmacological and family therapy. In J. F. Clarkin, G. Haas, & I. Glick (Eds.), *Affective disorders and the family.* New York: Guilford Press.

Epstein, N. B., Ryan, C. E., Bishop, D. S., Miller, I. W., & Keitner, G. I. (2003). The McMaster Model: A view of healthy family functioning. In F. Walsh *Normal family processes growing diversity and complexity,* (3rd ed.,) (pp. 581–607). New York/London: The Guilford Press.

Falloon, I. R. H. (2003). Behavioral family therapy. In Sholevar G. P., & L. D. Schwoeri (Eds), *Textbook of family and couples therapy,* (pp. 147–172). Washington, DC: American Psychiatric Publishing, Inc.

Fenderson, D. A. (1984). Preface. In Halpern A. S., & Fuhrer M. J. (Eds.), *Functional assessment in rehabilitation,* (pp. x–xiii). Baltimore, Paul H. Brooks Publishing Co.

Forman, B. D., Aronson, J, & Combs, M. P. (2003). Family assessment. In. Sholevar G. P., & Schwoeri L. D. (Eds.), *Textbook of family and couples therapy clinical applications.* Washington, DC London, England: American Publishing, Inc.

Frey, W. D. (1984). Functional assessment in the 80's: A conceptual enigma, a technical challenge. In. Halpern A. S., & Fuhrer M. J. (Eds.), *Functional assessment in rehabilitation.* (pp 11–43). Baltimore: Paul H. Brookes Publishing Co.

Glass, T. A., Berkman, L. F., Hiltunen, E. F., Furie, K., Glymour, M. M., Fay, M. E., & Ware, J. (2004). The families in recovery from stroke trial (FIRST): Primary study results. *Psychosomatic Medicine, 66*(6), 889–897.

Gottman, J. M. (1999). *The marriage clinic: A scientifically-based marital therapy.* New York, London: W.W. Norton & Company.

Granger, C. V. (1997). Foreword. In S. S. Dittmar & G. E. Gresham (Eds.), Functional assessment and outcome measures for the rehabilitation health professional. (p.ix). Gaithersburg, MD: Aspen Publishers, Inc.

Halpern, A. S., & Fuhrer, M. J. (1984). *Functional assessment in rehabilitation.* Baltimore: Paul H. Brookes.

Heru, A. M., & Ryan C. E. (2002). Depressive symptoms and family functioning in the caregivers of recently hospitalized patients with chronic/recurrent mood disorders. *International Journal of Psychosocial Rehabilitation, 7*(53), 53–60.

Heru, A. M., Ryan, C. E., & Iqbal, A. (2004). Family functioning in the caregivers of patients with dementia. *International Journal Geriatric Psychiatry, 19,* 533–537.

Heru, A. M., Ryan, C. E., & Vlastos, K. (2004). Quality of life and family functioning in caregivers of relatives with mood disorders. *Psychiatric Rehabilitation Journal, 28*(1), 67–71.

Hooley, J. M., & Teasdale, J. D. (1989). Predictors of relapse in unipolar depressive: Expressed emotion, marital distress, and perceived criticism. *Journal of Abnormal Psychology, 98*(3), 229–235.

Hurst, R. (2003). The international disability rights movement and the ICF. *Disability and Rehabilitation, 25,* 572–576.

Jenkins, J. H., & Karno, M. (1992). The meaning of expressed emotion: Theoretical issues raised by cross-cultural research. *American Journal of Psychiatry 149,* 9–21.

Kearney, P. M., & Pryor, J. (2004). The international classification of functioning, disability and health (ICF) and nursing. *Journal of Advanced Nursing, 46*(2), 162–170.

Keitner, G. I., (2005). Family therapy in the treatment of depression. *Psychiatric Times October,* 40–42.

Keitner, G. I., Archambault, R., & Ryan, C. E. (2003). Family therapy and chronic depression. In *Journal of Clinical Psychology/In Session: 59,* 873–884.

Keitner, G. I., & Miller, I. W. (1990). Family functioning and depression: An overview. *American Journal of Psychiatry, 147*(9), 1128–1137.

Keitner, G. I., Miller, I. W., & Ryan, C. E. (1993). The role of the family in major depressive illness. *Psychiatric Annals, 23*(9), 500–507.

Keitner, G. I., Miller, I. W., & Ryan, C. E. (1994). DC: *Family functioning in severe depressive disorders.* Washington, *American Psychiatric Press, Inc.*

Keitner, G. I., Ryan. C. E., & Epstein, N. B. (2006). Family assessment. In D. Goldbloom, (Ed.), *Psychiatric clinical skills.* (pp. 327–338.) Philadelphia, PA: Mosby Elsevier.

Keitner, G. I., Ryan, C. E., Miller, I. W., & Norman, W. H. (1992). Recovery and major depression factors associated with twelve-month outcome. *American Journal of Psychiatry, 149*, 93–99.

Keitner, G. I., Ryan, C. E., & Solomon, D. A. (2006). Realistic expectations and a disease management model for depressed patients with persistent symptoms. *Journal of Clinical Psychiatry, 67*, 1412–1421.

Kleinman, A, & Good, B. (1985). *Culture and depression studies in the anthropology and cross-cultural psychiatry of affect and disorder.* Berkeley/Los Angeles/London: University of California Press.

Lawton, M. P. (1971). The functional assessment of elderly people. *Journal of the American Geriatric Society, 19*(6), 465–481.

Leff, J. R., & Vaughn, C. E. (1985) *Expressed emotion in families.* London: Guilford Press.

Lewis, J. M., Beavers, W. R., Gossett, J. T., & Phillips, V. A. (1976). *No single thread: Psychological health in family systems.* New York, Brunner/Mazel.

McCubbin, H. I., Joy, C. B., & Cauble A. E. (1980). Family stress and coping: A decade review. *Journal of Marriage and the Family, 42*, 855–871.

McCubbin, H. I., & Thompson, A. I. (1991). *Family assessment inventories for research and practice* (2nd ed.). Madison: University of Winconsin.

McCubbin, M. A., McCubbin, H. I., and Thompson, A. I. (1987). Family Hardiness Index. In H. I. McCubbin & A. I. Thompson (Eds.), *Family assessment inventories for research and practice* (pp. 125–130). Madison: University of Wisconsin

McDowell, I., & Newell, C. (1996). *Measuring health: A guide to rating scales and questionnaires* (2nd ed.). New York: Oxford University Press.

Mengel, M. B. (1988). Functional assessment of families with a diabetic person. *Primary Care 15*(2), 297–310.

Miklowitz, D. J., & Clarkin J. F. (2003). Diagnosis of family relational disorders. In. G. P. Sholevar & L. D. Schwoeri (Eds.),. *Textbook of family and couples therapy.* (pp. 341–366). Washington, DC: American Psychiatric Publishing, Inc.

Miller I. W., Keitner G. I., Ryan C. E., Solomon D. A., Cardamil E. V., & Beevers C. G. (2005). Treatment matching in the posthospital care of depressed patients. *American Journal of Psychiatry, 162*, 2131–2138.

Moos R. H., Cronkite R. C., & Moos B. S. (1998). Family and extrafamily resources and the 10-year course of treated depression. *Journal of Abnormal Psychology, 107*(3), 450–460.

Moos, R., & Moos B. (1981). *Family Environment Scale manual.* Palo Alto, CA: Consulting Psychologists Press.

Moos, R., & Moos B. (1994) Family Environment Scale manual: Development, applications, research (3rd ed.). Palo, Alto, CA: Consulting Psychologists Press.

Olson, D. H. (2000). Circumplex model of martial and family systems. *Journal of Family Therapy, 22*(2), 144–167.

Olson, D. H., & Gorall D. M. (2003). Circumplex model of marital and family systems. In F. Walsh (Ed.), *Normal family processes growing diversity and complexity.* (3rd ed. pp. 514–548). New York/London: The Guilford Press.

Olson, D. H., Russell C. S., & Sprenkle D. H. (1989). *Circumplex model: Systemic assessment and treatment of families.* New York: Haworth Press.

Peterson, D. B. (2005). International classification of functioning, disability and health: An introduction for rehabilitation psychologists. *Rehabilitation Psychology 50*(2), 105–112.

Reed, G. M., Lux, J. B., Trask, C., Peterson, D. B., Stark, S., Threats, T. T., Jacobson, J. W., & Hawley J. A. (2005). Operationalizing the international classification of functioning, disability and health in clinical settings. *Rehabilitation Psychology, 50*(2), 122–131.

Ryan, C. E. (2002). Clinical and research issues in the evaluation and treatment of families. *Medicine and Health/Rhode Island, 89*(9), 278–280.

Ryan, C. E., Epstein, N. B, Keitner, G. I., Miller, I. W., & Bishop, D. S. (2005). *Evaluating and treating families: The McMaster Approach.* New York: Routledge Taylor & Francis Group.

Sander, A. J., Caroselli, J. S., High, W. M. Jr., Becker, C., Neese, L., & Scheibel, R. (2002). Relationship of family functioning to progress in a post-acute rehabilitation programme following traumatic brain injury. *Brain Injury, 16*(8), 649–657.

Sander, A. M., Sherer, M., Malec, J. F., High, W. M. Jr., Thompson, R. N., Moessner, A. M., & Josey, J. (2003). Preinjury emotional and family functioning in caregivers of persons with traumatic brain injury. *Archives of Physical Medicine and Rehabilitation, 84*(2), 197–203.

Sawin, K. J., & Harrigan, M. P. (1995). *Measures of family functioning for research and practice.* New York: Springer Publishing Company.

Scherer, M. J., & Cushman, L. A. (1997). A functional approach to psychological and psychosocial factors and their assessment in rehabilitation. In S. S. Dittmar & G. E. Gresham (Eds.), *Functional assessment and outcome measures for the rehabilitation health professional.* Gaithersbury, MD: Aspen Publishers, Inc.

Schlote, A., Richter, M., Frank, B., & Wallesch, C. W. (2006). A longitudinal study of health-related quality of life of first stroke survivors' close relatives. *Cerebrovascular Disease, 22*(2–3), 137–142.

Sholevar, G. P. (2003). Family theory and therapy: An overview. In G. P. Sholevar & L. D. Schwoeri (Eds.), *Textbook of Family and Couples Therapy Clinical Applications.*

Washington, DC, and London, England: American Psychiatric Publishing, Inc.

Stancin, T., Kaugars, A. S., Thompson, G. H., Taylor, H. G., Yeates, K. O., Wade, S. L., & Drotar, D. (2001). Child and family functioning 6 and 12 months after a serious pediatric fracture. *The Journal of Trauma, 51*(1), 69–76.

Stucki, G., & Kroeling, P. (2000). Physical therapy and rehabilitation in the management of rheumatic disorders. *Baillieres Best Practice Research Clinical Rheumatology,*14, 751–771.

Thoits, P. A. (1982). Conceptual, methodological, and theoretical problems in studying social support as a buffer against life stress. *Journal of Health and Social Behavior, 23*, 145–159.

Thoits, P. A. (1995). Stress, coping, and social support processes: Where are we? What's next? *Journal of Health and Social Behavior* Extra Issue, 53–79.

Üstün, T. B., Chatterji, S., Bickenbach, J., Kostanjsek, N., & Schneider M. (2003). The international classification of functioning, disability and health: A new tool for understanding disability and health. *Disability and Rehabilitation, 25*(11–12), 565–571.

Van Humbeeck, G., Van Audenhove, C. H., De Hert, M., Pieters, G., & Storms, G. (2002). Expressed emotion a review of assessment instruments. *Clinical Psychology Review,* 22, 321–341.

Vaughn, C. E., & Leff, J. R. (1976). The influence of family and social factors on the course of psychiatric illness: A comparison of schizophrenic and depressed patients. *British Journal of Psychiatry, 129*, 125–137.

Walsh, F. (2003). *Normal family processes growing diversity and complexity* (3rd ed.). New York/London: The Guildford Press.

WHO (2002). *Towards a Common Language for Functioning, Disability and Health ICF.* Geneva, Author.

30

Consumer Satisfaction

Lynn Koch
University of Arkansas, Fayetteville

OVERVIEW

This chapter explores issues related to the assessment of consumer satisfaction with rehabilitation and health-care services. First, the author provides an overview of the history and importance of assessing consumer satisfaction. Challenges and issues in assessing consumer satisfaction are then addressed. This section is followed by a review of commonly used assessment instruments, approaches, and contemporary satisfaction research studies. Finally, specific guidelines for conducting assessments of consumer satisfaction using both qualitative and quantitative approaches are outlined.

LEARNING OBJECTIVES
By the end of the chapter, readers should be able to:

- Understand the history and importance of assessing consumer satisfaction in rehabilitation and related health care settings
- Describe issues/challenges that need to be addressed to improve the assessment of consumer satisfaction
- Identify commonly used instruments and approaches to assessing consumer satisfaction in rehabilitation and health care settings
- Examine contemporary trends and research in the assessment of consumer satisfaction
- List key issues that must be considered in assessing consumer satisfaction

INTRODUCTION

The importance of assessing consumer satisfaction with rehabilitation and health care has been well-recognized for more than half a century (Di Palo, 1997; Keith, 1998). Historically, the assessment of satisfaction is rooted in social sciences and consumer research (Di Palo). In recent years, the construct of consumer satisfaction has gained increasing attention because of trends such as managed care and its emphasis on documenting effectiveness and efficiency of services, legal mandates requiring increased accountability among federally-funded programs, and the growing emphasis placed on consumer participation in all aspects of rehabilitation and health care service design and delivery. Despite its importance, consumer satisfaction is a complex construct that continues to challenge researchers and practitioners who investigate consumers' overall satisfaction with services and their degree of satisfaction with specific service components.

The purpose of this chapter is to provide a detailed overview of the strategies used and challenges confronted in assessing consumer satisfaction, as well as approaches that can be implemented to overcome these challenges. In the first section, the author describes the history and importance of the assessment of consumer satisfaction. Specific challenges in the assessment of consumer satisfaction are then detailed, followed by an overview of several commonly used satisfaction instruments, assessment strategies, and satisfaction research studies. The author concludes this chapter with a list of key considerations in assessing consumer satisfaction that have implications for program evaluation and future research.

HISTORY AND IMPORTANCE OF ASSESSING CONSUMER SATISFACTION IN REHABILITATION AND HEALTH CARE SETTINGS

Consumer satisfaction has been defined as the degree to which health care and rehabilitation service recipients find service providers and services that they receive to be acceptable and appealing (Nelson & Steele, 2006). The assessment of consumer satisfaction has numerous purposes, including: (a) service improvement, (b) program planning and revision, (c) in-service training, and (d) agency or program performance appraisal in relation to accreditation standards and governmental regulations (Kosciulek, 2003). Consumer satisfaction comprises both affective (positive or negative feelings) and cognitive (what is important and how it is evaluated) components (Keith, 1998). It has been described as the consumer's evaluation or opinion of services received, as well as the results of those services, and is based on whether these are consistent with his or her preferences (Williams, Coyle, & Healy, 1998). Expanding on this notion, Di Palo (1997) noted that:

> These evaluations are based on the [consumer's] expectations (set of beliefs), values (whether aspects of the health care encounter are important) and the sense of entitlement (believing he or she has a right to expect a particular outcome). [Consumers] bring these attitudes to the health care encounter. Satisfaction is determined by the interaction of this system of beliefs, the actual occurrences of the encounter, and the comparison of that encounter to others like it (p. 421).

Early satisfaction research was conducted as part of broader sociological research examining satisfaction with different aspects of individuals' lives (Di Palo, 1997). In the 1960s and 1970s, medical sociology emerged as a subdiscipline of sociology, and medical sociologists conducted research to better understand the behaviors of "the principle actors in medical care—physicians and patients" (DiPalo, 1997, p. 423). Consumer satisfaction was of interest to them, both as an outcome, and as an intervening factor that influenced adherence to medical treatment. Researchers, during this period, also explored the relationship of sociodemographic characteristics (e.g., age, social class, sex, race, income, educational level, occupation, religion) to consumer satisfaction, but found most demographic variables to be unrelated to satisfaction. With the emergence of managed care in the 1980s, research began to shift its focus to the relationship between satisfaction and the organization of health care, rehabilitation, and medical care.

Today, the emphasis in rehabilitation and health care on evidence-based practice underscores the need for research demonstrating the effectiveness of interventions and programs designed to assist people with disabilities to achieve the goals of increased independence in functioning and improved quality of life. Although the need to determine the efficacy and effectiveness of interventions is the primary focus in evaluating evidence-based practices, the examination of other areas, such as consumer satisfaction, contribute to a more comprehensive assessment (Nelson & Steel, 2006).

Philosophical Rationale for Assessing Consumer Satisfaction

The current movements in patient, mental health, and rehabilitation consumer empowerment provide powerful justification for assessing consumer satisfaction because of its direct link to self-empowerment. Emener (1991) defined empowerment as a guiding philosophy underlying rehabilitation practice that emphasizes the rights of individuals with disabilities to make informed choices, take risks, and assume control of rehabilitation planning. Title I of the Rehabilitation Act emphasizes consumer empowerment through informed choice in the selection of vocational goals, employment outcomes, services and supports, and service providers (Council of State Administrators of Vocational Rehabilitation, 2002). Despite this legislative emphasis, West and Parent (1992) reported that choice, a fundamental component of empowerment, is severely restricted in the delivery of services to rehabilitation consumers with severe disabilities.

Kosciulek, Vessell, Rosenthal, Accardo, and Merz (1997) suggested that a primary vehicle for promoting consumer empowerment is through the provision of effective rehabilitation services, and it has been further noted that health care and rehabilitation services are only empowering to the extent that they are responsive to views of consumers regarding both their needs and the ability of services to address their needs in ways that are acceptable and effective (Powell, Holloway, Lee, & Sitzia 2004). Satisfaction research has the potential to empower consumers by treating them as consultants whose opinions exert a powerful influence on the evaluation of services and providers (WHO, 2000). This potential is realized when (a) consumers are brought into satisfaction research studies as partners, not just subjects; (b) their knowledge is used to understand health and rehabilitation issues and to improve rehabilitation and health care interventions; and (c) the immediate benefits of the results of satisfaction studies are provided to participants (Agency for Healthcare Research and Quality [AHRQ], 2007). The potential outcomes of such research are (a) the identification and application of interventions that are mutually beneficial to consumers and service providers, and (b) increased confidence among consumers that services will result in desired outcomes.

Legal and Professional Rationale for Assessing Consumer Satisfaction

The importance of assessing consumer satisfaction is also directly linked to the objective of improving quality of life and increasing independent functioning among people with disabilities. Powell and associates (2004, p. 13) noted that "with effectiveness increasingly being measured according to economic—rather than clinical—criteria, the inclusion of [consumers'] opinions in assessments of services has gradually gained prominence." In this respect,

---

DISCUSSION BOX 30.1

Although the importance of assessing consumer satisfaction with rehabilitation and health care services has been well-recognized for more than 50 years, recent trends in rehabilitation and health care (e.g., expanding clienteles and patient bases, managed care and its emphasis on documenting effectiveness and efficiency of services, legal mandates requiring increased accountability among federally-funded programs, the growing emphasis placed on consumer/patient choice in all aspects of rehabilitation and health care service design and delivery) have resulted in renewed interest in this construct. Accompanying this renewed interest is an evolved recognition of the complexity of consumer satisfaction and the many challenges that it presents to researchers and program evaluators who investigate it.

Questions

In small groups, discuss the issues related to assessing consumer satisfaction with rehabilitation and healthcare services. Use the following questions to direct your group's discussion:

1. What are the purposes of assessing consumer satisfaction in rehabilitation and health care settings?
2. What are the issues/challenges that researchers and program evaluators confront in attempting to evaluate consumer satisfaction? What strategies can be implemented in the design of satisfaction research to address these issues/challenges?
3. Provide examples of each of the following approaches to assessing consumer satisfaction:
   a. quantitative
   b. qualitative
   c. mixed methods
4. Describe both the strengths and the weaknesses of each of the following approaches to assessing consumer satisfaction:
   a. quantitative
   b. qualitative
   c. mixed methods

consumer satisfaction is a key component of program evaluation (the systematic process of making judgments about the merit, value, or worth of rehabilitation and health care services; Schnelker & Rumrill, 2001). In fact, consumer satisfaction has been identified as one of four core facets of treatment evaluation (Nelson & Steele, 2006), the other three being outcome evaluation, provider evaluation, and economic evaluation.

Assessment of consumer satisfaction as a component of program evaluation is prioritized in the Rehabilitation Act of 1973 and its amendments. The Act includes nine program evaluation standards, one of which requires that federally funded agencies routinely evaluate consumer satisfaction (Koch & Merz, 1995). Similarly, assessment of consumer satisfaction is a priority in other rehabilitation and health care settings due to contemporary trends in programming, such as managed care and increased demands for fiscal accountability, that require providers to document the effectiveness and efficiency of their efforts. Although treatment outcomes (e.g., employment status, improvement in functional abilities) have traditionally been the prominent indicator of programmatic effectiveness and efficiency, the increasing level of involvement in services that rehabilitation and health care consumers are demanding in the current era of postmodern medicine calls for the consideration of other quality indicators such as consumer satisfaction. (Powell et al., 2004, p. 13).

The need to routinely evaluate consumer satisfaction is further justified by research documenting disparities among minority populations in comparison to majority populations regarding access to health care and vocational rehabilitation services, quality of those services, and service outcomes (Agency for Healthcare Research and Quality [AHRQ], 2005; Capella, 2002; Lurie, Zhan, Sangl, Bierman, & Sekscenski, 2003; Rosenthal, Wilson, Ferrin, & Frain, 2005). Research sponsored by the AHRQ (2005) has documented pervasive disparities related to race, ethnicity, gender, and socioeconomic status in virtually all aspects of health care including: (a) the dimensions of effectiveness, patient safety, timeliness, and patient centeredness; (b) facilitators and barriers to health care utilization; (c) levels and types of care including preventative care, treatment of acute conditions, and management of chronic disease; (d) medical conditions such as cancer diabetes, end stage renal disease, heart disease, HIV disease, mental health and substance abuse disorders, and respiratory diseases; (e) care settings including primary care, dental care, home health care, emergency departments, hospitals, and nursing homes; and (f) subpopulations such as women, children, elderly, residents of rural areas, and individuals with disabilities. In comparison to whites, ethnic minority groups report greater difficulties with access to and use of health care (Fongwa, Cunningham, Weech-Maldonado, Gutierrez, & Hays, 2006; Lurie et al., 2003). Similarly, research has illuminated the presence of disparities in access to vocational rehabilitation services, types and number of services provided, case dollar expenditures, and rehabilitation outcomes that are related to race, ethnicity, and gender (Capella, 2002; Rosenthal et al., 2005). Both the United States Department of Health and Human Services and Section 21 of the 1992 Rehabilitation Act Amendments call for substantial improvement in the delivery of services to these underserved populations, and satisfaction research provides a much needed mechanism, to be used in combination with behavioral or functional indicators, for evaluating progress toward achieving this goal.

Consumer Satisfaction and International Classification of Functioning, Disability, and Health

The World Health Organization (WHO; 2000) identified the following key components of service delivery that can be assessed in the evaluation of consumer satisfaction: (a) the reliability of services, or the assurance that services are provided in a consistent and dependable manner; (b) the responsiveness of services or the willingness of providers to meet client/customer needs; (c) the courtesy of providers; and (d) the security of services, including the security of records (p. 7). WHO further suggested that in assessing consumer satisfaction, specific inquiries should be made about the physical setting of services, the helpfulness of support staff, information resources, the competence of service providers, the costs of services, the relevance of services to consumers' needs, the accessibility of services, waiting time for services, frequency of appointments, time spent with service provider, the "humaneness" of services, and the effectiveness of services in ameliorating consumers' problems.

A final rationale for evaluating consumer satisfaction is offered by the World Health Organization's introduction of the *International Classification of Functioning, Disability and Health* (ICF) as a new paradigm for rehabilitation and health care providers to use to better understand and address health and health-related conditions (Bruyere, 2005; Peterson, 2005). In addition to its use as a clinical tool, the ICF was designed for use as a research tool to measure outcomes, quality of life, and environmental factors affecting disability and health. As a classification system, it provides a framework for assessing satisfaction

DISCUSSION BOX 30.2

Pervasive disparities in consumer access to rehabilitation and health care services related to race, ethnicity, gender, and socioeconomic status have been well documented. These disparities underscore the crucial need for (a) vast improvements in the delivery of rehabilitation and health care services to underserved populations, and (b) satisfaction research to evaluate consumer opinions regarding progress toward achieving this goal. However, collecting valid satisfaction data has proven to be a difficult challenge. Because cultural norms regarding the appropriateness of providing feedback to researchers and program evaluators may limit the number and range of responses to inquiries about consumer satisfaction, it is crucial that culturally appropriate methods are used to assess consumer beliefs and opinions. Otherwise, it is unlikely that research findings will be representative of underserved populations.

Questions

With these challenges in mind, complete the following research exercise:

You are rehabilitation or health care professionals employed by a nonprofit agency that provides community-based mental health and vocational rehabilitation services to urban consumers in an ethnically-diverse Midwestern community. Your agency must submit a program evaluation plan to their accrediting body. As a result, your supervisor has assigned you to a committee that has been charged with the task of designing a study to evaluate consumer satisfaction as one component of the program evaluation plan. In planning the design of this study, you want to ensure that you obtain a representative sample of consumers. Develop a research plan addressing the following questions:

1. What stakeholders will you involve in designing your study and how will they be involved?
2. What potential sources of data will be used to evaluate consumer satisfaction?
3. What methods, measurement instruments, and/or approaches will you use to collect satisfaction data?
4. What types of questions will you ask consumers?
5. How will you interpret the data?
6. How will you ensure that the data you collect provide you with both a breadth and depth of consumer perspectives?
7. How will you use the data you collect to improve the quality of services your agency provides?

with services designed to enhance functioning within the various domains representing an individual's functioning, disability, and health. Because the ICF framework "exemplifies the interactive and multidimensional character of the biopsychosocial factors involved in the rehabilitation process" (Homa & Peterson, 2005, p. 120), it is compatible with a multidimensional approach to assessing consumer satisfaction. Specifically, its interactive components of body function and body structure, activities and participation, and environmental factors provide targets for assessment of satisfaction with services tailored to ameliorate problems and improve functioning in each of these areas. An assessment of consumer satisfaction with these components can be used in combination with clinical performance indicators of each area of functioning to obtain an evaluation of overall quality of care and areas to target for quality improvement.

METHODOLOGICAL CONCERNS IN THE ASSESSMENT OF CONSUMER SATISFACTION

Before proceeding with a review of commonly used assessment approaches, readers should be aware of the challenges that clinicians and researchers confront in attempting to evaluate consumer satisfaction with rehabilitation and health care. With this understanding, readers will be able to consider the variety of options for assessing satisfaction in light of the potential limitations and strengths associated with each. The challenges to be discussed in the following paragraphs encompass issues such as: (a) construct validity, (b) acquiescence and social desirability, (c) structure of consumer satisfaction measures, (d) sampling bias, (e) psychometric properties, and (f) the relevance of satisfaction indicators to service users.

Construct Validity

Foremost among the challenges in assessing consumer satisfaction is the lack of a theoretical basis for the construct of satisfaction and the methods for assessing it (Williams et al., 1998). Rarely do researchers explicitly define consumer satisfaction, and the process whereby consumers arrive at assessments of the services they receive is seldom explored. Several theories and models have been proposed to explain the construct of consumer satisfaction (e.g., value-expectancy model, discrepancy theory, fulfillment theory, equity theory; Williams et al., 1998). However, when empirically tested, these models have failed to adequately explain the construct of consumer satisfaction. Subsequently, the development of tools to assess satisfaction has been plagued with problems.

Also related to the problem of construct validity, or lack thereof, is the tendency to equate consumer satisfaction with service efficiency and effectiveness. On the contrary, consumers sometimes report dissatisfaction with services that, according to other more direct measures, prove to be quite effective at ameliorating their problems (Sitzia, 1999). Conversely, consumers may report satisfaction with service providers or services that are characterized by other measures as ineffective. The satisfaction they express is often unrelated to the quality of technical care they receive and more often related to the manner in which those services are delivered (e.g., amount of time health care provider or rehabilitation professional spends with consumer; Chang et. al, 2006; Fowler, 1997).

Acquiescence and Social Desirability

Regardless of the instrument being used, consumers are regularly uncritical of the services they receive, and quantitative ratings of consumer satisfaction tend to be high and to lack variability (Capella & Turner, 2004; Powell et al., 2004; Sitzia, 1999). Two potential causes for this phenomenon are social desirability effects and acquiescent response sets (Capella & Turner). Social desirability effects occur when individuals respond to survey items with what they think is the "correct" or socially acceptable answer. Socially desirable responses are likely to be obtained if consumers fear that services will be discontinued if they express any dissatisfaction or if they believe that nothing will change as a result of complaining (Powell et al., 2004). Acquiescence occurs when respondents answer questions affirmatively regardless of the content. It is most likely to be a problematic issue when survey items are all positively worded. The tendency of respondents to agree with every statement is reduced when instruments contain both positively-worded and negatively-worded items (Capella & Turner).

Sampling Bias

Response rates tend to be low in satisfaction research, introducing an additional challenge in this line of inquiry—sampling bias (Capella & Turner, 2004; De Wilde & Hendriks, 2005). Sampling bias is of concern when people who respond to consumer satisfaction surveys or other data collection instruments are characteristically different from those who do not respond. For example, numerous studies have indicated that older patients, women, individuals with less education, and healthier patients are more likely to report satisfaction with their health care (Carlson, Blustein, Fiorentino, & Prestianni, 2000). Consumers who are dissatisfied with services may be less likely to respond to satisfaction instruments, whereas consumers who do respond may have a greater tendency to follow through with tasks and thus have more positive experiences in the rehabilitation process (Kosciulek et al., 1997). As Powell et al. (2004) pointed out, "without a representative sample from which to generalize survey findings, one risks basing future services on a self-selecting group whose characteristics could differ significantly from fellow service users (e.g., those most satisfied with, and therefore unlikely to be critical of, services," p. 14). A related challenge occurs because rarely do researchers directly seek out input from consumers regarding areas of dissatisfaction (Capella & Turner).

Structure of Consumer Satisfaction Measures

Another challenge is the unidimensionality of some measurement instruments. Unidimensional instruments only measure overall satisfaction and fail to provide a means for respondents to indicate their degree of satisfaction with specific aspects of services or components of programs (Koch & Merz, 1995). Many satisfaction instruments only provide a global score. For example, the Client Satisfaction Questionnaire-8 (CSQ-8; Larsen, Attkisson, Hargreaves, & Nguyen, 1979), one of the most popular satisfaction instruments used in human service settings today (Capella & Turner, 2004), only provides a single score representing general satisfaction. Researchers have demonstrated that, when asked to evaluate services on a general level, consumers tend to provide higher ratings than when asked more specific questions (Capella & Turner; Williams et al., 1998).

Today, satisfaction researchers are in general agreement that consumer satisfaction has a variety of dimensions, and numerous instruments and assessment approaches have been designed to evaluate this construct. However, although there is overlap in the dimensions identified by different investigators, these dimensions still tend to be as varied as the procedures used in data collection. For example, Ware, Snyder, Wright, and Davies (1983) identified the following domains of satisfaction in medical, mental health, and human service settings: interpersonal manner, technical quality, efficacy/outcomes, accessibility/convenience, finances, physical environment, and availability. Kosciulek (2003) identified two dimensions of consumer satisfaction

(satisfaction with case management versus employment and satisfaction related to consumer choice versus customer service) with vocational rehabilitation. In a related study, Schwab, DiNitto, Aureala, Simmons, & Smith (1999) classified the core dimensions they discovered as responsiveness to client, client participation or involvement in the rehabilitation process, satisfaction with services, and satisfaction with employment. In a third study, Capella and Turner (2004) conceptualized the dimensions of satisfaction with vocational rehabilitation as the interpersonal relationship with the counselor and his or her effectiveness in handling the consumer's case, the services received, and the agency's characteristics.

Similarly, researchers assessing satisfaction with other human and health care services have identified different, although overlapping, dimensions. With respect to satisfaction with service providers, some have argued that there are two distinct dimensions of technical skills versus interpersonal skills (Fung, Elliot, Hays, Kahn, Kanouse, & McGlynn et al. (2005). These findings, along with those of Capella and Turner (2004) support previous research indicating that consumer satisfaction is strongly related to the quality of the working alliance between the service provider and consumer (Horvath & Symonds, 1991).

In research investigating satisfaction with physical therapy, researchers identified the dimensions of: (a) treatment, admission, logistics, and global; (b) efficacy, convenience, comfort, and overall; and (c) enhancers, detractors, location, and cost (Monnin & Perneger, 2002). Although there appear to be similarities in the dimensions identified among these studies, direct comparisons across findings are difficult to make due to the researchers' use of different measurement instruments, data collection strategies, and data analysis procedures.

Some researchers have characterized consumer satisfaction as comprising a cognitive expectations component, and whether a consumer is satisfied or dissatisfied with a service is dependent as much upon that individual's expectations as it his upon his or her direct experience of the service (Powell et al. 2004). Consumers enter relationships with service providers with preconceptions about the nature of the relationship, and the failure of the rehabilitation, or health care professional to acknowledge and address these preconceptions (i.e., be responsive to the consumer's needs, identify and disprove negative expectations, educate the consumer about what can reasonably be expected, negotiate responsibilities, identify desired outcomes, monitor changes in consumer expectations over time) can result in dissatisfaction (Chan, Shaw, McMahon, Koch, &

Strauser, 1997). As Schwarz, Landis, Rowe, Janes, and Pullman (2000, p. 59) noted, "successfully improving quality depends on being able to understand customers' needs and expectations and then exceeding them." Research on counseling expectations has demonstrated that (a) congruence in consumer–counselor expectations is positively correlated with ratings of the working alliance (Al-Darmaki & Kivlighan, 1993); (b) consumers who enter the counseling relationship with low expectations due to prior unsatisfactory experiences are likely to prematurely terminate counseling (Alston & Mngadi, 1992); and (c) discrepancies between what the consumer expects and what actually occurs in counseling can also result in premature termination of the counseling relationship (Tinsely, Bowman, & Ray, 1988).

Given these findings, some researchers have noted the need to incorporate consideration of expectations into the assessment of satisfaction because, as marketing researchers have learned, "initial expectations must be equaled or exceeded by consumer perceptions of outcome before consumer satisfaction exists" (Richard, 2000, p. 39). Other researchers have noted that the constructs that we must consider are actually preferences and anticipations rather than expectations. Their rationale for this argument is that expectations are actually comprised of two distinct components—anticipations (what individuals think will happen) and preferences (what they want to happen). Because anticipations and preferences can vary substantially (i.e., an applicant for rehabilitation services may anticipate negative outcomes but prefer positive outcomes), consumer preferences are what we should target in satisfaction research because satisfaction with services is most likely to occur when services are consistent with consumers' preferences (Galassi, Crace, Martin, James, & Wallace, 1992; Koch, 2001).

Psychometric Properties

A further challenge is the plethora of "home made" satisfaction instruments that are used in rehabilitation and health care settings (Sitzia, 1999). Mail surveys, a frequently used method for assessing satisfaction with rehabilitation and health care services, are often developed for specific sites with scant attention given to their methodological rigor (Powell et al., 2004). In a review of 195 studies on health service user satisfaction, Sitzia (1999) found that 64% of the studies provided no data about the reliability and validity of the satisfaction instruments used. In many cases, reliability and validity data for "home made" instruments are not even collected, and when they do get collected, the reliability and validity of these instruments are significantly lower than they are for already existing instruments. Because of lack of standardization, comparisons between service sites and settings cannot be made.

Relevance of Satisfaction Indicators to Consumers

Another problem is that satisfaction instruments are often developed from a medical model perspective—"objectifying satisfaction as a 'thing' and ignoring the complexity of users' subjective appreciation of services" (Powell et al., 2004, p. 15). Such instruments represent providers' or researchers' views of the important dimensions of satisfaction, with the dimensions of satisfaction that consumers view as important given scant attention (Campbell, 1999; Richard, 2000). In many cases, instruments are developed by researchers and clinicians without any input from consumers. For example, Campbell (1994) conducted a survey of public mental health providers in one state to determine the extent to which mental health consumers were involved in the design and implementation of satisfaction instruments and found that consumers were involved in the development of the instruments only 25% of the time. Furthermore, it was found that few of the agencies involved consumers in any aspect of satisfaction research beyond instrument development. Consequently, such instruments restrict the range of potential responses and prohibit consumers from providing opinions that are outside of the instrument developers' view of what factors constitute consumer satisfaction. Failure to capture aspects of satisfaction that are relevant and important to consumers results in low content and face validity of measurement instruments (Meehan, Bergen, & Stedman, 2002).

METHODS FOR ASSESSING CONSUMER SATISFACTION

Approaches to collecting and analyzing satisfaction data in rehabilitation and health care disciplines include mail surveys, electronic surveys, telephone interviews, face-to-face interviews, focus group interviews, and combinations of these methods. In the following discussion, we organize these methods into the categories of (a) quantitative, (b) qualitative, and (c) mixed-methods approaches.

Quantitative Approaches

Quantitative consumer satisfaction surveys have emerged as the method of choice for eliciting the views of a relatively large number of people on the provision of health care, social services, counseling, and rehabilitation services (Powell et al., 2004; Schwarz et al., 2000). These instruments typically require respondents to rate their level of satisfaction with various aspects of service delivery on five- to six-point rating scales ranging from, for example, "very satisfied" to "very dissatisfied," "excellent" to "poor," or "strongly agree" to "strongly disagree" (Ware & Hays, 1988). While some of these instruments have been carefully developed with psychometric characteristics (e.g., reliability and validity) assessed and reported, and standard guidelines for administration, scoring, and interpretation provided, many of these instruments are psychometrically weak. Two examples of standardized quantitative consumer satisfaction instruments with established psychometric properties that are used in a variety of rehabilitation, social service, and health care settings are the Client Satisfaction Questionnaire-8 (CSQ-8; Larsen et al., 1979) and the Service Satisfaction Scale-30 (SSS-30; Greenfield & Attkisson, 1999).

THE CSQ-8.   One of the most popular quantitative instruments that has been developed for measuring consumer satisfaction in rehabilitation and related settings is the CSQ-8 (Attkisson & Greenfield, 2004; Larsen et al., 1979). The CSQ-8 is a self-completed paper-and-pencil instrument that contains 8 items that require respondents to rate the quality of services they have received on a scale of 1 to 4. Although it is usually self-administered, the CSQ-8 can be administered by an interviewer if respondents are unable to independently complete the instrument. Examples of items on the CSQ-8 include: How would you rate the quality of services received? If a friend were in need of similar help would you recommend our program to him or her? Have the services you received helped you to deal more effectively with your problems? The CSQ-8 provides a single, global score representing general satisfaction. Mean or modal levels of satisfaction can be compared with established norms or with norms obtained in a single organization or system of care. The CSQ-8 is available in English, Spanish, and Dutch versions. More recently it has been translated into Arabic, Chinese, Japanese, Laotian, Polish, Portuguese, Russian, Tagolog, Vietnamese, Korean, and Cambodian (Attkisson & Greenfield, 2004).

As a global measure of client satisfaction, the CSQ-8 has a substantial amount of evidence supporting its reliability and validity (Attkisson & Greenfield, 2004; DeWilde & Hendriks, 2005; Koch & Merz, 1995). Research studies report strong internal reliability with Cronbach's alphas ranging from .83 to .93. Correlations between the CSQ-8 and other satisfaction measures range from .60 to .80, indicating the CSQ-8 has good construct validity. Gaston and Sabourin (1992) provided support for the discriminant validity of the CSQ-8 in their research demonstrating that there was no association between CSQ-8 scores and scores on a scale to measure social desirability.

As has been established in a prior section of this chapter as problematic to satisfaction research in general, the CSQ-8 results in distributions of scores that tend to be negatively skewed by the production of highly positive responses. However, a benefit of the CSQ-8 is that it provides a core of generic items that can be applied to a variety of service settings and to which specific items can be added for acquiring satisfaction data about specific sites or populations (Koch & Merz, 1995).

THE SSS-30. The SSS-30 is a 30-item questionnaire used in a variety of rehabilitation and clinical settings including residential and outpatient alcohol or other drug dependency treatment facilities, employee assistance programs (EAPS), and managed behavioral health organizations (Greenfield & Atkkisson, 2004). It was specifically designed as a multifactorial scale to assess the various components of satisfaction with outpatient health or mental health services and substance abuse treatment programs. Written at a 6.4 grade reading level, the SSS-30 has four subscales, two of which are considered primary and two of which are secondary. The primary subscales are *Practitioner Manner and Skill* and *Perceived Outcome*. The secondary subscales are *Office Procedures* and *Access*. The SSS-30 also has a full scale that provides a score that serves as a general satisfaction measure. Norm groups for the SSS-30 include outpatients of four primary health care clinics, clients of two student mental health counseling services centers, mental health clients of a hospital-based EAP, clients of a community mental health clinic, psychiatric outpatients of an urban medical center, clients completing a mandatory chemical dependency treatment program for multiple driving under intoxication (DUI) offenders, clients of a methadone maintenance clinic, and clients of county-contracted substance abuse treatment programs (Greenfield & Attkisson, 2004).

Examples of items to assess different components of service satisfaction include: ability of your [practitioner/counselor] to listen to and understand your problem (assesses technical and interpersonal qualities); effect of services in helping relieve symptoms or reduce problems (assesses outcome); and availability of appointment times that fit your schedule (assesses accessibility of services; Greenfield & Atkkisson, 2004). Respondents self-administer the paper-and-pencil questionnaire, which

requires them to rate on a 5-point "delighted" to "terrible" scale how they feel about each of these service satisfaction items. In addition to the closed-ended items, the SSS-30 also includes open-ended items: "The thing I have liked best about my experience here is . . . ," "What I liked least was . . . ," and "If I could change one thing about the service it would be . . . " (Greenfield & Attkisson, 2004).

In terms of construct and content validity, the item content of the SSS-30 covers domains that have been established in the literature on consumer satisfaction (Greenfield & Attkisson, 2004). The validity of the SSS-30 as a general satisfaction measure has not been as well-established as that of the CSQ-8. However, in one study, the researchers found that the SSS-30 correlated .70 ($p < .0001$) with the CSQ-8 (Greenfield, 1989 as cited in Greenfield & Atkisson, 2004). In examining the SSS-30 in terms of its validity as a multidimensional measure of consumer satisfaction across settings, researchers have identified two major factors (manner and skill satisfaction and outcome satisfaction) with coefficients of congruence ranging from .88 to .97. Other factors (e.g., office procedures and personnel satisfaction and access satisfaction) have been found to be much less stable across service settings. Research examining the internal reliability of the SSS-30 subscales has reported reliability coefficients ranging from .60 to .93. (Greenfield & Attkisson, 2004; De Wilde & Hendricks, 2005).

Although quantitative approaches in the form of closed-ended, forced choice surveys yield satisfaction data from large numbers of people, they are not without their limitations. These include: (a) restriction of the information that can be yielded because associated expectations are typically not queried; (b) failure of surveys to tap into domains of satisfaction that are of greatest interest or importance to consumers; (c) limits on the range of possible responses that could result in overestimates of satisfaction; (d) failure of many surveys to solicit input into how services can be improved; and (e) potential of surveys to discriminate against consumers who are less literate or for whom English is not their first language (Schwarz et al, 2000).

Qualitative Approaches

Whereas quantitative approaches to assessing consumer satisfaction examine data that are measurable, qualitative approaches examine data that are reported in words. Because the aim of qualitative approaches is to make sense of participants' lived experiences, these approaches are particularly well-suited to exploring the construct of consumer satisfaction (Hein, Lustig, & Uruk, 2005). They tap into consumer opinions about service dimensions with which they are satisfied, as well as those with which they are dissatisfied, the value of different aspects of rehabilitation and health care services, and strategies to improve services to better meet their needs. Qualitative approaches provide research participants with opportunities to offer detailed opinions about their experiences and for researchers to uncover in-depth information such as *why* participants value certain programmatic components over others (Barbour, 2005).

A commonly used qualitative approach is the interview. Qualitative interviews generally entail the use of questioning to explore the phenomenon of interest from the interviewee's perspective. Interviews can either be structured (i.e., the interviewer has a set of questions to which he or she strictly adheres); unstructured or conversational (i.e., no questions are established *a-priori*); or semi-structured (i.e., the interviewer uses a loosely-structured interview protocol and probes, skips questions, or asks follow-up questions as needed; Sharma, 2004). Qualitative interviews can be conducted with individuals or groups. Interview data may be collected in person, telephonically, or electronically, and audiotaping and transcription are typically used (with the permission of the interviewee) to ensure accuracy in data collection and analysis. Examples of questions that could be used to guide qualitative interviews include: Describe your experiences with (provider). What aspects of services were particularly helpful? What aspects of services could be improved? How would you rate the overall quality of your experience with (provider)?

Focus groups are the most advantageous way to interview several participants at one time regarding their perceptions or opinions. The purpose of focus group research is to gather information about how people feel or think about an issue, product, or service from participants who share common characteristics or interests (Krueger & Casey, 2000). Focus groups are typically comprised of five to ten people and have proven to be useful in accessing the opinions of members of underserved populations, particularly if the groups are homogeneous (Barbour, 2005). Focus groups can uncover unanticipated issues that surveys cannot identify and explore the complexities of consumer satisfaction in greater depth (Schwarz et al., 2000).

In recent years, focus groups have become an increasingly popular method in satisfaction research in rehabilitation and health care (Barbour, 2005). For example, to examine the outcomes of nursing care during surgery and hospitalization from the perspectives of patients, Middleton and Lumby (1999) conducted focus groups with participants following a recent orthopedic inpatient admission to a large Australian teaching hospital. In their study, a total of 16 patients participated in one of several focus groups in which they responded to the following questions:

1. Were you satisfied with the level of health/well-being that you had achieved on the day of your discharge from hospital?
2. If you were not satisfied, what were your expectations prior to your operation about the level you could expect to achieve by the time of discharge from hospital?
3. What was done for you by the nursing staff that really made a difference to your outcome, both positive and negative?
4. What was not done for you by the nursing staff that you feel would have made a difference to your outcome? (p. 144)

In analyzing the audiotaped transcripts of the focus groups, the researchers identified five nursing activities (e.g., an explanation of pending operation, being informed about details of the treatment while in the hospital) that made a positive difference to patient outcomes; three activities (e.g., cranky nurses) that made a negative difference to patient outcomes; and seven activities (e.g., assistance from nurses at mealtime) not performed by nursing staff that participants believed would have made a positive difference to their outcomes.

In another focus group study investigating soldiers' experiences with military healthcare, the researchers only used two probes: What do you expect from the military health system? and Give me some ideas of what happens to you when you go to get health services (Jennings, Loan, Heiner, Hemman, & Swanson, 2005, p. 999). As a result of using these two broad probes, the researchers were able to identify factors (e.g., concerns about provider competence, challenges in getting appointments that don't conflict with their training schedules, the power of the command structure in supporting or thwarting their care, the prolonged recovery process) that may contribute to dissatisfaction with health care among active duty soldiers. The authors, in concluding that their research allowed them to explore sources of dissatisfaction that are typically not assessed in satisfaction research, highlight one of the benefits of focus group research.

To address gaps in the literature on client-centered service delivery models, Cott (2004) conducted focus groups with recipients of client-centered medical rehabilitation services in Ontario, Canada. She completed a total of six focus group interviews: one each with persons with spinal cord injuries ($n = 3$), acquired brain injury ($n = 4$), chronic respiratory conditions ($n = 5$), stroke ($n = 7$), and two with persons with arthritis and/or total joint replacement ($n = 14$). In the focus groups, nondirective, open-ended questions were used to encourage participants to identify issues of importance to them. They were first asked to discuss in general their experiences in rehabilitation and to identify what made the process easier or more difficult. As the discussion progressed, questions became more specific to issues of client-centeredness. The focus group interviews were audiotaped and transcribed verbatim.

Using inductive, qualitative procedures to analyze the transcribed interviews, Cott identified the themes of the individualization of services to the participants' particular needs; client participation in goal-setting and decision-making; client-centered education; preparation of clients for life in the real world; emotional support from family, peers, and staff; and isolation and abandonment as major influences on levels of satisfaction among the participants. The researcher concluded that client-centered rehabilitation service delivery models must extend beyond mere collaborative goalsetting and decision-making to encompass the expertise of the consumer more holistically and to shift from an acute illness curative model to one that takes into consideration the long-term impact of disability or chronic illness.

In addition to the studies cited above, focus group interviews have been used to elicit client opinions regarding the strengths and weaknesses of services provided in vocational training and rehabilitation settings (Packer, Race, & Hotch, 1994; Nalven, Oursler, & Green 2005); medical rehabilitation settings (Cott, 2004); community-based rehabilitation programs (Sharma, 2004); and one-stop career centers for job seekers with disabilities (Hall & Parker, 2005). Finally, focus groups have been used to develop user-friendly consumer reports summarizing the results of service user satisfaction studies (Smith, Gerteis, Downey, Lewy, & Edgman-Levitan 2001).

As with any approach to research, focus groups are not without their limitations—the most specific of which is the difficulty of identifying which participant or informant provided what specific data during the course of the discussion, particularly when parallel positions are being voiced (McReynolds & Koch, in press). This problem may be reduced by use of video- or audio-recording equipment. Other limitations result from the potential for the opinions of more dominant participants to be overrepresented in the research findings and the possibility that facilitators of the focus group may inadvertently provide cues (e.g., nonverbal gestures, voice inflection, follow-up questions) that influence how participants respond (Hatch, 2002). These potential limitations can be minimized by (a) providing participants with the opportunity to respond to focus group questions in writing as well as in the group interview; (b) including key stakeholders (e.g., other service users) as cofacilitators of the focus groups; and (c) purposefully seeking out divergent viewpoints in data collection and analysis.

Mixed Methods Approaches

Given the limitations inherent in both quantitative and qualitative assessment approaches, many researchers advocate that the best approach to acquiring a comprehensive understanding of the complexity of consumer satisfaction is through the use of multiple methods. High ratings on satisfaction surveys are often contradicted by more critical evaluations when researchers explore the experiences of consumers in greater depth (Powell et al., 2004). Multimethod approaches rely on the use of more than one instrument or data collection technique so that more critical evaluations of services can be elicited from consumers. These approaches allow researchers to obtain responses from numerous consumers (a strength of quantitative approaches), while also enabling them to explore the meaning of responses in greater depth (a strength of qualitative approaches). To capture the diverse aspects of consumer satisfaction, researchers can, for example, couple standardized quantitative instruments with focus group interviews or individual interviews (e.g., Kosciulek, 2003). Alternately, surveys with both open-ended and forced-choice response sets can be used to allow for the collection of both qualitative and quantitative data. Multimethod formats have been particularly instrumental in gathering consumer input into the development of satisfaction measurement instruments to ensure that the instruments are readily understandable, presented in a user-friendly format, and inclusive of survey items that are relevant to service users (Fowler, 1997).

Schwab, DiNitto, Aureala, Simmons, and Smith (1999) used a mixed-methods approach to address the "murkiness" of the construct of consumer satisfaction. These researchers analyzed responses to telephonic consumer satisfaction surveys completed by 11,959 Texas Rehabilitation Commission clients within 60 days of case closure. The 22-item survey they used included both forced-choice and open-ended items, inviting respondents to comment on the services that were most and least helpful to them and to suggest ways that services could be improved. Schwab and colleagues' data analysis resulted in the identification of four underlying dimensions of consumer satisfaction: satisfaction with employment, satisfaction with services, responsiveness to the client, and client participation in the process. The researchers also found that a combination of four variables was moderately successful in predicting satisfaction with services: the length of time it took to provide services, responsiveness to the client, closure status (i.e., successfully employed at case closure and not suitably employed at case closure), and understanding what services were available. Perhaps the most important discovery they made was that satisfaction with services is a multidimensional construct that rests more on the way clients are treated than any other variables, including whether or not their rehabilitation results in employment.

Addressing the need for greater consumer involvement in the design and conduct of satisfaction research, Kosciulek et al. (1997) relied on the use of a mixed-methods approach in the evaluation of data collected in a consumer satisfaction process developed by the Advisory Committee to the Missouri Division of Vocational Rehabilitation (VR). The researchers analyzed the responses to a mail survey card, developed by members of the agency's consumer advisory committee, that required respondents to rate seven statements (i.e., "As a result of the services provided by the Agency, my present work situation is better than it was before I began the program") in terms of their level of agreement ("strongly agree," "somewhat agree," "somewhat disagree," "strongly disagree"). The survey also included an item that required respondents to provide written feedback regarding their satisfaction with services. In addition, focus groups were conducted by advisory committee members to gather even more consumer satisfaction data. The percentage of consumers who strongly agreed with the survey card statements ranged from a high of 90% to a low of 69%, indicating that the majority of respondents were highly satisfied with all aspects of services. Respondents indicated that they received services in a timely manner, viewed the rehabilitation counselor as a critical component in the VR process, and obtained or anticipated obtaining employment as a result of VR services.

To address a number of limitations of existing satisfaction research, Capella and Turner (2004) incorporated several design features into their investigation of consumer satisfaction in a sample of 478 consumers of a state VR agency. To begin, they interviewed 9 current and former consumers for their input into the development of a 36-item instrument to ensure that the items reflected what consumers viewed as relevant to service user satisfaction, not what the researchers viewed as relevant. They also included importance ratings in their scoring procedure to ensure the relevance of the items to the respondents. In addition, half of the items on their instrument were negatively worded to address the problems in many satisfaction surveys of the presentation of acquiescent response sets.

Using a factor analysis procedure to assess its underlying structure, the researchers found support for three dimensions of consumer satisfaction: the interpersonal relationship with the counselor and the counselor's effectiveness in handling the consumer's case (as measured by 18 items on a counselor scale); the services received (as measured by 9 items on the service scale); and the agency's characteristics (as measured by 9 items on the agency scale; Capella & Turner, 2004). Sample items for each scale include "Counselor listened to me," "Counselor did not keep me informed about my case" (counselor scale); "Services I received helped prepare me for work," "Services were not provided as promised" (service scale); "I was treated courteously by DVR staff," and "Employees of DVR did not communicate well" (agency scale). As is typically the case in satisfaction research, the data were negatively skewed. However, although the majority of the respondents expressed satisfaction, there was notable variability in the degree of satisfaction reported along the three dimensions. Because the researchers had established norms and assessed the psychometric properties of their instrument, they recommended minor modifications to their instrument so that it could be used by all state VR agencies to address a common limitation in VR consumer satisfaction research in that each state tends to use its own instrument, making it impossible to compare findings across states.

FUTURE DIRECTIONS IN ASSESSING CONSUMER SATISFACTION

Although it would be impossible to design and conduct a research study without any of the limitations inherent in satisfaction research, readers should keep in mind that developing a thorough understanding of complex psychological constructs such as consumer satisfaction only occurs through "small, incremental steps with each successive primary research study building upon the one before it" (Rumrill & Fitzgerald, 2001, p. 165). Given the complexity of consumer satisfaction, coupled with the array of challenges associated with its assessment, the author would like to conclude this chapter with the following "best practices" recommendations for assessing this elusive construct.

To begin, rather than using a "homemade" consumer satisfaction instrument, it is preferable to use a validated instrument that can be coupled with context-specific items if necessary. Use of standardized instruments makes it possible to address issues that are generalizable across service settings and that allow for important comparisons between settings. Adding context-specific items allows for the incorporation of questions that address local needs and concerns (Sitzia, 1999). When using standardized instruments, it is also important to develop new norms so that comparisons can be made across service settings and clientele (Sitzia). To further validate quantitative measures of consumer satisfaction, ratings can be compared with actual behaviors that signify satisfaction with services such as the service user's record of keeping appointments, following through with "homework" assignments, completing treatment, and achieving outcome goals (WHO, 2000). If standardized instruments need to be modified to better assess consumer satisfaction in a particular setting or with a particular sample, or if new instruments must be developed, the reliability and validity of these instruments should also be evaluated (Sitzia).

Because most quantitative measures of consumer satisfaction produce negatively skewed distributions, efforts should be made to address the issue of sampling bias. One strategy that has been recommended is for satisfaction researchers to obtain higher response rates (DeWilde & Hendrix, 2005). It has also been pointed out that the assessment of satisfaction should not be limited to closed-ended surveys with dichotomous (i.e., agree/disagree) response sets or Likert-type scales. Rather, these data should be supplemented with open-ended survey questions and in-depth qualitative and quantitative analysis of areas of dissatisfaction (Powell et al., 2004).

Researchers should also consider conducting additional analyses by demographics (e.g., gender, race, ethnicity, age) and disability or disease condition to help identify quality improvement activities targeted at populations and programs associated with the largest degree of dissatisfaction (Smith et al., 2001). Furthermore, consumers should be assured that their anonymity will be protected; in written or verbal instructions for completing satisfaction surveys or participating in interviews or focus groups, that their honest feedback is being sought, and that no negative consequences will occur if they express dissatisfaction (Campbell, 1999).

Sources of dissatisfaction should be sought out by asking questions such as "are there any aspects of the program that you liked less than others?" and "do you have suggestions for ways that services can be improved?" (WHO, 2000). In addition to eliciting consumer opinions through satisfaction surveys, interviews, or focus groups, behavioral indicators of dissatisfaction (e.g., high drop-out or no-show rates within specific programs or for specific service providers) can provide supplemental information about areas of dissatisfaction (WHO, 2000). Important satisfaction data can also be derived from querying individuals about their reasons for dropping out of services (Campbell, 1999). Finally, because consumers may passively communicate their dissatisfaction by refusing to participate in satisfaction studies, the frequency of this type of participation refusal should be reported in research reports.

To better determine the relevance of survey items to research participants, instruments should include items regarding consumers' preferences and anticipations. Alternatively, they could include rankings of importance of the items in addition to ratings of degree of satisfaction (Capella & Turner, 2004; Powell et al., 2004). Survey items should also be both positively and negatively worded to reduce the tendency of respondents to agree with every statement (Capella & Turner). When using surveys or questionnaires, either open-ended items or space should be provided after each section for written comments so that consumers can relate their specific concerns on the survery or questionnaire (Sitzia, 1999).

Consumer focus groups should be utilized in the development of context-specific data collection tools as well as the interpretation of the research findings. Questions should address issues of importance from the consumer's perspective rather than those of researchers, service providers, or administrators (Powell et al., 2004), and consumers can provide meaningful input into the interpretation of research findings and implications for improving service delivery. Satisfaction researchers may want to consider employing former consumers as interviewers. These individuals can empathize with respondents and are likely to elicit more frank and honest responses than a researcher or service provider might (Powell et al., 2004).

In addition to assessing consumer satisfaction as an outcome, it should be assessed as a process variable (Koch & Merz, 1997). Gathering satisfaction data while individuals are still in the process of receiving services provides information that can be used to improve service quality while they can still benefit from these improvements. Because consumer preferences and opinions regarding services are likely to change over the course of time, periodically assessing consumer satisfaction rather than assessing it only at one point in time (i.e., at case closure) provides much more valuable data (Sitzia, 1999).

Capella, M. E., & Turner, R. (2004). Development of an instrument to measure consumer satisfaction in vocational rehabilitation. *Rehabilitation Counseling Bulletin, 47*(2), 76–85; Keith, R. A. (1998). Patient satisfaction and rehabilitation services. *Archives of Physical Medicine and Rehabilitation, 79*, 1122–1128; Sitzia, J. (1999). How valid and reliable are patient satisfaction data?: An analysis of 195 studies. *International Journal for Quality in Health Care, 11*, 319–328.

Objectives: Rehabilitation and health care researchers have selectively reviewed and assessed the large amount of literature on satisfaction with rehabilitation and health care services, paying particular attention to the psychometric properties of the measurement instruments used in these studies.

Method: These researchers have thoroughly examined and evaluated selected literature on consumer satisfaction published in various rehabilitation and allied health journals. They carried out these investigations by searching health literature and related databases (e.g., CINAHL, MedLine, PsycLIT, ERIC) and applying both qualitative and meta-analytic techniques to evaluate the psychometric characteristics of data collection instruments and to summarize the findings from a variety of satisfaction research studies.

Results: The researchers report that a diversity of satisfaction instruments are used to assess consumer satisfaction with rehabilitation and health care. Research generally reports high levels of consumer satisfaction. In addition,

researchers have found that higher satisfaction is associated with treatment compliance and better outcomes. Most satisfaction research is conducted using surveys that are typically administered by mail. A preponderance of studies use measurement instruments that demonstrate little evidence of reliability or validity, while many others provide limited information on the psychometric properties of the instruments used.

Conclusion: Lack of reliable and valid assessment instruments used in satisfaction research casts doubt on the credibility of satisfaction findings. If we are to adequately evaluate consumer satisfaction with rehabilitation and health care, we are in great need of standardized, valid measurement instruments that are appropriate for various settings.

Questions

1. What are potential explanations for the high levels of satisfaction that are generally reported by rehabilitation and health care consumers?
2. Why is it so important that researchers use instruments that demonstrate strong evidence of reliability and validity to measure consumer satisfaction?
3. What is the advantage of designing a measurement instrument that could be used in a variety (instead of just one) of settings?
4. Describe how qualitative approaches to assessing consumer satisfaction could be used in combination with quantitative approaches to address some of the concerns outlined above.

Summary and Conclusion

The importance of assessing consumer satisfaction with rehabilitation and health care services is a key component of program evaluation that provides consumers with the opportunity to directly influence how services are designed, implemented, and evaluated. Although consumer satisfaction has been studied for nearly half a decade, research in this area is still fraught with limitations. Prominent among these limitations are problems with construct validity, sampling bias, methodological rigor, and the relevance of satisfaction research to consumers. To address these limitations, contemporary researchers advocate the need to examine the construct of consumer satisfaction using a multimethod approach that includes both quantitative and qualitative design elements.

The specific examples of consumer satisfaction research cited in this chapter illustrate how investigators have attempted to improve the quality and utility of satisfaction research by addressing concerns such as the ambiguous nature of the construct of consumer satisfaction, the limited input of consumers into the design of assessment approaches, the lack of research based on consumer (rather than researcher) opinions regarding what constitutes satisfaction, the lack of research to determine the reliability and validity of instruments, the proliferation of surveys that only include positively worded items, and the lack of research that directly assesses areas of service user dissatisfaction.

It is hoped that an increased awareness of the many dilemmas inherent in attempts to obtain accurate portrayals of consumers' opinions of the services they receive will encourage readers of this volume to seek out and evaluate new methods for assessing consumer satisfaction. With this objective in mind, the author concluded the chapter with key considerations for designing future satisfaction research and program evaluation studies. As research investigating this crucial construct continues to evolve, the likelihood increases that rehabilitation and health care services will be delivered in a manner that is truly consumer-centered.

Self-Check Questions

1. Summarize why it is so challenging to obtain accurate and meaningful consumer satisfaction data.
2. What are the most salient findings of the satisfaction research described above?
3. List the reasons why it is important to assess consumer satisfaction with rehabilitation and health care services.
4. Describe three methodological challenges associated with assessing consumer satisfaction with rehabilitation and health care services.
5. Compare and contrast quantitative, qualitative, and mixed-method approaches to assessing consumer satisfaction.
6. Summarize the findings in current consumer satisfaction research investigations.
7. Develop a list of "best practices" to guide researchers and program evaluators who investigate consumer satisfaction with rehabilitation and health care practices.

Case Study

To self-appraise her job performance, Maria, a vocational case manager employed by a nonprofit rehabilitation agency, is interested in gathering and analyzing consumer assessment data. Although she is able to obtain outcome data from her agency's client data management system, she would also like to gather input from consumers regarding the quality of services that she provides. Her plan is to develop a structured protocol that she will use to conduct exit interviews with clients immediately prior to termination of services.

QUESTION

In developing the structured interview protocol, what are important design considerations that she must keep in mind?

References

Agency for Healthcare Research and Quality (2005). *National healthcare disparities report*. Rockville, MD: Author.

Agency for Healthcare Research and Quality (2007). Creating partnerships, improving health: The role of community-based participatory research. Retrieved 5/1/2007 from https://www.ahrq.gov

Al-Darmaki, F., & Kivlighan, D. M. (1993). Congruence in client–counselor expectations for relationship and the working alliance. *Journal of Counseling Psychology, 40*, 379–384.

Alston, R. J., & Mngadi, S. P. (1992). The interaction between disability status and the African American experience: Implications for rehabilitation counseling. *Journal of Applied Rehabilitation Counseling, 23*(2), 10–14.

Attkisson, C. C., & Greenfield, T. K. (2004). The UCSF Client Satisfaction Scales I. The Client Satisfaction Questionnaire-8. In M. E. Maruish (Ed.), *The use of psychological testing for treatment planning and outcomes research* (3rd ed., 799–811). Mahwah, NJ: Lawrence Erlbaum Associates.

Barbour, R. S. (2005). Making sense of focus groups. *Medical Education, 39*, 742–750.

Bruyere, S. M. (2005). Using the International Classification of Functioning, Disability and Health (ICF) to promote employment and community integration in rehabilitation. *Rehabilitation Education, 19*, 105–117.

Campbell, J. (1992). The well-being project: Mental health clients speak for themselves. In Third Annual Conference Proceedings on State Mental Health Agency Research (pp.21–32). Alexandra, VA: NASMHPD Research Institute.

Campbell, J. (1994). Consumerism, outcomes and satisfaction: A review of the literature. In R. W. Manderscheid & M. J. Henderson (Eds.), Mental health United States 1998 (pp. 11–26). U.S. Department of Health and Human Services.

Campbell, J. (1999). Exemplary practices for measuring consumer satisfaction: A review of the literature: Part one, two, and three. Retrieved 9/5/2006 from http://mimh200.mimh.edu/PieDb/01602.htm.

Capella, M. E. (2002). Inequities in the VR service system: Do they still exist? *Rehabilitation Counseling Bulletin, 45*(3), 143–153.

Capella, M. E., & Turner, R. (2004). Development of an instrument to measure consumer satisfaction in vocational rehabilitation. *Rehabilitation Counseling Bulletin, 47*(2), 76–85.

Carlson, M. J., Blustein, J., Fiorentino, N., & Prestianni, F. (2000). Socioeconomic status and dissatisfaction among HMO enrollees. *Medical Care, 38*(5), 508–516.

Chan, F., Shaw, L. R., McMahon, B. T., Koch, L., & Strauser, D. (1997). A model for enhancing rehabilitation counselor-consumer working relationships. *Rehabilitation Counseling Bulletin, 41*, 122–137.

Chang, J. T., Hays, R. D., Shekelle, P. G., MacLean, C. H., Solomon, D. H., Rueben, D. B., et al. (2006). Patients' global ratings of their health care are not associated with the technical quality of their care. *Annals of Internal Medicine, 144*(9), 665–672.

Cott, C. A. (2004). Client-centered rehabilitation: Client perspectives. *Disability and Rehabilitation, 26*(24), 1411–1422.

Council of State Administrators of Vocational Rehabilitation (2002, May). *Principles for the CSAVR during the 2003 reauthorization of the Rehabilitation Act* http://www.rehabnetwork.org/position_papers/rofrehabacthtm.

DeWilde, E. F., & Hendricks, V. M. (2005). The Client Satisfaction Questionnaire: Psychometric properties in a Dutch addict population. *European Addiction Research, 11*, 157–162.

Di Palo, M. T. (1997). Rating satisfaction research: Is it poor? Fair? Good? Very good? Excellent? *Arthritis Care and Research, 10*, 422–430.

Emener, W. G. (1991). An empowerment philosophy for rehabilitation in the 20th century. *Journal of Rehabilitation, 57*, 7–12.

Fongwa, M. N., Cunningham, W., Weech-Maldonado, R., Gutierrez, P. R., & Hays, R. (2006). Comparison of data quality for reports and ratings of ambulatory care by African American and White Medicare managed care enrollees. *Journal of Aging and Health, 18*(5), 707–721.

Fowler, F. J., (1997). Choosing questions to measure the quality of experience with medical care providers and health care plans. *Proceedings of the Section on Survey Research Methods*, 51–54.

Fung, C. H., Elliot, R. D., Hays, K. L., Kahn, D. E., Kanouse, E. A., McGlynn, E. A., et al. (2005). Patients' preferences for technical versus interpersonal quality when selecting a primary care physician. *Health Research and Educational Trust*, 957–977.

Galassi, J. P., Crace, R. K., Martin, G. A., James, R. M., & Wallace, R. L. (1992). Client preferences and anticipations in career counseling: A preliminary investigation. *Journal of Counseling Psychology, 39*, 46–55.

Gaston, L., & Sabourin, S. (1992). Client satisfaction and social desirability in psychotherapy. *Evaluation and Program Planning, 15*(3), 227–231.

Greenfield, T. K., & Attkisson, C. C. (1999). The UCSFS Scales: II. The Service Satisfaction Scale-30. In M. Maruish (Ed.), *The use of psychological testing for treatment planning and outcome assessment* (pp. 1347–1367). Mahwah, NJ: Lawrence Erlbaum Associates.

Greenfield, T. K., & Attkisson, C. C. (2004). The UCSF Client Satisfaction Scales; II. The Service Satisfaction Scale-30. In M.E. Maruish (Ed.), *The use of psychological testing for treatment planning and outcomes research* (3rd ed., 813–837). Mahwah, NJ: Lawrence Erlbaum Associates.

Hall, J. P., & Parker, K. (2005). One-stop career centers and job seekers with disabilities: Insights from Kansas. *Journal of Rehabilitation, 71*(4), 38–47.

Hatch, J. A. (2002). *Doing qualitative research in educational settings*. Albany, NY: State University of New York Press.

Hein, S., Lustig, D. C., & Uruk, A. (2005). Consumer recommendations to improve satisfaction with rehabilitation services: A qualitative study. *Rehabilitation Counseling Bulletin, 49*, 29–39.

Homa, D. B., & Peterson, D. B. (2005). Using the International Classification of Functioning, Disability and Health (ICF) in teaching rehabilitation client assessment. *Rehabilitation Education, 19*, 119–128.

Horvath, A. O., & Symonds, B. D. (1991). Relation between working alliance and outcome in psychotherapy: A meta-analysis. *Journal of Counseling Psychology, 38*, 139–149.

Jennings, B. M., Loan, L. A., Heiner, S. L., Hemman, E. A., & Swanson, K. M. (2005). Soldiers' experiences with military healthcare. *Military Medicine, 170*, 999–1004.

Keith, R. A. (1998). Patient satisfaction and rehabilitation services. *Archives of Physical Medicine and Rehabilitation, 79*, 1122–1128.

Koch, L. C. (2001). The preferences and anticipations of people referred to a vocational rehabilitation agency. *Rehabilitation Counseling Bulletin, 44*(2), 76–86.

Koch, L. C., & Merz, M. A. (1995). Assessing client satisfaction in vocational rehabilitation program evaluation: A review of instrumentation. *Journal of Rehabilitation, 61*(4), 24–30.

Kosciulek, J. F. (1999). The consumer-directed theory of empowerment. *Rehabilitation Counseling Bulletin, 42*, 196–214.

Kosciulek, J. F. (2003). A multidimensional approach to the structure of consumer satisfaction with vocational rehabilitation services. *Rehabilitation Counseling Bulletin, 46*(2), 92–97.

Kosciulek, J. F., Vessell, R., Rosenthal, D. A., Accardo, C. M., & Merz, M. (1997). Consumer satisfaction with vocational rehabilitation services. *Journal of Rehabilitation, 63*, 5–9.

Krueger, R. A., & Casey, M. A. (2000). *Focus groups* (3rd ed.). Thousand Oaks, CA: Sage Publications, Inc.

Larsen, D. L., Attkisson, C. C., Hargreaves, W. A., & Nguyen, T. D. (1979). Assessment of client/patient satisfaction: Development of a general scale. *Evaluation and Program Planning, 2*, 197–207.

Lurie, N., Zhan, C., Sangl, J., Bierman, A. S., & Sekscenski, E. S. (2003). Variation in racial and ethnic differences in consumer assessments of health care. *The American Journal of Managed Care, 9*(7), 502–509.

McReynolds, C. J., & Koch, L. C. (in press). Qualitative research designs. In J. Bellini & P. Rumrill (Eds.), *Research in rehabilitation counseling: A guide to design, methodology, and utilization* (2nd ed.). Springfield, IL: Charles C. Thomas.

Meehan, T., Bergen, H., & Stedman, T. (2002). Monitoring consumer satisfaction with inpatient service delivery: The Inpatient Evaluation of Service Questionnaire. *Australian and New Zealand Journal of Psychiatry, 36*, 807–811.

Middleton, S., & Lumby, J. (1999). Measuring outcomes from the patients' perspective. *International Journal of Nursing Practice, 5*, 143–146.

Monnin, D., & Perneger, T. P. (2002). Scale to measure patient satisfaction with physical therapy. *Physical Therapy, 82*(7), 682–691.

Nalven, E. B., Oursler, J., & Green, W. (2005). Assessing client satisfaction with vocational rehabilitation services: A focus group project. *American Journal of Psychiatric Rehabilitation, 8*, 63–79.

Nelson, T. D. & Steele, R. G. (2006). Beyond efficacy and effectiveness: A multi-faceted approach to treatment evaluation. *Professional Psychology: Research and Practice, 37*(4), 389–397.

Packer, T., Race, K. E. H., & Hotch, D. F. (1994). Focus groups: Consumer-based program evaluation in rehabilitation agency settings. *Journal of Rehabilitation, 60*, 30–33.

Patton, M. Q. (2002). *Qualitative research and evaluation techniques* (3rd Ed.). Thousand Oaks, CA: Sage Publications.

Peterson, D. B. (2005). International Classification of Functioning, Disability and Health: An introduction for rehabilitation psychologists. *Rehabilitation Psychology, 5*(2), 105–112.

Powell, R. A., Holloway, F., Lee, J., & Sitzia, J. (2004). Satisfaction research and the uncrowned king: Challenges and future directions. *Journal of Mental Health, 13*(1), 11–20.

Richard, M. A. (2000). A discrepancy model for measuring consumer satisfaction with rehabilitation services. *Journal of Rehabilitation, 66*(4), 37–43.

Rosenthal, D. A., Wilson, K., Ferrin, M. M., & Frain, M. (2005). Acceptance rates of African American versus white consumers of vocational rehabilitation services: A meta-analysis. *Journal of Rehabilitation, 71*(3), 36–44.

Rumrill, P. D., & Fitzgerald, S. M. (2001). Using narrative literature reviews to build a scientific knowledge base. *Work, 16*, 165–170.

Schnelker, D. L., & Rumrill, P. D. (2001). Program evaluation in rehabilitation. *Work, 16*, 171–175.

Schwab, A. J., DiNitto, D. M., Aureala, W., Simmons, J. F., & Smith, T. W. (1999). The dimensions of client satisfaction with rehabilitation services. *Journal of Vocational Rehabilitation, 13*, 183–194.

Schwandt, T. A. (2001). *Dictionary of qualitative inquiry* (2nd ed.). Thousand Oaks, CA: Sage Publications.

Schwarz, M., Landis, S., Rowe, J., Janes, C. L., & Pullman, N. (2000). Using focus groups to assess primary care patients' satisfaction. *Evaluation and the Health Professions, 23*(1), 58–71.

Sharma, M. (2004). Viable methods for evaluation of community-based rehabilitation programmes. *Disability and Rehabilitation, 26*(6), 326–334.

Sitzia, J. (1999). How valid and reliable are patient satisfaction data?: An analysis of 195 studies. *International Journal for Quality in Health Care, 11*, 319–328.

Smith, F., Gerteis, M., Downey, N., Lewy, J., & Edgman-Levitan, S. (2001). The effects of disseminating performance data to health plans: Results of qualitative research with the Medicare managed care plans. *Health Services Research, 36*(3), 643–663.

Tinsley, H. E. A., Bowman, S. L., & Ray, S. B. (1988). Manipulation of expectancies about counseling and psychotherapy: Review and analysis of expectancy manipulation strategies and results. *Journal of Counseling Psychology, 35*, 99–108.

Ware, J. R., Jr., & Hays, R. D. (1988). Methods for measuring patient satisfaction with specific medical encounters. *Medical Care, 26*(4), 393–402.

Ware, J. R., Jr., Snyder, M. K., Wright, W. R., & Davies, A. R. (1983). Defining and measuring patient satisfaction with medical care. *Evaluation and Program Planning, 6*, 242–264.

West, M. D., & Parent, W. S. (1992). Consumer choice and empowerment in supported employment services: Issues and strategies. *Journal of the Association for Persons with Severe Handicaps, 17*, 47–52.

Williams, B., Coyle, J., & Healy, D. (1998). The meaning of patient satisfaction: An explanation of high reported levels. *Social Science and Medicine, 47*, 1351–1359.

World Health Organization (2000). *Workbook 6: Client satisfaction evaluations.* Author.

PART

V

Looking Ahead

31

The Future of Assessment in Rehabilitation and Health

Elias Mpofu
University of Sydney
Thomas Oakland
University of Florida

INTRODUCTION

The development and refined use of tests and other assessment methods are likely to constitute a profession's most important technical contribution to practice. As this book clearly shows, professions involved in rehabilitation and other health care services are fortunate to have a wide range of assessment devices and methods that assist professionals in their work. Quality assessments also make it possible to provide health care interventions that are (a) patient driven in content and goals; (b) context sensitive; and (c) differentiated by consumer characteristics (e.g., by disability type, gender, race/ethnicity) (Davies & Cleary, 2005). The contents of this book are important by addressing, within each assessment procedure and the context in which it is used, client perspectives, personal variables that impact assessment procedures preferred, and contextual–environmental variables.

ASSESSMENTS ARE UNIVERSAL

Tests and other assessment methods are used in virtually every country, with newborns through the elderly, to describe current behaviors and other qualities, inform intervention methods, estimate future behaviors, assist guidance and counseling services, evaluate progress, screen for special needs, diagnose disorders, help prepare persons for jobs or programs, and assist in determining whether they should be credentialed, admitted/employed, retained, or promoted. Tests as assessments tools also are used widely in research and for various administrative and planning purposes. The benefits of assessments, including testing, clearly outweigh their limitations.

Society and professionals generally hold quality standardized assessment procedures in high regard, resulting in their frequent and varied uses. Such assessments provide objective information with known reliability and validity, typically in an efficient manner. Several strands of developments in rehabilitation and health assessment support quality of care-driven practices: multidisciplinary and interdisciplinary approaches, application of the *International Classification of Functioning, Disability and Heath* (ICF; WHO, 2001) guidelines, use of objective measures of rehabilitation and health outcomes, standards for testing and changes in the testing industry, and cost-consciousness in the health care industry.

EVOLVING MULTIDISCIPLINARY AND INTERDISCIPLINARY APPROACHES

This book brings together constructs in assessment for rehabilitation and health spanning professional issues; types of assessment; assessment procedures; and purposes in assessment in health psychology, rehabilitation, counseling, special education, law, engineering, and related professions. The authors of each chapter wrote from the perspective of health from their specific specialization, reflecting the multidisciplinary nature of rehabilitation and the health profession.

Historically, rehabilitation and health interventions have followed a service delivery model that resembles an assembly line, with a patient moving from one assessment specialist to another, perhaps seeing five or more professionals. All specialists have their assigned tasks, follow established protocol typical of their professional specialty, and, after administering their tests, attempt to pool their information. However, unlike the production of a car that rolls off the assembly line with integrated parts and displaying functional performance standards, the client may have been dissected, not integrated, with most attention directed to their body functions (i.e., physiological and psychological functions) and body structures (i.e., anatomical parts) and little attention paid to their functional life-styles and environmental variables. Discipline-oriented assessment services have tended to pay little attention to the dynamic interactions among body functions, body structures, activities (e.g., a person's display of a task or action), participation (i.e., their involvement in life activities), external environmental factors (i.e., a person's physical, social, and attitudinal environment), and personal (e.g., their gender, age, race, social, and economic status) qualities. Although professionals recognize limitations associated with this assessment process, various conditions reinforce its use, including traditions, professional affiliations, and health maintenance organizations capitation systems (see also chapter 1).

The intersection of several streams of expertise in rehabilitation and health assessment is testimony to the richness of models and practices that inform rehabilitation and health assessment. Assessments in rehabilitation and health increasingly are aligned to address aspects of health-related quality of life (see part 3 of the book). More points of intersection in disciplinary practices in health will evolve into truly interdisciplinary understanding of client treatment needs. Increased knowledge about assessment procedures for diverse rehabilitation and health needs will lead to the inclusion of other assessment procedures and functions in the tool kits of rehabilitation and health professionals.

APPLICATION OF THE ICF MODEL

Authors of this book applied the ICF to contextualize aspects of assessment within areas of client functional performance: individual and contextual factors. A focus on these factors is important in order to reinforce the fact that rehabilitation and health care outcomes are influenced by physical–bodily–psychological functions in their interaction with environmental factors. Improvement of care in health settings includes responsiveness by health service providers to client or patient characteristics, the environment of care, and the context of everyday participation in significant life areas: home-life, work, and community living (Institute of Health Improvement, 2006). To the extent possible, authors addressed personal factors that mediate rehabilitation and health outcomes within environments (e.g., activities of daily living, schooling, occupational–vocational, services, compensation systems).

The implementation of the ICF model is likely to lead to use of new assessment procedures that would address domains of activity and participation more adequately than current or existing procedures. Increasing use of the ICF guidelines for disability, health, and functioning also will lead to the application of established assessment procedures in new ways or their interpretation to support interventions to maximize function in specified activities and environments. The research sections of each chapter of this book variously address needs in assessment use for which cross-disciplinary conceptual frameworks, such as the ICF, would provide guidance in assessment procedure selection, use, and interpretation.

The ICF model suggests the need to utilize empirically-based services that are based on solid research evidence tailored to the patient's individual characteristics, including their environmental and personal qualities. Tests and other assessment methods, including observationally-acquired data, commonly will provide evidence of and be used to help justify needed services. These data also are likely to guide services when used as a baseline to evaluate treatment effectiveness. In effect, rehabilitation and health professionals will tend to use a test–intervene–test–intervene–test . . . model.

The ICF underscores and makes plain what professionals always have known: Behavior is a complex interaction among physical, psychological, social, personal, and environmental qualities. The ICF states this more clearly in the following way:

> [A]n individual's functioning in a specific domain (i.e., learning and applying knowledge,

general tasks and demands, communication, mobility, self-care, domestic life, interpersonal interactions and relationships, major life areas, and community, social, and civic life) is an interaction or complex relationship between the health condition and contextual factors (i.e., environmental and personal factors). There is a dynamic interaction among these entities: Interventions in one entity have the potential to modify one or more of the other entities. These interactions are specific and not always in a predictable one-to-one relationship. The interaction works in two directions; the presence of disability may even modify the health condition itself. To infer a limitation in capacity from one or more impairments, or a restriction of performance from one or more limitations, may often seem reasonable. It is important, however, to collect data on these constructs independently and thereafter explore associations and causal links between them. If the full health experience is to be described, all components are useful (World Health Organization, 2001, page 19).

The implementation of the ICF model poses a series of challenges for professionals. An understanding of its multipurpose classification system encourages professionals to rethink their services based on their understanding of new terminology and revised models of service delivery. In addition, all professionals are being asked to use a common language to describe health and health-related conditions. The ICF's de-emphasis on diagnosis and its emphasis on providing a scientific basis for understanding and studying health and health-related conditions, outcomes, and determinants also require changes, given the historic importance placed on diagnosis for describing health-related pathology and suggesting protocols for service. In addition, the implementation of the ICF in guiding assessment practices will increase as more rehabilitation and other health care services accept this model as authoritative, and adequately fund professional services based on the model.

CHALLENGES POSED BY ICF

The ICF model poses a series of challenges for test developers and users. We discuss two of these challenges.

Developing and Using Tests to Inform Interventions

Perhaps the greatest challenge for rehabilitation and health assessments lies in developing and using tests in ways that clearly inform intervention methods. Professionals generally have had two principal roles: to diagnose and to intervene. The importance of their diagnostic role is not being reduced. The importance of their intervention role is being increased. Support for this increased emphasis on interventions is found internationally and in all professions. The ICF's development reflects, in part, this worldwide emphasis on providing services that have lasting benefits while not stigmatizing the recipients of such services. Thus, rehabilitation and health professionals need tests that assess body functions and structures with sufficient specificity to assist them in identifying viable interventions and in evaluating the effects of services.

Health professionals need to know the links between assessment results and interventions. Among the thousands of assessments available in the medical and behavioral sciences, few have established these links. Thus, considerable research is needed to establish them. This book points to several areas for which research and other forms of scholarship would add to the value of assessment procedures within comprehensive rehabilitation and health interventions.

Developing and Using Assessment Methods to Identify Interactions Between Health and Contextual Conditions

An equally formidable challenge lies in developing and using assessment methods in ways that show the interaction between health (e.g., diseases, disorders, injury, trauma) and contextual (i.e., personal and environmental qualities) conditions. Treatment options, duration, prognosis, and other important clinical decisions depend on knowledge of a patient's history and other background qualities together with the physical, social, and attitudinal qualities that characterize the patient's environment.

For example, treatment options, duration, and prognosis differ for the following two males, both aged 45, who display moderate frontal lobe trauma following a motor vehicle accident 2 weeks ago. One lives alone, has no family support, and has few financial resources. The other lives in a loving and caring immediate and extended family that expresses strong expectations for full recovery. He also has good medical and psychological care insurance as well as disability coverage that can provide needed income for many years. Despite their common diagnosis, treatment options, duration, and prognosis are likely to differ.

Some day, computer models may be developed to help determine the complex interactions between health conditions and contextual conditions. These resources currently are in their early stages. However, for now and the foreseeable future, attempts to understand these complex interactions continue to rest on professional judgment. Thus, decisions as to the interactions between data describing health and contextual conditions rest on making artful interpretations by professionals who have an instrumental understanding of their specialty, as well as a good understanding of other key specialties.

USE OF OBJECTIVE METHODS OF ASSESSMENT

An attempt to adequately model a health care construct (e.g., community participation) useful for assessment and interventions for rehabilitation and health care requires consideration of a broad range of relevant indicators in the client's experiences that characterize the health care construct, the co-occurrence or overlap of the indicator construct, and related others contributing to a health outcome. Health indicators, with the qualities that sample health constructs broadly and within a measurement model sensitive to positioning health indicators in their salience to measuring the capacity or performance regardless of persons and contexts, have been labeled objective measures (Wright & Stone, 1979). Measurement models based on item response theory (IRT) characterize variation in the contribution of the individual test items to rehabilitation and health status outcomes, including their overlap and hierarchical positioning (see chapter 1).

Item Response Theory

Test development generally is guided by one of two psychometric methods: classical methods (see chapter 9 for a discussion of this method) and item response theory (IRT). Tests based on classical methods generally require the administration of the entire test. In contrast, tests based on IRT generally require the administration of only those items within the examinee's range of ability, thus providing a more accurate and efficient assessment. Its computer-based applications further increase IRT's attractiveness. One can expect tests and assessments in rehabilitation and health to increasingly apply IRT modeling.

The potential of IRT in rehabilitation outcome research is attested to by the growing body of literature that utilizes IRT methodology (e.g., Fisher, Harvey, Taylor, Kilgore, & Kelly, 1995; Hawley, Taylor, Hellawell, & Pentland 1999; Kilgore, Fisher, Silverstein, Harley, &

Harvey, 1993; Linn et al., 1999). Related studies on the more widely used medical rehabilitation outcome measures have investigated the following aspects: dimensionality (or factor structure) of scales (e.g., Hawley et al., 1999; Silverstein, Fisher, Kilgore, Harley, & Harvey, 1992); comparison of item difficulties as ability hierarchies (Fisher, 1999; Fisher, Eubanks & Marier, 1997); incremental value to predicting patient outcomes (e.g., Harvey et al., 1992; Hawley et al., 1999; Linn et al., 1999; Tesio & Cantagallo, 1998); rehabilitation measure equating (Fisher et al., 1995, Fisher et al., 1997); rehabilitation programming with various inpatient care facilities (Harvey et al., 1992); construct equivalence across instruments and samples (Fisher, 1997); and evaluating the reliability of rehabilitation outcome measure training systems (Granger, Deutsch, & Linn, 1998; Turner-Stokes, Nyein, Turner-Stokes, & Gatehouse 1999).

Studies by Fisher et al. (1995) and Bode, Lai, Cella, & Heinemann (2003) are among the few that demonstrate the use of IRT when examining applications of a rehabilitation outcome measure across disability types. Results were encouraging. For example, Bode and Colleagues investigated the usefulness of the 36-Item Short Form Health Survey for measuring physical functioning in four patient illness groups: cancer, HIV/AIDS, stroke, and multiple sclerosis. They concluded that the Short Form Health Survey could be reliably used with persons who display diverse chronic illness and disabilities. Various measures of physical and functional performance can be placed on a common metric scale using IRT procedures (Fisher et al., 1995, 1997). Although this book did not present a full chapter on IRT applications to rehabilitation and health outcomes, we perceive great potential in IRT models applied to assessment instruments in rehabilitation and health (see also Mpofu & Oakland, 2006).

Adaptive or Tailored Testing

Allied to use of IRT methodology is the use of adaptive or tailored testing. The use of adaptive or tailored testing is likely to be more prevalent over time in rehabilitation and health assessment. Health care professionals typically complete every question on a scale. This traditional process is inefficient in that most functional assessments contain items that either are too easy or too difficult or have items that subsume other responses. For example, using the *Functional Assessment Inventory* (Crewe & Athelstan, 1981), if we know a patient "has little ability to control and coordinate movements," then no additional information is gained by completing the ambulation or upper extremity functioning scales. The

information for each of these categories is already subsumed by the coordination rating.

Thus, rather than administer "fixed-item" measures on which all questions are rated, the selection of sequential items is possible, thus minimizing time, maximizing the collection of relevant data, enhancing the accuracy of measurement, and evaluating whether information is sufficient to terminate testing. This measurement procedure is called adaptive or tailored testing. In statistics, this procedure is called sequential testing. Tailored item selection can result in reduced errors and greater precision when using only a few properly selected items.

IRT may be ideal for the development of unbiased item and ability estimates. However, use of IRT on its own is not sufficient for ensuring mental processes that influence participant responses to individual items are compatible with the intent of the item. Cognitive interviewing (Bassili & Scott, 1996; Presser & Blair, 1994; Schober & Frederick, 1997) remains important for validating participant responses to questions that are consistent with evaluation goals and purposes.

Cognitive Interviewing

This approach provides a qualitative evaluation of sources of response error or information not germane to the intended purpose of specific test items. It focuses on understanding the specific thought processes that a question triggers in a respondent, including qualities that influence response choices. In using cognitive interviewing, volunteer participants from a target population are asked by a trained interviewer to verbalize their thoughts in response to a question. The interview is recorded and transcribed, and responses are analyzed for consistency with the keyed response. Cognitive interviewing helps map the mental processes that participants may take in arriving at a response choice, and explain either atypical responses or typical responses but for unexpected reasons. There is no record of cognitive interviewing being used in the design of rehabilitation outcome measures.

Use of Measures of Well-Being

Our discussion thus far has considered mainly the technical aspects of prospective applications to rehabilitation and health assessment. The future of rehabilitation and health assessment will see a greater use of measures of well-being, including those for spirituality, values, quality of life, and quality of rehabilitation care. Most of the newer measures will operationalize the environmental and personal factor domains of the ICF rather than of bodily function and structure domains. Rehabilitation and health professionals increasingly recognize that personal and environmental factors influence response to rehabilitation intervention more than the objective qualities of the chronic illness or disability. Within health conditions, there is likely to be greater development of ICF-based core sets of measures to inform rehabilitation interventions with those populations.

STANDARDS FOR ASSESSMENT AND CHANGES IN THE TESTING INDUSTRY

Various professions provide rehabilitation services, including but not limited to those who specialize in communication sciences, community health, counseling, kinesiology, occupational therapy, physical therapy, physiotherapy, physical medicine, psychology, and special education. The assessment procedures discussed in this book show variability in their standardization, a quality that is associated with reliable use and confidence in the use to which findings are put. We consider the extent to which standardized assessments are available across rehabilitation professions and the importance of adherence to standards of assessment for responsible or ethical use of assessments.

Availability of Standardized Assessments Are Not Uniform Among the Rehabilitation Professions

The availability and use of quality standardized tests (e.g., those normed on a large and representative sample and with good reliability and validity) differ among the various health care professionals. Although tests are available for use in all professions, their numbers differ. Psychology may have the most standardized tests, whereas those in occupational and physical therapy may have the least. In addition, the quality of tests commonly used by rehabilitation specialists differs. Some specialties have a wide array of quality standardized tests while other specialties rely more on clinical judgment, nonstandardized tests, and tests developed by health care agencies, researchers, practitioners, and others whose primary job is not test development. A test's norms, reliability, and validity typically are questionable when developed under these conditions.

Use of Uniform Standards for Assessment

Rehabilitation and health professionals may use standards for assessment that apply to their unique contexts of practice. However, the *Standards for Educational and*

Psychological Testing (American Educational Research Association, American Psychological Association, National Council for Measurement in Education, 1999) generally is recognized as providing the most authoritative set of standards governing test development and use. The *Standards* generally advocates for the use of multiple assessment methods (e.g., tests, observations, interviews, existing records) to acquire data on various pertinent personal qualities (e.g., body functions and structures, environmental qualities) based on information from various informed sources (e.g., the patient, significant others, supervisors) that lead to an understanding of the patient's behavior in various environments and over some period of time. Although these standards are ambitious and generally not characteristic of most existing practices, they are consistent with the implementation of the ICF. We believe that these standards will continue to be important for guiding assessment practices in rehabilitation and health.

LIMITED FINANCIAL RESOURCES

Assessment practices in rehabilitation and other health professions have benefited from resources in other sectors of our society, including a somewhat large number of testing companies willing to invest their financial and personnel resources to develop and market tests. Changes occurring in this sector may adversely impact assessment resources. Furthermore, the health care industry is under pressure to be more cost conscious to keep the cost of health care down and affordable to a greater number of people. Costs of health care from assessments will continue to be an important consideration in the future.

The Need for Additional Tests Yet Diminished Resources

The number of large testing companies, those with the most ample resources needed to develop and market tests, is being reduced due to mergers and acquisitions. This change has lead to fewer companies able and willing to assume the risks associated with test development. In addition, costs associated with test development are increasing. Given their profit-driven nature, companies that develop tests are likely to rely more on their existing test inventory and to develop fewer tests. Testing companies also are likely to rely more on test authors to acquire data or to assume a larger percent of costs associated with test development. Additionally, professionals who specialize at the graduate level, preferably the Ph.D level, in assessment are needed to direct this work.

However, few graduate programs prepare students for this work. Moreover, enrollment in these programs typically is low. In addition, the number of professors who teach these courses is decreasing through retirement, and few young scholars are being prepared to replace them.

Cost Consciousness by the Health Care Industry

All segments of the health care industry have experienced increased demands for services, increased costs, and decreased revenue from insurance and other third party sources. Thus, this industry is perceived to be curtailing services to better conform to existing financial resources.

The broad scope of the ICF suggests the need for additional professional resources. Their intended collaborative work may benefit the patient while increasing treatment expenses. The need to assess qualities other than the patient's body functions and structures further increases expenses. Efforts to provide services consistent with the ICF while maintaining fiscal integrity constitute a serious challenge to the health care industry and society. Assessment procedures that are perceived to be of little added value to fiscal austerity may be relegated. Professionals in rehabilitation and health assessment will need to continually demonstrate the worth of their specific procedures of assessment to cost reduction in health care provisions. A way to achieve that result is to use assessment procedures for which there is evidence of relevance to treatment outcomes.

CLIENT PERSPECTIVES MATTER

A convergence of views from rehabilitation service providers and patients may lead to the development of more equitable rehabilitation outcome measures (see also chapters 27, 30 and 31). This form of collaborative rehabilitation outcome measurement may result in rehabilitation outcome measures that are relevant to informing long-term rehabilitation success. The ICF provides constructs about disability, health, and functioning that both rehabilitation service providers and consumers understand, thus possibly facilitating the development of collaboration-based rehabilitation outcomes measures (Stucki, Üstün, & Melvin, 2005). There likely will be tremendous growth in the use of informal care assessments (Dooley, Shaffer, Lance, & Williamson, 2007) that capture the views of clients and caregivers in everyday contexts. Use of diaries (Bogler, Davis, & Rafaeli, 2003) and other reality-based measures also are likely to increase to address real-world issues and outcomes for clients in rehabilitation care.

Self-Check Questions

1. Based on your use of this book, what do you perceive to be trends in rehabilitation and health assessment that would influence practices in your particular area of expertise or in rehabilitation and health care?
2. What is the potential of the ICF as a framework for organizing assessment practices in rehabilitation and health?
   Discuss specific challenges in using the ICF framework in planning assessment interventions.
3. How do cost considerations influence use of rehabilitation and health assessments? What are some ways in which cost conscious health care providers could reduce the cost of health care from assessment?

References

American Educational Research Association, American Psychological Association, and National Council on Measurement in Education. (1999). *Standards for educational and psychological testing.* Washington, DC: Authors

Bassili, J. N., & Scott, B. S. (1996). Response latency as a signal to question problems in survey research. *Public Opinion Quarterly, 60,* 390–399.

Bode, R. K., Lai, J., Cella, D., & Heinemann, A. W. (2003). Issues in the development of an item bank. *Archives of Physical Medicine and Rehabilitation, 84,* 52–60.

Bogler, N., Davis, A., & Rafaeli, E. (2003). Diary methods: Capturing life as it is lived. *Annual Review of Psychology, 54,* 579–616.

Crewe, N. M., & Athelstan, G. T. (1981). Functional assessment in vocational rehabilitation: A systematic approach to diagnosis and goal setting. *Archives of Physical Medicine and Rehabilitation, 62,* 299–305.

Davies, E., & Cleary, P. D. (2005). Hearing the patient's voice? Factors affecting the use of patient survey data in quality improvement. *Quality and Safety in Health Care, 14*(6), 428–432.

Dooley, K. W., Shaffer, D. R., Lance, C. E., & Williamson, G. M. (2007). Informal care can be better than adequate: Development and evaluation of the exemplary care scale. *Rehabilitation Psychology, 52,* 359–369.

Fisher, W. P. (1997). Physical disability construct convergence across instruments: Towards a universal metric. *Journal of Outcomes Measurement, 1,* 87–113.

Fisher, W. P. (1999). Foundations for health status metrology: The stability of MOS, SF-36, PF-10 calibrations across samples. *Journal of the Louisiana State Medical Society, 151,* 566–578.

Fisher, W. P., Eubanks, R. L., & Marier, R. L. (1997). Equating the MOS, SF-36 and the LSU HIS physical functioning scales. *Journal of Outcomes Measurement, 1,* 329–362.

Fisher, W. P., Harvey, R. F., Taylor, P., Kilgore, K. M., & Kelly, C. K. (1995). Rehabits: A common language of functional assessment. *Archives of Physical Medicine & Rehabilitation, 76,* 113–122.

Granger, C. V., Deutsch, A., & Linn, R. T. (1998). Rasch analysis of the Functional Independence Measure (FIM) Mastery Test. *Archives of Physical Medicine and Rehabilitation, 79,* 52–57.

Harvey, R. E., Silverstein, B., Venzon, M. A., Kilgore, K. M., Fisher, W. P., Steiner, M., & Harley, J. P. (1992). Applying psychometric criteria to functional assessment in medical rehabilitation: III. Construct validity and predicting level of care. *Archives of Physical Medicine and Rehabilitation, 73,* 887–892.

Hawley, C. A., Taylor, R., Hellawell, D. J., & Pentland, B. (1999). Use of the functional assessment measure (FIM + FAM) in head injury rehabilitation: A psychometric analysis. *Journal of Neural Psychiatry, 67,* 749–754.

Institute of Health Improvement (2006). Patient-centered care: General. Retrieved April 19, 2006, from http://www.ihi.org/IHI/Topics/PatientCenteredCare/PatientCenteredCareGeneral/

Kilgore, K. M., Fisher, W. P., Silverstein, B., Harley, J. P., & Harvey, R. F. (1993). Application of Rasch analysis to the Patient Evaluation Conference System. *Physical Medicine and Rehabilitation Clinics of North America, 4,* 493–515.

Linn, R. T., Blair, R. S., Granger, C. V., Harper, D. W., O'Hara, D. W., & Maciura, E. (1999). Does the Functional Assessment Measure (FAM) extend the Functional Independence Measure (FIM) Instrument? A Rasch analysis of stroke inpatients. *Journal of Outcome Measurement, 3(4),* 339–359.

Mpofu, E., & Oakland, T (2006). Assessment of value change in adults with acquired disabilities. In M. Hersen (Ed.), *Clinician's handbook of adult behavioral assessment* (pp. 601–630). New York: Elsevier Press.

Presser, S., & Blair, J. (1994). Survey pretesting: Do different methods produce different results? *Sociological Methodology, 24,* 73–104.

Schober, M. F., & Frederick, G. C. (1997). Does conversational interviewing reduce survey measurement error? *Public Opinion Quarterly, 61,* 576–602.

Silverstein, B., Fisher, W. P., Kilgore, K. M., Harley, J. P., & Harvey, R. F. (1992). Applying psychometric criteria to functional assessment in medical rehabilitation: II. Defining interval measures. *Archives of Physical Medicine and Rehabilitation, 73,* 507–18.

Stucki G., Üstün B.T., & Melvin, J. (2005). Applying the ICF for the acute hospital and early postacute facilities. *Disability and Rehabilitation, 27,* 349–352.

Tesio, L., & Cantagallo, A. (1998). The functional Assessment measure (FAM) in closed traumatic brain injury outpatients: A Rasch based psychometric study. *Journal of Outcome Measurement, 2(2),* 79–96.

Turner-Stokes, L., Nyein, K., Turner-Stokes, T., & Gatehouse, C. (1999). The UK FIM+FAM: Development and evaluation. *Clinical Rehabilitation, 13,* 277–287.

World Health Organization. (2001). *International classification of functioning, disability and health.* Geneva, Switzerland: Authors

Wright, B. D., & Stone, M. H. (1979). *Best test design.* Chicago: MESA Press.

APPENDIX A

ARTICLES AND CHAPTERS ADDRESSING TEST SECURITY AND RELEASE OF RAW TEST DATA

Barth, J. T. (2000). Commentary on "Disclosure of tests and raw test data to the courts" by Paul Lees-Haley and John Courtney. *Neuropsychology Review, 10*(3), 179–180.

Behnke, S. (2003). Release of test data and APA's new ethics code. *Monitor on Psychology, 34*(7), 70–72.

Bush, S. S., & Lees-Haley, P. R. (2005). Threats to the validity of forensic neuropsychological data: Ethical considerations. *Journal of Forensic Neuropsychology, 4* (3), 45–66.

Bush, S. S., & Martin, T. A. (2006). The ethical and clinical practice of disclosing raw test data: Addressing the ongoing debate. *Applied Neuropsychology, 13*, 125–136.

Erard, R. E. (2004). "A raw deal" reheated: Reply to comments by Rogers, Fischer, Smith and Evans. *Journal of Personality Assessment, 82*(1), 44–47.

Fisher, C. B. (2003, January/February). Test data standard most notable change in new APA ethics code. *The National Psychologist*, 12–13.

Freides, D. (1993). Proposed standard of professional practice: Neuropsychological reports display all quantitative data. *The Clinical Neuropsychologist, 7*, 234–235.

Freides, D. (1995). Interpretations are more benign than data. *The Clinical Neuropsychologist, 9*, 248.

Holloway, J. D. (2003). A stop-gap in the flow of sensitive patient information. *Monitor on Psychology, 34*(3), 28.

Lees-Haley, P.R., & Courtney, J.C. (2000a). Disclosure of tests and raw test data to the courts: A need for reform. *Neuropsychology Review, 10*(3), 169–175.

Lees-Haley, P. R., & Courtney, J.C. (2000b). Reply to the commentary on "Disclosure of tests and raw test data to the courts." *Neuropsychology Review, 10*(3), 181–182.

Naugle, R. I., & McSweeny, A. J. (1995). On the practice of routinely appending neuropsychological data to reports, *The Clinical Neuropsychologist, 9*(3), 245–247.

Naugle, R. I., & McSweeny, A. J. (1996). More thoughts on the practice of routinely appending raw data to reports: Response to Freides and Matarazzo. *The Clinical Neuropsychologist, 10*, 313–314.

Piazza, N. J., & Baruth, N. E. (1990). Patient record guidelines. *Journal of Counseling & Development, 68*, 313–316.

Rapp, D. L., & Ferber, P. S. (2003). To release, or not to release raw test data, that is the question. In A. M. Horton, Jr. & L. C. Hartlage (Eds.), *Handbook of forensic neuropsychology* (pp. 337–368). New York: Springer Publishing Company.

Rapp, D. L., Ferber, P. S., & Bush, S. S. (in press). Unresolved issues about release of test data and test materials. In A. M. Horton, Jr., & L. C. Hartlage (Eds.), *Handbook of Forensic Neuropsychology* (2nd ed.). New York: Springer Publishing Co.

Rogers, R. (2004). APA 2002 ethic, amphibology, and the release of psychological test records: A counterperspective to Erard. *Journal of Personality Assessment, 82*(1), 31–34.

Shapiro, D. L. (2000). Commentary: Disclosure of tests and raw data to the courts. *Neuropsychology Review, 10*(3), 175–176.

Sweet, J. (1990). Further consideration of ethics in psychological testing: A broader perspective on releasing records. *Illinois Psychologist, 28*, 5–9.

INDEX

Note: Page numbers followed by "f" or "t" refer to figures or tables respectively.